W9-CTW-254

Twentieth-Century Literary Criticism

Topics Volume

Guide to Gale Literary Criticism Series

When you need to review criticism of literary works, these are the Gale series to use:

If the author's death date is:	You should turn to:
After Dec. 31, 1959 (or author is still living)	**_CONTEMPORARY LITERARY CRITICISM_** for example: Jorge Luis Borges, Anthony Burgess, William Faulkner, Mary Gordon, Ernest Hemingway, Iris Murdoch
1900 through 1959	**_TWENTIETH-CENTURY LITERARY CRITICISM_** for example: Willa Cather, F. Scott Fitzgerald, Henry James, Mark Twain, Virginia Woolf
1800 through 1899	**_NINETEENTH-CENTURY LITERATURE CRITICISM_** for example: Fyodor Dostoevsky, Nathaniel Hawthorne, George Sand, William Wordsworth
1400 through 1799	**_LITERATURE CRITICISM FROM 1400 TO 1800_** **_(excluding Shakespeare)_** for example: Anne Bradstreet, Daniel Defoe, Alexander Pope, François Rabelais, Jonathan Swift, Phillis Wheatley **_SHAKESPEAREAN CRITICISM_** Shakespeare's plays and poetry
Antiquity through 1399	**_CLASSICAL AND MEDIEVAL LITERATURE CRITICISM_** for example: Dante, Homer, Plato, Sophocles, Vergil, the Beowulf Poet

Gale also publishes related criticism series:

CHILDREN'S LITERATURE REVIEW

This series covers authors of all eras who have written for the preschool through high school audience.

SHORT STORY CRITICISM

This series covers the major short fiction writers of all nationalities and periods of literary history.

POETRY CRITICISM

This series covers poets of all nationalities and periods of literary history.

DRAMA CRITICISM

This series covers dramatists of all nationalities and periods of literary history.

ISSN 0276-8178

Volume 42

Twentieth-Century Literary Criticism

Topics Volume

Excerpts from Criticism of Various Topics in Twentieth-Century Literature, including Literary and Critical Movements, Prominent Themes and Genres, Anniversary Celebrations, and Surveys of National Literatures

Laurie DiMauro
Editor

David Kmenta
Marie Lazzari
Thomas Ligotti
Joann Prosyniuk
Bridget Travers
Thomas Votteler
Associate Editors

 Gale Research Inc. • DETROIT • LONDON

STAFF

Laurie DiMauro, *Editor*

David Kmenta, Marie Lazzari, Thomas Ligotti, Joann Prosyniuk, Bridget Travers, Thomas Votteler, *Associate Editors*

Ian A. Goodhall, Elizabeth P. Henry, James Poniewozik, Mark Swartz, *Assistant Editors*

Jeanne A. Gough, *Permissions & Production Manager*

Linda M. Pugliese, *Production Supervisor*
Lorna Mabunda, Maureen Puhl, Jennifer VanSickle, *Editorial Associates*
Donna Craft, Paul Lewon, Camille Robinson, Sheila Walencewicz,*Editorial Assistants*

Maureen Richards, *Research Supervisor*
Robin Lupa, Mary Beth McElmeel, *Editorial Associates*
Kathleen Jozwiak, Amy Kaechele, Julie Karmazin, Tamara C. Nott, Julie Synkonis, *Editorial Assistants*

Sandra C. Davis, *Permissions Supervisor (Text)*
Maria L. Franklin, Josephine M. Keene, Denise M. Singleton, Kimberly F. Smilay, *Permissions Associates*
Rebecca A. Hartford, Michele Lonoconus, Shelly Rakoczy (co-op), Shalice Shah, Nancy K. Sheridan, *Permissions Assistants*

Margaret A. Chamberlain, *Permissions Supervisor (Pictures)*
Pamela A. Hayes, *Permissions Associate*
Nancy Rattenbury, Karla Kulkis, Keith Reed, *Permissions Assistants*

Mary Beth Trimper, *Production Manager*
Mary Winterhalter, *Production Assistant*

Arthur Chartow, *Art Director*
C. J. Jonik, *Keyliner*

The paper used in this publication meets the minimum requirements of American National Standard for Information Sciences—Permanence Paper for Printed Library Materials, ANSI Z39.48-1984. ∞™

Library of Congress Catalog Card Number 76-46132
ISBN 0-8103-2424-5
ISSN 0276-8178

Printed in the United States of America

Published simultaneously in the United Kingdom
by Gale Research International Limited
(An affiliated company of Gale Research Inc.)

Contents

Preface

Since its inception more than ten years ago, *Twentieth-Century Literary Criticism* has been purchased and used by nearly 10,000 school, public, and college or university libraries. *TCLC* has covered more than 500 authors, representing 58 nationalities, and over 25,000 titles. No other reference source has surveyed the critical response to twentieth-century authors and literature as thoroughly as *TCLC*. In the words of one reviewer, "there is nothing comparable available." *TCLC* "is a gold mine of information—dates, pseudonyms, biographical information, and criticism from books and periodicals—which many libraries would have difficulty assembling on their own."

Scope of the Series

TCLC is designed to serve as an introduction to authors who died between 1900 and 1960 and to the most significant interpretations of these authors' works. The great poets, novelists, short story writers, playwrights, and philosophers of this period are frequently studied in high school and college literature courses. In organizing and excerpting the vast amount of critical material written on these authors, *TCLC* helps students develop valuable insight into literary history, promotes a better understanding of the texts, and sparks ideas for papers and assignments. Each entry in *TCLC* presents a comprehensive survey of an author's career or an individual work of literature and provides the user with a multiplicity of interpretations and assessments. Such variety allows students to pursue their own interests; furthermore, it fosters an awareness that literature is dynamic and responsive to many different opinions.

Every fourth volume of *TCLC* is devoted to literary topics that cannot be covered under the author approach used in the rest of the series. Such topics include literary movements, prominent themes in twentieth-century literature, literary reaction to political and historical events, significant eras in literary history, prominent literary anniversaries, and the literatures of cultures that are often overlooked by English-speaking readers.

TCLC is designed as a companion series to Gale's *Contemporary Literary Criticism,* which reprints commentary on authors now living or who have died since 1960. Because of the different periods under consideration, there is no duplication of material between *CLC* and *TCLC*. For additional information about *CLC* and Gale's other criticism titles, users should consult the Guide to Gale Literary Criticism Series preceding the title page in this volume.

Coverage

Each volume of *TCLC* is carefully compiled to present:

- criticism of authors, or literary topics, representing a variety of genres and nationalities

- both major and lesser-known writers and literary works of the period

- 12-16 authors or 4-6 topics per volume

- individual entries that survey critical response to each author's work or each topic in literary history, including early criticism to reflect initial reactions; later criticism to represent any rise or decline in reputation; and current retrospective analyses.

Organization of This Book

An author entry consists of the following elements: author heading, biographical and critical introduction, list of principal works, excerpts of criticism (each preceded by an annotation and followed by a bibliographic citation), and a bibliography of further reading.

- The **author heading** consists of the name under which the author most commonly wrote, followed by birth and death dates. If an author wrote consistently under a pseudonym, the pseudonym will be listed in the author heading and the real name given in parentheses on the first line of the biographical and critical introduction. Also located at the beginning of the introduction to the author entry are any name variations under which an author wrote, including transliterated forms for authors whose languages use nonroman alphabets.

- The **biographical and critical introduction** outlines the author's life and career, as well as the critical issues surrounding his or her work. References are provided to past volumes of *TCLC* and to other biographical and critical reference series published by Gale, including *Short Story Criticism, Children's Literature Review, Contemporary Authors, Dictionary of Literary Biography,* and *Something about the Author.*

- Most *TCLC* entries include **portraits** of the author. Many entries also contain reproductions of materials pertinent to an author's career, including manuscript pages, title pages, dust jackets, letters, and drawings, as well as photographs of important people, places, and events in an author's life.

- The **list of principal works** is chronological by date of first book publication and identifies the genre of each work. In the case of foreign authors with both foreign-language publications and English translations, the title and date of the first English-language edition are given in brackets. Unless otherwise indicated, dramas are dated by first performance, not first publication.

- **Criticism** is arranged chronologically in each author entry to provide a perspective on changes in critical evaluation over the years. All titles of works by the author featured in the entry are printed in boldface type to enable the user to easily locate discussion of particular works. Also for purposes of easier identification, the critic's name and the publication date of the essay are given at the beginning of each piece of criticism. Unsigned criticism is preceded by the title of the journal in which it appeared. Some of the excerpts in *TCLC* also contain translated material. Unless otherwise noted, translations in brackets are by the editors; translations in parentheses or continuous with the text are by the critic. Publication information (such as publisher names and book prices) and parenthetical numerical references (such as footnotes or page and line references to specific editions of works) have been deleted at the editors' discretion to provide smoother reading of the text.

- Critical excerpts are prefaced by **annotations** providing the reader with information about both the critic and the criticism that follows. Included are the critic's reputation, individual approach to literary criticism, and particular expertise in an author's works. Also noted are the relative importance of a work of criticism, the scope of the excerpt, and the growth of critical controversy or changes in critical trends regarding an author. In some cases, these annotations cross-reference excerpts by critics who discuss each other's commentary.

- A complete **bibliographic citation** designed to facilitate location of the original essay or book follows each piece of criticism.

- An annotated list of **further reading** appearing at the end of each author entry suggests secondary sources on the author. In some cases it includes essays for which the editors could not obtain reprint rights.

Cumulative Indexes

- Each volume of *TCLC* contains a cumulative **author index** listing all authors who have appeared in Gale's Literary Criticism Series, along with cross-references to such biographical series as *Contemporary Authors* and *Dictionary of Literary Biography.* For readers' convenience, a complete list of Gale titles included appears on the first page of the author index. Useful for locating authors within the various series, this index is particularly valuable for those authors who are identified by a certain period but who, because of their death dates, are placed in another, or for those authors whose careers span two periods. For example, F. Scott Fitzgerald is found in *TCLC,* yet a writer often associated with him, Ernest Hemingway, is found in *CLC.*

- Each *TCLC* volume includes a cumulative **nationality index** which lists all authors who have appeared in *TCLC* volumes, arranged alphabetically under their respective nationalities, as well as Topics volume entries devoted to particular national literatures.

- Each new volume in Gale's Literary Criticism Series includes a cumulative **topic index,** which lists all literary topics treated in *NCLC, TCLC, LC 1400-1800,* and the *CLC* Yearbook.

- Each new volume of *TCLC,* with the exception of the Topics volumes, contains a **title index** listing the titles of all literary works discussed in the volume. The first volume of *TCLC* published each year contains an index listing all titles discussed in the series since its inception. Titles discussed in the Topics volume entries are not included in the *TCLC* cumulative index.

A Note to the Reader

When writing papers, students who quote directly from any volume in Gale's Literary Criticism Series may use the following general forms to footnote reprinted criticism. The first example pertains to material drawn from periodicals, the second to material reprinted from books.

[1] T. S. Eliot, "John Donne," *The Nation and the Athenaeum,* 33 (9 June 1923), 321-32; excerpted and reprinted in *Literature Criticism from 1400 to 1800,* Vol. 10, ed. James E. Person, Jr. (Detroit: Gale Research, 1989), pp. 28-9.

[2] Clara G. Stillman, *Samuel Butler: A Mid-Victorian Modern* (Viking Press, 1932); excerpted and reprinted in *Twentieth-Century Literary Criticism,* Vol. 33, ed. Paula Kepos (Detroit: Gale Research, 1989), pp. 43-5.

Suggestions Are Welcome

In response to suggestions, several features have been added to *TCLC* since the series began, including annotations to excerpted criticism, a cumulative index to authors in all Gale literary criticism series, entries devoted to criticism on a single work by a major author, more extensive illustrations, and a title index listing all literary works discussed in the series since its inception.

Readers who wish to suggest authors or topics to appear in future volumes, or who have other suggestions, are cordially invited to write the editors.

Acknowledgments

The editors wish to thank the copyright holders of the excerpted criticism included in this volume, the permissions managers of many book and magazine publishing companies for assisting us in securing reprint rights, and Anthony Bogucki for assistance with copyright research. We are also grateful to the staffs of the Detroit Public Library, Wayne State University Purdy/Kresge Library Complex, and the University of Michigan Libraries for making their resources available to us. Following is a list of the copyright holders who have granted us permission to reprint material in this volume of *TCLC*. Every effort has been made to trace copyright, but if omissions have been made, please let us know.

COPYRIGHTED EXCERPTS IN *TCLC*, VOLUME 42, WERE REPRINTED FROM THE FOLLOWING PERIODICALS:

Books Abroad, v. 50, Spring, 1976. Copyright 1976 by the University of Oklahoma Press. Reprinted by permission of the publisher.—*Boston University Journal,* v. XXV, 1977 for "F. T. Marinetti: The Theory and Practice of Futurism" by Stephen Eric Bronner. Copyright © 1977 by the Trustees of Boston University. Reprinted by permission of the author.—*Comparative Literature Studies,* v. XI, June, 1974. Copyright © 1974 by The Pennsylvania State University Press. Reproduced by permission of The Pennsylvania State University Press.—*Contemporary Review,* v. 203, May, 1963. Reprinted by permission of the publisher.—*Dutch Quarterly Review of Anglo-American Letters,* v. 12, 1982. Reprinted by permission of the publisher.—*Harvard Slavic Studies,* v. II, 1954. © Copyright 1954 by the President and Fellows of Harvard College. All rights reserved. Excerpted by permission of the publishers.—*Jewish Book Annual,* v. 36, 1978-79. © 1978, by the JWB Jewish Book Council. Reprinted by permission of the publisher.—*Mosaic: A Journal for the Comparative Study of Literature and Ideas,* Vol. VI, Summer, 1973. Special Issue entitled *The Eastern European Imagination in Literature.* © *Mosaic* 1973. Acknowledgment of previous publication is herewith made.—*The Musical Quarterly,* v. LXII, January, 1976. Copyright © 1976 by Oxford University Press. Reprinted by permission of the publisher.—*The New York Times Book Review,* January 2, 1972 for "Beat Down and Beatific" by Wilfrid Sheed. Copyright © 1972 by Wilfred Sheed. Reprinted by permission of the author.—*The New York Times Magazine,* November 16, 1952 for "This Is the Beat Generation" by John Clellon Holmes. Copyright 1985 by John Clellon Holmes. Reprinted by permission of Sterling Lord Literistic, Inc.—*Panorama of Czech Literature,* No. 4439, 1986; No. 4541, 1987.—*Partisan Review,* v. XV, December, 1948 for "Does Existentialism Still Exist?" by Delmore Schwartz. Copyright © 1948 by *Partisan Review.* Reprinted by permission of the Literary Estate of the author.—*Playboy,* v. 6, June, 1959 for "The Origins of the Beat Generation" by Jack Kerouac. Copyright © 1959 by *Playboy.* Renewed 1987 by Playboy Enterprises, Inc. All rights reserved. Reprinted by permission of Sterling Lord Literistic, Inc.—*Poetry Review,* v. 80, Summer, 1990 for "Poetry against Absurdity" by Miroslav Holub, translated by Ian Milner and Jarmila Milner. Copyright © The Poetry Society 1990.—*Proceedings of the Comparative Literature Symposium,* v. 4, 1971. Reprinted by permission of Texas Tech University Press.—*Science-Fiction Studies,* v. 17, March, 1990. Copyright © 1990 by SFS Publications. Reprinted by permission of the publisher.—*Texas Studies in Literature and Language,* v. I, no. 2, Summer, 1959 for "Existentialism in Recent American Fiction: The Demonic Quest" by Richard Lehan. Copyright © 1959 by the University of Texas Press. Reprinted by permission of the publisher and the author.—*World Literature Today,* v. 59, Winter, 1985. Copyright 1985 by the University of Oklahoma Press. Reprinted by permission of the publisher.

COPYRIGHTED EXCERPTS IN *TCLC*, VOLUME 42, WERE REPRINTED FROM THE FOLLOWING BOOKS:

Aaron, Frieda W. From "Poetry in the Holocaust Dominion," in *Perspectives on the Holocaust.* Edited by Randolph L. Braham. Kluwer-Nijhoff Publishing, 1983. Copyright © 1983 by Kluwer-Nijhoff Publishing. Reprinted by permission of the publisher.—Barr, Alfred H., Jr. From "Early Futurism," in *Twentieth-Century Italian Art.* By James Thrall Soby and Alfred H. Barr, Jr. The Museum of Modern Art, 1949. Copyright, 1949, renewed 1977. The Museum of Modern Art. Reprinted by permission of the publisher.—Bosmajian, Hamida. From *Metaphors of Evil: Contemporary German Literature and the Shadow of Nazism.* University of Iowa Press, 1979. © 1979 by The University of Iowa. Reprinted by permission of the University of Iowa Press.—Cooper, David E. From *Existentialism: A Reconstruction.* Blackwell, 1990. Copyright © David E. Cooper 1990. All rights reserved. Reprinted by permission of Basil Blackwell Limited.—Davidson, Michael. From *The San Francisco Renaissance: Poetics and Community at Mid-Century.* Cambridge University Press, 1989. © Cambridge University Press 1989. Reprinted with permission of the publisher and the author.—Davies, Judy. From "The Futures Market: Marinetti and the Fascists of Milan," in *Visions and Blueprints: Avant-Garde Culture and Radical Politics in Early Twentieth-Century Europe.* Edited by Edward Timms and Peter Collier. Manchester University Press, 1988. Copyright ©

The Golden Age of American Popular Song

INTRODUCTION

Popular music in America underwent a period of unprecedented artistic development in the years between World War I and World War II, an era known as the Golden Age of American Popular Song. Characteristic songs of the period are collectively termed "Tin Pan Alley." These works share a tendency towards wordplay and an adroit coupling of lyrics and music that distinguish them from both the sentimental ballads and minstrel tunes of the nineteenth century and from the songs of the rock and roll era, which began in the 1950s. Often written for musical comedies, Tin Pan Alley songs now are perceived as independent works and are studied for the ways in which they define American culture.

Musicologists have traced the sources of Tin Pan Alley back to such African-American styles as blues and ragtime, and to such European traditions as the operetta and the art song, but most agree that its most direct ancestor was the sentimental ballad—characterized by simple, poignant melodies and typified by the songs of Stephen Foster. The expression "Tin Pan Alley" was invented in 1900 by the songwriter Monroe Rosenfeld in reference to the din produced by hundreds of composers in New York's song publishing district, though Charles K. Harris's "After the Ball" (1892) is often viewed as the first song of the genre. While popular music in the nineteenth century was introduced to the public in the form of stage revues and sheet music, the early years of the twentieth century witnessed the rise of musical comedy, an entertainment wherein the majority of Tin Pan Alley songs originated. Additionally, technological innovations, including the phonograph record and the "talking" motion picture, created the means to reach a larger audience. Such performers as Ethel Waters, Fred Astaire, and Al Jolson, whose interpretations of Tin Pan Alley songs are preserved in these media, helped define an era beset by two wars and an economic depression.

The most successful Tin Pan Alley songwriters exhibited particular genius for reinventing and popularizing existing music styles. Irving Berlin, the era's most successful composer despite his lack of formal musical education, had his first hit in 1911 with "Alexander's Ragtime Band," a song that was inspired by, but not technically related to, ragtime's syncopated meter. George Gershwin's enthusiasm for jazz and blues contributed to his musical ideas in composing the music for his opera *Porgy and Bess* (1935). Similarly, Cole Porter incorporated a variety of foreign styles into his melodies, ranging from the West Indian beguine ("Begin the Beguine," 1935) to the music he heard in the cafés of Paris ("I Love Paris," 1953).

The most distinctive feature of Tin Pan Alley songs is the ingenuity of their lyrics. Though the songs can be as nonsensical as Johnny Mercer and Harry Warren's "Jeepers Creepers" (1938), or as lyrical as Hoagy Carmichael and Mitchell Parish's "Stardust" (1929), they commonly celebrate romantic love and demonstrate a facility for wordplay and clever analogies. The poet Philip Larkin expressed particular admiration for the "middle eight" of Leo Robin and Lewis Gensler's "Love Is Just around the Corner" (1934): "Venus de Milo was noted for her charms. / Strictly between us, / You're cuter than Venus / And, what's more, you've got arms." Because the lyrics were usually written after the music, lyricists faced the challenge of writing words to fit a melody. The musicologist Charles Hamm has written, "One is reminded of similar restrictions embraced by writers of sonnets, by the Japanese poets of *haiku* verse, and by the great American bluesmen." Oscar Hammerstein II, the lyricist who collaborated with Jerome Kern on the landmark musical *Show Boat* (1927) and with Richard Rodgers on *Oklahoma!* (1943), concurred with this statement: "It is difficult to fit words into the rigid framework of a composer's meter, but this very confinement might also force an author into the concise eloquence which is the very essence of poetry." While some of the era's most popular lyricists, especially Cole Porter and Ira Gershwin, strongly resisted the idea that they were writing poetry, established literary figures have expressed admiration for Tin Pan Alley lyrics. Many examples are included in the *Oxford Book of American Light Verse*, and recording artists continue to perform material from the Golden Age, affirming the lasting appeal of the songs.

*REPRESENTATIVE WORKS

"After the Ball," by Charles K. Harris, 1892

"Alexander's Ragtime Band," by Irving Berlin, 1911

"All the Things You Are," by Jerome Kern and Oscar Hammerstein II, 1939

"Always," by Irving Berlin, 1925

"Begin the Beguine," by Cole Porter, 1935

"Blue Moon," by Richard Rodgers and Lorenz Hart, 1934

"Brother, Can You Spare a Dime?" by Jay Gorney and E. Y. Harburg, 1932

"Embraceable You," by George and Ira Gershwin, 1930

"God Bless America," by Irving Berlin, 1911

"I Can't Get Started," by Vernon Duke and Ira Gershwin, 1936

"I Love Paris," by Cole Porter, 1953

"Jeepers Creepers," by Harry Warren and Johnny Mercer, 1938

"Let's Do It," by Cole Porter, 1928

†"Love Is Just around the Corner," by Leo Robin and Lewis Gensler, 1934

"My Funny Valentine," by Richard Rodgers and Lorenz Hart, 1937

"Ol' Man River," by Jerome Kern and Oscar Hammerstein II, 1927

"Over the Rainbow," by Harold Arlen and E. Y. Harburg, 1939

"People Will Say We're in Love," by Richard Rodgers and Oscar Hammerstein II, 1943

"Smoke Gets in Your Eyes," by Jerome Kern and Otto Harbach, 1933

"Someone to Watch over Me," by George and Ira Gershwin, 1926

"Stardust," by Hoagy Carmichael and Mitchell Parish, 1929

"Stormy Weather," by Harold Arlen and Ted Koehler, 1933

"Summertime," by George Gershwin and Du Bose Heyward, 1935

"They All Laughed," by George and Ira Gershwin, 1937

"White Christmas," by Irving Berlin, 1942

"Yesterdays," by Jerome Kern and Otto Harbach, 1933

"You Must Have Been a Beautiful Baby," by Harry Warren and Johnny Mercer, 1938

"You're the Top," by Cole Porter, 1934

*When two writers are credited, the name listed first indicates the composer of the music, the second the author of the lyrics.

†Robin and Gensler cowrote both lyrics and music.

BACKGROUND AND MAJOR FIGURES

David Ewen

[*Ewen was an American biographer and music critic who wrote extensively on popular music. In the following excerpt, he chronicles the trends in popular song that led to the flourishing of the form in the twenties and thirties.*]

There would have been no Tin Pan Alley if a new generation of song publishers had not come into being in or about 1880. These publishers had the courage to invade what thus far had been a conservative stronghold, and they had the foresight and the imagination to introduce into their business a new aggressive method of operation.

While there had always been publishers to issue popular songs and popular-song lyrics, most of the song hits before 1880 came from music-publishing establishments specializing in serious music and in instruction books for students; others came out of print shops and music stores.

Stephen Foster was published by Firth, Pond and Company in New York until it was dissolved in 1863; and Firth, Pond and Company had been organized in 1831 to publish materials for serious musicians and students.

After 1837, the Oliver Ditson music store, in Boston, became one of America's leading publishers of classical music and instruction books. This firm also brought out, however, a good deal of popular material, including "The Battle Hymn of the Republic" and "Tenting on the Old Camp Ground" during the Civil War, the dusky ballad "Nicodemus Johnson" in 1865, and Harry Kennedy's tearjerker, "A Flower from Mother's Grave," in 1878.

Two other publishers of comparatively serious music in Boston brought out minstrel-show tunes on the side. They were C. H. Keith and John F. Perry, publishers of Dan Emmett and James Bland, respectively. John Church Company, still another Boston outfit, issued, together with their staples, the popular nonmilitary Civil War ballad "Aura Lee" and one of the leading sentimental ballads of the 1870's "I'll Take You Home Again, Kathleen."

Root and Cady in Chicago was also a publisher of musical classics, as well as a music shop, until it became a power in the song industry by issuing George F. Root's "Battle Cry of Freedom" in 1863 (George F. Root was a brother of one of the firm's partners). And Carr's was just a music store in Baltimore when in 1814 it published for the first time the song that was later to become America's national anthem—"The Star-Spangled Banner."

These were just a few of the publishing houses scattered all over the country who issued serious music with one hand and popular songs with the other. All such houses followed a pattern of operation that for many years left little room for initiative or experiment. These publishing executives sat in their offices waiting for successes to hatch. Composers, performers, even the public had to beat a path to their doors. To go out in search of song material, to manufacture songs for specific timely purposes or events, to find performers and even bribe them to introduce such songs, to devise ingenious strategy to get a public sufficiently interested in the songs to buy the sheet music—all this was not then in the philosophy of conducting a music-publishing venture. Song hits happened. Publishers themselves did little or nothing to create them.

A few early American song hits point up the rather apathetic way in which publishers seemed to go about their business. Measured by sheet-music sale—the yardstick that the industry used for many years—Stephen Foster's "Swanee River" and "My Old Kentucky Home" were substantial successes for their time. The *Musical World* of 1852 reported that "the publishers keep two presses running and sometimes three, yet they cannot supply the demand [for 'Swanee River']." "My Old Kentucky Home" sold over 50,000 copies of sheet music in less than a year after its publication in 1853. The publishing house of Firth, Pond and Company thus hit pay dirt, although it had done very little hand digging of its own. It was Stephen Foster himself, not his publishers, who interested the minstrel Ed Christy in using these songs in his shows.

The Hutchinsons—a popular troupe of singers touring the country in the middle 1850's—made "The Battle Cry of Freedom" a national success. But it was accident, not the planning of the publishers, that led the Hutchinsons to sing this patriotic ballad. The Hutchinsons had come across the song by sheer chance a few days after it had been introduced in Chicago by the Lombard Brothers.

The song chronicles of this period overflow with accounts of singers accidentally stumbling over numbers that they then introduced and made famous. The premières of many another popular song came about because their composers, such as Dan Emmett and Henry Russell, were performers as well. Certainly, the publishers took full advantage of the interest in sheet-music sale aroused by performance by popular singers. But finding ways and means of getting such performances, or stimulating public interest, did not come within the sphere of their activities. Advertising of popular songs was completely unknown. Promotion and song-plugging were nonexistent. To pay a performer to sing a song would have been regarded by some of these older die-hard publishers as an indiscretion only a degree higher than street soliciting.

But in or about 1880—and continuing right through the 1890's—a new concept of popular-song publishing was being crystallized. This unconventional, even revolutionary, concept could have come only from young men with the iconoclasm and the recklessness of the novice. Some of these new publishers had been printers, and some had worked as salesmen in other businesses. They came to popular-music publishing to seek out a rich area they shrewdly felt could reap a harvest if properly fertilized and tilled. Many of these new publishers were themselves songwriters who had grown weary of earning fifteen or twenty-five dollars from a number which later brought fortunes to the publisher. As publishers of their own creations, these neophytes would stop at no length to get their work across to audiences.

One of the first of the new publishing breed was Frank Harding, who took over the direction of his father's publishing establishment on the Bowery in New York City in 1879. Frank Harding represented the new age of music publishing for two reasons. He specialized in popular songs and through them became successful; and he was one of the first in the industry to realize that song composers had to be nursed and coddled into writing hits.

He had learned the music business by operating a hand printing press for a number of years in his father's firm, after which he became his father's assistant. Once he took over the control of the business, Frank Harding broke precedent by shattering the insularity of music publishing. He made his office a hangout for the city's composers and lyricists. They came there to drink liquor, play poker, or just to gab. But along the way they also wrote songs for Harding. Realizing that there was no stimulus so potent to creation as thirst, Harding would pay his writers the price of several rounds of drinks each time they handed him a manuscript. "It was no use giving them more than ten dollars at a time," he explained. "A man could get damned drunk on ten dollars. I used to buy beautiful songs from J. P. Skelly for from six to twenty-five dollars, excellent manuscripts." Skelly, James Thornton, Charles Graham, Monroe Rosenfeld—we'll talk a good deal more about them in pages to come—were some of those who could usually be found loitering around Harding's office. Thornton's celebrated ballad "My Sweetheart's the Man in the Moon" was published by Harding; so were Joseph J. Sulli-

van's "Where Did You Get That Hat?" and J. W. Kelly's "Throw Him Down, McCloskey."

T. B. Harms and Willis Woodward were two other young publishers to concentrate successfully on popular songs and to bring a new vision to their endeavor. Between 1881 and 1883, the firm of T. B. Harms had several minor hits to its credit, the most important of which was Frank Howard's "When the Robins Nest Again" in 1883. Introduced by Howard himself (a famous minstrel with Thatcher, Primrose, and West), this song immediately became a huge favorite with minstrel-show audiences.

The T. B. Harms company did not hit its full stride until Alex and Tom Harms, both of them perspicacious and indefatigable promoters, began tapping the New York musical theater for publications. Some publishers before Harms had issued stage music—William A. Pond, for example (successors in 1863 to Firth, Pond and Company) had released most of the songs that David Braham wrote for the Harrigan and Hart extravaganzas. But T. B. Harms exploited the sheet-music distribution of stage music more extensively than any publisher had done up to this point. Between 1885 and 1891, the firm published several songs from *Shane na Lawn* and *Wang,* the latter a spectacle starring DeWolf Hopper. Then, in 1892, Harms became the first Tin Pan Alley publisher to discover that the rights to the sheet music of a successful Broadway musical production were almost as profitable as striking oil. This valuable lesson was learned by Harms through *A Trip to Chinatown,* an extravaganza that had the longest run (650 performances) of any stage presentation in New York theatrical history up to this time; it also toured the country for more than a year. Among its songs—most of which were written by Percy Gaunt—were three winners in "Reuben, Reuben," "Push Dem Clouds Away," and "The Bowery." In fact, it was "The Bowery"—far more than Loie Fuller's sensational butterfly dance or the singing of J. Aldrich Libbey—that enabled *A Trip to Chinatown* to settle down for a long and prosperous run after a shaky beginning at the box office. For several weeks the show had floundered. Then, to bolster the material, Percy Gaunt wrote "The Bowery" and slipped the song into a scene in which Harry Conor impersonated a rube from the sticks who was surrounded by Bowery drunks and thieves. After he had delivered the six verses and chorus, the thunder of approbation compelled him to sing it again from the beginning. "The Bowery" is still remembered—one of a handful of songs by which the city of New York or districts of it have been immortalized.

In 1892, Harms published "The Bowery," "Reuben, Reuben," and "Push Dem Clouds Away," and sold what for that time was the astronomical figure of several hundred thousand copies of each of the three numbers. This was the first time in Broadway history, and in that of American popular music, that a stage production provided such a source of revenue for a publisher. Henceforth, following the lead of Harms, publishing houses would reach out to the musical theater ever more hungrily to cash in on its best musical numbers.

The sentimental ballad proved as rich a source of financial

rewards for the house of Willis Woodward & Company as the musical theater was for Harms.

The sentimental ballad was, to be sure, nothing new in the 1880's. As a matter of fact it was as old as America itself. America's first sentimental ballad and the Revolutionary War came hand in hand. "The Banks of the Dee"—John Tait wrote the lyrics and adapted them to the familiar Irish melody, "Langolee"—described a Scotsman's sad farewell to his lass before embarking with the British troops for the colonies. After that, the sentimental ballad flourished in the 1830's mainly through the efforts of Henry Russell, a visitor from England. He began his career as an American popular-song composer while he was touring the country as a concert singer. In his lyrics and music, Russell shed many a tear over a tree, Mother, an old family clock, a ship afire, alcoholics, the insane, and a gambler's wife. "The Old Arm Chair," one of Russell's most popular, is probably America's first "mammy" song. "Woodman, Spare That Tree!" was one of the most widely sung and best loved sentimental ballads before the Civil War.

After Russell's time, hardly a year passed when men did not sing to women who sighed, a sad tale of woe narrated by a popular ballad. These were some of the more celebrated of these songs: "Darling Nelly Gray" in 1856; "Aura Lee" in 1861; "When You and I Were Young, Maggie" in 1866; "Sweet Genevieve" in 1869; "Grandfather's Clock" in 1876; "A Flower from Mother's Grave" in 1878; and "Why Did They Dig Ma's Grave So Deep?" in 1880. (In 1956, Elvis Presley borrowed the melody of "Aura Lee" for his song "Love Me Tender," which he introduced in the motion picture of the same name, and recorded for Victor in a disk that sold more than a million copies.) To these, of course, must be added the sentimental ballads of Stephen Foster and those by other composers inspired by the Civil War.

Many a mighty publishing establishment in Tin Pan Alley, and many a fortune, was built on the foundation stones of the sentimental ballad, whose greatest era opened in 1890. Before 1890 it was Willis Woodward that became one of the first establishments to help bring about this development by concentrating its prime efforts on such ballads. One of the first releases of the then newly organized firm of Willis Woodward was "White Wings" by Banks Winter. Winter himself had previously introduced his song at Huber's Gardens, a German beer hall on Fourteenth Street. Though the song was well received, it found no takers along publisher's row—that is, not until Pat Howley, an employee at Willis Woodward, accepted it for publication in 1884. The song became a huge success after Banks Winter tried it out in Boston with the Thatcher, Primrose and West Minstrels. Soon after that it was heard and acclaimed at Niblo's Gardens in New York. There was still another hit ballad in the Willis Woodward catalogue in 1884—Jennie Lindsay's "Always Take Mother's Advice." Charles Graham's "If the Waters Could Speak as They Flow" was one of Willis Woodward's bestselling songs of 1887.

That year of 1887, as a matter of fact, proved providential for the Woodward publishing house. For in that year it released "The Outcast Unknown," thereby acquiring under its roof perhaps the most successful creator of sentimental ballads of his time, Paul Dresser.

His name originally was Paul Dreiser, and he was the brother of Theodore Dreiser, one of America's most distinguished novelists. Paul was born in Terre Haute, Indiana, in 1857. In his boyhood he learned to play the guitar and the piano. Because his father wanted him to become a priest—and because his own inclinations drew him to the stage—Paul ran away from home when he was sixteen and joined a medicine show that marketed a "wizard oil." One year later he became a member of a troupe making one-night stands, and from there he went on to a stock company by whom he was billed as "the sensational comique."

Already Paul Dresser was writing songs. His first, "Wide Wings," was issued by a small Indiana firm with profit to neither publisher nor author. Several of his other songs were grouped into the *Paul Dresser Songster* by a small Chicago publisher. Then, in 1885, while appearing as "Mr. Bones" with the Billy Rice Minstrels, Dresser started writing sentimental ballads for that company.

Dresser, a man who quivered with sentimentality in every tissue and muscle of his huge body, would burst into tears at the sound of a touching song, and especially at one he had written. Inspired by a frustrated love affair, he produced in 1886 the words and music of "The Letter That Never Came," which he sold to T. B. Harms for a few dollars. Though this ballad did not do well, Pat Howley of Willis Woodward was astute enough to buy Dresser's very next ballad, "The Outcast Unknown." The song brought in a profit. Now convinced he had a "find" in Dresser, Howley urged the composer to give up acting in minstrel shows and to become a staff composer at Willis Woodward. The wisdom of Howley's offer was proved decisively with two extraordinarily successful ballads issued by Willis Woodward in 1888 and 1891: "The Convict and the Bird" and "The Pardon Came Too Late."

If the Willis Woodward firm was directly responsible for the successful appearance of Paul Dresser in American popular music, it was also instrumental (though indirectly) in the founding of a new publishing organization. Because that house became one of the most adventurous in the early history of Tin Pan Alley, and was to set some of the patterns that would govern the Alley for many years, this achievement by Willis Woodward was no minor one. This is how it came about.

Willis Woodward had begun the practice of bribing performers to do his songs. He asked young Jay Witmark, a successful performer of ballads in variety and minstrel shows, to include in his repertory "Always Take Mother's Advice." Mainly due to Jay Witmark's effective rendition, the ballad amassed considerable sales. When the time of reckoning arrived, Willis Woodward, in place of the sizable sum he owed Witmark, presented him with a twentydollar gold piece. In retaliation, Jay Witmark swore he would enter publishing to become Willis Woodward's chief competitor.

At the time, together with his brothers Isidore and Julius,

Jay Witmark operated a little printing establishment at his home on West Fortieth Street. This firm did miscellaneous printing jobs such as Christmas cards and advertising throwaways. It now occured to Jay that if he was able to make songs into hits by singing them, he ought to go into music publishing and work this magic for himself. There was one obstacle, however: the Witmark boys had no songs to publish. The mother of invention—necessity—compelled them to produce one of their own. Seizing upon an announcement in the papers that President Grover Cleveland was to marry Frances Folsom, Isidore Witmark wrote the instrumental number *President Cleveland's Wedding March,* hoping that the publicity attending such an event might work to the sales advantage of his brain child. By the time the wedding ceremony took place at the White House in 1886, the young Witmarks had printed a "de luxe edition" of their march, ready for immediate distribution; they were the only publishers with such a timely item. They could hardly have realized it at the time, but with their maiden effort the Witmarks had begun a trend: to manufacture popular songs for a specific event.

Thus the house of M. Witmark and Sons stepped boldly into the publishing arena. (The letter "M" in the name stood for Marcus, the boys' father. Marcus had no interest in the firm, but his signature was needed for all business documents since the Witmark boys were all under age.)

The march did well enough to convince the Witmarks that they were in the song-publishing business for good. The better-established houses referred cynically to the new-comer as "The Hatchery," because its proprietors were just fledglings; indeed, Willis Woodward prophesied (with more bitterness than vision) that the Witmark establishment would collapse in less than six months. But having started out on a solid footing with a minor hit, the Witmark boys had no intention of losing ground.

Their second publication was an Isidore Witmark song, "I'll Answer That Question." Since Jay's experiences as a singer had taught the boys that the best way to make a song successful was to get it featured by some prominent performer, Isidore set for himself the task of placing his new song to its best advantage. He finally got Mademoiselle Renée—a foreign music-hall star then touring America—to use the song in her act. (Mademoiselle Renée became the wife of the Broadway producer William A. Brady and the mother of Alice Brady, star of stage and screen.) In the same persuasive way Isidore Witmark induced Daniel Sully, a vaudevillian, to interpolate the firm's "Sassy Nolan," into his comedy routine. "Sassy Nolan" sold even better than the preceding Witmark songs, not only because of Sully's popularity but also because Sully, whose act was also called "Sassy Nolan," helped swell the sheet-music sale by purchasing forty-five thousand copies for distribution among his friends and wellwishers.

It was not long before M. Witmark and Sons outgrew its little printing shop at home. In 1888 it opened an office for song publishing at 32 East 14th Street. It was not the first music-publishing house to come to the vicinity of Union Square. Willis Woodward had preceded them there by setting up shop in the Star Building on Thirteenth Street. But if the Witmarks were not the first, they were certainly among the first to come to Union Square. Here, too, they proved pioneers. For Union Square was about to become the mecca of American popular music, the birthplace of Tin Pan Alley. . . . (pp. 3-14)

The movement of popular-music publishers toward New York City's Union Square, begun just before 1890 by Willis Woodward and M. Witmark and Sons, continued throughout the 1890's. The trail blazers were joined by the better-established houses as well as most of the newcomers.

This was the first time that the popular-music-publishing business—formerly scattered all over the United States—became centralized. This, then, was the real beginning of Tin Pan Alley.

There were sound practical reasons why publishers should now want to settle in or near Union Square. The song industry had become fully cognizant of the importance of the entertainment world to the conduct of its affairs. The older publishers as well as the neophytes wanted to center their activities, and their very presence, in what was then the entertainment capital of America.

By 1890, here in Union Square could be found Tony Pastor's Music Hall, the foremost vaudeville theater in America. Its footlights were continually throwing their luminous glare on such fabled celebrities of show business as the Four Cohans, Lottie Gilson, the first Pat Rooney, May Irwin, Weber and Fields, Eddie Foy, Emma Carus, Maggie Cline, Ben Harney, Lillian Russell, and many others. In Union Square was located the Union Square Theater in which in 1886 Lillian Russell had dazzled her audiences with the operetta *Pepita,* the music of which was the work of her husband, Edward Solomon. Also in the Square, the Academy of Music was still the home of grand opera, even though in 1883 it had found a formidable competitor in the then newly opened Metropolitan Opera House "uptown" on Thirty-ninth Street.

In Union Square there was a proliferation of burlesque and sporting houses, beer halls, penny arcades, restaurants. Across the street from Tony Pastor's was the Dewey Theater, favored home of burlesque shows, and Theiss's Alhambra, for varied forms of live entertainment. A few doors from the Alhambra stood the street's most celebrated restaurant, Luchow's, to this day a landmark on Fourteenth Street. Huber's Prospect Gardens Music Hall (a replica of an English music hall, even though its staff was mainly German) catered to its faithful clientele at the corner of Fourth Avenue and Fourteenth Street.

Just a short distance from East Fourteenth Street were clustered a number of theaters in which minstrel-show and variety troupes performed regularly. Just around the corner from Irving Place and fashionable Gramercy Park were two hotels—the Trafalgar and the Academy—which, however rundown and weatherbeaten, were the homes of visiting entertainers.

In the Union Square of 1890, as elsewhere in the United States, one form of stage entertainment was on its way out and another was on its way in.

On a sharp decline was the minstrel show, which had been flourishing since 1846 when its format had been set and established for all time by Ed Christy and his Minstrels. The end men, Mr. Tambo and Mr. Bones, became for years just about the most famous pair of characters in the American theater. The sight of these performers—faces blackened by burnt cork; dressed in frock coats, striped trousers, white gloves; with large flowers in the lapel—was calculated to arouse in audiences anticipations of nostalgia, gaiety, and hilarity: gay double-entendres; puns; absurd answers to provocative questions, repartee; solo comedy songs and sentimental ballads; choral numbers; dances; and walkarounds (the last being the strut of a performer around the stage during the presentation of the concluding musical number). All this was blended into a wonderful triple melange: the "olio," the fantasia, and the burlesque. The "olio" consisted of variety entertainment with a standardized pattern; the fantasia, with no standard format, permitted individual performers to strut their stuff; the burlesque satirized some of the highlights of the earlier two parts.

During the first half-dozen years of its activities, the Ed Christy Minstrels gave more than twenty-five hundred performances. Its success inevitably inspired imitation. All over America, minstrel troupes sprang up like wild mushrooms. Cool White (John Hodges) was the head of one group; many considered him America's foremost minstrel after Ed Christy himself. The Bryant Minstrels was organized and led to success by Dan Emmett, the most important popular composer in America before Stephen Foster. Other groups included the Virginia Serenaders, the Ethiopian Minstrels, the Harrington Minstrels, the Ordway Minstrels.

But by 1890 the demise of the minstrel show was imminent. With the growing intrusion of girls and sex into the musical theater, all-male companies began to lose their hold. A few troupes were still able to keep the hallowed traditions of minstrelsy alive: the Lew Dockstader troupe, for example, or Thatcher, Primrose, and West (later called Primrose and West), or the last of the great minstrels, George "Honey" Evans and Eddie Leonard.

While it flourished, the minstrel show did more than please its audiences for a half-century with the most delightful stage entertainment; it also immeasurably enriched the storehouse of American popular music. Some of America's finest popular songs had been written for—and were introduced and made famous by—these great dusky-faced minstrels. Dan Emmett's "Dixie," today remembered mainly as the leading song of the Southland during the Civil War, started out as a "walkaround" for the Bryant Minstrels in 1859. Emmett wrote other delightful and famous songs for the minstrel show, some of them only slightly less familiar than his "Dixie." Among these are "Old Dan Tucker" and "The Blue Tail Fly," the latter probably better known to most people today as "Jim Crack Corn." Cool White introduced "Lubly Fan" (occasionally identified today as "Buffalo Gals") with the Virginia Serenaders. One of America's first successful nonsense songs was largely made popular by the minstrel Billy Emerson—"Polly Wolly Doodle" (author unknown). The first "hi-de-ho" song ever written was a minstrel-show tune called "De Boatman's Dance," introduced by the Virginia Minstrels. Stephen Foster wrote some of his immortal Negro ballads for Ed Christy, who was the first to bring them to their nationwide prominence—classics such as "Swanee River" and "My Old Kentucky Home." Some years after Foster, his most significant successor as creator of immortal Negro ballads, James A. Bland, himself a Negro, produced "Carry Me Back to Old Virginny," "Hand Me Down My Walking Stick," and "Oh, Dem Golden Slippers"—all of them staples in the minstrel-show repertory throughout the country. Banks Winter's "White Wings," as we said before, achieved its first success with the Thatcher, Primrose, and West Minstrels. And even as the minstrel show was gasping its last breaths, it had enough vitality to contribute several more permanent additions to our song literature—such favorites, for example, as songwriter Eddie Leonard's "Ida" and "Roly, Boly Eyes."

Eddie Leonard had just become a member of the Primrose and West Minstrels when, in 1903, he wrote "Ida." The manager of the company, Jim Decker, did not think highly of Leonard and was planning to fire him. When, therefore, Leonard insisted upon singing his new number, "Ida," in place of one previously selected for him, the company manager agreed as he fully expected this to be Eddie Leonard's last appearance. Singing with that slow drawl and those drawn-out vowels that were the salient characteristics of his style, Leonard created a furor. When he came back into the wings, Jim Decker told him: "Don't bother to pack, Eddie. You're staying with the company." Eddie Leonard now became the star of the troupe and stayed that way for over a decade. He always wore a white satin suit, white topper, and a frilled white shirt, a uniform that became as much a trademark of his as his slow drawl. His delivery of "Roly, Boly Eyes"—the last of his great song successes, published in 1912—was personalized by the way he drew out the words "eyes" to sound like "wa-wah-eyes." By the time "Roly, Boly Eyes" became popular, the minstrel show had lost its hold on theatergoers. But Eddie Leonard kept the song alive in vaudeville (where he was billed as "the last of the great minstrels").

While the minstrel show was dying out, vaudeville was beginning to reach a peak of national acceptance. It was to vaudeville, more than to any other branch of the musical theater, that the Tin Pan Alley of 1890 and the early 1900's owed its greatest debt. The history of vaudeville and Tin Pan Alley overlaps so frequently that it is hardly possible to speak of one without discussing the other.

Vaudeville (initially dubbed "variety") was a legitimate offspring of the minstrel show. Vaudeville, after all, was just a "fantasia" lifted out of the context of the minstrel show and stripped of minstrel costumes and burnt cork. The word "vaudeville" comes from *vau-de-Vire*, the French word that had taken on the meaning of "lively songs." The word "vaudeville" was used for the first time in the United States on February 23, 1871, at Weisiger's Hall in Louisville, Kentucky, when a troupe headed by H. J. Sargent presented a variety performance. In billboards and on programs the company identified itself as

"Sargent's Great Vaudeville Company from Chicago." In the 1880's a touring company of variety artists also used the term "vaudeville," to describe its entertainment; and the first theater to call itself a vaudeville house opened during the same period in San Antonio, Texas. . . . (pp. 20-5)

Vaudevillians, carrying a song on a circuit touching every major American city and many of the smaller ones, became a powerful agency for its promotion. Publishers could always tell when a certain vaudeville headliner played in a specific city: by the sudden spurt of sheet-music business from that place. And, because a vaudevillain retained a single act for a number of years (or until the circuit had been covered two or three times) a song could be kept alive in public interest for an indefinite period. The life span of a sheet-music publication was thereby extended. Even the older and more conservative publishers became convinced that it was important to place songs in vaudeville acts. And it was from their early experiences with vaudeville that the younger publishers in Tin Pan Alley came to realize that the first problem in their business was to get a vaudevillian to use their songs. (p. 29)

Second in importance to vaudeville (as far as placement of songs went) was burlesque. "To place a ballad . . . in a burlesque show was the infallible method in the nineties, and long afterward, of establishing a hit and insuring great profits," wrote Bernard Sobel, burlesque's distinguished historian. "The runs were long and by the time one show after another presented a song the whole country knew the tune by heart. Thus composers and song publishers went to great lengths to place their numbers and displace competitors." . . . (pp. 30-1)

Despite the immense popularity of the sentimental ballad in the 1890's, other kinds of songs, some of which were highly successful, were being produced in Tin Pan Alley in those years.

Still in a more or less sentimental vein—though much less so than dramatic ballads like "After the Ball" and "Mother Was a Lady"—were nostalgic little waltzes that projected a simply expressed sentiment rather than narrating an elaborate tale. In that style were such songs as "Daisy Bell" and "The Band Played On."

"Daisy Bell" (perhaps better known by its alternate title "A Bicycle Built for Two") was written by the Englishman Harry Dacre soon after he came to the United States in 1891. He arrived with a bicycle among his belongings, for which he was required to pay duty. Billy Jerome, a Tin Pan Alley lyricist, met him at the pier and remarked wryly: "It's lucky you don't have a bicycle built for two, otherwise you'd have to pay *double* duty." The phrase "bicycle built for two" stuck in Dacre's mind. He used it for the first song he wrote in America. Nobody in Tin Pan Alley was at first interested in it, since in 1891 cycling still had a limited appeal for Americans. But in England, where the song was introduced by Kate Lawrence, it struck home and became an instantaneous favorite.

Then, late in 1891, a revolution took place in the construction of bicycles in the United States. The former high wheel was made smaller, the frame was dropped, pneu-

matic tires were introduced. All this added up to a vehicle easier to handle and safer to ride. Women began leaving their kitchens to go cycling—encouraged by doctors who said the sport was beneficial to health and by ministers who maintained it was beneficial to the soul.

With cycling a national fad, "Daisy Bell" caught on. Tony Pastor was the first one to sing it in America—at his Music Hall. T. B. Harms published the song in 1892, and Jennie Lindsay caused a sensation when she sang it at the Atlantic Gardens on the Bowery. After that it seemed that the whole country was on wheels—and singing "Daisy Bell."

"The Band Played On" was inspired by the German brass bands that were roaming the streets of New York City in return for whatever coins appreciative listeners wished to shower upon them. Words and music were written by John E. Palmer after he had heard one of these bands playing outside his apartment. When Palmer's sister made a move to close the window he exclaimed: "Let the band play on." His sister replied: "That's a good song title for you." If this story is to be believed, Palmer agreed and went to work at once.

He showed his song to the vaudevillian Charles B. Ward. After Ward made some corrections and minor changes, he bought it from Palmer for a few dollars. Ward then published the song himself in 1895, taking credit for the music while crediting Palmer only with the lyrics. Ward introduced the song in a Harlem Theater. After that he used his influence among his stage friends to get it heard in leading vaudeville houses. The New York *World* also became interested in it, publishing both words and music in one of its Sunday issues and using its columns to publicize it. This was the first instance in which a Tin Pan Alley product was successfully promoted by a newspaper. The song sold a million copies within a few years, and Ward (much to Palmer's chagrin) was made wealthy by it. . . . (pp. 77-9)

A new century had arrived. It was rich in achievements and richer still in promises for the future. America had just emerged from the brief Spanish-American War victoriously, with flying banners and few casualties. It was about to extend its sphere of influence by leasing for perpetuity the Canal Zone on the Isthmus of Panama for the building of a canal linking the Atlantic and Pacific oceans.

Internally in the United States, expansion was the keynote. Industry, now grown to prodigious proportions, had created the billion-dollar trust. It was flourishing in spite of the efforts of the Sherman Antitrust Act to limit its giant growth. A survey early in the 1900's disclosed that more than five thousand organizations had been consolidated into three hundred trusts—one of the most powerful of these being U.S. Steel. These trusts were controlled by just a handful of financial barons, headed by the Rockefellers and the Morgans.

Prosperity was everywhere. In the West the successful application of science to agriculture had helped make the soil fertile and facilitated cultivation. Railroads linked hitherto widely separated and far-flung cities. In the South the rise of new factories and the development of natural resources increased job opportunities. In the East a fabulous extension of business opportunities came as the result of the invention of the automobile, telephone and telegraph, and the wider use of electricity. Exports to Europe soared as the demand for American-made machines and products exceeded the supply.

Growth and expansion penetrated into every possible area. The development of public education and growing literacy brought new strength to the press and made it a powerful instrument for the molding of public opinion. (Had not the press already proved its potency in 1898 by fomenting a war?) Large-circulation magazines and best-selling novels reached a larger public than ever before. The age was so sure of itself and its strength that it could now accept frank criticism: the "muckraking" magazine article and book were becoming popular.

It was an age able to think in terms of immense size—symbolized, perhaps, by the building of New York's first skyscraper, the Flatiron Building, in 1902. It was an age encouraging speed, first with the trolley car (in Boston in 1898), then with the subway (in Boston and New York in 1898 and 1900, respectively), finally with the automobile (14,000 of them on the road by 1900). As movement accelerated, man's age-old dream of flying was reaching fulfillment: In 1903 the Wright brothers lifted their airplane from the ground at Kitty Hawk.

Everyone seemed conscious of the promises of the new age; recognized how industry was continually opening new horizons; saw how seemingly limitless were the opportunities for favorable speculation and the amassing of wealth. Money was spent even more freely than in the 1890's, and by many more people. In an attempt to reap some of the economic harvest, con men, gold-brick merchants, and the city slicker enjoyed a heyday. People lived more opulently, lavishly, ornately than ever. They dressed more flashily. The dandy of the 1880's and 1890's was replaced by the dude with his loud-colored vest, peg-top trousers, stiff collar, and a hat, either derby or straw, that was attached to his coat lapel with a cord.

The national ego bulged; Americans were becoming increasingly chauvinistic. John Philip Sousa sang the praises of America's might and majesty in his stirring marches, of which "The Stars and Stripes Forever" in 1897 almost assumed the august status of a national anthem. Jack London, Edith Wharton, Frank Norris explored American backgrounds, experiences, and characters for their novels. Walter Damrosch wrote an American opera *The Scarlet Letter,* produced in 1896; and Edward MacDowell and Henry F. Gilbert tried to realize *American* symphonic music by using the melodies and rhythms of the American Indian. American drama was beginning to emerge from the cocoon with William Vaughn Moody's *The Great Divide* in 1906. Putting a forceful finger on American achievement, the Hall of Fame was instituted at New York University in New York, and the first volume of *Who's Who in America* was released, both in 1900. Charles Dana Gibson glorified the American girl in cartoons, as Ziegfeld was doing on the stage. In 1907, George M. Cohan—a real Yankee Doodle Dandy—strutted up and down the stage, a flag draped around his body, singing the praises of his country.

Like everything else in the United States, the musical theater was undergoing a radical metamorphosis. The slow-moving, static, girl-free minstrel show was on its way out. In its place came the revue, essentially vaudeville in fancy dress. The expanding American economy, with its partiality for gilding the lily, dictated that costume designs and staging be sumptuous; and to this dictation, the revue gave ready response.

The first revue—it was called *The Passing Show*—opened at the Casino Theater in 1894. It was the brainchild of George W. Lederer, who created it because he had become convinced that vaudeville, mounted with the magnificence of an extravaganza, could find a select audience willing to pay a far higher price of admission than the twenty-five and fifty cents charged by Tony Pastor. Lederer built up a program decked out with beautiful show girls posing in "living pictures," spectacles, acrobatic acts, sketches, songs. He brought down the curtain on a sensational divertissement that held the audience spellbound.

Like every other successful venture, *The Passing Show* inspired imitation. *The Merry Whirl* came in 1895, followed by *In Gay New York* in 1896, and *All of the Town* in 1897. By the end of the century the revue was a Broadway institution. It did not now have long to wait for a producer who combined showmanship with a dash of genius, imagination with a sprinkling of daring, taste with a flair for extravagance. Such a producer, destined to make the revue a true reflection of the times in the grandioseness of its concept and the magnificence of its realization, was Florenz Ziegfeld. His production—the *Ziegfeld Follies.*

Ziegfeld was a man who loved beauty in all its manifestations and deified it. No price, he felt, was too high to pay for its glorification, no obstacle too insurmountable for its successful fulfillment. Though his only experience in show business had been as manager of Sandow the Great, the strong man at the Chicago world fair of 1893, Ziegfeld soon was driven by the dream of producing an American show for Anna Held, the Parisian star. Penniless and without a reputation, he went to Paris and actually convinced her to sign a contract. Then he went about the necessary business of raising the funds for a sumptuous production. It was called *A Parlor Match* and it came to the Herald Square Theater on September 21, 1896. Here Anna Held sang "Won't You Come and Play With Me?" She was not a striking beauty, as Marjorie Farnsworth points out in *The Ziegfeld Follies.* "She had a plump little figure laced in at the waist until her hips jutted out horizontally. . . . She was a tiny girl, a little over five feet in height, with a halo of light brown hair and a nose a little too long to agree with an artist's ideal." But, Miss Farnsworth adds, "to Americans she was the epitome of Gallic spice and naughtiness." Her large, luminous dark eyes—filled with a baby innocence, "mischievous with a trace of naughtiness"—provided a tantalizing contrast to the suggestiveness of the lyrics, which her piquant French accent made all the more provocative.

She became Ziegfeld's wife in 1897, and continued to star

in other lavish Ziegfeld productions. In *Parisian Model* she sang "Delightful to Be Married" and "I Just Can't Make My Eyes Behave"; in *The Little Duchess,* "Maiden with the Dreamy Eyes." She consistently smashed the box-office records previously established at the Casino Theater by Lillian Russell—a fact that went a long way to prove that she was now Lillian Russell's successor as the darling of the stage. In fact, in line with this development, Lillian Russell's opulent figure—with its generous curves and ample swells—no longer was regarded as the criterion for feminine beauty. Women now sought to acquire the slim, petite, boyish contours of Anna Held. Whatever Anna Held did—or whatever her publicity maintained she did—the public followed. Even the taking of milk baths! For Ziegfeld, already a master at attracting newspaper interest, had been ordering gallons of milk delivered to his door each day for Anna Held's baths. He announced that Anna Held's perfect, satinlike skin was the product of these milk baths; he even brought reporters into the privacy of her bathroom to see for themselves how her skin was soaking in the milk. The stories that followed in the papers induced a new bathing cult among American womankind—who were already starving themselves in a desperate attempt to achieve Anna Held's "hand-spanned eighteen-inch waist."

By virtue of Anna Held's successes, Ziegfeld became a producer of wealth and influence. In the early 1900's he had the wherewithall to produce his stage masterpiece—the *Follies.* He wanted an American *Folies Bergères*—to create the most spectacular revue ever mounted in the United States, the setting for the most beautiful women ever to walk across an American stage.

On July 8, 1907 he presented the first such production—the *Follies of 1907,* at the Jardin de Paris (the roof of the New York Theater). There for the first time he glorified the American female with a chorus line of "Anna Held girls" in tableaux to stun the senses. One of these was a swimming pool routine simulating a motion-picture show. . . . (pp. 89-94)

In Union Square, M. Witmark and Sons had anticipated many of the later practices of Tin Pan Alley. Once again, in 1893, it became a pioneer by moving its offices out of the Fourteenth Street area to 49-51 West 28th Street. It was in the vanguard of a general movement on the part of publishing houses toward Twenty-eighth Street.

Publishers were moving uptown because show business was moving uptown. The Casino Theater, which had opened in 1882 (and which in the 1890's was the temple of musical productions in New York) was found in the Thirty-fourth Street district. So were the Herald Square Theater and the Manhattan Opera House, two other auditoriums in which musical shows were mounted. Nearby were the Knickerbocker and the Wallack theaters.

The finest restaurants were also drifting north. Delmonico's came to Forty-fourth Street and Fifth Avenue. Rector's migrated from Chicago to settle on Broadway between Forty-third and Forty-fourth streets. Café Martin, Café des Beaux-Arts, and the Metropole were some other luxurious eating and drinking places prospering near Forty-second Street.

Music publishers followed the trend. Howley and Haviland transferred to Broadway and Thirty-second Street; Leo Feist to Thirty-seventh Street. But most of the publishers followed Witmark's lead right into Twenty-eighth Street, between Fifth Avenue and Broadway. So did important out-of-town publishing houses, including Charles K. Harris from Milwaukee and Broder and Schlam from San Francisco. By 1900, Twenty-eighth Street knew the largest concentration of popular-music publishers any single street had known up to that time, Fourteenth Street not excluded. Two or three years more and Twenty-eighth Street would be baptized "Tin Pan Alley" by Monroe Rosenfeld.

It was on Twenty-eighth Street (in line with the over-all expansion taking place in all other facets of American life) that the song industry became big business. The year 1900 saw "A Bird in a Gilded Cage" selling two million copies of sheet music. By 1910 a five-million-copy sale had been realized several times—"Meet Me Tonight in Dreamland" made it in 1909, and "Down by the Old Mill Stream" and "Let Me Call You Sweetheart" in 1910. Between 1900 and 1910 almost each of a hundred songs sold more than a million copies and each of forty-odd had amassed a sale in excess of two hundred and fifty thousand copies. More than two billion copies of sheet music in all passed from counter to customer in 1910 alone!

The song industry, then, had by the turn of the century become a business in which publishers and songwriters could make fortunes. It cost a publisher about twenty-five hundred dollars to issue a number with an initial run of ten thousand copies, promotion and overhead expenses included. Since sheet music sold for fifty cents a copy in the early 1900's, a publisher could realize a profit of as much as one hundred thousand dollars from a million-copy sale. Songwriter-composers (who, for the most part, were now getting a five percent royalty instead of selling their work outright for a cash consideration) could share another one hundred thousand dollars.

The sheet-music market spread rapidly, from music stores to department stores. Siegel-Cooper's on Eighteenth Street and Sixth Avenue became the first department store to institute a sheet-music counter. This was in or about 1895 and, soon after that, competitive department stores including Macy's followed suit. In 1907 a fierce price war erupted between Siegel-Cooper's and Macy's, which had violent repercussions in Tin Pan Alley. During this competitive battle Macy's reduced the price on a piece of sheet music from fifty cents to six cents; Siegel-Cooper's did likewise. These moves threatened to throw the music-publishing business into confusion, possibly into disaster. Consequently, several Tin Pan Alley publishers formed an agency, the American Music Stores, Inc., to maintain the existing price structure in sheet music. This organization signed contracts with fifty department stores throughout the United States that guaranteed to maintain a fixed price. But Macy's and Siegel-Cooper's refused to join. To the horror of all other stores selling music, they insisted on retaining the six-cent price level.

The publishers were now driven to work out a carefully prepared maneuver to bring both stores into line. Secretly, they made arrangements with Rothenberg's, a store on Fourteenth Street, to sell a piece of sheet music for a penny, even though it cost the publisher twenty-three cents. The publishers agreed to foot the loss, and to provide Rothenberg's with all the stock it might need; they also guaranteed to keep the price war going for twenty weeks. On October 11, 1907, the bargain price was announced in the *Evening Journal.* The next morning enormous crowds swarmed into and overran Rothenberg's, creating havoc. At the same time the publishers arranged for fifty stooges to invade both Macy's and Siegel-Cooper's and cause pandemonium through their loud and angry insistence that these stores also sell sheet music for a penny apiece. In the hubbub, fixtures were smashed and the stock from other counters was thrown pell-mell over the floor.

The war lasted one day. Late that afternoon representatives from both Macy's and Siegel-Cooper's called the American Music Stores, Inc., to sign agreements protecting the existing price structure, and, the next day, the penny sale at Rothenberg's was called off. Once again the public in New York City had to dig into its pockets and pay fifty cents for every song it wanted to buy. . . . (pp. 121-24)

The ever-swelling ranks of songwriters-become-publishers on Twenty-eighth Street found an important recruit in Gus Edwards. He was born in Germany in 1879, where his name had been Gustav Edward Simon. When he was eight, his family moved to the United States, settling in the Williamsburg section of Brooklyn. The boy Gus was crazy about the theater. While working in his uncle's cigar store, he spent all his free time—and all his pocket money—at the Union Square shows. Lottie Gilson soon came to know him, and, impressed by the earnestness of his manner and his sensitive soprano voice, hired him as her singing stooge. She placed him in the balcony of Hurtig and Seamon's to follow her in singing refrains of popular songs.

Small, round-faced, eager-eyed—with a soaring voice whose vibrato was perfectly suited for the rendition of popular ballads—little Gus Edwards had no difficulty finding jobs in the theater. He worked with Imogene Comer, Helene Mora, Maggie Cline, Polly Moran, and Emma Carus—always as a boy stooge. At other times, he sang pop tunes in saloons, on ferry boats, at club meetings. Sometimes Witmark hired him for five dollars a week to plug its songs. For a while he sold sheet music in the lobby of the Circle Theater in New York City's Columbus Circle. Many years later he bought this same theater and renamed it the Gus Edwards Music Hall.

In 1896, Edwards was performing in a Brooklyn saloon when he attracted the interest of James Hyde, a vaudeville booking agent. Hyde conceived an act in which Edwards, with four other boys, appeared as newsboys. They were dressed in ragged clothes, had their faces smudged, and carried a bundle of newspapers under their arms. "The Newsboy Quintet," as this act was named, toured the vaudeville circuit in a presentation of current hit songs. George M. Cohan, who sometimes appeared on the same bill, went out of his way to coach Edwards in song deliv-

ery; at the same time he gave him valuable hints about songwriting. Paul Dresser also took an interest in him; since Edwards did not own a piano, Dresser arranged for him to use the one at the offices of Howley and Haviland.

In 1898, Edwards wrote his first popular song, "All I Want Is My Black Baby Back." Not knowing how to write down melodies, he asked Charles Frohman to do this for him. The song became a part of the Newsboy Quintet act.

During the Spanish-American War, when he was entertaining American soldiers at Camp Black, Edwards met Will Cobb, a young man with a gift for writing verses. They collaborated on "I Couldn't Stand to See My Baby Lose," which May Irwin introduced in vaudeville in 1899. That same year Edwards and Cobb had a hit with "I Can't Tell You Why I Love You, but I Do," published by Howley and Haviland. Before long, Edwards and Cobb had so many successful songs on the lists that they came to be known in Tin Pan Alley as "Words and Music."

In 1905, Gus Edwards became one of the ace composers of the firm of M. Witmark and Sons by producing three hits, all of them with lyrics by Vincent Bryan: "He's Me Pal," "In My Merry Oldsmobile," and "Tammany." "In My Merry Oldsmobile" was one of the first successful songs about the automobile. It was written to celebrate the successful completion of the first cross-country trip ever attempted by an automobile, a feat then accomplished by two Oldsmobiles. "Tammany," while supposedly a take-off on the Indian-type songs then so popular, was actually written for a party held at the National Democratic Club in New York, at which, even though it touched upon some of the less creditable practices of the Democratic Party, it proved to be a big hit. Soon after that, Lee Harrison sang it in the musical comedy *Fantana,* and Jefferson de Angelis made it extremely popular in vaudeville. Eventually it became the official song of New York City's Tammany Hall.

Weary of seeing the Witmarks reap such a financial harvest from his creative fruits, Edwards decided to open a publishing venture of his own. Late in 1905 he found an office on Twenty-eighth Street. One of the first songs, published, which he wrote with Cobb, was "I Just Can't Make My Eyes Behave," which Edwards convinced Ziegfeld to let Anna Held sing in *A Parisian Model.* Song and singer became so inextricably associated with one another that it became inconceivable to think of the number being sung without a provocative French accent. In 1906, Edwards and Cobb wrote the first number published by the new house of Edwards to realize a million-copy sale— "Sunbonnet Sue."

Having thus become a success as a composer and as a publisher, Edwards was ready in 1907 to conquer still another world, that of vaudeville. He wrote, directed, and starred in a revue which he initially called "School Boys and Girls." His role was that of a schoolteacher in a room filled with kids. They were allowed to sing, dance and mime—in short to bring to the vaudeville stage the welcome infiltration of the fresh, spontaneous gift of youngsters. "School Days," a song Edwards wrote for this revue, became the greatest success of his whole songwriting career, with three million copies sold.

Gus Edwards' kid act became a headliner in vaudeville that enjoyed a continuous booking on the circuit. Year after year Edwards searched for new talent; year after year he came up with remarkable youngsters who, after making their stage debuts in his act, went on to achieve the heights of success. The names of those who at one time or another were parts of his act read like a *Who's Who* of the American musical theater: Eddie Cantor, Georgie Jessel, Groucho Marx, Lila Lee, and Georgie Price. Edwards was so indefatigable in his search for new faces and fresh talent that before long the remark circulated freely along Broadway: "Pull your kids in, here comes Gus Edwards."

Of the songs that Edwards wrote for and popularized in his acts after 1907, the most important were "By the Light of the Silvery Moon" (which Georgie Price introduced in 1909), "If I Were a Millionaire" in 1910, and "Jimmy Valentine" in 1912. In 1940, the story of Gus Edwards' career was dramatized in the motion picture *The Star Maker,* in which Bing Crosby played the title role.

Then there was Ted Snyder.

In the early 1900's there was a small publishing firm in Tin Pan Alley called Rose and Snyder. The "Snyder" of this combination was a talented young composer who had been a café pianist, then a song plugger. Henry Waterson, a diamond merchant interested in going into the music-publishing business, kept his eye on Snyder for some time. Then in 1907 he offered to back him in a publishing venture. Ted Snyder formed the Seminary Music Company in 1908 (its name was soon changed to the Ted Snyder Company), and one of its first issues was the Ted Snyder song "If You Cared for Me." A year later the firm published Snyder's "Beautiful Eyes," which was interpolated into the stage musical *Mr. Hamlet of Broadway*. After that, Snyder published a number of substantial hits (which he helped to write), among which were "That Beautiful Rag," "That Mysterious Rag," "How'd You Like to Be My Daddy?" (which Al Jolson sang in *Sinbad*). "Who's Sorry Now?," written with Bert Kalmar and Harry Ruby in 1923, became a standard.

But despite the tremendous success of "Who's Sorry Now?" Ted Snyder's greatest contribution to Tin Pan Alley was not any one of his songs. His major contribution was the prominent role he played in the early songwriting history of Irving Berlin.

Like his parents and seven brothers and a sister, Irving Berlin (born Israel Baline) was a fugitive from a Russian pogrom. The family fled to America in 1892, when Israel, or Irving, was just four, and found a home in the Lower East Side of New York. There, where they had expected to encounter only milk and honey, they found overcrowded tenements, slums, poverty, long and hard work. Four of the children had to find jobs in sweatshops or sell papers in order to help support the family. The father—a part-time cantor in a synagogue and a part-time *shochet* in a kosher slaughter house—hardly earned enough to support his large brood.

Irving Berlin performing his "Oh! How I Hate to Get Up in the Morning."

When his father died, Irving, now aged eight, ran away from home. Since he had the gift of song, he made his way as best he could by singing. For a while he worked for Blind Sol, a singing beggar, whom he led into cafés and through the streets. Then he gave song renditions of his own. After leaving Blind Sol's employ, he found many opportunities to sing Tin Pan Alley's sentimental ballads in night spots and saloons on the Bowery or in Chinatown. He also worked for a while as Harry von Tilzer's song plugger at Tony Pastor's Music Hall.

In 1906 he found a job as a singing waiter in Pelham's Café in Chinatown. He served at the tables and cleaned up the café when it closed down for the night. But his main function was to entertain the guests with renditions of popular songs. It was there and then that he wrote his first published song.

Around the corner from Pelham's was Callahan's, which could boast that one of its waiters had written the lyrics for "My Mariuccia, Take a Steamboat" (music by Al Piantadosi, published by Shapiro-Bernstein). The proprietor of Pelham's, was convinced that what could be done at Callahan's could be done better at Pelham's. On his encouragement, the saloon pianist Nick Michaelson wrote a melody, and Israel Baline, who had proved himself adept in making up parodies, was asked to do the lyrics. In obvious imitation of their rivals around the corner, Michaelson and Baline called their song "Marie from Sunny Italy"—and the clientele of Pelham's loved it. Then in 1907 the song was published by Joseph W. Stern & Company. It was on this effort, for which Baline had contributed only the words, that the assumed name of Irving Berlin makes its first appearance. On a green and white cover on which was pictured a gondola and a photograph of Lillian Russell, the name Irving Berlin stood out bold and clear in large type. Berlin's total income from his first song was thirty cents in royalties. . . . (pp. 144-49)

> *David Ewen, in his* The Life and Death of Tin Pan Alley: The Golden Age of American Popular Music, *Funk and Wagnalls Company, Inc., 1964, 380 p.*

Charles Hamm

[*Hamm is an American composer, educator, and musicologist. In the following excerpt, he discusses the composers and lyricists that characterized Tin Pan Alley.*]

The era marked off roughly by America's involvement in the two great world wars of the twentieth century was one of the peaks of the entire 200-year history of popular song in America. Scores of talented songwriters and lyricists turned out hundreds of songs that delighted, charmed, and soothed not only their fellow Americans, but much of the rest of the Western world as well. This music penetrated deep into American culture; one need merely mention the names of several American songwriters of the period—George Gershwin, Irving Berlin, Jerome Kern, Cole Porter, Richard Rodgers, Harry Warren—to be reminded of the brilliance of this era and of the role these men and their songs played in the continuing emergence of a uniquely American culture.

Yet this era represents a single chapter in the continually unfolding story of popular song in America, linked at its beginning to the more-than-a-century-old tradition of American song and giving way at its conclusion to yet another musical style. (pp. 326-27)

Most eras of popular song in America have been dominated by one or another of the national or ethnic groups making up the complex web of American society—the English, the Irish, the Italians, the Germans, the Africans. The period [of the golden years of Tin Pan Alley] was no exception; it was dominated by Jewish Americans, and represents one of the first great contributions to American culture by the New York Jewish community, which was to be at the center of so much of America's cultural and artistic life in the twentieth century.

Jews had made up a tiny portion of the American population since shortly after the settling of the land. Coming mostly from Great Britain and the Germanic countries, they settled in urban areas, many of them becoming shopkeepers, merchants, and small-business men. Others were active in the arts, many as performing musicians and

teachers of music in various American cities and towns. Though scattered through various parts of the country, they were particularly prominent in New Orleans and in New York City, which had a Jewish population of some 80,000 by the 1880s.

They had been involved in popular song in this country almost from the beginning. John Braham, singer and songwriter of the early nineteenth century, and Henry Russell, the most important songwriter in America before Stephen Foster, were Jews. And they had played a particularly important role in the first decades of Tin Pan Alley: Charles K. Harris, Monroe Rosenfeld, and Edward B. Marks were successful composers in the first years of the era; and Harris, Marks, Lew Bernstein, and Maurice Shapiro were only the most notable of the American Jews who established successful music publishing houses in the formative years of Tin Pan Alley.

The Jewish population of the United States increased dramatically in the decades surrounding the turn of the century, as a result of a series of events set in motion by the assassination of Alexander II, czar of Russia, on March 1, 1881. The historic oppression of the Russian Jews had been moderated under Alexander, but his successor, Alexander III, did little to curb a rising tide of anti-Semitism sweeping over the land. Jews fled Russia by the millions, seeking refuge elsewhere; American immigration laws permitted several million to come to the States, and by 1910 there were more than a million Jews in New York City alone, making up more than a quarter of the population.

Most of these new immigrants were poorly schooled, and they encountered a certain amount of anti-Semitism even here. Life in New York was often desperate at first; but their native intelligence, aptitudes, skills, and determination enabled many of them to achieve financial and professional success within a decade or two, and soon entire fields—real estate, the clothing industry, entertainment— were dominated and altered by their successful pursuit of a sort of life denied them in Eastern Europe for so many centuries.

Vaudeville and other forms of popular American theater would have been quite different, and much poorer, without such entertainers as Sophie Tucker, Al Jolson, George Jessel, Eddie Cantor, Jack Benny, Ted Lewis, George Burns, Fanny Brice, Milton Berle, and hundreds of others. New York's vaudeville circuit was dominated largely by such ambitious and imaginative men as the Schuberts, Marcus Loewe, and Adolph Zukor. The Hollywood movie industry was built up mostly by the "Moguls," Jewish Americans such as Louis B. Mayer, Samuel Goldwyn, William Fox, the Warner brothers, and the Selznicks, described by a recent historian as

> Often vulgar, crude, and overbearing, they were brilliantly attuned to the needs of their business; they commanded and used to the full a profound instinct for the common denominator of taste; and they left a deep imprint on American popular culture. Trusting their own minds and hearts, shrewd enough not to pay too much attention to the talented or cultivated men they

hired, the Moguls knew which appeal to senti-ment, which twirl of fantasy, which touch of vio-lence, which innuendo of sexuality, would grasp native American audiences. It was something of a miracle and something of a joke. [Irving Howe, *World of Our Fathers*]

(pp. 327-28)

Jewish Americans had dominated another form of enter-tainment—popular song—for several decades before the Moguls built their movie dynasties, anticipating their as-tonishing grasp of "the common denominator of taste." Unlike the Moguls, these songwriters worked in a field with a long and successful tradition, which they carefully used as the basis for their own creations. And they were anything but "vulgar, crude, and overbearing."

Various theories have been set forward to explain the as-tonishing success of Jewish Americans in the various areas of entertainment in the first half of the twentieth century. They were, first of all, talented. Certainly another factor was that Jews already held important posts in the enter-tainment world, and thus the new immigrants did not en-counter the iron wall of anti-Semitism that met them else-where.

> Just as blacks would later turn to baseball and basketball knowing that here at least their skin color counted for less than their skills, so in the early 1900's young Jews broke into vaudeville because here too people asked not, who are you? but what can you do? It was a roughneck sort of egalitarianism, with little concern for those who might go under, but at best it gave people a chance to show their gifts. [Howe]

Even the most cursory biographical survey of the leading songwriters, lyricists, performers, and publishers of popu-lar song in the first half of the twentieth century underlines the domination of Jewish Americans. More important, their cultural and musical heritage colored their products, giving them a flavor quite different from that of earlier popular songs and bringing yet another ethnic strain to the already polygenous style of American song.

If a single songwriter were to be chosen to epitomize the era, it would certainly be Irving Berlin. He wrote songs from the very beginning of the period through to the end (and even into the next era); his songs represent all of the various types that characterized these years; and dozens of his songs were among the most popular products of the Tin Pan Alley years. Furthermore, his career and his music point up the strong links between the first and sec-ond generations of Tin Pan Alley, and the emergence of a somewhat different song style in the 1920s and '30s. (pp. 328-29)

Berlin's career spanned the time when several new media for the dissemination of popular song—the sound movie, radio, the phonograph record, television—brought about radical changes in the business of music, the several indus-tries concerned with the reproduction and marketing of the product produced by songwriter and lyricist. By the middle of the twentieth century, the size and wealth of the music industry had swollen to proportions unimaginable to even the most ambitious publishers in the early years

of Tin Pan Alley. But these new and sweeping technologi-cal developments sparked no new styles or forms of popu-lar song. Songs written by Irving Berlin in 1915 are essen-tially the same as those written thirty years later; continu-ity of musical style is one of the most striking features of the Tin Pan Alley era. One can hear this with one's own ears, or reflect on the many songs that have remained pop-ular for decades, or were revived after a long hiatus and were indistinguishable from the most recent inventions. For instance:

> *Variety* magazine, reviewing in its issue of De-cember 23, 1953, a newly released album, *The Eddie Cantor Story,* commented that "Cantor's singing style on the 1917 waxing was just about the same as it is today and the songs might easily be current pops."

> In 1946, Decca released an LP album, *Al Jolson,* with a song repertory mostly from the late 1910s an the1920s, which became the best-selling LP according to *Billboard's* popularity charts, re-mained in the No. 1 spot for 25 weeks, and was among the 10 most popular albums for 65 con-secutive weeks. *Al Jolson—Volume* 2 (1947) and *Al Jolson—Volume* 3 (1948) also became No. 1 hits, holding the top spot in *Billboard's* charts for 10 and 14 weeks, respectively.

> Irving Berlin's "God Bless America," one of the most popular songs of 1939-40 (and since), was actually written in 1917, in essentially the same form in which it was published more than twen-ty years later.

> "Peg o' My Heart," written by Fred Fisher in 1913, was revived in 1947, became a No. 1 single disc as performed by the Harmonicats, was fea-tured on "Your Hit Parade" for 20 weeks, and for 14 consecutive weeks held the first or second spot on this show.

> "You Belong to Me," written by Victor Herbert in 1916 for the operetta *The Century Girl,* be-came a top-selling single in 1952, as sung by Jo Stafford, appeared on "Your Hit Parade" for 19 consecutive weeks, and was also recorded suc-cessfully by Dean Martin and Pattie Page.

These are a mere handful of the examples that could be cited to support the contention that the style of Tin Pan Alley songs was constant throughout the creative lifetime of Irving Berlin and remained constant in the face of the most astounding technological changes yet experienced since popular song became part of American life shortly after the American Revolution. There would seem to be two explanations for this persistence of style at a time when every other aspect of the popular-music industry was fluid and even revolutionary, one political and one musical.

ASCAP (the American Society of Composers, Authors and Publishers) was founded in 1914 in an attempt to force restaurants, theaters, and other establishments fea-turing live music to pay fees for the public use of music. To that point, copyright protection covered only the pur-chase and mechanical reproduction of published composi-tions. Composers, lyricists, and publishers received no compensation from live performances of their music. After a series of legal battles eventually reaching the Supreme Court, the young organization won its case (in a ruling handed down on January 22, 1917), and all hotels, theaters, dance halls, cabarets, and restaurants were required to obtain a license from ASCAP—for a fee—before they could play a piece written by a composer or published by a publishing house belonging to the organization. In time, similar rulings were handed down in cases involving radio stations and motion picture studios. The ASCAP membership increased dramatically in the 1920s, eventually including all important publishing houses and almost all of the leading composers and lyricists of the day, and by the mid-1930s some $10,000,000 in licensing fees were paid annually, most of the money being distributed to the membership according to a complex rating system. The recording industry was already obligated to pay fees to composers and publishers, under the "mechanical reproduction" clause of the copyright law of 1909, which had fixed a fee of 2¢ per disc or cylinder to be paid to the copyright owner.

The net effect of these several developments was that each of the new media—the phonograph record, radio, the sound movie—obtained its music from ASCAP composers and publishers, whose chief concern, quite naturally, was with the type of music already being produced, rather than with the new types of music perhaps more appropriate to the several media. Putting matters in the simplest possible terms, the songs performed on radio and in the movies were written in a style born in vaudeville and other forms of musical theater in the late nineteenth and early twentieth centuries. There is no way to tell, from listening to a song by Irving Berlin or any of his contemporaries, whether it was written for vaudeville, musical comedy, the movies, or simply composed for radio play and possibly recording. The exploitation of the characteristic and differing potentials of each of the new media would wait for a later time.

The second reason for the persistence of a single musical style in the popular songs of the Tin Pan Alley era is simply that this style was a vital, viable, successful, somewhat flexible, and relatively new one. Changes in musical style, in popular song as in other forms of music, tend to come about when the prevailing style has been in use for a considerable period of time, when composers and audiences feel that it is beginning to be exhausted, when it has lost its "cutting edge," as Virgil Thomson once put it. The 1910s, '20s, and '30s saw a large number of extremely talented songwriters exploiting a song style that had not yet grown old, that still seemed to them to be perfectly suitable to express what they wanted to express, that could still be modified in its details enough for each of them to carve out a somewhat distinctive profile.

The first half of the twentieth century thus saw a conflict between two cycles—a musical one, still in its strong and formative stages, and a technological one, just beginning, that made possible, at least in theory, some radically new concepts in song. In this instance, musical impulses proved to be stronger than technology.

Irving Berlin's contribution to American song has been summed up thus:

> He represented, in song, every phase of musical fashion for forty-five years or more. . . . This is not to say that he was the best writer in each and every area of popular music. . . . Let it be said that he is the best all-around song writer America has ever had. In this area or that, I will say, and have said, that I believe so-and-so to be the master. But I can speak of only one composer as the master of the entire range of popular song—Irving Berlin. [Alec Wilder (see Further Reading)]

The range of his songs, in content and mood, if not in form, is enormous, from his early dialect and spirited "ragtime" songs, to his sentimental ballads, to the many songs written at all periods of his career that exploit one type of humor or another. Some take on a bit of the flavor of ragtime, of the blues, of country-western music, Latin-American music, or jazz. In an era that had almost forgotten the waltz, he wrote a succession of excellent, sentimental waltz-songs harking back to the first decades of Tin Pan Alley, including such perennial hits as "What'll I Do?," "Always," and "The Girl That I Marry." Some of his earliest songs represent the final phase in the century-long history of the minstrel song: his ragtime songs and such others as "I Want to Be in Dixie" (1912) and "When It's Night Time in Dixie Land" (1914) were written for Jewish blackface vaudeville performers ("Black became a mask for Jewish expressiveness, with one woe speaking through the voice of another." [Howe]). But through all of this, Berlin turned out a steady stream of slow, lyric, sentimental songs that have retained their popularity after other types have become dated and forgotten, songs that prompted his most recent biographer [Michael Freedland] to label him "America's Number One Balladeer," and that brought the following comment from a sympathetic contemporary:

> It may be the inheritance of his tribe in Irving Berlin that tinges so many of his songs with the mournfulness of solitude and self-pity. But somewhere within him the voice of the publisher also whispers reassuringly that sadness is rather apt to sell better than gayety in the song market. [Alexander Woolcott, *The Story of Irving Berlin*]

Though he was one of the few songwriters of the era to write his own lyrics, he has been sparing with words otherwise: he has had absolutely nothing to say about himself, his songs, his working methods, his opinions of the songs of other writers. It is said that he never learned to read music, that he works by ear at the piano, that he has always employed an assistant to write down and perhaps arrange his songs. Almost from the beginning of his songwritting career, there were persistant rumors that his songs were ghostwritten, or were at least heavily dependent on assistance from musicians with more technical knowledge. Characteristically, he has never acknowledged these rumors or commented on them; but several persons close to him have described his working methods in detail, reaching the conclusion,

So, though it is known that he has for years paid

a professional musician to harmonize his songs under close supervision, it is very nearly impossible, upon hearing some of these melodies, to believe that every chord was not an integral part of the creation of the tune. [Wilder]

The phenomenal and perennial success of so many of his songs cannot be explained in technical, musical terms, any more than can the similar success of Stephen Foster. The explanation lies in his innate talent and in his "profound instinct for the common denominator of taste." In the words of one of his peers [Jerome Kern]:

> He honestly absorbs the vibrations emanating from the people, manners and life of his time, and in turn, gives these impressions back to the world,—simplified,—clarified,—glorified.

Jerome Kern (1885-1945) was an almost exact contemporary of Berlin's, at least for the period when they were both creative; his songs were written in the same forms and in the same general harmonic and melodic language; many of his songs cannot be distinguished from those of Berlin by a listener who does not already know which of the two had written them. Despite all this, there are subtle and important differences in the careers and the compositions of the two, differences that remind us that even in a period when all songwriters willingly and comfortably fitted their compositions in the same molds, there was still room for different personalities and individual tastes to express themselves.

The most obvious differences between the two are that Kern had a sound education in music and that he wrote almost from the beginning of his career for operetta and musical comedy, rather than for vaudeville and revue.

Somewhat of a prodigy, Kern was given early instruction in piano and organ by his mother, then studied at the New York College of Music and briefly in London, where, in 1903, he had his first experience in writing for the musical stage, turning out musical filler material for various shows. Back in New York, he served a lengthy apprenticeship in Tin Pan Alley, working as a shipping clerk for E. B. Marks, as a song plugger, and as a rehearsal pianist for a succession of musical shows. Though his first successful song was published in 1905—"How'd You Like to Spoon With Me?," interpolated into *The Earl and the Girl*—it was another decade before he began writing genuinely successful songs and was recognized as an important songwriter in the musical and dramatic circles of New York City. He wrote his first complete score for a musical play in 1912, *The Red Petticoat,* and his first unqualified hit song came in 1914, with "They Wouldn't Believe Me," sung by Julia Sanders in *The Girl from Utah.*

Nobody Home (1915) marked his first collaboration with Guy Bolton in what became a long string of highly successful musical shows at the Princess Theatre; others were *Very Good, Eddie* (1916), *Oh, Boy!* (1917)—which ran for 463 performances and saw Kern's first songs with lyrics by P. G. Wodehouse—*Have a Heart* (1917), *Leave It to Jane* (1917), *The Riviera Girl* (1917), *Oh, Lady! Lady!* (1918), *Oh, My Dear!* (1918), *Sally* (1921, 570 performances), and *Sitting Pretty* (1924). *Sally* featured Kern's most popular song to that point, "Look for the Silver Lin-

ing," with lyrics by Bud De Sylva. The Princess shows enjoyed such lengthy runs that Kern had time to compose songs for other shows as well. He was, in fact, so much in demand and so well rewarded for his compositions that he commanded the highest annual income for songwriting alone of any American writer of the day; Edward B. Marks reported that during the period of World War I, Kern had an income of some $3,000 per week from his musical comedy scores alone.

These musical comedies were among the most successful works of the genre in the decade after George M. Cohan had revolutionized the musical stage with his "musical plays," and represent a further step in defining and popularizing the American musical theater style. Their indebtedness to European operetta was still apparent:

> Kern . . . had his musical roots in the fertile middle European and English school of operetta writing, and amalgamated it with everything that was fresh in the American scene to give us something wonderfully new and clear in music writing in the world. Actually he was a giant with one foot in Europe and the other in America.

Another immense stride forward came with *Show Boat* (1928), one of the great landmarks in American musical theater. American in theme and plot, its cast of characters included Southern belles, riverboat gamblers, wealthy plantation owners, and even blacks; it was an essentially serious work, leaving behind the gaiety and sophistication of so many earlier American musical comedies. The book and lyrics were by Oscar Hammerstein II, based on Edna Ferber's novel of the same name; Kern and Hammerstein had first worked together in *Sunny* (1925), which had a run of 517 performances and yielded the hit songs "Who?" and "Sunny." The sets and costumes of *Show Boat* were spectacular, the cast superb, the book tight and moving smoothly from large ensemble numbers involving the entire cast to effective dramatic climaxes, and Kern's score is arguably the best ever written for a musical comedy, with such superlative and perennially popular songs as "Why Do I Love You?," "Can't Help Lovin' dat Man," "Bill," "Make Believe," and "Ol' Man River." It opened at the Ziegfeld Theatre in New York on December 27, 1927, ran for 572 performances there, was revived for long and equally successful runs in 1932 and 1946, was made into a movie in 1929 and again in 1936, and has been singled out by critics and historians as pointing the way to a series of the most characteristically American musicals the stage has ever seen, in the ensuing half-century.

Unlike Stephen Foster and several other American songwriters who wrote their best pieces early in their careers, Kern became an even better and more successful composer as the years passed. *Show Boat* was followed by a succession of other successful musical comedies, each with superb songs: *The Cat and the Fiddle* (1931) brought such songs as "The Night Was Made for Love," to lyrics by Otto Harbach; *Music in the Air* (1932) featured songs written in collaboration with Hammerstein again, including "I've Told Ev'ry Little Star" and "The Song Is You"; *Roberta* (1933) introduced three of his very best songs— "Smoke Gets in Your Eyes," "Yesterdays," and "The

Touch of Your Hand"—with lyrics by Harbach; and his last stage score, for *Very Warm for May* (1939), included "All the Things You Are."

Like Berlin, Kern wrote for Hollywood sound movies almost from the beginning of the history of this new form of entertainment. *Show Boat* was made into a movie in 1929, and other musical comedies of his were filmed in succeeding years. Beginning with the film *I Dream Too Much* (1935), most of his new songs were written for the movies; almost every film for which he composed brought one or more new hit songs. *Swing Time* (1936), starring Fred Astaire and Ginger Rogers, featured such Kern/Dorothy Fields songs as "The Way You Look To-night" and "A Fine Romance." *High, Wide and Hand-some* had songs written to lyrics by Hammerstein, including "The Folks Who Live on the Hill"; *Joy of Living* (1938) introduced "You Couldn't Be Cuter"; *Lady Be Good* (1941) brought one of his finest songs, "The Last Time I Saw Paris"; *You Were Never Lovelier* (1942) yield-ed "Dearly Beloved." *Cover Girl* (1944) had Kern collabo-rating with Ira Gershwin to produce such songs as "Long Ago and Far Away" (one of the most successful songs in the entire history of "Your Hit Parade," remaining on the show for twenty consecutive weeks), and *Can't Help Sing-ing* (1944) brought yet more new Kern songs, including "More and More." *Centennial Summer* (1946), released after his death, showed that he had retained his skill and talent to the very end, with "All Through the Day."

Almost all of Kern's songs, then, were written for the mu-sical theater and films; he contributed one or more compo-sitions to some 120 of these. Almost without exception, his most successful songs were lyric ballads, drawing as much on the tradition of European operetta as on indigenous American song. The sentimental Waltz-song was all the rage when Kern began composing, but few of his songs were of this sort; when the ragtime craze swept over Tin Pan Alley, he mostly disdained it; few of his songs of the 1920s and '30s use the traces of jazz flavoring so popular with many of his peers. He was in this regard a much more limited composer than Berlin, yet by any method of calcu-lation his list of "top hit" songs is fully as long as Berlin's. In assessing the contribution of these two men to Ameri-can song style, it must be kept in mind that their first songs appeared several decades before those of most of the song-writers to be discussed and mentioned later—Gershwin, Porter, Rodgers, Nacio Herb Brown, Harry Warren—and to the extent that there is a general similarity of style in the songs of all these men, Berlin and Kern wrote the songs that served as models for their somewhat younger contemporaries.

There are technical differences between Kern's songs and those of Irving Berlin. Kern was more a master of pure melody, able to create tunes that progress, move, rise to peaks, and descend from these so naturally and effectively that his technique, mastered over so many years of ap-prenticeship, passes unnoticed. To [Wilder,] the writer who has most thoroughly studied the music of this era,

> Kern does exemplify the pure, uncontrived me-lodic line more characteristically than any other writer of American theater music. Long before

I knew the first thing about music, I knew his melodies. They pleased me, they even haunted me. . . . Even when he did use more elaborate harmony, and I had become involved myself in the excitement of lush harmonic patterns, I didn't need to know or hear his harmony in order to enjoy thoroughly his lovely melodic flights.

An even more obvious contribution to American song style, hinted at in the quotation above, was his use of more complex and sophisticated chords and harmonic changes than had been used by the first generation of Tin Pan Alley songwriters. (pp. 337-45)

Kern not only had one foot in Europe and the other in America, he also—like Berlin—had a thorough knowl-edge of, and a respect for, the songs of the American song-writers preceding him. The early songs of these two men were the strongest link connecting the first two genera-tions of Tin Pan Alley.

Parts of the story of George Gershwin (1898-1937) need not be told in detail here, since they so closely resemble those of so many other songwriters and lyricists of the era: birth, childhood, and early education in New York (Brooklyn, in Gershwin's case); early apprenticeship with a Tin Pan Alley publisher (Gershwin became a song plug-ger for the Jerome H. Remick Music Company in May of 1914); a thorough, practical knowledge of the song style of the day (Gershwin admired Irving Berlin, and one of his earliest compositions, "Ragging the Traumerei," was an emulation of Berlin's "That Mesmerizing Mendelssohn Tune"). An excellent pianist, Gershwin sometimes ac-companied such singers as Louise Dresser and Nora Bayes in his early professional years, and he cut some 125 player-piano rolls in 1915 and the years following. His first pub-lished song was "When You Want 'Em, You Can't Get 'Em, When You Got 'Em, You Don't Want 'Em," to a lyric by Murray Roth, brought out by the Harry Von Tilzer house in 1916. His first stage song, "Making of a Girl," was written for *The Passing Show of 1916,* and the following year he was signed to an exclusive contract as house songwriter for the T. B. Harms publishing firm.

Like so many songwriters throughout the entire history of popular song, he was almost unknown until a single song brought him instant fame and fortune. In Gershwin's case, it was "Swanee," written in 1919 to a lyric by Irving Cae-sar. The latter's account of the early career of the song un-derlines the role played by top performers in popularizing a new composition:

> Funny thing about "Swanee." It was received with great enthusiasm, but it wasn't a hit right off the bat. The Capitol opening [of *Demitasse Revue*] was tremendous, and it was the largest theater in the world at that time. Sixty girls danced to "Swanee"; they had electric lights in their shoes. Arthur Pryor's band played it. Sev-enty in the band. Everyone on stage sang it. Ev-eryone applauded. There were thousands of cop-ies in the lobby—but they didn't sell.

> One day Al Jolson gave a midnight party after a show at the Winter Garden. . . . George was invited up by Buddy De Sylva, with whom he

also wrote songs. Buddy was a great friend of Jolson's and asked George to play for Jolson. At that party George played "Swanee," among several other numbers, and Jolson at once adopted it and introduced it within three or four days, and the rest is history. Jolson made "Swanee" a hit, the biggest hit song George has ever had. If Jolson hadn't performed it with that great warmth he had, it probably wouldn't have happened.

The song rather quickly sold some million copies of sheet music for T. B. Harms; it also sold more than two million discs, as recorded by Jolson for Columbia, and by such other entertainers of the day as Yerke's Novelty Five, the All-Star Trio, and the Peerless Quartet. Gershwin was consequently in great demand to write for revues and other works for the musical theater. He wrote songs for *George White's Scandals* for the years 1920-24; one of his all-time hits, "Somebody Loves Me," was introduced in the last of these. 1924 also brought his first collaboration with his brother Ira as lyricist, in the show *Lady Be Good*; their partnership bore such immediate fruits as the title song and "Fascinating Rhythm," and the show—starring Fred and Adele Astaire—ran for 330 performances. *Tip Toes* (1925), *Oh, Kay!* (1926), *Funny Face* (1927), *Rosalie* (1928), *Treasure Girl* (1928), *Show Girl* (1929), *Strike Up the Band* (1930), *Girl Crazy* (1930), *Of Thee I Sing* (1931), *Let 'Em Eat Cake* (1933), and *Pardon My English* (1933) all had songs by the Gershwin brothers, including such classics as "Someone to Watch Over Me," " 'S Wonderful," "Soon," "I Got Rhythm," "But Not for Me," and "Of Thee I Sing." These shows, in their popularity and the sustained excellence of their songs, may be said to be the 1920s equivalent of the Princess Theatre shows (with their Kern/Wodehouse songs) of a decade earlier.

Caricature of Ira and George Gershwin (c) Al Hirschfeld. Drawing reproduced by special arrangement with Hirschfeld exclusive reproduction, The Margo Feiden Galleries Ltd., New York.

Like Berlin and Kern, Gershwin turned to writing for Hollywood movies in the 1930s. The film *Delicious* (1931) was the first to feature new songs by him; *A Damsel in Distress* (1937) introduced "A Foggy Day," *Shall We Dance?* included "They Can't Take That Away from Me" among its new songs, and *The Goldwyn Follies*, released in 1938 after his death, brought "Love Walked In."

Thus far, Gershwin's story reads like that of many other songwriters of the Tin Pan Alley era, distinguished only by the magnitude of his success and the quality of his songs. But two things set him apart from his peers: his involvement with classical music and with jazz.

His training and musical activity mixed popular and classical idioms from early in his life. He developed a serious interest in music after hearing a classmate at Public School 25, Maxie Rosenzweig, play Dvořák's *Humoresque* on the violin at a school assembly. His piano teacher, Charles Hambitzer, insisted on a sound classical training and helped him build a reliable technique while exposing him to the music of Bach, Beethoven, Liszt, Chopin, and the moderns of the day, Debussy and Ravel. Throughout his career, even during the periods of his greatest success as a writer of popular songs, he insisted that there need not be an irreconcilable gap between popular and serious music, and attempted to write music that would reach listeners of both persuasions. *Blue Monday Blues,* which he thought of as a one-act opera, was written for *George White's Scandals of 1922.* He accompanied the soprano Eva Gauthier for a recital in Aeolian Hall on November 1, 1923, on which she programmed songs by Byrd, Purcell, and Bellini, others by the contemporary composers Hindemith, Schoenberg, and Milhaud, and still others by Berlin, Kern, and Gershwin himself. His first large instrumental work, *Rhapsody in Blue,* written for "jazz" band and piano and orchestrated by Ferde Grofé, was premiered at Aeolian Hall on February 12, 1924, by Paul Whiteman's orchestra, with Gershwin as piano soloist. His *Concerto in F,* an even more ambitious work, was first done on December 3, 1925, at Carnegie Hall, by the New York Symphony Orchestra conducted by Walter Damrosch. He performed a set of piano preludes on a program given with the contralto Marguerite d'Alvarez in 1926; three of these were published and have been played often by concert pianists. A symphonic work, *An American in Paris,* was premiered on December 13, 1928, again by Damrosch; his *Second Rhapsody,* for piano and orchestra, was first done on January 29, 1932, by the Boston Symphony under Serge Koussevitzky. His most extended work, the full-length opera *Porgy and Bess*—based on a novel by Du Bose Heyward—was introduced at the Alvin Theater in New York on October 10, 1935.

The relevance of these pieces to the [popular song in America] is that Gershwin, through his involvement with classical music, brought more harmonic innovation and sophistication to his songs than any of his contemporary songwriters, even including Jerome Kern, and his harmonic experimentation helped expand the style of some of his peers, who listened to what he was doing and learned from it.

Equally distinctive in his career was his affinity for the music of blacks. Almost alone of the Tin Pan Alley songwriters, he sought out black musicians, befriended them, listened to their music, played with them. He knew James Reese Europe (1881-1919), who had organized the first bands specializing in syncopated dance music in New York in 1905 and had been an important figure in the early days of the dance craze that brought the fox trot and similar dances to prominence; he was a frequent visitor to "Black Bohemia," the center of fashionable black life in New York, on the West Side of Manhattan; he knew the black ragtime pianists James P. Johnson and Luckey Roberts. He was particularly close to Will Vodery (1885-1951), musical supervisor of Florenz Ziegfeld's productions; it was Vodery who orchestrated Gershwin's *Blue Monday,* his first attempt at a "negro" opera. Carl van Vechten recalled that he and Gershwin went together to parties, concerts, and other events in Harlem in the early 1920s. [In their *The Gershwin Years,* Robert Kimball and Alfred Simon comment]:

> George Gershwin was certainly one of the earliest to seek out black music purely from personal interest. He soaked himself in it, and this early enthusiasm would contribute mightily to that special fusion of European and Negro elements that is the Gershwin style.

Du Bose Heyward, author of the novel *Porgy* on which Gershwin's *Porgy and Bess* was based, recounted an incident occuring when Gershwin came South to discuss the libretto with him and to assimilate some of the flavor of that part of America:

> Under the baking suns of July and August we established ourselves on Folly Island, a small barrier island ten miles from Charleston. James Island with its large population of primitive Gullah Negroes lay adjacent, and furnished us with a laboratory in which to test our theories, as well as an inexhaustible source of folk material. But the most interesting discovery to me, as we sat listening to their spirituals, or watched a group shuffling before a cabin or country store, was that to George it was more like a homecoming than an exploration. . . . The Gullah Negro prides himself on what he calls "shouting." This is a complicated rhythmic pattern beaten out by feet and hands as an accomplishment to the spirituals and is indubitably an African survival. I shall never forget the night when, at a Negro meeting on a remote sea-island, George started "shouting" with them. And eventually to their huge delight stole the show from their champion "shouter." I think he is the only white man in America who could have done it.

It is no easy matter to pinpoint the precise stylistic details in Gershwin's songs that reflect his interest in, and involvement with, the music of black Americans. The matter is made more difficult by the fact that the music accepted by jazz historians today as "true" jazz was almost unknown in New York in the 1910s and '20s. Gershwin had little or no opportunity to hear country blues, or the urban blues developing in Chicago and other cities of the Midwest. New York heard little or no authentic New Orleans jazz in those days, and the territory bands of Kansas City and other such cities remained largely unknown in the

East. The term *jazz,* as used by such writers and critics as Gilbert Seldes, John Alden Carpenter, and Alexander Woollcott, referred to the ragtime songs of Irving Berlin and other New York composers, and to the syncopated dance music played by such white bands as those of Paul Whiteman, Isham Jones, and Ben Selvin. Thus in recent years, the research and attitudes of jazz historians have led to such judgments as:

> The *Rhapsody in Blue,* however, is not jazz, not even jazz dolled up. . . . Although he indicated that the *Rhapsody* was scored for "jazz band and piano," even the most cursory examination of the *Rhapsody* reveals it to be a work of symphonic music that owes far more to the influence of Tchaikovsky and Liszt . . . than of Buddy Bolden or King Oliver.

Admitting that this is true—and the same remarks would apply equally to Gershwin's other instrumental works, his operas, and even his songs—there still remains the fact that Gershwin knew and assimilated the music of various black musicians, and that his own music has had an appeal, over the years, to black musicians (singers and jazz instrumentalists alike)—an appeal not shared by the songs of other Tin Pan Alley composers. Certainly some specific details can be isolated; the syncopated rhythms in many of his songs go far beyond the rather elementary, Western European–bound rhythms of the songs of Berlin and Kern, and he made more frequent and telling use of "blue" notes than did most of his white contemporaries.

But the heart of the matter seems to be a point that cannot be well illustrated by the usual techniques of the music historian. There was something in the music of black Americans that struck a responsive chord somewhere deep in Gershwin, something about their music that he grasped in an instinctive way. In turn, this same indefinable quality found its way into many of his songs, to which black Americans responded in a similarly instinctive way.

Scholars and historians can point to evidence supporting this contention: almost any listing of repertories of black jazz musicians in the 1920's, '30s, and even '40s will include songs by Gershwin, and black singers have favored his songs ever since they were written. One can even suggest reasons for this affinity: both Jews and blacks have a long and sorry history as oppressed minorities (but why did blacks not respond to the songs of other Jewish songwriters such as Berlin and Kern? It is even possible to come full circle and suggest that the increased harmonic sophistication of jazz in the 1920s and '30s owed some small debt the the new chord changes black musicians learned from playing Gershwin tunes.) (pp. 345-52)

Cole Porter (1892-1964) . . . wrote songs that consistently matched those of Berlin, Kern, and Gershwin, with whom he is ranked by every writer concerned with this era. His career was exceptional for the era: he was born in Peru, Indiana (rather than New York); his musical training came at Yale and Harvard, and at the Schola Cantorum in Paris (rather than as an apprentice on Tin Pan Alley); he lived in Europe for several extended periods and was independently wealthy; success as a songwriter came late for him, not until he was in his middle thirties.

Writing mostly for the musical stage and the movies, he eventually produced songs that ranked, in quantity and quality, with those of any songwriter of the age, including the top hits "What Is This Thing Called Love?" (1930), "Night and Day" (1932), "Begin the Beguine" (1935), "Just One of Those Things" (1935), "I've Got You Under My Skin" (1936), "In the Still of the Night" (1937), "At Long Last Love" (1938), "You'd Be So Nice to Come Home To" (1943), "Don't Fence Me In" (1944), "Wunderbar" (1949), and "True Love" (1956), to mention only the most obvious. His lyrics—his own—are the equal of any of the era in cleverness, sophistication, and range of subject matter. Perhaps because of his unconventional background and training, and his independence of mind and spirit, many of his songs extend and even break the usual formal patterns of Tin Pan Alley, and his harmonic vocabulary was as rich and complex as that of Kern or Gershwin.

Richard Rodgers (1902-), in collaboration with a string of the outstanding lyricists of the day—Lorenz Hart, Oscar Hammerstein II, Stephen Sondheim—produced a number of the most successful musical comedies of the second quarter of this century, including the landmarks *A Connecticut Yankee* (1927), *On Your Toes* (1936), *Babes in Arms* (1937), *The Boys from Syracuse* (1938), *Oklahoma!* (1943), *Carousel* (1945), *South Pacific* (1949), and *The King and I* (1951). These works are the core of the Ameri-

can musical stage for this period. *Oklahoma!* became the most successful work of its sort—2, 212 performances after its opening on March 31, 1943, followed by a fifty-one-week tour to all parts of America; a road company took the show to an estimated 10,000,000 people in the course of a ten-year tour; its London run of three and one-half years was the second longest in the history of the English stage; the show grossed at least forty million dollars. *South Pacific* was scarcely less successful, with its opening run in New York of 1,925 performances, and comparable success on the road and as a movie. *Carousel* ran for a comparatively modest 890 performances, but was acclaimed as one of the most important, innovative stage works of the century, serious in theme, bridging the gap between musical comedy and opera.

The magnitude of Rodger's talent as a songwriter is apparent from the briefest listing of only the most sensationally successful of his songs, from his first big hit, "The Blue Room" (1926), through "My Heart Stood Still" (1927), "With a Song in My Heart" (1929), "Blue Moon" (1934), to "It's Easy to Remember" (1935). His popularity is easier to chart once "Your Hit Parade" came on the air: the No. 1 song on the very first broadcast, on the night of April 20, 1935, was his "Soon," from the movie *Mississippi;* later songs that were top favorites and featured on the show for many weeks were "This Can't Be Love" (1938), "People Will Say We're in Love" (1943, from *Oklahoma!,* broadcast for thirty consecutive weeks, a recorded second only to "White Christmas"), "Oh What a Beautiful Morning" (1943), "If I Loved You" (1945), "It Might As Well Be Spring" (1945, from the movie *State Fair*), "Some Enchanted Evening" (1949), "Bali Ha'i" (1949), and "No Other Love" (1953). *Variety's* list of the Golden 100 songs of Tin Pan Alley contains nine by Rodgers, Alec Wilder, in his extended study of songs of this era, finds "an extraordinary incidence of inventiveness in practically all of Rodgers's songs," and concludes that "of all the writers whose songs are considered and examined in this book, those of Rodgers show the highest degree of consistent excellence, inventiveness, and sophistication." He is, by any method of judgment, one of the two or three most talented and successful songwriters of his age, and is given less attention in the present book than several other composers only because his songs broke no new ground—but are superb examples of a song style established by several of his older contemporaries.

The seven songs by Harold Arlen on *Variety's* Golden 100 list entitle him to rank behind Berlin and Rodgers only. Born in Buffalo in 1905, Arlen gravitated toward black musicians and their music, as had Gershwin. In the early 1930s, he wrote the music for shows at the Cotton Club; many of his songs draw on the expressive content of the blues, if not on their structure. "Stormy Weather" (1933) was written for Cab Calloway and became a vehicle for such black singers as Ethel Waters and Lena Horne; "Blues in the Night" (1941) was featured in a movie of the same name, with a largely black cast; Pearl Bailey's first important stage role came in the Broadway musical *St. Louis Woman* (1944), with music by Arlen.

Cole Porter.

He was equally gifted in other kinds of songs, as well. His

first film song, "It's Only a Paper Moon" (1933), has been one of those rarities that retained its popularity into the 1970s. "Over the Rainbow," sung by Judy Garland in the original *Wizard of Oz* (1939), won an Academy Award as the best film song of the year and became one of the most enduring songs in the entire history of "Your Hit Parade." His success continued into the 1940s, with "That Old Black Magic" (1942), "Ac-cent-tchu-ate the Positive" (1944), and "Come Rain or Come Shine" (1946), to name but a few. He was surely the most talented and versatile songwriter in the third generation of Tin Pan Alley composers, those born several decades after Berlin and Kern.

The quality of invention scarcely drops off as one continues down the list of other songwriters of this period and their best songs: Harry Warren, matched only by Irving Berlin in the variety of types of songs and the high standard of professionalism he brought to them ("Shuffle Off to Buffalo," 1932; "Lullaby of Broadway," 1935; "Chattanooga Choo Choo," 1941; "You'll Never Know," 1943; "On the Atchison, Topeka & Santa Fe," 1945); Vincent Youmans ("Tea for Two," 1924; "Without a Song," 1929; "Orchids in the Moonlight," 1933); Jimmy McHugh ("I Can't Give You Anything But Love," 1928; "On the Sunny Side of the Street," 1930); Walter Donaldson ("My Blue Heaven," 1927; "Carolina in the Morning," 1922); Hoagy Carmichael ("Stardust," 1929; "Two Sleepy People," 1938; "Ole Buttermilk Sky," 1946); Arthur Schwartz ("Something to Remember You By," 1930; "Dancing in the Dark," 1931; "You and the Night and the Music," 1934; "They're Either Too Young or Too Old," 1943); and Duke Ellington ("Mood Indigo," 1931; "Don't Get Around Much Anymore," 1942).

This is an imposing list, and one that could be expanded further with little or no drop in quality or popular success. (pp. 352-57)

The era of Tin Pan Alley is the only one for which a detailed study of the musical style of its songs has been written: *American Popular Song. The Great Innovators, 1900-1950,* by Alec Wilder, a successful songwriter. The thesis of the book is stated in the first pages:

> Stephen Foster created the first truly native songs. . . . With his death something mysterious happened. The peculiarly native quality that he had brought to American popular song, a quality borrowed from Negro music, disappeared quite as suddenly as it had arrived. And it did not return until the 1880's. . . .
>
> Not until the Negro musicians and song writers were able, late in the century, to perform directly for the white community [did] the message slowly [come] through to white America that the Negro's musical talent was unique, and that something musically remarkable was emerging from the ghetto. . . .
>
> During the thirty-year period between 1885 and World War I, American popular music underwent many fundamental changes. Finally, when these changes—rhythmic, harmonic, melodic— were consolidated, a unique kind of song emerged: American song.

After saying that he considers the period with which he is dealing an age of "professional songwriters," and the period that followed (the era of rock 'n' roll and rock) to be a "flamboyant age in which it is unsurprising to read grotesquely extravagant tributes to the creations of untutored amateurs," Wilder proceeds to examine and discuss hundreds of Tin Pan Alley songs, concentrating chiefly on harmonic and rhythmic details, finding "more sophistication, more complex melody writing , much more involved harmonic patterns, shifting song form, greater elegance, and infinitely superior theater song writing"; but he concludes with a final tribute to "the early anonymous Negroes who, in spite of their dreadful, ignominious plight, had managed to create the beginning of an *entirely new music*" (italics mine).

His contention that uniquely American popular song came about only with the second generation of Tin Pan Alley composers is not new: the American composer John Alden Carpenter, for instance, observed in the 1920s, "I am strongly inclined to believe that the musical historians of the year 2000 will find the birthday of American music and that of Irving Berlin to have been the same." But the history of any kind of music can appear quite different when observed from the perspective of several decades, rather than from the present and the immediate past. . . . I question the role of "negro" music in the formation of the song styles of Stephen Foster and of the first generation of Tin Pan Alley writers. Similarly, I believe that only several quite superficial aspects of "negro" music were skimmed off by songwriters of the 1910s, '20s, and '30s, to add a touch of exotic seasoning to their products—and that emphasis on these details serves to detract attention from the more important fact that the chief stylistic features of the songs of the composers discussed in this [essay] . . . came from an earlier generation of American songwriters and from the music of Central and Eastern Europe. It does the history of music by black musicians no lasting good to insist on interpretations that are historically unsound, and it may also obscure the profound effect that black music had on American song in the mid-1950s and afterward.

In considering these points, a convenient place to start is with the shape of Tin Pan Alley songs. With almost no exceptions, they are in verse-chorus form, the verse sketching a dramatic situation or an emotional vignette,

> Time and again I've longed for adventure,
> Something to make my heart beat the faster.
> What did I long for? I never really knew.
>
> Finding your love I've found my adventure,
> Touching your hand, my heart beats the faster,
> All that I want in all of this world is you.

and the chorus following as a "set" piece, a more lyric section, elaborating on the situation set out by the verse:

> You are the promised kiss of springtime
> That makes the lonely winter seem long.
> You are the breathless hush of evening
> That trembles on the brink of a lovely song.
> You are the angel glow that lights a star,
> The dearest things I know are what you are.
> Some day my happy arms will hold you,

> And some day I'll know that moment divine,
> When all the things you are, are mine.
>   —"All the Things You Are" (1939), by Jerome Kern and Oscar Hammerstein II

Anyone who knows this song will be familiar with the chorus and will recognize it and perhaps even be able to whistle or sing it; few people will know, or even recognize, the verse. [The] . . . verse-chorus form of Tin Pan Alley songs functions in much the same way as the recitative-aria patterns in opera.

A musician in the early 1920s observed:

> Previous to 1897 every song had to have six or seven verses and each verse had eight or ten lines. Now there are two verses of a scant four lines each, and even at that, the second verse counts scarcely at all. The whole story must be told in the very first verse and chorus and usually there is very little to it anyway, the music being what matters. [Paul Whiteman and Mary Margaret McBride, *Jazz*]

In fact, a single verse became standard in the 1920s, and even this was often omitted in performance away from the stage, perhaps because the dramatic setting of a song was unimportant when it was heard over the radio or from a phonograph recording. And in less than a decade, composers themselves began treating the verse as an optional part of a song: though most songs of the '30s and '40s continued to be written in verse-chorus form, one need look no further than at the most popular songs (by Jerome Kern and Otto Harbach) in *Roberta* (1933)—"Smoke Gets in Your Eyes" and "Yesterdays"—for examples of verseless songs.

To summarize, Tin Pan Alley's verse (optional)–chorus songs represent a final step in a formal evolution that had taken place over a time span of more than a century:

> strophic solo songs, with many verses, sometimes with a refrain line or two at the end of each verse: late eighteenth and early nineteenth centuries;

> strophic solo songs, with many verses, and a refrain (sometimes sung by a chorus) at the end of each verse; the verse longer than the chorus, and containing the chief melodic material: early and mid-nineteenth century, minstrel songs, songs of the singing families, and the songs of Stephen Foster and his contemporaries;

> strophic solo songs, with several verses, and with quartet or choral refrain; verse and chorus of approximately equal length, either or both with chief melodic material: post-Civil War songs;

> strophic solo songs, with two or three verses, with a chorus after each verse sung by the solo singer; verse and chorus of approximately the same length, with the chief melody in the chorus: late nineteenth and early twentieth centuries, first generation of Tin Pan Alley songwriters;

> verse-chorus songs, one or two verses, most important melodic material always in the chorus;

the verse optional: 1920-55, second and third generations of Tin Pan Alley writers.

Formally, then, the songs of this era fall squarely into the continuing and evolving patterns of American popular song—and not, it might be added, into the patterns of Afro-American music, which most characteristically is built over harmonic patterns repeated an indeterminate number of times, as in the blues and the emerging jazz style.

The chorus of Tin Pan Alley songs is almost always cast in four sections of equal length. . . . [The] chorus is almost always 32 measures in length, the only exceptions coming from a doubling of measures in songs of lively tempos (to 64 measures) or from extensions of the last phrase. The four sections are most often in AABA or ABAC patterns, with occasional variants such as AABC and ABCA.

Thus the skill and genius of Tin Pan Alley composers (and lyricists) was revealed by what could be done within a tightly restricted formal structure, rather than by flights of fancy soaring to new and complex designs. One is reminded of similar restrictions embraced by writers of sonnets, by the Japanese poets of *haiku* verse, and by the great American bluesmen. (pp. 357-61)

The 1920s and '30s were an era of specialization in popular song. There were composers, lyricists, performers, and publishers—and it was rare for a single individual to be involved in more than one of these areas. Irving Berlin was the great exception, a throwback to the multitalented men of the first generation of Tin Pan Alley: he wrote his own lyrics, was a successful singer in the 1910s, and formed his own publishing house. Cole Porter wrote his own lyrics, also. Otherwise, the songwriters of the time depended on other people to furnish them with lyrics, sing their songs once they were written, and publish them.

It was the best era yet for lyricists. Only a generation earlier, the going price for a lyric had been five dollars, with no further claim on a song's earnings. But as Tin Pan Alley moved into a period of unprecedented prosperity, there was greater appreciation of the importance of a good lyric to the success of a song; and with the formation of ASCAP, lyricists were regarded as virtual equals of composers, sharing both publishers' royalties and the annual ASCAP fund accumulating from licensing fees and performance rights.

They came from the same milieu as the songwriters with whom they worked. The best and most successful of them, including Ira Gershwin, Oscar Hammerstein II, Lorenz Hart, E. Y. Harburg, Alan Jay Lerner, Billy Rose, Irving Caesar, Howard Dietz, and Dorothy Fields, were products of New York City; most came from families already involved in entertainment, or served early apprenticeships with Tin Pan Alley firms or on Broadway. Only Johnny Mercer, born in Savannah, Georgia, was an outsider, geographically.

The lyrics they produced dealt, at first, with a wide range of situations and emotions. No lyricists in the entire history of popular song in America produced texts of such variety—comic, sentimental, romantic, dramatic, ethnic, satirical—as did Irving Berlin in the first decade of his career. America's entry into World War I brought a rash of war songs, some of them rivaling the immediacy and intensity of the best songs of the Civil War: "Over There" (George M. Cohan, 1917), "The Rose of No Man's Land" (Joseph A. Brennan and Jack Caddingan, 1918), "Oh! How I Hate to Get Up in the Morning" (Irving Berlin, 1918), "Till We Meet Again" (Richard A. Whiting and Raymond B. Egan, 1918), and "Hello, Central! Give Me No Man's Land" (Jean Schwartz, Sam M. Lewis, and Joe Young) were among the most popular.

But somehow, as America moved into the 1920s and then the '30s, the expressive range of popular song narrowed. Texts began dealing almost exclusively with personal emotions, almost never with events outside of the person. An increasingly large percentage of the most popular songs was concerned with one aspect or another of romantic love. A glance at the titles on any representative list of the most popular songs of the period between 1920 and 1945, such as *Variety's* Golden 100 Tin Pan Alley songs, is enough to verify this generalization. Observers of the time were quite aware of this shift:

> The sentimental ballads before 1920 were often about babies, separation, death. The theme of the sentimental song two generations later was the impotence of the male. . . . They celebrated sadly the failure of the man to keep his woman.

And [Richard Rodgers] suggested that the preoccupation with personal love was a mirror of the times:

> The Twenties sang of carefree nights and the frenetic days that rushed headlong into the nightmare and fantasy of the Thirties. Both had their reality, both voiced it. This was a score of years in which love grew from an idle and pleasant pastime into a vital avocation—romance.

One searches almost in vain for songs touching in any way on the great social and political issues of those years—the continuing desperate plight of the black American in white America; the struggle of working class citizens to combat by unionization and strikes their exploitation by management; the worsening situation of ethnic minorities in Central and Eastern Europe and the inexorable rise to power of totalitarian regimes in many of these countries. A handful, a tiny handful, of popular songs deal with the Great Depression; "Brother, Can You Spare a Dime?" (Jay Gorney and E. Y. Harburg, 1932) stands virtually alone in its serious treatment of poverty. And no war in which America had been involved before produced so few songs as did World War II; such songs as "Praise the Lord and Pass the Ammunition" (Frank Loesser, 1942), "I Left My Heart at the Stage Door Canteen" (Irving Berlin, 1942), "We Did It Before and We Can Do It Again" (Cliff Friend and Charles Tobias, 1941), and "Comin' in on a Wing and a Prayer" (Jimmy McHugh and Harold Adamson, 1943) made up a tiny percentage of the songs written during the war years.

The perspective of history is helpful here, to remind us that other eras of song had similarly been concerned with subjective matters and personal feelings. Thomas Moore's *Irish Melodies* leap to mind as an earlier example of songs dealing with the inner workings of man, rather than with external events. And Tin Pan Alley's pose was a quite deliberate one, tied directly to the most powerful elements of the New York musical stage and the Hollywood sound film, which held that these media were best used to entertain people, to take their minds away from personal and national problems—not to remind them of such things.

The urbanization of American popular song, set in motion by events of the last decades of the nineteenth century, was effectively completed in the 1910s and '20s. Even more than had been the case during the formative years of Tin Pan Alley, the field was dominated by composers and lyricists born and trained in New York, writing songs for publishers who not only had their offices in New York, but were themselves products of the city. The style of the music and of the lyrics had become a New York style, and general attitudes as to what a song should be and where it should fit into American culture were also shaped by the climate and taste of New York. There was little effective cultural input from the rest of America into New York in these days, and to the extent that Tin Pan Alley songs reflected American culture in a broader sense, they did so because the rest of the country was willing to accept a uniquely urban, New York product, not because New York was absorbing elements of American culture from west of the Hudson River or south of Atlantic City. Hollywood was not a real exception to this, since it was musically a West Coast extension of New York. The songs of Kern, Gershwin, Porter, and their contemporaries were urban, sophisticated, and stylish, and they were intended for people who could be described by one or more of these adjectives—or aspired to be.

The result of all this was a product accepted all over America, true enough, but accepted by a more narrow range of Americans than had been the case in some earlier periods of popular song. The genre had been limited, before the advent of the phonograph record, radio, and the sound movie, to persons who were musically literate, who could purchase a piece of sheet music and either play or sing it in their homes. But ties to oral traditional music had resulted in dissemination even among people who did not read music. Moore's *Irish Melodies* and other Irish and Scottish songs of the early nineteenth century became known to nonliterate Americans whose own music was close enough in style for them to learn such new songs by ear. Songs from minstrel shows and the songs of Stephen Foster were disseminated both through sheet music and by ear; a Northern-born lady living in the South wrote:

> Although first published in the North, you there know nothing of the power and pathos given them [Negro melodies] here. The whites first learn them—the negroes catch the air and the words from once hearing, after which woods and fields resound with their strains—the whites catch the expression from these sable minstrels—thus Negro Melodies have an effect here not dreamed of at the North. [*Dwight's Journal of Music,* February 26, 1853.]

Ned Harrigan could still write, in the 1880s, of popular song helping to "lighten the toil of the working people" and to "admit sunshine into many a darkened life", and as late as the turn of the century, Theodore Dreiser was witness to the fact that popular songs reached "mansion and hovel . . . the blazing furnace of a steel mill . . . the open window of a farmland cottage." The word *populist* leaps to mind as an appropriate one for song throughout the nineteenth century. But the audience changed considerably during the first quarter of the twentieth century:

> *Progress of a popular song* (from fall in New York to summer throughout the country). Harlem cabarets, other cabarets, Reisenfeld's classical jazz, the Rascoe's private orchestra, the hand organs, the phonographs, the radio, the Webster Hall balls, other balls (college proms), men going home late at night whistling it on the street, picked out on Greenwich Village ukeleles, sung in late motor rides by boys and girls, in restaurants—hotel restaurants, Paul Whiteman and Lopez, vaudeville, played Sundays by girls at pianos from sheet music with small photographs on the cover, of both the composer and the person who first sang it—first sung in a popular musical comedy (introduced several times—at the end of the second act pathetically—and played as the audience are leaving the theater)—pervading the country through the movie pianists, danced to in private houses to the music of a phonograph—the Elks fair—thrown on a screen between the acts at the National Winter Garden Burlesque and sung by the male audience—Remey's Dancing Academy (decayed fairies).

It seems fair to generalize that Tin Pan Alley songs were for white, urban, literate, middle- and upper-class Americans. They remained practically unknown to large segments of American society, including most blacks (excepting musicians and a handful of urban blacks aspiring to a life-style approaching that of whites), and the millions of poor, white, rural Americans of English, Irish, and Scottish stock clustered in the South and scattered across the lower Midwest. These two groups had their own distinctive types of music, oral-tradition music that was given a tremendous boost in the 1920s and '30s by the new technology that brought commercial radio and wide dissemination of the phonograph record. (pp. 376-79)

> Charles Hamm, " 'It's Only a Paper Moon';
> or, The Golden Years of Tin Pan Alley," in his
> Yesterdays: Popular Song in America, *W. W.*
> *Norton & Company, 1979, pp. 326-90.*

David Ewen

[*In the following excerpt, Ewen focuses on the careers of George and Ira Gershwin.*]

The partnership of George and Ira Gershwin was a harmonious one, each being in full sympathy with and full understanding of the other's idiosyncrasies, each harboring a healthy admiration and affection for the other, each proving at once a stimulant and an inspiration to the other. Yet in behavior patterns, temperament, outlook, and personality they were worlds apart, as this writer had occasion to note in his biography of George Gershwin: "Where George was gregarious, a man who flourished at parties and other social affairs, and who thrived on move-

ment, activity, and work, Ira was reticent, shy, mild-mannered, somewhat slow moving. Where women were concerned George was the man of the world whereas Ira always had a disarming naïveté. Ira preferred the sedentary life. He was the kind for whom there's no regrettin' when he's settin' biding his time. It required genuine effort for him to go anywhere or do anything. There were periods . . . when he did not descend from his apartment into the street for days at a time. George had sensitive nerves, and he was given to emotional upheavals and hyperthyroid reactions. Ira was usually even-tempered, placid, soft spoken. George was the idealist, his head in the clouds. Ira was coldly logical and realistic, his feet planted solidly on the ground. George felt he had an artistic mission. Ira regarded himself only as a respectable workman, competent and methodical. George loved work, could work anywhere and anytime, frequently after coming home from a night-long party. To Ira, work was work—certainly less desirable than sprawling on a couch and smoking a series of Montecristo cigars, or spending the day at the races, or the evening at poker, or the late and sleepless hours of the night with books and magazines. He once said, 'I have a whole day's work ahead of me. I'm going to change the ribbon on my typewriter.' "

For thirteen years Ira wrote the lyrics for George's music. The influence of words on music was inestimable. The melody usually came before the lyric. Nevertheless, Ira's reservoir of fresh, new ideas for songs, for unusual titles, for intriguing colloquialisms and apt application of everyday phrases and speech, for slow and dry and subtle humor, for exciting rhythmic and rhyming patterns, for verbal euphony—all of this often sparked and inflamed George's creativity. In addition, Ira had a far-sighted, dynamic concept of what the musical theatre should be and could become; on the one or two occasions when he was allowed to try realizing this concept, he became a powerful factor in leading George toward new directions in stage music.

Lady, Be Good! starring Fred and Adele Astaire, inaugurated a skein of successes for the Gershwin brothers. Songs like the title number and "Fascinating Rhythm" are distinguished by rhythmic virtuosity: in the intriguing repeated triplets in cut time in the title song and the exciting changing meters of "Fascinating Rhythm." These—and "The Half of It, Dearie, Blues" with its unusual harmonies and the ballad "So Am I" with its haunting lyricism—were the highlights of the score, but they would have been thrown into a secondary position if still another song had been allowed to remain in the show. That song, "The Man I Love," had been written for the opening scene. But the producer felt it slowed up the action and during out-of-town tryouts it was dropped. It was never again destined to turn up in a stage production, but it did get heard extensively in London, Paris, and New York to become one of Gershwin's biggest hits since "Swanee." It was also one of his most original creations, in the haunting way in which a descending chromatic scale was used as a contrapuntal background to a six-note recurring blues progression.

As for Ira Gershwin's lyrics, they had already begun to

prove themselves to be in a class all their own, with few equals or rivals in 1924. As this writer commented in his Gershwin biography: "A line like 'I must win some winsome miss' demonstrates the easy way he now had with a well-turned, well-sounding phrase. A couplet like 'this is tulip weather, so let's put two and two together' pointed to a natural and charming simplicity. The chorus for 'Fascinating Rhythm' showed a verbal virtuosity in following the lead of the music in its intricate rhythmic movements."

With two exceptions, the Gershwin musicals following *Lady, Be Good!* did little to change either the character or the artistic goal of the musical theatre. They adhered to the accepted norm by conceiving the text as a convenient frame for good routines, star performances, skillful stage business. Productions were slick and the overall tone was frequently sophisticated, but the plot invariably remained both stilted and contrived, while characterization was most of the time nonexistent.

Some musicals proved significant because of individual performers. Fred and Adele Astaire starred not only in *Lady, Be Good!* but also in *Funny Face* in 1927. *Oh, Kay!* in 1926, was Gertrude Lawrence's first appearance in an American musical comedy. Secondary in importance to Miss Lawrence's all-important debut was the comedy of Victor Moore cast as a bootlegger disguised as butler in one of his inimitable Casper Milquetoast characterizations. This little sad-faced man with the broken high-pitched voice achieved what is the high-water mark in his

Betty Compton, Adele Astaire, Gertrude McDonald, and Fred Astaire in George and Ira Gershwin's Funny Face.

long and rich career as stage comedian with his never-to-be-forgotten delineation of Throttlebottom, the much-neglected vice-president in *Of Thee I Sing* in 1931.

And then, of course, there was Ethel Merman, whose stage debut in *Girl Crazy* in 1930 brought to musical comedy its reigning queen. As Kate Fothergrill, in a dude ranch in Custerville, Arizona, she injected the red blood of a lusty performance. She threw her big, brassy voice across the footlights in "I Got Rhythm," "Sam and Delilah," and "Boy! What Love Has Done to Me!" and brought audience and critics figuratively to their feet. They stayed on their feet for Miss Merman for the next quarter of a century.

Some of the Gershwin shows, even though failures, were important because they yielded song jewels. Out of *Tip-Toes* in 1925 came "Sweet and Lowdown" and "That Certain Feeling," each remarkable for its subtle accentuations and rhythmic patterns; out of the same show also came "Looking for a Boy," in which the distinguished English musicologist, Francis Toye, detected a Brahmsian personality. "How Long Has This Been Going On?" came out of *Rosalie* in 1929. "Liza," written in 1928 for *Show Girl*, was a song that was such a favorite with Gershwin himself that he used to improvise all kinds of variations to it at informal parties. "Liza" had a thoroughly spontaneous presentation when *Show Girl* opened at the Ziegfeld Theatre. Al Jolson's wife, Ruby Keeler, was the star of the show. On opening night, Jolson rose from his place in the audience to sing "Liza" to Ruby Keeler as she danced to its tantalizing rhythm on the stage.

"The Lorelei" was heard in one of the greatest failures the Gershwins sustained on Broadway, *Pardon My English* in 1933. Despite the distinction of the melody, this song is particularly notable in its lyrics for the use of the skat phrase "hey ho-de-ho" which, a year later or so, would become even more popular in the song "It Ain't Necessarily So" in *Porgy and Bess*.

Two Gershwin musicals suggested, and often realized, new horizons for the American musical theatre. *Strike Up the Band* (text by George S. Kaufman and Morrie Ryskind) was a bitter satire against war, big business, secret diplomacy, foreign intrigues. Everything else in the production was subservient to an overall theme in which America goes to war against Switzerland over the issue of chocolate tariffs. The hero of the American victory is Horace J. Fletcher, chocolate manufacturer, who in his dreams sees himself as the commander of the American forces. He falls from this high station, however, when the shocking news is spread that he uses only Grade B milk for his confections.

The book was most unusual for the time in sidestepping many of the accepted practices of musical comedy and reducing deadly serious issues to utter absurdity. Laughter was provoked by every element in the production: in the scintillating text and dialogue; in Ira Gershwin's consistently brilliant lyrics; in Gershwin's continually fresh approaches in his music. The title song and "Entrance of the Swiss Army," both of them takeoffs on pompous military music, the chauvinism of "A Typical Self-Made American," the nimble patter in "If I Became the President," all revealed a new deftness, as well as a new acidity, in Gershwin's musical writing. Gershwin also demonstrated a new expansiveness of thought and structure in his extended finales, in which song, choruses, recitatives, and instrumental episodes were woven into a single multicolored fabric.

Of Thee I Sing in 1931—the first musical ever to win the Pulitzer Prize in drama—was even more skillful in directing the keen-edged dart of satire into the bull's eye. The target here was American politics, specifically a presidential campaign, the Senate, the Supreme Court, and other follies in Washington, D.C., during the years of the Depression. Here, even more than in *Strike Up the Band,* music became a significant, at times even an inextricable, partner to the text in the projection of every situation, comment, and aside. Gershwin always had at his fingertips the right musical idiom or material for every suggestion and nuance of the play. The main songs were "Wintergreen for President," which made a mockery of political parades; the principal love song, the title number, which begins like a patriotic hymn but lapses into Tin Pan Alley sentimentality with the word "baby"; and "Love Is Sweeping the Country." Distinguished though each of these is in its own way, the three songs are hardly more important within the overall context than the choral episodes, orchestral interludes, extended vocal sequences, and quasi-operatic recitatives that go to make up Gershwin's most ambitious score for the popular musical stage. No wonder, then, that the critics found *Of Thee I Sing* "a landmark in American satirical musical comedy," in the words of George Jean Nathan; that the Pulitzer Prize committee broke all precedent by singling it out as the best play of the season; that the firm of Alfred A. Knopf also broke new ground by publishing the text in book form, the first time such a thing ever happened to a musical comedy; and that the production enjoyed the longest Broadway run of any Gershwin musical. (pp. 177-80)

Gershwin's last work for the stage was also his greatest: the folk opera *Porgy and Bess,* which the Theatre Guild produced with an all-Negro cast in Boston on September 30, 1935, and in New York on October 10. This run, the only one the opera had while Gershwin was still alive, had been more or less of a failure both at the box office and with the critics. But Gershwin knew with finality that he had here reached new heights, and not for a moment did he doubt that his faith would someday be fully justified. When the opera was given its first run-through, he beamed with joy. "It's even more wonderful than I thought it was," he said with a detachment as if he were speaking of somebody else's masterwork. After the unsuccessful New York run of 124 performances, Gershwin easily summoned facts and figures to prove that his opera had really enjoyed an unprecedented triumph. Here is how he figured it out: If a great opera by a Verdi or Puccini received 6 performances a season at the Metropolitan Opera, then the 124 performances enjoyed by *Porgy and Bess* represented a twenty-year run at one of the world's greatest opera houses. But even he, with all his supreme confidence in his masterwork, could not have anticipated the kind of acclaim that his opera would receive not only in America but in virtually every part of the civilized world; and that

many of the New York critics who had found fault with the opera when they first heard it would reverse themselves completely by hailing it as a masterwork, and the greatest opera by an American.

After *Porgy and Bess,* Gershwin's music was intended exclusively for motion pictures. He had written his first original score for the screen in 1931 for the Fox production *Delicious,* starring Janet Gaynor and Charles Farrell. In 1935 he went to Beverly Hills and set up residence with Ira and Ira's wife, Lee (Leonore), on North Roxbury Drive to work on *A Damsel in Distress,* an RKO production for Fred Astaire and Joan Fontaine. George lived to write only two more screen scores: *Shall We Dance,* with Fred Astaire and Ginger Rogers, and *The Goldwyn Follies.* For these films he produced songs with the unmistakable Gershwin fingerprints on them: "A Foggy Day," "Nice Work If You Can Get It," "Let's Call the Whole Thing Off," "They Can't Take That Away from Me," "Love Walked In," and "Love Is Here To Stay." Outstanding songs each, yet none capable of capturing an Academy Award.

George Gershwin died on July 11, 1937, from a tumor of the brain. He had been in excruciating physical pain and had been tormented by melancholia for a number of weeks before the real nature of his malady was properly diagnosed. Until this was done, he was believed to be suffering from a nervous breakdown and was being treated by a psychiatrist.

On July 9 he was rushed to the Cedars of Lebanon Hospital for preliminary and exploratory surgery. Then only was it discovered that he was the victim of a cystic degeneration of a tumor on the right temporal lobe of the brain. The major operation took four hours and proved unsuccessful: the tumor was found on that part of the brain that could not be touched. The prognosis was tragic. If he survived, which was doubtful, he would be disabled, blind, or both for life. Mercifully, George Gershwin died the following morning.

Due largely to his influence, the American popular song acquired a new identity, a new methodology, a new artistic status. As a matter of fact, the popular song had once and for all become liberated from the confining limitations previously imposed upon it by generations of composers on Broadway and in Tin Pan Alley. By virtue of that liberation, other and later writers could continue to endow the American popular song with new dimensions and new importance.

Gershwin may have died leaving many a masterwork unwritten, but not before he had achieved his destiny.

For Ira Gershwin, the death of George meant the loss of a brother, with whom he had been virtually inseparable, and a collaborator. Readjustment to new working habits, to new collaborators, in some ways to a new way of life, would not come easily. But it came. In the ensuing decade or so Ira Gershwin wrote lyrics for Jerome Kern, Harold Arlen, Harry Warren, and Kurt Weill. His lyric writing remained jeweled, as was attested by songs like "The Man That Got Away" and "Long Ago and Far Away" from the motion pictures *A Star Is Born* and *Cover Girl,* or "The

Saga of Jenny" and "My Ship" from the Broadway musical *Lady in the Dark*.

The flow of lyrics from his typewriter was reduced to a trickle by the 1960's, and there were more times than one when the well went altogether dry. Writing has always been a slow, painful process for a man who could accept for himself only the most fastidious craftsmanship and meet the most exacting standards of excellence and originality. And his approach to the discipline and routines of creativity had always been, to say the least, lackadaisical. Nevertheless, in 1959 he had published *Lyrics on Several Occasions* which had taken him several years to prepare, since this anthology of his lyrics was accompanied by at times brittle, at times amusing, and at times penetrating commentaries and verbal asides. (pp. 182-84)

No portrait of Ira can be complete without quoting his recipe for success in the art of lyric writing. It can be found in *Lyrics on Several Occasions* where he says: "Given a fondness for music, a feeling for rhyme, a sense of whimsy and humor, an eye for the balanced sentence, an ear for the current phrase, and the ability to imagine oneself a performer trying to put over a number in progress—given all this, I still would say it takes four or five years collaborating with knowledgeable composers to become a well-rounded lyricist. I could be wrong about the time element—there no doubt have been lyricists who knew their business from the start—but time and experiment and experience help." (p. 187)

> David Ewen, *"Songs of the 1920's and 1930's—1: George and Ira Gershwin,"* in his Great Men of American Popular Song, *revised edition, Prentice-Hall, Inc., 1972, pp. 169-87.*

Richard G. Hubler

[*Hubler is an American educator, biographer, and novelist. In the following excerpt, he delineates Cole Porter's aesthetics and affirms his importance as a songwriter.*]

Cole Porter blazed a path for himself through the jungle of an art that was peculiarly American and comparatively new. By the time he was tracing his infant compositions in Indiana, it was less than thirty years old—and, indeed, was not a recognizable genre at all. By the time it had firmed into its primitive patterns (about 1910), Porter was already launched on what might be called the seedbed of show music in his prep school and college careers. It was just coming into its own after World War I, and Porter was already contributing handsomely—and uniquely—to its final presence on the scene of entertainment.

All this is not to say that Porter was a pioneer or that musical comedy, as it is now known, was much more than a gathering-in of component parts which had existed for centuries. The very reason why Porter may claim to have had such a part in its creation was his love of organization, his high standards, and his adherence to his own brand of humor and high jinks, even though they brought at first nothing but disappointments. [Elsa] Maxwell told about some of the hours devoted to comforting him (while he paid the tab) in Paris:

> We used to spend long hours in all the night spots of Paris, discussing the reasons for his failures, and I remember saying to him:
>
> "The reason is as plain as the nose on my face: You are too good—your standards are too high; the wit and poetry of your lyrics are beyond them (the public) and you refuse to write down to the public. But one day you will haul the public up to your own level and then the world will be yours."

There was more to it than that. Porter's quality of output rarely varied very much; the quality of his lyrics, despite Miss Maxwell's approval, never got much better than trickery, but his tunes were always expert, musically, and creative and inventive in their melodic line. The quantity was always there; some of his college cronies insist he hoarded most of his hits—having written them during his undergraduate years and gradually leaked them out of his trunk to Broadway producers. What caused his original turndown by the public was his refusal to act the part of a Tin Pan Alley songsmith. He recognized the genius of Irving Berlin for the popular touch and often commented wistfully upon it. His rare moments of bitterness were reserved for those whom he felt would force him to become a hack in tune writing. (It should be noted here that Berlin disagreed with Porter about writing a hit every time his fingers touched the keys. Said Berlin: "Out of more than 600 songs I have written, no more than 50 have been hits. I miss eleven times for every time I succeed.")

Beyond this, like all the others in the growing musical comedy field, Porter suffered the pains of actually creating a medium expressly to fit his talents. In this sense, it was not his failure nor that of the public but the success of the isolated tune and the incredible mélanges of nonsense that passed for entertainment. The musical comedy had to come of age—and when it did, Porter stepped directly into his rightful niche.

It is enough to point out here that musical comedy has now become one of the mainstays of the stage and is likely to remain so. It is an entertainment, in a word, intended to give pleasure to the ear, eye, and innards of an audience—while imposing minimal demands upon its mentality. In the words of the critic George Jean Nathan (himself a musical comedy addict) written in 1931,

> The difference is the same difference that attaches to the mood of theatre-going in the instance of a music-show on the one hand and a dramatic play on the other. In the case of the music-show, a volitional predisposition to light pleasure and even gayety, a humor for intellect on the loose, a leaning to confetti criticism, are essential. The music-show is not for pundits in their punditical moments but for pundits, if at all, in such rare moments as they think and argue with laughter . . . (it invites one to watch) with top hat cocked saucily over his mind, with his ear filled with the hint of gay tunes, and with his eyes made merry by the imagined picture of all the relevant and appropriate clowns in the per-

sons of actors, of madly painted canvas, and of appetizing femininity. . . .

The world of musical comedy, like a satellite thrown off from more solid stuff, has ever had this basic relationship to music, comedy, and drama, but the manner and matter of its formation are lighter, more insubstantial, a kind of frozen effervescence. It has always meant moon travel, a drift to cloudcuckooland—in essence, a separation from self. Here it departs from opera, even from light- and folk-opera. Whereas such dramas with music endeavor to identify the audience with their themes and situations, musical comedy endeavors to set it free. It does not ask for a willing suspension of disbelief. It does not care. Its foremost symbol, one might speculate, came as early as 1905 with Eva Tanguay. She was the most uninhibited of her sex both in vaudeville and in the Follies. She was paid $125,000 yearly (an enormous sum in those days) for the most daring acts in show business—improvising Salome without veils, wearing forty-five-pound gowns made of coins, showing her fine legs, and shrieking her trademark song, "I Don't Care." As Miss Tanguay, the only I-Don't-Care Girl, she was paid the compliment of direct imitation and christening by the famous French musical comedy star, Mistinguette (Mees Tanguay).

Miss Tanguay never became a genuine musical comedy star—her assets were more exhibitionism than talent—but she helped set the scene for this American concoction. What resulted was a rough combination of plot and music, of costume and setting, of dialogue and diaphragm control, exercised over and smoothed out by a cooperative joining of musical and dramatic talents, individual in appeal yet fitting into a predetermined scheme of producer and director. What appeared to the spectator was a mass of glorious nonsense in which everything worked out improbably to the best result in the best of possible worlds. The audience left the theatre in a rosy aura, hoaxed into its momentary euphoria by the musical comedy "djinniuses." Any good musical comedy became the equivalent of an expert theatrical con game.

In his own lifetime, Porter witnessed three evolutionary changes in the chameleon styles of musical comedies. The first was *Of Thee I Sing* in 1931; the second, *Oklahoma!* in 1943; and the third, *West Side Story* in 1961. The trend was definitely toward a hard story line and a better book, less entertainment and more message, not so much glitter and glamor as sociological gilt. The old carefree attitude steadily changed toward didactic ditties and meaningful tunes. Entertainment for entertainment's sake was going out.

Porter in his personal style never paid the slightest obeisance to any of these demands. He went his own way, at his own pace—as if he were singing to himself, amusing himself with guests around the piano, not millions around the world. Traveling in Zanzibar in 1935, he had a drink in the patio of a little hotel. He found it crowded with burnoosed ivory dealers from East Africa, squatting about an old phonograph listening to a rendition of "Night and Day." "It was the greatest shock I ever had," he said, "hearing my own stuff in that out-of-the-way spot. I can't say I really liked it." He sometimes turned thumbs down

on an auditioning hopeful who had selected one of his tunes as a rendition, such a performance apparently having pained him as too public a display.

All of this came about largely because Porter never lost the ability to be self-critical. Where others heard the best in what he did, he often detected the weakness. He squirmed while his nimble musical memory scurried about with ideas to patch it up. But he never went back and tinkered with his tunes, once they appeared in public and a show was going well. He preferred to drive ahead into new fields of song.

He realized that the standard which is laboriously and anxiously erected by the composer and librettist is one which depends almost wholly upon the psychological reactions of the audience. In 1883 Oscar Wilde, in writing to Marie Prescott, an American actress who played the leading part in his play *Vera, the Duchess of Padua*, a high-flown poetic bit of nonsense, said

> Art is the mathematical result of the emotional desire for beauty. . . . The canons of each art depend on what they appeal to. Painting appeals to the eye and is founded on the science of optics. Music appeals to the ear and is founded on the science of acoustics. The drama appeals to human nature and must have as its ultimate basis the sciences of psychology and physiology. Now, one of the facts of physiology is the desire of any very intensified emotion to be relieved by some emotion that is opposite. Nature's example is the laughter of hysteria or the tears of joy. . . . The essence of good dialogue is interruption. All good dialogue should give the effect of its being made by the reaction of the personages on one another. It should never seem to be ready-made by the author and interruptions have not only their artistic effect but their physical value. They give the actors time to breathe and get new breath power.

Though Wilde would have indignantly denied he was writing a credo for musical comedy, his words have a good deal of force in the milieu which Porter found congenial. Wilde's definition of "dialogue" is explanatory chiefly of lyrics and their usage; Porter's feeling about his "lyrics" indicates that he thought of them really as musical dialogue.

In both cases, the authors were appealing to the only final judge of their art. The essence of musical comedy is what the audience is prepared to absorb, not what it is ready to accept. What pleases the eye and ear and makes for conscious enjoyment without cultural clutter (yet with some such overtones) is enough—and it is absolute. The function of a musical comedy is, basically, the art of producing happiness. It must be done in the fullness and generosity of the production, in the talent of the performers, and, most of all, in the astonishingly complex interaction of emotions within the audience itself. The post-Victorian playboys who used to buy out the whole of a performance and sit alone to enjoy it were as wretched as the actors on the stage. The audience is an indispensable part of the musical comedy; the form cannot live alone, even if it is subsidized by other sources until eternity.

Porter understood this within the framework of his own contribution. He knew its value very well; he once remarked to a friend while listening to the audience reaction to *Kiss Me, Kate:* "It's really terribly good, isn't it?" So it was. Porter was extremely flexible. He was, by all accounts, one of the great tunesmiths who was able to turn out a work of high talent and cosy composition with ease. He sometimes scribbled two or three songs for a particular part or episode and allowed someone else to select what he wanted or thought best.

It is this art of compromise which marks the best of musical comedy. There is a natural fitting together, which is the result of unnatural sweat and labor; which comes about only after infinite give-and-takes, massive rehearsals, bouts of temperament, and fits of despair. There is a joy which emerges like iridescence to the top of the boiling pot of rivalries, jealousies, and vying talents. It is this distillation which is skimmed off by the skillful director or producer and offered to the audience as the attar of performance.

Wilde's feeling about the importance of "interruption" in dialogue is reflected by musicians' feeling about the necessity of rests in musical expression. In another definition, musical comedy might be said to be dialogue or plot interrupted by song or dance or virtuoso exhibition. The "new breath power" described by Wilde is precisely what is necessary to the whole production, to give it renewed life and zest—for if anything comes close to the controlled energy of an atomic pile in real life it is the art of musical comedy.

Yet, as has been said, such a production does not really care about art in the abstract. The whole depends upon the efficacy of the effect, however achieved. Not in vain does Porter quote his mother as saying: "Wait for the second act." It is the creed of those who know that the second act is the last in musical comedy and that the applause for the first is meaningless unless it is topped at the end. The famous quotation from Francis Quarles might be the motto of all such patient preparers:

> My soul, sit thou a patient looker-on;
> Judge not the play before the play is done:
> Her plot hath many changes; every day
> Speaks a new scene; the last act crowns the play.

Thus, in the world which Porter chose from all others and which became peculiarly his own, the fact of success is everything. But it is nothing unless it is a success which is ostensibly achieved as lightheartedly and taken as high-handedly as if it did not matter at all. And this, of course, is the essence of snobbism.

Porter deliberately chose to be a snob, at least to all appearances. He inherited money and loved it; but he made much more by himself and loved it as well. He spent it freely and gained it freely; he even complained about taxes in a lighthearted vein. "My ninety-two per cent, I suppose, supports some unknown government bureau," he said. He was determined to be a gay divorcé from life and never abandoned the pose.

It was a pose. No one works as hard and revises as often—no one seeks for inspiration and chains it—no one fights for his place in the sun as desperately without being the opposite of a snob. Porter's life was a serious one—between his piano with its marked score paper and his worn rhyming dictionaries, which were always by his side. He valued the collection of a couple dozen jewelled cigarette cases given by him to his wife—one for each opening—above all other possessions, even his scores; he left them to posterity as some sort of sad symbol of what he had done.

No one can count the years that he was immersed in his work, sunk in a privacy that others took for aloofness and that he knew was necessary for creation. The landlord of the mansion he rented for years in Brentwood told of taking away more than twenty truckloads of trees and shrubbery that had grown up or been planted by Porter to screen himself from dilettantism. His friends complained of the "almost sinister ability" he had to detach himself and vanish from a party to do his work. Even his handwriting was that of a musician. He wrote left-handed but not horizontally—he wrote downward, one letter after another. When he relaxed, one of his pleasures was to read the biting theatre reviews of Beerbohm, that exquisite who asked and got a small place in classic critical literature.

Porter's originality did not need to be given impetus by an original story. The distinguishing traits of musical comedy had come to be that it was derivative in source and lightly satirical in tone. Great originals in the field—such as *Of Thee I Sing*—are atypical. This may be illustrated by the best representatives of musical comedy. *Oklahoma!* was derived from the play *Green Grow the Lilacs* by Lynn Riggs; *My Fair Lady* was lifted from *Pygmalion* by Shaw out of *Trilby* by du Maurier out of Greek legend; *West Side Story* was simply a modern retelling of the Romeo and Juliet legend from Shakespeare via Italian novellas. *Kiss Me, Kate,* had a similar ancestry. *Anything Goes,* another script that was hardly typical, was actually constructed (according to its rewriters, Lindsay and Crouse) around the score that Porter had already created.

Nor was much that was before this allowed to be original. In the words of Nathan, celebrating the birth of *Of Thee I Sing,*

> A glance backward over the modern American musical stage will disclose it to have followed, with little deviation, routine and rusty tracks. In endless succession that stage has given us the so-called romantic musical comedies with the proud princesses in love with humble naval lieutenants and their humble slaveys cinderellaed by proud princes, the revues with their vaudeville comedians and peafowl ladies, the shows laboriously manufactured out of dull comedies previously displayed on the legitimate stage, and the German and Austrian importations adapted to what has been believed to be the American taste by the insertion into their books of a sufficient number of facetious allusions. . . . Here and there, there has, occasionally, been a mild effort to break away from the established pattern but the effort has been so mild that it has come to naught and what has resulted has been, at bottom, much the same old thing.

Nathan went on to point out that, two years previously,

Kaufman, Ryskind, and Gershwin had invented a "novel bloom" of musical comedy satire called *Strike Up the Band* "that paved the way for the fuller and more highly perfumed sardonic hothouse" that was *Of Thee I Sing*. (pp. 99-109)

. . . . .

Cole Porter can be located in the world of musical comedy. Enough time has elapsed so that he may be seen clearly as what he was. It must be confessed at once that he was not original. He was deeply influenced by his times, by his colleagues in song writing, by the styles of the stage, by his acquisition of melody and rhythm on his travels. But Shakespeare had only one original plot out of thirty-nine plays and he never had to do with the frantic whims of musical comedy producers. An accusation of lack of originality is not an unduly serious charge against musical comedy artists. The imposition of tune and choreography, of wit and gaiety, upon a solid substratum of derivative story is almost a necessary reassurance to the audience—the enjoyment of something dimly familiar.

Nor can it be held against Porter that he was not serious. Satire, used as Jonathan Swift used it, may become a malign and destroying influence. This was far from Porter's intention: he preferred the fencing touch rather than cutlass and bludgeon. He did not even aspire to the home thrust; he preferred to flutter from flower to flower of inanity and leave only a momentary sting. It is possibly significant that his most skillful gift for the satiric point lies in his concepts of sexual relationships.

It is undeniable that he had a transforming effect upon his melding of words and music. As his friend Moss Hart said: "No one could write a Cole Porter song but Cole Porter. Each song had a design and a special felicity of its own that stamped it as uniquely his." He was inimitable. He had no disciples and wanted none.

Ten years after his first real success, Porter was acknowledged as an outstanding writer of musical comedy. He stuck to his last and never tried to alter the librettos. "Words and music are quite enough of a job," he said. He had achieved not only leadership, he had achieved innovation. His work had shifted musical comedy onto new and higher ground. He was, as one of his friends said, "a new musical voice of immense vigor and freshness . . . a forcible talent that was racy and bold but that had great elegance and a curious kind of purity." Another declared "he was to our generation what Gilbert and Sullivan were to theirs. His satire is just as merciless and he, too, hides the face of a philosopher and reformer behind the gay mask of a royal entertainer." Still another put it in the way that Porter might have liked best of all: "Cole knew more about the art of living than anyone else I've ever known. . . . He had a wonderful, wonderful sense of gaiety."

The critics were more analytical. One, Cecil Smith, pointed out that

> he made use of satirically-oriented books but preferred to employ as his weapon the barbed shaft of an individual line or song. . . . He developed his technique of acid comment only, slowly, contenting himself at first with a special urbanity of manner. . . . A *mot* or turn of phrase always meant more to him than anything else about his work; give him a choice between sacrificing the integrity of a character and sacrificing a rhyme and he would unhesitatingly sacrifice the character. He always was . . . primarily a *litterateur* and genteel pornographer.

The bluntness of this appraisal must be tempered somewhat with the judgment of Sigmund Spaeth, writing in 1948 just before Porter's ultimate triumph of *Kiss Me, Kate*. He described Porter as

> our most literate and sophisticated creator of popular songs . . . (showing) equal facility with text and tune, developing the two simultaneously in seemingly inevitable fashion. His only rivals in this respect are Irving Berlin and Stephen Foster himself. The group of trained musicians . . . beginning with Victor Herbert and including such names as Kern, Gershwin, Friml, Romberg, and Rodgers, can well single out Cole Porter as perhaps the most individual of them all. How he could turn out such a vast literature under the handicaps of his way of life remains an eternal mystery. He seems to have the power of absolute concentration, thinking out a complete composition, regardless of his surroundings, without going near a piano or a piece of music-paper.

Possibly the first summary is a little too harsh and the second is a little too generous. What they do is to illustrate the extremes of appreciation in which Porter was held. The upshot of it must be that throughout his life the composer dared to be himself, a person capable both of sentiment and scintillation, but always unique.

Cole Porter trusted his best self. He played his own part and spoke his message of music under his own name in his own way. He related it, without hesitation, to the style of his own day (which he molded into his own image) and made it correspond to the needs of the musical comedy art. He drew upon his life and experiences for its sustenance and operated in the milieu without the thought of an apology. Musical comedy was good enough for him; the only question in his mind was that he himself might not be good enough for it. He preached a gospel of detachment and hovered behind it. Nothing in this world was quite worth the winning: it was the work of the moment that was savory, that mattered.

What will make his creations live and thrive—as they have already proven—is their cool, wry objectivity. They have no special flavor, rather a kind of temperature and a dash of spice, a musical glass of cold water on an emotionally hot day. Because they really suit no one but Porter they have the facility of fitting everyone over the years. When Bianca, in *Kiss Me, Kate,* sings that "I never yet beheld that special face which I could fancy more than any other," she is singing Porter's own epitaph—and the universal reason why his fragile monument will stand. (pp. 121-24)

Richard G. Hubler, in The Cole Porter Story, *The World Publishing Company, 1965, 140 p.*

Sigmund Spaeth

[Spaeth was an American composer, critic, and educator. In the following excerpt from his 1948 study A History of Popular Music, *he defends popular music as a legitimate art form.]*

It has become a commonplace to say that popular music is an index to the life and history of a nation. Unfortunately, there are still too many people who do not really believe it. They are actually unaware of the extent to which the manners, customs and current events of every generation have been given expression in popular songs, particularly in the United States; nor do they realize how honestly, and often naively, such songs have reflected the changing character of our people.

Every period of American history has had its own characteristic songs, from the days of the Revolution, when patriotism and politics were the leading themes, to the reckless distortions of the Jazz Age, with its hysterical flouting of all convention or tradition. Slang, clothes, coiffures, inventions, games, food and drink, all have figured in popular song. When life was leisurely and slow, the songs were of the same type. With the increasing pace of recent years, our popular music kept time with the mood, dealt more and more in exaggerated effects of rhythm and tone color, the syncopation of ragtime leading to the improvised breaks and hot licks of jazz, and finally to the commercialized ecstasies of swing.

No matter what anyone thinks of such music, it is historically and racially important. The mere fact that millions of people sing a certain song, or listen to it with honest pleasure, gives it a significance that cannot be ignored. Artistic merit has nothing to do with the question.

If a popular hit or a folk-tune happens to possess some quality of permanent beauty, as is often the case, our listeners eventually discover it for themselves, and this law of the survival of the fittest applies to serious music as well as to the lighter type. There are good and bad symphonies and operas as well as good and bad popular songs. No individual critic has ever been able to decide that question. It remains for time and the general public to work out the answer. Even the artificial success frequently created by the commercial machinery of Tin Pan Alley cannot guarantee more than a short life for the average song of the people. Actually such desperately intensive exploitation may have an effect that is the exact opposite of permanence.

It is worth remembering that Stephen Foster, certainly America's best-known composer, was essentially a writer of popular songs, and these songs achieved permanence in the manner of true folk-music, without benefit of artificial exploitation or advertising. It may also be significant that one of Foster's most beautiful songs, "Jeanie with the Light-Brown Hair," was almost killed by the repeated assaults of radio at the time when most of our copyrighted music was kept off the air by the absurd battle between ASCAP and the broadcasting companies. Even so excellent a melody as that which opens the famous *Piano Concerto* of Tschaikowsky could not stand the strain of constant repetition when it was suddenly discovered by Broadway's arrangers.

The problems of the serious composer are quite different from those of the hit-writer. The former has a constant struggle to achieve performance of any kind, not to speak of publication, recording or broadcasting. The latter suffers from the quick turnover of big business, bowing to the necessity of concentrated "plugging," and happy to take his profits in a hurry and hope for a lucky repetition in the near future. If he is a "production man" (i.e. writing for the stage), perhaps with hopes of achieving the "standard" (permanent) catalogue, he may wisely insist on certain restrictions, so that his brain-child will not be flogged to death in the six weeks now considered a fair lifetime for a popular hit. So the attainment of anything like permanence in popular music has its delicate problems too, in spite of the well-established routine of the trade.

This routine is in any case a comparatively recent development, and has little to do with the innate vitality and universal appeal long ago established by perfectly natural processes, and still operating on a Darwinian basis. The artificial aids of commercial exploitation demand consideration in any history of popular music in America, but they are only a small part of the picture. Any great and lasting success must be traced to other causes, and can generally be analyzed from the standpoint of sincere and unaffected human reactions.

Here again popular music has a certain advantage over the serious type. The composer of an orchestral work, an art song or a piano sonata is generally convinced that his composition is a stroke of genius, or at least an expression of extraordinary talent. But it is quite possible that authoritative critics and musical scholars may not agree with him, and it is more than likely that the general public will never have enough opportunity to hear his music to form any opinion whatever concerning it. The great classics of musical literature achieved most of their reputation after their creators were dead, and among living composers of serious music the majority must continue to hope, perhaps in vain, for a hearing of any kind.

The immediate appraisal of serious music is at best a difficult matter, eternally handicapped by ignorance, prejudice, intolerance, snobbery and hypocrisy. America's concert audience has for years been limited to less than one per cent of the population (as is still the case in such a musical center as New York itself), and even with the help of radio, the phonograph and the screen, the great American public is just beginning to discover the established masterpieces of music, generally lumped under the damning title of "classical."

Can such an audience be expected to decide for itself what is good or bad in contemporary composition, especially when most of it is in an unfamiliar idiom, often unattractive or downright ugly in its immediate effect on the casual listener?

Popular music represents the line of least resistance. It is the easiest to remember and, perhaps consequently, the easiest to forget. When any of it arrives at some degree of permanence, it is a real tribute to its inherent qualities as well as to the skill and wisdom of its promoters.

The traditional contrast of "popular" and "classical" music seems rather absurd today, when the dividing line has been practically wiped out. A "classic" is after all nothing more than a work of art that has established its permanence, and in music such a masterpiece may prove to be more honestly popular than any hit song of the moment. A symphony like Beethoven's *Fifth* or Schubert's *Unfinished* has probably been played in some form more often during its lifetime than any "popular" piece. Conversely, a popular song may easily achieve the permanence that makes it in the best sense a classic, with the lyric inspirations of Stephen Foster as shining examples.

The tradition of serious music has been definitely aristocratic. That of popular music, including folk-music in general, is just as definitely democratic. Composers like Haydn, Mozart and Beethoven were dependent upon the patronage of a few well-born connoisseurs. Handel and Gluck gambled their success on the whims of an opera-conscious society. Wagner would never have written his greatest music-dramas if he had not been subsidized by the mad King Ludwig of Bavaria. Such modern composers as Sibelius and Ernest Bloch have profited by patronage, the first through governmental subsidies, and the second with the help of private contributions. We have our Guggenheim Fellowships and our Pulitzer Prizes, as well as the cooperation of such financially solid institutions as the Juilliard, Curtis and Eastman Schools of Music.

Our symphony orchestras, opera companies and concert courses have been largely aristocratic affairs, depending upon the support of moneyed social leaders, who have too often confused the power of underwriting with the responsibilities of aesthetic dictatorship. Even today, in a world made miserable by commercialism and individual selfishness, there persists a tendency toward rarification of the arts in favor of the few precious souls who presumably are able to appreciate them.

Snobbery and intolerance have consistently mated with honest artistic endeavor, and the offspring is not a happy one. Mild insincerity, with its gushing command of critical clichés, has often developed into rampant hypocrisy. The practitioners of these sly arts are determined only to conceal their fundamental ignorance and to jump upon any band-wagon that seems momentarily to be occupied by "the right people." It is fair to assume that a large proportion of the enthusiasm apparently created by modern serious music is completely dishonest and of no real significance. Yet there are plenty of well-intentioned artists, critics, teachers and music-lovers in general who continue to insist that their favorite art can be appreciated only by a few specially privileged and perhaps individually gifted souls.

To this picture of the domination of aristocracy over serious music throughout the world the history of popular music offers a violently refreshing contrast. Nobody has ever felt compelled to express enthusiasm over a popular song or tune that he or she secretly disliked. Nor has there ever been any inclination to hide the boredom that so often

followed the brief career of an enormously successful ditty. Just as the baseball fan alternates between ecstatic hero-worship and equally honest indignation with the same "bum," so the disciples of popular music are constantly hysterical over the perfection of their current favorite or scathingly contemptuous of the past hit that has died of overwork. There is no more dishonesty among the jitterbugs and hit-paraders than there is among the consumers of food and drink.

The very words "folk" and "popular," applied to music, suggest complete democracy. How could the music of the millions possibly be anything but democratic, as compared with the artificially nurtured, extra special delights of a small circle of connoisseurs?

The penalty of democracy in art is that it teeters too dangerously on the tight-rope between the sublime and the ridiculous. Pathos is constantly in danger of descending to bathos. The simple, naive sentiment of a great folk-song is far too easily replaced by the cheap sentimentality of a Broadway tunesmith; and the unabashed enthusiast, of open feelings openly arrived at, is too often unable to distinguish between the two. Therefore it is quite natural that many songs should have achieved tremendous popularity, and even a degree of permanence, in spite of the most obvious weaknesses of text or melody or both.

At their worst, however, our popular songs represent beliefs and emotions that are shared by the great majority of people. The expression may be commonplace, obvious, uninspired, but the basic ideas are completely honest. Thus there is no denying the enormous importance of love as a human experience, even though it may seldom attain true beauty of expression; and love has always been the most absorbing topic of the popular songwriter. It is equally true that most people are sincerely fond of their mothers and their children, deeply grieved by a death in the family, ready to laugh at even a bad joke, and frankly interested in other human beings and in the things that are going on about them. Of these common traits of human nature the popular songs of the world are made. They are not abstruse or deeply philosophical, seldom truly sophisticated, almost never vague or incoherent. They deal frequently in platitudes and they pay small heed to niceties of technique or felicities of expression. But they are as normal and universal as men, women and children. They give obvious and immediate expression to human experience of the most general kind. They continue endlessly because there is no end or limit to the fundamental truths with which they are concerned. Love ends in marriage or heartbreak, and marriage itself is an admirable convention. Woman is the natural object of masculine devotion, and if she is cruel, that is too bad. There are thousands of approaches to the relationship of the sexes, from gentle raillery to the abjectly maudlin. Death is the final tragedy, but the family and the home are still temporary buffers against the inevitable.

Even though every decade has shown marked changes in the life and character of the American people, these fundamentals of popular music have remained strangely constant. We still sing of love, though perhaps in different terms from those of a hundred or even fifty years ago. We are still sorry for ourselves in melancholy lyric vein. We still accept the dictum of Tin Pan Alley that a kiss is the ultimate in human ecstasy and that its logical and almost inevitable sequel is holy matrimony. Most decidedly do we continue to enjoy almost any touch of absurdity, even when it takes the form of mere nonsense syllables such as the early Elizabethans incorporated in their madrigals. From a "hey-nonny-nonny" to a modern scat-singer's "hi-de-ho," via *Ta-ra-ra-boom-der-é* and *Vo-deo-do,* is only a step, even though it covers nearly four centuries of time. The basic sameness of man's songwriting habits, combined with kaleidoscopic variations of detail, may be considered the chief justification for any serious, factual and analytical history of popular music, most of all in our own constantly changing yet fundamentally consistent country.

Let no musical scholar think for a moment that the creation of popular music is an easy matter, to be tossed off in an idle moment. Many a serious composer has been heard to lament his utter inability to turn out even one tune that people really want to whistle. When such musicians have occasionally decided to produce pot-boilers of the obvious type, or to take a flier in the popular field, under an assumed name, the results leaning toward the extremes of banality or totally unattractive melodic lines, have generally been deplorable. Musicianship and technical proficiency are often handicaps to the creation of popular material, even though they may prove tremendous assets when supported by the instinctive grasp of human values that is the mark of the great songwriter.

But it is equally wrong to assume that the composer of popular hits is necessarily an illiterate person, or that anyone able to hum a tune or to pick it out with one finger at the piano has the making of a melodic success, needing only the help of an arranger and some publicity. The fact that musically uneducated men and women, often boasting of their inability to read or write notes, have made a success of popular songwriting does not mean that such illiteracy is a help to their profession. The instinctive gift must be there to begin with, but the musical equipment of a Gershwin, a Kern or a Rodgers is not to be scorned. In most cases a truly successful song must be credited with a definite technique, conscious or unconscious, and many a listener would be surprised at the amount of thought, care and study expended on a seemingly obvious combination of words and melody.

While a few songwriters have been able to supply both text and tune, with such widely different men as Stephen Foster, Irving Berlin and Cole Porter as outstanding examples, most popular songs have been the result of collaboration, sometimes making use of the contributions of several individuals. In such collaboration the words and music are likely to develop together, as in the mind of a single creator, starting perhaps with a mere title or phrase, in which the verbal and the musical factors blend in the manner of a slogan. Whereas art song represents the setting of an already completed poem to music, popular song is not at all bound by this tradition. The words are perhaps more likely to be fitted to the music than vice-versa, with real collaboration still the ideal method.

Richard Rodgers (seated) and Oscar Hammerstein II in 1943.

The student of popular music is fairly sure to arrive in time at the recognition of certain basic patterns of melody, as well as common ideas and sentiments. This almost automatic repetition of tonal combinations often leads to suspicions of plagiarism, mostly unfounded, and to a general effect of reminiscence which must be considered an asset rather than a handicap. When quick and easy memorizing is essential, extreme originality is not always to be desired. The patterns of the scale and the common chord are eternally effective in music, and they have left their mark on popular songs as well as on the classic masterpieces. Our most successful hit-writers have often arrived at such patterns without the slightest consciousness of their affinity with the great music of the world.

It would seem permissible to place all popular songs in the general category of folk-music, for that is where they clearly belong. They have the same habit of being passed on by word of mouth, the same dependence on simplicity of melody, the same leaning toward monotony of rhythm, the same balance of responsibility between text and tune. Actually there are two kinds of folk-music; these can be conveniently tagged as rural and urban. The rural type is the more easily recognized and for some reason the more widely respected. But our slick city songwriters, who often sing yearningly of the country and of places they have never seen, have essentially the same attitude toward their urban surroundings and the same instinctive grasp of the moods and emotions of their fellow-men. It may be argued that a real folk-song is always of unknown authorship, but this is a rather specious contention when the ultimate effects are so clearly the same. Actually a great many songs are today considered as folk-music even though their creators are well known, as in the case of Stephen Foster. (The entire output of current "hill-billy" material can be traced to a few individuals, who grind it out with machine-like regularity.) Our best scholars have occasionally been deceived by the synthetic article in their search for authentic strains of the people.

The publishers themselves, like the record manufacturers, reserve a special catalogue for the rural types of "hill-billy" and "race" music, most of which is in dialect. But their chief dividing line is between "ballads" and "novelty songs." While a ballad was originally a song that told a definite story (which is still its correct definition), the term has come to be applied to any song of the conventionally sentimental type. "Novelty" can imply anything from uproarious humor or a nonsensical type of phrase (like "Yes, We Have No Bananas" or "Mairzy Doats") to subtle sophistication or a truly original idea. Among publishers the feeling is that a novelty song always has a chance of success, whereas a conventional ballad must not only possess inherent virtues of melody and words but must also receive special handling if it is to emerge successfully from the strenuous competition with other songs of the same type.

Regardless of its possible merits, musical or otherwise, a technically popular song, whether of the ballad or the novelty type, demands exploitation if it is to be a success. (This applies equally to "art songs" or to music of any kind, even though composers and publishers often seem totally unaware of the fact.) In any history of popular music the names of the promoters (publishers and "pluggers" or performers) must figure almost as prominently as those of the lyric-writers and composers themselves. The exploitation of popular songs has always been partly a deliberate art or science, perfected by the commercial machinery of the modern music business, and partly the result of gratuitous co-operation from singers, instrumentalists and conductors. In general it has been found necessary to create the initial demand through artificial publicity, aided by the personal friendship and confidence of a few important performers. (Today this includes the guarantee of an expensive promotion campaign, with a wide variety of direct and indirect bribery.) But once this first hurdle is passed and the popular appeal of a song is fairly well established, the performers themselves become willing and enthusiastic advertisers, insistently including the hit number in all their programs, making their own arrangements and giving it their individual interpretations, all free of charge to those most interested. When this natural exploitation has reached a saturation point, the song is likely to make a quick exit from the popular list.

In our early days the number of musical performers was limited, and a composer had to be his own promoter, as in the case of William Billings, the Colonial psalm-singer. Later there were musical families and other groups of artists who toured the country and popularized the music on

their programs. The next development was that of the minstrel shows, which did so much for the Foster songs, *Dixie,* etc. Then came the more elaborate productions of Harrigan & Hart, traveling shows like *A Trip to Chinatown* and the music-halls associated with the names of Tony Pastor, Koster & Bial, Weber & Fields and others. Meanwhile the circus, the county fair and the medicine show were doing their share of popular song-plugging, with the professional "buskers" in saloons and dives of every description keeping up a constant contribution through the exploitation of widely varying material. "Amateur nights" in the theatres proved a fertile field for planting new songs, and the family piano was kept busy in seconding the efforts of the professionals.

The coming of the phonograph caused a gradual decline in the sale of sheet-music, but made up for it in providing a new source of revenue and a far quicker and more effective method of musical promotion. The modern juke-box is still the best answer to a publisher's prayer, for a single record, incessantly played on these musical slot-machines, will always place a song in the hit class.

Radio went far beyond the phonograph in its possibilities of immediate exploitation, at the same time definitely shortening the life of the average popular song and still further cutting down sheet-music sales.

Tin Pan Alley now faced the problem of utilizing these enormous "plugs," while postponing the inevitable death of a hit as long as possible and capitalizing on the immediate volume of free publicity. A revision of the copyright law temporarily improved the situation so far as phonograph records were concerned, and the formation of the American Society of Composers, Authors and Publishers (ASCAP) led to new financial returns through the licensing of performing rights, more than offsetting the continued decrease in sheet-music royalties. The development of talking pictures added another significant angle to the exploitation of popular music, and the screen is now fully capable of moving a song single-handed into the current hit parade.

Today the relationship of musical creators, publishers and exploiters is a complicated one, handicapped by bickerings and legal technicalities. Popular music has become a big business, with huge investments and quick turnovers. The exact reasons for the success of any passing hit are not always easy to analyze. If anyone could consistently tell them in advance, he would be the highest-paid employee in the entire industry. Statistics are not always dependable, and commercial enthusiasms are sometimes misleading.

But the story of our popular music remains a fascinating one, intimately involved in our history as a nation. Out of a mass of material, often trivial and obvious, sometimes vulgar, there have emerged a few things of unquestioned musical importance, plus a wide variety of words and tunes that at least figured significantly in the life of each generation. Our wars and our political battles have had their songs, often with a deep and lasting effect upon the people. We have sung about our heroes and our villains, lyrically celebrating national calamities and disasters as well as the innocuous appeal of clothes, slang and everyday diversions. Always there has been the basis of human interest, an absorption in the current scene, and a willingness to express even the most commonplace thoughts and emotions in a naively honest fashion. Such habits and traditions must inevitably have produced occasional results that might qualify as Art. But far more significant is the universality of sentiment, no matter how obvious its expression, the inherent democracy and integrity of a vast literature of music that has grown up with the maturing of America itself. (pp. 3-14)

> *Sigmund Spaeth, in an introduction to his* A History of Popular Music in America, *Random House, 1948, pp. 3-14.*

THE LYRICS OF POPULAR SONGS

Philip Furia

[*In the following essay, Furia contends that the lyrics of popular music have gone unheralded, and underlines the cleverness and sophistication of the Tin Pan Alley lyricists.*]

Mrs. Oscar Hammerstein, so the story goes, once overheard someone praise "Ol' Man River" as a "great Kern song." "I beg your pardon," she said, "But Jerome Kern did not write 'Ol' Man River.' Mr. Kern wrote *dum dum dum da;* my husband wrote *ol' man river.*" It's easy to understand her frustration. While the years between World Wars I and II have long been hailed as the "golden age" of American popular song, it is the composers, not the lyricists, who always get top billing. "I love a Gershwin tune" too often means just that—the tune—even though George Gershwin wrote many unlovable tunes before he began working with his brother Ira in 1924. Few people realize that their favorite "Arlen" songs each had a different lyricist—Ted Koehler for "Stormy Weather," Yip Harburg for "Over the Rainbow," Johnny Mercer for "That Old Black Magic." Only Broadway or Hollywood buffs know which "Kern" songs get their wry touch from Dorothy Fields, who would flippantly rhyme "fellow" with "Jello," and which of Kern's sonorous melodies got even lusher from Otto Harbach, who preferred solemn rhymes like "truth" and "forsooth." Jazz critics sometimes pride themselves on ignoring the lyrics to Waller and Ellington "instrumentals," blithely consigning Andy Razaf or Don George to oblivion. Such Alley wordsmiths are forgotten even when their lyrics made all the difference: the most famous of all popular songs lay in limbo for years as a piano rag until Mitchell Parish put words to it, yet it is Hoagy Carmichael we think of when we hear "Star Dust."

The answer to the perennial question, "Which comes first—the music or the words?" seems all too clear. "In a well-wrought song," Susanne Langer has said, "the text is swallowed, hide and hair." Even in art song, where an existing poem is set to music, "the poem as a work of art is broken up. Its words, sound and sense alike, its phrases, its images, all become musical material." Thus even when the words are actually composed first, they still seem of only secondary importance.

If music swallows words in art song, how much more ravenous it must be in popular song, where words are written to already composed music. To Anthony Burgess the consumption seems so thorough he can argue that in a song lyric "what is said is not of great importance" [see Further Reading]. While Burgess pays lip service to the notion that in a good song words and music must "affirm a true marriage of equal partners," the sort of marriage he has in mind seems to be the old-fashioned kind with the lyricist, like a dutiful wife, "graciously obscuring the light of the words" to bring out and clarify the pattern of the music.

Because he regards the lyricist's role as playing second fiddle to the composer, Burgess, like many people, draws a firm distinction between song lyrics and poetry. "Poetry demands the concentration of the reader or listener on content, on originality of imagery or verbal trope; the true lyric deliberately damps the striking image." Instead of providing the "verbal shocks" of poetry, the lyricist's art, for Burgess, consists of the "matching of long vowels or diphthongs to long notes, the disposition of primary and secondary syllabic stress, and the management of climax."

However valid that distinction might be for poetry and song in general, it leaves Ira Gershwin, Cole Porter, and other lyricists of the golden age in limbo, since their lyrics, far from dampening witty tropes and striking imagery, bristle with the "verbal shocks" of poetry. Even Burgess confesses to finding Lorenz Hart's lyrics "brilliant" and quotes such gems as

> Beans could get no keener reception in a beanery.
> Bless our mountain greenery home!

While such a lyric skillfully matches long vowels to long notes and deftly disposes verbal to musical stresses, it also demands, like poetry, that the listener concentrate on the witty image and what Burgess himself calls the "ingenious" rhyme.

Yet such lyricists themselves have resisted attempts to celebrate these poetic qualities in their songs. George Balanchine, who choreographed several Rodgers and Hart shows in the 1930s, called Lorenz Hart the "Shelley of America" and urged him to publish his lyrics, without music, as a book of poetry. Like most lyricists of his era, however, Hart never seems to have considered such a project, regarding his art as one that was utterly dependent upon the music it set. Usually he could not even begin working until Rodgers had completed the melody, and, in typical Tin Pan Alley fashion, often started with a "dummy" lyric—banal, nonsensical, or even salacious phrases that helped him remember the rhythm and contour of the melodic line. Hart, in fact, acknowledged his subordinate role by breaking with theatrical tradition to allow the composer's name to precede his. Thus we speak of a Gilbert and Sullivan operetta but a Rodgers and Hart musical.

Paul Robeson (left) singing "Ol' Man River" in the 1936 film version of Jerome Kern and Oscar Hammerstein II's Showboat.

Even the few lyricists who did publish their lyrics separately made sure no one would accuse them of impersonating a poet. Ira Gershwin entitled his collection, with mock-pomposity, *Lyrics on Several Occasions by Ira Gershwin, Gent.* and posted a disclaimer as foreboding as Mark Twain's "Warning" to readers looking for a motive, moral, or plot in *Huckleberry Finn:*

> Since most of the lyrics in this lodgment were arrived at by fitting words mosaically to music already composed, any resemblance to actual poetry, living or dead, is highly improbable.

Even granting that much of the lyricist's craft rests in the artful fit of word to music, such an absolute distinction obscures the fact that lyrics also employ the elements of poetry—rhyme, imagery, metaphor—and some lyrics use these elements intricately enough to merit the same attention we give to poetry. A glance at any anthology will reveal that some of the most famous "poems" of the English language, such as "Drink to Me Only With Thine Eyes" and "A Red, Red Rose," are song lyrics—not "art" songs but lyrics, like Ira Gershwin's, that were set to already composed music.

There is simply no simple distinction between lyrics and poetry. Some lyrics, such as Stephen Foster's, so efface themselves before music that we would never try to "read" them as poetry. Others, like those of Robert Burns, present such subtle poetic features that we sometimes forget we are reading song lyrics. Occasionally the resemblance of lyrics to poetry, far from being "highly improbable," is so close it is hard to tell them apart. E. Y. "Yip" Harburg remembered how one day in high school he and a classmate found they shared an enthusiasm for poetry, especially for society verse. When Harburg recited some of his favorite poems, W. S. Gilbert's "Bab Ballads," the classmate informed him that those "poems" were actually song lyrics. "There's music to it?" asked an incredulous Harburg. "Sure is," replied the classmate, whose name was Ira, and invited him over to the Gershwin home to listen to Gilbert and Sullivan records on the family Victrola. "There were all the lines I knew by heart, put to music!" Harburg recalled, "I was dumbfounded, staggered."

One of their favorite books, he noted, was Carolyn Wells' *Vers de Société Anthology.* It contains hundreds of witty poems, from the elegant Cavalier works of Robert Herrick and Richard Lovelace to nineteenth-century verse by Ernest Dowson and Lewis Carroll. Yet many of those "poems" were song lyrics, and one frequently comes across a line that could pass for an ancestor of a Gershwin lyric, from "Your tiny little nose that turns up so pert and funny" to "I wonder if you wonder if I wonder if you wonder." The resemblance is hardly accidental, since society verse is based upon the same principles that underlie the lyrics of Hart, Gershwin, and Porter—principles spelled out by Carolyn Wells in the introduction to her anthology.

The "great distinction" of *vers de société,* she explains, is "ease" and "playful spontaneity." While it treats its subject with sophistication, the language is never formal and elevated but "terse and idiomatic, and rather in the conversational key." The rhymes are "frequent" and the rhythm "crisp and sparkling." Society verse, she cautions, must never be "ponderous" and sentimentality must be avoided: "enthusiasms are modified, emotions restrained." Its tone should be "playfully malicious," "tenderly ironical," or "satirically facetious."

But what better exemplifies those principles than a lyric by Lorenz Hart?

> When love congeals, it soon reveals
> the faint aroma of performing seals,
> the double-crossing of a pair of heels,
> I wish I were in love again!

Just as such a lyric closely resembles society verse, it is fundamentally different from the traditional song lyric, as described by Burgess, that "damps the striking image" and avoids the "verbal shocks" of poetry.

Yip Harburg and Ira Gershwin were not alone in their youthful admiration of society verse. Along with Howard Dietz, Dorothy Fields, and many other lyricists, they began their careers as writers of "smarty verse," their highest aspiration to place a poem in magazines like *The Smart Set, Vanity Fair,* or that pinnacle of verbal wit, Franklin Pierce Adams' (F. P. A.'s) column, the "Conning Tower," in the *New York World.* When these aspiring poets turned to the more lucrative art of songwriting, their lyrics still were rooted in *vers de société.* One of Ira Gershwin's wittiest lyrics, "Tschaikowsky," from his collaboration with Kurt Weill on *Lady in the Dark* in 1941, was based on a poem, consisting of the names of fifty-one Russian composers, which the fledgling poet had placed in *Life* magazine back in 1924. Gershwin was also inordinately pleased to find that some of his "improbably" poetic lyrics were selected for inclusion in the *Oxford Anthology of Light Verse,* along with lyrics by Cole Porter, Howard Dietz, Yip Harburg, and others.

The golden age of popular song, as John Updike reminds us in his tribute to Cole Porter [see Further Reading], was also a "heyday of light verse: there were book reviews in verse, and sports stories; there were droll ballades and rondeaux and triolets. The plenitudinous newspapers and magazines published Don Marquis, F. P. A., Louis Untermeyer, Arthur Guiterman, Christopher Morley, Dorothy Parker, Ogden Nash, E. B. White, Morris Bishop, and Phyllis McGinley." In some of those poems, the distinction between verse and song is virtually erased:

> If I were only dafter,
> I might be making hymns,
> To the liquor of your laughter

And the lacquer of your limbs.

How different is Witter Bynner's deft poetic daftness from Leo Robin's irreverent hymn to limbs?

> Venus de Milo was noted for her charms,
> but strictly between us,
> you're cuter than Venus
> and what's more you got arms!

Here the line between verse and lyric is a purely metrical one: Bynner's poem adheres to a regular metrical pattern, while Robin fits his meter to the irregular pattern of Ralph Rainger's musical accents. Such difficult fitting makes the witty achievements of the lyricist all the more admirable. "A light-verse writer," as Updike points out, "is not constrained to extend his inspiration through enough refrains to exhaust the chorus, to shape his syllables toward easy vocalization." Thus when Franklin Pierce Adams, the verbal wizard of the "Conning Tower," tried to turn his society verse talents to lyric writing, he found "This method of the lyrist" (fitting words to music) "infinitely harder." Yet following a musical rhythm with a metrically uneven line can have the advantage of producing, as Robin's does, a lyric with more colloquial ease than poetry—right down to the vernacular punch of "and what's more you got arms!" That conversational phrasing, in turn, makes the clever rhymes and imagery even more surprising when they seem to emerge from everyday American speech.

By blending the rigors of light verse with those of lyric writing, the songs of the golden age sparkled with a poetic wit that few songs, before or since, have displayed. Not all the lyrics of the age glitter, of course. Take, for example, a lyricist such as Oscar Hammerstein, who even at the height of the age was writing such sonorous paeans as

> You are the promised kiss of springtime
> that makes the lonely winter seem long.
> You are the breathless hush of evening
> that trembles on the brink of a lovely song

In setting Jerome Kern's soaring melody for "All the Things You Are," Hammerstein exemplifies the traditional lyricist's art as defined by Anthony Burgess: his rhymes are simple, his imagery is unobtrusive, and his skillful manipulation of long vowels and verbal phrasing brings out the musical pattern and makes the lyric eminently "singable."

Cole Porter, however, could take the same "You are . . ." formula of romantic compliment and fashion a lyric so full of the "verbal shocks" of society verse, "so overtly clever and wittily brilliant" that, as Gerald Mast observes, "they overwhelm the music"—a complete reversal of Burgess's formula for lyrical self-effacement:

> You're a rose,
> you're Inferno's Dante,
> you're the nose
> on the great Durante

In "You're the Top" the rhymes (*rose, nose,* Infer*no's*) are clever, the diction (right down to "you're" instead of Hammerstein's "You are . . .") casually colloquial, the sentiment flippantly antiromantic—all hallmarks of light verse. The images, moreover, are not only striking but demand the same concentration we give to poetry in order to see that what at first appears to be a clash of European classic and American vaudeville resolves into underlying harmony: superficially different, Dante and Durante both turn out to be Italian comedians, albeit the latter less divinely so.

Urbane yet casual, literate yet colloquial, sophisticated yet nonchalant, "You're the Top" (1934) epitomizes an era when song lyrics radiated the stylish verve of society verse. But the poets of Tin Pan Alley could also borrow features from the more avant-garde poetry emanating, a few blocks away, from Greenwich Village. The best Alley lyrics can be as ironically understated as a Millay sonnet or bristle with the linguistic by-play and foreplay of a cummings panegyric. [In his *The Well-Wrought Urn*] Cleanth Brooks, one of the few literary critics to take even passing note of song lyrics, once observed that the same striking images that characterized modern poetry—Eliot's comparison of the evening "spread out against the sky" to "a patient etherised upon a table," for example—could also be found in such popular songs as "You're the Cream in My Coffee." Had Brooks looked further into that or numerous other lyrics of the day, he would have found other features he praised in modern poetry: wit, paradox, "ironical tenderness," and a "sense of novelty and freshness with old and familiar objects."

In the wake of the famous Armory show of 1913, New York poets sought to adapt the techniques of such artistic movements as Cubism and Dadaism. Thus Marianne Moore could use the page as a canvas to arrange verbal fragments in rhyming shards:

> ac-
> cident—lack

In the same year, similarly, a lyricist like Lorenz Hart could use Richard Rodgers' music as a grid to break up words into equally clever rhyming fragments:

> sweet pushcarts gently gli-
> ding by

Just as e. e. cummings could construct a verbal collage where "Abraham Lincoln" was juxtaposed against an ad for "B. V. D" and "Lydia E. Pinkham" against "the girl with the Wrigley Eyes," Cole Porter's discordant list songs jarringly set "Botticelli" beside "Ovaltine," "Mahatma Gandhi" by "Napoleon Brandy."

When New York Dadaists began presenting ordinary "found" objects—a bicycle wheel, a snowshovel, a urinal—as "readymade" sculptures, poets like William Carlos Williams quickly followed suit, framing such prosaic objects as a red wheelbarrow or the "figure 5" in poetic lines. Poets also seized upon common verbal objects—ordinary catch-phrases like "so much depends upon" and "this is just to say"—and revealed their poetic qualities by fragmentation and juxtaposition.

Such "found" phrases were also the basis of many of the songs of the golden age, where the most banal colloquial idioms were lifted into the romantic space of a lyric. What could be less likely terms of endearment or heartache than these bits of vernacular junk: "I Guess I'll Have to Change My Plan," "I Can't Get Started," "What'll I Do?," "Sure Thing," "There'll Be Some Changes Made," "How About Me?," "How Long Has This Been Going On?," "It Never Entered My Mind," "It's All Right With Me," "Just One of Those Things," "You Took Advantage of Me," "I Didn't Know What Time It Was," "Say It With Music," "Say It Isn't So," "Don't Get Around Much Anymore," "I'm Beginning to See the Light," "You're Driving Me Crazy," "Ain't Misbehavin'," "I Should Care," "They Can't Take That Away From Me," "From This Moment On," "I Don't Stand a Ghost of a Chance," "Everything Happens to Me," "Day by Day," "Night and Day," "Day In—Day Out . . . ," a list that could go, as a more recent song has it, "On and On."

By the 1920s all of the arts emulated painting's emphasis upon its own medium, and the medium for Tin Pan Alley's lyricists, as it was for the poets of Greenwich Village, was what H. L. Mencken in 1919 pugnaciously dubbed *The American Language.* By adapting the techniques of modern poetry, as well as those of society verse, and wedding them to music, the lyricists of Tin Pan Alley took the American vernacular and made it sing.

Yet while much of their art resembles that of society verse and modern American poetry, much of it will be lost if we forget Ira Gershwin's warning. Since the lyricist's craft is one of fitting words "mosaically" to music, what we must notice is not only the witty image and cleverly fragmented rhyme but how well the lyricist works within musical constraints (or subverts them), how deftly he matches the composer's phrasing with verbal fits (or shrewd misfits). Seeing Ira Gershwin's lyric in print can reveal a clever pun like the one that closes "But Not for Me:"

> When ev'ry happy plot
> ends with the marriage knot—
> and there's no knot for me

But for other artful effects, we must read the words with the music in mind. Only then can we see why Ira loved the added restrictions of his brother's music, where abrupt, ragged phrases gave a lyricist little room to "turn around." In a song like "They All Laughed," for example, George Gershwin's melody starts out with a ten-note phrase, calling for a ten-syllable line,

> They all laughed at Christopher Columbus,

followed by a line of seven syllables:

> when he said the world was round.

Then the music seems to repeat the same pattern with another ten-syllable line,

> They all laughed when Edison recorded

But, instead of another seven-syllable line, it stops short on one note:

> sound.

Thus Ira fitted that tiny musical space with as much invention as the character he celebrated.

In *Lyrics on Several Occasions* Ira Gershwin traces the genealogy of this "mosaic" art back to the Elizabethan Age. However, he is careful to exclude the "great art-song writers," such as Dowland and Campion, since for them "the words always came first, even though many of these highly talented men were also fine composers and wrote their own lute accompaniments." Instead he looks to the "satirists and parodists" of the period "who, discarding the words of folk song and ballad, penned—quilled, if you like—new lyrics to the traditional tunes." This "practice of putting new words to pre-existent song" culminated in Gay's *The Beggar's Opera,* and continued a tradition that, for Gershwin, includes such unlikely precursors as Martin Luther, who put new, spiritual lyrics to old, worldly tunes. So severe is Gershwin in his insistence that the music must come first, he even excludes Gilbert and Sullivan operettas, since "practically all the lyrics were written first." Like a true purist, however, he includes Gilbert's earlier settings of music from Continental operas, cherishing their "tricky lyrics and recitatives loaded with puns."

Gershwin's thumbnail survey stops just before the twentieth century, but it was then, with the emergence of Tin Pan Alley, that lyricists faced musical constraints more severe than ever before—or since. One of the earliest industries geared to standardization and mass marketing, Tin Pan Alley quickly evolved a rigid formula for popular songs. Almost every song from the golden age is built upon the same musical pattern of a thirty-two-bar chorus structured in four eight-bar units, usually in an AABA sequence. That is, the main part of the song consists of a melody, eight measures long, repeated three times with only another eight-bar phrase to vary it. The formula made songs easy to write: think of a pleasant eight-bar melody, repeat it, shift briefly to another melody for the eight-bar B section, or "release," then return to the main melody for the final A section. The formula was also a model of efficient repetition, playing a melody, repeating it, varying it briefly, then, knowing that all listeners, like Shakespeare's Duke Orsino, want "that strain again," returning to the original eight-bar phrase.

For the lyricist this tight musical pattern was extraordinarily restrictive, and many lyrics from the period simply follow the musical repetitions with banal, box-like phrases: "you were meant for me; I was meant for you." Such restrictions, however, could spark the inventiveness of a lyricist like Gershwin, who could cleverly make the syntax of his lyric spill over the musical boundaries. In "They Can't Take That Away From Me," for example, he concludes the musical release with a dangling preposition:

> We may never, never meet again
> on the bumpy road to love,
> still I'll always, always keep
> the mem'ry of—

Only in the final A section is the lyrical thought completed with "the way you hold your knife"—a wryly tender image that understates, even as it affirms, romantic feeling.

The musical pattern also put constraints upon the lyricist's subject matter. In nineteenth-century songs, as well as in most contemporary rock and country songs, the musical pattern is a sequence of verses, punctuated by simple eight-or sixteen-bar refrains, and the lyrics often recount stories about a wide range of subjects, from "The Convict and the Bird" to "The Little Lost Child." But the rigid thirty-two-bar AABA chorus of the golden age allows no such freedom. Such a "seamless web" made narrative, characterization, or social commentary practically out of the question. What it did allow, demand, in fact, was the expression of "one moment's feeling in a fluid statement" of between fifty and seventy-five words. The feeling that lent itself best to such treatment was love—in, out of, or unrequited. Given such a musical formula, the problem for a lyricist was both simple and hard; as Doris Day puts it to Danny Thomas in the film biography of lyricist Gus Kahn, "Gus, ya gotta learn to say 'I love you' in thirty-two bars."

Little wonder, then, that between 1920 and 1940, 85 percent of popular songs were love songs—a substantially greater proportion than one finds in nineteenth-century songs or even in contemporary songs. Prohibition, the Depression—these are barely mentioned in the popular lyrics of the golden age. Such a constraint of subject matter put Tin Pan Alley lyricists in the same straitjacket as their medieval ancestors, the troubadours of Provence, who, after all, invented this thing called romantic love. To the modern reader, who looks to poetry for original insight, sincerely expressed, popular song lyrics, like medieval *chansons*, "all sound the same, . . . sweet but bland repetitions of the few basic clichés of courtly love" [James J. Wilhelm, *Seven Troubadours*]. What such readers miss is the cleverness, the inventiveness and, in the best sense of the word, artifice, that displays itself by ringing endless changes upon what are indeed the tiredest clichés, the tireder the better for the skillful artificers of Provence. In the lyrics of Tin Pan Alley, similarly, we must listen, not for new ideas or deep emotion, but for the deftness with which the lyricist solves the problem posed by a song of the 1930s: "What Can You Say in a Love Song That Hasn't Been Said Before?"

The great lyricists solved this problem tirelessly. Lorenz Hart could describe falling in love with skeptical masochism:

> this can't be love because I feel so well—
> no sobs, no sorrows, no sighs

Ira Gershwin could have a newly smitten lover react to a first passionate kiss with an angry demand, "How Long Has This Been Going On?"—a catch-phrase we associate more with an irate spouse discovering a mate's infidelity. Cole Porter could terminate an affair with an urbane shrug—"it was just one of those things"—then add a metaphoric afterthought that contradicts the very ordinariness it asserts: "a trip to the moon on gossamer wings—just one of those things."

Hart, Gershwin, and Porter set an unsentimental, even anti-romantic standard for song lyrics, a standard that emerged practically overnight, when "Manhattan," a "sophisticated" song from a little revue called *Garrick's Gaieties* became an enormous popular hit in 1925. "Suddenly in the middle Twenties," librettist Sig Herzig recalled,

I began to read about Larry [Hart] in the columns of the New York papers. . . . F.P.A., whose column, "The Conning Tower," was the arbiter of wit at the time, was mentioning Larry's lyrics, as were other columnists. It was a major breakthrough! Outside of a small coterie of Gilbert and Sullivan worshippers, a lyric was never noticed and the lyric writer remained anonymous. . . . Then other lyric writers started gaining attention and there was a gush of wonderful words and music

No one was more amazed at the popular success of such a witty song than Rodgers and Hart themselves, who had struggled for years to establish themselves on Broadway. At the same time, Ira and George Gershwin began their successful collaboration with *Lady, Be Good!* (1924), and their songs, too, quickly detached themselves from shows to become independent hits on Tin Pan Alley's sheet music and record sales markets. By 1928, Cole Porter, who had been trying unsuccessfully to write popular songs for years, finally had both a hit show and a hit song, with the insouciant "Let's Do It" from *Paris.* Just as Porter's star began to rise, Oscar Hammerstein, who eschewed sophistication and maintained the old lyrical tradition of effacing words before music, saw his career go into decline.

For nearly two decades, Hart, Gershwin, and Porter's casually sophisticated standard was emulated by other lyricists. Theater lyricists could sidestep the elevated, melodramatic strains of operetta to nonchalantly lament,

> I guess I'll have to change my plan
> I should have realized there'd be another man!
> Why did I buy those blue pajamas
> before the big affair began?

Hollywood lyricists, too, could sometimes transcend the banal fare of most film songs:

> Thanks for the memory
> of rainy afternoons,
> swingy Harlem tunes,
> and motor trips
> and burning lips
> and burning toast and prunes.

Even lyricists who wrote for Tin Pan Alley's straight popular market could occasionally turn a sensuously witty compliment:

> You go to my head
> like a sip of sparkling Burgundy brew
> and I find the very mention of you
> like the kicker in a julep or two

Such lyrics are, in a word, urbane, and Charles Hamm is right to observe that in the golden age the style of American popular song became a "New York style" [see excerpt above]:

> Even more than had been the case during the formative years of Tin Pan Alley, the field was dominated by composers and lyricists born and trained in New York, writing songs for publishers who not only had their offices in New York but were themselves products of the city. . . . There was little effective cultural input from the rest of America into New York in these days,

and to the extent that Tin Pan Alley songs reflected American culture in a broader sense, they did so because the rest of the country was willing to accept a uniquely urban, New York product. . . . The songs of Kern, Gershwin, Porter and their contemporaries were urban, sophisticated, and stylish, and they were intended for people who could be described by one or more of these adjectives—or aspired to be.

Thus listeners all over the country delighted in the urbane lyrics of Hart, Gershwin, and Porter with the same relish that "the little old lady in Dubuque" might await her copy of the *New Yorker* or a newspaper reader in Ohio might chuckle over the syndicated reports of Benchley and Parker witticisms at yesterday's luncheon at the Algonquin Round Table. What, after all, could be more deliciously ironic than the fact that Fred Astaire, the performer who most embodied that urbane style of casual elegance—and introduced many of the greatest songs of the golden age—was born in Omaha?

Such a homogeneous style, however, was bound to be short-lived. What Sig Herzig termed a "gush of wonderful words" crested in the late 1930s, then, with George Gershwin's death, Porter's crippling accident, and Hart's losing battle with alcoholism, it quickly began to subside. With World War II, sentimentality and nostalgia returned to displace nonchalant sophistication, and soon popular song began to reflect, as well as emanate from, other regions, races, and classes. Even in the heart of Manhattan the change was registered: when Richard Rodgers broke with Lorenz Hart, he turned to Oscar Hammerstein, whose lyrical style was the very antithesis of urbanity and sophistication. In 1943, when the curtain went up on *Oklahoma!,* an age that had begun with "Manhattan" was over.

Yet because the songs of the golden age set a new standard, not only in musical sophistication but in poetic artistry, they have continued to appeal to performers and audiences while songs from other eras have been relegated to period pieces. Many are as familiar today as when they were written, continually refreshed through interpretations by the most diverse performers in jazz, country, and rock idioms. Fittingly, we call such songs "standards"—though the poetic art that has helped them endure has, for too long, gone unsung. (pp. 3-18)

> *Philip Furia, "Blah, Blah, Blah, Blah Love: Alley Standards," in his* The Poets of Tin Pan Alley: A History of America's Great Lyricists, *Oxford University Press, 1990, pp. 3-18.*

S. I. Hayakawa

[*Hayakawa is an American philosopher and scholar, and a retired U.S. senator from California. In the following essay, he argues that the lyrics of popular songs, as exemplified by those of Tin Pan Alley, foster a harmfully idealistic view of love, and contrasts them with blues lyrics, which he finds express a realistic view of life.*]

Because I have long been interested in jazz—its history, its implications, its present developments—I also listen to some extent to popular songs, which are, of course, far from being the same thing. Up to now my interests in general semantics and in jazz have been kept fairly clear of each other. But since both interests are manifestations of the same nervous system, I suppose it was inevitable that some day I should talk about both jazz and semantics at the same time. My present subject is, therefore, an attempt to examine, from a semantic point of view, the *words* of popular songs and jazz songs in order to discover their underlying assumptions, orientations, and implied attitudes.

First, let me clarify the distinction between popular songs and jazz. In "true" jazz, as the jazz connoisseur understands the term, the basic interest on the part of both musician and listener is in the music as music. Originality and inventiveness in improvisation are highly prized, as are the qualities of instrumentation and of rhythm. Popular music, on the other hand, stands in about the same relationship to jazz as the so-called "semi-classics" stand in relation to Bach, Beethoven, and Brahms. Just as the musical ideas of the classics are diluted, often to a point of inanity, in the "semi-classics," so are the ideas of jazz (and of semi-classics) diluted in popular music—diluted, sweetened, sentimentalized, and trivialized.

Now the contrast between the musical sincerity of jazz and the musical slop of much of popular music is interestingly paralleled in the contrast between the literary sincerity of the words of blues songs (and the blues are the basic source of jazz inspiration) and the literary slop in the majority of popular songs. The words of true jazz songs, especially the Negro blues, tend to be unsentimental and realistic in their statements about life. (In saying "Negro blues," I should add that *most* of these are written by Negroes, but some have been written by whites under Negro inspiration.) The words of popular songs, on the other hand, largely (but not altogether) the product of white songwriters for predominantly white audiences, tend towards wishful thinking, dreamy and ineffectual nostalgia, unrealistic fantasy, self-pity, and sentimental clichés masquerading as emotion.

We have been taught—and rightly—to be more than cautious about making racial distinctions. Hence let me hasten to explain that the differences between (predominantly Negro) blues and (predominantly white) popular songs can, in my opinion, be satisfactorily accounted for without "racial" explanations. The blues arise from the experiences of a largely agricultural and working class Negro minority with a social and cultural history different from that of the white majority. Furthermore, the blues—a folk music which underwent urbanization (in New Orleans, Chicago, New York, Memphis, Kansas City, and elsewhere)—developed in an economic or market situation different from that in which popular songs, aimed at mass markets through mass entertainment media, developed. With these cultural and economic conditions in mind, let me restate the thesis of this paper, using this time the terminology of general semantics: *The blues tend to be extensionally oriented, while popular songs tend to exhibit grave, even pathological, intensional orientations.*

Perhaps I can make my thesis come to life by discussing a specific area of emotion about which songs are written,

namely, love, in the light of what Wendell Johnson calls the IFD disease—the triple-threat semantic disorder of Idealization (the making of impossible and ideal demands upon life), which leads to Frustration (as the result of the demands not being met), which in turn leads to Demoralization (or Disorganization, or Despair). What Johnson says in *People in Quandaries* is especially illustrated in the attitudes towards love expressed in popular songs.

First, in looking forward to love, there is an enormous amount of unrealistic idealization—the creation in one's mind, as the object of love's search, a dream girl (or dream boy) the fleshly counterpart of which never existed on earth:

> Will I ever find the girl in my mind,
> The girl who is my ideal?
> ["My Ideal," by Leo Robin, Richard Whiting,
>   and Newell Chase]

> Every night I dream a little dream,
> And of course Prince Charming is the theme,
> The he for me . . .
> ["The Man I Love," by George and Ira Gershwin]

Next, of course, one meets a not-altogether-unattractive person of the other sex, and the psychological process called projection begins, in which one attributes to a real individual the sum-total of the imaginary perfections one has dreamed about:

> I took one look at you,
> That's all I meant to do,
> And then my heart stood still . . .
> ["My Heart Stood Still," by Lorenz Hart and
>   Richard Rodgers]

> You were meant for me, and I was meant for
>   you.
> Nature fashioned you and when she was done,
> You were all the sweet things rolled up in
>   one . . .
> I confess, the angels must have sent you,
> And they meant you just for me.
> ["You Were Meant for Me," with lyrics by Arthur Freed, melody by Nacio Herb Brown]

Wendell Johnson has commented frequently on what he calls a prevalent belief in magic. Some of his clients in his speech clinic at the University of Iowa, he says, will do no drills, perform no exercises, read no books, carry out no recommendations; they simply seem to expect that now that they have come to THE right speech clinic their stuttering will somehow magically go away. The essence of magic is the belief that you don't have to do anything—the right magic makes all effort unnecessary.

Love is depicted in most popular songs as just this kind of magic. There is rarely an indication in the accounts of love-euphoria commonly to be found in these songs that, having found the dream-girl or dream-man, one's problems are just beginning. Rather it is explicitly stated that, having found one's ideal, *all* problems are solved:

> We'll have a blue room, a new room, for two
>   room,

Where every day's a holiday, because you're
  married to me . . .
["Blue Room," by Lorenz Hart and Richard
                                    Rodgers]

The "Blue Room" song hints at what other songs often state, namely, that not only are emotional problems (and apparently economic problems) automatically solved by finding "the sweetheart of all my dreams"; the housing problem is also solved:

You'll find a smiling face, a fireplace, a cozy
  room,
A little nest that's nestled where the roses
  bloom . . .
["My Blue Heaven," by George Whiting and
                            Walter Donaldson]

In a bungalow all covered with roses,
I will settle down I vow,
I'm looking at the world thru rose-colored glass-
  es,
And everything is rosy now.
["Looking at the World Thru Rose Colored
  Glasses," by Tommy Malie and Jimmy
                                    Steiger.]

That, then, is the idealization. And students of general semantics know from reading Wendell Johnson what *that* leads to. The unrealistic expectations—for love is never expected to last for any shorter a period than "forever"—result inevitably in disappointment, disenchantment, frustration, and, most importantly, self-pity. Hence:

I'm all alone every evening,
All alone, feeling blue,
Wondering where you are, and how you are,
And if you are all alone too.
              ["All Alone," by Irving Berlin]

What if it turns out that he wasn't all alone at all, but two-timing her? She complains bitterly:

You were only fooling,
While I was falling in love.
["You Were Only Fooling," with words by Billy
  Faber and Fred Meadows, music by Larry Fo-
                                        tine]

Little you care for the vows that you made,
Little you care how much I have paid . . .
["Somebody Else Is Taking My Place," by Dick
  Howard, Bob Ellsworth, and Russ Morgan]

But in spite of the disappointments he has caused, she still loves him:

Yesterday's kisses are bringing me pain,
Yesterday's sunshine has turned into rain,
I'm alone because I love you,
Love you with all my heart.
["I'm Alone Because I Love You," words and
                            music by Joe Young]

Am I blue, am I blue,
Ain't these tears in these eyes telling you?
["Am I Blue," by Grant Clarke and Harry Akst]

How can I go on living, now that we're apart?
["Have You Ever Been Lonely?" with words by
  George Brown (Billy Hill) and music by Peter
de Rose]

She admits vociferously, "I'm a fool to care," but she wallows nevertheless in self-commiseration:

No day or night goes by,
That I don't have my cry . . .
["I Need You Now," by Jimmy Crane and Al
                                        Jacobs]

The next stage in the progress from disenchantment to demoralization and despair is, of course, another popular song theme, "I'm through with love, I'll never love again"—a theme which has such variants as these:

I'll never love again,
I'm so in love with you.
I'll never thrill again
To somebody new . . .
["I'll Never Smile Again," with words and
                        music by Ruth Lowe]

And if I never fall in love again, that's soon
  enough for me,
I'm gonna lock my heart and throw away the
  key.
["I'm Gonna Lock My Heart," by Jimmy Eaton
                            and Terry Shand]

And what is the final stage? Students of general semantics are familiar enough with psychiatric concepts to know that when the world of reality proves unmanageable, a common practice is to retreat into a symbolic world, since symbols are more manageable and predictable than the extensional realities for which they stand. The psychiatric profession classifies this retreat as schizophrenia, but that does not prevent it from being the theme of a popular song:

I'm going to buy myself a paper doll to call my
  own,
A doll that other fellows cannot steal. . . .
When I come home at night she will be waiting,
She'll be the truest doll in all the world.
I'd rather have a paper doll to call my own
Than a fickle-minded real live girl.
              ["Paper Doll," by Johnny Black]

This, then, is the picture of love's unhappy progress, as presented by the song writers of the commercial song-publishing world. The unrealistic emotions and the bathos of popular songs have, of course, long been notorious. It may well be asked if songs can be otherwise and yet be popular.

In answer to this question, let me next present the problems of love as seen by the writers of blues songs, such as are the basis of jazz. The first thing to be noticed is that the object of love is not idealized, but is looked at fairly realistically. It is one thing to call a pretty girl an angel, but quite another to look at angels as they are seen in "Harlem Blues":

Now you can have your Broadway, give me
  Lenox Avenue,
Angels from the skies stroll Seventh, and for that
  thanks are due
To Madam Walker's Beauty Shops and the Poro
  System too,

That made them angels without any doubt.
                          ["Harlem Blues," by W. C. Handy]

Shortcomings of character or appearance in the object of one's love are candidly acknowledged:

The man I love's got lowdown ways for true,
Well, I am hinkty and I'm lowdown too.
               ["The Basement Blues," by W. C. Handy]

You're so mean and evil, you do things you
    ought not to do,
But you've got my brand of honey, so I guess I'll
    have to
put up with you.
    ["Goin' to Chicago Blues," by Jimmy Rushing
                          and Count Basie]

In other words, there is no to-do made about looking and looking for an ideal girl or man—one adjusts oneself to the kind of women and men that actually exist. Refraining from "always chasing rainbows," the people depicted in the blues appear to save themselves a vast amount of emotional energy.

The loved one's imperfections, however, do not appear to stand in the way either of the intensity or durability of one's affections, as is indicated in this lament over a woman's death:

I went down to St. James Infirmary,
Heard my baby groan,
I felt so broken-hearted,
She used to be my own.
I tried to keep from cryin',
My heart felt just like lead.
She was all I had to live for,
I wish that it was me instead . . .
Though she treated me mean and lowdown,
Somehow I didn't care.
My soul is sick and weary,
I hope we'll meet again up there.
               ["St. James Infirmary," by Joe Primrose]

Furthermore, there is no magical attitude towards love indicated in the blues. Love means a mutual human relationship, and therefore there are duties and responsibilities, no less than there are rewards. In its crudest and most elementary statement, the duty is financial:

You want to be my man you got to give me $40
    down,
If you don't be my man, your baby's gonna
    shake this town.
               ["The Memphis Blues," by W. C. Handy]

You sittin' down wonderin' what it's all about,
If you ain't got no money, they will put you out,
Why don't you do right, like other men do?
Get out of here, and get me some money too.
["Why Don't You Do Right?" by Joe McCoy]

In general the duties described are those of living up to one's obligations as a mate, of providing that minimum of dependability that makes, as they say, a house a home:

Kind treatment make me love you, be mean and
    you'll drive me away,
You're gonna long for me baby, one of these old
    rainy days.

Yes, I love you, baby, but you don't treat me
    right,
Walk the streets all day, baby, and never come
    home at night.
["Blues in the Dark," by Jimmy Rushing and
                          Count Basie]

And the famous blues singer, Bessie Smith, gives the following advice to girls—advice which is full of the sense of one's own responsibility in a love situation:

So if your man is nice, take my advice,
Hug him in the morning, kiss him every night,
Give him plenty loving, treat him right,
For a good man nowadays is hard to find.
["A Good Man Is Hard to Find," by Eddie
                          Green]

The physical basis of love is more candidly acknowledged in the blues than in most popular songs. I am indebted to Dr. Russell Meyers of the University of Iowa Hospitals for the following observation about Jelly Roll Morton's "Winin' Boy Blues," in which there occurs the line, "Pick it up and shake it, life's sweet stavin' chain." Dr. Meyers equates this line to Herrick's "Gather ye rosebuds while ye may," translating thus: "A 'stavin' chain' is the heavy chain used by loggers to bind together logs to be floated down river, so that it is metaphorically that which binds together, i.e., sexuality; the idea is, as in Herrick, that you shake it now, while you are still able."

Popular songs, to be sure, also refer to the physical basis of love, but usually in extremely abstract periphrasis, as in "All of me, why not take all of me?" In the blues, however, as in the Elizabethan lyric, the subject is treated metaphorically. The following is from a song made famous by Bessie Smith:

You better get yourself to a blacksmith shop to
    get yourself overhauled,
There ain't nothing about you to make a good
    woman bawl.
Nobody wants a baby when a real man can be
    found,
You been a good ol' wagon, daddy, but you done
    broke down.
["You've Been a Good Ole Wagon" (Smith-
                          Balcom), sung by Bessie Smith]

So there are disappointments in love in the blues, no less than in popular songs. But the quality of disappointment is different. The inevitability of change in a changing world appears to be accepted. Conditions change, people change, and in spite of all one can do to preserve a valued relationship, failure may result: . . .

I've got a hard-working man,
The way he treats me I can't understand,
He works hard every day,
And on Sat'day he throws away his pay.
Now I don't want that man,
Because he's done gone cold in hand.

Now I've tried hard to treat him kind,
But it seems to me his love has gone blind.
The man I've got must have lost his mind,
The way he treats me I can't understand.
I'm gonna get myself another man,
Because the one I've got done gone cold in hand.

["Cold in Hand Blues" (Gee-Longshaw), sung
by Bessie Smith]

The most vivid statement of a sudden change of situation, involving desertion and heartbreak, is made in "Young Woman's Blues," by Bessie Smith:

Woke up this morning when the chickens were
crowin' for day,
Looked on the right side of my pillow, my man
had gone away.
By the pillow he left a note,
Reading, "I'm sorry, Jane, you got my
goat" . . .

Her reaction to this blow, however, is not, as in popular songs, any giving away to self-pity. The song continues:

I'm a young woman, and I ain't done running
round.
["Young Woman's Blues" (Bessie Smith), sung
by Bessie Smith]

In other words, she may be hurt, but she is far from demoralized. This refusal to be demoralized under conditions which in popular songs call for the utmost in wailing and self-commiseration is repeatedly to be found in the blues. Instead of the self-abasement that we find in the "kick-me-in-the-face-again-because-I-love-you" school of thought, the heartbroken men and women of the blues songs regroup their emotional forces and carry on without breakdown of morale. The end of a love relationship is by no means the end of life. As Pearl Bailey has sung:

Gonna truck downtown and spend my moo,
Get some short-vamp shoes and a new guy
too , , ,
Cause I'm tired, mighty tired, of you.
["Tired" (Roberts and Fisher), sung by Pearl
Bailey]

There is, then, considerable tough-mindedness in the blues—a willingness, often absent in popular songs, to acknowledge the facts of life. Consequently, one finds in the blues comments of many problems other than those of love, for example, the problem of urban congestion, as in "I'm going to move to the outskirts of town," or of alcoholism, as in the song, "Ignorant Oil." There is also much folk wisdom in the blues, as in "Nobody knows you when you're down and out," or in such observations as:

Now if a woman gets the blues, Lawd, she hangs
her head and cries,
But if a man gets the blues, Lawd, he grabs a
train and rides.

I am often reminded by the words of blues songs of Kenneth Burke's famous description of poetry as "equipment for living." In the form in which they developed in Negro communities, the blues are equipment for living humble, laborious, and precarious lives of low social status or no status at all—nevertheless, they are valid equipment, in the sense that they are the opposite of escape literature. "Rock Pile Blues" states explicitly what the blues are for:

My hammer's heavy, feels just like a ton of lead,
If they keeps me slaving someone's gonna find
me dead.

Don't mind the rock pile, but the days are oh so
long,
Ain't no end of misery, that is why I sing this
song.
["Rock Pile Blues," by Spencer Williams]

As a student of general semantics, I am concerned here with two functions which literary and poetic symbols perform with respect to our emotional life. First, by means of literary symbols we may be introduced vicariously to the emotions and situations which we have not yet had occasion to experience; in this sense, literature is preparation. Secondly, symbols enable us to organize the experiences we have had, make us aware of them, and therefore help us to come to terms with them; in this sense, literature is learning.

If our symbolic representations give a false or misleading impression of what life is likely to be, we are *worse* prepared for life than we would have been had we not been exposed to them at all. The frustration and demoralization of which Wendell Johnson writes are of necessity preceded by the expectations created by unrealistic idealizations. This is not to say, of course, that idealizations are in themselves unhealthy; they are a necessary and inescapable product of the human processes of abstraction and symbolization, and without idealizations we should be swine indeed. But there is a world of difference in the semantogenic effects of *possible* and *impossible* ideals. The ideals of love, as depicted in popular songs, are usually impossible ideals.

Hence the question arises: do popular songs, listened to, often memorized and sung in the course of adolescent and youthful courtship, make the attainment of emotional maturity more difficult than it need be? It is almost impossible to resist having an opinion on this question, although it would be hard to substantiate one's opinion except on the basis of considerable experience in contact with the emotional problems of young people. Mr. Roy E. Dickerson, executive secretary of the Cincinnati Social Hygiene Society, who has had this experience, has offered the following comment on the thesis of this paper:

In my judgment there is no doubt about the unfortunate influence of IFD upon the younger generation today. I detected it, I think, in even such a highly selected group as the delegates to the Seventh National Hi-Y-Tri-Hi-Y Congress held under the auspices of the National Council of YMCA's at Miami University recently. I had the pleasure of handling the group of the section of the Congress which gave attention to courtship and marriage. It was still necessary to debunk some super-romantic concepts.

I am up to my eyes in marriage counseling. I feel that I am consulted again and again about ill-considered marriages based upon very superficial and inadequate ideas regarding the nature of love and how it is recognized.

The existence of the blues, like the existence of occasional popular songs with love themes which do not exhibit the IFD pattern, demonstrates that it is at least possible for songs to be *both* reasonably healthy in psychological content *and* widely sung and enjoyed. But the blues cannot, of course, take over the entire domain of popular song because, as widely known as some of them have been, their chief appeal, for cultural reasons, has been to Negro audiences—and even these audiences have been diminishing with the progressive advancement of Negroes and their assimilation of values and tastes in common with the white, middle-class majority. Furthermore, while there is lyricism to be found in blues *tunes* and their musical treatment, the *words* of blues songs are notoriously lacking in either lyricism or delicacy of sentiment—and it would seem that popular songs must, to some degree, supply the need for lyrical expression, especially about matters of love.

With all their limitations, however, the blues demonstrate that a popular art can function as "equipment for living." Cannot our poets and our song-writers try to do at least as much for our young people as Bessie Smith did for her audiences, namely, provide them with symbolic experiences which will help them understand, organize, and better cope with their problems? Or, if that is too much to ask (and perhaps it is, since Bessie Smith was, in her own way, an authentic genius), can they not at least cease and desist from further spreading the all-too-prevalent IFD disease? (pp. 83-95)

S. I. Hayakawa, "Popular Songs vs. The Facts of Life," in ETC.: A Review of General Semantics, *Vol. 12, No. 2, Winter, 1955, pp. 83-95.*

Dave Harker

[*In the following essay, Harker argues that popular Christmas songs reinforce society's dominant capitalist ideology.*]

According to crude market criteria, Irving Berlin's "White Christmas" is the most popular song ever recorded in the English language. Within a year of its first appearance in the film *Holiday Inn,* in 1942, it had won an Academy Award, and it had sold over a million copies in versions by both Freddie Martin and Frank Sinatra. Bing Crosby, who sang the piece in the film, had to wait until 1946 before his recorded version sold a million copies, however; and it wasn't until he sang it on film again in 1954, this time in a film named after it, that Crosby's success was fully assured. In 1955, Berlin earned over a million dollars in royalties from this one song; and by 1963 it had sold over 45,000,000 records, in one version or another. By 1975—even before the upsurge occasioned by Crosby's death, and the calculated re-release of his version of the song—"White Christmas" had sold over 135,000,000 records, almost one-quarter of which were of Crosby's rendition. If we are seriously trying to understand the nature of popularity, and whatever we might think about this particular song, we have to cope with the fact that over 135,000,000 men and women deliberately went into a shop and paid cash for "White Christmas." Similarly, we have to try to understand what it is about "Rudolph the Red-Nosed Reindeer" which caused over 110,000,000 people to buy it, and how "Winter Wonderland" has found over 45,000,000 willing customers. At the same time, we must remember that pieces like Hoagy Carmichael's "Stardust," W. C. Handy's "St. Louis Blues," Lennon and McCartney's "Yesterday" and Levin and Brown's "Tie a Yellow Ribbon" are said to have been recorded by over a thousand different artists, itself an indication of popularity amongst that obviously important section of the music industry; and we have to recognize the importance of the performer as well as the song, bearing in mind that the best-selling version of "Rudolph," that by Gene Autry, sold *only* 8,000,000 copies, or just over 7 per cent of the total sales of the song. Clearly, even the market criteria for popularity are not straight-forward; and we must be very careful when we are attempting to discover what sales figures of 100,000,000 *mean,* culturally.

Some generalizations are evident enough. It is surely significant, for example, that Christmas (and all it stands for in Western culture) is at the heart of these three best-selling recorded songs. What, though, is Christmas about? On the one hand, it retains a vestigial religious significance; but this element cannot be held to be important in a culture which, like Britain's, has seen a decline in religious observance since at least 1851 (when the first census question on the subject was included). On the other hand, Christmas hasn't yet been fully absorbed into the mainstream of holidays pure and simple. There remains suffi-

Ethel Waters in a scene from Irving Berlin's As Thousands Cheer.

cient official religiosity in the media and in certain areas of commerce to prop up key elements of the festival, so as to prevent its becoming wholly secular; though this is less the case in Scotland, for example, where New Year (Hogmanay) retains a large measure of its pre-Christian significance, and dwarfs 25 December altogether. In any case, it is the former importance of 26 December, Boxing Day, which dwarfs the day before, even though the customs of Boxing Day have now been eased back twenty-four hours, and in some cases to Christmas Eve.

Christmas, in our culture, is primarily about spending money, and not working. Presents are given and received, parties are held, camaraderie (real or feigned) usually predominates in the family (which, in turn, the ritual helps sustain) and in public. More basically, the holiday functions as a break in the long grind of winter work, the temporary release from the wet, the tedium, the insecurities of societies increasingly seen to be in crisis at shorter and shorter intervals. Conversely, to those many who have no real economic security—to the millions out of work or below the poverty line—Christmas serves to underline their relative deprivation. To an important extent then, Christmas highlights many of the contradictions of capitalist societies, and it would be surprising if songs like 'White Christmas,' 'Rudolph' and 'Winter Wonderland' did *not* articulate some of the key values (directly or indirectly) of the dominant ideology.

Every line of 'White Christmas' (unfortunately, we have been refused permission to print the lyrics) could fit inside a Christmas card. The second verse (as we know the song, without the introduction) even mentions those curious objects. Every line is, and is meant to be, evocative of those fantasy pictures on the front of Christmas cards—glistening tree tops, attentive, angelic children (usually boys, and more often than not, choir boys), elaborately wrapped parcels, and, of course, the superbly irrational reindeer and sleighs with bells and Santa. But when we think for a moment, it is clear that for these images to have any purchase on reality, there has to be an underlying assumption about a generally high level of material comfort in society. Only then could snow be seen, unequivocally, as attractive and welcome. To put the point baldly, how is snow perceived by the 100,000 or so old people in Britain who are at risk from hypothermia each winter? Then again, we have to suspend disbelief not only in the reindeer and all, but we must also ignore the relative infrequency of a Christmas Eve snowfall in most of the English-speaking world! But Christmas is *about* irrationality just as much as it is about sentimentality. It's about substituting the purchase of commodities for the effort of the year round affection and care. It's about throwing out anxieties and sympathy along with the wrapping paper and the heat-distorted, token cards. And it's about adding insult to injury, by twisting the emotional arms of those many who cannot really afford to indulge in the sentimentalities, but who are still driven to buy fripperies rather than food or heat. This is certainly the case in Britain; but perhaps it is less true in the affluent USA. Of course, this is not to put the finger on Irving Berlin for multiple crimes against humanity; but perhaps we can better understand how a song like 'White Christmas' has lent itself so easily to par-

ody, like many another commercially successful piece. What fitter subject for ironic inversion, overstatement, or hamming?

It's not Irving Berlin's fault, or Crosby's, if we choose to buy their work. What is important is the extent to which this song has been able to penetrate even working-class culture, as part of the general ideological success of capitalism's ruling class. Then again, it would be quite silly to accuse Berlin and Crosby of being part of some devious plot, and to place the onus for the song's success on the cleverness of our rulers. What we have to confront in songs like this is our own weakness, our own susceptibilities. For all Crosby's trite stutters, and in spite of the amazingly crude choirs of 'angels' who we *know* are on piece-work, it is the case that 'White Christmas' has permeated English-speaking cultures, perhaps permanently, over almost two generations. In analysing the song's appeal, then, we must of course bear in mind that Western working-class culture has to a large extent embraced the dominant capitalist ideology since the 1940s; but we must also beware of the conspiracy theory that workers have been unconsciously bamboozled into swallowing that ideology whole, uncritically, and in the prescribed manner.

It is no accident, for example, that the song was first sung, by Crosby, to US troops in the Philippines in 1942. As Berlin was well aware, by writing 'a peace song in wartime' and by having it included in a film which would be guaranteed to reach millions of people in the armed forces overseas, he was well on the way to commercial success. No doubt this is why in the film, 'White Christmas,' Crosby is pictured singing the title song on just such an occasion, near the front line, to a captive audience of army personnel (almost all of whom were men). Lovers apart is perhaps the dominant theme of most successful Western songs in any case, and what more poignant than separation by war? The answer to that question, of course, is just such a song set at Christmas time. If it were simply a question of these elements, suitably wrapped up by Berlin, the conspiracy theory might have some credibility; but, of course, the reality of being in the army and having a good time at Christmas are two activities which do not fit neatly into what our 'betters' would regard as appropriate working-class behaviour.

Christmas, in a working-class community, is by no means dictated by authority—by the state, by employers, or by commerce, let alone by the church or chapel. In practice, once the kids have got their presents—which are often bought at considerable economic sacrifice on the part of the parents, and which form a significant part of the yearly 'leisure' budget—Christmas is primarily about rest, food, drink and companionship. What differentiates working-class Christmases from those experienced by their 'betters', however, is the *public* character of much of the celebration. In spite of the fact that workers know the whole enterprise is horribly commercialized, and that their part in the business is to help keep cash registers tinkling by eating, drinking and buying strictly unnecessary products, they are still determined to enjoy themselves, not least because the return to 'normal' life is as inevitable as it is unwelcome. The apparent irrationality of over-eating and over-drinking, which leads 'sophisticated' commentators to recall the understandably all-but-paranoid pagan festivities during the crisis of the winter solstice, is socially *necessary*. So the irrationality of 'White Christmas' is to a large extent also a *necessary* irrationality. It is by now almost a traditional element in both the official and the unofficial Christmases, those quite different events—the former being what is publicly offered by those who control the major channels of transmission, and the other being how the official Christmas is *appropriated, and transformed,* by working-class people worldwide.

So, we can sleep easy. No propaganda expert could have produced a song such as this to keep the masses in the approved state of mindlessness. Fortunately, our leaders aren't that clever. What is true is that the Christmas evoked by Berlin's sparsely worded song and sentimental music does, indeed, have a fair degree of 'fit' with the dominant ideology; but what is also true is that those key elements of working-class culture which can so easily be trivialized, the compassion, the caring and the collectivity, are actively reinforced in the way in which the song is 'consumed'. It doesn't matter, then, though it is intriguing, that Berlin was once forced to admit 'I like sunny Christmases,' as he left for Florida. It doesn't matter, because it's not Berlin's fault or his responsibility how people behave in the market-place for music and song. If his song is manipulative—if it does effectively reinforce the values and assumptions of the ideology of capitalist individualism, taken straight—the point to remember is that 'White Christmas' is *never* taken straight. Even in the lyrics, Berlin recognizes that his song operates at the level of wish fulfilling fantasy: the best that can be hoped is that days *may* be merry and bright, and that Christmas *may* be white.

Compared to 'White Christmas,' 'Rudolph' (again, we have not been allowed to print the lyrics) is crude. It is also rather a nasty little song. It was written by Johnny Marks, and had its live debut at Madison Square Gardens in 1949, when it was sung by Hollywood cowboy, Gene Autry. His version went on to become the best-selling US record of 1949-50; and by 1964 the 300 recorded versions of the song had sold an aggregate of over 40,000,000 copies. The figure is now over 110,000,000. (Amongst others, Perry Como and Pinky and Perky have produced records of the piece, but it is perhaps in Autry's version that the song is best remembered, especially in Britain, where that version was most frequently used in radio broadcasts for children.)

Aimed as it is at children, the song's story line is simple enough. In fact, in Britain at any rate, it came across quite clearly as a Christmas version of that other 'Children's Hour' regular, the versified version of Hans Christian Andersen's tale 'The Ugly Duckling.' (At least, comic-grotesque was a change from wholehearted sentimentality.) But the assumptions on which both stories are based, and the bland manner in which quite extraordinary events are passed off as normal, deserve more than token analysis. Though it would in certain ways be comforting, and though we continually run the risk of becoming over earnest, there's no escaping that what 'Rudolph' sets out to

validate are peculiarly brutal examples of behaviour. So, while on the one hand it *is* a sad little story for kids, with the usual 'happy ending', on the other hand it offers itself as an account of 'human nature', thinly disguised as 'reindeer nature'.

Leaving aside the grand irrationality of the whole setting, for the moment, what can we learn of the social structure of Lapland/Greenland/the North Pole? We start with the isolated figure, Rudolph, who was a little out of the ordinary. The whole tone of the song suggests that, after all, its hero was *deformed;* and this is allowed to 'explain' why all of the other reindeer 'used to laugh and call him names'. So, while we are encouraged to sympathize with the deformed one, we are also invited to understand why Rudolph is treated vindictively by his fellows, even though (as verse two reveals) the whole reindeer community is equally subject to one authority figure, Santa. But it is surely disingenuous to believe that by transposing the scene to the fantasy world of Christmas, all moral distinctions are automatically invalid. Children *do* learn from a song that this kind of behaviour is allowed to go on—is, almost, acceptable—because it's allegedly 'reindeer nature'. And part of the potency of the song is the way in which all this is implied, never fully articulated. The 'absences', if you like, are more articulate than the lyrics.

The second verse reveals the social structure more fully. There is a single (human) authority figure who exercises a form of benevolent despotism over the remaining (non-human) reindeer population. But this is no *1984* scenario. Rather than see dissension in the ranks, Santa, the benevolent dictator, goes out of his way to find a practical use for Rudolph's 'deformity'. Ironically, by bringing this-worldly problems into an allegedly fantasy setting, Marks undermines the fantasy itself. After all, at the most obvious level, if we can imagine speaking reindeer, why should fog present any problems to Santa! Then comes the most crucial revelation. Immediately official approval is given, the four-faced reindeer bow, scrape and suck up to Rudolph (who, presumably, responds with a certain arrogance, now). Sycophancy, and implicit obedience, are as socially acceptable in this kind of society as is hypocrisy—'then how the reindeer *loved* him' indeed! Of course, the song offers no comment on this dramatic reversal of behaviour amongst the servile reindeer, let alone on the power of Santa. After all, it isn't meant to be a sociological treatise. But that's precisely the point: what *do* real, live human children make of this curious sequence of events? Do they learn that fickleness is part of reindeer (*read,* human) nature? Do they learn that truckling to individuals in authority—no matter how they came to be there, or whatever their behaviour—is not only acceptable, but necessary? Does the inculcation of servility—though I do not suggest for a moment that this was either Mark's or Autry's intention—in any case seem appropriate in societies where most children will remain in the working majority, the 'herd'? Or is this simply a happy little song for kids?

At least 'Winter Wonderland' is transparent. It was written by Felix Bernard and Dick Smith in 1934, and sold over a million copies in the version recorded by Guy Lombardo and his Royal Canadians with the Andrews Sisters. Amongst others, Ted Weems and his Orchestra, Perry Como, and the Ray Charles Singers have had successful recordings of the song; but it is probably the version produced by Johnny Mathis in the 1950s that is most familiar now, particularly to a British audience. (Though it is interesting that Mathis' version could reach only number seventeen in the British singles charts in 1958.) The scene is already familiar: sleigh bells, glistening snow, picturesque lanes and all; yet the courtship which is enacted in the song in terms of this fantasy landscape is notably revealing. It is not wholly preposterous to claim that 'Winter Wonderland' articulates the key fantasies not only about the Christmas period (though the festival is not referred to directly) but, crucially, about the pattern of sexual relations felt to be most appropriate for a particular social order.

We begin deep into fantasy, being asked to hear sleigh bells (which, of course, can be simulated on record); and then we're introduced into what is literally 'wonderland'. After all, the point about the situation is precisely that 'we're happy tonight', so there must clearly be something extraordinary going on! What could be more natural (or extraordinary, depending on your point of view) than to build a snowman—snow being a suitably chaste symbol, perhaps, until the thaw back to reality turns it to grey slush—and to pretend he is the parson? After the 'snowman' has asked an impertinent question, what more polite than to answer encouragingly, accepting his right not only to interfere, but also to perform the rites necessary to legalize the relationship? It goes without saying, in this 'wonderland', that courtship inevitably leads to marriage. But then look what happens. Once the couple return to their fireside, a little nearer the real world, they have to *'conspire'* to *'face unafraid'* the plans that they made in the first flush of their relationship. It's as though what had seemed like an opportunity, 'outside', had turned a little sour back 'inside'. So, whereas exuberance was possible—almost, demanded—in the 'wonderland', in the reality of marriage they recognize that a 'dream' is necessary to enable them to cope with their responsibilities. The relationship becomes the problem, not the opportunity it had once seemed. The heads go down, the brows furrow, and the possibility of a full and free relationship seems to recede rapidly, making the fantasy world of 'wonderland' ever more attractive as an intellectual bolt-hole. Ironically, it is 'sleigh bells land' which can seem more real than reality.

Getting married in a capitalist society is, indeed, a form of escape from the pressures of independence, and at the same time, more or less a deeper entry into the sentimental ideology favoured by that form of society. This is its basic contradiction, in the West. At its heart, of course, marriage is essentially a property relation; but it was usually seen (certainly in the 1930s and 1940s) as not only 'natural' but inevitable, almost as a precondition of adulthood. This is no longer the case, of course; but there is a residual irrationality in the notion that marriages or equivalent relationships *are* somehow 'made in heaven', or 'wonderland', or whatever. What remains genuinely extraordinary is the way in which marriage is seen as 'normal'—as, of course, is the family—even to the point where not being

married can often be taken as evidence of abnormality. The reasons for capitalist ideology's support of marriage and the family (as we know it) are transparent enough. Marriages tend to produce children, more often than not. Children are needed so as to increase the labour market, and thereby compete with each other as orthodox individualists. Without a surplus of potential producers, how could unemployment be a threat? And without that threat—without the divisions it fosters as part of the general antagonisms politely termed the 'market mechanism'—how could this form of society continue to exist? If the competitive individualistic system broke down, some half a million rich people in Britain alone would be worse off, and we can't have that, can we?

Yet, here again, there's no point in blaming Bernard and Smith for articulating elements of the dominant ideology in their song. It's hardly their fault if the song-buying public responds overwhelmingly to fantasy, any more than a capitalist ruling class can be blamed (in its terms, that is) for seeking to continue its dominance. If blame is appropriate, perhaps it ought first to be directed at the weakness in all of us which encourages us to wallow periodically in sentiment and nostalgia, rather than setting about changing a society in which such refuges are necessary. (pp. 42-50)

> *Dave Harker, "The Average Popular Song," in his* One for the Money: Politics and Popular Song, *Hutchinson, 1980, pp. 38-50.*

FURTHER READING

I. Anthologies

Harmon, William, ed. *The Oxford Book of American Light Verse.* New York: Oxford University Press, 1979, 540 p.
> Includes lyrics by Cole Porter, Oscar Hammerstein II, Lorenz Hart, Ira Gershwin, and Johnny Mercer.

II. Secondary Sources

Bergreen, Laurence. *As Thousands Cheer: The Life of Irving Berlin.* New York: Viking, 1990, 658 p.
> Recent biography of Berlin.

Burgess, Anthony. "Under the Bam." In his *This Man and Music,* pp. 96-116. London: Hutchinson, 1982.
> Comparison of song lyrics and poetry. Citing "Mamma, I Wanna Make Rhythm,"by Jerome Jerome, Richard Byron, and Walter Kent, Burgess writes, "Brash, yes, but not crude. Witty, but not rarefied. And exemplifying the possibility of a perfect marriage between colloquial speech rhythms and the rhythms of music."

Burton, Jack. *The Blue Book of Tin Pan Alley: A Human Interest Anthology of American Popular Music.* New York: Century House, 1950, 520 p.
> Chronological listing of songs and songwriters.

Chase, Gilbert. *America's Music: From the Pilgrims to the Present.* Urbana: University of Illinois Press, 1987, 712 p.

Views popular music from a cultural and historical perspective.

Craig, Warren. *Sweet and Lowdown: America's Popular Song Writers.* Metuchen, N.J.: The Scarecrow Press, 1978, 645 p.
> Comprehensive listing of songs and songwriters, including rankings of songwriters with the most "hits."

Ewen, David. *All the Years of American Popular Music.* Englewood Cliffs, N.J.: Prentice-Hall, 1977, 850 p.
> Exhaustive history of popular music, covering important songwriters, performers, and movements.

Gershwin, George. "The Relation of Jazz to American Music." In *American Composers on American Music: A Symposium,* edited by Henry Cowell, pp. 186-87. 1933. Reprint. New York: Frederick Ungar, 1962.
> Envisions the creation of an American music based on folk forms.

Gershwin, Ira. *Lyrics on Several Occasions.* New York: Alfred A. Knopf, 1959, 362 p.
> Lyrics for some of Gershwin's songs, supplemented with anecdotes and commentary.

Gill, Brendan. *Cole: A Biographical Essay.* New York: Holt, Rinehart & Winston, 1971, 283 p.
> Chronicles Porter's life and includes many of his lyrics.

Hammerstein, Oscar II. "Notes on Lyrics." In his *Lyrics,* pp. 3-48. New York: Simon & Schuster, 1949.
> Hammerstein discusses his attitudes about writing lyrics.

Harburg, E.Y. (Yip) "The Song." In Hard Times: An Oral History of the Great Depression, pp. 19-21. New York: Pantheon, 1970.
> Recounts the story behind his song, "Brother, Can You Spare a Dime?"

Horn, David. *The Literature of American Music in Books and Folk Music Collections: A Fully Annotated Bibliography.* Metuchen, N.J.: The Scarecrow Press, 1977, 556 p.
> Bibliography covering a wide variety of styles, periods, songs, and songwriters.

Jablonski, Edward and Stewart, Lawrence D., eds. *The Gershwin Years.* New York: Doubleday, 1958, 313 p.
> Photographic chronicle of George and Ira Gershwin.

Jasen, David. *Tin Pan Alley: The Composers, the Songs, the Performers and Their Times.* New York: Donald I. Fine, 1988, 312 p.
> History of "those songs that have become a most important part of our American heritage."

Kanter, Kenneth Aaron. *The Jews on Tin Pan Alley: The Jewish Contribution to American Popular Music, 1830-1940.* New York: Ktav, 1982, 226 p.
> Observes that such Jewish songwriters as Lorenz Hart, Jerome Kern, Irving Berlin, and George and Ira Gershwin "belonged to, or were not far from, a generation of immigrants who wanted nothing better than to be 'Americanized.'"

Kaufmann, Helen L. "Blacks and Blues and Ragtime, The Missing Link." In her *From Jehovah to Jazz: Music in America from Psalmody to the Present Day,* pp. 240-54. New York: Dodd, Mead & Company, 1937.
> Treats American popular music as a hybrid of the indigenous styles of blues and ragtime, and the European operetta.

Larkin, Philip. "Supreme Sophisticate." In his *Required Writing: Miscellaneous Pieces, 1955-1982,* pp. 225-27. New York: Farrar Straus Giroux, 1982.
> Celebrates Cole Porter's magnetic personality. Of Porter's lyrics, Larkin writes, "Cole Porter was well within the comic song/drawing-room ballad tradition that persisted into the Thirties from the previous century. Whether he influenced it is doubtful; the 'Cole Porter song', that feat of rhyme and reference, was rarely copied."

Mellers, Wilfrid. "From Pop to Art: Opera, the Musical and George Gershwin's *Porgy and Bess.*" In his *Music in a New Found Land: Themes and Developments in the History of American Music,* pp. 392-413. London: Barrie and Rockliff, 1964.
> Interprets *Porgy and Bess* as an opera about "the impact of the world of commerce on those who once led, would like to have led, may still lead, the 'good life,' based on a close relationship between man and nature."

Meyer, Hazel. *The Gold in Tin Pan Alley.* Philadelphia: J. B. Lippincott, 1958, 258 p.
> Focuses on the financial and legal aspects of popular song.

Montgomery, Elizabeth Rider. *The Story Behind Popular Songs.* New York: Dodd, Mead & Co., 1958, 253 p.
> Contains profiles of popular songwriters.

Mooney, H. F. "Popular Music since the 1920s: The Significance of Shifting Taste." *American Quarterly* 20, No. 1 (Spring 1968): 67-85.
> Calls the music audience between 1920 and 1950 "a generation of transition." Mooney contends that the audience "compromised between the gentility of the Victorian parlor and the libidinism of the beatnik's pad."

Pearsall, Ronald. *Popular Music of the Twenties.* Totowa, N.J.: Rowman and Littlefield, 1976, 176 p.
> Attributes the changes in popular music of the 1920s to the rise of the gramophone and the player piano.

Pessen, Edward. "The Great Songwriters of Tin Pan Alley's Golden Age: A Social, Occupational, and Aesthetic Inquiry." *American Music* 3, No. 2 (Summer 1985): 180-97.
> Calls for further inquiry into popular song based on the "universality of its appeal and the intrinsic qualities that account for this appeal." Pessen argues that "the melody, more than the lyrics, determines the quality of a song."

Porter, Cole. *The Complete Lyrics of Cole Porter,* edited by Robert Kimball. New York: Alfred A. Knopf, 1983, 354 p.
> Contains a foreword by John Updike crediting Porter for bringing "to the traditional and somewhat standardized tasks of songsmithing a great verbal ingenuity, a brave flexibility and resourcefulness . . . , a cosmopolitan's wide expertise in many mundane matters . . . , and a spirit that always kept something of collegiate innocence about it."

Rodgers, Richard. *Musical Stages: An Autobiography.* New York: Random House, 1975, 341 p.
> Reminisces about musical collaborations with Lorenz Hart and Oscar Hammerstein II.

Shapiro, Nat, and Pollock, Bruce, eds. *Popular Music, 1920-1979.* 3 vols. Detroit: Gale Research, 1985.
>   Annotated index of over 18,000 American songs.

Shaw, Arnold. "Popular Music from Minstrel Songs to Rock 'n' Roll." In *One Hundred Years of Music in America,* edited by Paul Henry Lang, pp. 140-68. New York: G. Schirmer, 1961.
>   Studies trends and styles in popular song and theorizes, "Although it has been maintained that the history of a country is written in its popular songs, American songwriters have not been too responsive to sociological developments, except, perhaps, for wars."

Spaeth, Sigmund. *The Facts of Life in Popular Song.* New York: Whittlesey House, 1934, 148 p.
>   Satirical study of the lyrics of popular songs.

Wilder, Alec. *American Popular Song: The Great Innovators, 1900-1950.* New York: Oxford University Press, 1972, 535 p.
>   Thorough study of both prominent and lesser-known songwriters, focusing on the music rather than the lyrics.

Wilk, Max. *They're Playing Our Song.* New York: Atheneum, 1973, 295 p.
>   Contains interviews with and personal reminiscences of American songwriters, including Jerome Kern, Ira Gershwin, and Stephen Sondheim.

The Literature of the Beat Generation

INTRODUCTION

The Beat Generation writers comprised a loosely affiliated group of American novelists and poets of the 1940s and 1950s who rejected the predominantly conservative middle-class values of the Cold War era. Adopting the slang of jazz musicians, Jack Kerouac, the chief literary figure and spokesperson of the movement, used the word "beat" to describe the world-weary yet optimistic attitude of his generation, signifying both the "beaten down" condition of disaffected youth of the time and their "beatific" quest for an existence unfettered by social conventions. The term "Beat" has been used to refer to the works of various avant-garde writers and artists of this period, but critics generally agree that Beat literature is best represented by the works of the novelists Kerouac and William S. Burroughs and the poets Allen Ginsberg, Gregory Corso, and Lawrence Ferlinghetti. While the Beats never formulated a consistent aesthetic or philosophical viewpoint, their works are most often characterized by experimental narrative and metrical forms, informal and frequently sexually explicit language, and uninhibited revelation of personal experiences.

Commentators date the inception of the Beat movement to 1944, when Kerouac, Ginsberg, and Burroughs met at Columbia University in New York; however, the Beat writers gained little attention until a widely publicized reading of Beat poetry in San Francisco in 1955 and the publication of Ginsberg's *Howl, and Other Poems* the following year. Unsuccessful attempts to ban the sale of *Howl* and Burroughs's *Naked Lunch* on charges of obscenity also brought notoriety to the Beat movement and later established important legal precedents for works of literature. During the late 1950s and early 1960s journalists and sociologists studied Beat communities in San Francisco and other cities, often focusing on the drug use, unconventional sexual mores, and apparent aimlessness of their bohemian life-style. Most commentators agree that by the mid-1960s the Beat movement had been largely superseded by the hippie counterculture.

Inspired by the improvisational style, harmonic structures, and argot of avant-garde jazz musicians, the Beats developed several experimental approaches to fiction and poetry, including Burroughs's "cut-up" and "fold-in" techniques for randomly juxtaposing passages of text to evoke new associations and Kerouac's composition of "spontaneous prose," in which he claimed to write without revision or concern for grammar and syntax. Recurring themes and subjects explored in Beat writing include the stifling conformity of American society, the horrors of nuclear war, attraction to Eastern philosophies, the use of marijuana and other drugs, sexual experimentation, and joy riding. Perhaps the most representative work of Beat literature is Kerouac's novel *On the Road,* a loosely structured, fictionalized account of the wanderings and reckless adventures of Kerouac and his friends. Many critics of the 1950s dismissed the experimental forms of Beat writing as incoherent babbling and considered the direct language and erotic content of their works obscene. Recognized today as an important development in American literature, Beat writing is considered a valuable commentary on the social and spiritual malaise of postwar America.

(See also *Dictionary of Literary Biography,* Vol. 16.)

REPRESENTATIVE WORKS

Bremser, Bonnie
   Troia: Mexican Memoirs (memoirs) 1969; also published as *For Love of Ray,* 1971
Bremser, Ray
   Poems of Madness (poetry) 1965
   Angel (poetry) 1967
Brossard, Chandler
   Who Walk in Darkness (novel) 1952
Burroughs, William S.
   Junkie: Confessions of an Unredeemed Drug Addict [as William Lee] (novel) 1953; also published as *Junky* [enlarged edition], 1977
   The Naked Lunch (novel) 1959; also published as *Naked Lunch,* 1962
Cassady, Neal
   The First Third, and Other Writings (autobiography) 1971; revised and enlarged edition, 1981
   As Ever: The Collected Correspondence of Allen Ginsberg and Neal Cassady (letters) 1977
Corso, Gregory
   In This Hung-Up Age (drama) 1955
   The Vestal Lady on Brattle, and Other Poems (poetry) 1955
   Gasoline (poetry) 1958
   The Happy Birthday of Death (poetry) 1960
DiPrima, Diane
   This Kind of Bird Flies Backward (poetry) 1958
   Dinners and Nightmares (prose and poetry) 1961; enlarged edition, 1974
   Memoirs of a Beatnik (autobiography) 1969
Ferlinghetti, Lawrence
   Pictures of the Gone World (poetry) 1955
   A Coney Island of the Mind (poetry) 1958; enlarged editions, 1959, 1968
Ginsberg, Allen
   Howl, and Other Poems (poetry) 1956
   Empty Mirror (poetry) 1961
   Kaddish, and Other Poems (poetry) 1961
   Reality Sandwiches: 1953-1960 (poetry) 1963
Holmes, John Clellon

Go   (novel)   1952; also published as *The Beat Boys,* 1959

Nothing More to Declare   (essays)   1967

Jones, Leroi (Amiri Baraka)

Preface to a Twenty Volume Suicide Note . . .   (poetry)   1961

Kaufman, Bob

Solitudes Crowded with Loneliness   (poetry)   1965

The Golden Sardine   (poetry)   1967

Kerouac, Jack

On the Road   (novel)   1957

The Dharma Bums   (novel)   1958

The Subterraneans   (novel)   1958

Mexico City Blues   (poetry)   1959

Big Sur   (novel)   1962

Visions of Gerard   (novel)   1963

Desolation Angels   (novel)   1965

Vanity of Duluoz: An Adventurous Education, 1935-1946   (novel)   1968

Visions of Cody   (novel)   1972

Micheline, Jack

River of Red Wine   (poetry)   1958

McClure, Michael

Passage   (poetry)   1956

Hymns to St. Geryon, and Other Poems   (poetry)   1959

Snyder, Gary

Riprap   (poetry)   1959

Myths & Texts   (poetry)   1960

OVERVIEWS

Wolfgang Bernard Fleischmann

[*In the following essay originally published in 1959, Fleischmann offers a contemporary overview of the Beat Generation.*]

We are all familiar with the term "beat generation." It has come, within the last three years, to connote a variety of American artistic and social phenomena. In its widest sense, "beat generation" describes a group of people involved in a way of life, the positive features of which are general resistance against the values and mores of the American middle class, a total acceptance of all types of sexual behavior, general predilection for "cool jazz," and the adoption of Oriental mysticism in the form of Zen Buddhism as a unifying metaphysics and philosophy of life. The negative features of the way of life described by the adjective "beat" are withdrawal from politics and from the responsibilities of citizenship, withdrawal from the universities and academies, and withdrawal of recognition from all institutions the State provides.

Less widely defined, the "beat generation" is thought of as a group of bohemians, made up of jazz-musicians, writers, artists, college students, and generally dislocated personalities who lead *la vie* "beat" in San Francisco, New York, or Boston—also, in a more isolated manner, in Mexican villages, on the beaches of Southern California, and at various spots in the Rocky and Smoky Mountains. The names of individuals play a larger role in this second visualization of a "beat generation" than in the first. We find grouped here jazz-musicians like Lennie Tristano, Dave Brubeck, and Lester Young, photographers like Harry Redly and Harold Feinstein, writers like the popular novelist Norman Mailer, as well as the poets and authors engaged in the more specifically literary contexts of the movement. These personalities often, though not always, gather in cafes of Bohemian character, surrounded by a coterie made up of the curious and interested. In some of the bars thus frequented, the central attraction is the reading, to the accompaniment of jazz, the works of the "beat generation's" writers and poets.

It is the fairly unorganized group made up of these authors which comprises the most narrow concept subsumed under the term "beat generation": the literary movement of that name which, so baptized by its main prose author Jack Kerouac, has attracted wide attention ever since some of its members gathered in a San Francisco art gallery in the fall of 1955 to rebel consciously against the academic tradition in American poetry.

Who are the "beat generation" authors? Even a cursory glance at their biographies shows that they are not a generation in terms of age, ranging, as they do, between the ages of twenty-odd and fifty-odd. Nor are their intellectual, social, and religious backgrounds of sufficient homogeneity to attribute to them a common denominator as to provenance. Are they, then, a "generation" in the sense of literary history—a unified movement of poetic innovation in style with a common philosophical set of beliefs? The answer to this question is not clear at first glance for, among certain ones of the group, a solidarity of style and ideas is readily apparent, though some salient differences also rise readily to view. It is hence necessary to take a closer look at the authors of the "beat generation" and at certain features some of these have in common.

Let us begin with the best known ones—Jack Kerouac and Allan Ginsberg. John (Jack) Kerouac is the author of thirteen novels, of which four, among them *On the Road, The Subterraneans,* and *The Dharma Bums,* are published. He is thirty-six years old, a former Columbia University football player and merchant marine sailor. According to Malcolm Cowley, publisher of *On the Road,* Kerouac works on typewriter strip-rolls without revising. He has defined, in the fifth issue of the *Evergreen Review,* a method of writing fiction based on Wilhelm Reich's theory of the orgasm. This method advocates self-expression in the total degree: the author creates his style by leaving his words and associations as they come from him in the hot pitch of creative frenzy.

Allen Ginsberg, four years Kerouac's junior, is the author of the "beat generation's" manifesto, the poem "Howl." Other major lyrics by Ginsberg include the poem "America," the opening lines of which

> America I've given you all and now I'm nothing.
> America two dollars and twenty-seven cents
>   January 17, 1956.

have endeared its author to European left-wing intellectuals, a long poem entitled "A Supermarket in California," and, more recently, a series of lyrics called *Siesta at Xbalba*. Unlike Kerouac, who claims total originality, Ginsberg openly declares himself in his poems to be an imitator of Walt Whitman, Maiakowsky, and Guillaume Apollinaire and a student both of Zen Buddhism and of Mayan mysticism. Like Kerouac, Ginsberg is a product of Columbia University.

In the second string of "beat generation" poets a great and diverse collection of individuals may be placed. To proceed here from the sublime to the ultra-terrestrial, we should start this list with William Everson, now Brother Antoninus, O.P., a forty-six year old lay brother. Brother Antoninus' verse speaks, in tones reminiscent of Gerard Manley Hopkins of the relations between man and God in a troubled universe. A second Roman Catholic poet, John Logan, has recently had verse of less eminent, but similar, sort published in the *Evergreen Review*. Philip Whalen, an ex-Reed College student and World War II veteran, closes, though in a different vein, the list of "beat generation metaphysicals." He is a Buddhist mystic who, after a period in a Japanese monastery, has settled down to write meditative verse in Berkeley, California.

The authors we may call the "beat generation ultra-terrestrials" seem to be, on the surface, in greatest contrast to the spiritually concerned group of poets just spoken of. But this contrast is superficial: while the poetry of Ginsberg and the prose of Kerouac dwell deliberately on the sordid, the unmentionable, and the socially controversial, they have a concern with values beyond the material ones which is rather clearly stated. Beyond Ginsberg's bloody toilets and Kerouac's bowls of unsanitary oatmeal served in truckers' cafes there lie visions of a peaceful world made strong by the love of comrades and the joys of mystic insight. Zen Buddhism and a kind of comradeship reminiscent of the *Wandervogel* movement in the German Weimar Republic's days, are its ideals.

The works of two other "beat generation" writers beside Ginsberg and Kerouac are in this "ultra-terrestrial" vein: the poetry of Lawrence Ferlinghetti and the prose of Michael Rumaker. Ferlinghetti, thirty-nine, is a San Francisco publisher and the owner of the City Lights Bookshop in that city. Like Ginsberg, he exalts emancipation and resistance to institutions; unlike "Howl," however, Ferlinghetti's *Pictures of the Gone World* and *A Coney Island of the Mind* are series of lyrics consciously imitative of William Carlos Williams' lighter verse and akin in technique to the work of E. E. Cummings. Rumaker, a twenty-six year old graduate of Black Mountain College, writes a prose highly reminiscent of Kerouac's but endowed with a distinctive gift for precise description. His story, "The Desert," printed in the second *Evergreen Review*, shows, as well, that even "beat" prose may gain value from proper punctuation.

Between the "beat generation metaphysicals" and its "ultra-terrestrials," a group of writers should be mentioned which might be termed "beat-generation experimentals." Here we have poets who share a predilection for jazz-rhythm and a certain mystic tone with Whalen, on

Front cover of Allen Ginsberg's Howl, and Other Poems *(1956).*

the one hand, and Ginsberg, on the other, but whose verse is neither topical nor philosophical but concentrated on a communication of images. A typical young "experimental" in this sense is Michael (Mike) McClure, like Rumaker twenty-six and a product of Black Mountain College, whose verse shows definite echoes of the American imagist movement (Amy Lowell, the early Pound) coupled with an imitation of "cool" jazz-rhythm. Another is Philip Lamantia, a fiftyish ex-anarchist and ex-surrealist. In Lamantia's poems, the strains of "way-out" jazz give motion to a world of Dali watches and William Carlos Williams guitars, melted together in a mystical—but undirected—way. Thirty-nine year old Robert Duncan boldly plays with the "Structure of Rime" in a long *Evergreen Review* poem of that name. Josephine Miles, a full professor of English at the University of California (Berkeley), endows her rather conventional imagist verse, the latest of some years' production, with startling touches evocative of jazz.

Robert Duncan, Josephine Miles—as well as several other less prominent poets published in the City Lights Press, the Jargon Press, and in the *Evergreen Review* make up a segment of the literary "beat generation" which shares with its "metaphysical" and "ultra-terrestrial" segments only a tolerance of unconventional form and language in poetry. Even more clearly than McClure and Lamantia, the minor "beat generation experimentals" are purely literary affiliates of the movement. Their presence within it indicates the "beat generation's" diverse poetic strains and its lack of a cohesive literary doctrine. For, upon further analysis, even my division of these authors into "metaphysicals," "experimentals," and "super-terrestrials" can be shown to be synthetic and arbitrary. Basically, the "beat generation's" authors are too distinctly individualistic to allow their work to be classified. Nor is there, in the maze of Zen Buddhism, Roman Catholicism, cynicism, hedonism, and surrealism which informs their work, any unified philosophical position, save, perhaps, that vague utopian and pacifist goal of man at ease with himself which is shared by both the religious and earthy "beat generation" writers.

We do not, then, have in the "beat generation," a literary movement as such a phenomenon as is understood by most historians of letters. What unifying factors which draw the "beat generation" authors together may be found? Is the "beat" way of life their only cohesive force? Surely not, for Brother Antoninus, Josephine Miles, and John Logan, to mention only three *Evergreen Review* poets, can scarcely (being, respectively, a Dominican lay brother, a nominee for the Executive Committee of the Modern Language Association, and a family-man teaching at Notre Dame) be associated with hot-rods, dope-peddling, or wandering *On the Road*. We must turn, for an answer to this question, to the critical prose of Kenneth Rexroth, the literary apologist for the "beat generation."

Rexroth, a fifty-three year old poet, ex-anarchist, ex-Marxist present-day radio announcer has, within the past two years, published several essays on the "beat generation" writers which treat of these in a sympathetic vein. Rexroth's essays are all fairly similar to one another and revolve about four central points:

> 1. The "beat generation" writers and poets are a unique and startlingly novel phenomenon in American literature.
>
> 2. The "beat-generation" writers revive a valuable—indeed the only real tradition in American letters.
>
> 3. The "beat generation" writers are the heroes of a long-needed revolution against academic and upper middle-brow writing and criticism in America.
>
> 4. The writers of the "beat generation" represent the true spirit of American youth today.

The last point we must leave to the sociologists and social philosophers; the first point is manifestly absurd. For a poet-critic like Rexroth, who has been reading American literature for some thirty-five years, must surely know that experiments in verse and prose have characterized it during that period. We need only recall Ezra Pound's *Cantos,* T. S. Eliot's *Four Quartets,* William Carlos Williams' *Paterson,* Hemingway's *Death in the Afternoon,* John Dos Passos' *42nd Parallel,* and Gertrude Stein's *Brewsie and Willie*—all eminent works with that characteristic published in the period 1923-1948 by authors of very diverse sensibilities, to be aware of that fact. To Rexroth's "San Francisco Renaissance" of the 'fifties we can oppose the fugitive agrarian movement of the "twenties" and the Marxist literary movement of the 'thirties—both, on the surface, collective efforts to bring American letters to a novel, startling, and unique re-birth.

Rexroth's other two assertions, however, that the "beat generation" poets revive a lost tradition in American literature and that theirs is a legitimate revolt against academic poetry and criticism contain enough truth to be looked into carefully. Though Rexroth may never have read Walt Whitman's late critical summary "A Backward Glance O'er Travel'd Roads," its last sentences are implicit in Rexroth's discussion of the "beat generation's" revival of the true American tradition. Whitman says here:

> Concluding with two items for the imaginative genius of the West, when it worthily rises—First, what Herder taught to the young Goethe, that really great poetry is always (like the Homeric or Biblical canticles) the result of a national spirit, and not the privilege of a polish'd and select few; Second, that the strongest and sweetest songs yet remain to be sung.

It is the democratic, rather than the aristocratic, the native, rather than the foreign tradition which are here, in 1891, praised as the desirable background for future American literature. And it is precisely the language of the native common man illuminating democratic sentiments which is, according to Rexroth, being revived in the prose of Rumaker and Kerouac, the verse of Ginsberg and of Ferlinghetti. The tradition which is revived by these is, according to Rexroth, that of Whitman's spontaneous and revolutionary verse, of Mark Twain's dialectal prose in *Huckleberry Finn,* and of Hart Crane's more energetic lyrics—all as set against the prose of Henry James and the poetry of T. S. Eliot which are condemned as foreign, formalistic, and artificial. There is, at first glance, much truth in Rexroth's assertions, especially as he is careful to allow those foreign authors in whom Ginsberg shows interest (Apollinaire, Beckett, and Maiakowsky) a place in the "beat generation's" tradition and freely admits that some *Evergreen Review* and City Lights Press poets draw on other experimental traditions in their work. Yet there is one factor which Rexroth eliminates from his assessment which, as we shall see, bears some striking resemblances to outstanding "beat generation work"—the Marxist literary effort of the 'thirties.

It is interesting, in this respect, to look at a volume entitled *Proletarian Literature in the United States* (1935). Here we find, for instance, a poem entitled "Thalassa, Thalassa" by James Neugass. It deals with a strike of Greek merchant seamen in the harbor of Buenos Aires and the last stanza of it reads:

> "Romance, travel, adventure." So what?—
>   saleswords for slavery.
> In Buenos Aires, they went out on strike and
>   they went out solid,
> They sat on deck and stared at their officers,
>   sang the Comintern.
> Two went under a third mate's Colt. The sharks
>   got another,
> They went out solid, they didn't scab, they
>   stayed out and they won
>   . . . . .

Struck once and won the first small part of what
    shall be theirs,
The Red Internationale of Seamen and Harbor-
    workers!

For comparison we turn to the madhouse scene in Ginsberg's *Howl,* Part III:

where there are twentyfive-thousand mad com-
    rades all
together singing the final stanzas of the Interna-
    tionale
       . . . . .
where we wake up electrified out of the coma by
    our own
souls' airplanes roaring over the roof they've
    come to
drop angelic bombs the hospital illuminates it-
    self imaginary
walls collapse O skinny legions run outside O
    starry-spangled
shock of mercy the eternal war is here O victory
    forget your
underwear we're free . . .

It is unlikely that Neugass influenced Ginsberg directly.
And Ginsberg's ideas differ from Neugass's: the latter's revolt is newspaper fact; the former's is a madmen's delusion. Yet the tone, the terms, and the form of the statements are remarkably alike.

The same volume which carries "Thalassa, Thalassa" also
brings a short story by Albert Maltz called "Man on a
Road." Here an anonymous man gives a poor worker a
ride and treats him to a cup of coffee:

We went inside. For the first time since I had
come upon him in the tunnel he seemed human.
He didn't talk, but he didn't slip inside himself
either. He just sat down at the counter and waited for his coffee. When it came, he drank it slowly, holding the cup in both hands as though to
warm them. When he had finished, I asked him
if he wouldn't like a sandwich. He turned
around to me and smiled. It was a very gentle,
a very patient smile. His big, lumpy face seemed
to light up with it and became understanding
and sweet and gentle.

The smile shook me all through. It didn't warm
me—it made me feel sick inside. It was like
watching a corpse begin to stir. I wanted to cry
out "My God, you poor man!"

And we turn to Jack Kerouac's *On the Road:*

all dead bums forever dead with nothing and all
finished and out—there—and this was the clientele in the Public Hair restaurant where I ate
many's the morn a 3-egg breakfast with almost
dry toast and oatmeal a little saucer of . . . my
26-cent breakfast, my pride—and that incredible
semiqueer counterman who dished out the food,
threw it at you, slammed it, has a languid frank
expression straight in your eyes like a 1930's
lunchcart heroine in Steinbeck . . .

where, once more, the resemblance between the Marxist
and the "beat generation" style is striking. Maltz and
Kerouac present the same mixture of dramatic human ex-

pression in similarly sordid surroundings. Their contexts
are, of course, different: Maltz's old man is dying of silico-
sis from working in a mining tunnel; Kerouac's protagonist is an intellectual earning a full professor's salary as a
railway brakeman who eats his 26-cent breakfast to prove
that it can still be eaten in the San Francisco of the 'fifties.

Proof that Marxist prose is of importance for understanding the "beat generation's" literary tradition does not invalidate the latter. Nor does the absence of a social purpose in the "beat generation's" writings force us to condemn these and brand them feeble, pointless imitators of
Marxist literature. For theirs is a different story, told to
a different age. But Rexroth's assertion that Whitman,
Twain, and Hart Crane make up the "beat generation's"
direct ancestry must here be modified to include Marxist
elements from the 'thirties.

Rexroth's statement that the "beat generation" writers are
the gadflies for a needed revolt against conventional academic poetry is perhaps the truest of his claims. For, since
the end of the American Marxist movement in literature,
no unified group of writers in present-day America has
dared to be scornful both of the popular media communication (the press, radio, and television) and of the conventional unconventionality of upper middle brow magazines
of the *Atlantic Monthly* variety, before the "beat generation" writers took this step. No frontal attack but the
"beat generation's" has been delivered recently, from an
outlook neither openly Marxist nor patently *bourgeois,*
against the control which the New Criticism and the
agrarian fugitive tradition exercise today over the emergence of younger literary talents. It is impossible, in
America today, to study American or English literature
on the university level without being indoctrinated, at one
point or the other, with the critical views of John Crowe
Ransom, Allen Tate, Randall Jarell, R. P. Blackmur, or
Lionel Trilling—to mention only the most prominent
names among the professor-poet-critics who control the
Kenyon Review, the *Hudson Review,* and the *Partisan Review.* It is very hard, by the same token, to break into print
as a young writer or critic without being, in some way, a
recognizable imitator of the older New Critics or ex-
fugitive agrarians. The "beat generation" writers attack
this rather rigid tradition, not because they oppose the creative and critical efforts of the Kenyon school, but because
they resent the control of vested academic and publishing
interests over the expression of the critical and creative
spirit. And in this they are, I feel, right. Unfortunately, the
"beat generation" has no unified critical doctrine, no poetics to support its polemic—the extreme individualism
which gave the "beat generation" writers strength to
launch their protest paradoxically negates the development of a strong intellectual point of view.

We have attempted, here, to give the "beat generation"
writers and poets a close look. What we found is a group
of young to middle-aged creative talents of some merit
who neither perform in a unified literary style nor defend
a common intellectual or spiritual point of view, save, perhaps, a tendency toward mysticism and pacifism cultivated by the metaphysical and ultra-terrestrial extremes of
the movement. We found that, in the light of the experi-

mental tradition in contemporary American poetry and prose, the "beat generation writers'" claims to uniqueness and originality within it are absurd. We saw, as well, that proletarian literature of the 'thirties plays a significant part in their literary ancestry and disqualifies Rexroth's claims that Ginsberg and Kerouac bring to a renaissance the dormant spirit of American folk-literature as exemplified by Whitman and Twain. Finally we saw that the "beat generation writers'" polemic against the strangleholds both of commercialism and of the cliquish spirit of New Critics and ex-fugitive agrarians is a healthy and positive feature of their approach to contemporary American letters. If they could only develop a unified point of view to spearhead their critical attack, the writers of the "beat generation" could bring great benefit to our literary scene. (pp. 13-20)

Wolfgang Bernard Fleischmann, "A Look at the 'Beat Generation' Writers," in Carolina Quarterly, *Vol. XI, No. 2, Spring, 1959, pp. 13-20.*

John Clellon Holmes

[*In the following essay, Holmes presents an introductory overview of Beat poetry.*]

QUERIES—Indifference to history is as American as the built-in obsolescence of our automobiles. Heirs of the past, we ignore it out of lust for the future—to the despair of our artists, marooned in the unfinished present, and thereby speaking in a language that is often unintelligible to their countrymen, who are bewitched by tomorrow or captive to yesterday.

For the "new" poets of the fifties and early sixties, those associated, directly or indirectly, with the so-called Beat Movement, dissertation-time, retrospective-time has come. Who were they? Where did they come from? Were they significant? Did they make any difference?

Above all, have they become *safe* enough—back there a few decades ago—for us to confront what they were saying so insistently?

GROUPS—I take this movement to include all those poets and writers who would agree, either whole-heartedly or with minor reservations, with William Carlos Williams' reaction to T. S. Eliot's *The Waste Land*. Williams felt that it would set American poetry back by twenty years, and by the late forties those twenty years were over, and the prophecy redeemed. I take this movement to embrace all those writers who rejected the formalism, conservatism, and "classicism" that Eliot's influence grafted on American writing; who went back to essential sources—in our national experience and in our earlier literature—to be renewed.

I take this movement to contain all those poets for whom Ezra Pound's injunction to "compose in the sequence of the musical phrase, not in the sequence of the metronome," embodied the beginning and the end of the only aesthetic on which most would agree, "Technique as the test of a man's sincerity."

There were loose groupings occasioned by geographical propinquity. The New York group, which included Allen Ginsberg, Jack Kerouac, Gregory Corso, and others, became officially known as the Beats. There was the so-called Black Mountain group, including Charles Olson, Robert Creeley, Robert Duncan, and others. In San Francisco, there were Lawrence Ferlinghetti, Gary Snyder, Philip Whalen, and Michael McClure. Another New York enclave, centered around the art scene there, was composed of Frank O'Hara, John Ashbery, and Kenneth Koch.

No artist, I suspect, is ever completely at ease finding himself shoved into a category. But I believe that all these writers more or less instantly recognized a similarity to life-attitude and aesthetic-direction in each other, and felt less alone, and drew fresh energy, from that recognition. Most of them found their ancestors in Melville and Whitman, rather than James and Hawthorne. Most of them believed that Ezra Pound and Hart Crane held out more hope for a new and vital American poetry than T. S. Eliot or Wallace Stevens. And most of them felt a fraternal kinship with William Carlos Williams that signalized the victory of his long struggle to establish a new poetics here. They were not a school, like the Imagists or the Surrealists. They were a tendency, a sort of continental drift, a barometric sign indicating the wind's direction. All at once it blew fair for strong feelings once again. It was a fine time to be alive.

ORIGINS—The roots of the attitudes that were peculiar to these writers are as random and diverse as American life in the forty years preceding their appearance. There are taproots in the movies, comic books, radio and big band music of the thirties that formed the images of the youth-mythos of that period before it was educated out of such trivia to higher "cultural" concerns. Think of such epiphanies as Chaplin eating his shoe, the sacred and profane dada of Harpo and Groucho, the lift towards ecstasy in a Basie riff, the princely cape beneath Clark Kent's plebian suit. Think of football twilights, the erotic secrecies of boys' rooms, the carnival of neighborhood streets, musing Huck Finn rivers—followed by the disintegrative uprootings of the war; death and euphoria kissing in a Kansas convertible, angels of excess haunting Terre Haute. Later, roots as well in the exegetical twitter of G. I. Bill classrooms, asphalted-pages of explication in the critical journals—all those sestinas and objective correlatives and analogies-to-myth and privileged moments—those suitcases-full of academic stones the young Sisyphuses of the time were forced to haul up Morningside Heights, and elsewhere.

More ongoing origins in the secret excitement of reading Blake, Lawrence, Rimbaud, Celine, Miller, Whitman—having no way to make them *respectable* to the New Critics, and thus long thoughts about the veracity of such respectability. At one point in 1949, for instance, *everyone* (as they later learned with astonishment) was reading Melville's *Pierre,* just re-published then for the first time in more than half a century, everyone's separate mind moving towards the same sources at some mysterious behest. Also, there was the eruptive, mobile, fluctuating nature of American postwar life—streets, bars, pads, bop, drugs, hipsters, sexual breakthroughs, urgings towards whatever was unknown.

Outrageous and unsettling questions started to shape themselves towards words. What did a sonnet really have to do with Hiroshima-Charlie Parker-upheavings in the spirit? What high rhetoric was equal to the "low deeds in Hungary" that characterized the times? Could you structure an account of cross-the-country-on-your-thumb by the old mechanical psychologies? Was poetic form simply an overlay you scissored the raw edges of content to fit? How close to the bones of usable truth could words cut, if stropped keen enough? Could seventeenth century meter and rhyme contain the syncopated accelerations of the actual reality of blaring radios and jackhammers and pavement-crowds and bomb-reverberations? Was John Donne the most reliable guide to past-midnight, cold-water-flat illuminations? How write about real death, under the bitter bridges, in the accents of madrigal? Was art no more than an afternoon teacup, after all?

Charles Olson wrote, dismantling Eliot's "classicism" in a sentence, "Verse now, 1950, if it is to go ahead, if it is to be of *essential* use, must, I take it, catch up and put into itself certain laws and possibilities of the breath, of the breathing of the man who writes as well as of his listenings." To go ahead. To be of essential use. The breathing of the man. One perception leading directly to a further perception. Spontaneous prose. First thought, best thought. Literature made by the whole man, writing. Rather remain silent than cheat the language.

Ultimate origins, there. A flowering, possible.

HISTORIES—The dismal early fifties, which Nelson Algren best characterized by saying that if *The Man in the Grey Flannel Suit* and *Marjorie Morningstar* were being married down the block he wouldn't go to the wedding, were "woodshed" years—a jazz musician's term for going off, and getting out of sight, and honing his axe alone.

In New York, Jack Kerouac wrote *On the Road,* and couldn't get it published, and set off back into America, freed by failure to write the books he himself would most like to read. Ferlinghetti migrated "overland" to San Francisco, going westward—which Thoreau had long ago divined to be the American intuitive direction—eventually to open City Lights Bookstore, the Shakespeare and Company of its generation. Ginsberg gave up writing murderously-compacted imitations of the Metaphysicals, and went to school to Williams, and then off to Yucatan to brood on prosody and invite new visions. Ex-streetboy Corso's *wanderjahr* took him to Harvard, Harvardman Creeley's to Mallorca, and Snyder's to logging camps and mountain-lookouts.

Poets were composing everywhere, most still unknown to each other, in that buried isolation of soul in which U.S. artists have immemorially labored, deprived even of the company of their fellow exiles, with no place to publish in the *Sewanee, Kenyon, Partisan* reviews of Academy America. So, a gradual budding of small presses and now-and-again little magazines—*Origin* in Boston, *Black Mountain Review* in North Carolina, the *Pocket Poets Series* in Fris-

co, and countless other fugitive blossoms appearing stubbornly between the paving stones of the official literature. There was general movement away from traditional centers, re-alignment in chance locations where the climate and vibrations were congenial, there to discover brother scriveners also on the move, writing the poems of actual, living-meat experience in Late Empire America, in our own true speech, and in forms as organic and mysterious as the seed-become-tree. All this ferment and innovation and creative flow not surfacing into the slumberous upper air until mid-decade.

As propitiously as the conjunction of Hawthorne, Emerson, Thoreau, Alcott, and Melville in the Massachusetts of a hundred years before (that first flowering of indigenous American writing), an astounding spectrum of writers converged in San Francisco by the felicities of chance, the breadth of that Bay (perhaps) corresponding to some enlargement within them—last margin of the continent, white clapboarded city of bridges that flung themselves, more audaciously than all of Crane's imaginings, in the direction of the Buddha-lands the Transcendentalists had been, themselves, an early bridge towards. It was the place, the time. Natural to these poets, for whom the life of the poem was the man breathing, was the urge to read in public—the wine-rich voice, the living people listening, the sound of streets as an antiphonal, and sometimes the skirl of sax or stutter of drum for punctuation.

At the Six Gallery, in 1955, Allen Ginsberg got up, after others, and began,

> "I saw the best minds of my generation destroyed by madness, starving hysterical naked, dragging themselves through the negro streets at dawn looking for an angry fix, angelheaded hipsters burning for the ancient heavenly connection to the starry dynamo in the machinery of night—",

raising his "Howl" against the cautious murmur of the times, and despite the bewilderment and outrage, it was clear (even to the *New York Times*) that something was happening: the first audible rumble of an immense underground river that had been building in volume and force for years. Whitman had said: "Unscrew the locks from the doors! Unscrew the doors themselves from their jambs!" and suddenly through the literature's doorless jambs the breath of whole men, writing, blew like a prairie wind.

It was as if the Indians were off the reservation, and the first instinct of the cowboys of the media and the academy was an attempt to corral them into a category, to stone them with epithets or bury them in non sequiturs. Following fast: *Partisan Review*'s "know-nothing bohemians," *Life* magazine's "only rebellion around," Kerouac's prose described as "typing not writing," and countless other idiocies that seemed to ironically acknowledge, by their very vehemence, the cultural wasteland in which these writers seemed so much more vivid. Following faster: public readings as scandalous, thronged, and disruptive as protest-rallies; obscenity trials that were the start of the long dismantling of American censorship laws; ugly and beautiful secrets about money, God, war, and sex let out of the psychic bag at last; and the discovery, as well, of the "great audiences" for which Whitman had called so long ago. But following fastest of all, the new literature itself: Ferlinghetti's *Coney Island of the Mind*, Olson's *The Maximus Poems*, Corso's *Gasoline*, Kerouac's *On the Road* (and thereafter a steady flow of all the other books he had written during his personal Diaspora), Levertov's *Here and Now*, Snyder's *Riprap*, Burrough's *Naked Lunch*, and books by Duncan, Creeley, McClure, Weiners, Whalen, O'Hara, and a dozen others. And finally, to plant a flag on the mountain and claim it as national territory, Don Allen's landmark anthology, *The New American Poetry* (1960), making apparent that, despite early obscurity and later notoriety, it had been a *decad mirabilis*, after all—its meanings and influences still, then, to be assessed.

CONTINUITIES—Most essentially, these poets were *American* poets, eschewing both the forms and attitudes that had characterized verse in English heretofore, and from which even Dickinson, Pound, Jeffers, and Frost had never wholly gotten free. They used American rhythms of speech, which, as Williams knew, were profoundly different from the British. They linked up again with the oldest American literary tradition—the rolling combers of Melville, the bardic inclusiveness of Whitman, the October tang of Thoreau, the lapidary apothegms of Emerson. And the westward-looking, open-souled, who-reads-this-encounters-a-man stance of these ancestors was *their* stance too. They shared, with Pound, a certain native crankishness and village-scholar erudition. Olson studied Mayan hieroglyphics, Ginsberg delved into mystical and pharmacological lore, Kerouac transliterated the Sutras, Whalen became a Zen acolyte, and Snyder an ecological consultant and *ombudsman* for the Great Globe itself. Nothing un-dehumanized was alien to them, and they wrote out of a passionate awareness of the unity of all knowledge, and that awe before undifferentiated nature that the presence of this continent, still untamed by thought, must have aroused in the earliest colonists.

They had connections, too, if looser, with existential ideas of being and becoming, of locating yourself (in the instant between breaths) and starting from there, of the freedom always imminent in ongoing time, the freedom to become free once you know you are, to transcend the Determined Ego into the Organic Self. "I am free: there is absolutely no more reason for living, all the ones I have tried have given way and I can't imagine any more of them. I am still fairly young, I still have enough strength to start again. But do I have to start again?" The Kerouac of *Desolation Angels*? No, Jean-Paul Sartre.

There was, as well, the powerful appeal of Oriental modes of thought, and these writers probably came closer to apprehending, across the mapless cultural Pacifics, the unique genius of the Eastern Mind than any westerners since Blyth and Fenollosa. Zen Buddhism, particularly, seemed to describe the fix they had perceived we were in, trapped in the absurdity of time-consciousness, only able to point at things, waiting for the sudden, blissful, silly flash to come. Both Zen and exsitentialism are ultimately concerned with the true nature of reality, which the formulating intelligence obscures. The purpose of *haiku*, to blow the mind; *satori*, perfect apprehension of what is *there*.

> Sweet is the swamp with its secrets,
> Until we meet a snake;
> 'Tis then we sigh for houses . . .

Bashō? Buson? Gary Snyder? No, Emily Dickinson. It is an old way of seeing among us.

Innovators? Yes. But, like all the most consequential innovators, these writers were concerned with the reconnection of broken circuits, insisting that body, mind, and soul are enmeshed, that corporeality is the "field" from which spirit emanates like the weather that is the protagonist in Turner's paintings. And so they were mostly affirming older continuities against contemporary relativisms, trying to annul alienation by passing through it to the other side, where (their faith implied) we all might enter into Blake's "lineaments of gratified desire." For which they were called nihilists, obscurantists, dope-and sex-fiends, and corrupters of literary values. Another hoary American tradition that American literature has always somehow survived. The popularity of their poetry attested to the fact that they were writing the poems the times demanded. They were unashamed to be articulating the signal themes of their era. Why not? Let poetry be at least as exciting and relevant as pop music. These poets still believed, in all their naiveté, that poetry had the power to redeem life.

TECHNICS—A few, glancing words about the nature of this writing—its tone, imagery, rhythm, and literary stance.

Gregory Corso writes: "O I would like to break my teeth / by means of expressing a radiator!" To comprehend, you must envision the iron-ribbed radiator, and the enamel-ribbed teeth, and the poet's mad need to *become* the radiator if he would seize it in his words. "I would like to drive a car / but I must *drive* it!" How often do people realize, in this way, that it is human intention that makes inert machinery go? The poem is called *Discord*, and moves forward towards the question: "Look—there must be a firing squad, yes, / but why a wolf?" And the discord clearly lies between what we automatically do, and what we intuitively know. One perception leading directly to a further perception, without the deadening losses that result from beaver-logic building dams against the flow. Instead, keep the mind and senses connected, and let them *go*. Then the movement will be natural, the way the consciousness actually works, with a consequent gain in richness, immediacy, and verisimilitude.

The image, "Fried shoes" (also from Corso), seems meaningless, arbitrary, and merely surrealistic, if you hold back and think about it. But if you let it enter your consciousness as effortlessly as butter in the mouth, further images and associations surface—charmingly different for everyone. I variously see Chaplin in his Arctic *Gold Rush* cabin, inferno-sidewalks of the city, leathery steaks in which you taste the real sole of life, and the actual shoe that comes to assume something of the *mana* of the wearer along the miles he has walked in it. Take your frying pan, melt your meager grease; fry up the shoe, and eat it—such are the secular communions of the starved, contemporary heart.

Of rhythm: most often staccato as the piano chords changing beneath a bop sax solo (the pianist acknowledging the soloist's shift of mind), or long and exfoliating like that soloist's try to contain everything, a *gloss* of his entire sentience, in a single unbroken line of melody. But, above all, *organic*—growing as natural things grow at the behest of their nature. Iambic? Yes, for sometimes we have emotions best expressed in the old, stately rhythms, so let them come. But rhythm seen as the instantaneous concatenation of blood-pulse, heartbeat, and eye-ear apprehension of the whole moment.

The old questions—How do we know what we know? Is the table really there? Am I a butterfly dreaming I'm a man?—are no longer merely intellectual conundrums in our time. Awareness of the precarious connection between sense-data and the reality "out there" is the common ground of most contemporary literary work. And these poets say: cleanse the senses in the morning and jog them in the evening, or vice versa—but always begin at the point of their intersection with a moment in time, in your world. Most aesthetic problems are solved the minute you vow never to lie about yourself seeing the gull fly.

EXEMPLARS—Richly diverse human voices—almost from the start; voices distinct enough, one from the other, in relation to the language that no single "company voice" ever emerged from among these poets. Who could ever mistake Frank O'Hara's happy, gossipy, Saturday-morning-in-the-world voice for one of Robert Creeley's precise, almost inaudible poetic tuning forks, delicate enough to register the faintest tremble in the modern heart? Much less for the percussive brutality of McClure's capitalized rant, screaming for love like a rapist in the throes of a shameful remorse? Who could fail to distinguish between Ferlinghetti's sadly hip anthems to the Lost Wonder without which all causes are empty coffins, and Philip Whalen's massive cartography of his ungainly, comic, Gulliver-like psyche in tones as sweet and winsome and self-derisive as a Shakespearean Puck? And once having heard them, who could ever mistake the poems of Gary Snyder—glints of hard light on mountain shale, words like gulps of bone-cold water, the clarities of immense distances, sojourner poems—from any other poems, short of those translated by Fenollosa?

There is a permanent body of work here, work that breaks ground and builds bridges, work that permanently expands the territories that our poetry will explore from now

Diane DiPrima reading poetry from her This Kind of Bird Flies Backward *(1958).*

on, work from which a uniquely American poetics might start to emerge at last.

Listen. It's *End of the Century Blues.*

AFTERMATHS—It's difficult to assess how many of the life styles, artforms, and attitudes of the sixties and seventies, both ongoing and counterproductive, proceeded directly from a kind of *contact-high* between these writers and the generation that matured after them. But rock lyrics show the distinct influence of this poetry in their insistence on reflecting more than just the callow insipidities of Moon-and-June, and Bob Dylan might never have come out of his fantasy of the hobo-thirties but for Allen Ginsberg, or the Beatles (their very name an indication) ever become more than just another Liverpool skiffle band without ex-Beatnik John Lennon. Also, of course, there were roses in the barrels of rifles, beards and beads and jeans, make love not war (a Beat one-liner), throw money at the stock exchange, don't be chicken talk turkey, if it feels good do it, and so many of the other first principles that motivated young people a little while ago.

Most knowledges that are worth their cost must be earned, not learned, and some of the behavior of these same young people smacked of rote. There were dirty needles, conversational impoverishment, minds blown to smithereens by the careless ingestion of psychic and chemical overkill, and nerves ruined by continual decibel feedback. There was, also, the violence that grows out of impatience and disappointment, campus Chés riffing on revolution like zapped-out guitarists who can only play three chords, the dumb romanticism of hitching with thirty dollars in your pocket, the parent-hatred, system-putdown, and square-baiting that were so often a pointless and debilitating irrelevance.

Some responsibility for all of this must end up at the doorstep of the Beats, and perhaps the immediate effects of the movement will turn out to be (as Lawrence said in another connection) "post-mortem effects." But literature for the next few years will probably never become the kind of cul-de-sac out of which these writers made their way. It is impossible to keep wind in burst balloons, or to back off from certain difficult admissions once made, or to forget the heady sniff of free air in the lungs. It will be no easier to write the truth, or even to appreciate it, but some obstacles, some hangovers from the past, have already been cleared away.

In 1974, an issue of *The New York Times Book Review,* which, on the front page, reviewed Ginsberg's *The Fall of America* (later to win the National Book Award), stated about the first biography of Kerouac: "This is a book about the men who changed everything." Only time will tell about that. But assuredly these writers left things different than they found them. They did honest work in the face of incomprehension and neglect, and they persisted in the name of their unique vision, as all true poets have.

That work, that vision, remains. (pp. 220-33)

> *John Clellon Holmes, "The Beat Poets: A Primer," in his* Passionate Opinions: The Cultural Essays, Vol. III, *The University of Arkansas Press, 1988, pp. 220-33.*

THE BEAT GENERATION AS A SOCIAL PHENOMENON

John Clellon Holmes

[*An American novelist, essayist, poet, and short story writer, Holmes wrote the novel* Go (1952), *one of earliest published works of Beat literature, and was considered the chief chronicler of the Beat phenomenon. In the following essay which originally appeared in the* New York Times Magazine *in November 1952, Holmes discusses the emergence of the Beat Generation in postwar American society and identifies prominent attitudes and characteristics that define it as a social phenomenon.*]

Several months ago, a national magazine ran a story under the heading "Youth" and the subhead "Mother Is Bugged at Me." It concerned an 18-year-old California girl who had been picked up for smoking marijuana and wanted to talk about it. While a reporter took down her ideas in the uptempo language of "tea," someone snapped a picture. In view of her contention that she was part of a whole new culture where one out of every five people you meet is a user, it was an arresting photograph. In the pale, attentive face, with its soft eyes and intelligent mouth, there was no hint of corruption. It was a face which could only be deemed criminal through an enormous effort of righteousness. Its only complaint seemed to be "Why don't people leave us alone?" It was the face of a Beat Generation.

That clean young face has been making the newspapers steadily since the war. Standing before a judge in a Bronx court house, being arraigned for stealing a car, it looked up into the camera with curious laughter and no guilt. The same face, with a more serious bent, stared from the pages of *Life* magazine, representing a graduating class of ex-G.I.'s, and said that as it believed small business to be dead, it intended to become a comfortable cog in the largest corporation it could find. A little younger, a little more bewildered, it was this same face that the photographers caught in Illinois when the first non-virgin club was uncovered. The young copywriter, leaning down the bar on Third Avenue, quietly drinking himself into relaxation, and the energetic hot-rod driver of Los Angeles, who plays Russian roulette with a jalopy, are separated only by a continent and a few years. They are the extremes. In between them fall the secretaries wondering whether to sleep with their boyfriends now or wait; the mechanics, beering up with the guys and driving off to Detroit on a whim; the models studiously name-dropping at a cocktail party. But the face is the same. Bright, level, realistic, challenging.

Any attempt to label an entire generation is unrewarding, and yet the generation which went through the last war, or at least could get a drink easily once it was over, seems to possess a uniform, general quality which demands an adjective. It was John Kerouac, the author of a fine, neglected novel *The Town and the City,* who finally came up with it. It was several years ago, when the face was harder to recognize, but he has a sharp, sympathetic eye, and one day he said, "You know, this is really a *beat* generation." The origins of the word "beat" are obscure, but the meaning is only too clear to most Americans. More than mere weariness, it implies the feeling of having been used, of being raw. It involves a sort of nakedness of mind, and, ultimately, of soul; a feeling of being reduced to the bedrock of consciousness. In short, it means being undramatically pushed up against the wall of oneself. A man is beat whenever he goes for broke and wagers the sum of his resources on a single number; and the young generation has done that continually from early youth.

Its members have an instinctive individuality, needing no bohemianism or imposed eccentricity to express it. Brought up during the collective bad circumstances of a dreary depression, weaned during the collective uprooting of a global war, they distrust collectivity. But they have never been able to keep the world out of their dreams. The fancies of their childhood inhabited the half-light of Munich, the Nazi-Soviet pact and the eventual blackout. Their adolescence was spent in a topsy-turvy world of war bonds, swing shifts and troop movements. They grew to independent mind on beachheads, in ginmills and U.S.O.'s, in past-midnight arrivals and pre-dawn departures. Their brothers, husbands, fathers or boy friends turned up dead one day at the other end of a telegram. At the four trembling corners of the world, or in the home town invaded by factories and lonely servicemen, they had intimate experience with the nadir and the zenith of human conduct, and little time for much that came between. The peace they inherited was only as secure as the next headline. It was a cold peace. Their own lust for freedom, and their ability to live at a pace that kills, to which war had adjusted them, led to black markets, bebop, narcotics, sexual promiscuity, hucksterism and Jean-Paul Sartre. The beatness set in later.

It is a postwar generation, and, in a world which seems to mark its cycles by its wars, it is already being compared to that other postwar generation, which dubbed itself "lost." The Roaring Twenties, and the generation that made them roar, are going through a sentimental revival, and the comparison is valuable. The Lost Generation was discovered in a roadster, laughing hysterically because nothing meant anything any more. It migrated to Europe, unsure whether it was looking for the "orgiastic future" or escaping from the "puritanical past." Its symbols were the flapper, the flask of bootleg whisky, and an attitude of desperate frivolity best expressed by Noel Coward's line: "Tennis, anyone?" It was caught up in the romance of disillusionment, until even that became an illusion. Every act in its drama of lostness was a tragic or an ironic third act, and T. S. Eliot's *The Wasteland* was more than the dead-end statement of a perceptive poet. The pervading atmosphere was an almost objectless sense of loss, through which the reader felt immediately that the cohesion of things had disappeared. It was, for an entire generation, an image which expressed, with dreadful accuracy, its own spiritual condition.

But the wild boys of today are not lost. Their flushed, often scoffing, always intent faces elude the word, and it would sound phony to them. For this generation conspic-

uously lacks that eloquent air of bereavement which made so many of the exploits of the Lost Generation symbolic actions. Furthermore, the repeated inventory of shattered ideals, and the laments about the mud in moral currents, which so obsessed the Lost Generation, does not concern young people today. They take it frighteningly for granted. They were brought up in these ruins and no longer notice them. They drink to "come down" or to "get high," not to illustrate anything. Their excursions into drugs or promiscuity come out of curiosity, not disillusionment.

Only the most bitter among them would call their reality a nightmare and protest that they have indeed lost something, the future. But ever since they were old enough to imagine one, that has been in jeopardy anyway. The absence of personal and social values is to them, not a revelation shaking the ground beneath them, but a problem demanding a day-to-day solution. *How* to live seems to them much more crucial than *why*. And it is precisely at this point that the copywriter and the hot-rod driver meet, and their identical beatness becomes significant, for, unlike the Lost Generation, which was occupied with the loss of faith, the Beat Generation is becoming more and more occupied with the need for it. As such, it is a disturbing illustration of Voltaire's reliable old joke: "If there were no God, it would be necessary to invent Him." Not content to bemoan His absence, they are busily and haphazardly inventing totems for Him on all sides.

For the giggling nihilist, eating up the highway at ninety miles an hour, and steering with his feet, is no Harry Crosby, the poet of the Lost Generation who flew his plane into the sun one day because he could no longer accept the modern world. On the contrary, the hot-rod driver invites death only to outwit it. He is affirming the life within him in the only way he knows how, at the extreme. The eager-faced girl, picked up on a dope charge, is not one of those "women and girls carried screaming with drink or drugs from public places," of whom Fitzgerald wrote. Instead, with persuasive seriousness, she describes the sense of community she has found in marijuana, which society never gave her. The copywriter, just as drunk by midnight as his Lost Generation counterpart, probably reads *God and Man at Yale* during his Sunday afternoon hangover. The difference is this almost exaggerated will to believe in something, if only in themselves. It is a *will* to believe, even in the face of an inability to do so in conventional terms. And that is bound to lead to excesses in one direction or another.

The shock that older people feel at the sight of this Beat Generation is, at its deepest level, not so much repugnance at the facts, as it is distress at the attitudes which move it. Though worried by this distress, they most often argue or legislate in terms of the facts rather than the attitudes. The newspaper reader, studying the eyes of young dope addicts, can only find an outlet for his horror and bewilderment in demands that passers be given the electric chair. Sociologists, with a more academic concern, are just as troubled by the legions of young men whose topmost ambition seems to be to find a secure berth in a monolithic corporation. Contemporary historians express mild surprise at the lack of organized movements, political, religious or otherwise, among the young. The articles they write remind us that being one's own boss and being a natural joiner are two of our most cherished national traits. Everywhere, people with tidy moralities shake their heads and wonder what is happening to the younger generation.

Perhaps they have not noticed that, behind the excess on the one hand, and the conformity on the other, lies that wait-and-see detachment that results from having to fall back for support more on one's human endurance than on one's philosophy of life. Not that the Beat Generation is immune to ideas: they fascinate it. Its wars, both past and future, were and will be wars of ideas. It knows, however, that in the final, private moment of conflict a man is really fighting another man, and not an idea. And that the same goes for love. So it is a generation with a greater facility for entertaining ideas than for believing in them. But it is also the first generation in several centuries for which the act of faith has been an obsessive problem, quite aside from the reasons for having a particular faith or not having it. It exhibits on every side, and in a bewildering number of facets, a perfect craving to believe. Though it is certainly a generation of extremes, including both the hipster and the "radical" young Republican in its ranks, it renders unto Caesar (i.e., society) what is Caesar's, and unto God what is God's. For in the wildest hipster, making a mystique of bop, drugs and the night life, there is no desire to shatter the "square" society in which he lives, only to elude it. To get on a soapbox or write a manifesto would seem to him absurd. Looking out at the normal world, where most everything is a "drag" for him, he nevertheless says: "Well, that's the Forest of Arden after all. And even it jumps if you look at it right." Equally, the young Republican, though often seeming to hold up Babbitt as the culture hero, is neither vulgar nor materialistic, as Babbitt was. He conforms because he believes it is socially practical, not necessarily virtuous. Both positions, however, are the result of more or less the same conviction—namely that the valueless abyss of modern life is unbearable.

A generation can sometimes be better understood by the books it reads, than by those it writes. The literary hero of the Lost Generation should have been Bazarov, the nihilist in Turgenev's *Fathers and Sons*. Bazarov sat around, usually in the homes of the people he professed to loathe, smashing every icon within his reach. He was a man stunned into irony and rage by the collapse of the moral and intellectual structure of his world.

But he did nothing. The literary hero of the Beat Generation, on the other hand, might be Stavrogin, that most enigmatic character in *The Possessed* by Dostoevski. He is also a nihilist, or at least intimately associated with them.

But there is a difference, for Stavrogin, behind a facade very much like Bazarov's, is possessed by a passion for faith, almost any faith. His very atheism, at its extreme, is metaphysical. But he knows that disbelief is fatal, and when he has failed in every way to overcome it, he commits suicide because he does not have what he calls "greatness of soul." The ground yawned beneath Bazarov, revealing a pit into which he fell: while Stavrogin struggled at the bottom of that pit, trying feverishly to get out. In

so far as it resembled Stavrogin, there have been few generations with as natural and profound a craving for convictions as this one, nor have there been many generations as ill-equipped to find them.

For beneath the excess and the conformity, there is something other than detachment. There are the stirrings of a quest. What the hipster is looking for in his "coolness" (withdrawal) or "flipness" (ecstasy) is, after all, a feeling of somewhereness, not just another diversion. The young Republican feels that there is a point beyond which change becomes chaos, and what he wants is not simply privilege or wealth, but a stable position from which to operate. Both have had enough of homelessness, valuelessness, faithlessness.

The variety and the extremity of their solutions is only a final indication that for today's young people there is not as yet a single external pivot around which they can, as a generation, group their observations and their aspirations. There is no single philosophy, no single party, no single attitude. The failure of most orthodox moral and social concepts to reflect fully the life they have known is probably the reason, but because of it each person becomes a walking, self-contained unit, compelled to meet the problem of being young in a seemingly helpless world in his own way, or at least to endure.

More than anything else, this is what is responsible for the generation's reluctance to name itself, its reluctance to discuss itself as a group, sometimes its reluctance to be itself. For invented gods invariably disappoint those who worship them. Only the need for them goes on, and it is this need, exhausting one object after another, which projects the Beat Generation forward into the future and will one day deprive it of its beatness.

Dostoevski wrote in the early 1880s, "Young Russia is talking of nothing but the eternal questions now." With appropriate changes, something very like this is beginning to happen in America, in an American way; a reevaluation of which the exploits and attitudes of this generation are only symptoms. No simple comparison of one generation against another can accurately measure effects, but it seems obvious that a Lost Generation, occupied with disillusionment and trying to keep busy among the broken stones, is poetically moving, not very dangerous. But a Beat Generation, driven by a desperate craving for belief and as yet unable to accept the moderations which are offered it, is quite another matter. Thirty years later, after all, the generation of which Dostoevski wrote, was meeting in cellars and making bombs.

This generation may make no bombs; it will probably be asked to drop some, and have some dropped on it, however, and this fact is never far from its mind. It is one of the pressures which created it and will play a large part in what will happen to it. There are those who believe that in generations such as this there is always the constant possibility of a great new moral idea, conceived in desperation, coming to life. Others note the self-indulgence, the waste, the apparent social irresponsibility, and disagree.

But its ability to keep its eyes open, and yet avoid cynicism; its ever-increasing conviction that the problem of modern life is essentially a spiritual problem; and that capacity for sudden wisdom which people who live hard and go far, possess, are assets and bear watching. And, anyway, the clear, challenging faces are worth it. (pp. 21-7)

John Clellon Holmes, "This Is the Beat Generation," in Kerouac and Friends: A Beat Generation Album, *edited by Fred W. McDarrah, William Morrow and Company, 1985, pp. 21-7.*

DEVELOPMENT

Jack Kerouac

[*An American novelist, Kerouac was the chief literary figure of the Beat Movement and is often credited with coining the term "Beat." In the following essay, he explains the origins of the Beat Generation.*]

This article necessarily'll have to be about myself. I'm going all out.

That nutty picture of me on the cover of *On the Road* results from the fact that I had just gotten down from a high mountain where I'd been for two months completely alone and usually I was in the habit of combing my hair of course because you have to get rides on the highway and all that and you usually want girls to look at you as though you were a man and not a wild beast but my poet friend Gregory Corso opened his shirt and took out a silver crucifix that was hanging from a chain and said "Wear this and wear it outside your shirt and don't comb your hair!" So I spent several days around San Francisco going around with him and others like that, to parties, arties, parts, jam sessions, bars, poetry readings, churches, walking talking poetry in the streets, walking talking God in the streets (and at one point a strange gang of hoodlums got mad and said "What right does he got to wear that?" and my own gang of musicians and poets told them to cool it) and finally on the third day *Mademoiselle* magazine wanted to take pictures of us all so I posed just like that, wild hair, crucifix, and all, with Gregory Corso, Allen Ginsberg and Phil Whalen, and the only publication which later did not erase the crucifix from my breast (from that plaid sleeveless cotton shirtfront) was *The New York Times,* therefore *The New York Times* is as beat as I am, and I'm glad I've got a friend. I mean it sincerely, God bless *The New York Times* for not erasing the crucifix from my picture as though it was something distasteful. As a matter of fact, who's *really* beat around here, I mean if you wanta talk of Beat as "beat down" the people who erased the crucifix are really the "beat down" ones and not *The New York Times,* myself, and Gregory Corso the poet. I am not ashamed to wear the crucifix of my Lord. It is because I am Beat, that is, I believe in beatitude and that God so loved the world that he gave his only begotten son to it. I am sure no priest would've condemned me for wearing the crucifix outside my shirt everywhere and *no*

matter where I went, even to have my picture taken by *Mademoiselle.* So you people don't believe in God. So you're all big smart know-it-all Marxists and Freudians, hey? Why don't you come back in a million years and tell me all about it, angels?

Recently Ben Hecht said to me on TV "Why are you afraid to speak out your mind, what's wrong with this country, what is everybody afraid of?" Was he talking to me? And all he wanted me to do was speak out my mind *against* people, he sneeringly brought up Dulles, Eisenhower, the Pope, all kinds of people like that habitually he would sneer at with Drew Pearson, *against* the world he wanted, this is his idea of freedom, he calls it freedom. Who knows, my God, but that the universe is not one vast sea of compassion actually, the veritable holy honey, beneath all this show of personality and cruelty. In fact who knows but that it isn't the solitude of the oneness of the essence of everything, the solitude of the actual oneness of the unbornness of the unborn essence of everything, nay the true pure foreverhood, that big blank potential that can ray forth anything it wants from its pure store, that blazing bliss, *Mattivajrakaruna* the Transcendental Diamond Compassion! No, I want to speak *for* things, for the crucifix I speak out, for the Star of Israel I speak out, for the divinest man who ever lived who was a German (Bach) I speak out, for sweet Mohammed I speak out, for Buddha I speak out, for Lao-tse and Chuang-tse I speak out, for D. T. Suzuki I speak out . . . why should I attack what I love out of life. This is Beat. Live your lives out? Naw, *love* your lives out. When they come and stone you at least you won't have a glass house, just your glassy flesh.

That wild eager picture of me on the cover of *On the Road* where I look so Beat goes back much further than 1948 when John Clellon Holmes (author of *Go* and *The Horn*) and I were sitting around trying to think up the meaning of the Lost Generation and the subsequent Existentialism and I said "You know, this is really a beat generation" and he leapt up and said "That's it, that's right!" It goes back to the 1880s when my grandfather Jean-Baptiste Kerouac used to go out on the porch in big thunderstorms and swing his kerosene lamp at the lightning and yell "Go ahead, go, if you're more powerful than I am strike me and put the light out!" while the mother and the children cowered in the kitchen. And the light never went out. Maybe since I'm supposed to be the spokesman of the Beat Generation (I *am* the originator of the term, and around it the term and the generation have taken shape) it should be pointed out that all this "Beat" guts therefore goes back to my ancestors who were Bretons who were the most independent group of nobles in all old Europe and kept fighting Latin France to the last wall (although a big blond bosun on a merchant ship snorted when I told him my ancestors were Bretons in Cornwall, Brittany, "Why, we Wikings used to swoop down and steal your nets!") Breton, Wiking, Irishman, Indian, madboy, it doesn't make any difference, there is no doubt about the Beat Generation, at least the core of it, being a swinging group of new American men intent on joy . . . Irresponsibility? Who wouldn't help a dying man on an empty road? No and the Beat Generation goes back to the wild parties my father

Hal Chase, Jack Kerouac, Allen Ginsberg, and William S. Burroughs in New York in 1944.

used to have at home in the 1920s and 1930s in New England that were so fantastically loud nobody could sleep for blocks around and when the cops came they always had a drink. It goes back to the wild and raving childhood of playing the Shadow under windswept trees of New England's gleeful autumn, and the howl of the Moon Man on the sandbank until we caught him in a tree (he was an "older" guy of 15), the maniacal laugh of certain neighborhood madboys, the furious humor of whole gangs playing basketball till long after dark in the park, it goes back to those crazy days before World War II when teenagers drank beer on Friday nights at Lake ballrooms and worked off their hangovers playing baseball on Saturday afternoon followed by a dive in the brook—and our fathers wore straw hats like W. C. Fields. It goes back to the completely senseless babble of the Three Stooges, the ravings of the Marx Brothers (the tenderness of Angel Harpo at harp, too).

It goes back to the inky ditties of old cartoons (Krazy Kat with the irrational brick)—to Laurel and Hardy in the Foreign Legion—to Count Dracula and his *smile* to Count Dracula shivering and hissing back before the Cross—to the Golem horrifying the persecutors of the Ghetto—to the quiet sage in a movie about India, unconcerned about the plot—to the giggling old Tao Chinaman trotting down the sidewalk of old Clark Gable Shanghai— to the holy old Arab warning the hotbloods that Ramadan is near. To the Werewolf of London a distinguished doctor in his velour smoking jacket smoking his pipe over a lamplit tome on botany and suddenly hairs grown on his hands, his cat hisses, and he slips out into the night with a cape and a slanty cap like the caps of people in breadlines—to Lamont Cranston so cool and sure suddenly becoming the frantic Shadow going mwee hee hee ha ha in the alleys of New York imagination. To Popeye the sailor and the Sea Hag and the meaty gunwales of boats, to Cap'n Easy and Wash Tubbs screaming with ecstasy over canned peaches on a cannibal isle, to Wimpy looking X-eyed for a juicy hamburger such as they make no more. To Jiggs ducking before a household of furniture flying through the air, to Jiggs and the boys at the bar and the corned beef and cabbage of old wood—fence moons—to King Kong his eyes looking into the hotel window with tender huge love for Fay Wray—nay, to Bruce Cabot in mate's cap leaning over the rail of a fogbound ship saying "Come aboard." It goes back to when grapefruits were thrown at crooners and harvestworkers at bar-rails slapped burlesque queens on the rump. To when fathers took their sons to the Twi League game. To the days of Babe Callahan on the waterfront, Dick Barthelmess camping under a London streetlamp. To dear old Basil Rathbone looking for the Hound of the Baskervilles (a dog big as the Gray Wolf who will destroy Odin)—to dear old bleary Doctor Watson with a brandy in his hand. To Joan Crawford her raw shanks in the fog, in striped blouse smoking a cigarette at sticky lips in the door of the waterfront dive. To train whistles of steam engines out above the moony pines. To Maw and Paw in the Model A clanking on to get a job in California selling used cars making a whole lotta money. To the glee of America, the honesty of America, the honesty of old-time grafters in straw hats as well as the honesty of oldtime waiters in line at the Brooklyn Bridge in *Winterset,* the funny spitelessness of old bigfisted America like Big Boy Williams saying "Hoo? Hee? Huh?" in a movie about Mack Trucks and slidingdoor lunchcarts. To Clark Gable, his certain smile, his confident leer. Like my grandfather this America was invested with wild selfbelieving individuality and this had begun to disappear around the end of World War II with so many great guys dead (I can think of half a dozen from my own boyhood groups) when suddenly it began to emerge again, the hipsters began to appear gliding around saying "Crazy, man."

When I first saw the hipsters creeping around Times Square in 1944 I didn't like them either. One of them, Huncke of Chicago, came up to me and said "Man, I'm beat." I knew right away what he meant somehow. At that time I still didn't like bop which was then being introduced by Bird Parker and Dizzy Gillespie and Bags Jackson (on vibes), the last of the great swing musicians was Don Byas who went to Spain right after, but then I began . . . but earlier I'd dug all my jazz in the old Minton Playhouse (Lester Young, Ben Webster, Joey Guy, Charlie Christian, others) and when I first heard Bird and Diz in the Three Deuces I knew they were serious musicians playing a goofy new sound and didn't care what I thought, or what my friend Seymour thought. In fact I was leaning against the bar with a beer when Dizzy came over for a glass of water from the bartender, put himself right against me and reached both arms around both sides of my head to get the glass and danced away, as though knowing I'd be singing about him someday, or that one of his arrangements would be named after me someday by some goofy circumstance. Charlie Parker was spoken of in Harlem as the greatest new musician since Chu Berry and Louis Armstrong.

Anyway, the hipsters, whose music was bop, they looked like criminals but they kept talking about the same things I liked, long outlines of personal experience and vision, nightlong confessions full of hope that had become illicit and repressed by War, stirrings, rumblings of a new soul (that same old human soul). And so Huncke appeared to us and said "I'm beat" with radiant light shining out of his despairing eyes . . . a word perhaps brought from some midwest carnival or junk cafeteria. It was a new language, actually spade (Negro) jargon but you soon learned it, like "hung up" couldn't be a more economical term to mean so many things. Some of these hipsters were raving mad and talked continually. It was jazzy. Symphony Sid's all-night modern jazz and bop show was always on. By 1948 it began to take shape. That was a wild vibrating year when a group of us would walk down the street and yell hello and even stop and talk to anybody that gave us a friendly look. The hipsters had eyes. That was the year I saw Montgomery Clift, unshaven, wearing a sloppy jacket, slouching down Madison Avenue with a companion. It was the year I saw Charley Bird Parker strolling down Eighth Avenue in a black turtleneck sweater with Babs Gonzales and a beautiful girl.

By 1948 the hipsters, or beatsters, were divided into cool and hot. Much of the misunderstanding about hipsters and the Beat Generation in general today derives from the fact that there are two distinct styles of hipsterism: the cool today is your bearded laconic sage, or schlerm, before a hardly touched beer in a beatnik dive, whose speech is low and unfriendly, whose girls say nothing and wear black: the "hot" today is the crazy talkative shining eyed (often innocent and openhearted) nut who runs from bar to bar, pad to pad looking for everybody, shouting, restless, lushy, trying to "make it" with the subterranean beatniks who ignore him. Most Beat Generation artists belong to the hot school, naturally since that hard gemlike flame needs a little heat. In many cases the mixture is 50-50. It was a hot hipster like myself who finally cooled it in Buddhist meditation, though when I go in a jazz joint I still feel like yelling "Blow baby blow!" to the musicians though nowadays I'd get 86d for this. In 1948 the "hot hipsters" were racing around in cars like in *On the Road* looking for wild brawling jazz like Willis Jackson or Lucky Thompson (the early) or Chubby Jackson's big band while the "cool hipsters" cooled it in dead silence before formal and excellent musical groups like Lennie Tristano or Miles Davis. It's still just about the same, except that it has begun to grow into a national generation and the name "Beat" has stuck (though all hipsters hate the word).

The word "beat" originally meant poor, down and out, deadbeat, on the bum, sad, sleeping in subways. Now that the word is belonging officially it is being made to stretch to include people who do not sleep in subways but have a certain new gesture, or attitude, which I can only describe as a new *more.* "Beat Generation" has simply become the slogan or label for a revolution in manners in America. Marlon Brando was not really first to portray it on the screen. Dane Clark with his pinched Dostoievskyan face and Brooklyn accent, and of course Garfield, were first. The private eyes were Beat, if you will recall. Bogart, Lorre was Beat. In *M,* Peter Lorre started a whole revival, I mean the slouchy street walk.

I wrote *On the Road* in three weeks in the beautiful month of May 1951 while living in the Chelsea district of lower West Side Manhattan, on a 100-foot roll and put the Beat Generation in words in there, saying at the point where I am taking part in a wild kind of collegiate party with a bunch of kids in an abandoned miner's shack "These kids are great but where are Dean Moriarty and Carlo Marx? Oh well I guess they wouldn't belong in this gang, they're too *dark,* too strange, too subterranean and I am slowly beginning to join a new kind of *beat* generation." The manuscript of *Road* was turned down on the grounds that it would displease the sales manager of my publisher at that time, though the editor, a very intelligent man, said "Jack this is just like Dostoievsky, but what can I do at this time?" It was too early. So for the next six years I was a bum, a brakeman, a seaman, a panhandler, a pseudo-Indian in Mexico, anything and everything, and went on writing because my hero was Goethe and I believed in art and hoped some day to write the third part of *Faust,* which I have done in *Doctor Sax.* Then in 1952 an article was published in *The New York Times* Sunday magazine saying, the headline, " 'This is a Beat Generation' " (in quotes like that) and in the article it said that I had come up with the term first "when the face was harder to recognize," the face of the generation. After that there was some talk of the Beat Generation but in 1955 I published an excerpt from *Road* (melling it with parts of *Visions of Neal*) under the pseudonym "Jean-Louis," it was entitled *Jazz of the Beat Generation* and was copyrighted as being an excerpt from a novel-in-progress entitled *Beat Generation* (which I later changed to *On the Road* at the insistence of my new editor) and so then the term moved a little faster. The term and the cats. Everywhere began to appear strange hepcats and even college kids went around hep and cool and using the terms I'd heard on Times Square in the early Forties, it was growing somehow. But when the publishers finally took a dare and published *On the Road* in 1957 it burst open, it mushroomed, everybody began yelling about a Beat Generation. I was being interviewed everywhere I went for "what I meant" by such a thing. People began to call themselves beatniks, beats, jazzniks, bopniks, bugniks and finally I was called the "avatar" of all this.

Yet it was as a Catholic, it was not at the insistence of any of those "niks" and certainly not with their approval either, that I went one afternoon to the church of my childhood (one of them). Ste. Jeanne d'Arc in Lowell, Mass., and suddenly with tears in my eyes and had a vision of what I must have really meant with "Beat" anyhow when I heard the holy silence in the church (I was the only one in there, it was five P.M., dogs were barking outside, children yelling, the fall leaves, the candles were flickering alone just for me), the vision of the word Beat as being to mean beatific . . . There's the priest preaching on Sunday morning, all of a sudden through a side door of the church comes a group of Beat Generation characters in strapped raincoats like the I.R.A. coming in silently to "dig" the religion . . . I knew it then.

But this was 1954, so then what horror I felt in 1957 and later 1958 naturally to suddenly see "Beat" being taken up by everybody, press and TV and Hollywood borscht circuit to include the "juvenile delinquency" shot and the horrors of a mad teeming billyclub New York and L.A. and they began to call *that* Beat, *that* beatific . . . bunch of fools marching against the San Francisco Giants protesting baseball, as if (now) in my name and I, my childhood ambition to be a big league baseball star hitter like Ted Williams so that when Bobby Thompson hit that homerun in 1951 I trembled with joy and couldn't get over it for days and wrote poems about how it is possible for the human spirit to win after all! Or, when a murder, a routine murder took place in North Beach, they labeled it a Beat Generation slaying although in my childhood I'd been famous as an eccentric in my block for stopping the younger kids from throwing rocks at the squirrels, for stopping them from frying snakes in cans or trying to blow up frogs with straws. Because my brother had died at the age of nine, his name was Gerard Kerouac, and he'd told me "Ti Jean never hurt any living being, all living beings whether it's just a little cat or squirrel or whatever, all, are going to heaven straight into God's snowy arms so never hurt anything and if you see anybody hurt anything stop them as best you can" and when he died a file of gloomy nuns in black from St. Louis de France parish had filed (1926) to his deathbed to hear his last words about Heaven. And my father too, Leon, had never lifted a hand to punish me, or to punish the little pets in our house, and this teaching was delivered to me by the men in my house and I have never had anything to do with violence, hatred, cruelty, and all that horrible nonsense which, nevertheless, because God is gracious beyond all human imagining, he will forgive in the long end . . . that million years I'm asking about you, America.

And so now they have beatnik routines on TV, starting with satires about girls in black and fellows in jeans with snap-knives and sweatshirts and swastikas tattooed under their armpits, it will come to respectable m.c.s. of spectaculars coming out nattily attired in Brooks Brothers jean-type tailoring and sweater-type pull-ons, in other words, it's a simple change in fashion and manners, just a history crust—like from the Age of Reason, from old Voltaire in a chair to romantic Chatterton in the moonlight—from Teddy Roosevelt to Scott Fitzgerald . . . So there's nothing to get excited about. Beat comes out, actually, of old American whoopee and it will only change a few dresses and pants and make chairs useless in the livingroom and pretty soon we'll have Beat Secretaries of State and there will be instituted new tinsels, in fact new reasons for malice and new reasons for virtue and new reasons for forgiveness . . .

But yet, but yet, woe, woe unto those who think that the Beat Generation means crime, delinquency, immorality, amorality . . . woe unto those who attack it on the grounds that they simply don't understand history and the yearnings of human souls . . . woe unto those who don't realize that America must, will, is, changing now, for the better I say. Woe unto those who believe in the atom bomb, who believe in hating mothers and fathers, who deny the most important of the Ten Commandments, woe unto those (though) who don't believe in the unbelievable sweetness of sex love, woe unto those who are the standard bearers of death, woe unto those who believe in conflict and horror and violence and fill our books and screens and livingrooms with all that crap, woe in fact unto those who make evil movies about the Beat Generation where innocent housewives are raped by beatniks! Woe unto those who are the real dreary sinners that even God finds room to forgive . . . woe unto those who spit on the Beat Generation, the wind'll blow it back. (pp. 31-2, 42, 79)

Jack Kerouac, "The Origins of the Beat Generation," in Playboy® *, Vol. 6, No. 6, June, 1959, pp. 31-2, 42, 79.*

BEAT LITERATURE

John Tytell

[*In the following excerpt, Tytell examines* Naked Lunch *by William S. Burroughs,* "Howl" *by Allen Ginsberg, and* On the Road *by Jack Kerouac as literary works that represent the reaction of Beat Generation writers to the conservative literary and social environment in America during the 1950s.*]

The Beat movement was a crystallization of a sweeping discontent with American "virtues" of progress and power. What began with an exploration of the bowels and entrails of the city—criminality, drugs, mental hospitals—evolved into an expression of the visionary sensibility. The romantic militancy of the Beats found its roots in American transcendentalism. Their spiritual ancestors were men like Thoreau with his aggressive idealism, his essentially conservative distrust of machines and industry, his desire to return to the origins of man's relations to the land; or Melville, with his adventurous tolerance of different tribal codes; or Whitman, optimistically proclaiming with egalitarian gusto the raw newness and velocity of self-renewing change in America while joyously admiring the potential of the common man.

Beginning in despair, the Beat vision was elevated through the shocks of experience to a realization of what was most perilous about American life. One of the images that best captures the motivating energy of this search is the nakedness that was expressed aesthetically in Jack Kerouac's idea of the writer committing himself irrevocably to the original impulses of his imagination, in Ginsberg's relentless self-exposure in a poem like "Kaddish," in Burroughs' refusal in *Naked Lunch* to disguise the demonic aspects of his addiction. But for the Beats nakedness did not exist simply as an aesthetic standard, it was to become a symbolic public and private stance, making art and action inseparable: thus Allen Ginsberg disrobed at poetry readings, and Kerouac once wrote that he wanted to be like the medieval Tibetan scholar-monk Milarepa who lived naked in caves—and as a supreme final statement Neal Cassady was found naked and dead near a railroad track in Mexico. This emphasis on baring the body and exposing the soul was an intuitive reaction to a betrayal the Beats felt because of mass acceptance of demeaning changes in the American idea of self-determination. Nakedness signified rebirth, the recovery of identity. (p. 4)

The postwar era was a time of extraordinary insecurity, of profound powerlessness as far as individual effort was concerned, when personal responsibility was being abdicated in favor of corporate largeness, when the catchwords were coordination and adjustment, as if we had defeated Germany only to become "good Germans" ourselves. The nuclear blasts in Japan had created new sources of terror, and the ideology of technology became paramount; science was seen as capable of totally dominating man and his environment. And the prospects of total annihilation through nuclear explosion, of mass conditioning through the media, only increased the awesome respect for scientific powers.

Few periods in our history have presented as much of an ordeal for artists and intellectuals. In *The Prisoner of Sex,* Norman Mailer has wondered how he survived those years without losing his mind. What Allen Ginsberg has called the Syndrome of Shutdown began in the late forties: the move toward a closed society where all decisions would be secret; the bureaucratic disease that Hannah Arendt has characterized as rule by Nobody where ultimately, as in Watergate, there is no final authority or responsibility; the paralysis caused by the use of technological devices that invade privacy; the increasing power of the Pentagon with its military bases designed to contain a new enemy supposedly (and suddenly) more threatening than the Nazis. The hysteria of rabid anticommunism was far more damaging, as Thomas Mann told the House Un-American Activities Committee, than any native communism; the patriotic blood-boiling became a convenient veil assuring a continued blindness to domestic social conditions that desperately needed attention. An internal freeze gripped America, an irrational hatred that created intense fear and repression, and since any repression feeds on oppression as its necessary rationalization, the red witch-hunts, the censorship of artists and filmmakers, the regimentation of the average man, began with unparalleled momentum and design. The contamination caused by this psychic and moral rigidity has been discussed by Allen Ginsberg in his *Paris Review* interview:

> The Cold War is the imposition of a vast mental barrier on everybody, a vast anti-natural psyche. A hardening, a shutting off of the perception of desire and tenderness which everybody *knows*. . . [creating] a self-consciousness which is a substitute for communication with the outside. This consciousness pushed back into the self and thinking of how it will hold its face and eyes and hands in order to make a mask to hide the flow that is going on. Which it's aware of, which everybody is aware of really! So let's say shyness. Fear. Fear of total feeling, really, total being is what it is.

With the exception of the Civil War period, never before had the sense of hopefulness usually associated with the American experience been so damaged. (pp. 5-6)

In three works particularly, *Naked Lunch,* "Howl," and *On the Road,* the Beats reacted to the embalming insecurities that had quelled the spirit of a generation. Each of these works represented a major departure in literary form as well as a courageous response to the dominating passivity of the age. In retrospect, these books can be seen as the confirmation that America was suffering a collective nervous breakdown in the fifties and that a new nervous system was a prerequisite to perception. In these three works, then, we will find the key to the cultural disorder of an era.

Nowhere was the fear of institutional power more pronounced than in the nightmarish collage of *Naked Lunch.* Burroughs pictured a future possibility far more dismal and terrifying then Orwell's *1984* or Huxley's *Brave New World,* a dystopia where technology strangles all vestiges of freedom, a police state where the human attributes of love and community are stripped away and defiled. *Naked Lunch* is a hallucinatory vision of the very worst expectations of the fifties. Burroughs' central figure is the junkie, the weakest, most despised and vulnerable of citizens, a Western version of India's untouchable caste. Ginsberg has written that to be a drug addict in America is like having been a Jew in Nazi Germany, and Burroughs reflects this idea of fascist control, magnifying its horror through the distorted lens of the junkie. Burroughs' image of the faceless addict counterpoints his view of a society that controls all its parts while remaining invisibly undetectable. The view of the drug experience is harshly antiromantic. Clinical, detached, almost scientifically cinematic, *Naked Lunch* is an educative warning against the horrors of addiction. It relentlessly parodies our institutional life, and at the same time makes apparent the deconditioning effects of drugs, which, like Dr. Benway's cures, are an end in themselves. Rarely has any novelist managed so explosive a struggle between the demands of total control and the nihilistic impulse to defeat those in control. The ensuing combat is so ferocious that the voice of the novelist, ordering experience, seems distant and lost, especially to the reader already distracted by Burroughs' experimental bias.

If there is an intellectual center in *Naked Lunch,* it will be found in a pervasive suspicion of the dangers inherent in technological organization:

> The end result of complete cellular representation is cancer. Democracy is cancerous, and bureaus are its cancer. A bureau takes root anywhere in the state, turns malignant like the Narcotics Bureau, and grows and grows, always reproducing more of its own kind, until it chokes the host if not controlled or excised. Bureaus cannot live without a host, being true parasitic organisms. (A cooperative on the other hand can live without the state. That is the road to follow. The building up of independent units to meet the needs of the people who participate in the functioning of the unit. A bureau operates on opposite principles of *inventing needs* to justify its existence.) Bureaucracy is wrong as a cancer, a turning away from the human evolutionary direction of infinite potentials and differentiation and independent spontaneous action to the complete parasitism of a virus.

This passage—anticipating the cancer metaphor in Mailer's *An American Dream*—exaggerates a social awareness into a political ideology. It is important because it is one of Burroughs' rare projections of anything that might resemble an ideal, for his usual mood is a disgust so intense, so voluptuously vicious as to make any ideal seem false and impossible, and American ideals, especially, precariously incompatible with the realities of world power.

Burroughs' disdain for future possibilities and his staunch antiromantic bitterness make him an exception among Beat writers. He represents a logical fulfillment of the despair of T. S. Eliot's "The Waste Land." Curiously enough, the backgrounds of the two writers are similar: both were born in St. Louis, both were descendants of old American families, and both attended Harvard. Both writers, especially in "The Waste Land" and *Naked Lunch,* share a destructive attitude toward form and structure. Conrad Aiken was the first to notice that the critics who took such great pains to discover the links and continuities of "The Waste Land" were misreading a poem that intended to reveal dissonance and kaleidoscopic confusion through violently contrasting fragments; Burroughs' discontinuity—his microcosmic focus on what frequently appear to be unrelatable experiences—is part of a similar attempt to deny the organic unities of nineteenth-century structure in poetry and fiction. Burroughs' use of the "cutup" method—an arbitrary juxtaposition of randomly selected words and phrases—is part of an attempt to restructure the grammar of perception; the new linguistic order that Burroughs invents initiates the Beats' assault on the conditioning influences of language.

Burroughs takes the motif of the unreal city from "The Waste Land" and compounds it with a nauseating imagery of hideous physical disintegration and degradation that promises a state of future plague. His hanged-men episodes in *Naked Lunch* are grotesque parodies of the talismanic material Eliot himself parodied with the grail legend in "The Waste Land." Burroughs presents these horrors with an unsettling calm, a cold earnestness reminiscent of Swift, a view of the psychological transformations latent in fantasy close to Kafka, and a picture of man as helpless victim that reminds us of Sartre, Beckett, and Genêt. Entering the absolute nadir of existence, Burroughs' fiction defines a purgatory of endless suffering—Beat in the sense of beaten, oppressed, and dehumanized. Yet Ginsberg's and Kerouac's pathway to beatitude stemmed from Burroughs' nightmare of devastation.

Burroughs' affinity with Eliot's objectivity and impersonality raises an aesthetic issue that is crucial for the Beats; because of this affinity, Burroughs once denied belonging to the Beat movement, and emphasized the differences in form among writers he considered more as friends than as literary compatriots. The effect of Burroughs' vision on Ginsberg and Kerouac—who both frequented Borroughs' apartment near Columbia University in 1944-45—cannot be denied; Kerouac, for example, makes Burroughs an oracular source of the wisdom of experience as Bull Lee in *On the Road.* But Burroughs' fiction, while capable of diagnosing what the Beats saw as threatening about American values—especially the worship of technology— did not project a sense of self strong enough to counter the debilitating apathy of the culture. Burroughs clarified his aesthetic of narrative near the end of *Naked Lunch*:

> There is only one thing a writer can write about: *what is in front of his senses at the moment of writing.* . . .I am a recording instrument . . . I do not presume to impose 'story' 'plot' 'continuity.' . . . Insofaras [sic] I succeed in *Direct* recording of certain areas of psychic process I may have limited function. . . . I am not an entertainer. . . .

In this respect, Burroughs is in accord with Eliot's notion that the artist's progress is measured by how well he transcends personality and private emotion.

While it is tempting to see this suppression of self as a classical imperative, it is partly an oversimplification to do so. As romantic a figure as Keats declared, in his letters, that the poet had no identity since he was constantly filling in for some other body. Keats was thinking of the poetic persona, the mask, which is the logical direction of artistic development in British poetry from Donne to Browning, and realized almost to perfection in Eliot. Ginsberg and Kerouac felt that the time had come to challenge this concept, as Whitman had previously, by making personality the center and subject of their work. Now this is a rather delicate and relative issue; it is really the *degree* of self allowed by the artist, and the extent to which an artistic mask subsumes the priorities of self. Henry James, reviewing Whitman's *Drumtaps* shortly after the Civil War, created a touchstone for the classical standard when he criticized Whitman and argued that "art requires above all things the suppression of oneself to an idea." Whitman's idea, which James to his credit later realized, was this expansive and cosmic sense of self: "what I give I give of myself," Whitman proclaimed in "Song of Myself." The classical temper will argue, however, that Whitman enters the atmosphere of emotion, not the terrain of idea. The tradition of Eliot and Pound suspected the manner in which feeling had been rendered in poetry, and attempted its subordination to ideas—thus, Eliot's theory of "objective correlative," a group of images standing in place of the direct expression of emotion. Partly as a result of this fear of statement, Pound and Eliot created a poetry that veered closer and closer to arcane scholarship, as both men, dependent on literary allusion, on other languages, fashioned poetry that became increasingly remote, intellectual, unintelligible, cryptically withdrawn. The seer/poet seemed extinct.

It would be wrong to suggest that the Beats rejected the legacy of Eliot or Pound. Ginsberg, in "Death to Van Gogh's Ear," makes Pound his secretary of economics, and "Howl" is a poem in the tradition of "The Waste Land." Pound, with his attacks on banking (Ginsberg: "Moloch whose soul is electricity and banks"), on the credit system to which most of the Western world is now in bondage, and with his devotion to the poetry of the East, is regarded with considerable admiration by the Beats. No, what was rejected was the tendency toward abstraction (which is ironic when we recall the original impulse of Pound's Imagism), and the abnegation of self that is suggested by the footnotes to "The Waste Land."

In the fifties, when the voice of personality seemed so endangered by an anonymity of sameness, the Beats discovered a natural counter for the silence of the day in a new sense of self, a renaissance of the romantic impulse to combat unbelievably superior forces. The Beats crashed through the restraining mask of the removed artist—the Flaubertian tradition that saw the artist as God, omnipresent but invisible—in a search for what Ginsberg termed "Unified Being." The objective camera eye of "The Waste Land" would be replaced by the "I" of the personal "Howl"; the difference can be felt simply by listening to the sound of Eliot reading his work—dry, unemotional, ironic, distant—and comparing that to Ginsberg's impassioned, arousing rhapsody of voice.

The Beats' denial of the artistic mask had extraordinary implications for the nature of language in literary art and the quality of experience to be expressed. Prematurely conscious of the potentials for lying on a national scale, the Beats raised the standard of honesty no matter what the artistic consequences. Art is created by the polar tensions of spontaneity and artifice, improvisation and contrivance, and the Beats passionately embraced the extreme of uncontained release and denounced superimposed and confining forms. Kerouac, in "The Essentials of Spontaneous Prose," attacked the concept of revision sacred to most writers as a kind of secondary moral censorship imposed by the unconscious, and compared the writer to the jazz saxophonist in a search for language as an undisturbed flow from the mind. In a sense, the nitrous oxide experiments of William James and Gertrude Stein at Harvard, which resulted in automatic writing, anticipated Kerouac's denial of the artist's traditional selectivity.

In *Sunday after the War,* Henry Miller had argued that art was only the path to reality, and that "man's task is to make of himself a work of art." In *Plexus,* he had anticipated the significance of natural speech, remembering that "some of my more honest friends, brutally candid as they often were, would occasionally remind me that in talking to them I was always myself but that in writing I was not. 'Why don't you write like you talk?' they would say." The desire to remove the literary superego was a sign of how the Beats would struggle with the conditioning influences of language; in many ways it represented a fulfillment of the romantic credo as formulated in the preface to the *Lyrical Ballads* in which Coleridge and Wordsworth promised to use the language of ordinary men.

Ginsberg has addressed this question in his *Paris Review* interview with great clarity:

> . . . what happens if you make a distinction between what you tell your friends and what you tell your Muse? The problem is to break down that distinction: when you approach the Muse to talk as frankly as you would talk with yourself or with your friends. So I began finding, in conversations with Burroughs and Kerouac and Gregory Corso, in conversations with people whom I knew well, whose souls I respected, that the things we were telling each other for real were different from what was already in literature. And that was Kerouac's great discovery in *On the Road.* The kind of things that he and Neal Cassady were talking about, he finally discovered were *the* subject matter for what he wanted to write down. That meant, at that minute, a complete revision of what literature was supposed to be, in *his* mind, and actually in the minds of the people that first read the book. . . . In other words, there's no distinction, there should be no distinction between what we write down, and what we really know to begin with. As we know it every day, with each other. And the hypocrisy of literature has been—you know like there's supposed to be a formal literature, which is supposed to be different from . . . in subject, in diction and even in organization, from our quotidian inspired lives.

The goal of complete self-revelation, of nakedness as Ginsberg has put it, was based on a fusion of bohemianism, psychoanalytic probing, and Dadaist fantasy in "Howl" that dragged the self through the slime of degradation to the sublime of exaltation. While the idea of self is the Beat focal point, it represents only a beginning, an involvement to be transcended. The movement in Ginsberg's poetry is from an intense assertion of personal identity to a merger with larger forces in the universe. The ensuing tension between the proclamation of self—evident in a poem like "America"—and an insistence upon man's eternal place in time creates a central dialectical opposition in Ginsberg's poetry. Believing that consciousness is infinite, and that modern man has been taught to suppress much of his potential awareness, Ginsberg has attempted to exorcise the shame, guilt, and fear that he sees as barriers to self-realization and total being. Ginsberg's work, generally, is an outgrowth of the tradition begun by Coleridge: to search for the source of dream, to release the unconscious in its pure state (avoiding literary simulation), to free the restraints on imagination and seek (as Blake did) for the potency and power of the visionary impulse.

Ginsberg sees his poetry as transmitting a sacred trust in human potentials, and he speaks in his *Paris Review* interview of how his mystical encounter with the spirit of Blake in 1948 revealed to him the nature and direction of his own search as a poet, making him see that his role would be to widen the area of consciousness, to open the doors of perception, to continue to transmit messages through time that could reach the enlightened and receptive.

Ginsberg's poetry is characteristic of the Beat desire *to be,* affirming existence as a positive value in a time of apathy. The quest for experience is as obsessive and all-consuming in "Howl" as in *On the Road.* Whether these experiences are destructive or not is of less importance than the fact of contact, especially the kind of experience that allows an individual to discover his own vulnerability, his humanness, without cowering. As Gary Snyder has argued in his essay "Why Tribe," to follow the grain of natural being "it is necessary to look exhaustively into the negative and demonic powers of the Unconscious, and by recognizing these powers—symbolically acting them out—one releases himself from these forces." This statement suggests the shamanistic implications of Beat literature; "Howl," like *Naked Lunch,* is an attempt to exorcise through release. While Burroughs' novel futuristically projects into fantasy, "Howl" naturalistically records the suffering and magnanimity of a hipster avant-garde, a group refusing to accept standard American values as permanent. The experiences in "Howl," certainly in the opening part of the poem, are hysterically excessive and frantically active. It is the sheer momentum of nightmare that unifies these accounts of jumping off bridges, of slashing wrists, of ecstatic copulations, of purgatorial subway rides and longer journeys, a momentum rendered by the propelling, torrential quality of Ginsberg's long line, a cumulative rhythm, dependent on parallelism and the repetition of initial sounds, that is biblical in origin.

While the pace and the autobiographical content of "Howl" shocked the sensibilities of Ginsberg's readers, the deeper significance of the poem was in its formal breakthrough. His long line was like a trip to the sun in the fifties: inconceivable, shattering prior expectations of what a poem could be like. Whitman had predicted that "the cleanest expression is that which finds no sphere worthy of itself and makes one." Rimbaud, discussing Baudelaire's poems, remarked that unknown discoveries demanded new form, and Kerouac had taught Ginsberg that "something that you feel will find its own form." In "Howl," Ginsberg proved that the organic basis of his prosody was neither the result of preconceived expectation nor imposed formal limitation, but an ability to flow with the natural: if "mind is shapely, art is shapely," he asserted.

Ginsberg's poetry ranges in tone from ecstatic joy to utter despair, soaring and plunging from one line to the next, confident, paranoid, always seeking ways to retain the ability to feel in numbing times, always insisting on a social vision that stresses transcendence and the need for spirit in the face of a materialistic culture. No wonder Bob Dylan has remarked that Ginsberg's poetry was for him the first sign of a new consciousness, of an awareness of regenerative possibilities in America. That Dylan shares Ginsberg's surrealistic imagination is evident in early recordings like "Subterranean Homesick Blues," but even more, Dylan participates in the Beat affinity for the road, the symbol of an attitude toward experience that braves anything as long as movement is encouraged.

The first account of this sensibility is found in Norman Mailer's essay "The White Negro." Mailer announced the appearance of a new man, whom he termed the "hipster," who found an existential model in the danger felt by the black man every time he walked down an American street. Seeking, sometimes psychopathically, the "rebellious imperatives of the Self," the hipster rejected the conformity of American life, and spread a "disbelief in the words of men who had too much money and controlled too many things." The hipster sought an apocalyptic answer to the demands of adjustment in the American pattern; he would become, Mailer promised, the thorn in an emerging totalitarian society. The hipster, in a constant attempt to change his nervous system, would always express forbidden impulses and actively violate social taboos; like Elvis Presley, Lenny Bruce, even Rojack in Mailer's *American Dream,* he would release primitive energies before a repressive society. Responding to a "burning consciousness of the present," the hipster stressed the energy of movement and magnified Hemingway's concentrated formula of "grace under pressure" to confront a state of perpetual crisis. Mailer's essay, besides defining the code hero of the Beat movement, was prophetic. He claimed that the hip consciousness would spread in proportion to our recognition of the Negro (the fruit of the civil-rights struggle in the sixties), and that as a result of the new forces caused by hip values, the complacent conformity of the fifties would be shattered by a time of violence, confusion, and rebellion.

The "angelheaded hipster," in the nomenclature of "Howl," staggered in the night journey of the Beat soul, answering a mysterious call from the dark, dragging "through the negro streets at dawn looking for an angry fix." The tortures of his damnation were like Orphic ordeals, sending him into an ecstatic song of destruction which ended in the radiance of secret knowledge. The hipster—affecting a looseness in body movement that was reflected in his judgment—was the connection between black and white cultures, the man whose being throbbed to the beat of bop music's variable rhythmic base. Ginsberg realized that Charlie Parker, the great saxophonist, had announced a new rhythm of thought, an extended breathing of the body in music and speech which led to the new awareness: when the mode of the music changes, the walls of the city shake, as Plato observed long ago. Since the hipster perceived differently, he presented himself in a new light, wearing strange combinations of clothing arranged in odd colors, pinks, purples, oranges. In the early fifties, Kerouac described the funeral of Al Sublette, a shipmate on a merchant freighter who had tutored him on the saxophone. Sublette was a one-eyed Negro who had once played drums with Jimmy Forest. He wore jackets without lapels, checkered pants, and wide-brimmed hats. He also snorted cocaine and had needle marks on his arms. What most impressed Kerouac about the funeral, however, was the black speech rhythms, the open rolling vowel sounds that seemed to follow a musical pattern in stark contrast to the clipped nasality of the white speech Kerouac was accustomed to hearing. Jive was a private code language that caricatured white power with hidden resentment and an incisive sense of the ridiculous. Jive was the ordinary black man's equivalent of the jazz musician's extraordinary improvisatory skills, the ability—resulting from years of practice and control of the medium—to invent endless variations on themes, countless combinations and new permutations of sound which signaled a return to the unconscious, the irrational and intuitive without any goal of permanence. As John Clellon Holmes maintained, jazz was a call from the dark to his generation. It was a euphoria of joy, dance let loose, the expression of an exuberance, an energy and untrammeled swinging style that blacks had developed, partially as a defense, partially as a continuation of a heritage that began in Africa and continued in the cotton fields of the South. The Beats eagerly responded to black music Holmes has stated because they "felt like blacks caught in a square world that wasn't enough for us," a world that was neither immediate, nor pleasurable, nor exciting enough.

Hip sensibility was in a process of constant mutation, Burroughs noted. Its language was subject to rapid change and new inflection; the very vocabulary was a register of fugitive intentions. The hipster, black or white, inhabited the world of the city street. His ideal was knowledge of how the regular world functioned so as to circumvent it. In one sense, he was the intellectual of the streets, but instead of the grounding of the academy, he would improvise his facts, confuse his cultural sources and levels by mixing languages of totally distinct kinds of experience. This "jive" was deliberate, part of a necessary disguise. Living in close contact with criminals, prostitutes, knowing the brutality of the police, the hipster acted as if he wanted to laugh the sadness of his world out of existence, always illuminating his despair or ecstasy with music and drugs. Searching for other modalities and inner pleasures, the hipster's secret initiation into consciousness was

through marijuana, cocaine, opiates, Benzedrine, anything that would depress or elevate, bring him to a "high" on a tingling continuum of significance to quicken the precious inner presence no matter how drab, routine, or oppressive the outer environment. Kerouac defined the hipster by his ability to procure drugs at any time. The lore of drugs ensured the hipster's position as the marginal man who nevertheless had to know how to penetrate the cosmopolitan center, with a ken for its rules and an instinct for self-preservation. The hipster was a case of the extreme—the man who steps so far out of the legal and civilized sphere as to depend exclusively on his own wits and resources, a survival lesson in an alien environment. The pursuit of drugs—what Ginsberg called the "ancient heavenly connection"—was as complex as it could be perilous, but it set a model of a life free from conventional expectations, and encouraged insidious attitudes to morality which were to have enormous social consequence. In 1953, Kerouac wrote Ginsberg that nearly every jazz genius had been jailed because of drugs, and he warned his friend that in the future writers would have to follow a similar route to prison or madhouse. The hip mentality became integral to Beat consciousness, and its seeds were to surprise the sixties, evident in the transformed values of American youth who actively challenged the socially accepted until change was sought as an end itself.

The new forces released by the discovery of the hipster consciousness form Kerouac's ideological focus in *On the Road,* a novel that seems characteristically American in its search for a fluid, unshaped life, free of preimposed patterns, fearing most the horrors of stasis, of staying in the same place without the possibility of change. The reviewers misread the novel almost without exception, finding it incoherent, unstructured, unsound as art, and unhappy as prophecy. Instead of seeing Dean Moriarty (in real life, Neal Cassady) as a genuine picaresque center, and thereby a source of unity in a novel about turbulence, the reviewers attacked the sensibility of nihilism. It is, perhaps, easier to see Dean today as a remarkable fusion of desperation and glee, as the "ragged and ecstatic joy of pure being" to borrow Kerouac's description, an utterly rootless individual who careens from coast to coast on sudden impulse, a man whose incredible energy makes a mockery of the false idol of security. Dean is drawn in the tradition of Huckleberry Finn but is untainted by Miss Watson's puritanism; as a result he is without guile or guilt. The sign of Dean's freedom is his infectious laughter. In the novel, laughter—even in the presence of despair—becomes a kind of life-force, a token of spirit; merely to laugh at the world, like the existentialist ability to say no, becomes a valuable source of inspiration for Kerouac. Dean has been in jail and reads Proust; but his defining quality is speed—in conversation, in a car, in his lifestyle. Kerouac, depicting Dean as a function of speed, has saliently tapped the distinguishing strain of American life in the second half of the twentieth century. This speed is reflected in an extraordinary hyperactivity that determines the atmosphere of the novel:

> the only people for me are the mad ones, the
> ones who are mad to live, mad to talk, mad to
> be saved, desirous of everything at the same

time, the ones who never yawn or say a commonplace thing but burn, burn, burn like fabulous yellow roman candles exploding like spiders across the stars.

But Kerouac himself, through the figure of his narrator, Sal Paradise, tries to offer a check on Dean's exuberant anarchism; indeed, one of the bases for scenic organization in the novel is the way in which other characters find fault with Dean after an episode. And Sal is inevitably drained by the momentum of experience, always aware of growing older and saddened by this; like Kerouac, he is an outsider, an imperfect man in an alien world, brooding, lonely, seized by moments of self-hatred. The refrain in *On the Road* of "everything is collapsing" is a reminder of the effects of disorder, of Kerouac's own vision of uncontained release, on himself. Clearly the endless celebrations, the pell-mell rushing from one scene to the next, create a hysteria that makes Sal want to withdraw from the world. This conflict between the demands of Self as expressed by Dean, and the need to extinguish Self as expressed by Sal, becomes the pivot of Kerouac's fiction. . . . (pp. 11-24)

[Books] like *On the Road, Howl,* and *Naked Lunch* were an apparent threat to the established literary as well as cultural order in the fifties. Critics began wondering in print about new barbarians, antiintellectual know-nothings, infidels of babel. The Beats as writers were either ignored, patronized, or condemned as exponents of a new nihilistic illiteracy. Kerouac, who wrote *On the Road* in 1951, could not get it published until 1957 because he resisted the demands of editors and publishers that he change the face of his manuscript; his best book, *Visions of Cody,* completed by 1952, did not appear in its entirety for another two decades. While Kerouac achieved popularity with *On the Road,* it was despite the literary establishment. Randall Jarrell, for example, accepting the National Book Award for poetry in 1960, commented on Kerouac's attempt to record everything that occurred in the action and in the mind of the author while writing. Jarrell argued that this might lead to a successful psychoanalysis, but the aim of art was concentration and the necessary elimination of everything that Kerouac insisted was most significant. Jarrell's analogy of analysis is interesting because many of Ginsberg's early critics felt his poetry was "therapeutic," and therefore valid only as personal exorcism. The literary critics, schooled in the "new criticism" inspired by T. S. Eliot, John Crowe Ransom of *The Kenyon Review,* Cleanth Brooks, and Austin Warren, expected a certain finesse of texture, strict formal adherance to convention, and proper taste in subject matter. They were conditioned to expect irony, self-deprecation, containment, craft; the romantic, especially any overt declaration of feeling, was suspect. The Beats, introducing new literary techniques, were flaunting their own raw personalities and rude vigors as subject matter, using a speech that employed obscenity as well as humor, ideologically responding to forces like Surrealism and Buddhism, and functioning generally on an entirely different idea of sanity than their critics.

"Howl," *On the Road,* and *Naked Lunch* dismayed many of these critics, causing them to respond with a ferocity of attack that resembled the reception of Henry Miller's *Tropics.* Miller is a key predecessor, stressing naturalness and freedom of composition, his aim being not to achieve "art" but an illusion of spontaneity. He saw himself as a literary outlaw, a "gangster author," as he inscribed a photograph in Paris in the early thirties. Miller suffered more from censorship than any American writer since Dreiser who fought in the courts for a decade to have *Sister Carrie* published as contracted. At the end of the fifties, the right to print "Howl" and *Naked Lunch* also had to be established in the courts. Of course, lines like Burroughs' "Gentle reader, we see God through our assholes in the flash bulb of orgasm" were not intended to appeal to readers with conservative tastes, and the resulting charges of editorial degeneracy and obscenity were resolved through judicial procedure. The trials proved to be a testimonial to the potency of the works, even as the resulting publicity enlarged the audience. That audience, small at first, was part of a broad artistic awakening: Jackson Pollock's automatism and his sprawling canvases of poured paint; John Cage's music, which like Kerouac's ideal of natural speech tried to capture every actual sound in the environment; Merce Cunningham in dance; Judith Malina and Julian Beck in the Living Theater performing Brecht and expressing the energy of immediate impulse; Charles Olson and Robert Creeley at Black Mountain College, poets also searching for a new personal voice, aware that the thought process need not be refined out of the poem, that the poet should not shy from his own action, randomness, or whimsy, but should, like the Beats, reach for the center of the subject rather than hover about it intellectually—working in obscurity, ignoring the hostility of the critics, these artists were the creative soul of the fifties. (pp. 29-30)

John Tytell, "The Broken Circuit," in his Naked Angels: The Lives & Literature of the Beat Generation, 1976. Reprint by Grove Press, Inc., 1986, pp. 1-30.

Michael Davidson

[*Davidson is an American educator and historian. In the following excerpt, he explores the tension between self-reflection and participation in life in the works of Jack Kerouac, Allen Ginsberg, and Michael McClure.*]

Like many literary movements, the Beat generation was largely the projection of the media, albeit aided by its participants. At the height of the period, the *San Francisco Chronicle* dressed one of its columnists in beard, beret, jeans, and workshirt and sent him undercover into the pads and jazz clubs of San Francisco's North Beach to report on the strange habits and sexual mores of these social misfits. And it was the *Chronicle's* feature columnist, Herb Caen, who added the suffix "nik" to the term "Beat," making a connection with the recently launched Russian satellite, *Sputnik.* The Beat*nik,* then, could be associated in the public mind not only with antisocial behavior but with things subversive and anti-American. For a while it was essential for comedians to have an arsenal of Beatnik jokes, and many of the television sitcoms of the day had a resident bearded bohemian. Adopting the period's red-baiting rhetoric, *Life* magazine announced that the Beat generation was under the direct influence of a few neurotic poets:

> This is not to say that the bums, hostile little females and part-time bohemians of the Beat Generation would not have been bums, hostile little females and part-time bohemians anyhow. But without the slightest missionary intent the poets have provided them with a name, the fuel of self-justification and attitudes guaranteed to "bug the squares."

Beatniks, the article goes on to say, are "talkers, loafers, passive little con men, lonely eccentrics, mom-haters, cophaters, exhibitionists with abused smiles and second mortgages on a bongo drum—writers who cannot write, painters who cannot paint, dancers with unfortunate malfunction of the fetlocks." Such vituperative language, in the context of a major journalistic exposé, did little to diminish the public ardor for a new fad and no doubt did much to bring about the very enthusiasm it lamented.

If the major tabloids' critical reception of the Beat generation was less than friendly, it was at least predictable. A more disturbing criticism came from writers of the Left, who might be thought to have shared some of the Beats' antiestablishment sentiments. These critics, writing in magazines like the *Partisan Review* and the *Nation,* saw in the Beat movement an apolitical and naive attempt to substitute for social commitment and activism a policy of retreat and egocentric self-absorption. Norman Podhoretz was representative of those critics who made invidious comparisons between the new bohemians and the "authentic bohemians" of the 1920s and 1930s. "The Bohemianism of the 1920's," according to Podhoretz [see Further Reading],

> represented a repudiation of the provinciality, philistinism, and moral hypocrisy of American life—a life, incidentally, which was still essentially small-town and rural in tone. Bohemia, in other words, was a movement created in the name of civilization: its ideals were intelligence, cultivation, spiritual refinement.

The bohemia of the 1950s, in contrast, "is quite another kettle of fish altogether."

> It is hostile to civilization; it worships primitivism, instinct, energy, "blood." To the extent that it has intellectual interests at all, they run to mystical doctrines, irrationalist philosophies, and left-wing Reichianism. The only art the new Bohemians have any use for is jazz, mainly of the cool variety. Their predilection for bop language is a way of demonstrating solidarity with the primitive vitality and spontaneity they find in jazz and of expressing contempt for coherent, rational discourse which, being a product of the mind, is in their view a form of death. To be articulate is to admit that you have no feelings (for how can real feelings be expressed in syntactical language?), that you can't respond to anything . . . and that you are probably impotent.

It is not that Podhoretz was necessarily wrong about specific attributes but that he was invoking these qualities negatively against such official abstractions as civilization,

coherent discourse, and feelings. And one wonders how the bohemians of the 1920s would have responded to Podhoretz's sunny picture of their "intelligence, cultivation, [and] spiritual refinement." The implication is that if one is going to reject the status quo, there is a series of self-evident standards by which one may do so.

To some extent this media coverage of the Beats, whether from the Luce organization or the *Partisan Review,* reflected a need, in the midst of the Eisenhower doldrums, to have a scapegoat for the anxieties facing mass society. The McCarthy committee had already provided a steady stream of such misfits, and the Beats became a more theatrical extension. And rather than repudiate their role as outsiders, they accepted it—even reveled in it—finding in the word "Beat" an immanent "beatitude" that would transform what critics saw as nihilism into a religious ideal. In doing so, they became projections of the very society they rejected—a fact that ultimately made life difficult (witness Jack Kerouac's sad later years) and that continues to make it almost impossible to untangle their writing from the fictions their writing created.

One of the most pervasive fictions surrounding the Beat writers is their cult of energy, a tendency to exalt the present over the past, action over reflection, movement over stasis. "Whooee," yells Dean Moriarity in *On the Road.*

> "Here we go!" And he hunched over the wheel and gunned her; he was back in his element, everybody could see that. We were all delighted, we all realized we were leaving confusion and nonsense behind and performing our one and noble function of the time, *move.*

In Beat argot, to "move," to be "hip," to "groove" are ways of participating with—not reflecting upon—the "natural" rhythms of life. Movement is not a means to an end but an end in itself. This cult of energy is buttressed by an Emersonian belief in the identity between natural forces and the mind, a relationship that may be activated by writing at great speed, without constraints and without revision. The correspondence between text and world is sustained by what Levy-Bruhl [in *Primitive Mentality*] calls a "participation mystique," in which the linguistic sign partakes directly of the natural sign in a relation of synecdoche. The word does not represent but incarnates powers latent in the world.

Though many remarks by Allen Ginsberg, Jack Kerouac, and Michael McClure would seem to support this view, one finds in their works a corresponding anxiety or self-consciousness about the difficulties of attaining such participation. For every Emersonian affirmation of the holiness of all being, there is a Poe-like skepticism about its realization in contemporary American life. In its extreme form, this anxiety turns into the bitter cynicism of William Burroughs, whose novels chronicle the various addictions of a society bent on authoritarian control.

If one wanted to characterize the tension between a "participation mystique" and reflectiveness in Beat poetry, one might look at Robert Creeley's well-known lyric "I Know a Man." Although Creeley is not usually associated with the San Francisco Beats, he was close to all of them, and his poetry of the period embodies much of what could be called a Beat "ethos."

> As I sd to my
> friend, because I am
> always talking,—John, I
>
> sd, which was not his
> name, the darkness sur-
> rounds us, what
>
> can we do against
> it, or else shall we &
> why not, buy a goddamn big car,
>
> drive, he sd, for
> christ's sake, look
> out where yr going.

The speaker is caught between two conflicting positions: whether to solve his existential despair by escaping from the world (by buying a "goddamn big car") or by paying a greater attention to what is immediately in front of him. Despite the poem's title, he cannot truly *know* anyone— either himself or another—because he is constantly talking and thus avoiding recognition of the other. He does not really know the other's name, nor is he able to differentiate himself from his interlocutor. His despair is generalized ("the darkness sur- / rounds us"), and to drive and thus escape such despair is an inadequate solution to a problem of much greater proportions.

The poem's last tercet introduces a voice of reason that urges the speaker to pay attention to what is happening: "for / christ's sake, look / out where yr going." But the terse and enjambed lines, the highly subordinated quality of the syntax, and the confusion of speaker and interlocutor conspire against the ostensible solutions these lines proffer. Adding to the general instability of the lines is the fact that the word "drive" could equally be a continuation of the previous lines (Why not buy a car and drive somewhere?), or it could be the beginning of an imperative spoken by "he" ("drive . . . look out where you're going"). Such ambiguities enact at a structural level the very conditions that prevent the "I" from "knowing" anyone. The poem, then, demonstrates one kind of attention—poetry's power to embody contradictory states of feelings and emotion—while denying another.

Creeley states in compressed form some of the dilemmas that can be found in the work of many Beat writers. The world is perceived as alien and hostile, an undifferentiated "darkness" created and maintained by forces beyond the individual's control. The hipster's endless talk becomes a tentative way of countering that darkness and of acknowledging, if inadequately, the need for dialogue. Another solution, one found in many another American literary work, from *Huckleberry Finn* and *Moby Dick* to *On the Road,* is to take the open road, "drive" away from Aunt Polly or the Man in the Grey Flannel Suit toward some indefinite freedom. Most accounts of the Beat myth stop here, at the edge of the highway, where the vast spaces of the West offer the illusion of escape. But Creeley's conclusion offers a salutary warning to pay attention in the midst of distraction and abstraction. This moment of self-consciousness, however tenuous, represents a side of the Beat myth seldom acknowledged: the recognition of solitude and vulnerability despite the competing claims of participation and communalism.

In terms of *On the Road* this quality of self-correction is embodied in the figure of Sal Paradise, who takes both a literal and a figurative "back seat" to the voluble, sociable Dean Moriarity. Or in the case of Ginsberg, it is the quality of loneliness and insecurity that pervades poems like "In a Supermarket in California" or "Kaddish." What Creeley offers in "I Know a Man" and what the Beats in general offer in their work is a demonstration, through a highly charged expressive vehicle, of extreme psychological and spiritual states, *including the limitations of those states.* If this corrective aspect of the Beats' writing has not been discussed, it is perhaps because their work has been valued for extraliterary qualities.

The imperative to "drive" away from (or more deeply into) the moment is reflected in the poetics of all the Beat writers. "First thought, best thought" is Ginsberg's condensed statement, and Kerouac's "Essentials of Spontaneous Prose" carries a similar message: "Never afterthink to 'improve' or defray impressions, as, the best writing is always the most painful personal wrung-out tossed from cradle warm protective mind—tap from yourself the song of yourself, BLOW! NOW!—YOUR WAY IS YOUR ONLY WAY." Kerouac seems to have carried his theory one step further by mythologizing his own compositional practice, just as he mythologized his life. According to an article he wrote for *Playboy,* [see excerpt above], *On the Road* was composed in "three weeks in the beautiful month of May 1951 while living in the Chelsea district of lower West Side Manhattan on a 100-foot roll" while taking ferocious amounts of benzedrine. But as recent studies have shown, Kerouac's method was considerably more crafted than he admitted. What we call *On the Road,* according to Tim Hunt [in *Kerouac's Crooked Road: Development of a Fiction*], is actually the fourth version of his "road" book, the final and ultimate text being *Visions of Cody.* Portions of *On the Road* appear in some of his other novels, and discarded segments from the early manuscript can be found in later books. As Kerouac wrote his "road" book, beginning sometime in 1947, he discovered new modes of composition that allowed him greater flexibility in his narrative and greater immediacy in rendering individual scenes. The manuscript of *On the Road* finally accepted by Malcolm Cowley was a considerably edited and reworked version of the famous teletype roll. None of this disqualifies Kerouac's remarks on spontaneity in prose; it simply points out certain discrepancies between theory and practice that are inevitable with a poetics dominated by such an expressive ideal.

The same could be said for Ginsberg's "Howl," the first section of which was composed, we have been told "madly in one afternoon, a huge sad comedy of wild phrasing, meaningless images for the beauty of abstract poetry of mind." James Breslin has pointed out [in *From Modern to Contemporary: American Poetry, 1945-1965*] that "Howl" was actually composed over a number of years, beginning as early as 1951 in notebooks in which were recorded the first catalogues of those destroyed "best minds" of his generation. In the Ginsberg archives at Columbia University, there are forty pages of worksheets for part II of "Howl" alone, in which "at some point [Ginsberg] went back and underlined those phrases [relating to Moloch] that struck him as most effective." We can trace the painstaking evolution of this manuscript by regarding a facsimile edition of *Howl* in which it is clear that Ginsberg made many drafts of each section and made liberal use of his editorial pencil. And when Ginsberg has discussed "Howl" publicly, he has always insisted upon the poem's formal structure. "It's built like a brick shithouse," he said to Richard Eberhart, and Ginsberg devotes the entire opening segment of his *Paris Review* interview ["The Art of Poetry VIII," 1966] to identifying the metrical structure of his poetic rhythms in "Howl." The fact that Kerouac's and Ginsberg's manuscripts reveal the kind of formal care that would seem to contradict their stated aesthetic beliefs indicates the difficulty of realizing a participation ethos without some of what Kerouac calls "afterthink."

This disparity between participation and reflection animates much Beat writing. In Kerouac's prose, it can be seen in his tendency to validate the present while secretly yearning for a state of permanent boyhood. In Ginsberg, it takes the form of an Emersonian involvement in the world mediated by a quality of loneliness and insecurity; and in the work of Michael McClure, it exists as a need to reach some primal, mammalian state while using traditional rhetorical modes. I would like to look briefly at these three writers and their attempts to deal with this tension between participation and reflection, between an idealization of the present and a desire for distance and detachment. I see this tension as both a limitation and a generative element of Beat writing, as something that animated much American writing during the hundred years between the first edition of *Leaves of Grass* and the publication of "Howl." (pp. 61-6)

Jack Kerouac's presence may seem somewhat out of place in a [discussion] . . . dealing largely with poets, but his importance to fellow Beat writers is seminal and his poetry, particularly that in *Mexico City Blues,* is significant in its own right. It was Kerouac's prose that initially influenced Allen Ginsberg's practice in poems like "Howl" and "Kaddish." And it was Kerouac's prose, rather than his poetry, that obviously captured the imagination of a larger readership. Other writers like Lew Welch, David Meltzer, Michael McClure, Ted Berrigan, and Clark Coolidge have commented on the importance of Kerouac's short-lined poetry—its go-for-broke goofiness and immediacy—but it is the novels in which the full richness of his visual and auditory imagination is displayed. And especially in a work like *Visions of Cody,* Kerouac challenges the generic designations of "novel" and "poem" by writing in a variety of voices and styles that make him much more than an ephebe of Wolfe or Twain and very much a part of the international avant garde.

Much journalistic copy has been devoted to Kerouac's invention of the term "Beat," a term that combines the hipster's qualities of existential malaise and world weariness with a "beatific" or angelic potentiality latent in that generation. Kerouac, however, associates the origins of the term with things very secular and very American. In his 1959 *Playboy* article, he first talks about Beat spirituality and identifies the generation's alliance with Christ, Lao Tzu, and Muhammad but then moves more directly into his own childhood sources in popular media. The Beat generation "goes back" to radio mysteries like "The Shadow" and to the comedies of W. C. Fields, the Three Stooges, and the Marx Brothers. Kerouac's central refrain, "it goes back," suggests that to be Beat is also to return to childhood. At this point "Beat" ceases to describe a religious or psychological condition and becomes a private signature for lost youth. It is this essentially boyhood state with its large-scale projections of danger, magic, power, and innocence that characterizes much of Kerouac's own work—the atmosphere of Tom Sawyer's gang with its secret signs, its antisocial nature (Kerouac later applauds the rascally Ignatz in the Krazy Kat cartoons), and fictionalized adventure. To be Beat, then, is to be innocent, to reclaim a time when the only danger is the maniacal sound of the Shadow's laughter on the radio.

The attraction of Tom Sawyer's gang is that it affords possibilities of community in a world dominated by authoritarian elders. If Kerouac's novels are "about" any one thing, it is the companionship of males and the pleasures of male bonding. Where fathers are noticeably absent, such fraternity replaces one kind of authority with another, one based less on filial than on sibling interrelationships. This bonding is particularly important for Kerouac as he seeks to find surrogates for his own brother, Gerard, who died at an early age. And just as bonding helps to create a sense of family, it also sanctions certain types of sexual experiences, whether hetero- or homosexual, that, as Catherine Stimpson points out [in "The Beat Generation and the Trials of Homosexual Liberation," *Salmagundi,* Fall 1982], "have the intensity of family life without the threat of incest or the taint of biological destiny." However liberated, the Beats often replicated many of the cultural stereotypes of power (passive-aggressive, masterslave) that their sexuality seemed to reject. As Stimpson points out, they were "heroic protagonists in cultural drama about homosexuality who exemplify how much harder it is to be free and to extend freedom than to be sexual, and homosexual."

This freedom is exemplified in Kerouac's novels by friends like Neal Cassady and Gary Snyder or by marginalized social types like the black jazzman, the skid row hobo, and the Zen eccentric. He projects these heroes as foils for his own confused relation to adulthood while he remains an endistanced observer:

> But then they danced down the streets like dingledodies, and I shambled after as I've been doing all my life after people who interest me, because the only people for me are the mad ones who are mad to live, mad to talk, mad to be saved, desirous of everything at the same time, the ones who never yawn or say a commonplace thing, but burn, burn, burn like fabulous yellow roman candles exploding like spiders across the stars. (*On the Road*)

Kerouac's characteristic position, shambling after the "mad ones," allows him both a narrative and an existential distance from his own story: He may act as first and third person, subject and observer of his own story, even while the ostensible focus is the wild, spontaneous life of others. For a novelist who set such stock in the uses of immediacy, his own narrative strategy is curiously Jamesian.

Although Kerouac is best known for individual novels, he essentially wrote one long novel all his life, a "vast book like Proust's, except that [his] remembrances are written on the run instead of in a sickbed." The name of this work is "The Legend of Duluoz" and it concerns the attempt by Jack Duluoz, alias Kerouac, to find a realm of vitality and comfort in the midst of modern, alienated American life. Occasionally he finds it among the "falaheen" people—the bums, Beat bohemians, blacks, and Indians—who live at the fringes of American life. The plot consists of a series of variations on incidents drawn from Kerouac's life (and, in the "road" book, from the life of Neal Cassady). The characters are projections of Kerouac's friends and family who represent the values and aspirations—and limitations—against which Duluoz must measure himself. If the "Legend" has a single social ethos, it is a blend of working-class, Roman Catholic, redneck American values combined, in the later novels, with ideals of compassion derived from Kerouac's idiosyncratic version of Buddhism.

The dominant theme of each novel is time—time passing and time regained: "Dreams of a kid and this whole world is nothing but a big sleep made of reawakened material (soon to reawake)." Kerouac's work comprises the "visions of the great remembrancer," and if a given passage seems familiar to us, it is usually because we have seen it recorded in another form in another novel or in an earlier passage. It is Kerouac's gift that he can use and reuse his incidents again and again, each time seeing them from different perspectives. Since incidents from the past illustrate rather than move the plot forward, they may be replayed again and again in order to intensify what are essentially timeless values. In this sense Kerouac's novels resemble those of his modernist predecessors, for whom time is cyclic, for whom the present is suffused with the past. A novel like *Desolation Angels,* for example, is an anthology of incidents taken from previous novels (hopping freights, living in San Francisco's skid row, hitchhiking cross-country with Cassady, etc.), which Duluoz remembers once again as he sits alone in his watchman's shack on the top of Desolation Peak. He recalls these incidents to sustain himself, just as Kerousac, the novelist, invokes them to cement events distant in time.

Compassion might well be the central theme of the Duluoz legend since it is the quality that the narrator most often admires in others, but an even more pervasive theme in the novels turns out to be loneliness. Kerouac "feels" for everyone but is terrified of solitude, of being unloved, of becoming swallowed by the void. Loneliness haunts his novels; his best moments occur when he evokes the solitude of bus stops, of wind in the trees, of winos on the skids, of a jazz saxophonist wailing in the night, of foghorns over the bay, of empty space itself:

> What is that feeling when you're driving away
> from people and they recede on the plain till you

see their specks dispersing?—it's the too-huge world vaulting us, and it's good-by. But we lean forward to the next crazy venture beneath the skies. (*On the Road*)

The only recourse against the "too-huge world" is to drive on to the "next crazy venture," although coming to the end of the road often involves returning to his East Coast home and his mother, where Jack can regroup and rekindle his restlessness.

On the Road is paradigmatic of Kerouac's thematics of youth and solitude. The narrator, Sal Paradise, respects and admires Dean Moriarity's sexual prowess, wild conversation, and muscular abandon, but he also recognizes in him vestiges of his long-lost brother and his own childhood "in those dye-dumps and swim holes and riversides of Paterson and the Passaic." Being with Dean represents a regression to a more immediate life, one free of adult cares and anxieties. But when Sal is on the road alone, he experiences his first pangs of aging, a moment of introspection that is associated immediately with the geography of America:

> I woke up as the sun was reddening; and that was the one distinct time in my life, the strangest moment of all, when I didn't know who I was—I was far away from home, haunted and tired with travel, in a cheap hotel room I'd never seen, hearing the hiss of steam outside, and the creak of the old wood of the hotel, and footsteps upstairs, and all the sad sounds, and I looked at the cracked high ceiling and really didn't know who I was for about fifteen strange seconds. I wasn't scared; I was just somebody else, some stranger, and my whole life was a haunted life, the life of a ghost. I was halfway across America, at the dividing line between the East of my youth and the West of my future.

Later, Dean's wild conversation and driving will distract Sal from such introspection. Dean invariably appears at a moment when Sal's life has become static, when he has been too long living at home or when a relationship threatens to tie him down. At this moment, Dean shows up and offers "the road" as a panacea.

But the road by itself is not enough. It provides adventure and change, but it also represents an escape from conditions that Sal is not willing to face. Before one trip with Dean, Sal tries to convince himself that he is going along only for the ride. His friends interrogate him about the reasons for his trip. Carlo Marx (Ginsberg) demands, "Now I'm not trying to take yo hincty sweets from you, but it seems to me the time has come to decide what you are and what you're going to do." And when the gang arrives at Old Bull Lee's (Burroughs) in New Orleans, Lee asks, "Sal, what are you going to the Coast for?" Sal's answer is oblique: "Only for a few days. I'm coming back to school." Even the ordinarily voluble Dean lacks a sufficient answer:

> Then a complete silence fell over everybody; where once Dean would have talked his way out, he now fell silent himself, but standing in front of everybody, ragged and broken and idiotic, right under the lightbulbs, his bony mad face

covered though tremendous revelations were pouring into him all the time now. . . . He was BEAT—the root, the soul of Beatific. What was he knowing? He tried all in his power to tell me what he was knowing, and they envied that about me, my position at his side, defending him and drinking him as they once tried to do. Then they looked at me. What was I, a stranger, doing on the West Coast this fair night? I recoiled from the thought.

"We're going to Italy," I said, I washed my hands of the whole matter. (*On the Road*)

Sal has relied too much on the road as a value in itself and on Dean's energy as a sustaining power. In this passage Sal tries to force a kind of spiritual presence on his "beat" friend, implying that Dean's silence betrays a kind of cryptic truth. But Sal's slightly hysterical answer—"We're going to Italy"—indicates how inadequate that projection is. The story of *On the Road* is not, as the book blurb describes, "an explosion of consciousness—a mind-expanding trip into emotion and sensation, drugs and liquor and sex," but a qualification of the limits of detachment. Kenneth Rexroth [see Further Reading] characterized the art of the Beat generation as "disengagement," but Kerouac's novels often point to the psychic toll that such disengagement takes.

In his essay on Walt Whitman, D. H. Lawrence comes to a similar conclusion about the American writer's tendency to become absorbed in the world. He complains that the end of Whitman's desire to penetrate all things, his amorous "ache," is death. The price of absorption is fragmentation and dissolution, and something of the same realization occurs in all of Kerouac's novels. In *On the Road* this realization is thematized in the dream of the "Shrouded Traveler," in which Sal Paradise encounters the mortality at stake in his desire to penetrate the world:

Something, someone, some spirit was pursuing all of us across the desert of life and was bound to catch us before we reached heaven. Naturally, now that I look back on it, this is only death: death will overtake us before heaven. The one thing that we yearn for in our living days, that makes us sigh and groan and undergo sweet nauseas of all kinds, is the remembrance of some lost bliss that was probably experienced in the womb and can only be reproduced (though we hate to admit it) in death. (*On the Road*)

The dream of the road, the lure of escape and motion is reseen as a metaphor of mortality. And instead of the romantic traveler in Dean, Sal suddenly sees in himself, like Blake's Mental Traveller, a figure hopelessly locked within the cyclic nature of life.

As Kerouac described in a letter, *On the Road* was a "horizontal account of travels on the road," presumably because it followed a more traditional, diachronic narrative. He thought of his next novel, *Visions of Cody,* as a "vertical, metaphysical study of Cody's [Cassady's] character in its relation to the general America." In order to achieve this "vertical" form, he developed a technique that he called "sketching," whereby he would render an incident on the spot, writing quickly while gaining as much particularity as possible. As he wrote to John Clellon Holmes:

What I'm beginning to discover now is something beyond the novel and beyond the arbitrary confines of the story . . . into realms of revealed Picture . . . *wild form,* man, wild form. Wild form's the only form holds what I have to say— my mind is exploding to say something about every image and every memory. . . . I have an irrational lust to set down everything I know . . . at this time I'm making myself sick to find the wild form that can grow with my wild heart.

In practice, sketching allowed Kerouac the freedom to describe Cody from a number of vantages without providing the usual rhetorical connectives. He could finally dissolve the distance between Jack and Cody, narrator and subject, into one multiple consciousness.

Kerouac's new "wild" narrative moves paratactically from one observation to another with a breathless, improvisatory quality. Unlike surrealist automism, sketching keeps the focus steadily on the scene—its shifting patterns of light, its ambient noise, its distractions:

An immense plate glass window in this white cafeteria on a cold November evening in New York faces the street (Sixth Avenue) but with inside neon tubular lights reflected in the window and they in turn illuminating the Japanese garden walls which are therefore also reflected and hang in the street with the tubular neons (and with other things illuminated and reflected such as that enormous twenty-foot green door with its red and white exit sign reflected near the drapes to the left, a mirror pillar from deep inside, vaguely the white plumbing and at the top of things upper right hand and the signs that are low in the window looking out, that say *Vegetarian Plate 60 cents, Fish Cakes with Spaghetti, Bread and Butter* (no price) and are also reflected and hanging but only low on the sidewalk because also they're practically against it)—so that a great scene of New York at night with cars and cabs and people rushing by and *Amusement Center, Bookstore, Leo's Clothing, Printing,* and *Ward's Hamburger* and all of it November clear and dark is riddled by these diaphanous hanging neons, japanese walls, door, exit signs. (*Visions of Cody*)

In this passage Kerouac describes the way that various surfaces in a brightly lit cafeteria—a plate glass window, neon lights, walls, a mirror pillar, signs—reflect each other so that inside and outside are constantly confused. The "enormous twenty-foot green door" across the street from the cafeteria suddenly appears to be inside among the "Japanese garden" wallpaper and neon lights. Menus hanging in the window itself seem to project outside among the "cars and cabs and people rushing by." Everything hangs tentatively in the air like a giant urban mobile while Kerouac adds to its "diaphanous" quality by intruding into his description with parenthetical remarks and qualifications. Duluoz is juxtaposed to this plethora of details as both observer and as object of observation. To some extent the constant shifting of perspective from near to far, inside to outside, mirrors the larger problem of subjectivity in the novel itself as Duluoz seeks to gain a perspective on his main character while understanding his complicity in Cody's life. Although this is but one sketch among many in the novel's opening two sections, it functions to create the character of Duluoz by studying *how* as well as *what* he sees.

At a larger structural level *Visions of Cody* makes use of this distortion of perspectives in five separate sections, each of which captures Cody from a different angle and by means of a different narrative strategy. The first section consists of sketches like the one above, which relate, as Gerald Nicosia observes [in *Memory Babe: A Critical Biography of Jack Kerouac*], "the narrator's psychological preparation to meet the hero." In the second, Cody himself is introduced through a straightforward description of his youth in Denver. The third section changes the narrative once again by presenting transcripts of tapes made by Kerouac and Cassady in the early 1950s. These tapes were originally made to provide material for a novel that Cassady intended to write, but Kerouac appropriates them as another level in his own narrative. The fourth section, "Imitation of the Tape," parodies many of the narrative techniques already developed and imitates (or mocks) a wide range of modern literary styles. The final section, subtitled "Joan Rawshanks in the Fog," takes many of the incidents encountered in *On the Road* but reframes them from the standpoint of an older and more self-critical Sal Paradise. By using the frame of the movie ("Joan Rawshanks in the Fog" parodies the Joan Crawford movie *Sudden Fear*), Jack Duluoz may suggest his own role in directing Cody's life as a fiction. All of these narrative techniques help to frame Cody not as a fictional character but as the site of Duluoz's own speculations on himself and on "the general America."

Whereas in *On the Road* Cody's actions are valued in themselves as signs of primitive vitality, in *Visions of Cody* they are part of a phenomenological matrix that depends on Duluoz's role as interpreter. At one point he says, "So I not only took care of Cody's understanding but protected him from horrors which he, unlike me, was not capable of absorbing." A remark such as this indicates that Duluoz's role in this novel will not be one of patient scribe but one of active agent in his friend's life. This position is very different from that of Sal Paradise, who trusts Dean's intuitions and perceptions without understanding his own complicity in fictionalizing them. Duluoz, unlike Sal, celebrates Cody's Faustian excesses but also qualifies them with parenthetical remarks—reminders that it is he, Duluoz, who is capable of providing a frame.

At times the sheer density and speed of sensations threaten to overwhelm him. He often complains that he cannot keep pace with the welter of events and wishes for a "peaceful hacienda or Proust-bed" from which to "recall in toto." But such a position is too passive and hermetic for Duluoz, who becomes increasingly anxious when he has such a vantage. At one point Duluoz says, "I wish God had made me vaster myself—I wish I had ten personalities" in order to take it all in, but then he qualifies that he "must struggle to live it all, and *on foot* and in these lit-

tle crepesole shoes." This is a version of Creeley's warning that, however ambiguous or threatening the territory, one lives within certain economies; one still must pay attention to the road. Kerouac desires the scope of Whitman's "I" (or Proust's memory) while retaining the perspective of a single, historical individual.

The tension between participation and critical distance is most thoroughly apparent in section 3, in which the tape transcripts offer what appears to be the unmediated interaction between narrator and subject. Ostensibly, it is a chance to hear Cody's fast-paced, energetic speech, but it becomes a demonstration of the ways Duluoz appropriates that speech in order to "create" his friend. Part of this appropriation is performed by editorial remarks that Duluoz provides in order to establish the context of the conversation:

> JACK. How can I be eating on Benzedrine? (*eating at table*)
>
> CODY. (*laughs*) That tea'll overcome anything. (*pause*) . . . Why don't you let me read John's letter? (*playing whiny little boy*)

Although we hear Jack's voice as the interlocutor, we also see him as editor, qualifying and shaping the conversation in its particular mood and tone by means of parenthetical stage directions. I see these editorial remarks not as refinements of Cody's speech but as introjections to indicate the narrator's role as transcriber.

As one can readily tell, much of the conversation and editorializing concern the drugs that are being consumed while the sessions are in process:

> JACK. See, did you dig this here? I didn't notice that till I played it back
>
> CODY. (*after long silence*) . . . (*laughing*) . . . It's like last night—ah damn thing
>
> JACK. Hmmm boy that was good. That was a good one wasn't it? (*Visions of Cody*)

The "good one," of course, is a hit of pot, which the two consume in large quantities. Such references to pot—the rituals of lighting up, passing the joint, blowing out smoke—provide yet another frame to the entire section as Cody attempts to remember events from his past. And this attempt to "get it down" as accurately as possible is frustrated by distractions that are both chemically and rhetorically induced. The constant interchange between drug talk and Cody's memories creates a counterpoint of present and past, observation and reflection that make section 3 the most charged part of the novel.

As I said, the ostensible purpose of the transcripts is to provide an accurate record of Cody's speech, but the result, curiously enough, is a metadiscourse on the problem of representation. Jack poses as the faithful recorder, but it quickly becomes obvious that he is as interested in the difficulty of recording as he is in Cody's actual stories. Much of the conversation, in fact, concerns Cody's comments on previous transcripts. Rather than tell a story, Cody must also critique his own telling of it as it appears in Duluoz's typed version. At one point Cody describes his first visit to Old Bull Lee in Texas, a conversation that describes Lee's accidental shooting of his wife June:

> Here's this Bull, he's so high, he's just sittin there with his bad order high, see he can't see a hundred yards, y'know, that sonofabitch, no wonder he hit June and killed her, imagine, no shit, he can't see with them glasses. (*Visions of Cody*)

But Cody, whether or not because of the pot, quickly becomes involved with his difficulties in remembering the event clearly:

> Phew! naw, but man, what I'd tell you is, I didn't know that I'd appreciate remembering these things more, so therefore when I was there I didn't pay much attention to any of this, I was hung up on something else, you know so I can't remember, say, like for example, I can remember NOW for example, but now that I CAN remember it doesn't do any good, because . . . man . . . I can't get it down. You know . . . I just remember it, I can remember it well, what happened 'cause I'M not doing nothin, see?
>
> JACK. You don't have to get it down
>
> CODY. (*demurely downward look*) But I can't remember what happened there, man, except I remember certain things. . . . But I'm saying like Huck [Herbert Hunke], me and Irwin [Ginsberg] goin out in the middle of the Louisiana bayou on a particular New York kick (*Visions of Cody*)

This incident is discussed at the next session, at which point Cody begins to qualify phrases from the previous transcript like "bad order high" and "can't get it down." He is especially concerned with Duluoz's parenthetical description of him as looking "demurely downward":

> And, so—that's what I say when I say "I can't get it down," and then . . . "two minutes"—but you picked up on that, of all the different things I was sayin, and so you said, "But you don't *have* to get it down," you know, that's what you said . . . and so the demure downward look . . . was simply in the same tone and the same fashion . . . as my reaction and feeling was when I said the words "but you can't get it down" you know. (*Visions of Cody*)

Much of the third section consists of this kind of wandering interrogation of individual phrases. If Cody has trouble "getting it down," Duluoz is always present to help him remember, to goad him on, to fill in the gaps. And Cody recognizes the crucial role of his friend in articulating his thought:

> . . . because see that's what happened, see, and I'm describin now, see, nowhere I'm going through the process of telling *you,* and you're the one who *wrote* it down, see, so I'm saying, you know, you know more about it than *I* do—
>
> JACK. I didn't punctuate it
>
> CODY. No, you know more about it than I do . . . no—well, it *was* unpunctuated talk anyhow (*Visions of Cody*)

Cody acknowledges that his "describin" depends on its textualization by his friend. Jack's modest disclaimer, "I didn't punctuate it," claims a kind of authorial neutrality—that he does not tinker with or modify the recorded speech—but Cody understands what Jack's modesty conceals: that to "know" more about an incident is to give it narrative shape. Cody may be the hero of the novel, but he lacks this essential ability to translate his life into a story, a failure that Duluoz quietly records while placing his friend on a pedestal.

Kerouac described this novel as "visions of the great rememberer," and while certainly this applies to Cody, it also applies to Duluoz. The novel presents visions (sketches) of Cody, but their accuracy depends on the narrator's ability to see through his subject's eyes. Hence the novel's title, *Visions of Cody,* contains the very problem with which its author had to contend: how to fuse subjective and objective poles in a single narrative. Kerouac seems to have realized that he could no longer represent his main character from a detached position but had to intrude himself as mediator of that life. *On the Road* remained, as he said, horizontal and linear, lacking the crucial "wildness" that would transform a historical chronicle of Cassady into what Allen Ginsberg, in his introduction to the novel, called "the sacramentalization of everyday reality."

Kerouac himself underwent the same fictionalization process to which he subjected Cassady. He became the official representative of a certain lifestyle that he was able to describe but was ultimately unable to live. His depressed, alcoholic decline (perhaps like Cassady's anonymous death near the Mexican border) testifies to the toll that society exacts from the writer who reaches a wide audience. It also testifies to the human toll exacted by the writer

Neal Cassady and Jack Kerouac.

caught between a desire to be "on" the road and to retain his ability to drive the car. (pp. 66-76)

Allen Ginsberg was not so sanguine about *Visions of Cody* as one might have anticipated. He complained to Kerouac that it "sounds like you were just blowing and tacking things together, personally unrelating them, just for madness sake." He was also concerned about the book's publishability: "I don't see how [*Visions of Cody*] will ever be published, it's so personal, it's so full of sex language, so full of our local mythological references." Given Ginsberg's own commitment to personal confession, such qualms about Kerouac's explicit description of sex comes as a surprise. The letter in which these remarks were made was written in 1952 at a point when Ginsberg was trying to assimilate both the lessons of his current master, William Carlos Williams, and the more academic influence of Mark Van Doren or Lionel Trilling, with whom he studied at Columbia. It is a letter that expresses a side of the young poet that varies strikingly with the portrait of him that has been painted by the media. It shows a Ginsberg concerned with literary proprieties which, despite his own comments to the contrary, never left him. Kerouac's example was a challenge—perhaps even a threat—that pushed Ginsberg into his own highly autobiographical mode.

Crucial to this change from the early Williams-derived poems in *Gates of Wrath* and *Empty Mirror* to the more recognizable long lines of "Howl" and "Kaddish" was the example of Kerouac's sketching. Although Ginsberg had already seen a draft of *Visions of Cody* (at that point still called *On the Road*), he learned of its new compositional mode in a letter that Kerouac mailed from Mexico in May 1952. In this letter Kerouac advocates a kind of verbal "sketching" in which the writer imitates the painter's rendering. Kerouac's ideas of honesty, spontaneity, and immediacy quickly became a model for Ginsberg, who likened Kerouac's method to the improvisatory style of jazz musicians. This "spontaneous bop prosody" allowed Ginsberg to turn aside from his shorter-lined poems and "follow [his] romantic inspiration—Hebraic—Melvillian bardic breath." And it was very much the matter of "breath" that attracted Ginsberg. In a letter to his father, Ginsberg described Kerouac's contribution as one of reinstating the speech base to prose:

> It has the same syntactical structure of fast excited spoken talking—this is an interesting event in prose development, and it's no less communicative to me than heard speech, mine, yours, his,—when you speak *you* also talk a little like that, especially when you're moved, excited, angry, or dizzy with happiness etc. etc.—heightened speech in other words.

In more recent years, Ginsberg has elaborated his poetics of breath and speech to include Charles Olson's ideas of the breath line in "Projective Verse," mantric breathing, and chanting. What is central to all of his statements is a need to return language to the body, to the physiology and musculature of the writer. Poetry thus approaches the condition of mantra, which "refocuses mental and physiological activity right back into the present in a world of frankly physical sound, pure sound, body sound, a continuous humming body sound that wakes up the body to some extent." The poem should not be a demonstration or description of states of consciousness, but should itself manifest the energies of those states.

Another necessary component of this poetics of the body is some agency that will circumvent traditional rhetorical and syntactic structures by which ideas are subordinated one to the next. While a student of Meyer Shapiro's at Columbia University, Ginsberg found such an agency in the paintings of Cezanne. Ginsberg studied the way that the painter recovered the "petites sensations" of the phenomenal field. According to Ginsberg's account, Cezanne painted a landscape or object by recording the moment-by-moment impressions of his own optical field. Rather than synthesize a single Mt. St. Victoire in virtual, three-dimensional space, Cezanne painted the history of his individual perceptions of that mountain, registering each one separately so that the painting gained its own mass and volume equivalent to the landscape. With the aid of Cezanne's letters, Ginsberg saw a strong symbolist impulse in the painter's landscapes; the images Cezanne painted were not re-creations of actual mountains, card players, or apples but the outward surfaces of spiritual and eternal states. The reconstitution of "petites sensations" led to nothing less than a vision of *pater omnipotens aeterna deus,* a phrase that has become more familiar to us in the conclusion to part I of "Howl." In these same lines, Ginsberg turns from his long catalogue of suffering individuals and invokes the verbal art, "the syntax and measure of poor human prose," by which his own poem is being written. It is an act of self-reflexiveness necessary if he is to move beyond the elegiac to some critical posture in relation to those "best minds." Ginsberg makes "incarnate gaps" in his text in which he—both as representative man and as poet—may stand before his readers, "speechless and intelligent and shaking with shame."

According to Ginsberg, Cezanne's ability to juxtapose two dissimilar images (or perspectives) creates a third image that partakes of the two but that is freed from the here and now. Such ideas are derived as well from Fenollosa's ideas of the ideogram and Pound's imagist tenets. In "Howl" this practice can be seen in the word clusters that make up Ginsberg's catalogues:

> who sank all night in submarine light of Bickford's floated and sat through the stale beer afternoon in desolate Fugazzi's, listening to the crack of doom on the hydrogen jukebox.

A phrase like "hydrogen jukebox" makes use of the associations attached to the hydrogen bomb and combines them with something as ordinary as a jukebox to give the feel of anxiety and paranoia that pervades the lies of Ginsberg's generation. A phrase like "submarine light" helps create the vague, floating quality of mind that is felt while one sits all night in Bickford's cafeteria. Many of these word clusters resemble T. S. Eliot's slightly surreal metaphors ("sawdust afternoons," "a patient etherized upon a table") in his early poetry, an identification that, at least in 1955, would have made Allen Ginsberg wince.

If individual phrases resemble Eliot's, whole clusters of them, as used in Ginsberg's catalogues, create a rather different effect. Relations between parts of speech are dissolved, substantives are jammed together, adjectives and nouns become intermixed:

> Peyote solidities of halls, backyard green tree cemetery dawns, wine drunkenness over the rooftops, storefront boroughs of teahead joyride neon blinking traffic light, sun and moon and tree vibrations in the roaring winter dusks of Brooklyn, ashcan rantings and kind king light of mind,

Marjorie Perloff has pointed out that such clusters of substantives, however indebted they are to Whitman's catalogues, also resemble the dada styles of Apollinaire and Cendrars. Their effect is to keep things in motion by linking powerful, percussive sounds ("kind king light of mind") with words from multiple semantic fields ("teahead joyride neon").

In a poem like "Sunflower Sutra," this use of noun clusters is particularly effective in rendering the specific incarnational moment that is the poem's subject. Ginsberg describes a walk with Jack Kerouac through a railroad yard when, all of a sudden, they come upon a sunflower covered with the grime of a thousand passing locomotives. This sad flower stirs memories of Ginsberg's Blake visions of the 1940s:

> —I rushed up enchanted—it was my first sunflower, memories of Blake—my visions—Harlem

> and Hells of the Eastern rivers, bridges clanking Joes Greasy Sandwiches, dead baby carriages, black treadless tires forgotten and unretreaded, the poem of the riverbank, condoms & pots, steel knives, nothing stainless, only the dank muck and the razor sharp artifacts passing into the past—

Here the detritus of the contemporary wasteland combines with the detritus of memory; there is little difference between the Harlem of the 1940s and the railroad yard of the present, though the sunflower has provided the first step in what is to become a visionary awakening. Ginsberg then addresses the sunflower, urging it to forget its grime and poverty and see itself as a living, growing thing. And because it has taken Ginsberg back in time, it provides him with an opportunity to regard his own "sunflower existence" beyond the quotidian moment. In the poem's last (and longest) line, Ginsberg uses his substantive clusters to create the visionary moment:

> We're not our skin of grime, we're not our dread bleak dusty imageless locomotive, we're all beautiful golden sunflowers inside, we're blessed by our own seed & golden hairy naked accomplishment—bodies growing into mad black formal sunflowers in the sunset, spied on by our eyes under the shadow of the mad locomotive riverbank sunset Frisco hilly tincan evening sitdown vision.

This vision recorded in the poem is not of an airy world beyond this one; it is made out of things—locomotives, riverbanks, sunsets, San Francisco, hills—that in themselves have a spiritual potential. Only through their "incarnation" in Ginsberg's vision can they lose their isolation and become part of a single experience. Ginsberg links them, without the usual syntactic connectives, to both enact and invoke their common universe.

To recover the body in poetry through a return to speech rhythms, through the disordering of conventional syntax, through a lineation based on the breath, we now recognize as pervasive features of postwar poetry. Charles Olson's inaugural formulation of these qualities in "Projective Verse" in 1950 was only the first of many statements advocating a poetics of "embodiment." But if his gesture seemed unique in 1950 or 1955 it was only so against the backdrop of the then-reigning New Critical orthodoxy that valued detachment and ironic distance. We see from a later vantage that it was less a new direction than a recuperation of certain aspects of romanticism that could be found in Blake, Wordsworth, Shelley, and Whitman. Ginsberg, like Olson, Duncan, Creeley, and others, was aware of this heritage and invoked such predecessors often and loudly.

However anxious Ginsberg may have been to develop a purely physical poetry, he was no less anxious to ascribe intention to his procedures. The burden of his essays on poetry and poetics, his interviews, and his correspondence is to clarify his knowledge of formal prosody and poetic structure. In doing so he reveals some ambivalence about the source of his inspiration: Although poetry presumably emerges from the poet's physiology, it often appears in the trappings of Greek classical meters. The distinction he makes is between a poetry written from a pre-established pattern and one discovered in the process of writing that may, after the fact, have a recognizable form: "Nobody's got any objection to even iambic pentameter if it comes from a source deeper than the mind; That is to say if it comes from the breathing and the belly and the lungs." By appealing to concepts like depth and surface, mind and body, Ginsberg reinstates their opposition while appearing to dissolve their boundaries. Iambic pentameter is permissible so long as its source lies in the internal organs and not in the regular count of a metronome.

The return of, and to, the body in poetry arises out of a more profound desire to rejoin the larger body of the world:

> yes, yes,
>   that's what
> I wanted,
>   I always wanted,
> I always wanted,
>   to return
> to the body
>   where I was born.

This participation carries with it the attendant dangers of solipsism and self-consciousness that proved so troubling to Wordsworth and Shelley. Ginsberg most often identifies this crisis of participation with Whitman:

> I saw you, Walt Whitman, childless, lonely old grubber, poking among the meats in the refrigerator and eyeing the grocery boys.

> I heard you asking questions of each: Who killed

the pork chops? What price bananas? Are you
my Angel?

This vision of a latter-day Whitman rummaging among
the cornucopia of foods available in a modern supermarket is wonderfully funny and tragic at the same time.
Whitman becomes an alter ego for Ginsberg, who himself
is "self-conscious" and "shopping for images." Ginsberg's
invocation of Whitman (and perhaps of Garcia Lorca)
"eyeing the grocery boys" emphasizes that this loneliness
is also the historical lot of the homosexual who is denied
the opportunity to participate in the bounty of "normal"
American life. The sight of Whitman in a modern-day supermarket reminds Ginsberg of the "lost America of love"
in which Whitman could fervently believe:

> Ah, dear father, graybeard, lonely old courage-
> teacher, what America did you have when
> Charon quit poling his ferry and you got out
> on a smoking bank and stood watching the
> boat disappear on the black waters of Lethe

Whitman is placed in Hell, curiously enough, not by his
disbelief but because of his extreme faith. But if Whitman
lives among the shades, his realm may still be glimpsed by
the poet who inherits his mantle.

The price of participation is loneliness, and Ginsberg has
been anxious to point out the importance of this theme to
those who see in his poetry only a wail of despair or else
a celebration of oneness. In a letter to John Hollander,
who had written a review condemning *Howl* (a "dreadful
little volume"), Ginsberg attempted to set the record
straight:

> . . . and some jerk named Brustein who
> TEACHES at columbia writing . . . drooling
> on about how I express every degradation but
> the one human one loneliness—I mean some
> completely inaccurate irrelevant piece of jour-
> nalism! ignoring big queer lonely lyrics about
> Whitman and Moloch in whom I sit lonely cock-
> sucking.

Ginsberg is referring to part II of "Howl" in which he catalogues the collective force that has appropriated and
neutralized the creative spirit of his generation. If
"Brustein" were correct, if "Howl" were simply an enumeration of certain members of society who "purgatoried
their torsos night after night," it would not have the power
that it has. But as Ginsberg observes, Moloch gains its
power not because it lives beyond human will but because
we willingly, if blindly, participate in its authority.

At the beginning of part II, Ginsberg asks "what sphinx
of cement and aluminum bashed open their skulls and ate
up their brains and imagination." He then answers his
own question: "Solitude! Filth! Ugliness! Ashcans and un-
obtainable dollars!" But at the point where this decalogue
threatens to remain a list of Moloch's attributes, Ginsberg
turns the poem on himself:

> Moloch in whom I sit lonely! Moloch in whom
> I dream Angels! Crazy in Moloch! Cocksuck-
> er in Moloch! Lacklove and manless in Mo-
> loch!

> Moloch who entered my soul early! Moloch in

> whom I am a consciousness without a body!
> Moloch who frightened me out of my natural
> ectasy! Moloch whom I abandon! Wake up in
> Moloch! Light streaming out of the sky!

The imperative is Blakean: to "wake up" within the "mind
forged manacles" of an absolute devouring power and recognize one's complicity in the very systems in which one
is bound. Here Ginsberg is not the happy bard, piping
songs of visionary delight, but a more troubled poet who
recognizes that the road to "natural ecstasy" is paved with
self-deception. The consciousness, once separated from
the body, creates specters that in turn become accusers.
Only by first identifying with Moloch can the speaker
truly "wake up" and alert others.

We can see the workings of Ginsberg's participation ethos
best in a poem like "Wales Visitation," in which the poet,
in order to testify to the unity of all things, must first separate himself from nature and address himself as another:
"Bardic, O Self, Visitacione, tell naught / but what seen
by one man in a vale in Albion." The rhetoric is exalted
and the diction archaic in order to give a tone of lofty seriousness and depth to what is, in actuality, an acid trip on
a hillside in Wales. Ginsberg establishes kinship with his
romantic precursors in order to collapse historical time
into poetic eternity: "the lambs on the tree-nooked hillside
this day bleating" are the same "heard in Blake's old ear."
The clouds become "the silent thought of Wordsworth in
eld Stillness" of Tintern Abbey. And Ginsberg even establishes kinship with himself, now "160 miles from London's symmetrical thorned tower," where recently he had
appeared on television. He remembers the television
screen "flashing bearded your Self" and addresses himself
from the standpoint of a viewer. These gestures, while removing Ginsberg from historical time, also tend to distance him from any specific location so that he may literally "visit" where he is.

Aided by LSD, the poet observes a nature quivering with
life:

> All the Valley quivered, one extended motion,
> wind
>   undulating on mossy hills
> a giant wash that sank white fog delicately down
> red runnels
>   on the mountainside
> whose leaf-branch tendrils moved asway
>   in granitic undertow down—
> and lifted the floating Nebulous upward, and
> lifted the arms of the trees
>
>
> and lifted the grasses an instant in balance
>   and lifted the lambs to hold still
> and lifted the green of the hill, in one solemn
> wave

Ginsberg, like Wordsworth, hears in this wind a "correspondent breeze" pertaining to himself; he cannot simply
remain "Crosslegged on a rock," observing nature; he
must embrace the landscape physically; he must "Fall on
the ground," "Stare close . . . ," "Kneel before the
foxglove . . . ," "look in the eyes of the branded lambs."
Each of these admonitions suggests that although he expe-

riences a great affinity for the land and seeks to participate with it, he still remains an observer, addressing himself as another.

When he speaks for the first time in the first person, it is as if he is answering the prophetic bard's injunctions:

> I lay down mixing my beard with the wet hair
> of the mountainside, smelling the brown vagi-
> na-moist ground, harmless, tasting the violet
> thistle-hair, sweetness—
> One being so balanced, so vast, that its softest
> breath moves every floweret in the stillness on
> the valley floor, trembles lamb-hair hung gos-
> samer rain-beaded in the grass,
> lifts trees on their roots, birds in the great
> draught hiding their strength in the rain, bear-
> ing same weight

The problem with passages like these is that Ginsberg must assert affinities that he finds in nature instead of letting them grow naturally out of the physical circumstance. He must name "One being so balanced, so vast" at the point where he had successfully "created" an omnipotent vantage. Another way of stating this limitation is to say that once Ginsberg fully inhabits his "I," he loses sight of the problematics of observation that dominates the first half of the poem.

The conclusion of "Wales Visitation" is a kind of coda, written from the vantage of London a week later, a vantage that is now informed by his new awareness:

> What did I notice? Particulars! The
> vision of the great One is myriad—
> smoke curls upward from ashtray,
> house fire burned low,
> The night, still wet & moody black heaven
> starless
> upward in motion with wet wind.
> *July 29, 1967 (LSD)—August 3, 1967*
> *(London)*

The dating of the poem becomes an important dimension of the experience described: that he wrote the poem in two places, LSD and London, the sacred (or at least psychedelic) and secular combined much as the poem unites the particulars of the Welsh landscape with a reincarnated Albion. The smoke curling "upward from ashtray" in London is now invested with the same upward drafts of air that he had observed during his psychedelic trip. And just as Wordsworth revisited Tintern Abbey while living "'mid the din / Of towns and cities" far from that enriching landscape, so Ginsberg will be able to revisit Wales, not as place but as visitation.

"Wales Visitation" is not Ginsberg's best poem, but it illustrates his awareness of the double self that mediates participation in the largeness of nature. One side of him "sees" with great accuracy while the other observes himself seeing. It is as though he has adopted the role of bardic poet in order to see at all, to become "one man in a vale in Albion." Ginsberg adds an interesting twist to the romantic pastoral ode that sets it off from its predecessors: his use of LSD. But the poem is not so much about the drug experience as it is about the "wisdom of earthly relations" glimpsed through a particularly heightened sensory moment. This moment is the product of specific images, recorded by a local "eye" willing to "Stare close." The moment is expanded when Ginsberg filters his observations through his visionary "I," which recognizes "no imperfection in the grass."

What links "Wales Visitation" to all of his other poems is its quality of testimony, its sense of witness and observation. Throughout his career, Ginsberg has asserted his participation in all aspects of American life, and in his best poems this assertion is combined with wry humor and self-deprecation. Whatever the tone, however, the poem is invariably about Allen Ginsberg being present at events that his presence ultimately affects. During the 1960s he became a sort of populist chronicler, providing, as he titled one book, "planet news" of contemporary history: the Chicago convention, the Human Be-In, various antiwar marches, May Day in Prague. Ginsberg was both the reporter and the antennae through which these events were received; his physical body (and, by extension, his physicalized long line) was the instrument on which history played, and his romantic rhetoric acted, in part, to dramatize the importance of the music. But Ginsberg has suffered the same difficulty as all romantic poets—that of participating so much in the world that he often lacks a vantage from which to speak. At its best, Ginsberg's work recognizes the vantage as well as the field before him. (pp. 76-85)

One of the most remarkable films made by National Educational Television in its "Poetry USA" series features Michael McClure reading his *Ghost Tantras* in the lion house of the San Francisco Zoo. While the big cats pace back and forth in their cages, McClure is seen pacing himself, reading in a rich, resonant voice. *Ghost Tantras* is written partially in what the poet calls "beast language," a language somewhere between human speech and animal sounds. As McClure reads, the lions become increasingly animated and begin roaring—whether in response or annoyance—to the poet's own voice:

> I LOVE TO THINK OF THE RED
> PURPLE ROSE
> IN THE DARKNESS COOLED BY THE
> NIGHT
> We are served by machines making stains
> of sounds
> Each blot of sound is a bud or a stahr.
> Body eats bouquets of the ear's vista.
> Gahhhrrr boody eers noze eyes deem thou.
> NOH. NAH-OHH
> hrooor. VOOOR-NAH-GAHROOOOO
> ME.
> Nah droooooh seerch. NAH THEE!
> The machines are too dull when we
> are lion-poems that move & breathe.
> WHAN WE GROOOOOOOOOOOOOOOR
> hann dree myketoth sharoo sree thah noh
> deeeeeemed ez.
> Whan eeeethooze hrohh.

Obvious precedents for this kind of poetry—and its performance—could be found in futurist and dadaist sound poetry, although McClure maintains a closer bond to some source language than do poets like Vladimir Khlebnikov or Kurt Schwitters. If one could speak of the "diction" of beast language, one might point to its incorporation of Anglo-Saxon and Middle English words. When McClure reads *Ghost Tantras* in public performances, he often prefaces his reading by quoting the opening lines of Chaucer's *Canterbury Tales* to suggest the origins of his poetry in early English verse. Beast language oscillates back and forth between modern and archaic speech, between recognizable words and expressive utterances.

Besides the language, another distinctive thing about the poem above is its presentation on the page. Like most of McClure's poems, it obeys a center margin, its lines built around a central axis. McClure compares the physical shape of his poems to biological organisms. "[The poems] look like a little whirlwind or a gyre. They have the bilateral symmetry, of an organism. . . . I've come to intuitively think in terms of the centered line. We are centered organisms, in the sense that we're bilaterally symmetrical, so poems come out that way with ease and naturalness." Not only does the poem imitate beast sounds (or hypothesize the beast sounds that humans might make) but it replicates on the page the skeletal structure of vertebrates. The center "spine" emphasizes, as well, the line as a physical entity on the page. Instead of returning to the left margin, the line asserts itself boldly as a free image, connected to the other lines like ribs to the spinal column. Instead of the line as a score for the voice, it becomes a separate object among other objects.

McClure's formulation of poetry as beast language and as biographical grid represents the most radical example of a physiological or "embodied" poetics that we have seen so far. Where Kerouac and Ginsberg base their remarks on an appeal to speech rhythms and breath, McClure carries poetry further back to the cellular and genetic basis of human life. He wants a poetry that lives at the borders of articulate speech, a poetry that manifests in its structure the nature of all organisms. For McClure, humans are meat, and one's expression—in its ideal state—is an incarnation of one's mammal nature. We are part of a biological, not a logical or rational, universe and our intercommunication involves the sharing of our biological heritage: "The biological energy of ourselves is extensions or tentacles of the universe of meat."

McClure's biological poetics is linked to the idea that every organism bears the imprint of its entire genetic history. Words are like DNA in the sense that they derive from the earliest human communication as well as from childhood babble. To speak is to gesture from a primordial position, one locked inside rationality. Since we have lost sight of this mammalian and genetic heritage, the only way to reclaim it is by testifying as directly as possible to our emotional states. And if this testimony takes the form of nonverbal expression, so much the better. To this end, McClure has always been interested in language at its most expressive—at moments when its semantic and performative characteristics merge. He devotes an entire essay, "Phi Upsilon Kappa," to the word "fuck" and to its liberating potential in poetry. The characters in his plays often spend a good deal of their time giggling, shouting, groaning, and expostulating for the sheer pleasure of physical sound. "Part of a man is the words leaping from his lips. They are made by his real meat lips and throat and signalled by his real physical hands of spirit sending them on their way."

McClure gained support for such ideas from poets like Blake, Shelley, and Artaud, but perhaps even more from the action painters whom he studied as an art student in the early 1950s. The big drip and splatter canvases of Pollock, de Kooning, and Kline gave McClure a sense of the importance of gesture and spontaneity in creation whereby the physical act of manipulating paint (or writing words on paper) was itself a psychologically cathartic act. His early poems often seem to be attempts to effect the same "gestural" style on the page that he admired in painters of the heroic period of abstract expressionism:

> OH FUCKING LOVER ROAR WITH
> JOY—I, LION MAN!
> I GROAN, I AM, UPON THE CONE
> SHAPED BREASTS
> & tossing thighs!
> . . . .
> And I am some simple cub
> with plump muscles, loving immortality!
> THE SHEETS ARE WHITE.
> THE PILLOW SOFT.
> JESUS HOW I HATE THE MIDDLE
> COURSE!

The heavy use of upper-case letters, the prominence of exclamation marks, the presence of numerous expletives and imperatives provide signposts for feeling. If the reader has any doubts as to McClure's hatred of the "middle course," the bold typographic display will dispel them. At the same time, McClure eschews any rhetorical subtlety or irony by making direct assertions ("I GROAN, I AM . . . ," "And I am some simple cub / with plump muscles . . . ," "THE SHEETS ARE WHITE"). By wearing his heart on his sleeve, as it were, he attempts to recover a kind of Blakean drama of declaration.

Despite this appeal to the biological and gestural basis of poetry and language, McClure's own rhetoric is quite formal. The poems tend to proceed by declarative sentences and assertions with little subordination or modification. His lineation is most often end-stopped. The above "Ghost Tantra 51," for example, is based on five declarative sentences, spread out over fifteen lines. Only two lines are enjambed, and the meter is quite regular—iambic, with an occasional anapestic substitution. Given the mystery and strangeness surrounding the poem's subject, one would expect a considerably more broken syntax, but in fact the sentencing is relatively conventional. Each "nonbeast" sentence is a regular declarative period, and passive constructions tend to dominate. Even the "theme" of the poem seems rather civilized. The idea that if we recognize our "beast" nature we can conquer the inhuman world of machines is a timid version of what poets have been saying since the early eighteenth century. Blake found infinite variations on the theme, and it is a standard part of every romantic and Victorian poet's repertoire.

What *is* radical about McClure's poetry is his extreme faith in the power of bald statement and gesture. In his plays and his poetry, he explores the thematics of innocence and naiveté in ways that make Jack Kerouac's pronouncements seem Augustan in comparison. The impetus to move in this direction was certainly inspired by the poets in San Francisco who were searching for a more direct and personal statement, but McClure [in "Mozart and the Apple," *Scratching the Beat Surface*, 1982] pushes an expressive poetics even further to suggest that naming and declaration are essentially animal acts:

> An animal does not specialize in a discipline. He puts the large chunks that will not pass through the sieve into an aggregate to ensure his survival. The wolf is not a wandering scholar but a wandering minstrel—with the whole prairie for an auditorium and world field to work upon. He can visualize a universe of sound as a field on which to conceive and topologize his personal statements.

A statement such as this helps explain McClure's willingness to "name his states" in a fairly bald-faced manner and to do so with childlike gusto:

> I AM MY ABSTRACT ALCHEMIST OF
> FLESH
> made real!
> I AM MY ABSTRACT ALCHEMIST OF
> FLESH
> made real!
> I AM MY ABSTRACT ALCHEMIST OF
> FLESH
> made real!
> And nothing more!
> NO LESS THAN A STAR—
> a chamber and a vacuole.
> Without sense! A Thing! I feel!

The problem with this kind of statement is that the reader has no room in which to participate or evaluate. The entire poem depends for its authority on the poet's sincerity of expression, his gesture in saying rather than the specific words he uses. Words are only the outward signs of internal states even though they are foregrounded as objects on the page. The lack of semantic or syntactic complexity further frustrates the reader's participation by closing off all alternative or divergent readings. One is left with an assertion that must be accepted by its sheer intensity. The poems, despite their energetic surface and dramatic rhetoric, remain relatively static and two-dimensional. In the terms outlined in my introduction, McClure's is a performative poetics that stresses only the performance and not its reception.

It is in his plays that McClure has managed to diversify his poetics and provide a more complex arena for working out his mammalian poetics. In works like *Gargoyle Cartoons, Gorf, The Beard,* and *The Blossom,* he has created a kind of alchemical theater in which his biological and ecological concerns are given vivid—and often comic—form. Like his poetry, his plays represent a direct manifestation of organic life. He conceives of each play as a cell. "It has its organelles, its ribosomes, and its DNA and RNA, and a good enactment of it is harmonically and biochemically in balance." McClure's early plays, now collected in *The Mammals,* tend to have some of the same static qualities as his poetry. "The Feast," for example, is

written for thirteen actors who sit around a table drinking black wine and eating bread. They speak, for the most part, in beast language, and their interaction is limited almost entirely to expressive grunts and roars with an occasional interruption of "human" speech:

> Thantar:
> KRYBEKK ALL MEOOOOGRR
> GEOOWWW
> GREEEEEAAKORRS KROOOOOOO
> Yeorg:
> . . . NOTHING AIR
> /GROOMSHAKTARBYMETH!
> TORNTORP!! CEREMENT!
> MARIGOLD
> OF MAMMAL'S EAR. WE ARE
> BANNERS! . . .
> Thantar:
> AHH! EEEH OOOOH AKKKKORR!
> GROOOOOOOOO!

At this stage in his writing, McClure was strongly influenced by Artaud's "theater of cruelty" and with the possibility of using the stage as "projective verse turned to theater." Characters do not speak so much as give testimony, retaining something of the hieratic posture of figures in religious allegory. With *The Beard* in 1965, however, McClure begins to give voices and identities to his obsessional world. The play's main characters, Billy the Kid and Jean Harlow, represent American folk heroes whose actions occur in some Elysian Fields of the wide screen. Their conflicts and sexual ectasies resemble those of tragic theater or, more appropriately, modern westerns with their "high noon" shootouts and overdrawn characters. And in McClure's subsequent plays, giant penguins, comic book superheroes, odd forest creatures, and fairy sprites come to populate the stage in a theater that resembles, on the one hand, baroque masque and, on the other, the absurdist dramas of Beckett and Ionesco. Like the works of other experimental theater movements of the 1960s, McClure's plays attempt to break the frame of the proscenium by engaging the audience in some form of participation, whether through direct address or by extending elements of the dramatic mise en scène into the larger theater space.

McClure's plays extend and develop many of the themes of the poetry but do so with a degree of complexity that the poetry seldom approaches. And whereas in the poetry, claims for authority and participation depend on a unitary "I," the plays displace such claims among several characters. Billy the Kid's posturing and primping are always qualified by Jean Harlow's sardonic retorts. In *The Meatball,* McClure's tendency toward grand pronouncement is undermined by hysterical passages of nonsense, new-age language:

> YOWEEEEEEEEEEEEEEEEEEEEE!   IN-
> CREDIBLE! [*Ecstatically*] YOWEE! WOW!
> [*Clasping hands together in a transport.*] OH
> WOW, WOW, WOW, WOW, WOW, WOW,
> WOW! [*Falls off chair. Rolls in joy.*] OW WOW
> WOW WOW! Look at it, man. It is a whole
> UNIVERSE! [*Getting up and staring into flowers.*] WOW! A UNIVERSE! A UNIVERSE!
> THE MAGIC IS GETTING STRONGER,
> MAN. SLEEK HEY, SLEEK . . . WE'VE

GOT TO HAVE MAGIC MUSIC WITH
THIS!

In *Spider Rabbit,* this debunking, comic spirit is combined
with a powerful antiwar polemic. The play was written
during the Vietnam War at a point when political double
talk allowed for massive human suffering under the neutral rhetoric of Washington bureaucratese. McClure's
central figure—a cross between a blood-drinking spider
and a soft, cuddly rabbit—embodies this duality by alternately endearing himself to the audience and pulling hand
grenades, electric saws, and human organs from a sack.
His standard refrain is "I HATE WAR!" but his actions
(usually involving forms of torture and cannibalism) contradict his statements. The play sustains the tension between a rhetoric of childhood play and the considerably
darker rhetoric of political genocide. In such plays, Mc-
Clure reveals an awareness of the tone of hypocrisy found
in the public sphere and yet uses the stage for all of its possibilities of entertainment, spectacle, humor, and display.

The most complex realization of McClure's biopolitical
theater is found in *Gorf,* a multilevel spectacle that, on the
one hand, resembles classical comedies like those of Euripides and, on the other, seems made out of television soap
operas. Its star is a winged phallus named Gorf, whose
function is to alert the world to the great "bump"—a kind
of Atlantean shift into mythical time—and who helps to
reunite the realm of the sacred to a scattered and secular
world. The other principal characters, Mert and Gert,
have lost their child—known as the Shitfer—to the cosmos, and they, with the help of Gorf, try to find him
throughout the play. Mert and Gert represent the lumpen
American couple straight out of "All in the Family" who
lead unenlightened lives—until they are sat upon by, of all
things, the hindquarters of a giant, hairy elephant. This
mock apotheosis projects them into mythical time, in
which they encounter figures like the Blind Dyke, a naked
girl with fairy wings, a pair of dancing television sets, and
the Giant Penguin, all of whom serve as cosmic guides
through the astral realm.

If all this seems preposterous, it is not without its ethical
point, provided by what I perceive as McClure's alter ego
in the play, the Giant Penguin. This wonderful creation
articulates the positive ecological ethos that will reunite
the particles of the Shitfer that have been scattered
throughout time and space in some gnostic dispersion.
When the penguin invokes this reunification, he does so
in McClure's favored Shelleyan rhetoric:

> JOY, JOY, JOY SUBLIME—
> FEEL THE NEARING OF TIME.
> JOY, JOY, JOY WITHOUT CRIME—
> SENSE THE PASSING OF SPACE.

But when the penguin attempts to be interpretive—for example, when he tries to explain the transformation from
real time to mythical time—his speech is slightly buffoon-
ish:

> Before the sqwunch of Time and Space, before
> the abyss was Abyssinia . . . [Pause] Before the
> giant hairy elephant sat on Mert and Gert. . . .
> [Pause] In the olden times that precede these
> days of myth. [Pause] When things were real.

> [Pause] When the snooty-rootian movements
> still jiggled in all the bumps that matter is made
> up of. . . . Then. . . . [Pause] Then the Shitfer
> was one. Then the Shitfer was just one thing. Ev-
> erything else as well, and whole, and happy, and
> the olive grew, and the duck fell down with a
> heart attack at the foot of the hunter.

In some sense, the Giant Penguin represents McClure's
own tendencies toward cosmic statement and visionary
pronouncement, but unlike the voice in the poems the
rather bombastic and portentous voice of the penguin is
treated with humor.

It is the Giant Penguin who recognizes that he, and the
other characters in the play, are all particles of the Shitfer.
At the end, the entire cast gathers with him in a huge
"Tableau of the Shitfer," which represents the lifting of
mythical time and the return to a redeemed "real" time.
The allegory here resembles Gnostic and Orphic cosmolo-
gies (the story of Atlantis, the Orphic theogony of Phanes)
but its application to the current ecological crisis tempers
its metaphysical trappings and makes it a particularly topical play.

Gorf, like McClure's other plays, provides an important
polemical and political dimension that, in the poems, is
often handled by means of sheer assertion:

> YES! THERE IS BUT ONE
> POLITICS AND THAT
> IS BIOLOGY.
> BIOLOGY
> IS
> POLITICS

In those lines, the force of declaration and statement is
spatialized into an icon. An essentially prose statement is
divided into a series of lines that, however urgent the message, depend upon rather simple equations. *Gorf,* by contrast, draws from a number of rhetorical frames (television
sitcoms, mystical literature, comic books) to give flesh to
the political and ecological dramas of our day.

Michael McClure's poetry represents all of the daring as
well as some of the limitations of the Beat ethos. He wants
the poem to dissolve into nature—to become transparent
to the world of which it is a part. He would like his individual words to free themselves from language and attain
an autonomous presence like so many protozoans on a mi-
croscope slide. McClure's belief in the mammalian base of
human consciousness leads him to exceed the normal or-
thographic conventions of poetry and, in the case of "beast
language," normal semantic patterns. The result is a language act caught somewhere between physical gesture and
shout, between act and object. At the same time, his sense
of language remains essentially passive and static. In an
attempt to personalize his poetry more radically, he relies
on a two-dimensional concept of the subject whose identity is largely dependent upon the sincerity of his expressive
gesture. In the plays, however, this problem of unitary
subject is eliminated by the creation of multiple roles and
qualities of self-reflection and self-mockery that make for
a considerably richer surface.

"Do I contradict myself?" asked Whitman one hundred

years before "Howl." "Very well then I contradict my-self." The author of *Leaves of Grass* envisioned an art large enough to contain contradiction, and in a sense this was his great legacy to the Beat writers. They appeared on the scene at a time when contradiction was a matter of rhetorical tension rather than existential disclosure. However therapeutic their appeal to openness and spontaneity may have been, their practice risked calling into question its own status as writing. McClure's desire to write words of meat and spirit means that we are asked to accept his poem as a metaphor—that is, as other than a collection of words. When Ginsberg and Kerouac ask that writing have the speed and energy of consciousness, they unwittingly detach the mind from the body they are so anxious to rejoin. And when the Beat writers elevate personal testimony to a value in its own right, they limit their ability to assess and measure the nature of their testimony. I have defined this problem as one of participation in which the desire to make the poem transparent before the world often leaves the poet without adequate grounds for self-reflection. In their best work, the Beat writers were aware of the dangers of such participation and made *that* a generative element of their work.

When making qualifications about Beat writing, it is necessary to remember the literary climate circa 1950, when this personalist poetics made its first appearance. It was a time of careful, modulated responses to Eliot's famous "dissociation of sensibility," and any attempt to cut the Gordian knot of form and content by anything less than a sonnet in blank verse was considered bad form. The Beats did not make distinctions. They raised the unwholesome specter of romanticism to center stage, talked about their personal lives in distinctly nonmetaphoric terms, and appeared to live the lives that their writing described. Their impact was immediate—if grudgingly admitted—causing even the sons and daughters of Ransom and Tate to examine the "life" in their "life studies." If we, in retrospect, find contradictions between their stated goals and their practice, it should not obscure the necessity of their attack.

The first intelligent critique of Beat writing *qua* writing occurred not in a professional journal or review but in Judge Clayton Horn's San Francisco Municipal Courtroom, where a half-dozen local academic critics and journalists (Kenneth Rexroth among them) testified in behalf of "Howl." It may have been the most appropriate forum. Today "Howl" finds itself in rather odd company: It is taught in classrooms, discussed in journals, and printed in college anthologies complete with footnotes on arcane subjects like "Bickford's," "Bellevue," and the "Bowery." Ginsberg's poetry has been collected into a massive *Collected Poems* with appendixes and notes. The manuscript of "Howl" has been printed in an expensive facsimile edition, complete with scholarly apparatus, notes, and transcription. There is a Norton Critical Edition of *On the Road* with critical commentary appended, and Kerouac is now the subject of six biographies. Documentaries on the Beats have been made by public television and Hollywood studios. Michael McClure's plays have been produced all over the world by distinguished companies, and several have won prestigious awards. Gale Research has

devoted a two-volume reference encyclopedia to the Beats [*Dictionary of Literary Biography*, Volume 16: *The Beats: Literary Bohemians in Postwar America*], and university libraries pay lavish amounts of money for their papers. In Europe, the Beats are regularly invited to international conferences and symposia, and their books are translated into practically every language.

This accommodation to the canon should not come as a surprise. To some extent it is a belated response to the fact that the Beats were *from the outset* part of American culture, not alienated from it. Kerouac's identification of his "gang" with the Marx Brothers or Ginsberg's and McClure's appearances at rock concerts and in Bob Dylan's *Rolling Thunder* movie are but some of the manifestations of this tendency. If the Beats attacked American life, they certainly identified with its antinomian and individualistic spirit. In their eyes, the social "darkness" that surrounded everyone during the 1950s represented a betrayal of a Whitmanian democratic spirit gone astray. The Beats saw their function as modern Jeremiahs walking a populace too easily swayed by the rhetoric of consensus and accommodation.

"O but there are times SHAZAM is not enough," Gregory Corso reminds us [in "Power"]. "There is a brutality in the rabbit / That leads the way to Paradise—far from God." The darkness that surrounded Americans could not be solved by driving away from it. The Beats realized that there are no magic passwords to eternity, even though they often found them by accident in sunflowers, sutras, and the wind along the highway. In their permission to remain open to quotidean experience they most resembled Whitman and followed the lessons of Huck Finn. (pp. 85-94)

> *Michael Davidson, " 'The Darkness Surrounds Us': Participation and Reflection among the Beat Writers," in his* The San Francisco Renaissance: Poetics and Community at Mid-Century, *Cambridge University Press, 1989, pp. 60-94.*

Geoffrey Thurley

[*Thurley is an English educator and critic. In the following excerpt, he examines the development of "Beat consciousness" in the poetry of Michael McClure, Philip Whalen, and Gregory Corso.*]

Even if we see Ginsberg as a wren who used the cover of Whitman's wingspan to fly higher than he could have flown unaided, the fact is that he *did* fly higher—higher than he could have flown had he not had the intelligence and the energy to exploit the various influences that lay in the background; higher than his older contemporaries, the liberal academics who were still cramped and twisted up with the self-consciousness endemic to the ironist tradition. He evaded the grip of the attitudes which were stifling the creative forces of American and English poets—the obligatory alienation, the by now stultifying isolationism, the cowardice of irony, the negativity which eventually congealed into the poetry of nervous breakdown. Ginsberg's breakthrough, such as it was, was a matter not so much of technique as of ideology. The cult of the nervous breakdown is . . . a phenomenon of affluence, like the extreme self-consciousness of modern America. In this sense it seems relevant to describe the cult of the nervous breakdown in poets like Lowell, Berryman, Roethke, Sexton as ideological symptoms; their varying academicism is only secondarily a technical matter. It is primarily a question of outlook, purpose and belief. If we turn to Allen Ginsberg's poetry or Kerouac's fiction we shall not need to look far for evidence of the spiritual suffering and nervous exhaustion which are part of life in an over-organized but chaotic society like America. The first line of "Howl" prepares us for the saga of sickness and pointless debauch we duly get; Kerouac's novels are the reverse of orgiastic: *Big Sur,* for instance, offers one of the most harrowing experiences available to the modern reader. Yet still, "Howl" is as different in purpose and impact from Berryman's *Dream Songs,* or a more recent work, like Galway Kinnell's *Book of Nightmares,* as *Big Sur* is from *Herzog.* Ideologically, Ginsberg and Kerouac are in a different age from Berryman and Bellow. And this difference is to be understood less through technical analysis than through an appreciation of a subtle, decisive shift in emphasis and direction. The nightmare is no longer hugged, as providing identity; the isolation no longer clutched, the alienation no longer cherished, the agony no longer needed. (pp. 187-88)

The use so many Beat poets made of drugs clearly formed part of its basic orientation towards non-striving, passivity and femininity. The experimentation with different drugs carries on the long tradition of *avant garde* spiritual exploration. But the ideal of the narcotic mandarin is a passive world, in which people do nothing because there's nothing they want to do but turn on. It's at this point that one usually starts talking about a new consciousness. It would be better to talk about a new orientation than a new consciousness. Consciousness does not alter: the psychedelic facts still have to be sorted somewhere in the human control-tower. An interesting confirmation of this is Michael McClure's first "Peyote Poem," written down the day after the experience:

> I KNOW EVERYTHING! I PASS INTO
> THE ROOM
> there is a golden bed radiating all light
> the air is full of silver hangings and sheathes
> I smile to myself. I know
> all that there is to know. I see all there
> is to feel. I am friendly with the ache
> in my belly. The answer
> to love is my voice. There is no Time!
> No answers. The answer to feeling is my
> feeling.

It is exhilarating and the moral authority assumed by the poet guarantees a consistent air of seriousness. It also brought McClure a following: he seemed in the mid-1960s the poet closest in intention to Timothy Leary. But this poem is really not typical of the sort of effusion it helped to encourage from so many other poets.

There is of course a sameness about all mystical and narcotic experience—or at least about the reports mystics and drug-users have given of it. Whether the experience is

gained through a natural oddity of bodily chemistry, whether it is deliberately induced or involuntary, whether it is celebrated in awe or suffered in terror, whether it is mystical or schizophrenic—the experience of the world we are here concerned with has certain unvarying properties: we may be familiar with McClure's intense lighting effects, his sense of great significance and his feeling of being at the center of the universe from the works of Blake, De Quincey, Boehme, Swedenborg, Strindberg—or from a psychiatrist's casebook. Mysticism and extreme schizophrenia depends as much on the body's chemistry as the hallucinations of the drug-user. The important variable is the intellectual context in which they take place—the use, in other words, which the victim of these bodily states makes of them. This is not the place to discuss the implications of these ideas. Whether a poet uses hallucinogens or not, the only question that concerns the reader of what purports to be poetry is, is the poetry produced good, bad or indifferent? Nor need this inquiry stay academic. It may be more significant than at first appears likely, for instance, that Michael McClure's poetry is by no means always as good as its tone suggests it must be. Poetry—for Michael McClure as well as for F. R. Leavis—is important beyond the performance of certain linguistic skills. If, to put it bluntly, poetry fails certain acid-tests, the conclusion critic and reader are justified in drawing is that there is something more radically wrong with the utterance than some technical incompetence. This is commonplace. But it needs re-stating here, I think: for Michael McClure, in the volumes that followed the poem quoted above, makes certain assumptions, certain claims, which, if justified, undercut a great deal of conventional intellectual and spiritual life: the poet, it is claimed, is able with the use of hallucinogens to penetrate to a layer of experience, of reality, which lies within or beneath "normal" vision, and is in some sense "more true," more real. So the normal version of the dogma runs. I have already indicated my opinion of the metaphysical bases of this dogma: hallucinogens cannot be said to make contact with reality, or truth. They simply change the body's chemistry and thereby its perception, which reverts, unless the equipment is damaged in the process, back to its former state (which we may therefore call "normal") upon the cessation of the narcotic effect. The most that could be claimed is that it is somehow morally better or healthier to perceive and experience hallucinogenically than in the ordinary way. Rimbaud's *Une saison en enfer,* the decline of Coleridge, and the testimony of William Burroughs suggest otherwise, but this is not, as I have said, the place to discuss that question. What is relevant here is the question, how do the aesthetic facts bear out the metaphysics? Why, and how, does McClure's verse fail? What are the moral implications of the aesthetic facts?

If McClure had been right, he ought to have hit a poetic gusher: there ought to be no difference between one poem and the next, whereas in fact there are enormous differences—of quality, tone, effect—even within one passage of one poem. Excellent as McClure's best drug poems are, there is little evidence of his having achieved the goal of every poetic mineralogist: the level of his verse fluctuates wildly, it moves from near-sublimity to near-bathos from one one to the next. This is so in the peyote poem already quoted. This, for instance, is the note hit so monotonously by psychosis—"I KNOW EVERYTHING!" McClure's poetry, like Christopher Smart's, moves into and out of relevance, while itself apparently remaining convinced of its own oracular profundity. The nuttiness of "I KNOW EVERYTHING!" is familiar to many users of hallucinogens, to say nothing of alcohol. Everyone who has ever been drunk or high knows this feeling of *significance:* the things said in this state—afterwards recollected to have been quite trivial—seem at the time to be tremendously, ultimately, profound. Later, in the same poem, McClure tones it down and drops the block capitals—"I know all that I need to know"—arrogant still perhaps, but not absurd. The second statement occurs after a passage of considerable beauty—

> The dark brown space behind the door is pre-
>   cious,
> intimate, silent, still. The birth-place
> of Brahms.
>
>   ("Peyote Poem")

That is an adjective sequence, we feel, which might have come into being without the peyote, though it's unlikely that the actual instigation—the space behind the door—would have caused it. Not so the Nerval-ish pretensions of "I read the meaning of scratched walls and cracked ceilings." This is surely private—an attestation only. Poetry comes into existence in the space between the poet and the world, between his experience and ours. McClure's overuse of upper-case type is a telltale sign of exasperation, an inability to communicate. But poetry, to say it another way, is not—much pseudo-symbolist claptrap to the contrary—concerned with the incommunicable, but with the *otherwise incommunicable.* Chairs are inexpressible, if you like, but our experience of them, or what this experience means to us, is not. In the same way, McClure's poetry succeeds when it is not trying to gesticulate towards the INEXPRESSIBLE, but precisely when it concerns itself with the frontierland between the experience of drugs and his own waking consciousness, between his extraordinary experience and our own more ordinary. It is, in other words, half-critical, half-comparative. It is blasphemous to seek to "say" God, to say what should be left unsaid. The true mystic's concern is what his experience teaches him and his readers about the whole meaning and conduct of life itself. Much of McClure's poetry invalidates itself in trying to declare the undeclarable. So, in the peyote poem under discussion, the interesting and comprehensible statement,

> Here in my Apartment I think tribal thoughts

(we think of Wise Indians smoking pipes of peace, of the wholeness the white man has lost), is followed by a straight line rules across the page, and then the single word "STOMACHE!!!" It is hard to know which is funnier, the upper-case type or the triple exclamation marks. Here, truly, is the absurd of drunkenness, the ludicrous conviction of *significance.* It is a phenomenon which could be illustrated at random from any of McClure's longer poems, those sprawling numinous extravaganzas. This is the sort of thing "poor Kit Smart" stumbled on in his madness: "STOMACHE!" In this instance, McClure immediately goes on to fish out a genuinely fascinating emblem from the unconscious—

> I am visited by a man
> who is the god of foxes
> there is dirt under the nails of his paw
>   fresh from his den.
> We smile at one another in recognition.

The episode is strangely meaningful, though its significance is hard to define without talking in Jungian terms about archetypes and collective memories. Anyway, McClure's memory becomes ours here: the weirdly alarming beauty of childhood is skillfully conjured up. Almost at once—so drastic are McClure's transitions—the scene vanishes: the poet closes his eyes—"Closing my eyes there are flashes of light—My eyes won't focus but leap." The reporting here is interesting and to the point: the physiological facts are relevant at this juncture. We want to know what it feels like, what actually happens, and he tells us, with a frank courage which is an important part of McClure's make-up. It doesn't seem important in the same way to know that he then felt he had three feet. But the odd detail—"I see seven places at once"—has a factual authenticity which tells us something we ought to know about the trip. Throughout this passage, indeed, the reporting is absorbing and pointful, probably because it keeps the inner narrative closely related to the outside world. "Seeing the loose chaos of words on the page"—we all know that aspect of language. In the middle of the passage there is another hilarious interjection—"STOM?ACHE!"—which must, but can't, be ironical; then, after another line ruled across the page, McClure again tells us solemnly of his feelings about his belly:

> My belly and I are two individuals
>   joined together
>   in life.

The conclusion of the poem, however, returns to the archetypal world to which it is McClure's peculiar gift and privilege to be able to penetrate:

> I stare into clouds seeing
>   their misty convolutions.
>
> The whirls of vapor
> I will small clouds out of existence.
>
> They become fish devouring each other.
> And change like Dante's holy spirits
>   becoming an osprey frozen skyhigh
>   to challenge me.
>
>   ("Peyote Poem")

Those ospreys, like the fox-man earlier and the lion men in the beautiful short poem "The Child," come from an impersonal realm, a timeless symbol-bank, which sets all the rest of the hallucination in a meaningful context. All McClure's best verse connects his drug-experience with some deeper, broader metaphoric layer, and in just this connection lies the poetry:

> COLD COLD COLD COLD COLD COLD
>   COLD COLD
>   COLD AND FAR AWAY
> and we are not cold in our space and not cool
>   and not different. And I do

not mean this as a metaphor or fact.
    Even the strained act it is.

Bending by the brook and filling cups.
          ("Peyote Depression")

The last line suddenly makes contact with Chinese religious thought; at the same time, it provides a metaphor for life itself which is at once ancient and original. The "fact-act" echo here reminds us again of McClure's verbal subtlety, subtlety evident more in a non-narcotic piece, like "Canoe: Explication" which reveals most strikingly McClure's provenance from Robert Duncan:

    it's the imagined song, the concept
        of anarchy set to music
    Wavering, symmetrical, unsymmetrical
    Pointed and strange as a matchflame
        Held in sunlight.

The almost invisible image (so much more apt than Olson's shot at the same thing) beautifully captures the elusiveness of the thought. The same delicacy is applied later to the motion of the canoe:

    A volta appears—the serene charged pause.
    Thought alone wonders
    At the connection
    And the duet begins again.

The simple yet subtle physical event—canoeing—has been "explicated" by the metaphor of music, just as the experience of hearing music has been enlarged by the physical analogy. The slightness of the theme produces a poetry of equal delicacy. McClure is a poet with or without drugs.

Whether he has realized his enormous potential is another matter. Since he came down from his narcotics plateau—a decade ago now—McClure has written a great deal of good poetry. Its sheer quantity indeed makes it impossible for this kind of survey to do it anything like justice. It is enough to say that at its best it achieves a poise and a sinewy delicacy rarely to be found in recent American writing. Its essence is a clarification and refinement of the archetypal symbolism which emerged so excitingly from the highs and lows of his peyote poems.

His best poems balance on a needle-point, yet are as sure as rock. What we might perhaps question is that power to engage our deepest human interest. Here is a more recent instance of this quasi-Blakean mode:

        EACH
        MAMMAL
          does
           a
       small perfect
         thing
         like
      to be himself
       or herself
   and to hold a new creation
     on a shining platter
        as he
       (or she)
      steps towards
     the waiting car.
        ("For Robert Creeley")

A derivative of Duncan's pedestal pieces, this poem has the shape of a baroque fountain. But one wonders whether it doesn't also share that non-problematicness essential to Duncan's often rather bland celebrations. The central assertion of the poem—that each created mammal (especially, by implication, man) is in itself perfect and in need of celebration—is finely illustrated by the final clause—the step towards the waiting car. No matter how trivial or transient the act, the poem asserts, we are in ourselves at any point perfect. But little of that complexity of all good poetry is generated out of the combination of the two major elements of the poem: we look in vain for that tension of contraries that gives Blake's smallest poems such force. Beat poetry offered Blakean celebration as opposed to existentialist nihilism. But it also offered at its best—in McClure's best peyote poems, in "Howl," in Corso's "Mutation of the Spirit"—an awareness of the foulness and complexity of the conditions against which the capacity for joy has to strive. . . . Whitman himself shortcircuited exploration by the expedient of mass-acceptance—acceptance which really accepted nothing, since it did not *know* what it was claiming to accept. Much of Michael McClure's later poetry, like much of Duncan's, seems to me to limit itself by a desire to say "Yea," or, still worse, to tell the rest of us that *we* ought to say "Yea"—yet without admitting all the facts. There is a feeling that the affirmativeness has been too easily acquired.

That vital intelligence characteristic of the best Beat poetry of the 1960s has gradually gone under to an elegant and stylish blandness. The impression is reinforced rather than gainsaid by the obligatory abuse of easy targets—the Pentagon, the Man in the Grey Flannel Suit, and so on. But McClure is still—comparatively—young, and we have not seen his best.

No poet illustrates the sophistication of Beat poetry more strikingly than Philip Whalen. Whalen's stock-in-trade is an attractive self-awareness, a wry, biting humor, a negligent familiarity with the numinous that contrasts interestingly with Michael McClure's solemnity:

    The trouble with you is
    That sitting on a bench in the back yard
    You see an old plank in the fence become
    A jewelled honeycomb of golden wires
    Discoursing music, etc.
        ("Denunciation, Or, Unfrock'd Again")

The subject-matter of the poem is much the same as in McClure's verse; but the psychedelic experience, the mind-changing effect of the drug, is not dashed down in rapt awe. It becomes a source of self-mockery:

    The trouble is aggravated by the grass
    Flashing alternately green and invisible
    Green and non-existent
    While the piano in the house plays
    The Stars and Stripes Forever

The self-mockery is more fertile, more purposeful than we had been accustomed to expect in modern verse. There is no covert self-satisfaction in the self-unmasking:

    The trouble with you is you keep acting
    Like a genius: Now you're not a genius

You're nothing but a prick . . . in fact you're
Not even that, you're nothing but a son-of-a-
    bitch
        GET OUT OF MY HOUSE!

Whalen obviously does find himself absurd, yet remains quite confident of the significance of what he has experienced:

    What plant put out those
    Tall thin stiff green leaves? Lines
    Drawn from the tip of each one
    Would describe the surface of what
    Regular solid polyhedron?
    You don't dare invent a name.

So closely are Whalen's satiric wit and his intellectual insight related. Once again, we are reminded of the significance of the new release of humor and wit: here something like the wholeness of sensibility it was the design of intellectualist criticism to guarantee with irony? Behind Whalen, as behind Leroi Jones, is the complex efficiency of Black Mountain imagism, with its subtle sense of vegetable life:

    Bud-clusters hang straight down from the sharp-
        ly crooked
    Geranium stem like strawberries, the wild
        mountain kind
    These flowers almost as wild right here
    Barbarous thick-jointed tangle, waist-high
    Escaped once for all from the green-houses of
        the north
    A weed, its heavy stalks jointing upwards and
        winding out
    In all directions, too heavy to stand straight
    The neighbors clipped some out of their yard
    The stalks lay in the gutter and grew for days
    In the rain water, flowering
    Ignorant of their disconnection.
                        ("Soufflé—Take IX")

The endless "takes" and jottings do, to some extent, betray a disorganized mind. Whalen has never produced the *magnum opus* he seems intellectually qualified to have written. Instead, there are the shorter ironic pieces ("For C," "Fond Farewell to the *Chicago Quarterly*") which are often perfect, and the longer, fragmented works which only occasionally achieve the moments of penetrating insight:

    The wind increases as the sun goes down
    The weight of that star pulling air after it
    Naturally the prune trees blossom now
    And some kind of bush with pink trumpet flow-
        ers
    All the other trees except acacias have quit.
                        ("Soufflé—Take III")

It seems to have been Whalen's destiny, his function perhaps, to accept a kind of failure. We may speculate once again on the influence of the feminization of the mind encouraged by Buddhism. It is unlikely that a forthright Christian ethic of duty, obligation and striving would have been able to give us the things Whalen has given. If we compare him with Roethke, for instance, whom he resembles in many ways (they write the tragicomedy of obesity), Roethke's labor and strain seem inadequate recompense

for the loss of the humor and the play of mind Whalen's detachment affords him:

    All day Christmas the sea whirled this tangle—
    Spruce logs, redwood stumps, fishboxes and
        lightglobes—
    A big eddy at the creek mouth
    Carting back several tons of debris back and
        forth
        across a hundred feet of beach
    In water maybe a foot and a half in depth.
                    ("Letter to Mme E T S, 2. 1. 58")

Curiously, many of Whalen's most strange and powerful perceptions are, like this, entirely unmetaphoric. It is enough, he intimates, merely to observe. There is, in my opinion, nothing in Carlos Williams or Olson to match the eerie reality of these things in Whalen. "All that comparison ever does," Olson had observed, "is set up a series of reference points: to compare is to take one thing and try to understand it by marking its similarities to or differences from another thing." Yet Olson's own verse swills around pointlessly, unless some metaphor creeps in. It is to Whalen that we must turn for evidence of the power of annotated reality.

This is especially true of the earlier work. *Like I Say* (1950-58) still seems his best collection. The wryness is already there. But the intelligence about himself (what we have come to regard as intelligent behavior in a poet this century being largely a matter of laughing at himself) is displayed as much in the mental energy that vaults beyond itself in order to see itself as it is in the self-depreciation. Whalen notes his failure—his obesity, his never getting anything done—with an athletic intellectuality strangely inconsistent with it and with the image of himself that he otherwise projects in his verse. This intellectual energy was what made possible the notation of unadorned reality just noted as being so important in Whalen's verse: the logs swilling about in the tide, the cut-off flowers still growing—these things are comprehended by an act of the imagination, in Coleridge's understanding of the term, not copied by a prose-camera. In his best pieces Whalen sets these natural images in a sound-pattern of considerable subtlety and a very complex intellectual frame. "Homage to Lucretius" (written in 1952, printed in the *Evergreen Review* of 1956, included in *Monday in the Evening,* 1961) suggests a systematic scheme in the title which is belied in the characteristic throw-away manner:

    It all depends on how fast you're going
    Tending towards light, sound
    Or the quiet of mere polarity

But the casual manner is supported here (or it supports) a very wide-ranging and economically presented argument. "We want crystals," he observes, but "can't easily imagine another world"—and the reason is that this one (we remember at this point the atoms of Lucretius) is itself "barely / Visible." Enough to say that this genuinely philosophical inquiry lacks altogether the portentuousness of Robert Duncan's pronouncements, but also that it succeeds in giving the abstract speculation a natural expression: the root-experience, which, I imagine, gave rise to the poem in the first place, is now disclosed, to fill out and illustrate the Lucretian speculations which were in fact suggested by it:

> We lined up and pissed in a snowbank
> A slight thaw would expose
> Three tubes of yellow ice. . . .
> And so on. . . .

The last phrase is disarming, and—of course—charming: we are meant to be delighted by the performance, and we are. This seems to me to be close in many ways to William Empson's more successfully philosophical explorations. What is characteristic of Whalen is not just the colloquial casualness which he shares with Empson, but the ease with which he succeeds in giving the insights—the piss frozen into tubes yields an insight into "A world not entirely new, But realized . . . "—a greater context of meaning. And the point is this meaning, not the attractive casualness, which is merely instrumental.

At his best, Whalen succeeds in relating this order of intelligence to the random events of a life—wasted, according to the world's view, in meditations, reading, and staring out of the window—and in holding it all in one perspective. The best of these complex efforts to marshal everything is, in my opinion, "Sourdough Mountain Lookout" (1955-1956), which displays, in its moments of inertia and fatigue, as much as in its explosions of mental energy, a wholeness rare in contemporary writing:

> Then I'm alone in a glass house on a ridge
> Encircled by chiming mountains
> With one sun roaring through the house all day
> & the others crashing through the glass all night
> Conscious even while sleeping. . . .

The poem exercises a fine virtuosity of feeling, moving from sharp imagist observation, instinct with life, to the inward world, the relations between which are Whalen's real theme. The intellectual vitality which holds together the details and the percepts is revealed also in the apparently random reading which structures the poem: Heraclitus, Byron, Empedocles, Buddha—the sources and influences file into and out of the poem according to a rhythm of walking, resting, climbing and reflection. When he is tired ("pooping out, exhausted"), the ironic awareness of himself comes to the surface ("Remember smart guy there's something / Bigger, something smarter than you"). And this wry self-ridicule—what a reader fresh to Whalen is most likely to take away from the experience—is a product of his intellectual vigor as much as the ability to "get round"—come round the back of—his wider intellectual interests. He concludes with a generalization that holds the whole of what has gone before easily within itself:

> What we see of the world is the mind's
>   Invention and the mind
> Though stained by it, becoming
> Rivers, sun, mule-dung, flies—
> Can shift instantly
> A dirty bird in a square time. . . .
>   ("Sourdough Mountain Lookout")

Such reflections upon the relations between the mind and the outer world constitute Whalen's major theme. It is a slippery ramp to get on: it is easy to feel, in moving through *On Bear's Head*, that Whalen is too clever for his own good. He does not work up the excitement in the face of the world which we see in the best of McClure; he cannot, it could be, put all the bits together right. He finds it easier to negate what he has just said than to find reasons for moving from it onto something greater. Scepticism is his essence.

It was Gregory Corso, perhaps, who suggested most powerfully what Beat was to be capable of. He stands in relation to Allen Ginsberg as Burroughs does to Kerouac. Where Ginsberg is all expression and voice, Corso is calm and quick, whimsical often, witty rather than humourous, semantically swift rather than prophetically incantatory. His early verse carries on the wit of Dickinson, with a fine surrealist fantasy:

> The light that makes us a friend of eagles
>   has made our poor wounds an interval of
>   clouds,
> slow and creeping, calm and sad,
> in the skyful dungeon of things.
>   ("One Day")

The surrealism is taken as lightly and deftly as it should be: collocations like "pie glue," "telephone snow," "cat shovel," "Firestones! Gas! Couch!," "old Dutch shoes," "nineteen twenties Norwegian stamps," "twig smear," "Roman coin soup," "Christmas teeth," "apple deaf," are meant to throw light on things, to illuminate the experiences of which they are severally composed. This has been commonplace poetic practice since the symbolists: Rimbaud's violent yoking together of opposites was applied systematically by the surrealists, and in essentially the same spirit. But Corso's orientation is quite different: the surrealist, following the symbolist, built up a hermetic wall around his sensibility: his creative identity depended upon the mysteriousness of his own words. He was afraid he would cease to exist—in his own mind—if his utterances became less cryptic. The Romantic poet's claim to be an unacknowledged legislator of the world had become strangely transmuted over the intervening hundred years. From the time of the symbolists, the poet had taken to cherishing his alienation as his last surviving claim to existence. The *avant garde*—for all its affectation of disgust for bourgeois obtuseness—had in fact always striven rigorously to repulse any attempted bourgeois fraternization: the public's acceptance of an *avant garde* idiom was always the sign for a rapid withdrawal to higher ground. The artist since Flaubert and Baudelaire has not tried to make himself understood by the bourgeois: on the contrary, he has worked hard to preserve his obscurity, while all the time capitalizing on the bourgeois's sociopolitical guilt to make the bourgeois itself feel responsible for the "gap." The gap has now been obliterated: there was no going beyond Pollock's painting and Cage's "music." It was the Beats who first made possible the *rapprochement* which has transformed art and literature over the past decade. The Beats were never an alienation movement in the *avant garde* tradition. On the contrary, theirs was primarily a spirit of acceptance, of celebration, of optimism. It was openly enthusiastic for a way of life of the yielded more spiritual substenance, more sheer well-being than the life of the organization man. But it avoided the limiting non-alignment of the liberal intellectual; because he really subscribes to (that is, coheres with, lives in, fails radically enough to dissent from) the values of the society he is intellectually committed to deploring, the liberal intellectual is thrown back upon irony. The question is, again, basically ideological. The tortuous (ironical) writings of writers like Bellow, Lowell, Roethke, Auden and Empson can be explained satisfactorily only in terms of ideology. And only ideological considerations can make complete sense of poetry like Gregory Corso's.

This could be illustrated in some of the poems from which the already cited neo-surrealist collocations are taken—"Marriage," for instance or "One Day." In the first, we find that the relations between poet and society are quite different from what we find to be the case in T. S. Eliot: the poet's satiric humor allows compassion for "Mrs. Kindhead," whose community chest *is* well-meaning and, as far as it goes, admirable. The poet's rejection of marriage does not have the muted bitterness of Eliot's "Prufrock." Its laughter is, indeed, infectious.

But the point will emerge more impressively from a consideration of a later, more mature poem.

Mutation of the Spirit (1967) synthesizes his best qualities

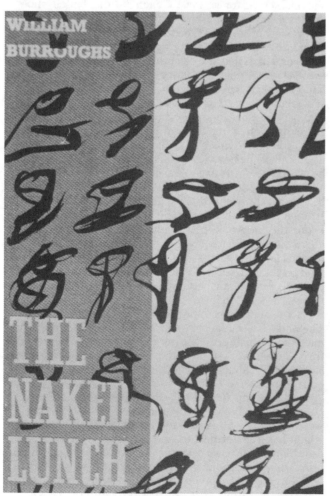

Dust jacket from William S. Burroughs's novel The Naked Lunch *(1959).*

with a new seriousness. It opens with a breathtaking paragraph that seems almost the only verse since written to rival the ease, poise, sophistication and rapidity of *The Waste Land's* opening run-in:

> Last night a white apple fell from the loneliest
> tree in the world.
> Today the field is green the sun bright and warm
> knit
> Children attend their spirits the old knit knit
> Chicken cries Sacramental sobs from the chapel
> a window closes
> Loneliness grandeur and blue lambs whorled
> eyes rinsed light
> Swimming deer and now the long hike back to
> the city
> Smells of rats and pasty poisons horizons of fuming
> domes dynamos
> Vast sick sense smudgepots gasping black-
> smoke
> Cheese-cloth faces dead carts bells a white arm
> A long pale arm falls across the port.

The section that follows provides a list of Blake-Smart definitions that imply a maturation of Beat ideals: instead of the usual opting for craziness and the mad, Corso's definitions insist on a severe normality:

> Imperfection may discredit the rare the odd
> Yet shall perfection honor the typical
> Blemishes humiliate the outlandish the unique
> the strange
> Yet excellence extols the orthodox the natural

Corso's direction at the head of the poem claims that these pages of verse may be read in whatever order one chooses. Yet I fancy he would rather have it read in the order in which it is printed. The first line *is* a first line if ever there was one, and the alternation of lucid density in the first paragraph with the abstract norms of the second recalls the procedures of *The Waste Land*. The action of the poem is also a setting of lands in order, like Eliot's poem:

> It's no longer When will I break through this
> dream
> suddened upon my by questioning life
> No longer is it A life unquestioned
> did well enough unquestioned
> No the signals are clear I can hear
> and I can ask
> Who is that man whose snip-snap
> makes him more than that mark madcap
> Please who is he tell wild salvo

The mutations involve pop mythology ("Dusty Bright"—a sexually ambiguous figure who "is to the sun what the sun is to the earth the sun's sun") and sinister figures from the declining days of Rome. In fact the whole poem is poised between a sense of civic disaster ("S is axed from P, and Q from R is tore") and an extraordinary elation of spirit, exulting in symbols and images of ecstatic cool transcendence:

> O there is burning snow flickering the air
> and white velvet sloths in the falling sun
> and flamewhite bears tip-toeing across the trees
> and oh there are streams of luminous fish in
> mountain winds
> and seldom beasts winking in snowclouds

O zero zoo invisibility

There is throughout a sense of having to make the final decisions—"come standby spirit my spirit fails"—in other words, a mature but not disabused reckoning, the kind of spiritual setting forth John Bunyan made once. As in Kerouac's *Big Sur,* the Beat life itself, which is what is in a way being placed (if not rejected,) enabled Corso to get to this starting-out point.

The basic elements of his earlier work appear transformed in this poem. There are the mythic personages—the Ares, for instance, of "Ares Comes and Goes" becomes "real opportunity," the new friend the poet says he's "gonna follow to the end." By means of such devices Corso has much freer access to regions of behavior and decision than is afforded by conventional introspective methods. In fact Corso had always shown great sophistication in his use of archaism, allegorical figures, fantasy and wit. All these elements of his art lend their weight to *Mutation of the Spirit.* The peculiar balance of the poem—its intensity and coolness, its force and delicacy, its urgent expectancy and moral seriousness—expresses Corso's own sensibility. But it expresses as well the intelligent flexibility of the poetic tradition to which it seems at the moment something like an apogee.

Ten years before it would have been unrealistic to expect from poetry in English a statement as mature and yet as joyously alive, as generally relevant and yet as unpompous as this:

> Everywhere here and way beyond there
>   suns glow with accordant liberties
> Paradise even pervades Hell cleansing like a bell
> The final gong deafens the sacrosanct room from
>   its door
>   from its halls its rooms Paradise evermore
>   glowed with laughing liberties
> A hell-less universe is on its knees
>   (*Mutation of the Spirit*)

This seems to me to possess the classic strength, the clear joyous clash of great poetry. Every poem today is written under the eye of the Bomb. Between the fake demonic celebrations of Doom, and the sturdy pretense that it isn't there, between shaggy Beat gloom-consciousness and square commonsense, Corso's poem finds what seems to be the only true path. It is saturated with an awareness of imminent destruction, that emerges in a halo of ultimate purity (the "burning snow," "blue lambs," "rinsed light," "swimming deer"). Yet it enjoins neither *carpe diem,* nor despair, nor carelessness, nor irresponsibility. "Come adorned in sun foliage in the final mutation in this God-closed age," Corso exhorts. "Ahead is black" and "The decencies of life have lost their way," but still, total engagement is all that can be urged. As the poem begins, surely and beautifully, so it closes on a sure final cadence:

> Arise new spirit unroll a nadir wool
> From tip to top the source is measured full
> The eternal exists as well in the ephemeral
> Air is everywhere and life is changeable
> In the yard of the old sun retired spirits sleep
> Into the pool of night the swimmer of light leaps.

(*Mutation of the Spirit*)
(pp. 195-209.)

Geoffrey Thurley. From The American Moment: American Poetry in the Mid-Century. *Arnold, 1977, St. Martin's Press, 1978. (c) 1977 by Geoffrey Thurley. Reprinted by permission of St. Martin's Press, Inc. In Canada by Edward Arnold (Publishers) Limited.*

Koos van der Wilt

[*In the following essay, Wilt discusses the autobiographical characterization of narrators and protagonists in several Beat novels.*]

One major sub-genre of the British, the French, as well the American novel features a novelist as protagonist and his/her writing as a central action; more peculiar to American fiction, according to one tradition in criticism, is that it is more consistently romantic and exploratory than its European counterpart. Four beat novels discussed here, Jack Kerouac's *On the Road* (1957), William Burroughs' *Naked Lunch* (1957), and to a lesser degree two little known examples of the genre, Lawrence Ferlinghetti's *Her* (1960), and Alexander Trocchi's *Cain's Book* (1961), suggest that most beat writing belongs to the sub-genre in which the protagonist works on a novel featuring himself as a character. Furthermore, if these novels are representative of the beat genre, then beat writing is a mid-twentieth-century extension of an inherently American tradition in literature.

The term "beat" has literary as well as social connotations that cannot easily be separated. On the one hand, members of the beat generation, beatniks, were Bohemians with a way of life characterized by free love, drugs, jazz, and material simplicity. On the other, the term applies to a group of American poets and novelists of the 1950s and 1960s who were in romantic rebellion against the value systems of American society. On the surface, the rebellion of beat authors involves the search for new forms of prose. Holding that "beat" refers to authors who use the milieu of members of the beat generation as their subject, Thomas F. Parkinson persuasively explains the relation between the social and the literary, suggesting that the social side of the beat movement provides plots, themes and characters for its literary counterpart.

Arguing that beat novels belong to an important sub-genre and are part of an American literary tradition does not in itself lead to any conclusions about the significance of beat writing. However, placing the beats in a generic and traditional perspective will help us to examine the structure and the meaning of beat novels and, with that, their value. Past criticism, focussing too much on the unorthodox lives of beatniks and beat authors, has failed to deal with beat fiction and the works of Kerouac and Burroughs have too easily been dismissed as garrulous and incoherent. Critics sympathetic to beat writing seem intent on defending the beats' unorthodox socio-political views and ways of life rather than on analyzing their literature. Now, some twenty years after the beat flourished as a movement, the distance in time should allow us to make a deeper examination of the relation between form and meaning in the beat novel.

In his recent study *The Self-Begetting Novel*, Steven G. Kellman defines a novelistic sub-genre in which the protagonist writes a novel featuring his *persona* as a character. By employing such a device, Kellman argues, such authors as Samuel Beckett, James Joyce, and Henry Miller enable their protagonists to create a new self through and in a work of literature. Three of the four beat novels studied here belong to this sub-genre. Moreover, the beat novel is part of a specifically American literary tradition. The publication of D. H. Lawrence's *Studies in Classical American Literature* (1923) has given birth to a school of criticism that claims the uniqueness of American literature in various respects. Some critics contend that American fiction is exploratory or romantic in nature. According to these critics, a longing for a new place and a new state of mind is pervasive in the American novel. One consequence of romanticism in American fiction is, as Richard P. Chase puts it, that explorers see privately. Whether or not Chase is talking about authors or their protagonists is unclear. Yet, if applied to both authors and protagonists, Chase's observation identifies the personal nature of works in the American romantic tradition, and so the lack of aesthetic distance between the writer and the main character.

The beat novel derives its strength and organic unity from a unique fusion of these generic and traditional characteristics. The search for a new place and a new state of mind is aided by the protagonist's recreation of himself; he casts himself in the role of an author who explores new ways of writing. The personal nature of the beat novel implies that the author's experiences and concern with new ways of writing are their protagonists' experiences and concern with new literary forms. Finally, that beat novels are written in an experimental prose style is itself in keeping with the exploratory tradition of the American novel. Therefore, the beat novel is autobiographical in character (although an author must never be fully identified with his *persona*), innovative in prose style, and is complicated by the fragmentary personal experiences the author has transferred to his protagonist.

One of the most striking characteristics of *On the Road* is Kerouac's use of what he labels "spontaneous prose". One example involves an unusual transition from a discussion of bop, a form of jazz, to a discussion of a trip the narrator, Sal Paradise, is planning. The transition occurs from one sentence to the next within one paragraph. Originally, the entire novel was written in this shifting manner, but Kerouac's publisher, Viking, compelled him to accept major revisions.

We find remnants of Kerouac's idiosyncratic style throughout the novel:

> In the daytime [Boncoeur, a friend of Paradise's] and I went out with the gun and tried to shoot quail in the hills. [Boncoeur] sneaked up to within three feet of the clucking birds and let go a blast of the .32. He missed. His tremendous laugh roared over the California woods and over

America. "The time has come for you and me to go and find the Banana King."

This passage is inadequate as a straightforward account of a hunting party. The author sketches the hunting scene in three lines, and next, in one sentence, the reader is rocketed to heights from which he gets an overview of the woods of California and then of all of America, the world rapidly receding beneath him. Next, the reader is suddenly presented with an encounter between Paradise and his friend, and an uncanny banana vendor in downtown San Francisco. In this passage, the pace is extraordinarily fast in comparison to the immediately preceding part of the narrative, an even-paced account of Paradise's stay at Boncoeur's.

The author defines spontaneous prose as a technique of writing without

> "selectivity" of expression but following free deviation (association) of mind into limitless blow-on-subjects seas of thought, swimming in a sea of English with no discipline other than rhythms of rhetorical exhalation and expostulated statements . . . Blow as deep as you want— write as deeply, fish as far down as you want, satisfy yourself first.

As Ann Charters remarks, spontaneous prose is inspired by jazz. Spontaneous prose enables the author to write in whatever direction his emotions lead him, much as a jazz-musician improvises according to his emotions. The use of a first-person narrator best meets the demand of a spontaneous prose style that a text should be written from the depths of the self: "Blow as deep as you want, write as deeply . . . satisfy yourself first." Kerouac deems himself and his own spontaneous impressions the proper subject of literature and his view of authorship is in this respect in keeping with the American brand of romanticism.

Related to Kerouac's private vision is what might be termed the "telescope effect" in *On the Road*. The author writes from his own experiences and as a consequence *On the Road* is largely autobiographical: it is not hard to recognize Jack Kerouac in the narrator or Kerouac's friend Neal Cassady in the character Dean Moriarty. Kerouac travels widely, is fond of jazz, and writes a novel which shows little aesthetic distance from his world. The main character of this novel likewise travels widely, is fond of jazz, and writes a novel. *On the Road*, then, is about an author whose novel is contained within *On the Road* just as one section of a telescope is contained within another.

Because of this telescope effect, the reader is presented with spontaneous prose in two ways. Not only is it a formalistic feature of *On the Road*, but it is also a thematic concern because Paradise, like Kerouac, practices its principles. That he does so is clear from what Moriarty exclaims as he looks over Paradise's shoulder while the latter is busy writing: " 'So many things to write! . . . How to even begin to get it all down and without modified restraints and all hung up on like literary inhibitions and grammatical fears'." This unity of form and content underlines an important point of such prose: to be liberated from writing conventions so as to be able to write more freely and directly about personal experiences.

Kerouac's actual experiences provide unity of form and content at other points in *On the Road.* Jazz, the music that was so central to Kerouac's life, for instance, is not only subject matter but also a factor of the prose style. Admittedly it is difficult to trace the influence of a musical genre on prose, but there is evidence in *On the Road* for Charters's contention that the spontaneous style in the novel is jazz-based. For example, the unusual transition from a discussion of bop to a trip the narrator is to make achieves the effect of improvisation. Secondly, the prose in *On the Road* features an occasional rapid increase in pace, for instance, in the hunting scene. Comparable to such an accelerando is the increase in the rhythm of the jazz that Paradise and Moriarty exalt over when they attend a performance by the jazz-musician George Shearing. The influence of jazz on the book's prose style is also evident in the vocabulary. The text occasionally replaces conventional words or phrases with allusions to jazz, for example "jazzbo" for black and "moaning along" for plodding along. The narrator describes a party as "roaring" and he says of one of the guests: "excitement *blew* out of his eyes [and] he lisped, he *writhed,* he flopped, he *moaned,* he howled" (italics added). The verbs used to describe a performance of Shearing and his band show that the jazz-vocabulary partially overlaps with that applied to the guest: the band "*writhed* and twisted and *blew* . . . they *moaned* (italics added).

In its disregard for more conventional writing, the role of spontaneous prose is not confined to one of protest against the academically oriented New Critics of the 1950s. Spontaneous prose gives *On the Road* its iconicity, its similarity between meaning and text with which this meaning is conveyed. Spontaneous prose is the technique that explains much about the minimal aesthetic distance between Kerouac and Paradise—and the former's recreation of himself as a writer/protagonist. After all, an experimental prose style effectively communicates the search for a new self. At the same time, spontaneous prose emphasizes the novel's place in an exploratory American tradition—as, of course, does the novel's plot, an account of Paradise's journeys across the North-American continent.

Like Kerouac in *On the Road,* Burroughs is given to prose experiments and displays a private vision in *Naked Lunch.* Although the two novels differ in many respects, the confessional character of *Naked Lunch* and its experimental prose ensure that the form and the content of the novel cohere. Some critics see the importance of Burroughs' prose style for his message, although they do not examine it in detail.

The description of a group of mental patients, the Irreversible Neural Damages, from a mental ward, the Annexia government Reconditioning Center, exemplifies Burroughs' shifting writing. Two characters, Dr Benway and protagonist Lee Williams, witness the escape from the roof of the mental ward. The Irreversible Neural Damages, a "batallion of rampant bores [that] prowls the streets . . . in search of victims" bring about horrors that grow ghastlier and larger than life line by line. Through this description sounds the voice of a scantily introduced British colonial: " 'I was the only white man ever initiated into the in-

famous Agouti society . . . ' " Next, the narrative cuts to youths preparing to fight among themselves, trooping out to a battlefield. The narrator, who has not previously introduced the youths, fails to specify what battle they are engaged in on the previously unmentioned battlefield. Now the narrator cuts in with his own voice: "Gentle Reader, the ugliness of that spectacle buggers description". This narrator answers for his nauseating description of the Irreversible Neural Damages and subsequently, without any form of transition, paragraph indention or any other signal, shifts to a statement by a young hooligan, who, incidentally, turns into a "Rock and Roll hoodlum". The description of a hoodlum is a volatile sketch of a participant in a scantily described battle. Again, the narrator comes in, this time virtually inaudibly: " 'So leave us return to the [battle] field' ". The book abounds with such shifting writing.

Two collage-like techniques, the "cut-up" and "fold-in", along with Burroughs' drug-addiction, account for this prose style. The "cut-up" technique consists of putting together at random fragments from the author's own writing and other texts, varying from newspaper items to quotations from literary works. Burroughs did not fully develop this technique until after *Naked Lunch,* but felt he was working towards it while editing the original thousand-page manuscript down to its present two hundred and fifty pages. Burroughs supplements the "cut-up" with the "fold-in" technique, whereby the author folds a page of his own work and a page of someone else's down the middle and places them side by side as one page.

That *Naked Lunch* is a frame narrative further contributes to its complexity. Burroughs' own voice constitutes the novel's outermost frame, consisting of an Introduction and an Appendix. The Introduction is part of the novel: it resembles the main body as regards content and style. With slight variations, motifs from the Introduction recur in the book's main body; also, the use of ellipses, capitalization, and syntax in the Introduction resembles that in the main body. The Appendix, Burroughs' letters to a British medical doctor about the author's addiction, is likewise part of *Naked Lunch,* since Burroughs refers to it inside the novel.

The clue to the identity of the narrator in *Naked Lunch* lies in one of the novel's last chapters, the "Atrophied Preface". Here the narrator establishes his credentials: he introduces himself as William Seward and states that he "will unlock [his] word horde", that is, begin his narrative. Such stilted phrases as "Gentle Reader" or "So leave us return to the [battle] field" are reminiscent of Seward's "Gentle Reader" or "My Viking heart fares over the great brown river" in the "Atrophied Preface". Seward, then, is the narrator in *Naked Lunch.*

The aesthetic distance between this narrator and Burroughs is minimal. Apart from their identical Christian names, their last names suggest synonyms: "burrow" and "sewer" both refer to an underground network. It is fitting that the name "Burroughs" should reappear in a version suggesting processes of festering, "Seward", in the "Atrophied Preface". Secondly, Burroughs' middle initial and the first letter of Seward's last name are the same. Thirdly,

Seward reveals that he, too, has written a novel entitled *Naked Lunch.* In the fourth place, Seward, like Burroughs, is a junkie, a drug-addict. Seward, therefore, is to a great extent identifiable with Burroughs.

There is also minimal aesthetic distance between Burroughs and protagonist Lee Williams. Again a similarity in names (the author's first and the protagonist's last) indicates this. More evidence suggests that Williams is Burroughs' *persona.* Williams travels through the United States of America and such chimerical areas as the Republic of Freeland, or Annexia, and the City of Interzone. The author's journeys through the U.S.A. and Latin America may have served as a model for Williams' trip.

Promising that he will be an "Honest" author in the Introduction, Burroughs makes clear the autobiographical aspects of the narrative in the inner frames of the novel: "*Bill's Naked Lunch Room* . . . Step right up [to] take a look around with Honest Bill". Burroughs' promise implies that he wears no fictional disguise in *Naked Lunch,* or that he is "speaking personally" in his novel, and the poet Allen Ginsberg has suggested that the word "naked" in the title signifies as much. *Naked Lunch,* then, is an account of the adventures of Burroughs' *persona* Williams, narrated by yet another of the author's *personae,* Seward. The three layers in *Naked Lunch* account for Seward's statement that "the writer sees himself reading to the mirror . . .": in this novel, Burroughs observes Seward reading the story of Williams, Burroughs' and Seward's common mirror image, his *personae.*

Layered structure, discontinuous narrative, and the personal nature of *Naked Lunch* combine to produce unity of form and content in the novel, as Seward's notions about writing reflect the purposely erratic prose in *Naked Lunch.* Seward writes that he does not "presume to impose 'story' 'plot' 'continuity' " upon his *Naked Lunch,* which accords with Burroughs' writing technique. Seward's novel, like Burroughs', "spill[s] off the page in all directions [being a] kaleidoscope of vistas". Presumably, Seward's novel is every bit as experimental as Burroughs'. Seward's statement that a reader may "cut into *Naked Lunch* at any intersection point. . . . I have written many prefaces. They atrophy and amputate . . . " underlines Burroughs' application of the "cut-up" technique and his placement of the "Atrophied Preface" near the end of the novel. Seward also states the personal nature of the novel: "there is only one thing a writer can write about: *what is in front of his senses at the moment of writing* . . . I am a recording instrument".

This is one aspect of a broader unity of form and content in *Naked Lunch.* Seward's interpretation of the craft of writing concerns not just his ideas about language as a literary medium, but about language in general. Seward both puts into words Burroughs' refusal to "impose . . . 'continuity' " upon his novel and his refusal to make his language cohere altogether. Capitalizing "Word" to equate it with language in general, Seward warns the reader that "The Word will leap upon you . . . it will cut off fingers and toes . . . it will hang you". These dismal properties of language are destroyed if, Seward writes, "The World [which] is divided into units which be all in one peace and

should be so taken [are instead] had in any order". In numerous passages in the novel incomplete sentences and a fading away into ellipses indicate a breakdown of language: Burroughs destroys syntax according to Seward's rules for an anti-language.

Burroughs' distorted prose results in part from an excessive use of drugs. In the intermediate frame, narrated by Seward, drugs producing an incoherent prose style is an explicit concern. One passage in the book's main body describes the Market of Interzone in an extremely incoherent manner. The narrator cuts in parenthetically to account for this lack of style by saying that he wrote the passage under the influence of a drug, yage. So the destructive influence of drugs is at the same time a factor of the form of *Naked Lunch* and part of its content.

This unity, the underlying principle of which is fragmentation, in turn underlines some themes in the account of Williams' travels in the innermost section. One such theme is the restraint of modern man by such institutions as the welfare state. *Naked Lunch* contains numerous allusions and references to the welfare state and bureaucracy, bureaucracy likened to cancer, the oppression of homosexuals and drug addicts disguised as benevolence, and travel to Sweden, paragon of welfare states. The fragmented treatment of the welfare state is the author's attack on the manipulation of individuals by such controlling institutions. (The welfare state is only one example of what the author regards as an oppressive institution; organized religion is another. Burroughs' fragmented treatment of the welfare state and religion according to Seward's writing practices has as its thematic aim the rendering of these institutions powerless. In *Naked Lunch,* Burroughs presents a mirror image of his life and the forces that exert control over it, but, as his new self, the author/*persona* Seward suggests, Burroughs shatters the mirror. For the reader to be able to rearrange the shards in his/her own way is the author's corollary for freedom from whatever oppressive forces the mirror reflects. Burroughs' writing is inspired by anarchism.

How do such lesser known examples of the beat novel such as Trocchi's *Cain's Book* and Ferlinghetti's *Her* fare with regard to the above structures and characteristics of *On the Road* and *Naked Lunch?* The protagonist of *Cain's Book* is an author working on a novel entitled *Cain's Book.* There is little aesthetic distance between the author, Trocchi, and the protagonist, Necchi. Apparently, both are of Italian ancestry, both are drug addicts, and both live in New York. Trocchi is easily recognizable in Necchi. Much evidence points to the protagonist's view that literary conventions must be done away with and a new sort of writing must be created. In an epigraph to one chapter, Trocchi asserts that "there is no story to tell" and in the same chapter Necchi remarks that, as an author, he is not "concerned with the events which lead up to this or that", in other words, a plot. Necchi disparagingly refers to contemporary authors and literary scholars as the "Shakespeare industry," and, somewhat bluntly, likens traditional writing to excrement. In Necchi's view there is only one way for literature to redeem itself: to abide by the principles of Jack Kerouac's spontaneous prose. However, the novel displays quite a discrepancy between form and content. Many passages show how well Trocchi is able to write the sort of prose that Necchi despises. In this respect, the theme of a new self through innovative prose is not realized in the technique of *Cain's Book.*

In Ferlinghetti's *Her,* the protagonist, Fatso Raffine, takes a long journey by train in order to find his "witless self anew." Raffine realizes that the goal of his quest is not fulfilled and commits suicide. *Her* is not written in a traditional prose style. There is no evidence, however, that Raffine can be closely identified with the author of *Her,* or that the narrative draws heavily on Ferlinghetti's own experiences. Raffine is not an author—certainly not of a novelette *Her,* as Seward and Necchi are authors of novels entitled respectively *Naked Lunch* and *Cain's Book. Her,* then, does not belong to the novelistic sub-genre in which the main character is working on a novel, nor is Raffine necessarily Ferlinghetti's *persona.* Although, in a sense, *Her* belongs to an exploratory tradition as far as theme and plot go, Ferlinghetti has not created a new self in Raffine. *Cain's Book* and *Her,* therefore, lack the organic unity that is characteristic of *On the Road* and *Naked Lunch.* (pp. 113-24)

> *Koos van der Wilt, "The Author's Recreation of Himself as Narrator and Protagonist in Fragmented Prose: A New Look at Some Beat Novels," in* Dutch Quarterly Review of Anglo-American Letters, *Vol. 12, No. 2, 1982, pp. 113-24.*

INFLUENCE

Wilfrid Sheed

[Sheed is an English-born American critic and fiction writer. In the following essay, he appraises the accomplishments of the Beat writers.]

"Did you catch Kerouac tonight? He was wild." "Yeah, well, we had Kerouac last week. Equally wild, man." Columbia forties-fifties, long before *On the Road.* As a neighborhood kibitzer, I kept missing him by five minutes, with the new smell, marijuana, still heavy on the air, like Satan's home-brewed incense. You probably had such a hot dog at your school—the country was starved for hot dogs then. But this one, in the media capital, produced with just one formidable friend and a few assorted spear-carriers, the Beat Generation.

I was reminded, sight and smell, of that period of Bruce Cook's *The Beat Generation* [see Further Reading]. The Beats belonged to their time and place as firmly as the 1920 flappers to theirs. The streets round Columbia had just been cleared of naval cadets singing "I've Got Sixpence." The veterans were back, of no mind to settle down with Greer Garson, or Philip Wylie's Mom, or the propaganda-sodden homefront. Jewish writers were enrolling at

Montana and Iowa to discover the country they'd been fighting for. Kerouac and his pals were pounding the highways—aimlessly, said the old man, who could understand traveling so long as you dropped a bomb when you got there—to find something commensurate with their war-primed excitement. It could have happened anywhere, there were two to six guys like that on every campus; but it happened at Columbia, with San Francisco as matchbox: two places beautifully prepared for it.

At that, what happened was only a happening, never a real generation. The two coasts were away out of sync. The omelet fell apart, as with such eggs it must. Kenneth Patchen didn't like the Easterners from the start. Rexroth approved on principle but wound up slashing Kerouac in *The New York Times* (for *Mexico City Blues*). Kerouac, for his part, thought that Rexroth was "just a crazy old anarchist anyway, who might twist the Beat thing into something political." The Westerners, tracing through Jack London and the Wobblies, always carried the germs of social action; and the Easterners had struck West, as usual, to escape just that. Within a year of *On the Road* word has it that Kerouac was being laughed at in the Bay Area for his drunken, mystagogical caperings: and only Allen Ginsberg, with his superior sense of history and Napoleonic gifts for organization, was able to establish even the appearance of solidarity.

And, in time, even the Eastern half of the omelet proved none too solid. The establishing documents, *On the Road* and Ginsberg's *Howl,* were as unlike as two cries from the depths can be. Kerouac insisted on ecstasy, an imperative that would eventually drain him dry. Jack loved America more than any country deserves, and it was through no inconsistency that he would end up as paranoid about it as a Minute Man. Ginsberg saw mostly woodworm, dry rot, and tears in the same material.

At first, it didn't matter. Ginsberg maintained that his "Howl" was really for hope, a spring canticle. Kerouac allowed that, while Beat stood for beatific, it also meant beat down and furtive. What they were really celebrating was their own brand of open, swinging friendship, as opposed to the stiff sexual arrangements and resolutely loveless male friendship of commercial America, and trifling points of dogma could be overlooked. By the first frost of middle age, though, Kerouac had turned from Ginsberg, manic rejecting depressive; except that by then the parts were reversed. Ginsberg had faced his despair earlier, when he still had the strength to cope with it. Kerouac had postponed his too long.

The last days of Kerouac are enough to strike terror in any writer's heart. I tend to believe he handled his tormented, overloaded temperament as well as it could be handled, squeezing out what joy he could and retiring to his tent when his liver clouded over, trying to write to the end. But let's stick to such of his story as affected the Beat phenomenon.

His most famous contribution, besides the Compulsory Joy, was Automatic Writing—a theory of speed composition calculated, like psychoanalysis (another postwar toy), to surprise the subconscious and shake out the real stuff.

Beat Generation gathering in front of Lawrence Ferlinghetti's City Lights Book Store, 1965.

It now seems possible that Kerouac wanted to bypass the subconscious by outrunning it. There is little in all those speed books that doesn't confirm his elected persona again and yet again. The words on the top of one's head do not necessarily come from anywhere near the subconscious.

Kerouac's manicness was a necessary strategy for fighting off the forest-dark, French-American glooms. He had been mustered out of the Navy in 1942 as a schizoid personality; and even allowing for the pin-the-tail-on-the-diagnoses of those days, the Navy may have been onto something. But what for him was therapy became for himself and others aesthetic doctrine. Everybody else was buying electric gadgets and pressure cookers, so why not pressure poetry? Charles Olson of the Black Mountain school talked about poems in terms of pure energy discharge. Ginsberg and Burroughs were fascinated with electronics, neural patterns, molecular structures, etc.; and it seemed for a while that the years that gave us IBM would also give us an electromagnetic literature to match, with readers fried and hopping to volts of poetenergy.

Kerouac's type of manicness could also be harnessed by a generation to another preoccupation of the time—the advertising style. Burroughs for one was fascinated by Madison Avenue and talked of a merger between art and selling—of artistic commercials, packed with glittering juxtapositions. Beat euphoria fit beautifully into the spiel of the postwar pitchman. *Howl,* for all its originality, has some of the cadence of advertising slogans. And such Ginsbergian combos as "hydrogen jukebox" or "skin of machinery" are just what copywriters still grope for through the Westport night.

There were other things in the air that could use Kerouacian energy for booster fuel. The celebration of the low-life ordinary, after the neurasthenic strangeness of war, was one such; the need to sell, to convert, to make like Bishop Sheen or Arthur Godfrey was another. Poetry could be used for incantation, and Ginsberg worked out a theory of metrics based on breath and body rhythm that would have also been ideal for pop preaching. It suited him, so long as he was there to read the poems himself. But the tyranny of breath had bad effects on less gifted cantors. It meant that poems could be read only one way. It also meant that what the eye, moving faster than the lungs, saw on the page was flat as a song lyric without music. (Traditional metrics also allowed for breath, but gave you a greater choice of tempos.)

The hottest thing on the 1940-1950s' agenda was the urge to defy the Academy, which had grown flabby and remote as academies will, and had made the practice of Art seem a hopelessly difficult penance. But just as the first Reformers spoke excellent Latin, so were the first Beats well-read Ivy Leaguers. Burroughs of Harvard was the teacher, Ginsberg, with straight A's in history, and Kerouac, a bilingual dropout and campus-sniffer, willing to talk literary theory forever, were the pupils. Later they picked their own Villon, Gregory Corso, troubador, boy-criminal, prison, *and* a trace of Harvard, an exquisite literary touch.

But once the walls were down, there were plenty of visi-Goths ready to swarm in. Why shouldn't everyone write poetry? It went with the GI Bill and the open roads. Never mind Ginsberg's breath metrics (a new academy in the making) or the rigors of the best Black Mountaineers. They dug Kerouac's mood and Ginsberg's use of private subject matter and thought that was all there was to it. The air was thick with confessions right then, movie stars becoming nuns, Communists becoming pigeons, everyone cleaning the plate for the New Age, so there was subject matter to burn. And the new open-admissions policy to poetry produced a situation comparable only to the land grab in Oklahoma: Sooners racing each other for the big homosexual admission turf or the junk and jazz concession. Philip Lamantia, reaching far out, was knocked off a park bench by an angel.

The hip Sooners grabbed up the earth in no time and reached for the sky. Kerouac still led the charge, war-whooping through Zen Buddhism, opening up Hinduism for trade, and wheeling back to Christianity. But when there was no sky left for the untalented, a plague fell on his young followers; and the speechless poet, the cool beatnik, with nothing to offer but Attitude, landed amoung them. The postwar world was over, and all the balloons came down together. Kerouac turned away in disgust. "I don't want any beatniks on my milk route," he muttered and stomped back to his beginnings in Lowell, Massachusetts. He couldn't even stop off at a university as an over-the-hill romantic should. "Success means 5,000 English instructors sneering at you," he said. There was no place to go but home.

I wouldn't propose this is strict chronological history. These things were happening at once, or backward, depending on which coffee house you went to. But the Beautiful Dream of everyone being a poet woke to an awful hangover at some point. Where it might have led to a love of poetry, whether you could write it or not, it led to a lofty, if-I-can't-do-it,-it-can't-be-worth-doing silence. The Beats had always been too clannish, listening to each other in indigestible earfuls, and they wound up bored stiff with poetry. Since they were too loyal to blame each other (only an older man like Rexroth could do that) they, or their young imitators, blamed poetry instead and said that words were just inadequate and even called on the wisdom of the East to bear them out (though no one chatters like an Indian holy man with a head of steam).

LSD completed the route, blasting away the last vestiges of the neurotic perfectionism that even a speed writer needs, only needs faster. Acid-heads may or may not continue to write—their tongues are sometimes loosed to flapping point—but they don't sweat so hard for the word that will make *you* see: because they see it so easily, and you'll never see it.

Writers afflicted with vocation would refuse to enter heaven itself if they couldn't describe it afterwards. They'd rather stay in hell with words. So the Beats dropped out of their own movement. Burroughs, the ex-junkie, shied away from LSD and insists you can't write anything on drugs. Kerouac stuck with his port jug, trying to find the word in a million that would save him; and Corso still plugs along on his own, no part of Timothy Leary's drug spectacular. The Beats were, goddamit, a literary movement, of whatever quality; and whatever Leary's running, it isn't literary. Just talkative.

That leaves the other founding father, Allen Ginsberg, in charge of the old ship, Beat. Ginsberg is quoted in Cook's book trendily pooh-poohing verbal communication and, more dishearteningly, prating about ecology. (Couldn't a poet find another word?) Allen may just be trying something new, his hair-trigger sense of history responding to every feather breath of fashion, or he may be happy to be out of the hell of words at last.

Watching him lately on TV chanting like a beaming choir master to a group of baffled self-conscious-looking kids, I thought how far he'd come from the blind-rat maze of *Howl* and the screaming nightsweats of *Kaddish*. He thought he'd seen the best minds of his generation destroyed even before he'd started and, since then, he'd seen Kerouac's destroyed for real and had wept at his friend's grave and had seen his own very nearly destroyed several times over; and I thought, you've probably earned your chant, even if the audience hasn't.

And there in the background, doing anonymous penance on the guitar, was Bob Dylan. By current change rates, the Beats actually had some staying power. The gelatinous Eisenhower years could have slowed down mercury itself. And the Beats outlasted any pop fashion we are likely to see soon. (pp. 110-15)

> *Wilfrid Sheed, "Beat Down and Beatific," in his* The Good Word & Other Words, *E. P. Dutton, 1978, pp. 110-15.*

FURTHER READING

I. Anthologies

Feldman, Gene, and Gartenberg, Max, eds. *The Beat Generation and the Angry Young Men.* New York: Citadel Press, 1958, 384 p.
> Reprints selections from the works of such Beat writers as John Clellon Holmes, Jack Kerouac, Chandler Brossard, William S. Burroughs, Carl Solomon, and Allen Ginsberg. Also includes critical essays by Kenneth Rexroth, Walter Allen, Norman Mailer, John Holloway, and Geoffrey Gorer.

Krim, Seymour, ed. *The Beats.* Greenwich, Conn.: Fawcett Publications, 1960, 339 p.
> Selections from the works of various Beat writers and critical essays about the Beats.

Meltzer, David, ed. *The San Francisco Poets.* New York: Ballantine Books, 1971, 224 p.
> Interviews with and selections from the works of Kenneth Rexroth, William Everson (Brother Antoninus), Lawrence Ferlinghetti, Lew Welch, Michael McClure, and Richard Brautigan.

Parkinson, Thomas, ed. *A Casebook on the Beat.* New York: Thomas Y. Crowell Co., 1961, 326 p.

> Reprints selections from the works of Allen Ginsberg, Jack Kerouac, Gregory Corso, William S. Burroughs, Lawrence Ferlinghetti, Gary Snyder, Philip Whalen, Michael McClure, and John Wieners, as well as criticism and commentary on the Beat movement by various authors.

Wilentz, Elias, ed. *The Beat Scene.* New York: Corinth Books, 1960, 185 p.
> Selections from the works of forty-five Beat writers with an introduction by the editor and photographs by Fred McDarrah.

II. Secondary Sources

Bartlett, Lee, ed. *The Beats: Essays in Criticism.* Jefferson, N.C.: McFarland, 1981, 237 p.
> Reprints critical essays on Beat writers by John Clellon Holmes, William L. Stull, R. G. Peterson, Albert Gelpi, L. A. Ianni, James Breslin, Thomas S. Merrill, Barbara Christian, George Dardess, Thomas Parkinson, Robert Kern, Geoffrey Thurley, and William Everson.

Berrigan, Ted. "The Art of Fiction XLI: Jack Kerouac." *The Paris Review* 11, No. 43 (Summer 1968): 61-105.
> Interview with Jack Kerouac, who discusses *On the Road,* fiction, poetry, religion, and the disintegration of the Beat movement.

Burns, Jim. "Yugen." *Poetry Information,* London 16 (Winter 1976/77): 39-41.
> Publication history of the journal *Yugen,* in which the editor Amiri Baraka (then LeRoi Jones) published works of many Beat writers between 1958 and 1962.

Butler, Frank A. "On the Beat Nature of Beat." *The American Scholar* 30, No. 1 (Winter 1960-61): 79-92.
> Unfavorable assessment of the Beat writers. Butler comments: "May the Beat Generation dissolve in its froth, and may its members find something sane to do with themselves."

Cassady, Carolyn. *Heart Beat: My Life with Jack & Neal.* Berkeley, Calif.: Creative Arts Book Co., 1976, 93 p.
> Recalls her involvement with Beat Generation in the early 1950s when she was married to Neal Cassady.

———. *Off the Road: My Years with Cassady, Kerouac, and Ginsberg.* New York: William Morrow and Co., 1990, 436 p.
> Autobiography by the former wife of Neal Cassady, who recounts her association with Cassady, Jack Kerouac, and Allen Ginsberg.

Charters, Samuel. *Some Poems/Poets: Studies in American Underground Poetry since 1945.* Berkeley, Calif.: Oyez, 1971, 118 p.
> Collection of essays focusing on the poetry of Charles Olson, Jack Spicer, Robert Duncan, Gary Snyder, Lew Welch, Allen Ginsberg, Lawrence Ferlinghetti, Robert Creeley, William Everson (Brother Antoninus), and Larry Eigner.

Cherkovski, Neeli. *Whitman's Wild Children.* Venice, Calif.: Lapis Press, 1988, 261 p.
> Discusses the influence of Walt Whitman on ten poets, including such writers associated with the Beat movement as John Wieners, Philip Lamantia, Bob Kaufman, Allen Ginsberg, William Everson (Brother Antoninus),

Gregory Corso, Harold Norse, and Lawrence Ferlinghetti.

Ciardi, John. "Epitaph for the Dead Beats." *The Saturday Review* 43, No. 6 (6 February 1960): 11-13, 42.
Unfavorable assessment of the Beat movement as both an intellectual and literary revolution.

Cook, Bruce. *The Beat Generation.* New York: Charles Scribner's Sons, 1971, 248 p.
History of the Beat movement.

Esler, Anthony. " 'I Saw the Best Minds of My Generation Starving Hysterical Naked . . . ': The Beats and the Angries, Both Sides of the Iron Curtain, 1950." In his *Bombs, Beards, and Barricades: 150 Years of Youth in Revolt,* pp. 214-34. New York: Stein and Day, 1971.
Discusses the youth revolution around the world during the 1950s and the Beat movement in the United States, noting that a number of supposed "squares" shared the beatnik contempt for middle-class values.

Glicksberg, Charles I. "The Rage of Repudiation: Polemic of Beats." *Southwest Review* 45, No. 4 (Autumn 1960): 338-44.
Criticizes the Beat writers for their opposition to tradition and restraint and for their fascination with criminal behavior. Glicksberg asserts that "with the exception of Clellon Holmes, the beat generation writers lack the patience that creation demands. Their epiphanies are born of marijuana or neurosis. There is no promise of flowering and fulfilment in a literature that springs from psychopathic negation" and predicts that the Beat literature will be forgotten by 1975.

Holmes, John Clellon. *Representative Men: The Biographical Essays.* Selected Essays, vol. 2. Fayetteville: University of Arkansas Press, 1988, 277 p.
Includes essays on Allen Ginsberg, Jack Kerouac, and Neal Cassady.

————. *Passionate Opinions: The Cultural Essays.* Selected Essays, vol. 3. Fayetteville: University of Arkansas Press, 1988, 273 p.
Reprints essays discussing various aspects of the Beat movement, including "The Name of the Game," "This Is the Beat Generation," "The Philosophy of the Beat Generation," "The Game of the Name," and "The Beat Poets."

Hynes, Sam. "The Beat and the Angry." *The Commonweal* 68, No. 23 (5 September 1958): 559-61.
Argues that the tendency to classify American and British writers of the 1950s as "Beat" and "Angry" is oversimplistic and arises from a desire to provide convenient labels for complex social changes.

Jacobson, Dan. "America's 'Angry Young Men': How Rebellious Are the San Francisco Rebels?" *Commentary* 24, No. 6 (December 1957): 475-79.
Asserts that the Beat writers have failed to perceive American life accurately, and that their rebellious lifestyle is based on these faulty observations.

Jones, LeRoi; Fitelson, David; and Podhoretz, Norman. "Correspondence: The Beat Generation." *Partisan Review* 25, No. 3 (Summer 1958): 472-79.
Letters by Jones and Fitelson criticizing Podhoretz's essay "The Know-Nothing Bohemians" (cited below), followed by a rebuttal from Podhoretz.

Kherdian, David. *Six Poets of the San Francisco Renaissance: Portraits and Checklists.* Fresno, Calif.: Giligia Press, 1967, 183 p.
Character sketches and bibliographies of primary and secondary sources for Lawrence Ferlinghetti, Gary Snyder, Philip Whalen, David Meltzer, Michael McClure, and William Everson (Brother Antoninus).

Knight, Arthur, and Knight, Kit, eds. *Kerouac and the Beats: A Primary Sourcebook.* New York: Paragon House, 1988, 272 p.
Collection of interviews with, letters by, and statements about the Beat movement with a foreword by John Tytell.

Krim, Seymour. "A Backward Glance O'er Beatnik Roads." *TriQuarterly* 43 (Fall 1978): 324-37.
Discusses Krim's involvement with Beat publishing and editing, including his anthology *The Beats* (cited above), and the Beat influence on contemporary prose, poetry, and journalism.

La Barre, Weston. "Countertransference and the Beatniks." In his *Culture in Context: Selected Writings of Weston La Barre,* pp. 276-85. Durham, N.C.: Duke University Press, 1980.
Discusses Beatnik subculture from an anthropological point of view.

Lipton, Lawrence. *The Holy Barbarians.* New York: Julian Messner, 1959, 328 p.
Examines life among "disaffiliated" members of the Beat Generation in Venice, California.

McClure, Michael. *Scratching the Beat Surface.* San Francisco: North Point Press, 1982, 175 p.
Collection of essays discussing Beat poetry.

McDarrah, Fred W., ed. *Kerouac and Friends: A Beat Generation Album.* New York: William Morrow, 1985, 338 p.
Reprints various journalistic and critical essays on the Beat Generation by such writers as Art Buchwald, John Clellon Holmes, Lawrence Lipton, Jack Kerouac, Diana Trilling, Norman Podhoretz. Also includes photographs by the editor and a *Mad Magazine* satire on the Beats.

Michelson, Peter. "On *The Purple Sage, Chicago Review,* and *Big Table.*" *TriQuarterly* 43 (Fall 1978): 340-75.
Explains how University of Chicago censorship of the *Chicago Review* for publishing the works of Beat writers led to the foundation of the journal *Big Table.*

O'Neil, Paul. "The Only Rebellion Around: But the Shabby Beats Bungle the Job in Arguing, Sulking and Bad Poetry." *Life* 47, No. 22 (30 November 1959): 114-16, 119-20, 123-24, 126, 129-30.
Unfavorable assessment of the Beat movement. O'Neil characterizes the majority of Beat writers as "undisciplined and slovenly amateurs who have deluded themselves into believing their lugubrious absurdities are art" and concludes his examination of the Beat life-style by commenting "A hundred million squares must ask themselves: 'What have we done to deserve this?' "

Plummer, William. *The Holy Goof: A Biography of Neal Cassady.* Englewood Cliffs, N.J.: Prentice-Hall, 1981, 162 p.
Study focusing on Cassady, "the muse of the Beat Generation," whose madcap adventures and rambling letters

influenced the style and subject matter of Beat literature, especially the works of Kerouac and Ginsberg.

Podell, Albert N. "Censorship on the Campus: The Case of the *Chicago Review*." *San Francisco Review* 1, No. 2 (Spring 1959): 71-87.
Recounts the circumstances surrounding the censorship of the *Chicago Review,* which was criticized for publishing "obscene" works by Beat writers.

Podhoretz, Norman. "The Know-Nothing Bohemians." *Partisan Review* 25, No. 2 (Spring 1958): 305-11, 313-16, 318.
Condemns the anti-intellectual stance of Beat writers and the criminal delinquency of the Beat Generation.

Pritchett, V. S. "The Beat Generation." *The New Statesman* 56, No. 1434 (6 September 1958): 292, 294, 296.
Unfavorable overview of the Beat writers that contrasts the Beat Generation with the earlier Lost Generation.

Rexroth, Kenneth. "San Francisco's Mature Bohemians." *Nation,* New York 184, No. 8 (23 February 1957): 159-62.
Describes the social environment of the San Francisco poetry renaissance and discusses the works of several major poets associated with the area, including William Everson (Brother Antoninus), Robert Duncan, Allen Ginsberg, Philip Lamantia, Lawrence Ferlinghetti, and Michael McClure.

————. "Disengagement: The Art of the Beat Generation." *New World Writing,* No. 11 (May 1957): 28-41.
Traces the influence of music, art, and literature on works by members of the Beat Generation.

Rigney, Francis J., and Smith, L. Douglas. *The Real Bohemia.* New York: Basic Books, 1961, 250 p.
Sociological study of Beats living in San Francisco. Using observations from field work in the Beat "scene" and the results of individual psychological testing, the authors examine the relationship between Beats and society and the creativity of Beat artists.

Snyder, Gary. " 'Notes on the Beat Generation' and 'The New Wind'. " *American Poetry* 2, No. 1 (Fall 1984): 44-51.
Reprints two essays originally published in Japanese in 1960 that were "written to introduce the poetry and cultural phenomena of the beat generation to the Japanese intelligentsia of the very early sixties."

Stephenson, Gregory. *The Daybreak Boys: Essays on the Literature of the Beat Generation.* Carbondale and Edwardsville: Southern Illinois University Press, 1990, 216 p.
Critical essays focusing on the works of Jack Kerouac, Allen Ginsberg, William S. Burroughs, Gregory Corso, John Clellon Holmes, Michael McClure, Richard Fariña, and Lawrence Ferlinghetti. Also includes an introductory overview of the development of the Beat movement and a study of fictional characters based on Neal Cassady.

Tytell, John. "The Beat Brotherhood." In *Essaying Biography: A Celebration for Leon Edel,* edited by Gloria G. Fromm, pp. 105-23. Hawaii: University of Hawaii Press, 1986.
Biographical discussion of William S. Burroughs, Jack Kerouac, and Allen Ginsberg.

Van Ghent, Dorothy. *Wagner Literary Magazine* (Spring 1959): 27-8.
Briefly describes the archetypal Beat protagonist.

Wilentz, Ted, and Zavatsky, Bill. "Behind the Writer, Ahead of the Reader: A Short History of Corinth Books." *Tri-Quarterly* 43 (Fall 1978): 595-613.
History of Corinth Books, which published the works of many writers associated with the Beat movement between 1959 and 1973.

Czechoslovakian Literature of the Twentieth Century

INTRODUCTION

Twentieth-century Czechoslovakian literature has been highly influenced by the nation's turbulent political history. Located between more militarily powerful countries, the Czechs and Slovaks have experienced annexations, occupations, and political coercion during various periods of the century by the Austro-Hungarian Empire, Nazi Germany, and the Soviet Union, circumstances which led to the frequent suppression of works of Czechoslovakian authors as well as the creation of subcultures of émigré and underground Czech writers. In the country's eras of democratic autonomy and liberalized communist government, however, Czech literature has flourished and contributed openly and influentially to modern European culture. The modern history of Czechoslovakia, some critics assert, has shaped characteristic qualities of the nation's literature, including a distrust of centralized authority and official language, and a prevalence of black humor and irony.

The regions that comprise the nation of Czechoslovakia—Bohemia, Moravia, and Slovakia—were governed by the dual monarchy of the Austro-Hungarian Empire through World War I, and commentators generally refer to the attainment of Czechoslovakia's political independence in 1918 as resulting in the first significant works of the nation's modern literature. During the next decade novels by Jaroslav Hašek and Franz Kafka, the latter a Jewish author who lived in Prague and wrote primarily in German, were published, and these works significantly influenced subsequent Czech fiction. In Hašek's picaresque novel *Osudy dobrého vojáka Švejka za světové války* (1921-23; *The Good Soldier Švejk and His Fortunes in the World War*), the protagonist outwits the Austrian army into which he has been conscripted, and he has been viewed by many as representative of the average Czech who sought to undermine foreign authority. The major novels by Kafka, *Der Prozess* (1925; *The Trial*) and *Das Schloss* (1926; *The Castle*), present central characters who futilely attempt to comprehend labyrinthine organizations and bureaucracies that circumscribe their lives. For such works Kafka is considered one of the most prominent authors of twentieth-century literature. The most significant Czech literary figure during the interwar era was Karel Čapek, a friend of the First Republic president, Tomáš Garrigue Masaryk, and an advocate of moderate, democratic politics who warned of the capacity of technology to undermine humanity in works that include the drama *R.U.R. (Rossum's Universal Robots)* (1921) and the novel *Válka s mloky* (1936; *War with the Newts*). Throughout the 1920s and 1930s the works of other Czech authors blended avant-garde trends that predominated in Western Europe and Soviet Russia, incorporating the aesthetics of Dadaism, Russian Futurism, and Proletarianism in such Czech variations as the literary circle Devětsil and the

movements of Vitalism and Poetism, all of which stressed the unconscious, spontaneous imagination, the literary use of popular culture, and Marxist-Leninist politics. The poetry of Vítězslav Nezval perhaps best characterizes these currents in Czech literature and, eventually affiliated with Surrealism, Nezval emphasized the revolutionary nature of both experimental literature and communism. A number of authors, including the novelists Marie Majerová, Marie Pujmanová, and Vladislav Vančura, and the poets Jaroslav Seifert and Jiří Wolker, similarly focused on proletarian protagonists and espoused left-wing politics.

Nazi Germany invaded and occupied Bohemia and Moravia in 1939, and the government that they established there, as well as the quisling government in Slovakia, proscribed the works of and frequently imprisoned Czechoslovakian authors. As a result, few significant works of literature were published in the nation during this period. Following the Second World War, Czechoslovakia was liberated from the Nazis by the Soviet Union and in 1948 engaged in a political alliance with the USSR. Subsequently, under the cultural policies of Soviet leader Joseph Stalin, censorship of literature in Czechoslovakia and the other Soviet-controlled states in Central and Eastern Europe was stringent, and Czech authors were compelled to adhere to the literary tenets of Socialist Realism. This state-sanctioned school of fiction emphasized the role of literature as an educational, propagandistic tool, requiring literary works to feature straightforward support of the Communist party, conventional literary techniques clearly comprehensible to a lower-class reading public, proletarian characters, and optimistic denouements. As with Czech literature produced during Nazi rule, few noteworthy works by Czech authors were published during the Stalinist period. Stalin died in 1953 and was denounced three years later by his successor, Nikita Khrushchev, an event that served to gradually relax many of the prohibitions placed on literature in Eastern bloc countries during the late 1950s. In Czechoslovakia, however, partially due to the publication of Josef Škvorecký's irreverent portrayal of national events during the conclusion of World War II in his novel *Zbabělci* (1958; *The Cowards*), governmental censorship of literature and the purging of cultural institutions were reimplemented.

Throughout the 1960s the Czechoslovakian government liberalized its policies on literature and the arts, and the period from the middle of the decade until August 1968 is considered one of the most fruitful in twentieth-century Czech literature. Czech drama in particular contributed significantly to European avant-garde art during these years, and works by Václav Havel, Ivan Klíma, Milan Kundera, and Josef Topol are noted for experimental techniques that reflect the dark humor characteristic of the Theater of the Absurd, as well as the influence of Kafka's fiction. Novels of the period, such as Kundera's

Žert (1967; *The Joke*) and Ludvík Vaculík's *Sekyra* (1966; *The Axe*), feature previously proscribed experimentation with literary technique and convey a strong disillusionment with the Communist government of the Stalinist era. Commentators observe that major works of these years, combined with the demands for uncensored artistic expression and political freedom by writers within the Union of Czechoslovak Writers, considerably influenced the replacement of Antonín Novotny as head of the Communist party with the more moderate Alexander Dubček in January 1968. This event commenced what has been denoted the "Prague Spring," a period between January and August of 1968 when both political and cultural constraints on Czechoslovakian citizens were greatly lessened.

Under the Dubček government the Prague Spring resulted in an unprecedented number of publications and productions of internationally acclaimed Czech fiction and drama. Russian and East European armies, however, invaded Czechoslovakia in August under the orders of the Soviet government, terminating the liberalization period and initiating the emigration of numerous Czech authors and intellectuals to Western European and North American countries. Throughout the 1970s and 1980s émigré writers produced much of what critics regard as the most significant contemporary Czech literature, including novels by Kundera and Škvorecký, and the dramas of Pavel Kohout. Within Czechoslovakia the cultural policies of the Soviet-supported president, Gustáv Husák, severely curtailed the ability of authors to publish uncensored works, creating what have been termed "parallel cultures": the "official" Czech culture, consisting of authors and journalists condoned by the government and permitted to publish, and a "dissident" culture of writers frequently silenced by the state. The latter group of authors typically had their works published abroad in translation, or in Czech through such publishing houses as Sixty-Eight Publishers, founded in Toronto by Škvorecký's wife, Zdena Salivarová. In Czechoslovakia banned works were often clandestinely produced through carbon-copied *samizdat* ("self-made") editions, the most notable written as part of the *Edice petlice* ("Edition Padlock") series. Critics note that in spite of the restrictive cultural climate of the nation during this time, works by "dissident" writers, including dramas by Havel and the fiction and plays of Klíma, have significantly contributed to contemporary Czech literature. While many commentators view works by Czech authors writing in exile and those published in *samizdat* form as comprising the country's most praiseworthy literature of the 1970s and 1980s, some also maintain that "official" Czech literature need not be automatically discounted. Authors approved by the Communist government, most notably the poet Miroslav Holub and the novelist and short story writer Bohumil Hrabal, have also received praise for creditable works of contemporary literature.

In January 1977, numerous Czech authors and intellectuals formed Charter 77, an organization which demanded governmental adherence to the human rights of Czechoslovakian citizens. Many of the writers who supported Charter 77, including spokesperson Havel, were sentenced to prison terms as a result of their democratic activism, and state censorship heightened throughout the next ten years. During the late 1980s, however, the government of the Soviet Union became liberalized under Mikhail Gorbachev through processes termed *glasnost* ("openness") and *perestroika* ("restructuring"), which subsequently loosened Soviet control over Czechoslovakia's internal affairs. Political pressures in Czechoslovakia from university students, liberal members of the country's Communist party, and public demonstrators in 1989 instigated what has been termed the "Velvet Revolution" of that year, during which the Communist leaders resigned and the country adopted a democratic form of government. In the national election that followed Havel was voted president of the country. The literary results of the Velvet Revolution in Czechoslovakia have included the abolishment of censorship laws and of state restrictions on publishing houses, allowing numerous previously banned works to appear.

CZECH LITERATURE THROUGH WORLD WAR II

Jiří Škvor

[*In the following essay, Škvor examines the influence of World War I on the fiction, poetry, and drama of early twentieth-century Czech authors.*]

The 19th century has been called the "Age of Anxiety". The First World War was, in a way, an echo of this anxiety. Social instability and anxiety always take the upper hand when spiritual support is lacking. The time shortly before the First World War was just such a time in the history of mankind.

World War I shook European cultural life. It undermined spiritual and material stability, caused cultural and social chaos, and introduced into the whole civilized world a revolution of mind and thought. From the horror and misery of war sprang a realization of the absurdity of life. Nihilism spread into other spheres of life besides the purely cultural. It appeared that humanity lost its inner security and unity; that it was split into several personalities in conflict with one other, and that the obscure powers of the subconscious predominated.

If we analyze the main works of literature from the era of World War I, we find a spontaneous negation of war, of its absurdity and cruelty. Let me mention, for instance, the novels by Erich Maria Remarque (*All Quiet on the Western Front*), by Arnold Zweig (*Die Erziehung vor Verdun*), by Ernest Hemingway (*A Farewell to Arms*), by Romain Rolland (*Lucienne*), Henri Barbusse (*Le feu*), Georges Duhamel's *Vie des martyrs,* and *Les croix de bois* by Roland Dorgeles.

The First World War tested the ethical equilibrium of a great part of the world. Many times it appeared that a materialistic concept of life had come to dominate each individual soul. The writers engaged on the battlefield and the writers on the "home front" both felt that they fought not only for themselves, but also for the collective soul of the nation.

The role of Czech writers was even more difficult since they had to fight on two fronts without betraying their real aims. On the home front, Czech poets had to make a pretence of supporting the "Two-headed eagle", the symbol of Austro-Hungarian monarchy. In the trenches of the battlefield, Czech writers were paradoxically fighting for their own defeat. Deceit and passivity, so well exposed by Jaroslav Hašek in his *Good Soldier Schweik,* became the most powerful weapon of the Czech soldier dressed in the Austro-Hungarian uniform.

In contrast to many other national literatures, the first literature produced in independent Czechoslovakia was not affected by the influence of decadence, nihilism, or direct morality to the extent that it interrupted the existing character of Christian humanism, religion, or patriotic tradition. The sober, rather analytical Czech spirit submitted all foreign literary influences to a rigorous acid test.

The War brought the old controversy between individualism and collectivism to a climax. In the immense "war machine", the human being became a smaller cog than ever. Armies consisting of millions of such cogs influenced the individual by their very massiveness. Under these circumstances, soldier-writers lost the sense of being separate individuals. They felt that even birth, conflict, and death were events which happened collectively. The War thus helped in the formation of "herds"; in dehumanization and de-individualization. A mass psychosis captured the human soul and its influence was clearly evident for a long time after the First World War.

Let us briefly examine some of the main themes, trends, and problems of the Czech war and first postwar literature. 1) The concept of a collective soul of the nation. 2) The love for the Czech country. 3) The active humanism of love of one's neighbour. (This humanism produced new heroes in Czech novels: doctors, nurses, priests, or just common soldiers as representatives of true "Kamaradschaft".) 4) The conflict between individualism and collectivism. 5) The new concept of Christian morality. (Many Czech writers turned toward the supernatural for salvation. They turned to the Omnipresent God who sees everything; to the Merciful God who is always close to the wounded soldiers.) 6) The conflict between Slavonic humanism and messianism, on one hand, and German expansionism on the other. 7) Finally, the War witnessed the conflict between nationalistic and international ideas. (The main scene of this ideological fight was the Russian front, and a good documentary of the struggle is the so-called "Czech legionary literature.")

. . . . .

Poetry, primarily lyric poetry, very often gave a better picture of the tragedy of war than did prose. The political nature of Josef Svatopluk Machar's poetry and the nationalism in the poetry of Viktor Dyk, written during the most fateful hours of the war, are among the best testimonials to the close ties between Czech poets and the whole na-

tion. The patriotic voice of Karel Toman's poems belongs to the purest melodies ever produced in Czech poetry. The war not only emphasized the political duty of Czech poets, but also assisted in warming the lyrical melody which sounded in the war-verses of Petr Křička, Fráňa Šrámek, and Božena Benešová.

Czech poetry of the First World War proved again that each historical period has its own poets, and that it is poetry which most accurately reflects the state of mind and the feelings of a whole nation. That War marked the end of the decadent, introspective poetry which had flourished at the turn of the nineteenth century. It also heralded the advent of new literary trends and forms, such as surrealism, cubism, dadaism, poetism, and other foreign imports, the representative of which was especially Vítězslav Nezval.

The War gave quite a shock to the prevailing social order. A new social class—the proletariat—emerged to claim its right in literature. The proletarian note of the poetry of S. K. Neumann, Petr Bezruč, Jiří Wolker, and Josef Hora sounded with a revolutionary spirit and stressed the realistic relation between a worker and his personal environment.

The ordinary, simple man became the focal point of Czech war poetry. During the War, it was impossible "to dream, while sitting on the cloud of dreaming" (with Vítězslav Nezval), or to look for literary themes in an artificially constructed situation. The poets tried to soothe and heal the wounds; they tried to effect moral reforms which would preclude any future war.

During the First World War, their analytic spirit made Czech poets aware of the fact that in the future the Czech nation would play an important part in the cultural exchange between the West and the East. The traditional preference for Western ideas could be explained also by Czech interest in new poetical forms. Nevertheless, new currents started intruding from the East. The Russian October Revolution and the influence of Blok, Maiakovsky, Briusov, and Lunacharsky could be given most of the credit for the birth and growth of the new trend in Czech proletarian poetry.

The lyric note in the proletarian poetry of Josef Hora and Jiří Wolker on one hand, and the proletarian cosmopolitanism and technical civilization depicted most clearly in the poetry of S. K. Neumann, on the other were direct products of the social changes caused by the War.

From the pressure of war there also grew a new wave of humanism. This, however, became mostly the domain of poets of the older generation. The poetry of Christian humanism dreamed about the "holiness of poverty", about a world in which there would be no more hunger, no more suffering, no more war. To this group of Czech poets belong the Catholic poets Jaroslav Durych and Jan Zahradníček, and partly, also the mystic, Otakar Březina, as well as Božena Benešová, and Jan Čep.

A new resurgence of vitalism in poetry was the natural reaction of men whose lives had often been saved by hardly a hair's breadth. Many poets advocated full enjoyment of life. This tendency was complemented by a renewed cult of the "return to the nature", which resounded so vigorously in the poems of sensitive sensuality by Fráňa Šrámek, and S. K. Neumann.

The First World War enriched Czech poetry in many ways; it brought new themes, new scenery, new dynamics of imagination, new, subtle, lyrical half-tones. From a true picture of social reality to the most complicated feelings which are difficult to express in words, the gamut of Czech poetry rapidly broadened.

. . . . .

The First World War also exerted a remarkable influence on the development of Czech prose. It gave birth to a thematically new and ethically significant "literature of legions", which showed clearly the contribution of the Czech and Slovak people to their nations' fight for liberation and political self-determination. The literary works of Rudolf Medek, Josef Kopta, František Langer, and F. V. Krejčí are descriptions of an enforced war, a glorification of the just and victorious fight of Czech and Slovak soldiers. Czech patriotism and idealism clashed here with Marxist internationalism, the ideals of humanitarian democracy faced godless Communism and violence.

A unique product of Czech war prose is Jaroslav Hašek's *Good Soldier Schweik*. This work is just the opposite of the "literature of legions" in its ethos and morality.

The main works of Czech prose dating from the period of the First World War show the penetrating influence of war on the typical individual environment: urban, rural, proletarian. Many of the Czech war novels, as, for instance, *Pole orná a válečná* (*The Ploughed Fields and the Battlefields*) by Vladislav Vančura, the war-trilogy *Železný kruh*, (*The Iron Circle*) by Karel Nový, and *Černá země* (*Black Earth*) by Vojtěch Martínek, belong to the best of modern Czech literature.

Under the impact of war, Czech writers focused their sights on particular strata of Czech society and on its structure. In contrast to the criteria which served the realists of the sixties and the later years of the nineteenth century, the judgment of postwar authors was much more realistic and critical.

War revealed the deepest inner character of the Czech peasants—not only their sacrifices, but also their egotism and greed; the desire to become rich to the detriment of their fellow men. A critical look at the authors of the war period reveals all these vices and shows the foundation for the development of the modern Czech rural novel. The war offered the same opportunity to authors depicting urban life. They captured the disintegration of bourgeois classes and the forming of the industrial proletariat. In this respect, the writings of Marie Majerová and Marie Pujmanová are typical. The literary study of war by both these talented authors produced monumental social novels, as, for instance, *Lidé na křižovatce* (*The Men at the Crossroad*) by Marie Pujmanová and *Siréna* (*The Siren*) by Marie Majerová. The portrayal of a particular social environment and the analysis of the soul of the urban dweller, which are also characteristic of Czech war novels, are found in the works of Ivan Olbracht, Jaroslav Durych, J.

V. Rosůlek, Čestmír Jeřábek, Edmond Konrád, and several other authors.

The First World War thus contributed to a great diversification in theme and form. Ivan Olbracht showed intensified interest in the fate of disinherited human society in his novel, *O zlých samotářích* (*About Bad Misanthropes*); the war evoked interest in the social and family life of women, as, for example, in *Advent* by Jarmila Glazarová, or in *Úder* (*The Blow*), by Božena Benešová. Václav Řezáč was concerned with the fate of the young Czech generation growing up during the war in his novel *Větrná setba* (*Sowing in the Wind*). Jaromír John's memories of war are captured in a collection of short stories called *Večery na slamníku,* (*Evenings on a Palliasse*).

Catholic writers like Jaroslav Durych and Jakub Deml were inspired by war to seek deeply for solutions to metaphysical problems. The rural milieu which played such an important role, especially in the war novels of Karel Nový and Vladislav Vančura, attracted the attention of adherents of ruralism such as Josef Knap, František Křelina, Jan Čarek, J. V. Sedlák, Václav Prokůpek, and others. The first echo of this literary movement was heard in A. C. Nor's war novel, *Bürkental*. The ruralists emphasized the traditional elements and created a counterweight to the conventional urban literature.

The enormous upheaval of the war years almost completely suppressed a tendency toward a new type of romanticism and classicism. Historicism, as represented by Alois Jirásek, whose literary work was a source of national faith and belief in a national resurrection, was another trend of the postwar novel.

One of the most characteristic features of the early postwar Czech novels was the decline of pathetic heroism. Every pose was radically rejected and condemned. The heroism shown by the soldiers on the battlefield was more convincing than any type of artificial literary pathos.

Generally speaking, the Czech war novel was broader in scope; it described, not only the new social problems and the growing complexity of the whole social development, but also the relations and conflicts between those in different spheres of life and classes, and the characteristic problems of the new generation. Refined and daring analysis and poetic imagination started to throw light into the dark corners of human life, and one can read in war prose of issues like loss of memory, "split personality", and other psychological problems.

. . . . .

Relatively speaking, the First World War produced a poor harvest in Czech drama. Except for František Langer's *Jízdní hlídka* (*The Mounted Patrol*) and some works by Stanislav Lom, Jaroslav Hilbert, Viktor Dyk, Jiří Mahen, and Otokar Fischer, Czech drama had to await the pragmatic generation of Karel Čapek and its positive achievements.

Unfavourable political circumstances long prevented Czech drama from reaching the heart of the nation, since it was almost impossible to produce the plays. Austro-

Hungarian censorship was very much aware of the potential political impact of drama on the Czech people.

With a few exceptions, like Hilbert's *Job* and a few plays by Josef Kopta, Rudolf Medek, and Zdeněk Štěpánek, the War influenced Czech drama very little as far as the thematic point of view was concerned. Nevertheless, the tension and environment of war created an emotional setting for a great many dramas. In some of them, the historical theme was used only as a background against which problems of current national importance were set. On the other hand, what Czech drama lacked in abundance or dramatic vigour, it gained in lofty ethical views.

· · · · ·

Many new literary forms were developed immediately after the War. The War evoked these literary methods and forms by changing the current form of the individualistic novel and poetry. The War itself was an enormous collective act, sweeping away individualism, subjectivism, and decadence. It evoked multivocal social, class, and collective symphonies. The loosening of social and state barriers was followed by the invasion of a "new life". Man became part of higher national and international units, and this new trend left its imprint on literature. In the nineteenth century, the bourgeois type of individualistic novel reached its peak. The First World War caused the awakening of a new social class, the proletariat.

Another result of the War was an "epidemic" of literary pluralism; the switching of literary themes, scenes, and time designed for the purpose of capturing as much of life as possible. World literature, immediately after the War, was flooded with such "pluralistic" novels, as, for example, works by Sinclair Lewis, John Dos Passos, Lion Feuchtwanger, and others.

The War also brought forth a new wave of literary expressionism. To the expressionists, the entire world was in a chaotic state which was growing worse every day. The human soul, shattered to its very foundations, had transformed the world into a hectic vision which expressed horror on one hand and the desire for redemption on the other. In a formal sense, expressionism was the bridge to a number of other literary trends. Some of them were occasionally found in Czech literature before the First World War. The First World War created the opportunity for them to broaden and develop. This was especially true of surrealism, dadaism, cubism, and some other trends which never actually became deeply rooted in Czech literature. The works of Gide, Proust, Joyce, and Breton to mention a few of their main representatives, had a strong influence primarily on Czech poets like Nezval, Biebl, Halas, and Holan and on the early poems of Seifert. Their influence on Czech prose, however, was comparatively weak.

A more important influence was the pragmatism of scholars like William James. Pragmatism supplied Czech authors with material for the psychological analysis of the lives of war heroes. Its favorite subjects were the reconstruction of man's life, and the different versions of "truth" which pragmatism brought to this reconstruction.

Similarly, the subjects and images of symbolist poetry suggested a great deal. Symbolism was the revival of an apparently exhausted poetic vocabulary. The associative quality of symbolism was occasionally called "impressionism", a word used with a meaning analogous to its meaning in the music of the same period.

The First World War somewhat delayed the impact of foreign influence on Czech literature, as far as literary forms were concerned. Immediately after the War, the "Manifesto of Czech Poetism" appeared in Prague. Poetry became a kind of imaginative game in which there appeared chain associations — often illogical and paradoxical — and the association of ideas, images, and words.

There was a new emphasis on the lyrical, subjective, and spiritual elements of poetry, with a disposition to view its imaginative processes as existing, not merely to give pleasure, but for the pursuit of truth by means of intuition. There was a corresponding disposition to discard the formal rules of poetic art which had been taught since the period of romanticism, and to exalt in their stead an individual freedom and novelty of literary form. Extraordinary metrical variety, in contrast with the regularity and conservatism of the neoclassical schools, was also characteristic of the Czech poetry of the first postwar period. (pp. 962-69)

> *Jiří Škvor, "Czech Literature and the First World War," in* Čzechoslovakia Past and Present: Essays on the Arts and Sciences, Vol. II, *edited by Miloslav Rechcigl, Jr., Mouton, 1968, pp. 962-71.*

Milada Součková

[*In the following essay, Součková surveys Czech fiction and poetry from 1918 to 1950.*]

Czech literature reached a high point in its cultural development in the 1930's. It achieved a kind of balance as between Eastern and Western influences, a position that Czech political leaders later tried to recapture with the slogan "a bridge between East and West." In the Thirties, translations of Valéry as well as of Mayakovsky were under way; Czech intellectuals were as familiar with Šklovskij and Formalism as with Surrealism. The most important Czech poets of this period were: Vítězslav Nezval, Jaroslav Seifert, and František Halas.

In 1928, Vítězslav Nezval published a long poem, *Edison,* into which he projected his own boyhood dreams about the exotic land of Michigan and which he integrated by an "object," an image of antiquated technology, the first incandescent electric lamp, which for him was packed with associations. The novelty of Nezval's poem lay in its emancipation from the rhetorics of Parnassian and impressionist poetry; the effect of its trochaic meters, melodiously rhymed, was immediate. The critics, the public, and the poets themselves realized that those verses opened a new period of Czech poetry.

Shortly after the publication of *Edison,* however, partly under the influence of his friend Karel Teige (a literary and art critic), Nezval aligned himself with Surrealism.

For Nezval Surrealism facilitated an escape into adolescence, an escape in which the objects and places of the past spontaneously created a poetic mood. Surrealist dream-fantasy and the surrealistic arrangement of odd fragments of reality provided him with rich material for his work. Also the surrealist sentimentality, set off by the counterpoint of monstrous fantasy, suited Nezval's artistic temperament to perfection. Nezval became overly prolific, due perhaps to his too easy success, his lack of self-criticism, and he produced many second-rate works.

Nezval and Teige greatly furthered the inroads of Surrealism into Czech art. Surrealism became the rage in poetry, in stage settings, in art exhibitions, and in critical aesthetics. Translations from André Breton, as well as personal contacts with him, were part of the common experience of the new artistic *avant-garde.*

The leading figure of Czech prose was Karel Čapek, whose reputation paralleled that of Nezval in poetry. He dominated the literary scene, as writer, as an influential editor of the daily *Lidové noviny,* and as a political figure, the personal friend of President Masaryk. Indeed, the literary portrait *President Masaryk Tells His Story* will perhaps be read longer than any other of Čapek's works. With Masaryk, Čapek shared an attitude which the Czechoslovak president and scholar would call "realistic," and Čapek himself "pragmatist."

Čapek's pragmatic approach to life sustained his *Tales from One Pocket* and *Tales from the Other Pocket* (1929). As an artist, however, Čapek turned out to be too much the sophisticated intellectual to identify himself successfully with the behavior of the common man of his civilization. Čapek certainly observed common behavior intelligently, and had an ear for the colloquial. But there was always a deprecating smile behind his display of sympathy for human failings and virtues. His casual style, picked up in the street or in the editor's office, challenged the stiff literary cliché; but it did not explore beneath the surface of the everyday. Perhaps for this very reason, Čapek was more successful, artistically, in his abstract utopian novels, *The Absolute at Large, An Atomic Fantasy* (1924), or in his ideological dramas *R.U.R.* and *The Life of Insects* (1920).

Highly honored, unrivalled in reputation, he was nevertheless challenged by two men. They were Vladislav Vančura and Jaroslav Durych, who for different reasons sharply opposed Karel Čapek's *Weltanschauung.* Čapek's hero, the common man, implied for him a level of common sense that might serve as a corrective for both intellectual abstraction and emotional irrationality. What lay either below or above this common sense level was to be distrusted. There might be a kind of heroism hidden in some common deed, yet it should not be exaggerated. Vančura and Durych had quite another view. Vančura stressed extremity, both in emotion and language, as signs of vitality, and Durych saw a way of achieving either sanctity or damnation. Vančura's short stories *The Bow of Queen Dorothy* were published in the same year as Čapek's *Tales from One Pocket.* The very titles symbolize the oppositeness of the authors. Indeed, Vančura's *The Bow* often sounded like a distant echo of medieval prose. Mod-

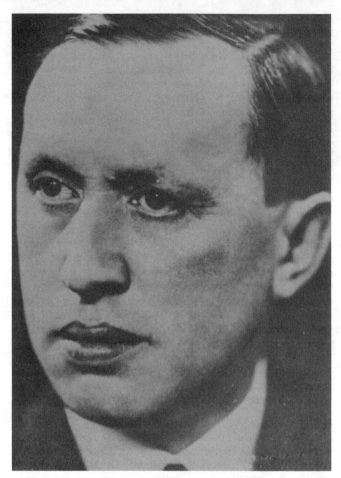

Karel Čapek.

ern Czech authors, following their temperaments and needs, aligned themselves under those two influences. Those who wrote traditional novels gladly accepted the rejuvenating influence of Čapek's colloquial style; others, reaching for a more monumental effect, or a more highly organized style, chose Vančura as a model.

Although there was a certain tendency to speak of Durych in the same breath as Čapek and Vančura, he never really attained their widespread popularity. His opposition to everything that was "official" in Czech literature deepened after the publication of his major work, *Bloudění* (1929), a Wallenstein trilogy, in which he stood for the unpopular view that the period of the Counter-Reformation in the Czech lands had not been an age of utter darkness. In 1938, after the collapse of the Czechoslovak state, Durych violently denounced Czech leftist intellectuals. Whatever might be said against him, particularly with regard to his verbal assault on T. G. Masaryk, he was never, at any rate, an opportunist.

The world political situation, especially since the German events of 1933, drove home to Czech writers that threats to their freedom were not remotely situated in some realm of pure ideology, but were on the very boundaries of their own country. Although they continued to write novels and poetry not very different from works of the previous decade, they became acutely aware of the danger. The year 1937 brought vague symptoms and forebodings into immediate focus. It was the year of T. G. Masaryk's death. Together with the headlines announcing this event, Jaroslav Seifert published a poem, "September the Fourteenth," which commemorated Masaryk's death as a prelude to impending European catastrophe.

In 1937 Karel Čapek wrote a play, called *The White Plague,* a pacifistic protest against the totalitarian state, obviously directed at Hitler's Germany. The play was produced on the stage of the National Theater, and was interpreted as a defense of Czech democracy. However, not only totalitarian Germany, or Italy, but the democratic Western powers, and especially the economic system of capitalism came under the suspicion of imperialism, which suffered totalitarian methods to be used in Abyssinia and in Spain.

In 1937, Bedřich Václavek published *Tvorbou k realitě* (*Reality and Creativity*), an orthodox Communist exposition of socialist realism. At that time, Czech writers saw in "socialist realism" a stress on content, as far as literature was concerned, as opposed to form; a counter to the aloofness of "art for art's sake." They thought fiction might help solve contemporary problems, might help provide the right kind of intellectual orientation. They never suspected socialist realism would some day become a compulsory totalitarian doctrine. Although many a Czech artist might have been apprehensive about Stalinist Russia's *volte-face* from progressive to reactionary art, Russian cultural policy, opportunist then as now, supporting Picasso in France, and Nezval or Vančura in Czechoslovakia, managed to veil the real meaning of Stalinist literary theory. Czech Communist writers were, on occasion, officially invited to Russia, and, unlike André Gide, returned with enthusiastic reports about the Communist country, its people and institutions. One of these was Marie Pujmanová. Her conversion to socialist realism, though not so spectacular and abrupt as that of Louis Aragon, was similar in character. Marie Pujmanová was one of the most talented of contemporary Czech writers, with a rare and unconventional vision of reality. In 1937, she published *The People at the Crossroads,* the first volume of a trilogy expounding socialism-communism in Czechoslovakia. The book was a literary event, hailed by critics, and awarded the state prize bestowed on honored artists.

Annexation of Austria, and Czech mobilization in May 1938, rocked the well-established foundations of the Czech literary world. The "pragmatic man" of Karel Čapek, the psychological introspection of some other novelists, seemed out of place: The country needed a hero. In 1938, in the year of his death, Karel Čapek wrote a play called *The Mother,* an outcry for the defense of his country. It was too late. In September, 1938, the Czech state collapsed, and literature sank into a state of desperate confusion. Nezval described the atmosphere of these days under the shadow of Munich: "The old country fell apart . . . Our old honor was being pawned."

The poet who seemed born for this particular situation was not so much Nezval himself but his younger contemporary, František Halas, whose poetry was often as raw as the humiliating experiences of the Czechs in the years 1938-1945. In general, the poetry written during this period intoned a continuous lament, interrupted by violent protests and accusations, and this was true of Halas, Nezval, and Holan, as well as less prominent poets. Except for Russia at the time of the Revolution, no other nation has produced in modern times a poetry so spontaneously and directly related to contemporary historical events. Halas was obsessed by the vision of a decaying Western Europe, old and thoroughly corrupted. The more the national sorrow of 1938 receded, the more his hatred turned against the Germans. His Underground mood, his fanatic resentment, his Communist sympathies with Russia were shared by men and women in prisons and concentration camps, some of them literary men, and many of them people who had never before thought of expressing themselves in poetry.

The poetry and prose written in prisons and concentration camps form one anonymous epic, one symptomatic document of our age. Written either by skilled writers such as Josef Čapek (the brother of Karel Čapek) or by an anonymous woman before entering a gas chamber, it testifies equally to the cruel degeneration of the jailers and the human integrity of their prisoners. This poetry was written under the menace of heavy punishment, often smuggled out by a warden, and has survived in anthologies, or in volumes of individual poetry, published after World War Two. The best known Czech document of this type *Notes from the Gallows* (translated into English, Russian, and French) was written by the Communist Julius Fučík who was executed in Berlin in 1943. In its documentary part and its strong self-discipline, *Notes from the Gallows* show that in our times neither the "right to happiness" nor intellectual aloofness are ideals that can make heroes.

A part of the Czech literary world suffered and died in German prisons and concentration camps, but the other part, in spite of the hardships of the German occupation, enjoyed a comparatively prosperous period. There were two reasons for this. First, Czech patriotism, barred from other modes of expression, fastened on the national literature as a kind of vicarious manifestation of the national spirit. Secondly, the [nation's] inflation created a very favorable market for books. At this time *Czech Gothic Painting,* an impressive folio with costly reproductions, was published and sold well. Popular novels like Eduard Bass's *Circus Umberto* were prized on the black market.

Many a better writer was silenced because of his previous involvement with the Communist party, or because of his Jewish origin, or again because of his close affiliation with the government of the First Czechoslovak Republic. Some of the authors used pseudonyms; others published little, and only with caution. Also many a new name rose to a doubtful prominence. In general, literature sought an escape either into a remote historical past that preserved encouraging examples of great exploits of the Czech nation or into the Victorian age, which on its side offered the soothing atmosphere of things harmless and innocent. Strangely enough, Czech literary interest in history was paralleled by an analogous tendency in Germany. For opposite reasons, both literatures explored their medieval history—the Germans for symbols supporting German ideology, the Czechs for symbols to fight it. Vančura's *Pictures from the History of the Czech Nation,* published in 1939 and 1940, represents the most characteristic and best work of this kind. Written in a manner which reminds one of the Czech renaissance style, *Pictures from the History of the Czech Nation* brought to the enslaved nation's vision the story of its past grandeur and also its sublimation, the grandeur of well-balanced, sonorous sentences. Other novels and stories fictionalizing history had far less merit, yet this genre continued to be popular with many writers, even after the liberation of Czechoslovakia in 1945.

When the day of liberation came, Czech literature greeted it in transports. In newspapers, which after six years of occupation were again free of German censorship, poems saluted Freedom and the Russian army. In verse as in newspaper headlines, the name of Stalin appeared. The enthusiasm of writers, such as Nezval, Seifert, Halas, Pujmanová, was quite sincere, at least in the first hours and days of the new freedom. After six years they were free to express their resentment with regard to the events of 1938-1945, and their hopes for a better future. The leading poets, joined by other, less prominent authors, greeted the Russian liberators, and the Revolution of May Fifth. František Hrubín, before the war an inconspicuous poet, figured as a centurion of the Revolution, a position he owed to his unreserved praise of Soviet Russia.

World War Two changed the Czech literary scene entirely. Čapek and Vančura were dead, Durych was branded a Fascist, and was as good as dead. Other writers of the older generation (such as Ivan Olbracht, who during the First Czechoslovak Republic was considered one of the finest stylists) were too old to produce; what they could still do and what some of them actually did, was to propagandize for the Communists.

In addition to those authors with an established name, there was a multitude of writers who had the ambition to fill in vacancies left by age, death, and change of situation. Many of them felt that now the writer's main task was to relate the events of recent history. The years 1938-1945 inside Czechoslovakia alone were regarded as matter sufficient for writing novels or short stories. The problem for the writer was therefore not subject matter but its presentation. Some authors chose documentary form; others, fiction. One wrote a novel about the May Revolution in the setting of a railway station in Prague, another published minutes of the Prague uprising. The Czech mobilization of 1938, the German occupation of the Sudetenland, or even more the story of the Czech Underground of World War Two were common subjects. Novels, instead of [depicting] individual characters, portrayed an anonymous newsreel crowd.

Another resolution for contemporary fiction lay in the direction of the "socialization" of the novel. The writer, either sincerely or opportunistically, believed that a socialist tendency inserted in the traditional form of the novel would speak for his "artistic responsibility," or protect him from negative Marxist criticism. Thus, authors sought to relate their novels to the nineteenth century socialism, or simply to create a socialist-oriented hero. The

present president of Czechoslovakia, Antonín Zápotocký, while he was still Premier, himself produced one of the worst examples of this kind of literature.

The political developments of the years 1945-1948 continued to affect Czech cultural affairs. In this period, during which the Iron Curtain was being drawn, a struggle went on, not between the Czech cultural Left and Right, as might have been expected, but between a kind of Titoist cultural resistance and the Comintern dictatorship. The polemic as to whether Czechs should accept Eastern-Soviet or Western cultural orientation served as a screen for the actual Communist drive for power. The literary critic Václav Černý fought gallantly for the Western tradition of Czech culture, opposed by the vigilant Communist press and by some obliging Czech scholars and literati. Parallel with Černý's articles, a group of young poets and critics, centered on the nonconformist new quarterly *Listy,* manifested their allegiance to the West, i.e., to the right to have access to Western culture. This *avant-garde* translated T. S. Eliot, discussed Existentialism, and wrote modern poetry. Ivan Blatný, who later sought asylum in London, was the outstanding poet of this group. Although under a strain, such "opposition" to the Communist dictate continued until the Communist coup of 1948, when Western heretics and cultural "Titoists" were wiped out.

From 1945, and even more strongly after 1948, the leader of the Communist *Kulturkampf* was Ladislav Štoll. A Moscow-trained party man, with a thorough experience of the Czech literary milieu (before the war he had been the editor of the influential Communist magazine *Tvorba*), he published in 1950 *The Thirty Years' Struggle for Czech Socialist Poetry.* His book attacked even Halas, the proletarian poet, the Underground worker, the tribune for the Communist cause. At that time Halas was dead, but Nezval and Seifert with whom Halas had fought in the struggle for modern Czech poetry, had to listen to Štoll's threats and blandishments: "There is no poetry without a fervent faith in the victory of socialism and Soviet Russia."

The Surrealist Nezval saved his skin by composing obligatory poems for Gottwald's and Stalin's birthdays, and unexpectedly succeeded in writing one or two poems in which his craft and talent were still evident; but, on the whole, his poetry and that of his entire generation sank to an unbelievably low level. The cultural leaders of the People's Republic were not concerned, however, with the artistic qualities of poetry; they were satisfied with short lines resembling a verse or a strophe, and commemorating a meeting of Communist youth, or praising love between a man and a woman in connection with their record output in a factory.

Fiction, on the other hand, presented a more burning problem, because in the Communist state-organization it acquired an important propaganda value. Communist Russia provided Czech writers with a ready-made blueprint for fiction, worked out in theory and practice by Russian intellectuals and writers. Czech authors on their side, entangled as they were in the traditional methods of "bourgeois" fiction, could realize only with difficulty that socialist realism's aim was not to describe or praise life in the Communist state, but *to make its intricate machine work.* Not all of the authors who were willing enough to follow the tenets of socialist realism were able to fulfill its demands. Neither the prominent Marie Pujmanová nor the public man Jan Drda succeeded in pleasing Communist critics, as in fact very few did—among them, Alena Bernášková, a young journalist, whose work received attention even in the Russian press. The title of her novel *The Road Is Open* designated a road in the direction of the new world—socialism and its happy life.

The literary development which took place in Russia from 1918 until the Fifties has been repeated on an abridged and reduced scale in Czechoslovakia from 1945 to 1950. The end of the Stalinist era found the façade of Czech literature as orthodox and as conformist to Russian socialist realism as the Russians could wish. The literary language itself froze into a kind of journalistic and propaganda idiom, unfit to produce a single sound sentence or a line of real poetry. (pp. 21-6)

> Milada Součková, *"The Critical Years in Czech Literature,"* in Books Abroad, *Vol. 30, No. 1, Winter, 1956, pp. 21-6.*

A. French

[*French is an English-born Australian educator who specializes in classical studies and has written several book-length works on Czech literature. In the following excerpt from his* Czech Writers and Politics, 1945-1969, *he discusses the interrelationship of Czech literature and politics from the turn of the century through World War II.*]

Future historians may note how closely the cultural scene of today has come to resemble our physical habitat. The mounting output of printed matter, which is a measure of our enlightenment, now clogs the transmission of its message to the receivers. The freeways of the mind are jammed with speeding traffic, heading relentlessly towards who-knows-what targets. The toxic fumes create an immense miasma, confusing the signs and concealing the known ways.

The goals of our hurtling automobiles are multifarious and apparently self-cancelling: their general impact upon the society they serve seems highly destructive. What is the impact of our equally uncomputed cultural vehicles? To what extent, and in what ways does literature affect human behaviour? What are the writers trying to do, anyway? How important or negligible, planned or unforeseen are their effects? It would be unrealistic to imagine that in this age the main function of literature is mere entertainment: a glance at the contents of any large bookshop should dispose of that idea. No novel can compete in sales with the text book or the bible. Literature has a wide range of functions—doctrinal, cathartic, scientific, imaginative, denotative, educative, persuasive. There are some who believe that the book has little effect on the organisation of man's world: this is quite evidently not the view of those who have long preached the message of the *Good Book;* or, at a different level of aim, those who practise or approve of the censorship of literature. In their eyes it can

improve, and does deprave—morally and politically. The gospeller with his bible, the censor with his blue pencil, manifest the belief that the printed word can bend man's judgement, appoint his goal, and direct his steps. (p. 1)

How exactly does art and literature change society? At the most obvious level their social function seems primarily persuasive—almost, one might say, pseudo-commercial. The twentieth century has perfected the techniques of selling: (its efforts have been especially heroic on behalf of goods which do not sell themselves, because they are unwanted, or actively harmful.) Literature has not kept pace with the spectacular advance of television advertising technique; it seems that it is harder to sell unwanted ideas than to sell plastic gadgets or lung cancer. What then are the commodities retailed by serious, creative literature? Ethical standards? New living styles? Blue-prints for a changed society?

Any change, even for the better, is subversive of the old. Artists of all types have long been under suspicion of being by their very nature inclined to subversion. The writer's non-conformism is taken for granted. A creature of subtle intuitions, a visionary of strange dreams from which ordinary folk are excluded, an irredeemable, unteachable champion of lost causes—always he seems to be looking for trouble. A profession dominated by freaks, neurotics, and social misfits?

If writers were really like this, one would properly expect imaginative literature to be a seed-bed of rebellion and a seismograph of social change. One might see in the literature of the years preceding revolution, the great wave swelling to its climax: by studying current literary trends, one might even predict social changes. Such an idea is as unrealistic as is the picture of the artist suggested above. A few writers, at certain times, see themselves as heralds of social reform or even of violent revolution. But as a matter of fact, when such cataclysmic events occur, the literary sector of society seems to be as surprised and bewildered as others. Socially oriented histories of literature earnestly seek the signs of things that were to come, in the output of the years preceding them: they are careful to stress the forward-looking character of books published on the eve of great changes. Such a selection consigns to oblivion the enormous mass of work which shows no sign of awareness that changes were afoot. Looking back at Russian literature in the years preceding the revolution, who can say, without hopeless distortion, that Russian writers were in the vanguard of rebellion? It is at least as plausible to argue that literary radicalism actually diminished in Russia after the reforms of 1907. During the war years 1914-17 Russian literature was more under the inspiration of patriotism and Messianism than revolutionary fervour. One thinks of the few works of Blok and Majakovsky as symptomatic of a literary trend: but how many talented Russian writers fled abroad, or later struggled to come to terms with the new system, often with little success! The literary output of an era rarely gives ground for generalisation of social trends. Its lines of approach, aims, methods, outlooks and presuppositions are bewilderingly diversified. That part which could by any standards be regarded as socially avant-garde is quantitatively insignificant: its social significance is acquired only in retrospect. The mass of imaginative literature seems in fact incorrigibly conservative. Rarely does it see as its task the submission of social blueprints: it is rather the transmitter of cultural tradition: and this is the function which it carries out with varied fidelity and grace. At its best, creative literature, by its re-interpretation of inherited values, preserves the momentum of cultural development. It is this role which, though in no sense revolutionary, gives it the characteristics of an avant-garde movement.

The literature of social ferment can therefore be conceived as operating in a hostile literary, as well as social, environment. Outnumbered, ignored, rejected, divided, and self-consciously ineffectual, the heralds of revolution have themselves little expectation of actually changing society. Their very feeling of impotence at times increases their irresponsibility and helps to give them immunity from reprisals. Society can afford an indulgent smile at the fierce predictions and colourful threats of what is manifestly a literary circus. Politicians collect with secret pride the caricatures which vilify them: rich men promote the sale of books which preach the overthrow of their system. The literary rebel may even combine a proud contempt for society's rewards with a modest private affluence. Attaining the distinction he affects to despise, he may accept from crown or commissar the reward of his lovable mischief. There is a danger of overestimating the leadership qualities of writers: it is easy to oversimplify their social role. So far from dictating the pace of change, it is they who frequently suffer dictation. At times they make the bullets to be fired by others: at other times they fire bullets made for them: sometimes they are the target.

Modern studies of East European literature tend to stress its ideological and overtly political aspect: in this, western critics have much in common with the communists. But the social functions of literature are more than merely political. Those who advocate the censorship of literature in our own society rarely mention politics. They are concerned that books affect life by setting patterns of moral behaviour which are imitated by readers. Such a notion is not demonstrable to the satisfaction of a sceptic; but it is probably accepted by a majority of those who think about it at all. The more superficial aspects of human behaviour, such as talk, dress, hair styles etc. seem to be influenced by the public media, as they are so susceptible to imitation. The influence of books on individual behaviour has been documented by some curious illustrations. When Goethe published his novel *Werther,* even he could hardly have anticipated that men would not only adopt the dress of his hero, but would actually shoot themselves in his fashion. Although Kipling spent so little time in India, his work seems to have left an indelible impact upon Anglo-Indian society. (As one of the oddest ripples from that literary venture one may quote the extraordinary career of Kim Philby, so mesmerised by the literary associations of his upbringing and name that he actually lived the part of a Kiplingesque spy). One wonders how many adventurous souls have illegally crossed frontiers in the self-conscious imitation of the Scarlet Pimpernel. During the Second World War German security officers are said to have combed the work of a certain English writer of thrillers

to discover the secrets of the British Intelligence Service; while members of the latter organisation were doing the same to gain inspiration for their own efforts. Young Nazi Germans participating in the romantic, medieval rallies around Rhine castles in the 'thirties were living the legends written for them by writers of the Weimar Republic: the superman of blood and iron was conceived by Nietzsche before he was made flesh by the SS. Hitler himself modelled his career on Napoleon: Napoleon thought of himself as another Caesar: Caesar trod in the steps of Alexander the Great: and Alexander enacted the role of Achilles; who never existed outside poetry.

It appears that styles of behaviour, made famous in literature, are so convincing that they become true. Once a national or group portrait is established, people live up to the legend. The national image which the Czechs had of themselves before 1920 can be well documented from literature. The legendary Czech was a peasant, serious, long-suffering, protestant, with a passionate longing for freedom and social justice. Then, after Hašek published his novel *The Good Soldier Schweik,* the image changed. Czechs began to see in themselves unsuspected resources of broad humour. The national hero (or anti-hero) became a stumpy figure whose imbecillic expression concealed unplumbable depths of low cunning. Hašek's character has so stamped himself upon Czech consciousness that without reading the book one can scarcely understand why his fellow countrymen still regard with such amusement and pride the ruinous tactics of the industrial go-slow, the inextricable muddling of directives, and the cultivated, ob-

Jaroslav Hašek.

stinate incomprehension of even the simplest bureaucratic procedures.

It is possible to argue that Czech history has been profoundly influenced by national legends created by modern writers. During the nineteenth century a small group of Czech writers made the theme of a national revival the central motif of their work. The smallness of the group is illustrated by the anecdote that, at one of their regular meetings it was said: 'If the ceiling fell in upon us, it would be the end of the Czech national movement'. By the end of the century the movement dominated both art and political thinking in Bohemia. In 1918 the legend became a political reality. Needless to say, the Czech national revival was not entirely the work of writers: had economic, social, and political conditions been different, their work would have taken its place with other romantic visions. But the poetry of Kollár and Svatopluk Čech, the novels of Rais and Jirásek, the journalistic sketches of Havlíček and Neruda, built up so consistent, so insistent, a picture of a Czech nation struggling to revive past glories, that they lent an aura of inevitability to a movement towards independence. A great Moravian kingdom of pre-history; a centre of medieval culture in the fourteenth century; a bearer of protestant freedom, and a torch of humane enlightenment to Europe, crushed by Austria and plunged into a dark age by German oppression and Jesuit witch-hunting—such was the past of the nation, as portrayed by nineteenth century romantic writers. It was a past that clamoured for a resurrection of national pride and freedom. The whole sequence reached a definitive form in the masterly and exhaustive *History* of Palacký, which stood for decades as the classic reconstruction of the Czech past.

The history of a nation is open to varied interpretations, and in the last fifty years Palacký's version has often been challenged. His picture of the early Hussite community was rather idealised: the idea that the humanist literature of the fifteenth century marked a peak is hard to substantiate: the representation of the Counter-reformation as a dark age for Czech art is hard to reconcile with the surviving masterpieces of baroque literature, including the sublime lyrics of Kadlický, Michna, and Bridel. The Romantics seem to have exaggerated the effects of the decay in order to make more dramatic the revival; the early Czech peasant art which they idealised did not always possess the antiquity which they attributed to it. But the gap between history and legend is small; it is the nature of all who re-create the past to select and elaborate. So the Czech national legend was savoured, improved, refined, and took its place of honour in the consciousness of the community. Those who preach of the second coming of Christ prepare public opinion one day to receive a new mystic, if his gospel is convincing. The literary apostles of nihilism who proclaim the coming collapse of civilisation induce in their readers not only an agreeable thrill of horror, but also a state of mind that is ready (in theory) to accept such a cataclysmic end. For a century Czech literature prepared public opinion in the homeland for a new era of political independence: the legend became itself a fact of history and an inspiration for men of action. Masaryk, Beneš, and Štefánik were all under its spell. In 1918, when the independent Czechoslovak republic was established from the collapsing fabric of Austro-Hungary, it seemed that the legend had come true. Art had dictated a pattern to life.

But even as those who give intellectual assent to prophesies of doom would be astounded by their literal fulfilment, so the fulfilment of the Czech legend was received by writers with a more qualified enthusiasm than might have been predicted. Fanfares of nationalistic triumph, hymns of noble gratitude, the deep consciousness of national fulfilment—such are the motifs which might have been expected to dominate the early post-war literature of Czechoslovakia. Work of this kind was written; but for the most part it has been ignored and long forgotten. The literature of the time reflected prevailing attitudes—or rather, the attitudes which the writers *thought* were prevailing—but triumph seems to have played little part in them. If one must single out one dominant mood amid the bewildering tangle of Czech literary trends after 1918, it would perhaps be the mood of *expectation*—a belief that tremendous social changes were afoot, and a new world was coming to replace one which was bled white by the war, and so manifestly discredited. War as a tremendous crime against humanity (a crime to which, regrettably, Czechoslovakia owed its political renaissance) demanded some great expiation. While nothing could justify the unparalleled suffering which war had created, it could at least be understood, if it were a prelude to some great change for the better in the human condition. The first President, the writer and philosopher T. G. Masaryk, regarded the war as merely an episode in a larger sequence, which he termed the 'era of world revolution'.

In the Czech lands the struggle for independence had been led by the so-called Young Czechs, with Dr Kramář at their head. After presiding over the first provisional government after independence, he and his party found themselves rejected by the electorate at the first elections arranged under the new constitution. The rejection of old leaders in favour of more radical ideas was symptomatic of public feeling in Czechoslovakia once war was over. Those who had thought themselves to be in the vanguard of a movement suddenly found that their leadership was not required: the ideas which had been regarded as so progressive were already outdated. The actual achievement of national independence ended its interest as a moral cause and a theme of art. At a time when progressive thinkers all over Europe were raising the cry of internationalism, the assertion of Czech nationalism seemed an anachronism. The mood expressed by the mushrooming periodicals of radical student groups was closer in sympathy to pacifism than to patriotism: the call of anarchy was sweeter than that of the discipline so necessary for the tasks of reconstruction. Those who had fought for freedom in the Czech legions abroad came home almost as strangers to the sons who had grown up in their absence. Fighting and the resistance are themes which soon become boring to those who have not participated in them: the young found it easy to ridicule Czech jingoism, cruelly identifying the liberationists with the imperial era from which they had emerged.

Only the legionaries had first-hand knowledge of the revolution which had overturned the social order in Russia;

but here, if anywhere, seemed the shape of things to come. A deep note of Messianism sounded in the most modern Czech post-war poetry: in holy Russia, motherland of the Slavs, a new lamp of hope seemed to have been kindled. Together with these touching hopes went an almost mystical belief that the coming era belonged to the common man. The new hero of war was not the general on his white horse, but the Unknown Soldier in his tomb. The sympathies of men went out not to the triumphal cavalcades, but to the legions of the dispossessed and displaced, the poor and the oppressed: for virtue was in them. In the youngest Czech literature a new school appeared, that of the so-called Proletarian poets, of whom the most gifted were Hora and Wolker. Reviving the folk ballad in modern form, Wolker portrayed social issues in an industrial setting: Hora pictured the Madonna as a woman of the slums, and the new Christ-child as the appointed leader of the workers in the hour of their liberation. The young poets wrote almost with reverence of the power and solidarity of the proletarian class, identifying themselves with it in the pictured panoramas of revolt. The writers who saluted the spirit and the coming triumph of the workers, were themselves almost without exception of middle-class origin and upbringing. Inspired by the slogans of Marxism they appointed themselves as spokesmen of the soon-to-be victorious proletariat, and claimed for the poet his historic role as a teacher and prophet. In retrospect such poems seem romantic and naive, imaginative without a touch of scepticism. They are dated by their adherence to a passing phase; yet at their best they reached a high level of art; and their effect on later work was to be great.

An advantage of Proletarian poetry was that it had the appeal of literature addressed to immediate, contemporary issues; lacking the thoughtful scepticism of much prose work of the time, it aimed straight for the heart rather than the intellect. Whatever else the Proletarians lacked, they had plenty of faith, an endearing quality in poetry. The prophetic writer can claim for his visions an authority which rests on revelation rather than argument; and his views can assume a startling, apocalyptic air. Yet his themes, though on the grand scale, are built not on personal experience but on hearsay, reading, and the doctrines of others. As he calls for assent to a doctrine, his presentation tends to be simplistic, sweeping away his readers on a wave of emotion. The exploitation of mass emotion opens the way to theatrical and embarrassing posing: the limitation of doubt and intellectual reservation can lead to shallow vulgarisation. Such are the pitfalls of prophetic literature. They were avoided by the leaders of the Czech Proletarian movement, but their later followers were not so circumspect. They set an example which was to have a delayed, but appalling harvest some thirty years later. In their theoretical work, as well as in their imaginative creations, the early Proletarians took a rash step. Proclaiming that the prime duty of literature was to change life by the liberation of industrial man, they placed their art unreservedly at the service of the radical cause, rejecting all claims for the autonomy of art. While the poems of Wolker himself reflect more the spirit of the evangelist than the agitator, he supplied a doctrine and an example for those who later were to declare that literature is properly the servant of politics, and that the criteria of literary value are social and political, rather than aesthetic. The Proletarian movement, as a trend of serious literature, lasted only a few years; its demise was aided no doubt by the tragic death of Wolker at the age of 24.

The strength of the movement lay in poetry; but a number of serious, attractive novels were also written in this style, notably by Olbracht, Vančura, and Marie Majerová. But in their popularity and influence they were dwarfed by Hašek's realist satire *The Good Soldier Schweik*. Critics denounced it for its crude vulgarity and technical defects of composition: its disorganisation and corrosive humour seemed typical of its author, who had once actually been expelled from the anarchist party for indiscipline. Hašek portrayed in his hero the underdog of modern industrial society, as Wolker had done, but with much greater skill and insight. Compared to the schematic, heroic worker of the Proletarians, Schweik really comes to life; and this unflattering portrayal of the Czech 'little man' won acceptance for its endearing realism. Set next to Schweik, the hero of Proletarian literature seems romantic—a nineteenth century 'noble peasant' dressed in the garb of a modern industrial workman.

Far more subtle and intellectual was the exploration of social themes in the work of Karel Čapek. In his play *R.U.R.*, first produced in 1921, he portrayed the collapse of man's society through the revolt of the robots against their creators. While the Futurists, with their Czech apostles, were glorifying the theme of technical progress—the 'miracles of the electric century' as they termed it—Čapek explored the theme of man's capacity to destroy himself; combining it with the contemporary theme of revolution. In his play the humans lose their capacity to reproduce themselves: but after the fall of man the robots take upon themselves human characteristics, and a new Adam and Eve commence a fresh cycle of life. The humans become as robots, the robots humans: so the current of life flows on, too powerful for human folly to destroy. *In spite of* science, *in spite of* revolution, the spirit of man survives.

From his plays, novels, essays, and criticism Karel Čapek, together with his brother Josef, became identified with a definite social philosophy, that of American pragmatism. The best-known of the Czech pragmatists, who carried his philosophy directly into politics, was the President, T. G. Masaryk himself. The trend of thought in the Čapeks' writing, the personal association between Karel and Masaryk, and the fact that the former published several books of intimate *Conversations with T. G. M.*, all contributed to give to Karel Čapek the air of a spokesman for the existing regime, and consequently a defender of the political status quo. Perhaps it would be truer to say that Čapek reflected attitudes widespread among the intelligentsia of post-war Czechoslovakia. These attitudes were:—an attachment to the values of western democracy; a dislike of crude nationalism and militarism; a feeling for rational compromise and the organisation of affairs according to enlightened, but businesslike, principles; above all a deep distrust of all forms of fanaticism, either in politics or religion. Karel Čapek's early novels, *Factory for the Absolute* and *Krakatit,* were both science-fiction essays on the theme of the deadly danger to humanity of man's release of energy, either spiritual or physical, which would be beyond his control. Čapek thus displayed, in both fiction and drama, a warning distrust of the miracles of experimental science: no less intense was his scepticism towards the current revolutionary faiths which promised to solve man's social problems by reorganising his economic and institutional arrangements. Though Čapek thought highly of Wolker as a poet, he deflated the wild pretensions of Proletarian art, regarding the literary revolutionaries as neo-Romantics.

Čapek's reservations toward religion made him unpopular with Catholic writers, who found in his liberal humanism a form of moral neutrality; the humanists were accused of putting man, not God, at the centre of their world. On the other hand strong nationalists, like the poet Viktor Dyk, found Čapek's work insipid, excessively cosmopolitan, and lacking in idealism. Of the Pragmatists it was said that they loved the whole world, and believed in nothing. They were identified with the prevailing system and with the political philosophy of the ruling group: as such they were the target for attack by dissenters of all types.

Distrust of the government, and dissent from official views, has been a commonly observed attitude of the Czech intelligentsia. No doubt the attitude had good historical reasons, stemming from the fact that for centuries their culture represented a minority struggling for recognition against alien rule. After the Czechs became masters in their own land, attitudes were slow to change. Czech politicians merely replaced Austrian officials as targets of abuse. People were so accustomed to seeing public policy managed from abroad that they regarded with suspicion and incredulity Czechoslovakia's independent role, and claimed that the Republic was a virtual puppet of the Western powers. Every political compromise, every rumour of corruption, added to the suspicions of the dissenters. It was claimed that the ideals of the pre-war struggle had somewhere been lost: the legend of Czech revival had been a noble one; the reality somewhat disappointing. Public life seemed more commercialised, materialistic, more smug and inequitable than was appropriate to an ideal republic.

For writers of principle political independence brought fresh problems. Before the war pacifism had been a patriotic ideal, combining humanism with a practical determination not to fight Austria's wars for it: ideals and national interests thus happily coincided. But when the first Czechoslovak army was formed, the issue changed. The poet Šrámek had made the hatred of militarism a theme of his art: after 1918 he altered his stance and abandoned pacifism. The ex-legionaries Medek and Kopta wrote a vigorous prose literature based on their wartime experiences. The Czechoslovak state had benefitted by the war, which had brought its independence; and militarism seemed to have been rehabilitated now that it was in Czech national interests. Such an attitude seemed to the young radicals quite unprincipled. The dilemma of Šrámek was that of his generation. Those who, in their youth had been the dissenters, had become in their middle years a new Establishment. The political leaders of the new Czechoslovakia were accused of selling their ideals for a mess of Western pottage—in particular of abandoning their anti-imperialist views in consideration of loans, credits, and military assistance from imperial France. In the old legend the historic model for a revived Czech state had been Tábor, the fifteenth century Hussite brotherhood. Then the Czech protestants had faced the scorn and enmity of Europe for the sake of their principles. Now the one state which seemed to be following in the steps of Tábor was not Czechoslovakia, but Russia. Even through the later years of disillusion with the realities of Soviet life, this image of an idealistic, struggling, persecuted community prevailed, while Czechoslovak political leaders, not excluding the President-Liberator T. G. Masaryk himself, were a target for criticism from all sides. Radical and Catholic writers alike used the freedom of the liberal democratic system to denounce its humbug, hypocrisy, and spiritual impotence.

Critics were fond of referring to the 'official' literature of Prague, and by this they meant especially that of the Pragmatists. Just as the left-wing writers were in close personal touch with communist political organisers, so the Pragmatist writers tended to associate with politicians of the liberal persuasion. While the radicals openly advocated social revolution in their writings, the Čapeks and their friend F. Peroutka, threw their weight behind the 'state-building' programme common to the democratic parties. A conscious effort to bring together men of literature and politics was made by Karel Čapek, when he organised a literary salon at his house in Prague. The salon, composed of artists, intellectuals, and public figures, met regularly. Dr. E. Beneš and T. G. Masaryk were among its members. Inevitably this association caused Čapek to be regarded as something of a spokesman for official cultural policy; and this unfortunate impression was increased when he became president of the Czech branch of the International P.E.N. Club.

But those critics who vigilantly espied political influence in the literary salon, or the corridors of powers in the Čapeks' suburban villa, seem to have been deceiving themselves. There is no reason to suspect that the co-operation of Čapek and other Pragmatists with politicians had any direct influence on public policy. How far their literary efforts aided policies made by others is doubtful. Čapek and his friends did more to propagate the liberal viewpoint in general than the platform of any political party, and their appeal was always more to intellectuals than to the common voter. At the other end of the political spectrum the fiery communist writers who plunged so eagerly into political affairs in the early twenties found their efforts crowned with futility. The avant-gardists soon abandoned the cause of politically committed literature, and proclaimed the total autonomy of art. Poetism was the name they gave to their new love—art devoid of all ideological content. They ridiculed all didactic art as a relic of medieval scholasticism, and gaily swept into oblivion the literary-political tenets they had themselves defended a short time before. Beginning like the French Dadaists they produced a stunning impression with their verbal pyrotechnics, dazzling surprises, and the literary exploitation of techniques derived from vaudeville and films. The Poetists, whose most splendid example was V. Nezval, had emerged from a revolutionary tradition, and the chaotic or barbaric element so natural to revolutionary art, became their guiding principle. They contributed some astonishing and brilliant work to the repertoire of Czech modern literature, but in its final stages their work descended into macabre surrealism, which unkind critics likened to infantile exhibitionism.

Although wedded to the idea of 'pure' art, the radical modernists in literature consistently proclaimed their adherence in politics to the communist cause: but radical principles were one thing, Party organisation another. Left wing artists and communist functionaries became increasingly exasperated with each other. To the latter the writers seemed irresponsible, undisciplined, uninterested in day-to-day problems of assisting the revolution. To the writers party officials seemed dreary, unimaginative, often officious and ruthless. Above all, the leaders who professed the cause of political revolution showed themselves in matters of art hopelessly conservative, not to say reactionary. The uneasy marriage between party revolutionaries and avant-garde art broke down in 1929, when a group of writers was expelled from the Party for gross violation of discipline. The attitude of the artists was that they had not abandoned their principles, as they were accused of doing; communist principles were more important than the Communist Party. They declared that the present Party leadership was hopelessly out of touch with reality—mouthing trite slogans, publishing unreadable journals, and lacking all understanding of, or influence over, the working people.

The crisis brought to light some of the problems faced by writers who attempt to engage their talents directly in politics. Where Čapek and the Pragmatists found frustration, the communist writers ran into even more exasperating conflicts, which brought them to the depths of disillusion. Between the revolutionary artists and the political revolutionaries the intellectual gulf was immense. The political leaders found it impossible to fit the artists into their plans; the artists found that the behests of the Party, the needs of vigilance in the 'class struggle', were empty phrases of little relevance to their literary work. By hard experience they discovered that the connection between literature and society is much more complex than they had imagined. Literary critics had committed the crude error of supposing that a writer was a mere reflection of his society. It was left for communist journalists to proclaim that the writer's true function was to propagate the social blueprints of the theoreticians. It thus appeared that the writers had seriously overestimated the political importance of their own efforts. Instead of leading the cause, they were being led; and at times manipulated. The dedication of the young poets to the communist cause was basically on ethical and aesthetic grounds: they rarely attempted to demonstrate to others, or even to themselves, the economic advantages of a socialised system, and it is unlikely that they ever bothered to study the complex economic and sociological arguments in favour of it. Their adherence to the cause was an act of faith, based on revulsion from social injustice, and on a desire to help build a better world. To them therefore principles were everything, expediency nothing. When they thought that the party leadership was itself acting in an unprincipled way, they appealed over its head to the members; and this was the unforgivable crime for which the writers were driven from the fold in 1929; their fault was disloyalty to party leadership. The point was well taken by one of the victims, who declared that for a writer, loyalty to principle must come before loyalty to a committee. When conflict arose, an artist must adhere to his own vision of truth, which no party boss could dictate to him.

Yet in spite of conflict and disillusion the cause of communism retained its appeal for many young Czech artists in the period between the wars. By their talents they graced the movement and lent it intellectual respectability. The Party was glad of their support and proud of the progressive and intellectual air which they gave to it. The sensitive social consciences of the writers were applauded by communist theoreticians, who even extended a mild tolerance to artistic deviations which would not have been permitted in Russia itself. But when the artists put their intuitions above political directives, and refused to toe the party line, they were reproved and disciplined. When the writers defiantly asserted their right to dissent from the Party, as well as from the government, then they were denounced as social-fascists, their work was described as unhealthy and reactionary, and the faithful were instructed not to read their books. The shape of things to come already cast its long shadow over Czech literary life.

During the twenties the cause of world revolution through the Third International seemed to have been quietly abandoned by Moscow, and news from Russia gave no reason to suppose that a millennium of human happiness had been achieved. It might reasonably have been expected that the cause of social revolution, embraced by humanists all over Europe with such enthusiasm in the early postwar years, would also wither away. In fact despite tremendous disillusion this did not happen. Partly the credit for the active survival of the communist faith abroad must be given to its resolute opponents. The abuse directed at the Bolsheviks attained such hysterical proportions, and the anti-communist cause was espoused by such manifestly reactionary elements that an air of injury and persecution lay like a halo on the Reds. It seemed that some good must lie on a cause which attracted the hostility of such an anachronistic troupe of dispossessed aristocrats, political primitives, Nazis, Jew baiters, and Fascists. A tremendous incentive to the radical cause was provided by the great financial depression which hit Europe about 1930. The situation was construed as the imminent breakdown of the whole capitalist system, and the darkest hour before a new dawn. Once more the banners of socialism appeared in full array on the streets of Western Europe. Socialism, as an idea, became a magic word, conjuring up hopes for a better world washed clean of the greed and folly of the old. It was in 1931 that an eminent English journalist returned from Moscow with the slogan: 'I have seen the future—and it works'. An international movement developed whereby brain-workers of all kinds sought to link up with the working class in the hope of ousting the bourgeoisie from power. French, British, and American artists themselves proclaimed the need to put their talents at the service of the cause, and give their work a social content. It was the era of international writers' congresses, when Europe grew accustomed to slogans such as 'Artists for Peace', 'Writers for Progress'. Seeking for support from the Socialist world, the writers turned hopefully to Moscow: but the Russians, already insulated for a decade from the intellectual ferment abroad, were slow to respond.

In 1930 a Writers' Congress had been held at Kharkov which effectively ended official support for a pluralist conception of literature in the USSR. The past rivalry between the Proletarian and the non-Proletarian schools concluded with the total rout of the latter. The liberal doctrine that no literary current could speak in the name of the Party, or monopolise literary production, was finally and completely abandoned. The Revolutionary Association of Proletarian Writers (R.A.P.P.) was founded on an international basis, proclaiming the doctrine that literature was merely a superstructure of economic relations, and the class struggle was the key to artistic criteria. The crude doctrine of the Rappists found little sympathy outside the USSR, even among the dedicated admirers of communism; and the Rappist branch set up in Prague was joined by hardly any serious writers. But by 1932 R.A.P.P. was abolished in Russia, and a single Union of Soviet Writers was formed, with Gorky at its head. This appeared to be a dramatic liberalisation of policy, and there was a keen response from abroad.

Hoping for closer co-operation with their Russian colleagues a group of Czech artists attended the Moscow Writers' Congress in 1934. By this time the book burnings in Germany had begun: there was street fighting in Paris between Communists and Fascists: a liberal left-wing movement in Vienna had been ruthlessly suppressed: and the danger of a new European war had drawn closer. The conference assumed the nature of an international anti-Fascist demonstration. The French had sent a powerful delegation, and the presence of artists of the calibre of Aragon, Malraux, and Bloch, and the participation of Russian non-conformists like Pasternak and Ehrenburg made a great impression on the Czechs. The Russian Futurists had apparently been rehabilitated, and when the name of Majakovsky was mentioned, the audience broke into a storm of applause.

Bukharin, who had been for some time under the shadow of official disfavour, made a long, well argued speech which included fearless criticism of certain trends in Soviet literature. He had recently become the editor of the influential newspaper *Izvestia,* and to the Czechs his liberal views seemed to represent a new Soviet cultural policy, one with which they would be happy to co-operate. (Evidence of such co-operation was the formation of an Anti-Fascist group of Czechoslovak writers.)

But the optimism was premature. Although the Russians had abandoned the sterile policy of the Proletkult period, it soon became depressingly clear that the change was one of doctrine, not of outlook. What had divided the communists from their liberal allies was the question of whether artists should choose their own way of aiding the cause, or whether they should operate according to directives laid down by the Party. Only the former alternative was acceptable to the Western writers, who included the

Czechs. The policy of the Russian literary establishment was unequivocally in favour of a Party line to be followed by the artists. The new guidelines had been enunciated by Zhdanov at the Congress: the doctrine of the Proletkult had been dropped, and that of Socialist-Realism had been put in its place.

Among the radical Czech writers an issue of the time was the adherence of certain artists to the international literary movement of Surrealism. In Prague, as elsewhere, the Surrealist movement was espoused by artists who were in fact among the strongest supporters of the Communist Party; the leading figures were the poets Nezval and Biebl, and the theoretician Karel Teige, who had been the leading spirit of the Poetist movement. From the outset the Czech Surrealist group aroused the hostility of orthodox Marxist critics, who denounced it as an example of bourgeois decadence and a betrayal of the methods of dialectical materialism. When the Surrealists spiritedly defended their methods, arguing in strictly Marxist terms, they were declared to be Trotskyists, and ordered peremptorily to follow the line dictated from Moscow. Meanwhile the atmosphere in Prague grew more tense as news came in of the Russian political trials: the Meierhold theatre closed; attacks on Shostakovich and Eisenstein; Bukharin, the hero of the thaw, arrested and shot. The more depressing was the news, the more unquestioning was the loyalty demanded by the Party and its cultural spokesmen. Finally they had their way with the Surrealist group, which was liquidated by Nezval after a violent quarrel with Teige. For twenty years Nezval had been the typical avantgardist, a rebel on principle, gaily rejecting restraints imposed by convention or doctrine. In 1938 he stifled all doubts and insisted on the need for loyalty to party policy, even in face of the Russian political trials and the suppression of cultural freedom in the USSR.

But despite their intolerance of so-called decadents, Trotskyists, and deviationists within their own camp, the Czech communists were, in the late thirties, eager to co-operate with elements of other political persuasions. During the period 1929-35 the Party, under a new young leadership, and under instructions from Moscow, had isolated itself from other parties, and openly worked for the destruction of the Czechoslovak political system. But as the German threat increased, with the signing of the Czech-Soviet military pact in 1935 and following the VIIth Congress of the Comintern the Party line again changed. Now the Czech communists were eager to co-operate in a wide anti-Fascist front, and welcomed the adhesion even of right-wing elements. The switch of support to the very nationalism which had been previously denounced, was welcomed by liberal elements. The new policy was symbolised by the slogan proclaimed by a Soviet literary delegation, 'Not Schweik but Žižka', as a model of behaviour for the Czech people. (Žižka was the high-born, nationalist champion of the medieval Hussites.) It was a strange paradox that Soviet intellectuals in their choice of a literary stereotype for Czech social behaviour, gave their preference to a nationalistic feudal knight rather than to the proletarian anti-hero of the anarchist Hašek.

The threat of war in 1938 brought together Czech writers

of the most diverse views into a common national front: amid the crisis old quarrels were temporarily laid aside. In a joint appeal to the outside world the Czech writers implored intellectuals everywhere to save their country. They won sympathy, but no help; and Czechoslovakia, abandoned by its allies, was mercilessly struck down by the Germans. The hopes of Russian intervention had proved as abortive as the earlier dreams of world revolution. But the greatest disillusion was with the policies of the democratic leaders, for it was the reigning government which took upon itself the responsibility of capitulation. Its careful plans and dearly bought alliances had collapsed like a house of cards. The cautious pragmatism and liberal faith which had for twenty years sustained official state policies and formed its political outlook, had been exposed as powerless before the elemental violence of the Nazis. To men like Čapek, whose whole work had been impregnated with faith in the power of human reason, the catastrophe was stunning. Karel died on Christmas Day 1938; his brother perished in wartime in a German concentration camp. The ending of this talented and humane pair of writers seemed tragically and curiously appropriate. Their democratic ideals of reason and tolerance were made to appear futile and utopian in a world dominated by organised fanaticism. The German occupation not only put an end to the First Czechoslovak Republic, it dimmed Czech faith in democratic institutions and in the civilised values which they represented. The occupation of the land symbolised the triumph of unreason, the practical vindication of the barbaric principles represented by the Nazi New Order. For many Czechs in those bitter days faith in liberal ideas wilted and died, together with their long and frustrating love affair with France. Those who sought to understand the Czech tragedy in a wider context saw in the Nazi movement the end of an era in Europe, the final collapse of the hopes of the Enlightenment and Humanism. The revival of the pogrom, the everyday use of torture, the book burnings and public executions, seemed to indicate that barbarism had won a perhaps final triumph over the civilised values of Europe.

Under German occupation all the media of instruction and propaganda were naturally employed in the Nazi cause; censorship was ruthless and efficient. One result of this state of affairs, which continued for six years, was to interpose between writer and reader a division which later became known as the credibility gap. Scepticism was sharpened to the extent that men acquired the habit of believing the opposite of the official pronouncement: together with incredulity there developed the custom of reading the written word as a code, to detect hidden allusions and cryptic messages. 'A withdrawal to prepared positions' meant a rout; a 'temporary setback' meant a catastrophe: 'Bolshevik terrorists' meant Czech resistance workers; 'traitors' meant patriots: 'official information' meant misinformation; 'justice' meant injustice; 'truth' meant lies. War brings in its trail a reversal of criteria; and once readers have lost faith in the public media, it is difficult to restore it. One legacy of the German occupation has been a lasting feeling of scepticism on the part of Czech readers, a disinclination to take anything at its face value, and the acceptance of the idea that any published work is likely to conceal political allusions and messages which only the eyes of the initiated can perceive.

There were other literary legacies of wartime occupation. Their language, literature, and traditions were the one unifying element of the Czech people, the kernel of their resistance, the only light to sustain the nation through the new Dark Age. Literature became the more precious because it was almost all that the Czechs had left in common; it provided a symbolic refuge from Germanisation. The social function of literature increased, and the role of the writer became over-valued by ordinary standards; in the post-war period men credited artists with real power to change the world. Writers could rejoice in their newfound importance: but the notion that imaginative writers could do immense good or harm to political causes was fatal to their independence, and later was to make them a prime target for political bosses.

A favourite theme of the Nazis was the doctrine of historical inevitability. The New Order was a logical, and inevitable consequence of long historical development. In 1941 the German empire stretched from the Pyrenees to the Near East; and even those who hated the Nazis with all their hearts feared the truth of the prediction that the German Reich was on the crest of a wave that nothing on earth could stop. Even intellectuals fell into a kind of fatalism, acknowledging the existence of irresistible historical forces to which nations must accommodate themselves. Then as the tide of success turned, faith in ultimate German victory ebbed, but the fatalistic attitude remained. Those who had seen the Nazis as carried on an irresistible wave of history, now saw the communists in a similar position. As so often with wartime propaganda, readers dismissed the details presented to them, but accepted the logic behind them. One of the sad intellectual legacies of the war was the belief that certain groups were 'on the side of history', and that common prudence indicated the folly of opposing them. Previously, to win support for a movement it had been necessary to indicate that it was wise, beneficial, or well-motivated: since 1939 it has been sufficient to argue that it is on the side of history, hence inevitable, and its opponents accordingly blind or corrupt reactionaries.

The years of enemy occupation subtly changed the mental climate of the Czechs, and the resulting attitudes were to show themselves in later literature. During the occupation new Czech poems, novels and plays were still published, provided they gave no offence to the occupiers, but the real issues of the time could not be the subject of controversial writing. Czech wartime literature has its own neutral style, and is like an intermezzo between the ferment of pre-war and post-war. A number of young and talented poets made their debut in this period, and among their most endearing legacy is the picture they have left of wartime Prague. Its aspect, like the lives of its dwellers, is humdrum, shabby, austere. The children of hard times and material shortages are strangers to the romantic world of grand gestures and flamboyant heroism. The young poets' obsession with mundane details and down-at-heel reality, their disinclination for romantic escapism, is a mark of their anxiety to convey the bare truth. They wrote of empty streets, stairs that lead nowhere, endless walks through faded suburbs, the sight of buildings which have long since been demolished: a lost world of childhood is conjured up by the sight of a battered textbook, or a childish treasure. Their work avoids pathos as much as it shuns politics: heroism, rhetoric, and sentimentality are rigidly excluded from their narrow world, which is not without a sense of its own absurdity. Kamil Bednář, Ivan Blatný, Jiřina Hauková, Jiří Orten are the stars of this brief period. Their work had common features which mark them off as a group—the so-called lost wartime generation. Orten was killed in 1941; the others survived but never gained the place in Czech literature which they had the right to expect. Their later work, which should have been their triumph, was to be a melancholy post-script to that of the war.

There was a curious gap between the deliberately humdrum world of new writing and the cataclysmic changes going on outside. The incongruity was carried into the lives of the writers themselves. While the critic Václav Černý was editing the austerely intellectual, literary journal *Critical Monthly* he was, until his arrest, active in the resistance, together with the novelist Vančura. Normal life was like a facade covering a network of deadly peril which touched the lives of all. No man was safe from arrest, not even the highest officials of the Protectorate government. No one could be sure that he would not be challenged at any moment to make a terrible decision—to assist the Nazis, or to resist them. In either case refusal could have fatal consequences. Emotions which in normal times are exceptional—intense anguish, searing fear and hatred—became commonplace. The normal had become bizarre, and the bizarre normal. Neutrality was impossible: there was no way to avoid involvement. What took away all security was the necessity to make hazardous choices; the freedom to choose was like a millstone round men's necks. How many people in wartime positively envied prisoners of war, because they alone were absolved from all choice! Exempted from the struggle, they were blessed with non-involvement. Under enemy occupation even the dead at times became objects of envy, and the grave a kind of refuge. The living were inexorably *condemned to be free.* The hero was driven into heroism, the coward into cowardice. The deadly burden of involvement paradoxically reversed the values of freedom and captivity: lacking choice the prisoner attained a desperate kind of security; the free man, able to collaborate or resist, to invite future reprisals or immediate execution, was in the trap. Freedom, like truth and justice, had suffered a curious inversion of meaning. The human experience of wartime was to be the future material of literature: it was a topsy-turvy world, in which many things were the opposite of what they seemed, and words meant the reverse of what they said. In this world was reality to be found in the apparent normalcy of everyday life, or in the anguished conflicts which lay behind it? In the thousand imaginary dangers that beset each day, or in the deadening routine which filled it? And when the day of liberation came, what would be *its* reality?

By May 1945 the fighting was virtually over in Western Europe: Prague, almost undamaged by warfare, awaited her deliverers. The pent-up hatred of the Czechs was about to be released upon the occupiers, but warned by experience, the resistance movement waited until the last minute. The rising began on the morning of May 5 when American help was within an hour's distance from the city. The radio station was seized, and the Germans were ordered to surrender. The American troops, apparently at the orders of the high command and in accordance with a secret agreement with the Russians, made no move towards Prague. Efforts by Czech moderates to effect a peaceful handover of power failed, and all compromise was rejected by the armed resistance movement, which now came into the open. So the heavy fighting began, as German tanks rolled into the city centre, and shelled public buildings. The lovely Spring sunshine witnessed a scene so often foreshadowed in revolutionary Czech poems, the sight of men desperately fighting at the barricades. It was four days before the first units of the Red Army fought their way into the Prague suburbs: meanwhile the city had experienced unprecedented scenes of savagery and carnage, in which prisoners were hanged in the streets and doused in burning petrol. So the German occupation, begun in March 1939 amid heavy omens, ended six years later in a crescendo of violence and horror. (pp. 2-22)

A. French, "Legends and History," in his Czech Writers and Politics, 1945-1969, *East European Monographs, 1982, pp. 1-22.*

Peter Hruby

[*In the following excerpt, Hruby focuses on the relation of Czech poetry of the interwar era to trends of the period in avant-garde French literature and to Communist politics.*]

It has often been remarked, how unusually great a role Czech poets and writers played in the creation of a national ethos and aspirations to establish an independent state. However, when the Czechoslovak state was finally formed, at the end of World War One, many of them did not show any lasting devotion to it. They very soon began to dream about another revolution that would destroy the democracy and, following Lenin, would install a "proletarian dictatorship." They were not at all interested in helping to build the new state and, in spite of the fact that its coalition Government was led by a strong Social Democratic Party and had implemented many social reforms, they imagined the time was ripe for a much more radical solution.

Politically, their ideal was represented by the Bolsheviks in the East. Artistically, they were influenced by modern trends that had, for several generations, flowed from the West—mainly from Paris, to Prague.

They were certain that an artistic revolution against bourgeois art and life would be meaningless without a proletarian revolution in matters of economics and politics. Their revolutionary fervor was thus poetical and political. They refused to compromise with forces which in their eyes exhibited either cautious moderation or outright reaction: nothing should contain the common march of artists and workers toward a completely new society to be born out of a bloody revolution. The true liberation of Prague, they held, could come only from a program which united artistic Paris and political Moscow. Since many French artists were on the extreme Left of the political spectrum, and Russian culture took part in the avant-garde it seemed to be a plausible connection.

Almost all the poets [that I will discuss] are listed among my favorites and I still enjoy as much of their verse as I did when I read them for the first time in my distant youth. If in the following portraits they appear rather foolish, my criticism / sarcasm is due to the obvious truth that politics and poetry do not mix well, and that getting enthusiastic about some political movement, or worse, a political party, can have disastrous consequences for both poetry and politics.

Since the Germans had been responsible for both political domination and social exploitation in Czech lands for centuries, there had arisen a strong pro-Russian, pan-Slav orientation as well as a tradition of radical social attitudes. In the raptured mood of the post-war period even the "old" lyric poet, Antonín Sova (born 1864), was inspired to pen verbose revolutionary lines:

> I want our flag to flap in red.
> And a mighty red flag it should be. . . .
> A flag to have a blood red laugh,
> and courage to rend the cowardly chains of pacts
> 　　　　　　　　　　　　　　　to pieces.
> Let the flag flap in red. Let it lash the face
> like a claw of caked blood, let it inflict pain!
> Fail to follow it and you will be trampled to
> 　　　　　　　　　　　　　　　death.
> And you, you pacifying and compromising lack-
> 　　eys
> of the gentry who practice usury of the spirit,
> keep your reformist and ridiculous alms!

Another older poet, Stanislav Kostka Neumann, born in 1875, the son of a lawyer and Imperial deputy in Vienna, became one of the most fierce propagandists for a bloody revolution. Until this time his career, both in politics and poetry, had led him through a rich sequence of contradictory poses. In 1893 he had taken part in anarchist riots and been condemned to fourteen months in prison. In 1896 he published his poetry under the title *I Am an Apostle of New Life,* and the next year followed it with *Satan's Glory Among Us.* He saw himself as a proud Nietzschean individualist:

> I sprouted above the mire. . . .
> Alone,
> haughty
> I declared eternal enmity to reptiles
> who all around vegetate through the dirt of their
> 　　　　　　　　　　　　　　　days in venom
> and elevated my hatred as a bright shield
> and expect blows.

Neumann, the future apostle of collectivism, wrote: "I sing of my pride / amidst the rabble." And then next, influenced by the Polish decadent, Przybyszewski, he addressed the Devil who defeats God in a poem called "Ave Satan." He became a poet of paganism and proclaimed himself to be a decadent: "When I will drag myself through the mud of the street, a scraggy decadent, cynical talker, with a swollen face." In 1903 in a poem entitled "A Dream About a Desperate Crowd" he declares the necessity for a strong leader and for a revolutionary change in the world. In this poem God is dead and the desperate crowd addresses itself to Satan who is "Life, . . . strength and lust and pride and mutiny."

Neumann went on to publish a lyrical and naturalistic collection of, mainly erotic, verse, *Book of Forests, Waters and Slopes,* in 1914 and followed this in 1918 with *New Songs,* which was full of so-called civilization poetry. His love for nature had been supplanted by its opposite—a love for modern technology embracing the whole planet in networks of electrical wires, telephones and telegraphs. Sixty years after Walt Whitman he admired the dynamic modern world and—for a change—loved the crowds.

Entering the post-war National Assembly as deputy for the anarchist faction of the Czech Socialist Party, he became ministerial counsel in the Ministry for Education and Culture. However, his erratic nature could not take it for long and he gave up both positions. After this his earnings from books and the editorship of a radically Left-wing literary journal, *Červen (June)*, provided just a modest income, but his, admittedly bourgeois, friends always tried to help him with State prizes or fellowships.

Although in 1918 he had written "Enough of Russia!", three years later he changed this to: "Oh, Russia, come!" At that time Neumann belonged to a Bolshevik faction of the Social Democratic Party and in September 1920 he took a leading part in a march on the party paper *Právo lidu (People's Right)*. The building was forcefully occupied by a so-called "action committee of the Prague workers' class," and the writer, Ivan Olbracht, who had just returned from Moscow, was installed as the new editor of the daily. (This was a man who, during the terrible famine, consistently wrote reports on the marvelous development of his promised land, and on the abundance of food supplies.) The paper was renamed *Rudé právo (Red Justice)* when a court forbade the occupiers to use the old name. Abetted by Neumann and other writers, this crisis finally led in 1921 to a split in the Social Democratic Party, and to the establishment of the Communist Party of Czechoslovakia. One of the Party's main spokesmen was Karl Kreibich. Kreibich was a German, and German Communists in Czechoslovakia were generally much more radical than their Czech counterparts and interested in the breakup of the new state. He urged revolution: "The only way to seizure of power is violence. There is either violence and dictatorship—or there is no socialism."

Neumann who, in 1920, had published an essay called "Proletarian Culture," aligned himself with this form of German radicalism and, in 1921, provoked his Czech compatriots with this poem:

> Father,
> my father,
> even as a boy
> I felt so immensely alone
> in a nation where people won't face
> action, thought, beauty and light
> and struggle. . . .
> How estranged I am now

from this lethargic nation
a stranger here!
We'll never agree nor come to terms.
I am moulded of other blood and fibre. . . .
This foetid land confines me. . . .
Insignificant Czech puddle, I am not of you!
Father,
my father,
why did you become a Czech?

By 1920 several younger poets had attempted to create a "Proletarian poetry" that would help workers on their road to power. Josef Hora published the first collection of Proletarian verse, *Pracující den* (*The Working Day*). Jindřich Hořejši followed the next year with *Hudba na náměstí* (*Music on the Square*), Jaroslav Seifert with *Město v slzách* (*A City in Tears*) and Jiří Wolker with *Host do domu* (*A Guest at Home*).

Also in 1920 a group of revolutionary poets and artists called *Devětsil* (Nine Forces), began to publish manifestos of the new Proletarian, anti-bourgeois art. Most of them were of bourgeois origin and although as "voluntary proletarians" they wrote verse on class struggle and barricades, they spent most of their days and nights in Prague cafés and bars, drinking coffee or wine—naturally red, and discussed art, poetry, girls and revolution. Since they did not know Russian but had access to an influential collection of excellent translations of modern French poetry published by Karel Čapek, their poetic imagination often mirrored the Parisian atmosphere rather than that of Moscow. Nevertheless, they believed that both revolutionary trends could be united.

In a typical poem of the future Nobel prize winner for literature, Jaroslav Seifert, expressed the revolutionary exhilaration of these habitués of bars and cafés:

> Loving ourselves
> we are the crowd
> that invades the streets,
> we are the cascade of humanity
> and passion at a boil,
> we are wine, purling in the goblet of the street:
> we are a crowd
> one hundred thousand heads,
> we are two hundred thousand hands
> passionately beating at the gates of the kingdom
>   of God,
> we are the miracle of miracles,
> crowds rejoicing,
> from the void we will create
> a world. . . . We are a crowd,
> should we choose to spit at the sun,
> it would shrivel.

Seifert enjoyed himself as a dandy and was to appear in Hora's later novel, *Dech na skle* (*Breath on Glass*), as Jaroslav Mydlář. (The Czech term for soap is "mýdlo" and in German it is "Seife.") Mydlář is a proletarian poet who out of his first royalty he receives for his "Proletarian poetry," buys himself a fashionable bamboo-cane and a foppish tie. Although the poets no doubt considered their sentiments genuine, it is hard to avoid the impression that the proletarian prose was just one of the carnival masks of the Bohemian bohème.

"Leaning against the wall of a factory, I choke with smoke and sing my song," is how the twenty year old Seifert depicts himself in his first book of poetry—a much more appropriate proletarian image than leaning against a bar choking on cigarettes and cigar fumes.

In another poem of social protest, he had a handless soldier regret his condition for the first time when he cannot throw stones at policemen! And in a prayer the poet asks: "Virgin Mary, . . . grant it that I will die on a lovely day at the barricades of the revolution with a rifle in my hand." In a similar vein Seifert imagines the coming "Revolution":

> We color with blood,
> stitch red flags,
> expound to heavens, houses and flowers,
> . . . that the revolution will come
> perhaps tomorrow.

His poem "Good News" builds up to end in a religious exultation:

> . . . good news
> that in the East there lies a beautiful country,
> giving birth to justice . . .
> a hammer and sickle. . . .
> Glory, glory to God in Heaven
> and to people on earth revolution.

Poetic titanism comes through the lines of his "The Most Humble Poem":

> . . . I act as a prophet pointing the way
> and predicting a glorious morrow for the poor.
> I am their sage advising in a hopeless day
> holding in my hand a bloom that will fade never
>   more.
> In the revolution I will be the first to shoot
> and I will also be the first one killed. . . .
> marvelous as god
> and mighty as god,
> I am more,
> I am much more,
> and still I am nothing
> humbly devoted to the grace of the masses
> a poet
> Jaroslav Seifert.

Two years later the second volume of Seifert's verse, *Nothing but Love,* was mostly amorous, with just traces of the revolutionary dream: "When the revolution comes, my sweetheart and I will go together to the barricades, to the barricades." But revolutionary blood was still on his mind when sitting in his Communist Party office or in the café Union, a favorite drinking place of the revolutionary poets, he was writing verse:

> "A Lullaby"
>
> . . . Just sleep and doze so you will not hear . . .
> as by the window all the poor will pass
> —your daddy will be with them—
> as over their heads the red flag will flutter
> as shots resound and the smoke will hover
> and one will fall with a bloodied forehead.

But, in his next book of poetry, *Svatební cesta* (*A Honeymoon Trip*), Marxist reviewers looked in vain for any trace of the revolutionary motif, or even for some interest in social problems. For some time, then, Seifert used his lyric talent only for poems of love and enchantment with the individual as focus. This was soon after the publication, in 1922, of a manifesto called "The New Proletarian Art" which Seifert had signed, and in which it was claimed that the major signpost of Proletarian culture was collectivism. A co-signatory was Karel Teige, a zealous composer of such proclamations of revolutionary modernism.

Another, and much more talented, practitioner of Proletarian poetry, Jiří Wolker, read, and then published, the manifesto in the name of the artistic group *Devětsil:*

> We feel the untenability and injustice of today's order and believe in a better reconstruction of society. Finding a solid and concrete plan for it in Marxist theses, we regard the world through historical materialism. Therefore, the new art is for us a *class, proletarian and communist* art. . . . The basic mark of the new art is its revolutionary spirit . . . The artist throws away the cult of everything personalized. He unites with a multitude of similarly fighting people. . . . Against individualism rises *collectivism,* against l'art-pour-l'artism—*tendency.* . . . Practically, collectivism means the consciousness of class solidarity.

French unanimism and Ch. L. Philippe were named as the inspirations for this new art. Six months later Wolker stressed the manifesto's intention to be *"propagation and provocation."* He answered critics who did not like the manifest class hatred by saying that to eliminate it would hurt proletarians because hate preserves human dignity: "Let Proletarian art be like proletarian life: aggressive, non-humanistic, dogmatic." In a famous poem, "X-Rays," he diagnosed hatred to be at the bottom of the poorman's heart. But otherwise in his verse, despite a preoccupation with the often sad life of the poor, Wolker—who was soon to die of TB—was a poet of warmth and optimism, and abundantly used religious images to convey his social message of compassion. *He was very popular.* Interestingly, in one of his plays, *Hrob (The Grave),* a priest said (prophetically): "He who desires a paradise on earth—will create hell!"

The journal S. K. Neumann edited between 1922 and 1924 was called, in the Soviet style, *Proletkult,* and during that period his inspiration came from Mayakovsky. "On Our Inner Battleground," one of the poems in *Rudé zpěvy (Red Songs),* a collection he published in 1923, is patterned on old Christian exhortations to defeat the devil within:

> Each one of us is a battleground. . . .
> The heart must groan and the mind must wrestle
> to crush the enemy within,
> to crush the bourgeois,
> to crush him at the core,
> to crush him, the traitor.

He no longer called himself "son of a bitch" as he had during his Satanic period, but "son of the revolution," and in his poem "To Socialist Women" he advises them that:

> . . . the revolution isn't a rhetorical jaunt:
> learn to shoot!

> Away with feminity!
> . . . Those who laugh now,
> will later wail:
> Learn to shoot! . . .
> Let each woman with the purpose of an arrow
> and like a bloody bitch
> set upon the dogs!

The *enfant terrible* of the Communist movement and its poetic vanguard was a gifted but un-self-critical poet, Vítězslav Nezval. This *bonvivant* needed the red flag of collectivism to save himself from suicidal tendencies and obsessive and terrifying hallucinations. A long poem of his, written in 1921, was published the next year in his first collection of verse, *Most (Bridge),* under the title *Podivuhodný kouzelník (Amazing Magician).* Karel Teige used this poem as a demonstration of the new movement, Poetism, which was replacing the short Proletarian phase. In it Nezval wildly combines strong eroticism with revolution. The fourth canto is called "Revolution":

> A green table supports the hands of the old government
> fifteen thousand revolutionaries stand at the barricade. . . .
> Give me a weapon so I may also stand!
> Order me the largest cockade.
> Something overcomes me, something is amiss.
> I really like the Communist Manifesto . . .
> The magician has once more laid aside his grief
> and mixes with his comrades. . . .
> Nursing hatred in their hearts
> one two
> Nursing hatred in their hearts
> who will feed the little ones?

Nezval later admitted that his "holy man" had been the anarchist Kropotkin, who supposedly helped him to understand Marx's and Engels' "Communist Manifesto" which he, rather incongruously, claimed he read and reread until he managed to lead his life in accordance with it.

But as the chances of a revolution in Czechoslovakia receded and Proletarian poets discovered that the workers were much less interested in poetry about factories than their bourgeois readers and publishers were, the poets now claimed that the task of writers was to prepare a socially liberated man for the future. They would free him from inhibitions of logic, form, tradition and any other order. Still swearing allegiance to Marx and Lenin, to the red flag and revolution, they proclaimed *hedonism* to be their goal. As an Australian observer remarked, "with this freedom went that touch of irresponsibility, of anarchy, so typical of Nezval, the atmosphere of the pantomime, the circus, and the harlequinade."

The poets of Prague were, in reality, much more influenced by modern trends in film, visual arts, jazz and literature, coming from Western countries, than by the Leninist revolution and its promises *cum* horrors. But for these typical bourgeois addicts of Prague night life it was tempting to fight, with their pens, for the new world that would emerge from revolution. In the style of *Proletkult* Nezval wrote a "March of the Red International":

> . . . Proletariat

```
        already
              marching
                     terrible
                            rebellion

Europe
      is
         cracking
               Europe
                     is
                         crumbling

Barbarian
        comes
             against
                   barbarian
                           resist
                                 resist

Barbarism
        the
           weapon
                barbarism
                        the
                           weapon

Barbarism
        the
           weapon
                barbarism
                        the
                           weapon

So will flee
        the
           burning
                 bourgeois
                         moth

So will come
         the dictatorship
                      so will come
                               the dictatorship
```

[Two times more the same slogan, etc.]

The Marxist literary critic Bedřich Václavek, in 1925, welcomed "in the art of Vítězslav Nezval . . . a barbarian invasion of creative, indeed poetic energy into art. This invasion of barbarians into art, prophesized by Ch. L. Philippe, spiritually parallels the vital energy of the revolutionary masses awakened by war and the Russian Revolution." (It was to take the years from 1945 to 1954, and again from August 1968 on, for the less poetical side of barbarism to be experienced.)

The more cautious and moderate Communist believers tried to combine Nezval's exuberant excesses with the march of the Russian proletariat. Thus in 1924 Josef Hora wrote:

> Lenin—according to Nezval a modern Dionysus! Dionysus, god of wine and lust! And yet—isn't it just here, in this conception of Lenin, that there emerges a key to understanding what links the "Poetism" of our young ones with the revolutionary social faith, seemingly so foreign to their almost voluptuous conception of art?

But other left-wing, and even Marxist, reviewers were not amused. A Slovak group of Communist poets and writers,

DAV (Crowd), condemned Poetism as a "manifestation of the bourgeois world which finds itself in deathlike decomposition." F. X. Šalda was "bored," and A. M. Píša denounced the "rococo effeteness of his [Nezval's] inspiration."

As usual in Marxist circles, both groups, the writers and their critics, were badly divided. They resembled herds of prickly porcupines more than a united brotherhood, often hating each other and mutually exchanging the worst possible epithet they could use, namely "bourgeois." (The touching part, of course, is that all of them were really bourgeois people, pretending to be proletarians; at best, they were sometimes charming, and often irresponsible, bourgeois Bohemians.)

Nezval who sometimes came with a few other Communist artists to the famous Friday discussions at Karel Čapek's house, provoked a hilarious reaction from President Masaryk by seriously claiming—with his usual impulsive enthusiasm—that the smaller the bourgeois, the more danger he presented.

The followers of Apollinaire and Lenin, however, listened to the advice and changing prescriptions of Karel Teige who continued putting out manifestos of civism, primitivism, futurism, cubism, modernism, imagism, constructivism, proletarianism, poetism, barbarism, artificialism, abstractivism, and so on. In 1930, in another of the periodically produced programmatic articles, Teige decided to "give the new society a new type of man . . . a harmonious total man." That was at least an appropriate program in the age of totalitarian movements. In a world in crisis, it was fashionable to imagine a new, "total" man.

But, in 1929, Josef Hora and the other Czech poets, Jaroslav Seifert and S. K. Neumann, were among seven writers who were expelled from the Party because they dared to criticize the new Bolshevik leadership imposed by Moscow. They realized that the bridge that Teige had been attempting to create between the artistic avantgarde and Communism had collapsed. Hora wrote then: "We have poets who profess social revolution but by their whole lifestyle they belong in a bourgeois drawing-room." And in 1930 he commented on another basic illusion of the group: "The worker we believed in is different from the worker we know."

In 1927 Teige had begun publishing a new journal, called *ReD*. The title was an abbreviation of "*Revue Devětsilu.*" It was an imitation of the Soviet obsession with acronyms, e.g. CHEKA which hid the long name of the secret police. Proudly displayed on the first page of the 1921 slogan of Devětsil: "New is the star of Communism and without it there is no modernism." Teige now attacked Hora in this journal in the barbaric style that was considered proper for 'decisive' revolutionaries. Hora responded in another journal:

> On the cover of *Red* this quote is underlined: New is the star of Communism and without it there is no modernism. However, that modernism, whether real or imaginary, has nothing in common with Communism. It is fully a child of refined French bourgeois culture. I take excep-

tion to people who powder their faces and glaze themselves with perfumes to call me a social fascist. . . . I lived my communism, did not merely mouth it: I embodied it in my work. For me it was an inner drama but for many of you, dear Teige & Co., no more than an aesthetic mask.

The next fashionable toy brought to Prague from Paris by Nezval and Teige was Surrealism. The Freudian subconscious marvelously suited Nezval's imagination, haunted, as it was, by images of death and suicide or overflowing with all the trappings of carnivals, fairs, circuses, magic and childish playfulness. In 1929 Teige created the "Left Front" of artists, writing its manifesto, and in 1930, he did the same thing for Surrealism. Nezval translated André Breton and Paul Eluard. Proclaiming his Communist purity he published, in 1931, three books of poetry with the titles *Sexuální nokturno* (*Sexual Nocturne*), *Tyranie nebo láska* (*Tyranny or Love*) and *Dolce far niente* (*Sweet Doing Nothing*). When his vigorous defence of Surrealism at Soviet or other world congresses of writers, serving Soviet interests, was not welcomed or even permitted by Russian apparatchiks, responsible for the "cultural front," he was gravely disappointed.

"It became clear that the hoped-for co-operation between Marxist and experimental art was doomed," commented a well informed Australian observer quoting S. K. Neumann:

> It is now quite clear to me that the so-called avantgarde . . . is the direct descendant of the so-called idealistic world attitude, and the recognizably bastard offspring of bourgeois decadence. Their sterile efforts to become the bedfellow of the avantgarde of social revolution, which recognizes one method and one truth—dialectical materialism—is an irresponsible farce.

The growing danger of Fascism and Nazism brought Leftwing writers closer together and they began signing manifestos, even with non-socialist writers. But political processes and show trials in the Soviet Union continued to divide them. S. K. Neumann was always of the opinion that "means are not important, but aims are decisive." He refuted bourgeois criticism of the 119 new executions in the USSR in the winter of 1934/35 by stating: "It is a most insignificant sacrifice if it prevented a bloody attempt at a civil war."

In August 1936 Záviš Kalandra, a member of the Surrealist group, in conjunction with a prominent Communist, Josef Guttman, published a paper, "The Revealed Secret of the Moscow Trial," condemning the show trial of Kamenev, Zinoviev and others. "In Moscow," he wrote, "a crime was committed against the world proletarian revolution." Denounced as Trotskyites, both authors were expelled from the Communist Party—and the democratic Republic, naturally, protected them from anything worse, at least for the moment. Kalandra began to edit a new anti-Stalinist fortnightly called *Proletář* (*The Proletarian*). This catchword of postwar Leftism was still in use but how its connection with Soviet Communism had changed.

The translation of André Gide's *Return from the USSR* provoked a sharp exchange of views and split the cultural Communists into two camps. In 1936, after its serial publication in *Literární noviny,* fifty thousand copies in seven editions were published in a few weeks. The famous French writer's condemnation of the lack of freedom in the Soviet Union, of the cult of Stalin and of the Soviet campaign against modernism in the arts and literature were welcomed by Leftist critics of Stalinism. During a public discussion of the book in January 1937, with Záviš Kalandra, Josef Gutman and Vlado Clementis, Karel Teige denounced Soviet cultural practices as anti-socialist:

> Socialist thought can develop only in a democratic atmosphere of free criticism. . . . Suppression of criticism . . . would mean really a swing towards a disgusting police State.

The Stalinist battler S. K. Neumann did not have such scruples. In May 1937 he published his answer to Gide under the title *Anti-Gide; or, Optimism without Superstition and Illusions.* The poet and propagandist was short of arguments but strong in scornful abuse and vituperations in his address of "decadent poets and artists":

> Go to hell! . . . Even though pseudo-intelligents flirt with some Leftist ideology, after all in their lifestyle and character of their creation they are mycological "flora" of a bourgeois hothouse. . . . [It is] a childish supposition that the so-called artistic avantgarde forms a part of the revolutionary proletarian vanguard. . . . The socialist revolution does not have anything in common with today's aesthetic "revolutions" in the intelligentsia's glass of water which is only a metropolis, coffee-house, lukewarm, badly filtered, in all sorts of ways sweetened, perfumed and colored liquid for the spoiled stomach of an isolated caste.

Because Neumann hit the Communist intellectuals in their very sensitive underbelly of self-doubts and because they felt the need for political alliance with the Soviet Union against Nazism, the reaction to his vulgar pamphlet was mild. It was up to a non-Communist to remark that "unlike the French writer who wrote what he saw and felt, Neumann wrote what he imagines and what he believes."

Vítězslav Nezval supported Neumann by an idolatrous ode, according to which Stalin was "a great tuner of pianos" who "tore up rotted strings."

In October 1937 Soviet censorship drastically eliminated many paintings from the official exhibition of Czech visual arts. Again, the Communists in Prague accepted the humiliation without any public protest. The Soviet campaign against Meyerhold and the closing of his celebrated theater evoked at least a sharp reaction from Karel Teige, Roman Jakobson and the Czech avantgarde theater director E. F. Burian. This Communist then became a target for concentrated attacks by his comrades for his poetical and imaginative productions. Burian defended artistic freedom against these vulgar criticisms and accused Julius Fučik as "a deterrent sinking to the level of a wild bourgeois capable of cutting pictures he does not understand or burning books that disturb him."

In the democratic Republic Burian dared to defend principles which ten or twenty years later he would find difficult if not impossible to repeat:

> The working people of Czechoslovakia must know that no external power of any state has the right to interfere in the cultural politics of this country. . . . Here in Czechoslovakia we will solve our cultural and social questions ourselves. We, inheritors of a famous cultural tradition reaching far back into the Middle Ages will solve our problems as we will see fit on our way to general social progress. . . . In our conditions so-called "socialist realism" is a theoretical bluff. In the first place, it is a false term. It concerns Soviet realism and not at all socialist realism.

> If in the name of Soviet realism, S. K. Neumann is hellbent on calling for bolts and lightnings on every art created in our own traditions, it would be appropriate to remind this bard of dilettantism and masked naturalism that his poetic practice does not at all correspond with his strange theory that he is calling Marxism.

When an attempt to induce members of Burian's theater to denounce their director misfired since they unanimously supported his stance, another theater director from a provincial city attacked him viciously and threatened to close down his hall the way it happened to Meyerhold: "Then we will really sweep the stage!" The spirit of liquidation that would carry the day in February 1948 was already present in the Party.

The confrontation continued in cultural and political magazines. S. K. Neumann kept attacking formalism and other supposedly decadent trends and stigmatized as absolutely incorrect "the old liberal and individualistic superstition that an artistic work should be judged only by artistic criteria."

Novelist Vladislav Vančura . . . defended artists' freedom and remarked:

> S. K. Neumann is an idyllic rebelling against his own idyllic nature. Youth, love, Satan, communism and revolution are only props used by the poet to interweave in his tapestries. These disproportions between stormy will power and his own peaceful feeling probably create the poet's charm, and gives the impression of titanism. However, it surely does not protect the author from an objection of formalism.

Karel Teige went further than that and called attention to similarities between Hitlerism and Stalinism:

> Aesthetic kinship binds together socialist realism and Nazi realism. . . . [Neumann] took over his terminology of "perverse art" from people who reach for a gun when they hear the word culture.

Vítězslav Nezval unilaterally declared the Surrealist group dissolved and claimed that Meyerhold's theater had to be closed down because it was hiding spies. When Teige systematically criticized Soviet "reactionary censorship, . . . scientific stagnation and decline, . . . reaction-

ary culture," in a long study *Surrealism against the Current* (1938), Nezval called his old friend "this aged avantgardist and Trotskyite intellectual" and addressed him and his friends:

> Oh, paper galley-slaves! Soap bubbles! Puffed-up buffoons! These monsters!

Although the majority of Czech men and women of culture, including many Communists, refused to accept Soviet barbaric treatment of its artists, it was obvious that even in Czechoslovakia there was a group of simpleminded and determined liquidators who just needed to come to total power in order to display their anti-cultural terrorism.

Záviš Kalandra, Karel Teige and many other Communist enthusiasts, not only Surrealists, had to pay for their criticism of Soviet crimes after the Communist coup d'état of 1948 when they experienced for themselves revolutionary barbarism and its progressive "scientific torture" once it reached Prague from Moscow. Others would have constant problems because they did not adopt the Stalinist line and believed in democratic socialism. That would be the case of Jaroslav Seifert who grew wiser and in 1937 published a poem called "In Lenin's Mausoleum":

> Beneath the red wall, beneath the domes
> golden and gleaming
> on his catafalque in sweet repose,
> as if just dreaming,
> in a glass coffin Lenin lies,
> as though by death unmarred,
> watching with half-closed eyes
> the soldier who stands on guard. . . .
> The red flag's still there
> but where is the revolution—where?
> The Kremlin wall, red like a field of poppies,
> its teeth bare in ire.
> There comrade Stalin has his office,
> but no revolutionary fire.
> Suddenly the silence is shattered
> by the sound of shooting—
> at the Lubyanka enemies and traitors
> they are executing.
> Now Lenin seems to awaken.
> He stretches out his hand:
> "Why do I lie here forsaken?
> Tell me that my friend.
> When out there in the streets they need me
> I cannot stay.
> Don't leave me here to sleep, but lead me
> to join the fray."
> But the soldier shook his head and pressed
> the lid down tight.
> "No, you just lie here quietly and rest.
> Why go and fight?
> Sleep, comrade, and be glad you're here.
> These days it's best to keep
> your nose clean, don't you interfere.
> Good night, go back to sleep."
> Lenin falls asleep. In his quiet tomb
> the shadows gather in,
> his tranquil face permeated
> with wax and paraffin.

Kalandra, Teige, Seifert, Clementis and many others would never be forgiven for having expressed doubts or criticism of Stalin's activities. Communist commissars once they assumed total power in Prague would remind them of it and punish them while S. K. Neumann would be extolled as a model poet and man to be followed by all. (pp. 21-39)

> Peter Hruby, "Czech Poets' Post-World War I Mésalliance: French Avantgarde and Russian Communism," in his Daydreams and Nightmares: Czech Communist and Ex-Communist Literature, 1917-1987, *East European Monographs, 1990, pp. 21-39.*

Wilma Iggers

[*Iggers is a Czech-born American critic and educator. In the following excerpt, she discusses the relationship of Jewish authors living in Bohemia during the early twentieth century to Czech society and to their own Jewish heritage.*]

The literature written by German-speaking Bohemian Jews has recently been receiving, deservedly, an increasing amount of attention. This cannot be said of Czech-Jewish literature, partly because it is less accessible than literature written in German. A more important factor seems to be, however, that since the emergence of Jews in Bohemian *belles lettres,* conditions have been more favorable to those writing in German than in Czech.

The families of both groups were generally small-town businessmen who spoke the local language; by governmental decree, however, they were forced to have German religious services and instruction, business contracts, and even names.

We encounter the first generation of Jewish writers in Bohemia before the middle of the nineteenth century; Leopold Kompert, Ludwig August Frankl, and Moritz Hartmann were the best-known among them. They wrote in German and considered themselves Austrian Germans of liberal Jewish belief. (p. 88)

About the turn of the century, there were German-Jewish writers, such as Friedrich Adler, the philosopher, Fritz Mauthner and Hugo Salus, who wrote lyric poetry and fiction, while their Czech-Jewish counterparts were preoccupied with the theme of nationality, like many of their successors. They wrote mostly for the Czech-Jewish publications which originated in the 1880's: *Českožidovsky kalendář, Českožidovské listy,* and *Rozvoj.* Although these periodicals contained cultural sections and strove for the mutual understanding of Czechs and Jews, their chief aim was to transform their readers into Czechs who happened to be of the Jewish faith. Their editors and writers also fought against assimilationism, which, to them, meant the abandonment of all Jewish ties; they fought against the use of the German language, especially in the religious schools, against anti-Semitism, and, later, against Zionism. For the literary sections, contributions with a Czech patriotic tendency were clearly preferred.

Some of the writers and editors wrote exclusively for these publications; others, like Edvard Lederer, known under the pen name of Leda, and Viktor Vohryzek, also wrote novels and stories, mostly of village life. Only Vojtěch Ra-

kous reached a wider reading Czech public; his work was translated into German, and (less extensively) into English. Among the writers of the Czech-Jewish movement, Vohryzek was most outstanding as a cultural leader and humanitarian, as an advocate of tolerance and peace among the factions. Together with a coworker, he was accused of high treason and jailed during World War I by the Austro-Hungarian government. Even he, however, wasted much energy on relatively trivial problems such as, for example, whether a certain colleague preferred his Czechness or his Jewishness. The Czech-Jewish movement was also concerned with its relationship to the Czechs as Christians. Jindřich Kohn stressed the importance of understanding the Christianity of the Czechs, in view of the Christian character of the noblest parts of Czech national tradition.

The Czech-Jewish movement also tried to show a thirteenth-century foundation for its views. Its members were able to point to a thirteenth-century scholar, surnamed "Chládek," who supplied a Czech glossary for Hebrew writings, as well as two Jews among the vernacular translators of the *Kralická bible.* Moreover, since the Bohemian Jews had been forced to adopt the German language which language that had replaced—Czech, Hebrew or, perhaps, Judendeutsch—became a major topic of discussion.

It seems strange that so many intelligent people should have put so much effort into discussing the identity of a group. The very timing and suddenness of the rise of such an intellectual group is puzzling; the political reasons of 1918 and later were then absent and, by the same token, the argument that one suppressed people was being loyal to another would have been equally valid for the earlier period. Nor does German anti-Semitism constitute a valid explanation. Masaryk's claim that there was never a Czech theorist of anti-Semitism comparable to Chamberlain in Germany is not valid. There were books in the 1890's, such as Březnovský's *Ujařmeni Světa Židy* [*The Subjugation of the World by the Jews*] and Rudolf Vrba's *Národni sebeochrana: Úvahy o hmotném a mravnim upádku národa českèho. [National Self-Protection: Reflections on the Material and Moral Decay of the Czech Nation*].

At that time, Czech anti-Semitism seems to have been at least as strong as the German. It was during the period of the most intense Czech-Jewish activity that anti-Semitic riots were most frequent in Bohemia. In fact, there was still violence against Jews in the midst of the rejoicing over newly-won freedom in 1918 and after. At that time, again, the question of whether Jews should be writing in Czech, particularly patriotic literature, received considerable notice in the Czech press.

Czech anti-Semitism was further aggravated by the fact that Jews, who had left the ghettos so recently, quickly became prosperous. The difficulty of the situation was compounded by the Austrian government's attempted suppression of the Czech language, as well as by the presence of a sizable German population. The Jews had long felt like, and had been felt as, aliens to whom the idea of national solidarity—Czech or German—was irrelevant;

since they were hardly in a position to quibble with the Austrian Imperial government about language, they often did speak the language which symbolized to the Czechs *the* threat to their national survival.

In general, even the philo-Semitic Czechs, such as Machar and Prof. J. V. Krejčí, viewed the Jews as members, not only of a religious group, but also of a nationality, and felt they should be preserved as such. There are statements like this, as one might expect, not only from Havlíček, but also from Thomas Masaryk, who emphatically disapproved of changing one's nationality as a means to an end.

It may seem strange that we have not yet mentioned Jewish religion *per se*. Among the major Bohemian-Jewish writers, Czech or German, there is not one who accepted the orthodoxy of his ancestors. Relatively few, mostly German-speaking Jews, took the final step and declared themselves non-Jews, while the majority seems to have taken it for granted that all religion was on the decline. Thus, the advocates of *Československví* dealt more extensively with their Czechness than with their Jewishness. This rejection of traditional Judaism was one of the rare instances of similarity between the Czech Jews and the German Jews.

There was a sudden general decline in Jewish learning toward the end of the nineteenth century. For the first two-thirds of the century, there had been high esteem for religious institutions, for rabbis and teachers of religion. Then there followed the gradual abolition of German-Jewish schools in Czech-speaking areas and their replacement by a few hours of Jewish religious instruction each week; finally, with few exceptions, there was nothing left but the observance of the most essential ritual and the high holi days. About 1900, attitudes within the Jewish communities ranged from those who welcomed these developments to those who regretted them as signs of the impending end of the Jews *as Jews*.

Various explanations suggest themselves: There was the abolition of the ghettos, and the new freedom of the Jews to move, to choose their occupations, and to enter the professions. There was also, as Hugo Hermann pointed out, the rationalistic, secular, liberal, and anti-religious tone which prevailed in the Austrian schools. One wonders whether the recent closer association with the Czech gentiles was not an additional important factor; they themselves, trapped between enforced Catholicism and forbidden Protestantism, had long since become lukewarm toward religion. Both Czech and German Jewish writers were aware of this decline, and trusted that the vacuum was going to be filled somehow.

Among the Czech-Jewish writers, it was Rakous who felt most bitter about his experience with Jewish schools and synagogues, and expressed himself about them repeatedly in his autobiographical cycle of sketches, *Lojza Kiesler*. Here we must take into account the humiliation Rakous experienced as the son of a near-beggar among the rich, and as a village Czech among prosperous town Germans. While his work is full of nostalgia about village practices, which to him had the folkloristic freshness of rural Catholicism, his work also abounds with accounts of the in-

humanity and formality of German "city" Judaism. Most moving is Rakous' description of young Lojza accompanying his father to synagogue: "Only those . . . went to the altar who sat in the front seats . . . The sacred parchment was only for the people who had golden chains . . . " Rakous still felt bitter after many years; "I would like to tell how happy the children of poor Jews felt in those glorified schools. The teacher, a man without any education coarse and greedy, was used to generous gifts . . . From us, he could hope—at the most—for a loaf of black bread. So my poverty was the cause of much rejection . . . "

In Rakous' comments, there is often even hate as well as regret; " . . . Look at the rabbi . . . a man who looks in the synagogue as if he wanted to eat the dear Lord, but outside is full of greed and gossip. And the religious services . . . What good is this constant rising and bowing and beating of one's breast? In those prayers, how much praise is brought to God! And praise which is actually repulsive in its obtrusiveness . . . "

That this attitude persisted, with some variations, can be seen in an article by Kamil Kohn, several decades later: "Religion taught by Jewish teachers in the old way, without any human understanding of the young, strengthens them in the view that it (religion) is old and outmoded." And, almost literally like his German-Jewish contemporary, Willy Haas, he continues: "The parents cannot give the ritual a vital foundation, because they lack the basic sources of the human spirit."

Since the German Jews lived in Prague, and the Czech Jews mostly in small towns, their paths rarely crossed. But they shared the same awareness of the meaninglessness and formalism of organized Judaism. Max Brod expressed this in his largely autobiographical *Beinahe ein Vorzugsschüler:*

> We pupils of "Mosaic confession" gathered . . . for a ridiculous undertaking which bore the name of instruction . . . for there we learned nothing at all. I have rarely seen a more pronounced indifference than that with which "Rebbe Bloch" treated his subject and his pupils . . . He was bored no less than he bored us . . . One can imagine what an effect these sloppy procedures had on us . . . The literary documents which were to be studied were obviously not . . . worthy of serious consideration . . . One chatted shamelessly threw paper ships filled with ink . . . Others openly wrote their assignments for the following, so-called "worldly" class . . .

Brod seems to have accepted this situation without particularly strong feelings. He was a proud Jew and an early Zionist, who, although he felt that he owed the greatest debt to German culture, and expected to continue writing in German, at least as long as he lived in the "diaspora," nevertheless advocated what he called "Distanzliebe" toward the Germans. With the Czechs he lived in mutual esteem, but the possibility of Czech identity never seems to have entered his mind, although he enthusiastically promoted Czech music (Janacek's especially). Brod was emotionally involved with his Jewishness, but it constituted no problem for him. He was, therefore, able to write, on the one hand, clear statements of faith without grinding propagandistic axes, and on the other hand, stories in which he drew from his own background.

It is striking how many writers of that generation left similar testimony concerning their own experience of organized religion. Willy Haas said briefly: "Nothing had remained to us of the faith of our ancestors," and "Thus we were neither Christians nor Jews . . . "

Kafka's letter to his father is well-known, especially the reproaches he heaped on him for the meaninglessness of the Jewish religious services, which his father was, after all, powerless to change.

> It was really . . . a nothing, a joke, not even a joke. You went to temple four days a year, and were there . . . closer to the indifferent than to those who took it seriously, patiently went through the prayers as a formality; you astonished me sometimes by being able to show me the passage in the prayerbook which was just being recited, . . . I was permitted to "hang around" wherever I wanted, as long as I was in the temple. I yawned and dozed through the many hours . . . Preparing for Bar Mitzvah was ridiculous memorizing . . . at home it was perhaps even more miserable. The eve of Pass-over was a comedy with laughing cramps. This then was the religious material which was handed down to me. I did not understand how one could do anything better . . . than to get rid of it as

quickly as possible . . . It was impossible to make plausible to a . . . child that the few insignificant gestures which you carried out in the name of Judaism, with an insignificance in keeping with that insignificance, could have a higher meaning.

Yet Kafka not only accepted the fact that he was a Jew—he wanted to be more so. He was interested in the Eastern Jewish actors who came to Prague, as much for their Jewishness as for their acting, and he spent a considerable amount of time studying Hebrew. There was also his relationship with Dora Dymant, the Eastern European Jewish friend of the last period of his life, and his frequently-expressed regrets at not being the father of a family, another circumstance setting him apart from the chain of generations descended from biblical times.

Kafka wrote in German, but his German contained "Prague-isms," occasional affinities with Czech expressions and forms. He regretted not knowing Czech perfectly, feeling that language was "nearer to his heart" than German. Realizing that nothing could make up for the strong Jewish tradition that was lacking in his childhood, he was tortured by not "belonging."

This does not mean that I agree with the frequently-repeated attribution of insularity to the Prague German Jewish writers, especially the triple isolation of Kafka—religious, national, and social—as proclaimed by Pavel Eisner. If Kafka's anxiety was really an expression, no matter how creative, of a limited social situation, rather than a universal expression of the human condition, at least of his and our time, we would merely be following a moribund fad in considering him as a literary figure. To be sure, most of the Prague German writers, almost all of whom were Jewish, were almost completely isolated from Czech, and from what there was of Sudenten German culture, but certainly not from that of the German-speaking world. They did not, as Lore Foltin claims in her book about Werfel, live in a ghetto. Hans Kohn, who was close to the Prague German Jewish writers, and may have been aware of such claims, wrote in his autobiography; " . . . The German-speaking minority among whom I grew up maintained a fully-developed, separate cultural and social life of its own. We did not feel isolated. We felt at home in Prague and in the Czech countryside around the city. All this was our land, too. We breathed its air and loved its contours."

From childhood to maturity, Jewishness played a relatively small role in Franz Werfel's life. His background was somewhat more upper-class than that of the other Prague writers. If we take into consideration the many accounts of contemporaries about the coldness and impersonality of the Werfel home (by Brod, Haas, etc.), Werfel's later religious development becomes plausible. As Judaism does not seem to have been a force at all, in the entirely assimilated Werfel family, he approached religious feeling of a kind, a sympathy for Catholicism, by way of the human warmth of the Czech maids who cared for him in his childhood. His feeling of brotherhood with all mankind, as found in his expressionistic poetry and later in his novels, was certainly religious, but not specifically Jewish.

Franz Kafka.

Still, it seems to have been because of solidarity with the persecuted Jews that he never actually joined the Catholic Church. All his life, Werfel felt nostalgic for Prague, but he certainly felt no more at home in any one of the countries in which he lived and of which he wrote than in another. Perhaps his last, utopistic work, *Star of the Unborn,* dealing with life on a supranational planet, provides a clue.

Before the turn of the century, another current joined this complex stream of literatures; the Zionists. For the most part disinterested in traditional religion, they hoped for a Jewish community in Palestine, where old values would be translated into modern secular terms. Here again, there were actually two currents, Czech and German, and again they differed in character.

The Czech-Zionist writers, like the earlier Czech-Jewish ones, were largely represented in focal publications; *Zidovskè zprávy, Židovskè listy* and *Židovský kalendář.* These were of a rather high literary level, and also had non-Jewish contributors. This Czech-Zionist group derived much of its impetus from the anti-Jewish riots in Bohemia, chiefly at the time of the Hilsner affair, and from the Dreyfus affair. Its most important writer was František Gottlieb. In comparing him with Brod, his German counterpart, one is again struck by the fact that Gottlieb's writings, even his lyric poetry, are largely propagandistically Zionist, while Brod's literary works are free of ideological elements.

Love of the Czech homeland was also a frequent note with the Czech Zionists. In the words of Irma Poláková, one of the few Czech-Jewish women writers: "I love two worlds. I shall never stop thinking of you, little village on the Vltava [Moldau]; may my right hand wither if I stop longing for you, Jerusalem."

On the other hand, the Zionists often blamed their love of the Czech fatherland for the Jewish decline, as when Oskar Kraus (not to be confused with the Prague German writer of the same name), a frequent contributor to *Ceskozidovsky kalendář,* stated that he had been mistaking his love of "cěšstvi" (Czechness) for a sense of belonging.

During the first decades of the twentieth century, a very important generation of Czech-Jewish writers developed. The best of the new writers were complex, quite interesting, and highly individualistic. What they had in common was their Jewish family background and the fact that they either ignored, rejected, or only reluctantly and belatedly accepted it. Nothing was of less interest to them than organized Judaism.

One of the writers least concerned with the Jewish Problem was František Langer, one of the greatest Czech dramatists, who achieved an international reputation with *Velbloud uchem jehly.* Langer wanted the Jews to become non-Jewish Czechs, and exhorted them to suppress their Jewish characteristics. Consequently, almost no Jewish characters appear in his works.

František Gellner went further, being a violent anti-Semitic Jew. In *The New Cult* of 1904, he stated that, unlike Catholic clericalism, Jewish clericalism does not strive to increase its religious status, but works, rather, for the economic advantage of the "chosen people" over the impractical "natives". He was sceptical of the motives of Jews, whether Zionists, assimilationists, patriots, or liberals, and claimed that he considered them quite capable of ritual murder. Often denying his own Jewish origin, he also suggested that there be pogroms against the Jews of Moravian Brno for their pro-German sentiments. In the light of these opinions, it is significant that Gellner, the best example of Jewish self-hatred among the Czechs, was acceptable as a staff member to *Lidové noviny,* perhaps the most respected Czech daily.

Karel Poláček, born in 1892 and ten years younger than Gellner, was a satirist storyteller of *genre,* frequently of Jewish characters from the full range of the middle class. Their spoken Czech is mixed with German-Jewish phrases and they partake of all the faults generally attributed to Jews. If Rakous endeared his characters to the Czech Gentiles, the opposite is sometimes true of Poláček. Some of his stories, therefore, have the same appeal as anti-Semitic jokes.

A recently rediscovered figure is Richard Weiner, a Czech-Jewish writer of the same generation. His works are now being republished in Czechoslovakia. In him, we find an amazing number of parallels with Kafka; they were born at the same time, and in both we find a strong psychological emphasis. Like Kafka, Weiner is often a difficult writer, expressing himself in symbols and allegories. Many of his characters are young men with split personalities. In his novel, *Smrt Jakuba Ondřicha,* a rich man tries to destroy a poor friend, and if we replace poverty with Judaism, we can understand the feelings of an estranged Jew. Where the poor boy, that is, the Jew, passively accepts insults—poverty—he is that much less poor, or less a Jew. When Jakub talks to his parents about prejudice against the poor, it is clear that prejudice against Jews is meant. As in Kafka's work, the Jewish problem as such is rarely mentioned. Only one Jew, a positive figure, appears, yet Jewishness is present in Weiner's intellectuality, in his inclination toward irony, and in his critical and journalistic talent. He considered much of his own character typically Jewish, such as his pretense of indifference and self-irony in the face of strong feelings. Weiner regarded it as a Jewish characteristic that he was not carried away in political fights and that peace was always his goal. Then again, he hated himself for being self-critical, yet conciliatory toward others, which he also considered typically Jewish.

Weiner felt a little more drawn toward the Zionists than toward the Czech Jews, and contributed to their publications. He called himself a Czech because he felt closer to Czech artists than others, yet he expressed the insecurity of this stand when he spoke of the tragedy of the Jew trying to merge with his surroundings as being "that he doesn't feel like what he is, and isn't quite what he feels." After some anti-Semitic riots in Bohemia in 1919, Weiner advised (in *Socialistické listy*) that there be an end to the Czech-Jewish movement, "which wears its Czechness as a joy and its Jewishness as a bitter drop in it." Undoubtedly, of all the writers of his generation, Weiner had the most intellectual appeal.

The most creative man, of many facets, was Otokar Fischer, who lived through many years of self-torture before coming to terms with his Jewishness. Carrying away from his native Kolín a strong dislike of its Jewish community, he studied Germanics in Berlin, became Professor of German Literature at Charles University and, later, "dramaturg" at the National Theater. As a translator, he was probably the most important mediator between Czech and foreign literatures, especially German. He translated into Czech works by Goethe, Heine, Kleist, Nietzsche, and others. Above all, Fischer was an outstanding lyric poet and dramatist.

Even early poetry reflected his feelings about his Jewish origin:

> "who am I"? A descendant of sensuous races—yet without feeling for their children, thrown by life like a ball from one century to another . . . my place a crossroads . . . my home; the labyrinth of the ages . . . I am of the blood from which Ahasver emerged.

When Fischer fell in love with a Jewish woman, that love seemed to him incestuous and he fled from it.

He remained separated from the Jews by a personal dislike of them and by lack of a religious faith. At the same time, he realized that he had tried to become a member of another people which did not accept him; "I am one of them. And yet less and more. I am chosen . . . only a newcomer, a guest, a half-breed. Thus different from those whose songs I sing, a renegade from those whose blood I have . . . " After having long evaded Jewish environment, ideas, and culture, and even after going so far as to be baptized, he came to believe that one cannot escape one's race. Although aware of differences, Fischer felt akin to Heine and esteemed him as the foremost modern Jewish poet. He probably suffered for his Jewishness much more than Heine: he was reminded of its inescapability every time he heard a lively dance and felt a stranger to its spirit.

When Fischer's play, *Přemyslovci,* appeared, it was praised highly by some, and rejected by others, who denied the appropriateness of a Czech patriotic play written by a Jew, as they also had in the case of some of Langer's plays.

It is a strange coincidence that Kapper, the first Jew to write in Czech, and Fischer, the greatest of the last generation before World War II, met with the same fate (at least, from some critics); rejection as Jews. It is an ironic situation in which a man of intensely cosmopolitan intellect, with the soul of the eternally searching Jew, fulfills the hopes of generations of his fellows in writing a great work of literature for his host nation, only to be rebuffed. If there is a lesson to be learned from this, it is that injustice—in this case, against the Czechs—produces feelings of insecurity which seem to result in greater injustices more often than in just retribution against guilty. (pp. 89-101)

> *Wilma Iggers, "The Bohemian Jewish Writers: Their Attitude toward Their Roots," in* Studies in Czechoslovak History, Vol. II, *edited by Miloslav Rechcigl, Jr., Sadhna Prakashan, 1976, pp. 88-101.*

René Wellek

[*An American critic who grew up in Vienna and Prague, Wellek is noted for his literary criticism as outlined in such works as his* Theory of Literature *(1949) and the multivolume* History of Modern Criticism *(1955-1986). At the center of Wellek's theories lies his differentiation between an "extrinsic" and "intrinsic" approach to critical analysis. He maintains the necessity of viewing a work of art as an entity in and of itself rather than as a result of such properties extrinsic to the work as the social or cultural environment in which it was created. In the following excerpt, Wellek surveys the works of major Czech literary critics of the interwar era.*]

During the last twenty or twenty-five years, we have witnessed a remarkable revival of criticism in the United States. Criticism has successfully invaded the academic groves: academic historians themselves have adopted methods of criticism, a union of scholarship with critical sensitivity and acumen has been accomplished in many instances. This happy marriage, good for both scholarship and criticism, occurred but rarely at other times: we can think of Ferdinand Brunetière and other "professional critics" in France; we might name De Sanctis who was Professor of Comparative Literature at the University of Naples; we might consider Matthew Arnold or A. C. Bradley who were, for a time, Professors of Poetry at Oxford. But these are isolated instances. The most striking example of an almost unique collaboration between criticism and scholarship was the Czechoslovakia of between the two world wars. There critics were professors and professors critics, almost as a matter of course.

The leading figure in the whole history of modern Czech criticism is F. X. Šalda (1867-1937) who had joined the University of Prague, comparatively late in his life, in 1917, as *Docent* and later as professor of Western literatures. He was always an unacademic person: the critic who had come to the university from the outside, from journalism of a high level.

Šalda had begun writing criticism in 1892, at a crucial time in Czech literary history. His first ambitious article, "Synthetism in the New Art", opened entirely new vistas to the Czechs. It was an exposition of the French symbolist view of poetry, interpreted rather freely, not merely in the terms of the actual symbolist coterie. Šalda speaks of "synthesis", of "concrete symbolism", slogans which allow him both a rejection of mysticism, of high-flown claims for art as a way to the Absolute, and of naturalism as advocated by Zola. Poetry is symbolic, both concrete and intuitive; style is expressive, individual, a psychological sign, something purely subjective which allows the writer to go against his own language because he wants to evoke an exact shade of feeling. There is no divorce between form and content, image and idea, subject and meaning, and ultimately, while not mystical insight, art is a way of knowing, of grasping essences, of seeing into the nature of things. In retrospect, this article seems today rather too obviously derivative: it is heavily overloaded with references and footnotes, tortuously self-conscious in its striving for an exact abstract terminology. Its sources, even for the formulas on synthesis and concrete symbolism, are writers now little known in France: Charles Morice, Émile Hennequin, and an Italian, Vittorio Pica, who wrote on Mallarmé in the *Revue indépendante* (vol. 18, 1891). It is characteristic for the cultural situation of the Czechs at the time that Šalda's knowledge of and enthusiasm for English poetry, for Shelley and Whitman, comes from French sources (such as Gabriel Sarrazin) and that even his quotations from German writers (from Wagner and Goethe) are lifted from his French models.

But Šalda, as a practising critic, reviewing current Czech books, indulging in polemics with his contemporaries, quickly emancipated himself from any close dependence on his sources and developed a critical personality of great strength and sharply defined character. Soon nobody could mistake his style. It fuses the most diverse elements in the furnace of a fiery temperament: learned terminology, abstract concepts jostle there cheek by jowl with trivial colloquialisms, hymnical passages of florid metaphors with coarse sarcasms and surprising *ad hoc* personal applications. The earlier mannerisms of the end of the century, the aristocratic pose, were slowly abandoned, and late in life Šalda managed to speak more forthrightly, more directly and colloquially without losing his subtlety or brilliance. In 1928, when he was 61, Šalda started a monthly magazine, *Šalda's Notebook,* which he wrote from cover to cover up to his death at the age of 70, in 1937. There he found the right medium for his temperament, the possibility of publishing descriptive, analytical, historical articles alongside reviews of current productions, comments on political and social events, and personal polemics. But though we can observe this change of style, and can see a change of fronts during the forty-five years of Šalda's writing life, we cannot speak of any complete break, of any lack of unity or coherence in his outlook. A close discussion of his evolution as a writer would have to distinguish different stages, but we need not do so here where we want to describe only his central position and concrete merits.

Šalda's strength is hardly literary theory, if we demand of a critic that he should have elaborated a theoretical system of aesthetics and poetics (as Taine or Croce did). But Šalda has an astonishing grasp of essentials, a sane and balanced creed, which, in spite of his violent temperament and even frequent bad temper, is quite free of the fanaticism of a single school or of any pussyfooting eclecticism and colorless compromises. He thinks as a true dialectician in terms of opposites which can be reconciled in a higher synthesis, knowing that either extreme side is true in part, and neither is true as a whole. He firmly holds fast to both handles of a question.

Thus his theory of criticism seems to oscillate between the poles: the critic, he says, is both an artist and a scholar, both a man of passion and personal involvement and a patient describer and observer of things, both a historian who knows the past and a prophet who anticipates the future. There is nothing irreconcilable in these demands which Šalda made, with different emphasis, at different times, without ever giving up either of these sides. In an early piece, he disparages method which only distracts attention from the one necessary condition of criticism: the personality of the critic, his equipment, his qualification. The critic must first have a passionate regard, a personal experience of art, sensitivity both of the mind and the senses. He must be an artist who creates a new work, and he must be a judge who asks: do I want the life which the artist wants? Even in the late papers, in the *Notebook,* there is this emphasis on personality, sympathy, and this distrust of any fixed table of values. He can say that "the critic must find his criteria in the last moment with the same act of intuition with which the poet creates", and that subjectivism means not caprice but, if developed in its full strength, an actual way to objectivity. Thus Šalda early rejected scientific theories which seem to account for literature by external causes such as Taine's system of determinism, not because he does not see literature as part of society and was not a keen student of social psychology and history, but because he realized that finally all these theories are confronted with something they cannot cope with: individuality, creativity. Similarly, late in life, he rejected Marxism for the very same reasons: both as a theory of literature and its application in Russia where he saw it stifled creation and suppressed the freedom of the artist. But he saw the advantages of a more systematic analysis of literature and came to view a more coherent "science of art" (*Kunstwissenschaft*) as an ideal of the future. He always believed in the central function of the critic: the necessity of judging, of deciding what is art and what is not art, what is life and what is death. The critic, he says, is like a horse in the Alps, preceding a sleigh, trying the snow to see whether it can carry a human load. He is the advance rider, the man with a feel for the future, just because he knows and loves the past.

Thus there is no contradiction between Šalda's frequent defense of tradition and even classicism (which must not be academicism), of order, discipline, and form, and his search for the new, the revolutionary, his sympathy for the young who want to do something different, to strike out in new directions. Šalda simply had a very concrete grasp of the nature of poetry and literature which was to him not limited to any one kind of art and still exacting enough to exclude anything which seemed to him lifeless, derivative, merely photographic, or merely rhetorical and tendentious. Basically, he kept to his very earliest sympathies, which were with the symbolism he helped to introduce to his countrymen. He always believed that "poetic experience is a way of knowing, of the highest, essential kind, which penetrates like lightning into the very nature of a thing, into the very texture of life by direct intuition". He always believed that poetry is not merely experience, sincerity, good intentions, but that it is primarily creation: complete, synthetic vision by a complete man, who uses his imagination and feelings, intellect and will, body and soul. But the poem, Šalda realizes very early, is made up of words which the poet must handle with skill and daring to create a coherent structure. There is something like an "alchemy of words", a "laboratory of the word" which makes it essential for the critic to analyze style and form.

Šalda was hardly and could hardly be a technical "formalist": but even in early essays we can find a constant regard for technique, frequent attention to subtle shades of meaning, of diction, syntax, and metaphor. Such remarks are rarely there for their own sake; they serve as a means towards a general characterization, as a way of entering into the mind and soul of the author, as Šalda believes in the unity of content and form, soul and art. But he conceives of personality as something *in* art, not as something outside in the empirical life of the author. He recognizes that the greatest experience of an artist is his work, and that there he may build up a fictional person, accomplish an "autostylization", as Šalda called the process. But this personality of the author or rather this search for personality which is a search for the work and its fullest realization, is not meant to be something purely individualistic and egotistical. Šalda knows that the poet is simultaneously trying to find something superpersonal—call it truth or beauty or life—and that in expressing himself he is expressing humanity and thus serving it. Though in early pronouncements, in agreement with his time, Šalda seems to lean occasionally to an art for art's sake point of view, reacting against the utilitarian demands of patriots, he increasingly came to stress the artist's responsibility to society. In the years after the war, he praised many professedly socialist and communist poets without being frightened by their ostensible purpose. But he always firmly kept to his central view that art must be art first, before it can be considered for social usefulness. Just as he had opposed the patriots and nationalists who wanted everything to serve an immediate national purpose, so he came to oppose the recipes for "proletarian" art and to protest against Gorky and local advocates of uniformity and immediate social utility.

He could do so because he understood the nature of art as an aesthetic fact and also saw its intimate connection with religion. "Art and religion agree on one thing: they kindle and preserve the belief in the reality of the individual and his infinite value". Šalda's religion is something highly individualistic, personal, internal, though he recognizes the symbolical and practical value of dogma and ritual and, in words written shortly before his death, knows that God is the God of everybody and all and cannot be "private". He saw the social role of art as an almost religious act of love, of human solidarity. In a remarkable essay "On the So-Called Immortality of the Work of Art", Šalda indulges in melancholy reflections on the transience of glory, on the errors and misunderstandings of fame, on the terrible struggle which the living wage with the dead for a piece of free life: for there are so many of the dead! And so many are constantly being added to them, all the time. And they rob the living of so much life! But against this inevitable decay of the "immortality" of even the greatest works, Šalda puts the eternity of values as the true and only result of creation.

Šalda's importance as a critic is, however, less in these general reflections and attitudes than in his concrete evaluations and analyses of particular authors and works. Inevitably, his main interest was focussed on the Czech literary tradition, which he revalued with great severity, but also genuine sympathy and fervor. His judgments will stand the test of time, even though in detail he changed some of his opinions and, in some contexts, overrated some contemporaries, or will seem needlessly harsh in his polemical fervor. He has refused to share the enthusiasm for the Czech baroque which was discovered and overpraised in the thirties, though he showed considerable understanding for its mentality. He has rejected the attempt to find genuine classicism in the early nineteenth-century poetry, especially in Čelakovský, and he has rightly concentrated on the rediscovery of the greatest of the Czech romantic poets, Karel Hynek Mácha. An early essay on Mácha (in *Duše a dílo,* 1912) successfully combines an analysis of ideas with a close study of style: Mácha's unreconciled "dialectics of dissonances" is shown to be exemplified also in his style: his rhythms, his metaphors, his use of verbs. Šalda sees Mácha in the light of modern stylistics, without ever losing his grip on the critical question of Mácha's true poetic greatness.

Similarly sane and true was Šalda's attitude toward the most famous Czech poet of the nineteenth century, Jaroslav Vrchlický. Some of Šalda's early reviews of Vrchlický's numerous collections of poems, plays, and translations—as the masterly slashing of Vrchlický's translation of Baudelaire—caused a great deal of offense in their time, as they show how shoddy and cheap Vrchlický's vaunted techniques and ideas could be. But Šalda always acknowledged the enormous cultural role of Vrchlický's break with the German tradition in favor of the French and Italian; he always recognized his representative position and, increasingly, came to value both the early erotic poetry and the late intimate lyrics of disappointment, bitter sorrow, and spiritual loneliness. Šalda said both the harshest and the kindest things which can be said about Vrchlický's poetry, *pro* and *contra.* There is no contradiction in Šalda's views; the rifts and contrasts are in Vrchlický's work itself.

Šalda earned his critical spurs as the champion of the new Czech literature arising in the nineties. He did most for the reputation of the two symbolist poets, recognized as leading even today: for Otokar Březina, the visionary mystic, and for Antonín Sova, a quieter, more restrained, more impressionist poet. One cannot, I think, deny that Šalda overpraised these poets and several of his contemporaries, especially Růžena Svobodová, a woman novelist who became a close personal friend. But, on the whole, Šalda proved his wonderful flair for the new and valuable, also after the first World War. He picked the good poets from the "proletarian" and "poetist" groups: he analyzed and classified the novelists, and again and again surveyed the whole development of modern Czech literature, probing into its sociological implications, its national characteristics and its artistic values.

It was in the nature of Šalda's position that his critical work on foreign literatures loomed less in bulk and was less original. He conceived his role as that of a mediator and expounder and less so as a critic. But also in discussing the other literatures, though less systematically than Czech, he preserved his own point of view, made his own selection and enforced his own taste. (pp. 179-85)

The overwhelming personality of Šalda changed the whole

atmosphere and raised the level of Czech criticism immeasurably. Šalda was so vividly conscious of the whole spiritual map of Europe, was so keenly aware of all the implications, demands and diverse methods of criticism, practised so many in so different forms himself, that nobody after him could be quite as provincial, untheoretical or impersonal as critics had been before. But nobody also could quite live up to his ideal of complete criticism. Specialization, after Šalda, became a necessity: not only because most critics were far more limited in range, but because it seemed valuable to demonstrate one method, one taste, one attitude against what seemed to the time the bewildering variety or even eclecticism of Šalda.

Among the critics who began their careers in the years before the first World War and who were in prominent academic positions after it, we must single out three: Arne Novák, Otokar Fischer, and František Chudoba. Arne Novák (1880-1939) was primarily a historian of Czech literature, Fischer of German, and Chudoba of English. Novák wrote several general histories of Czech literature: the first published in German in 1907 attracted much attention and aroused much ill feeling by its brilliantly and acidly formulated judgments on local celebrities (such as the historical novelist, Jirásek). But after this first youthful foray, Arne Novák developed, mostly under the impression of the first World War, in a direction which can be described as conservative, nationalist, and traditionalist. He became increasingly cool toward modernist, left-wing literature and stressed the Catholic tradition of his nation. He tried to enhance the value of early nineteenth-century poetry by tracing neoclassical elements in it. He studied most thoroughly a poet, Svatopluk Čech, who by his Pan-Slavism and clumsy rhetoric had repelled the subtler modern critics. He exalted many contemporary writers who met his demands for national pathos and his interest in a return to the soil. One cannot help feeling that this rediscovery of the values of the national tradition required a frequent sacrifice of critical standards. But Novák, we must recognize, had considerable insight into the evolution of the art of literature and a remarkable power of characterization and analysis. Especially the last edition of his *History of Czech Literature* (1936-1939) is a superb achievement in combining psychological portraiture, biography, sketches of long evolutions, characterizations of periods and backgrounds, all under one cover. One feels that frequently too much has been attempted: the desire for encyclopedic information clashes with an ambition to give a philosophy of Czech literature. Also Novák's style ranges disconcertingly from the factualism of a chronicler to elaborate and even ornate passages which sound sometimes bombastic and affected.

With Novák we can associate Otokar Fischer (1883-1938), who was primarily a historian of German literature besides being a fine poet and superb translator of poetry. Goethe's *Faust* is possibly his best achievement, but he also translated Shakespeare's *Macbeth*, Nietzsche's *Zarathustra*, and much of Heine, Kleist, and Villon, most successfully. Fischer began as a historian specializing in German literature: his first publications were in German, such as his edition of reviews by the eighteenth-century critic Gerstenberg which he was the first to identify, his analysis

of Immermann's *Merlin*, or his monograph on Kleist's dramatic fragment, *Robert Guiscard*, for which he gave a convincing interpretation and forecast of its probable continuation. In later years, Fischer published three large books on German authors: on Kleist (1912), on Nietzsche (1913), and on Heine (1926). The last book is the best: it retells the life very critically and revalues the work in detail, stressing the newness and boldness of the last phase of Heine's poetry. In later years Fischer's interests turned more and more to Czech literature, to subtle analyses of style and rhyme, which are always used as keys to the mind and soul of the author. Fischer's main interest in literature is psychological, in difficult, twisted, divided personalities and works which allowed him to go beyond the surface to their sources in the subconscious mind of the author. Fischer was, I believe, the very first man to apply psychoanalysis to literature (in an analysis of the dreams of Keller's *Grüner Heinrich*, in 1908); he certainly was one of the first to pay close attention to such problems of literary psychology as synaesthesia (the seeing of colors and hearing of sounds), or the "double" in literature, to phenomena like "déjà vu" or "fausse reconnaissance". The extreme brilliance of Fischer's work, his extraordinary combination of scholarship and poetic sensibility, psychological insight and knowledge of verbal craftsmanship, far outweigh the limitations of his type of mind: his comparative lack of interest in philosophical thought, an excessive tolerance, and a historical relativism which follows from the preoccupation with the variety of human psychology.

František Chudoba (1878-1941), the third of our group of critic-scholars began his literary career with a little book on Wordsworth, whom he described sympathetically, concluding with a violent attack on the overestimation of Byron on the Continent. Later Chudoba published several series of essays on the main nineteenth-century English poets and thinkers. They are very well written, reproduce and evoke the originals skillfully, but show little power of analysis or criticism. His main interests were the Pre-Raphaelites, Tennyson, Hardy, etc. and, late in his life, Chudoba wrote a very large book on Shakespeare which disappointed even his admirers. It is a diffuse compilation—learned, but derivative and undistinguished as criticism. Novák, Fischer, and especially Chudoba did not altogether avoid the limitations of the historical orientation, the dangers of academicism.

After the first World War, the union of scholarship and criticism became rarer among the younger men entering literary life. Many of the new voices outside the Academy became strident propagandists of one contemporary movement. František Götz (born in 1894) was probably the most ambitious and pretentious of these new critics who diagnosed all the newest poetic movements and fads, but he also used his wide acquaintance with German philosophy, Russian theories, and French aesthetics to reduce the contemporary situation of literature to a bewildering welter of abstract formulas and -isms. His books on recent Czech poetry and fiction are preferable in their concreteness to his excursions into a philosophy of history in the style, though not on the scale of Spengler. Orthodox Marxist criticism was increasingly represented. Bedřich Václavek (1897-1943), who was to become a victim of the

Nazis, was its best practitioner. He used the sociological approach rigidly and dogmatically in describing recent Czech literature, but also explored folklore and folk poetry by his methods. The Catholic revival had its best critic probably in Albert Vyskočil (born 1890) who wrote a difficult, labored book on Mácha, and one on recent Catholic writers in Czechoslovakia, which show a speculative, highly introverted, meditative turn of mind.

In the universities a movement which called itself "Structuralism" proved most fruitful and influential for the study of literature. It emanated from the Prague Linguistic Circle, a group organized by Vilém Mathesius (1882-1945) in 1926. Mathesius was primarily a linguist, but early in his career he had written a sober descriptive *History of English Literature,* which reached only the end of the Middle Ages. The Prague Linguistic Circle, whose greatest achievements are in linguistics, originally transferred the methods of the so-called Russian formalists to Czechoslovakia. Russian formalism found the ground prepared by the native tradition of Herbartian aesthetics and met with the ready welcome of a group of younger scholars profoundly dissatisfied with the conventional methods of literary scholarship, its excessive factualism, and stress on ideology. A Russian by birth, Roman Jakobson (born 1896), was the moving spirit of the group, and a Czech, Mukařovský, the member who contributed most to literary theory. Jakobson is primarily a linguist, but he did important work on Czech metrics and the analysis of Czech medieval and Romantic poetry. Jan Mukařovský (born 1891) started with minute and very technical analyses of individual works of art such as Mácha's main poem, *May,* but later advanced bold theories on the evolution of literature, the relations between literature and society and the nature of poetry conceived as a part of general semantics or a theory of signs.

The sight of these scholars, who had a small but vigorous following, was consistently fixed on an analysis of the actual work of art as a formal structure. They minimized biography, psychology, and the study of external sources and influences. They conceived of the work of art as a whole system of closely knit signs, where the old distinction of content and form is completely abolished. A close relation with modern linguistics, especially phonemics, was sought for the analysis of euphony, metrics, and semantics. This concentration on the individual work of art and its artistic devices was, however, balanced by an intense interest in the history of literature conceived of as an internal evolution. Evolution to them was a Hegelian dialectical evolution of forms and patterns, *genres* and devices which, however, evolve in close relationship to the social situation of the time. The group around the Linguistic Circle represented a remarkable parallel to the so-called New Critics in the United States. There is the same intense preoccupation with the actual text of the work of art and its minute analysis; there is the same suspicion toward the biographical and psychological approach to literature and the same endeavor to link literary theory with semantics. But the Czech movement was far more conscious of its philosophical implications and was far more closely related to technical linguistics than its American counterpart. The Americans seem quite uninterested in the problem of literary evolution, while the Czech group differs from them in its critical relativism, its lack of interest in critical judgment as such. But both movements were healthy developments, as they made literary scholarship centrally literary, returned attention to the actual works of art and to the theory of literature, away from both factual antiquarianism and flimsy aesthetic "appreciation".

Practically all the younger men who practised literary history attempted to combine scholarship with criticism, and several showed the influence of the teachings of the Prague Linguistic Circle. The most gifted of them was Vojtěch Jirát (1902-1945) who, as a pupil of Otokar Fischer, studied the technique of translation, analyzed most thoroughly the style of a German poet (A. Platen) and late in his brief life, wrote sensitively on Czech poetry, expressing at first shyly, but more and more openly his strange personality: his love for the quiet back-waters of history, his melancholy, and his cynicism.

The German occupation of 1939 slowly strangled all Czech cultural activities. During the early part of the war, up to the assassination of Heydrich, in 1942, Czech critical periodicals continued to appear. Some of the activities of the Linguistic Circle continued and a new critical monthly, founded by Václav Černý (born 1905), a Romance scholar, kept on with surprising vigor until its suppression. Černý had written in French an *Essay on Romantic Titanism* (1935), a study of ideas and attitudes of Romantic poets, mostly in France and England, and had published a little book on the baroque in literature (1937). His general critical outlook was similar to Šalda's in ambition and tone, though the emphasis on Bergsonism and socialism was more pronounced. After the liberation in 1945, the critical reviews were re-established and Černý reassumed his role as a mouthpiece of the non-Communist intelligentsia. He published since a very valuable study of the *Czech Medieval Love Lyric,* with many side-glances on its relations to the Provençal, Italian, and German parallel movements, but he got increasingly involved in the polemics about the cultural orientation of Czechoslovakia, siding vigorously with the West. The Prague Linguistic Circle resumed its activities, but on a reduced scale, with increasing defections. Actual scholarly production suffered during a period of unrest and transition. The Communist seizure of power, in February 1948, soon sealed the fate of anything which was not strictly in line with the new official creed. Černý and his magazine were silenced. Mukařovský, who had been the leading exponent of formalism, recanted publicly, pretending that structuralism can be fused with Marxism. New Marxist theoreticians began to lay down the law; but it seems characteristic of the general paralysis of independent thought that even they did not produce any systematic reinterpretation of the Czech literary tradition and had to be content with exalting such minor figures of the past as the second-rate historical novelist Alois Jirásek. The attempt to annex Šalda for their purposes has apparently been given up, to judge from the fact that the publication of the collected edition, in progress since 1947, has been suspended. The prospects for criticism and literary scholarship are very dim: some innocuous work of historical research can continue, but, on the whole, a dreary uniformity of doctrinaire dogmatism, with all results fixed in advance, has been imposed. Criticism, as an act of understanding and free judgment, is dead. (pp. 187-92)

René Wellek, "Modern Czech Criticism and Literary Scholarship," in his Essays on Czech Literature, *Mouton & Co., 1963, pp. 179-93.*

DE-STALINIZATION, THE PRAGUE SPRING, AND CONTEMPORARY LITERATURE

Miroslav Holub

[*Holub is a Czech poet as well as a scientist specializing in clinical pathology. His poems are marked by free verse forms that have been compared with those of American poet William Carlos Williams and frequently use scientific metaphors to, as Holub states, "find poetic equivalents for the new reality of the micro-world." In the following essay, he describes his and other Czech poets' reactions to World War II and to the governmental censorship of authors in Czechoslovakia in subsequent decades under Communism.*]

We began to write poetry in war-time, hiding somewhere and somehow from the German *Arbeitsamt* (labour administration) and *Totaleinsatz* (forced labour) and from the Allied bombs. The bombs were one of the few positive and promising features of life, as were Seifert's love poems.

The inner landscape could have been defined as a little corner in Picasso's *Guernica.*

In 1945-46, after the liberation, there was hardly time to draw breath and find one's own way of getting beyond Adorno's pronouncement: After Auschwitz there can't be any poetry. No poetry after Auschwitz. In my view, an alternative statement or programme was: No more words. Just sharp, concrete, viable, bleeding images, partly inherited from the surrealist imagery of the thirties.

Personally, I was attracted by the heritage of Czech 'civilian' poetry, Group 42, and would have liked to write something like Josef Kainar's 'Taxidermist' (*New Myths,* 1946):

. . . . .

Bird's guts are wrapped in fat
fat is wiped off on a glass plate

Something is torn off
With two fingers it is torn off
From time to time something crackles in the
palm

. . . . .

Nevermore will it find the finest branch
To be rocked on it by the beat
Of its tiny heart
In the calm
They took its life away
And the taxidermist

He took away even its death

It will never more burn in the wind

And if I wrote my poem
If I am stuffing the unknown bird . . .

But before we could identify ourselves with anybody or anything, before the beginner and outsider could catch his breath, there was 1948, which I can best illustrate by personal experience. I had just won the third prize in poetry and the fifth prize for an 'Essay on the Present Moment' in the nationwide students' competition. After days and nights of student street protests against the Communist coup, there was a meeting at the Students' Union Headquarters where we were supposed to receive our prizes. Instead, the leader of the Communist students announced that the Union had just been dissolved and a blind, hysterical sort of *yurodivy* ('visionary') young man began screaming about his vision of the May Day parade in which we would all march and sing the Russian songs.

At that moment I realized that there is no poetry not only because of Auschwitz, that there are no words, that there is no identity, that we are completely isolated in the crowds of quasi *yurodivy* colleagues, that there is no 'civilian' poetry, no Walt Whitman nor Carl Sandburg, no Group 42, and no programme except to shut up.

So we entered literature by shutting up. By complete silence. By a complete distrust of everybody.

It was a perfect lesson in Creative Non-writing. It was a short-cut to an almost biological feeling of the absurdity of everything, including one's inner self.

Wittgenstein's view that 'in the arts it is difficult to say something which would be as good as to say nothing' was pushed to its extreme.

Whatever was published as admissible poetry was in the guise of Russian socialist realism, with a minimal number of personal, private positive deviations.

The mainstream of poetry, rather than any new language, was merely a cover-up of reality, in which opportunities for humans shrank and opportunities for statues expanded.

The statues rose up above the shabby and peeling facades of buildings in which countless Kafka trials took place. In the streets something would run that was later ascertained to be Ionesco's rhinoceroses, and in private something went on that was later defined as waiting for Godot.

Thus quite involuntarily, without the assistance of any sort of literary programme, a perfect situation of inner and outer absurdity was being created, and was created. It was only a question of poetic nature and a question of context as to who would record it and when.

However, one could instinctively feel that 'recording' was

not the thing. Literature and art in general are always a counterpoint to the state of affairs. In a tidy society, literature is inclined to get unruly, uncombed, flourishing underground; in a complete mess, literature believes in (and is believed to create) traces of order and seeds of value. In absurd conditions, literature must have a rational grain and programme. What was written on the walls were metaphors, not entire poems. What was to be recorded was the feeling of human responsibility in the overwhelming absurdity, using its images.

As it happened, the official socialist realism was a frank recording of irresponsibility and nihilism and isolation. Looked at from the outside, it was something like the vision of a sentimental romantic bureaucrat. A romantic bureaucrat is himself a Beckettian hero belonging in *Endgame*. Socialist realism was an integral part of general absurdity.

Anything else that happened in literature could not even be named. It was not modernism, nor postmodernism. It was plain self-defence; when you are drowning, you may not care for theoretical, linguistic and literary denotations of your words or bubbles.

Against the vast official nothingness, any kind of minimal personal or group programme was a step forward, in accordance with Kainar's words in 1960: 'A grain of truth is the entire universe'. But the most radical programme in my view was provided by Kolář and Holan: in Holan's case, his poetry from the time when he 'spoke to the wall—and it replied'. In the lyric-epic *Pribehy* (*Episodes*) he achieved a certain magic matter-of-factness, based on the self-reliant fates of his heroes and a drastic counterpointing of image and meaning. As it is in the 'Ode to Joy', which is about a girl burnt alive. As it is in the key line of the poem 'Flight' ('Utek'):

> Only when we kneel, we become life-size.

And 'Ode to Joy' starts with a comprehensive statement of the situation:

> A sweet summery early evening . . . Summery,
> because summery,
> and absurd, because sweet . . . Everything is
> light
> and everything is elevated and the elephant's
> dance
> is the most elevated . . .

and a later poem ('Again') reads:

> Without death life is impossible to feel,
> with it, life is just thinkable,
> and therefore absurd . . .

Matter-of-factness as the basic defence against emptiness, concreteness as the counterweight to a lie—before our 'poetry of the everyday'—is actually defined in Holan's poem 'Resurrection':

> After this life here, we're to be awakened one
> day
> by the terrible screams of trumpets and bugles?
> Forgive me, Lord, but I trust
> that the beginning and the resurrection of us,
> the dead,

> will be announced by the crowing of a
> rooster . . .

> We'll lie on for a little longer . . .
> The first one to rise
> will be mother . . . We'll hear her
> quietly making the fire
> quietly putting the kettle on,
> and cozily taking the coffee grinder out of the
> cupboard.
> We'll be at home again.

Holan's magic matter-of-factness was one form of defence against absurdity. In virtually hopeless situations defence of course becomes attack from the outset.

The second radical record, and a decisive and inspirational one, was the poetry of Jiří Kolář. From the poetry of the town he came, in the circumstances of general absurdity, to the mirror. He discovered that authenticity, living everyday authenticity, plain human speech, and the most ordinary human situation of these years were not only poetically viable but also the most telling argument. By conviction. It was poetry as a project and at the same time as testimony. Poetry as an escape from the book to the street, where now and then a rhinoceros would run past.

Kolář himself defined it as 'to be where life is heaviest'. Methodologically important here is what Marco Polo said to Mr. A.:

> We have now reached the heart of the country
> In whose terrible frosts live people spangled
> with eyes
> The nobler the creature
> The more eyes it has
> The more it sees . . .

(One must note that Kolář's Mr. A. preceded Herbert's Mr Cogito.)

Kolář's authenticity reaches its climax in the *Czech Suite* in which the poems are made up only of free verse lines from the letters of Czech artists of the last century, including compulsive scribblers and including the reports of agents appointed to keep artists under surveillance.

For me it is poetry-which-is-more-than poetry, for instance in this quotation from the report of the secret agent Novotny concerning the obtaining of a woman informer among the acquaintances of the Czech writer Božena Němcová:

> Guided by the desire to fulfill my mission
> responsibly
> I found a person
> suitable for confidential service of the given
> kind
> in a daughter of our corps of discreet informers
> working under the name of Chemist . . .
> having regard to the level of her education . . .
> . . . and the delicate nature of the assignment
> allow me
> to recommend a monthly salary of A2 of the
> second grade.

In a situation where almost every Czech writer had behind him, beside or in front of him somebody with the monthly salary of A2 of the second grade, this is poetry of maximal impact and minimal stylization.

In the given context it's impossible to achieve a greater effect.

I consider that both Holan's and Kolář's testimony was a poetic act of more than national importance. During the 'sixties and 'seventies the concrete situation proved to be a model: the Czech experience was an epitome of the age-old struggle of intellect with codified stupidity.

Nothing we did since the 'fifties in Czech poetry and its struggle against the absurdity of the social order surpassed the limits defined by Holan and Kolář.

All we were doing was only serving within these limits.

If I may call to mind the years 1969-71 as a repetition of 1948, I see the editor-in-chief of a 'steam-rollered' socialist realist publishing house who was explaining to me why my book on E. A. Poe could not come out under my name: 'You know, comrade, it's like catching a cold. If it's not taken care of in time, it has lasting effects'.

According to this poet's conception, a neglected cold was not merely the basic concept of why-and-what for poetry and why-and-what for man, but also Kantian Pure Reason itself. At the time of making this prediction the National Artist didn't have that *yurodivy* expression. But this demonstrated that the situation was now even worse because here was absurdity in which even the *yurodivost* was faked.

And so it ended.

I don't know how successful we are going to appear from the standpoint of later history. But we were certainly not short of proposals. (pp. 4-6)

Miroslav Holub, "Poetry against Absurdity," translated by Ian Milner and Jarmila Milner, in Poetry Review, *Vol. 80, No. 2, Summer, 1990, pp. 4-6.*

William E. Harkins

[*Harkins is an American educator who specializes in Slavic languages and literature. In the following excerpt, he discusses major Czech novels of the 1960s and 1970s.*]

Though less celebrated abroad than the contemporary Czech "new-wave" film and the theater, the Czech novel achieved during the [1960s and 1970s] a richness and variety unparalleled in the history of Czech literature. The only possible exception is the epoch between the two World Wars, which saw the emergence of such giants of fiction as Karel Čapek, Vladislav Vančura and Ivan Olbracht. Some of this legacy of new creativity was translated into other languages, particularly German and French as well as English, and doubtless much more would have been translated had the Prague Spring not come to such an abrupt and unhappy end. In the work of emigré writers such as Josef Škvorecký and his wife, Zdena Salivarová, and in Czech novels sent abroad and published there either in Czech or in translation, including works by

Vaculík and Šotola, as well as unpublished works circulated in Czechoslovakia in manuscript, we have a promise of continuing fresh creative development. On the other hand, the spectacle of the officially approved writing published in Czechoslovakia since 1968 shows, even in the works of such talented writers as Fuks and Páral, both artistic impoverishment and a drying up of the creative imagination.

Before looking more closely at recent and contemporary Czech fiction, we might note its generational character. With the single exception of Bohumil Hrabal, who is older, all the writers I shall discuss were born between the years 1924 and 1930. They were born into the middle class society of the Czechoslovak Republic and into middle class families, had begun to attend school by the beginning of World War II; they experienced the postwar period of Popular Front style government, and had reached adulthood (though barely) by the time of the country's turn to Communism in 1948. Hrabal is an exception in that he did not follow a typically bourgeois pattern in which high school and university schooling were part of normal development; he did receive a doctor's degree in law at Charles University, but only in 1946, when he was thirty years of age, and he entered literature only in the mid-fifties, when he was in his forties. This background shared by the younger generation of writers encouraged a sense of political and social instability, bringing mistrust in social and political institutions as well as in change itself; at the same time it left a kind of dream of a better life in the placid middle-class world of the 1930's, satisfied and contented so long as it was secure from the rigors of economic depression and so long as it was not torn away from its roots by the horrors of Nazism and war. At the same time we may note that, save for poets such as Seifert, Holan and Hrubín, there were almost no older writers left to compete with this younger generation, particularly in the realm of fiction. World War II and the turn of political events in February, 1948, resembled a great watershed that cut off for a time the development of Czech fiction: those major talents, such as Olbracht and Majerová, who survived, turned to children's fiction, as if to proclaim that it was too difficult for them in their old age to adjust to the demands of socialist realism; younger established writers such as Pujmanová and Řezáč who sought to make the adjustment to the new regime only destroyed themselves creatively. But even they were now gone. True, several promising younger writers did emerge during the 1950's, particularly those, such as Arnošt Lustig and Norbert Frýd, who could draw on their concentration camp experiences for moving literary material, or those, such as Ludvík Aškenazy, who could treat the humorous and childlike aspects of the building of socialism in the new state. But these promising talents of the 1950's largely failed to develop, even during the more favorable conditions of the 1960's. True, one author of this older generation, Edvard Valenta, did succeed in producing an interesting study of the psychology of a weak, selfish egoist who is converted to the cause of anti-Nazi resistance: the novel, *Follow the Green Light* (*Jdi za zeleným světlem*, 1956), employed a series of highly subjective interchapters or "intermezzi" which far exceeded the limits formerly imposed on this technique by the dogmas of socialist realist writing. But Valenta's psychologism was not destined to start a pro-

CZECHOSLOVAKIAN LITERATURE   ***TWENTIETH-CENTURY LITERARY CRITICISM, Vol. 42***

ductive new trend; thus the arena of fiction was wide open for the younger generation, and there was little or no past tradition of continuity to dominate or shape it.

We can identify three main trends which the Czech novel has followed in its development since 1963: the first two are largely predictable; the third one less so. Predictable, first of all, is the formula of inverting or parodying the socialist realist novel to produce irony or satire. A novel may take the form of a socialist realist production novel, for instance, but as it proceeds the expected socialist pathos fails to materialize, and irony or humor at the expense of socialism results. The second formula (one actually less employed than one might have anticipated) is that of allegory. In this formula any of the devices of allegory (the most obvious one is the selection of a subject from past time in a historical novel) can be used to point out the contradictions of the present. The third tendency, one which at times overlaps the first two, but which was itself intrinsically less predictable (unless we take into account world literary trends as well as political developments in Czechoslovakia and other countries of Eastern Europe), is the very great influence of the work of Franz Kafka, and a broader interest in the grotesque, the fantastic, and the absurd. Finally, we may note a number of miscellaneous trends which help to bring Czech fiction up to a par with its contemporary counterparts over the world: these include the modern cult of sexual freedom, the use of black humor as a comic and expressive style, and some interaction (though perhaps not so much as we might have expected) with the techniques of the modern film.

The first trend, and actually the first one, chronologically, to appear, was that of inversion of the values and formulas of socialist realism. Such inversion could be carried out in a straightforward manner (though with a certain degree of irony implicit), or it could be done with great exaggeration or humor. The more straightforward way is the earlier style of the two, probably because creative restrictions eased only gradually, but partly too, no doubt, because the authors themselves originally tended to take socialism and its ideas seriously.

The first of the new novels to gain prominence abroad, Josef Škvorecký's *The Cowards* (*Zbabělci,* 1958), showed

Milan Kundera (center) and Josef Škvorecký (right) at the Slavonic Conference at the University of Pennsylvania in 1980.

certain limited elements of this inverted socialist realism. The work depicts a local uprising in Northern Bohemia in 1945 at the time of the German withdrawal and the advance of the Russians. The novel ignores the heroes of the uprising and rather chooses as its protagonists the sons of the middle class, pro-Western in their attitudes, who go in for jazz music and who talk in a frank, scatological manner till then taboo in Czech fiction. The most marked elements of inversion, perhaps, concern the treatment of the Russian liberation forces: they arrive later than expected, and are unruly, brutal and drunken. Škvorecký's novel was promptly withdrawn as too extreme, and could not be republished again until as late as 1964, well after the second "thaw" of the 1960's was under way.

A more complete example of the technique of inversion, where the social dogmas of socialist realism itself are inverted, is Ivan Klíma's novel, *An Hour of Silence* (*Hodina ticha,* 1963). This work literally gives the impression of having been taken up by its author as a straight work of socialist realism, but then changing in mid-stream as the atmosphere of increasing liberalization made such a change possible. The novel describes the work of an engineer, a Party member, who attempts to improve living conditions in the countryside in Moravian Slovakia, particularly by damming up swamp areas where malaria is rampant and where no crops can be raised. The subject is of course typical for the socialist realist novel, and in the hero's service to the people he is a typical socialist realist hero, but in the end he is defeated by the apathy and indifference of the very Party and government officials who are supposed to help him. Instead of individual deviation corrected by the Party, a customary formula of orthodox socialist realism, we have Party indifference and error opposed to the correct ethical stand of the individual; instead of the obligatory optimistic ending, the hero gives up here in total defeat.

The masterpiece of this genre is doubtless Ludvík Vaculík's *The Axe* (*Sekyra,* 1966). Vaculík was a Party member (he was excluded from the Party after 1968) who in 1968 gained world attention as author of the celebrated "2,000 Words" manifesto which called on the Czech citizenry to bring pressure on the regime for liberalization. *The Axe* is subtler in its use of the inversion formula than is Klíma's novel. The main theme of the work is the conflict of generations, itself a major theme of East European "thaw" literature, since the younger generation saw in Stalinism the betrayal of socialist idealism by its elders. In Vaculík's novel a boy grows up to adore his father, a minor Party official, but gradually comes to realize that the father, decent enough in his dealings with his family, has been corrupted by his petty share of power and is unjust and officious in his treatment of the villagers whom he is organizing into a collective (like Klíma's novel, Vaculík's also takes place in Moravian Slovakia). At the same time the son, a journalist, discovers that to follow the correct Party line in his work means to suppress the truth and even to lie hypocritically. In an open ending to the novel the hero seems to be on the verge of opting out of the system entirely.

Here the inversion is again one of values as well as formulas: the "correct" application of the Party line leads to results which contradict the very ethical premises on which it claims to be based. More, perhaps, than any other novel, Vaculík's is preoccupied with the question of justice: how can justice be realized under socialism? Hence it is not strange that he came to be identified so closely with the Prague Spring movement, which sought to bring in "socialism with a human face."

As time went on and the pace of liberalization increased, it became possible to do more than question the justice of the Party's progress on the road to socialism; it became possible to mock that progress by showing up and burlesquing its contradictions and exaggerations. Škvorecký's novel *The Lion Cub* (*Lvíče,* 1969; English translation as *Miss Silver's Past,* 1974), belongs to this category. The work is ostensibly a detective novel (Škvorecký is much interested in the rules of detective fiction and the ways in which they can be violated) as well as an erotic novel, but the author has incorporated a good deal of experience in the publishing business, no doubt his own, for the novel is presumably a *roman à clèf* in spite of Škvorecký's routine disclaimer to the contrary. The action of the novel dates from a time which is uncertain but which must be either 1957-58 or 1963, i.e., the time when a literary "thaw" is getting under way, but when the entrenched officials of the Party are using their powers and the forces of inertia to resist liberalization. The subplot concerns the drive of younger members of the staff of a publishing house to bring out a liberal novel on life in reform schools against the wishes of their chief, whose task it is to suppress such evidences of "contradictions" on the face of socialist reality. A number of comic anecdotes are told concerning events which no doubt actually occurred: one tells how a translator is forbidden to use slang, since slang does not in fact exist; the concept is only an invention of bourgeois scholars! Another tells how a press was stopped because a photo caption read, "On the right sits so-and-so," which was ideologically unacceptable; this was yanked from the presses and changed to read: "So-and-so sits to the left of so-and-so."

The Lion Cub was confiscated in its second edition of 1970 following the writer's emigration to Canada. There Škvorecký published his next novel, *The Tank Batallion* (*Tankový prapor,* 1971) in his own publishing house, Sixty-Eight Publishers; only short portions from this novel had been published in Czechoslovakia. The work is a comic portrayal of life in the Czechoslovak army in the early 1950's (when the author did his own military service): in spite of all the zealous attempts by the officers to create an effective socialist fighting force, their efforts are sabotaged by the unwillingness, naïve or deliberate, of the draftees under their command. Hilarious and especially effective is a long scene of an examination on Communist *belles lettres* given to the men in spite of the fact that the books on the required reading list have never been supplied and the men have no interest in reading them even if they had been. The novel recalls Hašek's celebrated *Good Soldier Schweik* in its portrayals of passive resistance by the men; it is reported to circulate illegally among enlisted men in the Czechoslovak army today, who may be

sentenced to terms in solitary for its possession; even officers have been punished for having copies on their person.

Škvorecký's . . . novel, *The Miracle* (*Mirákl,* 1972), was published in Canada. It embodies a detective plot, the attempt to unriddle the mystery of a supposedly faked miracle which takes place in a Czech country church and which is "exposed" by the secret police to discredit religion; evidence that the "miracle" is a fake must be reconciled with the priest's apparent strong conviction that some real miracle had taken place. Various solutions (à la Karel Čapek) are proposed but none is finally accepted; the whole event is evidently to be left in the realm of mystery. To this plot Škvorecký adds reminiscences of the Prague Spring movement and life in emigration. Rather diffuse, the novel can hardly be said to be entirely successful, and raises by implication the somewhat ominous question of where its author can go from here: the role of the writer in exile is obviously not an easy one.

Black humor is the specialty of Vladimír Páral, one of the most imaginative and creative writers of the new generation, though his work is uneven. Páral depicts the "new" managerial class that has come to power under socialism, its relatively luxurious and totally indolent way of life. His chief subject is sex, treated erotically and somewhat frenetically; the exaggeration of his characters' sexual frenzies is relieved by the liberal doses of black humor with which Páral invests his novels, and their sexual excesses, especially of sadism, are frequently turned about in ridicule by the author. In a sense Páral is "apolitical," and the world of meaningless values he depicts could be capitalist as well as socialist. But the reader can hardly help asking himself: if the new socialist managerial class is so rotten, what are the political leaders like? And since Páral, himself a chemical engineer, fills his novel with details from the world of factories and industrial production, his novels very strongly, if only peripherally, suggest a burlesque of these aspects of the classic socialist realist factory novel. Typical is Páral's most ambitious attempt, *Lovers and Murderers* (*Milenci a vrazi,* 1969), but it is spoiled by its excessive naturalism, and much better are two earlier, shorter works: *The Private Whirlwind* (*Soukromá vichřice,* 1966) and *Catapult* (*Katapult,* 1967). The first, using many of the techniques of the French "new-wave" novel, depicts the meaningless triviality of the professional, social and sexual lives of the managers and workers of a textile factory; the main device is endless repetition of patterns; even when these vary, nothing essentially is changed. *Catapult* is without question the author's masterpiece, and deals with the complex love life of a Don Juan business traveller, who organizes an entire network of mistresses along the route of his travels. Amid the rich black picaresque humor of the novel one gets rare but gripping insights into the hero's inner agony as he strives vainly to live contentedly and happily in a world devoid of spiritual values.

Weaker are Páral's later novels. *The Career Woman* (*Profesionální žena,* 1971) is a burlesque retelling of the Cinderella tale with a modern setting. *The Young Man and the White Whale* (*Mladý muž a bílá velryba,* 1973) constitutes a pallid attempt on the part of the author to find positive heroes among the industrial workers to compensate for the bankruptcy of the corrupt managerial class. Finally, *Joy till Morning* (*Radost až do rána,* 1975) describes the reform of two social misfits.

Last in this group of inversions of socialist realism may be mentioned the novel *Honzlová,* by the actress and writer Zdena Salivarová (the wife of Josef Škvorecký), published in 1972 in Canada (English translation as *A Summer in Prague,* 1973). The novel is a somewhat Chaplinesque mixture of comedy and pathos, sometimes overly sentimental and overdrawn, but excelling in its attention to the details of everyday life under the Novotný regime, with its widespread espionage, bureaucratic difficulties and petty frustrations, aspects of everyday existence which often go unmentioned in works of literature, and thus it unmasks the hypocrisy of Czech socialist society.

To conclude . . . , it must be said that there was rather less "journalistic" reporting and exposes of conditions under the Stalinist terror than might have been expected. Still, a novel by Jiří Mucha on concentration camp life did appear, *A Likely Appearance* (*Pravděpodobná tvář,* 1963); Karel Pecka's *The Fever* (*Horečka,* 1967) pursued the same subject; while abroad the young writer Jan Beneš published, in English, a novel called *Second Breath* (1969), also concerned with life in the camps. Mucha's memoir of prison life, *The Midnight Sun* (*Půlnoční slunce,* 1968; English translation as *Living and Partly Living*) gained considerable fame abroad.

Our second category, one which likewise appears as predictable, is that of the allegory. The allegory serves as an age-old traditional form of criticism in which attack is veiled, at least in part, by shifting the subject in time or space, or in altering the conditions to which reality is normally subject, e.g., in the use of animal characters, Martians, fantastic countries or worlds, etc. Well-known allegories include *Everyman* and Bunyan's *Pilgrim's Progress;* the device is common in Soviet writing of the twenties and includes such works as Zamyatin's futurist utopia, *We* and his play on the Spanish Inquisition, *The Fires of St. Dominic.*

In view of the classic character of this genre, and its adaptability for political and social satire, it seems odd that we cannot find very many examples of its use in Czech fiction after 1956. Stalinist critics and their successors were relatively sensitive to this form of satire, of course, and after the 1920's it is not very easy to find clear examples of its use in Soviet literature either; nor does it figure much in the writing of the other satellite states of Eastern Europe, though the work of the Polish playwright Mrożek constitutes a notable exception.

Probably the best example of an allegory on Czech Stalinism is found in Jiří Šotola's novel, *The Society of Jesus* (*Tovaryšstvo Ježíšovo,* 1969). This is a long novel about the work of the Jesuit Order in Bohemia during the Counter-Reformation and the loss of Czech independence which followed the defeat at the White Mountain in 1620. The parallels between the Society of Jesus and the Communist Party seem rather obvious, and they are further emphasized by the author, who highlights the discrepancy between the spiritual idealism of the Order and its practices, which embody the techniques of propaganda, espionage and enforced compulsion, as well as utter indifference to the welfare of the people themselves. A second novel by Šotola, *Chicken on the Spit* (*Kuře na rožni*—the title is actually an untranslatable pun, since the leading character is named Matěj Kuře—"Matthew Chicken"), first appeared in German translation, but ultimately in the original (Prague, 1976). The novel tells the life of a poor itinerant actor of the Napoleonic era; the allegorical element, if one is indeed present, concerns art as a questing for truth, a quest which never succeeds, but which does lead its practitioners to find freedom, even when the external political order is harsh and despotic. Thus the novel can be read as an assertion of the artist's inner freedom under the present regime.

Ludvík Vaculík's second novel, *The Guinea Pigs* (*Morčata*), has likewise been published only outside Czechoslovakia; an American edition appeared in 1973 and Sixty-Eight Publishers issued it in Czech in 1977. It differs almost totally in method from Vaculík's earlier masterpiece, *The Axe,* which was essentially realistic while being at the same time lyrically poetic. *The Guinea Pigs,* in marked contrast, is a Kafkaesque allegory set in a madly grotesque world. The novel is rich in diverse themes: the clearest element of allegorization involves the pet guinea pigs: their owner treats them at first benevolently but, as time passes and he gets little reaction from them, his treatment turns increasingly malevolent and even sadistic. Thus the novel may be read as an expressionistic parable of the narrow line distinguishing tyranny from idealism, and the extreme fragility of individual freedom.

Allegory may involve a grotesque world different from the real world, and hence this second category blends with our third category of the grotesque and fantastic, and Vaculík's novel actually belongs to both.

It is noteworthy that of all writers it is probably Franz Kafka who constitutes the major influence on Czech literature of the sixties. For the Marxist Revisionists Kafka's writing served as a vivid symbol of individual alienation, and the struggle to publish Kafka in Czech translation became the major ideological battle waged by the Czech intelligentsia in the early 1960's. Why this was the case is not entirely clear, but Kafka had lived in Prague, and the prohibition of his works seemed manifestly and egregiously unnecessary, at the least, as a condition for the development of socialism. The battle came to a head in 1963, when a conference on Kafka was held at Liblice, near Prague, with delegates attending from a number of East European countries, though not from the Soviet Union.

Kafka's influence was not alone, of course, in bringing an interest in the grotesque and absurd. Kafka's contemporary and fellow Praguer, Jaroslav Hašek, author of the celebrated *Good Soldier Schweik,* was another influence, as well as the older literary trends of dada and surrealism. Theater of the absurd was another current and finally, the Czech literary avant-garde of the 1920's, especially of Deml and Richard Weiner.

The work of the writer Bohumil Hrabal shows an interesting blend of the influences of Hašek and of surrealism in his stories of wildly eccentric middle-class and proletarian types told in a crude, slangy but highly expressive manner. Hrabal is essentially a story writer, but he has published one short novel, *Closely Watched Trains* (*Ostře sledované vlaky,* 1965; English translation, 1968). The film version of the novel was one of the most popular Czech "new-wave" films of the mid-sixties. The book is a Chaplinesque blend of pathos and black humor, the story of a nondescript youth who finally overcomes his sexual impotence to become a hero of the Czech underground resistance, but is himself blown to pieces in the explosion he sets to blow up a German train (the phallic character of this "explosion," after impotence, is unmistakable). Also notable is another long story or very short novella, *Dancing Lessons for Older and Advanced Pupils* (*Taneční hodiny pro starší a pokročilé,* 1965). This is an interior monologue cast in the form of a single prolonged sentence, the erotic thoughts and fantasies of one of Hrabal's typical bathetic characters; in its way the work is a kind of parody of the final chapter of James Joyce's *Ulysses.*

The principal practitioner of Kafkaesque grotesque in Czech fiction is no doubt the novelist Ladislav Fuks. Fuks is obsessed with the theme of death, in its comic as well as its grotesque aspects. He gained an international reputation with his novel, *Mr. Theodore Mundstock* (*Pan Theodor Mundstock,* 1963; English translation, 1968), the story of a Jew doomed to go to a concentration camp who systematically trains himself to endure the rigors of life there. He is killed, ironically, run over by one of the very trucks come to take him and others to the camp. The high-point of Fuks' creation is probably the long novel, *Variations for a Dark String* (*Variace pro temnou strunu,* 1966). It tells the story of the fall of Czechoslovakia to the Nazis; this is blended, expressionistically, with a family horror story with overtones of vampirism and lycanthropy. A short novel, *The Burner of Corpses* (*Spalovač mrtvol,* 1967), also made into a notable film, depicts the grisly career of an undertaker who kills his own wife and children, ostensibly because they are partly Jewish, and disposes of their bodies in his own crematory; he ends up serving as an exterminator of Jews in the gas chambers, and finally goes mad.

The Death of a Guinea Pig (*Smrt morčete,* 1969) is a collection of stories which treat death more humorously, but a long final story, "The Trip to the Promised Land" ("Cesta do zaslíbené země") is actually a novella with a strongly cinematic quality: it relates the flight of a group of wealthy Jews down the Danube to escape the Nazi terror; their boat is wrecked in the shoals of the lower Danube, and they perish wandering back and forth over the wastes of the large sand islands of the river in a now insane quest for the "promised land."

The Mice of Natalie Mooshaber (*Myši Natalie Mooshabrové,* 1970) shows great technical skill and inventiveness, but a certain decline in artistic conception and an increasing lack of any connection with reality. It deals, in almost fairy tale fashion, with a lost princess who falls victim to the compulsion to punish wicked children by murdering

them, lest they become as delinquent as her own son had once been. The setting is ostensibly the world of the future, but the details lack conviction. The novel is perhaps the most Kafka-like of Fuks' works. Fuks' . . . *Return from the Rye-Field* (*Návrat z žitného pole,* 1974), is far more pallid, the story of a country boy who, after the events of February, 1948, decides to escape abroad, but finally changes his mind after he comes in contact with some young people in his own homeland who are involved in brigade construction. The novel has many loose ends; obviously it is the torso left from a more ambitious conception on the author's part which events did not permit him to realize.

Finally, we come to the name that is perhaps best known outside Czechoslovakia today: this is Milan Kundera. Kundera does not fit any of our categories really (though some of his stories could no doubt be made to fit our first category). Like Páral, he is obsessed with erotic subject matter, but he is more consistently tongue-in-cheek in his treatment of such subjects than Páral, if less imaginative and less felicitous as a stylist and pure artist of words and images.

Kundera's first novel is *The Joke* (*Žert,* 1967; English edition, 1969), but the author had earlier written some lyric poetry and drama. A student is sentenced to a number of years at hard labor in a punitive unit of the Army because he had sent his girlfriend a postcard greeting which contained the frivolous sentence "Long Live Trotsky!" After his release he seeks to revenge himself on the former fellow student who was responsible for his punishment. His planned vengeance takes an ingenious form: he will seduce the man's wife and then present the husband with the evidence of the wife's infidelity. The seduction is easy enough, but after it takes place the hero realizes that the husband in fact could not care less: he is exclusively occupied with his own mistress. And finally the hero grasps what is the novel's point: because of the violent shifts in ethical values and standards under socialism, it is wrong to try to hold individuals responsible for wrongdoing: not only do they not deserve punishment (the man in question was convinced at the time that he was doing right), but the punishment would have no meaning in retrospect, for the moral basis on which it would have been carried out has long since vanished. This is the real, ironic "joke" of the novel's title.

Kundera's second novel, *Life Is Elsewhere* (*Život je jinde*), has never been published in Czechoslovakia, but has appeared in French and in English (English translation, 1974). It is the story of a narcissistic young poet who grows up under socialism and is destroyed, both spiritually and literally, by his collaboration with the Stalinist regime. The title is taken from a slogan scratched on a wall during the student uprising at the Sorbonne in 1968. Efforts to relate the youth's spiritual tragedy to the fate of great poets of the past, particularly those who perished young, such as Shelley, Keats, Pushkin, Lermontov and Rimbaud, seem a bit pretentious, perhaps, as does the incorporation of passages from a novel which the poet is writing.

Kundera's . . . novel . . . *The Farewell Party* (*Valčík na rozloučenou*), has also never appeared in Czechoslovakia, but has been published in English in 1976. It is a kind of charade-like comedy dealing with themes of murder and paternity; the treatment is in Kundera's typical ironic, even cynical manner, and this of his novels is the closest to his popular series of ironic tales about eroticism, *Laughable Loves* (*Směšné lásky,* 1963). The novel ends without resolution of its themes, and it is difficult to say what it "means," if in fact it does mean anything precise.

Most of the novelists mentioned above fall into one of two roughly equal groups. One group, including Klíma, Vaculík, Škvorecký and Šotola, is essentially ethical and political, and emphasizes the betrayal which Stalinism represented. Common to these writers is a basic concern for ethical values, whether relating to the individual or the entire society, and a sense that the betrayal of ethical values by the society is one source of modern man's estrangement and unhappiness. It does not matter essentially whether these writers are leftists (Vaculík, Šotola) or further to the right in ideology: they are joined by a common concern for ideals and a disapproval at the betrayal of ideals by either extreme left or right. Thus, in his *The Miracle* Škvorecký expresses his alarm at the excesses of the revisionists and their persecution of "good" adherents of the Novotný regime.

On the other hand, we have a group of novelists, including Hrabal, Páral, Kundera and Fuks, who are essentially non-ideological and who refrain from ideological commitment (Páral's and Fuks' latest attempts to publish works acceptable to the regime are scarcely sincere and need not be taken seriously). No world of spiritual ideals appears in their works; they are profoundly pessimistic and deeply estranged. And hence these writers are not essentially political: they seem unable to imagine a world organized in satisfactory fashion, since man himself lacks the spiritual force to achieve such a world. All of them are essentially humorists, with the partial exception of Fuks, yet all of them are deeply pessimistic.

Finally, one trend shared by most of these writers is a pronounced absence of psychologizing, a trait shared with much of contemporary Western fiction and even drama, to be sure. Though one of the first works of the post-Stalinist thaw was Valenta's *Follow the Green Light*, a work of intense psychological analysis, and though one can find a good deal of introspection in the novels of Vaculík and Šotola, the fact is that the basic trend is directly away from psychologism. This is in part a cyclical, natural reaction, in part, perhaps, an implicit declaration of the abandonment of a quest for the alienated self, whose alienation is thus made to appear objective rather than subjective. Even in the drama, in spite of the popularity of the work of such Western writers as Tennessee Williams, Arthur Miller, or John Osborne, psychologism has hardly been a strong trend in recent Czech drama.

If we raise the issue of national tradition versus cosmopolitanism (a dichotomy that has been of immense importance in Czech literary history), we also obtain very divergent results. Some of these novelists, such as Hrabal and Vaculík, are very Czech; others, such as Páral and Fuks, are cosmopolitans and almost free of specifically Czech literary influences (Páral has undergone the schooling of the French "new-wave" novel; Fuks absorbed the influence of Kafka and of melodramatic horror fiction). Škvorecký occupies an intermediate position: he is strongly influenced by Hemingway, whom he translated, but his humor betrays a strong, authentic Czech popular note.

Yet one thing is clear. In abjuring the cult of socialist realism, with its compulsory optimism and political rhetoric, Czech fiction has once again found itself and regained and reasserted the classical role which Matthew Arnold assigned to literature: the criticism of life. For a brief decade and a half it, along with the Czech film and Czech theater, came to the forefront of European cultural progress. Whether this new role and this new excellence can be sustained under the conditions of an emigré literature or through underground publication abroad, is still too early to say. (pp. 3-15)

> *William E. Harkins, "The Czech Novel since 1956: At Home and Abroad," in* Czech Literature since 1956: A Symposium, *edited by William E. Harkins and Paul I. Trenský, Bohemica, 1980, pp. 3-15.*

Thomas G. Winner

[*A Czech-born American educator and critic, Winner specializes in Slavic languages and literature, as well as in semiotics. In the following essay, he examines major works of Czech avant-garde fiction from the 1960s.*]

In the interwar period, Czech literary and artistic development could no longer be understood apart from the European art community. Such avant-garde movements as dadaism, cubism, futurism and surrealism were all strongly represented, and even dominated the Czech arts, but these stimulating cultural exchanges were interrupted by the Second World War and—after a brief period of fertile experimentation after the war—were followed by the sterility of communist orthodoxy. In the 1960's, after two decades of isolation, Czech art again recaptured its spirit of experimentation, although much of this has now ceased. The explosion of creative activity in the 1960's encompassed all modes of artistic expression, theater, film, the graphic and plastic arts, and literature. The new Czech prose forms suggested the French *nouveau roman,* but also returned to, and further developed, the earlier Czech traditions of surrealism of the 1930's. In a brief, but brilliant, burst of energy, Czech art had again demonstrated the rich heterogeneity of the avant-garde art of the 1920's and 1930's.

Throughout Europe one witnessed similar revitalizations of the aesthetic values of the avant-garde movement of four or five decades ago. In discussing these characteristics distinctive to the Czech development, we must first attempt to define the avant-garde movement which was born in the 1920's. Various terms, such as Avant-gardism, Modernism, and even Post-modernism, all suggest a movement forward from a previous position. But by the early twentieth century, these terms also implied a specific iconoclastic attitude to past art forms, linking avant-garde art to the general crisis of humanity. By the turn of the century, scientific discoveries had put into question past certainties and suggested man's impotence. Darwin's evolutionary theory had attacked man's anthropocentrism, just as Galileo's discoveries had, centuries earlier, destroyed the belief of terrocentricity; and in the early twentieth century Einstein and Heisenberg had demonstrated the feebleness of the traditional principle of causality. Freud dramatised the importance of unconscious forces, threatening the concept of the free and rational will of man. Marx wrote of underlying economic structures which determined man's fate. Industrialization and the growth of urban centers, first a source of liberation, now seemed to bring alienation and deculturation. Accompanying these conceptual revolutions was an equally exigent crisis in the arts, which questioned and destroyed traditional aesthetic attitudes: music discarded conventional harmony for new tonal relationships; the visual arts found the principle of mimesis lacking in significance; and, of course, literature also relegated to the past the principle that art represented an objective reality, as it was exemplified in the "transmind" (*zaum*) poetry of the Russian futurist Xlebnikov who experimented with poetry as pure sound, or the art of German poet Kurt Schwitters. Prose organizations based on linear time and traditional dichotomies between narrator's speech and the speech of the characters, traditional plot forms and settings, all lost significance in the face of newer conceptions of reality, defying earlier compartmentalizations.

In Czechoslovakia in the interwar period, a group of poets, painters, dramatists and architects self-named *Devĕtsil*, (a curative plant *tussilago farfara*), called for a non-engaged art: art, far from reflecting historical reality, was to be pure play, its only aim the exciting of the sensibilities of its viewers. In their first programmatic declaration, the group called for non-tendencious art, championing Mallarmé's experiments with the sounds and typographical arrangements of poetic language, and declaring allegiance to Marinetti's futurism and to dadaism. In the theatrical arts, *Devĕtsil* rejected psychological drama for a stage opened to clowneries, the grotesque and the absurd, so vividly developed in the thirties in the circus review atmosphere of Voskovec and Werich's "Liberated Theatre" (*Osvobozené divadlo*). In prose, linguistic experimentation fully exploited the various colloquial levels of the Czech language, a fertile field since the Czech language exhibits an unusually wide gulf between the written and the spoken subcodes. This is true because after the battle of the White Mountain (1620), the Czech language effectively ceased to exist as the language of literature and of the upper classes, and was replaced by Latin and German; consequently, when early in the last century the Czech reformers undertook the recodification of the Czech language, they turned to the norms of the language of the seventeenth century, whereas during the past two centuries the spoken language had undergone vast changes. Following Jaroslav Hašek's *Adventures of the Good Soldier Švejk* (*Osudy dobrého vojáka Švejka*), avant-garde prose of the thirties occupied itself with the colloquial levels of Czech. Notably, the prose of Karel Poláček developed the linguistic subcode of the Czech lower middle classes, and the work of Marie Půjmanová extensively utilized colloquialism and slang.

After its brief florescence and freedom, Czech literature entered the long period of stagnation beginning with the German occupation and continuing—with a brief interruption—almost through the 1950's. The monotony of orthodox socialist realism was only momentarily broken in the early postwar years; but in 1949 the first Congress of the Union of Czechoslovak Writers warned against the brief flirtation with formal experimentation, labelling all avant-garde art as "cosmopolitan." Thus there triumphed the so-called "construction novel" (*budovatelský roman*), a kind of *Erziehungsroman* in which the hero's ideological evolution is traced from a politically "wrong" position to a constructive one which supports the building of socialism.

Socialist realism as an ideology burned itself out by the end of the fifties. In 1957, the break with the strictures of ideology was heralded by the publication of Josef Škvorecký's *The Cowards* (*Zbabĕlci*). The novel, which created a sensation, was immediately proscribed, setting off a new, but shorter, period of repression of artistic freedom. When the work was finally allowed to be republished in 1963, it became, as it were, a programmatic declaration. Its edition of 100,000 was enormous for a country the size of Czechoslovakia; and it became the *cause célèbre* around which the new movements of literary experimentation began to organize. What is it in this novel that so excited the Czech reading public? The novel depicts the internal events in a small Czech town before and after its liberation by the Russians. However, the expected heroic resistance is composed not of heroes, but only of selfish and petty souls; the events are seen through the story's narrator, Danny Smiřický, a jazz-loving non-political teenager drawn into the struggle inadvertently, who is more interested in his vain attempts at seducing a reluctant girl friend than in politics. The Russian liberators also receive a realistic treatment. Teenage slang and jazz language and a skillful use of an oral style of narration (*skaz*) render grotesque the potentially heroic. By the early 1960's the new wave in Czech literature could no longer be ignored; in 1963 the third Congress of Czechoslovak Writers outlined new and more lenient guidelines, ushering in a period of fertile artistic experimentation.

This most recent avant-garde movement was less ideological and more negative than was its interwar predecessor. The ideological fervor of the interwar avant-garde movement is gone, as is its predominantly leftist trend. Now faith in the future of socialism and in the Soviet Union, the former model, was shaken. Experimentation with new forms expressing the dominant mood of skepticism and irony inherited from the Kafkaesque tradition predominated.

What were the general characteristics of the new art? Old forms and themes which had dominated the "construction novel" were abandoned, while more attention began to be paid to *Ich-form* narration and to *skaz* which had a strong tradition in Czech literature since Jaroslav Hašek, as well as to *Erlebte Rede*. Surrealist practices remained strong and were further developed. All this led to a new relationship of author, reader and protagonist, which attempted to force the reader to participate in the creative process by means of what the Russian Formalists called the novel's "difficult construction."

I shall now turn to a discussion of a few of the most significant writers of the new generation who have experimented in interesting ways with both new themes and new forms. Those artists who have relied primarily on traditional techniques, such as Weil, Grossman and others, in their powerful depictions of the Jewish experience during the German occupation, are not discussed here since we limit ourselves to those writers we can identify as avant-garde.

Josef Škvorecký, who now lives in Toronto, has continued to experiment with new forms as a novelist and a film writer (he wrote the scenarios for the Czech films *Murder in the Bar* and *The End of the Priest*). Early influences were contributed by his translations of Joyce, Hemingway, James, and Lewis. A particularly interesting work, entitled *From the Life of Good Society* (*Ze života lepší společnosti*), continues the verbal experimentation and the utilization of sub-standard language levels which Škvorecký developed in *The Cowards*. This collection of loosely connected texts, originally written for presentation at a Prague nightclub, is presented in the form of school compositions by young children from the "better families" of a Czech provincial town. These texts give a fine opportunity for exploiting the wide gulf between written and colloquial Czech; for the "school exercises" are written in stilted and cumbersome "high" Czech style, inadvertently mixed with teenage colloquialisms. The mock pompous style, the puns and word games, all parody philistinism and patriotism, and all that is required of schoolboys to write "correct" Czech. Škvorecký's latest novel, *The Tank Brigade* (*Tankový prápor*), published in Canada in 1971, is a satiric treatment of Czech army life which fully utilized Czech slang.

Milan Kundera (b. 1929) demonstrates the broad syncretic interest in all the arts typical of the Czech avant-garde of both the 1920's and the 1960's. Kundera's works provide fewer obstacles to the translator than do those of Škvorecký, since Kundera relies less heavily on the use of the complex interplay between different language styles and levels. Kundera began his literary career as a poet. His first collection, *Man, an Open Garden* (*Člověk, zahrada širá*, 1953), and his . . . *Monologues* (*Monology*, 1957), were both attacked for their eroticism during the puritanical Novotný era. In Kundera's first collection of short stories, which appeared in 1963 and was entitled *Ridiculous Loves* (*Směšné lásky*), traditional love themes were parodied. However, Kundera's fame in Czechoslovakia and abroad rests primarily on his novel *The Joke* (*Žert*, 1967) which has been translated into English, but hardly successfully, since important sections are omitted and the internal order has been disturbed. The opening of the novel places us first in the immediate post-Novotný period, while flashbacks take us to the repressive 1950's following upon one seemingly small incident. Ludvík Jahn, the hero of the novel and a student leader, sends a postcard to his girlfriend who is at a camp for "cadre schooling" with the following message: "Optimism is the opium of the people! The healthy atmosphere stinks! Long live Trotzky!" When Ludvík's joke is intercepted, he is accused of anti-

revolutionary activities and expelled from the university. In the disciplinary army battalion, where he is sent, he falls in love with a girl who shortly rejects him. As the novel opens, Ludvík has been "rehabilitated" and works in a scientific institute, having returned to the university to complete his degree. He meets a journalist, Helena, the wife of the opportunist Zemánek whose betrayal contributed to Ludvík's disgrace and downfall. Ludvík decides to revenge himself for Zemánek's earlier betrayal by a meaningless seduction of Helena, only to discover in the end that Zemánek has a young mistress and is grateful to Ludvík for having helped him to be rid of his wife. Thus, unwittingly, Ludvík has provided means for his enemy to obtain a divorce. When Helena understands the true motives of Ludvík's seduction, she attempts suicide; but, in a final joke she mistakenly takes laxatives, instead of sleeping pills.

While the central theme of the novel is simple and superficially conceived, it is inventive because of its skillful montage-like construction, its deft use of narrational perspectives and shifting points of view, which all present a multi-dimensional view of the events involved. The four narrators, who relate essentially the same story, are: Ludvík, the chief narrator and main protagonist; Helena, Zemánek's wife and Ludvík's victim; Jaroslav, a visionary dedicated to the preservation of Moravian folk art and the folk "soul," as artificially cultivated in the 1950's; and Kostka, Ludvík's idealistic friend who believes in a mystical synthesis of Christianity and Marxism. Of the seven chapters, three (chapters one, three and five) are narrated by Ludvík; Helena, Jaroslav, and Kostka narrate one chapter each (two, four, and six respectively), and the last chapter is divided into three segments, narrated by Ludvík, Helena, and Jaroslav. Since each of the four narrators is also described by the other narrators, a multi-dimensional narrational perspective is created. The theme which the juxtaposed narration of the individual characters reveals is simply that of small persons working relatively fruitlessly for narrow ends. Thus, in the final analysis nothing works. Romantically counterposed to this world of insignificant people and the fakery of the "official folklore" of the party, suggested by the young girls who dance folk dances at May-day marches, is Kundera's view of genuine folklore expressing true emotions, expressed in a theme which permeates the novel and which is fully and explicitly expressed in Jaroslav's monologue encompassing one chapter which is unfortunately omitted in the English translation.

Another leader of the Czech avant-garde movement is Bohumil Hrabal (b. 1914), well known as the author of the scenario of the Czech film *Closely Watched Trains*. His approach, both less ideological and more experimental and original than Kundera's, encompasses the stream of consciousness, surrealist elements and experimentation with the oral forms of the Czech language. His first published work, a collection of texts entitled *The Little Pearl at the Bottom* (*Perlička na dno*, 1963) is composed of a plotless collage-like series of small events and recollections recorded in oral style. Innumerable digressions by the narrator are strung together in an associative contiguity, recalling Švejk's recounting of seemingly irrelevant trifles of which he is "reminded," but which are quite unconnected with the story he is telling. Hrabal's next text, published in 1964, *Dancing Lessons for Adults and Advanced Students* (*Taneční hodiny pro starší a pokročilé,* 1964) experiments further. It is composed of one undivided syntactic unit, one sentence being over ninety pages in length. In a monologue, an old man reminisces as he addresses an inattentive young girl who crochets or picks cherries as he tells his endless story. The old man, who fancies he still has an eye for a young girl, restitutes an epic of his nation and of the Austro-Hungarian monarchy. In this montage-like confrontation of heterogeneous semantic materials and the juxtaposition of disharmonious and distinct language levels, Hrabal has blurred the distinction between oral folk art and "high" art. We are reminded that Mukařovský, and Propp before him, had pointed out that motifs in folk art are relatively independent and moveable, and freely arranged, thus allowing them to move from one folk creation to another, and even permitting the regrouping of motifs within one and the same work of art, in contrast to the structure of "high" art in which motifs are mutually interdependent. Now high art, like folk art, assumes just such a free movement of motifs, their relation being only the contiguity of free association. Further innovations are the expressions of surrealist themes in substandard language and the grotesque use of Communist jargon for quite inappropriate themes. Here is an example:

> . . . once the priest gave me a picture of Jesus with the chalice, that used to be kind of fashionable in the Austrian days, they had their screenings (*prověrky*) and their personal dossier interviews (*kádrování*), who is the Father and the Son and the Holy Ghost? one priest was even hauled into court because the Ulman sisters could not say what the Holy Trinity was? and the priest made them sit on the heated stove on their bare behinds, and then them gals couldn't get married, nobody wanted nothing to do with them, Jesus, if they didn't even know what the Holy Trinity was, well nobody knew it nohow, but they all pretended that they knew, so them sisters raised sunflowers, in those days there were godawful many murders and robberies, everyone closed the windows at night on the farms and kept axes and shooting arms, and then one quiet night this miller sees in the moonlight as how someone starts to cut away at the door with a saw to stick in his hand and undo the latch, and that miller steals quietly up with his axe, and when the hand begins to come through the crack of the door, bang! off comes the hand, then the gendarmes looked and looked, but couldn't find noone without that hand, then the priest got mad, because he had to bury the hand in the churchyard, he had to buy a tiny little coffin. Jesus-holy virgin (*panenkomarjá*)! a soldier stands guard in Olomouc and looks, something is burning in the churchyard, so he runs, opens the door to the dead-house, and what do you think he sees? the grave digger with a kettle, and from that kettle stick out human arms and legs, and the fat is burning, and there the gendarmes take him, they says he dug up dead corpses and cooked them as pigfood, and later the Prostějov

kids used to sing a song, there are the little arms and legs of that little girlie . . .

Another innovator, Ivan Vyskočil (b. 1929), composes short, almost plotless texts which he used to read aloud in Prague nightclubs in programs called "text appeals." Later, these little sketches, skits, bits of music and songs were assembled in a volume entitled *Flying, After All, Is Easy* (*Vždyt' přece létat je snadné,* 1963). They are characterized by linguistic deformations, neologisms, and grotesque juxtaposition of incongruous language levels; their dominating theme is the failure of communication which dominates Western literature as well.

In his brief prose works, Vladimir Páral depicts the alienation of modern consumer-oriented society. *A Private Hurricane* (*Soukromá vichřice,* 1966), subtitled *A Laboratory Report on Insect Life,* describes the emptiness and stereotyped mechanics of sexual relations, marital and nonmarital, reduced to habit and convention. A similar theme is struck in Páral's earlier *Fair of Fulfilled Wishes* (*Veletrh splněných přání,* 1964). Again in *The Catapult* (*Katapult,* 1967) Páral relates the empty love life of a self-destructive hedonist. Faceless, mechanical humans who lead monotonous lives and repeat stereotyped thoughts and acts people Páral's novels. Such humans are dwarfed by a modern society in which man-made objects increasingly control the lives of their makers. This view is conveyed by an obsessive dwelling on the concreteness of objects, details and realia which, as in Chaplin's *Modern Times,* or in the novels

Bohumil Hrabal in a Czech pub.

145

by Robbe-Grillet, reverses the traditional hierarchy of man and things.

Perhaps the most significant of contemporary Czech prose writers is Ladislav Fuks (b. 1923) who lives in Prague, the locus of many of his writings. He holds a doctorate in philosophy and psychology from Charles University, but has devoted his creative career to writing. His first novel, *Mr. Theodore Mundstock* (*Pan Theodor Mundstock,* 1963) which has been translated into many languages, including English, is an ironic treatment of the tragedy which, like so many of Fuks' works, is focused on the inner life of the protagonist. The novel is set in German-occupied Prague. Its hero is an elderly Jewish man who, while awaiting transport to the concentration camp, attempts to prepare himself by training in advance for its rigors, thus hoping to be able to endure the ordeal he knows will befall him. But he is run over by a German military truck on his way to the collection point for the transport. The novel has been interpreted philosophically as an exposition of the hopelessness of man's attempt to transform a reality which eventually defeats him in a world based on force and injustice.

The hero of the novel, Mr. Theodore Mundstock, is isolated by his world of illusions and hallucinations. His separation from the outside world is expressed stylistically by the limitation of dialogue to only a few very specific situations. For even when Mundstock is addressed directly, he can answer only indirectly through a form of internal monologue. Mundstock's effort to live a "normal" life in a world shown as insane results in the tragic and grotesque admixture of horror and the ridiculous, the elevated and the low, despair and hope. Structurally, this grotesque quality is expressed through a semantic ambivalence; only an indefinite border separates physical reality and imagination and, consequently, reality is fragmented. Fragmentation, which is perhaps the constant characteristic of Fuks' art, is expressed on all levels of the novel: on that of plot a continuous plot line is replaced by an aggregate of episodes; on the level of characterization there is no clear distinction between reality and unreality (for instance Mundstock has constant conversations with an imaginary double whom he calls "Mon"); and on the level of speech the line between objective narrational information and the character's monologue becomes indistinct by the employment of the various gradations of *Erlebte Rede.* The intellectual and emotional substructure of the novel is one of paradox, a paradox which turns all goals into their opposites. Thus the novel systematizes, as does so much of contemporary absurd drama, the paradox of modern society, where rationality leads to the irrational, and where communication becomes lack of communication.

Fuks' next work, *My Dark-Haired Brethren* (*Mojí černovlasí bratří*) appeared in 1964. Composed of a series of short stories, all related in the first person by a young high school student, it is set in the early years of the German occupation of Prague and depicts the plight of the Jewish fellow students of the narrator who are tortured by a brutal geography teacher.

In 1967, there appeared a short novel grotesquely entitled *The Burner of Corpses* (*Spalovač mrtvol*). In this modern horror story the anti-hero is the crematorium official Kopferkringl, who professes kindliness and harmlessness, but is in fact a murderer. He begins by killing his part-Jewish wife and children, and ends by becoming a mass operator of concentration camp gas chambers.

This novel is again built on a paradox: the protagonist does not appear to be an evil man; rather, he appears perfectly normal and quite human even. He upholds the normal platitudes of decency, believes that man should not suffer, and is obedient to law and order. And yet, he commits murders; not out of hate, but because circumstances of his time lead him to crime. His violent acts, he explains, will save his victims from an even worse fate. This paradox is played on all the levels of the novel, and we find again the fragmentation achieved primarily through many repetitions and variations of key episodes and phrases.

Fuks' most significant work to date is doubtlessly his third novel, published in 1966, entitled *Variations for a Dark String* (*Variace pro temnou strunu*), which continues the theme of the threatened German occupation and violence begun in *My Dark-Haired Brethren.* In the novel, Michal, a boy of high school age, describes in the first person the experiences of his childhood and adolescence. We learn of his unresponsive family, his friends and his school, but essentially we read of Michal's inner world, his dreams and fears. In the background, but persistently and threateningly felt, is an ever-present consciousness of violence, a feeling of approaching danger and doom. The novel ends with the German occupation of Czechoslovakia in 1939.

While externally the novel is about the political events which lead to the destruction of the Czechoslovak Republic, the underlying themes pertain to death treated on various planes, from the metaphysical to the ironic and even to burlesque, and the related themes of alienation and isolation. Fuks' characters strive to escape from their lonely prisons. Michal's house is surrounded by secret police; his father is faceless and nameless, identified only by the third person pronoun *on.* The atmosphere Fuks wishes to portray is metaphorically expressed in the ballad of the Czech romantic poet J. Erben, "The Wedding Shirt" ("Svatební košile") recited and commented upon in the following fashion by the Czech literature teacher:

> " . . . the dead man is neither dead nor is he alive . . . The dead man is a creature without a soul. Do you know how this is said in German? Soulless? Michal . . . Michal . . . "

Michal does not know the German word, no one knows it; but the search for the word recurs and becomes as it were a *leitmotif* of the novel; and at the end of the novel the secret word emerges. It characterizes the SS man: he is *seelenlos.* Finally, Michal finds himself to be neither dead nor alive, hence a *seelenlos* creature.

> I was supposed to be dead and yet alive and in this world, I was supposed to be alive, and yet dead for the world and life.

All these themes express unpredictability and terror, metaphorically expressed throughout the work by the harp on which man and the uncontrollable winds play the "dance of life." The dark string, perhaps the *id,* forever threatens the individual, for it may be played fortuitously. This is explained to Michal by his Jewish school friend Katz:

> ". . . .Man is like a harp, *on which the wind plays, but on which he also plays himself.* He plays on himself, isn't that strange, life is . . . is like a *dance.* Well, and just as there are many different strings on the harp, so are they on man. He has very high strings, but those are the weakest, as on the harp, so that man sometimes does not even hear them, and sometimes he does not touch them all his life, they never sound all his life, or if they sound, then only occasionally, like a tinkle or ringing which immediately fades out into the lower strings. Man has, however, also deeper and deepest strings, and then [. . . .] then there is in every man also a *dark string.* . . . One dark string [. . . .] and that dark string man must not touch. He can play on all strings, but not on that dark string."
>
> "And what if *the wind* plays on it," I said. . . . "What will happen then?"
>
> "You know," said Katz and smiled, "I haven't thought about that." And a little later, he became serious and said: "That could perhaps result in a tragedy."

The metaphor of the harp sets the atmosphere for the entire novel, one of tension and foreboding. How is this mood conveyed? Here we can isolate a central, organizing principle of the work, that of fragmentation of reality. This fragmentation pervades all levels of the novel. First, on the most realistic plane, the story is about fragmentation and uncertainty. This is the import of the political events, of the disturbed human relations, and of all the action. But fragmentation is portrayed not only on the level of plot meaning but also on stylistic levels, from syntax to methods of discourse, images and motifs.

How does Fuks articulate the principle of fragmentation, and how does it dominate the novel's structure? We note that fragments in Fuks' world have their own structures, composing a kind of haunting symmetry and circular repetition. It is as though, in Fuks' works, splintered echoes, each differing slightly from all others, reach the inner ear. Words, phrases, sentences, images, motifs, small pieces of action and description occur repeatedly, until they become almost obsessive. Each time they occur, they are illuminated from a different angle because of the shifting context. Fuks uses the term "resonances" to describe his technique. He says that resonances

> function both independently and in their mutual interrelations; thus they are provided with a context, and the book obtains a second and third level. . . . The detail resounds in different fashions and repeatedly throughout the work, and thus it is raised to a higher power.

By these interacting resonances Fuks constructs a fragile world of psychological and poetic reality. Its implicit opposition to the world of logic and common sense imparts a pervasive and constant underlying tension. We know this method from the new film art. In a recent article, S. B. Purdy compares the cinematographic method of Robbe-Grillet's film *Last Year at Marienbad,* which is

characterized by overlapping repetitions of words, phrases and visual images, to the repetitions in the poetry of Gertrude Stein. He even quotes Gertrude Stein as recognizing the relationship of what she was trying to do to the cinema of her day; however, Fuks has developed the technique of resonances far beyond Stein's interesting experiments. For his technique pervades not only the linguistic pattern, but all other levels of the novel as well. We now discuss some applications of Fuks' techniques to the various levels of the novel.

We turn first to the level of syntax. The central construction of the novel revolves around the narration by Michal. But in Fuks' typical fragmentation, there seems to be an apparent shifting of narrational perspective. The narrator tells of events observed, and in which he is a participant. The entire world of the novel is centered around Michal and, with the exception of Růžena the maid, none of the other characters are developed independently from Michal's view of them. Nevertheless, the construction of the narrative patterns in the novel is characterized by a blurring of the boundary line between information provided by the narrator and that provided by other characters, causing a marked interpenetration of external and internal events. One way this is achieved is by the weakening of the grammatical distinctions of verbal persons and numbers. The speech of the narrator is interpenetrated at times with that of the characters. This leads, as the Czech critic Zdeněk Kožmín observes, to a situation in which individual utterances about reality are constantly placed in question by being shifted into other types of utterances in which their meaning and stylistic weight is altered. Sometimes discourse is given multiple perspective by repetition of the same utterance in a different person or, in Fuks' terminology, certain details are viewed from more than one perspective, causing resonances. For example:

> . . . Mrs. Hron smiled and shook her head. "Wait, first I'll give you some hip wine (wild rose wine?), we live like in a storm," she said. And Hron. . . . sat down at the table opposite us. "First she'll give you some hip wine, we live like in a storm," . . .

Another technique contributing to fragmentation is that of shifts between direct, indirect, and reported discourse, as in the following example:

> "Oh, piano lessons," she sighed and continued to stand at the cold kitchen stove, "I am not sure whether I am not going crazy." And then she asked me, whether I had ever noted that when I meet a stranger, he reminds me of someone I know, and that I either don't know whom he reminds me of, or why he reminds me of him, or that I don't know at all that he reminds me of someone. . . . Don't I know why that is? When I didn't know, she said:
>
> "It is simply because the two persons do not look alike."

The quoted conversation between the maid and Michal opens with direct discourse, which is immediately followed by indirect discourse. The sentence beginning with

"Don't I know" (*Nenapadlo mě*) is reported discourse. It stands between direct and indirect discourse, having marks of both: it is not graphically marked as direct speech, but lacks the syntactic features of indirect discourse (it does not say "she said that . . ."), though it contains some of its grammatical features (the addressee is in the first person; but then it is he who narrates).

There is throughout the novel an uncertainty as to who is speaking or reflecting. This confusion of individual consciousnesses, by omitting the grammatical marks of individual identities, suggests the general loss of identity in Fuks' world, where all traditional systems and orderings seem to fail.

Still another aspect of Fuks' syntax, contributing to the fragmentation of reality, is a further obliteration of boundaries, this time between imagination and the external world. This is achieved by the frequent use of aposiopesis, the sudden interruption of an utterance usually graphically indicated by dots, as though the speaker were unable or unwilling to complete the statement. This allows the text to sound into a void, to express forlornness, indefiniteness, uncertainty, and to make it unclear whether the sentences are actually spoken or exist only in the internal world of the narrator, and thus to express the isolation of man.

The existential background of the French *nouveau roman,* felicitously described recently by a German critic, might as well have been directed at Fuks. The critic notes that the reality of modern times has taken on an opaqueness which man can not bear. For in this fragmented reality, bearing unsolvable problems, man no longer can find a rational order nor a meaningful center, for such "centers" as God or Reason have lost their validity. This destruction of a finite world image and the accompanying loss of a sense of the unity of the world is a part of Fuks' reality, which we perceive as a conglomerate of incongruous and dissonant elements and fragments, and which form a confusing chaos ordered only by Fuks' system of resonances.

In 1970 a new novel by Fuks was published, entitled *The Mice of Mrs. Mooshaber (Myší paní Mooshabrovê),* which continues the grotesque and absurd works of the last decade and is a brilliant piece of writing. It is a horror novel of the absurd in which fairytale elements mingle with realistic scenes of horror and with surrealist pictures. The novel is an allegory of the dark forces that act on man in its intermixture of a picture of a modern dictatorship and medieval formulae of evil and witchcraft and miracles. Again the principle of fragmentation is predominant, expressed in repetitions of plot segments, syntactic units, imagery, and persistent words.

A new novel by Fuks, *The Incident of the Criminal Inspector (Příběh kriminálníko rady),* published in 1971, is a Dürrenmatt-like detective story with allegorical overtones, which shows little of Fuks' usual brilliance.

Today many Czech writers have found no alternative than to go into exile, and to continue their work under the difficult conditions of separation from their reading public. Of the writers discussed in this essay, only Páral and Fuks continue to be active in Czechoslovakia. Inside of Czechoslovakia, the vibrant experimentation of the 1960's has been halted; the Czech Writers' Union has been dissolved and has so far not been replaced by a viable organization. But, assuredly, many writers continue to write "for the drawer" where their works must remain until a freer climate again makes possible the open flourishing of the Czech creative literary traditions. (pp. 107-19)

Thomas G. Winner, "Czech Avant-garde Prose of the Sixties," in Mosaic: A Journal for the Comparative Study of Literature and Ideas, *Vol. VI, No. 4, Summer 1973, pp. 107-19.*

Josef Škvorecký

[*A Czech novelist, editor, translator, and screenwriter, Škvorecký is one of the most highly noted contemporary Czech authors. The publication of his first major novel* Zbabělci (The Cowards) *in 1958 gained Škvorecký both political notoriety and national popularity for what Czech government authorities deemed an irreverent portrayal of the Soviet army and the use of coarse colloquialisms. The* Cowards *and such major works by Škvorecký as* Příběh inženýra lidských duší (*1977;* The Engineer of Human Souls) *reflect the influence of American jazz music and the fiction of Ernest Hemingway and William Faulkner, and typically satirize and denounce rigid forms of political and philosophical dogma. A member of the Czechoslovak Writers Union during the 1960s, Škvorecký emigrated to Canada following the Prague Spring. In Toronto he has worked as an educator and has assisted his wife in establishing Sixty-Eight Publishers, a firm that has issued numerous texts that had been banned in Czechoslovakia during the 1970s and 1980s. In the following excerpt, Škvorecký addresses the difficulties experienced by Czech authors exiled in the West after 1968, surveying several of their works from the 1970s.*]

If Ovid had been a Christian, he would have been the best candidate for the patron-saintship of writers. The barbaric punishment that became his lot and that some equally afflicted writers considered to be more severe than outright execution, this cutting off—to speak as the Russians do—of the roots which connect the writer's creative soul with the nourishing juices of the fatherland and the mother tongue, shamefully enough survives in some countries to this very day.

However, Ovid, the blabbering, homesick wreck of a great poet, is the pagan patron saint of only *one* kind of exiled writer. There is also Joseph Conrad; he obviously was in no great need of the "nourishing juices of the fatherland" and thrived very well in an acquired tongue. Exile is a hard experience, but it is not all gloom, despair and inevitable suicide. It depends on certain things. To Ovid, the poet laureate of a huge empire, the gates of the world were wide open. He, however, preferred to stay at home, where fame flattered his ego and the friendship of shapely matrons kept him busy (and in the end probably proved his undoing). He was thrown out of the cozy, warm, glittering crystal nest of the Capital of the World and banished to a barbaric corner of the empire. The only literate men there were some of the better-educated centurions, and soldiers, even in that day, probably did not hold poetic fame in high esteem. As for the local ladies, we can hardly assume they were very proficient in the sophisticated, cosmetic and highly ritualized Roman *ars amandi.*

Joseph Conrad, on the other hand, grew up in a country [Poland] that had been cruelly subjugated by a far less enlightened superpower. He was the son of an intellectual father, doomed to die the death of the disobedient serfs in the North of insensitive Russia, and of a mother who, with her young son, returned from that hopeless Ultima Thule, only to die the death of the sensitive and the fragile, a victim of tuberculosis. Conrad was the heir of a complex tradition strangled by the medieval hand of Russia, and so he ran away into exile. Exile to him was not the barren Tomis of Ovid. It was free Britannia and her worldwide waves, her sophisticated system of legal security, the society of her free-living, free-thinking intellectuals—also poverty and hard struggle, to be sure, but with no obstacles that could not be surmounted by one's talent and efforts. No all-powerful censor, no arbitrary judge, no firing squad.

These, then, are the two sides of the same coin called "writer in exile." You will notice that I omit exiles of the notorious American Lost Generation type. These are not exiles. These are vacationers in countries where a dollar simply lasts longer. And you will also notice that the above statement is not an attempt on my side to join the numerous and clamourous ranks of America's detractors. To my mind, it is a statement in praise of the poor, selfless, open-armed land of the Yankees.

When we Czech and Slovak writers went into exile in 1968-69, we were somewhere halfway between Ovid and Conrad. We still vividly remembered the glorious mid-sixties, the lovely girls begging for autographs, the feeling of being a part of the collective effort to put our nation back on the map of the world's honest art, the subconscious knowledge that, apart from all private ambition, we were doing this basically *ad maiorem populi Boiohemi gloriam.* But the stench of the armored diesel engines was in our nostrils too. The war cries of the left-fascist Jodasites, the militant neo-Stalinists claiming our heads and demanding that we be handed over to the KGB resounded in our ears louder than the more distant songs of the Spring of 1968. The specter of the Gulag Archipelago, the long journey east of the Hungarian rebels of 1956, the dark shadow of imperial Russia swallowing our tiny Western Slavic island of a tradition so alien to that of Muscovy—all these overshadowed our future. So we were both Ovids and Conrads, some of us habitually inclined to be more of the former, some happily able to be more of the latter. We prospered accordingly.

Common to all of us was the experience of a reverted Alice in Wonderland. We were veterans of Nazism, Stalinism, neo-Stalinism and the periodic thaws and freezes—and suddenly we found ourselves in a world incredibly innocent of our knowledge. The old and truistic truth dawned on us with a strange intensity: that the only experience that matters, except for a few exceptional cases, is *personal* experience, not the experience of books or hearsay. Each of us knows the utter frustration when, after an hour's recital of the restrictions, habits and horrors of dictatorship,

the pretty, carefully made-up American hostess stares at you with wide eyes and asks: "Have you ever been back for a visit, since you left your country?"; the frustration of reading in big, glossy American magazines that the late Jacquelin Susann was bored by that highly recommended "novel" *The Gulag Archipelago;* the helpless anger when an Angela Davis swears she will dedicate her life to the freeing of all political prisoners anywhere in the world, and then adds, with a logic worthy of purest Orwellian Marxism, that political prisoners in the socialist countries are of course not included in her noble efforts: they are against socialism, i.e., against the People, and therefore deserve to pine away in jails; the painful allergy we suffer from, to the very capital *P* in People, for we know that in Stalinese it denotes: Police.

Our first common reaction was to attempt to square the circle and succeed where the giants of literature had not succeeded before us, to tell, to explain, to show, to persuade, to write "the novel that would open Western eyes." I shall not mention those of my generation of literary exiles who tried and failed. Quite a few tried, and invariably they failed. They failed even artistically, no matter how good they had been. The nut is too hard to crack, the emotions too strong to be tamed into a work composed of disciplined words. I know of only one case so far which, in the Faulknerian sense, is at least a splendid failure. I harbor no illusion that the novel will change anything in the Western psyche; but it portrays it well, with healthy cynicism and with penetrating sarcasm. The novel is *The Report of the Death of Rosenkavalier,* and the writer is a Czech-Canadian writer from Vancouver, Jan Drábek. This youngish man had the good fortune of having come to this continent as an adolescent, and so he managed what Conrad had managed: he mastered the foreign tongue. His novels two of them by now, the first being the remarkable *Whatever Happened to Wenceslas?* (1975)—were written in English, but their spirit and vision are Czech: an émigré imagination, not of the Ovidian but of the Conradian type, somewhat like the vision of *Under Western Eyes,* a portrait of the exile's mind, of his human situation among other humans who, by experience and even if older than himself, are one generation younger and consequently so much less knowledgeable.

This is probably the best way open to us: to catch the flavor of our situation, its sadness and frustration, but also its chances, its feeling of *safety* never experienced before; the old-fashioned, much-ridiculed, yet to us so concrete and sweet sense of *freedom.* Two authors of the 1968 emigration wave have so far and to my knowledge succeeded in this field, this mode, this subject matter—the poet Stanislav Mareš and the short story writer Jaroslav Vejvoda. Mareš's approach is that of a mellowed, more sophisticated Ovid. He has even made use of the ancient Roman form of the hexameter, has sprinkled his verse with allusions to the pagan patron saint and, in my opinion, has given us in his *Báje z noveho světa (A Fable of the New World,* 1975) one of the very best long poems in modern Czech literature. He is a truly Czech Ovid residing in, of all places, the unlikely town of Wollongong in New South Wales. His is an Ovidian past as the son of a farmer expropriated by the regime in 1948, a brilliant translator of W. H. Auden, T.

S. Eliot, Vachel Lindsay and other modern Americans, and the author of a play banned in the late fifties which had been inspired by the dense atmosphere of Tennessee Williams and by the even denser atmosphere of Charles University in the years following the Trials. All that perhaps explains why there is little homesickness in the haunting long poem. There is sarcasm for those who remained, unaware of or ignoring Joyce's "Non serviam!"; an informed, slightly amazed wisdom with which the poet views the arid new home in the land of the grotesque platypus; a rich and perhaps provocative resignation of the man who, in imitating Conrad's wish to do the highest justice to the world, chose for his epigraph the lines from an early nineteenth-century convicts' song, "True patriots we, for, be it understood, / We left our country for our country's good."

In Jaroslav Vejvoda's collection of short stories, with its title reminiscent of Marc Chagall's pictures, *Plující andělé, letící ryby* (*Swimming Angels, Flying Fish,* 1974), the reader meets the youngest generation of the 1968 exiles: the former supporters of Dubček, both students and young apprentices, in their new home—conservative, stuffy, stingy and xenophobic Switzerland. Some of these stories are Conradian, capturing the spirit of adventure that besets the young, until recently restricted by the infamous exit visas of their now-occupied homeland, hitchhiking thirstily through the southern regions of Europe to prohibited Spain and to the warm sands of the Mediterranean. Others examine the conflict between the Western and Eastern consciousness objectively, evocatively and with an understanding for both sides in a fashion worthy of *Under Western Eyes,* their prototype. Some selections, on the other hand, are almost pure Ovid: for example, that touching tour de force, "Granny, Mail Me the Blue Elephant," the soliloquy of a child in an alien universe who finds her Paradise Lost of home embodied in an absurd toy left behind in Prague. One story, "The Little Feather," is, to my mind, truly universal, symbolic of the situation of all exiles. It tells of the Christmas odyssey of an adolescent boy through wintry Switzerland to spend Christmas Eve with a Czech girl in a prudish Swiss pension in one of the distant cantons. Blind to the charms of the Schwyzer-Deutsch-twittering lasses, frozen and hungry, the boy arrives at the home of the girl—who bears the poetically unpoetic name of M. Linhartová—and is clandestinely smuggled into her room, where gentlemen's visits are strictly forbidden, only to fall asleep from exhaustion and spiritual happiness on the girl's narrow couch. Vejvoda's book was awarded the annual Egon Hostovský Prize for 1974 for the best fiction written by a Czech or Slovak writer in exile.

There have been a few other remarkable works esthetically defining exile, particularly Antonín Brousek's book of poems, *Contraband* (1975), or the late Vratislav Blažek's collection of letters, *Mariáš v Reykjaviku* (*A Card Game in Reykjavik,* 1975). But the majority of the truly good books of fiction written or published in exile returned for their subjects to the pre-exile days. The most widely acclaimed of these was a novel by Zdena Salivarová entitled *Honzlová,* (1972), which also appeared in English as *Summer in Prague* (1973). If anything can, however slightly, open the eyes of the West, then it is this story of an average young woman from an average family who finds herself in an average predicament. The heroine is a working girl. Two members of her family—the father and an older brother—are in exile and in a concentration camp respectively, and the protagonist, Jana, suffers from the attentions of a Secret Political Police agent, who first tries to turn her into a police informer, then later himself becomes a victim of amatory affection. The love, however, is unrequited—the girl is too distrustful of her unlikely suitor's intentions—and the black farce of the unique love story changes into a tragedy of fate.

But Salivarová's novel is no naturalistic chronicle of life in a police state. It is, as the author, a singer by profession, has subtitled it, a "protest song." There are distinct motifs often borrowed from folk songs, the structure represents a point-counterpoint of reversed values, the language is terse and poetically slangy, and an almost biblical symbolism of the story of the fallen angels underlies the plot. Exiles and Westerners alike love this gem of a narrative, and even critics as well read as George Steiner writing in a journal as sophisticated as *The New Yorker* (12 May 1973) have found words of highest praise for it: "the modulations of feeling . . . belong almost to the Dostoevskian world." The author has just finished another work, the short novel *Nebe, peklo, ráj* (*Heaven, Hell and Paradise*), a kind of answer to Erich Segal's *Love Story* in which the man dies, or better, disappears into the Gulag. The work is a variation on the Romeo and Juliet theme wherein the feuding families are two socialist states, tied—theoretically—by bonds of mutual friendship and immersed in indivisible freedom.

Another excellent author who has emerged in exile is Ota Filip, whose *Nanebevzetí Lojzka Lapáčka ze slezské ostravy* (*Lojzek Lapáček's Ascension to Heaven,* 1975) is probably the most substantial novel in the category of books about the pre-exile past. Filip, a man of great personal courage, spent the first post-invasion years in jail in Czechoslovakia. As an undesirable he was dispatched into involuntary exile in 1974, preceeded by the German edition of *Lojzek Lapáček.* This long and complex novel is a detailed history of the common man caught in the bedlam of Central Europe in the epoch of dictatorships. Centering on the history of a soccer team, Filip's contemporary Human Comedy grows in intensity—and absurdity—and assumes an original symbolism which leaves the reader with the distinct impression that although the common man survives, he does so only after much suffering. Two more narratives have appeared from the prolific pen of this author since his departure from Czechoslovakia: *Blázen v městě* (*A Fool Is in the Town,* 1975) and *Paskvrněné početí* (*The Non-Immaculate Conception,* 1976). The second, portraying the post-invasion Marxist farce in a small Moravian town, probably has the distinction of being the culmination point of black comedy in Czech literature.

Naturally enough, many of the works in the category of exile writing are stories of life in concentration camps or, to use the official term, correctional establishments. Two stand out: Jan Beneš's novel *Druhý dech* (*Second Breath,* 1974) and Minka Rybáková's *Útěk z rekreace* (*Escape from Recuperation,* 1974). Interestingly enough, they represent two diametrically opposed approaches to this well-known theme: Beneš's book is an artistic reshaping of personal experience, whereas Rybáková's novel is a tour de force by a woman who has never been in the camps. Her story of a Jew who finds himself in a situation similar to that of his compatriots under a former dictatorship is based on meticulously checked documents and on the narratives of others. Also, interestingly enough, both novels are rich in texture and realistic detail, breathtaking in dramatic sweep and redeeming in their portrayal of invincible humanity. Beneš's novel has also appeared in English (1969); Graham Greene, after reading it, wrote that although naturally all novels about concentration camps stand in the shadow of *One Day in the Life of Ivan Denisovich,* he found *Second Breath* the better novel of the two. It is probably superfluous to add more praise to this, so let me just say that Minka Rybáková's book also deserves translation.

There have also been a few good political satires, the two most memorable ones from the pen of journalist Jiří Hochman, entitled *Jelení brod* (Stagford, 1971) and *Český happening* (1976). *Stagford* became one of the most widely-read books in exile and was produced with considerable success in a dramatized version by the BBC in England and by the CBC in Canada. In essence, it is a utopian story employing the device of an unexplainable journey into a kind of fourth dimension, where a group of bureaucratic Stalinist autocrats find themselves facing a true "people's democracy." *Czech Happening* is much richer and more ambitious and carries the tragic story of Soviet occupation to the present time under the disguise of a hilariously absurd chronicle of a contemporary Czech *Krähwinkel* [The editor of Škvorecký's essay states that this Czech term is "the Central European equivalent of 'the boondocks' "].

I must omit here the many nonfiction books—mainly volumes of memoirs—that have been published in exile in the past five years. Some of these, such as Julius Firt's memoirs *Knihy a osudy* (Books and Fates, 1972), will undoubtedly remain among the most important documents of our times, and some are even available in English, as in the case of Heda Kovály's unique account of persecutions under two dictatorships, *The Victors and the Vanquished* (1973; Czech edition, *Na vlastní kuži,* 1973). The latter work, written with Erazim V. Kohák, recounts the author's life first at Auschwitz, then later as the wife of Rudolf Margolius, one of the executed victims of the infamous culmination of Stalinist insanity, the trial of Slánský et al. Also not included are scholarly books such as Otto Ulč's brilliant dissection of everyday Stalinist justice *The Judge in a Communist State* (1972; Czech edition, *Malá doznání okresního soudce,* 1974).

But I cannot omit one cultural phenomenon that also became a typical feature of the Czech seventies, the other exile, the inner one—namely, those writers who have remained at home and who either do not want or are not allowed to publish along with the subservient and truly reactionary hacks of the occupational regime in Prague such as Alexej Pludek, the author of the viciously anti-Semitic novel *Va banque.* This remarkable group undoubtedly includes some of the best and most courageous Czech literary artists, many of them world-renowned, such as Václav Havel, Ludvík Vaculík, Jaroslav Seifert, Milan Kundera, Karel Pecka, Pavel Kohout, Josef Topol and many others. [Kundera has since emigrated to France; Kohout to Austria.] Together they have started an underground *samizdat* enterprise called Edice Petlice (Edition Padlock), which to date has published some sixty titles. Together with the more than one hundred titles published by the several Czechoslovak publishing houses in exile, these books constitute a very satisfactory crop indeed. Many of them will certainly still be read when the works of the laureates of the Soviet occupation have long been forgotten.

Together also, the two exiles, the internal and the external, have proved that Aragon's Biafra of the Mind and Böll's Cemetery of Culture pertain only to the field of contemporary Czech officialdom. Czech literature is alive and well, at home in exile. (pp. 308-13)

> *Josef Škvorecký, "At Home in Exile: Czech Writers in the West," in* Books Abroad, *Vol. 50, No. 2, Spring, 1976, pp. 308-13.*

Paul I. Trenský

[Born in the Moravian region of Czechoslovakia, Trenský is an American educator with special interests in Slavic literatures and comparative literature. In the following excerpt, he surveys Czech drama of the 1950s and 1960s.]

[The] renaissance of the Czech theater had begun well before 1956. The fall of the Stalinist cult accelerated developments as accumulated artistic energies found application with much less effort. An important feature of the post-1956 era is the very rapid diversification of theater life. Previous years were characterized by rigid conformity, and the work of the director, actor, and playwright was under the close supervision of a highly centralized system. The theater, like other arts, followed the canons of dogmatic teaching, and only minute differences could be observed between individual companies. This policy prevented the theater from evolving into independent units with clearly defined artistic goals. In the second half of the 1950's this sort of homogeneity becomes a thing of the past: the centralized machinery is replaced by numerous, substantially autonomous centers with specific artistic creeds. This diversification was given official sanction by the establishment, which, with the exception of a brief hiatus from 1958 through 1961, was usually satisfied with perfunctory assurances that a given production, play, or creative idea was not intended as a denial of Marxist principles. The Minister of Education and Culture, František Kahuda, who held jurisdiction over the whole of theater life in Czechoslovakia, defined the new policy as follows: "We are in favor of every artist choosing his own way, one that is most suitable to his individuality. It is important, of course, that he does not wander astray. We wish him to create as a socialist man who speaks to the people and who does not become a practitioner of art for its own sake." Under the umbrella of a loosely defined concept of social utility, not only was some of the most esoteric theater allowed to flourish, but in later years even some patently antiestablishment plays were tolerated. Their production was permitted because of their authors' token claims that they were attacking adverse aspects of the system rather than the system itself.

Most theater companies attempted to define their own program. Those that succeeded were usually headed by one or two strong personalities—most often by the director and the dramaturg (literary adviser)—who were able to organize a group of individuals with common artistic views, including actors, scenographers, and playwrights. The first such company to gain prominence was the National Theater in Prague (Národní divadlo) under the leadership of Otomar Krejča. Krejča's artistic program called for a theater aiming at the exploration of the complex psyche of modern man. Its resident playwrights were František Hrubín, Josef Topol, Milan Kundera, František Pavlíček, and Zdeněk Mahler. A conscious opposition to the esthetics of the National Theater was centered in the Mahen Theater of Brno, under the leadership of the triumvirate of Miroslav Hynšt, Evžen Sokolovský, and Bořivoj Srba. It was a politically engagé theater, whose most important playwright was Ludvík Kundera. Very close to the tenets of the Brno Theater was the Regional Theater in Hradec Králové, under Milan Pásek. Regional theaters were in general quite important in the revival of the theater life in Czechoslovakia thanks to generous subsidies given them and also to considerable attention paid by metropolitan critics, who reviewed their productions on a regular basis. In the small industrial town of Ostrava, for example, Jan Kačer organized in 1959 a young repertory company whose success attracted such a degree of nationwide attention that in the 1960's Kačer went to Prague, taking with him some of his most important actors.

In the early 1960's the center of gravity of the Czech theater moved from large established institutions to the so-called "small theaters" (*malá divadla*), which provided a more favorable ambience for experimentation and a better opportunity for a well-delineated repertory. Small theaters virtually mushroomed throughout the country; by 1963 there were some fifty companies in Prague alone, performing drama, musical comedy, pantomime, dance, as well as a mixture of various forms. The life of some of these companies was ephemeral, but others quickly acquired prominent roles in Czech cultural life. The prototype of the small theaters was Reduta, founded by Jiří Suchý and Ivan Vyskočil in 1957. It produced loosely structured shows combining casual entertainment with a demanding intellectual element. In later years the small theater movement developed in two different directions. One continued to base its repertoire on a blending of heterogeneous cabaretlike forms with a strong emphasis on musical content. The most important of these theaters was Semafor, founded in 1959 by Jiří Suchý and Jiří Šlitr. Other small theaters veered toward more traditional dramaturgy and made the literary text the cornerstone of the repertoire. This trend began in the early 1960's with the Ballustrade Theater (Divadlo na zábradlí), under the leadership of the famed critic and director Jan Grossman, who transformed this small theater into a showplace of the so-called drama of the absurd, both domestic and foreign. Václav Havel

was its most important resident playwright. In 1965 Jan Kačer, together with the critic Jaroslav Vostrý and the playwrights Ladislav Smoček and Alena Vostrá, founded the Drama Club (Cinoherní klub). Unlike most other theaters of this period, the Drama Club professed no complex world view. It was an actor-oriented company that conceived of the theater as a forum for the exploration of man through the art of acting. It deliberately deemphasized all rational and ideological elements, attempting to present "man in play" (Vostrý). After prolonged harassment by Prague's cultural bosses, in 1965 even Krejča left the National Theater to found a small theater called Behind the Gate (Za branou). Among the small theaters outside Prague, the most important one was Evening Brno (Večerní Brno), which staged plays with satirical content. It had a pleiad of authors, of whom Milan Uhde was the most brilliant. In general it was the trend of the late 1950's and early 1960's for the playwright to associate himself with a particular company, in contrast to the previous years, when the playwright wrote for "all theaters." Such associations were pursued even when a particular company did not have a clearly defined artistic program. Pavel Kohout, for example, had most of his plays staged at the Central Theater of the Army (Divadlo armády, also called Na vinohradech), as well as at the Realistic Theater. Associations were formed as much on a personal level as on an ideological or artistic one, in a climate conducive to cooperation and conviviality.

The large majority of plays written after 1956 came from the pens of new, often entirely inexperienced authors who sought the expert guidance of the director and his dramaturg. Eventually, many dramatists later entered into a genuine employer-employee relationship with a specific theater company. Topol, Smoček, and Kohout, for example, were active as directors; Havel, Pavlíček, and Ludvík Kundera were dramaturgs. This closeness, while contributing substantially to the development of the specific style of a particular company, resulted sometimes in difficulties when other theaters attempted to stage some of the plays. Again and again critics observed the remarkable decline in the artistic level of productions once they were removed from their original ambience.

The Czech drama of the late 1950's and early 1960's changes as rapidly as the entire character of the Czech stage. The changes are wide-ranging in theme as well as in technique. During the first half decade following 1956 the dramatists generally shy away from polythematic plays with broad social and political implications. Man is once again regarded as an individual rather than as a social type, and his private, frequently his most intimate concerns are the center of attention. Parallelling new developments in poetry, whose main stream is represented in the second half of the 1950's by the so-called Květen (May) group, the drama is interested in the exploration of the "everyday." Action moves from public meetings to private houses, from factories, fields, and offices to inns, dormitories, and other mundane, "private" locales. People cease to be merely workers, collective farmers, directors, party functionaries, soldiers, and youth-league members; they also become fathers, mothers, husbands, wives, and lovers. Ideological problems are not necessarily avoided, but they are shown as they affect characters, rather than characters being personifications of ideological standpoints. The trend is from the political toward the ethical, with an individual's worth considered empirically rather than according to preconceived ideological formulas. Even in dramas dealing with social problems, playwrights prefer an intimate atmosphere. The domestic setting becomes the most frequently used one of this period in dramas, comedies, and satires as well. The pseudo-optimistic tenor of the dogmatic period is replaced by a more somber mood. Playwrights refuse to take anything for granted and embark on a dogged probing of the social environment, in which they discover serious flaws. One of the central themes of the second half of the 1950's is the abuse of power due to insensibility, incompetence, or even malice. This theme, which was touched on first by Daněk and Kohout before 1956, now begins to be explored with greater courage in Milan Jariš's *The Intellectuals* (1956), Ilja Prachař's *Your Home Is Here* (1956), Pavel Kohout's *They Called Me Comrade* (1961), and František Pavlíček's *Struggle with the Angel* (1961).

A theme either directly or indirectly related to many of these plays, but which can be found in many others as well, is the generation conflict. It ought to be pointed out that Stalinist dogmatic esthetics tended to exclude the generation conflict from literature, regarding it as unessential and distracting from other more important ones. Ideological differences were regarded as cutting across borderlines of generations, and as a result little attention was given to the different historical experiences of individual generations and to their different psychological and political dispositions. During the period of the thaw the dualistic concept is replaced by a pluralistic one. The idea that people can be divided into two camps according to their attitudes toward the revolution gives way to the understanding that human conflicts are varied and inexhaustible. The emphasis on the generation conflict in the post-1956 Czech drama has been the subject of numerous controversies, yet there does not seem to be a simple explanation for its occurrence. The interest of the dramatists may be interpreted as being simply a part of the trend toward the refocusing of their works on eternal, timeless themes. The generation theme parallels the introduction of other timeless themes neglected during the dogmatic period, such as love and death. It can also be explained as being part of the new tendency of Czech drama to absorb impulses from the West, where the generation conflict had been prominent during previous decades in plays ranging from Anouilh's *Antigone* to those of the "angry young men" of the 1950's. The occurrence of the generation gap theme in the Czech drama, however, also appears to have some concrete sociopolitical causes, as pointed out by the Slovak dramatist and critic Peter Karvaš.

Initially the generation conflict that took place during the 1950's seemed to have been induced by the different backgrounds of the Communist fathers and their children. The fathers felt that they had carried all the burden of history on their shoulders in the 1930's and 1940's, the time of the depression and the war, and were resentful of the young generation's lack of appreciation for their accomplishments. The "sons," on the other hand, felt that develop-

ments after 1948 had effectively excluded them from any constructive participation in public life and regarded themselves as stifled by the rigor and monotony of the regime. While the young generation was on the defensive during the early 1950's, the fall of the Stalinist cult brought about a sudden reversal in the situation. The older generation, which had actively participated in the maintenance of the cult, was suddenly discredited, and the former inferiority feelings of the younger generation changed into those of superiority. The fact that the older generation lost much of its confidence not only in itself but in the ideals it had fought for resulted in the younger generation's increasing aggressiveness.

In dramas of this period the conflict is not expressed in a manner directly revealing its historical causes. It is rather revealed in codes and symbols, the generation gap frequently manifesting itself in trivial domestic conflicts seldom leading to open ideological confrontations. Nearly all plays featuring the generation conflict, no matter whether written by young or old playwrights, portray the younger generation with much greater sympathy than the older one. The young people may at first sight appear as cynical, politically indifferent, or openly hostile to Communism, but inside them there is a healthy, honest core. Their negativism is only a mask for their frustrated ideals. The members of the older generation are, on the contrary, portrayed as careerists, parasites, cowards, and self-satisfied opportunists. In their family life they tend to be insensitive, tyrannical, and unfaithful. The motif of children as touchstone of their parents' moral fiber becomes a virtual stereotype in this period and can be found in plays by authors of such varied artistic persuasions as Kohout, Blažek, Hrubín, Březovský, Topol, Pavlíček, and others. Only very few exceptions to this pattern can be found, one being Daněk's somber morality *A Look into the Eyes* (1959), a play which portrays the older generation with iconographic reverence. Even here, however, it is contrasted to the middle rather than to the youngest generation. There can be no doubt that the preference for youth on the part of the authors reflects the generally forward-looking mood immediately following the fall of the cult. In the mid-1960's, when a pessimistic wave is on the rise in Czech drama, the theme of generation conflict virtually disappears, and the younger generation ceases to be treated with the same favor it had been shown in previous years. Young people, too, are engulfed by the materialistic alienated world, as, for example, in the plays of Havel, Uhde, Vostrá, and others.

Characteristic of the new trend is the rapid disappearance of the central hero, featured prominently in the plays of the dogmatic period. The mainstream of the Czech playwrights embarks on the "deheroization" of the drama, a tendency that seems to be motivated philosophically as well as by esthetic considerations. Immediately after 1956 a new figure appears, the passive hero-victim, now no longer the victim of bourgeois society or its vestiges but of socialist society itself. The most important plays containing this theme are Jariš's *The Intellectuals* and Kohout's *Such a Love* (1957), both featuring suicides of young women with a calculated emotional impact. The plays differ significantly, however, in the development of the theme. In

Jariš's play the chain of tragic events has political causes; in Kohout's, specific political considerations are deliberately excluded. The death of the female protagonist has an intentionally "banal" motivation—unrequited love—but the dramatist makes out of the play a broad indictment against the insensitive society that drives valuable human beings to destruction. Curiously, this theme of tragic victimization, echoing the terror of the early 1950's, is absent in the Czech drama in later years. Exceptions may be seen in Topol's *The End of Carnival* (1963), Březovský's *All the Bells of the World* (1967), and Klíma's *The Jury* (1968). With the exception of Topol's play, however, these plays feature antiheroes rather than heroes in the traditional sense of the word. The disappearance of the active hero as the ideological as well as compositional focal point occurs in spite of opposition on the part of some leading critics (Kopecký, Karvaš, Hájek, Fuchs, Machonin, and others). Their concept of the hero is of course no longer confined to the canons of socialist-realist principles, their arguments resembling rather those of some modern theoreticians of neoclassicism. "Deheroization . . . leads to the death of the drama," writes, for example, Karvaš. "The urgent call for a hero and the call for a genuine drama are one and the same. . . . Heroism is always a deed, an act in a critical situation, coming on the crest of social and psychological developments." And Jan Kopecký writes:

> The solution of our problem is the real dramatic hero who comes on the stage to join the other dramatis personae. It is not sufficient for the author to stand in the background of his characters, substituting with his sympathies or aversions a hero who is present on the stage. We, that is, the audience, our society, and our time, yearn to meet a hero in a drama and live through his struggle. I use the term hero because I cannot find any other expression in dramatic terminology which denotes a figure who *acts* in the drama in a certain way in contrast to one who merely passively exists.

There are only very few, generally unsuccessful attempts to create a hero within the meaning of these definitions. Some of them appear around 1960, when Stehlík, in *For Crown and for Love* (1961), attempts to reinstate the character of a positive hero-worker, or in Kohout's *The Third Sister* (1960), which presents an isolated example of a central character, an attractive Communist activist. Hrubín, also yielding to pressures of the time, in *Crystal Night* (1961) makes a half-hearted effort to create a "positive" protagonist. A different kind of attempt is made by the same playwright in his last play, *Oldřich and Božena* (1968), in which he revives a hero-centered drama by means of a legendary theme treated with an openly romantic and somewhat decorative pathos. The mainstream of the Czech drama, however, is much more memorable for its characters with deeply seated inner conflicts, for its social misfits, sterile intellectuals, and rebels against society, whose rage is manifested in passive withdrawal rather than in action. The Czech drama of the 1960's is populated with decomposed individuals, mechanical puppetlike figures who are symbols of an alienated world. The growingly relativistic and skeptical vantage point from which most dramatists observe reality made the hero-centered drama impossible.

The radical shift in the thematic orientation of the drama in the second half of the 1950's is accompanied by an even more radical expansion in form. Experimentation becomes the rule of the day, and playwrights are engaged in what appears in retrospect as a frantic search for new techniques. This exploration of new forms was much more uninhibited than that of new themes, since while the playwright had to keep looking over his shoulders at the establishment so far as the content of his plays was concerned, he felt reasonably assured of relative freedom in questions of technique. After 1956 the establishment ceased to demand adherence to old norms and never again attempted to formulate new ones. Experimentation should be understood here as first consisting of attempts to utilize techniques existing in the Western world. Only later, in the mid-1960's, can one find independent innovative designs.

The general trend of the Czech drama after 1956 is toward the destruction of the classical linear structures that had been prevalent during the dogmatic period. Instead of contrived plots, developed in a traditional manner linearly from act to act, playwrights now generally prefer a loose composition of short, rapidly changing scenes not necessarily related to each other according to the principle of cause and effect so far as action is concerned. Free composition makes possible closer scrutiny of the characters, who are now explored in specifically circumscribed situations. Characters are not developed merely through a chain of events to which they are forced to react but also in static scenes in which their inner lives are manifested in all their complexities and ambivalences. The drama thus acquires an increasingly lyrical character, with the invisible and the implied being of the greatest significance. The dramatic technique of Chekhov was extremely influential on the new plays written by Hrubín, Topol, Pavlíček, Kohout, and others.

Simultaneously we can observe an increasingly epic tendency in the drama. The technique of free montage, especially suitable for the subjective organization of thematic material, is preferred by many authors. The pioneering work in this regard is Kohout's *Such a Love,* in which linear time is entirely eliminated. The author structures the play on a pattern of flashbacks disregarding chronology, the story being developed as a post-mortem examination of the life of the tragically deceased woman. While the play suggests the influence of Pirandello, Wilder, and A. Miller, Kohout's next play, *The Third Sister,* uses discernibly Brechtian devices. A less felicitous application of the epic method is Daněk's *A Look into the Eyes,* in which the generation conflict takes the form of a confrontation between a young woman of loose morals and her dead father, whose past is revived in brief snapshotlike images. While the above plays are representative of the anti-illusionary epic theater, other plays are based on illusionary principles; the most important of them is Stehlík's drama-reportage, *For Crown and for Love.* In this play the epic subject does not serve the purpose of creating the pathos of distance between the action and the audience. On the contrary, its purpose is to enhance the illusion by insisting on the documentary nature of events.

The use of various scenic effects with the aid of music and other nonverbal media in order to destroy the conventional dramatic modes is widespread. Frequently the authors emphasize experimentation in form by refusing to place their works into acknowledged dramatic genres. *The Third Sister* is thus called "A New Variation on an Old Theme"; Vyskočil-Suchý's *Thousand Clarinets* (1958), "A Leporello"; Březovský's *A Dangerous Age* (1961), "A Serious Comedy"; Uhde's *King Vávra* (1964), "Non-stop Nonsense"; Smoček's *Picnic* (1965), "A Tale in the Forest"; and so on.

In the early 1960's the mainstream of the Czech drama undergoes a distinct change. Plays featuring intimate conflicts are on the retreat as authors begin to be interested in encompassing broader thematic concepts in their works. The genre of the domestic drama becomes inadequate for the new objectives. The crisis of the domestic type of drama is reflected, for example, in Blažek's *A Much Too Merry Christmas* (1960), in which the family setting is an obvious obstacle to the dramatist's intentions. He resolves the problem only half successfully by the device of an overlengthy narrative describing events that occur outside the family home. Another tenuous solution can be found in Kohout's *The Third Sister,* in which the dramatist's need for a large cast of characters within the domestic setting results in his making each sister the offspring of a different father, with the mother a prostitute. An open revival of the polythematic, pluralistic drama comes about with Ludvík Kundera's *Total Cockcrow* (1961), in which he attempts to reflect broad historical currents by applying Brechtian dramaturgy. Another key play of this period is Milan Kundera's *The Keepers of the Keys* (1962?), which abandons psychology for the sake of dramatizing philosophical concepts.

Kundera's play starts a trend toward a more abstract theater in which characters are less individuals and more types. This development is manifested in works by playwrights of various persuasions and in all genres, whether drama, comedy, or satire (although not necessarily in the same manner). Thus in the plays of Topol, who in *Their Day* (1959) aimed at an illusionary, detailed portrayal of reality, the trend is first reflected in the multileveled symbolic design evident in *The End of Carnival* (1963). In Topol's subsequent one-act plays the dramatic pattern is based on condensed existential situations devoid of any sociohistorical context. In the plays of other authors the trend is even more pronounced. Most playwrights abstain from the method of a direct portrayal of life. They shy away from using realistic plots, structuring their plays on ideas, on philosophical concepts, and not on the behavior of man as an individual. Striking is the extensive use of literary, legendary, Biblical, and mythological sources by numerous playwrights: Uhde's *King Vávra* and *The Wench from the Town of Thebes* (1967); Ludvík Kundera's *Corsair* (1963) and *Nonjoke* (1963); Daněk's *Forty Scoundrels and One Little Innocent* (1966); Šotola's *Anti-Orpheus* (1965); Toman's *Don Juan* (1967); Hrubín's *Oldřich and Božena* (1968); Pavlíček's *The Heavenly As-*

cension of Sashka Christ (1967) as well as his adaptation of Karel Čapek; and Kohout's adaptations of Jules Verne, Čapek, and Hašek. Other plays are built on artificial, rationally constructed situations. The setting and the action become nonrealistic, visionary, and dreamlike as the anti-illusionary convention begins entirely to dominate. The Czech drama becomes especially influenced by the technique of the so-called theater of the absurd, in particular Ionesco, as well as by Dürrenmatt (Havel, Smoček, Uhde, Klíma, Daněk, and others). Drama is conceived of as a "model" with an internal logic of its own, and associations with the outside world can be achieved only indirectly, *per analogiam.* The stage becomes highly intellectualized, the dramatis personae being pieces in a chess game, and the playwright showing little concern whether they come to life as characters.

It is interesting to note that even the conscious attempts at deintellectualization of the theater rely on literary sources. The most famous were Jan Kopecký's adaptations of seventeenth- and eighteenth-century folk dramas dealing with Biblical subjects: *A Play about the Martyrdom and Glorious Resurrection of Our Lord and Savior Jesus Christ* (1966) and *A Play about the Star* (1967).

The overall character of the Czech drama of this period is particularly well reflected in the commentary by Sergej Machonin on the occasion of the staging of Uhde's *The Wench from the Town of Thebes:*

> So Czechoslovakia is richer by an additional play-parable. I am sitting in the audience and racking my brains in order to figure out what Antigone stands for in this "model," what Creon means, what Haimon, what Chorus I and Chorus II. I leave the theater with feelings of inadequacy and guilt that I did not figure everything out sufficiently, that some kind of a metaphor has escaped my attention, and that I should take a careful look at myself. And deep inside I have a secret and sinful desire to go sometime again to the theater and see there a bit of simple life, a few strange or joyful people who do not try to solve anything but are merely themselves. Maybe, when they are their true, ordinary, nonsymbolic selves, their significance will somehow expand by itself, and I will have no trouble recognizing it.

There can be no question that an important factor in the playwrights' utilization of these methods was the desire to take a disguised critical position toward the existing social and political system. The principal theme of the period is the demonstration of the destructive mechanisms of power and bureaucracy leading to the decomposition of human values. Most important dramatists became opposed not only to the establishment but to Marxism in general.

During the second half of the 1960's the trend begins to take a new form. While playwrights continue to use the same methods, on the thematic level they move still more toward the abstract. The emphasis is progressively more on the philosophical and the universal rather than on the political. Kundera's *The Keepers of the Keys,* Havel's *The Garden Party* (1963) and *The Memorandum* (1965), or Uhde's *King Vávra* were after all engagé plays par excellence. In later years, however, Havel moves from pointedly satirical plays with political overtones to a satire that might be called indirect or general, dealing not with dehumanization amidst a specific sociopolitical environment but rather with the universal theme of alienation of modern man (*The Increased Difficulty of Concentration,* 1968). Similarly Uhde's second play, *The Wench from the Town of Thebes,* describing the general decline of values, is filled with resignation and devoid of a specific polemical target. While Milan Kundera's first play was built on a clearly defined ideological design and had a distinct sociopolitical relevance, in *Cock-a-Doodle* (1969) he creates a grotesque parable of man as a victim of his own desire for power and sexual gratification. Even Kohout, the most engagé of the Czech playwrights, resorts to the form of a parable containing a general commentary on the paradoxical nature of human endeavor (*August August, the Clown,* 1967).

The decline of the politically committed drama was commented on interestingly by Pavlíček, who wrote in 1967:

> The answer is simple, I believe, and goes to the very roots of our concept of artistic commitment. We did not realize that artistic and civic activism is first of all influenced by its effectiveness and therefore by its demonstrable consequences in practice. The decline of the new wave and the weakening of interest on the part of the spectator can be explained not only as a result of the repetitiveness of this genre but also as a disillusionment with the lack of repercussions in practical life.

This commentary on the part of one of the most prominent playwrights of the period reflects the pessimistic and resigned mood prevalent on the eve of the Prague Spring of 1968, an event that seems to have surprised those who had helped bring it into existence perhaps most of all. Pavlíček's statement, however, only partly explains the phenomenon discussed above. There appears to be another reason for the decline in the interest in the type of dramatic art to which Pavlíček refers. It seems to have stemmed from the general feeling of dissatisfaction with an art related too specifically to a small country under very closely constricted historical circumstances. The extensive contact of the Czech theater with the West made it conscious, perhaps excessively so, of its limitations. The interest on the part of the playwrights in more universal themes was related to their desire for international recognition. While in the second half of the 1960's Czech drama indeed began to be staged abroad to an extent unparalleled in its history, at home it was undergoing a crisis that was not to be found in the development of other literary genres of this period. The zenith of the Czech postwar drama was not reached during the period of the Prague Spring but several years earlier, approximately in the period 1963-65. In later years the productivity of the leading playwrights generally declined not only in quantity but in quality as well, with no truly new significant talents on the horizon. The crisis was not limited to playwriting alone but was reflected in other aspects of theater life. Some old alliances began to dissolve: the Krejča circle of playwrights began to disintegrate, and after he moved to the theater Behind the Gate in 1965, only Topol remained from the original

group of playwrights. During the 1967-68 season, Grossman and Havel left the Ballustrade Theater; Sokolovský and Srba resigned their posts at the Mahen Theater. Whether this crisis was a temporary one to be followed by a second wave will never be known, as the Soviet intervention of 1968 was shortly followed by a complete standstill in the cultural life of the country. Those playwrights who continue to write solely for export have basically not changed their style, and with the exception of Kohout, they have not surpassed their earlier accomplishments. (pp. 12-24)

> *Paul I. Trenský, "The Spirit of the 'Thaw'," in his* Czech Drama Since World War II, *M. E. Sharpe, Inc., 1978, pp. 12-24.*

Marketa Goetz-Stankiewicz

[*A Czech-born Canadian educator and critic, Goetz-Stankiewicz has written* The Silenced Theatre: Czech Playwrights without a Stage *(1979) and has edited the volume* The Vaněk Plays: Four Authors, One Character. *In the following excerpt from her introduction to that collection, she discusses portrayals of the fictional Czech playwright Ferdinand Vaněk, the protagonist of dramas by Jiří Dienstbier, Václav Havel, Pavel Kohout, and Pavel Landovský, as he represents the role of the Czech dissident writer.*]

When the main character of Kafka's novel *America* was asked by a woman employee of the Hotel Occidental where he came from and when he answered "from Prague," she called out with delight: "Oh, then we are countrymen. . . . I'm from Vienna!" This was—in fictional as well as historical time—about 1912. Today, an immigrant from Vienna would react very differently in the same situation. The two imperial cities, Vienna and Prague, related for hundreds of years by their political fate as well as cultural development, are now separated by a border which is not merely the border between two countries (like, say, that between France and Germany or Canada and the United States) but between two vastly different political systems which divide Europe into an Eastern and a Western half. Though a short distance apart, the two cities belong to two dramatically distinct societies— the open society of the democratic West and the coercive society of the totalitarian East. Of the four playwrights [who wrote the Vaněk plays], two live in Prague (Havel and Dienstbier) and two, since 1978, in Vienna (Kohout and Landovský). In other words, two are still "at home," surrounded by their own language and culture (though that culture is being put to a hard test of survival); the other two have had to make the adjustment to another language and a culture which, though growing from related roots, has undergone the same changes that all the consumer societies of Western Europe have undergone since the Second World War.

The life stories of all four writers—future biographers are likely to fill many pages with aspects of these true-to-life accounts—have the components of political thrillers. There are prisons and enforced labour, house-searches, constant watches, exile, ruthless acts of censorship, ostracism, harassment, confiscation of valuable manuscripts, and even a poisoned dachshund. However, these life stories also contain (and perhaps in this sense, too, they strangely resemble the generally optimistic tenor of popular thrillers) brotherly sacrifice, noble deeds of friendship, patterns of deep loyalties, and unshakable ethics which transcend not only the authors' above-mentioned difficulties in living but also—on a less tangible level—the tightly closed political border.

Václav Havel (born 1936), the recipient of several literary prizes, including, in 1986, the prestigious Erasmus Prize awarded by the Netherlands, is a well-known international writer whose plays are staged in the many languages in London and New York, Stockholm and Paris, Tel Aviv and Vienna, Zurich and, surprisingly, Warsaw. In addition to more than a dozen plays, of which *The Memorandum* (1966) is perhaps the best known and of which the most recent, *Temptation* (1985), is possibly the most profound and challenging—intellectually, philosophically, and dramatically—Havel has been writing a steadily increasing number of essays on topics of urgent concern to our modern world, from peace to power, from ecology to the nature of faith. The best known of these essays is "The Power of the Powerless" (1978), in which Havel eloquently analyses the pressures exerted on an individual in a totalitarian society.

In his plays, Havel demonstrates over and over again how a phrase or a slogan can be employed—consciously as well as unconsciously, strategically, as well as carelessly—to destroy a reasoning process, to obfuscate reality. In his essays written with circumspect, thoughtful clarity, Havel has provided the contemporary international politico-cultural scene with aphoristic formulations which have already spawned commentaries by others. Apart from the above mentioned "the power of the powerless," the reader may take note of his musings on modern man's need for "a renewed rootedness in the universe"; ponder the implications of "totalitarianism entering every vein and artery of the social organism"; or the "rut of seriousness" eroding causes, no matter how just. The reader may also consider the tragedy of a society, albeit well fed and adequately clothed, which is "living in a lie"; as well as Havel's own attempt—shared by his character Vaněk . . .—at "living in truth" (a title given to a selection of twenty essays, six by Havel himself, the others by friends and colleagues, which appeared in 1987 [see Further Reading]).

Havel's *Letters to Olga,* written to his wife during his four-and-a-half-years' prison sentence between 1979 and 1983, are eloquent documents of a thinking man's attempt to formulate and to try to answer—under very difficult physical and spiritual circumstances—some of the most private but also the most general questions of human life, from the salutary results of tea-drinking to the nature of human identity; from the quality of a man's moods to the essence of truth. His autobiographical *Dálkové rozhovory* of 1986 is another artistic document, rousing for its intellect, moving for its unassuming honesty.

Pavel Kohout (born 1928) is a writer of many talents. Less philosophical and searching than his colleague Havel, he has written an extraordinary number of lively dramatic texts and prose works, many of which have been translated into other languages and performed from Germany to Greece and the United States, from Finland to Japan and Canada. In the late 1970's, after having spent a year in Vienna, where he had been invited to act as consultant and director at the venerable Wiener Burgtheater, he was forcibly prevented from re-entering Czechoslovakia and was thus compelled to start life "in exile." With unfading energy and resourcefulness Kohout has managed to continue writing, even while surrounded by a new language. His dramatic adaptations still catch the imagination of countless audiences. Just as his dramatization of Jules Verne's *Around the World in Eighty Days* delighted Prague audiences in 1962, so his version of Rostand's *Cyrano de Bergerac* delights audiences in Brussels today.

Of his original plays, *August August, August* (its English language première took place in Minneapolis, in May 1986) is the most popular (to date it has had over 2,400 performances in several languages); though his *Poor Murderer,* an adaptation of a short story by Andrejev, had a successful run on Broadway in the 1976-77 season. A Czech literary critic once wrote that "Kohout was given to the Czech theatre, so that there would not be any peace and quiet." There is truth in this ironic adage: Kohout does keep things on the move. He is every inch a man of the theatre, happy to direct his own plays as well as those

Pavel Kohout.

of others because his whole work (including his prose writings, of which several have been published in English translation) is permeated by the intense awareness that the actual text is only one part of the whole structure of the play, that the word is only one of the many means to reach an audience. This is where Kohout, despite his exile from his native environment, has a professional advantage over his colleagues in Prague, one that is as obvious as it is absurd: he is able to see his plays performed on stage. Pavel Kohout is also the only playwright represented here who has begun to write in another language: *Safari* is the first play he has actually composed in German. Kohout's work glows in many colours, some of them loud, even gaudy. Yet one thing is certain: with an uncanny sense for topicality, he uses every aspect of the stage with unfailing histrionic intuition.

For Pavel Landovský (born 1936), who also now lives in Vienna without the possibility of returning to Prague, exile presents a particular problem: he is an actor turned playwright. In Prague, Landovský was an eminent member of the theatre Činoherní Klub, starred in several films, and immortalized the image of several dramatic characters. His unforgettable features were well-known to Prague theatre audiences from the late 1950's to the late 1970's. Since language is the most important professional tool for an actor, Landovský's talents have obviously been severely curbed. However, with half a dozen exhilarating comedies to his credit, Landovský's claim as a playwright is substantiated. His spirited farce *Detour,* which appeared in English translation in *Dramacontemporary: Czechoslovakia* (1985), is as lively a proof of this as is [the Vaněk play] *Arrest.* . . . As Landovský writes in his note on the Vaněk plays, he was actually the first to "borrow" the dramatic figure of the shy and polite forbidden writer Vaněk from his friend and colleague Havel, and introduce it in 1976 into his biting comedy *Sanitární noc* (which I have translated elsewhere as *Closed for Disinfection).*

There circulates a story which, if it is not true, ought to be because it vividly illustrates the nature of Landovský's ebullient talents and character. When he complained to Pavel Kohout in Vienna that he was never considered for more prominent parts at the Burgtheater because of his deficiency in German, Kohout, with typical resourcefulness, suggested that Landovský write a dramatic text with a mute character in it and thus create a role for himself. Landovský did just that, and we now have *Arrest* with its wordless but magnificently theatrical character of the gypsy Matte.

Jiří Dienstbier's (born 1937) writing career has many aspects to it. After working as editor with the Czechoslovak broadcasting network, he became its Far Eastern correspondent in the 1960's and subsequently correspondent in the United States. Apart from the many essays and commentaries he wrote in his capacity as correspondent and observer in many countries, he contributed to a number of journals of opinion and literary publications, and wrote a book on events in Indonesia. Forbidden to publish since 1969 and fired from broadcasting, he became spokesman for Charter 77 in 1979. Three of his plays, a number of essays, and a collection of international political essays circulate in Czechoslovakia in *samizdat* editions. As he notes in his comment on the Vaněk figure, he was imprisoned together with Havel and spent the years from 1979 to 1982 in prison. His play *Reception* is inspired by this experience.

. . . . .

In his essay ["Light on a Landscape"], Václav Havel tells us that *Audience* and *Unveiling,* the two plays in which the character Vaněk first appeared, were originally written to entertain a few friends. It did not then occur to the author that these private playful musings would conquer the international theatre scene. Their unexpected success taught Havel, as he writes in the "Afterword" to the Czech edition of his plays (published by Sixty-Eight Publishers in Toronto in 1977), that it was essential for him to write with a concrete audience in mind, rather than envisaging a faceless international reader; that he must "lean on what I know, on my own concrete living background, and that only by means of this authenticity I could—perhaps—provide a more general comment as witness of a certain period." And so, drawing on his personal experience, he wrote the three one-act plays that have come to be produced more often and in more countries than any other of his plays. They are also the works which inspired Havel's three colleagues to "borrow" his central character and write their own plays around him—truly an uncommon, if not a unique, occurrence in modern theatre.

The eight plays, written in an unplanned, indeed an impulsive way in the course of a decade, surprisingly fall into what seems a logical pattern of development as if they were part of a preconceived scheme. In Havel's *Audience,* Vaněk is working in a brewery, still living at home, though already regarded and watched as a subversive person, harmful to the state and noxious to its community of citizens (as a result, his boss, the Brewmaster, is faced with an unusual professional problem: he is expected to inform the authorities about the "subversive" activities of the suspect employee—a difficult task indeed, if it is to be performed regularly).

In *Unveiling,* Vaněk is visiting successful and "normalized" friends, who distinguish themselves from him by being able to travel abroad to the West, by serving international exotic food, and by being generally well adapted and definitely "with it," politically and in every other way. In *Protest,* the playwright meets a "colleague"—a writer who is successful in the society that has ostracized Vaněk. Their hour-long discussion—containing Staněk's masterly display of "dialectically argued objectivity"—is resolved by a change in the momentary but by no means in the basic situation. In Havel's three plays Vaněk deals with private individuals. However, their weaknesses, strategies, and blunders—which become blatantly obvious during the action—are soon revealed as the meek echoes of the workings of a vast hierarchy of powers, the upper echelons of which remain unfathomable and hence, like the power-structure referred to by Kafka's gatekeeper, unchallenged and unassailable. Kohout's Vaněk (*Permit* and *Morass*) no longer copes with private individuals; he is obliged to tackle the authorities, a dog-licence office, on the one hand, and a bureau for drivers licences *cum* police station, on the other. In these plays, the power structure becomes more concrete and with it the employees' need to conform dutifully.

In Landovský's *Arrest* and Dienstbier's *Reception,* Vaněk has ended up where his steadfastness has inevitably led him—in prison. Again, it is the other prisoners who catch and hold our attention. Not only are they interesting characters in themselves, but they also provide a fascinating picture of the Czech variety of a police-state prison. As we laugh our way through the rambunctious comedies, the dark shadows of more serious, indeed tragic, issues retreat into the background, only to emerge more insistently when we become aware that the hilarious goings-on on stage are a comic reflection of the vast political and social issues which hover over our divided world.

In *Safari,* Pavel Kohout's play . . ., Vaněk is for the first time exposed to the "liberal" society of a Western democracy. Having been spirited to Vienna, Vaněk now faces a panel of artists and intellectuals who have been invited by the media to take part in a televised talk-show and interview with the famous "dissident" writer from the neighbouring "Eastern bloc" country. Again, the playwright is more interested in revealing Vaněk's surroundings than in the amiable "anti-hero" himself. In a rollicking hour of acerbic fun, Kohout explores standard types of mass-media minds: their relativistic values, their confused notions of freedom, their clichéd ideas of what a "forbidden" writer is all about, and their adamant refusal to learn anything that would rock their respective ideological boats.

And so we realize that, despite their unplanned nature, the Vaněk plays have come full circle and thus reflect the shape of some of the plays themselves (say, *Audience, Unveiling, Moruss*), which are structured in such a way that at the end they could begin again, thus forming a circular link in an endless chain reminiscent of Beckett's *Waiting for Godot.* At the end of *Safari,* the hapless writer Vaněk goes back to his home country where—the thought is inevitable—he will again embark on a cycle of similar experiences. In fact, he might, if permitted by the authorities, again begin working as a labourer, say, in a brewery. . . .

. . . . .

Vaněk is a shy, unpretentious man whose intelligence never really shows, although it is often referred to by the other characters. After all, most of them know—for better or for worse—that although he has been ostracized by the régime, he is a formidable writer. However, although Vaněk knows how to put words on paper, he cannot handle them in conversation. It is the others who talk and tell him what they want, know, hope, and fear. Sometimes they even tell him what he himself is all about, and he never manages to counter their arguments. None of the four authors gives Vaněk the chance to show verbally what he is supposed to stand for. His spoken part inevitably consists of unfinished sentences, fragmentary apologies, murmured remarks, repetitions. The venerable Viennese actor Joachim Bissmeier (who acted the enormously difficult part of Vaněk in all three Havel plays as well as in Kohout's *Permit* with the subtle understanding and meticulous control it requires) said in an interview that "the

rules of the part are established very precisely"; Vaněk is "the catalyst, it is the others who bring the problems."

In a way Vaněk practices what George Steiner called the "retreat from the word." Vaněk's experience has taught him that he can no longer be committed to the resources of language as a dependable instrument with which to convey reality. When he tries to use language with precision and circumspect caution, in order not to formulate anything that might not correspond to the truth, he is met by torrents of language, obfuscating and void-filling, or strategic and calculated to produce a certain effect. Language as the instrument that can bring the mind into contact with reality—as classic and medieval philosophy have taught us—is no longer valid. Silence becomes the chief defence against the falseness of language. The silence that Vaněk practices becomes a more eloquent tool of communication than the thousands of words used by the others.

It is this largely silent man who gradually reveals himself as controlling the situation on a deeper level, though, on the surface, he seems to be manipulated by it. While the other characters psychologically—and therefore also linguistically—twist and turn, Vaněk remains himself and emerges from each play unchanged in his basic attitudes. Soon it dawns on the audience that this awkward, fumbling man could not be moved by ten horses, nor by a powerful political hierarchy, to do something he considers wrong. This strength in weakness, this "power of the powerless" (in the words of Havel's famous essay), becomes the intellectual focus as well as the moving spirit of the plays.

There is another interesting thing that happens in the receptive process. As we watch (or read) the plays, we are bound to realize that we steadily give more attention to the characters who surround Vaněk rather than to him. He somehow takes on the quality of the quiet eye of a hurricane where things remain the way they were and where there is shelter from the roaring and shifting turmoil all around. And yet we must be cautious about the implications of this image. A hurricane wreaks destruction; there is no doubt about it. But the people who surround Vaněk are not really evil. They are merely all too human in their pathetic weakness, their petty greeds, their creeping fears, their anxious hearts trained on the passing chances to grasp a shred of an advantage for themselves. There are, let it be quite clear, no "villains" in the Vaněk plays. And it is in part this very fact that makes the plays such good and challenging pieces of theatre. To be sure, it would be less disturbing to watch a clear display of evil as the counterpart of the gentle, movingly awkward, and obviously sorely wronged writer Vaněk, who is bound to draw sympathy, even affection, from readers or audience. However, this is not what we get. None of the four writers provides the comforting service of pitching poor nice Vaněk against brutal representatives of political power. If that were the case, we would be free to lodge our righteous resentment fairly and squarely on the representatives of the "other" side—the persecutors, oppressors, exploiters. We would place ourselves just as fairly and squarely in Vaněk's camp, certain of what is good and bad, our ethical judgments supported by an uncluttered, streamlined view of good against evil. But such a reassuring, cowboy-movie pattern does not emerge from the intensely searching literature of Central Europe.

In this way, as if despite himself, Havel has created a new hero for Czech literature, an antipode to Hašek's Good Soldier Švejk, who is silent where Švejk talks, whose stories, unlike Švejk's are never told, whose unsung life, unlike Švejk's colourful adventures, remains concealed in the background. In recent years Švejk has been variously compared and contrasted with Kafka's characters, and it has been said, by the eminent Czech philosopher Karel Kosík, that one posits the positive and the other the negative scale of human values. Vaněk also posits a scale of human values by not subscribing to the false values of those who surround him. It is the others who spout "values": a good life, a safe income, a need to make do with the powers that be (after all, a wise old proverb teaches us that one ought to make the best of any situation), plus a dash of cynicism about the messiness of human affairs. What's wrong with these values? Ferdinand Vaněk does not voice criticism of them, but he makes it perfectly clear that he will not live by them. Thus, without expounding "right" values but by constantly, yet modestly, even unconsciously, displaying the absence of "wrong" values, Vaněk posits his own scale of values, which can best be defined by what it is *not:* it is not materialistic, not opportunistic; it is not intolerant and not arrogant; it is the very opposite of facile conformism and strategic reasoning.

. . . . .

The word "dissident" is used frequently and largely unthinkingly by the Western press and media. What exactly is meant by it? If we try to suggest an image behind the modish word, we might envisage, say, a frowning young man with a placard, pacing up and down in front of a government building; or perhaps a fiery-eyed young woman in a humid cellar, late at night, editing human-rights activist pamphlets; or else a venerable grey-haired citizen, standing upright at court, defying a bribed judge's verdict; or else . . . ? Perhaps the only fair thing is to allow every reader to choose the image that fits the word "dissident" in his or her own mind. Of course, the cases of famous "dissidents"—no matter under which régime—contribute to moulding the popular image. We might think of the renowned physicist Andrei Sakharov's "internal exile" in the Soviet Union imposed in 1980; of Polish labour leader Lech Wałęsa addressing a crowd of workers in the shipyards of Gdansk during the strike of 1980; of the Czech student Jan Palach setting himself on fire to protest the invasion of his country by Soviet troops in 1968. Yet these examples, vivid as they are, do not really define the concept of "dissident" either. They refer to drastically different situations, and their common denominator is too abstract to yield a useful definition.

There is another problem which clouds the issue. If a "dissident" happens to be a writer—as is often the case—there exist many designations for what he produces. We find references to "parallel," "underground," "uncensored," "illegal," "independent" or *samizdat* literature. Each of these designations leads to problems in connotation and inevitably creates confusion. For example, "unofficial" literature means something different in each age and political situation; "underground" literature gives the impression that it is non-literary (we may think of pamphlets); "illegal" literature is confusing in the sense that, for example, the works of some Czech writers (though very few) have appeared both in *samizdat* typescripts and in works issued by state-sponsored publishing houses.

If such uncertainty reigns with regard to what to call their writings, what are we to call the authors themselves? Does the word "dissident" not add to the confusion rather than lessen it? Besides, neither the forbidden writers of Central-Eastern Europe nor those who have emigrated and now write in the West feel comfortable with the term "dissident," although they are surely aware of the fact that this label has been given with the best intentions to point out their difficult and courageous attitude and behaviour.

I will mention three examples of writers' attempts to illuminate the misleading nature of the word "dissident." Milan Kundera, who left Czechoslovakia in 1975 and now lives and writes in Paris, said in an interview (*Index on Censorship* 6:6, 1977):

> I must confess I don't like the word "dissident," particularly when applied to art. It is part and parcel of that same politicising, ideological distortion which cripples a work of art. . . . The importance of this art (the art that comes from Prague or Budapest) does not lie in the fact that it accuses this or that political régime, but in the fact that on the strength of social and human experience . . . it offers new testimony about human conditions.

Secondly, there is Josef Škvorecký, now living and writing in Toronto, Canada, who in his note on the "Writer / Dissident" (in *Na Brigádě,* 1979) argues with typical wry irony that the true "dissident" writer should actually be called a "socialist writer" in Marxist terminology: he acts according to the dictates of the freedom of will which, as Hegel taught the Marxists, is the understanding of necessity. The "dissident," after all, does just that—he understands this necessity and behaves according to it—namely, he says and writes what he perceives to be the truth.

The third voice in this context comes from Czechoslovakia, from [a writer] . . . who himself is being constantly referred to as a "dissident" writer. Václav Havel, less ironic than Škvorecký, less aphoristic than Kundera, and guided by his usual circumspect rationality as well as first-hand experience of the circumstances, tries in "The Power of the Powerless" (1978) to define the main qualities of people who are called "dissidents" by the Western mass media. Havel's main points are the following: Firstly, such persons make their critical opinions known publicly, albeit within the severely limited possibilities at their disposal. Secondly, they have reached a stage in which they are taken more or less seriously by their government, and even their persecution causes certain complications for this government. Thirdly, their critical engagement extends beyond a narrow circle and has therefore taken on a political character. Fourthly, these people are for the most part intellectuals (Havel calls them "men of the pen") whose only political means is their writing; the attempts of others, namely, non-writers, to "live in truth" rarely penetrate beyond their country's borders and are by and large unknown in the West. Fifthly, Westerners refer more frequently to the political engagement of these people than to their activity as writers. Havel himself knows from personal experience that at some point—and he did not realize exactly when this came about—people in the West began to regard him less as a writer than as a "dissident" who in his spare time also wrote some plays. "Dissidentism," Havel writes, "somehow creates the impression that it is a kind of profession rather than a state of mind that makes a person reason and act in a certain way." In fact, it usually happens that it is only after a person has consistently behaved in a certain way, and has done so from an inner urge and conviction, that he suddenly realizes that this will probably earn him the label of "dissident." People with first-hand experience of Central-Eastern Europe are aware of this. In his essay "Does Central Europe Exist?" (*New York Review of Books,* 9 October 1986) Timothy Garton Ash calls Havel "a playwright catapulted by circumstances and the dictates of conscience into the role of dissident but not at all by temperament a political activist." To be a dissident, we conclude, therefore, is an existential attitude arising from certain ethical convictions or, as Havel puts it, from the conscious decision "to live in truth."

. . . . .

It is important to realize that [the Vaněk] plays are related to each other not merely by the figure of Vaněk but by the whole surrounding social context. The audience (or reader) is constantly made to feel that there are real lives being lived, say, on the street running past the apartment where Vaněk visits his well-adjusted friends; beyond the office where he tries to obtain breeding papers for his dog; in the village near the brewery where he rolls beer barrels; outside the prison where he serves a sentence for "subversive activities." Throughout the text, moreover, there are references to other Czech writers (forbidden as well as "official" ones); popular singers (those banned from their profession as well as those successfully pursuing it); we are made aware of a world that contains political dissidents like Sakharov, literary figures of the past like Ibsen and of the present like Samuel Beckett. Moreover, there are references to the authors who wrote the very plays we are watching or reading and to events from their real lives which become part of the plays. We are, for example, amused by references to Pavel Landovský's not-too-restrained drinking habits (*Audience*); we are made to wonder about Pavel Kohout's youthful flirtation (or more?) with Communism (*Morass*); we learn about the official offer made to Václav Havel by the Czech authorities to leave the country (taking along his possessions) and about his decision to refuse to do so and to go to prison instead if his friends were not released as well (*Reception*); and we hear about Kohout's poisoned dachshund (*Permit*) and Vaněk's (or Havel's?) never "giving a damn about what the others did" (*Arrest*). Real figures and true occurrences thus merge with the events on the stage in what seems a singular blend of fact and fiction, of the world as a stage and the stage as a world reflecting in its concentrating mirror images the complex, personal, political, and

ethical issues of the contemporary world. Yet, it must be stressed again, the plays bear their burden of ideas exceedingly lightly. Never weighed down by the serious issues they raise, they vibrate with the histrionic and intellectual exuberance of the playwrights' comic genius.

The fictional figures, too, provide a connecting line by re-emerging in the play of a different author or flashing across its background. For example, Staněk, the well-adjusted playwright who manages to provide the most convincing arguments for not signing the dissident letter in Havel's *Protest,* is referred to in Kohout's *Permit* as having attended a formal occasion in the Czech National Theatre; the gypsy Sherkezy, who rolls barrels in *Audience* and tends to arrive at work tipsy (though we never actually see him on stage), has ended up in prison in *Reception,* where he tattoos the prisoners with imaginative variations of the Hradčany Castle; in fact, we have the pleasure of seeing his artwork on the Brewmaster's hairy chest. In *Audience,* Vaněk is warned not to associate with Kohout, in *Protest* and *Morass,* he is told not to go drinking with Landovský, whom Michael, the impeccable host of *Unveiling,* calls "a failure." The Brewmaster, who in *Audience* repeatedly asks Vaněk to bring the actress Bohdalová for a visit to the brewery, complains in *Reception* when he meets Vaněk in prison that the latter had not kept his promise, had not brought the actress, and he, poor Brewmaster, had never had the pleasure of seeing her in person. An early Stalinist poem written by Kohout as a young man is quoted by an apparatchik twenty-five years later as the very work that influenced him to embark on a marriage that had turned out less than ideal (*Morass*). The Brewmaster, who in *Audience* tried (unsuccessfully) to make Vaněk help him to compose reports on his, Vaněk's, subversive activities, has become more efficient in *Reception;* he suggests that Vaněk write an "ideologically clean" skit for the prison May celebrations, to be submitted to the authorities under the Brewmaster's name and subsequently performed by the prisoners in one of their classroom hours. A film about the liberation by the Soviets in 1945—which is being shot in the next prison compound and causes havoc during the final stages of *Arrest*—is likely to be the kind of film that was shown to the leftist poet in *Safari* on one of his red carpet visits to Prague. (pp. xv-xxvi)

. . . . .

[Comments by the four authors] certainly reveal the different artistic temperaments and intellects of the playwrights, but they also express varying perceptions of the Vaněk figure. Václav Havel, who was the first to conceive Vaněk, emphasizes that, though he has some of the author's personal traits and represents some of his experiences, Vaněk is not a self-portrait. Rather he is a dramatic principle which causes his environment to react and reveal itself. However, the other three writers, all aware that they have put the stamp of their own artistic personalities on their Vaněk figures, are obviously not able to remove their conception of the character from their experience of Václav Havel himself. Kohout, calling Vaněk Havel's "fictional twin brother," stresses the character's childlike soul and "chastity" (Kohout insisted on using this word, perhaps in order to express the timeless and rarefied nature of this quality). Landovský sees Vaněk as a "symbol" of Havel: instead of delving into past layers of the language, he expands Vaněk's quality by abstracting it. Dienstbier, who is possibly less intense in his thoughts about Havel (perhaps because he not only currently shares his fate as "dissident" but also has personal contact with him that is denied to the writers who live abroad) tells us that he has taken up two of Havel's dramatic figures (he also revived the Brewmaster from *Audience*) because he wanted to make a point about true ethical commitment having to be practical rather than remaining suspended in abstract theory.

What all this boils down to is that the figure of Ferdinand Vaněk—actually a dramatic paradox because he does not wield the word, a dubious hero because he hardly acts, a suspect model because he knows better what *not* to do than what to do—provokes by merely existing and proving to a corrupt world that a "good" existence is still possible. It is the way to show this possibility of "goodness" which the other three writers absorbed into their work. Karl Kraus once wrote that one must "dig up words by their roots" in order not to be drawn into the murky pool of cliché. In that sense, the word "goodness" is to be taken here. By resisting the use of the language gone dead under the weight of facile, unexamined usage, Vaněk proves the falseness (the "deadness" to truth) of the language by which most of the other characters in the plays live. This is what the three writers who borrowed the figure of Vaněk inherited from Havel. This is why in their comments they try, by different means, to stress the general aspect of the figure. That Vaněk captured their attention because he not only came from the pen of their colleague and friend but also resembled him in a basic way, is a lucky incident both for Czech literature and for contemporary literature and theatre as such. Without this incident we would not have this remarkable string of plays. It also shows that in a time when every writer strives for individualism, there exists—no matter how fragile—a common idea of human value. That this idea reaches beyond the stringent calls for human rights whirling agonizingly around our globe is clear. That it comes from a country situated precariously at the very borderline of a vast division is a fact that deserves more thought. (pp. xxvii-xxviii)

A scene from Václav Havel's drama Audience *produced in Munich in 1977.*

Marketa Goetz-Stankiewicz, in an introduction to The Vaněk Plays: Four Authors, One Character, *edited by Marketa Goetz-Stankiewicz, University of British Columbia Press, 1987, pp. xv-xxviii.*

Hana Hrzalová

[*The following essay was published in* Panorama of Czech Literature, *an English-language journal published in Prague under the auspices of the Union of Czech Writers which frequently reflected the official aesthetic dictates of the nation's former Communist government. Here, Hrzalová surveys Czech fiction of the early and middle 1980s.*]

Prose today boasts a large and varied community of readers in Bohemia. Not infrequently a new title of fiction is sold out swiftly a few days after reaching the bookshop counter. Providing a good indicator of readers' preferences, such rapid sales reflect the need for larger editions of the novels, collections of short stories or longer narratives dominating the best-seller list. Re-editions of fictional steady-sellers and readers' favourites in the Klíč (Key) series of the Knihovna lidové četby (People's Library) editorial programme of the Československý spisovatel Publishing House often reach the staggering volume of thirty, forty or even ninety thousand copies. (Thus in 1985 the fourth edition of Jan Otčenášek's novel *When the Rains Swept Paradise* was published in the Klíč series in 99,000 copies.) As a rule, a successful novel today qualifies for Klíč re-edition status one to two years after its first publication. Historical fiction and nonfiction are widely read. The boom in science fiction—and this applies to both original Czech fiction and translations from other languages—continues unabated (as it happens, interest in science-fiction literature easily becomes a matter of authors' speculation). Constantly in demand is the social novel or any brand of fiction inspired by contemporary life, prose commenting on temporal and "eternal" problems, on human ideals and aspirations, on the longings, joys and sorrows of contemporary humanity.

The Czech reader is a discriminating reader. His taste has been shaped by the numerous re-editions of the masterpieces of Czech and Slovak interwar and postwar literature; his aesthetic sensibility and ideological acumen were made subtler by the dozens and hundreds of translations from European and world literature. Although books in a lighter vein—primarily books of entertainment and pastime literature—do get a fair amount of attention, world classics and modern literature figure prominently in the current publishing programmes. These criteria—just as the criterion of life practice and experience—determine public response to each new work of Czech prose.

Czech prose published within the span of the past two to three years shows an interesting constellation of authors, themes and genre varieties. Thus 1984 put the spotlight on novels dealing with the problems of the young and middle-aged generations—the type of fiction Oldřich Rafaj, critic and editor-in-chief of *Literární měsíčník* (*Literary Monthly*), fittingly described as the "prose of moral conflict". Although the prose works then published fuelled a lively debate and polemics, one thing was certain—they gave a new lease of life to contemporary Czech literature, more dynamism, a spirit of new freshness. The choice of hero and the new approach to conflict-depiction reflected with greater fidelity the ethically demanding, creative social climate of the day. As a result, Czech fiction broadened its own range of impact within society. Interestingly, the change was associated with authors belonging to different generations. Jaromíra Kolárová, the author of the ever-popular *My Boy and Me* (a novel published in the mid-1970s), called her new novel *I Wish I Had That Tree*. The central theme is the conception of love as professed and practised by some of the youngsters of today. The message Kolárová addresses to the young generation strikes a note of warning: the growth of genuine affection cannot be rushed. Therefore, do not deprive yourself by hasty and inconsiderate action of your wonderful chance to love and be loved, the chance of lifelong partnership. Kolárová's novel bristles with wit and humour. Her insight into the life style of the young generation (cf. her impressive command of teenage idiom) betrays a compassionate observer of contemporary adolescence—a quality to which readers and critics (with two or three exceptions) responded with much sympathy and acclaim. The milieu and atmosphere shaping the attitudes and ideals of the technical intelligentsia provided inspiration for Jiří Křenek's novel *Tomáš and Markéta*. Křenek's hero is a young engineer employed in a research institute, who seeks and finally finds his true role in life and society, regains personal confidence and asserts his professional integrity and scientific competence. Painfully aware of his own shortcomings, the hero experiences moments of scepticism, overcomes them and realizes his responsibility vis-à-vis himself and other people, his responsibility for the quality of relations governing personal human contact and the professional code of behavior. Jan Kostrhun, a South Moravian author, published a new novel portraying the people and problems he knows so well from his own profession (for many years he has worked as an engineer in agriculture). *Wedding of the Century* confirms Kostrhun's spontaneous, dynamic style of narration, his sense of humour, irony and self-irony, his knowledge of human nature, his insight into the intellectual outlook and emotional life of his own generation. Kostrhun's young hero, an agricultural engineer exercising for some time the function of chairman in a large-scale farming cooperative, lives through many disillusions, encounters bureaucracy and careerism, but he too, in the final analysis, triumphantly asserts his committed approach to the cause he pursues with passionate zeal. Consistently differentiating between social interest and strictly personal interests, he successfully pools his knowledge, talent and personal conviction for the sake of the victory of common labour, the prosperity of socialist agriculture, in support of new farming technology and progressive farming methods. Kolárová's (but especially Křenek's and Kostrhun's) novels ushered a new type of hero into Czech literature—the young engagé hero expressing the life style of the middle-aged generation, its attitude to life and the present, its conception of social responsibility and commitment. The fresh impulse emerging in Czech fiction in late 1984 never slackened. The following year brought a rich harvest. New books came from experienced and es-

tablished writers, but a distinctive share of merit must be acknowledged for the middle-aged generation and there were several entirely new names, an impressive array of fiction debuts—some promising, others less promising, some immature, others even misconceived.

Zdeněk Pluhař broke the silence of three years which had elapsed from the publication of his novel *Six O'Clock in the Astoria* (State Prize award) with a new novel. As the title suggests, *Curtain without Applause* is a story of theatre life concentrating on problems of art, the artist's role and function in society, problems of love, individual and social responsibility, and professional and personal conflicts. The new novel confirms Pluhař's narrative flair, his great powers of psychological description, solid knowledge of the setting and fine verbal craftsmanship. In the value-hierarchy of new Czech fiction published in 1985, Pluhař's novel is bound to occupy one of the leading positions.

To find a common denominator for Czech prose published in 1985 is a challenging task. The picture confronting us is remarkably complex and the complexity is compounded by works differing in genre and value. The dozens of new titles include, of course, books just to be read and forgotten. But there are also more ambitious ventures, bolder forays into the present, books probing the surface of everyday life, the problems and phenomena which, though conspicuous, prove to be less relevant when viewed in the strong light of reality. Some of the books strike a distinctly confessional note communicating the author's deep concern. A good example is Petr Prouza's new novel *Life Alternates with Death*—an arresting account of human courage in which the young heroine, mother of two children, is dying of leukaemia. Jiří Marek's *Tristan; or, A Tale of Love* evokes the magic mood of the Lesser Town of Prague and is basically about the vigour and vulnerability of love. Zdeněk Pluhař and Jiří Marek are exponents of the generation of writers whose fictional debut dates back to the 1940s. In Jaromír Tomeček's fiction life and letters never fail to match. The give-and-take of man and nature, ecological risks and threatened wild life are the keynote of his multi-episode chronicle *The Burning Mountain*. Bearing the subtitle "Ballad of the King of Clubs" and set in North Moravia (on the Moravian-Slovak border), Tomeček's novel contrasts the crowding and racket of the town with nature's serenity and order. It is a passionate plea for belief in human reason and the final victory of knowledge that wild life and the countryside have always formed an inalienable part of the world man inhabits. Two other writers of the older generation are completing wide-range historical novels: Alena Vrbová, better known for her poetry, and Helena Šmahelová, a novelist of distinction. Both share intense interest in their ancestral history and both use the form of trilogy. Alena Vrbová's three-volume novel opens with an account of the history of the Thirty Years' War and traces events up to the 19th century (*When the Cock Stopped Crowing—The Cardinal's Seal—Sprouting*). Helena Šmahelová depicts the period of feudal serfdom and her epic of Bohemian history has so far brought us to the age of reforms under the Emperor Joseph (*The Ancestral Trail*). Well researched and conceived in the spirit of realism, both novels recapture the greatness, drama and tragedy of man's battle for happiness and dignity. Vrbová and Šmahelová develop the tradition of the Czech historical novel from the vantage point of the present. Their interpretation of the past is an interpretation of a writer of our day and age and, in this sense, they are worthy representatives of Czech historical fiction of 1985. An exponent of the middle-aged generation is Miroslav Rafaj. After his earlier novels (cf. *Salt Snow*), Rafaj's interest has in recent years shifted towards shorter narratives. The short story—or rather a closely-knit set of short stories well premeditated in theme, effect and conception—is now his favourite medium. *Surrounded by Blessed Figures* is Rafaj's tribute to the ordinary "unheroic" working man and his "unobtrusive greatness", his magnanimity and moral fibre. The message of Rafaj's rural and urban stories is that none of these qualities can be acquired and retained without a deliberate effort. Moral growth is the reward of man's daily struggle, thoughts and deeds. Rafaj's new collection of short stories—just as Křenek's and Kostrhun's novels—documents the consistent endeavour of contemporary Czech fiction to portray the "positive hero" with all his human attributes, a man of flesh and bones, a fallible and vulnerable creature treasuring the cause of truth, a man constantly longing and striving to live according to the moral code he respects—for himself, for other people, for society, for the sake of a good creative cause.

Other prose writers, who thanks to their systematic creative involvement have gained a niche of their own in Czech literature and ought to be mentioned in connection with the 1985 upsurge of new writing, largely hail from the ranks of the middle-aged generation first emerging in the literary limelight in the 1970s. Josef Frais published his second novel *The Tree at the End of the Road* in 1985. The theme is theatre life and the message highlights man's creative urge and the chances open to his revitalization and inner growth. Ilona Borská's *Minuet in the Hangar* is a gripping and utterly convincing story set in the days of wartime Nazi occupation. New contributions to Czech fiction came from Stanislav Rudolf (*All My Loves*) and Jana Moravcov (*The Gate to Understanding*). Both turned in a solid job of work. Rudolf's novel deals with professional and family problems. Moravcová writes with the sovereign detachment of a story-teller cultivating the tale of the fantastic and mysterious. Petr Pavlík, a native of South Bohemia, gave us much food for thought in his novel *The Private Air Show*. Miroslav Ivanov's lasting preoccupation with non-fiction is well documented by his latest book on Antonín Dvořák's American period. Ivanov's account of the American inspiration of the eminent Czech composer (*The New World Symphony*) is based on authentic first-hand sources the author studied in America. A travelogue exploring life in Czechoslovakia is Jan Suchl's *No Waiting for Happiness*. Critics have praised Ladislav Pecháček's new novel *Good Pigeons Return Home*. Pecháček, a member of the medical profession, has so far published several prose works which thanks to their humorous slant and delight in satirical deflation attracted much attention in the Czech film-making world. This time he has given us a haunting study of human loneliness, the drama of a lonely man who, searching for a way out of his labyrinth, cures himself of alcoholism, and struggles for

his own present and future through memories of his childhood and of good, brave people he has known. Pecháček formulates some disturbing questions concerning man's loneliness, hope and longing for togetherness, a knowledge of weakness and inconsistency, describing how people often meet and pass on, though he does not deny the possibility of catharsis, human understanding and solidarity. 1985 saw the publication of Ludvík Štěpán's novel *Sailing the Seas Is a Different Business,* a remarkable portrayal and well-orchestrated account of human destiny.

Science fiction proliferated on a spectacular scale in 1985. For some of the younger writers this brand of literature has obviously become preoccupation number one. Dedicated practitioners of science fiction include Zdeněk Volný (*The Gate to Eternity,* 1985) and Ondřej Neff, whose 1985 contribution was a set of shorter narratives *The Egg Inside Out.* Nevertheless, the reviewers' praise seems to be reserved for earlier masters of the form—in particular Karel Čapek, or—to quote a postwar exponent of Czech science fiction—Josef Nesvadba. Critics recall the skill, sense of proportion and high literary standard characterizing Ludvík Souček's science-fiction stories. And their final verdict runs as follows: what Czech science fiction needs in the first place is a more pungent social impact coupled with more perfect craftsmanship. The canon of principles evolved for this genre of writing at home and abroad can neither be ignored nor circumvented. Respect for the discoveries of science should be dovetailed with the inner logic of the hero and the story.

The development of Czech prose continues and the territory so far covered shows a lively pattern of different themes, genres and authors. The contemporary identity of Czech prose is shaped by dozens of distinguished writers. New names come to the front and each new aspiring writer contributes his own experience, his own angle of vision, his own depiction of the different social and professional settings influencing man's life, character, thought and action. The inner continuity of Czech prose is not impaired. On the contrary, works of fiction created in the past decade are now appreciated as to their true intellectual and aesthetic merits. The reader's receptive mind registers all the books recently recognized as worthy of them: the historical metaphor of Ladislav Fuks's fin-de-siècle novel *The Duchess and the Housekeeper;* Jan Kozák's modern romantic epic *Adam and Eve,* unfolding against the background of the Řip countryside; Zdeněk Pluhař's abovementioned novel *Six O'Clock in the Astoria;* Věra Adlová's *Autumn's Bitter Fragrance* (now sold out)—a novel set partly in wartime Czechoslovakia, partly in the present. Other writers like Vladimír Páral are busy working on new fictional projects and the Československý spisovatel Publishing House plans to publish Bohumil Hrabal's new prose shortly. The talent of young writers of promise—only recently revealed—is now crystallizing in more appreciable form. Thus František Mandát, winner of the 1984 Jiří Wolker Literary Contest for budding authors, has presented another portrayal of army life in his second novel *Barriers,* published in late 1985.

Prose today responds to a wide range of topical problems. The relevant is being separated from the irrelevant, the substantive from the ephemeral. Literature becomes the testing ground of man's historic experience and only sterling qualities of the past survive the test: the struggle of preceding generations, the path traversed by society in the march towards freedom, towards the ideal of man enjoying all possibilities of creative development. Hence the permanent topicality of inspiration drawn from World War II, from personal wartime experience and active involvement in the antifascist struggle. Prose responding to the challenge of contemporary life expresses in its best works the humanist conception of man and the world, the social issues and moral consciousness of our age, the supreme value of human talent and labour, and the will and longing to preserve peace for the sake of human life, happiness and creativity. (pp. 5-9)

> Hana Hrzalová, *"Contemporary Czech Prose," in* Panorama of Czech Literature, *No. 4541, 1987, pp. 5-9.*

Igor Hájek

[*In the following essay, Hájek rebukes Czech fiction approved and published by the nation's government during the 1980s. While he deems such works trivial in content and form, Hájek also observes that, compared to Czech fiction of the 1970s, they more effectively disclose corruption and materialism within Communist Czechoslovakia.*]

It is generally acknowledged that Czech literature, namely and in particular that which is published under official auspices in Czechoslovakia, is in the doldrums. In Czechoslovakia itself, the admission is made grudgingly and one has often to read between the lines to find it. The true picture of stagnation is obscured by boastful quotations of figures: the number of books published, the size of total printings, the number of titles published in translation into foreign languages. Such figures are of course meaningless as they tell us little of the quality of the writing; at best they could be viewed as interesting indices of a literary stagflation.

In the West, there is a tendency to praise works written by banned and exiled authors, while literature officially allowed to be published at home is almost instinctively dismissed. An exception is usually made in the case of one or two of the "old masters"; the names of Bohumil Hrabal and Vladimír Páral are most often mentioned in this connection, disregarding the fact that they both have recently produced quite mediocre work. On the other hand, some younger writers of considerable talent tend to be overlooked, as if being published officially were in itself a mark of inferiority. True, there are not too many of the latter and raw talent is often the only attribute of their work.

Due to such divisions imposed by political circumstances, a comprehensive approach at present may be unrealistic, and we would perhaps do better to reconcile ourselves to only partial views of the scene until Czech literature is once again reunited. That point, alas, is likely to be reached only in the distant future, if ever.

Examination of contemporary Czech literary production

by sections can be justified on the ground that they do differ in many important respects. Officially published authors, for instance, write for a far larger readership than the banned and exiled writers can hope to reach; their attitudes are frequently close to or identical with those of the holders of power; they reflect in their style and method critical and political demands which the banned and exiled writers can afford to ignore; in general they can describe aspects of everyday life from their own experience and in greater detail, as they are fully integrated in it.

The character of the examination has to be adjusted accordingly. It would be a waste of time to apply aesthetic criteria to material which from that point of view is completely uninteresting. But even writing which is trivial or close to being trivial may be worthy of examination for its content.

Of those writers who publish their short stories and novels in Czechoslovakia today, up to two-thirds in my estimation produce literature to which the term "trivial" can be applied. They do not necessarily embark on that road from the very outset. A good example is Josef Frais (b. 1946). Having worked as a miner, he used the experience in his first short novel, *Muži z podzemního kontinentu* (*Men from the Underground Continent,* 1978), which was in many respects quite promising. But his subsequent books have only been a record of a downhill slide. The latest one, *Strom na konci cesty* (*The Tree at the End of the Road,* 1985), a confused and concocted paraphrase of *Hamlet,* makes one wonder about the professional judgement of the editor who sent it to the printers. Or is it too naïve to think that there must be a limit, a standard below which things must not be allowed to sink, at least not in the prestigious publishing house of the Writers' Union?

Such startling inconsistency in the quality of writing is a characteristic of much of Czech writing and Frais's case is far from unique. The high wastage rate may be explained by the fact that due to a shortage of good writers, many *new* writers have half-baked novels accepted for publication without ever having had an opportunity properly to test their foothold in literature with a short story. But there seems to be at the same time something else at work which causes that rapid deterioration. It is as if there were a monster at large that devours talent or a pestilence that makes it disintegrate. Of those who came to the fore in the mid-1970s as the North Bohemian epic school, Jiří Švejda (b. 1949) was the most prominent. Less sophisticated than his mentor Páral, he possesed a ferocious energy that drove him to explore some of the less attractive aspects of life in his region. Considering the circumstances, he wrote fearlessly. Yet a few books later his dynamism was nearly spent, and he was drowning in triviality. Was this the consequence of having come against a barrier that proved impossible to penetrate, of having reached the permitted limits of exploration? Was his talent being thwarted by external pressures? There are signs of a crisis in the banal *Dlouhé dny* (*Long Days,* 1981), but Švejda, unlike many others, managed to recover from it as his more recent work, in particular *Moloch I: Hledání roznováhy* (*In Search of Balance,* 1983) and perhaps even *Moloch II: Ko-*

nets sezóny (*End of the Season,* 1985), suggest. This, however, can be regarded as an exception rather than the rule.

It seems that in a country like Czechoslovakia, with a tradition of its writers' involvement in national, social, and political issues, inability to explore the depths drives them to drown in the shallow waters of triviality. A similar process can, of course, be observed in the West, where no subject is taboo, but where the media have pre-empted serious treatment of many issues. It may be no coincidence that the majority of prose writers who publish their work in Czechoslovakia today fit perfectly the description of the work of a contemporary American writer formulated by an American critic twenty years ago. In our quotation the plural is substituted for the singular:

> They have none of the attributes we conventionally associate with major literary talent. They do not have interesting minds. They do not possess remarkable narrative gifts or a distinguished style. They do not create dynamic or colorful or deeply meaningful characters. They do not confront the reader with dramatic situations that bear the mark of an original or unique manner of seeing and responding to experience. They do not challenge the imagination or stimulate, shock, or educate it. In fact, one of the problems they pose for the critic is that they engage the imagination so little that one has real difficulty remembering their work long enough to think clearly about it. It has an annoying way of slipping out of the mind before one has had time to take hold of it, and of blending back into the commonplace and banal surfaces of reality, which are so monotonous a part of our daily awareness that the mind instinctively rejects them as not worth remembering.

There are exceptions, of course. From time to time a more ambitious work slips through, but seldom without some difficulty either before or after publication. Such delays are a reliable indication that the author or the book are not to the authorities' liking. According to a recent interview in *Tvorba,* Petr Skarlant (b. 1939) had to wait four years for the publication of his latest novel *Věk náruživosti* (*Age of Passion,* 1985). And a full ten years elapsed between the writing and the publication in 1981 of *Semestr života* (*A Term of Life*) by Jana Červenková, and even then it was provided with an apologetic editorial postscript.

We can thus obtain a fairly good idea of which subjects are considered to be too delicate and what image of personal or social life the political authorities do not wish to have projected. It seems that what is particularly unwelcome is any attempt to place personal shortcomings and social aberrations in a wider context, and any suggestion that they could be linked to the political sphere.

On the other hand, what is the picture of contemporary Czech society that the authorities would like to see in literature? That can be gleaned from various official pronouncements as well as from the never-ending stream of theoretical articles outlining the road to be taken by writers and postulating ever anew the principles of socialist realism. Futile theorizing is one of the aspects of a decaying literature. However, there are very few works which could

be pointed out as examples of socialist realism. Writing in a recent issue of *Česká literatura* [Vol. XXXIII, No. 1 (1985)] on the past forty years of Czech prose, Hana Hrzalová (b. 1929) quotes only a handful of names, presumably because not many writers would conform to her definition of Socialist literature. She refers to Václav Řezáč, Jan Otčenášek, Norbert Frýd, Ladislav Fuks, Josef Nesvadba, Bohumil Hrabal, Vladimír Páral, and repeatedly to Bohumil Říha, Jaromíra Kolárová and of course Jan Kozák. Completely omitted are the few—and she stresses *few*—novels of the 1960s, whose heroes were allegedly conceived so as to "demonstrate the helplessness of man in the face of history." With the above exceptions, there is hardly any mention of the prose of the 1970s and 1980s, either.

Hrzalová's extremely selective treatment of Czech prose may be explained by the fact that her conception is demonstrably rooted in the ideology of the 1950s. Her sectarian and complacent view of the recent past contrasts with the observations of a much younger critic. In his hopelessly verbose, although—within the limits of the possible—honest book *Prozaická skutečnost* (*Prosaic Reality,* 1982), Jan Lukeš (b. 1950) writes about the "ruthlessly ambitious and institutionalized grand snobbery" and of the "spreading careerism, reckless race after profit and the rise of petty bourgeois attitudes in interpersonal and work relationships" as aspects of the 1970s that are at the root of the skepticism of his generation. These remarks seem to be at considerable variance with Hrzalová's presentation of a world of socialist achievements, ever perfecting itself, the process of perpetual improvement being reflected in the work of a few chosen writers.

Neither one nor the other critic, however, pays much attention to the bulk of current production. For an ideological critic like Hrzalová, it may not be sufficiently imbued with "passionate love for socialism" (quoting the poet Vítězslav Nezval) or because its shortcomings are too conspicuous and embarrassing. A younger, seriously oriented critic like Lukeš may regard it as part of the aggressively self-advancing environment and, since he deals exclusively with writers of his own generation, as being outside his brief. Should we, too, disregard those unpleasant, dreary, and often poorly written novels and short stories that do not really lend themselves to critical analysis and any of the games academics like to play with works of art, mainly because they cannot aspire to belong in that category? Do we dismiss them as literary rubbish, which some of them undoubtedly are, or do they, like all human activity, contain elements of genuine and useful information?

The fact that they have been passed for publication in an authoritarian system where permission of some sort is always required, does not in itself mean that they present an ideal picture of life as officialdom would like to see it. It seems that, despite the unflattering comment some of them make on it, they are being tolerated—for various reasons. One of them may be the financial profit they bring to the publishers. Indeed, in number of copies printed quite a few compete successfully with bestsellers such as, say, the Czech translations of Joseph Heller or Edgar Doctorow, while the authors need not be paid in foreign currency. Or the powers that be may simply be more enlightened and sophisticated than we think, and do not mind the reading public being provided with entertainment: people always find watching themselves fascinating. Hampered by their inexperience, lack of talent, or ineptitude, our authors seldom create; instead, they describe. Spontaneous naturalists that they are, they pick facts and details off Aldridge's "commonplace and banal surfaces of reality," and with the help of simple plots weave them into novels and short stories. In a letter to Margaret Harkness, Friedrich Engels wrote how from Balzac, whom he regarded as "a far greater master of realism than all the Zolas, past, present, or future," he learned more about French society than "from all the professional historians, economists, and statisticians of the period together." Some claim that Engels himself was laboring under an illusion: that the world which Balzac described was in fact his own fantasy. The contemporary Czech prose writers whom we have in mind are no neo-Balzacs; not even neo-Trollopes. And they do not possess an imagination strong enough to create a fantasy world. The picture they paint of their environment may thus be closer to reality than had it come from Balzac. It could even cause embarrassment to the ideologists and theorists who still battle for the virtues of the romantic fiction of socialist realism. In contemporary socialism, facts of life seem to be prevailing over ideology.

What kind of reality does then emerge from these books? One that is very different both from the fictional reality of the 1950s and 1960s as well as from the postulated reality of the 1970s and 1980s. First, the working class has all but disappeared. The hero of the literature of actually existing socialism is more often than not a research worker, a doctor, a director of a factory or institute, in short a well-established middleclass citizen. True, in the works of younger writers we sometimes encounter young men who make a living by manual work, but these are mostly uprooted, restless characters who may yet end up as publishers' editors in the capital. Genuine workers seem to have been relegated to the role of chain-smoking, coffee-drinking, ill and aged Party branch chairmen, who come to the help of the director with a few words of wisdom. We can find a cardboard figure of this kind in the novel *Druhý dech* (*Second Breath*, 1975) by Stanislav Vácha (b. 1930), where the director has to face an onslaught of assorted careerists who have discovered his weak point. Sometimes the wisdom dispensed by the Party man can be rather surprising. In *Formule I* (*Formula 1*, 1981) by Stanislav Rudolf (b. 1932) the director is in the habit of signing his name on research papers, patent applications, and even learned articles prepared and written by his subordinates, and he also pockets any fees paid for them. (This is not the author's fantasy: publishers actually do pay fees for learned articles in Czechoslovakia.) When a young research worker points out the infamous practice to the Party chairman, he explains that the director is a world-renowned expert and that undermining his position at home would have repercussions abroad. Moreover, he helped the partisans during the War . . . However, the chairman promises to raise the matter at the next committee meeting.

Vácha and Rudolf are two of the very few authors who still acknowledge the existence of the Party and politically identify with it. In most cases, the hero is politically amorphous. In the novel *Tomáš a Markéta* (*Thomas and Margaret,* 1984) by Jiří Křenek (b. 1933) personal data concerning the hero appear from a computer printout on the very first page. Under the heading *Political Affiliation* the answer stands out almost provocatively: "Without political affiliation." Despite this shortcoming the hero proceeds to become the head of a new project in a large research institute. It may be purely coincidental that he first marries the daughter of the institute's director. The only person who may be suspected of having an affiliation is a frightful old hag who retires to the hero's native village which he likes to visit. An inexhaustible activist, she pesters everybody, calls boring meetings, makes speeches, and sends reports of them to the papers. Her undoing comes when her son falls in love with a black girl, a visiting student of Czech from the United States, and the politically "progressive" mother turns out to be a racist at heart. A cardboard figure once again, cut out of 1950s material, but this time the purpose is ridicule.

While the population at large is depicted as being at best lackadaisical in relation to politics, it reveals great passion for all aspects of consumption, including the conspicuous variety, shared, one suspects, by the authors themselves. In this area status symbols are rife. When describing rooms or dress, or when referring to shopping, every item is meticulously listed, usually by its brand name; sometimes even the price is included, either in Czechoslovak crowns or in Tuzex coupons. People do not wake up to the ringing of any old alarm clock, but to the buzz of a miniature battery operated one. They do not throw away the blanket and get up, but they carefully push off the lightweight *larisa* and then have a shower and treat themselves with *tabacspray*. They do not get into a car and drive off to work. The make has to be mentioned. In just two pages of the novel *Poslední knížka o dětství* (*Last Book of Childhood,* 1982) by Zdeněk Zapletal (b. 1951) we find four car models: Lada 1500, Wartburg 353W, Škoda 120L and Simca Chrysler 1307GLS. Color is frequently mentioned, metallic paint serving as a mark of luxury and success. Luckily there is little chance of these books being translated into many foreign languages, otherwise they would cause their translators problems similar to those which American writers of the late fifties and early sixties, intoxicated with affluence and consumerism, caused their foreign translators. How could a Czech translator at that time be expected to know what the author had in mind when he wrote, "She put it in the bendix?" (compare also references to items such as "G-Plan" in John Braine and others).

The Czech variety of consumer society which we see reflected here, is not quite the result of high productivity and affluence that would put the dazzling new products within the reach of nearly everybody. More than money is needed to acquire the status symbols so useful to writers as a sign language. In a planned economy, bound by import controls and beset by chronic production and distribution bottlenecks, one does not just buy goods, one has to hunt for them or obtain them with the help of bribes and services rendered in return. Even items of everyday use may thus become status symbols or fetishes of a kind when they are in short supply. An excellent description of such a hunting chain appears in Zapletal's book *Pozdě na hlasitou hudbu* (*Too Late for Loud Music,* 1983). Here is a condensed version of it.

As the manager of a stationery shop receives his supplies one morning, he is pleased to find that they include not only toilet paper (normally sold in stationery shops in Czechoslovakia), but also colored crayons which the local doctor wants for her granddaughter. In return for the crayons he gets a prescription for diazepam (a Czech version of valium), while for the promise of diazepam the butcher will put aside for him two kilos of pork and two kilos of beef. The butcher uses diazepam to obtain cotton children's underwear for a friend whose children are allergic to man-made fibers. The friend, manager of a food shop, offers to the butcher in return lentils, another item in short supply. The butcher does not really need lentils, but he needs brake linings and window wipers for his car. The car parts shop manager is glad to supply them in exchange for lentils, which he trades for a carton of Sparta cigarettes in hard packs and the popular magazine *Mladý svět* at the tobacconist's. The tobacconist barters her lentils for cloth buttons and long zippers from the haberdashery. There the manager lets one of her shop assistants have the lentils. The shop assistant knows that her friend who works at the chemist's has been hunting for lentils, and this is her opportunity to acquire two much sought after items, *peromat* and *batul*—whatever they may be. The lady at the chemist's no longer needs lentils, but remembers that the manager of the stationery shop has been looking for lentils and so she passes them on to him in exchange for toilet paper and colored crayons. We leave the manager of the stationery shop wondering what to do with the lentils, as he already has a year's supply at home.

Engels would have been pleased, no doubt. Such passages in contemporary Czech fiction (fiction?) explain more about the mysteries of socialist distribution and the preoccupations of the citizen, than any economist or statistician could hope to do. It should be explained that this is not barter in the traditional sense. All goods are paid for with money; it is the opportunity to purchase them which constitutes the privilege.

Not everybody, however, is in the enviable position of being able to offer rare services or goods in order to obtain similar in exchange. Take for instance people in intellectual professions, writers, and editors. What do they do when in need of lentils or a good dentist? We may learn from a lecture on this subject in the novel *Vrabčí hnízdo* (*Sparrows' Nest,* 1983), a half-hearted satire by Roman Ráž (b. 1935), where two such characters discuss their predicament:

> That's what the world is like today, neither of us has made it that way, that's how it is and whatever we may do, we won't change it. The dentists have it good, the butchers, too, and the plumbers. Everybody is happy to do something for them. For a car mechanic, too. They are all doing well. But what are we supposed to do? We, who with our own hands cannot even fix a toilet

seat properly? We just have to pay through the nose. At the dentist's, at the butcher's. We cannot start any kind of barter. From us they ask cash on the nail. That is why we have to make more money than the others. And how can we do that? Only by scratching each other's back like the others do. Are we supposed to be different from the others?

Besides providing a potential explanation why so many writers in Czechoslovakia are remarkably prolific and how it is possible that novels like *Vrabčí hnízdo* get published, this manifesto of conformity in corruption implies that a strong stomach and a degree of callousness are required to get by in the existing jungle. Indeed, ruthlessness, even brutality in private and public human relations, often the consequence of greed or thwarted ambition, are foremost among the features of daily life mirrored in this literature which one hesitates to call fiction. There are numerous examples of such behavior, in fact it is the essential ingredient in many books. There may be, of course, some influence of crude Western fiction, but more often than not the experience is purely Czech.

In the collection of short stories *Proč ulovit chřástala* (*Why Catch a Sprite?,* 1983) by Bohuslav Trojan (b. 1946), a woman falls in love with an Air Force lieutenant who passes her home on the way to his base. The lieutenant is quite unaware of her infatuation. When he marries, she out of spite writes a letter to the military authorities and accuses him of having kept secret from them that two of his relatives are living abroad. The lieutenant is investigated and this accusation proves to be false. During the investigation, however, it is discovered, to his surprise, that a distant relative of his brother-in-law has lived in Canada since 1969—and he is in trouble. In vain does he claim not to have known of this relative. "You should have known," they tell him.

Far from being the subject of the short story, this episode is allowed hardly more than a paragraph, mentioned almost in passing to characterize the hero's wife. That the military authorities acted the way they did is regarded as natural, and on the whole the incident is presented as being quite commonplace. In other books there is equally casual treatment of many aspects of life that even in Czechoslovakia two decades before would have aroused concern or would have been expected to exist only in the depraved West. What is so disquieting is that "the rise of petty bourgeois attitudes," Jan Lukeš's euphemism for brutalization and *embourgeoisement,* is viewed as the norm and no attempt is made by the authors to approach it from an ethical standpoint.

Naturally, this attitude also affects sex. Long gone are the times when a Czech writer was charged with pornography because he dared to mention such parts of the human body as the bosom—and then only in connection with heaving. A new record must have been set by Antonín Bajaja who has managed to squeeze onto the very first page of his novel *Mluviti stříbro* (*Silver for Talking,* 1982) the description of those acts of mutual adoration between man and woman which are usually referred to by two long Latin names. But at least it is executed with some skill and it has a place and purpose in the story. Explicit or joyful sex is not found in the work of other writers. As if they were unable to deal in prose with genuine emotions of any kind, they operate mostly with allusions and lascivious remarks in poor taste, which indicate minds not only uninteresting, but also vulgar. Very often sexual relations are presented almost as a slightly boring part of the office routine or are reduced to the level of crude pleasure seeking.

There are many other repulsive aspects of the contemporary way of life which these Czech writers describe, as far as we can judge, quite faithfully. One of them is an attitude to women which would have all Western feminists up in arms. In many ways, the picture they present contains more unattractive details than we find, for instance, in the collection of short stories *Má veselá jitra* (*My Merry Mornings,* 1979) by the banned writer Ivan Klíma (b. 1931). The difference is that they do not use such facts of life for critical exposure, for the questioning of attitudes, for satire or for social analysis. They only record them. What sounds most true in their books is not what they dwell upon, but what they mention casually, as a matter of course, a generally accepted fact or an internalized attitude, whether it is the ubiquitous presence of *veksláci* (illegal foreign currency changers) or behavior which by any other standards would be regarded as knavish.

There is no doubt that this substantial part of current Czech book production brings a particular testimony about contemporary Czechoslovakia, and that we can learn more from this prose than from the press which reflects a much more closely controlled and censored reality. In a decade or two there may be enough of this literature to provide for a study of the values of existing socialism similar to that undertaken by Vera Dunham in her book *In Stalin's Time.* Although these writers have "none of the attributes we conventionally associate with major literary talent," they may yet supply academics with something to play with. (pp. 214-23)

> *Igor Hájek, "Changing Attitudes in Recent Czech Fiction: Towards a Typology of Actually Existing Socialism," in* Aspects of Modern Russian and Czech Literature: Selected Papers of the Third World Congress for Soviet and East European Studies, *edited by Arnold McMillin, Slavica Publishers, Inc., 1989, pp. 214-24.*

Maria Němcová Banerjee

[*In the following excerpt, Banerjee explores the nature of humor in contemporary Czech literature, observing precedents in the novels of Franz Kafka and Jaroslav Hašek.*]

Laughter, in all its nearly infinite variety, is essentially a choric phenomenon. Explosively communicative and communal, it unifies by momentarily simplifying the complexities of life. Yet, underneath the illusion of spontaneity it projects, humor conceals a complicated, double-edged impulse to disturb the order of the universe while also seeking to reconcile us to it. This ambivalence is most aggressive in grotesque or black humor, which often pits laughter against the threat of annihilation. The ancient

compulsion to exorcise death by laughter is alive in the sophisticated clowning of the *poétes maudits,* as in the gallows humor of their populist brethren and the lowbrow obscenities of their ancestral wakes.

Black humor thrives on catastrophe, and a culture like the Czech one, with a history of living perpetually on the edge of extinction, naturally develops a certain virtuosity in it. After all, humor is the best revenge of the powerless, and it was a Czech, Jaroslav Hašek (1883-1923), who wrote the great comic novel of World War I, *Osudy dobrého vojáka Švejka* (*The Good Soldier Schweik;* 1921-23). Paradoxically, at the time when Czech readers were first laughing over the games Schweik plays with the Austrian military machine, the nation was on the upswing, experiencing one of the most positive moments of its history. Newly independent and democratically governed, the Czechoslovak Republic had emerged from the Great War as one of its few real victors. Moreover, this was achieved by skillful negotiations rather than by the force of arms. In those days Hašek's humor could be enjoyed as pure satire directed at something external to oneself. Josef Lada's celebrated illustrations established the folk image of a rotund, almost peasant Schweik, beaming at the world with the benign, crafty-idiotic smile of a sure winner.

However, as a very recent article by a Czech critic argues, this image of Schweik, so close to the Czech heart, may be incongruous with Hašek's text. The good soldier could and indeed was drawn differently, with a grimace that evokes the chill of horror instead of laughter, as in George Grosz's illustrations. An updated Czech reading of Hašek agrees with the German expressionist. No longer the happy clown, today's Schweik is a homeless wanderer without a steady occupation, like his creator almost a tragic cynic with nothing to hold on to but his belly in a world which has suddenly become alien and where laughter no longer renews. It now makes sense that Hašek was an exact contemporary of Franz Kafka (1883-1924), born in the same city and into an empire on its last legs, whose ruling people, as Robert Musil has shown in the first part of his novel *Der Mann ohne Eigenschaften* (*The Man without Qualities;* 1930), suffered in desperate frivolity from a feeling that they lacked sufficient reasons for their existence.

A similar illegitimacy stalks the more plebeian Soviet Empire of Central Europe in the fourth decade of its existence, but the historical fatigue seems to afflict the subjects. In an interview with Philip Roth, Milan Kundera has observed:

> If someone had told me as a boy: one day you will see your nation vanish from the world, I would have considered it nonsense, something I couldn't possibly imagine. A man knows he is mortal, but he takes it for granted that his nation possesses a kind of eternal life. But after the Russian invasion of 1968, every Czech was confronted with the thought that his nation could be quietly erased from Europe.

Even more recently, Kundera has talked of his country and the cultural zone he persists in calling Central and *not* Eastern Europe as if they were already a lost Atlantis under the Russian sea. Russian civilization, he warns, is alien to Europe, having known "another way of laughing, living and dying" in the immensity of its all-devouring space, where time moves so slowly. Still, the real tragedy of his homeland, Kundera charges, is not Russia with its armies, but Western Europe, which in its rush to "bow out" of culture has disowned the smaller nations to its east. He sees no becoming modesty in this scaling down of European cultural horizons, only a remnant of cynicism left over from the grand marches of former ambitions.

Kundera would argue that Central Europe is more precious than ever for Europe, having become the twentieth-century home of the nonserious spirit of skepticism, which he considers the heart of the European civilization. Rabelais, in his *Tiers livre* (*Third Book;* 1546), had celebrated the young strength and courage of joyous knowledge by rolling his Diogenic tub up and down the hill Cranium while others armed for religious conflict. The Czechs, whom Karl Marx classified among the nonhistorical Slavs, also learned something of that wisdom in the course of their experience at the receiving end of history. Their most binding memory is of the collective death they suffered in the seventeenth century and of their rebirth in the nineteenth. As Kundera reminds us, the Czech nation owes its very existence to the Pascalian wager against the powers of oblivion made by those who re-created Czech culture out of the linguistic and musical memories rooted in the village. The anguish about the enforced forgetting of the Husák era, expressed in his novel *Kniha smíchu a zapomnění* (*The Book of Laughter and Forgetting;* 1980), is a theme deeply embedded in the ethos of Czech literature.

Kundera's unique vision as a novelist seems to derive from his ability to perceive the comic side of every human situation, no matter how pathetic. Having placed the art of the novel under the aegis of *gai savoir,* he deploys all the resources of laughter against everything that would make man less human. In *The Book of Laughter and Forgetting* he distinguishes between two kinds of laughter, forever competing to hold the stage and rarely kept in balance. The yes-saying laughter of the angels, the eternal partisans of the divine creation, threatens to degenerate into the unisonous handclapping and footstamping of the fanatical celebrants of "uncontested meaning." Whenever that happens, it is time for the devil, the eternal subversive, to laugh. In his second novel, *Život je jinde* (*Life is Elsewhere;* 1974), Kundera forthrightly took the devil's side in order to demystify the lyric attitude of the poets of revolution, those angelic adolescents of all ages like Jaromil and Paul Eluard, whose ecstasies rise from and above murder committed in the name of the good. The other side of Kundera's conundrum about laughter is that "if the world loses all its meaning (the reign of the demons), life is every bit as impossible." How is man to live then? The novelist denies himself the temptation of answering the questions with which he riddles his texts.

In his . . . novel, *Nesnesitelná lehkost bytí* (*The Unbearable Lightness of Being;* 1984) Kundera has found still another expression for his puzzling manysidedness. He confronts the artistically and erotically brilliant Sabina, her lightness in moving through time and place by way of personal betrayals, with Tereza's burdensome commitment to a single love. Tomas, the successful Czech neurosurgeon and Don Juan, who loves both women, is alternately oppressed by too little and too much meaning in his life. In a decision that shapes his future, he chooses to follow Tereza, his wife, from Switzerland back to a Prague in the grips of postinvasion normalization. There, the logic of the responsibilities he keeps assuming for himself and for his past (he refuses to denounce an article he once wrote about Oedipus), at odds with that scoundrel time, drives him to divest himself gradually of all the attributes of his former position. He and Tereza take on menial jobs in a village, where they eventually die together in a humdrum version of the death of exemplary lovers when the truck Tomas is driving after an evening out dancing overturns in a ditch. In those last quiet months of enforced fidelity, as the mold of his life began to harden perceptibly, Tomas's memory rearranged the unraveling reel of his past experience—the chance encounters, the questionable decisions, the splintering moments of sexual excitement and mystery—into a pattern of rhythmic repetitions that endowed it with a beauty and a significance which no longer oppressed him.

Kundera has said that each of the characters in that novel developed a set of the author's own possibilities. In allowing Tomas to create for himself the ineffable music of being, he may have been giving freer rein to his angelic mirth. He was also using Tomas to lay bare the novel's musical form of articulation, which relies on the recurrence of certain narrative and philosophical motifs to relate the interlocking stories of Tomas, Tereza, Sabina, and her Swiss lover Franz. For playing such games with his characters, a tongue-in-cheek reviewer has accused the author of manipulating them like a puppeteer [Robert Taylor, *Boston Sunday Globe,* 6 May 1984].

In truth, however, nothing is more unlike the mature and ironic Kundera than to aspire to a dictatorial or divine overview. His inherent skepticism about all absolutes places him at the opposite pole from Kafka, this "Tantalus of Prague" who spent his life as a "marginal settler" looking in vain for a supremely sanctioned legitimacy. It was Kundera who drew attention to the prophetic way in which Hašek and Kafka managed to embody in their archetypal personages the two opposing twentieth-century attitudes toward a totally manipulative power. Schweik's way out is that of the knowing fool, who destroys the legitimacy of the authority he confronts by an exaggerated mimicry of conformism. Joseph K.'s attempts at intellectual identification with the incomprehensible power that would judge him brings it crushing down upon his head. It is tempting to see the difference between the two postures in terms of the classical comic/tragic dichotomy. The comic solution, after all, hinges on survival by various means, while tragedy resolves its conflicts through death accompanied by increased knowledge.

In our world these distinctions have become murky, however. The latest reading from Central Europe sees a dark Schweik, whose "play is in vain," crowning Hašek as "the tragic bard of twentieth-century nihilism." On the other hand, Thomas Mann, in introducing *Das Schloß* (*The Cas-*

tle; 1926) to the American public, called Kafka a "religious humorist," whose theme is "the grotesque unconnection between the human being and the transcendental." In his religiously positive interpretation of the novel, Mann ranged himself with Kafka's friend and literary executor Max Brod, who, while conceding that Justice is presented in *Der Prozeß* (*The Trial;* 1925) "under the image of a machine planned with an inhuman, an almost fiendish refinement of cruelty," nevertheless maintained that, in spite of an utter lack of illusions about the Absolute, Kafka's faith in it was unshakable. The psychoanalytical interpreters of Kafka can point out that this new Isaac's pathetic complicity under Abraham's knife, the double-edged shame and loathing of it, had at least as much to do with the perceived majesty of the earthly father, to whom Kafka once wrote that he possessed "that mysterious quality which all tyrants have, whose privilege is based on their personality and not on reason."

To separate the private metaphor from the powerful and simple design of the controlling myth in Kafka's fictions is like pulling apart a seamless garment. The metaphysics and the psychology both seem irrelevant if one looks at Kafka from the perspective of present-day Czechoslovakia. Paul Trenský has noted [in *Czech Drama since World War II*, 1978] that the Czech public has a tendency to interpret all dramas of the absurd as political satire. That explains in part the remarkable run of popularity Kafka had in Prague, when transplanted to the Czech stage of the sixties. In 1963 the experimental director Jan Grossman adapted *The Trial* for his Divadlo na Zábradlí (Ballustrade Theatre) as one among a series of dramas of the absurd, where it played alongside Václav Havel's *Zahradní slavnost* (*The Garden Party*). A year later, Ivan Klíma rewrote *The Castle* for the stage of the Divadlo na Vinohradech (Vinohrady Theatre). *Zámek* is an original play, conceived by Klíma more in parody than in imitation of Kafka, deliberately reducing the tragicomedy of cross-purposes between the ways of God and man to the grotesquely low level of farce. The land surveyor K., renamed Josef Kahn by contamination from *The Trial,* is what Trenský calls "the archetypal fool incapable of accepting the nobility of the castle as a myth," even though, unlike K., he has been allowed to see it from the inside. The seeming optimism of this update in the quester's old story is derided by a macabre twist in the plot. The new acolyte is strangled in the castle, as others were before him, and the play ends as it had begun: with the shrieks of a dying victim. This transposition of the hauntingly silent execution scene from *The Trial* into the serialized violence of a loud farce has the effect of endowing Kafka's fantastic image with a raw vitality. In a country where socialist realism had temporarily banished everything real from literature, the truth of life managed to sneak back in the most unexpectedly subversive guise.

Josef Škvorecký tells us [in *Cross Currents*] how much critical cunning was expended in Prague to smuggle Kafka into the officially approved pantheon of socialist writers. This process of legitimization and nationalization, which culminated in the Liblice Conference of 1962, was not without its own ironies. As Škvorecký recounts it, they pulled a fast one on the bureaucrats of culture. It is both

laughable and moving to contemplate the thought that almost half a century later, Schweik did find a place for Kafka, in the tavern of the Czech low life. Škvorecký concludes: "I wonder if the atmosphere of a country where anonymous people coined the untranslatable word *kafkárna* to denote the craziness produced daily by totalitarian *Besserwisser,* cannot be identified with the atmosphere of the great Bohemian's [Kafka's] stories."

The curious Czech mixture of *švejkovina* and *kafkárna* is uniquely alive in Ludvík Vaculík's third novel, *Morčata* (*The Guinea Pigs;* 1973), which was awarded the Orwell Prize by Penguin Books in 1976. In Czechoslovakia it could only appear in the underground Edice Petlice (Padlock Press), which Vaculík directs.

The Guinea Pigs is a novel of great linguistic virtuosity, oscillating between humor and gothic horror and bristling with irony aimed at the corruption inherent in a totalitarian society as well as the self-delusions to which man is prone. The action is told in diary form by the inquisitive bank clerk Vašek, father of two irrepressible boys. Writing ostensibly for the children's instruction, he records meticulously his observations of the family's two pet guinea pigs, which he is subjecting to increasingly sadistic experiments. His ideal is the supreme objectivity of the perfect scientist. "The exemplary observer," he remarks "would be God himself," but the neutrality which he attributes to absolute power keeps eluding him. He remains mired in subjectivism, and his behavioristic investigations of animals drift irresistibly into introspection.

It all began with a casual but, as it turned out, rather problematic impulse, when Vašek saved a grass snake from drowning in a stream during a walk outside Prague. That gesture, or rather the consciousness of his own magnanimity ("I was only sorry the children weren't there"), launched him. Now, as he stands at night in his bathroom, hands pressing down the little rodent's struggling head into a tub filled with water, Vašek thrills under the crisscrossing charges of the ultimate brinkmanship. He can regain control only by shifting the gear of his consciousness from the first-person confessional to the third professional. Surprisingly, the pet Ruprecht saves himself this time, emerging with his snout above the water. It is too late for Vašek, however, who was the real guinea pig of that moral experiment. The diarist, or "the banker," as he now calls himself, concludes that "God is guilty, even if no one in this world, not even a mouse, believes in him."

The father fares no better in his pursuit of domestic authority. The self-confident didacticism of the nightly diary is parried successfully in the daytime by the two boys. In the endless verbal give-and-take which characterizes this—when all is said—happy family, the sons' talent for repartee more than matches the father's formidable wit.

It is the outside world that most frustrates Vašek. His work, like that of all his colleagues, is marked by utter futility. The bank clerks spend the office hours counting the money that belongs to the official circulation. Then they regularly purloin a portion of it for their unofficial uses, only to have it confiscated by the policemen who routinely search them at the street door. The Central Bank serves as a Kafkaesque metaphor for the society, where "effects are absurdly cut away from their causes, and values are turned upside down." The great secret of the economy is what Vašek has classified as "the third circulation." No one knows what happens to the confiscated currency, which never returns into the official channel. Vašek's anxiety is fueled by a colleague who warns that the nation is about to be sucked into the whirlpool of crisis created by the mysterious circulation of money. "It is a maelstrom!", he shouts. Engineer Maelström, as he is instantly dubbed, is a strange old man kept at the bank because he knows the Lombard system of accounting, something as mythical now as the First Republic when it was in use. The ever-resourceful Vašek locates Maelström on the map of the real world, where it figures as Moskoeström. The connotation of Moscow, the abyss of destruction, is unavoidable in a novel written two years after the invasion. The violent resolution of Vašek's quest into the meaning of the mystery symbol, however, reaches deeper than the immediate context.

In a climax of terror which parallels the execution scene at the end of *The Trial,* Vašek is murdered in Maelström's suburban cottage. To dispatch his hero, Vaculík uses the mechanism of the duel in place of Kafka's ritualistic immolation. The identity of the monstrous foe remains in doubt nonetheless, as in *The Trial.* There are really two foes, with the second, victorious opponent materializing at the moment Vašek sinks his knife into the belly of his original target. This doubling is the essence of the horror. It blurs the categories of murderer and murdered and equalizes the labels variously applied to the nightmarish combatants: man, monster, assassin.

After the liquidation of the father figure, the narrative closes with the image of the remaining family. The intimate circle made up of mother, two boys, and two new pets seems alive with comic possibilities. The sacrifice of Abraham in place of Isaac has cleaned the air. It is a fittingly irreverent resolution for a novel that has been laughing at man's pretension of playing God. The feeling that lingers is best summed up in the words of Max Brod, reacting to a stage adaptation of *Schweik.* "Is man good?" the Prague Jew asked, and the Czech fool prompted, "No, that sounds improbable. . . . Man is indestructible." (pp. 14-17)

> *Maria Němcová Banerjee, "Czech Laughter between Hašek and Kafka," in* World Literature Today, *Vol. 59, No. 1, Winter, 1985, pp. 14-17.*

SLOVAK LITERATURE

František Vnuk

[*In the following essay, Vnuk surveys literature written by exiled Slovak authors from 1945 to 1965.*]

A nation with such a tormented past as the Slovak nation will always have an exiled and a self-exiled minority among which the men of letters will form the most noticeable group. In the days of the Counter-Reformation, for example, there were some well-known writers among the Protestant émigrés. Forcible suppression of the rising Slovak nationalism in pre-1918 Hungary, coupled with economic misery, caused extensive migration of the Slovak population, especially to the United States. The most distinguished migrant-writer of the period was Martin Kukučín (in South America), while, in the United States, there lived several other noted authors (Bielik, Maršall-Petrovský, etc.). During the Second World War, some more literary personalities chose to live in exile (G. Vámoš, J. Slávik-Neresnický, V. Clementis-Hron, T. Herkel-Florin, and V. Szatmáry-Vlčková but—apart from Florin (who published two small volumes of poetry)— they did not show many signs of literary creativeness.

The end of war in 1945 spelled disaster for Slovak literature at home and ushered in an era of Slovak exile literature on a massive scale. To escape the advancing Red Army, some 3,000 Slovak intellectuals, with their families, sought refuge in the West. Among them were many of the best-known Slovak poets (A. Žarnov, R. Dilong, K. Strmeň), prose writers (M. Urban, J. C. Hronský, T. J. Gašpar), and literary critics and historians (J. Ambruš, J. E. Bor, S. Mečiar, J. Mešťančík). Their ranks swelled further when, after the Communist *coup* in 1948, more Slovaks fled to the West, including such literary figures as M. Žiar, G. Zvonický, and P. Hrtús-Jurina.

A writer-in-exile is an age-old phenomenon. Ovid, Dante, Hugo—to mention but a few—went through this experience and left us an artistic record of their feelings and sentiments. At one time, Paris was the capital city of Polish literature, and only recently, both Russian and German literature had their foremost representatives in exile (Bunin, Merezhkovskiy . . . Mann, Brecht . . .). On a modest scale, a similar situation befell Slovak literature after 1949, when the fury of Socialist realism paralysed all artistic creativity at home. With the forcible imposition of silence on such authors as E. B. Lukáč, V. Beniak, and J. Silan, the imprisonment of the old Communist writers (L. Novomeský, I. Horváth), and the severe censure of the younger ones (V. Mináč, D. Tatarka), literary life in Slovakia came to a standstill. Those years were remorsefully called, after the Twelfth Party Congress, "barren" or "lost" by the Communists themselves. It is thanks to the Slovak writers in exile that they were not completely lost or entirely barren. The fifty-odd Slovak men of letters living on this side of the Iron Curtain kept the lights of Slovak culture burning when they had been extinguished in the writers' native country. This may sound emotional or sentimental, yet it is a sad truth that in the years 1950-55, there appeared in Slovakia hardly a single book worth rereading. In those years, indeed, émigré literature was *the* contemporary Slovak literature.

The productivity of the Slovak exile writers does not match the number of books published at home. It exceeds the domestic production in quality, however, possessing those attributes of artistic works which are so destructive-

Ivan Klíma.

ly absent from a literature with its function defined, its themes prescribed, its style predetermined, its production quotas planned and fulfilled.

This does not mean that the Slovak writer in exile had smooth sailing. The fact is that here, also, many a writer was passing through a minor or even major crisis of his own, and for some of them, the obstructions were nearly insurmountable. Torn from their natural habitat and thrown into the hard and inhospitable life of exile, the Slovak writers recovered only slowly, perhaps never completely. Being too much the true sons of their own nation, they failed, as a rule, to strike roots in new surroundings. Continuously mindful of the foreign environment and longing for their native enslaved country, they excelled chiefly at expressing the nostalgia and melancholy which are ever-present in their work.

The concept of the writer as the conscience of his nation which was so often (and justly) applied to the Slovak writers of the past was revived very quickly among the exile writers. They, too, saw themselves in this noble role, and as the voice of a silenced and oppressed people, they went on registering their agonized sighs, protests, and bitter complaints. This is reflected in one of the first poems written in exile, by an anonymous author. (The poem is a paraphrase of T. Milkin's famous hymn of thanksgiving, which was set to music by M. Schneider-Trnavský and was subsequently sung in churches as a national anthem.)

Bože, ráč zhliadnuť na slovenský ľud svoj,
pod bičom krivdy ako zasa hynie:

doma i v svete octovsky pri ňom stoj,
v súžení svojom ked sa k Tebe vinie.
K modlitbe vrúcnej spínajú sa dlane:
Dedičstvo otcov zachovaj nám, Pane!

(O God, be pleased to look down on your Slovak nation as it lies prostrate again under the whip of injustice:
As a kind Father, stand at the side of those at home and those in exile
when they in their suffering are seeking your protection.
They lift their hands in fervent prayer:
O Lord, preserve the spiritual inheritance of our fathers!)

In the first postwar years (1945-48), Rome was the centre and, as it were, the rallying point for the exiled Slovak writers. But their exodus was not to finish there. It was followed by a diaspora: some emigrated to the United States, others to the Argentine, Canada, Australia, Germany, etc. In January 1956, they founded their organization, "Spolok slovenských spisovateľov a umelcov" (The Association of Slovak Writers and Artists), and the quarterly, *Most* (*The Bridge*), became their official organ, published in Cleveland, Ohio. This journal, appearing since 1954 under the able editorship of M. Šprinc, became the principal forum of Slovak writers and intellectuals and a reliable chronicle of the cultural life among the Slovak emigrés of the last decade. Other writers (J. Slávik, F. Mikula, M. Zlámal, etc.) were active members of the Czechoslovak Society of Arts and Sciences in America ("Spoločnosť pre vedy a umenie") and published their contributions in its quarterly, *Proměny* (*Transformations*). The Slovak writers also contributed in no small measure to the journals and papers established by the prewar Slovak emigrants in the United States, Canada, and elsewhere, or started numerous publishing ventures of their own. These last-named attempts, almost without exception, were usually of short duration.

By far the most significant literary activity occurred in the field of poetry. Emigré poetry—especially lyrical poetry—mirrors with seismographic accuracy the reactions of the poet's sensitive heart, both to the events at home and to the happenings in his new, strange, and often cold surroundings.

The Nestor of the Slovak émigré writers is Miloš K. Mlynarovič (1887-). He migrated to the United States in 1914 as a young priest and spent most of his life in intense pastoral activity among the Slovak immigrants there. Though he wrote sporadically from his early years, it is only in the last two decades that his poems and prose works have appeared in book form. As a poet, Mlynarovič writes with Franciscan simplicity, his verse almost untouched by the fashionable poetic achievements of the present century. Religious zeal, charitable compassion for the downtrodden and humble, and captivating sincerity make him what, in one of his poems, he claims to be: "nový Eliáš" (a new Elias). His books of verse include *Boha hľadm (In Search of God)*, 1948, *Z ľudu-za ľud (From the People—For the People)*, 1956, *Dejiny srdca (Story of a Heart)*, 1964. In his prose, Mlynarovič is a writer of social protest, boldly revealing the hidden and festering wounds of modern society. His collection of short stories, *Borba s osudom (Struggle with Destiny)*, 1952, is interesting. His best novel is *Vtáčence vo víchrici* (*The Birds in a Maelstrom*), 1956.

Among the poets a prominent place is held by Karol Strmeň (1921-), now living in the United States. This promising poet and capable translator has matured in exile, widening his outlook and bringing new qualities into his poetry. His two books of verse show him to be a truly European poet of great sensitivity. The first collection, *Básne neprevrených* (*Poems of the Dispossessed*), 1948, still reflects the poet's personal sadness over his own and his nation's tragedy. *Strieborná legenda* (*The Silver Legend*), 1950, contains some of the most beautiful love poems in the Slovak language. In his recent book of poems, *Čakajú nivy jar* (*The Meadows Await the Spring*), 1963, he repeatedly displays an astounding skill and mastery of the Slovak word. Strmeň is also an outstanding translator from English, French, Spanish, Italian, German, and other languages. His new translation of Dante's *Inferno* (*Peklo*), 1965, bears eloquent testimony to his talent and ability.

Rudolf Dilong (1905-) is a Franciscan friar who in 1965 moved from the Argentine to the United States where he is editor of the popular religious magazine, *Listy sv. Františka* (*Leaflets of St. Francis*). He is one of the most prolific writers of the Slovak diaspora (ten publications, to date). The centre of gravity of his work is in poetry, but he also writes prose works and plays. Dilong is a very versatile poet, but the wide scope of his activity is often at the expense of depth (though one must say that what is good—especially in his poetry—is very good). Noteworthy among his volumes are: a novel, *Pieseň lásky* (*The Song of Love*), 1953, another novel—partly autobiographical—*Bez matky* (*Without a Mother*), 1955, a collection of religious legends, *Golgota* (*Golgotha*), 1956, and several books of poems, *Balady* (*Ballads*), 1953, *Za svetlom* (*In the Pursuit of Light*), 1954, *Na vrchu nádejí* (*On the Crest of Hope*), 1955 and *Dotyk s večnost'ou* (*Contact with Eternity*), 1961.

Mikuláš Šprinc (1914-), the secretary of the Slovak Writers Association and the editor of its organ, *Most*, was known before 1945 mainly as a translator of Papini, Rilke, and other Western authors of the Catholic Revival. In 1949, he surprised his reading public with an unusual and most readable account of his Odyssey to the United States, *K slobodným pobrežiam* (*To the Coasts of Freedom*). His poetry bears unmistakable influences of the Spanish, French, and Italian poets, culture and scenery. His verse is at its best in *Vinohrad* (*Vineyard*), 1950, written partly in Italy. Other notable products of Šprinc's many-sided activity are: collections of poems, *Tvárou proti slnku* (*Face Towards the Sun*), 1956, *Z poludnia a polnoci* (*From South and from North*), 1960, *Mladost' orla* (*Eagle's Youth*), 1962; lyrical religious meditations, *Matka krásneho milovania* (*Mother of Fair Love*), 1954; translations from G. Papini, etc.

Andrej Žarnov (the pen-name of František Šubík, 1903-) is one of the best-known Slovak poets of intense nationalist sentiment. A doctor by profession, he now lives in the United States where he settled in 1952. His literary output is not very large, yet one of his poems, *Slovenský žial'* (*Slovak Sorrow*), 1954, represents émigré poetry at its best. In a terse, elegiac tune, he expressed poetically a most powerful lamentation over the sorrowful Slovak present. Recently, Žarnov transcribed and adapted a number of poems by J. Hollý (originally written in the West Slovak dialect, one hundred and fifty years ago) and published them under the title, *Hlas matky Tatry* (*The Voice of Mother Tatra*), 1963.

Gorazd Zvonický (the pen-name of Andrej Šándor, 1913-) is a priest of the Salesian order who survived the Communist closing of monasteries in Slovakia and subsequently escaped. He typifies, perhaps most strikingly, the emotions of an emigrant for whom there is no substitute for his native land. His book of verse, *S ukazovákom na mraku* (*Index-Finger on the Cloud*), 1958 is a passionate outburst of protest, accusation, and pleas for the Lord's vengeance. His other works of poetry include: *Prebúdza sa zem* (*The Awakening Earth*), 1964, and *Na jubilejné víno* (*The Wine for Jubilee Celebrations*), 1965. He lives in Italy.

Marián Žiar (the pen-name of Imrich Kružliak, 1914-), a highly articulate poet, lives in Germany. His poems appear mainly in *Most* and bear witness to an alert eye for the contemporary literary scene in the West. But Žiar is also a keen and sympathetic observer of literary events behind the Iron Curtain. He has published translations of East European poetry of the post-Stalinist thaw, *Podaj nám ruku, Europa!* (*Grasp our Hand, Europe*), 1956. In 1955, he edited *Modlitby a putách* (*Prayers of Those in Chains*), a most remarkable and deeply touching collection of poems of anonymous prisoners of the Communist régime.

Other poets whose contributions occasionally appear (or used to appear) in the Slovak press abroad are: Ján Okál', author of a small volume of poems, *Kronika Slovákov* (*Chronicle of the Slovaks*), 1954, and of a satirical novel, *Blíženci* (*Gemini*), 1962; Jozef Varínsky, author of *Krvavé roráty* (*Bloody Rorate-Mass*), 1961; Miloslav Zlámal, author of *Zpěvy z modrých hor* (*Songs from the Blue Mountains*), 1964; Dominik Valko, L'udo Bešeňovský, Cyril Ondruš, Maruša Jusková, Jožo Zvonár-Tieň, Ján Doránsky, Fero Zobor, Jozef Vágovič, Jozef Dragoš-Alžbetínčan, Andrej Gemerský, Ján Vetva, L. Šebesta, M. Chudoba, A. Brázda, and others.

Among prose writers, the most outstanding artist was Jozef Cíger-Hronský (1896-1960), an incomparable master of the Slovak language. His profound knowledge of the psyche of the Slovak "little man" enabled him to depict the complex pattern of Slovak village life with unique and inimitable artistry. In exile, in addition to a number of short stories, he wrote a historical novel, *Andreas Búr, majster* (*Magister Andreas Bur*), 1948. His most ambitious project, a novel, *Svet na Trasovisku* (*The Little World at Trasovisko*), 1960, did not reach the standard of his best pre-1945 writings. The novel deals with the memorable and dramatic events of the last months of the war immediately before the author's escape from Slovakia. As the testimony of a refugee writer, the novel has both artistic and social value.

Juraj Slávik (1890-) returned to literary activity after 1948, having resigned his post as Czechoslovak Ambassador to the United States (in protest against the Communist *coup* of February 1948). In 1952, he started the serialized publication, in *Newyorský denník* (*The New York Daily*), of his memoirs; the first volume *Detstvo, chlapectvo, mládenectvo* (*Infancy, Boyhood, Youth*), appeared in book form in 1955. It is a delightful series of personal reminiscences of persons, events, and places, narrated in a simple, unassuming style. The book contains many passages of lyrical beauty, betraying the author's earlier poetic career (in his youth, Slávik used to write poetry under the pseudonym of Neresnický).

Pavol Hrtús-Jurina (1919-) started as an author of very great promise. Since his emigration to Australia in 1949 these expectations have been only partly realized. He has published a few short stories of imaginative vividness and rich lyrical undertones. In his most recent book, *Z reči do reči* (*Heart-to-Heart Talks,* 1964, he gives lively literary interpretations of the first experiences of the Slovak settlers who migrated to Australia in the 1920's.

Draga Divínska (the pen-name of Draga Paučová, 1922-) wrote a number of short stories in which she displayed delicate sensitivity and a keen talent for observation. Her stories have true feminine freshness and show signs of her search for an expressive individuality.

Norin (the pen-name of Juraj Cíger) published his first and, so far, only novel, *Tri stoličky* (*Three Chairs*), 1947, followed by a few humorous stories. Then he withdrew into silence.

Among other writers of prose one could mention Michal Gerdelán, author of a novel, *Kráľ otrokov* (*The King of Slaves*), 1962; Rudolf Kalenčík, who wrote a satirical novel, *Doktor Šáša* (*Doctor Šáša*), 1964, Jozef Detvan, author of *Osudy jedného z nás* (*Fortunes of One of Us*), 1963; Ján Dafčík, Felix Mikula, Teodóra Rjachinová, Marián Dafčík, Andrej Kalnik, and others.

Certain Slovak writers considered their personal experiences sufficiently interesting for English readers, and drew on their eventful past as authors or coauthors of several semi-documentary books in English. Since they are not written in Slovak, these books are not strictly within the scope of our topic but one should mention at least these writers: Sister Cecilia Baráth, L. M. Telepun, L. Lahola, S. Ilok, and J. Paučo. J. Paučo's two books were later published in Slovak (*Unconquerables,* 1958—*Neporaziteľní,* 1961; *Flight to Wonderland,* 1963—*Na úteku,* 1965).

There is no significant accomplishment among the dramatic pieces written by Slovak émigré playwrights. Dramatic works which originated in exile reflect most plainly the emigrants' obsession with nostalgia for the past. Even Milan Novák (the pen-name of K. Strmeň), in his dramatic attempt, *Krvavý kríž* (*Cross of Blood*), 1950, turned out a languishing melodrama.

Ján Doránsky (1911-), now living in Canada, wrote several plays, of which the most successful, *Stará mat', neopúšťajte nás!* (*Grandmother, Do Not Leave Us Alone!*) 1956, was staged by various Slovak dramatic societies in Canada, Argentina, and the United States, J. Zvonár-Tieň published, in Canada in 1956, his drama in Alexandrine verse, *Ohne* (*Flames*), which was originally written in 1942 and which deals with incidents of the revolutionary years 1848-49.

Some writers tried to revive in their dramas the remote history of the ninth century, when Slovakia was the setting for glorious and fondly-remembered historical events. Thus, Cyril Ondruš wrote a play in 1956 named after a celebrated ruler of the Great Moravian kingdom, *Rastislav;* and Rudolf Dilong called his dramatic experiment after a Slovak disciple of Sts. Cyril and Methodius, *Gorazd* (1963).

Other playwrights among the émigré authors include J. Martinec (*Pašeráci slobody—The Smugglers of Freedom,* 1957), M. Dafčík (*A hviezdy zhasli—The Light of the Stars Faded Out,* 1956), and M. Veleš (the pen-name of K. Čulen).

Slovak exile literature is somewhat deficient in workers engaged in the literary "sciences" (criticism, theory, history). It is true that the conditions for this kind of work are most unfavourable, and even those few who are thus active often deal with problems remote from the realities of the exile literary life. Stanislav Mečiar wrote a two-volume treatise on M. Kukučín (*Kukučín živý—Living Kukučín,* 1960), J. E. Bor is the author of several monographs on both well- and lesser-known Slovak writers (e.g., Mlynarovič, Dilong, Zelenka). Among the writers of articles and studies in literary history and criticism, one may also name Ján Mešťančík, Imrich Kružliak, Jozef Kirschbaum, and others.

Such, in brief outline, is the picture of Slovak literature in exile during the two decades from 1945 to 1965. Its achievements, if measured by the amount published, may not look very impressive. But when measured against the heavy odds it has had to overcome, these accomplishments will have an honourable and lasting place in future histories of Slovak literature. (pp. 869-78)

> *František Vnuk, "Slovak Exile Literature," in* Czechoslovakia Past and Present: Political, International, Social, and Economic Aspects, *Vol. I, edited by Miloslav Rechcigl, Jr., Mouton, 1968, pp. 869-78.*

Antonín Měšťan

[In the following excerpt, Měšťan discusses Slovak poetry, fiction, and drama, focusing on works written from the end of World War II through the early 1970s.]

Nineteenth-century Slovak literature performed many of the same extra-literary functions as did Czech literature. But conditions in Hungary, of which Slovakia was then a region, were much less favorable than in Austrian-controlled Bohemia and Moravia, and this oppression impeded the development of Slovak literature. After Bohemia, Moravia, and Slovakia were united into the new nation of Czechoslovakia in 1918, Slovak literature rapidly began to catch up with the Czech lead.

Toward the end of the nineteenth century, Slovak writers, like Czech writers, became more interested in literature as an art form; the establishment of the state of Czechoslovakia in 1918 held out the promise to Slovak writers, as it did to Czech writers, that they could now leave literature's paraesthetic functions to other institutions of the state. But Slovak writers realized quite soon after World War I that circumstances demanded that they write politically committed works. A special incentive in Slovakia for committed literature was a resentment of Czech domination in national politics and a need to assert their own—Slovak—identity.

When Hitler annexed Bohemia and Moravia in 1939, he created a nominally independent state of Slovakia; and the Nazis did not directly influence Slovak cultural life until 1944. Thus, during the war Slovak literature enjoyed better conditions for development than did Czech literature. The activity of the surrealists had special significance, because it was interpreted by the Slovak people as democratic opposition to the German-sponsored fascist regime. Between 1945 and 1948, Slovak writers shared with their Czech counterparts the same enthusiasm and the same illusions, and surrealism still dominated Slovak literature. The communist takeover in 1948 brought quick disenchantment in Slovakia. The situation was aggravated by the return of centralizing pressure from Prague. Dissatisfaction with the state of affairs in public life and with the enforced socialist realism in art imposed from above became even more intense in Slovakia than it did in Bohemia and Moravia, but the dissatisfaction could not express itself to any extent in literature.

After a brief period of relaxation after Stalin's death, Slovaks were disillusioned by the renewed repressions following the Hungarian revolution and by the anti-Slovak policy of Novotný and his cohorts, despite the fact that some Slovaks exerted considerable influence in the national government. The tension over the anti-Slovak attitudes began to be aired about 1963, especially in Slovak literary journals. From 1963 to 1967 Slovak writers spearheaded the resistance to Novotný, making headway against dogma much sooner than the Czechs. Yet what they preached most of all was the legitimacy of Slovakia's ethnic interests. Only secondarily did they stress the need for a general democratization in public life.

Slovak nationalism was also apparent during the "Prague spring" of 1968. Until today, it has not become clear why the Slovak writers failed to take an active part in the historic Fourth Congress of the Czechoslovak Writers' Association in June, 1967, in which decisive struggle against Novotný was embarked upon.

Today the west is the home for émigré Slovak writers, both those who left during the 1940s and those who left after 1968. Slovak literature in exile, however, is not particularly rich. Some of the émigré writers, such as Ladislav Mňačko (born 1919) now publish almost exclusively in languages other than Slovak.

Unlike Czech poets, the most important Slovak lyric poets did not become politically committed during the period 1945-48. The surrealists, the most outstanding Slovak

Poster in Prague of Václav Havel, president-elect in 1989 of the democratic Czecho-Slovak Federal Republic.

poets, continued to go their own way. Consequently, when Slovak surrealists after 1948 joined in panegyrics to Stalin, industrial production, and the collectivization of agriculture, the rupture with the past was much more striking than in Czech literature. It was not until 1960, and even more conspicuously after 1963, that Slovak poetry returned to its pre-1948 voice.

Štefan Žáry (born 1918), one of the most talented Slovak surrealists, was, like so many of his colleagues, influenced by the great Czech poet Vítězslav Nezval. Also fluent in French and Spanish poetry, loyal to his own poetic origins, and maintaining his surrealistic idiom, Žáry wrote in an antimilitaristic, humanist vein in his first postwar collections—*Pavúk pútnik* (1946, *The Wandering Spider*) and *Zasl'úbená zem* (1947, *The Promised Land*). But in 1948 he glorified the Slovak heroes of the nineteenth and twentieth centuries in his *Meč a vavrín* (*Sword and Laurels*), using the verse forms of Slovak folk poetry and the Slovak romantics.

Žáry's collection *Cesta* (1952, *The Road*) linked him with those writers who endeavored to comply with the demands of socialist realism without suppressing their own creativity. But in 1960 he returned much more thoroughly to his earlier poetic goals. *Zázračný triezvy koráb* (*The Magic Sober Ship*) and *Ikar večne živý* (*The Immortal Ica-*

rus) contained poems in which he soared freely over the philosophical and human problems of space flights.

Another surrealist, Pavel Bunčák (born 1915), published in 1946 the collection *S tebou a sám* (*With You and Alone*), one of the major works of postwar Slovak surrealism. Since *Zomierat' zakázané* (1948, *Dying Is Forbidden*) he has been writing dull, dutifully optimistic works. His interest in Polish poetry and his translations from Polish were the sole evidence for many years that Bunčák was not dead as a poet. But *Prostá reč* (1963, *Simple Speech*) signified a turning point in that it gave evidence of his renewed creative power.

Ján Rak's (1915-1969) postwar poetry followed a path similar to that of so many Slovak surrealists. In his first postwar works—*Nezanechajte nádeje* (1946, *Don't Give Up Hope*) and *V údolí slnka* (1946, *In the Valley of the Sun*)—he was still writing surrealistic poems. But the title of his next work, *Pieseň mierových rúk* (1949, *Song of the Hands of Peace*), indicated that after 1948 he switched to political poetry. Not until the poems in *Plenér* (1962, *In the Open*), which could be called impressionistic, was there an indication that Rak had veered in a new direction. The poems collected in *Poslední gladiátori* (1970, *The Last Gladiators*), which appeared only after his death, showed very clearly that he, too, wished to return to his poetic beginnings.

Vladimír Reisel (born 1919), a prominent theorist and champion of surrealism, was still developing his own definition of surrealism in 1946, in the poems in *Zrkadlo a za zrkadlom* (*The Mirror and Behind It*). After 1948 he, like so many others, abandoned his predilections, and his collection *Svet bez pánov* (1951, *The World without Masters*) contained pallid poems. He lost his leadership without gaining favor with the official critics. Only gradually did his poetry regain resonance and color. Since his collection *More bez odlivu* (1960, *The Tideless Sea*) he has taken his place once more among major Slovak poets. Love has been the central theme of Reisel's more recent works: *Láska na posledný pohl'ad* (1964, *Love at Last Sight*) and *Smutné rozkoše* (1966, *Melancholy Rapture*). In them his poetic talent was again evident.

Laco Novomeský (born 1904), before the war an avantgarde poet, a communist journalist and politician, for a long time published nothing after the war except the collection *Pašovanou ceruzkou* (1948, *With a Smuggled Pencil*), which he had written during the war. His prewar work was influenced by Nezval, Mayakovski, and Yesenin. His experience as an important cultural organizer and a politician seemed to assure him great authority and influence after the war. He was indeed active in various party and state offices after 1945, but during the period in which the party line hardened, he was condemned as a nationalist and imprisoned. For a time after his release, he was forbidden from partaking in political activity. Not until 1963 could he publish his long poem *Vila Tereza* (*Villa Tereza*), in which he described his ties with the Soviet Union. In *Stamodtial, a iné* (1964, *From Yonder, and Other Poems*) he wrote about his experiences after 1945. In recent years Novomeský has again become politically active in Slovakia.

Ján Kostra's (born 1910) first postwar collection, *Presila smútku* (1946, *The Overwhelming Sorrow*), reminiscent of Czech proletarian poetry of the 1920s, was followed by the poem *Na Stalina* (1949, *On Stalin*). But by 1953, in *Javorový list* (*Maple Leaf*), Kostra was once again writing pure poetry. He showed considerable virtuosity by his translations of Nezval, Hrubín, and Baudelaire, as well as by his later original works: *Šípky a slnečnice* (1958, *Hedge Roses and Sunflowers*) and *Báseň, dielo tvoje* (1960, *The Poem, Your Work*). In recent years he has devoted himself to eternal themes of poetry—love and friendship—as can be seen in *Len raz* (1968, *Only Once*).

Andrej Plávka (born 1907), a conservative in art, has linked himself consciously to the Slovak poets of the nineteenth century. His first book of poetry, *Ohne na horách* (1947, *Fire on the Peaks*), took as its subject the Slovak uprising of 1944. For a while he wrote party propaganda, an example of which is *Sláva života* (1955, *The Glory of Life*). His later works, such as *Korene* (1965, *Roots*), are far more appealing, but he still continued to use poetic techniques of the past.

A number of poets after 1948 considered the artist's mission that of political agitation. Pavol Horov (born 1914) attempted to write propagandistic poetry in *Slnce nad námi* (1954, *The Sun above Us*). Then there was a striking change in his work. His volumes of poetry *Vysoké letné nebo* (1960, *The High Sky of Summer*) and *Koráby z Janova* (1966, *The Ships from Genoa*) revealed a reflective poetry with a touch of sentimentality akin to his mature writing during World War II.

Those Slovak poets who entered literary life shortly after 1945 shared the dilemma of their Czech contemporaries. Between 1945 and 1948 the young writers, fascinated by Slovak surrealism, were only just beginning to find their poetic voices. But after 1948 they had to conform for a number of years to the prescriptions of socialist realism if they wished to see their works in print. Some of the younger writers themselves believed in the value of socialist realism. Among them was Milan Lajčiak (born 1926), a party official and diplomat, who pleased the officials of the party more than he did his readers with his first book, *Súdružka moja zem* (1949, *My Comrade, My Country*). He published similar poetic products in rapid succession. His collection *Kniha istoty* (1960, *Book of Certainty*) made it clear that the political and cultural thaws in Czechoslovakia since Stalin's death had affected him little.

The poems of Vojtech Mihálik's (born 1926) first book, *Anjeli* (1947, *The Angels*), were in the spirit of Christian humanism. But *Plebejská košel'a* (1950, *Plebeian's Shirt*) showed a radical change. He wrote many poems devoted to the "building of socialism." Later, however, Mihálik turned to other themes and showed himself to be a very competent craftsman, especially in *Útek za Orfeom* (1965, *Flight after Orpheus*). At the end of August, 1968, he attacked the Soviet Union vigorously in the poem *Rekviem* (*Requiem*), but in 1969, in *Čierna jeseň* (*Black Autumn*), he took a stand against the ideas of democratization that were gaining such force in 1968. Mihálik has been very active politically since 1969; at present he is chairman of a chamber of the Czechoslovak Parliament.

The writers who have come to the fore since around 1960 have had it much easier because of the retreat during the 1950s from the extremes of dogmatism. Miroslav Válek (born 1929) elicited astonishment with his surprisingly mature collection *Dotyky* (1959, *Touches*), which was rapidly followed by other equally accomplished works. His poetry was quickly appreciated by the young and found many imitators. Válek has avoided false pathos, but traces of sorrow and fear of the unknown, instead of the false optimism required by the official line, can be found in his poems. He later became an official in the Slovak Writers' Association. Today he is the Slovak minister of culture.

Slovak writers of fiction, like their Czech counterparts and those of other eastern-bloc nations, were more disturbed by the developments after 1948 than the poets were. There was an additional hindrance in Slovakia: Hungarian tyranny during the nineteenth century prevented the complete unfolding of critical realism in fiction. Because it came so late to Slovakia, critical realism dominated fiction well into the twentieth century, even after 1945. After 1948 novelists shifted to the "higher plane" of socialist realism. Many long-winded works were written during the early years of communist rule, among which were a number of trilogies (most of which were never completed) in the leisurely tradition of the nineteenth century. Few of these works succeeded in achieving more than superficial descriptions. The representative writers of the early postwar years were Peter Jilemnický (1901-1949) and Fraňo Kráľ (1903-1955).

Peter Jilemnický, an early communist, began his writing career in his native Czech, but, after becoming a teacher in Slovakia he published only in Slovak. Even before the war he had been an uncompromising champion of socialist realism, to which his stay of two years in the Soviet Union contributed. His novel *Kronika* (1947, *Chronicles*) described the anti-German uprising in Slovakia in August, 1944, in which, however, Jilemnický had not taken part because he was in a concentration camp. He pictured the communists as the chief organizers of the uprisings, and his glorification of the communists became adopted as canon in other works about the uprising.

Fraňo Kráľ became a high party official after 1945. In his novel *Za krajší život* (1949, *Toward a Better Life*) he offered an autobiographical account of the life of a party official. In his last novel, *Bude ako nebolo* (1950, *It Will Be As It Has Not Been*), he wrote the typical tedious story of the "building of socialism." For a number of years this work was prescribed to young Slovak writers as the model they had to copy in dealing with contemporary problems. Slowly, however, both Jilemnický and Kráľ lost their binding power on Slovak novelists.

The first novel of František Hečko (1905-1960), *Červené víno* (1948, *Red Wine*), about life in a tiny wine-growing village in western Slovakia, was written completely in the objective spirit of critical realism. But in his second novel, *Drevená dedina* (1951, *The Wooden Village*), whose theme was the collectivization of agriculture in northern Slovakia, Hečko attempted to meet all requirements of socialist realism. Only his storytelling talent saved this work from oblivion. Hečko planned a trilogy of novels about life in

Slovakia during World War II, but he died soon after finishing the first part, *Svätá tma* (1958, *Sacred Darkness*), in which he criticized sharply, from the communist viewpoint, the Nazi-supported Tiso regime that ruled "independent" Slovakia during the war.

The writing career of Rudolf Jašík (1919-1960) lasted only five years. In his first novel, *Na brehu priezračnej rieky* (1956, *On the Bank of a Clear Stream*), he described life in one of the most impoverished regions of Slovakia before 1939. The novel *Námestie svätej Alžbety* (1958, *St. Elizabeth's Square*), about the love of a Slovak man for a Jewish girl during the war, was one of the most widely read books of its day. *Mŕtvi nespievajú* (1961, *The Dead Don't Sing*), about the fate of Slovak soldiers fighting against the Soviet Union, was unfinished when Jašík died.

Dominik Tatarka (born 1913) has been one of the most individual Slovak writers. His novel *Farská republika* (1948, *The Republic of Priests*), about the church-dominated fascist state in Slovakia, was a deeply penetrating psychological analysis of his people during World War II. Tatarka's works after 1950 were no longer marked by psychological analysis, an omission that did not exactly increase their worth. Yet, he was one of the first in Slovakia to criticize Stalinism, in the political satire *Démon súhlasu* (1956, *The Demon of Consent*). At first, the work was permitted to appear only in a magazine; it was not published as a book until 1963. Since then Tatarka has published well-balanced works of psychological depth, such as *Prútené kreslá* (1963, *The Wicker Armchair*), which described the atmosphere in Paris just before World War II.

Ladislav Mňačko was for a long time extolled by the communists as a writer to be emulated. After some completely unsuccessful poetic efforts and some too-obviously-plotted plays, he published a novel, *Smrť sa volá Engelchen* (1959, *Death Is Called Engelchen* [Little Angel]), about the battles of the Czech and Slovak partisans on the border of Moravia and Slovakia during the closing phases of World War II. During the less restrictive atmosphere of the early 1960s, Mňačko wrote *Oneskorené reportáže* (1963, *Belated Reportage*), in which he condemned the methods of Stalinism. This work led to a rift with the Novotný group. After being deprived of his citizenship and living for a while in the west, Mňačko returned to Czechoslovakia and published the novel *Ako chutí moc* (1968, *How Power Tastes*), which had previously appeared in translation in the west. After the disastrous events of August, 1968, he went abroad again and wrote in German an attack against the Russian invasion in the novel *Die siebente Nacht* (1968, *The Seventh Night*). This work and another novel, *Vorgang* (1970, *An Occurrence*), could not be published in Slovakia. Mňačko's lively journalistic style, combined with a decided knack for sensationalism and publicity, has made him one of today's most widely known contemporary Czechoslovak writers.

Alfonz Bednár (born 1914), an accomplished translator from the English, surprised the public by publishing his own novel, *Sklený vrch* (1954, *The Glass Mountain*). At its appearance it caused a sensation; it was regarded as an attack on the tedious novels extolling production records. In succeeding works Bednár began to make cautious analyses of postwar developments. But it was not until 1968, in the short novel *Balkón bol privysoko* (*The Balcony Was Too High*), that he more openly criticized the postwar period, especially the manipulation of the whole society. More recently, he has turned in part to surrealism.

The writer who won perhaps the greatest popularity during the relaxation of the political atmosphere after 1963 was Ladislav Ťažký (born 1921). After some works that attracted little attention he published the novel *Amenmária* (1964, *Mother of God!*), which can be described as a story of the fate of the Slovaks during World War II, especially of Slovak soldiers in the Soviet Union. In his later works Ťažký has continued to focus on World War II, as in the novel *Pivnica plná vlkov* (1969, *Cellar Full of Wolves*), which described the life of Slovak peasants during the war and after 1945. Ťažký has tried to open up the techniques of realistic narration and has also experimented with language itself.

Slovak poetry, and to some extent also Slovak fiction, underwent exciting growth after the founding of the state of Czechoslovakia in 1918. But this was not true of the drama. Before 1918 there was practically no professional theater in Slovakia. The consequences of this have not yet been overcome. After World War II the older Slovak playwrights wrote practically nothing. After 1948 the Slovak stage presented, in addition to works of non-Slovak playwrights, a few new plays by its own writers; only the titles of these works are remembered today.

The only Slovak playwright who has won wider than local recognition is Peter Karvaš (born 1920). His sharp criticism of the Slovak petty bourgeoisie and its conduct during the war, as revealed in *Polnočná omša* (1959, *Midnight Mass*), brought his work to the attention of readers abroad. Karvaš showed himself to be a perceptive psychologist in *Antigona a tí druhí* (1962, *Antigone and the Others*), a play he wrote in a concentration camp during the war. His play *Jizva* (1963, *The Scar*) caused an international sensation; it was the first play in Slovakia to picture the persecution of innocent people after the communist takeover. Karvaš is also a fine writer of fiction, as he demonstrated in the stories in *Nedokončená pre detský hlas* (1968, *The Unfinished for a Child's Voice*).

In recent years little theaters have sprung up in Slovakia, especially in Bratislava, on the pattern of those in Prague. Suffering from the lack of original Slovak works, the repertory of such theaters as the Divadlo na Korze (Theater on the Boulevard) in Bratislava consists predominantly of foreign plays. The interesting cabaret theater called Tatra-Revue in Bratislava was closed down in February, 1970, for political reasons—just one more example of the dominance of politics over literature in Czechoslovakia since 1948. (pp. 146-53)

> Antonín Měšťan, "Czech and Slovak Literature," in World Literature since 1945: Critical Surveys of the Contemporary Literatures of Europe and the Americas, *edited by Ivar Ivask and Gero von Wilpert, Frederick Ungar Publishing Co., 1973, pp. 136-54.*

J. M. Kirschbaum

[*In the following excerpt, Kirschbaum discusses the influence of Communism on Slovak literature throughout the twentieth century.*]

The Soviet occupation of Slovakia affected the social and political structure of Slovak life more radically than political occupations and social changes used to do in the past. The totalitarian character of Communism affects all important sectors of national life, be it religion, philosophy, the arts, or literature.

Due to the peculiar circumstances under which the Slovak people were subjected to Communism, cultural life in Slovakia experienced probably the strongest impact of all the Soviet satellites. The reasons are many. First of all, the character of Slovak literature. . . . Slovak literature and Slovak culture had developed from the fall of Great Morava primarily under the Western influences. Literature in the Slovak vernacular had originated in the seventeenth century mainly in the classical climate of the Catholic University of Trnava, and with the exception of the Gothic period, we find in Slovak literature all the literary currents from Humanism through Baroque to Classicism, Romanticism, Realism, Catholic "moderne" and Surrealism. In fact, the classical reminiscences, the era of the Enlightenment and Romanticism gave birth to Slovak poetry and prose. Some of the Western influences appeared later, or lasted longer, or else their form was not pure—a phenomenon to be found in all Slavic literatures, with the exception of the Russian.

Western influences and the Western orientation of Slovak literature has been more evident in the content and in the mission that poetry and prose aimed to accomplish in the life of the Slovak people than in poetic and literary forms. Slovak poets and novelists, beginning with Ján Hollý in the eighteenth century, and the group around Ľudovít Štúr in the nineteenth century to Hviezdoslav, Vajanský, Rázus, Žarnov, Urban, Hronský, Beniak and other Slovak poets and writers in the twentieth century, saw the real function of Slovak literature primarily in equipping the Slovak people with the spiritual resources necessary for survival and the fight for freedom. They endeavoured to bring to the Slovak people an awareness of their spiritual and national individuality and fought for their political and social rights. Just as the poetry of Mickiewicz, Krasinski and Slowacki, "summoned the Poles from political enslavement to a spiritual life and revealed to them entirely new perspectives of moral responsibility resulting from the nation's political situation," so in the same way the Slovaks learned through the works of their poets and novelists to regard the national cause as a question of honour and as the supreme moral criterion around which the entire spiritual life of the nation was crystallized.

Slovak poets and novelists who regarded their mission from this perspective could not nourish any illusion about their fate under Communist rule. They knew that literature, as a means of expression of the national soul and as the most efficient instrument in reshaping the nation's patterns of thinking, would be the first cultural field to undergo substantial change. Furthermore, they knew that exiled Czech politicians returning with the Red Army would take revenge on all Slovaks who had claimed the right of self-determination for the Slovak people, and who had applied or advocated this when the occasion had presented itself.

Thousands of Slovak intellectuals, therefore, preferred exile with all its uncertainties and miseries to Czech and Communist rule. Among these emigré intellectuals were numerous writers and poets who had been the representatives of Slovak literature between the wars and who had made a name for themselves. There were, at the beginning, not only the two most popular novelists of the inter-war period, Milo Urban and J. C. Hronský, whose works were translated into several European languages, but also Andrej Žarnov, T. J. Gašpar, R. Dilong, M. Šprinc, K. Strmeň and many others. They all preferred exile to Communist rule and they have continued to write far from Slovakia, in Argentina, in the U.S.A., in Canada, in Australia, and elsewhere.

However, Slovak literature was not only affected by the departure of writers and poets into exile. Many poets and writers were also silenced. Within a decade of the inclusion of Slovakia within the Soviet orbit, literature in Slovakia went through some of the most peculiar transformations. Those Slovak novelists and poets who did not leave the country or choose silence, were abruptly compelled to adapt their literary creeds, forms and subjects to the new line of "Socialist Realism" and to an exclusively Eastern orientation. This happened against all Slovak literary traditions; for . . . the main characteristics of Slovak literature were patriotism, universalism, Pan-Slavism, and a deep religious spirit. The generation which followed Holly, namely, Ján Kollár and the group of L'. Štúr, had turned their eyes, as founders of nineteenth century Pan-Slavism, to Russia; but their literary works, education and philosophy were fundamentally Western. They were educated at German universities and, while Kollár's *Daughter of Sláva* was modelled on Dante and Petrarca, L'. Štúr and his group were under the influence of German Romanticism, having for masters in their philosophy Herder and Hegel. Kollár's idea of Slavic reciprocity refrained from any attempt to mould a political ideology. His philosophy was deeply humanistic: "He only is worthy of liberty who respects the liberty of others; he who forges the chains for others is himself a slave; when thou callest for a Slav, there must respond a man."

According to many foreign scholars, Slovakia can be considered as the classical country of the Slavic idea, with several conceptions of Pan-Slavism based on the equality of the Slavic peoples. However, an identification of the idea of a Slavic cooperation with Russophilism was rare; it appeared as a result of national and depression despair. Such was the case of L'. Štúr, for whom "Pan-Slavism in the political sense was a chimera," but who later, according to W. Lednicki, formulated about 1850 "the most complete and consistently-developed program for the subjugation of Slavs to Russia" in his book *Slavdom and the World of the Future.* Štúr had written his book in German in a period of national depression and despair, and the book never appeared in Slovak.

During the last decades of the nineteenth century and the

years before and during the first World War, Slovak literary and cultural life was dominated to some extent by Slovak Russophiles like S. H. Vajanský and Škultéty. However, this was merely an interlude. After the war, the influence of French, English and even Scandinavian writers, which was manifest among the younger poets and novelists (I. Krasko, V. Roy, P. O. Hviezdoslav, M. Rázus), firmly gained ground. The Russophile orientation in Slovak literature was chiefly due to the political situation following the Austro-Hungarian compromise of 1867, when the Slovaks were left at the mercy of the Magyar efforts at assimilation. As Slovak poets and novelists saw that the only hope for a Slovak national survival was in Russia's power, they gave full expression to this belief in their literary works. But they did not mean to exchange one oppression for another, and they were opposed to Communism.

The Bolshevik Revolution and the First World War changed this Russophilism. The Revolution destroyed the Panslavic and Russophile dreams of Slovak poets. The Western Powers and not Russia helped to fulfill the hopes for emancipation from Magyar rule by creating the Czecho-Slovak Republic. Even if Prague dominated Slovakia politically and economically, the Slovaks were left free to choose their own cultural orientation. They either turned again to the West or they used their own spiritual and moral traditions for creative inspiration. The general trend of Slovak literature in poetry as well as in prose was to broaden its range of interests and to become responsive to European literary currents. The main representatives of Slovak literature between the two Wars were uninterested in Soviet Russia, except for a small group of "proletarian" or left-wing poets and writers under Czech influence of whom only three or four acquired literary recognition. The older generation of Slovak poets, headed by P. O. Hviezdoslav, V. Roy, Ivan Krasko and Martin Rázus, continued to create in the traditional forms or used European literary forms and currents corresponding to their talents and creativeness. In prose, we find the realists Kukučín, Tajovský, T. Vansová, Timrava and L'. Podjavorinská.

The younger generation looked to foreign literatures for new forms. The really successful literary works of more than ephemeral value were, however, those which drew their motives from Slovak life, their inspiration from Slovak national traditions and their art from their own spiritual sources. Among the outstanding writers of this school are J. C. Hronský, Milo Urban, V. Beniak, J. Smrek, E. Boleslav Lukáč, A. Žarnov, Š. Krčméry, T. J. Gašpar, J. Hrušovský. Consciously or unconsciously they belonged both to the West, and to their country's social and ideological evolution. Their orientation was continental in form, in philosophy, and in motivation. All the European currents and literary schools, from Symbolism and Impressionism to Catholic Modernism (especially French) and Surrealism, characterized Slovak literature between the wars.

The Second World War did not substantially change the orientation of Slovak literature. Being an island of relative peace where until the fall of 1944, the German impact on cultural life was neither violent nor apparent, Slovakia experienced a strong literary and cultural development. Though after the War this period was depicted as oppressive for poets and writers, there is a lot of evidence to show that even known Communists (Novomeský, Poničan, Tatarka) freely published their works. The general trend of Slovak literature remained Western, nationalist, conservative and traditional. But with the "liberation" of the country, the shock of the Soviet impact was violent, spreading deep and wide throughout the literary and cultural life of Slovakia.

For the first three years after the restoration of Czecho-Slovakia Slovak poets and writers were waging a lost battle for a free literature. Those who believed the pronouncement of politicians about the building of a new, free democratic, humanistic and socially just Slovakia attempted not only to write according to their own artistic criteria and the dictates of their own conscience, but they also fought with the left-wing writers for freedom of expression in Slovak cultural life. Literary journals like *Verbum, Elán, Nová práca* and *Slovenské pohl'ady* bear witness to the courage as well as to the political naiveté of many Slovak writers and poets who did not leave Slovakia to go into exile.

In Slovak prose and even more significantly in the poetry of this period, one can clearly see two general trends; an attempt at continuing the literary tradition which had evolved in Slovakia under the West European influence, and the ruthless tendency of a handful of left-wing writers and critics to impose a revolutionary romanticism according to Zhdanov's Socialist Realism. Since the general mood in Slovakia was not pro-communist (as it became clear in the elections in 1946, in which the democratic forces won 62% of the votes) it was still possible to publish literary works in the Western tradition. In prose we find the novels by Margita Figuli (*Babylon*), J. Bodenek (*Kríž Profesora Munku*), J. Hrtús-Jurina (*Kameň na kameni*) F. Hečko (*Červené víno*) and others. In poetry, long-established poets like Ján Smrek, later silenced for many years, published a collection of lyrics *Studňa* (*The Well*) and poets of the Catholic "moderna," Ján Haranta, P. G. Hbina and Janko Silan made a bold attempt at keeping Slovak literary tradition alive. The ranks of established poets and writers seemed to be strengthened in poetry with the debut of Vojtech Mihálik (*Anjeli*) and in drama, with the writings of Peter Karvaš; but both succumbed later to the regimentation imposed by the Communist Party.

As a result, there were several literary trends in this period. The monthly *Elán,* edited for nearly two decades by the poet Ján Smrek, defended the principle that politics should not interfere in the arts and literature. Other writers spoke in favour of freedom of expression and a Christian *Weltanschauung* in *Verbum* and *Nová práca*. They used these outlets to fight against the falsification of Slovak literary history and for a free cultural orientation, stressing the role of moral forces against materialism in intellectual activities. At the same time, contributors to these journals opposed the tendency to isolate Slovak literature and Slovak cultural life in general from the West. The oldest and the most prestigious of Slovak literary journals, *Slovenské pohl'ady* however, began to waver in the struggle against the imposition of Marxist literary methods and criteria.

The main Slovak cultural institutions, like the *Matica slovenská, Spolok sv. Vojtecha, Slovenská Katolícka Akademia, Tranoscius* and *Slovenská Liga,* made the same efforts as literary and cultural journals. There was in all these institutions a strong revival of cultural activities which had been interrupted in the fall of 1944, first by Soviet partizan actions and a military uprising and then by the actions of Soviet military forces. Leading representatives of all these institutions also believed in the possibility of democratic fair-play on the part of the Communists, and they tried to pursue their cultural activities despite violent attacks by the Communist press. The value of the publications of these cultural institutions was even greater than before because the new régime had forbidden publication of students' periodicals and of the religious press, mainly Catholic, shortly after the end of the war.

The victory of the Marxist parties in Bohemia-Moravia in 1946 (42% of the vote) not only made all the efforts of Slovak writers and cultural institutions more difficult, but soon made it evident that they were fighting a losing battle. The Communists used all available means and methods to stifle the appeal of non-Communists. Some writers became frightened, whereas others joined the ranks of the Communists. When the Communist Party took over the country in February 1948 by a *coup d'etat,* those writers and poets who were not willing to adjust were silenced. Among them were not only the representatives of Catholic modernism including Valentin Beniak, but also the Protestant pastor, E. B. Lukáč, the poet of lyrical eroticism Ján Smrek, and many others.

After 1948, a small group of "proletarian" poets, surrealists and left-wing critics or novelists, headed by L. Novomeský, (who along with J. Rob-Poničan, was the only known poet of this group before 1945), took over Slovak literary and cultural life, and decided who would be allowed to continue as writer, poet, journalist or scientist and what kind of literature they would be allowed to create. If the writers wished to continue their work, they had to become members of the Writers' Association, which was organized on the Soviet model. Their main duties were to extirpate the "corrupting" influence of Western "bourgeois and Fascist" writers, and to follow the line of "the great Socialist Soviet literature inspired by the ideals brought to reality by Stalinism." The slogan was "progress," and the name of the new current was "Socialist Realism." Yet many of the main actors in this "revolutionary reshaping" of Slovak literature had been the former imitators of prewar French Surrealism (R. Fabry, V. Reisel, M. Mittelman). Soviet literature, "with its surpassing wealth of ideas, its burning socialist patriotism, its new humanism," was destined to be the highest ideal of Slovak literature.

This reshaping of Slovak cultural life was radical, and it was put into practice not only without regard for tradition, but also without those who had previously been the true representatives of Slovak literature. Neither the best novelist of the period 1918-1939, Milo Hurban (b. 1904) whose *Living Whip* was translated into several European languages, nor poets such as Valentin Beniak, Ján Smrek, E. B. Lukáč, and Andrej Žarnov, took part in the new trend. They preferred to be silent. (Žarnov, who was under constant threat of arrest and deportation and many times imprisoned; later he left his country). Tido J. Gašpar (b. 1893), author of splendid short novels and exotic tales, was also silenced in prison.

To understand the vast change brought about by this "re-shaping" of Slovak literature, we must remember that the "proletarian" poets, like the surrealists, were only a small group alien to Slovak literary traditions and spiritual atmosphere. For the most part, they grew up under the influence of Czech Marxist or Communist intellectuals and writers (J. Wolker, V. Nezval, J. Fučík, I. Sekanina). Their movement, with its journal *Dav,* originated in Prague. L. Novomeský, J. Poničan, D. Okáli, V. Clementis and others brought their revolutionary ideas and left-wing orientation into the Slovak puritan literary atmosphere as university students in the Czech capital. Poničan declared this proudly during the "Congress of National Culture" held in Prague in 1948. At the same time, however, he condemned "Czech cultural imperialism" and its tendency to assimilate the Slovaks. This latter policy, according to him, was the consistent aim of Prague's bourgeois régimes between the Wars.

During the twenties, the proletarian group had tried to transplant into Slovakia Communist literary aesthetics. They made appeals to break from traditional themes and forms, and they favoured collectivism rather than individualism, materialism instead of idealism. They often hurt the religious feelings of the population by their youthful revolt against God and Christian traditions. In the thirties the group had direct contact with Moscow (Novomeský attended the Congress of Writers in Moscow and Ilja Ehrenburg appeared in Bratislava), but it was still Prague whose Czech Marxist poets and intellectuals (around the journal *Tvorba*) ideologically nourished Slovak proletarian literature and prescribed its aesthetics.

After 1945, the group, strengthened by surrealists and young intellectuals reared during World War II, continued their revolt against individualism, subjectivism, art for art's sake, petty-bourgeois realism and clericalism. Their concept of "Socialist Realism," based on the philosophy of dialectical materialism, the Marx-Lenin-Stalinism theory of literature, a new approach to "reality" and the active participation in building a new Socialist society, was this time imposed by the political power of the Communist Party. In periodicals and in the daily press, the literary critics asked for conformity with Russian literature, condemned all "apolitical" approaches, and proudly declared that the struggle for socialism was a struggle for a new and true art.

As the Communist Party had unlimited control over all newspapers, periodicals and publishing firms and the exclusive right to permit or prohibit publication, traditional Slovak literature abruptly disappeared. Literary production was organized by the Party and its organs; literature was so planned as to obtain a rapid spiritual re-orientation, *i.e.,* sovietization and conformity with Russia as well as mental Russification.

Under such circumstances, Slovak literature was not only impoverished—it became an imitation of Soviet literature, rather than an expression of the Slovak soul. Filled with slogans and praise for Communism and its leaders, exaggerating social differences and struggling against religion and old traditions, "Socialist Realism" had little in common with real artistic values or true realism.

The sovietization of Slovakia brought with it a steadily-increasing flood of translations of Soviet books with the aim of sovietizing the literary life of Slovakia, not only in form but in spirit.

An analysis of books published . . . shows that at the end of 1953 and in the first month of 1954, forty-one translations of poetry and prose had been published in Slovakia. Twenty-two of those translations were from Russian literature, nineteen from all others. Modern Soviet writers were represented by sixteen works, the Russian classics by five. Of nineteen translations from non-Russian literature, thirteen works were written by Communists; the others, except for a translation of Ovid, are the works of Mark Twain, Maupassant, Bendel and others, depicting the moral decadence of Western society.

The picture is similar in the production of books for children and youth. Of forty-three books published in the same period (the end of 1953 and the beginning of 1954) twenty-one works were written by Slovak writers, eighteen by Russians and the rest by Czech, Hungarian and Rumanian authors. No Western writers were represented. Six Slovak original works and fourteen translations from Russian were pure propaganda.

Sovietization and mental Russification did not appear only in the number of translations from Russian and Soviet satellite languages. By the exclusion of Western literature, a sort of "cultural iron curtain' was built in Slovakia.

Under the heading "Marx-Leninism" one finds sixty-nine publications, twenty-five Slovak originals, thirty-eight translations from Russian, two from German (the works of Marx and Engels), one from Hungarian and one from Bulgarian. Though some Slovak intellectuals had mastered the Western languages, there was no translation from French, English or any other Western tongue.

If we consider that books translated from the Russian are published in tens of thousands and that they are sold at reduced prices, the picture is clear. Mental Russification and sovietization was promoted by every available method.

Following the theory given to Marxist philology by J. V. Stalin in his work *Marxism and Philological Questions* and *The Economic Problems of Socialism in the USSR* the new Slovak "working intelligentsia" not only changed the spirit, structure, and forms of literature but also reformed the language. Some of the changes effected by the Communists were proposed before and during World War II by Prof. H. Bartek, in order to simplify Slovak orthography. A gifted philologist and linguist, Bartek advocated his reforms on the grounds of scientific research and the evolution of the Slovak language. Consequently, not all the initial changes introduced by Marxist philologists can be regarded as harmful or unnecessary. Slovak exiles as well as the Slovak press in the free world basically accepted this reform. In the 1950's, however, there appeared harmful tendencies towards Russification and Czechization of the Slovak language under the pressure of Prague and Moscow. Stalinist cultural policy in Slovakia was, fortunately, later to be opposed by a majority of Slovak linguists and philologists. Just as Slovak intellectuals had been convinced in the past that the very existence of the nation depended upon the preservation of its language, and that national identity was bound up with language, so Marxist intellectuals became aware of the importance of the purity and preservation of the Slovak language. There has always been a kind of "sanctity of language" among the Slovaks. Applying a reform by referring to the rules laid down for Marxist philosophy by J. V. Stalin, therefore, could not but hurt the Slovaks in their most sensitive spot. Hence, the reform brought about a reaction against itself.

Very soon after the Communists took over the direction of cultural affairs in Slovakia and the potential opposition had either fled the country or been silenced, Slovak literary history also was re-examined. The first revaluation was made as early as 1948, when the Slovak Academy of Sciences and Arts, founded during the Slovak Republic, published a *History of Slovak Literature.* The author, Professor Andrej Mráz, had not been a Communist before the War. During the War he had published in German another history of Slovak literature. His new work mirrored in many respects the new situation in the cultural life of Slovakia.

Aware that the "Eastern orientation" of Slovakia's cultural life had been made a *fait accompli* by the Košice Programme (which clearly stated the Slavic, *i.e.* Russian orientation of Slovak culture), Mráz adapted his work to the new situation. He revised his previous judgment of writers and poets who were now in prisons or in exile, while "proletarian" and surrealist poets on the other hand became more talented, their novels and poetry of greater importance and artistic value. On the whole, however, his book was still written in the manner of pre-war literary schools. His phraseology shows little similarity with Marxist-Leninist literary critics of the years following L. Novomeský's imprisonment and the condemnation to the gallows of V. Clementis, the intellectual leader of the Slovak Communists.

The revaluation of Slovak history by Mráz must be seen in a more general context. The Košice Programme had defined the ideological orientation for the future and had put an end to an old controversy about Slovak national, cultural and literary individuality. The Programme stated that "the relation between Czechs and Slovaks should be that of separate nations joined in common interest in a single State," even though a year before Slovak Communist intellectuals had proudly manifested their desire to see Slovakia as an autonomous Soviet Republic rather than as a province dominated by Prague. Mráz adapted his *History of Slovak Literature* to this nationalist atmosphere, and consequently he included *ex cathedra* in the Slovak cultural and literary heritage not only the writings of Sts. Cyril and Methodius and those of their disciples (which had

been consistently, though erroneously, claimed by the Czechs); he also included the Latin works of all scholars and writers who were of Slovak origin. He also took an objective and favourable view, considering the circumstances, of the Slovak literature created by Catholics in the seventeenth and eighteenth century, a literature which in the inter-war period had been either minimized or passed over in silence.

The thesis that the Slovaks and not the Czechs are the true heirs of Great Moravia, that there existed a clear distinction, during the centuries between Czechs and Slovaks and their language, and that the Slovaks preserved a consciousness of their ethnic and cultural individuality and their continuity with the Slovak kingdom of Great Moravia—these were accepted as historical facts by Mráz. He supported his position by quotations from, and references to the works of Slovak writers of the seventeenth and eighteenth centuries. Mráz also accepted the point of view that the archaic Czech language, which was brought into Slovakia by the Czech Protestants "who found shelter in Slovakia and even printed books in Czech for the purpose of smuggling them into Bohemia," was merely a borrowed language, and that the Slovak Protestants used it for literature and liturgy in the same way as the Catholics used Latin. Though this thesis had previously been supported by many experts in Slovak language, literature and history, the universities in pre-war Czechoslovakia tried to impose a theory of a common language with the Czechs until the Štúr reform of 1844. In his book Mráz stated, "The Slovak cultural and literary sphere was never blended or identified with the Czech; it always had its specific needs and set of rules." From these premises, Mráz judged favourable the activities of the Jesuit University of Trnava (1635), the Catholic writers of the era of Enlightenment, and the generation of 1848, who created modern Slovak nationalism in letters and in political life.

Mráz's *History of Slovak Literature,* probably written during the Second World War and adapted to the political climate of the first post-War years, expressed the changed situation only partly by its method and criteria. The book remained basically within the framework of values, terminology and concepts established earlier in Slovakia. The "revolutionary revaluation" was undertaken soon after 1948 by a young group of militant members of the Communist Party (A. Bakoš, K. Rosenbaum, R. Mrlian, J. Horvát, J. Noge, and others), who made a fanatical reappraisal of Slovak literature and "purged" the libraries to bring them in line with the Party ideology and the Marxist-Leninist theory of literature. When L. Novomeský was also "purged" as a "bourgeois nationalist and deviationist," the new school of "Socialist Realism" was firmly established. Consequently, only those books and writers serving the new social order were regarded as representative of true literary values. The rest were rejected as reactionary, deviationist, rightist, and petty-bourgeois. As Slovak literature was also integrated into the structure of the new Communist order and destined to be subordinated to the Party and its ideology, the poet and novelist, literary critic and scientist would have to contribute by their talents and works to the building of a Communist society. The model: Soviet Russia.

After seven years of "Socialist Realism" which made Slovak literature a tool of the Communist Party's policy and poets and writers "engineers of human souls," there grew suddenly in 1955 a strong need to analyze what kind of literature and what kind of artistic and moral values were being created in Slovakia under Communism. At the same time, poets and writers began to call for a change, for a revision of ways and methods by which literature was regimented and creative energy stifled. Except for a few literary critics who blindly served the régime, Slovak poets and writers began to rebel against the strait-jacket of Party censorship and interference with writers' freedom to follow their own inspiration and choose what subjects they liked, or to express their opinions freely.

On behalf of the silenced poets and writers the first to protest was Ján Smrek who expressed his opposition in

"The Awesome Poem"

A mercenary is no knight.
A mercenary kills for gain.
The knight defends his weapon's honour
Drawing it only when constrained.
So does the poet draw the word,
In knightly fashion. Should he deprave
His art, let him vie with dogs,—
He is no better than a devil's slave.
Some of them have written scores.
Rhymes they boast, and metaphors.
But liars playing troubadors
Succeed in being sickening bores.
The awesome poem is a nought,
In market-value hardly worth
A coin, and yet it pierces hearts
In scattered corners of the earth.
Utter no slogans illustrious,
Shun metaphysical display,
And when you simply say Good Morning,
Let people see the break of day.
                    (Translation by Jaroslav Vajda)

Following an exchange of opinions in the pages of the official organ of the Union of Slovak Writers, *Kultúrny život,* the forums which served for the examination and evaluation of Slovak post-war literature were the conference on Slovak poetry and five months later the conference on Slovak prose, held in Bratislava on December 21, 1955. Even though the Party organ *Pravda* strongly sided with some critics who accused poets and writers of irresponsible and anti-socialist stagnation, Slovak poets and writers fought back and pointed to the reasons which caused stagnation, sectarianism and low artistic standards in Slovak literature. The heated debates at the conference did not, however, solve the problem. The discussion continued for some time in *Kultúrny život,* but the first steps had been taken.

Among the first to put his fingers on the malaise in *Kultúrny život* was Ivan Kupec. In October 1955, he wrote: "The art of some authors and artists is dominated by a lack of courage and there is an unhealthy atmosphere of sectarianism in our art. We are obliged to say that a vulgar critique by one-sided requirements of 'Party line' and 'truthfulness' caused much damage."

Alexander Matuška, one of the leading Marxist literary critics who had sided with the régime already in 1945, expressed his views as follows: "In the average Slovak literary works the practice of a certain socialist realistic style spread and it is characterized namely by such qualities as imitation and lack of personal touch, greyness and dullness, overload of phraseology and anti-poetism. This lack of taste in style, the impersonalism and lack of personality extended equally into such outstanding works of Slovak prose as is, for instance, the novel *Osie hniezdo (Hornet's Nest)* by Katarina Lazarová."

Dominik Tatarka, the most favoured novelist of the régime, was no less critical: "I consider the situation in our literature as very serious, and not only in literature. The events, the great storm winds which shattered the world and namely the people's democracies, blew away also our illusions. Or do you think that nothing happened here? Something did happen. Much. Very much. There is a fundamental change in the thoughts of people. Even in literature we cannot build on illusions anything except a house of cards."

Another novelist, Ferinand Gabaj, joined Tatarka in his criticism and wrote: "Too much printed paper, but very few words and sentences for the souls of the people who honestly work day after day. And this is due to the fact that various 'personalities' urged us to write. . . . Please let us cry out and sing out our feelings in order that we may deserve the name of 'conscience of parents, of ourselves and of our children' which we have lost over ten years." According to Vladimir Mináč, a writer who supported the régime quite blindly, "the last two years have been unfertile in the Slovak prose. Only a few works appeared and even those which appeared do not bring any substantial contribution either for readers or for the development of our literature."

"Many of our writers did not take their literary work seriously," wrote another critic. "There have been some who misused the mission of the arts, created sick, dead works which do not affect substantially our life. We have often declared as valuable literary works such literature which was far from life, dry and lifeless works in which life acquired grotesque forms and in which the truth of the class struggle was replaced by a subjective valuation of reality, multiplied by non-artistic composition. For this incorrect creation and destruction of values are responsible both the literary critics and the literary theory, at fault are the editors and the institutions publishing books . . . ."

This prolonged exchange of views only slowly helped Slovak literature to come out of stagnation. Three years later a review of books published in *Slovenské pohl'ady* indicated that Slovak poets and writers still had not found the climate suitable for creating literature of artistic value, or for writing at all.

The revision and re-examination of the Slovak literary and cultural life in 1955-1956 was part of the general trend of the "thaw" in the Soviet orbit after Stalin's death. In all satellite countries efforts to revise "Socialist Realism" appeared almost simultaneously, and they were accompanied by discussions of "self expression" and sincerity. In the Soviet Union the "thaw" started with the appearance of Ehrenburg's *Otepel* and V. Panova's *Vremena Goda.* In

Slovakia, the "thaw" contained some specific features pertaining to the fact that Slovakia was being ruled since 1948 from Prague. Slovak poets and writers had, as a result, a two-fold task to accomplish: to cultivate "brotherhood and unity" between Czechs and Slovaks, and to create a new socialist literature which would introduce socialist consciousness among the Slovaks.

Though the "pseudo-literature," to which "Socialist Realism" necessarily degenerated, may use any of the technical devices and forms used by literature, and though the quality of writing in pseudo-literature is not infrequently quite good, Communist writers in Slovakia came to the conclusion that their literature of the first decade after the War was little more than poor and unsuccessful.

Since the Congress of Slovak Writers in 1956 there had been mounting dissatisfaction in Slovakia among the writers and journalists who remained, after the imprisonment of the political leaders accused of "bourgeois nationalism," the only spokesmen for the Slovak people. In 1963, the spark for open criticism and an insistence on reforms was given by the release of these "bourgeois nationalists." Their later accounts of the brutality they underwent in prison shook the conscience of Slovak writers and journalists, some of whom had contributed to their condemnation, while others had praised the régime and its iron grip, ignoring the brutality and persecution of innocent people in all walks of life. They now wanted to repair the damage and from L. Mňačko, who became well-known abroad, to M. Hysko, V. Mihálik, V. Mináč, R. Kaliský, and others, the writers and intellectuals denounced the Stalinist régime and its brutality, and asked for reforms.

The Congresses of Slovak Writers became more than a mere meeting for discussing literary and cultural problems. This was the beginning of a serious effort to change the ruling system, to clear the atmosphere of the suffocating fear of oppression, and to correct injustices and crimes of the period of the cult of personality. Slovak writers and journalists again played the role of the "conscience of the nation." The Stalinist terror had not only silenced them for many years but had found some eager collaborators among the writers. The editorials in *Kultúrny život* before the Congress of Slovak Writers in 1963 were entitled "Literature in the Struggle for Truth," and the participants proved that they meant to have it thus. Furthermore, after the congress they asked for "a clean slate" and stated that "everything is not in order."

At the Congress of the Union of Czechoslovak Writers, held in Prague 22-24 May, 1963, Slovak writers used the same fighting spirit to speak against terror and for a "cult of truth," instead of a cult of personality. The words fear, falsification of facts, abuse of confidence were repeated time and again. Especially noteworthy were the outspoken speeches by the poets Vojtech Mihálik and Laco Novomeský, the dramatist Peter Karvaš, the novelist V. Mináč, the essayist M. Chorvath, Zora Jesenská, and others. Mihálik spoke of the duty of writers to be the "conscience of the nation" and bitterly criticized the period of the cult of personality. L. Mňačko, whose series, "Belated Reports," well-known for their exposure of the terror and injustices, began to appear in *Kultúrny život*, spoke of the

"mousetrap" and the "unrosy economic, political and moral situation of the country." L. Novomeský, whose contribution to the discussion was published under the heading "With Comrade Reason," and the contributions by Zora Jesenská and Karvaš "About One Source of Dogmatism" completed the picture of dissatisfaction with the past and present, insisting on the necessity for change and reform.

These congresses, as we now know, launched Czechoslovakia upon a new course, with consequences unpredictable at that time. If until the early 1960's the Communist Party of Czechoslovakia could have served as "a laboratory specimen of diehard dogmatism and appeared practically untouched by the winds of change stirring in the international Communist movement" after these meetings this was no longer true. (pp. 215-34)

> *J. M. Kirschbaum, "Slovak Literature under the Soviet Impact," in his* Slovak Language and Literature: Essays, *University of Manitoba, 1975, pp. 215-35.*

CZECH SCIENCE FICTION

Ivan Adamovič

[In the following excerpt, Adamovič surveys Czech science fiction of the twentieth century.]

A continuous SF tradition in Czechoslovakia goes back to the beginning of this century, though it has not for that long been clearly distinguishable from fantastic literature. The first Czech work identifiable as SF is Karel Pleskač's *Život na Měsíci* (*Life on the Moon*, 1881), whose narrator mentally transports himself to a lunar utopia and falls in love with the daughter of an astronomer whom he encounters there. The SF of the first four decades of the 20th century in effect carries on in Pleskač's vein of anticipating some future society, but it is also rich in adventure stories centering on explorations of space, mad scientists, lost civilizations in the heart of Africa, and mysterious technological inventions. SF was mainly a field for "pulp" writers, but with honorable exceptions—most notably, of course, Karel Čapek.

The age of SF tales of adventure comes to an end with the 1940s. "J. M. Troska," an enormously popular writer of space operas, published his last book in 1947, and the same is true of one of the deans of Czech hardcore SF, "R. V. Fauchar." The next decade, with which I begin a somewhat more detailed account of developments to date, was largely a period of retreat, a farewell to "the Golden Age."

An atmosphere inhospitable to SF began to prevail in 1948, when private publishing houses vanished, their operations taken over by the State. New editors were installed who demanded realistic prose, and a new generation of writers appeared willing to oblige them. As a result,

SF production diminished from ten titles in 1948 to two the following year. Furthermore, the character of the genre changed. Authors limited their use of fantastic motifs; and if they speculated in the future at all, they kept to the near future. All of this constitutes a still-persisting departure from previous Czech tradition; so that many readers continue to look with pious nostalgia to the "Golden Age" of the 1920s and '30s.

The situation became bleak quickly but not instantly. At least one book from the late '40s is worth singling out: Hanuš Sedáček's curious *Krtoryt contra ptakolet* (*Moledigger Contra Birdflier*, 1948), which dramatizes the rivalry between the owners of flying machines and the operators of subways in a Prague of the future. But by 1950 it had become virtually impossible to get any such SF printed. Indeed, that year was the first since 1914 wherein no SF title whatever appeared, chiefly because the ideological conviction that all literature should serve the immediate project of building the Czech socialist republic became a matter of publishing policy—a development hardly conducive to the kind of future imaginings that are the staple of SF.

A number of already-established authors were not able to adapt to the new demands of (state) publishers. Jan Weiss (1892-1972) is a typical example. His *Dům o 1000 patrech* (*A Thousand-Storey House*, 1929) is widely regarded as being one of the best examples of Czech fantastic fiction; but the beauty of its dream-like qualities is almost entirely absent from his post-World War II efforts at writing SF: *Země vnuků* (*The Country of Our Grandchildren*, 1957) and two other books from the '60s not even worth mentioning.

SF regained some visibility only in 1955, when Vladimír Babula (1919-66), the editor of *Science and Technology for Young Readers*, began publishing his *Signály z vesmíru* (*Signals from Space*). This turned out to be an epic trilogy, which Babula subsequently revised and brought out in a single volume as *Oceánem světelných let* (*Through the Ocean of Light Years*, 1963). Strongly influenced by optimism about the future in the Soviet SF, *Oceánem* can hardly be called a well-crafted or stylistically ingratiating piece of work; but for the '50s, it was a significant contribution to the genre and attracted many readers.

In the later '50s, the production of juvenile SF began to spread, under the leadership of František Běhounek (1898-1973). Běhounek was a well-known scientist and member of the Czech Academy of Sciences who had participated in Amundsen's and Nobile's expeditions to the North Pole. He also authored nine hard-tech SF novels between 1942 and 1968, and two of these remain quite popular and have been reprinted several times. One of them, *Akce L* (*Operation L*, 1956), describes the colonization of the Moon; in the other, *Robinsoni vesmíru* (*The Space Robinsons*, 1958), the protagonists attempt to destroy a comet before it can collide with Earth.

The Space Robinsons came out in the same year as the short-story collection *Tarzanova smrt* (*The Death of Tarzan*). Its author, until then an unknown psychiatrist and playwright named Josef Nesvadba (b. 1926), would inaugurate a new era in Czech SF.

The success of *The Death of Tarzan* encouraged Nesvadba in a number of similar ventures: *Einsteinův mozek* (*Einstein's Brain*, 1960), *Výprava opačným směrem* (*An Expedition in the Opposite Direction*, 1962), *Poslední cesty kapitána Nema* (*The Last Travels of Captain Nemo*, 1966), and so forth. The short stories brought together in these volumes focus on character rather than on the usual paraphernalia of SF; and they also show Nesvadba to be adept at connecting plot to a philosophical meaning. His fictions, many of which were translated into English and published in the US and/or the UK, are thus of the sort that adults can read without the discomfort of feeling that they are indulging themselves in the puerile fantasies about outer space written to appeal to their children.

Jiří Brabenec (b. 1911) and Zdeněk Veselý (b. 1927) collaborated to carry on the "classic" SF tradition in such of their jointly-authored works as *Dobrodružství v Eridanu* (*An Adventure in Eridan*, 1961) and *Zločin v Duhovém zálivu* (*Crime at the Rainbow Bay*, 1966). Meanwhile, Ivan Foustka (b. 1928) came up with one of the best "hard" SF novels of the 1960s, *Vzpoura proti času* (*The Mutiny Against Time*, 1965), an SF thriller about a group of astronauts imprisoned inside an artificial cosmic body ruled by an evil computer. Foustka's next book is entirely different. *Výlet k Pánubohu* (*A Trip to God*, 1968) is a biting satire about a cosmic expedition from the Vatican to a distant planet. The zealots introduce a new order there—and in consequence contrive to turn (its) Heaven into a more horrific place than Hell itself.

Czech SF visions of the 1960s are noticeably darker than those of the previous decade. Indeed, the bright optimism of the '50s loses whatever credibility, or power of conviction, it may once have had and generally gives way to pessimistic warnings about the future. Achille Gregor's *Odnikud nikam* (*From Nowhere to Nowhere*) and Vladimír Straka's *Druhá potopa světa* (*The Second World Deluge*) together constitute a striking instance: both depict catastrophes resulting from deadly radiation, and both came out in the same year (1964). Equally characteristic of the time are two dystopian works: Jiří Jobánek's *Stříbrné ostrovy* (*The Silver Islands*, 1965) and *Blažený věk* (*Blessed Ages*, 1967) by the prolific mainstream writer Jiří Marek (b. 1914). The latter, a classic dystopia, takes place in an urban future over which "equitable order" presides. Everywhere banners proclaim the principles of this order: "Citizen of the City: The Happiest Man in the World," "Citizens, Stay in the Streets. Private Happiness is the Happiness of the Past!," "We Know that towards Real Freedom Many People Must Be Compelled," and "Citizens of the City! Say Your 'Yes.'" And the citizens dutifully say their "yes" daily to express their loyalty and as a sign of their unquestioning obedience.

Another work from this period, Čestmír Vejdělek's *Návrat z ráje* (*Return from Paradise*, 1961) is, in the judgment of many (including myself), the best Czech SF novel. Its claim to that distinction rests primarily with its character portrayal and its humanity. Its hero, Řehoř, is no superman, just an ordinary guy making ordinary mistakes. As a news reporter, he secretly visits the planet Lucie to (dis)cover the mystery of its civilization. He goes through one "reality" level after another, only to find out in the end that what had appeared to be a very attractive utopia is in fact a moribund dystopic society whose inhabitants are unaware of being slaves to the central computer which rules over them. With its detailed description of the layout and history of Lucie, *Return from Paradise* is a very complex fiction. Nor does its moral message come down to a simple black/white; indeed, it demonstrates that even truth and happiness are relative matters.

Also making his debut at this time was Ludvík Souček (1926-78). Formerly a doctor and then an editor, he published his first SF novel, *Cesta slepých ptáků* (*Voyage of the Blind Birds*) in 1964. Over the next decade, he became the most popular Czech writer in the genre, though more so among young readers than with adults. In the course of a 17-year long career, he wrote some 40-odd volumes, not only SF but books about photography, communications, the drama, astronomy, history, and—above all—his beloved "Dänikenology." Almost all of his SF is informed by his ideas about Ancient Visitors from Space and flying saucers from the future—though "non-believers" could also find his works entertaining.

To *Blind Birds* Souček added two sequels: *Runa Rider* (1967) and *Sluneční jezero* (*The Sun Lake*, 1968). The trilogy begins with the search for mysterious messages in Icelandic caves and ends with the discovery of a Viking colony on Mars. (To judge from the letters that he got, he apparently convinced a number of his readers that he was dealing in facts.) Other SF titles of his include *Krotitelé ďáblů* (*The Devil-Tamers*, 1965), *Případ Baskervilského psa* (*The Case of the Hound of the Baskervilles*, 1972), and *Pevnost bílých mravenců* (*Fortress of the White Ants,* 1972), plus two collections of short stories: *Bratři Černé planety* (*Brothers of the Black Planet,* 1969) and *Zájem galaxie* (*For the Benefit of the Galaxy,* 1973).

A multitude of SF stories also began appearing in various magazines during this decade, which saw as well the first Czech translations of contemporary Anglo-American SF. Among the authors the latter introduced to Czech readers were Robert Heinlein, A. E. van Vogt, Clifford Simak, Lewis Padgett, and Arthur C. Clarke.

In the early '70s, Czech SF went through its second crisis. This one wasn't as profound as that of the early 50s; but still, the number of SF titles decreased from 13 in 1970 to four in 1974. This reflected the bleak conditions prevailing throughout Czech culture at that time—conditions imposed by the neo-Stalinist regime that came to power following the Warsaw Pact invasion of 1968. The second half of the decade was a different story. In those years, a new group of promising writers emerged. And unlike the SF of the '60s, which came largely from mainstream authors, theirs indicated that this new generation had grown up on SF.

The leading figure of this period was Jaroslav Veis (b. 1946). He made his reputation with two collections of short stories: *Experiment pro třetí planetu* (*Experiment for a Third Planet,* 1976) and *Pandořina skříňka* (*Pandora's Box,* 1979). Veis is notable as a stylist; his stories are not formulaic; and he is capable of masterly psychological dramas as well as cheerful prose with philosophical implications. Now that he serves as editor for the Mladá Fronta Publishing House, his own literary output has slowed down, but he is still considered to be Czechoslovakia's best SF short-story writer.

Two other authors worth singling out from Veis's generation are Ludmila Vaňková (b. 1927) and Karel Blažek (b. 1948). Vaňková, popular for her historical romances, published a long SF novel in 1976 called *Mosty pres propasti času* (*Bridges Over the Abysses of Time*). Premised on a global catastrophe that caused an ancient technologically advanced civilization to vanish, it recapitulates Earth's history as the product of subsequent visitations by cosmic explorers descended from that civilization (i.e., à la van Däniken). Blažek, though he is as prolific as Vaňková, has not been nearly as successful. His *Přistání* (*The Landing,* 1979) was not particularly well-received, though that did not deter him from attempting a much more ambitious work called *Nejlepší století* (*The Best Century,* 1982), which pictures in detail a future utopia. The result is interesting, but it suffers from being overly "talkative" and lacking in action.

Souček, too, was a presence in this decade, and not just through his SF. An article of his, "Interpellation for the Future," created a stir for expressing his bitter dissatisfaction with the state of both Czech SF and fandom—one of the consequences of which protest was the foundation of several SF fan clubs. Shortly after "Interpellation . . . " came out, the author died of a heart attack (his ninth), leaving behind *Blázni z Hepteridy* (*The Madmen from Hepteris,* 1980). That book, its brevity notwithstanding, is perhaps the best Czech space opera since the pre-war efforts in that line by Troska.

Along with some other East European countries, Czechoslovakia experienced an SF boom at the start of the '80s. Not only was SF "in" again; but now serious literary critics began to accept it, the Czech Writers' Union established an SF section, and legions of SF writers were flooding into any number of popular magazines, ranging from those tailoring themselves to soldiers, motorists, or women to the prestigious "slicks." And not to be left out, Czechoslovak television produced several SF series.

In the first of these vintage years, three young writers, Miloš Kratochvíl, Zdeněk Rosenbaum, and Ladislav Szalai, each made himself known via a short-story gathering; and so, too, did the translator and editor Zdeněk Volný, who exhibited his precise, cold style to advantage. The publication of a double anthology edited by Vojtěch Kantor—*Lidé ze souhvězdí Lva/Železo přichází z hvězd* (*People from the Constellation Leo/The Iron Comes from the Sky*)—was also an important event, especially for Zbynek Černík, Miroslav Kostka, Ondřej Neff, and Jiří Čihař, all of whom debuted in hard covers there. But more important still were the next such collections of mostly hitherto unpublished authors: *Stalo se zítra* (*It Happened Tomorrow,* 1984) and *Návrat na planetu Zemi* (*Return to the Planet Earth,* 1985). Compiled by Ivo Železný, the two contained 90 original short stories altogether, thus evincing both the genre's broad authorial base and its popularity (the print-run for the second volume was 83,000).

Of the writers just mentioned, at least two deserve some further attention. One of them is Szalai (b. 1951). In *Cesta do bláznovy zahrady* (*A Way to the Madman's Garden*, 1984) and three other collections of his short stories, he showed a neverending inventiveness, imagination, and sense of absurdity that earned him the sobriquet, "the Czech Lem." The only obstacle between him and literary greatness is his prolificness, the superiority of quantity over quality in his work.

The other is Neff (b. 1945). His star has been fast rising over the last five years—to the point where he has become, along with Veis, the most popular living Czech practitioner of SF. A journalist by occupation, Neff has been enormously active also as a literary theorist, translator, lecturer, photographer, and fan. He wrote the first history of Czech SF, *Něco je jinak* (*Something Is Otherwise*, 1982), and following on this pioneering work came a thick volume on foreign SF called *Všchno je jinak* (*Everything Is Otherwise*, 1987).

Neff's first SF novel, *Jádro pudla* (*The Heart of the Matter*, 1984), was set on a colonized Mars, owed something to E. R. Burroughs and *Brave New World* . . . and went largely unnoticed. But the next year, his *Vejce naruby* (*Inverted Egg*) proved an instant success and went on to win many awards. The short stories comprising the volume range from hard, fast-paced thrillers ("The Wildest Guy in the History of Swang," "The .38 Calibre White Stick"), through taboo-breaking humorous pieces ("Peter and Lucy," "The Monument"), to serious excursions bearing on ecology ("The Tree") and human nature ("The Puzzle," "String of Life"). After publishing a second collection of such short stories (*Čtvrtý den až navěky*—i.e., *The Fourth Day Forever*, 1987), he put out another novel, this one about a colony of Moon miners, called *Měsíc mého života* (*The Moon of My Life*, 1988). Written in the hardboiled and ironic style typical of him, the book was markedly more successful than his first such venture.

Meanwhile, three established authors made (re)appearances. In 1986, Veis published his third collection, *Moře času* (*The Sea of Time*). The stories there are not as original as those in his previous volumes, and their tone is more pessimistic. The highlight of the book is "Šest měsíců, in ulna" ("Six Months in Ulna"), a bitter tale about a young mugger, Akbar Ibn Kato, who resides in a future oriental metropolis where the punishment for all crimes is amputation. This novella-length story was rightfully awarded the prize for the year's best work of short fiction.

Nesvadba was heard from again too, but a Nesvadba who had undergone a considerable metamorphosis since the 1960s. In his recent works, he has reduced the number of SF elements and drawn more upon everyday reality, especially from his experiences as a practicing psychiatrist. He remains a best-selling author: his latest novel, *Hledám za manžela muže* (*I Seek a Male as a Husband*, 1986), with a print-run of 92,000 copies, was sold out in the space of a few weeks. But by bringing himself closer to the mainstream, he also of course took himself farther from the SF field.

Conversely, and to the great surprise of everyone acquainted with the literary scene, the most acclaimed contemporary Czech mainstream writer, Vladimír Páral, was turning to the SF genre just as Nesvadba was distancing himself from it. In 1982, he published two SF novels, *Pokušení A-ZZ* (*Temptation A-ZZ*) and *Romeo a Julie 2300* (*Romeo and Juliet 2300*), which were soon followed by his third—and best: *Válka s mnohozvířetem* (*The War with a Multibeast*, 1983). The "multibeast" of that last title is initially a half-intelligent form of smog. But in the second half of the book, this smog transforms itself into a parasite capable of influencing the mind of its host. Naturally, this complicates the struggle, since those fighting the "multibeast" must also fight their own will.

In his SF, Páral has the same concerns as in his mainstream fictions. He continues to analyze the morals, manners, and negative aspects of contemporary life, except that he now tests his findings under new generic conditions. His latest offering, *Země žen* (*The Country of Women*, 1987), is a powerful dystopian parable about a society where women rule and men are kept in concentration camps. Yet his pursuing of his mainstream interests into the realm of SF was something of a risk for him inasmuch as the genre is still thought of as one which "serious" authors shouldn't care about. On the other hand, while he brings to SF the virtuosity of a skilled writer and fills his SF with living, believable characters, he is not alone among established authors using SF motifs in their work. This constitutes a proof of sorts that the genre can speak to all manner of readers and stand respectably beside "great contemporary prose"—or, as some of the more radical SF fans would have it, that the latter can stand respectably beside SF. (pp. 50-6)

Ivan Adamovič, "Czech Science Fiction in the Last Forty Years," in Science-Fiction Studies, *Vol. 17, No. 1, March, 1990, pp. 50-9.*

Ondřej Neff

[*In the following excerpt, Neff describes developmental stages of twentieth-century Czech science fiction, including discussion of works by Karel Čapek written during the interwar period and of Czech science fiction novels from the mid-1950s through the mid-1980s.*]

In the eighteen-nineties, works of foreign writers of the SF genre began to be translated in the Czech Lands. The greatest popularity was achieved, of course, by Jules Verne. By the beginning of the 20th century, all his significant works so far published were available to Czech readers, and publication of his books has continued to the present day without interruptions except perhaps for the war years. Translations of Verne's contemporaries and imitators also appeared on the market, of the Frenchmen Laurie, Galopide, d'Ivoi, de la Hire, and of the "Italian Verne" Luigi Motta. Starting in 1905, two fantastic works by H. G. Wells appeared *The Time Machine* and *The First Men in the Moon,* and gradually all Wells's fantastic writings were published. Also popular were books by H. Rider

Haggard, whose most famous novel *She* appeared for the first time in 1907. These literary achievements could not but influence Czech culture. Nevertheless, the beginnings were not much to speak of. The not very talented writer Karel Hloucha, a café owner by profession, tried to become famous as the "Czech Verne". His first fantastic book *Little George's Remarkable Travels* (1907) was intended for children; for grown-ups he wrote a science-fiction travelogue *The Land Under a Spell* (1910), about wanderings to a mysterious land in the Far North, inhabited by troglodytes. Later, in the interwar period, he published some more novels and short-story collections but with good reason he fell into oblivion. Two other pioneers who had their works printed at little-known publishers are almost unknown: Metod Suchdolský, whose novel *The Russian on Mars* (1909) is still remarkable in many respects today, and František Pavlovský, who wrote two none too successful novels *By Land* (1911) and *By Air* (1921), which are today much-sought-after collector's titbits for their charming naivety.

Truly significant writers began to write fantastic books only in the interwar period.

Jiří Haussmann, who published the extraordinarily gifted *Wild Stories* (1922) and, in the same year, the fantastic novel *The Large-Scale Production of Virtue,* had a tragic fate. Both these works are sharply satirical. Haussmann (though he denied it) had the talent to match one day that giant of Czech satire, Jaroslav Hašek, author of the world-famous *Good Soldier Švejk*. Sadly, at the beginning of 1923, Jiří Haussmann died at the age of only twenty-four. Both his works are still read today and are counted among the greatest values of interwar Czech prose.

Karel Čapek belongs without doubt to the most important Czech writers of the interwar period. He was born in 1890, graduated from the Philosophical Faculty of Charles University in Prague, but gave preference to journalism and literature. Spiritually he was influenced, above all, by the philosophy of pragmatism, which he of course remoulded in his own way and on whose foundations he built up his typically "Čapekian" philosophy of mutual human decency. G. B. Shaw and G. K. Chesterton were the world authors who were closest to him. Especially the latter influenced Karel Čapek and led him to fantastic literature.

The greatest success was scored by Čapek's first signifi-

A scene from a 1922 American production of Čapek's drama R.U.R. (Rossum's Universal Robots).

cant play *R.U.R.,* which appeared in book form in 1920 and a year later was staged in the National Theatre in Prague. The drama describes a victorious rebellion of robots and is, besides, remarkable for the first use of the word "robot". This word was invented by Čapek's brother, the painter Josef Čapek, who wrote himself and later participated with Karel on several dramas. The word "robot" comes from the old Czech expression "robota", meaning forced labour of the village inhabitants of the feudal estates. It is still used for hard physical toil today. From the viewpoint of truly professional SF terminology, Čapek's robots were in fact androids, as their basis was biological. This too is the point of the drama: the victorious robot-rebels do not know the secret of production and are threatened with extinction. Fortunately, there exists a "zero series" of improved robots, capable of love and physical reproduction, which becomes the nucleus of the future mankind. In the space of just a few years, Čapek's play *R.U.R.* was staged in many countries all over the world. A modified version of it was filmed in the Soviet Union. Surprisingly, however, no later film version has been made. In 1922 Karel Čapek published a novel, or rather a series of essays, called *The Manufacture of the Absolute.* In grotesque hyperbole, the author describes the invention of a machine capable of the perfect conversion of matter into energy. What remains is God, present, according to pantheistic teachings, in every particle of matter. However, this liberated God will do no good to mankind, on the contrary he will hurl it into a horrible world war. No wonder that the machine is forbidden after the war and all copies of it are destroyed. . . . Čapek returned to the motif of the threat of war in his novel *Krakatit* (1924). This concerns an explosive named after the Krakatoa volcano, the effects of which remind one of contemporary nuclear weapons. The author especially examines ethical questions connected with scientific work on weapons. Čapek's novel *The War with the Newts* (1936) had a particularly strong impact. In it he reacted to the immediate threat of fascism felt especially strongly in the Czechoslovakia of that time, because literally all the neighbouring countries were controlled by totalitarian fascist regimes. Čapek allegorized the fascists in his vision of the newts, remarkably gifted amphibians who are capable of building up their own civilization. Just as the Western democracies were not able to stand up effectively to the Hitlerite threat before it was too late, so the Great Powers in *The War with the Newts* too not only do not resist the newts but even help them liquidate their own dry land and build up a newts' world without continents, in which there will be no place for man. Čapek quite openly opposed fascism in his play *The White Disease* (1937): in a fictional totalitarian state, the population of people over fifty is attacked by a fatal disease the external sign of which is a whitening of the skin. A certain philanthropic doctor discovers a medicine for the "white disease", but he is willing to use it for a cure of the sick dictator on condition that he abandons his militaristic policy. In 1937, however, Čapek no longer cherished the optimistic hopes he expressed in *The War with the Newts.* At the close of the play, a hysterical crowd simply tramples the doctor to death. In vain did Čapek rouse the people against Hitlerism. The government of the then Czechoslovakia submitted to the Munich Dictate without resistance and the desperate Karel Čapek died in 1938. The Nazis deported his brother Josef to a concentration camp where he died at the very end of the war.

The third interesting author of Czech interwar fantastic writings was Jan Weiss, born in 1892. During the First World War he was taken prisoner by the Russians. His feet were frost-bitten, he fell ill of typhus and nearly died. Delirious visions of a swooning state persecuted Weiss all his life long. The most impressive passages of his short stories and novels usually move along a dream level. Weiss's supreme work is the allegorical novel *A Thousand-Storey House* (1929), in which, among other things, the author foretells with horrifying details the death ovens of the Hitlerite concentration camps. Weiss continued writing until the beginning of the nineteen-sixties, though the standard of his works dropped markedly in the post-war period.

Besides the above-mentioned three authors, of course, other writers also dealt with fantastic and SF themes in the interwar period. The standard of their works was, however, usually rather poor. Some chose the field of mystical and occult prose, sometimes with an erotic tinge. Many novels were published on the theme of the next world war and the consequent destruction of mankind—let us at least mention the trilogy *The Decline of Mankind* by Tomas Hrubý, which achieved a certain popularity in its time. Novels with cosmic themes came out sporadically until the end of the nineteen-thirties, when Jan Matzal started his author's career under the pen-name of J. M. Troska. This "nom de guerre" was symbolic because the word "troska" means "ruin" in Czech, and the writer was on a disability pension from the age of forty. He was born in 1881 but only published regularly from 1937. He wrote an eight-volume novel cycle set partly in the ocean depths and to a larger extent in space. It is an analogy of a sort of naively-written prose of the type of a "space opera" of low literary value, but composed so skilfully that Troska still has many readers or even idolizers in our country today. His last big novel appeared in 1943; after the war he only occasionally published in magazines and soon ceased writing.

Czech SF prose underwent a great renaissance in the second half of the nineteen-fifties mainly in consequence of the beginning of mankind's cosmic era. Vladimír Babula was very promising, inspiring young readers with a trilogy of adventurous cosmic SF books—*Signal from Space, The Planet of Three Suns* and *Friends from the Serpens* (1956-63). Unfortunately Babula died young and it took eight years to find his follower in the person of Ludvík Souček, about whom we shall hear more later. The novels by František Běhounek still have a great response among young readers today. He was born in 1885 and became famous even before the Second World War when, together with Umberto Nobile, he took part in his flights to the North Pole aboard the airship Norge in 1926, that time successfully, and aboard the airship Italia in 1928. This expedition ended in disaster and the crew lived through a polar Robinsonlike adventure, which, for some of its members, ended fatally. František Běhounek became an outstanding scientist who worked in radiology and was a member of the Czechoslovak Academy of Sciences. He al-

ready wrote adventure science fiction in the nineteen-forties, but the greatest success was scored by his cosmic novels *Operation L* (1956) and *The Space Robinsons* (1958). The critics accused Běhounek of weak plots and flat characters, but child readers liked the precise and mainly credible descriptions of various technical wonders of the near future.

The Czech SF of the nineteen-sixties was dominated by two authors who were close to each other in age and profession—both of them being doctors, even fellow-students at the Medical Faculty—but quite different in their creative methods. One of them, Josef Nesvadba is known to a wide circle of fans of the SF genre even abroad, whereas Ludvík Souček is almost unknown beyond the frontiers of our country.

Josef Nesvadba drew the public's attention in 1958 with his short-story collection *The Death of Tarzan,* which contains a short story "The Island of Pirates." It is important because it was the first short story written in a socialist country which was published in the United States in *The Magazine of Fantasy and Science Fiction* in February 1962. Nesvadba chose a different way than Babula or Běhounek and concentrated mainly on ethical and psychical problems, and when he did mention machines and inventions, it was, as a rule, to make fun of them. And because Josef Nesvadba is a psychiatric specialist and still works in psychiatry, he is first of all interested in the psychic reasons of anomalous deeds. In his later creative development, Nesvadba stopped writing pure SF or speculative prose. His interest in man took the upper hand in his work and he used fantastic motives just to express his ideas more vividly and colourfully. His books *The Absolute Machine* (1972), *Driver's Licence for Parents* (1979) and *The Return of Minnehawa* (1981) met the greatest response. (pp. 40-6)

Ludvík Souček, like Josef Nesvadba, was born in 1926. He died at the close of 1978 after a stormy and extraordinarily successful literary career, which he started relatively late at the age of thirty-five. He devoted the greater part of his work to the popularization of technology, especially photography, though nearly all his fiction belongs entirely to the SF genre, starting with his first extensive work, the trilogy *The Way of the Blind Birds* (1964-68), and ending with *The Gods of Atlantis,* which appeared posthumously in 1983. Let us also at least mention his *Devil-Tamers* (1965), the short-story collections *Brothers of the Black Planet* (1969) and *For the Benefit of the Galaxy* (1973), and the posthumously published novel *The Madmen from Hepteris* (1980), which is perhaps the most-read and most ingeniously conceived prose work Souček ever wrote. The readers, however, evaluate most highly his nonfiction— the "Dänikenlike" articles on the past of our planet— compiled into the books *A Foreboding of the Shadow* (1975) and *A Foreboding of the Connection* (1978).

At the beginning of the nineteen-seventies, the interest in science fiction in Czechoslovakia slackened. There were many reasons for this. A certain role was played by the space programmes of both the Soviet Union and the U.S.A. being taken more for granted and deromanticized. Further the fact must be taken into account that a considerable percentage of SF readers is made up of young people and children. It had obviously happened that one generation of readers had outgrown it and the oncoming generation probably preferred other genres such as detective stories. Only Ludvík Souček remained accessible to young readers, whereas the more intellectual works by Josef Nesvadba were intended for older readers. Fewer and fewer SF books were published in smaller editions for there was no interest in science fiction, and even such classics as *Guardians of Time* by Poul Anderson were left unsold on the booksellers' counters. On the basis of this experience, the booksellers came to the conclusion that SF literature was done for, a thing of the past, and they succeeded in passing on the idea to publishing editors.

The situation gradually changed in the second half of the nineteen-seventies. There were many reasons for this too: readers and authors realized that science fiction did not by far have to draw inspiration and encouragement only from space events. Together with the outbreak of the energy crisis, the broad masses of the population began to observe other problems closely too—questions of ecology, pollution, transport, mass-media influence and the moral state of youth. Readers realized that what Josef Nesvadba wrote ten, fifteen years ago, though not only him but also Václav Kajdoš and Jaroslav Zýka, who were close to him from the creative viewpoint, was not just idle abuse of the imagination, amusing and good for training the brain cells, but a significant and clairvoyant testimony of people who knew their way about the world and saw in time where it was heading. This was a shocking realization especially for many intellectuals. Some of them reacted quite simply by starting to hunt for books published earlier and reading them. Others decided that they would do something positive for science fiction, as they had reached the conclusion that this was a serious kind of literature capable of reaching the heart of problems often more directly than other literary genres and fields.

One of them was the young journalist Jaroslav Veis, who in his short-story collections *Experiment for a Third Planet* (1976) and *Pandora's Box* (1979) embarked on the line of speculative prose, to which Josef Nesvadba kept at the beginning of the nineteen-sixties and later Václav Kajdoš and Jaroslav Zýka, who, of course, themselves followed the legacy of Jiří Haussmann, Karel Čapek and Jan Weiss. Naturally, Jaroslav Veis was not alone. When Zdeněk Volný became editor-in-chief of the notable literary revue *Světová literatura,* he began to print outstanding foreign authors regularly and started to write science fiction himself. In 1980 his *Sunday for Sale* appeared and in 1983 his *Golden Trap Full of Time.* The further development of SF literature owes much to two publishing houses specializing in children's books (Albatros) and books for young people (Mladá fronta). In 1981 I published in Albatros the book *Something Is Different,* dealing with the most important authors of Czech fantastic writing, and in 1980 Albatros published the first anthology of Czech science fiction, called *The Invisible Thieves,* and, in the same year, an extensive anthology of Czech and foreign authors, entitled *The Creators of New Worlds* and accompanied by the authors' biographies and a brief history of the genre from the pen of the translator and editor Ivo Železný. Mladá

fronta reacted to *The Invisible Thieves* by publishing in 1983 a two-volume anthology *Iron Comes from the Stars.* The Svoboda publishing house did not stand aside either—in 1982 it put out the first volume of a five-volume anthology series of world SF, named *Terrestrials and Extraterrestrials.*

Thus, at the beginning of the nineteen-eighties, a quite different situation arose from what had existed five years earlier. In a short time a very eager circle of readers had formed, ensuring a large number of copies for every good SF book, and so publishing success, too. Important steps were also taken in the theoretical field. In 1980 Miroslava Genčiová published a comparative study *Science Fiction* and, in the same year, a similar work by Dušan Slobodník, called *The Genesis and Poetics of Science Fiction,* appeared in Slovakia. A Czech translation was published of an important work by the Soviet researcher Yuly Kagarlitski entitled *SF, Utopia, Antiutopia* (1983). A significant step was taken in 1982 by the Union of Czech Writers, when it founded the specialized Section of SF Authors, which systematically explores and supports this literary branch.

If we were to characterize briefly the three stages of Czech fantastic literature, then we should perhaps have to state that the best works of the early and interwar fantastic prose were created by authors who did not take much account of the existence of the SF genre and used fantastic motives to express their thoughts allegorically. The science fiction of the nineteen-fifties and -sixties, and to some extent of the seventies, emphasized technological prognosis or, on the speculative level, the moral consequences of technological development, the limits of which only few people then realized, and all this, if possible, written in adventure story style with an eventful plot. In contemporary science fiction, technological prognosis is almost absent and the authors aim, above all, at those "growth limits" whose increasing pressure we feel ever more urgently.

That was perhaps the reason why Czech SF literature, concentrating on problems that concerned literally the whole of society, ceased to be—as far as it ever had been in our country—a matter of a narrow, limited circle of authors and readers writing and reading nothing but science fiction. This new trend was already indicated in 1973 by Jana Moravcová in her short story collection *The Infallibles' Club,* in which short stories of an undoubtedly SF character alternated with little prose pieces of other literary genres. At that time, many readers thought that this was merely accidental and the authoress had just involuntarily wandered into a sphere she was unfamiliar with. The collection *The Fallibles' Club,* which appeared ten years later, confirmed her clear-cut intention. The authoress uses SF motives when it suits her intentions, but she is not going to be forced into a situation when a writer writes only science fiction and nothing else. Lubomír Macháček does the same thing and in his best-known collection *Sand in the Teeth* (1978) SF short stories also alternate with ghost and social-satirical stories.

Science fiction is also dealt with in an individual way by authors who have gained popularity in main-stream literature too. Otakar Chaloupka, a writer and well-known theorist of children's literature, surprised readers with his allegorical novel *The Blue President* (1980), in which he expressed his belief in the victory of freedom in a dictatorial society having at its disposal even the most sophisticated means of violent oppression. Ota Dub, a favourite author of stories from the world of medicine, one of the many literary doctors in Czech literature, published in 1982 his *Fantastic Transplantations,* in which he explored moral questions of transplanting human organs in a society corrupted by money. Alexej Pludek first became known as the author of historical prose. His two longest and most important novels about the Egyptian and Indian civilizations became a trilogy together with the novel *The Enemy from Atlantis* (1982), set in a fictitious empire. His original views of the sense of human history and the role played in it by an individual, are expressed in a colourful plot inevitably resulting in the destruction of Atlantis. The story's allegory is evident. Bohumil Nohejl too, who has usually drawn inspiration for his prose work from his deep personal experiences of the situation in Czech villages, published a humoristic novel *Sinful Václav* (1979), based on an SF plot.

The broad reading public was most surprised by the "conversion" of Vladimír Páral. The fifty-two-year-old writer has, for almost twenty years, been writing social novels in which he critically analysed many negative features of society that had remained outside the sphere of interest of the writers' community. In 1982 he surprised his readers when he published two SF novels: *Temptation A-ZZ* and *Romeo and Juliet 2300.* He took a courageous step and, in a way, risky too. The readers, who were used to his realistic critical prose, all of a sudden found themselves faced with novels in which extraterrestrials appeared, where society was run according to the principles of eugenics, about problems having nothing in common with modern everyday life. Only when they looked more closely, the readers found that Páral had not changed and still wrote about the same things. He used SF set-up as a sort of crooked mirror, which stresses those features of the human character that had attracted him for twenty years: egoism, careerism, stupidity, and mendacity to others and oneself as well. In 1983 he published his third and so far best SF novel *The War with the Multibeast,* in which he dealt with ecological questions, but first and again with moral ones. The idea is that pollution fallout, under favourable conditions, creates a paravital organism, all-devouring and all-destructive. In the first part of the novel, the multibeast is an individual being with whom war must be waged according to all the rules. In this situation people prove themselves excellently competent. The multibeast then passes through a mutation and penetrates into the human organism, so that man is attacked from inside. This is an immensely harder test of character, because the multibeast acts a little like a drug and suits people with a hedonistic tendency. The author examines the course of this unusual war in detail and convincingly, and I think it is no exaggeration when I rank *The War with the Multibeast* among the foremost works of Czech SF literature.

Besides these authors, there are of course also writers, especially the younger ones, who have made SF prose their main line. We have already mentioned the names of Jaroslav Veis and Zdeněk Volný. The novels by Ludmila Freiová, written in a gentle mood, are intended for young people. In a space of just a few years, she has published three novels and is preparing a fourth one. Very promising too are Zdeněk Rosenbaum and Ladislav Szalai, who in 1983 made their common SF début with a book of short stories, entitled *A Double Double,* already remarkable for its basic principle, according to which the authors each wrote their own short stories on a given theme so that a unique anthology of short-story pairs came into existence. Miloš Kratochvíl drew attention to himself in the anthology already mentioned, *Iron Comes from the Stars.* Now he has published an independent collection *Pavilion J* (1983). The broad public became acquainted with other talented writers in an extensive anthology of Czech and Slovak science fiction, issued in 1984 by the Svoboda publishing house. Here, for the first time in book form, were works by young authors who had so far published their stories only in magazines.

The time has come to ask whether the present upsurge of Czech SF is a temporary phenomenon, a passing fashion trend, or an expression of some long-term tendency in the heart of literature as such. Similar discussions are often held in the literary world, and I will not conceal the fact that critical voices can often be heard: What will the future of Czech SF be? Will it disappear from the world when the wave of interest has ebbed away, as the critics assert, or will interest in it grow and its quality improve, as the optimists hope? Naturally, it is my wish that the optimists are right and that Czech science fiction, on a world scale, will take a place beside the Soviet or Polish. You may think that I incline to this optimistic view because I write science fiction myself. Besides my belief, however, I have got arguments too, and one of them I think is really important.

When we examined the origin of the present wave of Czech SF at the end of the nineteen-seventies, we first of all talked about literary realities, authors and anthologies, about editors and publishers. Only briefly did we mention the really important fundamental cause of such an interest in science fiction in our country. This fundamental cause is in fact identical with the reason why SF and speculative literature exists in the world. Its existence was necessitated by the objective reality of the contemporary world. If literature as such is a reflection of the development of society, if it is a self-reflection of this society, dialectically in turn influencing its development, then there inevitably must exist literary trends within literature, reflectively aimed at significant civilizational moments and problems, and at a hypothetical examination of different variants of their solutions. Today, not only a technician, scientist, ecologist and urbanist, but also a psychologist and pedagogue must think in this way. Not even a man of letters can think otherwise, if he is to express himself relevantly on the time in which he lives.

And as long as he thinks that way, he stands on the threshold of SF literature, speculative, reflective and fantastic in the broadest sense of the word. The wave of interest in SF in our country may fall and some of the next years will certainly be scantier in quantity of output. Science fiction, however, will never disappear from our literature. It takes its place there not because we care for it so much, but because the time itself has forced it on us. (pp. 46-50)

> *Ondřej Neff, "A Third Wave of Czech Science Fiction," in* Panorama of Czech Literature, *No. 4439, 1986, pp. 40-50.*

FURTHER READING

I. Anthologies

Cincura, Andrew, ed. *An Anthology of Slovak Literature.* Riverside, Calif.: University Hardcovers, 1976, 425 p.
   Extensive volume of translated Slovak literature, including poetry as well as dramas and "excerpts from the works of the most important American writers of Slovak descent."

Goetz-Stankiewicz, Marketa, ed. *The Vaněk Plays: Four Authors, One Character.* Vancouver: University of British Columbia Press, 1987, 258 p.
   Collects eight plays by Dienstbier, Havel, Kohout, and Landovský that feature the fictionalized Czech "dissident" dramatist Ferdinand Vaněk. Goetz-Stankiewicz's introduction to the works is excerpted above.

Mihailovich, Vasa D., ed. *White Stones and Fir Trees: An Anthology of Contemporary Slavic Literature.* Rutherford, N.J.: Fairleigh Dickinson University Press, 1977, 603 p.
   Contains numerous selections of translated Czech and Slovak prose and verse in thematically organized sections of Slavic literature.

Němcová, Jeanne W., ed. *Czech and Slovak Short Stories.* Translated by Jeanne W. Němcová. London: Oxford University Press, 1967, 296 p.
   Offers Czechoslovakian short fiction by such authors of the early twentieth century as Karel Čapek, Jaroslav Hašek, Marie Pujmanová, and that of contemporary writers, including Jan Drda, Bohumil Hrabal, Ivan Klíma, and Josef Škvorecký. Němcová provides an introductory survey of modern Czechoslovakian literature.

Otruba, Mojmir, and Pešat, Zdeněk, eds. *The Linden Tree: An Anthology of Czech and Slovak Literature, 1890-1960.* Translated by Edith Pargeter, et al. Prague: Artia, 1962, 403 p.
   Features fiction and poetry by major Czech and Slovak authors of the period.

Selver, Paul, ed. *An Anthology of Czechoslovak Literature.* Translated by Paul Selver. New York: Kraus Reprint Co., 1969, 302 p.
   Provides "English renderings from the works of Czech and Slovak authors of prose and verse, mostly modern and many of them contemporary."

Theiner, George, ed. *New Writing in Czechoslovakia.* Baltimore: Penguin Books, 1969, 247 p.
   Selection of Czech and Slovak short stories and poetry, consisting primarily of translations of works published in Czechoslovakia during the 1960s.

Weiskopf, F. C., ed. *Hundred Towers: A Czechoslovak Anthology of Creative Writing.* New York: L. B. Fischer, 1945, 277 p.
   Features translated Czech and Slovak poetry, short fiction, and essays by major national authors published prior to and through the Second World War.

II. Secondary Sources

Alvarez, A. "Czechoslovakia (1962)." In his *Under Pressure: The Writer in Society—Eastern Europe and the U.S.A.,* pp. 50-76. Baltimore: Penguin Books, 1965.
   Transcript of a 1962 BBC radio broadcast, including conversations with Czechoslovakian authors who comment on the nation's culture, and on societal and political pressures placed on contemporary Czech writers.

Blumenfeld, Yorick. "Off Wenceslas." In his *Seasaw: Cultural Life in Eastern Europe,* pp. 232-51. New York: Harcourt, Brace & World, 1968.
   Discusses Prague theater of the 1960s, including conversations with contemporary directors and a discussion of the dramas of Václav Havel, Ivan Klíma, and Josef Topol.

Burian, Jarka M. "Art and Relevance: The Small Theatres of Prague, 1958-1970." *Educational Theatre Journal* 23, No. 3 (October 1971): 229-57.
   Details the productions of "the small, artistically independent theatres of Prague," focusing on their contributions to European avant-garde drama during the 1960s.

———. "Post-War Drama in Czechoslovakia." *Educational Theatre Journal* 25, No. 3 (October 1973): 299-317.
   Surveys major Czech dramas of the 1950s and 1960s.

———. "High Points of Theatre in the First Czechoslovak Republic." *Modern Drama* 27, No. 1 (March 1984): 98-111.
   Examines Czech theater of the 1920s and 1930s. Burian maintains that interwar Czech drama, "especially in the 1930s, . . . was able to respond vitally to events affecting the life of the young state and the fate of its people."

———. "Czech Theatre, 1988: Neo-*Glasnost* and *Perestroika.*" *Theatre Journal* 41, No. 3 (October 1989): 381-95.
   Describes 1988 productions of Prague theaters, asserting that a "slow revival" of Czech drama occurred during the period of Soviet political liberalization in the late 1980s.

Čulík, Jan. "Breaking the Rule of the Average: A Review of Recent Czech Fiction." *Irish Slavonic Studies,* No. 4 (1983): 123-35.
   Outlines Czech fiction from the mid-1970s to the early 1980s, focusing on authors approved by the Communist government.

Czerwinski, E. J., and Piekalkiewicz, Jaroslaw, eds. *The Soviet Invasion of Czechoslovakia: Its Effects on Eastern Europe.* New York: Praeger Publishers, 1972, 210 p.
   Offers essays on Czech literature during and following the Prague Spring: Hana Benesova examines the role of the nation's authors in Czechoslovakian political reform of the 1960s and Czerwinski discusses Czech and Yugoslavian drama from 1968 and 1969.

Dvořáček, Jaroslav. *The Museum of Czech Literature.* Translated by Iris Urwin. Rev. ed. Prague: Orbis, 1963, 74 p.
   Details the history of the national museum and library

situated in the Strahov monastery in Prague, summarizing the history of Czech literature from the thirteenth century through the mid-twentieth century.

Eekman, Thomas. "Rhyme in Czech and Slovak Poetry." In his *The Realm of Rhyme: A Study of Rhyme in the Poetry of the Slavs,* pp. 210-34. Amsterdam: Verlag Adolf M. Hakkert, 1974.

> Contains discussion of the development of rhyme techniques in modern Czech and Slovak poetry.

French, Alfred. *The Poets of Prague: Czech Poetry between the Wars.* London: Oxford University Press, 1969, 129 p.

> Extensive analysis of interwar Czech poetry, detailing the development of Proletarianism, Poetism, and Surrealism, as well as that of other movements of the era.

————. *Czech Writers and Politics, 1945-1969.* Boulder, Colo.: East European Monographs, 1982, 435 p.

> Analyzes the role of Czech authors and critics in national politics after World War II. French's introductory essay on Czech literature and politics during the first half of the twentieth century is excerpted above.

Goetz-Stankiewicz, Marketa. "A Revealing Encounter: The Theatre of the Absurd in Czechoslovakia." *Survey: A Journal of East and West Studies* 21, Nos. 1-2 (Winter-Spring 1975): 85-100.

> Discusses the critical reception and literary influence in Czechoslovakia during the 1960s of productions of dramas by Samuel Beckett, Eugène Ionesco, and other dramatists associated with the Theater of the Absurd.

————. *The Silenced Theatre: Czech Playwrights without a Stage.* Toronto: University of Toronto Press, 1979, 319 p.

> Extensive study of Czech drama of the 1960s and 1970s, including individual chapters on the works of Václav Havel, Pavel Kohout, Ivan Klíma, Josef Topol, and Ladislav Smoček, as well as general critical analyses.

Hájek, Igor. "The Rule of the Average: Czech Official Literature in the 1970s." *International Journal* 33, No. 3 (Summer 1978): 702-19.

> Concludes that "in the 1970s, political pressure divided [Czechoslovakian literature] into two separate streams; while its official branch suffers from lack of creativity and vision, its creative core, denied official recognition but capable of providing a stimulus for further development, has continued an active existence both at home and abroad."

————. "Precarious Survival." *Formations* 1, No. 1 (Spring 1984): 114-21.

> Examines the effects of the Prague Spring on subsequent Czech literature, delineating characteristics of fiction written by governmentally sanctioned, dissident, and exiled Czech authors.

Harkins, William E., and Trenský, Paul I., eds. *Czech Literature since 1956: A Symposium.* New York: Bohemica, 1980, 161 p.

> Includes ten essays on contemporary Czech fiction, culture, politics, and semiotics by such critics as Antonín J. Liehm, Trenský, and Thomas G. Winner. Harkins's discussion of Czech novels of the 1950s and 1960s is excerpted above.

Havel, Václav. *Living in Truth: Twenty-Two Essays Published on the Occasion of the Award of the Erasmus Prize to Václav Havel.* Edited by Jan Vladislav. London: Faber and Faber, 1987, 315 p.

> Contains essays by the Czechoslovakian president and dramatist on the nation's literature, culture, and politics. Major Czech and West European authors also contribute laudatory essays and fiction.

Hedbávný, Zdeněk. "Dramaturgs in Czechoslovakia." *Slavic and East European Arts* 4, No. 1 (Spring 1986): 31-4.

> Hedbávný discusses his role in Czech theater as a dramaturg, or production organizer, and outlines the influence of dramaturgs in formulating the ideological and aesthetic program of Czechoslovakia's theater since World War II.

Heythum, Antonín, and Heythum, Charlotte. "A National Theatre in Action: Prague—Before May, 1939." *Theatre Arts* 24, No. 2 (February 1940): 136-46.

> Traces the history of Prague's Municipal and Nobility theaters through the early twentieth century.

Hostovský, Egon. "The Czech Novel between the Two World Wars." *Slavonic and East European Review* 21, No. 57 (November 1943): 78-96.

> Examines reactions of Czech novelists to World War I in works written during the interwar era. Hostovský includes analyses of the novels of Karel Čapek, Jaroslav Hašek, and Vladislav Vančura.

Hruby, Peter. *Daydreams and Nightmares: Czech Communist and Ex-Communist Literature, 1917-1987.* Boulder, Colo.: East European Monographs, 1990, 362 p.

> Discusses major twentieth-century Czech authors and their political affiliations, particularly in relation to Soviet Communism. Hruby's essay on Czech poetry of the interwar period is excerpted above.

Jerabek, Esther. *Czechs and Slovaks in North America: A Bibliography.* New York: Czechoslovak Society of Arts & Sciences in America, 1976, 447 p.

> Bibliography of over 7,600 entries that cites works by Czechoslovakian authors living in North America.

The Jewish Publication Society of America. *The Jews of Czechoslovakia, Vol. I: Historical Studies and Surveys.* Philadelphia: Jewish Publication Society of America, 1968, 583 p.

> Contains a section of essays on Jewish Czech contributions to the nation's modern literature, journalism, and publishing industry.

Kárnet, George. "Flowers from the Graveyard: Morbidity, Necrophilia and Baroque Feelings in Present-Day Czechoslovak Poetry." *East Europe* 10, No. 1 (January 1961): 26-32.

> Elaborates on the treatment of the theme of death in Czech poetry from 1959 and 1960. Kárnet observes, "With a monotonous certainty we find words like death, cemetery, burial, tombstone, gravedigger, Hamlet, shrouds, shins, skeletons, widows, decay, coffins, etc."

Kovtun, George J. *Czech and Slovak Literature in English: A Bibliography.* Washington, D.C.: Library of Congress, European Division, 1984, 132 p.

> Extensive list of primary sources in anthologies and of full-length works, as well as secondary sources.

Kucera, Henry, and Kovtun, Emil. "Literature." In *Czechoslovakia,* edited by Vratislav Busek and Nicholas Spulber, pp. 173-97. New York: Frederick A. Praeger, 1957.

> Includes discussion of Czech and Slovak literature of the

interwar era and of that written during Czechoslovakia's first five years under Soviet Communism.

Kundera, Milan. "Somewhere Behind." In his *The Art of the Novel,* translated by Linda Asher, pp. 99-117. New York: Grove Press, 1988.

Discusses the novels of Franz Kafka, describing what Kundera characterizes as "the *Kafkan*" in relation to life in Prague under Communism.

Liehm, Antonín J. *The Politics of Culture.* Translated by Peter Kussi. New York: Grove Press, 1970, 412 p.

Offers excerpts from interviews with such contemporary Czech authors as Václav Havel, Ivan Klíma, Milan Kundera, Josef Škvorecký, and Ludvík Vaculík, who discuss Czech culture, politics, and their literary aesthetics. Liehm also includes a translation of Jean-Paul Sartre's essay "The Socialism That Came in from the Cold," which addresses events of the Prague Spring.

Nejedlá, Jaromíra. "An Auspicious Beginning." *Panorama of Czech Literature* 6 (1984): 5-10.

Surveys Czech poetry and fiction of the early 1980s, focusing on writers officially sanctioned by the Communist government. Nejedlá asserts that "the determining factor of this stratified and many-faceted organism is the authors' awareness of responsibility to a socialist society whose citizens they are and in whose womb their work originates."

Novák, Arne. *Czech Literature.* Edited by William E. Harkins. Translated by Peter Kussi. Ann Arbor: Michigan Slavic Publications, 1976, 375 p.

Contains a section that surveys major Czech literary figures of the early twentieth century in a study originally published in Czech in 1932. A supplement by Harkins addresses the works of Czech authors writing between 1946 and 1974.

Pynsent, R. B. "Assimilation, Childhood and Death: New Czech Fiction-Writers of the 1970s." *Slavonic and East European Review* 59, No. 3 (July 1981): 370-84.

Argues that the interest of Czechoslovakian authors born during and after World War II in "the assimilation of outsiders leads them to an interest in the pre-assimilated state, childhood, and the post-assimilated state, old age," rather than to an exclusive concern with the concept of socialist responsibility.

Rechcigl, Miloslav, Jr., ed. *The Czechoslovak Contribution to World Culture.* The Hague: Mouton & Co., 1964, 682 p.

Presents transcripts of the first congress of the Czechoslovak Society of the Arts and Sciences in America, held in Washington, D.C., in 1962. The volume contains a section on Czech literature and literary criticism, including essays by Jiří Škvor and René Wellek.

———, ed. *Czechoslovakia: Past and Present.* 2 vols. The Hague: Mouton & Co., 1968.

Comprises transcripts of the second congress of the Czechoslovak Society of the Arts and Sciences in America, held at Columbia University in 1964. Both volumes include several essays on twentieth-century Czech literature and culture by such critics as Alfred French, William E. Harkins, George Kárnet, and René Wellek. Discussions by Jiří Škvor and František Vnuk are excerpted above.

Rzounek, Vítězslav. "The Developmental Rhythm of Post-War Czech Literature." *Panorama of Czech Literature* 7 (1985): 96-111.

Surveys Czech literature written in the decades after the 1948 Soviet occupation, maintaining that works of that era reflect an "undiminished intensity of the boundless joy in regained freedom, achieved through the crushing of fascism in the first place by the Red Army."

Schamschula, Walter. "The Contemporary Czech Historical Novel and Its Political Inspiration." In *East European Literature: Selected Papers from the Second World Congress for Soviet and East European Studies,* edited by Evelyn Bristol, pp. 57-68. Berkeley, Calif.: Berkeley Slavic Specialties, 1982.

Explores the influence of Czechoslovakian politics on the manner in which contemporary Czech novelists select historical settings and the protagonists of their works.

Škvorecký, Josef. "Panorama of (Unionized) Czech Writers." *World Literature Today* 57, No. 1 (Winter 1983): 50-3.

Condemns the Czech English-language journal *Panorama of Czech Literature* for publishing almost exclusively what Škvorecký deems inferior Czech literature through the auspices of the Union of Czech Writers, a group politically affiliated with the Communist government.

———. "A Cabaret of Censorship." *Index on Censorship* 13, No. 5 (October 1984): 38-41.

Details the effects of governmental censorship on literature written in Czechoslovakia under Soviet Communism after the Prague Spring.

Součková, Milada. "Marxist Theory in Czech Literature." *Harvard Slavic Studies* 1 (1953): 335-61.

Discusses the influence of Communism and the aesthetics of socialist realism on Czech literary criticism during the first half of the twentieth century.

———. *Literature in Crisis: Czech Literature, 1938-1950.* New York: National Committee for a Free Europe, 1954, 158 p.

Offers an extensive analysis of Czechoslovakian literature during "the German occupation up to 1945; the false freedom to 1948; and the Russian occupation" during its initial years.

———. *A Literary Satellite: Czechoslovak-Russian Literary Relations.* Chicago: University of Chicago Press, 1970, 179 p.

Examines Czech literature of the twentieth century, focusing on "the 'pro-Russian' sentiment and its literary traditions" and investigates "its most characteristic groupings as they appear in various authors who were in direct contact with Russia."

Sziklay, László. "The Prague School." In *Literature and Its Interpretation,* edited by Lajos Nyírő, pp. 69-111. The Hague: Mouton Publishers, 1979.

Outlines major tenets of the interwar movement, particularly the linguistic and aesthetic theories of structuralist Jan Mukařovský in relation to the poetry of Vítězslav Nezval.

Viney, D. E. "Czech Culture and the 'New Spirit', 1948-52." *Slavonic and East European Review* 31, No. 77 (June 1953): 466-94.

Extensive discussion of Czechoslovakian culture during

the nation's first four years under Soviet Communism. The essay includes a detailed analysis of national aesthetic and ideological conflicts in relation to literary criticism and journalism.

Vočadlo, Otakar. "The Theater and Drama of Czechoslovakia." In *The Theater in a Changing Europe,* edited by Thomas H. Dickinson, pp. 330-63. New York: Henry Holt and Co., 1937.

Survey of leading Czech theaters of the early twentieth century, their directors, and the dramas that they produced.

Volek, Bronislava, and Volek, Emil. "*Guinea Pigs* and the Czech Novel 'Under Padlock' in the 1970s: From Modern Absolutism to the Postmodernist Absolute." *Rocky Mountain Review of Language and Literature* 37, Nos. 1-2 (1983): 20-52.

Discusses Czech novels of the 1970s, noting the role of the *samizdat* publications of the series *Edice petlice* ("Edition Padlock"). The Voleks particularly praise Ludvík Vaculík's novel *Morčata* (*Guinea Pigs*) as "one of the finest experiments and achievements of the 1970s."

Wellek, René. "The Two Traditions of Czech Literature." In *Slavic Studies,* edited by Alexander Kaun and Ernest J. Simmons, pp. 213-28. Ithaca, N.Y.: Cornell University Press, 1943.

Elaborates on the historical roots of twentieth-century Czech literature, observing a "dualism between an idealist, imaginative tradition and an empirical, rationalist trend [that] is not peculiarly Czech."

———. "Modern Czech Criticism and Literary Scholarship." *Harvard Slavic Studies* 2 (1954): 343-58.

Examines the theories of Czech literary critics of the first half of the twentieth century, particularly those of F. X. Šalda.

———. *The Literary Theory and Aesthetics of the Prague School.* Ann Arbor: Department of Slavic Languages and Literature, University of Michigan, 1969, 37 p.

Traces the development of the theory of the Prague movement, focusing on the works of structuralist Jan Mukařovský.

Existentialism and Literature

INTRODUCTION

Although Existentialism is widely considered one of the most important shaping influences on the thought and literature of the post–World War II era, there is little consensus as to which authors and what beliefs comprise this school of philosophy. While some critics limit the Existentialist period to the 1930s and 1940s, when such philosopher-authors as Jean-Paul Sartre and Albert Camus began writing on human existence in a purposeless, absurd universe, others trace its beginnings to the mid 1800s, when a radical reevaluation of Christian theology was presented in the works of Søren Kierkegaard and Fyodor Dostoevsky. Complicating any attempt to precisely define Existentialist philosophy is the fact that most of its major proponents, including Camus and Martin Heidegger, have denied being Existentialists, seeking to avoid being associated with the often contradictory ideologies the term "Existentialism" came to encompass.

There are, however, certain themes and ideas which occur throughout Existentialist literature. Prominent among these is the concept of "absurdity"—the feeling of dissonance and unsettlement resulting from the perception of the universe as random and nonrational, in spite of humanity's desire for order and purpose. A corollary of this belief is the idea that "existence precedes essence," that is, that the world has no meaning except that which individuals impose upon it, and that there are no absolute moral values, only those created by human beings. From this concept stems another concern of Existentialism: that of human freedom. Existentialist philosophy holds that, in the absence of an absolute moral authority, individuals have the power to choose how they will act and must take responsibility for those choices. In Sartre's terminology, human existence is initially that of dead objects, *en-soi* existence or "being in-itself"; by giving purpose to one's life through vital, committed action, one achieves *pour-soi* existence or "being for-itself." Most people, however, live in "bad faith," believing themselves controlled by metaphysical forces such as God or fate. Individuals must therefore rebel against all constraints on liberty, even those of reason; this idea is exemplified by the protagonist of Dostoevsky's *Notes from the Underground*, who insists on irrationally believing that two plus two equals five in order to demonstrate his free will. These Existentialist tenets reflect Friedrich Nietzsche's declaration that God is dead and that people alone are responsible for giving order to the universe. However, while most Existentialists took an atheist or agnostic view of the universe, there also developed a branch of religious Existentialism led by such philosophers as Martin Buber and Paul Tillich, who maintained that individuals could overcome their essential isolation by believing in God through an irrational "leap of faith."

The philosophy and literature of Existentialism are closely related. Many of the principal Existentialist philosophers also wrote creatively, expressing some of their most important philosophical convictions in novels. The protagonist of an Existentialist novel most frequently is an individual who feels estranged from other people and comes to a realization of the indeterminate nature of being and the falseness of social and intellectual orthodoxies. Among the most noted of these characters are Roquentin of Sartre's *La nausée* (*Nausea*), who rejects his life in academia after an epiphanic revelation of the superfluousness of existence, and Meursault of Camus's *L'étranger* (*The Stranger*), who is tried for murder and sentenced to death not so much for his crime as for his atheism and his disregard for social conventions. Plots in Existentialist literature often involve a gratuitous action which demonstrates free will or a character facing death; only by being aware of one's mortality and being confronted with the void, the authors contend, can one realize the need to act purposefully and freely while still alive.

In the aftermath of the worldwide Great Depression and World War II, Existentialism was a popular intellectual and literary phenomenon throughout Europe and to a lesser extent in the United States. In the 1950s, however, the movement's major figures began to drift away from Existentialism in favor of Marxist politics, other philosophies, or more aesthetic approaches to writing. Nevertheless, Existentialism remains a significant influence on contemporary philosophy, and its concepts of the absurd, irrationality, the loss of meaning, and the aloneness of the individual became major components of the Theater of the Absurd and literary postmodernism.

REPRESENTATIVE WORKS

De Beauvoir, Simone
   L'existentialisme et la sagesse des nations   (essays)
      1948
   Les mandarins   (novel)   1954
   [*The Mandarins,* 1956]
Camus, Albert
   L'étranger   (novel)   1942
   [*The Stranger,* 1946]
   Le mythe de Sisyphe   (essay)   1942
   [*The Myth of Sisyphus,* 1955]
   Caligula   (drama)   1944
   [*Caligula* published in *Caligula and Three Other Plays,* 1958]
   La peste   (novel)   1947
   [*The Plague,* 1948]
   Les justes   (drama)   1950
   [*The Just Assassins* published in *Caligula and Three Other Plays,* 1958]
   L'homme révolté   (essay)   1951

[*The Rebel*, 1953]
La chute   (novel)   1956
   [*The Fall*, 1956]
L'exil et le royaume   (short stories)   1957
   [*Exile and the Kingdom*, 1958]
Dostoevsky, Fyodor
Zapiski iz myortvogo doma   (novel)   1862
   [*Notes from the Underground*, 1912; also published
      as *Letters from the Underworld*, 1913]
Besy   (novel)   1873
   [*The Possessed*, 1913; also published as *The Devils*,
      1953]
Brat'ya Karamazovy   (novel)   1880
   [*The Brothers Karamazov*, 1912]
Heidegger, Martin
Sein und Zeit   (treatise)   1927
   [*Being and Time*, 1962]
Existence and Being   (essays)   1949
Jaspers, Karl
Philosophie. 3 vols.   (treatise)   1932
   [*Philosophy*, 1969-71]
Vernuft und Existenz   (treatise)   1935
   [*Reason and Existence*, 1953]
Existenzphilosophie   (treatise)   1937
   [*Philosophy of Existence*, 1971]
Kafka, Franz
Die Verwandlung   (novella)   1915
   [*The Metamorphosis*, 1937]
Der Prozess   (novel)   1925
   [*The Trial*, 1935]
Das Schloß   (novel)   1926
   [*The Castle*, 1930]
Kierkegaard, Søren
*Enten-eller: Et Livs Fragment udgivet af Victor
      Eremita*   (essay)   1843
   [*Either/Or: A Fragment of Life*, 1944]
*Frygt og Bæven. Dialektisk Lyrik af Johannes de
      Silentio*   (essay)   1843
   [*Fear and Trembling: A Dialectical Lyric by
      Johannes de Silentio*, 1939]
Malraux, André
La condition humaine   (novel)   1933
   [*Man's Fate*, 1934]
Nietzsche, Friedrich
*Also sprach Zarathustra: Ein Buch für Alle und
      Keinen*. 4 vols.   (prose)   1883-85
   [*Thus Spoke Zarathustra: A Book for All and None*,
      1909]
*Jenseits von Gut und Böse: Vorspiel einer Philosophie
      der Zukunft*   (essays and aphorisms)   1886
   [*Beyond Good and Evil: Prelude to a Philosophy of
      the Future*, 1907]
Zur Genealogie der Moral   (essays and aphorisms)
      1887
   [*On the Genealogy of Morals* published in *The
      Complete Works of Friedrich Nietzsche*, Vol. 13,
      1910]
*Die Götzendämmerung; oder, Wie man mit dem
      Hammer philosophiert*   (essays)   1889
   [*The Twilight of the Idols*, published in *The
      Complete Works of Friedrich Nietzsche*, Vol. 16,
      1911]
Rilke, Rainer Maria

Die Aufzeichnungen des Malte Laurids Brigge
   (novel)   1910
   [*The Notebooks of Malte Laurids Brigge*, 1930; also
      published as *The Journal of My Other Self*,
      1930]
Sartre, Jean-Paul
La nausée   (novel)   1938
   [*Nausea*, 1949; also published as *The Diary of
      Antoine Roquentin*, 1949]
L'être et le néant: Essai d'ontologie phénoménologique
   (essay)   1943
   [*Being and Nothingness: An Essay on
      Phenomenological Ontology*, 1956]
Les mouches   (drama)   1943
   [*The Flies* published in *The Flies and In Camera*,
      1946]
L'âge de la raison   (novel)   1945; revised edition,
      1960
   [*The Age of Reason*, 1947]
Huis clos   (drama)   1945
   [*In Camera* published in *The Flies and In Camera*,
      1946; also published as *No Exit*, 1947]
Le sursis   (novel)   1945
   [*The Reprieve*, 1947]
L'existentialisme est un humanisme   (essay)   1946
   [*Existentialism*, 1947; also published as
      Existentialism and Humanism, 1948]
Qu'est-ce que la littérature?   (essay)   1948
   [*What is Literature?*, 1949; also published as
      Literature and Existentialism, 1962]
Wright, Richard
The Outsider   (novel)   1953

OVERVIEWS AND DEFINITIONS

Henri Peyre

[*Peyre is a French-born critic who has lived and taught
in the United States for most of his career. One of the
foremost American critics of French literature, he has
written extensively on modern French literature in
works that blend superb scholarship with a clear style accessible to the non-specialist reader, most notably in*
French Novelists of Today, *from which the following
excerpt is taken. Peyre is a staunch defender of traditional forms of literature that examine the meaning of
life in modern society and the role of individual destiny
in an indifferent universe; he dislikes experimentalism
for its own sake, noting that "many experimenters are
the martyrs of a lost cause." In the following excerpt,
Peyre provides a history of the Existentialist movement
and outlines five of its major precepts.*]

Existentialism is a metaphysics, a psychology relying
upon phenomenology, a sociology of literature, a thera-
peutics, and, probably more than anything else, an ethics.
Clouds of confusion, due in part to the complexity of the
issues and to a failure to agree on clear definitions of
words, but in part also sedulously thickened by the rival
high-priests of existentialism, have turned it into a myth,
surrounded it by a cult, but created in others a bitter ani-

madversion. Far too much publicity, not always sought by the German or French champions of that philosophy, has surrounded the movement. Many among the early detractors of existentialism in France, even more in Britain and America where the movement was branded for ten or fifteen years as a systematic debasement of all values and as obscene scatology, have tried to discredit it as erotic titillation and delight in coarseness. After two or three decades of discussion, we may not necessarily be much clearer as to the meaning of existentialism. There will never be a consensus among philosophers as to what 'existence,' 'nothingness,' 'the absurd,' 'a project,' or our moral duty as discovered by our own derelict self and still valid for other men, may signify. But it is possible to relate existentialism to its precursors, to its age, and even to assess, as Croce did for Hegel and as has been done for other philosophy, what in that system is dead or moribund and what, from it, is likely to survive.

The general context in which several of the existentialist moods and ideas appeared antedates World War II. Indeed, like much that permeates the second half of the twentieth century, it can be traced back to the general failure of reason's claims to explain the world, around 1910-15, and to the growing lack of faith in science as affording absolute certainties. The earliest printed expression of Sartre's anguish is probably found in an 'Enquête auprès des étudiants d'aujourd'hui,' reported in *Les nouvelles littéraires* on February 2, 1929. Sartre, then at the Ecole Normale and preparing for the Agregation of Philosophy (where he was to be admitted number one that very year, after having failed the previous year for inadequate knowledge of history of philosophy), said: 'At the bottom of the human creature as at the bottom of nature, I see sadness and boredom. . . . Good and Evil, ideas of man working on man: vain ideas. Vain also is that determinism which strangely attempts to effect the synthesis of existence and of being. We are as free as you wish, but powerless. . . . There is no will to power. All is too weak: all things tend to die. . . . ' Comparing his generation, which regarded itself as sick with 'le mal du siècle,' to previous generations, Sartre concluded, at twenty-four: 'We are more unhappy, but more "sympathiques." '

Soon after, an economic and social depression was to darken the prospects of Western man. Unemployment was to grow catastrophically. Nationalism became resurgent in Europe and tyrannies ruled over half of its area. Traditional humanism had become inadequate. Faith in the future had collapsed; so had faith in fraternity and faith in the moral and sexual liberation which, after Freud and the breakdown of old taboos, had seemed to promise happiness. Man felt desperately alone and knew he would have to rely upon himself, a derelict. 'Leave us alone without books, and we shall be lost in confusion at once,' had written Dostoevski, then eagerly read in France. 'We are oppressed at being men, men with a real individual body and blood. We are ashamed of it, and we try to continue being some sort of impossible generalized man.' Another Russian, who lived in Paris and who is often called a Christian existentialist (he was an Orthodox, but the friend of many French Catholic thinkers), Nicholas Berdiaev, wrote in *Solitude and Society* (1938): 'Sex is one

of the chief causes of human solitude. Man is a sexual being, that is, half a being, divided and incomplete.' The comfort which the young people of France had derived first from the philosophy of Bergson, mostly influential between 1905 and 1925, then from that of Maritain, appeared of little avail to the intellectuals of 1935-38. Disappointed with Stalinist Russia, estranged from the new Messiah (which the surrealists, André Gide and others had naïvely hoped to hail in 'Cette grande lueur à l'est,' as the French title of Romains's *Men of Good Will,* volume 19, puts it), they were seeking elsewhere. Bergson, it is true, had sketched a distinction between the 'deeper self' and the 'superficial self' that was to be formulated anew and with greater rigor by the existentialists when they contrasted the authentic with the inauthentic self. But he had not stressed the recoiling before anguish which led man to take refuge in the inauthentic. Moreover he tended to explain man by what had preceded him, an *élan vital* of which God was the prime mover, and he had declared the notion of nothingness to be unthinkable. Not without much injustice to the moving developments of *Les deux sources de la morale et de la religion* (1935), the existentialists, in their claim to hold a monopoly over anguish, resented Bergson's apparent serenity. Merleau-Ponty, however, made amends to Bergson in his inaugural lecture at the Collège de France, *Eloge de la philosophie,* in 1953.

The existentialists were attracted by phenomenology, of which Merleau-Ponty, for many years a close friend of Sartre and his collaborator at the helm of *Les temps modernes,* was the chief exponent in France. Husserl, its founder, conceived it as a method which, in presence of an object, seizes only the appearance according to which we think it and which it assumes in our consciousness, and a method which remains unconcerned with the reality which may not correspond to that appearance. Such a method, intent on grasping the meaning of the world directly, would resort to literary description as preferable to abstruse and abstract speculation. It sought an ally in fiction and drama and another one in political and social 'engagement' or involvement. 'The world is not what I think, but what I live,' declared Merleau-Ponty, echoing Kierkegaard. Sartre, like him a professional metaphysician, but one who is equally at home in the novel, the drama, polemics, and criticism, stated: 'Metaphysics is not a barren discussion on abstract notions which lie beyond the reach of experience; it is a living effort to embrace, from the inside, the human condition in its totality.'

The later volumes of Sartre and of his friends have been acclaimed in the Anglo-American world. A skillful but minor masterpiece, *Les mots,* was rapturously overpraised in 1963-64. *Time* and *Newsweek,* which had at one time mocked him as decadent, devote respectful articles to him. *Playboy* publishes reverential interviews with him, and grave essays by him. Camus has had more worshippers in the United States than any writer since Harriet Beecher Stowe and was mourned upon his death as a saint. Simone de Beauvoir ventured to suggest, after one of her trips to this country, that America was *the* land for existentialism *par excellence;* the youth of the United States has certainly, since 1960, been far more drawn to that ethics of freedom and of action than that of France, and more philosophical and literary volumes on Sartre and on Camus appear in the United States than in the whole rest of the world. Some of the Sartrian formulas ring like echoes of pragmatist compatriots of William James and of John Dewey: 'To understand the abstract concretely'; 'The world is not what I think, but what I live'; or 'Freedom is nothing else than a choice which creates for itself its own possibilities.' Even Sartrian professions of atheism have failed to dismay Unitarians, Episcopalians, or the Catholics of 1965 who are advised by the Ecumenical Council to understand atheism and to learn from it. 'If you admit God,' said Sartre, 'it is because you are afraid to be what you are, simply men, and to be self-sufficient. I say: God is not, man is sufficient unto himself'; or (in *Action*, on December 29, 1944), 'A motto for man: to do and through doing, to "do" himself [*Faire et en faisant, se faire et n'être rien que ce qu'il s'est fait*] and to be nothing but what he has made of himself. . . . True optimism is to be glad to count on oneself alone, and to act alone for the good of all.' The change in Anglo-American opinion reflects a deeper transformation in the moods of the English-speaking nations. During and just after World War II, the Anglo-Saxon allies, spared invasion or bombing of their own lands, holding high their courage and determined to save the rest of the free world, looked down upon the oppressed and demoralized Europeans of the continent as doomed to misery for years, unable to solve their problems and therefore seeking an escape in grandiose abstract speculations. They compared their weakened allies whom they were rescuing to the Germans who, in 1917-18, sensing that they were going to lose the war which they had at first hailed as 'fresh and joyous,' concluded that their collapse was a gigantic 'Decline of the West.' Many an American commentator then contended that existentialism, a philosophy of decadence emanating from a Europe that had lost all faith in herself and in the future, was as such discredited and would never seduce a healthy and optimistic New World. Such however was not the case. Much of what is significant in that philosophy was already latent in the nineteen-twenties and 'thirties, not only in Germany but in an early volume by Malraux and in Sartre's first philosophical writings, which antedated and did not foresee the capitulation of Munich and the collapse of the ruling classes in France in 1940. However, even if the subsequent formulation of existentialism, on the absurd, on the necessity for anguish, and on the need for man to formulate his own immanent values himself and to conquer his own freedom, had been inspired by the catastrophes which shook Europe in 1940, by the gas chambers, and by the bombings of civilian populations, such a lived source for emotions and ideas would in no way impair the validity of that philosophy. It would, on the contrary, be revolting that thinkers could have then ignored the breakdown of values around them, could have polished words and systems as Goethe had done, singing wine, women, young men, and the delights of art in his *West-Östliche Divan* while Napoleon was trampling Germany under foot, and could indeed have remained deaf to the clamor of oppressed people who then hoped in vain to hear clear and militant encouragement from the Pope or from their religious and academic leaders. The existentialists then lived their ethics with courage. They bid farewell to universals and chose to concentrate on the way in which traditional and general truths presented themselves to them *hic et tunc,* then and there.

Sartre, like Camus, like Genet whom Sartre has ironically transfigured into a saint, and like the leader of surrealism, Breton, before him, considers moral issues alone as important and has said so in the presentation of his own ethical thought by his friend Francis Jeanson. But a moralist is not a teacher of lay Sunday school precepts for obedient little boys. Somewhat provokingly, and as a part of his anti-bourgeois obsession, he has sought to give some jolts to the decorum of middle class ethics; because of this some of the Parisian reviewers of his novels even classified him with the naturalists of the last century. Their perspective was faulty and Sartre is certainly no Zola. His occasional incursions into scatology in one or two of his short stories and in the second volume of *Les chemins de la liberté* (*Roads to Freedom*) are more the 'canulars' or practical jokes of a 'Normalien' and of a bachelor dwelling among books and ideas than a systematic attempt at portraying the lower realities of life. There is no doubt a negative aspect to Sartrian philosophy, and with it some reveling and wallowing in the mud. But, as Leibnitz and Renan liked to assert, any philosophy is false in what it negates and true in what it asserts. With a perspective of several decades, we may now safely disregard the few negative, superficial, and ephemeral aspects of Sartrian existentialism and assert that his most lasting contribution may well lie in the psychological acuteness of his descriptions of moods and states of consciousness (of the *café* waiter, the caress, the 'inauthentic' and frigid woman in *L'être et le néant,* of the Spanish soldier afraid of death in *Le mur,* and of the schizophrenic couple in *La chambre*), in his search for an ethics, in his achievement as a novelist, and, at his best, as the most superb essayist of our age.

Existential thought was more profound perhaps in Kierkegaard, certainly in Husserl, who remains the primary and the earliest advocate of a return to things ('Wie wollen auf die Sachen selbst zurückgehen') and of the project (or intentionality) as being the very nature of consciousness. Heidegger was probably not known to Sartre when he began elaborating his own system of thought in the early nineteen-thirties and there always remained many differences between his thought, called in French *existentiale,* and that of Jaspers, dubbed *existentielle.* Heidegger himself always carefully separated his own doctrine (or successive doctrines) from French existentialism and deplored Sartre's dualism, as radical and ill-founded in his view as that of Descartes. His own ambition is to restore a link between the object and the subject: his concern is with existence, or, as he puts in the Latin plural in *existentialia,* in what is. But the originality and the force of French existentialism is that it did not stay enclosed in university seminars of philosophy and wrapped in abstruse language. As an English commentator of that French literature has called it, it was from the start 'literature as philosophy' (Everett Knight [see Further Reading]) and the work of the 'Novelist as Philosopher' as another Englishman, John Cruickshank, entitled his volume.

The movement of ideas, derived in part from German predecessors and, to a lesser extent, from Pascal, Kierkegaard, Nietzsche, and Unamuno, made a momentous commotion in France and elsewhere, shaking most of the branches of literature, our response to poetry, painting, and music, and affecting the lives of thousands of individuals. As had been the case once with Cartesianism, then with the Enlightenment and with Bergsonism, philosophy sprang to a new life in attempting to seize the individual and the concrete. It coincided once again with life, fulfilling the wish formulated by Kierkegaard when he took issue with Hegelian philosophy turned obstinately backward: 'We live forward, but we understand backward.' This correspondence between philosophy and an *Erlebnis*, a lived experience, proved a boon to literature. The latter could no longer be reduced to seductive stories, skillful comedies, and pleasing garlands of imagery and of words. Such literature has been treated contemptuously by Sartre, even when it was written by his former close friend, Camus, or (as he repeated in *Les mots*) by himself. The French readers of 1940-60 insisted upon literature facing the anguish of modern man. Everything had crumbled down around them and they knew that all had to be called in question, with the feeling—termed by the poet Henri Michaux the most precious asset of modern man—'irrespect.' That literature of years of distress had to attempt what Marx had defined, in his *Critique of Hegel's Philosophy*, as being radical: going to the very roots. And, Marx added, the root of everything is in man himself.

The importance of a movement, ideological, aesthetic, and even political, cannot be measured clearly by the number of persons who present themselves as belonging to it, but by the quality of their sensibility and the power of their ideas. Surrealism has influenced scores of painters, sculptors and poets, in and outside France, from René Char to Giacometti and Arshile Gorki, who never bowed to the iron rod of André Breton. There may well never have been more than sixty existentialists or sixty surrealists; nevertheless those movements constituted the marching wing of French literature for several decades. None rivaled them in importance. The years 1940-65 may well be labeled, in future histories of taste, the existentialist era. Nor does it seem of much consequence to debate at length on who was, or was not, a genuine existentialist, or an authentic surrealist, or a true romantic. Existentialism never constituted a chapel, or a school, from which a heretic or an unruly child is expelled: it is a mood. Camus repeatedly refused to be labeled an existentialist; but in spite of his technical differences on the respective role of essence and existence and on the meaning of the absurd, or his attitude toward concentration camps in Russia or toward the Algerian war, Camus nevertheless grew up in the same climate of sensibility, acclaimed the same masters (Dostoevski, Kierkegaard, Nietzsche, Kafka), fought the same battles as other existentialists; the very bitterness of his later quarrel with Sartre and Jeanson testifies to his closeness to his 'frères ennemis' and to the passionate dialectics required to distinguish him from his former allies. Along with Camus, and besides the high-priestess of existentialist altars, Simone de Beauvoir, the leading French phenomenologist Merleau-Ponty, from whom Sartre became estranged and on whom he wrote a moving essay after his friend's death in *Situations IV*, played a significant role in existentialism. Jean Genet, Violette Leduc, J.-M. Le Clézio, even Robbe-Grillet (reluctant as he would be to be thrust into a pigeonhole with other phenomenological doves), Colette Audry, and others have been or are close to existentialism. So are a number of critics and moralists, such as Jean Pouillon, Francis Jeanson, and Bernard Dort. Unlike Breton, Sartre has never attempted to imprison any disciples in his own system or to impose his technique to them. He is too intelligent not to be aware of the danger of epigoni, who would soon degrade his most original artistic devices by turning them into mere tricks. The chief existentialist review, *Les temps modernes*, after bidding fair to renovate literary life in the nineteen-fifties, has become monotonous, obsessed with a few political and sociological themes and remote from literature and art. It has been too long under Sartre's exclusive control and has failed to draw outstanding young talent. But if a movement is worth as much as its leader is, existentialism remains very considerable. Sartre stands out, 'above the rest proudly eminent,' as the most extraordinary intelligence of his generation, as a novelist and storyteller of the first order, as a successful playwright, as a brilliant essayist and critic of literature, art, life, even as a political thinker, and, of course, as a psychologist and as a philosopher. Like Voltaire and Diderot, he unites an amazing variety of gifts in one person; and he has occasional flashes of insight into poetry and into religion, of which his eighteenth-century predecessors had not proved capable.

'A fictional technique,' Sartre wrote, 'always sends us back to the novelist's metaphysics. The critic's task is to elucidate the latter before appraising the former.' The assertion may lead to erroneous conclusions if all literature comes to be interpreted as nothing but philosophy in another form. But since so much confusion has clouded the few vital principles that existentialism has upheld, it is useful to state the fundamental points which Sartre and his friends put forward. But the imaginative works of Sartre preceded his most important philosophical treatises. So did *Caligula*, in an earlier version, *L'étranger*, and the essays in which Camus voiced his pagan lust for life, which all came before the murky dissertations of *Le mythe de Sisyphe* and of *L'homme révolté*.

The first notion stressed by existentialism is that of nothingness. That notion was discarded by most philosphers, and again not long ago by Bergson, as untenable. But the existentialists stress it, at least negatively, and, outdoing or contradicting Pascal, they establish a colloquy with the absence of God. We experience, according to Heidegger, the utter nothingness of not being; existence (*Dasein*) is steeped in it. Sartre contends that the concept of nothingness comes into the world through man. Why do I exist? Why does anything exist? Why is there not just nothingness? If the idea of nothingness does not lend itself to analysis, it can at least be experienced in fear and trembling. The *Angst* or anguish, of which Kierkegaard made so much, is the starting point of a personal philosophical reflection. Thanks to it, we pass from the superficial level of conventions lazily observed to the deeper level of individual reflection which accompanies man's awareness of his dreadful freedom.

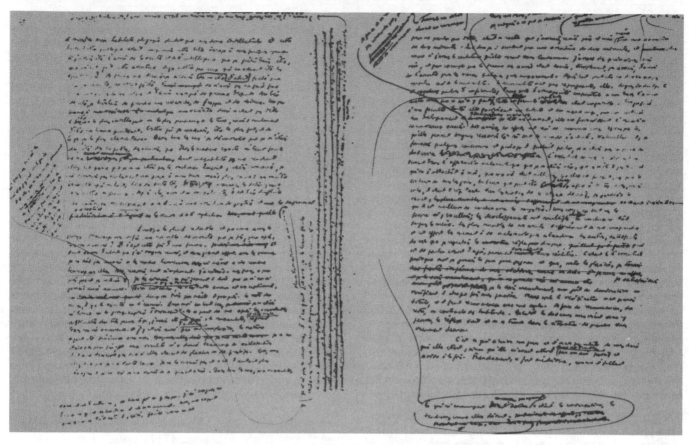

Camus's manuscript for his last novel La chute (The Fall).

Man facing nothingness undergoes the revelation of the absurd. No word has been more misinterpreted, partly through lack of a neat definition of what was meant by it on the part of Kafka and Malraux, who first threw the notion among us, then through the same indefinition on the part of Sartre and Camus. The word itself has retained in French its Latin meaning of 'dissonant,' 'discordant' (*ab* intensifying *surdus,* deaf or insufferable to the ear), 'inharmonius,' hence 'foolish' and 'unreasonable.' For Kafka, man is surrounded with mysterious signs which he cannot decipher and which appear to be hostile to him. For Sartre, the absurd is what in a being is 'given,' injustifiable, the weight of all that is contingent and makes man feel 'de trop,' superfluous, unwanted. But Camus made the most of the notion of absurdity which, to him, lies in a relationship between man and the world which is jarringly dissonant. Man is athirst for rationality yet he continually stumbles upon irrationality. He harbors in him 'a wild need for clarity' and he is confronted with darkness and confusion. He wishes happiness but the conditions of life seldom or never bring happiness within his reach. He would like a presence to watch over him and guide him through perils, but the eternal silence of the heavens fills him with dread. 'Men die and they are not happy' is the realization which prompts Caligula to commit his insensate crimes. The absurd is the conflict between human nostalgia for a reasonable order and the ubiquitous presence of the irrational.

That lag between man's wild wishes and 'reality's dark dream,' as Coleridge called it, fills the brain and the stomach of the existentialist with nausea. His temptation at first is to resort to what Camus, after Novalis, calls the only truly philosophical gesture, suicide. But suicide would merely amount to doing away with the one element, rational, courageous, and capable of clarity, that protests against the absurd irrationality of a blind universe: man. Camus rejects suicide, anxiously but with a little of the same sophistry with which Schopenhauer had eluded it. He welcomes the paradoxes that Kierkegaard, in his *Journal* for the year 1838, had lauded as the true privilege of intellectual life and the hallmark of great thinkers, the ability to proclaim the truths of tomorrow. Sartre and Camus will not, as did Kierkegaard, resort to the leap of faith to reach 'the absolute paradox, Christianity.' Their move of transcendence will not be toward a nonexistent God, but toward the world, other men, and toward the future.

Atheism is the third postulate. Existentialists waste no time attempting to prove a negative, which is deemed impossible in logic. What is gratuitously asserted may, in any case, be just as gratuitously negated; as old logicians ruled, 'quod gratis asseritur gratis negatur.' Their placid assumption is that everything takes place as if God did not exist, and they drive the famous Nietzschean 'death of God' to its consequences. They spurn the facile solaces of deism ('the deist is he who lacks the nerve to be an atheist,' said the French Catholic writer, De Bonald) and of pantheism, the latter being one of the most glittering diamonds in that jewel-case of synonyms that Renan hinted the modern had substituted for God. For too many moderns, God is merely a convenient symbol to whom we transfer the burden of our problems in order to evade solving them ourselves as religious thinkers, grateful to atheistic existentialism for its forthrightness, have pointed out. 'Man is a being that projects to be God. . . . Man loses himself as man in order that God may be born. But the idea of God is contradictory and we lose ourselves in vain. Man is a useless passion': thus concluded the philosopher of *L'être et le néant.* Let us transcend ourselves, not vertically, seeking a heaven above, but horizontally, like the doctor and his friend in *La peste,* assume our human condition fully and, most difficult of all, our freedom. Existentialist philosophy has been praised by its devotees as a liberation, albeit a frightening one. There is indeed more stoicism and optimism (or 'muscular and constructive pessimism') in existentialism than there is apathy or irresponsibility. Again and again, its partisans have stressed their difference from Kirilov who, in Dostoevski's *The Demons* (or *The Possessed*), exclaimed: 'If God does not exist, everything is allowed.' In their view, on the contrary, man must unflinchingly assume his duties to himself and to his fellow-beings. Since God does not exist, or since everything happens as if He did not exist, nothing is permitted. Man will set himself up as the creator of values, in the place of an absent or silent God. It is up to him to create his own essence and accept his total freedom.

The fourth credo of the existentialists is the well-known assertion that existence precedes essence. Man was not created according to a preexisting mold or pattern, like a table or a paper-knife. He is not just one sample of a general entity pompously dubbed 'human nature.' He is not a shadow in Plato's cave, aspiring to the noble and stable Idea. He was thrown into the world, a derelict; he exists. No properties were assigned to him beforehand. He is what he conceives himself to be and what he makes of himself; but he does not have to fulfill any pre-established plan. Only as he is here and now, does anything begin for him. He enjoys a 'morose delectation' in feeling thus forlorn, a prey to care or *Sorge,* shorn of God and of a Redeemer. From his very dereliction he will draw audacity. He will create his own human nature and his own values, through transcending the past and the present, throwing himself into the future and pursuing his project. 'One is nothing else but one's own life.' Man, thrown into this world through a sudden and random *Geworfenheit,* does not long dwell in gloom. He accepts himself and looks forward. Sartre summed up his ethical message as 'You are free. Choose, that is to say, invent.'

Subjectivity is the obvious starting point for such a doctrine, and here again the ancestor is Kierkegaard. *Sum* has become the foe of *cogito. Sum, ergo cogito* proposed the disgruntled Hegelian from Denmark, who added: 'A thinker cannot prove his existence through thought, for insofar as he thinks abstractly, he forgets precisely this: that he exists.' Man is a subject with a self to acquire, and not an object to be known. The literature of existentialism does not proceed through generalities about man, nature,

passions, the world. It attempts to seize man in the quick, to grasp him in the irreducible uniqueness of his existence. Man is described *en situation,* in certain conditions that happen to constitute the framework of his existence, and in his project. He fulfills himself, through living, in a world and with a consciousness inextricably welded to each other. *Sein* is *Zeit* for him.

The fifth postulate is man's freedom, fundamental in Sartre's view of things and totally unproved, but a necessary postulate. Man has the freedom to become free. He chooses and projects himself toward his choice. He does not want that freedom, which is a heavy burden; the creature who has realized how momentous his freely assumed burden is becomes seized with dread. But that freedom also constitutes man's greatest single asset. It entails involvement, the duty of bringing a similar awareness of man's potential and dynamic freedom to others, through political, journalistic, and literary action. That freedom is always in danger of being lost and must incessantly be reconquered.

The individual, thus nondetermined, condemned to be totally free, does not turn into an anti-social anarchist, intoxicated with his individualism—or so Sartre assumes. He chooses the good and rejects vice, crime, oppression. He would not treat any person as a thing. Existentialism, gratuitously, almost mystically, considers freedom as the basis for responsibility and formulates what amounts to a new categorical imperative. The free person avoids becoming the mere captive of former decisions, for the irreplaceable quality of individual existence would then be dried up, and he must also heroically extend his responsibility to the awakening of placid unprivileged mortals who have not yet assumed the burden of their freedom. One of the favorite existentialist maxims is none other than the declaration in *The Brothers Karamazov:* 'Everyone is responsible for everything before everybody.' (pp. 244-56)

[Much] has been written, often glibly, on the pessimism of existentialist fiction. There is far more pessimism in Thomas Mann's stories of decrepitude and of the inevitable unbalance of genius, in Cesare Pavese's and in Alberto Moravia's novels, indeed in almost all modern Italian literature, and in three-fourths of American letters, Mark Twain and John Dos Passos not excepted, and William Faulkner himself included in spite of his official speeches, than there is in recent French literature. There was infinitely more obsession with decadence and death in Flaubert and his contemporaries, between 1850 and 1870, than there has been in our own age.

To be sure, some form of pessimism is rampant around us today. But it is, we believe, a very different pessimism from that of the nineteen-twenties, much less cynical and complacent, more courageous and more constructive. The men and women of 1920-30 had tried to forget a war they considered as a huge mistake and to resume, freed from all remnants of Puritanism and from bourgeois morality, a search for happiness, often conceived as mere pleasure, once hampered and then interrupted. Their literature refused *engagement* and closed its eyes to tragedy. It took the American depression, the advent of Hitler in Germany, the vogue of Russia as the new land of promise, and the threat of an impending new war to arouse the writers of the early 'thirties out of the shallow optimism of the preceding years. The Spanish civil war and the defeat and occupation of France were then the two great creative events in thought and literature. Catastrophes had not been forestalled. They had to be lived through.

Existentialism does not ignore despair. But it attempts to lead away from it after having drunk from its cup to the dregs. "The gravest form of despair,' said Kierkegaard, 'is not to be desperate, not to be aware of one's despair.' Faith in a divine providence is rejected. Faith in progress is rejected likewise, or at least critically re-examined. Faith in the innate goodness of man has been exploded by the spectacle of wars, of concentration camps, of man's inhumanity to man. Fear is with us, and it has spread to the New World, once immune from it. Like the conscience in existentialist doctrines, it gnaws like a worm in the fruit, at our unequaled prosperity and at our worship of science, education, and good neighborliness.

The usefulness of existentialist literature, regardless of its aesthetic value, is in its rejection of the delusions through which modern man often attempts to forget the duties he must assume. It is deliberately modern, and, as Sartre put it in a famous manifesto, one must write for one's own time. It thus spurns the easy escape of many scholars who, heirs to a nineteenth-century tradition, seek the explanation of the present in the past and of modern man in the study of primitive societies—the matriarchate among the Polynesians, incest among the Amazon tribes, or the swaddling clothes of Russian babies. Existentialism is a socially conscious literature, which fights with equal ardor communism on its left and the middle class on its right; the one has abdicated critical spirit and freedom, the other suffers from a Hegelian bad conscience and dares not face the future; it is pitiful in its good will and in its maze of contradictions, but it is sterile. 'The freedom to write,' Sartre asserts in his remarkable *Qu'est-ce que la littérature?,* 'presupposes the freedom of the citizen. One does not write for slaves. Prose-writing is bound up in solidarity with the only regime in which prose retains a meaning: democracy . . . To write is another way of wanting freedom.' Marxist materialism has been dealt grievous blows by Sartre and Merleau-Ponty, for the existentialists reject the acrobatics through which good and evil play off against each other in the dialectical pursuit of the synthesis. But they stand equally firm against the easy solace of religion or the comfort of philosophical idealism, for which evil is merely a shadow necessarily accompanying the good. If elsewhere Sartre may be charged with excessive *virtuosité* and even with sophistry, he has written, in *Qu'est-ce que la littérature?* and in *Réflexions sur la question juive,* some of the most moving and most definitive pages of our age. Better than any other French writer since Bergson, or earlier still, since Renan and Voltaire, he has combined clarity and depth, a tragic feeling for life and the conviction that man has not yet said his last word. Through revolting against God, or against one of the successive conceptions of God that man has made for himself, the modern hero who has plumbed the depths of absurdity and of anxiety and discarded the illusions of mechanical

progress teaches and practices self-reliance and holds out a beacon in the night, which threatens, or lures, us today.

In words that aptly render the moral attitude that was then Sartre's as well as his own, Camus has stated the existentialist position, deprived of all philosophical subtleties and expressed with forthrightness and nobleness.

> We refuse to despair of man. Without having any exaggerated ambition to save him, we hold at least to the idea of serving him . . . To the last we shall reject a divine charity that would deprive men of the justice which is their due.

And elsewhere, after defining his position:

> Is this pessimism? No. This is an honest effort to determine what is wanted, what is unwanted . . . We, young Frenchmen, label as pessimists those who say that all goes well and that nothing changes human nature. We call them pessimists, because they are among those from whom nothing can be expected. *They* will be to blame if the world indeed never changes. But there are among us enough men of decision pledged to do all that is within their power to cure the world and themselves of their present sickness.

(pp. 270-72)

Henri Peyre, "Existentialism and French Literature: Jean-Paul Sartre's Novels," in his French Novelists of Today, *revised edition, Oxford University Press, 1967, pp. 244-74.*

F. McEachran

[*In the following excerpt, McEachran surveys the principal elements of Existentialism as embodied in the works of several Existentialist authors.*]

Existentialism has a reasonably long history behind it, even if we do not take it back as far as St. Augustine. Certainly, in so far as it may be regarded as a criticism of metaphysics, Blaise Pascal shows signs of it in his attack on Descartes. With all his metaphysicising, says Pascal, Descartes could not avoid starting off the world with a little "push". Later, a good deal later, came Kierkegaard with his onslaught on Hegel and his doctrine of the *absurd,* and for completely opposite reasons his successor in the same century, Friedrich Nietzsche was also a firm supporter. The *absurdity* of life lies in the contrast, the perceptual and the conceptual, life and death, time and eternity, which no Hegelian "mediation", i.e. synthesizing, can possibly iron out. Nietzsche did not exactly talk this language, but he so emphasized the particular in contrast to the general, the immediate present against past and future, time against eternity, that his doctrine has a strange resemblance to that of Kierkegaard.

These three men, and possibly St. Augustine too, were the loneliest men in history and their writings, particularly those of Kierkegaard and Nietzsche, reflect this fact. If you stress the here and now, the concrete immediate, to the extent Nietzsche did, in contrast to the world of imagination and conceptual thought, a gulf widens round you and it may be terrifying. Nietzsche hammered on the fact that we have only this life to live and this body to live in it, this life here and now, with no hereafter to cushion and protect it, and in the end it frightened him. To cover up his fear he invented the doctrine of *ewige Wiederkunft* or "eternal recurrence" which is simply the old immortality under a new name, that of living the same life an infinite number of times. He even served up a new morality with it (modelled on Kant's categorical imperative), exhorting his followers to live this present life so well that it would be worth while living an infinite number of times (since in any case it will have to be lived). Kierkegaard was aware of the same gulf. He closed it with a "leap of faith". This immediate life is "absurd"—life against death, time against eternity—so close down on your reason, leap into the unknown by an act of faith and God will do the rest. So also more remotely did Pascal, but less hysterically, when he advised the unbelieving freethinker to *s'abêtir* to become a docile animal till the grace of God fell upon him.

I want now to develop the argument, not as it stands in the works of the philosophers such as Jaspers or Heidegger, valuable though their contribution has been, but as it has worked itself out in literary masterpieces in Anouilh, Camus and Sartre. Simply expressed, the argument runs that man is alone in the universe, a creature able to make decisions, and by making decisions (and sticking to them) becomes free. I may add that by making decisions he passes from *existence,* which he shares with inanimate objects (the *en soi* according to Sartre), to essence where he lives with a purpose (*pour soi*) whether the purpose is being a poet, or a revolutionary or a bourgeois Tory, and so on. In his creation of an *essence for himself* man aims at the pure stability of objects (the *en soi*), which, of course, he can never achieve—to achieve it he would have to become deity—which he can never do.

So man is destined first to endless frustration and then to shipwreck in death (to use Heidegger's word) in the universe, but by accepting this shipwreck, this ultimate *absurdity* of having aims which cannot be achieved, he demonstrates his supreme freedom. Over against man is the world of matter, an amorphous and disorganised chaos which can only engender *nausea* in man by its very formlessness, and which man alone can inject with meaning—a new interpretation, if you like, of the *raw matter* of Aristotle. Man can also fail to act freely in the world around him and then he is guilty of *mauvaise foi,* the situation of most of us in actual experience, when we turn a blind eye to our own purposes. A strong vein of pessimism runs through all this doctrine, which in fact is nothing but religion taking on a new and original form.

This vein of pessimism is clearly to be seen in some of the *Pièces noires* of Anouilh, still more perhaps in the *Huis clos* of Sartre and his film script *Les jeux sont faits,* less perhaps in *Les mouches* and *Les chemins de la liberté,* and perhaps least of all in *L'étranger* and *La peste* of Camus, but in one form or another it is present most of the time. Anouilh, by his own contention, is not strictly speaking an existentialist, but his work is strongly influenced by it none the less. Take, for example, his *Antigone* and consider the existentialist contents—man alone in the world in the figure of Antigone—alone against Creon, against her sister,

against the city mob. She makes her decision and in the end she sticks to it. She is determined to bury the body of her brother Polynice which, by order of the king, should be exposed to the vultures—a terrible fate to anyone nurtured in the Greek religion. Creon had his good reasons for ordering it thus. Polynice had attacked his native town with the help of foreigners. True, he had been unjustly expelled from Thebes, but treachery is worse than injustice. An example had to be made and Creon had made it.

So far the story is strictly Sophoclean. But wait a little—there is a difference—and a new strikingly pessimistic note. Creon does something he does not do in Sophocles. He completely destroys Antigone's moral values. He compels her to admit that she does not really believe in the hocus pocus of the priests, in their hastily mumbled incantations at so much a time, nor even in her own hocus pocus of shovelling a little earth on to the corpses. He points out to her in addition something she did not know. That is how contemptible both brothers were, how in fact both were really traitors, and worst of all the brute fact that he himself, Creon, who had buried Eteocle with honours and outlawed the corpse of Polynice, did not even know which body he had buried, so mangled and mutilated were the corpses in the final *mêlée*.

He nearly wins her over and she is just about to retire to her room and give up the struggle when he lets drop the word which reverses the situation. *Bonheur* (happiness). Let her live, marry his son Hemon, whom she loves and who loves her, and be happy ever after. Now he has put his foot into it once for all. She is not asking for *bonheur,* nor the daily round of triviality. What she wants (and this is the religious aspect of it) is an intense decision, a final decisive act, and now her meaningless, motiveless deed receives a new sanctification. She acts, even without a content. She does the deed for no purpose, for herself—*l'acte gratuit* of Gide. So, as in Sophocles, but not for the same reason, she has to die, and Creon, like a modern dictator, goes back to his *besogne,* his job of work.

The image of human life presented in the less serious play (tragi-comedy) of *Point de départ* (Eurydice) is still more pessimistic. Orpheus meets Eurydice at a railway station and enchants her, as he should, with his music, causing her to desert her former lover, who throws himself under a train. The loving couple are contrasted with their vulgar parents, in particular the father of Orpheus, whose obsession with trivial comforts and satisfactions reflects human life at its lowest level. The play takes the life-denial a step further than Antigone, in that the desire for death is the main theme. Antigone had at least seen something to live for and she did at least die in action, so to speak. Orpheus dies because life is too trivial, too mean, too vile—death is better. Life as represented by his father, by the mother of Eurydice, by her lover Vincent, is just not worth it.

A more serious point of view is put forward in *L'étranger* of Camus, which despite the trivial outlook of the hero, is not in the least life denying. The hero, Mersault, is the plum opposite of the Cornelian hero, if such can be imagined. Gone is the classical hero of *Le cid,* with his lofty view of life, his magnanimity, his obsession with moral values, *le point d'honneur,* the rhetorical flourish, the wonderful *"justes causes"* for which men fight and die. The life chockful of *essences,* so to speak. Here in *L'étranger* there are no moral ends, no just causes, no cultural or religious views on life, no pattern or indeed essence really at all. The hero just lives, and nothing more. He is Flaubert's *homme moyen* sensual on the lowest worker's level, bereft of culture, of religion, of any point of view at all. He is not even a good Marxist, or failing that, a good Trade Unionist. If he belonged to the ETU he would certainly have stayed in bed instead of going to vote and so let the Communists in. At the same time he presents something more subtle.

He stands for no essence in the world that matters, except just one thing—integrity on his own existentialist level, integrity on the lowest level if you like, just existence, but nevertheless integrity. He does what he feels like doing, and stands by it. The story, in a sense, works backward. By what is almost an *acte gratuit*—a momentary impulse—a shaft of sunlight in the eye—a touch of sunstroke, he kills an Arab, having been led into bad company by a casual friend. He is arrested, imprisoned and brought to justice. What in the end condemns him is not his act of murder, if indeed it was murder, but the trivial acts which had preceded it. The story began with the death of his mother whom, for quite adequate reasons, he had put away in a home. He is summoned to her burial. He does not wish to see her for a last time. He smokes by her coffin during the vigil. He goes swimming with his mistress the following day. All these small acts are done quite innocently and reflect exactly his feelings.

He loved his mother but not all that much. He makes no pretence, as most of us would do, to love her more, or to pretend that smoking by her coffin makes any real difference. All this is innocent, but unconventional, and because he offends against the conventions he must die. The prosecution works up a tremendous feeling of hostility towards this unnatural son, almost forgetting the actual deed of murder with which he is charaged. The young man dies for his sins against convention, not for murder. But there is this feature which relieves the general pessimism of the story. Just before he dies, in a last outburst, to which he has been slowly working up during the attempts of the Christian judge and the chaplain to convert him, he accepts in full Nietzschean sense, the world and all that therein is. He makes one last convincing speech of affirmation. Nothing can take from him the fact that he has lived; nothing can change it; nothing can diminish it. He is supremely content with his life, and his only desire is that when he dies, as many of the world's people shall see him die as possible.

In *L'étranger* we have the philosophy of the *absurd* in its purest form with the hero solving the engima by his own (Nietzschean) affirmation. In the novel *La peste* men also suffer injustice, senseless evil, but it is that of the whole universe, not that of man, and the conclusion is different. The town of Oran in Algeria is visited by a plague, largely symbolizing the evils of the German occupation, and the whole scene is shown through the eyes of Dr. Rieux, whose identity is only disclosed at the end of the story. The *absurd* here has no definite cause; it comes out of the unknown as (what used to be called) an act of God and in consequence men must suffer and die. As compared with *L'étranger,* the reactions, varied as they are, seem to be on a more human level. Dr. Rieux, for example, sympathizes with the journalist who wants to escape in order to go back to his mistress in Paris. In the end the man renounces this aim, and stays behind to help fight the plague, but an important point comes out in a remark he had made before making this decision: "I've had enough of people who die for an idea. I don't believe in heroism. I know that it is easy and I've learned that it is murderous." As a critique of *Les justes causes* this is a sound and healing statement.

In Sartre we have a still more subtle development. His earliest novel, *La nausée,* inspired by the Malte Laurids Briggs of Rilke, takes the form of a philosophical autobiography. The author is doing research on an eighteenth century French diplomat in a small French seaport, Bouville-sur-Mer, which looks suspiciously like Le Havre. He spends his working time in the public library doing his research, and his leisure in seedy cafés and restaurants, and suffers from an intense sense of loneliness. Almost the only person he meets is the *Autodidacte,* who also spends his time in the library reading the encyclopaedia—I forget which—from A to Z. He still believes like a humanist of the nineteenth century that more knowledge will heal the world and symbolizes what is left—for existentialists—of the old humanitarian ideals of humanity, justice, etc. In other words he is a symbol of derision. Gradually, after examining the past in the light of his research, Roquentin the hero, comes to the conclusion that there is no reality but the present, and the present forces itself upon him with tremendous impact.

A *locus classicus* of existentialism is the passage where Roquentin discovers for the first time the true nature of existence, the nauseating *thingness* of objects when once abstracted from the meaning men have given to them, their sheer *contingency,* their sheer lack of any meaning—a pebble on the beach, the braces of Adolphe the waiter, his own face in a mirror, a root in the public gardens.

> Absurdity was not an idea in my head nor the sound of a voice. It was this long, dead, wooden snake curled up at my feet, snake or claw or talon or root, it was all the same. Without formulating anything I knew that I had at last found the clue to my existence, to my nausea, to my life. And indeed, everything I have ever grasped since that moment comes back to this fundamental absurdity.

The climax of the book is the famous passage where Roquentin walks through the municipal portrait gallery, examining critically the portraits of the tinpot notables who had been the great benefactors of the town. (Let us praise famous men and our fathers that begat us, etc.) He penetrates to their essence, stripped of its portentous but artificial décor and finds nothing there—*Salauds, salauds* is his final judgment. The only reality he acheives is his mental *Odyssey,* that of the melody on the gramophone (*Some of These Days*). This is clear cut, does not nauseate, presents a Platonic ultimate which gives him relief.

In the slighter work *Les jeux sont faits,* which reads like a film script, the theme is the impossibility, in one lifetime, of forming a genuine "essence" and in the same lifetime, changing it. The hero, Pierre, a Marxist workman, leading a revolt against a Fascist dictator, is shot by a malcontent follower and in the next world meets the wife of the Fascist secretary of militia, who has just been poisoned by her husband. They fall in love in the *au-delà,* and by virtue of a charming fantasy a mistake on the part of the management provides an excuse for their return to earth. The management, in fact, acknowledging its responsibility, offers them a new lease of life to allow them to fulfil their thwarted destinies. If they can sustain for twenty-four hours their newly-found essence—she as the bourgeois lover of a Marxist worker—he as the Marxist worker living a private life with his bourgeois beloved—they will be allowed to live out their lives to the end.

In fact, of course they find this impossible to do. Pierre is *engagé* (committed) to his revolutionary mates—he cannot detach himself from them. Eve, for her part, cannot strip off her bourgeois *milieu.* The fundamental pessimism shows itself in the fact that in the next world Pierre discovers how his own well-organized plot of rebellion was already known to the Fascist dictator in detail, who was only waiting for the signal to arrest him and his mates—was annoyed by his, Pierre's, inopportune death. Back on earth Pierre finds it hard to explain all this to his comrades when time moves back, although this is presumably the fault of the fantasy. In the epilogue at the end, Pierre and Eve are once again dead and thwarted in their desire to live again. Pierre sums up the atmosphere in one remark: *Tout le monde rate sa vie* (Everyone misfires in life).

Sartre's most serious works (apart from the philosophical work *L'être et le néant,* which I do not propose to consider here) are *Les mouches, Huis clos* and *Les chemins de la liberté,* with *Huis clos* as perhaps the most pessimistic of all. But also it is the most illustrative of the existentialist philosophy which seems to fit the theme like a glove. Recasting the *Oresteia,* Sartre brings before us an existentialist exile, Oreste, returning to his country, Argos, hoping to strike roots, *commit* himself and create an essence. Urged on by his elder sister Electre, who plays a rôle not unlike that of Lady Macbeth, Oreste murders his mother, Clytemnestre, in order to avenge his father, Agamemnon, previously slain by Aegisthus and Clytemnestre. All this is in the true Greek vein of vendetta, but as in Antigone, there is going to be a difference. Jupiter, the Almighty God who has brought Oreste to Argos precisely for this purpose, is delighted. For twenty years *Les mouches* (*The Flies*), symbol of contrition and remorse, have clouded the skies of Argos, and Jupiter has had the double pleasure of having, as a just God, instigated the murder (since Agamemnon deserved it and it was in some sense just) and of having lapped up the atoning sacrifices of those who connived it or at least did nothing to prevent the death. Now the situation will repeat itself.

Oreste, following his destiny and urged by his sister, will kill his mother and Egisthe in order to avenge his father, and he too will feel contrition. Jupiter will again get it both ways and is looking forward to the prospect of a double delectation. Unfortunately Oreste has read his Nietzsche,

Also Sprach Zarathustra, and knows that God is dead; he rejects Jupiter's offer to place him on the throne of Argos, if only he will wallow, like his predecessors, in remorse for his dreadful (though also just) crime. He remembers his Nietzsche *le plus lâche des assassins, c'est celui qui a du remords.* He rejects the phanton god. (pp. 257-62)

And at the very end it is Electre, who, like Lady Macbeth, breaks down and cannot sustain the mental struggle. She accepts the long plague of *Les mouches* once again while Oreste departs triumphant from the stage. He takes upon himself (as God did once) the weight of all the crimes of Argos and leaves the town for ever, an exile, an outsider, an intruder—but free.

Sartre's masterpiece, for dramatic construction and philosophical content, is undoubtedly *Huis clos*. Here we have three human beings, Garcin, Inez, Estelle, one male and two females in hell, or at least in the next world which they are going to transform quite quickly into hell. The situation only gradually reveals itself in three series of conversations, the first being largely lies (since they are afraid to betray their real essence to each other and of course are affected by each other), the second partly true and the third entirely true and completely hopeless. Thus there is a dramatic development through three crises. Three essences are chasing each other in the drama and will (we finally realize) chase each other for ever. Inez, the most intelligent of the three, is a lesbian and at once falls in love with Estelle. Unfortunately she can never have her because Estelle is a completely natural, frivolous heterosexual who just wants a man, any man, any time. Naturally enough Estelle would like to find her satisfaction in Garcin, but Garcin is preoccupied with his own essence which pursues other ends. He deserted from the army as a pacifist and was shot for it, dying an ignoble and cowardly death, from which mortality he will never recover.

He wants one thing and one thing only, and that is to be thought a brave man by somebody he respects. If he could find only one human being in the world who would do this for him he would be happy for ever. He would have achieved his essence. Estelle tries to do it for him, but reveals only too clearly that she doesn't care a damn how he died, nobly or ignobly, provided only that he loves her. Inez could do it, but her interests are elsewhere, and in any case she is too honest to pretend what she knows is untrue. So none of the three can have what they want, or will ever have what they want, and there they are together, for ever tormenting each other in vain. *L'enfer, c'est les autres. . .* Here again it is the eternal present which is the insoluble problem, and meanwhile there, on the mantelshelf, sits *La nausée,* in the form of a bronze ornament, quite irrelevant, quite irresponsible, staring at them, with a completely meaningless stare, for ever.

Although not finished, mention must be made of *Les chemins de la liberté,* which is Sartre's main attempt in the form of the traditional novel. In the first volume, *L'âge de la raison,* we are presented with various types of people whose fortunes intertwine and who are contrasted in their different attitudes towards the question of existential freedom. Mathieu, the hero, cannot come to any decision, either about the approaching war (it is 1936) or about what he shall do with his mistress, who is *enceinte*. He is contrasted with Brunet, a good Marxist, who is committed (*engagé*) to the good cause and with Gomez, a Spanish loyalist fighting in Spain—contrasts which heighten his own sense of indecision.

Mathieu's own personal problem is solved by the action of a third person, Daniel, in eventually taking his mistress off his hands by marrying her, and in the second volume *Le sursis* (*The Reprieve*) Munich is looming up, and the various characters are scattered round France. The Crisis (for Mathieu) comes in the third volume (*La morte dans l'âme*) in which the French are defeated and a contrast drawn between Mathieu and Brunet. The latter, taken prisoner, continues to play his Marxist rôle clandestinely in the German prison camp. Mathieu, on the other hand, despite the defeat, makes a last desperate stand in a church tower with a few friends, and in one last *élan* of decision and *engagement* (commitment) makes atonement for the irresolution of his protracted youth.

> He approached the parapet and standing up began to shoot. It was a mighty revenge. Each shot avenged some former irresolution. There's one shot for Lola whom I didn't dare rob, another for Marcelle whom I ought to have left in the lurch, another for Odette whom I didn't wish to kiss. This one for the books I never dared write, that one for the journeys I never allowed myself to take, that one for all those chaps whom I wanted to dislike and yet tried to understand. He fired. Laws collapsed into fragments. 'Thou shalt love thy neighbour as thyself', bang into that clot-like gob. 'Thou shalt not kill'—bang into that sneaking face opposite. He fired on Man, on Virtue, on the whole world. Freedom is Terror-Fire. Terror Fire burned in the town hall and also in his head. Bullets whistled as free as the air. The world will blow up, and me too. He shot. He looked at his watch. 14 minutes 10 seconds. He wanted nothing now but a reprieve of half a minute, just time enough to fire at that handsome officer running so proudly towards the church—he fired at the handsome officer, on all the beauty of the world, on the street, on the flowers, on the gardens, on everything which he had loved. Beauty ducked its head in an obscene fashion. Mathieu shot again. He fired. He was pure. He was omnipotent. He was free!

The existentialist philosophy, as I see it, reduces to this. There is only the empirical present *here and now,* and nothing at all allows us to escape from it. We must accept it and act, and our action is the sign of our freedom, maturing into integrity. (pp. 262-64)

> *F. McEachran, "The Literature of Existentialism," in* Contemporary Review, *Vol. 203, May, 1963, pp. 257-64.*

Delmore Schwartz

[An American poet, short story writer, and critic, Schwartz was among the most prominent figures in American letters of the mid-twentieth century. His poems and short stories draw heavily on the experiences of American Jewish immigrants and their children. A prolific and deeply troubled writer who served as the model for the protagonist of Saul Bellow's novel Humboldt's Gift, Schwartz also served as an editor of Partisan Review and like many of the magazine's staff was associated with the leftist "New York intellectual" movement of the 1940s. In the following essay, Schwartz offers a personal interpretation of the implications of Existentialist philosophy.]

Let me explain this question. Is it not true that the discussion of the meaning of existentialism has been dying down? or at any rate is being taken more and more for granted, like cynicism, optimism, surrealism, alcoholism, and practically all the other well-known topics of conversation?

If so, this is a dangerous state of affairs. For as soon as a philosophy is taken for granted, as soon as its meaning is assumed, then it begins to be misunderstood and misinterpreted. Philosophical idealism is a good example. It was once just as fashionable as existentialism and is now generally thought to have to do with those impractical people who believe in ideals and never amount to anything.

I propose a revival of interest in the meaning of existentialism because when everyone asks what something means, the possibilities of misunderstanding are, if not lessened, more controllable. Having studied existentialism in an offhand way since 1935, I become more and more convinced that its meaning can be reduced to the following formulation: *Existentialism means that no one else can take a bath for you.*

This example is suggested by Heidegger, who points out that no one else can die for you. You must die your own death. But the same is true of taking a bath. And I prefer the bath as an example to death because, as Heidegger further observes, no one likes to think very much about death, except indigent undertakers perhaps. Death is for most a distant event, however unpleasant and inevitable.

A bath, however, is a daily affair, at least in America. Thus it is something you have to think about somewhat everyday, and while you are thinking about it, and while, perforce, you are taking a bath, you might just as well be thinking about what existentialism means. Otherwise you will probably just be thinking about yourself, which is narcissism; or about other human beings, which is likely to be malicious, unless you are feeling very good; or worst of all, you may not be thinking at all, which is senseless and a waste of time.

Of course, there are other acts which each human being must perform for himself, such as eating, breathing, sleeping, making love, etc. But taking a bath seems to me the best of the lot because it involves the vital existentialist emphasis on choice: you can choose *not* to take a bath, you can waver in your choice, you can finally decide to take a bath, the whole drama of human freedom can become quite hectic or for that matter quite boring. But eating is hardly a matter of choice, except for the menu itself, nor is breathing which can be done not only without taking thought but while one is quite unconscious. As for making love, taking a bath is a better example because you can keep it clean, simple, free of fixations, perversions, inhibitions, and an overpowering sense of guilt.

Now despite the fact that most of the bathtubs which exist are in America, some Americans are not in the habit of taking baths for granted. I know of one American (formerly an existentialist, by the way) who avoids taking frequent baths because he feels that the taking of a bath is an *extreme situation*. (He is not averse to using existentialist arguments when it suits his purpose, though in company he attacks existentialism.) He says that taking a bath is an extreme situation because God knows what may occur to you when you are in the tub, you may decide to drown yourself because existence, as existentialists say, is essentially *absurd;* you may decide to become a narcissist because of the pleasures of the warm and loving water; you may decide to join the Roman Catholic Church because it too is quite comforting and comfortable. But there's no use listing all the catastrophes this fellow thinks may occur to anyone in the extreme situation of taking a bath.

So too with the bathtaking of a close friend of mine, who finds the taking of baths a matter of no little thought. He takes two baths a day, but he has to force himself to do so because there are so many other more important things to do (so it seems to him!) or which he feels he ought to do during the time occupied in taking a bath (note how the question of moral value enters at this point). It is a matter for much thought also because he has to decide whether to take a bath or a shower. He is afraid that sooner or later he will break his neck slipping on a cake of soap while taking a shower (which he prefers to a bath), although, on the other hand, he feels that in some ways it is better to take a shower than a bath because then he does not have to wash out the tub for others *(the others are always important, as* Sartre has observed), and in short the taking of baths is not a simple matter for him. Once I visited him while he was taking a shower, and while I was conversing with his wife in their handsome living-room, he kept crying out through the downpour of the shower: "Say, you know it's mighty lonesome in here." He wanted me to visit with him and keep him company (note the *aloneness* of the human situation as depicted by the existentialists), to converse with him. Consequently, after he had shouted his fourth appeal for my company, I had to go in and point out to him that we would have to shout at each other because of the noise of the shower and we shouted at each other often enough for more justifiable reasons.

In the upper class, as is well known, it is customary (I am told by friends who have soared to these circles at times ho, ho!) to take at least two baths a day, while in the lower middle class and working class this is less true, an observation I bring forward to show how important social and economic factors are, or, as the existentialists say, how all being is being-in-the-world, although they seem to think that the social and economic aspects of being-in-the-world are not so important as I am forced to think they are. Of course, some of the existentialists may have changed their minds during the second World War and the recent so-called peace.

The real difficulty in explaining what existentialism means flows from the basis of this philosophy, a basis which can be summarized in the following proposition: *Human beings exist.* They have an existence which is human and thus different from that of stones, trees, animals, cigar store Indians, and numerous human beings who are trying their best not to exist or not to be human.

If you are really human, if you really exist as a human being, you have no need of any explanation of existence or existentialism. In the meantime, the best thing to do is to keep on reading explanations of existentialism and existence. (pp. 408-11)

> *Delmore Schwartz, "Does Existentialism Still Exist?" in* Selected Essays of Delmore Schwartz, *edited by Donald A. Dike and David H. Zucker, The University of Chicago Press, 1970, pp. 408-11.*

HISTORY AND INFLUENCES

William Barrett

[*An American critic and nonfiction writer, Barrett served as associate editor of* Partisan Review *during the flourishing of that magazine's intellectual influence in the 1940s and 1950s, and was its leading proponent of the newly emerging philosophy of Existentialism. His book* The Truants (*1982*)*, a memoir of his days spent at that journal, was highly praised for its vivid and lucid depictions of such literary figures as Delmore Schwartz, Philip Rahv, and Mary McCarthy. Known for his engaging and unpretentious prose style, Barrett has written and edited a number of works on Existentialism and other contemporary philosophical issues. In the following excerpt, Barrett examines Existentialists' efforts to create a philosophy that wholly engages individuals and restores passion and purpose to their lives.*]

Nowadays we speak quite easily and naturally of the crisis through which our civilization is passing. Without questioning the assumption that we are in the midst of a crisis, I should like to ask whether this feeling of crisis is not something inseparable from human life in any historical period. The more closely we examine the past, the more we find that it, too, is uneasy with its own sense of historical crisis and urgency. Sometimes, in retrospect, these crises look illusory, for mankind has survived some of its worst apprehensions; and then we have to remind ourselves that these men and women of the past felt that bygone crisis in their bones, with the same intimate uneasiness with which we feel ours. We begin to suspect that to live itself is to exist in crisis (more or less actual at any moment), and that only in periods of real historic somnolence and lethargy—real decadence, in short—has mankind been without a sense of crisis. No doubt, there are important differences of degree, and one age may be more plainly a period of breakdown than another; it would be folly to neglect such differences of degree, but the thought that crisis, or the sense of it is a permanent part of human life, does fortify us to see our own contemporary crisis in a much broader light—as a total human condition.

This thought will explain why I prefer to discuss existential philosophy as a symptom, rather than a solution, of our present crisis. For to the degree that we see our crisis as a total and concrete condition, to that degree we shall doubt that any philosophy, no matter how ambitious, can propose itself as the unique path of salvation. Anyone who has had any personal experience of a spiritual crisis will know that recovery does not come through the acquisition of any new abstract ideas. The progress from health to sickness is a change of being, rather than a change in thought. So, if we agree that our civilization is spiritually sick, we should also expect that the recovery will not come through any single set of ideas, or philosophy, but only through a transformation of our whole existence—thus requiring social, economic, and religious change. A new philosophy would be only a necessary *part* of this total change.

Moreover, it is the very characteristic of Existentialism as a philosophy that it must look with irony upon any system of thought that proposes itself as *the* solution for all of life's crises. Let us remember that Kierkegaard, the founder of Existentialism, began to philosophize with the purpose of discovering difficulties, rather than offering easy and readymade solutions. Existentialism as a philosophy attempts to make man aware of certain basic realities of his life. In this sense it seeks to increase, rather than minimize, our human difficulties. The business of finding solutions must come only after a man is aware of the whole depth, import, and, therefore, difficulty, of his human life.

This preliminary definition of existential philosophy will be understood better, if we contrast it with the usual kinds of philosophy now taught in our academies. The various schools of philosophy are distinguished from each other by different beliefs. Thus it comes about that a philosophy is understood as a set of beliefs, or propositions, to which a man gives intellectual assent. A man is said to have a philosophy, then, if he has a system of propositions which he holds to be true on purely intellectual or rational grounds. This is the understanding of philosophy that has prevailed particularly in our period of the departmentalization of all human knowledge. But Existentialism seeks to restore a much more primitive sense of the word, "philosophy," than this: namely, the ancient sense of philosophy as a concrete way of life, rather than an abstract set of propositions. Nietzsche, also an Existentialist, pointed out that for ancient man, and even the modern Oriental, the business of achieving a philosophy is one that engaged the whole man, his total being, and was not pursued simply as one specialized department of knowledge among others. Kierkegaard attacked the Hegelian professors of his time as being philosophers without any real philosophic existence: they had a system of propositions to teach, but the system itself was a means of forgetting the concrete realities of human life. For us in America today the philosopher is merely a "professional" savant among many others.

Existentialism, on the contrary, understands philosophy as a thing that is to be lived, and not merely a body of knowledge to be taught to pupils. I have said that Existentialism attempts to bring to human consciousness the basic, even banal, realities of human life: realities such as death, anxiety, choice, love, freedom, guilt, conscience, the willing acceptance of anxiety, etc., etc. In American academic philosophy today these are not the prevailing concepts: philosophers discuss concepts relating to science, knowledge, logic. Existential concepts are thought to belong to literature, perhaps to poetry. This rejection is an evidence of how far one particular tradition among the intellectual elite of our society has tended to set knowledge above life. If the philosopher exists professionally as a member of a department in a university, and if he accepts his role as one that deals with one special department of knowledge among others, then he is inevitably drawn to devote himself to those very special and technical problems that seem to be the peculiar province of the "expert." Our technological civilization has tended more and more to worship the expert, and the philosopher, assimilated to his civilization, strives more and more to justify his own professional existence by a high technical competence in the special problems of logic and philosophical analysis. The result is that a great deal of modern philosophy has tended to become divorced from life. Hence it is only natural that Existentialism, which struggles against this tendency, is looked on somewhat askance by a great many American philosophers.

All this has been by way of explaining why it seemed preferable to discuss Existentialism as a symptom, rather than a solution, of our contemporary crisis. But there has also been in the background of my remarks another, and much more drastic point, which will be substantiated by my further discussion, but can be announced now: the point, quite simply, that there is never a solution to any of life's crises. This is one of the cardinal points in existential philosophy itself. The word, "solution," belongs to the vocabulary of science and engineering, suggesting some kind of blueprint that would immediately deliver us from the pain and muddle of suffering, when, in fact, we know that our really deep crises in life are precisely those that we have to live through. Our deepest personal problems do not in the least resemble any problem of engineering, and it is the same, we suggest, with the sickness of civilization, even though the "cure" of a sick civilization might require vast exploits of engineering.

That movement in thought should be a symptom of its time, is not in the least a condemnation of this movement as a wild or trivial aberration. I am using the word, "symptom," in its simple and unprejudiced sense of a sign—something that instructs us about the state of the organism from which it arises. Thus Existentialism has a great deal to teach us—which we might otherwise not know—about the condition of the Western civilization that has brought it to birth.

Most Americans connect Existentialism with the current French movement, and particularly with the name of its most brilliant publicist, Jean Paul Sartre. Sartre's is an agile and energetic mind, but his doctrine represents, I believe, a dilution of existential philosophy, and in any case does not take us back to its original sources. These lie in the nineteenth century, and the great innovators are Kierkegaard and Nietzsche—though the latter, unlike Kierkegaard, is not fully aware of his existential point of departure. Existential themes are treated in the fiction of Tolstoi and Dostoievski. In this century the two most important existential philosophers have been the German professors, Martin Heidegger and Karl Jaspers. To these names we might add the considerable figure of the Spanish philosopher, José Ortega y Gasset, who has described his philosophy as one of "vital reason," though it is fundamentally existential in its directions. These names should indicate that Existentialism is not a momentary intellectual fad, derived from the French, but a much wider and deeper movement in Western thought, having roots indeed in the profound upheavals of this civilization during the past two centuries. To see what these roots are, we may find it more convenient to turn, not to an abstruse text in philosophy, but to a work of literature that takes a simpler and more direct grasp of the issues involved: Tolstoi's great story, *The Death of Ivan Ilyich,* which by this time has become something of a basic scripture for existential thought.

The plot of Tolstoi's story is slight and almost negligible. Ivan Ilyich is an amiable and undistinguished bourgeois, who has spent his whole life trying to be like everyone else in his social class: a successful and happy man, where happiness means only the absence of suffering. But one day Ivan Ilyich feels a pain in his side, which resists all treatment by doctors, and as his illness progresses, he suddenly realizes that he is going to die. For the first time in his life death becomes a reality for him. In the face of this awful presence, all his disguises fall away: confronting death for the first time in his life, he is also confronting himself for the first time. Hitherto in his life he had hid from himself amid the routine mechanisms of all his social, official, and familial functions. Now, as he is about to die, he asks himself the questions: Who am I? What has been the meaning of my life? In the end Ivan Ilyich dies content, because he has reached the point of knowing that the life he lived was empty, futile, and meaningless.

What Tolstoi is saying here, to put it now as a general thesis, is that modern life has alienated the individual from himself. The materialistic and rationalistic nineteenth century, with its emphasis upon all the bourgeois routines of life, has so externalized the individual that he has lost the feeling and the passion for his own personal existence. Modern man, Tolstoi is saying, has lost the meaning of life, and, as with Ivan Ilyich, it will take nothing less than the presence of death to restore this sense of life.

The sense of decadence haunts the nineteenth century, even at the moments of its most splendid optimism. There is a widespread uneasiness that life has lost its passion, intensity, and meaning; that there has been some secret decline in human vitality. Kierkegaard puts it as eloquently and compactly as one could wish:

> Let others complain that times are bad; I complain that they are petty because they lack passion. Men's thoughts are as flimsy as thin ice and men themselves as insignificant as the thin snow that covers it. Their thoughts are too petty to be sinful. A worm might consider such thoughts to be sinful, but not a man created in the image of God. Their pleasures are circumspect and boring; their passions, sleep; these materialistic souls fulfill their duties, but they collect their usury for it; they believe that although our Lord keeps His accounts in good order, they can hand Him counterfeit. Out with them! This is why my soul always hearkens back to Shakespeare and the Old Testament. There one feels that those who speak are men; there they hate; there they love; there they kill the enemy, curse their descendants for generations to come, there they sin.

This passage might almost have been written by Nietzsche, who launches his plea from the diametrically opposite anti-christian pole. Modern man, says Nietzsche, lacks a goal, and his existence is, therefore, purposeless and nihilistic. Similar themes appear also in such diverse writers as Stendhal and Burckhardt.

The twentieth century has no reason to forget these fears. Our technological civilization has become even more involved with elaborate apparatus to catch and smother the individual. We have gone beyond the nineteenth century in the development of a fantastic mass culture—in radio, movies, and television—that stamps out all individual differences. Modern society has become more and more a mass society. Cities grow larger, crowds become more and more potent factors, and the individual threatened more than ever by anonymity in the mass. The image of modern man lies in T. S. Eliot's line: "Men and bits of paper, whirled by the cold wind." These fears of the nineteenth century turn out to be prophetic for us: amid this general purposelessness of life, this mass drifting, we set ourselves the task of recapturing the sense and the meaning of life.

When Tolstoi speaks of a loss of the meaning of life, he is not referring to a loss of some rational explanation. Nor is the meaning that is to be restored an intellectual one, some new fact or discovery of the mind. On the contrary, the disorder in modern man that Tolstoi's story speaks of is a disorder in the more primitive and irrational, or non-rational, parts of man's being. Existentialism as a philosophy seeks to deal with these irrational parts of our existence in a way that philosophy has never done before, and by so doing gives reason itself a new place in the human hierarchy.

This is why existential philosophy has been frequently—and, I think, unjustly—criticized as anti-rational. One is not against reason, if one insists that the irrational is an inseparable part of life, and that it is precisely with the irrational parts of our being that modern civilization fails to deal adequately. This so-called "anti-rational" tendency in modern philosophy has now had a long history, from Rousseau to Bergson, Whitehead, and Heidegger in our century, and it embraces too many great names to be dismissed out of hand. Any future rationalism worth its salt will have to assimilate a great deal from these thinkers, and we ourselves would be less than rational, if we did not make an earnest effort to understand in detail how the irrational enters human life.

We gain some idea of the irrational character of life, if we turn back again to Tolstoi's *Ivan Ilyich.* As death appears to Ivan Ilyich, it presents itself as something altogether unreasonable and incomprehensible. Immersed in the comfortable structure of his life, he sees this strange and dark intruder creep in to destroy everything. Yes, death is a banal fact, and we know that all men have to die; Ivan Ilyich knows all this with his head, but his heart cannot grasp the incomprehensible fact that he, Ivan Ilyich, should have to die. This bewilderment may strike us as childish, but it is Tolstoi's means of showing us how the irrational, like death, may fall upon us in the most incalculable and unpredictable way, upsetting all our plans for life.

Kierkegaard has expounded the presence of the irrational in another area of human life—in the act of choice or decision. We do not doubt that some decisions are more rational than others, and we may even speak of a decision as being the only rational choice under the circumstances. But is a rational choice one from which the irrational is ever completely excluded? Is any choice, however rational it be, free from the uncertain contingencies of risk and adventure? Of course, there are certain trivial choices that we make every day, and that we may reverse the next day, if we are proved wrong. But these are choices that do not commit us deeply, that leave us relatively disengaged from the consequences. As soon, however, as a choice cuts deeply; as soon as it commits our whole life in a certain direction; so soon, then, do the immense difficulties appear, the balance of probabilities becomes harder, and each alternative appears, however we may canvass its possibilities, as a leap into the unknown.

The choice that personally involved Kierkegaard happened to be the question whether or not to marry. Engaged to a young woman in Copenhagen, he desired marriage intensely, but he felt in himself also a certain religious mission that would prevent him from giving himself completely in marriage. The particular psychological facts involved here are important for an understanding of Kierkegaard's biography, but the peculiarly personal difficulties should not obscure for us the fact that the pathos of choice Kierkegaard faced is universal. There are, in short, choices in life that are irreversible. Kierkegaard could not have made an *experimental* choice of marriage, in the expectation that if it "did not work out"—to use the expression that has become common among us these days—he could return to his religious vocation and its tasks, for the vocation might have been lost through his marriage. On the other hand, if he renounced marriage experimentally, he could not hope to return to the young lady, should the other alternative not work out. She might not be there (as in fact she was not) when he returned. Love has to be seized at the moment it is offered; our indecision pollutes and destroys it.

All of this points to the fact that the situation of human choice is not at all a situation of scientific experiment. A situation is experimental in science when certain scientific controls have been established, so that through these controls we can repeat the experiment at any time and place we choose, and indeed repeat it indefinitely. The more precisely scientific the experiment becomes, the more its features of accidental particularity become refined away, and the easier it becomes to repeat it in all its detail. But our

fundamental choices in life do not permit us this degree of control, because they do not permit us this degree of detachment. We have to choose here and now, and for the rest of our life, and the alternative we renounce is lost forever. We could be completely experimental about our own lives only if we were immortal, and so could repeat any situation or choice indefinitely.

But as death is real and our lives finite, every choice is also a renunciation, and this is why Kierkegaard speaks of the *pathos* of human choice. It was this sacrificial and pathetic aspect of choice that led Kierkegaard to his great polemic against the excessively rational philosophy of Hegel. The old adage puts the matter quite simply and adequately, "You cannot eat your cake and have it, too"; but Hegel devised a sophisticated dialectic by which it was possible to bring together two conflicting alternatives, thesis and antithesis, into a higher synthesis, so that the speculative philosopher, triumphing over life, could both have his cake and eat it, too. Such a reconciling of opposites is indeed possible in knowledge, where a more inclusive theory may embrace two conflicting alternatives; but it is not possible in life, where the suffering of renunciation cannot be altogether eliminated by reason. This opposition between knowledge and life has been one of the chief themes of Existentialism, as well as of a great deal of modern philosophy and literature.

These two brief illustrations of the irrational—death and human choice—which cannot be altogether expunged from our existence, also illustrate that science, and scientific experiment, cannot take over the whole of life. The fear that science might devour the whole of human life has been a very powerful current of thought in the West, from William Blake onward. Indeed, from the Enlightenment in the eighteenth century to the present day, two deeply opposed attitudes toward science have dominated Western thinking: along with the great hope in science and its possibilities of human liberation, there has developed a great fear that science would somehow mechanize and impoverish human life. This fear of science cannot be dismissed simply as a crude popular superstition, for it embraces too many great names of our culture: Blake, Wordsworth, Kierkegaard, Nietzsche, Dostoievski, Tolstoi, Bergson. Our task, rather, should be to disengage the philosophical traits that characterize this fear of science at its deepest level.

One of the best expressions of the fear of science is found in the first part of Dostoievski's great novel, *Notes from Underground*. The hero is afraid of the scientific society of the future, in which human life can be rationally controlled and ordered, down to the very last detail. When human life is so scientifically precise and predictable, nobody would want to live it. Dostoievski's hero would prefer to smash this machine that would seek to contain him—out of sheer spite, as he puts it—to show that his human will in its liberty transcends the mathematically predictable, even if he has to show this in a destructive way. We come back thus to our principal point: what Dostoievski is saying, through his tormented and oppressed little hero, is that human life must be more than pure reason, and to attempt to reduce it to the latter is to destroy it, even if we make that reduction in the name of universal enlightenment.

It would be a mistake to consider the Underground Man as merely a sick and neurotic individual produced by the stresses of modern society. He is that, of course, but he is also a universal human character. We are all the Underground Man, to some degree or other. He is that dark side of our being, with which we must try to live in peace, and if we take lightly his fulminations against a human regime completely controlled by science and reason, we do so at our own risk.

As he is thus universal, the Underground Man reappears, and perhaps I may drive home my point by turning to the rather extraordinary position advanced in the nineteen hundred and twenties by I. A. Richards, the British critic and psychologist—a position that seems to me to express the extreme of hope that science will master life. (In justice to Richards, however, we must point out that at the time he was much more enamored of the possibilities of psychology than he is today.) Richards contended nothing less than this: that we can anticipate the time when psychological science will have advanced to the point where we can have, if we choose, whatever minds we desire. In the perfectly scientific utopia, in short, you could order your personality at a psychological laboratory the way you might order a prescription at a druggist's. Select your label, follow the prescription carefully, and you will have the personality, or the mind, that you want. Science which has performed so many miracles in the transformation of matter, and has found synthetic substitutes for almost everything, would here have found at last a substitute for life itself. In this psychological utopia it would be possible for a man to have a certain character without living through the risks, anxieties, and uncertain struggles that make it. We need not live to become a certain kind of being; science would provide it readymade.

We notice that this possibility that once inspired Richards with such hopes, is precisely the possibility against which Dostoievski's Underground Man rebels. Sick and resentful though he may be, the Underground Man at least insists upon having his own human life, rather than some mechanized substitute for it. The science of psychology has gone on developing since Richards's remark, but it is now further from maintaining any such utopian claims as once enchanted him. Among some circles in America, psychoanalysis may be regarded as a kind of magic, but not by the analysts themselves. Some people tend to think of psychoanalysis as a process in which the analyst, somewhat like a mechanic, overhauls the patient and gives him a new engine or set of works. But the serious analyst, while hoping to transform the neurotic patient's fundamental orientations toward life, insists that the patient can solve his problems only in actual life and not in the psychoanalytic session. Life has to be lived, there is no substitute for living—not even psychoanalysis.

Existential philosophy, in its insistence that the categories of life cannot be reduced to science, carries this point further. It may seem a rather trivial platitude to say that there can be no substitute for living, but the saying may not strike us as so platitudinous when we reflect upon the vast

Martin Heidegger.

mechanized passivity that our civilization imposes upon so many of its members. In such circumstances the living rediscovery of certain banalities may represent an immense task and an immense triumph. Some of the greatest chapters in the history of philosophy are its discoveries of what lay obvious, but unnoticed, before every man's eyes. We may recall the great saying of Heraclitus, at the very dawn of philosophy in the sixth century B.C.: "Man is estranged from that with which he is most familiar, and he must continuously seek to rediscover it." This saying might serve as a very good motto for Existentialism. Among other things, it may make clear why the modern Existentialist, Heidegger, finds these early pre-Socratic Greeks his real forebears in the effort to confront human life and the whole life of nature with a primitive directness. The ancestry of existential philosophy thus turns out to be very ancient. I come back thus to a point made at the beginning, which should now be considerably clearer in its import: Existentialism, a modern movement in philosophy, is, in fact, an effort to recapture an old and very primitive sense of philosophy. Philosophy, here, is not the mere putting together of certain abstract propositions into a system; it is rather the concrete effort of the living individual to relate himself to his own life and the life of others around him. Quite literally, philosophy is a task that each individual has to perform for himself.

In this search for the primitive, Existentialism is in line with the most considerable movements in art and literature in this century. The word, "primitive," here is bound to arouse misunderstandings, if it is associated with the life of savages, barbarians, or big game hunters. Primitivism suggests to some the beat of tom-toms, Tahiti, maidens in sarongs, Gauguin; in short, an escape from modern civilization into the illusory simplicities of some South Sea island. These forms of primitivism have abounded, but they have always ended in a blind alley, because the desire for escape is itself a very non-primitive state of being. I am using the word, "primitive," in a much more basic—I almost wrote primitive—sense: the primitive is the primary; and the valid search for the primitive is a search for the sources of our being which a too routinized civilization tends to obscure. In this sense, nearly all the art and literature that matter in the past half century have been primitive.

Modern painting and sculpture, for example, have really succeeded in creating a new kind of vision. In these works we stand in a new and more direct relation to colors, shapes, and forms. It is a vision of things at once simpler and more complex than the Western art of the past. In its distorting simplifications, bold arbitrary forms, it often resembles primitive art, from which indeed it has consciously drawn inspiration in certain cases, though it could not exist without the whole tradition of Western art. Moreover, the artist himself seems to stand in a new and direct relation to the very materials of his art: he seeks naively to assert the presence of his paint, stone, or metal, and his art is no longer a device to conceal or transcend this presence.

In literature, in writers such as D. H. Lawrence, James Joyce, and Thomas Mann, we find similar and diverging efforts to deal with the primitive. In his Joseph stories, Mann seeks to restore the primitive mythic consciousness to literature. James Joyce, in his last work, uses the most sophisticated literary technique, drawing upon the whole past of Western literature for its resources, in order to render the most unconscious, inarticulate, and primitive parts of human experience. Of these writers perhaps Lawrence is the most explicitly programmatic in his search for the primitive simplicities that he believes modern life to have lost. The organic unity of being that Lawrence seeks through sexual experience, is something that existential philosophers have sought in other directions. As T. S. Eliot reminds us, Lawrence was a man with an intense spiritual vocation, and his interest in sex was not at all a message of sex-for-sex's sake. Nevertheless, his proposed solution to the sickness of modern civilization seems to us today to be rather onesided. His perception of the sickness was real enough, but his prescription for cure represents a kind of impatient rush toward a solution. We are reminded, again, that when a sickness is total, the recovery can come only through development along many avenues of being at once.

This list could be swelled indefinitely to show that this struggle for rebirth is one of the great themes of modern culture. I have appended these brief indications to my main discussion only to point to the total historical context in which we must try to see the development of modern existential philosophy; and to suggest that this philosophy is not an eccentric movement, but lies in the main stream of modern culture. Existentialism makes clearer the human tasks that our epoch confronts. Unless we realize what the tasks are, we can hardly work significantly toward any solution at all. (pp. 139-52)

> *William Barrett, "Existentialism as a Symptom of Man's Contemporary Crisis," in* Spiritual Problems in Contemporary Literature, *edited by Stanley Romaine Hopper, 1952. Reprint by Harper & Brothers, 1957, pp. 139-52.*

Richard Lehan

[*Lehan is an American educator and critic who has written extensively on the twentieth-century American novel. In the following excerpt, he discusses the impact of American novelists on Existentialist literature.*]

If Dostoyevsky prefigured modern existentialism in one way, the modern American novel prefigured it in another. Perhaps the most systematic and complete account of the American novel in postwar France has been made by Thelma Smith and Ward Miner in a book entitled *Transatlantic Migration, The Contemporary American Novel in France*. The book makes no pretense to being critical but rather is expressly historical and bibliographical, the authors concentrating upon the French critical studies of American fiction and the French reactions to the American novel.

Smith and Miner list almost two dozen books that were either fully or partially devoted to the American novel, as well as articles too numerous to count, all written between 1946 and 1950. The more important full-length studies of the American novel include Maurice Coindreau's *Aperçus de Littérature américaine* (1946), Pierre Brodin's *Les écrivains américains de l'entredeux-guerres* (1946), Jean Pouillon's *Temps et roman* (1946), Claude-Edmonde Magny's *L'âge du roman américain* (1948), and Jean Simon's *Le roman américain au XXe siècle*.

Perhaps the greatest encouragement to American fiction came from the popular magazines. During the war, for example, a number of Algerian magazines published anthologies of American fiction. In 1943, one such magaine, *Fontaine*, published an issue entitled "Ecrivains et Poètes des États-Unis," containing selections from the works of Hemingway, Steinbeck, Faulkner, and Caldwell. *Confluences*, another magazine of similar nature, got out an issue entitled "Problèmes du Roman" and discussed the American influence on the French novel. After the liberation of Paris, these special issues were printed in book form. Also at this time, special series containing selections from the American novel were issued by such other popular French journals as *L'arbalète, Cahiers des langues modernes, Espirit, Renaissances,* and *Les temps modernes*. The American Library in Paris undoubtedly also influenced the popularity of American fiction. The library contains over 80,000 American books and its subsidiary libraries are also well stocked. These libraries were established primarily for the American serviceman in France, but counts have shown that 60 per cent of its subscribers were French. The final encouragement to American fiction came from the National Ministry of Education. Before the war only the Sorbonne gave a course in American literature and civilization. Now such courses are being given at universities in Aix-Marseilles, Alger, Bordeaux, Caen, Clermont, Dijon, Rennes, and Strasbourg. Modern American literature is often featured prominently in French graduate literary studies, and symposiums on American literature have also been frequently given and popularly attended in France.

French enthusiasm over the American novel has been perhaps no better expressed than by Jean-Paul Sartre himself. Sartre maintains that

> The greatest literary development in France between 1929 and 1939 was the discovery of Faulkner, Dos Passos, Hemingway, Caldwell, and Steinbeck. . . . These authors have not had in France a popular success comparable to that of Sinclair Lewis. Their influence was far more restricted, but infinitely more profound. . . . To writers of my generation, the publication of the *42nd Parallel, Light in August, A Farewell to Arms* evoked a revolution similar to the one produced fifteen years earlier by the *Ulysses* of James Joyce. . . . At once, for thousands of young intellectuals, the American novel took its place together with jazz and the movies, among the best of the importations from the United States. The large frescoes of Vidor joined with the passion and violence of *The Sound and the Fury* and *Sanctuary* to compose for us the face of the United States—a face tragic, cruel, sublime.

American fiction was new and different to the French. It was distinct from any narrative genre France had yet known. On the one hand, it was removed from the deterministic, highly documented, socially determined naturalism of Zola. On the other hand, it was faster-paced and more down to earth than the bloodless, over-refined Proustian novel of psychological analysis, and more concrete and objectively rooted than the abstract or heavily symbolic writing of Gide, Valéry, and Giraudoux. In his *Atlantic Monthly* essay, Sartre maintained that the French did not want a heavily documented, ponderous, intellectual, or psychological novel in an age of Buchenwald and Hiroshima. The novel of intellectual analysis, he says, "was no longer anything but an old mechanism badly adapted to the needs of the time. . . . Could it take into account the brutal death of a Jew in Auschwitz, the bombardment of Madrid by the planes of France?" The French wanted a novel of action, and they found it in the repertoire of Hemingway, Dos Passos, and Faulkner. "Here," said Sartre, "a new literature presented its characters to us synthetically. It made them perform before our eyes acts which were complete in themselves, impossible to analyze, acts which it was necessary to grasp completely with all the obscure power of our souls." The success of Faulkner, Hemingway, and Dos Passos, Sartre says elsewhere, "was the defensive reflex of a literature which, feeling itself menaced because its techniques and its myths no longer permitted it to face the actual situation, grafted on itself

foreign methods in order to fulfill its function in dealing with the problems placed before it." The objectivity of presentation, the inversion of time, the collectivist view and wide social range, the extended intensity of emotion—all these literary qualities were new in France and account in part for the popularity of the American novel.

The existentialists also admired the American novel because it dramatized an organic world view. They stressed, in particular, what they called its sense of "dépaysement," which can be translated as "uprootedness" or as "deracination." As one French critic, Claude-Edmonde Magny, put it:

> Le roman américain est venu circuler un souffle plus large dans la République des Lettres. Aussi son charme est-il en particulier celui de l'exotisme non tant au sens banal de l'eloignement dans l'espace, que grâce au prestige plus profond du dépaysement social. Il nous montre des vagabonds, des chomeurs, des ivrogness invétéres; de mauvais garçons dénués de tout romantisme. . . .

America, still in the process of growth, was a relatively young country to the French. While America offered the individual much more freedom than the more fixed Continent, with its age-old traditions, for some it was a hostile and brutal prison. The novels of Faulkner, Dos Passos, Steinbeck, Hemingway, and Caldwell are populated with floundering expatriates or itinerant workers who live on the periphery of society and are forever looking for new adventure or for a new start. The Hemingway, Dos Passos, Faulkner hero is seldom cerebral or (with the obvious exception of characters like Quentin Compson) self-involved and often wanders alone and aimlessly through a land devoid of tradition, defining himself through immediate action. Sartre, in particular, calls attention to the solitary heroes of American fiction who seem to have lost contact with past tradition:

> What fascinated us all really—petty bourgeois that we were, sons of peasants securely attached to the earth of our farms, intellectuals entrenched in Paris for life—was the constant flow of men across a whole continent, the exodus of an entire village to the orchards of California, the hopeless wanderings of the hero in *Light in August,* and the uprooted people who drifted along at the mercy of the story in *The 42nd Parallel,* the dark murderous fury which sometimes swept through an entire city, the blind and criminal love in the novels of James Cain.

Sartre has admitted his debt in matters of technique to John Dos Passos's panoramic trilogy *U.S.A.* "It was after reading a book by Dos Passos," he said, "that I thought for the first time of weaving a novel out of various lives with characters who pass each other and who all contribute to the atmosphere of a historical period." Sartre has even gone as far as to say, "I regard Dos Passos as the greatest writer of our time." While Sartre's praise is excessive, there is little doubt that *U.S.A.* deeply influenced *Les chemins de la liberté.* The final effect of the two works is particularly similar. As Sartre himself has pointed out, Dos Passos' novel seems to take place in the present tense.

The reason for this is that it sustains a horizontal structure, a quantitative time, in which one action or event is made to seem as important as the next one. There are no real crises in *U.S.A.* Also one action never seems to be the result of another. As Sartre puts it, "not for an instant does the order of causality betray itself in chronological order. There is no narrative, but rather the jerky unreeling of a rough and uneven memory. . . . As a result of this, past things retain a flavour of the present." Furthermore, in both Dos Passos's and Sartre's novels, the reader must identify himself with various characters, must become a part of the social consciousness and conscience. If he is to read at all, he must piece together the fragmented images, link them in time, view them in relation to the main social problem, and pass jugment on himself at the same time he passes judgment on the characters. At least this is Sartre's hope and expectation: "If you name the behavior of an individual," Sartre has said, "you reveal it to him; he sees himself. And since you are at the same time naming it to all others he knows that he is *seen* at the same time he *sees* himself." The final image in these novels is supposed to be the reader himself, and the problem is one of identity—or so Sartre insists. Sartre used Dos Passos's technique to show man trying to define himself in the chaos of the modern world.

If the French existentialists admired the newness and the sense of *dépaysement* in American fiction in general, they admired the American detective story in particular. They linked under this category a number of writers that American critics do not often connect with each other—and they called this kind of fiction "la littérature noire." In 1946 Marcel Duhamel started a series of detective stories entitled *Série Noire.* Gallimard published three books in this series a month, selling for 220 francs each, about half to one-third the price of an ordinary novel. About 90 per cent of these books were translations from the American and included such writers as W. H. Burnett, Horace McCoy, James Cain, Dashiell Hammett, Raoul Whitfield, Don Tracy, and P. F. Wolfson.

These novels were popularly read and respected by even the most serious writers. In fact, until about mid-century, French criticism of American fiction tended to lack discretion and sensitivity, and it was not surprising to find a commentator seriously maintaining that a Hammett or a Cain was of the same literary magnitude as a Faulkner. In all fairness to the critics, the French saw the detective novel as a significant genre. Even Albert Camus expressed his debt to the form when he structured *L'étranger* on James M. Cain's *The Postman Always Rings Twice.* As I have shown elsewhere, Cain's novel—with its "innocent" victim—represented a point of departure and not an ideal conclusion for Camus who believed that the responsible man employed both his senses and his reason, and was thus able to interpret as well as immediately react to stimuli. Camus disliked the American "tough guy" who lived on the surface of life, lacked the dimension of interior reality, and whose behavior embodied the very indifference of nature itself. Camus saw, however, that in *L'étranger* he could use the fast narrative pace of the detective novel to secure the interest of the reader in a novel that would have philosophical implications. He further saw that the world

in the detective novel was not dissimilar from the violent world of the twentieth century and that it compactly organized and dramatically revealed a hostile and indifferent universe—the world of the absurd. Camus also saw that the world of the detective novel was the world of the outsider. The heroes of Cain's and Hammett's novels, for example, are social malcontents who live dynamically on the fringes of society. Finally, the dramatic structure and the extreme situation in the detective novel offered a narrative vehicle for Camus's ideas about the structure of society, the nature of motivation, the nature of guilt, and the general psychological makeup of the social rebel. Dostoyevsky's *Crime and Punishment* is a form of the detective novel in its highest sense. In *L'étranger,* Camus used a similar vehicle for dramatic speculation about the structure of existence and the need to live in the face of the absurd—questions discussed at length in *Le mythe de Sisyphe.*

Lastly, the French existentialists were interested in what they called the tragic world of American fiction. In his preface to *Sanctuary,* André Malraux maintained that Faulkner's novel is "l'intrusion de la tragédie grecque dans le roman policier." Unfortunately, Malraux did not elaborate. One might question the similarity of Faulkner's characters and the more noble and more enlightened characters of Aeschylus, Sophocles, and Euripides. But if Malraux is referring to the similarities between the dramatic world of Faulkner and that of the Greeks, his observations are suggestive and worthy of further investigation. Like the early Greeks, Faulkner constructs a moral world. His characters may not always seem to possess free will, but they are all obsessed with sin and guilt. Faulkner's sense of sin and guilt is, in fact, so strong that the French critics continually talk about his underlying Puritanism. Coindreau, for example, maintains that

> L'oeuvre de Faulkner est l'oeuvre d'un puritan qu'abide l'idée de la fatalité, la crainte et l'horreur du péché et de ses consequences. C'est un réquisitoire passionné centre le vice, et il serait aisé d'y démasquer un grand idéalisme. Alors que William Faulkner regrette que l'homme ne soit pas un ange, Caldwell voudrait qu'il fût le plus possible un bête.

While the tension and the complexity in much American literature stems, as Coindreau suggests, from an inability to reconcile a feeling about the natural baseness of man with that of his ultimate dignity, Faulkner's fiction goes beyond Coindreau's "l'idée de la fatalité." As Coindreau connects Faulkner directly with Puritanism, other critics have connected him with naturalism. If Faulkner's characters have "fallen," and if there is a sense of naturalistic darkness in his fiction, man seems to have caused his own fall, to have brought the naturalistic disorder down upon himself. In a novel like *Absalom, Absalom!* we see a pattern that can often be found in Faulkner's fiction. First we have a time of order and harmony, a kind of Eden before the Fall, when Thomas Sutpen was living in the mountains of West Virginia in a world where everyone was equal and one man was as good as the next. When his father takes him down from the mountains to the Tideland area of Virginia, the descent is both a metaphorical and a literal fall.

In Virginia, Sutpen is totally robbed of his innocence when he is turned away from the plantation door—an incident that violates everything that he had taken for granted, destroys his old way of looking at himself, and turns him toward his mono-maniacal design. The design, in time, leads him to repudiate his son, Charles Bon, which parallels what happened to him at the plantation door and which becomes an act of irreparable evil that is always at the center of Faulkner's fiction (this act varies in the novels but is usually connected with miscegenation). Sutpen's repudiating his son leads in turn to Henry Sutpen's murdering Bon (a fratricidal act which has parallels to the Civil War, the novel moving from the personal to a historical level of meaning). Throughout the novel, we have an inevitable sense of doom, Sutpen planting his own tragic seed, the fleur de mal. Although the chronology of the novel belies it, there is a tremendous sense of causality in *Absalom, Absalom!*: all *was is,* as we are told, the sins of the father are handed down to the sons, the past is contained in the present, even though Sutpen himself will not admit this. Thomas Sutpen is doomed, but he is doomed because of his own mono-mania—and this is what separates Faulkner from the naturalists who think of tragedy in purely environmental terms, and from Coindreau's Puritans who think of it in terms of God's will. If God's will is at work in the novel, it is working beyond man's ability to understand it. Faulkner's novels are often told by a young man (a Quentin Compson or an Isaac McCaslin) with a tormented consciousness, a young man who struggles to impose meaning on events that seem to defy meaning, events that go beyond explanation. For Camus, the world became absurd when man lost his power to give it meaning, when reason broke down in the face of the unknown. Like the existentialists, Faulkner continually demonstrates the void between an act and the narrator's ability to verbalize its meaning. An outer conflict creates an even deeper inner conflict; an act in the past short-circuits meaning in the present. When the flow of events lose meaning, time can only be endured—and meaning can only be found in the struggle. One can perhaps now better understand why Camus translated and adapted *Requiem for a Nun* for the Paris stage. Nancy Mannigoe was bound to fascinate him—Nancy, that mysterious, dark, brooding figure who solitarily stands under sentence of death and accepts the sentence with quiet heroism.

Faulkner, of course, was not an existentialist, and one can become carried away by Camus's and Sartre's interest in him. Even the existentialists did not give him total consent. Sartre disliked the way Faulkner made his characters victims of their memory, the way he created an inevitable sequence of events which man's will could not break, the way his characters became prisoners of time (strangely enough, in the very center of Yoknapatawpha County—on top of the courthouse—is a clock; again in the center of Yoknapatawpha County—in the basement of the courthouse—is the prison). While Faulkner saw the absurd struggle in terms of redeeming the past, the existentialists saw it in terms of living the present (Camus) or projecting oneself toward the future (Sartre). Faulkner's characters, cut off from an Edenic past, momentarily restore the initial order by finding the more simple and natural life, like Wilbourne and Charlotte in *The Wild Palms* when they escape to a timeless Eden deep in the Wisconsin woods. Perhaps this is why Faulkner put so much faith in such simple, often earthy, characters as Lena Grove, Byron Bunch, Horace Benbow, and Isaac McCaslin. Yet, if Faulkner postulated an ideal world in his fiction, his characters do not function in this ideal world but only in relation to it. If the ideal world is an Edenic past, the real world is a lost paradise, a world where a simple agrarian life is giving way to a more complex industrial one, a world without order, often violent and malevolent, moving with no seeming end or purpose. Within such a world, the individual can bring about his own destruction with the violence of a Meursault or a Joe Christmas, or he can fulfill himself with the love of a Dr. Rieux or a Lena Grove. And if Faulkner's characters seem helpless to change their fate, the events in the novel do not suggest a mechanistic and dehumanized universe because man—in one way or another—has planted his own seeds of ruin, is the source of his own fate, and remains the source of his own redemption. When the sins of the father are handed down to the son, time is humanized and becomes a personal burden. Like Dostoyevsky's Ivan, Faulkner's characters must become their own Christ. We can thus understand why, for this reason if no other, Sartre said, "Faulkner's humanism is probably the only acceptable kind." (pp. 190-98)

Richard Lehan, "American Fiction and French Literary Existentialism," in Themes and Directions in American Literature: Essays in Honor of Leon Howard, *edited by Ray B. Browne and Donald Pizer, Purdue University Studies, 1969, pp. 186-99.*

Hannah Arendt

[*A German-born American political philosopher and literary essayist, Arendt ranks among the most important political thinkers of the twentieth century. In her many works she considered the central issues of the times—war, revolution, political power, violence, anti-Semitism—with original, and at times controversial, insight. Perceiving the political thinker as a "truth-teller" who counters the lies of politicians, Arendt sought through her writings to expand the realm of human freedom and resist tyranny. In the following excerpt, Arendt comments on Existentialism's break with Western intellectual and philosophical tradition.*]

A lecture on philosophy provokes a riot, with hundreds crowding in and thousands turned away. Books on philosophical problems preaching no cheap creed and offering no panacea but, on the contrary, so difficult as to require actual thinking sell like detective stories. Plays in which the action is a matter of words, not a plot, and which offer a dialogue of reflections and ideas run for months and are attended by enthusiastic crowds. Analyses of the situation of man in the world, of the fundaments of human relationship, of Being and the Void not only give rise to a new literary movement but also figure as possible guides for a fresh political orientation. Philosophers become newspapermen, playwrights, novelists. They are not members of university faculties but "bohemians" who stay at hotels and live in the cafe—leading a public life to the point of renouncing privacy. And not even success, or so it seems, can turn them into respectable bores.

This is what is happening, from all reports, in Paris. If the Resistance has not achieved the European revolution, it seems to have brought about, at least in France, a genuine rebellion of the intellectuals, whose docility in relation to modern society was one of the saddest aspects of the sad spectacle of Europe between wars. And the French people, for the time being, appear to consider the arguments of their philosophers more important than the talk and the quarrels of their politicians. This may reflect, of course, a desire to escape from political action into some theory which merely talks about action, that is, into activism; but it may also signify that in the face of the spiritual bankruptcy of the left and the sterility of the old revolutionary élite—which have led to the desperate efforts at restoration of all political parties—more people than we might imagine have a feeling that the responsibility for political action is too heavy to assume until new foundations, ethical as well as political, are laid down, and that the old tradition of philosophy which is deeply imbedded even in the least philosophical individual is actually an impediment to new political thought.

The name of the new movement is "Existentialism," and its chief exponents are Jean-Paul Sartre and Albert Camus, but the term Existentialism has given rise to so many misunderstandings that Camus has already publicly stated why he is "not an Existentialist." The term comes from the modern German philosophy which had a revival immediately after the First World War and has strongly influenced French thought for more than a decade; but it would be irrelevant to trace and define the sources of Existentialism in national terms for the simple reason that both the German and the French manifestations came out of an identical period and a more or less identical cultural heritage.

The French Existentialists, though they differ widely among themselves, are united on two main lines of rebellion: first, the rigorous repudiation of what they call the *esprit sérieux;* and, second, the angry refusal to accept the world as it is as the natural, predestined milieu of man.

L'esprit sérieux, which is the original sin according to the new philosophy, may be equated with respectability. The "serious" man is one who thinks of himself *as* president of his business, *as* a member of the Legion of Honor, *as* a member of the faculty, but also *as* father, *as* husband, or as any other half-natural, half-social function. For by so doing he agrees to the identification of himself with an arbitrary function which society has bestowed. *L'esprit sérieux* is the very negation of freedom, because it leads man to agree to and accept the necessary deformation which every human being must undergo when he is fitted into society. Since everyone knows well enough in his own heart that he is not identical with his function, *l'esprit sérieux* indicates also bad faith in the sense of pretending. Kafka has already shown, in *Amerika,* how ridiculous and dangerous is the hollow dignity which grows out of identifying oneself with one's function: In that book the most dignified person in the hotel, upon whose word the hero's job

and daily bread depend, rules out the possibility that he can make an error by invoking the argument of the "serious" man: "How could I go on being the head porter if I mistook one person for another?"

This matter of *l'esprit sérieux* was first touched upon in Sartre's novel *La nausée,* in a delightful description of a gallery of portraits of the town's respectable citizens, *les salauds.* It then became the central topic of Camus's novel *L'étranger.* The hero of the book, the stranger, is an average man who simply refuses to submit to the serious-mindedness of society, who refuses to live as any of his allotted functions. He does not behave as a son at his mother's funeral—he does not weep; he does not behave as a husband—he declines to take marriage seriously even at the moment of his engagement. Because he does not pretend, he is a stranger whom no one understands, and he pays with his life for his affront to society. Since he refuses to play the game, he is isolated from his fellow-men to the point of incomprehensibility and isolated from himself to the point of becoming inarticulate. Only in a last scene, immediately before his death, does the hero arrive at some kind of explanation which conveys the impression that for him life itself was such a mystery and in its terrible way so beautiful that he did not see any necessity for "improving" upon it with the trimmings of good behavior and hollow pretensions.

Sartre's brilliant play *Huis clos* belongs to the same category. The play opens in hell, appropriately furnished in the style of the Second Empire. The three persons gathered in the room—"Hell is the Others"—set the diabolical torture in motion by trying to pretend. Since, however, their lives are closed and since "you are your life and nothing else," pretense no longer works, and we see what would go on behind closed doors if people actually were stripped of the sheltering cover of functions derived from society.

Both Sartre's play and Camus's novel deny the possibility of a genuine fellowship between men, of any relationship which would be direct, innocent, free of pretense. Love in Sartre's philosophy is the will to be loved, the need for a supreme confirmation of one's own existence. For Camus love is a somewhat awkward and hopeless attempt to break through the isolation of the individual.

The way out of pretense and serious-mindedness is to play at being what one really is. Again Kafka indicated in the last chapter of *Amerika* a new possibility of authentic life. The great "Nature Theater" where everyone is welcome and where everybody's unhappiness is resolved is not by accident a theater. Here everybody is invited to choose his role, to play at what he is or would like to be. The chosen role is the solution of the conflict between mere functioning and mere being, as well as between mere ambition and mere reality.

The new "ideal" becomes, in this context, the actor whose very profession is pretending, who constantly changes his role, and thus can never take any of his roles seriously. By playing at what one is, one guards one's freedom as a human being from the pretenses of one's functions; moreover, only by playing at what he really is, is man able to affirm that he is never identical with himself as a thing is identical with itself. An inkpot is always an inkpot. Man is his life and his actions, which are never finished until the very moment of his death. He *is* his existence.

The second common element of French Existentialism, the insistence upon the basic homelessness of man in the world, is the topic of Camus's *Le mythe de Sisyphe; essay sur l'absurde,* and of Sartre's *La nausée.* For Camus man is essentially the stranger because the world in general and man as man are not fitted for each other; that they are together in existence makes the human condition an absurdity. Man is the only "thing" in the world which obviously does not belong in it, for only man does not exist simply as a man among men in the way animals exist among animals and trees among trees—all of which necessarily exist, so to speak, in the plural. Man is basically alone with his "revolt" and his "clairvoyance," that is, with his reasoning, which makes him ridiculous because the gift of reason was bestowed upon him in a world "where everything is given and nothing ever explained."

Sartre's notion of the absurdity, the contingency, of existence is best represented in the chapter of *La nausée* which appears in the current issue of the *Partisan Review* under the title "The Root of the Chestnut Tree." Whatever exists, so far as we can see, has not the slightest reason for its existence. It is simply *de trop,* superfluous. The fact that I can't even imagine a world in which, instead of many too many things, there would be nothing only shows the hopelessness and senselessness of man's being eternally entangled in existence.

Here Sartre and Camus part company, if we may judge from the few works of theirs which have reached this country. The absurdity of existence and the repudiation of *l'esprit serieux* are only points of departure for each. Camus seems to have gone on to a philosophy of absurdity, whereas Sartre seems to be working toward some new positive philosophy and even a new humanism.

Camus has probably protested against being called an Existentialist because for him the absurdity does not lie in man as such or in the world as such but only in their being thrown together. Since man's life, being laid in the world, is absurd, it must be lived as absurdity—lived, that is, in a kind of proud defiance which insists on reason despite the experience of reason's failure to explain anything; insists on despair since man's pride will not allow him the hope of discovering a sense he cannot figure out by means of reason; insists, finally, that reason and human dignity, in spite of their senselessness, remain the supreme values. The absurd life then consists in constantly rebelling against all its conditions and in constantly refusing consolations. "This revolt is the price of life. Spread over the whole of an existence, it restores its grandeur." All that remains, all that one can say yes to, is chance itself, the *hasard roi* which has apparently played at putting man and world together. " 'I judge that everything is well,' said Oedipus, and this word is sacred. It resounds in the ferocious universe which is the limit of man. . . . It makes of destiny an affair of men which should be settled among men." This is precisely the point where Camus, without giving much explanation, leaves behind all modernistic attitudes and comes to insights which are genuinely modern,

the insight, for instance, that the moment may have arrived "when creation is no longer taken tragically; it is only taken seriously."

For Sartre, absurdity is of the essence of things as well as of man. Anything that exists is absurd simply because it exists. The salient difference between the things of the world and the human being is that things are unequivocally identical with themselves, whereas man—because he sees and knows that he sees, believes and knows that he believes—bears within his consciousness a negation which makes it impossible for him ever to become one with himself. In this single respect—in respect of his consciousness, which has the germ of negation in it—man is a creator. For this is of man's own making and not merely given, as the world and his existence are given. If man becomes aware of his own consciousness and its tremendous creative possibilities, and renounces the longing to be identical with himself as a thing is, he realizes that he depends upon nothing and nobody outside himself and that he can be free, the master of his own destiny. This seems to be the essential meaning of Sartre's novel *Les mouches* (*The Flies*), in which Orestes, by taking upon himself the responsibility for the necessary killing of which the town is afraid, liberates the town and takes the Flies—the Erinyes of bad conscience and of the dark fear of revenge—with him. He himself is immune because he does not feel guilty and regrets nothing.

It would be a cheap error to mistake this new trend in philosophy and literature for just another fashion of the day because its exponents refuse the respectability of institutions and do not even pretend to that seriousness which regards every achievement as a step in a career. Nor should we be put off by the loud journalistic success with which their work has been accompanied. This success, equivocal as it may be in itself, is nevertheless due to the quality of the work. It is also due to a definite modernity of attitude which does not try to hide the depth of the break in Western tradition. Camus especially has the courage not even to look for connections, for predecessors and the like. The good thing about Sartre and Camus is that they apparently suffer no longer from nostalgia for the good old days, even though they may know that in an abstract sense those days were actually better than ours. They do not believe in the magic of the old, and they are honest in that they make no compromises whatever.

Yet if the revolutionary élan of these writers is not broken by success, if, symbolically speaking, they stick to their hotel rooms and their cafes, the time may come when it will be necessary to point out "seriously" those aspects of their philosophy which indicate that they are still dangerously involved in old concepts. The nihilistic elements, which are obvious in spite of all protests to the contrary, are not the consequences of new insights but of some very old ideas. (pp. 253-58)

Hannah Arendt, "French Existentialism," in One Hundred Years of 'The Nation': A Centennial Anthology, *edited by Henry M. Christman, The Macmillan Company, 1965, pp. 253-58.*

EXISTENTIALISM CRITIQUED AND DEFENDED

Gaston Berger

[*In the following excerpt taken from a series of lectures on Existentialism, Berger criticizes Existentialism's implication that the world lacks inherent meaning and absolute moral or aesthetic values.*]

Existentialism seems to have spread out very rapidly. Its novels are read, its plays produced all over the world and it seems to be in France the philosophy of the moment. But this is only an appearance. Existentialism is not the philosophy of the post-war years; it is only a description of that period. It gives an expression to preexisting feelings. Its strength comes from its lack of originality. Existentialists do not lead anything, nor anybody; they follow a trend. That is why their importance is greater as novelists or as playwrights than as philosophers. Sartre is a kind of newspaperman of genius and his tactics are exactly those of a newspaperman: he puts the emphasis on the most shocking detail, even if it does not correspond to an important feature of the event. Or he exaggerates the facts, he brings them to the most extreme consequences.

This is not without importance. In social, as in individual life, to be conscious of a feeling and to express it give to that feeling a new power. A disclosed and proclaimed opinion possesses some rights which did not exist when it was concealed.

But the task of a philosopher is not to be a speaker. It is to be a guide. We have neither to sing the weary songs of despair nor to preach the suppression of laws to men who have already lost their rules . . . It was proper to expose the weaknesses of bourgeois capitalism in 1848, as Marx did, or to foretell nihilism at the end of the XIXth century, as did Nietzsche, at a moment when society had a solid structure.

What we have to do now is not to recall the dangers of yesterday but to announce the dangers of tomorrow. And, as we have experienced anxiety and despair, we have to go on the other side of despair and give again a meaning to human life.

The existentialists cannot bring any help for this constructive task, and if they want to propose a definite set of rules for our actions, they will have to drop their former statements. If man is an absolute liberty, if he is free to *create* himself right and wrong, and not simply to *choose* between right and wrong, then morality disappears. If "everything is allowed," as Dostoievsky said and as the existentialists repeat, why do you propose this behavior as better than that one?

Moreover the feeling of anxiety to which the existentialists give a great importance, is ridiculous in their doctrine. Why should I be concerned with my actions if there is neither right nor wrong? If there are no values, everything is unimportant. The suppression of all the rules should lead to indifference.

But anxiety is really a momentous aspect of human reflection, and that for two reasons. *First* because we have no absolute guaranty that God is really dead. Suppose my arguments were wrong? Suppose man has really a destiny? Suppose I am deliberately spoiling my eternal life? Considerations of this kind open the door to anxiety, but anxiety is here connected with the suspension of atheism. And *secondly,* and independently from any religious belief, because we feel that *something* should be done, without knowing exactly *what* should be done in the circumstances of the moment. And this is precisely human Fate. I have to do my duty, but I do not know, in all cases, what my duty is. And this happens particularly when the conditions are changing and when old duties lose their importance, while an exacting consciousness discovers new duties.

This explains quite well human anxiety and corresponds to an actual experience. I want to do my duty. I know that there is a good and an evil according to which the value of my action should be appreciated, but, even when I have general rules, I have to invent their application to a particular case, and I may be wrong. The reason for my anxiety is that "not everything is allowed." And this is really human consciousness: we know that there is a rule, and we do not know the rule.

I have witnessed a great many cases of this moral anxiety, with ever the same background: belief in the moral laws and ignorance of the proper duty. After the armistice of June 1940, Pétain had organized in the southern part of France, which was not occupied by the German troops until 1942, groups of young men called *Les Chantiers de Feunesse,* who, instead of getting military training, received physical training, acquired the habit of team-work and worked for the state or for the communities in timberyards or on road-building.

I had many talks with the officers and non-commissioned officers of this civilian army. My aim was to explain to them that a collaboration with the Nazis was an actual treason toward France. As a rule, these men had a great feeling for morality associated with a weak power of criticism. They did not lack courage. The problem was not, for them, to *perform* an evident duty. It was to *find out* where duty was. And I have seen men of honor tortured by the very idea of treason and by the difficulty of discovering where treason really was. One day, in a training camp for the staffs of these *Chantiers de Feunesse* I suggested giving a series of compositions on moral subjects such as: "Obedience and duty," and "How can you decide upon the conflict of different duties?" and so on. And I found in the answers the expression of a sincere and impressive anxiety.

Thus, if existentialism is based upon the experience of anxiety which is real, it gives to this experience a meaning entirely false. Instead of coming from the absence of moral rules, it comes from the ignorance of the true requirements of existing and exacting rules.

If the existentialist description of man as an absolutely free Being, creating the values, inventing and not discovering the good, the true, the beautiful, does not explain human uneasiness, it does not fit our actual experience either. Man does not live for life's sake. He does not care for the things or for the events. He lives for a particular quality of the events which is different in each case, but which can be designated by the general term of "Value." He lives for truth, or for beauty, or for God, or for love—or simply he lives for Happiness. And truth is not a fact, it is a quality of a certain particular event called judgment. Happiness is not a fact either. I cannot put the presence of my friend on one side and my happiness on the other. It is not correct either to say that my happiness *comes* from his presence—my happiness is his presence, it is the *value* of his presence.

It is not my purpose to develop here a theory of value. I shall be concerned only with the description of some important aspects which are not irrelevant to the present problem. First, let us emphasize the fact that a value has to be experienced. You can deduce a consequence from a principle; from a set of given facts, you can draw the conclusion that the reality of an event, outside the present experience, must be admitted. But value has to be felt. Otherwise it is nothing. Considered from outside, value disappears and we have just a particular behavior.

But let us try to sympathize with the man who actually experiences a value. Let us take this student bending over a problem. He looks for a solution, and first he looks for a correct formulation of his problem. What should be stated first? Into what smaller problems must the initial and massive difficulty be divided? What will be the convenient method? He does not know what he is looking for, otherwise he would already have discovered it. But he knows the *value* he is in search of: he wants to *understand,* and to understand *rightly.* He does not look for *one* solution, but for the *good* one. And his mind is filled with a particular form of anxiety, with an intellectual concern. He has forgotten the particular motives of his research, and they do not matter at all. Maybe the problem has been proposed by the professor as an exercise; maybe it is a trial the solution of which is very important for his career; or perhaps he has put the problem to himself, out of pure curiosity . . . All the remembrances of his psychological motivations are in the background. What remains only in the foreground is an intense effort toward understanding.

And look, here it is. He is smiling broadly. All tension has disappeared. He has got the *evidence* of the solution. And what is given to him is not a construction of his mind, but the truth *of the thing itself.* Of course his actions have preceded this invasion of his mind by the feeling of evidence: he has drawn some lines, tried ineffectual combinations, made some preparatory analyses. . . . But all these operations are just leading to a final aim: the evidence of the truth, the apprehension of an objective relation. Evidence is no more an action, it is an enlightenment.

Sometimes this fullness does not last very long. The student had forgotten a particular requirement of the problem. His solution is not valid. All the reasoning must be considered again, and perhaps it has to be abandoned. This does not mean that the importance of evidence is vanishing, but only that there is a conflict between opposing evidences: the evidence of the mistake or of the omission has overcome and annihilated the illusory evidence of the solution. And in human experience tension and plenitude are never absolutely separated, that is to say, never absolutely pure. In all our victories something remains of the anterior deceptions. As there have been, in the past, delusive evidences, there is always in my present evidences a small touch of apprehension. On the other hand, in my sad hours of despair, I cannot forget the fullness of anterior experiences. Human experience of value has the character of Plato's *Eros,* of this platonic love whose Father was Richness but whose Mother was Poverty.

And if you want to realize the meaning of truth, you must not be contented with studying the history of sciences, nor considering the successes and failures of somebody else. You have to try it yourself.

A few minutes ago, I was talking about the moral anxiety of those Frenchmen who were trying to decide whether the treason was to collaborate with the Germans or to be unfaithful to the government which, in France at that moment, seemed to be legal. Moral anxiety is not of course identical with intellectual concern, but it is analogous. And, in the same manner, the consciousness of duty is analogous to the requirements of truth: some acts are endowed with moral value, as some statements are endowed with intellectual value, and there is moral enlightenment, similar to the evidence of judgments, subject to the same phases of enthusiasm and disappointment.

The same remarks could be made with respect to the esthetical value, and here the many testimonies of the artists are in agreement. The myth of inspiration is a poetical manner of expressing this transcendence of beauty, the poet or the painter pretending to be solely the medium used by the beautiful in its realization. And so is the traditional theory of "nature," as unique guide of the artists. All the artists are in search of *something* but not of *anything.* They try . . . and when "it" comes on the canvas, they are not rejoiced by the successes of *their* procedures but by the actualization of a value coming from the outside.

I know many stories about the French painter Matisse, because two good friends of mine had worked, when young, in the same studio as Matisse, and remained afterward in close and friendly relation with him. One day in Spain Matisse had locked himself up in his attic, with food for many days, in order to avoid being disturbed while painting a canvas which seemed to require much time. After only two hours he came to the patio—it was in Seville—where his friend was having a cup of coffee. "Hello, did you forget anything?" his friend asked. "Oh, no!" he answered. "But I have been turned out of my painting. It has come." By these words Matisse meant that the thing was on the canvas, so completed that nothing else should be added. And the painting itself seemed to decide. Beauty was on the canvas. It had come *through* the artist, but it did not come *from* him.

And it happened frequently that Matisse looked at one of his paintings with admiration and shouted "How beautiful!" It was not vanity, nor self-complacency. He was not

Guests at the 1944 reading of the play Desire Caught by the Tail *by Pablo Picasso (arms folded), including Simone de Beauvoir (standing, second from right) Jean-Paul Sartre (sitting far left), and Albert Camus (kneeling, center).*

at all concerned with the man who did create the painting. The canvas was there, simply, as a "thing of beauty."

The difference between the creator and the spectator disappears when value is concerned. Admiration gives the same kind of rapture as inspiration, and evidence is as illuminating when somebody else has invented the proof as when you have discovered it yourself. The same happens in ethics. When something should be done, the value is in the thing to be done and not in your or in my personal feelings. The duty is to perform the deed and not to increase our personal merits.

If you want to talk about esthetical values don't try to criticize from the outside the statements of this or that theory of art. But remember your first visit to some museum and the shock you felt in your heart when you looked at a certain painting. You remained silent, shivering with an inexpressible joy, and the tears came to your eyes. There was no place in your mind for any question concerning the meaning of human life. The world was justified, just as it is justified by the sacrifice of a hero or by the discoveries of the scientist.

But all men are not sensitive to the same values: it is not

immediately perceptible because all men use the same words, and because also there are certain feelings which are conventionally expressed on certain occasions, even if they are not really experienced. In fact, there are people who are not at all interested in painting and who are bored by sculpture but who are deeply moved by music. Or even, there are people who have practically no feeling at all for any esthetical values. The same happens with intellectual and moral values. Children, for instance, are very seldom concerned with moral values. They generally feel much more definitely beauty than justice. They are above all sensitive to social values.

Because there are not only the three values, the truth, the good, and the beautiful, which have been emphasized by tradition. There are also social values; there are religious values, which have been frequently mistaken for the others, as they have been associated with them for centuries. And love is a value too, which gives to the mind the same feeling of transcendence as art or duty, but, of course, with quite original connotations. Life is always meaningful for the lover and the world is justified by the very presence of the woman I love . . .

We begin to understand that the reluctant feeling of the existentialists concerning life could express either the exhaustion of a deficient man who is not strong enough to be moved by the calls of the values, or rather the defeat of a man who could not succeed in a field of value, which was for him of a particular importance. The feeling of shame, for instance, which Sartre associates constantly with the experience of my fellow-men is nothing but a failure of love. But shame testifies to the value of love, as my revolt against absurdity proves the importance of evidence. And in this sense, Sartre's philosophy is a philosophy of love, but of powerless and ineffectual love. And this philosophy can be impressive because it is true that love is frequently unsuccessful. We can even say that love is never perfectly successful. When the lover holds his beloved in his arms, when he hears her voice whispering the sweetest words, he still is in search of something which is out of his grasp. Love wants union and can never go beyond any separation. Just as understanding looks for so clear and so distinct an evidence that no delusion could follow. But love does not want to *have;* it wants to *give,* and it is a sign of egoism which makes us concerned with the response of the partner. That last point expresses another aspect of the problem. Value is the way in which the Absolute presents itself to the human mind. The experience of value is never that of a creation, but that of a surrender. I never take possession of the Absolute, and when the existentialists are sorry for this impossibility, it is just because they did not reflect upon and did not give account of the characteristics of the Absolute. And this seems to me one of the most important gaps in the philosophy of today.

I can never reach the absolute, that is to say introduce it into my human experience. It would be contradictory. But I can recognize my dependence upon the Absolute, feel my own place in it and let it permeate all my being. And this is the meaning of human liberty: to say "no" or "yes." To put oneself in the very center of the universe or to accept to play a part in this immense universe "the center of which is everywhere and the limits of which are nowhere." But, if metaphysics is a necessary part of any coherent philosophy, it is not at all necessary to be a metaphysician to acknowledge the transcendence of the Absolute. This is realized in any experience of value.

You could perhaps remark, now, that the trends of contemporary thought seem to be directly opposed to my theory. Let us take modern painting as an example.

Modern painters emphasize their independence of the objects, and more generally from nature. They do not want to copy any more; they create. What happens then to inspiration, to the existence of a transcendent beauty? The promethean revolt is here quite clear. Beauty is not a ready made disposition of patterns, it is a free construction of the human mind.

I clearly recognize this change in the minds of some painters. But it seems to me that it is not a question of finding new rules, and perhaps a new definition for beauty. It is a deep change in the values for which painting is intended. And this is not only a personal theory, it is a fact confessed by the artists themselves. In the name of the surrealists

André Breton declared that beauty was no more the aim of art nor of poetry, and Picasso made similar statements. When after my lecture on modern art a lady, who was, I believe, a professor at the University of Chicago, came to me and explained that modern painters were not at all in search of beauty, I entirely agreed with her. But the drama of painting is that the painters do not yet see clearly the *other* value they want to express.

I do not pretend to predict now accurately which new values will be emphasized by the art of tomorrow. Maybe it will be something like the expression of an unconscious and magic world which poetry and art would give us the means to reach. Social values seem also to be at work in this conception of art. Surrealist art does not only express the unconscious life of an individual. It reaches a collective unconscious and affords to mankind the possibility of a new communication, which would be neither intellectual, nor properly religious . . .

Anyway what I see in modern art and in some modern theories of literature is not so much a different description of the value-experiences as a discovery of new values and a shift of the emphasis from one value to another.

And the value which is now prominent is the social value. The surrealist movement was closely connected with the idea of social revolution and the disagreement between the tenants of the doctrine is now only to determine if the communist party is really the representative of a valuable revolution. It is well known that the Marxists affirm the absolute prevalence of social life. For them, a good painting is, before all, a painting reinforcing the union of the proletarians in their common fight, and the traditional idea of beauty must be abandoned as a product of bourgeois society. But the existentialists themselves subordinate also literature to social action. If they consider poetry as one of the fine arts and do not urge the poet to "engage" himself into social problems, they maintain, on the other hand, that the author who writes in prose has nothing else to do but to reveal the social reality to his fellow-citizens. He is not morally free to write on the subjects he likes. Sartre hates Flaubert because he did not write against the bourgeois regime, and was not concerned with the revolution of 1848. There is something very attractive in the speech of the existentialists for liberty—even if their idea of liberty is highly disputable. At least they refuse any kind of dictatorship, as well a bourgeois-dictatorship as a communist totalitarianism.

But still, if we put too strongly the emphasis on the social values, as the existentialists do, we are opening the way to a totalitarian regime. Before being a form of government, totalitarianism is a turn of mind. It is a particular form of fanaticism, in which one type of value is placed, once for all, above all the others.

And thus we see existentialism hesitating between the two dangers which are now threatening our civilization: nihilism and fanaticism. On the one hand, we believe in nothing, on the other we believe in anything. At one moment, we are abandoned without any rules, before the impossible task of giving ourselves values out of nothing. At another moment, social values and political activity appear as the only aim deserving our efforts.

And it is not surprising to see nihilism in such a connection with fanaticism. Valuation is not an accidental activity of man. Human thought and even human life involve valuation. We can shift the emphasis from one value to another, we cannot suppress all value. When we believe that we do so, we are still attracted by a value, but without knowing it, that is to say without any possibility of criticism. As an example, Nazi fanaticism came directly from nihilism, as Rauschning explained in his famous book on Naziism, *Philosophy of Nihilism.*

Against this double danger, what can we do? What should we do?

I answer: return to the description and to a correct interpretation of experience.

Against a sad and exhausted nihilism there is no other remedy than to put the anxious or the skeptic in contact with men who experience themselves the call of the absolute on this or that field of values, with scientists in search of truth for its own sake, and not only engineers looking for a practical device, with enthusiastic artists, with heroes and saints. Youth is always ready to hear the call of the hero. But the heroes are few in a world spoiled by the war and dominated by mechanical technics and by social organization. This promotion by living example is—or more exactly—should be the main task of education. But in fact education is more and more technical, that is to say it just gives practical means for reaching the aims which are supposed to exist naturally in the heart of everybody.

Means, independent of any aims, are just a power. But power in itself is ambiguous. It can give both justice and injustice. It does not suppress the importance of value. It increases this importance. When a man has only his fists at his disposal, his anger, his bad temper, his wickedness are not very momentous. But when this man is the head of a big state, so carefully organized by the constraints of education, the seductions of propaganda and the control of the police, that all the people will obey his orders as a finger obeys the brains, when these people use the most terrible weapons, then the aims of the man and the values he appreciates are of the utmost importance.

The danger of technical training is not only in transforming man himself into a piece of machinery. It is also in diverting attention from the consideration of the values, in making believe that power in itself *has* value. It is important to go as fast as possible from one place to another if you can use the time you save in a profitable way. During the war, we could not use our cars at all. The Germans took the gas, took the tires, and sometimes took the cars too. Then everybody used bicycles and nothing was changed in the week-end or in the Sunday trips. In peace time, many people used to drive two hours in the morning, have lunch in a good restaurant, in a nice place, and come back in the afternoon. Nothing was changed with the bicycle, except that we rode thirty miles instead of driving three hundred miles and that the good restaurant was replaced by a poor sandwich. But the distance did not affect the program and its subjective value: and in the future,

when we take trips in a plane, we shall fly one thousand miles. What is the difference if we smoke the same cigar, after the same lunch, and read the same funnies in the same Sunday paper?

But we believe that we did something great and we forget the vanity of our purposeless activity because we are a little more busy today than yesterday.

Nihilism of the exhausted man, who finds activity tasteless and develops a philosophy of nausea. Nihilism of the busy man, who is always in a hurry and never wants to be here or there, but somewhere else. Both attitudes are identical: in both cases life is empty. And both have the same origin: men are not attentive to the call of value. This cannot be cured by arguments but by personal experience, encouraged by stimulating examples.

Frenchmen do not easily despair, and they are also too critical to be satisfied with sterile activity for long. French existentialism has not been very long nor very deeply a philosophy of nausea. It turned from that first aspect to a more active and positive doctrine. It pretends now to be a humanism, and to bring a political doctrine. What can bring, on this field, a philosophy endowing man with an absolute liberty, deprived of any ideal aim? Nothing else than change for change's sake and permanent revolution . . .

This is the great temptation of the moment. But I don't believe it will prevail in France. Of course, we have a very critical turn of mind and we cannot refrain from being impressed by a philosophy which encourages us to say "no" instead of saying "yes." A Frenchman is frequently like the man who came, one day, into a hall, where somebody was making a speech about something. He did not know at all the argument, but a few seconds after he was seated, he stood up and shouted "I disagree." And it is true also that now many things should raise some objections. And there were in the world, in the last decades, too many "yes" and not enough "no" . . .

But still we don't love in France the indefinite movement. We are not fascinated by the romanticism of "becoming," nor by cosmic, grandiloquent exaggerations. We keep to the moderate and to the human and we like limits. Our fields are closed by fences and walls as our ideas are fixed by precise definitions. Every Frenchman is something of an artisan. He likes handicraft and perfect work. Progress for him is not a permanent change, but the realization of different achieved works, each one of which is superior to the preceding. From this viewpoint progress is never an everchanging flood, but the succession of different orders, replacing one another. The maxim of the French positivist Auguste Comte: "Order and Progress," expresses a permanent feature of the French temperament. The emphasis may be shifted from one of the terms to the other, but both terms must remain.

I have talked of nihilism. Let us now turn to fanaticism. I believe that, on this point, a philosophical reflection on the nature of values could clear up many difficulties and avoid many dangers. It should point out, namely, that no human value is absolute, and that for two different reasons: First: The Absolute does not belong to this world.

If I speak the language of a theologian, I should remind you of the first words of a prayer: "Our Father, who art in Heaven." "God is in the heaven" is only the translation of a metaphysical statement which can be explained by purely rational arguments: nothing, on earth, in the world, is Absolute.

Human experience of value is precisely the feeling of this transcendence of the Absolute: it is up to us to endow this world of ours with value, in order to give it some perfection. Value is the call coming from the Absolute, as Le Senne explains. But it always reaches human ears and its meaning is elaborated in human understandings. And if the call comes from eternal values, the response is given by men living in time. A young and brilliant philosopher, working in the Cartesian tradition, and who is anxious not to confuse philosophy and theology, Ferdinand Alquié, says that we must at the same time believe in eternity and operate in time. By their deeds, men embody, incarnate the values.

I should add to this that the call of the value is always formal: we have to promote justice; we must repel the non-evident statements and yield to coherent demonstrations; we must surrender to beauty and so on . . . But the transcendent value never gives a criterion for our concrete difficulties. I never have to choose between justice and injustice; I only wonder whether there is more justice in this than in that. Nor do I hesitate to prefer beauty to ugliness: I am in suspense only because I do not know if this word is better than that, if this color has to be put in this or in that place. And this is one of the roots of our anxiety. The value does not give the solutions: we have to find them out with our poor human forces. The value does not even state the problems: those come from the circumstances. The value gives an order, and such an order that our heart recognizes in it its own vocation, so exacting an order that we understand we cannot fulfill entirely its requirements, and that still we must do it. In one word, the value gives Faith . . .

That is not all. There is another reason for us to be modest. The value is not only a general and "formal" call; it is also a multiple call. We are not confronted with one single value, but with a multiplicity of different, and generally opposing values. The absolute is not only veiled; it spreads out in different directions, and we can say that it is diffracted.

In primitive societies, the different values were so closely bound together that it was very difficult to distinguish them from one another and the sociologists are always biased when they try to derive the different values from one single so-called "primitive" value. It is unfair to say that social, or ethical, or religious values were the primitive ones. The war dance of a native tribe is *at the same time* loaded with social, moral, religious, and esthetical values. And so is the work of the medieval sculptor carving a virgin on the front gate of a cathedral. The analysis of the values is a discovery of the modern mind, and a very important one. Only a modern believer can enter a church and consider separately the holy character of the place and the esthetical value (positive or negative, of course) of the building.

And here is the problem. As the values are more and more dissociated, their conflicts become more and more frequent and serious. We have not only to choose between two actions from the same point of view of justice, or between two shapes from the single point of view of beauty, we have to compare beauty with justice, with happiness, with truth, with social unity and so on. And we have no means of determining once for all an absolute rank for each value. It would be very easy to show that it depends upon the circumstances. When the life of somebody is in danger you don't hesitate to offend his liberty or to break a social regulation in order to save him. And when a society is in a great danger it takes some drastic measures even if some values may be hurt. Let us take another example of the impossibility of sticking, in all cases, to a single value. The idea of punishment is very difficult to admit from a purely moral point of view, because we are never able to appreciate the real intentions of the culprit. But if we admit that punishment is established only on a social basis, we shall be led to certain conclusions which would be too unjust to be accepted, like the punishment of an innocent person "as an example" or like the execution of hostages. The justice of men is obliged to make compromises between the individual and society, that is to say between moral and social values.

Sartre is right when he says that to write a book is a social action. But a book is not only a social event, able to be considered as good or bad from the point of view of society. If a book were nothing more than a social action, perhaps Sartre's novels should be prohibited, because it is not sure that they have helped many people to discover the ways of liberty, while it is sure that they had a very bad effect on the morality of young and sensitive people.

Thus the task of man is to dispose of the values as an arbitrator. He has to determine which value will get the first place *according to circumstances*. And he will do that in using his liberty and at his own risk. Here is his responsibility. He is responsible because he is the agent of the choice and because the choice is important. Every value is an expression of the absolute. Every value is highly precious. We are not in front of the Nothingness, as the existentialists say. We are confronted with the fullness of Being, with an inexhaustible Richness. But limited as we are by time and space, we must, by our choice, kill an indefinite number of possibilities. To promote a value, we are obliged to push back the other values, and sometimes to destroy them.

And don't believe that certain values, for instance esthetical values, are evidently less important than the others, and that it would be very easy to determine once for all that they have to be sacrificed to the others, each time they come into conflict with them. Suppose all the works of art were suppressed. Suppose all the books were taken from our libraries except the purely technical ones. Let us destroy also the fine buildings and all the ornaments of our houses. No more museums, no more art galleries. Our children would be ignorant of the enchantment of a midsummer night's dream because they could not look through the eyes of Shakespeare; they would never hear the imposing harmony of Beethoven's symphonies; they would be deprived of the miracle of the light playing on blue and red, because there would be no Vermeer to open their eyes. And even—o, shame, let the charm of the women we love vanish, as it is essentially an esthetical value. Tell me now, would such a world retain some interest? Of course, we still could live. But what for? For saving life we should have suppressed all the charm of life.

And thus our responsibility is tremendous. We cannot act without running the risk of destroying many precious aspects of the world. Nothing is gratuitous. The human law is sacrifice, and our vocation is to determine what has to be sacrificed on each occasion. What I have to do is neither to apply mechanically a rule under all circumstances, nor to invent arbitrarily rules of my own. It is to find out the best balance of all the values in the particular situation in which I am placed.

And I believe that a strong feeling for the variety of the values and for the real importance of each of them is of particular moment in a world where fanaticism is growing—that is to say the belief in one single, in one unique value and the contempt for all the others—fanaticism which gives to a human aim the characteristics of the Absolute, fanaticism which brings to mankind tears and sorrow, wars and destruction.

Philosophy will be something more than a subject for academic addresses if it can help mankind to learn tolerance, a tolerance which would not come from indifference, but from the mutual respect for all sincere love. (pp. 172-86)

> *Gaston Berger, "Existentialism and Literature in Action," in* The University of Buffalo Studies, *Vol. 18, No. 4, December, 1948, pp. 157-86.*

Jean-Paul Sartre

[*In the following essay, titled "Existentialism Is a Humanism," Sartre defends Existentialism against charges of nihilism and amorality.*]

My purpose here is to offer a defence of existentialism against several reproaches that have been laid against it.

First, it has been reproached as an invitation to people to dwell in quietism of despair. For if every way to a solution is barred, one would have to regard any action in this world as entirely ineffective, and one would arrive finally at a contemplative philosophy. Moreover, since contemplation is a luxury, this would be only another bourgeois philosophy. This is, especially, the reproach made by the Communists.

From another quarter we are reproached for having underlined all that is ignominious in the human situation, for depicting what is mean, sordid or base to the neglect of certain things that possess charm and beauty and belong to the brighter side of human nature: for example, according to the Catholic critic, Mlle. Mercier, we forget how an infant smiles. Both from this side and from the other we are also reproached for leaving out of account the solidarity of mankind and considering man in isolation. And this, say the Communists, is because we base our doctrine upon pure subjectivity—upon the Cartesian "I think": which is the moment in which solitary man attains to himself; a position from which it is impossible to regain solidarity with other men who exist outside of the self. The *ego* cannot reach them through the *cogito*.

From the Christian side, we are reproached as people who deny the reality and seriousness of human affairs. For since we ignore the commandments of God and all values prescribed as eternal, nothing remains but what is strictly voluntary. Everyone can do what he likes, and will be incapable, from such a point of view, of condemning either the point of view or the action of anyone else.

It is to these various reproaches that I shall endeavour to reply to-day; that is why I have entitled this brief exposition "Existentialism and Humanism." Many may be surprised at the mention of humanism in this connection, but we shall try to see in what sense we understand it. In any case, we can begin by saying that existentialism, in our sense of the word, is a doctrine that does render human life possible; a doctrine, also, which affirms that every truth and every action imply both an environment and a human subjectivity. The essential charge laid against us is, of course, that of over-emphasis upon the evil side of human life. I have lately been told of a lady who, whenever she lets slip a vulgar expression in a moment of nervousness, excuses herself by exclaiming, "I believe I am becoming an existentialist." So it appears that ugliness is being identified with existentialism. That is why some people say we are "naturalistic," and if we are, it is strange to see how much we scandalise and horrify them, for no one seems to be much frightened or humiliated nowadays by what is properly called naturalism. Those who can quite well keep down a novel by Zola such as *La terre* are sickened as soon as they read an existentialist novel. Those who appeal to the wisdom of the people—which is a sad wisdom—find ours sadder still. And yet, what could be more disillusioned than such sayings as "Charity begins at home" or "Promote a rogue and he'll sue you for damage, knock him down and he'll do you homage"? We all know how many common sayings can be quoted to this effect, and they all mean much the same—that you must not oppose the powers-that-be; that you must not fight against superior force; must not meddle in matters that are above your station. Or that any action not in accordance with some tradition is mere romanticism; or that any undertaking which has not the support of proven experience is foredoomed to frustration; and that since experience has shown men to be invariably inclined to evil, there must be firm rules to restrain them, otherwise we shall have anarchy. It is, however, the people who are forever mouthing these dismal proverbs and, whenever they are told of some more or less repulsive action, say "How like human nature!"—it is these very people, always harping upon realism, who complain that existentialism is too gloomy a view of things. Indeed their excessive protests make me suspect that what is annoying them is not so much our pessimism, but, much more likely, our optimism. For at bottom, what is alarming in the doctrine that I am about to try to explain to you is—is it not?—that it confronts man with a possibility of choice. To verify this, let us review the whole question upon the strictly philosophic level. What, then, is this that we call existentialism?

Most of those who are making use of this word would be highly confused if required to explain its meaning. For since it has become fashionable, people cheerfully declare that this musician or that painter is "existentialist." A columnist in *Clartés* signs himself "The Existentialist," and, indeed, the word is now so loosely applied to so many things that it no longer means anything at all. It would appear that, for the lack of any novel doctrine such as that of surrealism, all those who are eager to join in the latest scandal or movement now seize upon this philosophy in which, however, they can find nothing to their purpose. For in truth this is of all teachings the least scandalous and the most austere: it is intended strictly for technicians and philosophers. All the same, it can easily be defined.

The question is only complicated because there are two kinds of existentialists. There are, on the one hand, the Christians, amongst whom I shall name Jaspers and Gabriel Marcel, both professed Catholics; and on the other the existential atheists, amongst whom we must place Heidegger as well as the French existentialists and myself. What they have in common is simply the fact that they believe that *existence* comes before *essence*—or, if you will, that we must begin from the subjective. What exactly do we mean by that?

If one considers an article of manufacture—as, for example, a book or a paper-knife—one sees that it has been made by an artisan who had a conception of it; and he has paid attention, equally, to the conception of a paper-knife and to the preexistent technique of production which is a part of that conception and is, at bottom, a formula. Thus the paper-knife is at the same time an article producible in a certain manner and one which, on the other hand, serves a definite purpose, for one cannot suppose that a man would produce a paper-knife without knowing what it was for. Let us say, then, of the paper-knife that its essence—that is to say the sum of the formulae and the qualities which made its production and its definition possible—precedes its existence. The presence of such-and-such a paper-knife or book is thus determined before my eyes. Here, then, we are viewing the world from a technical standpoint, and we can say that production precedes existence.

When we think of God as the creator, we are thinking of him, most of the time, as a supernal artisan. Whatever doctrine we may be considering, whether it be a doctrine like that of Descartes, or of Leibnitz himself, we always imply that the will follows, more or less, from the understanding or at least accompanies it, so that when God creates he knows precisely what he is creating. Thus, the conception of man in the mind of God is comparable to that of the paper-knife in the mind of the artisan: God makes man according to a procedure and a conception, exactly as the artisan manufactures a paper-knife, following a definition and a formula. Thus each individual man is the realisation of a certain conception which dwells in the divine understanding. In the philosophic atheism of the eighteenth century, the notion of God is suppressed, but not, for all that, the idea that essence is prior to existence;

something of that idea we still find everywhere, in Diderot, in Voltaire and even in Kant. Man possesses a human nature; that "human nature," which is the conception of human being, is found in every man; which means that each man is a particular example of an universal conception, the conception of Man. In Kant, this universality goes so far that the wild man of the woods, man in the state of nature and the bourgeois are all contained in the same definition and have the same fundamental qualities. Here again, the essence of man precedes that historic existence which we confront in experience.

Atheistic existentialism, of which I am a representative, declares with greater consistency that if God does not exist there is at least one being whose existence comes before its essence, a being which exists before it can be defined by any conception of it. That being is man or, as Heidegger has it, the human reality. What do we mean by saying that existence precedes essence? We mean that man first of all exists, encounters himself, surges up in the world—and defines himself afterwards. If man as the existentialist sees him is not definable, it is because to begin with he is nothing. He will not be anything until later, and then he will be what he makes of himself. Thus, there is no human nature, because there is no God to have a conception of it. Man simply is. Not that he is simply what he conceives himself to be, but he is what he wills, and as he conceives himself after already existing—as he wills to be after that leap towards existence. Man is nothing else but that which he makes of himself. That is the first principle of existentialism. And this is what people call its "subjectivity," using the word as a reproach against us. But what do we mean to say by this, but that man is of a greater dignity than a stone or a table? For we mean to say that man primarily exists—that man is, before all else, something which propels itself towards a future and is aware that it is doing so. Man is, indeed, a project which possesses a subjective life, instead of being a kind of moss, or a fungus or a cauliflower. Before that projection of the self nothing exists; not even in the heaven of intelligence: man will only attain existence when he is what he purposes to be. Not, however, what he may wish to be. For what we usually understand by wishing or willing is a conscious decision taken—much more often than not—after we have made ourselves what we are. I may wish to join a party, to write a book or to marry—but in such a case what is usually called my will is probably a manifestation of a prior and more spontaneous decision. If, however, it is true that existence is prior to essence, man is responsible for what he is. Thus, the first effect of existentialism is that it puts every man in possession of himself as he is, and places the entire responsibility for his existence squarely upon his own shoulders. And, when we say that man is responsible for himself, we do not mean that he is responsible only for his own individuality, but that he is responsible for all men. The word "subjectivism" is to be understood in two senses, and our adversaries play upon only one of them. Subjectivism means, on the one hand, the freedom of the individual subject and, on the other, that man cannot pass beyond human subjectivity. It is the latter which is the deeper meaning of existentialism. When we say that man chooses himself, we do mean that every one of us must choose himself; but by that we also mean that in choosing for himself he chooses for all men. For in effect, of all the actions a man may take in order to create himself as he wills to be, there is not one which is not creative, at the same time, of an image of man such as he believes he ought to be. To choose between this or that is at the same time to affirm the value of that which is chosen; for we are unable ever to choose the worse. What we choose is always the better; and nothing can be better for us unless it is better for all. If, moreover, existence precedes essence and we will to exist at the same time as we fashion our image, that image is valid for all and for the entire epoch in which we find ourselves. Our responsibility is thus much greater than we had supposed, for it concerns mankind as a whole. If I am a worker, for instance, I may choose to join a Christian rather than a Communist trade union. And if, by that membership, I choose to signify that resignation is, after all, the attitude that best becomes a man, that man's kingdom is not upon this earth, I do not commit myself alone to that view. Resignation is my will for everyone, and my action is, in consequence, a commitment on behalf of all mankind. Or if, to take a more personal case, I decide to marry and to have children, even though this decision proceeds simply from my situation, from my passion or my desire, I am thereby committing not only myself, but humanity as a whole, to the practice of monogamy. I am thus responsible for myself and for all men, and I am creating a certain image of man as I would have him to be. In fashioning myself I fashion man.

This may enable us to understand what is meant by such terms—perhaps a little grandiloquent—as anguish, abandonment and despair. As you will soon see, it is very simple. First, what do we mean by anguish? The existentialist frankly states that man is in anguish. His meaning is as follows—When a man commits himself to anything, fully realising that he is not only choosing what he will be, but is thereby at the same time a legislator deciding for the whole of mankind—in such a moment a man cannot escape from the sense of complete and profound responsibility. There are many, indeed, who show no such anxiety. But we affirm that they are merely disguising their anguish or are in flight from it. Certainly, many people think that in what they are doing they commit no one but themselves to anything: and if you ask them, "What would happen if everyone did so?" they shrug their shoulders and reply, "Everyone does not do so." But in truth, one ought always to ask oneself what would happen if everyone did as one is doing; nor can one escape from that disturbing thought except by a kind of self-deception. The man who lies in self-excuse, by saying "Everyone will not do it" must be ill at ease in his conscience, for the act of lying implies the universal value which it denies. By its very disguise his anguish reveals itself. This is the anguish that Kierkegaard called "the anguish of Abraham." You know the story: An angel commanded Abraham to sacrifice his son: and obedience was obligatory, if it really was an angel who had appeared and said, "Thou, Abraham, shalt sacrifice thy son." But anyone in such a case would wonder, first, whether it was indeed an angel and secondly, whether I am really Abraham. Where are the proofs? A certain mad woman who suffered from hallucinations said that people were telephoning to her, and giving her orders. The doctor

asked, "But who is it that speaks to you?" She replied: "He says it is God." And what, indeed, could prove to her that it was God? If an angel appears to me, what is the proof that it is an angel; or, if I hear voices, who can prove that they proceed from heaven and not from hell, or from my own subconsciousness or some pathological condition? Who can prove that they are really addressed to me?

Who, then, can prove that I am the proper person to impose, by my own choice, my conception of man upon mankind? I shall never find any proof whatever; there will be no sign to convince me of it. If a voice speaks to me, it is still I myself who must decide whether the voice is or is not that of an angel. If I regard a certain course of action as good, it is only I who choose to say that it is good and not bad. There is nothing to show that I am Abraham: nevertheless I also am obliged at every instant to perform actions which are examples. Everything happens to every man as though the whole human race had its eyes fixed upon what he is doing and regulated its conduct accordingly. So every man ought to say, "Am I really a man who has the right to act in such a manner that humanity regulates itself by what I do." If a man does not say that, he is dissembling his anguish. Clearly, the anguish with which we are concerned here is not one that could lead to quietism or inaction. It is anguish pure and simple, of the kind well known to all those who have borne responsibilities. When, for instance, a military leader takes upon himself the responsibility for an attack and sends a number of men to their death, he chooses to do it and at bottom he alone chooses. No doubt he acts under a higher command, but its orders, which are more general, require interpretation by him and upon that interpretation depends the life of ten, fourteen or twenty men. In making the decision, he cannot but feel a certain anguish. All leaders know that anguish. It does not prevent their acting, on the contrary it is the very condition of their action, for the action presupposes that there is a plurality of possibilities, and in choosing one of these, they realise that it has value only because it is chosen. Now it is anguish of that kind which existentialism describes, and moreover, as we shall see, makes explicit through direct responsibility towards other men who are concerned. Far from being a screen which could separate us from action, it is a condition of action itself.

And when we speak of "abandonment"—a favorite word of Heidegger—we only mean to say that God does not exist, and that it is necessary to draw the consequences of his absence right to the end. The existentialist is strongly opposed to a certain type of secular moralism which seeks to suppress God at the least possible expense. Towards 1880, when the French professors endeavoured to formulate a secular morality, they said something like this:— God is a useless and costly hypothesis, so we will do without it. However, if we are to have morality, a society and a law-abiding world, it is essential that certain values should be taken seriously; they must have an *à priori* existence ascribed to them. It must be considered obligatory *à priori* to be honest, not to lie, not to beat one's wife, to bring up children and so forth; so we are going to do a little work on this subject, which will enable us to show that these values exist all the same, inscribed in an intelligible heaven although, of course, there is no God. In other words—and this is, I believe, the purport of all that we in France call radicalism—nothing will be changed if God does not exist; we shall re-discover the same norms of honesty, progress and humanity, and we shall have disposed of God as an out-of-date hypothesis which will die away quietly of itself. The existentialist, on the contrary, finds it extremely embarrassing that God does not exist, for there disappears with Him all possibility of finding values in an intelligible heaven. There can no longer be any good *à priori,* since there is no infinite and perfect consciousness to think it. It is nowhere written that "the good" exists, that one must be honest or must not lie, since we are now upon the plane where there are only men. Dostoievsky once wrote "If God did not exist, everything would be permitted"; and that, for existentialism, is the starting point. Everything is indeed permitted if God does not exist, and man is in consequence forlorn, for he cannot find anything to depend upon either within or outside himself. He discovers forthwith, that he is without excuse. For if indeed existence precedes essence, one will never be able to explain one's action by reference to a given and specific human nature; in other words, there is no determinism—man is free, man *is* freedom. Nor, on the other hand, if God does not exist, are we provided with any values or commands that could legitimise our behaviour. Thus we have neither behind us, nor before us in a luminous realm of values, any means of justification or excuse. We are left alone, without excuse. That is what I mean when I say that man is condemned to be free. Condemned, because he did not create himself, yet is nevertheless at liberty, and from the moment that he is thrown into this world he is responsible for everything he does. The existentialist does not believe in the power of passion. He will never regard a grand passion as a destructive torrent upon which a man is swept into certain actions as by fate, and which, therefore, is an excuse for them. He thinks that man is responsible for his passion. Neither will an existentialist think that a man can find help through some sign being vouchsafed upon earth for his orientation: for he thinks that the man himself interprets the sign as he chooses. He thinks that every man, without any support or help whatever, is condemned at every instant to invent man. As Ponge has written in a very fine article, "Man is the future of man." That is exactly true. Only, if one took this to mean that the future is laid up in Heaven, that God knows what it is, it would be false, for then it would no longer even be a future. If, however, it means that, whatever man may now appear to be, there is a future to be fashioned, a virgin future that awaits him—then it is a true saying. But in the present one is forsaken.

As an example by which you may the better understand this state of abandonment, I will refer to the case of a pupil of mine, who sought me out in the following circumstances. His father was quarrelling with his mother and was also inclined to be a "collaborator"; his elder brother had been killed in the German offensive of 1940 and this young man, with a sentiment somewhat primitive but generous, burned to avenge him. His mother was living alone with him, deeply afflicted by the semi-treason of his father and by the death of her eldest son, and her one consolation was in this young man. But he, at this moment, had the choice between going to England to join the Free French Forces or of staying near his mother and helping her to live. He fully realised that this woman lived only for him and that his disappearance—or perhaps his death—would plunge her into despair. He also realised that, concretely and in fact, every action he performed on his mother's behalf would be sure of effect in the sense of aiding her to live, where as anything he did in order to go and fight would be an ambiguous action which might vanish like water into sand and serve no purpose. For instance, to set out for England he would have to wait indefinitely in a Spanish camp on the way through Spain; or, on arriving in England or in Algiers he might be put into an office to fill up forms. Consequently, he found himself confronted by two very different modes of action; the one concrete, immediate, but directed towards only one individual; and the other an action addressed to an end infinitely greater, a national collectivity, but for that very reason ambiguous—and it might be frustrated on the way. At the same time, he was hesitating between two kinds of morality; on the one side the morality of sympathy, of personal devotion and, on the other side, a morality of wider scope but of more debatable validity. He had to choose between those two. What could help him to choose? Could the Christian doctrine? No. Christian doctrine says: Act with charity, love your neighbour, deny yourself for others, choose the way which is hardest, and so forth. But which is the harder road? To whom does one owe the more brotherly love, the patriot or the mother? Which is the more useful aim, the general one of fighting in and for the whole community, or the precise aim of helping one particular person to live? Who can give an answer to that *à priori?* No one. Nor is it given in any ethical scripture. The Kantian ethic says, Never regard another as a means, but always as an end. Very well; if I remain with my mother, I shall be regarding her as the end and not as a means: but by the same token I am in danger of treating as means those who are fighting on my behalf; and the converse is also true, that if I go to the aid of the combatants I shall be treating them as the end at the risk of treating my mother as a means.

If values are uncertain, if they are still too abstract to determine the particular, concrete case under consideration, nothing remains but to trust in our instincts. That is what this young man tried to do; and when I saw him he said, "In the end, it is feeling that counts; the direction in which it is really pushing me is the one I ought to choose. If I feel that I love my mother enough to sacrifice everything else for her—my will to be avenged, all my longings for action and adventure—then I stay with her. If, on the contrary, I feel that my love for her is not enough, I go." But how does one estimate the strength of a feeling? The value of his feeling for his mother was determined precisely by the fact that he was standing by her. I may say that I love a certain friend enough to sacrifice such or such a sum of money for him, but I cannot prove that unless I have done it. I may say, "I love my mother enough to remain with her," if actually I have remained with her. I can only estimate the strength of this affection if I have performed an action by which it is defined and ratified. But if I then appeal to this affection to justify my action, I find myself drawn into a vicious circle.

Moreover, as Gide has very well said, a sentiment which is play-acting and one which is vital are two things that are hardly distinguishable one from another. To decide that I love my mother by staying beside her, and to play a comedy the upshot of which is that I do so—these are nearly the same thing. In other words, feeling is formed by the deeds that one does; therefore I cannot consult it as a guide to action. And that is to say that I can neither seek within myself for an authentic impulse to action, nor can I expect, from some ethic, formulae that will enable me to act. You may say that the youth did, at least, go to a professor to ask for advice. But if you seek counsel—from a priest, for example—you have selected that priest; and at bottom you already knew, more or less, what he would advise. In other words, to choose an adviser is nevertheless to commit oneself by that choice. If you are a Christian, you will say, Consult a priest; but there are collaborationists, priests who are resisters and priests who wait for the tide to turn: which will you choose? Had this young man chosen a priest of the resistance, or one of the collaboration, he would have decided beforehand the kind of advice he was to receive. Similarly, in coming to me, he knew what advice I should give him, and I had but one reply to make. You are free, therefore choose—that is to say, invent. No rule of general morality can show you what you ought to do: no signs are vouchsafed in this world. The Catholics will reply, "Oh, but they are!" Very well; still, it is I myself, in every case, who have to interpret the signs. Whilst I was imprisoned, I made the acquaintance of a somewhat remarkable man, a Jesuit, who had become a member of that order in the following manner. In his life he had suffered a succession of rather severe setbacks. His father had died when he was a child, leaving him in poverty, and he had been awarded a free scholarship in a religious institution, where he had been made continually to feel that he was accepted for charity's sake, and, in consequence, he had been denied several of those distinctions and honors which gratify children. Later, about the age of eighteen, he came to grief in a sentimental affair; and finally, at twenty-two—this was a trifle in itself, but it was the last drop that overflowed his cup—he failed in his military examination. This young man, then, could regard himself as a total failure: it was a sign—but a sign of what? He might have taken refuge in bitterness or despair. But he took it—very cleverly for him—as a sign that he was not intended for secular successes, and that only the attainments of religion, those of sanctity and of faith, were accessible to him. He interpreted his record as a message from God, and became a member of the Order. Who can doubt but that this decision as to the meaning of the sign was his, and his alone? One could have drawn quite different conclusions from such a series of reverses—as, for example, that he had better become a carpenter or a revolutionary. For the decipherment of the sign, however, he bears the entire responsibility. That is what "abandonment" implies, that we ourselves decide our being. And with this abandonment goes anguish.

As for "despair," the meaning of this expression is extremely simple. It merely means that we limit ourselves to a reliance upon that which is within our wills, or within the sum of the probabilities which render our action feasible. Whenever one wills anything, there are always these elements of probability. If I am counting upon a visit from a friend, who may be coming by train or by tram, I presuppose that the train will arrive at the appointed time, or that the tram will not be derailed. I remain in the realm of possibilities; but one does not rely upon any possibilities beyond those that are strictly concerned in one's action. Beyond the point at which the possibilities under consideration cease to affect my action, I ought to disinterest myself. For there is no God and no prevenient design, which can adapt the world and all its possibilities to my will. When Descartes said, "Conquer yourself rather than the world," what he meant was, at bottom, the same—that we should act without hope.

Marxists, to whom I have said this, have answered: "Your action is limited, obviously, by your death; but you can rely upon the help of others. That is, you can count both upon what the others are doing to help you elsewhere, as in China and in Russia, and upon what they will do later, after your death, to take up your action and carry it forward to its final accomplishment which will be the revolution. Moreover you must rely upon this; not to do so is immoral." To this I rejoin, first, that I shall always count upon my comrades-in-arms in the struggle, in so far as they are committed, as I am, to a definite, common cause; and in the unity of a party or a group which I can more or less control—that is, in which I am enrolled as a militant and whose movements at every moment are known to me. In that respect, to rely upon the unity and the will of the party is exactly like my reckoning that the train will run to time or that the tram will not be derailed. But I cannot count upon men whom I do not know, I cannot base my confidence upon human goodness or upon man's interest in the good of society, seeing that man is free and that there is no human nature which I can take as foundational. I do not know whither the Russian revolution will lead. I can admire it and take it as an example in so far as it is evident, to-day, that the proletariat plays a part in Russia which it has attained in no other nation. But I cannot affirm that this will necessarily lead to the triumph of the proletariat: I must confine myself to what I can see. Nor can I be sure that comrades-in-arms will take up my work after my death and carry it to the maximum perfection, seeing that those men are free agents and will freely decide, to-morrow, what man is then to be. To-morrow, after my death, some men may decide to establish Fascism, and the others may be so cowardly or so slack as to let them do so. If so, Fascism will then be the truth of man, and so much the worse for us. In reality, things will be such as men have decided they shall be. Does that mean that I should abandon myself to quietism? No. First I ought to commit myself and then act my commitment, according to the time-honoured formula that "one need not hope in order to undertake one's work." Nor does this mean that I should not belong to a party, but only that I should be without illusion and that I should do what I can. For instance, if I ask myself "Will the social ideal as such, ever become a reality?" I cannot tell, I only know that whatever may be in my power to make it so, I shall do; beyond that, I can count upon nothing.

Quietism is the attitude of people who say, "let others do what I cannot do." The doctrine I am presenting before you is precisely the opposite of this, since it declares that there is no reality except in action. It goes further, indeed, and adds, "Man is nothing else but what he purposes, he exists only in so far as he realises himself, he is therefore nothing else but the sum of his actions, nothing else but what his life is." Hence we can well understand why some people are horrified by our teaching. For many have but one resource to sustain them in their misery, and that is to think, "Circumstances have been against me, I was worthy to be something much better than I have been. I admit I have never had a great love or a great friendship; but that is because I never met a man or a woman who were worthy of it; if I have not written any very good books, it is because I had not the leisure to do so; or, if I have had no children to whom I could devote myself it is because I did not find the man I could have lived with. So there remains within me a wide range of abilities, inclinations and potentialities, unused but perfectly viable, which endow me with a worthiness that could never be inferred from the mere history of my actions." But in reality and for the existentialist, there is no love apart from the deeds of love; no potentiality of love other than that which is manifested in loving; there is no genius other than that which is expressed in works of art. The genius of Proust is the totality of the works of Proust; the genius of Racine is the series of his tragedies, outside of which there is nothing. Why should we attribute to Racine the capacity to write yet another tragedy when that is precisely what he did not write? In life, a man commits himself, draws his own portrait and there is nothing but that portrait. No doubt this thought may seem comfortless to one who has not made a success of his life. On the other hand, it puts everyone in a position to understand that reality alone is reliable; that dreams, expectations and hopes serve to define a man only as deceptive dreams, abortive hopes, expectations unfulfilled; that is to say, they define him negatively, not positively. Nevertheless, when one says, "You are nothing else but what you live," it does not imply that an artist is to be judged solely by his works of art, for a thousand other things contribute no less to his definition as a man. What we mean to say is that a man is no other than a series of undertakings, that he is the sum, the organisation, the set of relations that constitute these undertakings.

In the light of all this, what people reproach us with is not, after all, our pessimism, but the sternness of our optimism. If people condemn our works of fiction, in which we describe characters that are base, weak, cowardly and sometimes even frankly evil, it is not only because those characters are base, weak, cowardly or evil. For suppose that, like Zola, we showed that the behaviour of these characters was caused by their heredity, or by the action of their environment upon them, or by determining factors, psychic or organic. People would be reassured, they would say, "You see, that is what we are like, no one can do anything about it." But the existentialist, when he portrays a coward, shows him as responsible for his cowardice. He is not like that on account of a cowardly heart or lungs or cerebrum, he has not become like that through his physiological organism; he is like that because he has made himself into a coward by his actions. There is no such thing as a cowardly temperament. There are nervous temperaments; there is what is called impoverished blood, and there are also rich temperaments. But the man whose blood is poor is not a coward for all that, for what produces cowardice is the act of giving up or giving way; and a temperament is not an action. A coward is defined by the deed that he has done. What people feel obscurely, and with horror, is that the coward as we present him is guilty of being a coward. What people would prefer would be to be born either a coward or a hero. One of the charges most often laid against the *Chemins de la liberté* [a series of novels by Sartre] is something like this—"But, after all, these people being so base, how can you make them into heroes?" That objection is really rather comic, for it implies that people are born heroes: and that is, at bottom, what such people would like to think. If you are born cowards, you can be quite content, you can do nothing about it and you will be cowards all your lives whatever you do; and if you are born heroes you can again be quite content; you will be heroes all your lives, eating and drinking heroically. Whereas the existentialist says that the coward makes himself cowardly, the hero makes himself heroic; and that there is always a possibility for the coward to give up cowardice and for the hero to stop being a hero. What counts is the total commitment, and it is not by a particular case or particular action that you are committed altogether.

We have now, I think, dealt with a certain number of the reproaches against existentialism. You have seen that it cannot be regarded as a philosophy of quietism since it defines man by his action; nor as a pessimistic description of man, for no doctrine is more optimistic, the destiny of man is placed within himself. Nor is it an attempt to discourage man from action since it tells him that there is no hope except in his action, and that the one thing which permits him to have life is the deed. Upon this level therefore, what we are considering is an ethic of action and self-commitment. However, we are still reproached, upon these few data, for confining man within his individual subjectivity. There again people badly misunderstand us.

Our point of departure is, indeed, the subjectivity of the individual, and that for strictly philosophic reasons. It is not because we are bourgeois, but because we seek to base our teaching upon the truth, and not upon a collection of fine theories, full of hope but lacking real foundations. And at the point of departure there cannot be any other truth than this, *I think, therefore I am,* which is the absolute truth of consciousness as it attains to itself. Every theory which begins with man, outside of this moment of self-attainment, is a theory which thereby suppresses the truth, for outside of the Cartesian *cogito,* all objects are no more than probable, and any doctrine of probabilities which is not attached to a truth will crumble into nothing. In order to define the probable one must possess the true. Before there can be any truth whatever, then, there must be an absolute truth, and there is such a truth which is simple, easily attained and within the reach of everybody; it consists in one's immediate sense of one's self.

In the second place, this theory alone is compatible with the dignity of man, it is the only one which does not make man into an object. All kinds of materialism lead one to

Jean-Paul Sartre (far right) and Simone de Beauvoir (second from left) at an editorial meeting of Les temps modernes, *Sartre's journal which fostered Existentialist thought.*

treat every man including oneself as an object—that is, as a set of pre-determined reactions, in no way different from the patterns of qualities and phenomena which constitute a table, or a chair or a stone. Our aim is precisely to establish the human kingdom as a pattern of values in distinction from the material world. But the subjectivity which we thus postulate as the standard of truth is no narrowly individual subjectivism, for as we have demonstrated, it is not only one's own self that one discovers in the *cogito,* but those of others too. Contrary to the philosophy of Descartes, contrary to that of Kant, when we say "I think" we are attaining to ourselves in the presence of the other, and we are just as certain of the other as we are of ourselves. Thus the man who discovers himself directly in the *cogito* also discovers all the others, and discovers them as the condition of his own existence. He recognises that he cannot be anything (in the sense in which one says one is spiritual, or that one is wicked or jealous) unless others recognise him as such. I cannot obtain any truth whatsoever about myself, except through the mediation of another. The other is indispensable to my existence, and equally so to any knowledge I can have of myself. Under these conditions, the intimate discovery of myself is at the same time the revelation of the other as a freedom which confronts mine, and which cannot think or will without doing so either for or against me. Thus, at once, we find ourselves in

a world which is, let us say, that of "inter-subjectivity." It is in this world that man has to decide what he is and what others are.

Furthermore, although it is impossible to find in each and every man a universal essence that can be called human nature, there is nevertheless a human universality of *condition.* It is not by chance that the thinkers of to-day are so much more ready to speak of the condition than of the nature of man. By his condition they understand, with more or less clarity, all the *limitations* which *à priori* define man's fundamental situation in the universe. His historical situations are variable: man may be born a slave in a pagan society, or may be a feudal baron, or a proletarian. But what never vary are the necessities of being in the world, of having to labour and to die there. These limitations are neither subjective nor objective, or rather there is both a subjective and an objective aspect of them. Objective, because we meet with them everywhere and they are everywhere recognisable: and subjective because they are *lived* and are nothing if man does not live them—if, that is to say, he does not freely determine himself and his existence in relation to them. And, diverse though man's purposes may be, at least none of them is wholly foreign to me, since every human purpose presents itself as an attempt either to surpass these limitations, or to widen them, or else to deny or to accommodate oneself to them. Consequently every purpose, however individual it may be, is of universal value. Every purpose, even that of a Chinese, an Indian or a Negro, can be understood by a European. To say it can be understood, means that the European of 1945 may be striving out of a certain situation towards the same limitations in the same way, and that he may re-conceive in himself the purpose of the Chinese, of the Indian or the African. In every purpose there is universality, in this sense that every purpose is comprehensible to every man. Not that this or that purpose defines man for ever, but that it may be entertained again and again. There is always some way of understanding an idiot, a child, a primitive man or a foreigner if one has sufficient information. In this sense we may say that there is a human universality, but it is not something given; it is being perpetually made. I make this universality in choosing myself; I also make it by understanding the purpose of any other man, of whatever epoch. This absoluteness of the act of choice does not alter the relativity of each epoch.

What is at the very heart and centre of existentialism, is the absolute character of the free commitment, by which every man realises himself in realising a type of humanity—a commitment always understandable, to no matter whom in no matter what epoch—and its bearing upon the relativity of the cultural pattern which may result from such absolute commitment. One must observe equally the relativity of Cartesianism and the absolute character of the Cartesian commitment. In this sense you may say, if you like, that every one of us makes the absolute by breathing, by eating, by sleeping or by behaving in any fashion whatsoever. There is no difference between free being—being as self-committal, as existence choosing its essence—and absolute being. And there is no difference whatever between being as an absolute, temporarily localised—that is, localised in history—and universally intelligible being.

This does not completely refute the charge of subjectivism. Indeed that objection appears in several other forms, of which the first is as follows. People say to us, "Then it does not matter what you do," and they say this in various ways. First they tax us with anarchy; then they say, "You cannot judge others, for there is no reason for preferring one purpose to another"; finally, they may say, "Everything being merely voluntary in this choice of yours, you give away with one hand what you pretend to gain with the other." These three are not very serious objections. As to the first, to say that it matters not what you choose is not correct. In one sense choice is possible, but what is not possible is not to choose. I can always choose, but I must know that if I do not choose, that is still a choice. This, although it may appear merely formal, is of great importance as a limit to fantasy and caprice. For, when I confront a real situation—for example, that I am a sexual being, able to have relations with a being of the other sex and able to have children—I am obliged to choose my attitude to it, and in every respect I bear the responsibility of the choice which, in committing myself, also commits the whole of humanity. Even if my choice is determined by no *à priori* value whatever, it can have nothing to do with caprice: and if anyone thinks that this is only Gide's theory

of the *acte gratuit* over again, he has failed to see the enormous difference between this theory and that of Gide. Gide does not know what a situation is, his "act" is one of pure caprice. In our view, on the contrary, man finds himself in an organised situation in which he is himself involved: his choice involves mankind in its entirety, and he cannot avoid choosing. Either he must remain single, or he must marry without having children, or he must marry and have children. In any case, and whichever he may choose, it is impossible for him, in respect of this situation, not to take complete responsibility. Doubtless he chooses without reference to any pre-established values, but it is unjust to tax him with caprice. Rather let us say that the moral choice is comparable to the construction of a work of art.

But here I must at once digress to make it quite clear that we are not propounding an aesthetic morality, for our adversaries are disingenuous enough to reproach us even with that. I mention the work of art only by way of comparison. That being understood, does anyone reproach an artist when he paints a picture for not following rules established *à priori?* Does one ever ask what is the picture that he ought to paint? As everyone knows, there is no predefined picture for him to make; the artist applies himself to the composition of a picture, and the picture that ought to be made is precisely that which he will have made. As everyone knows, there are no aesthetic values *à priori,* but there are values which will appear in due course in the coherence of the picture, in the relation between the will to create and the finished work. No one can tell what the painting of to-morrow will be like; one cannot judge a painting until it is done. What has that to do with morality? We are in the same creative situation. We never speak of a work of art as irresponsible; when we are discussing a canvas by Picasso, we understand very well that the composition became what it is at the time when he was painting it, and that his works are part and parcel of his entire life.

It is the same upon the plane of morality. There is this in common between art and morality, that in both we have to do with creation and invention. We cannot decide *à priori* what it is that should be done. I think it was made sufficiently clear to you in the case of that student who came to see me, that to whatever ethical system he might appeal, the Kantian or any other, he could find no sort of guidance whatever; he was obliged to invent the law for himself. Certainly we cannot say that this man, in choosing to remain with his mother—that is, in taking sentiment, personal devotion and concrete charity as his moral foundations—would be making an irresponsible choice, nor could we do so if he preferred the sacrifice of going away to England. Man makes himself; he is not found ready-made; he makes himself by the choice of his morality, and he cannot but choose a morality, such is the pressure of circumstances upon him. We define man only in relation to his commitments; it is therefore absurd to reproach us for irresponsibility in our choice.

In the second place, people say to us; "You are unable to judge others." This is true in one sense and false in another. It is true in this sense, that whenever a man chooses his purpose and his commitment in all clearness and in all sincerity, whatever that purpose may be it is impossible to prefer another for him. It is true in the sense that we do not believe in progress. Progress implies amelioration; but man is always the same, facing a situation which is always changing, and choice remains always a choice in the situation. The moral problem has not changed since the time when it was a choice between slavery and antislavery—from the time of the war of Secession, for example, until the present moment when one chooses between the M.R.P. [Mouvement Républicain Populaire, a French political party] and the Communists.

We can judge, nevertheless, for, as I have said, one chooses in view of others, and in view of others one chooses himself. One can judge, first—and perhaps this is not a judgment of value, but it is a logical judgment—that in certain cases choice is founded upon an error, and in others upon the truth. One can judge a man by saying that he deceives himself. Since we have defined the situation of man as one of free choice, without excuse and without help, any man who takes refuge behind the excuse of his passions, or by inventing some deterministic doctrine, is a self-deceiver. One may object: "But why should he not choose to deceive himself?" I reply that it is not for me to judge him morally, but I define his self-deception as an error. Here one cannot avoid pronouncing a judgment of truth. The self-deception is evidently a falsehood, because it is a dissimulation of man's complete liberty of commitment. Upon this same level, I say that it is also a self-deception if I choose to declare that certain values are incumbent upon me; I am in contradiction with myself if I will these values and at the same time say that they impose themselves upon me. If anyone says to me, "And what if I wish to deceive myself?" I answer, "There is no reason why you should not, but I declare that you are doing so, and that the attitude of strict consistency alone is that of good faith. Furthermore, I can pronounce a moral judgment. For I declare that freedom, in respect of concrete circumstances, can have no other end and aim but itself; and when once a man has seen that values depend upon himself, in that state of forsakenness he can will only one thing, and that is freedom as the foundation of all values. That does not mean that he wills it in the abstract: it simply means that the actions of men of good faith have, as their ultimate significance, the quest of freedom itself as such. A man who belongs to some communist or revolutionary society wills certain concrete ends, which imply the will to freedom, but that freedom is willed in community. We will freedom for freedom's sake, and in and through particular circumstances. And in thus willing freedom, we discover that it depends entirely upon the freedom of others and that the freedom of others depends upon our own. Obviously, freedom as the definition of a man does not depend upon others, but as soon as there is a commitment, I am obliged to will the liberty of others at the same time as mine. I cannot make liberty my aim unless I make that of others equally my aim. Consequently, when I recognise, as entirely authentic, that man is a being whose existence precedes his essence, and that he is a free being who cannot, in any circumstances, but will his freedom, at the same time I realise that I cannot not will the freedom of others. Thus, in the name of that will to

freedom which is implied in freedom itself, I can form judgments upon those who seek to hide from themselves the wholly voluntary nature of their existence and its complete freedom. Those who hide from this total freedom, in a guise of solemnity or with deterministic excuses, I shall call cowards. Others, who try to show that their existence is necessary, when it is merely an accident of the appearance of the human race on earth,—I shall call scum. But neither cowards nor scum can be identified except upon the plane of strict authenticity. Thus, although the content of morality is variable, a certain form of this morality is universal. Kant declared that freedom is a will both to itself and to the freedom of others. Agreed: but he thinks that the formal and the universal suffice for the constitution of a morality. We think, on the contrary, that principles that are too abstract break down when we come to defining action. To take once again the case of that student; by what authority, in the name of what golden rule of morality, do you think he could have decided, in perfect peace of mind, either to abandon his mother or to remain with her? There are no means of judging. The content is always concrete, and therefore unpredictable; it has always to be invented. The one thing that counts, is to know whether the invention is made in the name of freedom.

Let us, for example, examine the two following cases, and you will see how far they are similar in spite of their difference. Let us take *The Mill on the Floss.* We find here a certain young woman, Maggie Tulliver, who is an incarnation of the value of passion and is aware of it. She is in love with a young man, Stephen, who is engaged to another, an insignificant young woman. This Maggie Tulliver, instead of heedlessly seeking her own happiness, chooses in the name of human solidarity to sacrifice herself and to give up the man she loves. On the other hand, La Sanseverina in Stendhal's *Chartreuse de Parme,* believing that it is passion which endows man with his real value, would have declared that a grand passion justifies its sacrifices, and must be preferred to the banality of such conjugal love as would unite Stephen to the little goose he was engaged to marry. It is the latter that she would have chosen to sacrifice in realising her own happiness, and, as Stendhal shows, she would also sacrifice herself upon the plane of passion if life made that demand upon her. Here we are facing two clearly opposed moralities; but I claim that they are equivalent, seeing that in both cases the overruling aim is freedom. You can imagine two attitudes exactly similar in effect, in that one girl might prefer, in resignation, to give up her lover whilst the other preferred, in fulfilment of sexual desire, to ignore the prior engagement of the man she loved; and, externally, these two cases might appear the same as the two we have just cited, while being in fact entirely different. The attitude of La Sanseverina is much nearer to that of Maggie Tulliver than to one of careless greed. Thus, you see, the second objection is at once true and false. One can choose anything, but only if it is upon the plane of free commitment.

The third objection, stated by saying, "You take with one hand what you give with the other," means, at bottom, "your values are not serious, since you choose them yourselves." To that I can only say that I am very sorry that it should be so; but if I have excluded God the Father, there must be somebody to invent values. We have to take things as they are. And moreover, to say that we invent values means neither more nor less than this; that there is no sense in life *à priori*. Life is nothing until it is lived; but it is yours to make sense of, and the value of it is nothing else but the sense that you choose. Therefore, you can see that there is a possibility of creating a human community. I have been reproached for suggesting that existentialism is a form of humanism: people have said to me, "But you have written in your *Nausée* that the humanists are wrong, you have even ridiculed a certain type of humanism, why do you now go back upon that?" In reality, the word humanism has two very different meanings. One may understand by humanism a theory which upholds man as the end-in-itself and as the supreme value. Humanism in this sense appears, for instance, in Cocteau's story *Round the World in 80 Hours,* in which one of the characters declares, because he is flying over mountains in an aeroplane, "Man is magnificent!" This signifies that although I, personally, have not built aeroplanes I have the benefit of those particular inventions and that I personally, being a man, can consider myself responsible for, and honoured by, achievements that are peculiar to some men. It is to assume that we can ascribe value to man according to the most distinguished deeds of certain men. That kind of humanism is absurd, for only the dog or the horse would be in a position to pronounce a general judgment upon man and declare that he is magnificent, which they have never been such fools as to do—at least, not as far as I know. But neither is it admissible that a man should pronounce judgment upon Man. Existentialism dispenses with any judgment of this sort: an existentialist will never take man as the end, since man is still to be determined. And we have no right to believe that humanity is something to which we could set up a cult, after the manner of Auguste Comte. The cult of humanity ends in Comtian humanism, shut-in upon itself, and—this must be said—in Fascism. We do not want a humanism like that.

But there is another sense of the word, of which the fundamental meaning is this: Man is all the time outside of himself: it is in projecting and losing himself beyond himself that he makes man to exist; and, on the other hand, it is by pursuing transcendent aims that he himself is able to exist. Since man is thus self-surpassing, and can grasp objects only in relation to his self-surpassing, he is himself the heart and centre of his transcendence. There is no other universe except the human universe, the universe of human subjectivity. This relation of transcendence as constitutive of man (not in the sense that God is transcendent, but in the sense of self-surpassing) with subjectivity (in such a sense that man is not shut up in himself but forever present in a human universe)—it is this that we call existential humanism. This is humanism, because we remind man that there is no legislator but himself; that he himself, thus abandoned, must decide for himself; also because we show that it is not by turning back upon himself, but always by seeking, beyond himself, an aim which is one of liberation or of some particular realisation, that man can realise himself as truly human.

You can see from these few reflections that nothing could be more unjust than the objections people raise against us.

Existentialism is nothing else but an attempt to draw the full conclusions from a consistently atheistic position. Its intention is not in the least that of plunging men into despair. And if by despair one means—as the Christians do—any attitude of unbelief, the despair of the existentialists is something different. Existentialism is not atheist in the sense that it would exhaust itself in demonstrations of the non-existence of God. It declares, rather, that even if God existed that would make no difference from its point of view. Not that we believe God does exist, but we think that the real problem is not that of His existence; what man needs is to find himself again and to understand that nothing can save him from himself, not even a valid proof of the existence of God. In this sense existentialism is optimistic, it is a doctrine of action, and it is only by self-deception, by confusing their own despair with ours that Christians can describe us as without hope. (pp. 391-416)

Jean-Paul Sartre, "Existentialism Is a Humanism," translated by Philip Mairet, in The Existentialist Tradition: Selected Writings, *edited by Nino Langiulli, Anchor Books, 1971, pp. 391-416.*

PHILOSOPHICAL AND RELIGIOUS PERSPECTIVES

Ralph Harper

[*In the following excerpt, Harper examines the concept of "the dead God" in Existentialist literature and philosophy.*]

Whoever believes in God cannot know ultimate loneliness. Whoever has not yet faced a future emptied of those who care for him does not know ultimate loneliness either, and is hardly likely to sense the void left by the passing of God. Not all existentialists have responded openly to this aspect of our recent cultural past. We must do it for them. Their insights into the spectrum of darkness are not as profound as those of Kafka, who in his "fear" felt the full force not only of human rejection but of cosmic indifference as well. He was not merely fearful, he was, except in his writing, disabled. It can be said that this is not an age of anxiety but an age of emotional and spiritual disability. The difference is considerable.

Buber, Marcel, Tillich, Jaspers—compared to Kafka and Heidegger—seem not even to have felt the irony of Pascal's skepticism, to say nothing of Nietzsche's nihilism. It is difficult to understand how anyone can mention God complacently after reading Pascal, how anyone can talk of God at all after reading Nietzsche. Does an experience of radical human loneliness have to precede the conclusion that there is no God, or is it possible to be immune to the spiritual climate of one's time? After all, Nietzsche had warned us that it would take time before the death of God would reach our ears.

Pascal, of course, did not believe God was dead. He knew he could not see or know him. God is, but is hidden. "If there is no God, He is infinitely incomprehensible. We are incapable of knowing either what He is or if He is." We are almost equally incapable of knowing what we are. We live in darkness, and we are ourselves full of darkness. Lost in some corner of a silent universe, we can only imagine a God who himself is lost, and whom only the heart can reach, reason being powerless and misleading.

Many years had to go by before men wondered whether there was any difference between a hidden God and no God at all—whether, if reason could not know, the heart could, whether longing was not wishful thinking. But when the question was finally clearly asked by Nietzsche, the answer came back fast enough. What is extraordinary is not that it took so long to ask but that it has taken so long to understand the question. Nietzsche has been read for seventy years now, and many of his admirers—among whom one would have to place many theologians—still are not willing to say "of course, it should have occurred to me long ago," so rooted are minds in the ideas of the past, or perhaps, as Nietzsche himself said, "I'm afraid we are still not rid of God because we still have faith in grammar."

At least Pascal—and Ingmar Bergman and Unamuno—understood their own ambivalence. As Lucien Goldmann has pointed out, for Pascal God was at all times both absent and present. This was the source of the conflict between his faith and his skepticism. Both were real, thus the Pascalian anguish. Bergman's Knight asks, "Why can't I kill God within me. . . . What is going to happen to those of us who want to believe but aren't able to?" The idea of God takes a distressingly long time to die, and yet when death comes it can come swiftly. Unamuno's life seems to have been devoted to the impossible task of promoting a concept of God which his reason could accept even less than Pascal's, in order to suggest a guarantee for the immortality of his consciousness, and immortality which his reason could also not accept. Pascal, at least, did believe from the heart; Unamuno could not.

Whatever the difference, and it is considerable, their sense of the abyss was quite distinct from Dostoevsky's and Nietzsche's. In spite of the superficial orthodoxy of Dostoevsky, he, not Nietzsche, was the first to outline the consequences of the absence of God and immortality. He had no illusions: absence meant void and vacuum. An abyss between head and heart may be infinite, but it is totally unlike the spiritual emptiness that surrounds one who no longer believes in the reality of God. Such a person is not easily convinced that the existence of other men will reduce the burden of his loneliness. If others like ourselves are all we can know, then we are truly alone, unless we are capable of responding to them and they to us, as true "religious" respond to God.

That is the problem, and it is as much a problem for the future as it was for Dostoevsky and Nietzsche. Can one live in a vacuum, a place from which God has been sucked out, and not be at the mercy of every slight and snub, each making the inner man more nervous and more vulnerable than the last? Nietzsche thought not: "you will never pray again, never adore again, never again rest in endless trust; you have no perpetual guardian and friend for your seven solitudes." We know that Buber, for one, had a different answer, but although we can respect his reply, he would be more convincing if we could feel that he knew the Nietzschean and Kafkan experiences from the inside. It is easy to introduce "the eternal Thou" when one has been able to experience presence with other human beings. But what has made this experience possible in a time of no God, no eternal Thou? Is it enough to say that Nietzsche was only doing what had to be done, killing off a God who was a conceptual It so that the true, the real God who is with You can be felt? Perhaps. But if so, we are left with the mystery of the disabled, of Nietzsche himself, of Kafka, and all the rest of those who, as Proust said, cannot emerge from themselves to meet someone and live with his presence.

Perhaps there is no mystery at all. Perhaps we should expect a gap here between the time when the mind suddenly loses faith in the incredible and the time when it becomes accustomed to looking for its health elsewhere. Who can adjust to such a change, such a debasement of his idea of God, and such an exaltation of his idea of his experience with another? However this may be, the certainty of the void coexists with the isolation of modern man, and it is unwise to assume too quickly that the coincidence is accidental.

It was some years before Dostoevsky realized that there might be a connection between a spiritual void and a moral vacuum. The moral symptoms he knew early, as early as *Notes from Underground,* but he seems to have concluded only that moral schizophrenia was a consequence of living in the nineteenth century. What it was about that century that made it so different he did not know—that is, not until he came to write *The Possessed* and *The Brothers Karamazov.* Then it was clear to him that a man who no longer believes in God (and, he always added, immortality) might feel free, might even feel obliged, in order to prove his freedom, to be a sadist or a masochist. Although we can say, with some degree of truth, that sadism and masochism were consequences of psychological defects in Dostoevsky himself, nevertheless he is not unconvincing when he asks what barriers are left once you have taken absolutes away. He then turns the question around and suggests that it is difficult to live in the nineteenth century and believe in God, and that once God's absence is admitted, a man is free to do as he pleases.

The Dostoevskian characters whose pleasure it is to be kind to their neighbors are no more impressive to us than to Dostoevsky. Those who admit their love for evil, for Sodom, for parricide, seduction of minors—for, in short, the worst their traditional sense of beauty and goodness could imagine—are also the most energetic. But once liberated by the death of the idea of God, free only to do evil, they either kill themselves or go mad.

There is a historical process at work here. The French revolutionaries were as conscious of the death of God and traditional morality as were Dostoevsky and Nietzsche a century later. Liberation has many meanings, and the least one can do is assume, until proof to the contrary is really available, that, causality aside, there are simultaneous associations among economic, political, psychological, philosophical, and religious liberations. It is the historian's unenviable task to try to unravel them. Philosophers should note that several centuries after radical skepticism first addressed itself to the question of the absolute of absolutes, it is still possible for educated men to act as though the question had never been raised. But then our part of the twentieth century might be characterized, for many people, by a "leave-of-absence" phenomenon, a waiting without hope, but without despair either.

In this respect Camus' notion of the absurd is timely, although not a complete parallel. For him man in our time—and he did not in theory exclude the possibility of the recovery of absolutes—was torn between the nostalgia of the heart for truth and justice and the unreasoning silence of a murderous world. He had no ultimate hope, and no illusions. He thought that the best living was the most living, and that revolt, passion, and intellectual lucidity alone could provide the vitality needed to keep the absurd tension from collapsing. If it were to collapse, then nostalgia would sink into despair or be humiliated by religious or metaphysical faith. He preferred the honesty of lucidity, a Kafkan honesty in the face of injustice and ambiguity.

But it must be pointed out that Camus' absurd is not the same as a vacuum. As he himself said, the rebel can say *no* because (in some way) he has already said *yes*. Camus is an affirmative thinker, he said *yes* to many things, to love as well as to justice, to the sand, sea, and sun, to many people, to the future of man. He was as fascinated by Kafka as Buber, for just as Buber could see the God of the concentration camps prefigured in the Law that Kafka hated and worshipped, so Camus could respond to what he thought was Kafka's nostalgia for a lost paradise even more than to his peculiar kind of resignation. How often we have found ourselves borrowing something from another mind and ignoring that mind's clear challenge to some illusion of our own.

In this sense even Kafka was not ready to listen to Nietzsche. The latter once quoted Epicurus, an apocryphal Epicurus, as saying "if there are gods they do not care for us." One might imagine Kafka saying "if there is God, he hates us." And yet it was Kafka who cared, not Nietzsche, who found the quotation amusing. Kafka's Law is real enough. He does not need to call it God; as the Law, it lives somewhere between God and human dignity; it challenges the latter, questions it, persuades it to seek conformation outside itself, and carefully avoids contact with it. This is a negative God, a God, that is, like a photographic negative, with all qualities in reverse except absoluteness, absolutely negative.

There is a distinction currently made between the experience of the absence of God and the absence of the experience of God. Camus and Sartre had no experience of God, and they could not be said to have experienced the absence of God. Bergman and Unamuno could. Kafka does not fit here at all. However radical his theology—putting aside the question of the appropriateness of using the word the-

ology—his experience was not so much of absence as of concrete, living, active rejection. The Law was his symbol for the authority of his life that convinced him that his being rejected was both justified and obscene. The negative God was not absent for Kafka but was part of his whole life and estimate of himself. He could not envisage life without its senseless governance.

It might well be asked which is worse, a dead God or a negative God, life in the shadow of rejection or life at the edge of the void, some attention or no attention. The choice is not usually ours to make, any more than it was for Kafka and Nietzsche. The life of neither is enviable enough to use as a model. The difference may be a philosophical one in any case. Can one live in a time of no God, as the theologians put it, and live with God, absent or negative, hidden or malevolent? Or is it just sleight of hand, so to speak, when someone raises rejection and self-rejection to the level of divinity? As Kafka said of the young man that it was not the Castle but only the daughter of the charwoman, so we can say that there was no Law but only a tyrannical father Kafka took too seriously. Let us not be too critical; by Kafka's stripes some of us may yet be healed.

Kierkegaard has reminded us that we love to hear the sweet anguish of the poet; we ask him to sing and suffer so that he may sing the more sweetly, not only for our pleasure but for our salvation as well! Across death, men like Kafka and Nietzsche are our companions; for all practical purposes they are presences. Their drama is our psychodrama; we act out our own illnesses through plotting the graphs of their diseases. Better an understanding of someone else than no understanding of ourselves? Rather some understanding of ourselves through understanding them. And yet how remote they actually are to us, the times in which they lived, their families, their dispositions, their friends, their talents. They were, we must remind ourselves, true isolates. If we are tempted to admire them because they did not continually weep for themselves—if we are disappointed because on occasion they did weep for themselves—we would be presumptuous to demand of them, most of all of Nietzsche, the strength to endure an experience of the void so overwhelming that even now we feel safe in contemplating it only when we admire the completeness and clarity of their insights.

From his first book, *The Birth of Tragedy,* to the end, before illness paralysed his mind, one thing above all was clear to Nietzsche; there was only Becoming, no Being. What he at first called "the Dionysian substratum of the world," individuation, terror and horror, flux, are the nature of reality. Mankind has had only two choices, to recognize and accept this or to deceive itself in order to avoid terror. Nietzsche spent his life uncovering the deceptions of history, the desperate and, to him, shameful attempts to believe in an order of reality for which only faith is evidence.

His own development of destructive criticism passed from a euphoric period when he depended on metaphors to express his discovery of the unreality of God, Being, Another World, to his later systematic criticism of the psychological motives for religious and metaphysical belief and the probable cause of its disappearance. It was one thing to say "God is dead," and another to show what that meant. What ought to be felt as relief was in fact experienced as a radical nihilism that would leave mankind homeless for many years to come and would be followed by a reexamination of all values.

How lightly and how gaily he sketched, in *The Twilight of the Idols,* the stages of disillusionment about a "true world," once "attainable for the sage, the pious, the virtuous man; he lives in it, he is it," to the day when it is "an idea which is no longer good for anything, not even obligating—an idea which has become useless and superfluous." But the sketch fails to bring to life the radical nihilism that opens up a psychological void for civilized men and women, accustomed to the consolation of what they thought were experiences of transcendence. For that matter, Nietzsche's rhetoric makes one wonder whether he fully understood, in his pride at being a pioneer, how desperately mankind had felt the need of something transcendent to cancel out the pain of individuation.

And yet when we read the notes in *The Will to Power* which outline the withdrawal of an assurance of meaning in all events, of a structure within events, of a permanence beyond empirical evidence, we can believe that he knew—regardless of what he may have felt—what he was talking about: "now one realizes that becoming aims at nothing and achieves nothing"; "at bottom man has lost the faith in his own value when no infinitely valuable whole works through him." This is a far cry from his earlier conclusion that life is "not all sad and dark, but rather like a new, scarcely describable kind of light, happiness, relief, exhilaration, encouragement, dawn. Indeed, we philosophers and 'free spirits' feel as if a new dawn were shining on us when we receive the tidings that 'the old god is dead'; our heart overflows with gratitude, amazement, anticipation, expectation." But not for long. Toward the end he was saying "night more and more surrounds me."

There is something unexpected, almost illogical—as if it should not have happened—in Nietzsche's collapse into an admission of homelessness. His position all along was quite different from Dostoevsky's, as illustrated by the sophistry of Kirillov. "I must affirm my unbelief, for there's nothing higher for me than the thought that there's no God. . . . Man kept inventing God in order to live. I am the first man in history to refuse to invent God." This may sound like Nietzsche, except that at no time did Nietzsche imagine that he was the first to refuse to invent God. When Kirillov goes on to say "it is my duty to make myself believe that I do not believe in God," the difference appears. We know he spoke for Dostoevsky when he added, "God has tormented me all my life." At no time was Nietzsche tormented by God, at no time was he unsure of his unbelief. But he was mistaken when he thought he had the strength to endure metaphysical loneliness and at the same time the inability on the part of his closest friends to understand him.

There might seem to be a similarity between Kirillov's reluctant God and Nietzsche's free spirits and Titans of the future. The reluctant God is a man who had demonstrated his freedom by killing himself. But it never occurred to

Nietzsche that these free spirits—of which he was surely one—or the new men of the future would be called upon to kill themselves. However crime and evil might be evaluated in the future, it seems not to have occurred to Nietzsche that suicide might be a necessary good. Unlike Kirillov, he had too historically oriented a mind to retreat into masochism.

Nevertheless, he arrived at a point of dangerous stillness, not only for his own life, but as a model for future generations. When we look back at him, and think of him as brother and fellow sufferer, we can forget that the void he uncovered in the mind of man remains, and that therefore it is unsafe to assume, as he did, that the seas are really open and the horizon clear. On the contrary, the dramatic literature of our time, even more than its philosophy, has made it evident that psychological nihilism is now a cultural fact so firmly established that the only way of living with it is, paradoxically, not to take it too seriously. This is the method and part of the point of the plays of Beckett and Pinter.

In Beckett's plays nothing happens; in Pinter's plays things do happen, the wrong things, terrible things. For both there is "nothing certain," "nothing to be done," for everyone is "alone in the midst of nothingness" [Beckett, *Waiting for Godot*]. It might seem that Beckett's characters are better off because even in their aimless shuffling of talk back and forth they can imagine they are Adam, made in the image of God, and can compare themselves to Christ. But the comparisons are not apt, for all they do is wait. If this is hope, as Beckett has said, it is hope based on wishful thinking rather than ministry, passion, and sacrifice. There is in Pinter much suffering, the suffering of the insulated and enclosed, living in a world where no one knows what is going on in another's mind, and where the only clues to one's own mind are recollections. These at least are often warm and loving, however distant they may be. Perhaps this is healthier, preferable to Beckett's more abstract insistence on hope where there would seem to be no point to hope. To say "I can't go on like this," and then to go on quite cheerfully, suggests that Beckett is concealing whatever it is that enables him to live a personal life which is not paralyzed by the sight of the void. Is it so simple, as his plays suggest, the old friendly hostility between head and heart, the silence of the world and the nostalgia of the human spirit? Or is there a real world to live in and think about and celebrate, as well as a metaphysical void? Marcel may have been right in insisting that we learn how to construct a concrete metaphysics, for whatever he may have meant by this, it should be possible to talk to the realities we care about and not be paralyzed by looking into the void of an impossible metaphysics.

We might imagine Beckett saying "if there is a God, I'll wait for him" and Pinter saying "if there's a God, he's not worth talking about." Sartre once said of himself, "I collared the Holy Ghost in the cellar and threw him out; atheism is a cruel and long-range affair; I think I've carried it through." Smart talk speaks for itself. Beckett's waiting, however unsupported, has the same air of seriousness that the later Heidegger's has. "The holy does indeed appear," announced Heidegger, "but the god remains far off." Beckett would agree to that. But he would not go so far as to speak of God's failure, and the need of man to remain near that failure. Indeed, it is difficult to make much sense of such talk. Whether God has withdrawn—and thus failed us—or whether we have failed him and ourselves is a secondary question in comparison with the suspicion that there is no God anyway, and void is his name.

Beckett's characters experience nothing and imagine something else. Pinter's remember reality and make no connections with each other. The loneliness of non-communication may in the end be no worse than the isolation of a mind that pretends reality where there is none. Hope without reality is only an excuse for not following evidence to a conclusion. That was not a mistake Camus was likely to make. He knew nothing of hope or reverberations from a distant God. He knew what men can do to each other in the name of reason, murder, betrayal, and these are worse evils than the inability of one man to know what is going on in another's mind. He did not hope; he did something better, he promised to work for a just world, in moderation, and with some kind of love for that world. He shared this affection for physical reality—including human beings—with Pinter, and carefully avoided abstractions, metaphysical or religious, unless they were in some way supported by what he knew to be possible. He did not expect justice to come to him like a returning God. He intended to go out and help bring it into the world. Compared to this attitude, there is a sterility in Beckett precisely in so far as an abstract hope matches an abstract void. There is more future—whatever the difference between future and hope may be—in a world where one is reminded of sea, sun, earth, lost loves, than in a world where nothing happens, and where nobody comes and nobody goes. To laugh at this world is to admit, with immense relief, that it is false. To laugh with Pinter is to realize that in spite of the fact that it is impossible much of the time to verify what goes on and why, things do happen, and some things are frightening, and some things are beautiful. (pp. 67-80)

> *Ralph Harper, "The Void," in his* The Existential Experience, *The Johns Hopkins University Press, 1972, pp. 65-83.*

David E. Cooper

[*In the following excerpt, Cooper discusses Existentialists' views on death and its importance in defining human freedom and giving meaning to existence.*]

Most existentialist writers have devoted attention to the topic of death. This is not, as popularly supposed, out of preoccupation with the gloomier side of the human condition, nor due to a belief that death renders life pointless. The attention is explained, rather, by the conviction that the phenomenon of death reveals authentic possibilities of human existence. (p. 133)

In at least two senses, it is not death as such which concerns The Existentialist [by "The Existentialist," Cooper means "the 'ideal' existentialist, who embodies the best wisdom . . . to be gleaned from actual existentialist writ-

ers"]. First, like Jaspers, he distinguishes 'existential' from 'vital non-being'. The latter ensues with clinical death, since I am no longer alive. But I could remain alive, yet cease to 'ex-ist': if, for example, I am rendered a hopeless vegetable by brain damage. The Existentialist is concerned with the finitude of existence, the fact that it ends, and not with the particular way—clinical death—in which that end normally comes. Second, he is not concerned with the event—death, brain damage or whatever—which ends my existence, but with my life in relation to the prospect of that event. This is what Heidegger means by calling death an 'existential phenomenon', and by saying, 'when we speak of death, [it] does not signify *Dasein*'s Being-at-an-end, . . . but a *Being-towards-the-end* . . . Death is a way to be.' [*Dasein* is Heidegger's name for the kind of Being possessed by human beings.] These remarks will occupy us later.

We will also need to clarify the several remarks by existentialists which give the impression that death is what gives meaning to life. De Beauvoir, for instance, notes with apparent approval Montaigne's dictum that 'the continuous work of life is to build death', while Jaspers refers to death as 'throwing us back upon the fulfilment of *Existenz*'. In a special sense it does turn out that, for The Existentialist, death or finitude is responsible for existence having meaning. But it is important, straightaway, to distinguish this from other senses. Jaspers, for example, makes it clear that death should never be thought of, in the *Liebestod* tradition, as the triumphant 'perfection' of the otherwise drab business of living. Nor, even with religious existentialists, is death the aim of life in the sense of a gateway to something better. The sentiment is not at all Mozart's, who wrote to his father. 'As death . . . is the real purpose of our life . . . [its] image is very soothing and comforting! And I thank God for affording me . . . the opportunity . . . of realizing that [it] is the key to our real happiness.' The sense in which, for The Existentialist, death may confer a meaning on life comes closer, as we shall see, to the thought attributed by Anthony Kenny to Wittgenstein: 'If death has meaning, it is precisely as an end, a final end, of life. Wittgenstein described his father's death as beautiful, as a death worth a whole life. Perhaps, indeed, the test of a good life was that it was one that issued in a good death.'

The main business is to explain why The Existentialist thinks the phenomenon of death—death as a prospect for each of us—reinforces and elaborates . . . the free, individualized character of existence. He has, I think, three points, the last of which is the most important one.

The first point is that a person's finitude is at least a necessary condition of his freedom and individuality. Sartre puts in unequivocally:

> Death is the limit, but also a constituent of freedom . . . If a being were endowed with temporal infinity, he could realize all his possibilities . . . he would disappear with respect both to individuality (the realization of some possibilities to the exclusion of others) and to freedom (dangerous and irremediable choice of certain possibilities).

If we lived for ever, each of us would eventually take up the same possibilities, so that no one could be individuated by the choices peculiar to him. Each of us would eventually taste everything on offer, so no real weight would attach to choosing this now rather than that later. 'Our lives would merge into universal indifference,' writes de Beauvoir, and 'there could be neither projects nor values.'

Put like this, the point requires us to speculate on how things might be for us if we lived for ever—a requirement that The Existentialist may be advised to avoid. However things may be for immortals, he can argue, our actual sense of ourselves as free individuals is tied to recognition of our finitude. Not all choices need be 'dangerous', but it would damage our image of our freedom if nothing of final moment ever turned on the choices we make. Now the idea of choices being of moment and weight would not arise, arguably, if our lives had no temporal limit and every decision could one day be remedied and replaced. Nor is it clear that notions deployed in characterizing a person's individuality—the *shape* of his life, say, or the *story* to be told of it—could gain purchase if lives never ended. Shape demands boundaries, and a story which *could* not end is not a story. To be sure, a novel, *Nausea* for example, may have no end in that things are 'left in the air'. But the reader knows that Roquentin is not going to turn into a frog, nor go backwards in time, nor live for ever. Without that silent knowledge, the story—the coherence and direction of the episodes—falls apart. We should have no way of identifying episodes as significant, for we should have no grip, however loose, on what is significant in the characters' lives. In fiction and in fact, we must assume that a person's life is going in some directions and not others, and that whatever the direction, it will come to an end.

The second of The Existentialist's points is that attention to a particular aspect of a person's fate after death throws into sharper relief how things stand with him when alive. Put differently, the error of some ways of thinking of human life is brought out by recognizing that they are properly true only of people whose lives are ended. . . . The bad faith in Garcin's whine [in Sartre's *Huis clos*] that his life had 'fallen into the public domain' is made apparent by the irony that now, since he is dead, the complaint is indeed warranted. The crucial significance of death, for Sartre, is that it is the 'transformation into otherness of the whole person'. Death, he nicely puts it, is the act of 'supreme generosity', whereby I place myself totally at the disposal of others. The dead man no longer has the opportunity, through future action, to give the lie to the Other's summation of him, nor to pit his own interpretation and evaluation of his life against the Other's. Without further possibilities, his freedom and individuality are absolutely alienated in favour of those who remain. It is this which is at the heart of Sartre's and de Beauvoir's horror at '*my utter non-being*'. This particular kind of horror of what happens at death would be inexplicable if . . . we were always, even when alive, constituted by the place we occupy in the schemes and categorizations of others. An appreciation of the way that, at death, we are delivered over to others carries with it the perception that this is not how matters stand before that event.

The last of The Existentialist's claims is encapsulated in Heidegger's remark that 'anticipation [of death] utterly individualizes *Dasein*.' This individualization has two merging senses. . . . A person is individualized to the extent, first, that he withdraws from immersion in the world of the 'they' and, second, that he lends a wholeness and integrity to his life.

It was Kierkegaard who first focused on, and connected, these senses—not in relation to death, but to the 'despair' attendant on the 'aesthetic' way of life. By this last expression he does not have in mind only, or mainly, the kind of life led by an Oscar Wilde or Aubrey Beardsley. The 'aesthete'—whether in the shape of a dilettante, a Don Juan, or a busybody hopping from one activity to another—is a person 'sunk in immediacy'. He blows with the wind: following the latest fashion, chasing the latest girl, or indulging in the latest pursuit to cure his boredom. His is a life of 'despair', not because he is buried in gloom, but because his life 'hinges upon a condition outside of itself' [Kierkegaard, *Either/Or*]. Fashion, caprice, public opinion, external stimuli dictate the course of this life. The worst aspect of such an existence is that the person is dissolved into a 'multiplicity', and has lost 'the inmost and holiest thing of all in a person, the unifying power of personality' [*Either/Or*]. So the person who fails to follow Kierkegaard's imperative, 'Be an individual!', through drifting with the prevailing breeze which blows from the 'public', also fails to follow it through the absence of a 'unifying power' in his life.

Kierkegaard's conclusion, now in relation to death, is taken up by Heidegger and Jaspers. In anticipation of death, writes Heidegger, one is 'wrenched away from the "they"' and 'liberated from one's lostness in those possibilities which may be accidentally thrust upon one'. Only through this anticipation, furthermore, 'can it be made plain to what extent *Being-as-a-whole* . . . is possible in *Dasein* itself'. That is, I am 'individualized' through the prospect of my death, since it enables me both to 'wrench' myself away from the 'they' and to lend a wholeness to my life.

But how is this? By what process does anticipation of death enable this dual 'individualization'? An answer is suggested by Heidegger's badly misunderstood pronouncement, 'Death is *Dasein's* ownmost possibility.' Many critics have objected to both terms in this description. Death is 'ownmost', Heidegger seems to argue, because it is not 'delegatable'. 'Dying is something that every *Dasein* must take upon itself.' This, his critics argue, is either false or trivial. That it is false, taken one way, is shown by cases like Sydney Carton's 'standing in for' Charles Darnay at the scaffold. To be sure, Carton could not die Darnay's death in the sense that he could wear his hat, but nor, in that sense, could he have gone through Darnay's marriage or bout of flu. So, taken another way, it is trivially true of my death—as it is of my marriage and flu—that it is not 'delegatable'. Second, is it not absurd to describe death as a 'possibility'—unless one believes, as Heidegger does not, that there is also a possibility of immortality?

What these critics ignore is that the 'death' Heidegger describes as my 'ownmost possibility' is not the event of my demise, but what he calls my 'Being-towards-death'. And the 'dying' which cannot be 'delegated' is defined as a *way of Being* in which *Dasein* is towards death'. So it is a way of *living* in relation to the prospect of death, and not my execution or heart-attack, which is my 'ownmost possibility'—a possibility, in fact, which most people fail to take up, preferring as they do to be 'distracted' from, and 'anaesthetized' against, the prospect of their deaths.

This 'ownmost possibility' is none other than my living so as to become a totality, a Being-as-a-whole—a possibility whose realization requires a 'wrenching away' from those provided by the 'they'. But how, quite, is this possibility related to death, and why is it my 'ownmost'? The suspicion must lurk that Heidegger is punning on two senses of 'wholeness' or 'totality': that of having finite boundaries and that of being an integral unity. But the suspicion is not, I think, warranted. Heidegger is not punning, but trying to forge deep conceptual connections between the finitude and potential integrity of a life.

To begin with, it is my knowledge that there will be a final 'not yet' which enables me to range before it and order my other future and potential 'not yets'. And it is in virtue of this ability that I can stand back from my present passing embroilments. For without a sense of a future direction and pattern, I should be without a perspective for assessing the significance of what I am presently about—my work, say, or a romantic involvement. It is an irony that an immortal creature, lacking an idea of its possible demise, could not take the long-term view which, as Heidegger puts it, 'liberates' a person from immediate embroilments. Because a day will never come for such a creature when it can say, '*This* is how I judge the significance of my life as a whole, its direction, its success or failure', there cannot be a time when it stands back from its situation so as to assess the place it might occupy in that final judgement.

But we are still left without an explanation of why this possibility of wholeness is uniquely 'ownmost'. We get some help from Charles Guignon's remark: 'there is one possibility each of us has which is *not* delegatable . . . Although all the concrete roles I take over are public and not unique, there is one possibility that is mine alone: my Being-towards-death as the possibility of appropriating these public meanings in an integrated and coherent way.' I suggest we understand the point in the following terms. There is nothing I ordinarily do of which I can say, 'It is impossible that anyone else, however suitably placed, should have done that.' Someone else might have written this book or married my wife in place of me. In that sense, everything I do is delegatable and anonymous. The exercise of my capacity to draw together all the possibilities which I have, or will have, taken up and to import a significance to this totality is not, however, similarly delegatable.

To be sure, I can approach a friend or biographer and give to him the brief of providing an interpretation of my life: but this is not at all like entrusting to a doctor or a colleague judgement on the significance of my headaches or my latest book. Their verdict cannot alter the significance of headache or book, whereas my 'delegating' to a biographer an assessment of my life, as well as my response to that assessment, are themselves significant ingredients of that life. They are to be put in the melting-pot along with everything else that forms the object of the assessment I am to make. I may perhaps accept the biographer's judgement of my life as, say, a well intentioned failure: but that I accept it is itself a contribution to my life's significance. No biographer in the future could be entitled, in coming to a verdict on the significance of my life, to ignore the significance I myself attached to it, since this is an important part of the life which he is writing. I cannot, then, irredeemably transfer to others the 'appropriation' of the elements of my life in an 'integrated and coherent way', since any such provisional transfers, and their results, are further elements for an 'appropriation' which I alone can perform. It is in this sense that my Being-as-a-whole, whose possibility is provided by the prospect of death, is uniquely my 'ownmost'. (pp. 133-38)

[We] have already seen what The Existentialist could *not* mean by speaking of death as imparting meaning to a life. It is not, for example, that an heroic martyrdom can turn an otherwise worthless existence into a triumphant one. If The Existentialist is to have sympathy with Wittgenstein's thought that a beautiful death is worth a whole life, that a good death is the test of a good life, it must be along the following lines. Without at least the possibility of a final judgement as death comes close, there can be no good life—not because that judgement can transmute the bad into the good, but because, without the prospect of that judgement lying ahead, a person cannot lend to his life the integrity and direction upon which the judgement is passed. A beautiful death is worth a *whole* life—or, better, they are equivalent in value. For the possibilities of imparting wholeness to one's life and of recognizing, at the end, that this wholeness has indeed been sculpted, are not to be separated. (p. 139)

David E. Cooper, " 'Angst,' Death and Absurdity," in his Existentialism: A Reconstruction, *Basil Blackwell, 1990, pp. 127-46.*

EXISTENTIALIST FICTION AND DRAMA

Maxine Greene

[*An American educator and critic, Greene has written extensively on issues in education, pedagogy, and philosophy. In the following excerpt, Greene discusses the methods through which Existentialist authors used fiction to communicate their philosophy.*]

Since 1842, when Søren Kierkegaard made "indirect communication" one of the categories of communication, existential philosophers have been awakening individuals to a sense of their condition through the use of literary devices and forms. Kierkegaard's view of his own age had much to do with his decision to beguile people, to stir them up, to make their lives more difficult. "A revolutionary age is an age of action," he wrote, "ours is an age of advertisement and publicity. In the present age a rebellion is, of all things, the most unthinkable. Such an expression of strength would seem ridiculous to the calculating intelligence of our times." Concerned with making "an expression of strength" possible for individuals, he created a literature intended to challenge both calculating intelligence and the calculated enjoyments associated with the "aesthetic" approach to life. His project was to seduce his readers into asking the questions and making the choices that seemed to him to be the "proper and stringent expression of the ethical." But he could function neither as seducer nor as gadfly if he relied upon abstract argument. His readers had to be brought to participate imaginatively in situations where decisive choices were demanded and where there were never enough good reasons for saying that one alternative was absolutely right and the other wrong.

Either/Or involves a dialogue between the intellectually gifted aestheticist "A" and the less gifted but committed ethical thinker, Judge William. Between "A's" essays and the Judge's letters appears the "Diary of a Seducer," based upon Kierkegaard's own experiences with Regina Olsen: the love affair, the wooing, and the broken engagement. Kierkegaard had already decided to give Regina up when he began *Either/Or,* so the account cannot be regarded as diary or confession. Rather, it is a deliberate transmutation of actuality into fiction. The world in which Johannes pursues and then retreats from Cordelia is a concrete world full of ambiguities and open possibilities; moreover, it is suffused by the imaginary. The reader willing to enter into it cannot remain an indifferent spectator. His own consciousness becomes the subject of the Diary, his own awareness of the contradictions between romantic and conjugal love, the problem of fidelity, the discrepancies between the outward appearance of an engaged couple and their inner lives. He is there in person, confronting the necessity to choose either good *and* evil—or not to choose at all. The climax is reached not when Cordelia, repelled by a deliberately unpleasant Johannes, breaks the engagement herself. It is reached when the Judge writes: "If you will understand me aright, I should like to say that in making a choice it is not so much a question of choosing the right as of the energy, the earnestness, the pathos with which one chooses. Thereby the personality announces its inner infinity, and thereby, in turn, the personality is consolidated." Kierkegaard called the work an "incantation," not an argument. He was trying to arouse each reader to "earnestness of spirit," to the consolidation or creation of himself. And this could be done best by means of imaginative literature.

Kierkegaard, of course, was predominantly interested in becoming a Christian; and his primary purpose, as he said, was religious. He thought of himself as a teacher, which "in the right sense was to be a learner"; but he was an exemplary philosopher in the existential sense. He demonstrated this clearly enough when he wrote in *The Point of View for My Work as an Author:*

> I have nothing new to proclaim; I am without authority, being myself hidden in a deceit; I do

not go to work straightforwardly but with indirect cunning; I am not a holy man; in short, I am a spy who in his spying, in learning to know all about questionable conduct and illusions and suspicious characters, all the while he is making inspection is himself under the closest inspection.

As we shall see, this could describe any literary artist. The novelist, for example, has often been presented as a forger, a counterfeiter, a confidence man. In this case, however, the deceit, the cunning, and the indirection—not to speak of the self-inspection—appear to be distinctive characteristics of the existential philosopher; and they help to explain his use of literature.

Kierkegaard was not the only one. There was Nietzsche as well. He used metaphors, epigrams, plays on words, satires, aphorisms. "Whoever writes in blood and aphorisms," he says, "does not want to be read but to be learned by heart. In the mountains the shortest way is from peak to peak; but for that one must have long legs. Aphorisms should be peaks—and those who are addressed, tall and lofty. The air thin and pure, danger near, and the spirit full of gay sarcasm: these go well together." Later, talking about seeking the truth, learning and trying out himself, the character Zarathustra says: "A trying and questioning was my every move; and, verily, one must also learn to answer such questioning. That, however, is my taste—not good, not bad, but *my* taste of which I am no longer ashamed and which I have no wish to hide. 'This is *my* way; where is yours?'—thus I answered those who asked me 'the way.' For *the* way—that does not exist." Once again, the effort is (indirectly, through Zarathustra, the fictional "I") to arouse people to their own subjective awareness—and to awareness of that awareness—so they can seek *their* ways. *Thus Spake Zarathustra* has no more practical utility than a lyric; it cannot be summarized, paraphrased, or used for any end beyond itself. As Sartre puts it about literature in general, "the end to which it offers itself is the reader's freedom."

So it is with Sartre's imaginative works, Albert Camus', Simone de Beauvoir's, Martin Buber's, and those of other existential philosophers. Acting upon his or her existential commitment, each has been concerned with moving persons to reflection upon themselves and to choose what to make of themselves within their own historical situations. Free people write, as it were, their own histories; they are the authors of their own lives. But they must act and choose in terms of the reality given to them by way of consciousness. More often than not, they do not see their own reality. Conventions, presuppositions, proprieties, habitual automatisms, *idées fixés* of all kinds disguise or deform the impinging world; they prevent individuals from returning to "things in themselves." The artist is concerned with such returning, with renewing the reader's own world. "For this is quite the final goal of art:" writes Sartre, "to recover this world by giving it to be seen as it is, but as if it had its source in human freedom."

In *Being and Nothingness,* Sartre discusses "quality as a revelation of being" and the existential symbolism of things. He makes the point that the quality of a thing is nothing other than its being. "The yellow of the lemon, we said, is not a subjective mode of apprehending the lemon: it is the lemon. We have shown also that the whole lemon extends throughout its qualities and that each one of the qualities is spread over the others; that is what we have correctly called 'this.' Every quality of being is all of being; it is the presence of its absolute contingency; it is its indifferent irreducibility." In Sartre's novel, *Nausea,* Antoine Roquentin discovers the absolute contingency of the world. There are only qualities, appearances: there are only labels and abstract categories—nothing more. He is sitting on something named a seat in a tramcar. "I murmur: 'It's a seat,' a little like an exorcism. But the word stays on my lips; it refuses to go and put itself on the thing. . . . Things are divorced from their names. They are there, grotesque, headstrong, gigantic and it seems ridiculous to call them seats or say anything at all about them: I am in the midst of things, nameless things. Alone, without words, defenseless, they surround me, are beneath me, behind me, above me. They demand nothing, they don't impose themselves: they are there." He sees a man half-lying on the opposite seat; he watches his finger scratch his scalp with a nail. Then he jumps off the tram and finds himself in the park. "I drop onto a bench between great black tree-trunks, between the black, knotty hands reaching towards the sky. A tree scrapes at the earth under my feet with a black nail. I would so like to let myself go, forget myself, sleep. But I can't, I'm suffocating: existence penetrates me everywhere, through the eyes, the nose, the mouth. . . . And suddenly, suddenly, the veil is torn away, I have understood, I have seen."

In *Being and Nothingness,* the philosopher has much to say about the relation between things and human reality. He writes much about the psychic meaning of the slimy which is "identical with the symbolic value which the slimy has in relation to being-in-itself." For all his imagery, for all such terms as "sticky thickness," "the sucking of the slimy which I feel on my hands," and "the invisible suction of the past," the nature of the human situation is not revealed as it is in the novel. It is not made available for appropriation by a reader's consciousness in the same fashion, because the reader is not asked to apprehend it imaginatively. It has, therefore, nothing like the impact of Roquentin's metaphysical predicament when he has his vision in the park. "And then all of a sudden, there it was, clear as day: existence had suddenly unveiled itself. It had lost the harmless look of an abstract category: it was the very paste of things, this root was kneaded into existence. Or rather the root, the park gates, the bench, the sparse grass, all that had vanished: the diversity of things, their individuality, were only an appearance, a veneer. This veneer had melted, leaving soft, monstrous masses, all in disorder—naked, in a frightful, obscene nakedness." The terrible nausea experienced by the man who yearns for an orderly, intelligible universe and discovers that existence escapes the boundaries of language and science is the product of the consciousness disclosed in the novel. That nausea can only become significant, however, if the reader gives to it some of his own revulsion at contingency and arbitrariness. He can only give in this way if, for a moment at least, he contemplates existence from an inward and personal vantage point. Contemplating it in this fashion, he may be able to summon up his awareness of the there-

ness of things and the otherness of human beings, the opaqueness surrounding him, the imperviousness. The illusioned world that is *Nausea* can only be entered by way of his own consciousness at a time when he is capable of bracketing out his commonsense perceptions of benches, gates, trees, and trams. Having bracketed out or set aside what he has learned to see as the reliable particularities of daily life, he can (moving through his consciousness of the patterned events in *Nausea*) see his own reality in a strange nakedness. This means that he can look upon the world as it presents itself to him in its concreteness and immediacy, without the intervention of social recipes and schemata. In doing so, he may also perceive possibilities of human action unthinkable in his everyday world. If nothing else, he may suspect that, if existence is nameless or meaningless, it is up to human beings to restore meanings. Or he may discover what Anny means when she talks about living forward, outliving herself, avoiding fixities and bad faith. At the very least, dimensions of his life will be disclosed for the first time; he will have been helped to recover his world.

This is what happens when the existential philosopher decides to supplement his or her philosophic texts with indirect communication. We need only recall Simone de Beauvoir's *The Second Sex* with its call for the liberation of both men and women, its demand that people dare to be human and to live in good faith, and compare the work with her novel, *The Mandarins.* Here a woman struggles to live her married life in good faith, to confront aging and disillusionment, to choose against her own death because of the remorse of her family would suffer. "I am here," Anne thinks at the end of the book. "They are living, they speak to me, I am alive. Once more, I've jumped feet first into life. . . . Either one founders in apathy, or the earth becomes repeopled. I didn't founder. Since my heart continues to beat, it will have to beat for something, for someone. Since I'm not deaf, I'll once more hear people calling to me. Who knows? Perhaps one day I'll be happy again. Who knows?" We need only recall as well the difference between Albert Camus' lucid descriptions of the Absurd in *The Myth of Sisyphus* and such images as that of the "whole beach, pulsating with heat" pressing against Meusault's back in *The Stranger*—or "the benign indifference of the universe" and the "howls of execration" at the novel's end.

We do not suggest that the only effective existential novels are those created by philosophers eager to confront readers with their own reality. We suggest that imaginative literature holds a distinctive significance for the existential philosopher because of his dominating interest in human freedom, authenticity, and the elusiveness of Being. Idealist philosophers may cherish literature and the other arts for their mimetic function or (as Benedetto Croce does) for being themselves spiritual acts through which images and intuitions are clarified and expressed. Pragmatic philosophers may cherish literature and the other arts because they make possible paradigmatic experiences. "An object," wrote John Dewey, "is peculiarly and dominantly esthetic, yielding the enjoyment characteristic of esthetic perception, when the factors that determine anything which can be called an experience are lifted high above the threshold of perception and are made manifest for their own sake." In the one case, literature is expected to communicate a form of spiritual knowledge; in the other, an engagement with literature is expected to provide an experience characterized by wholeness, integration, and the fullest realization of qualitative particulars. Both idealists and pragmatists find in the arts a capacity to promote heightened sensitivity and awareness, perhaps an intensified perception of meaning. But existential philosophers are unique in their view that consciousness, in its intentionality, is as empty and as clear as the wind. This means that consciousness does not contain the ego. "In fact the consciousness which I have of the I never exhausts it, and the consciousness is not what causes it to come into existence; and I is always given as *having been there before* consciousness—and at the same time as possessing depths which have to be revealed gradually. Thus the ego appears to consciousness as a transcendent in-itself, as an existent in the human world, not as *belonging* to consciousness." The individual is therefore constantly in search of himself, encountering nothingness or the dread of nihilation, living among possibles. To find himself, he must become reflective about his situation; he must experience the anguish which is the manifestation of his freedom—which is also "the recognition of a possibility as *my* possibility." Because literature goads a reader to reflexiveness and, at once, to confrontation with his freedom, it becomes a potential means of self-discovery, an aid in the pursuit of being. For the existentialist, then, a literary encounter can be an encounter with the fundamental drama of an individual's life.

In a poem called "Torso of an Archaic Apollo," Rainer Maria Rilke describes a statue in the Louvre which bursts with light and gleams "until there is no place / that does not see you. You must change your life." Saying this about the impact of art upon the beholder, he is speaking for generations of writers who were not philosophers but whose awareness of the human condition was so similar to that of existential philosophers as to warrant the description "existentialist." In the first of the *Duino Elegies,* Rilke uses angels to represent either imagination or an ideal of undivided consciousness men aspire to and can seldom achieve. He writes:

> Each single angel is terrible. And so I keep down
> my heart, and swallow the call-note of depth-
> dark sobbing. Alas, who is there we can make
> use of? Not angels, not men; and already the
> knowing brutes are aware that we don't feel very
> securely at home within our interpreted world.

His perception of the void that exists after the death of God led him to the fearful recognition that men themselves, if they were able, would have to create new imaginative orders in empty space, horrified space. Not only did he present an awareness of what Sartre was later to call an indifferent, hostile, and restive world; he knew of homelessness and insecurity, even in the face of what was "interpreted" by the sciences and the old sterile faiths.

Fyodor Dostoyevsky knew as well, and had known long before the *Duino Elegies,* even before *Thus Spake Zarathustra.* In most of his novels—*The Possessed, Crime and Punishment, The Brothers Karamasov*—the recurring existential themes are sounded and explored: freedom, anguish, despair, boredom, guilt, loneliness, dread. We need only think back to *The Brothers Karamasov* in order to summon up that topsy-turvy world inhabited by people who seem to have no everyday reality. Living their lives in extreme situations, they are presented as thrusting consciousnesses; the fiction is composed of what they intend. Ivan Karamasov's "poem" about the Grand Inquisitor suggests some of this and at once reminds us of certain perplexities which have become obsessions in the modern world. In the "poem," the Grand Inquisitor blames Jesus for destroying His own kingdom. He destroyed it by insisting on receiving love that was freely offered "and not the base raptures of the slave." He rejected, therefore, the forces of miracle, mystery, and authority, all of which could have been counted upon "to hold captive forever" the consciences of rebellious men.

> Instead of taking men's freedom away from
> them, Thou didst make it greater than ever!
> Didst Thou forget that man prefers peace, and
> even death, to freedom of choice in the knowl-
> edge of good and evil? Nothing is more seductive
> for man than his freedom of conscience, but
> nothing is a greater cause of suffering. And be-
> hold, instead of giving a firm foundation for set-
> ting the conscience of man at rest for ever, Thou
> didst choose all that is exceptional, vague and
> enigmatic; Thou didst choose what was utterly
> beyond the strength of men, acting as though
> Thou didst not love them at all—Thou who
> didst come to give Thy life for them!

In Dostoyevsky's *Notes from Underground,* the reader discovers one of the most compelling enactments of self-confrontation ever created. Transmuting old conventions having to do with caverns, pits, and being buried alive, Dostoyevsky devised the metaphor of underground to communicate the sense of anguished inwardness or human subjectivity. The cellar inhabited by the Underground Man is located, significantly, in St. Petersburg, a shabby modern city shrouded in dingy, yellowish snow. Without support or attachment, the speaker is struggling to identify himself and at once to understand his being-in-the-world. Not only does he lash out at the Crystal Palace that represents progress and industry; not only does he rebel against abstract formulas, notions of the "normal" and the "reasonable," and the thought of being treated as a "piano-key." Breaking with all aspects of common-sense reality and morality, he has to face the terrible conundrums of anguish and free will; he has to find a way of coping with boredom and with "spite." In his predicament, he exudes the fear and trembling which accompany reflexiveness. To engage with his anguished consciousness is to plunge into the existential dilemma, to suffer free will.

> And yet I think man will never renounce real
> suffering, that is, destruction and chaos. Why
> suffering is the sole origin of consciousness.
> Though I did lay it down at the beginning that
> consciousness is the greatest misfortune for man,
> yet I know man prizes it and would not give it
> up for any satisfaction. Consciousness, for in-
> stance, is infinitely superior to twice two makes

Ranier Maria Rilke, seated at his desk in Paris at the time of the writing of The Notebooks of Malte Laurids Brigge.

four. Once you have mathematical certainty there is nothing left to do or to understand. There will be nothing left but to bottle up your five senses and plunge into contemplation. While if you stick to consciousness, even though the same result is attained, you can at least flog yourself at times, and that will, at any rate, liven you up. Reactionary as it is, corporal punishment is better than nothing.

To move from Dostoyevsky to Leo Tolstoy is ostensibly to move from the world of the outsider to the dense concreteness of social reality; but in Tolstoy's works too there are disturbing and incessant evocations of absurdity. In *The Death of Ivan Ilyich* existential preoccupations become increasingly manifest as the civil servant, Ivan Ilyich, is forced by terminal cancer to break with the natural attitude that sustained him throughout his life. An agreeable marriage, promotions in his ministry, a "delightful house," expensive confectioners, the "best people": all the accoutrements of bourgeois living shield him from his own reality. He injures himself slightly. There follows a certain absent-mindedness, a bad taste in the mouth, an ache in his side. Ivan Ilyich visits the doctor, who tells him only what is "necessary and proper." At length a chill comes with despair; he sees that he is going to die. He thinks of

the old syllogism, "Caius is a man, men are mortal, therefore Caius is mortal"; and he thinks that what was correct about Caius—"man in the abstract"—cannot be true of him, "a creature quite, quite separate from all others." This is his awakening in the face of death. Suddenly he perceives his own loneliness and forlornness in a place where those he knows best are receding and becoming "other" to him. On the verge of dying (here compared with being thrust into a black sack), he begins to question and to think of choice: " 'What is the right thing?'," he asks. Aware of his family's wretchedness, he feels sorry and thinks that "he must act so as not to hurt them: release them and free himself from these sufferings." In some manner, he has come to be on the very brink of dissoulution, of a nothingness where there is only light.

There is Joseph Conrad also, with his continual emphasis upon the inscrutable and the ambiguous and the darkness. In *Heart of Darkness,* there is a remarkable confrontation between the man who has seen reality unmasked and those who persist in living submerged in everyday life. Marlow is sitting on a yawl in the Thames river at a gathering hosted by the Director of Companies; he is moved to tell his companions with their "stay-at-home" minds a yarn about his confrontation with the wilderness. Describing the journey down the silent African river, he tells of how he had to watch for sunken stones and peices of dead wood. And then: " 'When you have to attend to things of that sort, to the mere incidents of the surface, the reality— the reality I tell you—fades. The inner truth is hidden— luckily, luckily. But I felt it all the same; I felt often its mysterious stillness watching me at my monkey tricks, just as it watches you fellows performing on your respective tight-ropes for—what is it? half a crown a tumble—' " The effect of this is felt by the one man who is awake and who growls, " 'Try to be civil, Marlow,' " as if it were somehow impolite to disclose absurdity. Later, Marlow (having told of the death of the black helmsman, the way his shoes filled up with blood, and his flinging the shoes overboard) becomes more specific.

> "Absurd!" he cried. "This is the worst of trying to tell. . . . Here you all are, each moored with two good addresses, like a hulk with two an- chors, a butcher around one corner, a policeman round another, excellent appetites, and tempera- ture normal—you hear—normal from year's end to year's end. And you say, Absurd! Absurd be—exploded! Absurd! My dear boys, what can you expect from a man who out of sheer ner- vousness had just flung overboard a new pair of shoes!"

To have a normal temperature is to be impervious to the hidden, to the "immense jabber . . . without any kind of sense." It is to be like the manager with his lack of care and concern, the man who never gets sick—and who can never, therefore, see his own reality. To be sick is to expe- rience extremity "in an impalpable grayness, with nothing underfoot, with nothing around, without spectators, with- out clamor, without glory, without the great desire of vic- tory, without the great fear of defeat." To be sick is to know one's being in the world.

Being in the world, in reality; being *there:* this becomes the ground of what is rendered in imaginative literature with increasing frequency as the twentieth century moves on. Franz Kafka evokes the philosophy of Kierkegaard in his presentations of an impenetrable web of institutions, offi- cials, codes, and authorities. In *The Trial,* for example, K. has a job in a bank; he has identity papers; he believes he exists in an ordinary world and in an ordinary network of relationships. Once he is accused and held to be guilty, once he tries without avail to reach the Judge and the High Court, at least to find out of what he has been accused, he falls out of the world. Realizing, on some level, that he in unutterably alone and homeless, he comes in touch with the ground of his own being as he moves closer and closer to the quarry where he is scheduled to die. Yet here, as in *The Castle,* the short stories, and the *Letter to My Father,* there is a sense of something transcendent and unknow- able, something expressed in one of Kafka's parables:

> He is a free and secure citizen of the world, for he is fettered to a chain which is long enough to give him the freedom of all earthly space, and yet only so long that nothing can drag him past the frontiers of the world. But simultaneously he is a free and secure citizen of Heaven as well, for he is also fettered by a similarly designed heav- enly chain. So that if he heads, say, for the earth,

his heavenly collar throttles him, and if he heads for Heaven, his earthly one does the same. And yet all the possibilities are his, and he feels it; more, he actually refuses to account for the deadlock by an error in the original fettering.

This peculiar fettering, too, is part of the existential situa- tion at a particular moment of time. Kafka wrote in the letter to his father that he was absorbing "the negative ele- ment of the age in which I live, an age that is, of course, very close to me." And it may be that what we discover in so much of contemporary literature is itself a response to a historical situation, a peculiar "present age."

André Malraux defined himself openly and repeatedly within a particular historical situation as he developed his perception of the absurd. *Man's Fate* (*La condition hu- maine*) is in one sense a specific response to an age of polit- ical violence, when the Shanghai Revolution could con- vincingly serve as an emblem of a boundary situation at its most extreme. In another, more profound sense, how- ever, *Man's Fate* deals with the desperate predicament of men and women adrift in a wholly absurd universe. Each one confronts his or her fate, which may be nothingness or death or simply an inevitable catastrophe. Because the situation is so extreme, each character has no choice but to defy nothingness through action or through a type of mania. Each one (because he is neither "normal," bour- geois, or even prudent) must struggle for self-assertion in the void. Ch'en combats the blankness with terror and self-destruction. Kyo commits himself to human dignity and makes that commitment his personal fate. Katov creates his meaning in a heroism rooted in fraternity; Gi- sors withdraws into the distancing of opium dreams. Fer- ral defies nihilation with eroticism and the wielding of power; Clappique gambles, renders his own life a myth and a game. Malraux renders them all as irreducibly pri- vate persons and engages the reader with their inwardness. He shows them to be persons fiercely aware of the gulf be- tween their subjectivity and the violent public world in which they must act in order to be. At the end, some of them are transfigured: solitary individuals converge—at the cost of their lives—in an image of Mankind. Katov, having sacrificed his own cyanide to aid a wounded young comrade, walks towards his execution in the boiler of a lo- comotive with an utterly hopeless dignity. The revolution- ary cause has been lost. There remains only death for those who fought.

> He began to walk. Silence fell, like a trapdoor, in spite of the moans. The lantern threw Katov's shadow, now very black, across the great win- dows framing the night; he walked heavily, with uneven steps, hindered by his wounds; when the swinging of his body brought him closer to the lantern, the silhouette of his head vanished into the ceiling. The whole darkness of the vast hall was alive, and followed him with its eyes, step by step. The silence had become so great that the ground resounded each time his foot fell heavily upon it; all the heads, with a slight movement, followed the rhythm of his walk, with love, with dread, with resignation. All kept their heads raised: the door was being closed. A sound of deep breathing, the same as that of sleep, began

to rise from the ground: breathing through their noses, their jaws clenched with anguish, motionless now, all those who were not yet dead were waiting for the whistle.

Existential heroism is heroism on the edge of the precipice, when the abyss yawns inexorably and there is no reason left for hope, no rational justification for bravery. Katov's is the dignity of extremity, and those who follow him with their eyes achieve the only real communion possible in an empty cosmos: a lucid awareness of a predicament they share. Malraux had Blaise Pascal in mind when he named his book *La condition humaine.* Pascal said that the human condition could best be represented by picturing a number of men in chains, all condemned to death and being executed one by one before the others' eyes. In their fate the remaining ones could only see a reflection of their own condition. That was what it meant to exist, to be alive.

Indeed, this seems to be the buried assumption in many twentieth century works of literary art. Terrence Des Pres, discussing some of the exemplary ones, writes of an "ethos of survival in extremity" and of a need for a kind of heroism "commensurate with the vastness of desolation in our time." No one who recalls the death camps in Germany, the mental institutions in the Soviet Union, the decimated village societies in Vietnam, the mass expulsions, or the violence of repression around the world, can deny that people in many places live against incredible odds, with death always a condition of their lives. Nor can anyone easily deny that anything is possible in his or her own life.

Des Pres talks about a heroism of survival, of the miracle of mere existence; and he reminds his readers of the many novels which have recently explored the theme of how to survive as a dignified human being under atrocious, antihuman circumstances. This literary thematic would not have come to be were it not for an initial concern with the human condition in the existential sense—the human condition rather than human psychology, the human condition rather than the social plights of men. So there have been books like Albert Camus' *The Plague,* Alexander Solzhenitsyn's *The First Circle,* Ralph Ellison's *Invisible Man,* and Bernard Malamud's *The Fixer,* all dealing with victims of dehumanizing forces over which no one has complete control. They are not passive victims, however; they are people who struggle to move beyond their victimization, no matter how extreme, in order to keep faith with themselves as men. Dr. Rieux, in *The Plague,* may speak for most of them when he tells Tarrou (the "Saint without God"): " 'I don't believe in heroism; I know it's easy and I've learned it can be murderous. What interests me is living and dying for what one loves.' "

Significantly, Dr. Rieux also asserts that he has seen enough of "people who die for an idea" and that man is not an idea. This scorn of the abstraction is another existential theme which has begun to permeate twentieth century novels. In *A Farewell to Arms,* written after the First World War, Ernest Hemingway's Lieutenant Henry talks about how embarrassed he has already been by the words "sacred, glorious, and sacrifice." And then: "Abstract words such as glory, honor, courage or hallow were ob-

scene beside the concrete names of villages, the numbers of roads, the names of rivers, the numbers of regiments and the dates." This challenge to empty abstractions became a leitmotif in ensuing years; the determination to return to the concreteness and contingency of "things themselves" has found expression in diverse important ways. Writers ranging from Alain Robbe-Grillet in France to John Barth in the United States have tried in idiosyncratic ways to demonstrate how myths, symbols, and metaphors falsify reality by obscuring its contingency. Robbe-Grillet's *Le Voyeur* does without any patterns but those the reader can impose. The story presents what is seen by the murderer, whose fears, gestures, memories, and plans are rendered with neither depth, temporal dimension, nor interpretation of any kind. Implicit questions are raised with regard to literature itself, to novelistic form and language, to character and imagery. In John Barth's *End of the Road,* the questions are made explicit; indeed, the novel itself has to do with roles, masks, abstractions, and a parody of existentialism called "mythotherapy." Jake Horner, the hero of the book, is trying to overcome his "weatherlessness" with role-playing, but has become aware of the way in which myth and language both tend to obscure reality and disguise the "raggedness of things."

> Articulation! There, by Joe, was *my* absolute, if I could be said to have one. At any rate, it is the only thing I can think of about which I ever had, with any frequency at all, the feelings one usually has for one's absolutes. To turn experience into speech—that is, to classify, to categorize, to conceptualize, to grammarize, to syntactify it—is always a betrayal of experience, a falsification of it; but only so betrayed can it be dealt with at all, and only in so dealing with it did I ever feel a man, alive and kicking. It is therefore that, when I had cause to think about it at all, I responded to this precise falsification, this adroit, careful myth-making, with all the upsetting exhilaration of any artist at his work. When my mythoplastic razors were sharply honed, it was unparalleled sport to lay about with them, to have at reality. In other senses, of course, I don't believe this at all.

The book concludes with an ambiguous and tearful yearning on Jake's part for the opportunity to take responsibility. He does not know what to do now that Rennie (who was Joe Horner's wife but may have become pregnant through sleeping with Jake) is dead after her abortion. But the book itself is an indication that he did something called "scriptotherapy"; he wrote about what had happened and thereby tried to give it meaning. Like Roquentin in Sartre's *Nausea,* he realized somehow that life as it goes on moment to moment has no meaning; it only takes on meaning later, when one tells a story about it, gives it form and point. Also, one falsifies; but so do Malraux's characters when they sacrifice their lives for the "fates" they choose. There remains a tension, as the individual struggles for authenticity, for the kind of heroism that derives from confrontation *in person* of the world as it presents itself to consciousness.

Authenticity and dignity are both unthinkable if the individual agrees to subordinate himself to a system or to define his belonging by locating himself in a hierarchy. Part of the rebellion against abstraction in literature becomes a rebellion against systems, controls, fixities of all kinds. In a tragicomical dimension, the system may resemble Catch-22, which says (as an old woman in Rome tells Yossarian in Joseph Heller's novel) that "they have a right to do anything we can't stop them from doing." "They" may refer to circumstance in general, to the air force, to flying formations, to the syndicate, or to any rigid pattern imposed on the particularities of existence. Yossarian, unable to cope in any reasonable fashion with anti-human forces that confuse identification papers with individual identity, eventually abandons the system by deserting from the army. " 'I'm not running away from my responsibilities. I'm running *to* them. There's nothing negative about running away to save my life.' " In Thomas Pynchon's mysterious *V,* the enemy is the "Inanimate," automatism or entropy. The danger permeating the novel is "rockhood," or the inability to care. In William Burroughs's *Nova Express,* "Reality" itself is a pattern imposed by "a power primarily oriented towards total control," and men's only hope is to retake the universe by restoring the reality that existed before they were manipulated and narcotized.

These novels—and the many others which reiterate the same or similar existential themes—may be thought of as responses to a particular historical situation, now more than a century old. It is characterized by urbanization, industrialization, bureaucracies, technological regularities, manipulations, incipient violence, and the persistence of the "crowd." The only way to become a survivor in such a situation is to rebel against systematic controls and endeavor to see through—or to bracket out—conventional schemata in order to confront one's own naked reality. The novels which present such predicaments are, most often, not the work of existential philosophers or even the work of writers who proclaim an existential orientation. Nevertheless, they give evidence of an increasing prevalence of existential perspectives and phenomenological themes. They make those themes available for inward appropriation by readers capable of grasping them. And it would appear that imaginative literature of this sort can only fulfill its purpose if it is inwardly appropriated, if it enables readers to see more and thus to change their lives. "My task which I am trying to achieve," wrote Joseph Conrad, "is, by the power of the written word to make you hear, to make you feel—it is, before all, to make you see. That—and no more, and it is everything. If I succeed, you shall find there according to your deserts: encouragement, consolation, fear, charm—all you demand—and, perhaps, also that glimpse of truth for which you have forgotten to ask." (pp. 63-76)

> *Maxine Greene, "Literature, Existentialism, and Education," in* Existentialism and Phenomenology in Education: Collected Essays, *edited by David E. Denton, New York: Teachers College Press, 1974, pp. 63-86.*

Ihab Hassan

[*An Egyptian-born American educator and critic, Hassan has written extensively on twentieth-century fiction,* *particularly the Postmodernist novel. In the following excerpt, he considers the Existentialist antihero as embodying several conflicts present in modern culture.*]

The baffling contradictions of Existentialism, which its current faddishness in America must seem to aggravate, need not deter us from perceiving its relevance. Contradictions are sometimes put in the service of truth. That much Nietzsche knew. And it was Nietzsche who forecast the advent of nihilism in our century "because nihilism represents the ultimate logical conclusion of our great values and ideals—because we must experience nihilism before we can find out what value these 'values' really had." The recoil of the self in passion (from which new values may be created) and its extension in gratuitous actions which refer to no accepted norm (the need to act precisely because action is no longer intrinsically meaningful) constitute the means by which modern man is forced to cope with the fact of nihilism. Man reclaims the devil in him to transcend the death of God and escape the death of man, to become at once better and more evil than himself. This is an extreme measure, but so is our literature reputed to be a literature of extreme situations. This, too, is the ultimate meaning of individualism as Kierkegaard, playing a Christ to Nietzsche's Anti-Christ, saw it. "The crowd is untruth. Therefore was Christ crucified. . . . And hence every one who truly would serve the truth is *eo ipso* . . . a martyr." Between nihilism and sainthood, the modern self wavers, seeking still the meaning of life. In its concrete encounter with absurdity, with dread and the obscene corporeality of death, with mystical anarchy and organized nothingness, with abstract truth and experienced reality, the modern self discovers ways of affirmation that heroes of yore did not envision. For better or worse, man's fate is now a *human* fate; and as Camus said in his conclusion to the *Myth of Sisyphus,* "One does not discover the absurd without being tempted to write a manual of happiness." If Existentialism is a symptom of an industrial society in process of dissolution, the existential self which modern literature reveals is one that reaches out to new conditions while recoiling to preserve a radical kind of innocence.

The alienation of the self, its response in martyrdom or rebellion or both to the modern experience, has been briefly observed in history, in the body politic, in man's psyche, and in his existence. History predicts no salvation for man and accords no meaning retrospectively to his efforts. The dominant political trend of the age fortifies the collective and technical organization of society. Freudian psychoanalysis reveals that the antagonism between instinct and civilization is founded on the more hopeless opposition between love and aggression. Existentialist philosophy exposes the absolute nudity of the self in a world devoid of preconceived values or significance. Is it proper, then, to infer that what the world may face is not only an end to individualism but a breakdown of the human form itself? What the world faces ultimately depends on man's response to the destructive elements in his experience. Nowhere is that response more richly articulated than in the modern novel, to which we must now turn.

"In its essence literature is concerned with the self," Lionel Trilling writes in *Freud and the Crisis of Our Culture,* "and the particular concern of the literature of the last two centuries has been with the self in its standing quarrel with culture." The image of the self in its standing, and recently embittered, quarrel with culture—indeed in its quarrel with itself, as Mr. Trilling neglects to say—comes to focus in the figure of the anti-hero.

In fiction, the unnerving rubric "anti-hero" refers to a ragged assembly of victims: the fool, the clown, the hipster, the criminal, the poor sod, the freak, the outsider, the scapegoat, the scrubby opportunist, the rebel without a cause, the "hero" in the ashcan and "hero" on the leash. If the anti-hero seems nowadays to hold us in his spell, it is because the deep and disquieting insights revealed to us by modern literature often require that we project ourselves into the predicament of victims.

The gradual process of atrophy of the hero may have begun with Don Quixote, or perhaps even Job, Orestes, and Christ. It enters the critical phase, however, only late in the eighteenth century. Goethe's Werther introduces the "tragic" Romantic hero who, in his inordinate conception of himself, severs the traditional bond between the hero and his society, and points the way to such extreme stances of alienation as were to find expression in the Byronic and Sadist hero, in the gothic and demonic protagonist, in werewolf, ghoul, and vampire. But as the new bourgeois order, which the Romantic hero rejected, became a powerful social reality, the strategy of opposition changed. The characters of Stendhal, Balzac, and Flaubert often seem, as Raymond Giraud has recognized, "heroes of ironies" whose "ideals, desires, and feelings are in disharmony" with their "adult conception of reality." Similarly, the subtitle for *Vanity Fair: A Novel Without a Hero,* suggests that Victorian fiction was quietly disposing of the heroic protagonist. The ambivalences of a bourgeois hero in an overwhelmingly middle-class society raise for him problems of estrangement and communion, sincerity and simulation, ambition and acquiescence, which we recognize as the patent themes of the great novels of the last century. The wretched fate of the lower-class hero, caught between malignant Heredity and crushing Environment in the *roman experimental* of Zola, and in the less experimental but more benign novels of the brothers Goncourt, reflects the familiar bias of Naturalism and marks a further stage in the disintegration of heroism. Victim to immitigable "cosmic laws," with little or no control over his fate in the world, man turns inward again. The next development is predictable. "The way was open from the realist to the intimist novel," Mario Praz concludes in *The Hero in Eclipse in Victorian Fiction.* "Disillusioned observation of life as it really was, led to the eclipse of the hero and the disclosure of man's swarming interior world, made up of disparate and contradictory things."

With the retrenchment of the individual, the drama of good and evil which the hero and villain once objectified in society becomes blurred. The traditional forms of moral conflict are so internalized that no victory or defeat, where self is divided against itself, can claim to be more than pyrrhic. Cunningly introspective, the modern novel redefines the identity of its central character and redirects his energies toward the virtues of love or self-discovery, virtues that are a good deal more personal than social. To become someone, to know who or what one is, to reach finally another human being with love, and to do so in terms that society may censure, this is the passionate, bitter concern of the modern anti-hero. But the modern identity proved an elusive thing to capture. "You mustn't look in my novel for the old stable *ego* of the character," D. H. Lawrence wrote to Edward Garnett. "There is another *ego,* according to whose action the individual is unrecognizable, and passes through, as it were, allotropic states. . . ." A new shifty ego, a new concept of man. The sad history of the anti-hero is nothing more than the history of man's changing awareness of himself. It is the record of his recoil.

The encounter between the new ego and the destructive element of experience, we have insisted, lies at the dramatic center of the modern novel in Europe and America. The encounter is further illumined by some striking European images which define the modern idea of the self and clarify its responses. We shall view some concrete instances of the anti-hero—whom in hope and charity we may simply call "hero." These instances are taken from writers of very different age and background, yet they add to a remarkably persistent theme.

To consider Dostoyevsky's *Notes from Underground,* 1864, modern is perhaps to stretch the idea of modernity to its permissible limit. The document so shrill and anxious, so full of spite and spleen, reveals, in any case, what the modern soul likes most to gnaw upon: itself. The dagger is turned inward, the most refined tortures are reserved for the self. Whom else are we really interested in? Listening for forty years from the crack under his floor, Dostoyevsky's hero looks at existence with a cringe and a snarl. He knows the intense pleasure of degradation and of despair, and knows, while gnashing his teeth, that "there is no one even for you to feel vindictive against, that you have not, and perhaps never will have, an object for your spite. . . . " Precisely the condition which Albert Camus calls, in *The Rebel,* metaphysical rebellion, and which our hero understands as a revolt against "the whole legal system of Nature." But no one is to blame; "consequently there is only the same outlet left again—that is, to beat the wall as hard as you can." This frenzy is not only meant to be a protest against the whole order of Nature, the terrible fact that "every sort of consciousness . . . is a disease," or merely a protest against the historical enemies of Dostoyevsky—rationalism, meliorism, and science, the coxcomb fact that two plus two equals four. The frenzy, in the form of caprice, is also directed against our individuality. That Dostoyevsky's "insect" can establish his identity only by forcing himself to collide ignominiously with an arrogant officer who does not even recognize his existence is of no importance. The important thing is that it is *he* who *forces* the recognition. This is freedom.

The grotesque image of this strange creature haunts modern literature and remains at the center of our dread. Its cracked reflections in some way or other penetrate the works of most European novelists. And its perverse truths, almost insupportable, infiltrate recent American fiction which does not stem only, as Hemingway claimed, from a book by Mark Twain called *Huckleberry Finn* but also from another, it may be argued with equal pertinence, by Dostoyevsky called *Notes from Underground.* The image, taken up, modified, and recreated by later novelists deserves further attention.

Conrad, we know, shared with Dostoyevsky more than the dubious heritage of a Slavic temper. His metaphysical romances of the seven seas subject the idea of heroism to an ironic rhetoric which is peculiarly modern, and his abiding interest in the theme of the double—his *Secret Sharer* and Dostoyevsky's *The Double* come to mind— probes the distempers of the modern self in a way that seems now familiar. While no character of his strictly reminds us of the hero of the *Notes,* the state of immersion, the desperation felt in the heart of darkness or in the underground habitations of consciousness, the surrender to the "destructive element," compel our terrified assent in the novels of both authors. Kurtz, in *Heart of Darkness,* had perhaps immersed himself too deeply, there where victim and victimizer become one, till he could distinguish only the horror. But Kurtz creeping on all fours in the night-time jungle and Lord Jim erect and dazzling in spotless white are still two sides of the same image, two sides separated really by the enormous distance between action and heroic intention. Conrad does not repudiate human striving. In a celebrated passage from *Lord Jim* he simply points to the way of fulfillment. "A man that is born falls into a dream like a man who falls into the sea," Conrad writes. "If he tries to climb out into the air as inexperienced people endeavor to do, he drowns. . . . The way is to the destructive element submit yourself. . . ." The unintelligent brutality of existence leaves man no other choice.

It is, of course, the unintelligent brutality of existence that dominates the Dublin of Joyce's *Ulysses;* the city becomes a focus, in Eliot's famous words, to "the immense panorama of futility and anarchy which is contemporary history." The proportions of the hero are further shrunken, his self pushed further underground in the world of memory and fantasy. The element to which Bloom submits himself, in humor and humility, is the ignominious element. Insult and pathos, loneliness and failure, are his familiars. Leopold Bloom, wandering Jew, mock Odysseus, and lowly Christ, finally appears to us, above all, as "Everyman or Noman." He stands between Stephen Dedalus and Molly Bloom, between intelligence and nature, as a bathetic monument to the generosity of suffering. For intelligence, in the person of Stephen—he is Lucifer and Hamlet and Dedalus—can only cry: *Non serviam!* And Nature, in the person of Molly—Ceres, Hera, eternal Mother Earth— must endlessly murmur: Yes I will Yes. Man, meanwhile, goes clowning his sentimental way into eternity, unable to reconcile himself completely to one or the other.

The two heroes of Joyce and of Dostoyevsky show that humility lies on the other side of spite. But the clown in man has many disguises. He is Bloom, "one lonely last sardine of summer." He is also, as we shall see, an insect, a sentient tubercle, at best a shaggy wolf. The self in recoil cannot afford to be choosy.

Dostoyevsky's metaphor of man as an insect inevitably calls to mind Kafka's story, "Metamorphosis," in which the narrator is transformed into a huge, hideous, and pathetic vermin. This, too, is self-degradation, a form of the self in recoil. This, too, is protest. The theme is everywhere in Kafka, in *The Castle,* in *The Trial,* in "The Penal Colony" or "The Judgment." Man is always judged, and found invariably guilty. He is the victim of an unappeasable power, a horrible and recurrent outrage, and even in his most serene moments he can only exclaim, like the Hunter Gracchus: "I am here, more than that I do not know, further than that I cannot go. My ship has no rudder, and it is driven by the wind that blows in the undermost regions of death." The vision of man is as grotesque as that of Dostoyevsky; but it goes farther, denying man freedom, the sheer horror of choice, and denying him grace. Indeed, of man Kafka can only say, "He found the Archimedean point, but he used it against himself; it seems that he was permitted to find it only under this condition." The lever which gives man mastery over his universe, moving worlds at the touch of a finger tip, is still the inbred dagger of the soul. In Kafka as in Dostoyevsky, the sense of compounded guilt and absurdity defines the point at which victimization and rebellion meet.

This view of the human predicament will no doubt seem to many both exigent and extreme. It borders, people argue, on disease. Exactly. In the panoramic view of Thomas Mann, whose sane vision did not prevent him from cultivating a lifelong interest in Kafka and Dostoyevsky, disease and even death become an ultimate response to life. The idea informs at least two of his masterpieces, *The Magic Mountain* and *Death in Venice,* and it hovers about his latest work, *The Confessions of Felix Krull.* Hans Castorp reflects, as if prompted by the hero of Dostoyevsky's *Notes,* "Disease was a perverse, a dissolute form of life. And life? Life itself? Was it perhaps only an infection, a sickening of matter? . . . The first step toward evil, toward desire and death, was taken precisely then, when there took place that first increase in the density of the spiritual, that pathologically luxuriant morbid growth. . . ." But the radical disease of consciousness, which the hero of Dostoyevsky resented to the end of his spite, and to which the Kafka hero finally submits in a lucid nightmare, is transmuted by Thomas Mann into a condition of spiritual refulgence. It is thus that Mann is able to claim, with Nietzsche and Dostoyevsky in mind, that "certain attainments of the soul and the intellect are impossible *without disease, without insanity, without spiritual crime,* and the *great invalids* are *crucified victims,* sacrificed to humanity and its advancement, to the broadening of its feeling and knowledge—in short, to its more *sublime health* [italics mine]." Man, we see, pitches himself at the terrible limit of experience, as Lucifer did.

Mann's statement reminds us that grace, if it is to be found at all, lies deep in the soft core of violence. The saint and the criminal stand back to back on either side of the demonic. Both are protestants, both victims. But pure violence, like the demonic, has no reality in the public realm, the domain of action. Pure violence, as we shall repeatedly observe in modern fiction, seems almost the ultimate form of introspection. That the saint and the criminal, the suppliant and psychopath—they are conjoined in the recent literature of hipsterism and in such enduring figures as Greene's Pinkie and Faulkner's Christmas—partake of violence compulsively is no surprise. For untrammelled violence is not an act, it is merely a state; it is the experience of world negation. As Miss Arendt saw, the saint and the criminal are both lonely figures: " . . . the one being for, the other against, all men; they, therefore, remain outside the pale of human intercourse and are, politically, marginal figures who usually enter the historical scene in times of corruption, disintegration, and political bankruptcy. Because of its inherent tendency to disclose the agent together with the act, action needs for its full appearance the shining brightness we once called glory, and which is possible only in the public realm."

It is perhaps unnecessary to recover for our age the Corneillian idea of glory, but when the focus of moral energy moves so far from the center of human effort in the world, losing itself in the domain of holy silence or demonic violence, then it is time to give vent to our anxiety. The dissociation of action from intelligence, we remember, is manifest in Dostoyevsky's *Notes* whose hero openly condemns the active life. The consequences of this attitude are not limited to the cult of inactivity, living in a hole, like the man from underground, or in a jar like the hero of Beckett's *The Unnamable,* living, if you will, in the "packing-box shanty on the city dump" thoughtfully reserved by the editors of *Life* for our most promising novelists. The consequences also involve the alienation of the moral and artistic imagination from things of this world, often leading to a criminal state of autonomy.

The rebel-victim, we see, is also the outsider in search of truth. Harry Haller, in Hermann Hesse's *Steppenwolf,* is still an isolate genius of suffering "whose fate it is to live the whole riddle of human destiny heightened to the pitch of a personal torture, a personal hell." He is still grappling with the radical multiplicities of the human ego, oscillating not merely between two poles, such as the body and the spirit, the saint and the sinner, but between "thousands and thousands." In the "Treatise on the Steppenwolf," however, the outsider is finally made to reckon with the fact that man may be nothing more than a temporary agreement between warring opposites, nothing more, in fact, than "a bourgeois compromise"—such as Bloom!

The idea of man as a transient compromise in the universe entails the acceptance of permanent outrage. Harry Haller could find some redemption of that condition in love or art, or even in humor which reconciles all opposites, and in whose "imaginary realm the intricate and many-facted ideal of all Steppenwolves finds its realization." Other writers—Mauriac, Bernanos, Graham Greene—sought for their characters a solution more commensurate with their religious faith; for, as Colin Wilson has loudly noted, the problems of modern man, rebel, victim, or outsider, lend themselves to an intense religious apprehension which need not be specifically Christian. Yet even the Christian novelists, so Jansenist they seem in their insistence on human depravity, manage to convey only the terrible intricacies of damnation. Thus, for instance, is the pursuit of damnation conceived in *Brighton Rock* as an ap-

palling manifestation of the mercy of God. The modern Christian martyr, it seems, can aspire only to perdition.

To the religious and the humanist solutions of man's plight in the universe must be added the Existentialist. The basic question here is still one of freedom, the search for identity under the aspects of violence or alienation. Freedom, we recall, is known to the hero of the *Notes* only as caprice; he understands that men, himself included, must seek freedom and must be repelled and horrified by it. The same ambivalence haunts the quest of Kafka's characters. Beginning with Gide, however, the ambivalence is seemingly resolved in favor of positive action. Man asserts his liberty in a gratuitous act of murder, as in Lafcadio's case, in acts of social repudiation, or ruthless heroism, as in the case of Michel and Theseus. Freedom consists of revolt, against morality, against the social order, against history. But the blood-curdling price is one that only heroes and supermen can afford. In this direction, the Existentialist novelists go farther than Gide was willing to go, and their view is correspondingly more special. Victory, in their novels, depends on the certainty of defeat, *is* the process of defeat. But unlike the heroes of classical tragedy, their protagonists act in full foreknowledge of their fatality, act *only* in *despite* of that fatality. And there is never any reconciliation.

It is thus that Sartre understands man—a creature *condemned* to be free. Antoine Roquentin, in *The Nausea,* suffers from metaphysical disgust. His consciousness is like a decayed trap door through which the sordid impressions of his world endlessly sift. Nothing happens in his life, nothing begins or ends; Phenomena merely change, and Things, grotesque, obdurate, and unnamable, simply exist. Roquentin thinks: "I have only my body: a man entirely alone, with his lonely body, cannot indulge in memories; they pass through him. I shouldn't complain: all I wanted was to be free." Thinking is his game, the famous Cartesian proof of existence his plaything. In Kafka's work, as Erich Heller perceived, a cursed Intelligence asserts its omnipresence; the Cartesian formula becomes: "I think, and therefore I am not." Such negation of being is inadmissible to Sartre; the proper formula should read: "My thought is *me*. . . . At this very moment—it's frightful—if I exist, it is because I am horrified at existing." The change is less of an improvement than it may seem. For as Roquentin comes to believe, existence is nothing if not superfluous. Everything is *de trop,* everything is rooted in the Absurd, the irreducible condition of all reality. Man, we see, is not only a clown or a transient compromise, he is a contingency of existence. The way to true being, seldom realized, lies through Nausea.

Sartre's doctrine that existence precedes essence, carried to its atheistic conclusion, defines no limit to the idea of freedom and gives no value to the concept of being. Camus, a far more accomplished artist if not a more systematic thinker, starts with his "absurdist" philosophy of man and reaches, in *The Rebel* and *The Fall,* a more complex awareness of freedom. In his early novel, *The Stranger,* Meursault surrenders to the absurd, the destructive element, and loses his life, it seems, without ever finding it. In the following novel, *The Plague,* a small light of hope, even of redemption, flickers through the night of human victimization. Doctor Rieux says: "All I maintain is that on this earth there are pestilences and there are victims, and it's up to us, as far as possible, not to join forces with the pestilences. . . . I decided to take, in every predicament, the victim's side, so as to reduce the damage done. Among them, I can at least try to understand how one attains to the third category: in other words, to peace." To join the victims is an act of rebellion against and alienation from the prevalent norm. But such an act is never purely nugatory. "Rebellion," Camus wrote, "though apparently negative, since it creates nothing, is profoundly positive in that it reveals the part of man which must always be defended." Rebellion is therefore an aspiration to order, a means of lifting pain and evil from personal to collective experience. For the rebel-victim, the Cartesian argument par excellence is: "I rebel—therefore *we* exist [italics mine]."

The problem of the anti-hero is essentially one of identity. His search is for existential fulfillment, that is, for freedom and self-definition. What he hopes to find is a position he can take within himself. Society may modulate his awareness of his situation, but only existence determines his stand. The recoil of the modern self is its way of taking a stand. The retreat weakens its involvement in the living world. It leads it in the ways of violence and alienation, augments its sense of guilt and absurdity, and affords it no objective standard for evaluating the worth of human action. But living in the world exclusively, living in what Ortega y Gasset has called the Other, is also brutish and deadening. Complete immersion in the otherness of things is a ghastlier form of alienation: it is alienation from the self. "Without a strategic retreat into the self," Ortega rightly notes, "without vigilant thought, human life is impossible." It is precisely in fear of the Other—total loss of selfhood—that the modern conscience has fallen back on its internal resources. The schizophrenic goes too far in that direction, the rebel-victim remains in the field of our vision.

Camus' statement, "I rebel—therefore we exist," brings to surface a dialectic that has been implicit in all the works we have viewed. In its naked form, the dialectic can be seen as an interplay between the essential Yes and the radical No, two piercing utterances beyond which the human voice cannot rise. Such utterances may sometimes blend. It is only silence they equally abhor. In the modern novel, man seems to overcome the contradictions of his experience, its destructive or demonic element, by assuming the role of the anti-hero, the rebel-victim. The rebel denies without saying No to life, the victim succumbs without saying Yes to oppression. Both acts are, in a sense, identical: they affirm the human against the nonhuman. The figure of modern man, when he chooses to assert his full manhood, always bears the brave indissoluble aspects of Prometheus and Sisyphus—the eternal rebel and the eternal victim. The paradox is resolved when man cries, in the ringing words of Jaspers, "Although I am an anvil, as a hammer I can consummate what I must suffer." Sparks from the same anvil were struck when Christ said to his disciples, "For whosoever will save his life shall lose it;

and whosoever will lose his life for my sake shall find it." (pp. 19-32)

Ihab Hassan, "The Modern Self in Recoil," in his Radical Innocence: Studies in the Contemporary American Novel, *Princeton University Press, 1961, pp. 11-33.*

Maja J. Goth

[*In the following excerpt, Goth traces Existentialist themes in the work of Franz Kafka and explores Kafka's influence on Jean-Paul Sartre and Albert Camus.*]

The first Kafka translation was published in France in 1928. But before World War II Kafka was known only among the surrealists and in the Gallimard milieu. During the war of 1939 and especially during the post-war period Kafka's writings became a mirror of people's sorrows, anxieties, and sufferings. As Pierre Klossowski, one of Kafka's best translators and critics, put it, Kafka captivated people with the existential truth of his writings. What struck them particularly were the prophetic element and the atmosphere of anguish, subdued terror, and concentration camps. The Czech writer who died in 1924 seems to have foreseen the sufferings of his own people and of all the victims of Nazi Germany. The world he created is their world; those who survived are fascinated by this coincidence of experience and thought.

Therefore, a suitable climate for the reception of Kafka's works in France was created by historical circumstances. Sartre, while working out an ontology that deprives the world of all values and confronts man with nothingness, found in Kafka the confirmation of a fundamental world perception: the feeling of having been thrown arbitrarily into a world without essence. Sartre, with whom I spoke about Kafka in 1949, said at that time that one could not talk about an "influence" of Kafka on French writers of the post-war period, but rather of "rencontres," spiritual encounters which made them recognize themselves in certain aspects of his writings.

Nevertheless Sartre said that he himself had been deeply influenced ("profondément influencé") by Kafka. This might have been an overstatement expressing the admiration of a great writer for another whom he considered a model. But he went on to explain that it would be quite difficult to determine this influence since his conception of life was fundamentally atheistic while Kafka's was religious; therefore, he added, he had the tendency to laicize Kafka's world. Sartre's emphasis on the religious aspect of Kafka's writings was notable during our conversation. Kafka's world is deeply Israelitic, a mysterious world whose transcendence can be felt everywhere but can never be attained. Talking about surrealism and its affinity to Kafka, he remarked that the surrealist element of fantasy ("le fantastique") is of this world and therefore is accessible to the one who is receptive to it, whereas Kafka's fantasy is not immanent, but rather relates to a transcendent being. The surrealist concern with fantasy is much more bourgeois, he said, more French, while Kafka's is marked by a religious depth of Central European character. And Sartre added that Kafka's raw realism is corroded by fantasy; being becomes questionable. On the other hand, fantasy enriches Breton's reality with new experiences and turns it into a magical, but nevertheless actual, surreality.

Turning to the philosophical impact which Kafka's works had on him, Sartre pointed out that the Kafkan atmosphere gave him access to the world of Kierkegaard and Hegel. Generalizing his particular case, he said that the French had discovered Kierkegaard and Hegel through Kafka and that as late as 1949 Hegel's name barely appeared on the program of the "agrégation." Sartre stressed the influence which he thought Kierkegaard had had on Kafka. He quoted the episode of Amalia's rejection of Sortini's advances in *The Castle* and firmly adhered to Max Brod's interpretation of this passage: Amalia, like Kierkegaard's Abraham, is unable to take the existential leap, she dreads the absurd and therefore clings to ethical values and by doing so she fails to establish her Self. Thus Sartre sees Kafka as rooted in existential thinking. And Kierkegaard, who originated the philosophy of existence, is the common point of reference which helps to establish the affinity between Sartre and Kafka.

A common atmosphere of despair, emptiness, and absurdity prevails in the novels of both Kafka and Sartre. In these works there is no traditional predetermined system of values upon which man can rely, no metaphysical or ethical world whose authority he will accept. World War II and the post-war period leave Sartre's man all alone, in a world emptied of meaning. His metaphysical interrogation sends him back to his own subjectivity. But again he loses himself in a totally impersonal, technical world. His individuality is threatened with a loss of meaning; he becomes a mere cog in a machine the finality of which escapes him. Thus the return to his own Self reveals to him the privation of his Self; again he faces a void.

The experience of nothingness is the starting point for all three writers. Kierkegaard, in his conception of anguish, calls it "the immense nothingness of ignorance." Being conscious of nothingness, says Sartre, brings up the question of being.

> C'est la possibilité permanente du non-être, hors de nous et en nous, qui conditionne nos questions sur l'être.

Matthieu, Antoine Roquentin, all of Sartre's heroes, are questioners who try to avoid false affirmations and who are ready to go through the experience of nothingness. The same is true for Kafka's heroes. Without formulating precise questions they are nevertheless in a state of perpetual questioning.

Nothingness can be experienced as a threatening power which can submerge existence. . . . Kafka sometimes illustrates this loss of Self by using the experience of a plunge into the world of the lower animals. The animal symbolizes the degradation and deprivation of Self and, ultimately, the loss of Self. Man finds himself deprived of his uniqueness. He glides into a nameless vegetating state or changes into a mere insect as in the *Metamorphosis,* or again conceives himself as a dog, a mole or an ape right from the beginning. "I miss nothing except myself" Kafka wrote in 1911. Both Kafka and Sartre, then, experi-

ence the loss of what is essentially "I" as an estrangement from the body.

To feel alienated from the world and its objects, to feel alienated from one's Self, these are the manifestations of the process of nihilation. It begins in me and expands into my surroundings: I discover the world as being "fragile," I discover in it an "appearance of a permanent possibility of non-being." Nothingness "haunts being." Even objects are seized by this wave of instability. (pp. 51-4)

Since nothingness emerges from being, it was born within "me" and I carry it around with me. Nothingness is "au sein même de l'être, en son coeur, comme un ver" for Antoine Roquentin as well as for K. The world in which they live keeps its every day appearance, yet it is seen from a nihilating viewpoint; severed from the order of casuality impressed upon it by society, it suddenly shows its reverse side. The world shows a face hitherto unknown to the hero: vanishing, incoherent, and gratuitous. Bouville in the fog, the café Mably, Antoine's hotel room—everything becomes diffuse in Antoine's eyes, everything has lost its *raison d'être*. Antoine is perfectly conscious of this change within himself. "Quelque chose m'est arrivé, je ne peux plus en douter" he says, and, as he scrutinizes himself, he comes to discover what causes the vanishing of meaningful reality. K., on the other hand, never thinks of analyzing himself. His world does not change, for it is incoherent from the very beginning. Antoine comes upon the fundamental gratuity of being, K. finds himself in the midst of it. The awakening of Joseph K. in *The Trial* or of Gregor Samsa in *The Metamorphosis* shows man faced with the *fait accompli*. This shady world of a court in the attic and of administration offices in *The Castle* is there. He does not question it; he needs all his strength to cope with it. Although Roquentin and K. share the same experience, Sartre's ontological preoccupation always interrupts the narration with philosophical reflection. Antoine not only illustrates the experience of being; he also gives a critique of the structure of being. K. is, on the contrary, completely absorbed by the experience and therefore desists from any analytical attempt to cope with it. Roquentin and K. live their alienated existence in an alien world. They are unmarried, lonely, friendless, they live in a furnished room. They are in effect outlaws—outsiders. Roquentin accepts his status, but K. tries to find his way back into society.

Kafka's conception of nothingness has religious connotations when he evokes absolute authority: the supreme judge in *The Trial* and the Lord in *The Castle*. God and nothingness then would come to synthesis, as in the cabala and the writings of the mystics. Kafka has read the cabala and Master Eckhardt. However, his fusion of God and nothingness lacks the emotional implication of the mystics, for their *unio mystica* means blissful solution of all opposites in God and complete abandonment of the Self in its union with God. Kafka's nothingness seems often to identify itself with non-value, with moral negativity comparable to Plato's coordination of truth and being, error and non-being. Kafka's nothingness corrodes and caricatures the image of God so that God becomes an ambiguous force, half God, half demon. K. never sees him or even perceives him because God is absent, remote—an abstraction in the abstract. But his power is nevertheless omnipresent. He supposedly dwells in a castle-like, ridiculously shaped building or appears as a supreme judge in a painting. K. will never attain him; it is even suggested that He does not exist. Yet this non-being is almighty, and K. cannot withdraw from it. He accepts its power a priori.

Before giving in, however, K. struggles with this negative deity. Like Job, he would like to know the cause of his suffering. He is ready to endure this anguish if God can justify its necessity. Should his suffering be unfounded, it would mean that he simply had to surrender to the arbitrariness of God. And like Job, he is unable to accept this. But whereas Job finally recovers his faith and trusts God's wisdom, K. is unable to believe in God. He persists in reflecting upon the ethical meaning of the divine will and requires from God the justification of his *ens absconditus.* He tries to oppose God by negation, but his efforts are in vain. God persists and the nothingness K. invokes turns against him.

This is the religious aspect of Kafka's nothingness. It is, of course, totally absent from Sartre's thought.

Nothingness or non-being is at the root of that anxiety so peculiar to Kafka and Sartre. How can one defend oneself against non-being? How can one fear it? Non-being could not inspire fear—it would be a fear without object. It can only inspire anguish, which is precisely, as Kiekegaard defines it, fear of nothing.

Anguish is a fundamental disposition of Kafka's and Sartre's thought; Kierkegaard calls it a "fundamental tonality." It "distinguishes itself from fear by the fact that fear is fear of world beings and anguish refers to myself," says Sartre referring to Kierkegaard. Anguish reveals to man that he is separated from his essence by nothingness. He becomes conscious of the fact that he is free. (pp. 55-6)

The fear of nothing is an "angoisse devant moi-même," a realization of one's freedom.

Unlike Sartre's, however, Kafka's anguish implies guilt. Anguish is a fundamental mood, a *Grundstimmung,* as Heidegger defines it; Kafka simply adds to it the sense of guilt. By fearing guilt, Kafka's heroes become guilty. Anguish related to sin gives birth to sin. Because K. is afraid to be pronounced guilty, he is also afraid of becoming guilty. So the "rien" of anguish is not "rien" anymore; it is fault, it is sin. And it is in this religious sense that Kafka's conception of anguish is closer to Kierkegaard's than to Sartre's. *Any* first sin, not just that of Adam, brings sin into the world, Kierkegaard says in his *Concept of Anguish.*

Kierkegaard's existential meditation is centered around the notion of anguish. He shows that fault originates from that specific psychological condition that is anguish. Original sin could not be the object of a scientific analysis: it defies any ethical definition since it is the exception in the causal system of knowledge of fault and repentance. Original sin is beyond knowledge. And that is precisely what Kafka wants to express by creating guilt in characters who are not guilty of specific crimes. Sin cannot be grasped.

The qualitative element of Adam's sin consists of the fact that sin came into the world through a sin. Reason finds it difficult to grasp this idea since it implies the consequence that fault is self-implied. When he sinned, Adam simply entered the chain of being and by doing so assumed his human destiny.

This predetermination of existence by *peccabilitas* is the foundation of Kierkegaard's thought. Likewise in Kafka it is the point of departure of existence. To exist, for Kierkegaard and Kafka, means to live in relation to guilt. Joseph K. knows that he is guilty. His quest for justice stems from the desire for clarification concerning the condition of the sinner, a condition which fatally must be his. The possibility of existence depends entirely on man's ability to reconcile the Self with its propensity to sin. This will constitute the foundation of the "être-soi." Kierkegaard's "qualitative leap" realizes the "être-soi" by establishing the transition from innocence to guilt.

This substitution of fault for nothingness is peculiar to the Judeo-Christian psyche. Therein fault is directly related to anguish: it attracts man; it arouses in him the desire to sin and, at the same time, the fear of sin. Consequently, the religious person will always be driven by the need to redeem his fault and to sacrifice himself. He is subject to masochism or inclined to cultivate a methodical asceticism; in both cases he submits to his desire for self-punishment. Kierkegaard and Kafka are both marked by a tendency to torment themselves and take an ascetic approach to life. As for Kafka's heroes, they are literally eaten by inner suffering. Joy does not even present itself to them as a possibility.

The awakening of Joseph K. at the beginning of *The Trial* symbolizes the awakening of the Self. The moment he opens his eyes, his being is called into question. He thinks himself guilty and he feels anguish. His first reaction is to escape. He concentrates on everyday work and his professional life as he tries to pretend that nothing has happened. But at the same time he tries to put his life in order under the law by finding out where the court of justice is located, for he must prove his innocence. Hoping to be justified, he puts the law into motion. Finally, he must acknowledge that he is unable to satisfy the postulate of the quest of Self. The dizziness produced by his looking into the abyss of nothingness (that is, the abyss of guilt) overcomes him. Again, in the *Metamorphosis,* the sudden knowledge of Gregor's own Self is so monstruous that he cannot accept it. He tries to escape into his past by clinging to the memory of his fulfilled obligations. But in the end the unveiling of his guilt, now symbolized by the metamorphosis of his body, is so overwhelming that he is annihilated.

What is the attitude of these anguished heroes towards existence? The mechanism of "bad faith" which directs negation upon the Self, the "mensonge à soi" as Sartre calls it, helps man to avoid facing his own truth. The duplicity of being, that is to say, the division of being between "être-pour-soi" and "être-pour-autrui" permits the evasion of the Self from the "pour-soi" to the "pour-autrui." In trying to establish the Self being-in-itself, one avoids facing nihilation; one believes that one is what one is. To believe that one can hold onto being means to yield to the need

Dust jacket for the first edition of Franz Kafka's A Hunger Artist.

to fill the void and escape anguish, to free oneself from one's fragility, to believe in one's essence.

Antoine Roquentin is Sartre's prototype of good faith. He remains entirely clairvoyant as far as his condition of existing is concerned. He accepts the oscillation of being between stability and instability; he agrees to live in anguish, in nausea. But the affirmation of this ontological factuality requires a rupture with all traditional values. Neither science nor the framework of a structured society nor religion nor any other established value can protect him from his anguish. If any one could, it would have become to him an absolute value to which he conformed in order to escape anguish. He would have exchanged his freedom for these values and would have given up his responsibility.

Like Erostrate or Pedro in *Le mur,* Antoine is lucid. But Pierre in *La chambre* uses his mental illness in order to avoid the deceitful world of the righteous. His morbid asceticism is a finality in itself. Because Pierre believes in its essence, he fails to achieve his freedom. The same is true for Kafka's fasting champion [in "A Hunger Artist"] who, locked up into his cage, thinks that in his world of total abstinence he possesses being. To him abstinence is the magic way of attaining *être-en-soi,* just as remaining day

and night on a trapeze is absolute being to the acrobat in "First Sorrow." (pp. 58-61)

The absurd is the meeting point of Kafka, Sartre, and Camus. The absurd determines the lives of Roquentin, Meursault, and K.; it is part of the banalities of their every-day lives. However, the absence of anguish differentiates Camus' *absurdum* from that of Kafka and Sartre. The Supreme Judge has no place in Camus' world. For his part, Kafka is miles away from Meursault's delights in the pleasures of the sea and the earth.

Camus expressed his views on Kafka's novels in the appendix to his *Myth of Sisyphus.* He compared Kafka and Dostoevsky as the only writers who dared envisage the problem of the absurd. Camus stressed first of all the natural quality of Kafka's absurd, which is the presupposition of its authenticity. In Camus this quality is obvious, for nothing in his works transgresses the rational; there is no fantasy, no oneirie vision, no escapade of the imagination. Sartre has pointed out that incoherence in Camus derives from a technique that registers gestures in their appearance only, gestures deprived of meaning. In addition, each action is seen separately in a strange extra-causal isolation. There is a glass wall between the characters in the novel and the reader: "on l'a construite de telle sorte qu'elle soit transparente aux choses et opaque aux significations." There are frequent irrational moments in Kafka: fantasy and dream are not excluded from his universe. Likewise, a supernatural and absurd power intervenes in the destiny of his protagonists. But Kafka's sobriety of style, his moderate presentation of fantasy, and the trivial appearance of his characters lend the most extraordinary happenings an air of naturalness which is strange only to the reader, not to the characters themselves, for whom the absurd is as natural as the air they breathe. In the final analysis, Meursault's arrest is as "natural" as Joseph K.'s: it is the consequence of the encounter with the absurd which for Meursault results in a gratuitous action and for K. in the confrontation with the absurd transcendance.

The extraordinary element in the midst of natural phenomena characterizes the absurd in art. The absurd dwells in every-day reality: "l'esprit projette dans le concret sa tragédie spirituelle," Camus says. Fantasy and concrete reality alternate constantly in the same way as "le naturel et l'extraordinaire," "le tragique et le quotidien, l'absurde et le logique." The two worlds exist side by side; it is the function of absurd art to make them coincide, and Kafka's art certainly succeeds in doing so.

Camus understands the function of the work of art to be a description of the writer's conscious experience— sentimental, spiritual, or physical:

> l'oeuvre est alors la chance unique de maintenir
> sa conscience et d'en fixer les aventures.

The event lived is stressed at the expense of interpretation. According to Camus, experience subjected to intellectual analysis is no longer authentic; therefore, writing must duplicate experience. The artist is not to explain it or try to give it a solution. His function is "d'écrire en images plutôt qu'en raisonnements." Camus refuses to consider the work of art as a symbol since the work must not contain any solution. If it is a symbol, then it must be a silent or a polyvalent symbol. It does not mean anything; yet it means everything. The work of art itself, then, "is a phenomenon of the absurd."

In this sense, Kafka is a novelist of the absurd. He is a philosopher as, according to Camus, all great novelists are philosophers; his thought examines concrete experience and tries to enlighten it, not systematically, but with images. The reader then, will understand that each attempt at elucidation is meant to prod him forever into renewed interpretations. If a work has symbolic meaning it invites a plurality of interpretations. A symbol transcends not only its author's intentions but also his consciousness. As Camus writes, a symbol reveals the author's Self to him and at the same time leads the reader to enlarge upon its contents. The reader is aware of the variety of possible interpretations; therefore, while elaborating his own, it is himself he finds in it. Thus, the absurd is a risk for authors and readers alike. For to create and to interpret art is to commit oneself.

Critics have maintained highly controversial views about Kafka. They have seen in him an obsession with God and total atheism, a gratuitous phenomenology and a vigorous symbolism, a cabalistic thinker and a mental patient trying to liberate himself from his anxieties. Kafka has served all his commentators. But he probably would have been at a loss to give us the key to *The Trial* or to *The Castle,* for there simply is no key; there are only different approaches.

Like all artists, Kafka creates his own atmosphere, which remains the same throughout his work. In this sense, Camus concludes, Kafka is certainly a creator of the absurd. He repeats his interior experience, he subjects it to the penetration of thought without, however, holding it to any one single explanation. "La pensée abstraite rejoint . . . son support de chair" in any great creator, whether novelist or philosopher. Passion, not a given system, directs thought.

At this point, it is pertinent to ask whether Camus himself followed his theoretical model. *L'étranger* is indeed a novel that does not explain; it describes and estranges. When seen in the light of the *Myth of Sisyphus* however, it becomes transparent. The novel is the application of the theory of the absurd. The incoherent and unrelated facts convey the gratuity of existence, the opacity of reality, a taste for a great variety of experiences, and the abolition of all values and of causality. Each sentence is part of the structure of the absurd. Consequently, as Sartre points out: "*L'étranger* est une oeuvre classique, une oeuvre d'ordre, composée à propos de l'absurde et contre l'absurde." Camus' novelistic world is beyond intelligibility but the key to it lies in the *Myth of Sisyphus,* where the logical substructure of *L'étranger* and the necessity for the absurd are revealed. *L'étranger* is a novel in which practice illustrates theory. As such, it is both a service and a disservice to the cause of the absurd. Kafka has not, however, written a *Myth of Sisyphus;* therefore, despite his passion for logic, his novels must remain opaque. Since there is no key to them, Kafka is essentially more a creator of the absurd than is Camus, the theoretician of the absurd.

But Camus sees a loophole in Kafka's system of the absurd. While *The Trial* posits the problem of absurdity by making evident the absurd condition of man. *The Castle* offers a solution to it. Joseph K. drowns in anxiety caused by irrational guilt and the remoteness of the elusive Judge. On the other hand, K. will find divine grace in the Lord of the castle. Grace will put an end to the absurdity of his being. Camus here adopts Max Brod's hypothetical ending of Kafka's unfinished novel. He compares Kafka to Kierkegaard and blames him for having betrayed the *absurdum.* Kafka, like Kierkegaard, opts for "the deification of the absurd"; he escapes from the absurd by taking the "leap."

Kafka's critics have pointed out many times that Max Brod's interpretation is inconsistent. There is indeed a pronounced continuity in *The Trial* and *The Castle.* Joseph K. is condemned, K. is outlawed; in both novels the presence of Authority, unnamable and transcendental, is equally powerful, equally absurd, and consequently, equally revolt-provoking. Camus demands that man revolt against the capacity of his condition:

> l'absurde n'a de sens que dans la mesure où l'on n'y consent pas.

But in order to maintain the permanence of revolt, the motivating force of such revolt must be constantly preserved. Therefore, revolt is in this sense self-consuming and sterile; it leads to a state of non-revolt which is acceptance:

> Il s'agissait précédemment de savoir si la vie devait avoir un sens pour être vécue. Il apparaît au contraire qu'elle sera d'autant mieux vécue qu'elle n'aura pas de sens. Vivre une expérience, un destin, c'est l'accepter pleinement.

Is it possible, however, to fulfill the absurd requirement of revolt and acceptance at one and the same time? Just as Camus found a loophole in Kafka's system, might one not find a loophole in Camus' position at his point? A revolt which contains its own finality is also an escape from the absurd in the sense that it ceases to be a revolt. However this may be, revolt for the sake of revolt is certainly less exhausting than Kafka's revolt against a paradoxical and cruel Authority. In fairness to Camus, it might be well to mention here that, after the *Myth of Sisyphus,* he changed his views on the nature of revolt and gave it an ethical content.

To conclude, Sartre and Camus have recognized themselves in Kafka. They have been especially drawn to Kafka's figuration of absurdity, nothingness, and anguished freedom. And, finally, they have admired the authenticity of his existential commitment as a writer. (pp. 65-8)

Maja J. Goth, "Existentialism and Franz Kafka: Jean-Paul Sartre, Albert Camus, and Their Relationship to Kafka," in Proceedings of the Comparative Literature Symposium: Franz Kafka, His Place in World Literature, *Vol. 4, 1971, pp. 51-69.*

Richard Lehan

[In the following excerpt, Lehan examines the influence of Existentialist fiction on American novelists.]

Jean-Paul Sartre has commented on the literary debt that he and Albert Camus owe the American novel. Sartre has outlined the influence Hemingway had on Camus' *L'étranger* and the effect of Dos Passos' *U.S.A.* on Sartre's own *Les chemins de la liberté* (*The Roads to Freedom*). Thelma Smith and Ward Miner as well as Claude Magny have called detailed attention to the popularity of American fiction in France after the Second World War. No one, however, has yet attempted to demonstrate the influence the postwar French novel has had on new American novelists. Paul Bowles, for example, has translated Sartre's *Huis clos* (*No Exit*) for the Broadway stage. Bowles has attached the same emotional and intellectual significance to North Africa as has Camus, and uses this scene in a way remarkably similar to the way Camus uses it in his fiction. Moving to Paris in 1946, Richard Wright has come under the direct influence of Sartre, who published part of Wright's *Black Boy* in *Les temps modernes,* a literary and philosophical journal edited by Sartre. Cross Damon, the hero of Wright's *The Outsider,* uses an existential jargon and acts out of obvious existential motives. Recent novels by Ralph Ellison and Saul Bellow also seem to employ an existential hero in search of existential values.

Yet the problem is not entirely one of influence. The influence of Continental fiction on Bellow and Ellison is most remote, and it would be indeed difficult to prove that they have written conscious existential fiction. The problem is more one of an affinity of mind or spirit. The Americans are preoccupied with the same problems and themes that fascinate and puzzle the French writers. Sartre, Camus, Bowles, Bellow, Wright, Ellison—all are concerned with the meaning of identity in the modern world, the nature of good and evil, the possibility of fulfilment in the contemporary society, the source of values in a world without God, and the possibility and meaning of action in an ethical vacuum. The new American hero is similar to the French existential hero because he shares a common world and a similar world view. (pp. 63-4)

No one has illustrated the tenets of existential philosophy better than Paul Bowles. The principal characters in *The Sheltering Sky,* Bowles' first novel, are Port and Kit Moresby, both ineffectual and overcivilized Americans who discover new depths of being after several months of primitive life in the desert. The novel functions in terms of Camus' vital universe and Sartre's theories of consciousness. It reveals Camus' belief in the destructive power of creation and Sartre's belief in the destructive nature of self-fulfilment. The novel takes place in Camus' North Africa, in and around the borders of the Sahara. The land is completely antihuman: the sun burns without mercy; the sky cracks with heat; the wind singes the skin like a gust from a blast furnace; and the red earth burns like an ember of molten lead. These elements are manifest extensions of the destructive powers lying behind the protective shield of the sky. The sky is a thin veil protecting man from the cosmic violence beyond; it "shelters the person beneath from the horror that lies above." Port and Kit find new depths of being in an elemental contact with the desert before they are eventually consumed by the vital but destructive forces that sustain life.

Port's death functions in a dual capacity—symbolic and structural. Attempting to transcend the human condition, he refused to recognize the reality of death; he also founded his existence upon a cold antihumanism, "was unable to break out of the cage into which he shut himself, the cage he had built long ago to save him from love." It is dramatically appropriate that Port dies of meningitis, shaken with chills. The chills are the objective equivalent of his cold antihumanism, his impersonal being. In *The Plague* Father Paneloux died a "metaphysical death." Port also dies of the plague to demonstrate an existential truth—that one cannot be so completely self-contained that he can transcend physical reality or be protected from the malevolent element that lies beyond the sheltering sky. Port's death also has a structural significance. Since Kit relied completely on Port, she is suddenly thrown totally upon herself. When this happens, she becomes aware of the absurd, the gratuity of her existence, the "sudden surfeit of time, the momentary sensation of drowning in an element become too rich and too plentiful to be consumed, and thereby made meaningless." Kit desires to exist within Sartrean states of mutually destructive being—to maintain a free yet rocklike consciousness, to live within the world but outside of death, to possess the joys of sensual being in a state of godlike eternality. Her quest functions within the existential vocabulary, its dramatic pattern, and its tragic finale. As Sartre would explain it, she tries to push her freedom to a form of perfect completion; she desires to be one with pure consciousness and yet still be one with a sensual world, to be pure thought and pure sensation at the same time, to be both in and out of the world. As a result she becomes so self-involved that the delicate balance between consciousness and reality gives way to an extreme form of dementia. As Camus would put it, Kit finds new regions of sensual being only by becoming one with the universe and establishing a contact with the element that ultimately destroys her sanity.

Let It Come Down, Bowles' second novel, repeats almost exactly the general pattern of action in *The Sheltering Sky* and also functions within terms of a destructive and demonic element. Nelson Dyar (the surname hints at an element of the demonic suggesting "dare" and "desire") comes to Tangier to escape the limitations of life in America. He also finds a new life in a physical and elemental relationship with the natural life. Although Dyar wants to be the sole source of his being, he lives in anguish, knowing that existence is completely fluid and unfixed. He attempts to secure a rigidity of being—first by stealing Jack Wilcox's money and then by murdering the Arab Thami—through acts of commitment so extreme that they transfix his being in relation to himself and the world. The scene that leads Dyar to this extreme action has most remarkable parallels to the beach scene in *The Stranger.* One morning as Dyar walks down a sun-drenched beach, he feels an explicit kinship with the world. He is suddenly at one with the universe. His very breath becomes part of the wind; the natural life "cleanses" him and washes away his bitter futility; his strength "came out of the earth, nothing which would not go back into it. He was an animated extension of the sunbaked earth itself."

As we have seen, Meursault also incarnates the universe and becomes a very extension of a destructive element when he murders the Arab. Since Dyar and Meursault are both sensual neopagans, both are primitivists who refuse to go beyond the world of matter; both maintain a completely unilateral view of life; one act, one situation, has no more meaning or importance than the next. "The whole of life does not equal the sum of the parts," Dyar maintains. "It equals one of the parts; there is no sum." Life is purposeless; existence has no meaning outside of itself. There is no grand design, no transcendent justification. Dyar and Meursault make no attempt to restrain their actions in this ethical void. By refusing to limit their extreme action, they become complicit with the destructive element, immersed in an evil which eventually consumes them.

Let It Come Down takes its title from the rain that continues to fall throughout the story. The rain—along with the wind, the sun, the violent sea—is the dramatic incarnation of the unseen forces which constitute the conditions hostile to man. The desire of the beetle to destroy the ant is only "infinity in a grain of sand." Dyar wants to be so self-involved that nothing from this hostile world can harm him. To use Sartre's vocabulary, he desires to be his own *causa sui*—pure being and pure consciousness at one and the same time. After he has stolen Wilcox's money, Dyar flees with Thami to a small Arab town, high in the Spanish mountains, where they find sanctuary in Thami's small cabin. As Dyar tries to sleep at night, the wind bangs the door back and forth. The rattling door reminds him of outside reality: "the loose door was equivalent to an open door. A little piece of wood, a hammer and one nail could arrange everything: the barrier between himself and the world outside would be much more real." The next night—thoroughly fortified with *kif,* exhilarated by vicarious participation in a frenetic native dance—Dyar is again awakened by the banging door. He gets up to drive a nail into the door—instead he drives the nail into Thami's head. With this drastic act, Dyar bolts the door between him and humanity and seals himself within his own consciousness: "his existence, along with everything in it was real, solid, undeniable . . . he was conscious of the instantaneous raising of a great barrier that had not been there a moment before, and now suddenly was there, impenetrable and merciless." At this moment Dyar incarnates the absurd and becomes the source of his own being—a modern satanic hero, an avatar of malevolence driven by essentially demonic motives to be his own *causa sui.* Now outside the realm of humanity, his being has all the fixity of death. Like other existential heroes Dyar destroys himself at the moment he fulfills himself.

The Spider's House, Bowles' latest novel, has oblique parallels to Camus' *The Plague.* The novel takes place in Fez, at the time in a virtual state of siege. Morocco is being torn in half by two factions, the relentless French colonialists and the greedy Istiqlal nationalists. Like Camus' Oran, the stock way of life has been violently interrupted, the old order has suddenly given way, and the individual is forced to construct a new way of life in an extreme and absurd world that has no moral base or center. As in Camus' fiction, the suffering and violence in Fez has no meaning outside of itself and is meant to be taken as an indivisible part of the total human condition. Again, as in Camus' fiction, the world of Bowles is without causal links. Existence is completely gratuitous. An object has no meaning except in and for itself. As the protagonist, John Stenham, puts it, this is a world of "and then" rather than of "because"; "one thing doesn't come from another thing. Nothing is the result of anything." A world without links defies coherence. Since the world of Fez is both irrational and malevolent, it is by necessity absurd. In this cause *The Spider's House* is an oblique commentary on the psychological state of mind that motivated action in Bowles' earlier fiction. Port and Kit Moresby and Nelson Dyar sought protection from the absurd forces around them within the well of consciousness. John Stenham tells Lee Veyron that the populace of Morocco also wants to dissociate itself from "the whole world outside [which] is hostile and dangerous." Camus and Sartre never carried their concept of the absurd to the extreme conclusions of Bowles, but it certainly seems evident that the existentialists and Bowles start out with the same general premise and that there is an explicit relationship between their two orders of fiction.

The relationship between Saul Bellow and French existentialism is more difficult to determine precisely. Yet *Dangling Man,* Bellow's first novel, is very similar to Sartre's *Nausea* and Camus' *The Stranger.* Joseph, Bellow's hero, is suddenly tumbled out of a comfortable way of life when he receives an induction notice from his draft board. While Joseph knows he will eventually be called into the army, his immediate induction is postponed and he is left dangling. Joseph resembles Meursault and Roquentin in many ways: he is a minor clerk (like Meursault); initially he is caught up in the stifling ritual of daily activity; he is most susceptible to physical stimuli; he is an empiricist; he lives in a world divested of ends; he grows from philosophical innocence to a state where he questions the nature of creation and human existence; he records this progress in a journal (like Roquentin). In sum, *Dangling Man* follows the dramatic pattern of *The Stranger* and *Nausea*—reveals an innocent mind coming in contact with the absurd and portrays the effect this has on the hero and his relationship with others.

In *The Myth of Sisyphus* Camus outlined the psychological process that precedes and follows awareness of absurdity. Joseph develops in relation to this pattern. He is caught up initially in the mechanical pattern of daily activity; his induction notice suddenly interrupts this routine; life thereupon is robbed of all meaning. Joseph begins to live at a distance from the world, outside the realms of ordinary men, carrying the full weight of his undirected existence. " 'I am forced,' he says, 'to pass judgments on myself and to ask questions I would far rather not ask: "What is this for?" and "What am I for?" and "Am I for this?" My beliefs are inadequate, they do not guard me.' " Like Meursault and Roquentin, Joseph journeys a path of continued anxiety. His quest for identity takes him outside the order of men to a point of self-autonomy so complete that he almost is unable ever again to accept his original world view, to return to society, or to reaffirm his initial identity.

Meursault and Roquentin are unable to find any meaning in the communal life. Joseph also rejects the order of men when, at Mitta's party, he suddenly realizes that his friends band together for mutual protection, behave the way the group expects them to behave, assert the group values, scorn all that is outside the clique, and ridicule all that threatens the general definition. He also rejects his materially minded brother, Amos, and Amos' daughter, Etta. Joseph even begins to reject Iva, his wife, who is sympathetic but not really understanding of his sudden deracination.

Joseph's disillusionment in people prefaces his disillusionment with the whole nature of creation; the world suddenly becomes a very indifferent thing, and he is no longer willing to live in a passive relationship with it. "The world comes after you," he says, and there is a "feeling of strangeness, of not quite belonging to the world at large." An indifferent world precludes a beneficent and personal God, and Joseph asserts that "there are no values outside of life. There is nothing outside of life." Joseph rejects God for the same reasons as do Meursault and Roquentin; he insists that God is born out of "a miserable surrender . . . out of fear, bodily and imperious . . . I could not [he says] accept the existence of something greater than myself."

Once he has rejected society, the world, and God, Joseph, like all existential heroes, longs for the purity of the completely self-contained existence, the very internal necessity of an art object. "We need," he says, "to give ourselves some exclusive focus, passionate and engulfing." In *Nausea* Roquentin is fascinated by a jazz tune, "Some of These Days," he hears on a phonograph in the café, Railwaymen's Rendezvous. He longs for the constituted fixity of an art form. "When the voice was heard in the silence," he says, "I felt my body harden and the Nausea vanish. Suddenly: it was almost unbearable to become so hard, so brilliant . . . the music . . . filled the room with its metallic transparency, crushing out miserable time against the walls." Without transcending the human condition, the music unifies a shapeless reality, orders a discordant flux of time, and lends intensity and meaning to human suffering:

> A glorious little suffering has just been born, an exemplary suffering [says Roquentin]. Four notes on the saxophone. They come and go, they seem to say: "You must be like us, suffer in rhythm."

Joseph listens to a Haydn *divertimento* with the same intensity as Roquentin listened to his jazz tune. Joseph also wants to give his life the integrity of an art object, his suffering the brilliance of formal arrangement, and his existence the inner necessity and proportion of a harmonious order of creation. It is difficult to believe that Bellow wrote this scene without conscious recall of Sartre's *Nausea*. Joseph echoes the exact sentiments and ideas of Roquentin:

> It was the first movement, the adagio, that I cared most about. Its sober opening notes, preliminaries to a thoughtful confession, showed me that I was still an apprentice in suffering and

humiliation. I had not even begun. I had, furthermore, no right to expect to avoid them. So much was immediately clear. Surely no one could plead for exception; that was not a human privilege. What I should do with them, how to meet them, was answered in the second declaration: with grace, without meanness. And though I could not as yet apply that answer to myself, I recognized its rightness and was vehemently moved by it. Not until I was a whole man could it be my answer, too. And was I to become this whole man alone, without aid?

Like the existentialists, Bellow is not only trying to depict the emotion of abandonment that accompanies the loss of fixed traditional values; he is also trying to depict the motives that lead to the self-enclosed hero. In a prolapsed world, in a state of continued suspension, the hero carries his personal existence in its total weight. He can live in terms of no future reality—except death. He can act in terms of no emblem—except self-definition. All of his actions have no meaning outside of themselves; his existence is completely autonomous and self-enclosed.

The dichotomy of self-affirmation and self-negation—of total rejection of a fixed social order and total acceptance of unfounded existence—almost destroys Joseph, as it destroys Kit Moresby and Nelson Dyar. Like other existential heroes, Joseph desires an ideal existence almost at the expense of his real existence. The Spirit of Alternatives, Joseph's alter ego, is the voice of "Unreason" which keeps him dangling between irreconcilable orders—hope and actuality, the ideal and the real, life and death:

> "The vastest experience of your time doesn't have much to do with living. Have you thought of preparing yourself for that?" [says the Spirit of Alternatives]
>
> "Dying? . . . "
>
> "I mean it."
> "What is there to prepare for? You can't prepare for anything but living. You don't have to know anything to be dead. You have merely to learn that you will one day be dead. I learned that long ago. No, we're both joking. I know you didn't mean that."
>
> "Whatever I mean, you get it twisted up."
> "No. But I'm half-serious. You want me to worship the anti-life. I'm saying that there are no values outside of life. There is nothing outside life."
>
> "Apparently we need to give ourselves some exclusive focus, passionate and engulfing."
>
> "One might say that."
> "But what of the gap between the ideal construction and the real world, the truth?"
>
> "Yes . . . "
>
> "How are they related?"
>
> "An interesting problem."
> "Then there's this: the obsession exhausts the man. It can become his enemy. It often does."
>
> "H'm."

"What do you say to all this?"

"What do I say?"
"Yes, what do you think? You just sit there, looking at the ceiling and giving equivocal answers."

"I haven't answered. I'm not supposed to give answers."

The Spirit of Alternatives brings out rather clearly the difficulty of being a law unto oneself when every possible course of action suggests an alternative. Bellow, of course, is here expressing an existential idea—the ambiguity of ethics, the difficulty of choice between two courses of action that are not morally exclusive of each other.

Joseph's discussion with the Spirit of Alternatives calls to mind Ivan's talk with the Devil. It is a rather curious coincidence that Joseph's journey leads to a form of demonic union. Mrs. Harscha calls him Mephistopheles, and Joseph says, "She had seen through me—by some instinct, I thought then—and, where others saw nothing wrong, she had discovered evil. For a long time I believed there was a diabolic part to me." I believe that Bellow is merely playing with ideas here. Joseph is not a thoroughgoing satanic hero, and he himself rejects the label. The interesting thing is that Bellow and Camus are both concerned with the possibility of life outside the social order, and both are willing to recognize that such a life borders upon a satanic existence—the rebel in the underground.

Bellow's hero dangles between accepting and rejecting his freedom, is torn by the nature of alternatives (as his alter-ego signifies). Like other existential heroes, once Joseph has divested the world of meaning he finds it impossible to act in terms of commitment. Joseph's state of suspended activity is a form of death in life; his new identity brings him to the edge of a peculiar kind of self-destruction. As Sartre has pointed out, matter has to be infused with consciousness before it assumes a momentary meaning; freedom too must be directed outside itself in a form of (say) political commitment before it takes on meaning. Joseph is the completely autonomous hero who is unable to direct his energy outside of himself and almost burns himself out in fits of insignificant restlessness. He is like the character in *The Plague* who spends all his time counting a bushel of peas from one basket into another, or the one who spends all his time rewriting the first sentence of his novel, or the character who appears each noon, calls the neighborhood cats to his balcony, and then spits upon them with great accuracy.

The *Dangling Man* is similar to *The Plague* in another rather significant way. The plague brings Camus' characters to a moment of self-awareness. The majority of Camus' characters invest their freedom with a kind of meaning by fighting the plague (even though they know that their efforts will have no permanent avail). Joseph, however, does not invest his freedom with any outside meaning and, as a result, dangles between a kind of existential integrity and bad faith. The close of the plague marks the end of a forced awareness; the end of Joseph's waiting marks the end of an imposed consciousness. It is interesting to note that both Joseph and the plague-stricken are able to reaffirm their initial identity and to return to the original community. The quest stops short of self-destruction because it stops short of any kind of cosmic identification or total autonomy. Joseph welcomes release from his unfixed state of being, and his surrender is marked by a refreshing breath of air—almost the sea-blown air that greets Diego after the termination of the plague in Camus' play, *State of Siege*. Joseph was on the threshold of freedom, but recognized that its consequences were too great:

> We are afraid to govern ourselves [he declares]. Of course. It is too hard. We soon want to give up our freedom. It is not even real freedom, because it is not accompanied by comprehension. It is only a preliminary condition of freedom. But we hate it. And soon we run out, we choose a master, roll over on our backs and ask for the leash . . . That's what happens. It isn't love that give us weariness of life. It's our inability to be free.

Freedom imposes too great a burden; it can lead to extremes, and extremes can lead to self-destruction. "I am no longer to be held accountable for myself," Joseph concludes upon entering the army. "I am grateful for that. I am in other hands, relieved of self-determination, freedom cancelled. Hurray for regular hours! and for the supervision of the spirit! Long live regimentation!" It is noteworthy that Joseph's journey stops short of social alienation, and that Bellow possibly saves Joseph from the fate of Nelson Dyar.

Cross Damon, the hero of Richard Wright's *The Outsider,* is another modern hero whose existential motives lead to overreaching and personal disaster. *The Outsider* is the most express treatment of the existential theme in American fiction. The novel, however, does not reveal a major talent and has most serious limitations: it is a philosophical *tour de force,* exploits the sensational, relies upon existential ideology to fill out character motivation, and editorializes far more than the most tendentious Continental existential novels. Wright, however, does understand the basic philosophies of both Sartre and Camus, and his portrait of the modern satanic hero is documented in existential terms.

Cross Damon is also in search of a new identity. When he is listed by mistake among the dead of a horrible train wreck, he repudiates an identity in which he can no longer believe. His problems are supposed to be the problems of modern man: he is "the twentieth-century writ large." He rejects the common values because he can find no meaning in society, and because he is unable "to relate himself to others."

Damon's dilemma is in a way also Meursault's—"the dilemma of the ethical criminal, the millions of men who lived in the tiny crevices of industrial society completely cut off from humanity, the multitudes of little gods who ruled their own private worlds and acknowledged no outside authority." Like Meursault, once Damon is outside the social order he enters into a diabolical cosmic relationship, becomes a law unto his own undefined nature, and becomes the source of all good and all evil:

Damned is the man who must invent his own
god! [says Damon, anticipating his own ultimate
damnation] Shun that man, for he is part of the
vast cosmos; he is akin to it and he can no more
know himself than he can know the world of
which he is in some mysterious way a part . . .
what does this mean—that I don't believe in
God? It means that I, and you too, can do what
we please on this earth.

Damon's cosmic identity becomes licence for murder. Although both Meursault and Damon are metaphysical murderers, they are also "innocents"—innocent because society is guilty. Meursault kills the Arab because he is an automaton and merely reacts to an unpleasant series of sensations. The point is that Meursault is an automaton because of the meaningless workaday world: the rising at seven, breakfast, tram, work, lunch, work, tram, dinner, the rising at seven again. The robot woman in Céleste's restaurant, who mechanically wolfs her way through dinner so that she can get home to the evening radio programs, is meant to be read as society writ small. Damon is also innocent because society has given him no values in which he can believe and by which he can live. Damon murders with impunity because, as Wright puts it, "there was a kind of innocence that made him want to shape for himself the kind of life he felt he wanted." Damon protests his innocence at the end of the novel, after he has been shot and is about to die. "In my heart," he says, "I felt . . . I'm innocent . . . That's what made the horror."

The Stranger is constructed on a strict ironic framework since society is both at the source of Meursault's murder and of his death sentence. Meursault is a victim; he thinks of himself as a martyr, the new Christ. Cross Damon continually refers to himself as a victim also. Like Meursault, Damon is also an inverted Christ-figure. His very name suggests that he is both satan and saviour—that "a genuine atheist is a real Christian turned upside down." Named by his mother after the cross of Christ, Damon is indifferent to his mother (Meursault is similarly indifferent to his mother) and follows the wayward footsteps of his father (Camus also sees the destructive principle in terms of the father or the judge). The name "Cross" is significant because it suggests the hero's godlike desire to be the autonomous and self-enclosed martyr. Damon wants to be either pure consciousness or pure matter, *pour-soi* or *en-soi,* to use Sartre's terms for the Godhead. He wishes "to swap the burden of this sorry consciousness for something else! To be a God who could master feelings! If not that, then a towering rock that could feel nothing at all." The name "Damon" is significant because it represents "the quality of the demonical in him." Near the end of the novel, Damon tells Sarah, "Remember, He said: 'Come unto me, all ye that labor and are heavy laden, and I will give you rest'?"

> "But you don't believe that," [Sarah] protested,
> baffled, halfscared. "I know you don't. Do you?"
>
> "No." He could not resist telling her the truth.
>
> "Then why do you tell *me* that?"
> "Perhaps God uses the Devil to guide people
> home," he told her. . . .

"You are the *devil*!" she burst out bitterly.

Like Roquentin, Damon listens to jazz music in an attempt to realize a new identity. Roquentin envies the internal necessity of the art form. Cross Damon believes that by listening to jazz he can systematize his sensual impulses and become a kind of God. He refers to its "demonic contagions" and, as Wright tells us, the "blue-jazz became his only emotional home . . . He came to feel that this music was the rhythmic flauntings of guilty feelings, the syncopated outpourings of frightened joy existing in guises forbidden and despised by others."

As we have seen, the dichotomy between rejection of a fixed social order and acceptance of an unfixed existence almost destroys Joseph. Once Damon becomes self-enclosed, he finds that there is no return to the community, and his plight becomes that of the Moresbys and Nelson Dyar. Damon, a variation of Camus' Jean-Baptiste, finds no redemption from modern hell. He is exposed by Bob Houston, the District Attorney, a hunchback who has the psychological makeup to understand the motives of a satanic hero:

> Houston, a hunchback, an outsider, a man
> whose physical deformity had forced him to live
> in but not of the normal rounds of ritualized life,

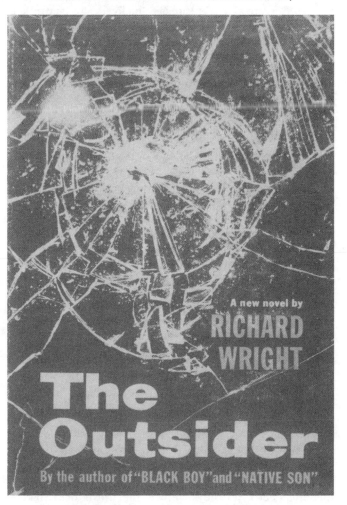

Dust jacket for The Outsider, *by Richard Wright.*

knew the demonic feelings of men who played god because he himself was of the demon clan, having hidden his kinship with the rebellious by publicly upholding the laws and promises that men live by.

One demonic consciousness upends another; and when Damon recants at the end of the novel, he is in essence expressing the tragic consequence of existentialism—the cosmic hero becomes self-enclosed only by traveling the path of self-destruction. Like Kit Moresby and Nelson Dyar, Damon's end was in his beginning. Nietzsche's man of power assumes a satanic mask, and the flight toward identity leads up a road that never turns back to man.

The hero of Ralph Ellison's novel, *Invisible Man,* also destroys his original identity and quests unsuccessfully to reaffirm another one. He is still another contemporary hero who is unable to redeem himself from a fallen world, a modern hell. While relationship between Ellison and the existentialists is most remote, they are bound together by definite preoccupations with the nature of identity in the absurd world. Ellison's hero ultimately comes to very existential attitudes toward life: "I knew it was better," he says at the end of his journey, "to live out one's own absurdity than to die for that of others." "Our task is making ourselves individuals," he says elsewhere. "We create the race by creating ourselves." "Life is to be lived, not controlled, and humanity is won by continuing to play in face of certain defeat." Sisyphus could not have expressed himself more clearly, or in more distinct existential terms. If he is speaking for himself, Ellison certainly does not overstate the case when he says that Sartre, Kierkegaard, and Unamuno are the chief literary heroes of the modern world.

Ellison's unnamed hero loses his identity when he is expelled from a small Southern Negro college. His only offense is to expose a wealthy northern philanthropist to the realities of Negro life in the South. Mr. Norton thinks of the Negro as an abstract extension of his personal destiny. Dr. Bledsoe, the president of the college, endeavors to preserve this God-subject relationship between Norton and the Negro. By keeping Norton in contact with only the most idealistic aspects of Negro existence, Bledsoe is able to keep him in contact with a non-entity, an abstraction, an invisible generic animal.

Norton is a symbolic Godhead; the college is a symbolic Garden of Paradise. Nameless and without precise location, the college has an air of otherworldliness. Norton visits the school each spring; his presence accompanies the cycles of life, and the campus is beautifully in bloom; yet beneath the appearance of life and fecundity is the stark reality of arid death. "Why is it," the hero asks, "that I can recall in all that greenness no fountain but one that was broken, corroded and dry?" A forbidden road runs through this paradise on "past the buildings, with the southern verandas half-a-city block long, to the sudden forking, barren of buildings, birds, or grass, where the road turned off to the insane asylum." Here again is the familiar road, the possibility of the journey outside society, the insane asylum at journey's end.

Ellison's hero journeys down the forbidden road—bringing Mr. Norton with him. Once Norton sees Jim

Trueblood and the veterans at the Golden Day, he can no longer think of the Negro as an extension of his beneficent nature, and Ellison's protagonist can no longer think of Norton as God. As the protagonist leaves the college, never more to return, he notices a snake crossing the highway. The loss of the old identity is worked out in terms of the Fall. The quest for the new identity is both frenetic and unsuccessful, and the hero eventually ends up alone, abandoned, on an underground coal pile. There is a humor here—but rather a demonic humor, a kind of satanic glee, the shrill laugh of Dostoyevski's possessed or underground hero with whom Ellison's protagonist is indeed blood brother. After he killed the Arab, Meursault tells us that he feels doomed. Ellison's hero also recognizes a kind of inevitability in his flight outside of man. "My end," he tells us, "was in the beginning."

The coal pile becomes a retreat from both society and self. Like Kit Moresby and Nelson Dyar, Ellison's hero ends in a state between being and non-being. "All dreamers and sleepwalkers must pay the price," he says, "and even the invisible victim is responsible for the fate of all. But I shirked that responsibility; I became too snarled in the incompatible notions that buzzed within my brain. I was a coward." No writer, on either side of the Atlantic, has found a more powerful image to convey Sartre's concept of bad faith. Yet it is a bad faith which follows from the tenets of existentialism itself. Existential choice and freedom are constructed along asocial lines; existential commitment, on the other hand, is a principle of social involvement. The hero is thus torn between the instinct to live outside society and the guilt which follows such a choice. These two positions are mutually exclusive—and yet to see them both in existential philosophy is only to place Sartre's *No Exit* next to his *What Is Literature?* Like Mathieu, Brunet, Jean-Baptiste, Invisible Man—aware of both necessities, unable to act in terms of either—frustrates his will and is consumed by his very logic.

Destruction—either death or a kind of insanity—is at the end of the existential quest. And yet the quest, the dramatic means of revealing a free will in search of identity, is absolutely necessary to existential literature. The existential hero believes at times that hell is other people. He also believes that there is no longer a dichotomy between good and evil and that evil is a gratuity, a latent part of existence. The existential hero desires to master the malevolent element rather than let it master him. These motives—the desire to be a moral or social law unto himself, the desire to be so self-involved that the outside world is no longer a threat—lead to the flight, the quest, towards a new identity in which the hero is completely autonomous and creation is a mere extension of his will. This explains why the existential hero often assumes the guise of the sensualist, the man who is able to say *no* to death by making an eternity of the moment, the atheist who is able to fill the moral void by making the all-consuming experience the end of existence. "To feel" is often the first step in the desire "to power." The sensualist is the satanic hero who has incarnated the Nietzschean will.

Ivan collaborated with the Devil, and Camus (perhaps unjustly) maintains that Ivan is the character who most captivated Dostoyevski's imagination. Certainly Ivan, the rôle Camus played in his dramatic adaptation of *The Brothers Karamazov,* is the character who most captivates Camus' imagination. American novelists have also been fascinated with the figure of Satan. Young Goodman Brown and Ethan Brand meet him. It is not, however, until Faulkner's Joe Christmas that the American hero actually *becomes* the Devil. Christmas is explicitly referred to as the Devil ten times, and the label is certainly consistent with his nature. The Moresbys, Nelson Dyar, Joseph, Cross Damon, Invisible Man—all, in various ways, continue the tradition of the demonic hero. Without family, outsiders, physically dislocated, they are the sensualists who desire the all-consuming experience. Save Joseph, they are plagued by the emotions of loneliness which haunt their journey. Like Satan, they are their own destroyers; they reject society, plot against it, seek a new reality, a supreme identity, and thereby destroy themselves.

The modern hero stands at a crossroads—one path leads to the society, the other away from the community. Joseph, torn by the struggle of choice, almost burns himself out trying to reconcile the alternatives. The Moresbys, Nelson Dyar, Invisible Man—all take the path outside the community and pursue it to a form of ultimate doom. Along with Meursault and Joe Christmas, they are the first of the existential martyrs. The irony of their deaths is part of the absurdity of their lives. Society makes them and then destroys them for what they are.

It is interesting to note that the existential hero of late is taking the path to the community. Camus' Rieux, Tarrou, D'Arrest, Sartre's Brunet, Bellow's Leventhal and Wilhelm—all possess a new compassion, and the existential struggle is not quite so antiheroic, so satanic in character. Perhaps this is only the natural difference between the underground existence of Sartre and Camus during the Resistance and their rather prominent social positions after the war.

Perhaps the death of the satanic hero anticipated this return to society all along. In *The Rebel* Camus says "the individualist cannot accept history as it is: he must destroy reality not collaborate with it, in order to affirm his own existence." The modern writer destroys reality by destroying the modern hero who incarnates it in its most malevolent form. The modern novel exorcises the devil in a very real way and thereby establishes a sense of what *should be* rather than what *is.* The death of the antihero is a form of protest as well as a form of hope—a way of saying that the world *should* and perhaps *could* be a better place in which to live, that the world cannot be changed but that man can as long as he is free to choose and act. This is only saying, in sum, that existence precedes essence. The death of the modern hero is an instance in which art subsumes reality and perfects it. Malraux, Camus, Sartre, Hemingway, Bellow, Wright—all give deference to the artist in his many manifestations. Is it any wonder the artist has become a supreme figure, the very hope of the modern world?

It would be misleading to leave the impression that the treatment of the existential theme in America is of a piece. The handling of the theme varies radically. Bowles' novels

are constructed around a symbolic scene. There is an objective correlative between the violence of the scene and the violence of the action. Bellow's four novels are so different that it is difficult to generalize about his methods. *Dangling Man*—similar in character presentation, dramatic pattern, tone and point of view to *The Stranger* and *Nausea*—is a masterpiece of compression, probably the closest American adaptation of existential techniques. Wright has never recovered from the influence of Dreiser. In *Black Boy* he tells us

> I read Dreiser's *Jennie Gerhardt* and *Sister Carrie* and they revived in me a vivid sense of my mother's suffering; I was overwhelmed . . . It would have been impossible for me to have told anyone what I derived from these novels, for it was nothing else than a sense of life itself. All of my life had shaped me for realism, the naturalism of the modern novel, and I could not read enough of them. Steeped in new moods and ideas, I bought a ream of paper and tried to write.

In *How Bigger Was Born,* Wright tells us that he worked on *Native Son* like a "scientist in a laboratory," inventing "test-tube situations [and placing] Bigger in them." *Native Son* is indeed a naturalistic novel. Wright assumes his theme as a scientific fact (that man is determined by his society), invents a situation to control this theme (Bigger's murder), and then documents excessively (cf. the long speech of the lawyer at the end). *The Outsider* uses the same methods. Wright assumes his theme as a scientific fact (that modern men, especially Negroes, are unable to accept social values), invents a situation to control this theme (Cross' murder), and then documents at length (cf. Cross' long speech at the end). Wright, in other words, has used exactly the same structure in an avowed existential novel that he used in an avowed naturalistic work. The technique of *The Outsider* contradicts the philosophical position of the work itself. Wright insists that one's existence is limited to one's situation; yet *The Outsider* is written from an omniscient point of view. The novel employs the familiar "block method." The narrator, outside the action, accumulates a great mass of material and arranges it into blocks or units. There is little relationship between these units, and the progression of the novel stems from a necessity no greater than that of chronology. Each unit is related to another only because it is related to the main theme, and each block repeats or enlarges the central theme. *The Outsider* employs the repetitive form of the naturalistic novel.

Invisible Man employs a diametrically different technique. Ellison constructs his novel in terms of a number of key symbols, images or metaphors. The metaphor of invisibility correlates the position of the Negro with the properties of glass: one can look through the Negro as one can look through a pane of glass without being aware of a substance, a property of existence. The metaphor of blindness reinforces the major metaphor: Homer A. Barbee, who extols the work of Bledsoe, is blind. Jack, the Communist who sees the Negro in terms of a group caught in a dialectical process, has a glass eye. The hero himself is initially blinded by his ambitions; at the town meeting he is appropriately blindfolded, sent out to box a number of his companions; he does not begin to see until Mr. Emerson shows him Bledsoe's letter. Appearance hides reality in this myopic world, and the impostor reigns supreme. The images of darkness and light complement the metaphor of blindness. On the coal pile, the hero cannot see; yet he no longer lives in the world of blindness. He secures light, first by burning his high-school diploma (thereby rejects white man's institutions), then by burning a Negro doll (rejects stereotype Negro), and finally by burning his party correspondence and name tag (rejects political abstractions). He manages to tap an electric line and wires his underground home with lights. Light itself is an objective manifestation of his new-found intellectual repository for various objects the narrator picks up on his journey—a toy bank in the image of a Negro, a Negro puppet manipulated by an invisible black string, a link in a leg chain. The objects symbolically depict the Negro as an economic pawn.

As the variety in technique would indicate, the American writers did not go to the French novelists in any systematic or inclusive way. The Americans, in fact, often use elements from the writings of both Sartre and Camus, seemingly unaware that Sartre and Camus split in 1952 in an argument over Communism. Despite the variety of technique, despite the electric nature of American existentialism, there is a distinct similarity of theme in Continental and American fiction which, it seems to me, goes beyond mere accident. Both orders of fiction reveal the hero functioning in a moral vacuum, a law unto himself, the society a prison restraining his free and natural impulses; both orders of fiction depict the reality of death, a centripetal universe folding in upon the hero, and the feeling of ethical abandonment which accompanies the realization that all activity is directed toward no ethical purpose; both depict the shock of moral recognition which accompanies the realization that the world is absurd and that one has been complicit in its malfunctioning; both extol the sensualist who tries to order his sensations in such a way that the moment says no to death; both express the feelings of loneliness and abandonment which come with the loss of the family and traditional beliefs and values; both employ forms of the demonic and dislocated hero, the Antichrist and conqueror of God, the outsider in search of identity.

These preoccupations, of course, exist in a historical framework more inclusive than existentialism:

> The man of the future [writes Nietzsche], who in this wise will redeem us from the old ideal, as he will form that ideal's necessary corollary of great nausea, will to nothingness, and Nihilism; this tocsin of noon and of the great verdict, which renders the will again free, who gives back to the world its goal and to man his hope, this Antichrist and Antinihilist, this conqueror of God and of Nothingness—*he must one day come.*

The preoccupations of existentialism are the preoccupations of an age. Sartre and Camus have major talents and their contributions are significant. They have continued the tradition of the nineteenth-century thinkers and turned modern man back to the truths of Nietzsche, Dos-

toyevski, and Kirkegaard. Existentialism as a modern philosophical theme has now gone beyond the limits of a specific country or even continent. Sartre and Camus will undoubtedly continue to go their separate ways. Sartre no longer has the popular appeal he had fifteen years ago. Camus, however, has captured the imagination of today's young intellectuals and writers in an almost unprecedented way. American criticism of Camus' fiction is continually growing. *The Stranger* has been adapted for translation in American French courses, and is bound to have a certain effect on many promising writers now in the college classroom. Camus died without fully realizing his talent. His later works, especially *Exile and the Kingdom,* reveal a falling off. Yet Camus made his mark, and his presence is still felt. One can hear the language of the rebel in William Styron's *Set This House on Fire.* One can detect the influence of *L'étranger* on Walker Percy's *The Moviegoer.* Undoubtedly Camus will continue to influence many new novelists—both on the continent and in America. (pp. 66-83)

> Richard Lehan, *"Existentialism in Recent American Fiction: The Demonic Quest,"* in Recent American Fiction: Some Critical Views, *edited by Joseph J. Waldmeir, Houghton Mifflin Company, 1963, pp. 63-83.*

J. L. Styan

[*Styan is an English educator and critic who has written numerous studies of the theater, including the three-volume* Modern Drama in Theory and Practice. *In the following excerpt from that work, Styan examines the drama of Jean-Paul Sartre, Albert Camus, and Jean Anouilh, offering an explanation for the relatively brief flourishing of Existentialist theater.*]

Intellectual leaders in France have traditionally turned to the theatre to promulgate their views, and so it was during the Second World War and just after. During the German occupation in Paris, a uniquely French series of plays reflected the moral dilemma of an audience suspicious of the collaborator and shaken by the pent-up fear and hate of years of war, torture and execution. A people close to exhaustion found release in the drama, and for a short time a most uncommon theatre came about. The names of Jean-Paul Sartre and Albert Camus became a secret rallying cry, and attending their plays was like joining a conspiracy against the enemy right under their noses.

When the theatres were allowed to re-open after the fall of France in 1940, the unlikely *Saint Joan* by Bernard Shaw was permitted a production by the German censor because it appeared to be anti-British. Did it not, after all, show the English putting the French national heroine to the flames? As it turned out, the Paris audience automatically perceived the campaign to expel the English from France as analogous with their desire to be rid of the German forces of occupation. When Sartre came to write *Les mouches* (*The Flies,* 1942), he took care to choose a mythological subject in order to conceal the subject of the play from the censor, and at the same time to bring to a beleaguered public a sense that the French situation was not new, but as old as the human race. Then in 1943, the

Antigone of Jean Anouilh began a record run at the Atelier because his little heroine stubbornly refused all comfort and compromise. The French audience felt her stance to be its own. When Antigone declared that nothing would stop her burying her brother, the audience heard the voice of the Resistance and exulted. 'What is your reason for doing this?', she is asked. 'For myself', is her unabashed reply. A few spectators were troubled by the fact that the tyrant Creon, who was otherwise perceived as the Nazi oppressor, was given so eloquent a defence on the need for compromise, but it was in vain that the author denied the intention of introducing any political satire into his play. Anouilh was a dramatist before he was a politician, and it was a matter of pure chance that *Antigone* met the need for an anti-Nazi play. Such is the force of political circumstance that it can determine a success or a failure on the stage.

Sartre had been a prisoner of war in Germany in 1940, when he was released by a lucky mistake. In the prison camp, he had written and produced a Biblical play for his fellow prisoners. This was never published, but during the performance Sartre remarked the intense concern and concentration of his audience under the unnatural circumstances of their confinement. The occasion taught him, he said, the nature and virtue of a collective experience in the theatre, and justified his pursuit, in terms of drama, of the philosophy he had been formulating before the war. 'Existentialism' proposed that man was a lonely creature of anxiety and despair living in a meaningless world, and that he was merely existing until he made a decisive and critical choice about his own future course of action. By such a choice, a person would acquire an identity, a purpose and dignity as a human being. For preference, existential man should adopt some social or political cause in order to acquire this dignity and purpose, and in translating these ideas into dramatic form, Sartre's name became synonymous with the *théâtre engagée,* the theatre 'committed', that is, to positive social or political action. Each of his plays is representative of his philosophical concerns as an existentialist. *Huis clos* (*In Camera* in Britain, *No Exit* in America, 1944) is a carefully structured drama about the manoeuvring of three people forced to share a small room together in hell. *Morts sans sépulture* (*Men without Shadows,* 1946) is a play which explores the extreme predicament of men facing physical torture. *Les mains sales* (*Crime Passionnel* in Britain, *Dirty Hands* or *The Assassins* in America, 1948) is a play which tests a man's true motives in committing a political assassination.

Like Anouilh, Camus also became an inadvertent spokesman for the spirit of the French Underground when he published a long philosophical essay, *Le mythe de Sisyphe* (*The Myth of Sisyphus*) in 1942. For Camus, the legendary figure of Sisyphus was the prototype of an 'absurd' hero, condemned by the gods forever to roll a rock to the top of a mountain, only to have it roll back down again by its own weight. He represented the epitome of futile labour and pointless existence. Although Camus denied any connection with Sartre's existentialism, the book became a manifesto for the new existentialist drama, and later for the theatre of the absurd. In it, Camus asserted that it was legitimate and necessary to wonder whether life had any

meaning. He described how man felt himself to be a stranger in an alien world, and believed that this divorce between man and life was properly 'le sentiment de l'absurdité', the feeling of absurdity. Was suicide the way to end this feeling? No. In the confrontation with the irrational, it was possible to proceed beyond nihilism, for there was a 'wild longing for clarity' in the human heart: 'If the world were clear, art would not exist.' In both his novels and his plays, Camus protested on behalf of the war-torn generation against man's fear of death and his helplessness in the face of a meaningless universe.

The plays which pleased Parisian audiences during the war have in common a classical austerity and a fierce moral purpose, both of which proved less attractive after the tension of the war had eased. When, for example, *Antigone* was produced in New York by Katherine Cornell under very different circumstances in 1946, the public found the return to Greek myth unaccountable and the play deficient in realistic characterization, a quality it had come to expect on the American stage. Sartre came to the play's defence in *Theatre Arts,* and followed up his arguments in *Qu'est-ce que la littérature?* (*What is Literature?,* 1948). The common quality that Sartre recognized as existentialist in the French plays of this period may be regarded in the context of this history as yet another variant of symbolism in the modern theatre. The new philosophical drama, Sartre maintained, had knowingly turned away from psychological realism, and rejected the kind of theatre for which a dramatic situation was chosen and developed only to exhibit characters. Anouilh's *Antigone,* for example, was not a study of 'human nature' in the usual sense, and not 'naturalistic' by the nineteenth-century definition. The character Antigone was not in the play to demonstrate the concerns of her society, or display the symptoms of a particular heredity and environment. The play was essentially one of 'situation', and Antigone represented 'a naked will' in a universal situation selected to throw light on 'la condition humaine', not the condition of society but the state of mankind. The dramatic interest was not in the person or personality of a young Greek princess, but rather in the choice she makes and why she makes it. Any directorial emphasis, therefore, on the characters of Antigone or Creon would be wholly misplaced.

This account of Anouilh's *Antigone* emerged rather blatantly as a formula for an existentialist play after Sartre's own heart. It is true, however, as Sartre contended, that his was a scheme for a 'theatre of situation', one dealing in general experience, collective human rights, universal conflicts, inevitable passions and final values. It was a return to the elements of classicism in the Corneillean tradition. Like Greek or French classical tragedy, existentialist drama quickly precipitates its central character into the symbolic conflict. In its brevity and its focus on a single event, its form approximates to the classical unities. And at its best its dialogue is simple and economical, even to the point of being dry and terse. Such a drama had no need to use visual or verbal symbols *per se,* but it emerged as a symbolic theatre of the ideal, intent on defining a kind of modern mythology. If its characters appeared to be of flesh and blood, this was only to lead the audience towards a conviction of their reality before the play went on to assert or imply their universality.

Luckily for all parties, author, actor and audience, the strong conflict of interests implicit in an existentialist choice lends itself wonderfully well to a dramatic expression that is full of challenge and suspense, and while Sartre's plots are symbolic of his personal philosophy, his plays are otherwise naturalistic in treatment. Their existentialist content did not alter one whit the fact that the actors had to play by the principles of Stanislavsky like those in any realistic drama. Indeed, some playgoers have been attracted to the existentialist play merely as a philosophical thriller, and the thread of violence running through many of Sartre's plays has supported this claim to their popularity.

The Flies is a specially interesting example of what was done. The play loosely modernizes Aeschylus's *Oresteia* to provide Parisians with a story of resistance against the German occupation and the Vichy government. It was first produced by Dullin at the Théâtre Sarah-Bernhardt in 1943, with sets, masks and statues designed by Henri-Georges Adam. In disguise, Orestes has returned home to Argos where his father Agamemnon was murdered by his wife, Orestes's mother, Clytemnestra, fifteen years before. He comes upon a spine-chilling scene. The city is afflicted with a plague of avenging flies, because the people have been cleverly persuaded by Zeus (played by Dullin himself) that they are responsible for the murder: in this way the gods have enslaved them. The mask of Zeus was designed to have a vacant stare and a bloody head, and the movements of the insect-like old women of Argos may be suggested by Sartre's description of the old woman of Bouville in his novel *La nausée* (*Nausea*, 1938):

> Suddenly she grows bolder, she scuttles across the courtyard as fast as her legs will move, stops for an instant before the statue, her mandibles quivering. Then she scurries off, black against the pink pavement, and disappears into a crack in the wall.

Orestes also witnesses the degradation of his sister Electra, who has been living at home in an atmosphere of hate with her mother and her stepfather Aegisthus. Act II depicts the Argives' grand festival of guilt and penitence, at which Electra must dance in an attempt to dispel the people's self-indulgent misery. This is the moment when Orestes chooses to reveal his identity and kill Clytemnestra and Aegisthus for the sake of the city. However, urged on by Zeus, the loathsome flies remain and flourish, a little like the plague in Camus's novel, and then as Furies they pursue Orestes and Electra to the shrine of Apollo. Electra is the weak one, and she succumbs to repentance and returns to Zeus's power, but the strong Orestes defies Zeus and declares that he is free. He has committed matricide without regret, and has chosen to stand alone. The play ends with a triumphant Orestes leaving the city with the swarm of flies and Furies at his heels.

This exit of Orestes is not far short of comic, and was characteristic of the risks taken by so theatrical and spectacular a conception. The play also sagged under an abundance of ponderous polemical speeches, in which Sartre's ideas resisted full dramatization and simply had to be mouthed. But the play's story, and therefore the symbolism in its situation, were simple and strong, making a plain moral statement in allegorical terms. If *The Flies* does not persuade an audience of the validity of existentialism, it is nearly acceptable as a modern drama of individual heroism in the face of the enemy and of social disapproval. But none of this detracts from the urgency and importance of the play's first production in 1943, the integrity of the dramatic event in its historical context. Sartre himself has commented upon Dullin's courage in putting the play on in occupied Paris:

> It was 1943 and Vichy wanted to drive us into repentance and shame. In writing *The Flies* I tried to contribute as best I could to the extirpation of this sickness of repentance, this abandonment to shame that Vichy was soliciting from us. The collaborators made no mistake about it. Violent press campaigns rapidly forced the Sarah Bernhardt theatre to withdraw the play, and the remarkable work of the man who was our greatest director was not rewarded (in *La Croix,* 20 January 1951, translated Dorothy McCall).

A philosophical approach to playwriting also inhibited the complete success of the plays of Camus in the theatre, although he was a great admirer of Copeau and, unlike Sartre, had gathered experience as an actor and a director. He had established the communist Théâtre du Travail in 1936-7, and when he broke with the party he created the Théâtre de l'Équipe, which lasted from 1937 to 1939. *Caligula,* which was also produced during the war years, was directed by Paul Oettly at the Théâtre Hébertot in 1945. This play had been written in 1939, and Camus evidently intended the title part for himself. With Gérard Philipe in the lead in 1945, it ran for nearly a year, and it will possibly be Camus's most enduring play. Certainly it is one of his more successful plays in dramatizing his philosophy of existential absurdity.

Camus called *Caligula* 'a tragedy of the intelligence', and made of it a very free treatment of Roman history. In Caligula's grief over the death of his sister, with whom he had enjoyed an incestuous love, the young emperor decreed that Rome should be ruled by the ugly logic of a purposeless universe. All patricians had to leave their wealth to the state and be prepared to die. At first a man of gentle disposition, Caligula now becomes a cruel despot in order to show others what a monstrous world they live in. He starves the poor and decimates the rich, and even strangles his mistress. But for all the illogic of absurdity, he achieves no happiness, and before he is stabbed to death, the only logical thing that happens in the play, he screams at his own image in the mirror and flings a stool at it.

The play was acceptable to the Paris audience because it readily identified Caligula's philosophical absolutism with the hated Nazism and Fascism, and his megalomania with Hitler's and Mussolini's. Nevertheless, as drama, the play reproduces a series of horrors, and for all its philosophical underpinning, it fails to dramatize any moral conflict in Caligula himself. But then, did not the existential dramatist wish to avoid the narrow limitations of psychological realism? Perhaps the one redeeming feature of the play might have been some probing of the human mind. But just as Sisyphus loved life and was absurdly punished, so Caligula dies without hope for the future, and the statement of the play is wholly negative.

Intractable ideas, and the unsatisfying message they conveyed, must account for the short life of the existentialist drama, and for its failure to be exported far from Paris. It is as unwise to enter the theatre as a writer with a philosophical theory as it is to act in a tragedy with a theory of tragedy in mind. (pp. 117-24)

> *J. L. Styan, "The Existentialist Play: Sartre and Camus," in his* Modern Drama in Theory and Practice: Symbolism, Surrealism and the Absurd, Vol. II, *Cambridge University Press, 1981, pp. 117-24.*

FURTHER READING

I. Anthologies

Kaufmann, Walter, ed. *Existentialism: From Dostoevsky to Sartre.* New York: Meridian, 1975, 384 p.
   Anthology of several seminal texts of Existentialist philosophy and literature, including excerpts from Sartre's *Being and Nothingness,* Kafka's *The Trial,* Heidegger's *Being and Time,* and Nietzsche's *Ecce Homo,* with a comprehensive introductory overview by Kaufmann.

Solomon, Robert C., ed. *Existentialism.* New York: Modern Library, 1974, 363 p.
   Contains selections from a wide variety of Existentialist and Existentialist-influenced texts, ranging from philosophical essays by Kierkegaard to excerpts from John Barth's *The End of the Road* and Arthur Miller's *Death of a Salesman.*

II. Secondary Sources

Adams, Laura. "Existentialist Aesthetics: An Interview with Norman Mailer." *Partisan Review* 42 (1975): 197-214.
   Interview in which Mailer expounds on the importance of Existentialism to his work and his recurring theme that God and the devil are at war for control of the universe. Mailer says he considers himself an Existentialist, but differentiates his writings from those with "roots in atheistic philosophers like Sartre. . . . [That] has become the basic concept of Existentialism in America. But it's not mine."

Barrett, William. *Irrational Man: A Study in Existential Philosophy.* Garden City, N.Y.: Doubleday, 1958, 278 p.
   Historical and critical overview of Existentialism.

Breisach, Ernst. *Introduction to Modern Existentialism.* New York: Grove Press, 1962, 247 p.
   Historical overview and assessment of Existentialism, with lengthy sections on the religious Existentialists and the relation of Existentialism to "The American Dream."

Chiaromonte, Nicola. "Paris Letter: Sartre versus Camus."

Partisan Review 19, No. 6 (November-December 1952): 680-86.
   Delineates the causes of the intellectual and political break between Sartre and Camus over communism, charging Sartre with "spreading intellectual confusion" and avoiding response to issues raised by Camus.

Clive, Geoffrey. *The Broken Icon: Intuitive Existentialism in Classical Russian Fiction.* New York: Macmillan Co., 1972, 233 p.
   Considers Existentialist themes in the works of several Russian authors, including Dostoevsky, Gogol, and Tolstoy.

Finkelstein, Sidney. *Existentialism and Alienation in American Literature.* New York: International Publishers, 1965, 314 p.
   Examines the development of existential themes and concerns in American fiction from the 1920s to the mid-1960s.

Glicksberg, Charles I. "Jean-Paul Sartre: From Existentialism to Communism." In his *The Literature of Commitment,* p. 222-35. Lewisburg, Pa.: Bucknell University Press, 1976.
   Critique of Sartre's attempt to combine Existentialist theory and Marxist politics, arguing that it decreased his authority and effectiveness as a theorist.

———. *The Tragic Vision in Twentieth-Century Literature.* Carbondale: Southern Illinois University Press, 1963, 187 p.
   Contains several chapters examining the philosophical, religious, and political themes of such authors as Kafka, Kierkegaard, and Sartre.

Hanna, Thomas. *The Lyrical Existentialists.* New York: Atheneum, 1962, 299 p.
   Examines parallels in the lives and works of Camus, Kierkegaard, and Nietzsche. Hanna argues that the three writers are united not only by their philosophical and metaphysical opinions, but also by their lyrical prose styles.

Hatzfield, Helmut. "Existentialist *Engagement.*" In his *Trends & Styles in Twentieth Century French Literature,* pp. 137-59. Washington, D.C.: The Catholic University of America Press, 1957.
   Argues that, despite their claims to the contrary, Existentialist writers are greatly concerned with God and Christianity.

Kaufmann, Walter. "The Reception of Existentialism in the United States." In *The Legacy of the German Refugee Intellectuals,* edited by Robert Boyers, pp. 69-96. New York: Schocken, 1968.
   Discusses the impact of Central European emigrés of the 1930s and 1940s on the acceptance of Existentialist writers and philosophy by American intellectuals. Kaufmann concludes that while many of the emigrés were strong adherents of the philosophy, they did surprisingly little to advance Existentialism in the United States.

Keefe, Terry. *French Existentialist Fiction: Changing Moral Perspectives.* London: Croom Helm, 1986, 250 p.
   Extended analysis of the fiction of de Beauvoir, Camus, and Sartre written before, during, and after the Second World War.

Kern, Edith. "Existential Humanism and Literary Modes." In *Writing in a Modern Temper: Essays on French Literature*

and Thought in Honor of Henri Peyre, edited by Mary Ann Caws, pp. 240-57. Saratoga, Calif.: ANMA Libri, 1984.
> Contrasts Sartre and Heidegger in their philosophical views concerning humanism.

Kerr, Walter. "The Playwright as Existentialist." In his *God on the Gymnasium Floor and Other Theatrical Adventures,* pp. 127-58. New York: Simon and Schuster, 1971.
> Contends that Harold Pinter is the only absurdist dramatist to have written according to an Existentialist structure, through which he introduces abstract ideas late in his plays rather than grounding his works in them from the beginning in the manner of Beckett, thus mirroring the Existentialist belief that existence precedes essence.

Knight, Everett. "From Baudelaire to Sartre." In his *Literature Considered as Philosophy: The French Example,* pp. 34-87. London: Routledge & Kegan Paul, 1957.
> Places Existentialist writing, especially that of Sartre, in the context of what Knight identifies as a tradition of philosophically oriented modern French literature.

Langford, Michele K. "The Concept of Freedom in Surrealism, Existentialism, and Science Fiction." *Extrapolation* 26, No. 3 (Fall 1985): 249-56.
> Examines the influence of Existentialist philosophy on contemporary science fiction, particularly that of the French author Gérard Klein.

Lehan, Richard. *A Dangerous Crossing: French Literary Existentialism and the Modern Novel.* Carbondale: Southern Illinois University Press, 1973, 198 p.
> Examines the relationship between the works of the writers of the French Existentialist movement and those of such later American novelists as Norman Mailer, Joseph Heller, and Thomas Pynchon.

McElroy, Davis Dunbar. *Existentialism and Modern Literature.* New York: Citadel Press, 1963, 58 p.
> Collection of lectures relating the works of several Existentialist and post-Existentialist writers to a sense of crisis in modern civilization.

Palumbo, Donald. "Sadomasochism and Modern Existential Fiction." *West Virginia University Philological Papers* 28 (1982): 49-61.
> Explores themes of sadomasochism in the works of Sartre, Dostoevsky, and Faulkner, arguing that sexual alienation depicted in their fiction symbolizes man's alienation from God.

Rabil, Albert, Jr. "Existentialist Philosophy and Literature: Evolution of an Historical Movement: Parts I and II." *Southern Humanities Review* 16, Nos. 3, 4 (Summer 1982; Fall 1982): 235-55, 303-15.
> Comprehensive outline of the history, development, and philosophical influences of Existentialism, covering the period from Kierkegaard to Merleau-Ponty.

Schwartz, Kessel. "Jacinto Grau and the Meaning of Existence." In his *The Meaning of Existence in Contemporary Hispanic Literature,* pp. 133-43. Coral Gables, Fla.: University of Miami Press, 1969.
> Finds in the work of Spanish playwright Jacinto Grau (1877-1958) several Existentialist themes, including the creation of one's own environment through will, the need to act, and man's effort to cope with the absurdity of death.

Sinfield, Alan. "Varieties of Religion." In his *Society and Literature: 1945-1970,* pp. 87-117. New York: Holmes and Meier, 1983.
> Includes Existentialist literature in a general discussion of religious issues in the society of post–World War II England.

Slote, Michael A. "Existentialism and the Fear of Dying." In *Language, Metaphysics, and Death,* edited by John Donnelly, pp. 69-87. New York: Fordham University Press, 1978.
> Examines the manner in which various Existentialist philosophers treat the subject of death.

Whitman, Cedric H. "Existentialism and the Classic Hero." In his *The Heroic Paradox: Essays on Homer, Sophocles, and Aristophanes,* pp. 44-65. Ithaca: Cornell University Press, 1982.
> Considers several classical Greek tragedies as embodying concepts of Existentialist philosophy.

Wilson, Colin. "The Existential Temper in the Modern Novel." In *Christian Faith and the Contemporary Arts,* pp. 115-20. New York: Abingdon, 1957.
> Criticizes some Existential writers for not addressing issues of morality and religion in their work.

———. *The Outsider.* Boston: Houghton Mifflin, 1956, 288 p.
> Traces in nineteenth- and twentieth-century fiction a type of character which Wilson terms "The Outsider," a misfit who rejects the predominant philosophies and values of society in favor of a life of passion and revolt. Wilson cites a number of Existentialist protagonists as examples of this character.

———. *Religion and the Rebel.* Boston: Houghton Mifflin, 1957, 338 p.
> Examines Existentialist authors and their characters as "Outsiders," estranged from society through their rejection of conventional models of material and spiritual reality.

Winchell, Mark. "Beyond Existentialism; or, the American Novel at the End of the Road." In *Modern American Fiction: Form and Function,* edited by Thomas Daniel Young, pp. 225-36. Baton Rouge: Louisiana State University Press, 1989.
> Examines the development of existential themes in the novels of John Barth, arguing that he debunks earlier Existentialist writers who Winchell contends worked contrived affirmations of life into their writing. Winchell states: "It is perhaps Barth's greatest achievement to make us regard . . . romantic Existentialism as old hat, really a concealed 'yes' posing as a 'no' in thunder."

Witt, Mary Ann Frese. *Existential Prisons: Captivity in Mid-Twentieth-Century French Literature.* Durham, N.C.: Duke University Press, 1985, 231 p.
> Discusses the use in Existentialist literature of the image of the prison to symbolize the Existentialist conception of existence, with chapters focusing on the works of Camus, Genet, Malraux, and Sartre.

Yale French Studies, No. 16 (1955-56): 3-145.
> Special issues devoted to essays on Existentialism, including a study of Existentialism in Italian literature, an examination of the works of Maurice Blanchot, and a discussion of Camus's political writings.

Italian Futurism

INTRODUCTION

Italian Futurism was one of the most influential cultural movements of the early twentieth century. Organized and publicized by Italian poet and dramatist Filippo Tommaso Marinetti, the movement encompassed virtually every aspect of literature and the fine arts. Demonstrating contempt for the values and institutions of the past, the Futurists rejected not only traditional art forms but the conventions of Western society in general, most prominently the traditions of reason and romantic love. By contrast, they glorified war, technology, and the modern urban milieu in works characterized by dynamic movement, alogical juxtaposition, and intuitive, often violent expression.

Critics generally divide Italian Futurism into two periods: the first and more significant phase spanning from 1909 until Italy's entrance into World War I in 1915; the second beginning during the war and declining steadily until Marinetti's death in 1944. The Futurist movement originated with the publication in 1909 of Marinetti's *Manifeste du futurisme* (*The Founding and Manifesto of Futurism*) in the Parisian journal *Le Figaro*. This document established the movement's ideal of aggressive modernity, providing the ideological principles for subsequent Futurist works. The founding manifesto attracted a number of visual artists to the movement, and the *Manifesto dei pittori futuristi* (*Manifesto of the Futurist Painters*) was issued in 1910 by painter and sculptor Umberto Boccioni, along with painters Gino Severini, Carlo Carrà, Giacomo Balla, and Luigi Russolo, who was also a Futurist composer. Numerous manifestos were published by the Futurists over the next five years on aspects of culture ranging from architecture to men's clothing. Futurist writings received exposure through Marinetti's journal *Poesia,* based in Milan, and were translated into the major European languages. The movement gained cohesiveness in 1913 through the support of the Florentine journal *Lacerba,* founded by Ardengo Soffici and Giovanni Papini, who remained Futurists until 1915.

Traveling exhibitions by Futurist painters, in conjunction with lectures by Marinetti, earned Italian Futurism widespread international attention in 1912 and 1914. These tours were highly publicized and their confrontational stance acquired notoriety in major cities throughout western Europe. In Italy the Futurists received additional publicity through *serate,* or evening performances, which comprised spontaneous readings and dramatic performances in urban cafés and theaters. Often deriding the audience and provoking food barrages and riots, the Futurist *serate,* with the manifestos *Il teatro di varietà* (*The Variety Theatre*) and *Il teatro futurista sintetico* (*The Futurist Synthetic Theatre*), provided the basis for Futurist drama. Best exemplified by the *syntesi,* or synthesis drama, Futurist theater condemned the dramatic conventions of plot development and character psychology, emphasizing instead the provocation of the audience, depersonalized characters, brevity, and an ironic, anti-art viewpoint.

Italy's entrance into World War I, although strongly supported by the Futurists, signaled a decline in Futurism's popularity. Boccioni and architectural designer Antonio Sant'Elia were killed during the war, and most of the movement's major figures renounced Futurism during this time. In the succeeding decades, Marinetti continued to publicize the movement and recruited a second generation of adherents, yet his ongoing affiliation with Benito Mussolini and the developing Fascist movement in Italy detracted significantly from Futurism's status as an avant-garde movement. The Futurist impulse was gradually assimilated into the totalitarian government, illustrated perhaps most strongly by Marinetti's appointment by Mussolini to the Italian Academy in 1929. Of note among the contributions of Futurism's second phase are the innovations in mechanized stage settings by Enrico Prampolini and Fortunato Depero.

Although criticized for maintaining an alliance with Fascism, for espousing an antihumanist philosophy, and for overemphasizing technological novelty, Italian Futurism has been the object of renewed critical interest since the 1960s. The movement is chiefly esteemed for its dynamic visual artwork and for the inflammatory expression of its manifestos, while the innovative techniques of Futurist drama are considered to have greatly influenced subsequent anti-art movements in modern theater. Of Italian Futurism, critic Stephen Eric Bronner observes, "There was barely an aspect of culture which the Futurists did not call into question, and no later avant-garde group has failed to take up their challenge to create a new experience of existence."

(For further discussion of Italian Futurism, see the entry on F. T. Marinetti in *TCLC,* Volume 10.)

REPRESENTATIVE WORKS

Balla, Giacomo

Per comprendere il pianto (drama) [first publication] 1916; published in journal *Gli avvenimenti*
   [*To Understand Weeping* published in *Futurist Performance,* 1971]
Sconcertazione di stati d'animo (drama) [first publication] 1916; published in journal *Gli avvenimenti*
   [*Disconcerted States of Mind* published in *Futurist Performance,* 1971]

Boccioni, Umberto

Manifesto tecnico della scultura futurista (manifesto) 1912

[*Technical Manifesto of Futurist Sculpture* published in *The Documents of 20th-Century Art: Futurist Manifestos*, 1973]
La scultura futurista (manifesto) 1912
Dinamismo plastico (lecture) 1913; published in journal *Lacerba*
[*Plastic Dynamism* (partial translation) published in *The Documents of 20th-Century Art: Futurist Manifestos*, 1973]
Pittura scultura futuriste (essay) 1914; published in journal *Poesia*
[*Futurist Painting and Sculpture* (partial translation) in *The Documents of 20th-Century Art: Futurist Manifestos*, 1973]
Il corpo che sale (drama) [first publication] 1916; published in journal *Gli avvenimenti*
[*The Body That Ascends* published in *Futurist Performance*, 1971]
La garçonnière (drama) [first publication] 1916; published in journal *Gli avvenimenti*
[*Bachelor Apartment* published in *Futurist Performance*, 1971]
Genio e coltura (drama) [first publication] 1916; published in journal *Gli avvenimenti*
[*Genius and Culture* published in *Futurist Performance*, 1971]

Boccioni, Umberto; Carrà, Carlo; Russolo, Luigi; Balla, Giacomo; and Severini, Gino

Manifesto dei pittori futuristi (manifesto) 1910
[*Manifesto of the Futurist Painters* published in *The Documents of 20th-Century Art: Futurist Manifestos*, 1973]
La pittura futurista: Manifesto tecnico (manifesto) 1910
[*Futurist Painting: Technical Manifesto* published in *Exhibition of Works by the Italian Futurist Painters*, 1912]

Buzzi, Paolo

Parallelepipedo (drama) [first publication] 1916; published in journal *Gli avvenimenti*
[*Parallelepiped* published in *Futurist Performance*, 1971]
Il premio di futurismo (drama) [first publication] 1916; published in journal *Gli avvenimenti*
[*The Futurist Prize* published in *Futurist Performance*, 1971]

Cangiullo, Francesco

Detonazione (drama) [first publication] 1915; published in journal *Gli avvenimenti*
[*Detonation* published in journal *The Drama Review*, 1970]
Luce! (drama) [first publication] 1919; published in journal *Dinamo*
[*Lights!* published in *Futurist Performance*, 1971]

Carrà, Carlo

La pittura dei suoni, rumori e odori (manifesto) 1913; published in journal *Lacerba*
[*The Painting of Sounds, Noises and Smells* published

in *The Documents of 20th-Century Art: Futurist Manifestos*, 1973]

Corra, Bruno, and Settimelli, Emilio

Atto negativo (drama) [first publication] 1915; published in journal *Gli avvenimenti*
[*Negative Act* published in journal *The Drama Review*, 1970]
Davanti all'infinito (drama) [first publication] 1915; published in journal *Gli avvenimenti*
[*Faced with the Infinite* published in *Futurist Performance*, 1971]
Dissonanza (drama) [first publication] 1915; published in journal *Gli avvenimenti*
[*Dissonance* published in *Futurist Performance*, 1971]
Passatismo (drama) [first publication] 1915; published in journal *Gli avvenimenti*
[*Old Age* published in *Futurist Performance*, 1971]

Depero, Fortunato

Colori (drama) [first publication] 1916; published in journal *Gli avvenimenti*
[*Colors* published in journal *The Drama Review*, 1970]

Marinetti, Filippo Tommaso

Mafarka le futuriste (novel) 1909; also published as *Mafarka il futurista*, 1910
Manifeste du futurisme (manifesto) 1909; published in newspaper *Le Figaro;* also published as *Fondazione e manifesto del futurismo* in journal *Poesia*, 1909
[*The Founding and Manifesto of Futurism* published in *Marinetti: Selected Writings*, 1972]
Poupées électrique (drama) 1909
Le roi Bombance (drama) 1909
Manifesto tecnico della letterature futurista (manifesto) 1912
[*Technical Manifesto of Futurist Literature* published in *Marinetti: Selected Writings*, 1972]
Distruzione della syntassi—Immaginazione senza fili—Parole in libertà (manifesto) 1913; published in journal *Lacerba*
[*Destruction of Syntax—Imagination without Strings—Words-in-Freedom* published in *The Documents of 20th-Century Art: Futurist Manifestos*, 1973]
Il teatro di varietà (manifesto) 1913; published in journal *Lacerba*
[*The Variety Theatre* published in newspaper *Daily Mail*, 1913]
Zang tumb tuum (poetry) 1914
Le basi (drama) [first publication] 1915; published in journal *Gli avvenimenti*
[*Feet* published in journal *The Drama Review*, 1970]
Simultaneità (drama) 1915
[*Simultaneity* published in journal *Drama Review*, 1963]
Manifesti del futurismo. 4 vols. (manifestos) 1919
Elletricita sessuale (drama) 1920
Futurismo e Fascismo (essay) 1922
Gli indomabili (novel) 1922
[*The Untamables* (partial translation) published in *Marinetti: Selected Writings*, 1972]

Marinetti: Selected Writings (essays, manifestos, memoirs, and novel) 1972

Marinetti, Filippo Tommaso; Settimelli, Emilio; and Corra, Bruno

Il teatro futurista sintetico (manifesto) 1915
[*The Futurist Synthetic Theatre* published in *Art and Stage in the Twentieth Century,* 1968]

Prampolini, Enrico

Scenografia e coreografia futurista (manifesto) 1914; published in journal *La balza futurista*
[*Futurist Scenography* published in *Total Theatre: A Critical Anthology,* 1969]

Pratella, Balilla

Manifesto dei musicisti futuristi (manifesto) 1910
[*The Manifesto of the Futurist Musicians* published in journal *Musical Courier,* 1915]
Musica futurista: Manifesto tecnico (manifesto) 1911
[*Technical Manifesto of Futurist Music* published in *Music since 1900,* 1971]

Rognoni, Angelo

Stanchezza (drama) [first publication] 1916; published in journal *Gli avvenimenti*
[*Weariness* published in journal *The Drama Review,* 1970]

Russolo, Luigi

L'arte dei rumori (manifesto) 1913
[*The Art of Noise* published in *Futurist Performance,* 1971]

Sant'Elia, Antonio

L'architettura futurista (manifesto) 1914; published in journal *Lacerba*
[*Manifesto of Futurist Architecture* published in *The Documents of 20th-Century Art: Futurist Manifestos,* 1973]
Città nuova (drawings) 1914

This work also contains manifestos by other authors.

PRINCIPLES AND FORMATIVE INFLUENCES

Stephen Eric Bronner

[*Bronner is an American critic, educator, and novelist who has written extensively on modern political science and political theory. In the following excerpt, he discusses the central aesthetic, social, and political tenets of Italian Futurism.*]

The importance of Futurism is no longer in question. Few cultural movements have been as broad in scope and as forceful in their demands for a sweeping transformation in the style and quality of everyday life. From painting to language to architecture to men's clothing, there was barely an aspect of culture which the Futurists did not call into question, and no later avant-garde group has failed to take up their challenge to create a new experience of existence. Yet, coincidental with their firmly articulated cultural-aesthetic vision, the Futurists exhibited an irresponsible, almost nihilistic, view of social reality. Nowhere does this troubling combination emerge with greater clarity than in the work and life of the founder and organizer of the movement as a whole: F. T. Marinetti.

Looking back on Marinetti today, what is particularly interesting, given the influence he exerted, is that he was not an extraordinary poet; even as a pamphleteer, his works possess neither the theoretical richness and political acumen of Lenin's polemical pieces, nor the striking imagery and aesthetic relevance of Breton's. Still, in an era which was marked by a new concern with the subject, it is not difficult to understand how this charismatic personality could incarnate the cultural rebelliousness of the Italian avant-garde. Even more than with his contemporaries D'Annunzio and Stefan George, Marinetti's greatest asset was his personality; through his flamboyance, and the controversy which followed him wherever he went, he spread the ideas and works of truly gifted artists beyond the confines of an elite few to a larger public.

Of course, Marinetti had other assets. To begin with, he recognized talent and was generous, supporting such artists as Boccioni, Carrà, Russolo, and others for years at a time. Moreover, through magazines such as *Poesia* and *Lacerba,* he was able to unify various disparate artists into a self-conscious group. But, perhaps most importantly, he could capture a cultural sensibility in a few words. Thus, Marinetti could greet the modern technological epoch with his famous claim that a racing car was, in fact, "more beautiful than the *Victory of Samothrace.*"

This very characteristic statement points up several of Futurism's most arresting features: its desire to break completely with the past, to value unequivocally the dynamic and the new, and to transmit the avant-garde message through shocking effects. Many of Marinetti's contemporaries considered the statement scandalous, and scandal, too, became part of the avant-garde repertoire: duels were started in public and leaflets were dropped from rooftops. In Marinetti's Futurist *soirées,* which later turned into anti-neutrality demonstrations with the onset of World War I, notoriety became a virtual end unto itself.

The Futurist position was, of course, formed by the social conditions which emerged at the turn of the century. During this period of tremendous technological advance, the rise of the cities as the focal points of existence and the concomitant rise of the masses through the expansion of the bourgeois society changed the face of traditional existence. In relatively advanced capitalist societies where a proletarian movement was entrenched, and had differentiated itself from the right, the response was clear: fascists and proto-fascists stood in complete opposition as befitted the anachronistic classes—such as the petty-bourgeoisie and the peasantry—which they represented; on the other hand, the proletariat wished to channel this progress into new directions. In Italy, however, which was not highly industrialized but rather still fundamentally agrarian, the response was more confused. Lacking a solidly based socialist-workers' movement, the left and the right, the anarchists and the fascists, intersected. This intersection was mirrored and refracted by the Futurists in the ambivalence of their response to the changes which were emerging around them. Consequently, they were thrilled with the "frenetic life of the great cities and the exciting new psychology of night life; the feverish figures of the bon viveur, the cocotte, the apache and the absinthe drinker." Yet, they were opposed to the degradation and routinization of "everyday life" which the bourgeoisie fostered through its extension of bureaucracy and bureaucratic rationality. As the Futurists were inspired by technology and the extraordinary increase in inventions which emerged around the turn of the century, they were simultaneously horrified by "all the slovenly and facile commercialism." Then too, they shared the renewed enthusiasm for science, but, at the same time, they opposed the positivist's denial of the subject and the uniqueness of his experience. Furthermore, they praised "the masses" inasmuch as they served as a threat to the traditional cultural order, and yet attacked notions such as democracy, equality, and humanism insofar as these notions contributed to the extermination of grandeur and the rise of "mediocrity."

From the first, a concrete social analysis was lacking through which the interconnection of these phenomena could be perceived. Instead, following Bergson, Sorel, and, above all, Nietzsche, Marinetti opposed to bourgeois rationality and traditional humanism a vitalistic activism which exalted the unique experience. The result was the demand for a type of catharsis which would purge society of its accumulated traditions and which would allow the individual to manifest his grandeur. Thus Marinetti became the advocate of war—the "world's only hygiene"—while championing notions of the artist as humanity's savior since only the artist could fully understand and articulate mankind's new experiential needs. In this respect, however, Marinetti was not a hypocrite. He went off to serve as a war correspondent in 1911 to cover the Italo-Turkish war. Then he went to the Balkans in 1912 to cover the conflict there. (These experiences were the basis for poems such as "La bataille de Tripoli.") Finally, Marinetti served honorably in the First World War.

Politically, what emerged from all this was a curious mixture of elitism and rebellion. This combination, however, has aesthetic roots in the cultural influences upon Futurism. Though Futurism considered itself unique and self-contained, there emerged from the Cubists a formalist-elitist "l'art pour l'art" ["art for art's sake"] mentality while the experimentation of the Fauves and the Expressionists tended to spur on the Futurist dynamism.

These, however, were contemporary movements; the world of the past had nothing to offer, and so Marinetti could challenge those who would seek to revitalize the past with the remark: "and what is there to see in an old picture except the laborious contortions of an artist throwing himself against the barriers that thwart his desire to express his dream completely." Such barriers were to be destroyed: the nude was to be expelled from painting, photographic naturalism was to be denied in favor of an artistic mode whose fundamental purpose was to reveal the spontaneous gesture of the individual. Instead of the rational analysis demanded by classicism and naturalism, empathy was to become the crucial element; an empathy through which the original distance between subject and object was to be broken through the unconscious irrational identification of the subject with the painting, with the result that the spectator would take his place at the center of the work.

The notion of art as the exploration into the unknown, as the continuous project of elaborating and defining the new, is perhaps the most lasting contribution of the Futurists. The rest of their politically radical, or pseudo-radical, cultural tendencies have been assimilated. This is particularly the case with Marinetti's *cult of the new,* the worship of change without purpose, which has proved itself to be quite compatible with the imperatives of the capitalist state. Especially at present, both for the bourgeois of advanced industrial society and the parasitical avant-gardist, whatever appears as new, different, or technically innovative, becomes ipso facto progressive—provided, naturally, that it is commercially viable for the one and aesthetically pleasing for the other.

The trend itself is part of a planned obsolescence which reaches into the very heart of cultural creation and appreciation. Questions of how the content, the style, the given innovation, not to speak of the work as a whole, are to relate themselves to the elaboration of a potential for human happiness—to a practical "realm of freedom"—are forgotten in the name of a fetishization of the new. Through this fetish, even what Adorno conceived of as the "negative moment" can be turned into its opposite. Precisely because the new is deprived of any emancipatory norm, the *demand for liberation* becomes lost in a relativized contentless chaos while, simultaneously, the *demand for the new*—which no longer concedes any truth to the accomplishments of the past—becomes a ritualized need that imposes itself upon the spontaneous creative experience. Nowhere is this more noticeable than in Antonio Sant'Elia's *Manifesto of Futurist Architecture 1914* where he claims that "the fundamental characteristics of Futurist architecture will be its impermanence and transience. Things will endure less than us. Every generation must build its own cities."

The "must" is what undermines the free decision and that utopian novum which does not seek a mechanistic abolition of the past, but rather its transformation. This injunction of Sant'Elia's, however, is quintessentially tied to a demand for self-realization, current at the time, which also lacked any humanistic emancipatory norm. Thus, Marinetti could take Nietzsche's cry literally: "Do whatever you will, but first be such as are able to will!" The only way to realize this mystifying will was through dynamic action—in its extreme, the "gratuitous act"; that act which, by its very singularity, would transcend existence and so become the product of the "highest will."

Today it is clear that the gratuitous act has already given rise to a tradition. Its beginnings are to be found in Dostoyevsky, but it was Gide who fully formulated the notion which then became a central tenet of Surrealist thought and important even to Sartre and the Existentialists. But, where Dostoyevsky, Gide, and Sartre were horrified, and where Breton wished only to *épater le bourgeoisie* ["shock the bourgeoisie"], Marinetti took up the notion as a guiding principle. In fact, in his play *Le roi Bombance,* he viewed the gratuitous action as marking the artist who would confer a new breath of meaning on society and who thereby would justify himself as the one who could lead a state.

Through this notion, art and action become fused into a grand politics. The work of art is to serve as the spectacle which an elite can experience in such a way that rational understanding cannot serve as a check. For Marinetti, the work of art was not supposed to be "understood." Why should that fat little bourgeois understand, if the Futurists themselves "didn't want to understand. . . . [And, what's more] woe to anyone who says those infamous words to us again!" For the bourgeois could only understand that which wasn't worth explaining. If the break with the past was to be complete, it had to call into question and deny the very act of rational cognition itself. Language? Marinetti wanted to explore a new mode of communication through his "Words in Freedom." Feelings? It was time to discover a new unsentimental way of perceiving objects and oneself as well. Art? It could only reflect a world which the past controlled; art, true art,—as the painter Carrà said—would only begin with Futurism.

The Futurists didn't want to "understand" because they had already understood—intuitively, irrationally, spiritually; and this understanding was strengthened by that closeness which is inherent amongst the members of any avant garde movement vis-à-vis the group's estrangement from society at large. But, precisely because of their isolated social position, and in the intense mutual reinforcement of their respective egos, what the avant-garde sought to communicate came to be infected with an extraordinary verve and a consistently elitist pomposity. The Futurists always detested the placid and the sober; their desire was to infuse a dazzling, vibrant, excitement into society at large. [In a footnote Bronner observes that "this concern with the sparkling gaiety which should mark existence is fundamental to Futurism and emerges as one of its most progressive traits. The best examples of this aspect are to be found in the works of Marinetti, and Boccioni, as well as in the little pieces by Giacomo Balla such as *The Futurist Manifesto of Men's Clothing 1913.*"] Thus, Marinetti could recall that "an immense pride was buoying us up, because we felt ourselves alone at that hour, alone, awake and on our feet, like proud beacons or forward sentries against an army of hostile stars glaring down at us from their celestial encampments."

Marinetti drew the battle lines against this staid, establishmentarian, "army of hostile stars." Against them, the Futurist "beacons" would project the true demands of youth—the demand for an apocalypse which would result in a new man, a "multiplied man." There is no question but that the Futurist concern for a "multiplied man" and a "multiplication of values" served to oppose the stultify-

ing specialization caused by the division of labor as well as the routine of "everyday life" and the objectivism of positivist rationality; aesthetically, as the Futurist musician Pratella put it in his *Manifesto of Futurist Musicians 1910,* a perception would arise "capable of enriching any fact with a more imposing personality." Still, the thrust of the Futurist notion, as Marinetti and the majority of the Futurists conceived it, held no humanistic content, but rather an illusory emancipation insofar as this

> multiplied man we dream of will never know the tragedy of old age! To this end the young modern male, finally nauseated by erotic books and the double alcohol of lust and sentiment, finally inoculated against the disease of Amore, will methodically learn to destroy in himself all the sorrows of the heart, daily lacerating his affections and infinitely distracting his sex with swift casual contacts with women.

Freedom thus became the freedom of the conqueror, or the "hero." This was a vision which, later, would become part and parcel of the fascist ideology. In the beginning however, the Futurists were not sure to whom they would hand on their vision. In this respect, Marinetti lingered in the abstract; he would speak to *all* Italians, just as in his famous pamphlet "Let's Murder the Moonshine!" he had spoken to *all* Venetians. Yet, since Futurism rejected the status quo, since Futurism lacked a coherent view of the world and even of the future which it wished to impose, and since it didn't wish to be "understood"—because complete understanding would already imply a bond to the given—it could not choose a group or class to which it could direct its appeals.

Because the Futurists spoke to all, but chose no one, they—albeit unintentionally—became an integral part of that society which they were reacting against. Subjectively antagonistic to it, objectively the Futurists found themselves incorporated within it. Totally averse to social analysis, Marinetti abstracted the concept of the "bourgeois" from its determinate social context, leaving the concept devoid of class content; ultimately, then, he could only view the bourgeois as an abstract type. At the same time, he feared the political intrusion of the proletariat because of the "mediocrity" which would result from the equalizing tendencies which it would propagate. Thus, it was no accident that, when Marinetti did speak of the "proletariat," it was characteristically as an abstraction, as the "proletariat of gifted men." Once again, Marinetti fostered a notion—in this case of arbitrary elitism—which would converge with the ideology of Mussolini.

However, what the Futurists subjectively opposed comes out splendidly in the impressionistic picture which Marinetti painted of prewar Italy. From his writings, it is easy to see the type of bourgeois whom Marinetti and the Futurists mechanistically reacted against and, to a certain extent, why the group was so blatantly bellicose and antihumanist. For Marinetti saw this bourgeois as enraptured with the glories of an ancient past, as an effete cosmopolitan, a dilettante obsessed with eroticism and sentimentality, with "tango-teas" and appearing chic. Resting on the laurels of a bygone age, this bourgeois seemed decadent and diseased, no longer capable of creating anything except by virtue of foreign influences. Moreover, this bourgeois was a hypocrite: espousing his rationalist materialism, he still could accept a respectable Christianity.

To all this, Marinetti responded with his call for virility, daring, nationalism, and callousness. Liberalism, enlightenment, rationalism, and its products, as well as Christianity, were seen as nothing but relics from the past and were to be denied through intuition, instinct, aggressiveness, and pitilessness. Defined by what he opposed, Marinetti was trapped; furthermore, the special vehicle which he posited as that which would transform and overcome this old-world decadence only made clear the contradiction between life and art which the Futurists wished to resolve.

That vehicle was to be speed. An aesthetically abstracted result of the new technology, speed was to turn into the principal source which would open up a wealth of new possibilities. This notion would become the fundamental principle for an aesthetic which would take its inspiration from "the barbaric element of modern life" (Boccioni). Unlike other avant-garde movements, the Futurists always started out with the realistic object; yet "absolute motion is a dynamic law inherent in an object. The plastic construction of the object must here concern itself with the motion which an object has within itself, whether it be at rest or in movement." These words of Boccioni's, from his pamphlet *Absolute Motion + Relative Motion = Dynamism,* lies at the base of his attempts to abolish finite lines and the self-contained statue. Then too, absolute motion would make possible the experience of "dynamic sensation" in the spectator's encounter with the painting. The dynamization of objects and the experience of the spectator is what undermines the routine, boredom, and commodity fetishism of capitalist production.

As an artistic concept, the principle proved free and invigorating, providing one of the theoretical grounds for modern abstractivism and the growth of the modern imagination. In fact, this aesthetic breakthrough helped express the new existential relation between man and his world, in terms of a new experiential perception; thus, as Boccioni explains in the same pamphlet, "a horse in movement is not a motionless horse which is moving but a horse in movement, which makes it another sort of thing altogether, and it should be conceived and expressed as something simply varied." Consequently, time and space, subject and object, come to take on new dimensions in the attempt to create the aesthetic ideal of pure motion.

But Marinetti and the Futurists were not satisfied with the aesthetic; they wished to extrapolate the notion of speed, as a guiding principle, on to the social realm in a direct fashion. For Marinetti, speed was virtually to take the place of fate. Therefore, in accordance with his vitalistic activism, speed would finally force men to know the moment fully; through speed they would see that "they must stake their lives on a single cast, not on the lookout for cheating croupiers or trying to control the wheels." Speed, motion, and incessant activity for the sake of activity were to become the contents of Marinetti's "multiplied man."

This incessant activity to no purpose other than that of continuous inhuman self-transformation is one of the hallmarks of a fascist bureaucracy. Individuals, groups, races, and classes must all take subservience to the demands of an abstract mystical ideal. In social terms, Marinetti's concept of speed justifies such activity insofar as it becomes the horrific agent of purification. As he says himself, "the sick and weak [will be] crushed, crumbled, pulverized by the vehement wheels of intense civilization. The green beards of provincial back alleys [will be] shaved clean by the cruel razors of speed." From this position, the anti-humanism of the Futurists emerges; once motion, speed, and transformation become ends unto themselves, duration comes to mean as little for an individual as for a machine. Consequently, in the *Futurist Painting: Technical Manifesto 1910,* the Futurists could proclaim that "the suffering of a man is of the same interest to us as the suffering of an electric lamp which, with spasmodic starts, shrieks out the most heartrending expressions of color."

As speed becomes the abstract vehicle of purgation through which the unfit can be destroyed, existence is propelled into a situation in which the past—even in its most progressive aspects—comes to be abolished. In this way, the Futurist goal finally assumes a type of clarity: existence as a perpetual future without a past or present; a completely uncontrolled, unreflective movement along a self-negating horizon.

In the absence of a mass-based political movement, however, the goal could only remain suspended, and thus the Futurists waited for a political agent which could put their dreams for transforming Europe into effect. That agent came in the form of Italian fascism which seemed to laud the same qualities as the Futurists. In 1914, Marinetti encountered Mussolini, and ultimately became part of that nationalist-militarist contingent from which the Blackshirts were recruited. A bond was established between Futurists and fascists and, suddenly, the Futurists were no longer to be lightly dismissed as crazy bohemians or simply relegated to the aesthetic realm. Unfortunately, however, the alliance was between unequal partners. Though both movements were bellicose, ultra-nationalistic, irrationalist, and activistic, Futurism's emphasis upon abstraction and its contempt for the "public" contradicted the fascists' pseudo-classical kitsch and their pseudo-revolutionary populism. While the Blackshirts were on the rise, Marinetti's unreflective apocalyptic radicalism served them well. But Futurism's dynamism could potentially threaten any established order and Mussolini recognized its subversive elements. Thus, as the fascists became secure, Futurism was forced to tone down; the Futurists became less visible and, even aesthetically, the movement declined as its leaders started to concern themselves with nonsense such as "tactilism." For all practical purposes, Futurism's program was politically fulfilled as it became aesthetically nullified; the movement became institutionalized and academic, and this spelled its demise. (pp. 48-55)

Stephen Eric Bronner, "F. T. Marinetti: The Theory and Practice of Futurism," in Boston University Journal, *Vol. XXV, No. 2, 1977, pp. 48-56.*

Caroline Tisdall and Angelo Bozzolla

[*The following excerpt is from Tisdall and Bozzolla's*
Futurism, *a comprehensive study of the Italian cultural
movement. Here, they discuss the aesthetic and ideological sources of Futurism in literature and the visual arts.*]

The roots of Futurism are a tangled web of turn-of-the-
century political, cultural and philosophical currents that
come to light, unacknowledged, in *The Founding and
Manifesto.* Few, if any, of the ideas in it are totally original. Violence, war, anarchy, nationalism, the cult of the
superman, glorification of urban life, of technology and of
speed, together with hatred of the past and scorn of academic values, had all been voiced before. What was new
was the way in which they were all brought together and
synthesized into one inflammatory cultural document ripe
for distribution.

Violence of course was uppermost:

> We intend to sing the love of danger, the habit
> of energy and fearlessness. . . . Courage, au-
> dacity and revolt will be the essential elements
> of our poetry. . . . There is no more beauty ex-
> cept in strife. No work without an aggressive
> character can be a masterpiece. Poetry must be
> conceived as a violent attack on unknown forces,
> to reduce and prostrate them before man.

Love of violence and professed belief in the virtue of destruction were the hallmarks of the French Symbolist literary circles which had been the main formative influence
on the young Marinetti. Writers from J. K. Huysmans to
Stéphane Mallarmé and Paul Valéry expressed their hatred of the mean, vulgar and money-grubbing life of the
modern bourgeois through their elevation of the extraordinary, the gloriously immoral and the adventurous. In
the last decade of the nineteenth century events caught up
with literature in a series of daring raids and exploits that
brought anarchy and Symbolism even closer together. The
destructive gesture of the anarchist' advocated by Marinetti in 1909 had found its real-life expression in the
bombs of Emile Henry, Auguste Vaillant and Ravachol
(which gave the French language a new verb beloved of
Symbolists, *ravacholer*), in the exploits and bank raids of
the Bonnot and Marius Jacob gangs, and in a wave of out-
rages and assassinations that swept the capital. The poets'
reactions were calculated to shock. Octave Mirbeau saw
in Ravachol's explosions 'the roll of thunder preceding the
joy of sun and peaceful skies'. Anarchist reviews and
newspapers, the most famous of which was *Les temps nou-
veaux,* published sympathetic writings by Valéry, Mallarmé, Saint-Pol Roux, Emile Verhaeren, Paul Adam and
Laurent Tailhade, who was infamous for the phrase
['What do the victims matter, if the gesture be
beautiful?']. . . . (pp. 17-18)

The writings of Pierre-Joseph Proudhon, Mikhail Baku-
nin, Friedrich Nietzsche and Georges Sorel informed this
cultural anarchism. Most influential of all was Sorel's elevation of violence to a political doctrine. He had come to
the conclusion that class struggle contributed to the vigour and health of society, and that only violence could
produce the 'extreme moments', the moments of true freedom when 'we make an effort to create a new man within

ourselves'. Such ideas, pursued at length in Sorel's *Reflections on Violence,* found their cultural expression in a manifesto of 1907 (two years before *The Founding and Manifesto of Futurism*) published by the Parisian group, the
Compagnons de l'Action d'Art, in which violence was advocated as the means to preserve the dignity of art, under
the slogan 'Long live violence against all that makes life
ugly!'

What attracted a restless generation to the theories of
Sorel was the seductive equation of violence and freedom.
Second only to his influence on the Symbolist climate of
Marinetti's Parisian youth was that of Nietzsche. Both
were later to be the subjects of essays by the young Socialist schoolmaster, and erstwhile anarchist, Benito Mussolini, whose study of Nietzsche was published in the Florentine magazine *La voce* in 1911. Mussolini's interpretation
of the philosophy of Nietzsche was symptomatic of the
process of oversimplification and distortion to which his
work has been subjected. In this interpretation Nietzschean ideas of the aesthetic superman, his advocacy of a
war of opinions, his rejection of the market place and his
misanthropy were taken out of context to serve the interpreter's own ends. 'To understand Nietzsche', Mussolini
wrote, 'we must envisage a new race of "free spirits",
strengthened in war, in solitude, in great danger . . . spirits endowed with a kind of sublime perversity, spirits
which will liberate us from the love of our neighbour.'

The shrugging off of neighbourly love emerges in that contradictory marriage of anarchy and nationalism which
characterizes this period, and which re-emerges so stri-
dently in *The Founding and Manifesto.* Eleven years later,
in 'Futurist Democracy' of 1919, Marinetti commented on
the effect of this association:

> One of the sentences of the first manifesto, . . .
> glorifying at the same time patriotism and the
> destructive gesture of the libertarian, seemed
> madness or simply joking to political mentali-
> ties. Everyone found it absurd or ridiculous that
> the libertarian idea went hand in hand with that
> of the Fatherland for the first time. . . . How
> come the idea, 'destructive gesture of the liber-
> tarian', was not accompanied by its inseparable
> friend, anti-patriotism? Enormous shock for
> those brains, so-called political, nourished on
> commonplaces and bookish ideologies, absolute-
> ly unable to understand life, race, crowds, indi-
> viduals. But their shock was even greater when,
> during that glorious May of 1915, they again
> saw the strange couple walking the streets of
> Milan and Rome: Destructive Gesture of the
> Libertarians and Patriotism, with the new
> names of Mussolini, Corridoni, Corradini, Gari-
> baldi, Marinetti, to the cry of 'War on
> Revolution'. . . . We today separate the idea of
> the Fatherland from that of reactionary, clerical
> Monarchy. We unite the idea of Fatherland with
> that of daring Progress and of anti-police revolu-
> tionary democracy.

It was on just these points, of course, that Marinetti and
Mussolini were to fall out.

Marinetti would have been loath to admit it, but this turbulent nationalism had its precedents too. In Italy it had

already been processed into a justification for Italian imperialism by 1900, when Giovanni Pascoli's oration 'Una Sacra' made the African wars respectable by presenting them as 'patriotic socialism'—the shifting of class struggle from internal to foreign politics, from classes to nations, so that the fight was between rich nations and poor ones. Much the same kind of reasoning, coupled with hatred of the past, lay behind the Futurists' later 'Interventionist' campaign for Italy's entry into the First World War, presented as Italy and France against the old tyrants of Europe, Germany and Austria.

Politicians were not alone in seeing the twin policies of nationalism and imperialism as a means of galvanizing the Italian people into acting as a nation rather than as separate states. Italy had been united as a country only since 1861, and regional allegiance, or provincialism, in culture as in politics, still came before the sense of 'Italianness'. The most vocal and energetic exponent of Italian nationalism in culture before Marinetti was Gabriele D'Annunzio, the prolific writer and man of action who prefigured Marinetti in appropriating Nietzschean ideas of grandeur and the superman to become what the sculptor Medardo Rosso called *il Presidente della Casa Io* (President of Maison Ego). The lifelong rivalry between Marinetti and D'Annunzio certainly had something to do with the larger-than-life egos of both men, but it must have been particularly irksome to Marinetti that through his poetry and plays D'Annunzio had already expressed many of the themes that seemed so innovatory in *The Founding and Manifesto*.

With a facility for catching on to the latest cultural currents and moods that was in contrast to the heaviness of his style, D'Annunzio had as early as 1892 sung the praises of the machinery of modern warfare in his 'naval ode', 'To a Torpedo Boat on the Adriatic'. Both D'Annunzio and Marinetti had a thematic precedent in the elegiac Symbolist verse of the Belgian poet Emile Verhaeren, whose *Villes tentaculaires* included themes of factories, stock exchanges, revolts and the future. (pp. 18-20)

In 1903, D'Annunzio's highly coloured poem 'Laus vitae' ('Praise of Life') celebrated the confrontations between striking workers and charging cavalry that were a frequent event in those years of social upheaval. The poem was couched in an epic style and romantic tone that would be unacceptable to Marinetti a few years later, but the theme found a clear echo in *The Founding and Manifesto*: 'We will sing of the multicoloured polyphonic tides of revolution in the modern capitals. . . .' And to top it all, in 1910 D'Annunzio was among the first to see the poetic possibilities of the aeroplane in 'Perhaps So, Perhaps Not'. But, most important as a precedent for the Futurist espousal of war was D'Annunzio's excited reaction to the prospect of war in Africa. It was typical of the poet that this should emerge as a confusion of populism and imperialism with the glory of ancient Rome that was to be a keynote of D'Annunzio's later poetry and a foretaste of the official Fascist penchant for the re-creation of the style and architecture of the Roman Empire. . . . (p. 21)

So close did the paths of the two poets move that in 1906

they both produced equally obnoxious superman heroes in works inspired by the 'African passion'. Corrado Brando, the expeditionary adventurer in D'Annunzio's tragedy *More than Love,* lives and kills for glory in the service of imperialism, his slogan being, 'If this be a crime, I wish all my virtues to kneel before my crime.' Mafarka the Futurist, hero of Marinetti's novel, is even more bumptious in his pretensions. Born, of course, without the aid of woman, Mafarka in Africa swashbuckles his way through every variation of exotic and erotic experience armed with the mighty penis that was to be the subject of Marinetti's trial for obscenity in 1910; he exits only when he has compelled his slaves to build him 'a gigantic invincible bird'—a sailplane—on which to set off for even greater adventures.

Such extravagant manifestations of intransigent aggression in literature bore fruit a few years later. When the Libyan War was declared in 1911, a massive press campaign and popular feeling won over not only the Socialist party and the government headed by Giovanni Giolitti but also the revolutionary syndicalists who were now prepared to maintain that colonialism and syndicalism could go hand in hand. While D'Annunzio greeted this as the vindication of Latin-Italic history, the 'martial eagle' and the 'Libyan Sibyl', Marinetti saw in it the 'great Futurist hour' and urged the government to 'become Futurist, to enlarge all national ambitions, disdaining the stupid accusations of piracy and proclaiming the birth of Panitalianism'. Reality is sometimes even sillier than literature.

Underlying the Futurist emphasis on the will to change was the philosophy of Henri Bergson (1859-1941). Bergsonian ideas of *élan vital,* universal flux, dynamism, and the importance of intuition, coloured the general theoretical tone of Futurism, while his theories of perception were to find something approaching visual interpretation in Futurist paintings. In Bergson, Marinetti recognized an antideterminist philosopher proposing a future formed not by the unchangeable forces of the past, but by the action of men in the here and now: a voluntarist philosophy as expressed in *Creative Evolution* (1907). Added to this was Bergson's belief in the universality of art and the sheer vitality of creativity, made all the more relevant by his exploration of the relationships between mind and body, material and memory, time and movement, and the fact that all of these were considered in the light of contemporary scientific knowledge.

Italian painting of the second half of the nineteenth century had also reflected the course of social and political events, though in a much less overt and aggressive way than literature. Among the painters, too, the romantic spirit of the Risorgimento found its expression in realism and rebellion both against traditional academic standards of beauty and against the cultural domination of France. Italian critics were to continue to despise the home product and ignore the achievements of Italian artists, but the painters themselves proved that Italian art could be more than just a feeble imitation of French Realism, Impressionism or Post-Impressionism. The Futurists, grudging in their recognition of literary precedents, were glad to hail Italian artists like the painters Giovanni Segantini,

1909 cover of the journal Poesia, *the first issue to feature the subtitle "Il futurismo."*

Gaetano Previati and Giuseppe Pellizza da Volpedo, and the sculptor Medardo Rosso, as their predecessors, because they were Italian and because they had all been victims of critical Francophile snobbery.

What was new in Futurism was the will to establish an Italian national art. Groups and movements of the nineteenth century had been firmly centred in one city or another—Naples, Florence, Rome or Milan—and their character had been local rather than national or international. While Futurism was certainly a product of the industrialized and urban north, Marinetti's internationalism brought a new dimension of experience and a firmer sense of identity to artists trapped between the achievements of the ever-present Renaissance and a shaky knowledge of contemporary developments abroad. (pp. 21-2)

Initially Boccioni certainly owed almost everything to Previati, stylistically as well as in terms of Symbolist subject matter. Although he was to discard Previati's religious feeling, he retained more than a trace of his symbolism to the end, and his penchant for the monumental figure of his mother could well have been a leftover from Previati's favourite theme of maternity. Previati's most famous work, *Fall of the Angels,* extravagantly combines the

two apparently contradictory sides of his nature. A colossal cascade of angels reminiscent of Rodin's *Gates of Hell,* silhouetted against the brilliant rays of the sun, brings together Previati the mystical illustrator of the *Divine Comedy* and Previati the rationalist, author of books on the science of colour and light, the technicalities of painting, and the physiological phenomena of Divisionism.

Previati's symbolically loaded anti-realism was to have a great effect on the early work of the Futurist painters. So too was the almost cult-like worship of light and sun suggested by the intensity of the *Fall of the Angels.* The theme recurs in an extraordinary painting by another artist admired and defended by the Futurists. Pellizza da Volpedo's *Sun* of 1904 is a study of iridescent light, an equivalent in painting to a photograph taken looking into the sun. Composition is drastically simplified to the contrast of light and dark zones so that the shimmering beams of the sun obliterate the foreground rather than illuminate it. While *Sun* was painted in strictly Divisionist technique, Pellizza's most influential canvas, much admired by the Futurists for its social theme, was the huge *Fourth Estate* of 1896-1901, in which the treatment is closer to Impressionism, and the compositional focus centres on a powerful grouping of massed and organized workers: the new Italy.

The *Technical Manifesto of Futurist Painting* ends with a clear statement: 'We conclude that painting cannot exist today without Divisionism.' It was from the vocabulary of Segantini, Previati and Pellizza that the young Futurists were to build up their repertoire of themes and techniques. The Divisionist style was well in evidence in their work for some time after the publication of *The Founding and Manifesto* in 1909 and their own *Technical Manifesto of Futurist Painting* in 1910.

Divisionist themes of city life, working life, intimist interiors and the study of light were the natural choice for a generation born, with the exception of the older Balla, in the early 1880s. Boccioni, still searching for a personal style and approach, was the only one who had been strongly attracted to the loaded symbolism of Previati, and this mostly in his graphic work (*Crowd Surrounding Equestrian Monument* and *Ex-libris,* both of 1908). Boccioni painted the *Suburbs of Milan: Factories at Porta Romana* of 1908 in strictly Divisionist style; Carrà was seduced by the nocturnal lights of Piazza Beccaria into transforming the suns of Pellizza and Previati into glittering impressions of artificial light and city life. Severini in Paris applied a cheerful Post-Impressionism, with none of the drama of Boccioni and Carrà, to carefree scenes like the 1908 *Boulevard* (its Métro sign hinting at the future) and the Divisionist *Spring in Montmartre.* Perhaps the most significant individual development was Balla's extraordinary marriage of Divisionist touch, realist approach and social concern in large-scale canvases like *Work* and *Bankrupt* of 1902.

The *Manifesto of the Futurist Painters,* published on 11 February 1910, adds another name to the list of Italian artists overlooked and neglected by the critics, that of the sculptor Medardo Rosso: 'Ask these priests of a veritable religious cult, these guardians of old aesthetic laws, where we can go and see the works of Giovanni Segantini today. Ask them why the officials of the commission have never heard of the existence of Gaetano Previati. Ask them where they can see Medardo Rosso's sculpture. . . .'

Two years later, when Boccioni turned his interest to sculpture, his *Technical Manifesto of Futurist Sculpture,* published on 11 April 1912, described 'the genius of Medardo Rosso, an Italian, the only great modern sculptor who has tried to open up a whole new field of sculpture by his representation in plastic art of the influences of the environment and the atmospheric links which bind it to his subject'.

Medardo Rosso (1858-1928) had been an outstanding victim of Italian neglect, and, discouraged, had virtually stopped work in 1907. Born in Turin, he spent most of his relatively few working years in Paris, where he met Soffici in 1904. During his lifetime and after, his extraordinary breakthrough in sculpture was blindly underrated as simply a sculptural form of Impressionism, or as a small-scale shadow of Rodin. Soffici and the Futurists were the first to recognize, in 1909-10, the significance of his attempt to break down the solidity of sculpture, not just through Impressionistic play of light on the surface, increased by the wax coating he evolved to enhance the fluidity of his forms, but also by expressing both the interdependence of figures and surroundings, and the unity of space, light and air. A small group of works like *Kiss under the Lamp Post* (1882), *Impressions of an Omnibus* (1883-84) and *Conversation in a Garden* (1893) show how he evolved a unique genre of sculpture in which fleeting gestures and psychological moods were caught with the perceptiveness and wit of the city-dweller turning for inspiration to the life around him on the streets. (pp. 24-7)

The relationship between such perception and the 'dynamic interpenetration' described by the Futurist painters in their *Technical Manifesto* is clear: 'To paint a human figure you must not paint it—you must render the whole of its surrounding atmosphere. . . . Our bodies penetrate the sofas on which we sit, and the sofas penetrate our bodies.'

Marinetti's group of Milanese Futurists were not the only intellectuals to defend Italian art in general and grotesquely underrated personalities like Medardo Rosso in particular. For several years magazines and scholarly yet polemical journals had provided a platform for trenchant attacks on the stagnant state of official Italian culture. The most sustained and impressive of these had come from Florence, through the pages of the two magazines sponsored by Giuseppe Prezzolini (1882-?) and Giovanni Papini (1881-1956)—the self-styled 'villains of philosophy' who introduced themselves to their public as pagans, idealists and individualists. *Leonardo,* the first of these magazines, was published from January 1903 to August 1907. During these years it faithfully mirrored the ambivalent position of its editors and contributors. In the name of creative freedom, idealist philosophy was flaunted in the face of the prevailing positivism of Italian culture. Here there was in fact a similarity with the thinking of their rival in philosophy, and *bête noire,* Benedetto Croce, whose writings on aesthetics, although showing affinities with the *élan vital* of Bergson, were in general too 'Hegelian', too idealist (old style), and too officially academic, for the younger generation.

In the pages of *Leonardo* the mysticism of Prezzolini and Papini found its place with the provincial nationalism of Adolfo De Carolis, attacks on and defence of the aesthetic of Art Nouveau, and enthusiasm for Symbolist literature and painting. In 1907 they were joined by the young painter and writer Ardengo Soffici (1879-1964). Soffici had lived in Paris since 1904, and had an intimate knowledge of the latest developments in French painting. His accounts of Cubism were to be the most stimulating and lucid writings on the movement to appear in Italy, while his own painting. Futurist though the titles may have been (e.g. *Lines and Volumes of a Person,* 1912; *Decomposition of Plastic Planes,* 1913), was a closely observed personal rendering of the Cubist aesthetic.

Fifteen months after the demise of *Leonardo* it was replaced by *La voce,* which attempted to put into practice Prezzolini's tale of a young man possessed by a mysterious voice which urges him on to a campaign of moral purification. In the first issue the ultimatum was delivered in an article entitled 'Innovation and Junk': 'Old age and rubbish must not have an everlasting domain. We must make room for the young.'

The limitations of *Leonardo* had yielded to a breadth of approach that covered social, political, moral and cultural issues. The aim was nothing less than 'an integral education of man', and Croce was now back in favour as 'the poet of philosophy'. While the emphasis was firmly 'Nationalists no, but Italians yes', some of the most significant articles were Soffici's on French developments, though he sprang to the attack in 1909 when the Venice Biennale once more failed to honour Medardo Rosso. In 1911 another contributor was Benito Mussolini, still a socialist, writing on the linguistic struggle in the Austrian-ruled Trentino. Gradually, however, a split developed in *La voce* between Prezzolini, who was increasingly concerned with political and social practicalities, and Papini and Soffici whose commitment was to poetry and art. This was eventually to result in their departure from *La voce* at the end of 1912 to found *Lacerba*. This 'act of liberation', as Papini and Soffici called it, belongs to [another discussion]. . . . Although the group in Florence did become to some extent the victims of what Papini called the 'provincial narrow-mindedness' of that city, and lacked the outrageously iconoclastic internationalism of Marinetti, their activities as expressed through the pages of *La voce* were essential yeast to the fermentation of Futurism. (pp. 28-9)

> *Caroline Tisdall and Angelo Bozzolla, in their* Futurism, *1977. Reprint by Oxford University Press, Inc., 1978, 216 p.*

MANIFESTOS

Filippo Tommaso Marinetti

[*What follows is the 1909 essay* The Founding and Manifesto of Futurism, *in which Marinetti expresses in narrative form the impulse behind Futurism and establishes the movement's central precepts.*]

We had stayed up all night, my friends and I, under hanging mosque lamps with domes of filigreed brass, domes starred like our spirits, shining like them with the prisoned radiance of electric hearts. For hours we had trampled our atavistic ennui into rich oriental rugs, arguing up to the last confines of logic and blackening many reams of paper with our frenzied scribbling.

An immense pride was buoying us up, because we felt ourselves alone at that hour, alone, awake, and on our feet, like proud beacons or forward sentries against an army of hostile stars glaring down at us from their celestial encampments. Alone with stokers feeding the hellish fires of great ships, alone with the black specters who grope in the red-hot bellies of locomotives launched down their crazy courses, alone with drunkards reeling like wounded birds along the city walls.

Suddenly we jumped, hearing the mighty noise of the huge double-decker trams that rumbled by outside, ablaze with colored lights, like villages on holiday suddenly struck and uprooted by the flooding Po and dragged over falls and through gorges to the sea.

Then the silence deepened. But, as we listened to the old canal muttering its feeble prayers and the creaking bones of sickly palaces above their damp green beards, under the windows we suddenly heard the famished roar of automobiles.

"Let's go!" I said. "Friends, away! Let's go! Mythology and the Mystic Ideal are defeated at last. We're about to see the Centaur's birth and, soon after, the first flight of Angels! . . . We must shake the gates of life, test the bolts and hinges. Let's go! Look there, on the earth, the very first dawn! There's nothing to match the splendor of the sun's red sword, slashing for the first time through our millennial gloom!"

We went up to the three snorting beasts, to lay amorous hands on their torrid breasts. I stretched out on my car like a corpse on its bier, but revived at once under the steering wheel, a guillotine blade that threatened my stomach.

The raging broom of madness swept us out of ourselves and drove us through streets as rough and deep as the beds of torrents. Here and there, sick lamplight through window glass taught us to distrust the deceitful mathematics of our perishing eyes.

I cried, "The scent, the scent alone is enough for our beasts."

And like young lions we ran after Death, its dark pelt blotched with pale crosses as it escaped down the vast violet living and throbbing sky.

But we had no ideal Mistress raising her divine form to the clouds, nor any cruel Queen to whom to offer our bodies, twisted like Byzantine rings! There was nothing to make us wish for death, unless the wish to be free at last from the weight of our courage!

And on we raced, hurling watchdogs against doorsteps, curling them under our burning tires like collars under a flatiron. Death, domesticated, met me at every turn, gracefully holding out a paw, or once in a while hunkering down, making velvety caressing eyes at me from every puddle.

"Let's break out of the horrible shell of wisdom and throw ourselves like pride-ripened fruit into the wide, contorted mouth of the wind! Let's give ourselves utterly to the Unknown, not in desperation but only to replenish the deep wells of the Absurd!!"

The words were scarcely out of my mouth when I spun my car around with the frenzy of a dog trying to bite its tail, and there, suddenly, were two cyclists coming toward me, shaking their fists, wobbling like two equally convincing but nevertheless contradictory arguments. Their stupid dilemma was blocking my way—damn! Ouch! . . . I stopped short and to my disgust rolled over into a ditch with my wheels in the air. . . .

Oh! Maternal ditch, almost full of muddy water! Fair factory drain! I gulped down your nourishing sludge; and I remembered the blessed black breast of my Sudanese nurse. . . . When I came up—torn, filthy, and stinking—from under the capsized car, I felt the white-hot iron of joy deliciously pass through my heart!

A crowd of fishermen with handlines and gouty naturalists were already swarming around the prodigy. With patient, loving care those people rigged a tall derrick and iron grapnels to fish out my car, like a big beached shark. Up it came from the ditch, slowly, leaving in the bottom like scales its heavy framework of good sense and its soft upholstery of comfort.

They thought it was dead, my beautiful shark, but a caress from me was enough to revive it; and there it was, alive again, running on its powerful fins!

And so, faces smeared with good factory muck—plastered with metallic waste, with senseless sweat, with celestial soot—we, bruised, our arms in slings, but unafraid, declared our high intentions to all the *living* of the earth:

MANIFESTO OF FUTURISM

1. We intend to sing the love of danger, the habit of energy and fearlessness.

2. Courage, audacity, and revolt will be essential elements of our poetry.

3. Up to now literature has exalted a pensive immobility, ecstasy, and sleep. We intend to exalt aggressive action, a feverish insomnia, the racer's stride, the mortal leap, the punch and the slap.

4. We say that the world's magnificence has been enriched by a new beauty; the beauty of speed. A racing car whose hood is adorned with great pipes, like serpents of explosive breath—a roaring car that seems to ride on grapeshot—is more beautiful than the *Victory of Samothrace.*

5. We want to hymn the man at the wheel, who hurls the lance of his spirit across the Earth, along the circle of its orbit.

6. The poet must spend himself with ardor, splendor, and generosity, to swell the enthusiastic fervor of the primordial elements.

7. Except in struggle, there is no more beauty. No work without an aggressive character can be a masterpiece. Poetry must be conceived as a violent attack on unknown forces, to reduce and prostrate them before man.

8. We stand on the last promontory of the centuries! . . . Why should we look back, when what we want is to break down the mysterious doors of the Impossible? Time and Space died yesterday. We already live in the absolute, because we have created eternal, omnipresent speed.

9. We will glorify war—the world's only hygiene—militarism, patriotism, the destructive gesture of freedom-bringers, beautiful ideas worth dying for, and scorn for woman.

10. We will destroy the museums, libraries, academies of every kind, will fight moralism, feminism, every opportunistic or utilitarian cowardice.

11. We will sing of great crowds excited by work, by pleasure, and by riot; we will sing of the multicolored, polyphonic tides of revolution in the modern capitals; we will sing of the vibrant nightly fervor of arsenals and shipyards blazing with violent electric moons; greedy railway stations that devour smoke-plumed serpents; factories hung on clouds by the crooked lines of their smoke; bridges that stride the rivers like giant gymnasts, flashing in the sun with a glitter of knives; adventurous steamers that sniff the horizon; deep-chested locomotives whose wheels paw the tracks like the hooves of enormous steel horses bridled by tubing; and the sleek flight of planes whose propellers chatter in the wind like banners and seem to cheer like an enthusiastic crowd.

It is from Italy that we launch through the world this violently upsetting, incendiary manifesto of ours. With it, today, we establish *Futurism* because we want to free this land from its smelly gangrene of professors, archaeologists, ciceroni, and antiquarians. For too long has Italy been a dealer in secondhand clothes. We mean to free her from the numberless museums that cover her like so many graveyards.

Museums: cemeteries! . . . Identical, surely, in the sinister promiscuity of so many bodies unknown to one another. Museums: public dormitories where one lies forever beside hated or unknown beings. Museums: absurd abattoirs of painters and sculptors ferociously macerating each other with color-blows and line-blows, the length of the fought-over walls!

That one should make an annual pilgrimage, just as one goes to the graveyard on All Souls' Day—that I grant. That once a year one should leave a floral tribute beneath the *Gioconda,* I grant you that. . . . But I don't admit that our sorrows, our fragile courage, our morbid restlessness should be given a daily conducted tour through the museums. Why poison ourselves? Why rot?

And what is there to see in an old picture except the laborious contortions of an artist throwing himself against the barriers that thwart his desire to express his dream completely? . . . Admiring an old picture is the same as pouring our sensibility into a funerary urn instead of hurling it far off, in violent spasms of action and creation.

Do you, then, wish to waste all your best powers in this eternal and futile worship of the past, from which you emerge fatally exhausted, shrunken, beaten down?

In truth I tell you that daily visits to museums, libraries, and academies (cemeteries of empty exertion, calvaries of crucified dreams, registries of aborted beginnings!) is, for artists, as damaging as the prolonged supervision by parents of certain young people drunk with their talent and their ambitious wills. When the future is barred to them, the admirable past may be a solace for the ills of the moribund, the sickly, the prisoner. . . . But we want no part of it, the past, we the young and strong *Futurists!*

So let them come, the gay incendiaries with charred fingers! Here they are! Here they are! . . . Come on! set fire to the library shelves! Turn aside the canals to flood the museums! . . . Oh, the joy of seeing the glorious old canvases bobbing adrift on those waters, discolored and shredded! . . . Take up your pickaxes, your axes and hammers, and wreck, wreck the venerable cities, pitilessly!

The oldest of us is thirty: so we have at least a decade for finishing our work. When we are forty, other younger and stronger men will probably throw us in the wastebasket like useless manuscripts—we want it to happen!

They will come against us, our successors, will come from far away, from every quarter, dancing to the winged cadence of their first songs, flexing the hooked claws of predators, sniffing doglike at the academy doors the strong odor of our decaying minds, which already will have been promised to the literary catacombs.

But we won't be there. . . . At last they'll find us—one winter's night—in open country, beneath a sad roof drummed by a monotonous rain. They'll see us crouched beside our trembling airplanes in the act of warming our hands at the poor little blaze that our books of today will give out when they take fire from the flight of our images.

They'll storm around us, panting with scorn and anguish, and all of them, exasperated by our proud daring, will hurtle to kill us, driven by hatred: the more implacable it is, the more their hearts will be drunk with love and admiration for us.

Injustice, strong and sane, will break out radiantly in their eyes.

Art, in fact, can be nothing but violence, cruelty, and injustice.

The oldest of us is thirty: even so we have already scattered treasures, a thousand treasures of force, love, courage, astuteness, and raw will power; have thrown them impatiently away, with fury, carelessly, unhesitatingly, breathless and unresting. . . . Look at us! We are still untired! Our hearts know no weariness because they are fed with fire, hatred, and speed! . . . Does that amaze you? It should, because you can never remember having lived! Erect on the summit of the world, once again we hurl our defiance at the stars!

You have objections?—Enough! Enough! We know them . . . we've understood! . . . Our fine deceitful intelligence tells us that we are the revival and extension of our ancestors—perhaps! . . . If only it were so!—But who cares? We don't want to understand! . . . Woe to anyone who says those infamous words to us again!

Lift up your heads!

Erect on the summit of the world, once again we hurl defiance to the stars! (pp. 39-44)

> *Filippo Tommaso Marinetti, "The Founding and Manifesto of Futurism," in his* Marinetti: Selected Writings, *edited by R. W. Flint,*

translated by R. W. Flint and Arthur A. Coppotelli, Farrar, Straus and Giroux, 1972, pp. 39-44.

Filippo Tommaso Marinetti

[*The following 1912 essay comprises the* Technical Manifesto of Futurist Literature, *in which Marinetti outlines the fundamental literary tenets and techniques of Futurism.*]

Sitting on the gas tank of an airplane, my stomach warmed by the pilot's head, I sensed the ridiculous inanity of the old syntax inherited from Homer. A pressing need to liberate words, to drag them out of their prison in the Latin period! Like all imbeciles, this period naturally has a canny head, a stomach, two legs, and two flat feet, but it will never have two wings. Just enough to walk, to take a short run and then stop short, panting!

This is what the whirling propeller told me, when I flew two hundred meters above the mighty chimney pots of Milan. And the propeller added:

1. One must destroy syntax and scatter one's nouns at random, just as they are born.

2. One should use infinitives, because they adapt themselves elastically to nouns and don't subordinate them to the writer's *I* that observes or imagines. Alone, the infinitive can provide a sense of the continuity of life and the elasticity of the intuition that perceives it.

3. One must abolish the adjective, to allow the naked noun to preserve its essential color. The adjective, tending of itself toward the shadows, is incompatible with our dynamic vision, because it supposes a pause, a meditation.

4. One must abolish the adverb, old belt buckle that holds two words together. The adverb preserves a tedious unity of tone within a phrase.

5. Every noun should have its double; that is, the noun should be followed, with no conjunction, by the noun to which it is related by analogy. Example: man–torpedo-boat, woman-gulf, crowd-surf, piazza-funnel, door-faucet.

Just as aerial speed has multiplied our knowledge of the world, the perception of analogy becomes ever more natural for man. One must suppress the *like,* the *as,* the *so,* the *similar to.* Still better, one should deliberately confound the object with the image that it evokes, foreshortening the image to a single essential word.

6. Abolish even the punctuation. After adjectives, adverbs, and conjunctions have been suppressed, punctuation is naturally annulled, in the varying continuity of a *living* style that creates itself without the foolish pauses made by commas and periods. To accentuate certain movements and indicate their directions, mathematical symbols will be used: $+ - \times : =$ and the musical symbols.

7. Up to now writers have been restricted to immediate analogies. For instance, they have compared an animal to a man or to another animal, which is almost the same as a kind of photography. (They have compared, for example, a fox terrier to a very small thoroughbred. Others,

more advanced, might compare that same trembling fox terrier to a little Morse Code machine. I, on the other hand, compare it to gurgling water. In this there is *an ever-vaster gradation of analogies,* there are ever-deeper and more solid affinities, however remote.)

Analogy is nothing more than the deep love that assembles distant, seemingly diverse and hostile things. An orchestral style, at once polychromatic, polyphonic, and polymorphous, can embrace the life of matter only by means of the most extensive analogies.

When, in my "Battle of Tripoli," I compared a trench bristling with bayonets to an orchestra, a machine gun to a fatal woman, I intuitively introduced a large part of the universe into a short episode of African battle.

Images are not flowers to be chosen and picked with parsimony, as Voltaire said. They are the very lifeblood of poetry. Poetry should be an uninterrupted sequence of new images, or it is mere anemia and green-sickness.

The broader their affinities, the longer will images keep their power to amaze. One must—people say—spare the reader's capacity for wonder. Nonsense! Let us rather worry about the fatal corrosion of time that not only destroys the expressive value of a masterpiece but also its power to amaze. Too often stimulated, have our old ears perhaps not already destroyed Beethoven and Wagner? We must therefore eliminate from our language everything it contains in the way of stereotyped images, faded metaphors; and that means almost everything.

8. There are no categories of images, noble or gross or vulgar, eccentric or natural. The intuition that grasps them has no preferences or *partis pris* ["prejudice"]. Therefore the analogical style is absolute master of all matter and its intense life.

9. To render the successive motions of an object, one must render the *chain of analogies* that it evokes, each condensed and concentrated into one essential word.

Here is an expressive example of a chain of analogies still masked and weighed down by traditional syntax:

> Ah yes! you, little machine gun, are a fascinating woman, and sinister, and divine, at the driving wheel of an invisible hundred horsepower, roaring and exploding with impatience. Oh! soon you will leap into the circuit of death, to a shattering somersault or to victory! . . . Do you want me to make you some madrigals full of grace and color? As you wish, *signora*. . . . To me you resemble a lawyer before the bar, whose tireless eloquent tongue strikes his circle of listeners to the heart, moving them profoundly. . . . At this moment you are an omnipotent trepan that cuts rings around the too hard skull of this stubborn night. . . . And you are also a rolling mill, an electric lathe, and what else? A great blowtorch that sears, chisels, and slowly melts the metal points of the last stars! . . . ["Battle of Tripoli"]

In some cases one must join the images two by two, like those chained iron balls that level a whole grove of trees in their flight.

10. To catch and gather whatever is most fugitive and ungraspable in matter, one must shape *strict nets of images or analogies,* to be cast into the mysterious sea of phenomena. Except for the traditional festoons of its form, the following passage from my *Mafarka the Futurist* is an example of such a strict net of images:

> All the bitter sweetness of past youth mounted in his throat, as the cheerful cries of boys rose from the schoolyard toward their teachers leaning on the parapets of the terraces from which ships could be seen taking flight. . . .

And here are two more nets of images:

> Around the well of Bumeliana, beneath the thick olive trees, three camels squatting comfortably on the sand were gargling with contentment, like old stone gutters, mixing the *chak-chak* of their spitting with the steady beat of the steam pump that supplies water to the city. Cries and Futurist dissonances, in the deep orchestra of the trenches with their winding depths and noisy cellars, as the bayonets pass and repass, violin bows that the sunset's ruddy baton inflames with enthusiasm. . . .

> It is the sunset-conductor whose wide sweep gathers the scattered flutes of tree-bound birds, the grieving harps of insects, the creak of branches, and the crunch of stones. It is he who suddenly stops the mess-tïn kettledrums and the rifles' clash, to let the muted instruments sing out above the orchestra, all the golden stars, upright, open-armed, across the footlights of the sky. And here is the *grande dame* of the play. . . . Prodigiously bare, it is indeed the desert who displays her immense bosom in its liquefied curves, all glowing in rosy lacquer beneath the mighty night's cascading jewels. ["Battle of Tripoli"]

11. Destroy the *I* in literature: that is, all psychology. The man sidetracked by the library and the museum, subjected to a logic and wisdom of fear, is of absolutely no interest. We must therefore drive him from literature and finally put matter in his place, matter whose essence must be grasped by strokes of intuition, the kind of thing that the physicists and chemists can never do.

To capture the breath, the sensibility, and the instincts of metals, stones, wood, and so on, through the medium of free objects and whimsical motors. To substitute for human psychology, now exhausted, the lyric obsession with matter.

Be careful not to force human feelings onto matter. Instead, divine its different governing impulses, its forces of compression, dilation, cohesion, and disaggregation, its crowds of massed molecules and whirling electrons. We are not interested in offering dramas of humanized matter. The solidity of a strip of steel interests us for itself; that is, the incomprehensible and nonhuman alliance of its molecules or its electrons that oppose, for instance, the penetration of a howitzer. The warmth of a piece of iron or wood is in our opinion more impassioned than the smile or tears of a woman.

We want to make literature out of the life of a motor, a new instinctive animal whose general instincts we will know when we have learned the instincts of the different forces that make it up.

For a Futurist poet, nothing is more interesting than the action of a mechanical piano's keyboard. The cinema offers us the dance of an object that divides and recomposes without human intervention. It also offers us the backward sweep of a diver whose feet leave the ocean and bounce violently back on the diving board. Finally, it shows us a man driving at two hundred miles an hour. These are likewise movements of matter, outside the laws of intelligence and therefore of a more significant essence.

Three elements hitherto overlooked in literature must be introduced:

1. Sound (manifestation of the dynamism of objects).

2. Weight (objects' faculty of flight).

3. Smell (objects' faculty of dispersing themselves).

To force oneself, for example, to render the landscape of smells that a dog perceives. To listen to motors and to reproduce their conversations.

Material has always been contemplated by a cold, distracted *I*, too preoccupied with itself, full of preconceived wisdom and human obsessions.

Man tends to foul matter with his youthful joy or elderly sorrows; matter has an admirable continuity of impulse toward greater warmth, greater movement, a greater subdivision of itself. Matter is neither sad nor gay. Its essence is courage, will power, and absolute force. It belongs entirely to the intuitive poet who can free himself from traditional, heavy, limited syntax that is stuck in the ground, armless and wingless, being merely intelligent. Only the unsyntactical poet who unlinks his words can penetrate the essence of matter and destroy the dumb hostility that separates it from us.

The Latin period that has served us up to now was a pretentious gesture with which the myopic and overweening imagination forced itself to master the multiform and mysterious life of matter. The Latin period, consequently, was born dead.

Deep intuitions of life joined to one another, word for word according to their illogical birth, will give us the general lines of an *intuitive psychology of matter*. This was revealed to me when I was flying in an airplane. As I looked at objects from a new point of view, no longer head on or from behind, but straight down, foreshortened, that is, I was able to break apart the old shackles of logic and the plumb lines of the ancient way of thinking.

All you Futurist poets who have loved and followed me up to now have, like me, been frenzied makers of images and courageous explorers of analogies. But your strict nets of metaphor are too disgracefully weighed down by the plumb line of logic. I advise you to lighten them, in order that your immensified gesture may speed them farther, cast them over a vaster ocean.

Together we will invent what I call *the imagination without strings* [*l'immaginazione senza fili*]. Someday we will achieve a yet more essential art, when we dare to suppress all the first terms of our analogies and render no more than an uninterrupted sequence of second terms. To achieve this we must renounce being understood. It is not necessary to be understood. Moreover we did without it when we were expressing fragments of the Futurist sensibility by means of traditional and intellective syntax.

Syntax was a kind of abstract cipher that poets used to inform the crowd about the color, musicality, plasticity, and architecture of the universe. Syntax was a kind of interpreter or monotonous cicerone. This intermediary must be suppressed, in order that literature may enter directly into the universe and become one body with it.

They shout at us, "Your literature won't be beautiful! Where is your verbal symphony, your harmonious swaying back and forth, your tranquilizing cadences?" Their loss we take for granted! And how lucky! We make use, instead, of every ugly sound, every expressive cry from the violent life that surrounds us. We bravely create the "ugly" in literature, and everywhere we murder solemnity. Come! Don't put on these grand priestly airs when you listen to me! Each day we must spit on the *Altar of Art*. We are entering the unbounded domain of free intuition. After free verse, here finally are *words-in-freedom*.

In this there is nothing absolute or systematic. Genius has impetuous gusts and muddy torrents. Sometimes it imposes analytic and explanatory longueurs. No one can suddenly renovate his own sensibility. Dead cells are mixed with the living. Art is a need to destroy and scatter oneself, a great watering can of heroism that drowns the world. Microbes—don't forget—are essential to the health of the intestines and stomach. There is also a microbe essential to the vitality of *art, this extension of the forest of our veins,* that pours out, beyond the body, into the infinity of space and time.

Futurist poets! I have taught you to hate libraries and museums, to prepare you *to hate the intelligence,* reawakening in you divine intuition, the characteristic gift of the Latin races. Through intuition we will conquer the seemingly unconquerable hostility that separates out human flesh from the metal of motors. (pp. 84-9)

> *Filippo Tommaso Marinetti, "Technical Manifesto of Futurist Literature," in his* Marinetti: Selected Writings, *edited by R. W. Flint, translated by R. W. Flint and Arthur A. Coppotelli, Farrar, Straus and Giroux, 1972, pp. 84-9.*

Filippo Tommaso Marinetti

[*The following excerpt is from the 1913 manifesto* The Variety Theater, *in which Marinetti characterizes the basis of Futurist performance.*]

We are deeply disgusted with the contemporary theater (verse, prose, and musical) because it vacillates stupidly between historical reconstruction (pastiche or plagiarism) and photographic reproduction of our daily life; a finicking, slow, analytic, and diluted theater worthy, all in all, of the age of the oil lamp.

Futurism exalts the Variety Theater because:

1. The Variety Theater, born as we are from electricity, is lucky in having no tradition, no masters, no dogma, and it is fed by swift actuality.

2. The Variety Theater is absolutely practical, because it proposes to distract and amuse the public with comic effects, erotic stimulation, or imaginative astonishment.

3. The authors, actors, and technicians of the Variety Theater have only one reason for existing and triumphing: incessantly to invent new elements of astonishment. Hence the absolute impossibility of arresting or repeating oneself, hence an excited competition of brains and muscles to conquer the various records of agility, speed, force, complication, and elegance.

4. The Variety Theater is unique today in its use of the cinema, which enriches it with an incalculable number of visions and otherwise unrealizable spectacles (battles, riots, horse races, automobile and airplane meets, trips, voyages, depths of the city, the countryside, oceans, and skies).

5. The Variety Theater, being a profitable show window for countless inventive forces, naturally generates what I call "the Futurist marvelous," produced by modern mechanics. Here are some of the elements of this "marvelous": (a) powerful caricatures; (b) abysses of the ridiculous; (c) delicious, impalpable ironies; (d) all-embracing, definitive symbols; (e) cascades of uncontrollable hilarity; (f) profound analogies between humanity, the animal, vegetable, and mechanical worlds; (g) flashes of revealing cynicism; (h) plots full of the wit, repartee, and conundrums that aerate the intelligence; (i) the whole gamut of laughter and smiles, to flex the nerves; (j) the whole gamut of stupidity, imbecility, doltishness, and absurdity, insensibly pushing the intelligence to the very border of madness; (k) all the new significations of light, sound, noise, and language, with their mysterious and inexplicable extensions into the least-explored part of our sensibility; (l) a cumulus of events unfolded at great speed, of stage characters pushed from right to left in two minutes ("and now let's have a look at the Balkans": King Nicholas, Enver-Bey, Daneff, Venizelos, belly-blows and fistfights between Serbs and Bulgars, a *couplet,* and everything vanishes); (m) instructive, satirical pantomimes; (n) caricatures of suffering and nostalgia, strongly impressed on the sensibility through gestures exasperating in their spasmodic, hesitant, weary slowness; grave words made ridiculous by funny gestures, bizarre disguises, mutilated words, ugly faces, pratfalls.

6. Today the Variety Theater is the crucible in which the elements of an emergent new sensibility are seething. Here you find an ironic decomposition of all the worn-out prototypes of the Beautiful, the Grand, the Solemn, the Religious, the Ferocious, the Seductive, and the Terrifying, and also the abstract elaboration of the new prototypes that will succeed these.

The Variety Theater is thus the synthesis of everything that humanity has up to now refined in its nerves to divert itself by laughing at material and moral grief; it is also the bubbling fusion of all the laughter, all the smiles, all the mocking grins, all the contortions and grimaces of future humanity. Here you sample the joy that will shake men for another century, their poetry, painting, philosophy, and the leaps of their architecture.

7. The Variety Theater offers the healthiest of all spectacles in its dynamism of form and color (simultaneous movement of jugglers, ballerinas, gymnasts, colorful riding masters, spiral cyclones of dancers spinning on the points of their feet). In its swift, overpowering dance rhythms the Variety Theater forcibly drags the slowest souls out of their torpor and forces them to run and jump.

8. The Variety Theater is alone in seeking the audience's collaboration. It doesn't remain static like a stupid voyeur, but joins noisily in the action, in the singing, accompanying the orchestra, communicating with the actors in surprising actions and bizarre dialogues. And the actors bicker clownishly with the musicians.

The Variety Theater uses the smoke of cigars and cigarettes to join the atmosphere of the theater to that of the stage. And because the audience cooperates in this way with the actors' fantasy, the action develops simultaneously on the stage, in the boxes, and in the orchestra. It continues to the end of the performance, among the battalions of fans, the honeyed dandies who crowd the stage door to fight over the *star;* double final victory: chic dinner and bed.

9. The Variety Theater is a school of sincerity for man because it exalts his rapacious instincts and snatches every veil from woman, all the phrases, all the sighs, all the romantic sobs that mask and deform her. On the other hand it brings to light all woman's marvelous animal qualities, her grasp, her powers of seduction, her faithlessness, and her resistance.

10. The Variety Theater is a school of heroism in the difficulty of setting records and conquering resistances, and it creates on the stage the strong, sane atmosphere of danger. (E.g., death-diving, "looping the loop" on bicycles, in cars, and on horseback.)

11. The Variety Theater is a school of subtlety, complication, and mental synthesis, in its clowns, magicians, mind readers, brilliant calculators, writers of skits, imitators and parodists, its musical jugglers and eccentric Americans, its fantastic pregnancies that give birth to objects and weird mechanisms.

12. The Variety Theater is the only school that one can recommend to adolescents and to talented young men, because it explains, quickly and incisively, the most abstruse problems and most complicated political events. Example: a year ago at the Folies-Bergère, two dancers were acting out the meandering discussions between Cambon and Kinderlen-Watcher on the question of Morocco and the Congo in a revealing symbolic dance that was equivalent to at least three years' study of foreign affairs. Facing the audience, their arms entwined, glued together, they kept making mutual territorial concessions, jumping back and forth, to left and right, never separating, neither of them

ever losing sight of his goal, which was to become more and more entangled. They gave an impression of extreme courtesy, of skillful, flawlessly diplomatic vacillation, ferocity, diffidence, stubbornness, meticulousness.

Furthermore the Variety Theater luminously explains the governing laws of life:

> a) the necessity of complication and varying rhythms;
>
> b) the fatality of the lie and the contradiction (e.g., two-faced English *danseuses:* little shepherd girl and fearful soldier);
>
> c) the omnipotence of a methodical will that modifies human powers;
>
> d) a synthesis of speed + transformations.

13. The Variety Theater systematically disparages ideal love and its romantic obsession that repeats the nostalgic languors of passion to satiety, with the robotlike monotony of a daily profession. It whimsically mechanizes sentiment, disparages and healthily tramples down the compulsion toward carnal possession, lowers lust to the natural function of coitus, deprives it of every mystery, every crippling anxiety, every unhealthy idealism.

Instead, the Variety Theater gives a feeling and a taste for easy, light, and ironic loves. Café-concert performances in the open air on the terraces of casinos offer a most amusing battle between spasmodic moonlight, tormented by infinite desperations, and the electric light that bounces off the fake jewelry, painted flesh, multicolored petticoats, velvets, tinsel, the counterfeit color of lips. Naturally the energetic electric light triumphs and the soft decadent moonlight is defeated.

14. The Variety Theater is naturally antiacademic, primitive, and naïve, hence the more significant for the unexpectedness of its discoveries and the simplicity of its means. (E.g., the systematic tour of the stage that the *chanteuses* make, like caged animals, at the end of every *couplet.*)

15. The Variety Theater destroys the Solemn, the Sacred, the Serious, and the Sublime in Art with a capital *A.* It cooperates in the Futurist destruction of immortal masterworks, plagiarizing them, parodying them, making them look commonplace by stripping them of their solemn apparatus as if they were mere *attractions.* So we unconditionally endorse the performance of *Parsifal* in forty minutes, now in rehearsal in a great London music hall.

16. The Variety Theater destroys all our conceptions of perspective, proportion, time, and space. (E.g., a little doorway and gate, thirty centimeters high, alone in the middle of the stage, which certain eccentric Americans open and close as they pass and repass, very seriously as if they couldn't do otherwise.)

17. The Variety Theater offers us all the records so far attained: the greatest speed and the finest gymnastics and acrobatics of the Japanese, the greatest muscular frenzy of the Negroes, the greatest development of animal intelligence (horses, elephants, seals, dogs, trained birds), the finest melodic inspiration of the Gulf of Naples and the Russian steppes, the best Parisian wit, the greatest competitive force of different races (boxing and wrestling), the greatest anatomical monstrosity, the greatest female beauty.

18. The conventional theater exalts the inner life, professorial meditation, libraries, museums, monotonous crisis of conscience, stupid analyses of feelings, in other words (dirty thing and dirty word), *psychology,* whereas, on the other hand, the Variety Theater exalts action, heroism, life in the open air, dexterity, the authority of instinct and intuition. To psychology it opposes what I call "body-madness" [*fisicofollia*].

19. Finally, the Variety Theater offers to every country (like Italy) that has no great single capital city a brilliant résumé of Paris considered as the one magnetic center of luxury and ultrarefined pleasure.

FUTURISM WANTS TO TRANSFORM THE VARIETY THEATER INTO A THEATER OF AMAZEMENT, RECORD-SETTING, AND BODY-MADNESS.

1. One must completely destroy all logic in Variety Theater performances, exaggerate their luxuriousness in strange ways, multiply contrasts, and make the absurd and the unlifelike complete masters of the stage. (Example: Oblige the *chanteuses* to dye their décolletage, their arms, and especially their hair, in all the colors hitherto neglected as means of seduction. Green hair, violet arms, blue décolletage, orange chignon, etc. Interrupt a song and continue with a revolutionary speech. Spew out a *romanza* of insults and profanity, etc.)

2. Prevent a set of traditions from establishing itself in the Variety Theater. Therefore oppose and abolish the stupid Parisian "Revues," as tedious as Greek tragedy with their *Compère* and *Commére* playing the part of the ancient chorus, their parade of political personalities and events set off by wisecracks in a most irritating logical sequence. The Variety Theater, in fact, must not be what it unfortunately still is today, nearly always a more or less amusing newspaper.

3. Introduce surprise and the need to move among the spectators of the orchestra, boxes, and balcony. Some random suggestions: spread a powerful glue on some of the seats, so that the male or female spectator will stay glued down and make everyone laugh (the damaged frock coat or toilette will naturally be paid for at the door)—sell the same ticket to ten people: traffic jam, bickering, and wrangling—offer free tickets to gentlemen or ladies who are notoriously unbalanced, irritable, or eccentric and likely to provoke uproars with obscene gestures, pinching women, or other freakishness. Sprinkle the seats with dust to make people itch and sneeze, etc.

4. Systematically prostitute all of classic art on the stage, performing for example all the Greek, French, and Italian tragedies, condensed and comically mixed up, in a single evening—put life into the works of Beethoven, Wagner, Bach, Bellini, Chopin by inserting Neapolitan songs—put Duse, Sarah Bernhardt, Zacconi, Mayol, and Fregoli side by side on the stage—play a Beethoven symphony back-

ward, beginning with the last note—boil all of Shakespeare down to a single act—do the same with all the most venerated actors—have actors recite *Hernani* tied in sacks up to their necks—soap the floorboards to cause amusing tumbles at the most tragic moments.

5. In every way encourage the *type* of the eccentric American, the impression he gives of exciting grotesquerie, of frightening dynamism; his crude jokes, his enormous brutalities, his trick weskits and pants as deep as a ship's hold out of which, with a thousand other things, will come the great Futurist hilarity that should make the world's face young again. (pp. 116-21)

> Filippo Tommaso Marinetti, "The Variety Theater," in his Marinetti: Selected Writings, edited by R. W. Flint, translated by R. W. Flint and Arthur A. Coppotelli, Farrar, Straus and Giroux, 1972, pp. 116-22.

Filippo Tommaso Marinetti, Emilio Settimelli, and Bruno Corra

[*What follows is the 1915 manifesto* The Futurist Synthetic Theater, *which corroborates the renunciation of traditional dramatic forms in* The Variety Theater (*excerpted above) and elaborates on major techniques of Futurist drama.*]

As we await our much-prayed-for great war, we Futurists carry out violent antineutralist action from city square to university and back again, using our art to prepare the Italian sensibility for the great hour of maximum danger. Italy must be fearless, eager, as swift and elastic as a fencer, as indifferent to blows as a boxer, as impassive at the news of a victory that may have cost fifty thousand dead as at the news of a defeat.

For Italy to learn to make up its mind with lightning speed, to hurl itself into battle, to sustain every undertaking and every possible calamity, books and reviews are unnecessary. They interest and concern only a minority, are more or less tedious, obstructive, and relaxing. They cannot help chilling enthusiasm, aborting impulses, and poisoning with doubt a people at war. War—Futurism intensified—obliges us to march and not to rot [*marciare, non marcire*] in libraries and reading rooms. THEREFORE WE THINK THAT THE ONLY WAY TO INSPIRE ITALY WITH THE WARLIKE SPIRIT TODAY IS THROUGH THE THEATER. In fact 90 percent of Italians go to the theater, whereas only 10 percent read books and reviews. But what is needed is a FUTURIST THEATER, completely opposed to the passéist theater that drags its monotonous, depressing processions around the sleepy Italian stages.

Not to dwell on the historical theater, a sickening genre already abandoned by the passéist public, we condemn the whole contemporary theater because it is too prolix, analytic, pedantically psychological, explanatory, diluted, finicking, static, as full of prohibitions as a police station, as cut up into cells as a monastery, as moss-grown as an old abandoned house. In other words it is a pacifistic, neutralist theater, the antithesis of the fierce, overwhelming, synthesizing velocity of the war.

Our Futurist theater will be

Synthetic. That is, very brief. To compress into a few minutes, into a few words and gestures, innumerable situations, sensibilities, ideas, sensations, facts, and symbols.

The writers who wanted to renew the theater (Ibsen, Maeterlinck, Andreyev, Claudel, Shaw) never thought of arriving at a true synthesis, of freeing themselves from a technique that involves prolixity, meticulous analysis, drawn-out preparation. Before the works of these authors, the audience is in the indignant attitude of a circle of bystanders who swallow their anguish and pity as they watch the slow agony of a horse that has collapsed on the pavement. The sigh of applause that finally breaks out frees the audience's stomach from all the indigestible time it has swallowed. Each act is as painful as having to wait patiently in an antichamber for the minister (*coup de théâtre:* kiss, pistol shot, verbal revelation, etc.) to receive you. All this passéist or semi-Futurist theater, instead of synthesizing fact and idea in the smallest number of words and gestures, savagely destroys the variety of place (source of dynamism and amazement), stuffs many city squares, landscapes, streets, into the sausage of a single room. For this reason this theater is entirely static.

We are convinced that mechanically, by force of brevity, we can achieve an entirely new theater perfectly in tune with our swift and laconic Futurist sensibility. Our acts can also be moments [*atti—attimi*] only a few seconds long. With this essential and synthetic brevity the theater can bear and even overcome competition from the *cinema*.

Atechnical. The passéist theater is the literary form that most distorts and diminishes an author's talent. This form, much more than lyric poetry or the novel, is subject to *the demands of technique:* (1) to omit every notion that doesn't conform to public taste; (2) once a theatrical idea has been found (expressible in a few pages), to stretch it out over two, three, or four acts; (3) to surround an interesting character with many pointless types: coat-holders, door-openers, all sorts of bizarre comic turns; (4) to make the length of each act vary between half and three-quarters of an hour; (5) to construct each act taking care to (a) begin with seven or eight absolutely useless pages, (b) introduce a tenth of your idea in the first act, five-tenths in the second, four-tenths in the third, (c) shape your acts for rising excitement, each act being no more than a preparation for the finale, (d) always make the first act *a little boring* so that the second can be *amusing* and the third *devouring:* (6) to set off every *essential* line with a hundred or more insignificant *preparatory* lines; (7) never to devote less than a page to explaining an entrance or an exit minutely; (8) to apply systematically to the whole play *the rule of a superficial variety,* to the acts, scenes, and lines. For instance, to make one act a day, another an evening, another deep night; to make one act pathetic, another anguished, another sublime; when you have to prolong a dialogue between two actors, make something happen to interrupt it, a falling vase, a passing mandolin player. . . . Or else have the actors constantly move around from sitting to standing, from right to left, and meanwhile vary the dialogue to make it seem as if a bomb might explode outside at any moment (e.g., the betrayed husband might catch his wife red-handed) when actually nothing is going to explode until the end of the act; (9) to be enormously careful about the *verisimilitude of the plot;* (10) to write your play in such a manner that *the audience understands in the finest detail the how and why of everything that takes place on the stage, above all that it knows by the last act how the protagonists will end up.*

With our synthetist movement in the theater, we want to destroy the Technique that from the Greeks until now, instead of simplifying itself, has become more and more dogmatic, stupid, logical, meticulous, pedantic, strangling. THEREFORE:

1. *It's stupid to write one hundred pages where one would do,* only because the audience through habit and infantile instinct wants to see character in a play result from a series of events, wants to fool itself into thinking that the character really exists in order to admire the beauties of Art, meanwhile refusing to acknowledge any art if the author limits himself to sketching out a few of the character's traits.

2. *It's stupid* not to rebel against the prejudice of theatricality when life itself (which consists *of actions vastly more awkward, uniform, and predictable* than those that unfold in the world of art) is for the most part *antitheatrical* and even in this offers *innumerable possibilities for the stage.* EVERYTHING OF ANY VALUE IS THEATRICAL.

3. *It's stupid* to pander to the primitivism of the crowd, which, in the last analysis, wants to see the bad guy lose and the good guy win.

4. *It's stupid* to worry about verisimilitude (absurd because talent and worth have little to do with it).

5. *It's stupid* to want to explain with logical minuteness everything taking place on the stage, when even in life one never grasps an event entirely in all its causes and consequences, because reality throbs around us, bombards us *with squalls of fragments of interconnected events, mortised and tenoned together, confused, mixed up, chaotic.* E.g., it's stupid to act out a contest between two persons *always* in an orderly, clear, and logical way, since in daily life we nearly always encounter mere *flashes of argument* made *momentary* by our modern experience, in a tram, a café,

a railway station, which remain cinematic in our minds like fragmentary dynamic symphonies of gestures, words, lights, and sounds.

6. *It's stupid* to submit to obligatory *crescendi, prepared effects, and postponed climaxes.*

7. *It's stupid* to allow one's talent to be burdened with the weight of a technique that *anyone* (even imbeciles) *can acquire by study, practice, and patience.*

8. IT'S STUPID TO RENOUNCE THE DYNAMIC LEAP IN THE VOID OF TOTAL CREATION, BEYOND THE RANGE OF TERRITORY PREVIOUSLY EXPLORED.

Dynamic, simultaneous. That is, born of improvisation, lightninglike intuition, from suggestive and revealing actuality. We believe that a thing is valuable to the extent that it is improvised (hours, minutes, seconds), not extensively prepared (months, years, centuries).

We feel an unconquerable repugnance for desk work, a priori, that fails to respect the ambience of the theater itself. THE GREATER NUMBER OF OUR WORKS HAVE BEEN WRITTEN IN THE THEATER. The theatrical ambience is our inexhaustible reservoir of inspirations: the magnetic circular sensation invading our tired brains during morning rehearsal in an empty gilded theater; an actor's intonation that suggests the possibility of constructing a cluster of paradoxical thoughts on top of it; a movement of scenery that hints at a symphony of lights; an actress's fleshiness that fills our minds with genially full-bodied notions.

We overran Italy at the head of a heroic battalion of comedians who imposed on audiences *Electricità* and other Futurist syntheses (alive yesterday, today surpassed and condemned by us) that were revolutions imprisoned in auditoriums—from the Politeama Garibaldi of Palermo to the Dal Verme of Milan. The Italian theaters smoothed the wrinkles in the raging massage of the crowd and rocked with bursts of volcanic laughter. We fraternized with the actors. Then, on sleepless nights in trains, we argued, goading each other to heights of genius to the rhythm of tunnels and stations. Our Futurist theater jeers at Shakespeare but pays attention to the gossip of actors, is put to sleep by a line from Ibsen but is inspired by red or green reflections from the stalls. WE ACHIEVE AN ABSOLUTE DYNAMISM THROUGH THE INTERPENETRATION OF DIFFERENT ATMOSPHERES AND TIMES. E.g., whereas in a drama like *Più che l'amore* [D'Annunzio], the important events (for instance, the murder of the gambling house keeper) don't take place on the stage but are narrated with a complete lack of dynamism; in the first act of *La figlia di jorio* [D'Annunzio] the events take place against a simple background with no jumps in space or time; and in the Futurist synthesis, *Simultaneità,* there are two ambiences that interpenetrate and many different times put into action simultaneously.

Autonomous, alogical, unreal. The Futurist theatrical synthesis will not be subject to logic, will pay no attention to photography; it will be *autonomous,* will resemble nothing but itself, although it will take elements from reality and combine them as its whim dictates. Above all, just as the painter and composer discover, scattered through the out-

Caricature by Boccioni of a Futurist evening performance in 1911.

side world, a narrower but more intense life, made up of colors, forms, sounds, and noises, the same is true *for the man gifted with theatrical sensibility, for whom a specialized reality exists that violently assaults his nerves:* it consists of what is called THE THEATRICAL WORLD.

THE FUTURIST THEATER IS BORN OF THE TWO MOST VITAL CURRENTS in the Futurist sensibility, defined in the two manifestos *The Variety Theater* [see excerpt above] and *Weights, Measures, and Prices of Artistic Genius,* which are: (1) our frenzied passion for real, swift, elegant, complicated, cynical, muscular, fugitive, Futurist life; (2) our very modern cerebral definition of art according to which no logic, no tradition, no aesthetic, no technique, no opportunity can be imposed on the artist's natural talent; he must be preoccupied only with creating synthetic expressions of cerebral energy that have THE ABSOLUTE VALUE OF NOVELTY.

The *Futurist theater* will be able to excite its audience, that is, make it forget the monotony of daily life, by sweeping it through *a labyrinth of sensations imprinted on the most exacerbated originality and combined in unpredictable ways.*

Every night the *Futurist theater* will be a gymnasium to train our race's spirit to the swift, dangerous enthusiasms made necessary by this Futurist year.

CONCLUSIONS

1. Totally abolish the technique that is killing the passéist theater.

2. Dramatize all the discoveries (no matter how unlikely, weird, and antitheatrical) that our talent is discovering in the subconscious, in ill-defined forces, in pure abstraction, in the purely cerebral, the purely fantastic, in record-setting and body-madness. (E.g., *Vengono,* F. T. Marinetti's first drama of objects, a new vein of theatrical sensibility discovered by Futurism.)

3. Symphonize the audience's sensibility by exploring it, stirring up its laziest layers with every means possible; eliminate the preconception of the footlights by throwing nets of sensation between stage and audience; the stage action will invade the orchestra seats, the audience.

4. Fraternize warmly with the actors who are among the few thinkers who flee from every deforming cultural enterprise.

5. Abolish the farce, the vaudeville, the sketch, the comedy, the serious drama, and the tragedy, and create in their place the many forms of Futurist theater, such as: lines written in free words, simultaneity, compenetration, the short, acted-out poem, the dramatized sensation, comic dialogue, the negative act, the reechoing line, "extralogical" discussion, synthetic deformation, the scientific outburst that clears the air.

6. Through unbroken contact, create between us and the crowd a current of confidence rather than respectfulness, in order to instill in our audiences the dynamic vivacity of a new Futurist theatricality.

These are the *first* words on the theater. Our first eleven theatrical syntheses (by Marinetti, Settimelli, Bruno Corra, R. Chiti, Balilla Pratella) were victoriously imposed on crowded theaters in Ancona, Bologna, Padua, Naples, Venice, Verona, Florence, and Rome, by Ettore Berti, Zoncada, and Petrolini. In Milan we shall soon have the great metal building, enlivened by all the electromechanical inventions that alone will permit us to realize our most free conceptions on the stage. (pp. 123-29)

> *Filippo Tommaso Marinetti, Emilio Settimelli, and Bruno Corra, "The Futurist Synthetic Theater," in* Marinetti: Selected Writings *by Filippo Tommaso Marinetti, edited by R. W. Flint, translated by R. W. Flint and Arthur A. Coppotelli, Farrar, Straus and Giroux, 1972, pp. 123-29.*

FUTURIST LITERATURE

Rosa Trillo Clough

[*Clough is an American educator and critic specializing in Romance languages. In the following excerpt, she outlines the thematic and technical characteristics of Italian Futurism in literature.*]

It has been observed that the reason [the Futurists'] noisy denunciation of poetical tradition was made in Italy was that the literature of this country suffered more than others from bookish influences. In this connection we must bear in mind that while the poetry of other lands has always been enlivened by renewed contacts with life and nature, Italian literature from its inception developed an autonomous and isolated life of its own. Poets acquired from the very beginning the habit of turning for inspiration to their favorite authors and not to brooks and woods and mountains. Nature and life were admitted only in the form in which preceding artists had left them. In fact, appreciation of Italian poetry is impossible unless approached with the full equipment of literary history.

Dante set the example. He reshaped, lyrically, the lines of the ancient writers; he wove his most touching episode around a famous line of Virgil, and translated into poetry the philosophical theories of Aristotle. Petrarch changed the subject but not the tune; his sources are different, but the lyrical stream is none the less one of secondary derivation. His imitators, in the centuries that followed, went even further and bequeathed to Italy a second classicism, and with it the art of kindling a torch from an already borrowed light. This practice was faithfully adhered to throughout the course of Italian literature.

The Futurists' invitation to destroy libraries, academies, museums, universities, constituted what we might call the negative side of Marinetti's famous Magna Carta, the *Manifesto* published in the Paris *Figaro* on February 20, 1909. Professors and old-fashioned critics were, indeed, systematically reviled; but, fortunately, no Caliph Omar ever arose to put the torch to the Vatican Library.

The positive side of this document deals only with the necessity of introducing up-to-date materials in place of old themes. Obviously Marinetti was convinced that quality in literature depends upon the nature of the subject matter, and that consequently the modernization of themes was the necessary and sufficient condition for the production of poetical masterpieces.

This "transformation of topics" was described somewhat as follows: Love for women was to be banished from literature: enough of adultery, triangles, mystic alcoves. The passion to be sublimated in Futurist art was blind love of danger, inordinate worship of action.

The most glorious of literary themes was therefore to be War—the consummation of all activity, the end of all desires. Consequently the calling to be poetically exalted above all others was that of the soldier.

A ban was pronounced against the individual characters which exist only in the pages of old books. Living masses alone can interest the new poets: masses of working people, swarming in factories, deafened by the roar of machines, themselves mechanized and motorized by the contact with metals and by the exigencies of speed. In the course of time even these throngs will lose their prestige and be replaced by the "solemn solidarity of attentive, zealous, orderly motors." But that will come at a later period, on the auspicious day "when the Animal Kingdom comes to its end and the Mechanical Realm begins."

Speed was to be the principle and also the criterion of all things, the goal and measure of poetry, the Alpha and Omega of life, the new absolute of Futurist ontology. "Nous vivons déjà," said the *Manifesto* [excerpted above], "dans l'absolu, puisque nous avons créé l'éternelle vitesse omniprésente . . . le temps et l'espace sont morts hier" ["We already live in the absolute, since we have created eternal, omnipresent speed . . . time and space died yesterday"]. A new transcendental: by the side of *Goodness* and *Truth* there must be *Speed,* and *Rapidity* must become the property of *Beauty.* (pp. 40-1)

The insistence upon the importance of subject matter, the advisability for artists to engage in up-to-date pursuits, and the artistic advantages of a mechanical mentality, were not without foundation. There was something to Marinetti's contention that the experience of flying transforms our intuitive faculties. "Devouring rapidity" tends to blur the outlines of the landscape. Quasi-instantaneous apparitions and disappearances which occur when we travel at high speed destroy, perhaps, the sharp individuality of objects. It is quite possible that the flying poet may come to respond more to "change" and less to "things." He may, in the absorbing survey of a limitless expanse, rise to that kinetic ecstasy, to that pantheistic assimilation which is so dear to the heart of the new estheticians. And none can deny that a rapidly accelerated course of life may result in a more rapid rhythm of expression.

In any case the young Italian writers who fluttered helplessly from a "pure page of Shelley" to the "obscenities of the French stage," from "Scandinavian decay" to "Latin corruption," may have been helped by the indignant fury of Marinetti who pronounced a solemn interdict against "the primitive and the savage, the sylvan and the rustic; against the adoration of the gloomy, the moldy, the filthy, and decrepit; against the exaltation of decay, disease, failure, suicide."

The emphasis on new subject matter was interpreted as a revolt against the dominant role of traditional poetry. "Remplacer la psychologie de l'homme désormais exposée par l'obsession lyrique de la matière"—that was the great poetical revolution: to discover the activity of matter, which had always been considered inert; to sing the instincts of ores, stones, wood; to marvel at the group instinct, the aversions, and attractions not of men, but of metals—their alloys, fusions, and combinations; to discover new sources of passion in the dramas of the chemical laboratory or the tragedy of the blast furnaces. These are the biddings of Futurism whose followers considered the mechanical piano more interesting than the ordinary one, and the cinema infinitely superior to the stage because of the mechanical arts whereby its action may be reversed, increased in size and speed, and transformed in color.

It soon became obvious to the innovators, however, that change of subject did not carry them very far and that the revolution would have to be directed into the fields of formal esthetics, metrics, and style.

Futurist critics directed their weapons first against intellectualistic literature, then against intelligible poetry. Marinetti's poetical [*Technical Manifesto of Futurist Literature,* 1912, excerpted above] closed with this proclamation: "Poets of Futurism, I have taught you to loathe the libraries and the museums in order to cultivate in you the hatred of intelligence, and to reawaken that divine intuition which is the characteristic gift of the Latin races. By means of intuition we plan to overcome the apparently irreducible hostility which still separates our human flesh from the metal of motors."

In commenting on the above *Manifesto* Marinetti's critics reminded him that his denunciation of intelligence seemed to be an echo of popularized Bergsonianism. It was the time, moreover, when everyone was quoting Croce's *Estetica* and particularly the first sentence. "Cognition," said Croce, "is twofold; either intuitive or logical, either imaginative or intellectual, either of the individual or of the universal, either a producer of images or a maker of concepts."

Marinetti resented these comparisons, and in his *Supplemento al manifesto* he stated that his anti-intellectualism was inspired by Dante's denunciation of syllogistic reasonings and also by Poe in "The Colloquy of Monos and Una." The latter reference reads as follows: " . . . the poetic intellect—that intellect which we now feel to have been the most exalted of all—since those truths which to us were of the most enduring importance could only be reached by that analogy which speaks in proof-tones to the *imagination alone, and to the unaided reason bears no weight.*"

This opposition to intellect, which at times seemed to

point to a complete mechanization of man, was rather effectively restated in the concluding remarks of the article mentioned above. "It is impossible to determine exactly," said Marinetti,

> when unconscious inspiration ends and lucid volition begins. At times, the latter abruptly resolves itself into the former; at others, the two are found side by side. After hours of relentless toil, the creative spirit seems suddenly to shake off its shackles and become prey to an incomprehensible spontaneity of conception and execution. The hand that writes seems to break away from the body and move off into the distance, far from the brain that likewise has freed itself and looks down from its lofty station with awe-inspiring lucidity on the images that unwittingly flow from the pen.

The anti-intellectual issue, and the incomprehensibility of art were also treated by Soffici. Poetry and the other arts display values which cannot be accounted for in abstract logical terms. There is no appraising system of esthetics outside the terms of art itself; and every attempt to construct one has resulted in the evaluation not of artistic qualities but of extraneous matters. Poetry does not proceed from knowledge and knowledge can in no way be made its aim, unless by knowledge we mean the inspired intuitional enjoyment of the reader which is but a resonance of the original superrational creative act of the poet.

Intuition, for the Futurists, is the poet's peculiar quality in that it enables him to discover *analogies* which, hidden to reason, are yet the essentials of art. For this precious realization the Futurists declared themselves indebted to Poe, whose authority "Monos and Una" was somewhat arbitrarily invoked. "Analogical discovery" in Futurist criticism was that inspired vision which penetrates to the essence of reality and discloses the communion of all things by indicating the identity of their source. "Analogy," Marinetti explained, "is but another name for that immense love which brings distant things into close relationship." Poets, he held, have always been aware of the possibilities of analogy. Their only difficulty was that they kept too close to external resemblances and did not venture to take those daring leaps which join in an ineffable union clashing and contrasting moods.

The scope of analogy should therefore become greater as *rapports* are enhanced by increasing distances; and its efficacy varies directly in proportion to logical remoteness. Analogy therefore offers a touchstone to gauge poetical values, viz., the power to startle. The artistic criterion derived from analogy is stupefaction.

Marinetti and his followers were not slow in becoming aware of this *passéist* slip, but smilingly they accepted its inherent implications. Soffici's apology was as follows:

> Pure sensation, which in our esthetics is the basis of all artistic creation, turns out to be, upon close scrutiny, nothing more than a prolonged shock of astonishment experienced before a reality which continually reveals itself under new and unpredictable aspects. The expression of this surprise, the communication of it through signs and *rapports* is the inescapable end of artistic ac-

tivity. Marino who, like all the baroque artists, was a creator of new forms and a pioneer of modernism, wrote a line which expresses the fundamental truth at the basis of our esthetics: "E del poeta il fin la meraviglia" ("the poet's aim is to surprise").

Soffici explained that the similarity between Marinism and Futurism was due to their common possession of a trait essential to poetical expression. Ordinary mortals, he said, see things with other people's eyes: their vision is influenced by convention, and determined by usage. This usage and this convention are destructive and mortifying simplifications. They reduce the world to a rigid structure of abstract formulas. The ever-changing aspect of things, the significance of their infinitely varying details, the value of their caressing lusters are done away with, and are replaced by a mass of insignificant labels. The poet, however, in his childlike, impatient curiosity brushes away all these concealing tags, and gazes with astonishment upon the eternally renovated spectacle of reality. The communication of his astonishment is art; the reaction to this discovery is that poetic stupefaction so dear to Marino and to his followers. This is Soffici's apology for the baroque.

But when the baroque poet would surprise us by dwelling on incongruous *rapproachements,* the case is different. His "chariot of the sun" remains a hackneyed image even after he has taken us through the "stable" in which it is stored for the night. The line: "Sudate fuochi a liquefar metalli," ("Sweat, oh fires, at liquefying metals"), was admired because the poet in his search for the unexpected, out of all the possible traits by which furnaces might be personified as toiling bodies, selected the one (sweat) which could be reconstructed into a startling *rapprochement* of two contrasting elements: fire and water. Though such comparisons tended to be ridiculous, they were all the more acceptable to the Futurists who were in arms against the sublime and reveled in bathos.

These analogies, the Futurists insisted, constitute the entire essence of poetry. Their multiplicity responds to life's versatility. Marinetti spoke of them as though they constituted a net through which the imagination flows leaving a catch behind; he pictured them as a "chain of images created by the poet's fantasy." He exemplified his view of the successive analogical unfoldings by referring to his [novel *Mafarka le futuriste*] and to the following description: "All the sharp sweetness of his youth rose to his throat just as from the school courtyards the merry cries of children rise toward the old teachers who look from the balcony toward the sea covered with rapidly moving ships." The shift of images is, however, not particularly Futuristic. Dante and many before and after him have given startling examples of this flowing of pictures in utter defiance of logical coherence and in perfect compliance with lyrical consistency.

This view of analogy as the power that discovers identity in diversity and establishes the unity in the manifold, was accepted by the Futurists in their frequent endeavors to identify human sensation with the "living feel of matter." Their analogical sensitiveness was supposed to react to the impulses of metals, to the inner force of matter, to elemental compression, cohesion, and expansion, to the "swarming of molecules, to the whirling of electrons." As Marinetti said:

> It is not a question of dramatizing and humanizing matter, but rather the reverse. The compactness of a metal plate moves us for its own sake. We identify ourselves with that incomprehensible and inhuman combination of molecules which, for instance, blocks the way of a cannon shell. The red heat of iron is more entrancing for us than a woman's smile.

This analogical pervasiveness enabled the Futurists, as stated above, to do away with the *passéist Ego,* the bookish memories on which it fed, and the dreary logical scaffolding on which it rested. Intuition in its unconscious, unreflecting, spontaneous vivacity is what sends the poet down the stream of motion, synchronizes his breathing with the rhythm of the motor and his pulse-beat with the throbs of metals, of stones, of wood. "It substitutes for exhausted human psychology the lyrical obsession of metals."

This esthetics of analogy was adapted by Soffici to a philosophy of *irony.* The old romantic doctrine must have found its way into the readings of these Futurist critics, who were not slow in discovering its utility. The conception of the artist as one who forever hovers above and beyond a subject that is endlessly made and unmade by the annulling power of fancy, a poetic fancy that grins as it gazes upon the ruins of its own structure—all this was re-echoed by the Tuscan critic. He asserted that irony is the manner of seeing of those who realize the absolute futility of what they have zealously labored at, who suddenly discover the disproportion between expectation and realization, and save themselves from tragic pessimism by retreating into the citadel of poetry from whose heights they can look down and laugh at the futile spectacle of man's ambitions.

These were the fundamental principles of the new esthetics. But intuition had long been pressed into the service of enthusiastic critics. Analogy had always been the rationale of all figurative expression. As for irony, it was so old and forgotten that it looked almost new when the dust was brushed away from it. What was new and untried, at least more so than their principles and theories, were the Futurists' stylistic devices.

The Poetics of Futurism enjoined the following: 1) Abolition of traditional syntax; 2) Elimination of punctuation; 3) Introduction of mathematical and musical notations; 4) Complete repudiation of metrics; 5) Generalization of onomatopoeia to justify introduction of new sounds, modifications of accepted words, readoption of antiquated ones; 6) Utilization of the pictorial possibilities of typography.

The fundamental postulates of this stylistic reform were the exigencies of speed and liberty. These postulates and their applications were fully set forth in the manifestoes already quoted, in the polemical articles of *Lacerba,* in *Les mots en liberté* and in the *Zang-tumb-tuum* of Marinetti.

In the theory of the Futurists, the conditions of modern life and the state of excitement they produce in our minds can no longer put up with the old retarding syntax. Substantives must be strewn about freely, and solely in accordance with the law of analogical relationship. Ordinary familiarity with instinctive actions provides us with a clue, with a remote but fruitful notion of what may eventually be done along this line.

> The man who has witnessed an explosion does not stop to connect his sentences grammatically. He hurls at his listeners shrieks and substantives. Let us imitate his example! This release from grammatical subserviency will also enable the artist to do what no one, so far, has succeeded in doing: to communicate by words the sensation of weight and the power of diffusion by which he can express odors. It is a new field which is opened to asyntactical writers.

The adjective was normally discarded because it drags and because it introduces nuances in a universe which is, and must remain, black and white. Exceptions were tolerated, particularly if the adjective was employed for distinction and not for adornment, in the same way that railroads use white, green, and red signals—merely to regulate the speed of the substantives. Another exception was made in favor of adjectives used as headlights. For example the modifiers: *gray, stormy, disgusting,* placed together in parentheses at the beginning of a clause, throw a flash of light on all the substantives that follow: *passengers, sea, ship, sky, decks, nausea.* The *Passéists* say: *the sky is gray; the sea is stormy.* Here, instead, the adjectives are all agglomerated and conjoined by reciprocal reflections in order to make the reader feel the disgusting nausea of the passengers, the grayness of the sky, the rolling of the billows. The adverb, too, must go—that "vieille et fastidieuse agrafe qui tient attachés des mots qui ont envie de s'éparpiller" ["old and tedious buckle that keeps words attached that are longing to be scattered"].

Conjugations, for the most part, were doomed; one verbal form sufficed; the infinitive; all the others were but hindrances. "The infinitive is round, and like a wheel it may be applied to all the cars of the analogical train; by making stops impossible it provides style with speed. Moods and tenses are triangular, square, or oval. The infinitive alone is circular."

Each substantive must have its double; that is, it must be followed immediately (and without any such retarding words as: "like," "as if," etc.) by the substantive to which it is linked by the divine law of analogy, e.g., man-bomber, woman-bay, door-faucet. More complex juxtapositions were rendered necessary by the widening circles of analogical emanations.

The signs of punctuation which are a corollary to the coordination and subordination of cases, moods, and tenses disappeared along with these forms. They were partly replaced by mathematical signs $\times + : - = > <$ and by certain well-known musical indications such as: *più presto, rallentando, due tempi* ["more quickly," "slow down," "two times"].

Metrical rules, in the sense in which the term is used in traditional prosody, had no longer any meaning. Futurism began by accepting and even recommending the use of free verse, but soon realized its inadequacy. This was, however, a first step in the right direction; it showed a desire to liberate poetry from the shackles of prosody and its retinue of fixed feet, alternating syllables, rigid rhyme schemes; but it did not go far enough. It was too thoroughly bound up with tradition and too fond of producing the stale effects of *passéist* cadences, rhythmic responses, balances, etc. Its existence moreover implied the maintenance of syntax and the consequent clogging of all the sources of free inspiration. Thus they went a step further and resorted to poetical composition described by the term: *parole in libertà* (word autonomy). Futurist imagination freely expressed itself in the new language, no longer bound by the exigencies of syntax, punctuation, and metrics.

The Futurist reform consisted in the distortion of words as a part of "integral onomatopoeia" and in response to analogical purification. Marinetti claimed that: "lyrical intoxication allows us, or rather forces us, to deform and reshape words; to lengthen and shorten them; to reinforce their center or their extremities by increasing or diminishing the number of vowels and consonants."

Distortion was but a small part of their onomatopoetic system which covered the introduction of any and every sound irrespective of its similarity to significant words. Onomatopoeia, we are told, may be direct (i.e. realistic), and imitative. In this guise it had always been known: *Boom; Miau,* etc. The Futurists further systematized the practice and developed its possibilities. Said Marinetti (*Mots en liberté*): "In my *Zang-tumb-tuum* the strident onomatopoeia *ssiii,* which reproduces the whistle of a tugboat on the Meuse, is followed by the muffled *fiiii fiiii* coming from the other bank. These two onomatopoeias have enabled me to dispense with a description of the breadth of the river which is thus measured by contrasting the consonants *s* and *f.*"

In addition to this imitative word formation, the Futurists recommended the use of what they described as indirect onomatopoeia. It was to be employed to express the subjective responses to external conditions. They also had a third process called abstract onomatopoeia, which served to echo the complex and recondite movement of the soul without reference to external sounds or movements.

The poetry embodying these principles was called *essential* and *synthetic lyricism: essential* because superfluous items had been eliminated; *synthetic* because the utmost compression had been introduced.

Marinetti began to compose in this new jargon in 1912. Before the end of the year he had declaimed synthetic poems in the principal cities of Italy. Subsequently he held forth in Paris, Brussels, London, and Moscow. For a while this style enjoyed a certain popularity. *Lacerba* boasted many synthetic compositions; even other publications accepted them. They were also imitated for the purpose of ridicule. Soffici himself had regaled the public with several dozen pages of liberated words. However, when he changed his mind and began to make fun of the principles of Futurism, many thought he was still speaking seriously. And the readers of *Lacerba* wondered if Apollinaire in his "Lettre-Océan" was joking or not.

The Futurists also introduced a typographic reform—the utilization of type as an element of artistic expression. The diversification of letters: Italic, Roman, Gothic; small, medium, large; in different color schemes, and in varying formations, was considered a novel and precious instrument of Parnassus. It "welded painting to poetry just as onomatopoeia had wedded lyricism to music." Some of this printing is imitative art. We have for example the balloon typographically designed in Marinetti's *Zang-tumb-tuum.* But the Futurists went beyond this imitative typographic figuration and attempted to show their invincible faith in distortion. This non-imitative typographic painting they called symphonic typing. Marinetti described it in *Zang-tumb-tuum:*

> The poet will hurl along parallel lines several chains of colors, sounds, odors, noises, weights, thicknesses, analogies. One of these lines can be the pictorial one; another, the musical one; the third, odorous. Let us suppose that the chain of pictorial analogies dominates all the others. It will then be printed in larger type than the second and third lines which contain, let us say, musical and odorous analogies.

This arrangement is further complicated by strophic repetition. Soffici, in his *Primi principii,* gives us the rationale of these typographic devices. The letters themselves are beautiful; in fact their beauty as an ideographic sign remains after it has become stereotyped in the alphabetic series. They have an extraordinary power of suggestion; they evoke past civilizations, dead languages. Their beauty may be enhanced by pictorial practices which, however, do not go beyond the means and instruments of the type-setter. Changes in size, arrangement, and color give the requisite movement to a page which then may, with justification, be called a work of art.

Marinetti was very proud of his typographic revolution on which he staked many of his claims to originality. When critics accused him of copying the worst features of Mallarmé's poetic art, he answered:

> This new array of type, this variety of colors, this original use of characters enable me to increase many times the expressive power of words. By this practice I combat the decorative and "precious" style of Mallarmé, his *recherché* language. I also combat Mallarmé's static ideal. My reformed typesetting allows me to treat words like torpedoes and to hurl them forth at all speeds: at the velocity of stars, clouds, aeroplanes, trains, waves, explosives, molecules, atoms.

(pp. 42-52)

[In poetry] the ideal of Futurist composition is abbreviation—a more and more condensed form of expression, a super-dispatch style. In his [*Les mots en liberté (Destruction of Syntax—Imagination without Strings—Words-in-Freedom*)] of May 11, 1913, Marinetti insisted upon "a telegraphic lyricism which must appear very unpoetic to the *passéists,*—a style which partakes little of books and much of life." In this same publication, and both before and after it, he did not hesitate to state in unmistakable terms that the excellence of poetry depended upon its terseness: "Everything brief, in two words," was his compendious recipe for this Tironian composition.

Of the many daily exercises offered by Marinetti to his disciples, the one that was deemed most important was "to spit upon the altar of art." One of his constant exhortations was: "Let us courageously produce ugly literature." He intended only to convey the necessity of being sharp and rapid, asyntactical and concise, cacophonous and brutal, for these are the qualities of life, and the final goal of art is to lose itself in life. "The limit of musical development is the roar of the diving plane."

Marinetti, the abbreviator, was not a voice crying in the wilderness. His disciples studied these apocalyptic visions of the artistic Future, spread the word, and some of them even brought arguments of reason in support of these dictates of faith. Soffici in particular wrote some interesting pages on the twilight of poetry. In his *Principii,* the work in which he had gathered, somewhat systematically, his esthetic creed, he stated:

> Art tends fatally toward its own destruction.
>
> For, admitting that the function of art is to refine, to sharpen sensibility, it follows:
>
> 1. that both the poet and his public will develop a steadily increasing impressionability and consequently a greater facility of communication.
>
> 2. as a result of this highly developed susceptibility there will come about such a state of perfect communion between the creator and the contemplator, that one word from the former, one sign, will reveal everything to the latter.
>
> 3. consequently the modes of artistic expression tend to be more and more compendious, or rather we should say, synthetic; they become more and more intimate, more abstract until they finally reach the point of a conventional cipher, of an hermetic cryptography intelligible only to the initiated.
>
> 4. hence, by virtue of this hyper-susceptibility, both the artist and the beholder will find satisfaction, not in the common elaboration of a lyrical reality, but in the devising of a representative symbol. . . . The destiny of art is therefore to refine general sensibility to the point of making useless any outward manifestations. Art's final masterpiece will be its own destruction.

Of course Soffici could invoke the authority of those who had said, long before his time, that the supreme expression of music is silence.

This doctrine of the Futurists formed part of a diffused state of mind and of a general and widespread tendency to attack the fine arts and the beauty which for two thousand years had inspired, consoled, and dignified humanity. In this work of destruction the Futurists had their predecessors, but they also exercised a notable and "beneficent" influence on those who came after them. They may have learned much from Lautréamont, Rimbaud, and Apollinaire who was a sort of *nympha egeria* ["instructor"] to Soffici, and from others, but they surely taught the Dadaists and the Surrealists. (pp. 56-8)

Rosa Trillo Clough, in her Futurism: The Story of a Modern Art Movement, *Philosophical Library, 1961, 297 p.*

Caroline Tisdall and Angelo Bozzolla

[*In the following excerpt, the critics elaborate on the influence of Marinetti's technique of "words-in-freedom" on the development of Futurist poetry.*]

In February 1905 Marinetti began his cultural crusade in Italy with the first appearance of the literary magazine *Poesia*. Through the pages of *Poesia,* to the cover of which was later added the red-printed name of *Il futurismo,* Marinetti brought to Italy the best of the new masters, descendants of Mallarmé and Verlaine: Verhaeren, Paul Fort, Gustave Kahn, Swinburne, Yeats, Jarry and Georges Duhamel, plus a new Italian generation who were to become Marinetti's Futurist poets: Gian Pietro Lucini, Aldo Palazzeschi, Corrado Govoni, Paolo Buzzi, Armando Mazza and Enrico Cavacchioli. The highly Symbolist cover of *Poesia,* by Alberto Martini, figured a stout Muse slaying a dragon from the top of a mountain. *Poesia* was published from Marinetti's luxurious flat in Milan, where *The Founding and Manifesto* was penned a few years later. The name of the publishing company was retained until the early 1920s, and it was under the imprint of *Poesia* that many books by Futurist writers and poets were to appear, as well as the immaculately printed and distributed manifestos of Futurism in leaflet form.

It may seem curious that a young writer who had already won a certain respect in the cultural capital of Europe should choose to return to Italy. But Marinetti was nothing if not a superb tactician. He probably realized that he could get so far and no further in Paris, while in Italy he would be outstanding. He wished to rival D'Annunzio's monopoly in Italy of themes both Nietzschean and modern. More positively, he did have the crusading fervour of the exile: *Poesia* served the double function of offering a much-needed platform to the young Italian poets, for whom Marinetti had an infallible nose, and educating its public on international developments. Politically, too, Italy offered much more excitement with its rumbles of foreign wars, campaigns to oust the Austrian tyrant, and the new possibilities that emerged in the climate of tension generated in the newly industrialized northern cities. (p. 91)

In October 1910, the year in which the Futurist Evenings had first appeared, Marinetti had been brought to trial for obscenity and affront to public morals. The offending book was *Mafarka the Futurist.* Marinetti's epic answer to D'Annunzio's 'African passion'. The aim seems to have been not just to accuse Marinetti, but to discredit the entire Futurist movement in the eyes of the art world by outlawing them as pornographers. Marinetti was able to transform the trial into a theatrical performance in which the roles of accuser and accused were exchanged, the decadence and partiality of Italian justice were exposed, and, with the aid of a public that was vociferously pro-Marinetti, a victory was gained over the passéists of the law.

Although *Mafarka* was deliberately offensive in both content and language, Marinetti had still retained the traditional use of grammar and syntax. Between the appearance of *Mafarka* and his next major work, *Zang tumb tuum,* in 1914 he dedicated most of his energy to a number of scintillating manifestos which laid the ground for the liberation of Futurist literature and theatre from its Symbolist heritage. In poetry this meant farewell to the *vers libre* ['free verse'] and welcome to the new and liberated form of 'Words-in-freedom'. In prose it heralded the abolition of syntax and passéist grammatical conventions. And in theatre it meant that the speed and inventiveness of variety theatre and music hall could be extended into the new Futurist forms of Synthetic Theatre.

The *Technical Manifesto of Futurist Literature* appeared on 11 May 1912, dedicated, at the behest of a whirling propeller, to the liberation of words from their Latin prison. In this state of freedom, nouns would be scattered at random, infinitives with their greater elasticity would replace the pedantic old indicative and would free nouns from the domination of the writer's ego. Out too was the 'old belt-buckle' of an adverb. Punctuation was, of course, annulled, and the 'foolish pauses made by commas and full stops' replaced by musical or mathematical signs ($+ - \times : =$) to indicate movement and direction. Now each noun would have its double: the noun to which it is related by analogy. 'Example: man-torpedoboat/woman-gulf'. The principle of analogy itself was not new, being held in common with Baudelaire ('Correspondances'), with Bergson and with Mallarmé, for whom the detachment of objects from rational control allows the free play of imagination, as in 'Un coup de dés . . .'. (pp. 93-4)

The idea was to describe the life of matter (the universal *materia* that Boccioni too was attempting to express in paint). The life of matter was to replace the ego of the writer, whose function now would be to shape the nets of analogy that would capture elusive matter in the mysterious sea of phenomena: 'Destroy the *I* in literature, i.e. all psychology. The man side-tracked by the library and the museum is of absolutely no interest. We must drive him out of literature, and in his place establish *matter,* the essence of which can be grasped only by flashes of inspiration: something physicists and chemists will never be able to do.'

This lyrical obsession with matter was to protect it from the anthropomorphic emotions with which romantic poets and pantheists had endowed it: 'The solidity of a strip of steel interests us for itself.' The life of massed molecules and whirling electrons would form the modern poet's inspiration: 'The warmth of a piece of iron or wood is in our opinion more impassioned than the smile or tears of a woman.' Matter, for the Futurists, was to be 'neither happy nor sad'.

To capture even more faithfully the sense of matter, three neglected elements were to be introduced into poetry:

> (1) Sound (manifestation of the dynamism of objects);
>
> (2) Weight (faculty of flight inherent in objects);

> (3) Smell (means by which objects spread and disperse).

By such means a landscape could be described as it is perceived by a dog, and the conversations of motors be reproduced, in much the same way as proposed by Carrà in his manifesto *The Painting of Sounds, Noises and Smells* a year later, and in the dramas of objects that were to be a feature of the Futurist Synthetic Theatre.

All this would lead in turn to what Marinetti called 'Imagination without Strings' (*Immaginazione senza fili,* 'wireless imagination' or 'untrammelled fantasy')—the stage at which the first term of each analogy could be omitted to leave no more than an uninterrupted sequence of second terms. For this of course both the need to be understood and the pursuit of traditional beauty could be abandoned; 'It is not necessary to be understood. . . . We bravely create the "ugly" in literature and murder the solemn on all sides. . . . Every day we must spit on the Altar of Art.' Free intuition was the rule, where once logic and rationalism had inhibited the creativity of the poet. A year later a further manifesto, *Destruction of Syntax—Imagination without Strings—Words-in-Freedom,* reinforced the message, with further examples of the 'animalization, vegetabilization, mineralization, electrification or liquefication of style. For example, to give life to a blade of grass, I say: "I will be greener tomorrow"'.

The first example of Words-in-freedom appeared as an appendix to the *Technical Manifesto of Futurist Literature.* 'Battle Weight + Smell' of 1912, like many of the Words-in-freedom pieces, is an account of a battle, in which not only smells and noises, but arms too, acquire a life of their own. An example of the use of analogy is this presentation of the green, white and red Italian flag: 'meadows sky—white-with-heat-blood'. But the masterpiece of Words-in-freedom and of Marinetti's literary career was the novel *Zang tumb tuum.* It was not published until 1914, though various parts of it were declaimed in February 1913 in Berlin and Rome. *Zang tumb tuum* is the story of the siege by the Bulgarians of Turkish Adrianople in the Balkan War, which Marinetti had witnessed as a war reporter. The dynamic rhythms and onomatopoetic possibilities that the new form offered were made even more effective through the revolutionary use of different typefaces, forms and graphic arrangements and sizes that became a distinctive part of Futurism. In *Zang tumb tuum* they are used to express an extraordinary range of different moods and speeds, quite apart from the noise and chaos of battle. The story has three poetic high points: the mobilization of the troops and departure for the front, the siege itself, and the harrowing fate of a trainload of injured soldiers left to die in the heat.

Audiences in London, Berlin and Rome alike were bowled over by the tongue-twisting vitality with which Marinetti declaimed *Zang tumb tuum.* As an extended sound poem it stands as one of the monuments of experimental literature, its telegraphic barrage of nouns, colours, exclamations and directions pouring out in the screeching of trains, the rat-a-tat-tat of gunfire, and the clatter of telegraphic messages.

It would be a misinterpretation to assume that it is an unqualified glorification of war: there are tragic interludes, too, and reflective passages in which Marinetti describes how war affects not only soldiers but the entire population—men, women and animals. The life of molecules, evoked ironically in the manifestos as a shared characteristic of the intestines and the poetic urge, now joins all forms of life in the vibration and heat of war:

> I counted the 6 milliard shocks my molecule sisters gave me I obeyed them 6 milliard times taking 6 milliard different directions . . . within the cells of my body (diameter 1 micromille of a millimetre) are contained 4 races of indivisible atoms this jolt = loss of weight of 6000 atoms leaving my right arm but 5000 atoms re-enter my left foot.

This minute molecular study continues in the passages describing cholera and the trainload of sick soldiers:

> Karagath Station banging of opening doors at end of carriage doctors nurses stretchers carriers breeze lanced like this Anatolian captain's blister dysentery trembling of weary hand bringing bottle of milk to mouth [here the typographic changes indicate the reaction of the milk as it encounters the body] furnace of microbes putrefaction of intestinal tube instal themselves multiply quickly attack putrify the walls avalanche of milk 6000 lactic fermentations onslaught tumult visceral battle. . . .

After this myopic drama comes the large-scale battle:

> sshhooouuuutttt of 1500 sick men trapped by locked doors in front of 18 Turkish artillery lightning struck rags tatters coats officers thrown on to the rails

—and in the distance, the sound of a flute carried downwind.

The final chapter is Marinetti's apotheosis of war as the 'sole hygiene of the world', the bombardment in which noises, weights, smells, turbines, molecules and chains are linked in a network of analogy and offered to his Futurist friends.

In the following years, Words-in-freedom became the house style of Futurism, for poets and painters alike. Boccioni, Carrà, Cangiullo, Balla and Soffici all experimented with the form. Each adapted it to his own interests. An article by Carrà attacking art critics, subtitled 'Words-in-freedom', appeared in *Lacerba* on 1 January 1914; it was little more than a series of words strung together with little of Marinetti's inventiveness. Boccioni's Words-in-freedom piece 'Society Shoe + Urine', again in *Lacerba,* was another strange exploration of his guilt-ridden attitude to women—with his girl-friend Inez somewhere in between the world of prostitutes and the purity of his sister.

For the writers it offered tremendous typographic possibilities, and meant a stimulating combination of visual art and poetry. Palazzeschi was a master of the art of the evocative onomatopoeia demonstrated in his evolution of a 'sick fountain':

> clof, clop, cloch,
> cloffete
> cloppete
> clocchete
> chchch . . .

This—now used in the Italian primary school curriculum—was greeted by Marinetti as 'the first glorious gob of spit which Futurism let fall on the ridiculous altar of Art with a capital A'. Other poets adapted the new typographic freedom to themes that were as far from war as Palazzeschi's fountain. 'The Sea', of 1915, by Govoni, is a lyrical example of the kind of precursor of concrete poetry that now appeared in the pages of *Lacerba* and in immaculately printed Futurist editions. In these the visual quality of print was explored to the full, employing 'if necessary, 3 or 4 different inks and 20 different typefaces', in an extension of the possibilities offered by Apollinaire's *Ideograms.* At the same time it was a literary equivalent of Boccioni's demands for '20 different materials' in a single work of sculpture, and disrupted what Marinetti ungratefully called 'the static state of Mallarmé', just as the Futurist painters had suggested that *The Street Enters the House* [the title of a painting by Boccioni].

The artists in turn extended the possibilities of the visual forms of Words-in-freedom into their 'free-word paintings' (*tavole parolibere*), including Balla's *Trelsi trelno,* Carrà's *Interventionist Manifesto,* his illustrations for his own book *Guerrapittura* (*Warpainting*), and Soffici's *BIF ZF + 18* series of *Simultaneities* and *Lyrical Chemistries* of 1915, which succeed in imposing a certain amount of Cubist order on the exuberance of Marinetti's exploding word-clusters. Meanwhile, Severini applied Marinetti's principle of extended analogies to painting, in works like *Sea = Dancer + Vase of Flowers* of 1913.

Francesco Cangiullo, a Neapolitan adherent to the movement, was actually the most successful in adapting Words-in-freedom to a whole range of activities in painting, poetry and theatre. In *Dance of the Serpent,* printed in *Lacerba* in 1914, Severini had used blocks of evocative or onomatopoetic words to indicate colours and rhythms, fitting them into the abstracted Cubist planes of his painting. A year later Cangiullo took the much more radical step, in his *Free-Word Painting,* of making the words themselves, painted in various colours, supply subject, composition and directional flow. (pp. 94-101)

[In presenting Futurist poetry on stage, as] outlined in the *Manifesto of Dynamic and Synoptic Declamation* published [in 1916], the idea was to vary speed and rhythm, using the whole range of voice tone, bodily movement and all parts of the theatre too, so that the spectator could no longer remain in a cool position of critical detachment—an idea which recurs a few years later, though in a calmer and more rational way, in the stage sets of the Russians Stepanova and Popova.

At the Doré Gallery in London on 28 April [1914], extracts from *Zang tumb tuum* became the basis of Marinetti's Dynamic and Synoptic Declamation in a room 'hung with many specimens of the ultra-modern school of art', according to *The Times,* 8 May 1914. This time there were fewer actors, but Marinetti made up for that in a rendering of the Siege of Adrianople, accompanied by the extra ingredients described in the manifesto. To begin with, he did not stay put in one place facing the audience but 'marched through the hall with dynamic gestures', as the *Observer* of 3 May reported. Three blackboards were placed at various points in the room, and during the declamation he 'alternately walked and ran' to them, drawing diagrams, theorems, equations and synoptic visualizations of the Words-in-freedom he was reciting, so that the audience had to keep swinging round to follow the rhythm of the words as their physical space was invaded. According to his account, 'the listeners turned continually to follow me in all my evolutions, participating with their whole bodies'. Sound, too, was stage-managed so that it came from different directions. On the table in front of him Marinetti had a telephone over which to pass the Turkish general's orders to [English futurist painter C. R. W.] Nevinson in the next room, ready and waiting to strike two enormous drums, while Marinetti beat out the sound of machine-gun fire with hammers: these were the 'imitations of artillery' picked up by *The Times* and the sound which 'boomed like guns heard across the hills' heard by the *Observer* correspondent. According to Nevinson's account of the Evening, Marinetti was so disappointed by the meagre amount of audience participation that he rushed back on to the stage at the end and roared: 'This was a very imperfect rendering. There should be no passive listeners. Everyone should take part and act the poem.'

It seems unlikely that Marinetti put into practice the manifesto's recommendation that the performer should move towards the elimination of idiosyncratic detail and towards a depersonalized, 'abstract' and mechanical delivery: what people remembered was his own magnetic personality.

The distinguished war correspondent Henry Nevinson, father of the artist, had this to say in the *Newark Evening News:* 'Antiquity exploded. Tradition ceased to breathe . . . I have heard many recitations and have tried to describe many battles. But listen to Marinetti's recitation of one of his battle scenes . . . the noise, the confusion, the surprise of death, the terror and courage, the shouting, curses, blood and agony—all were recalled by that amazing succession of words, performed or enacted by the poet with such passion of abandonment that no one could escape the spell of listening.' (pp. 103-04)

Belief in innovation was both the strength and weakness of Futurism. The strength lay in the freedom it gave the inventor—relief from the tyranny of the idea of the 'masterwork', and the freedom to be prodigal with ideas and energy, to move on constantly to the next thing. This was the speed and momentum that Marinetti demanded, and which he was able to sustain for a surprisingly long time. But this constant search for innovation played against Futurism too, and perhaps more so in the scattered and ephemeral media of literature and theatre than in any other field.

Almost every twentieth-century attempt to release language from traditional rules and restrictions has a precedent somewhere in Futurism. So, too, do the various typographic experiments in marrying words and the visual qualities of print and poetic line, from the Vorticists' short-lived magazine *Blast* in 1914, strongly influenced by

Lacerba, to the more recent developments in concrete poetry where typography is used to bring out the meaning of words, as in Govoni's 'The Sea' of 1915. . . . But the precedents set by Futurism find little recognition in either literary or theatrical histories. History is as wary of ceaseless innovations as it is of prankish jokes, and apart from the recognized transformation of the Futurist Evening into Dada cabaret by Tristan Tzara in Zurich in 1916, the rest was largely ignored or forgotten until the 1960s. It was then, too, that interest in Marinetti was revived from the shadowy legacy of Fascism, and *Zang tumb tuum* reinstated as his one concession to that despised phenomenon, the masterpiece. (pp. 108-09)

> *Caroline Tisdall and Angelo Bozzolla, in their* Futurism, *1977. Reprint by Oxford University Press, 1978, 216 p.*

Marjorie Perloff

[*Perloff is an Austrian-born American educator and critic who specializes in twentieth-century poetry. In the following excerpt, she examines the rhetorical and aesthetic use of the manifesto genre by the Italian Futurist movement.*]

In the autumn of 1913, at the height of the manifesto fever that swept across Europe in the years preceding the First World War, Gino Severini, then living in Paris, sent the manuscript of a projected manifesto to F. T. Marinetti in Milan. Spurred on by the example of his fellow Futurist painters, Severini evidently wanted to participate in the new literary sport. His text did not, however, meet the standard of the movement's leader. Here is Marinetti's reply:

> I have read with great attention your manuscript, which contains extremely interesting things. But I must tell you that there is nothing of the *manifesto* in it.
>
> First of all, the title absolutely won't do because it is too generic, too derivative of the titles of other manifestos. In the second place, you must take out the part in which you restate the *merde* and *rose* of Apollinaire, this being, in absolute contrast to our type of manifesto, a way of praising a single artist by repeating his own eulogies and insults. Moreover . . . you must not repeat what I have already said, in *Futurism* and elsewhere, about the futurist sensibility. The rest of the material is very good and very important, but to publish it as is would be to publish an article that is excellent but not yet a manifesto. I therefore advise you to take it back and reword it, removing all that I have already mentioned, and intensifying and tightening it, recasting the whole new part in the form of *Manifesto* [*in forma di Manifesto*] and not in that of the review article about futurist painting. . . .
>
> I think I shall persuade you by all that I know about *the art of making manifestos* [*dall' arte di far manifesti*], which I possess, and by my desire to place in *full* light, not in *half* light, your own remarkable genius as a futurist.

To give one's text "the form of *Manifesto*"—a form Marinetti defined in an earlier letter to the Belgian painter Henry Maassen as requiring, above all, "de la violence et de la *précision*" ["*violence* and *precision*"]—this was to create what was essentially a new literary genre, a genre that might meet the needs of a mass audience even as, paradoxically, it insisted on the avant-garde, the esoteric, the antibourgeois. The Futurist manifesto marks the transformation of what had traditionally been a vehicle for political statement into a literary, one might say, a quasi-poetic construct.

Consider the following definition of *manifesto* in the *OED:* "A public declaration or proclamation, usually issued with the sanction of a sovereign prince or state, or by an individual or body of individuals whose proceedings are of public importance, for the purpose of making known past actions and explaining the reasons or motives for actions as forthcoming." This definition dates from 1647. By 1848, when Marx and Engels published anonymously the most famous of all manifestos, *Der Manifest der Kommunistischen Partei,* "the sanction of a sovereign prince or state" had become at best irrelevant and at worst a mockery. In the wake of the French Revolution, the manifesto had become the mode of agonism, the voice of those who are *contra*—whether against king or pope or ruling class or simply against the existing state of affairs. It is this agonistic mode of discourse that set the stage for what Marinetti called *l'arte di far manifesti.* Indeed, it is the curiously mixed rhetoric of the *Communist Manifesto,* its preamble itself something of a prose poem, that paved the way for the grafting of the poetic onto the political discourse that we find in Futurist, and later in Dada and Surrealist, manifesto. "Ein Gespenst geht über Europa—das Gespenst des Kommunismus" ("A specter is haunting Europe—the specter of Communism")—here is the paradigmatic opening shot—a kind of verbal *frisson*—that the Futurists would adapt to their own purposes.

The shrewd recipe that Marinetti sent to Henry Maassen—"l'accusation *précise,* l'insulte bien *définie*" ["the *precise* accusation, the well-*defined* insult"]—made its Marinettian debut in the *Fondation et manifeste du futurisme,* published in Paris on the front page of *Le Figaro* on 20 February 1909. The *Figaro* headnote reads:

> M. Marinetti, the young Italian and French poet, whose remarkable and fiery talent has been made known throughout the Latin countries by his notorious demonstrations and who has a galaxy of enthusiastic disciples, has just founded the school of "Futurism," whose theories surpass in daring all previous and contemporary schools. The *Figaro,* which has already provided a rostrum for a number of these schools, and by no means minor ones, today offers its readers the Manifesto of the "Futurists." Is it necessary to say that we assign to the author himself full responsibility for his singularly audacious ideas and his frequently unwarranted extravagance in the face of things that are eminently respectable and, happily, everywhere respected? But we thought it interesting to reserve for our readers the first publication of this manifesto, whatever their judgment of it will be.

This bit of mythmaking sets the tone for the brilliant propaganda machine to come. I say mythmaking because the fact is that Marinetti became a public figure as a result of, not prior to, the publication of the first Futurist manifesto. Even more ironic, the Marinetti whose "theories" were ostensibly more "daring" than those of "all previous and contemporary schools" was writing, as late as 1909, decadent versions of Baudelairean lyric like the following:

> Mon bel ange sensuel, brûlant et trempé
> des voluptés du ciel et de l'enfer! . . .
> Je tends les bras éperdument vers toi
> dans la profonde solitude
> de cette nuit étincelante qui m'inonde
> d'un flot d'étoiles glacées!
>
> My beautiful, sensual angel, burning and bathed
> in the pleasures of heaven and hell! . . .
> Madly, I hold out my arms to you
> in the deep solitude
> of this glittering night that floods me
> with a cascade of frozen stars!

This is the first stanza of "Le dompteur" ("The Vanquisher"), which appeared in *Akademos* just a month before the publication of Marinetti's first manifesto. It ends with the lines:

> Ta chair, ta chair et sa chaleur nue tout entière,
> et son arome qui embaume à jamais
> la terre en deuil où je vais
> creusant un sillon monotone,
> Ta chair, ta chair et sa saveur tout entière,
> je l'attends!
>
> Your flesh, your flesh and all its naked warmth
> and its scent that forever perfumes
> with mourning the earth where I wander
> cutting a monotonous path,
> your flesh, and all its deliverance,
> I wait for it!

Within a year, in *Futurist Painting: Technical Manifesto,* Umberto Boccioni and his fellow artists were to launch their attack on "the nude in painting, as nauseous and as tedious as adultery in literature." "Artists," Boccioni declared, "obsessed with the desire to expose the bodies of their mistresses have transformed the Salons into arrays of unwholesome flesh." He might have been talking about Marinetti's "Ta chair, ta chair et sa saveur tout entière."

The 1909 manifesto thus reflects Marinetti's program for the future rather than his own poetic practice. As a lyric poet, he was a mediocre late Symbolist; as a thinker, he was almost wholly derivative, his extravagant statements being easily traceable to Nietzsche and Henri Bergson, to Alfred Jarry and Georges Sorel. But as what we now call a conceptual artist, Marinetti was incomparable, the strategy of his manifestos, performances, recitations, and fictions being to transform politics into a kind of lyric theater. (pp. 81-4)

The novelty of Italian Futurist manifestos . . . is their brash refusal to remain in the expository or critical corner, their understanding that the group pronouncement, sufficiently aestheticized, can, in the eyes of the mass audience, all but take the place of the promised art work. Indeed, when a few months after its *Figaro* publication, Marinetti, preceding the performance of his play *Les poupées électriques,* declaimed the 1909 manifesto from the stage of the Teatro Alfieri in Torino, the audience all but disregarded the play itself (a fable of husband and wife, plagued by the mechanical puppets made by the former—puppets that, as allegorical embodiments of bourgeois duty, money, and old age, turn out to be the couple's own alter egos) and responded to the drama of the manifesto.

The typical manifestos of the period open with a particular assertion or generalization about the arts. For example [in Jean Schlumberger's *Considerations,* 1909]:

> There are, in art, problems of circumstance and problems that are essential. The former change every fifteen years, every thirty years, and every half-century, according to whether the issue is one of fashion, of taste, or of custom. The more ephemeral they are, the more they absorb the attention.

Or [as in R. Canudo's *L'Art cerebriste,* 1914]:

> Never has a time been more favorable to artistic disputes. The Athenian Republic of modern times takes a passionate interest in them, and judges and condemns five or six times a year, on the occasion of a Salon, a concert, or a play.

Here, by contrast, is the opening of Marinetti's 1909 manifesto [excerpted above]:

> We had stayed up all night, my friends and I, under hanging mosque lamps with domes of filigreed brass, domes starred like our spirits, shining like them with the prisoned radiance of electric hearts. For hours we had trampled our atavistic ennui into rich oriental rugs, arguing up to the last confines of logic and blackening many reams of paper with our frenzied scribbling.

Not exposition—the controversial statement, the daring generalization—but narrative: this invention was one of Marinetti's master strokes. For when the eleven "theses" that follow in the body of the manifesto are placed within the narrative frame, their "validity" has already, so to speak, been established. So Marinetti begins by telling us about a particular night in Milan when he and his poet-friends stayed up till dawn, planning for the glorious future that would include "stokers feeding the hellish fires of great ships," "black spectres who grope in the red-hot bellies of locomotives launched down their crazy courses," "drunkards reeling like wounded birds along the city walls." As the night comes to an end, the friends are drawn outdoors, not by bird song or moonlight but by the "mighty noise of the huge double-decker trams that rumbled outside, ablaze with coloured lights, like villages on holiday suddenly struck and uprooted by the flooding Po and dragged over falls and through gorges to the sea."

Violence and precision—here is Marinetti's formula put into action. The friends dash outside and take off in their three motor cars (called *fauves* in the French version), traveling with breakneck speed so that "Here and there, sick lamplight through window glass taught us to distrust the deceitful mathematics of our perishing eyes." In this newly discovered fantastic landscape, everything is trans-

formed. The "ideal Mistress" of Romantic and Symbolist poetry gives way to the poet's *macchina* (the Italian word for *automobile* is oddly appropriate, given the Futurist context), capable of "hurling watchdogs against doorsteps, curling them under our burning tires like collars under a flatiron." Marinetti himself almost meets the same fate: just when the drive is at its most exhilarating, his car comes up against two cyclists, swerves, and turns over in a womb-like ditch:

> Oh! Maternal ditch, almost full of muddy water! Fair factory drain! I gulped down your nourishing sludge; and I remembered the blessed black breast of my Sudanese nurse. . . . When I came up—torn, filthy, and stinking—from under the capsized car, I felt the white-hot iron of joy deliciously pass through my heart!

Capsized, the automobile is reborn: "Up it came from the ditch, slowly, leaving in the bottom, like scales, its heavy framework of good sense and its soft upholstery of comfort." Accordingly, their "faces smeared with good factory muck," with "celestial soot," the group can put forward its program.

Marinetti's narrative contains a good deal of intentional buffoonery and declamation. Everything is presented in the most extreme terms possible: the automobile as beautiful shark, "running on its powerful fins," the steering wheel like "a guilliotine blade that threatened my stomach," and so on. The language, as Luciano de Maria has noted, is still heavily Symbolist—the maternal ditch, the overturning of the car as rebirth metaphor, the "electric hearts" of the hanging mosque lamps. But these images do not point toward the self; they reflect neither inner struggle nor the contours of an individual consciousness. On the contrary, Marinetti's selfhood is subordinated to the communal "we" (the first word of the manifesto), addressing the "you" of the crowd, the mass audience whom he hopes to move as well as to delight. In its reliance on hyperbole and parody (the reference to the "maternal ditch" immediately leads to the memory of "the black breast of my Sudanese nurse"), Marinetti's *symbolisme* takes on something of a hard edge; his landscape of capsized cars and factory drains has less in common with, say, Mallarmé's "transparent glacier" than with the animated surface of the Walt Disney cartoon.

In its celebration of what D. H. Lawrence, an early admirer of Marinetti, called "the inhuman will," the 1909 manifesto strikes an oddly impersonal note. It is lyrical (in the sense of choric), declamatory, and oracular without being in the least self-revelatory or intimate. Not that Marinetti did not possess, as did Lawrence, an enormous ego, decry ego as he might. But in his manifestos and other writings, questions of individual psychology and personal emotion are consistently subordinated to the discourse's pathetic argument, its appeal to the audience to join the movement. Marinetti thus uses question, exhortation, repetition, digression, tropes, and rhetorical figures to draw the audience into his radius of discourse. For example:

> Che ci si vada in pellegrinaggio, una volta all'anno, come si va al Camposanto nel giorno dei morti . . . ve lo concedo. Che una volta

The Futurists Russolo, Carrà, Marinetti, Boccioni, and Severini in Paris, 1912.

all'anno sia deposto un omaggio di fiori davanti alla *Gioconda,* ve lo concedo . . . Ma non ammetto che si conducano quotidiamente a passeggio per i musei le nostre tristezze, il nostro fragile coraggio, la nostra morbosa inquietudine. Perché volersi avvelenare? Perché volere imputridire? (ellipses are Marinetti's)

That one should make an annual pilgrimage, just as one goes to the graveyard on All Souls' Day—that I grant. That once a year one should leave a floral tribute beneath the *Gioconda,* I grant you that. . . . But I don't admit that our sorrows, our fragile courage, our morbid restlessness should be given a daily conducted tour through the museums. Why poison ourselves? Why rot?

A man on his feet talking, Charles Olson might have said of this. Or again, "ONE PERCEPTION MUST IMMEDIATELY AND DIRECTLY LEAD TO A FURTHER PERCEPTION. . . . get on with it, keep moving, keep in, speed, the nerves, their speed."

Ci opponete delle obiezioni? . . . Basta! Basta! Le conosciamo . . . Abbiamo capito! . . . La nostra bella e mendace intelligenza ci afferma che noi siamo il riassunto e il prolungamento degli avi nostri.—Forse! . . . Sia pure! . . . Ma che importa? Non vogliamo intendere! . . .

Guai a chi ci ripeterà queste parole infami! . . . (ellipses are Marinetti's)

You have objections?—Enough! Enough! We know them . . . we've understood! . . . Our fine deceitful intelligence tells us that we are the revival and extension of our ancestors—perhaps! . . . If only it were so!—But who cares? We don't want to understand! . . . Woe to anyone who says those infamous words to us again!

I shall return to the question of the theatricality of Marinetti's manifestos below. But first, let us look at the theses he puts forward. Here are the first four:

1. We intend to sing the love of danger, the habit of energy and fearlessness.

2. Courage, audacity, and revolt will be essential elements of our poetry.

3. Up to now literature has exalted a pensive immobility, ecstasy, and sleep. We intend to exalt aggressive action, a feverish insomnia, the racer's stride, the mortal leap, the punch and the slap.

4. We affirm that the world's magnificence has been enriched by a new beauty: the beauty of speed. A racing car whose hood is adorned with

great pipes, like serpents of explosive breath—a roaring car that seems to ride on grapeshot is more beautiful than the *Victory of Samothrace*.

Marinetti's cult of energy, aggressiveness, violence, and heroism is not unlike that of such manifesto writers as de Bouhélier and Romains. But here the theses are not enumerated until the narrative has already presented them in action: we have witnessed the "feverish insomnia" of the poet and his friends, the "racer's stride" and the worship of the "roaring car that seems to ride on grapeshot." Accordingly, when we come to the ninth thesis, "We will glorify war—the world's only hygiene—militarism, patriotism, the destructive gesture of freedom-bringers, beautiful ideas worth dying for, and scorn of woman," we do not question it as closely as we might; indeed, war is made to look like the necessary prelude to a new world composed of "great crowds excited by work," of "polyphonic tides of revolution in the modern capitals," of the "vibrant nightly fervor of arsenals and shipyards blazing with violent electric moons." Images of sound, color, and kinetic motion are foregrounded, the rhetorical strategy of the manifesto being to minimize the possibilities for rumination on the reader's part.

Marinetti claimed to have received more than ten thousand letters and articles in response to the publication of his manifesto in *Le Figaro,* and although much of this mail was negative, even angry and jeering, the response tells us a great deal about manifesto art. The eleventh and final thesis, for example, is often cited as a description of what Boccioni, Balla, and Carrà were doing in their paintings, but, ironically, the painters had not yet produced a single "Futurist" painting at the time that Marinetti was writing his paean to "shipyards blazing with violent electric moons," to:

> greedy railway stations that devour smoke-plumed serpents; factories hung on clouds by the crooked lines of their smoke; bridges that stride the rivers like giant gymnasts, flashing in the sun with a glitter of knives; adventurous steamers that sniff the horizon; deep-chested locomotives whose wheels paw the tracks like the hooves of enormous steel horses bridled by tubing; and the sleek flight of planes whose propellers chatter in the wind like banners and seem to cheer like an enthusiastic crowd.

Just as Gertrude Stein began to resemble her portrait by Picasso only years after he had painted it, so the Futurist paintings (for example, Boccioni's *The City Rises* of 1910-11 or Carrà's *Funeral of the Anarchist Galli* of 1911-12) were painted only *after* the publication of the manifesto, as if Marinetti's Nietzschean prophecies ("In truth I tell you") had to be fulfilled.

But it is not enough to say of this and subsequent Futurist manifestos that theory preceded practice, that, say, Luigi Russolo's *The Art of Noises* (1913) outlined the new sounds of the "Futurist orchestra" before the machines made to produce these sounds had been invented. For the real point is that the theory, in Russolo's as in Marinetti's manifesto, *is* the practice in that the text foregrounds what Giovanni Lista calls "the problematic of the precedence of project to work, of metalanguages to creation." To talk

about art becomes equivalent to making it, and indeed most historians of Italian Futurism agree that the series of fifty-odd manifestos published between 1909 and Italy's entrance into the war in 1915 were the movement's literary form par excellence. Not only are Marinetti's manifestos more interesting than his poems, novels, or even than such experimental collage-texts as the problematic *Zang tumb tuuum;* his *arte di far manifesti* became a way of questioning the status of traditional genres and media, of denying the separation between, say, lyric poem and short story or even between poem and picture. (pp. 85-92)

. . . . .

The *Futurist Painting: Technical Manifesto* was published as a leaflet in Marinetti's journal *Poésia* on 11 February 1910. It was composed by Boccioni and Russolo (although the signatures of Carrà, Balla, and Severini were also affixed to it) in a single day, Marinetti joining the two artists in the evening to add the finishing touches. A few weeks later (18 March), the manifesto was declaimed from the stage of the Teatro Chiarella in Torino to an audience of approximately three thousand artists, students, and factory workers. Addressed "TO THE YOUNG ARTISTS OF ITALY!" it adopted the violent rhetoric of contemporary political manifestos:

> Comrades, we tell you now that the triumphant progress of science makes profound changes in humanity inevitable, changes which are hacking an abyss between those docile slaves of past tradition and us free moderns, who are confident in the radiant splendour of our future.

And again:

> In the eyes of other countries, Italy is still a land of the dead, a vast Pompeii white with sepulchres. But Italy is being reborn. Its political resurgence will be followed by a cultural resurgence. In the land inhabited by the illiterate peasant, schools will be set up; in the land where doing nothing in the sun (*nel paese del dolce far niente*) was the only available profession, millions of machines are already roaring.

The roaring machines are not only a prominent manifesto subject; they also provide the manifesto writers with a new typographic format, a format drawn from the world of advertising posters and newspapers, which was soon to find its way into the literature of the period. In the manifesto, the page supplants the stanza or the paragraph as the basic print unit, a situation that, when applied to lyric poetry, was to call into question the integrity of the verse line itself. (pp. 92-3)

The use of boldface headings, capital letters, numbered series, and aphorisms set off from the text can, of course, be traced back to the various communist manifestos and pamphlets of Marx and Engels, but the more immediate source of Futurist page design was the language of advertising of the late nineteenth century. As Arthur A. Cohen observes:

> The placard, the sandwich man, the poster, the sign, the advertisement, the leaflet, the broadside, prospectus, *prier d'insérer*, ticket, hand-

bill—all these methods of calling out, shouting, if you will, were devices of circumventing traditional language, imitating the sound of speech, and hence restoring to a kind of primacy, the original spoken rhythm which had been for millenia abstracted by written language. . . . Since its [advertising's] intentions were thought to be vulgar, its means could be untraditional. Garishness of color, juxtapositions of bold wood typefaces, the use of illustrative cuts . . . the mix of fonts, the stridency of exclamation points and underscorings, all these could be employed by the commercial arm of the reigning bourgeoisie to advertise a product and to sell it. Typographic novelty began, so to speak, in the marketplace, catching the accelerated pace of an urban culture.

L'arte di far manifesti was a way of infusing this commercial strain into the lyric fabric, the intent being to close the gap between "high" and "low" art. Titles, for example, became very important. When Moréas published his manifesto of 1886, he called it quite simply *Le Symbolisme;* again, Jules Romains called his *unanimiste* manifesto *Les sentiments unanimes de la poésie.* Here, by contrast, are some of Marinetti's titles, usually printed in big black block letters: *Uccidiamo il chiaro di luna!* (*Let's Murder the Moonshine*), *Contro Venezia passatista* (*Against Past-Loving Venice*), *Abbasso il tango e Parsifal!* (*Down with the Tango and Parsifal*), *Distruzione della syntassi—Immaginazione senza fili—Parole in libertà* (*Destruction of Syntax—Wireless Imagination—Words-in-Freedom*). To be memorable, Marinetti posited, a title must be concrete and provocative enough to catch the eye as well as the ear. Other Futurists followed suit: *Absolute Motion Plus Relative Motion Equals Dynamism* (Boccioni), *Futurist Reconstruction of the Universe* (Balla, Fortunato Depero), *Futurist Manifesto of Lust* (Valentine de Saint-Point), and so on.

Subtitles also play a big role. In *Destruction of Syntax—Wireless Imagination—Words-in-Freedom,* Marinetti introduces such subtitles as "The Semaphoric Adjective," "Typographical Revolution," "Death of Free Verse," and "Multilinear Lyricism." These subtitles are usually printed in italics or bold face, the model being the newspaper column. Under these headings, items are regularly numbered, again with boldface headings, as in *Futurist Painting: Technical Manifesto* where we read "WE DECLARE," followed by a list of nine items, and "WE FIGHT," followed by a list of four. Balilla Pratella's *Manifesto of Futurist Musicians* (1910) similarly lists eleven stated aims, all in the infinitive and in capital letters, beginning with the following:

> 1. TO CONVINCE YOUNG COMPOSERS TO DESERT SCHOOLS, CONSERVATORIES AND MUSICAL ACADEMIES, AND TO CONSIDER FREE STUDY AS THE ONLY MEANS OF REGENERATION.

Enumeration is, as the authors of political manifestos had long understood, a way of arresting the attention of the audience. The numbered principles or goals of the Futurists almost always shade into one another; they are all part of the same thrust. But numbering implies that the authors mean business, that the goals to be achieved are practical and specific. It also means that the individual units are

short and immediately perceivable by the reader, as in the following list from *Wireless Imagination:*

> 1. Acceleration of life to today's swift pace. . . .
>
> 2. Dread of the old and the known. Love of the new, the unexpected.
>
> 3. Dread of quiet living, love of danger and an attitude of daily heroism.
>
> 4. Destruction of a sense of the Beyond and an increased value of the individual whose desire is *vivre sa vie,* in Bonnot's phrase.
>
> 5. The multiplication and unbridling of human desires and ambitions.

Sometimes, as in Marinetti's *The Variety Theater,* first published in *Lacerba* in October 1913 and then in English in the *Daily Mail* that November, different print faces, large type, numerical listing in boldface, and the use of plus and equal signs are combined with *parole in libertà,* that is, a string of nouns or noun phrases (usually concrete images) in apposition, with no connectives between them, as well as with onomatopoeic articles.

Here Marinetti wants to present us with a graphic image of his thesis—that "The Variety Theater is absolutely practical, because it proposes to distract and amuse the public with comic effects, erotic stimulation, or imaginative astonishment." Accordingly, the page contains advertising slogans in large bold type ("FUMEZ FUMEZ MANOLI FUMEZ MANOLI CIGARETTES"; "GIOCONDA ACQUA PURGATIVA"); the phonetic representation of screeching ambulance sirens ("trrrr trrrr sulla testa trombeeebeeebeette fiiiiiiischi sirene d'autoambulanze | pompe elettriche"), and the burlesque cataloging of erotic measurements ("donna in camicia [50 m. + 120 altezza della casa = 170 m.]"). But, most important, the manifesto page substitutes white space or blanks for conventional punctuation so as to indicate an abrupt stop, a change of scene or image. The main effect is thus one of fragmentation. (pp. 94-6)

· · · · ·

In his manifesto *Futurist Painting and Sculpture* (1914), Boccioni declares:

> For us the picture is no longer an exterior scene, a stage for the depiction of a fact. A picture is not an irradiating architectural structure in which the artist, *rather than the object,* forms a central core. It is the emotive, architectural environment which creates sensation and completely involves the observer. . . . We therefore maintain, unlike Cézanne, that *the boundaries* of the object tend to retreat towards a periphery (the environment) *of which we are the centre.*

The "emotive architectural environment" that "involves the observer" is created, in Futurist manifesto, by a variety of theatrical strategies, the most important being the conception of the artist as *improvvisatore.* . . . Improvisation is . . . an art that depends not on revision in the interests of making the parts cohere in a unified formal structure, but on a prior readiness, a performative stance that leaves room for accident and surprise. Or at least, in the case of the Futurist manifesto, a stance that pretends to leave such room.

Thus Marinetti observes in *The Birth of Futurist Aesthetic* (1915):

> To a finished house we prefer the framework of a house in construction whose girders are the color of danger—landing platforms for airplanes—with its numberless arms that claw and comb out stars and comets, its aerial quarterdecks from which the eye embraces a vaster horizon. . . .
>
> The frame of a house in construction symbolizes our burning passion for the coming-into-being of things [*pel divenire delle cose*].

And in *The Futurist Synthetic Theatre,* written in collaboration with Emilio Settimelli and Bruno Corra, Marinetti declares:

> We believe that a thing is valuable to the extent that it is improvised (hours, minutes, seconds), not extensively prepared (months, years, centuries). . . . THE GREATER NUMBER OF OUR WORKS HAVE BEEN WRITTEN IN THE THEATRE. . . . Our Futurist theatre jeers at Shakespeare but pays attention to the gossip of actors, is put to sleep by a line from Ibsen but is inspired by red or green reflections from the stalls. WE ACHIEVE AN ABSOLUTE DYNAMISM THROUGH THE INTERPENETRATION OF DIFFERENT ATMOSPHERES AND TIMES.

"A thing is valuable to the extent that it is improvised"—this preference for the unfinished, the tentative, the potential, for "girders that are the color of danger," characterizes the form as well as the ideological stance of Futurist manifesto. (pp. 101-03)

When Marinetti told Henry Maassen that the formula for manifesto art was "violence and *precision,*" he might have added a third quality that he and his fellow manifesto writers had in abundance—namely wit. . . . [As exemplified by] the effect of comic hyperbole in *Contro Venezia passatista,* in which the inertia of the modern Venetian is defined by comparing the gondoliers to "gravediggers trying in cadence to dig ditches in a flooded cemetery." An even better example of Marinetti's proto-Dada sense of the absurd is found in the 1914 manifesto *Down with the Tango and Parsifal,* subtitled "Futurist Letter Circulated among Cosmopolitan Women Friends Who Give Tango-Teas and Parsifalize Themselves" (*Abbasso il tango e Parsifal!*: "Lettera futurista circolare ad alcune amiche cosmopolite che dànno dei thè-tango e si parsifalizzano").

Here the coinage *parsifalizzano* comically implies that the cult of Wagner is no more than the latest fashion in social dance, in this case the tango. But the equation of tango and Parsifal is also quite serious, Marinetti implying that the revolutionary and nationalist spirit must embrace all areas of cultural life, its fashions in dance or food or clothing as well as in the "high" arts. In order to deflate the high-society cult of both these exotic imports—tango and Parsifal—the manifesto again resorts to catalogs of absurd metaphors, to gigantism:

> Monotony of romantic haunches, amid the flashing eyes and Spanish daggers of de Musset, Hugo, and Gautier. Industrialization of Baudelaire, *Fleurs du mal* weaving around the taverns of Jean Lorrain for impotent voyeurs *à la* Huysmans and inverts like Oscar Wilde. Last crazy fling of a sentimental, decadent, paralytic romanticism toward the Fatal Woman of cardboard [*la Donna Fatale di cartapesta*].

The image is one of parody *fin de siècle,* of the final death throes of the Romantic tradition of Victor Hugo and Alfred de Musset, culminating, via J. K. Huysmans and Oscar Wilde—and, one might add, via the young Marinetti himself—in a mechanized ("Industrialization of Baudelaire") cardboard version of *Les fleurs du mal.* Such hyperbole is punctuated, as so often in Futurist manifesto, by aphorism:

> To possess a woman is not to rub against her but to penetrate her.

And again the poet adopts the dialogic mode, responding to his own cynical aphorism with the dismay of the outraged listener:

> "Barbarian!"
>
> "A knee between the thighs? Come! they want two!"
>
> "Barbarian!"
>
> Well, then, yes, we are barbarians!

Having declared his willingness to assume this adversary role, the performance artist can now invent increasingly absurd fantasies about the enraptured tango dancers:

> Is it amusing for you to look each other in the mouth and ecstatically examine each other's teeth, like two hallucinated dentists? To yank? . . . To lunge? . . . Is it so much fun to arch desperately over each other, trying to pop each other like two corked bottles, and never succeeding? (ellipses are Marinetti's)

And then, having made us laugh, the poet shifts tone abruptly, casting a cold eye on the concept of fashion in art, even as D. H. Lawrence was to do in manifestos like "Surgery for the Novel—or a Bomb" (1923). Here is Marinetti's indictment:

> Tristan and Isolde who withhold their climax to excite King Mark. Medicine dropper of love. Miniature of sexual anguish. Spun sugar of lust. Lechery out in the open. Delirium tremens. Cockeyed hands and feet. Pantomime coitus for the camera. Masturbated waltz. pouah! Down with the diplomatics of the skin!

Metaphor after metaphor, piled up in abrupt noun phrases, followed by renewed exhortation: down with . . . up with! The speaker's attention then turns to Richard Wagner and the same strictures are applied to *Parsifal,* with its "cloudbursts, puddles, and bogs of mystical tears." Again the tone is comic—"Tears and false pearls of Mary Magdalen in décolletage at Maxim's"—but the humor is savage, Marinetti making his case for an honest and open sexuality, for a rejection of romantic cant and coyness. His final rhetorical flourish—a sort of last twist of the knife—is to turn the significance of "tango" and "parsifalization" back on those who practice it by informing them that

> Furthermore, you forget *this final argument,* the only persuasive one *for you:* to love Wagner and *Parsifal* today, performed everywhere and especially in the provinces . . . to give tango-teas like all good bourgeois all over the world, come come, it's no longer CHIC! [NON È PIUUUÙ CHIC!]

This is a good example of the power of improvisation to outwit the reader. For Marinetti has declared, in the opening paragraph of the manifesto, just two pages earlier, that "This epidermic oscillation [the tango] is spreading little by little through the whole world." How, then, can the fashion already be over? Because, so the text implies, it is the very nature of fashion to disappear before it has fully taken hold. And accordingly the artist's role is to expose it.

Most readers would grant that *Down with the Tango and Parsifal* has great rhetorical ingenuity, that it is a stunning performance. Still, by the norms of Modernist aesthetic, such theatricality, insofar as it has pretentions to being "art," is suspect. As Michael Fried has put it in his essay "Art and Objecthood" (1967), which is itself a kind of manifesto attacking, in the name of Op or color-field painting, the new minimal and conceptual art of the sixties, *"art degenerates as it approaches the conditions of the-atre";* indeed, *"The success, even the survival of the arts has increasingly to depend on their ability to defeat theatre."* An artwork "defeats" theater when it is a self-contained, coherent formal structure, adhering to its own medium and genre. When, on the other hand, the artwork has no existence apart from a given situation or environment, when "it depends on the beholder, is incomplete without him . . . has been waiting for him . . . and refuses to stop confronting him, distancing him, isolating him," then it "degenerates" into "mere" theater. (pp. 107-09)

[A situational aesthetic] governs what Marinetti calls *l'arte di far manifesti.* Situational in the literal sense, of course, in that the Futurist manifesto has a practical purpose: to move an audience to action, or at least to assent, in a particular situation in, say, the "passéist" Venice of 1910. Again, the manifesto is situational in that it operates in real time and real space; thus *Down with the Tango and Parsifal* is an attack on the cultural and sexual hypocrisy of the Italian upper classes and their bourgeois followers. But the Futurist manifesto is also theatrical in a deeper sense, occupying as it does a "space that lies between the arts" and conflating verbal strategies that do not conventionally cohere: the ethical and pathetic arguments of classical rhetoric, the rhythm, metaphor, and hyperbole of Romantic lyric poetry, the journalistic narrative of everyday discourse, and the dialogic mode of drama which acts to draw the reader (or viewer) into its verbal orbit. (p. 111)

Manifesto art thus paves the way for the gradual erosion of the distinction between "literary" and "theoretical" texts that has become a central problematic in our own critical discourse.

Such generic rupture, like the cutting and intercalation of collage, is symptomatic of what we might call the new technopoetics of the twentieth century. It is a commonplace that the avant-garde movements of the 1910s and 1920s were by definition *anti,* that their informing spirit was one of rupture and reversal, of negation in defiance of the art of the dominant culture. But there can hardly be rupture without a compensatory addition: to cut out X inevitably means to make room for Y. In the case of Futurist experiment—whether with words-in-freedom or collage or performance—the urge is to include extraliterary (or extrapainterly) material that might situate the work in its actual context. "Les fenêtres de ma poésie," said Cendrars, "sont grand'ouvertes sur les boulevards" ["The windows of my poetry are large openings onto the boulevards"].

One way to achieve such an opening is to make language visible or, conversely, to make the visual what Roland Barthes has called *scriptible.* Writers such as Marinetti, artists such as Carrà and Severini, present us with important theorizing about the opening of the verbal-visual field. . . . (p. 115)

> *Marjorie Perloff, in her* The Futurist Moment: Avant-Garde, Avant Guerre, and the Language of Rupture, *The University of Chicago Press, 1986, 288 p.*

FUTURIST THEATER

Christiana J. Taylor

> [*In the following excerpt from her study* Futurism: Politics, Painting and Performance, *Taylor charts the development of Futurist theater.*]

Futurism as a movement consisted of two distinct phases. The first phase, which lasted from 1909 to 1915, was most important and influential in the areas of painting, literature and politics. The second phase, lasting from 1916 to 1929, was characterized by profuse and original theatrical activities while the influence of painting and literature declined. The absorption of Futurism into Fascism which occurred after the war, during 1919, 1920 and 1921, diminished both the potency and the international prestige of the Futurist movement except in the area of theatre art. During this period the Futurist theatre expanded its influence throughout Europe. Two factors caused the eclipse of Futurism under the Fascist regime. The Government exercised control and censorship over the arts, and the artists who had founded and fostered the movement had disavowed Futurism, leaving lesser known, more manipulatable men as standard bearers after 1920.

Activities of a theatrical nature had been customary among the Futurists since 1909, several years prior to the publication of a specific manifesto dealing with Futurist Theatre. The evenings spent declaiming and explicating

Futurist political and painting theory, . . . were in fact planned, staged, and orchestrated by Marinetti. These evenings, called 'serate,' were designed to outrage and provoke that favorite Futurist target "the passatista." Using techniques which the Futurists developed to publicize themselves, their movement and their political ideas, they rented halls or theatres in one city after another, selling tickets to a much touted "opening night." When the audience arrived the Futurists confronted them from the stage with a systematic, thorough and direct attack on their bourgeois mediocrity, passéist ideas and stupidity. The predictable response generally escalated into a melee of shouts, insults, fists, rotten vegetables and finally peaked with the arrival of harried local prefects. Francesco Cangiullo recalls one such 'serate' in Florence at the Verdi Theatre in 1914.

> . . . the showers of potatoes, oranges and bunches of fennel became infernal. Suddenly he [Marinetti] cried, 'Damn!' slapping his hand to his eye. We ran to help him; many in the public who had seen the missiles land protested indignantly against bestial cowardice, and, with what we shouted from the stage, the place became a ghetto market where things were said that cannot be repeated, much less written.
>
> I see Russolo again with saliva running from his mouth; I hear Carrà roaring, 'Throw an idea instead of potatoes, idiots!' And now the spectators shouted at Filiberto Scarpelli who, to demonstrate solidarity, wished to be with us on stage . . .
>
> I, with a table leg in my hand, wanted to look for a place . . . to support it in the audience.

These evenings, beginning in Turin in 1909, quickly became a Futurist trademark and drew hundreds of curious, angry and sympathetic Italians as the Futurists careened again and again from one end of Italy to the other. As the efficacy of the 'serate' as publicity mechanisms grew, they became more structured, more elaborate and more like performances. Marinetti, aware of the potential for declamation and explication, was also sensitive to an art form buried in the 'serate' which included elements of the cabaret, the theatre and the pulpit.

The first manifesto to deal specifically with Theatre, *The Variety Theatre Manifesto,* appeared October 1, 1913 in *Lacerba.* Often called the 'Café Concerto' manifesto, it has been republished more often than any other except the *Foundation Manifesto* in 1909 which it greatly resembles in style and spirit. The *Variety Theatre Manifesto,* written by Marinetti, was meant to illuminate the direction in which Futurist Theatre activity would proceed. As had been the case with the Futurist painters, comprehension of the task to be accomplished and the possible forms it would take preceeded the actual fact of accomplishment. (pp. 29-30)

In describing the Variety Theatre, Marinetti used the music-hall, cabaret, night club, athletic event and circus as models upon which the new theatre would be based. He did not call the Variety Theatre a Futurist Theatre, but rather the starting point for the formation of a Futurist Theatre which would contain many of the attributes synthesized from public entertainment as he saw it in 1913. In so far as many of these entertainment forms were thoroughly modern, complex and technical, they contained elements which Marinetti believed were useful and appropriate to Futurism. Marinetti intended these ersatz performance methods to provide a stimulus for the development of Futurist Theatre which would be synthesized from many sources. He called the Variety Theatre "the crucible in which the elements of a new sensibility that is coming into being are stirring." In this first theatre manifesto of 1913, Marinetti suggested a developmental growth of a Futurist Theatre which would be constantly regenerated and renovated, a theatre which would not remain fixed stylistically but which would evolve beyond any prescribed system, style or 'raison d'être'.

The basic philosophy underlying the *Variety Theatre Manifesto* and the Futurist Theatre forms which derived from it between the years 1913 and 1925 were inherent in the Foundation Manifesto of 1909. For example, Marinetti was particularly delighted with the physical, energetic, competitive aspects of the Variety Theatre; the robust humor of vaudeville, the speed and danger of death-diving, the grace and agility of gymnasts. In these he found reflections of the "aggressive movement, feverish insomnia, the running step, the somersault, the insult and pinches" of his Foundation Manifesto.

The spectacles provided by the Variety Theatre existed in and of themselves, irrespective of what preceeded or followed each segment of a performance. There was no necessary order of appearance, no thread or narrative carrying the spectator from one act to the next. This structure of unrelated activities strung together for the entertainment of the audience was fundamental to what Marinetti viewed as the true form which Futurist Theatre would eventually achieve.

In calling for an end to well made plays, contrivances, psychologies, denouements, and all the other accountrements of the established theatre, he proposed what has been termed 'illogical theatre'. Illogical theatre allowed events and incidents to occur without regard to their relationship to one another, or to their consequences. In effect, Marinetti initiated a theatre which eliminated cause and effect, where audience expectancy and rules of probability exerted no influence on stage actions. The concept of illogical structure which was articulated in the *Variety Theatre Manifesto* had been developed in Marinetti's poetry, from which it pervaded all forms of Futurist literature. Marinetti believed that the audience was not to be permitted to proceed in its accustomed manner of putting together information in a logical sequence. The new Futurist Theatre, which would come into being, would teach the audience to intuit information, sensation and understanding. The Variety Theatre's illogical structure was an elementary step towards the instruction of the intuitive approach to the audience.

The intuitive approach to art was one of the most important of Marinetti's dictums. It was fundamental to his literary, theatrical and cinematic manifestos, as well as to the manifestos of the painters and sculptors, although it was not always included formally in these works. For Marinetti and the Futurists, a paramount task was the stimulation of the passéist intuitive capability. (pp. 34-6)

Onomatopoeia, typography, 'parole in libertà' [Marinetti's literary concept of 'words-in-freedom'] and abolition of syntax were combined with several performance techniques which evolved from the 'serate,' with techniques for declaiming poetry and propaganda, and with elements of the Variety Theatre. All innovations worked out in one discipline were available to the Futurists of all of the other disciplines and there was an astounding amount of transfer and translation of information between artists. This practice of integrating principles from one art form with another and translating the fundamental ideas of the movement into usable artistic vocabularies gave Futurism a stylistic homogeneity.

The most obvious consequence of Futurist literary devices which were transposed into the writing of plays was the incoherence of the play when compared to traditional, explicit, dramatic literature. (Usually plays written in the new Futurist style were performed by the Futurists, or by closely tutored friends, who could comprehend the material and convey it properly.) However, the central purpose of these innovations in literature which had been adapted to playscripts was to begin the process of abstracting out of the play all the essential features. Characters lost their personalities and became abbreviated in a manner which imbued them with a mechanical aspect. This mechanical character concept, perhaps derived from Gordon Craig, developed into a major concern among the Futurists. Plot became shortened and intensified so that a single incident might be all the action utilized.

An early play of Marinetti's [Drama senza titolo] dated 1913, describes a young woman who enters an office, sits down and converses with a man of no description. The dialogue contains no information about either character, gives no reason for their activity and has only a faint resemblance to anything which might actually take place. On a sound from off stage, the young woman rises and leaves and the play ends. There are other signals which are indicated by marginal notes and which have ambiguous meanings. The diaglogue has the same sparseness of the 'parole in libertà'. Also at certain points the reader gets the feeling that they are about to begin talking with each other in a logical sequential way, but it never quite occurs. Very rich images are passed between them, but the images have no function. The mechanical nature of the actors is reinforced by the single author's note at the bottom of the script which requests that the actors move with deliberation and in no way express any emotion in what they are doing or saying.

These short early plays written between 1910 and 1914 had the illogical and non-sequential aspect called for in Marinetti's Variety Theatre Manifesto, and contained little psychological or character development. Some seemed to depict social types such as the wealthy art patron, the socialite, the debonair bachelor, and the fat politician. Plot was minimal, involving one or two incidents and no climactic event. Indeed, these plays had no clear message, no theme, no exposition, no denouement. The most that can

be said of them is that they occasionally had humor and that they were capable of rendering a very small vignette of some everyday aspect of life.

Prior to 1914, the performances given by the Futurists lacked a clearly recognizable form. Several types of structure were used for different purposes. The 'serate,' which constituted the major form of production, could consist of poetry readings, political discourses, lectures, art shows, riots or even plays. These performances, or 'serate,' were distinguished by their lack of form and by the inclusion of multiple performance techniques such as juggling, dancing, and contests of various sorts. This loose and unpredictable structure was in keeping with the style of performance which Marinetti found admirable in the Variety Theatre Manifesto.

Before 1914 there was no coherent production design guiding Futurist performances; many aspects of these performances were spontaneously arranged at the last moment. For example, arriving in Turin for an evening of lectures in 1913, Marinetti found that the rented hall had no curtain separating stage from auditorium. He had planned on having several Futurists, hidden from the audience, call out certain responses to questions in his lecture and later to appear and take part in the discussion which would follow. In order to provide himself with a means of carrying out his plan, he dashed out during the afternoon and bought ten folding Japanese screens which he lined up on stage behind his lectern. The effect was apparently hilarious as the audience had a view of the legs and shoes of the waiting Futurists. This same effect was later developed into a short theatre piece called Feet in which various lower legs performed improvisations together while the rest of the bodies were concealed behind a semi-lowered curtain.

The Futurists had discovered an effective and useful method of decorating the stage space during the early years of the movement. Wishing to display their work and surround themselves with a 'Futurist milieu,' they hung Futurist paintings along the drops to form a 'painted backdrop' against which the action occurred. . . . This custom continued through the history of the movement and has been cited by a number of journalists and scholars. The hanging paintings were often well received by critics and audiences and they were frequently sold after the performance. The custom of hanging paintings does not constitute a design scheme; the possibilities for stage design were not developed in these early performances. The only mention of concern for the stage space appears in the Variety Theatre Manifesto:

> 16. The Variety Theatre destroys all our conceptions of perspective, proportion, time and space. (E.g., a little doorway and gate, thirty centimetres high, alone in the middle of the stage, which certain eccentric Americans open and close as they pass and repass, very seriously as if they couldn't do otherwise.)

During 1914 Marinetti developed some of the areas of performance which had been neglected in the 'serate' and which are not expressly described in the Variety Theatre Manifesto. Marinetti, assisted by the Futurist painters, demonstrated a scenographic compliment to performance, a mode of dressing the stage which would be integral to whatever activity they planned. They were not consistent in their use of scenography, nor were they always original in their selection of scenographic elements. They were exploring the possibilities of the space and especially the relationship between the performance space and the audience which had been of central importance in Marinetti's *Variety Theatre Manifesto.*

An early example of the use of scenographic elements in a performance occurred in Rome in March and April of 1914. The Futurists performed what they termed an evening of 'dynamic and synoptic declamation,' or an evening of poetry readings sometimes accompanied by multiple voices and instrumental sounds. For this performance Marinetti read from the 'parole in libertà' poem *Piedigrotta* by Francesco Cangiullo. The performance was held at the Spovieri Gallery in Rome. The gallery was actually a large hall hung with numerous Futurist canvases and a large drop curtain painted by Balla, Boccioni, Severini, Carrà and Russolo. A large freestanding set-piece which depicted three 'Crocean philosophers' adorned one corner of the hall. The room was lit with lights covered with red paper which created an effect variously called 'adulterated chianti,' 'bloody and dim' and 'murky.' The light quality was given special attention by Marinetti who wished to use the light to 'erase the old distinctions between areas, compartments of people.' Consequently, the hall was treated as one space which contained both performers and patrons. The performers were the Futurists themselves attired in splendid costumes capped with rich and exotic hats. The declamation was carried out by Marinetti with various amounts of choral support from Balla and Cangiullo. Moreover, the recitation was enhanced by orchestration from several homemade instruments which were used to generate a panoply of sounds many of which were unmusical. Clearly the Futurist performances of 1914 had moved away from the Variety Theatre's casual production style in that these evenings had a cohesiveness and planned program which integrated the efforts of the poets and painters toward a production design. Moreover, performance space, ignored in the *Variety Theatre Manifesto,* had become an integral aspect of the Futurist performance, requiring some consideration and design. The introduction of Futurist 'noise' and a Futurist chorus into the performances aroused possibilities which were developed later as the full force of Futurist Theatre began to emerge.

Early in 1915, Marinetti, with Bruno Corra and Emilio Settimelli, wrote the *Futurist Synthetic Theatre Manifesto,* published in Milan on January 11. The *Futurist Synthetic Theatre Manifesto* announced and explicated the core of ideas from which theatre activity subsequently derived. Unlike the *Variety Theatre Manifesto* which had proposed tentative resources and possible directions to be explored in an effort to evolve a Futurist Theatre aesthetic, the *Futurist Synthetic Theatre Manifesto* was the definitive statement which had been promised two years earlier. (pp. 39-46)

The *Futurist Synthetic Theatre Manifesto* was by procla-mation the first word on the Futurist theatre. Combining elements from the *Variety Theatre Manifesto,* from the 'serate,' from other manifestos (e.g., *Weights and Measures, Photodynamism, Manifesto to Playwrights*) and from their experiences over the last two years, Marinetti, Corra and Settimelli defined the Futurist theatre aesthetic which had been promised in the *Variety Theatre Manifesto* which said, "Today the Variety Theatre is the crucible in which the elements of an emergent new sensibility are seething."

An important aspect of the *Futurist Synthetic Theatre Manifesto* was the political emphasis incorporated into it. Marinetti believed emphatically in the propaganda potential of theatre, potential which he and the Futurists were committed to exploiting in their efforts to engage Italy in the War. The Pact of London, officially allying Italy with England and France against the Triple Alliance Nations, an objective which was paramount to Marinetti and the Futurists, was signed just five months after the manifesto was written. Unmistakably the Manifesto was part of an all-out campaign launched by the Futurists between January 1915 and August 1916 to proselytize and promote the war through a barrage of activities, principally theatre. Futurist performers toured the length and breadth of the Italian peninsula, playing to generally receptive and boisterous audiences. During the months of February, March, April and May eight companies were recorded touring a repertory of Futurist productions.

Although the Futurists were pledged to preparing Italy for war, the activities which followed the publication of the manifesto were not confined to war themes or to propagandist content. The physical and intellectual revolution which the Futurists proposed was expedited by the imminence of the war but not dependent on it. Rather, Futurism at this vital, energetic stage of growth was greater in scope and ambition than is usually acknowledged by historians. The Futurists saw themselves as prophets struggling against a massive wave of inert humanity which must be jabbed and pummeled onward into the future and which must be able to advance unencumbered by vestigial pre-Futurist drawbacks such as religion, fear, education, conditioning and bourgeois value systems. In fact, the Futurists, with the jabbing and pummelling created an atmosphere of 'feverish creativity,' 'jarred awareness,' 'speed, noise and bodymadness' which involved all levels of society encouraging their participation and gaining their committment. The radical political motivation behind Marinetti's movement, with its attendant passion and zeal, ran contrary to the detached and effete intellectualism that had been characteristic of art groups before the emergence of Futurism. The Futurists were the vanguard of a new wave of art movements whose political philosophies would include the conversion of the masses through the arts, notably Dada and Surrealism.

For the Futurists, theatre was considered the most efficacious means for transmitting to the inert masses the new ideology: 'Every night the Futurist Theatre will be a gymnasium to train our race's spirit to the swift, dangerous enthusiasms made necessary by this Futurist year . . . The Futurist Theatre will be able to excite its audience, that is, make it forget the monotony of daily life, by sweeping it through a labyrinth of sensations imprinted on the most exacerbated originality and combined in unpredictable ways.' The *Futurist Synthetic Theatre Manifesto* described the techniques for accomplishing this objective.

The basic unit of the Futurist Synthetic Theatre was a short compressed script called a 'sintesi'. The essential feature of the 'sintesi' was its briefness, a few lines to a few pages at most.

> The Futurist Theatre was to express in a very few minutes and with a very few words and gestures innumerable situations, emotions, ideas, sensations and facts, and to present a tragedy in sixty acts of which the first fifty-nine need not be shown.

An example of the compression of time, character development and dialogue typical of the 'sintesi' occurs in *Education* by Angelo Rognoni.

> (*A classroom*)
>
> THE PROFESSOR. (*Thirty years old. He is reading to his students.*) Dante is a great poet. He wrote the "Divine Comedy" and . . .
>
> (*Several seconds of darkness*)
>
> THE PROFESSOR. (*Forty years old. He is reading with a bored voice.*) Dante is a great poet. He wrote the "Divine Comedy" and . . .
>
> (*Several seconds of silence*)
>
> THE PROFESSOR. (*Sixty years old. He is like a gramophone.*) Dante is a great poet . . .
>
> A PUPIL. (*Interrupting him*) Why?
>
> THE PROFESSOR. (*Surprised and embarrassed*) It is printed here. Sit down and be quiet. Dante is a great poet. He wrote . . .

CURTAIN

Furthermore, Marinetti denounced the unities of time, place and action and asserted the necessity for abolishing all conventions pertaining to the writing of dramatic literature. Although none of these pronouncements taken singly were innovative, the anti-Aristotelian aesthetic underlying Marinetti's vision went further than simply negating the established theatre of psychology, device and causal relationships in that it described an alternative, eclectic and energetic theatre. Furthermore, the degree to which the Futurists carried their program of renovation in both dramatic literature and performance techniques was innovative and consequential. The new manifesto called for an end to developmental, psychological, motivated characterization, preferring sparse, nonspecific characters similar to those depicted by the Symbolists and denoted as 'he' or 'women.' These characters were sharp and streamlined, sometimes eliciting recognition of a type of person or class, as in the example just cited, but more often simply portraying 'beings in action' which did not attempt to evoke complex responses based on empathy and character identity. By reducing and compressing identities, which also abolished certain facets of plot and entanglement associated with popular drama, the Futurists sheared away

the excess verbiage from the theatre and opened the performance to original, spontaneous, simultaneous assortments of input from actors and audience, such as actor-audience dialogue and improvisation.

Marinetti adhered emphatically to his earlier doctrine of entangling and involving the audience on as many levels as possible in the performance, and further, of provoking and encouraging the performance to continue on 'into the street, the café, the morning after, the rest of one's life . . .' For, 'Everything of any value is theatrical. . . . life itself . . . offers innumerable possibilities for the stage.' Marinetti believed that by intermingling actuality and performance the Futurist theatre would offer direct, concrete experience, an absolute antitheses to the vicarious illusion proffered by the theatre of realism, farce, melodrama or tragedy. The important Futurist principle of simultaneity was manifest in a theatre which could occur spontaneously in several areas of the auditorium and continue among diverse groups of people as they filtered out into the streets.

The intermingling of actuality and performance was often accomplished through devices which had little public exposure in established theatre. The most effective method the Futurists used for engaging the audience was spontaneous actor-audience dialogue. These dialogues were probably effective because the audiences, in Milan especially, tended to be made up of a number of critics and artists who were known personally to the Futurists and possibly to other members of the audience. The other effective device which the Futurists exploited was the structured and unstructured improvisation. The structured improvisation began with a scenario of activities and was carried to an agreed upon conclusion but was open to any interruption or digression which might occur from the audience. The unstructured improvisation apparently had no conclusion and only a brief description of activities to be included. Some of the 'sintesi' are believed to have been written after they had been performed as structured or unstructured improvisation. This speculation satisfies the wide margins of discrepancy between the written texts which are available for study and the descriptions from contemporary journals which assessed the same piece of material in performance.

Another technique for involving the spectator was subconscious as well as conscious involvement of the audience. This concept of cerebral stimulation had been translated from the *Painter's Manifesto* of 1911. . . . Just as the spectator standing in front of the Futurist canvas was stimulated to 'become one with Being' and to 'perceive the inner core of things,' so the participant in the Futurist Theatre was bombarded with sensations which were aimed at opening new areas of awareness, pride and confidence. The Futurist Synthetic Theatre intended to distill and compress life itself, to synthesize the sensations 'present for a moment in a tram, in a café, at a station, and which remain filmed on our minds as dynamic, fragmentary symphonies of gestures, words, noises, and lights.' The Futurist Synthetic Theatre used the same contemporary visual vocabulary which was at the foundation of Futurist painting (i.e., trains, trams, machines, physical ac-

Poster for Marinetti's 1914 appearance at the London Coliseum.

tivities, aeroplanes, guns, light). Moreover, this vocabulary was shaped in the Futurist Synthetic Theatre by the principle of simultaneity in much the same way that the painters had shaped this vocabulary in painting: where forms and lines had been overlapped and intermingled to explicate the interpenetration of objects and their reverberations, in Futurist painting overlapping and intermingling of activities, dialogue and ideas occurred in performance. One simple example, from Marinetti's play *The Communicating Vases,* written in 1916, demonstrates how the most rudimentary form of simultaneity operated on stage. Three different locations occupy the stage, in each of which the action goes on uninterrupted by or influenced by the actions of the other locations. Although the actions are fused at the end, they still have no logical relationship. Actors from one location break through the stage partitions into the other areas. Their action recalls the painter's device of force-lines, which were used to make visual the movement of objects in space and to describe their interpenetrability. The actions of these characters have no logical or sequential meaning: they simply obtrude into other compartments of the stage in the same sense that objects in Futurist paintings reverberate and interpenetrate with one another. In both cases the intention has been to stimu-

late the audience or spectator with various visual sensations (in the instance of performance, other auditory and tactile sensations could also be produced). Moreover, the simultaneous activities of the actors which overlap and interpenetrate because of the actual movement of bodies from one place to another described an event which was full of Futurist dynamism. In the stage performance the actual movement of bodies and objects could be accomplished without the use of painterly symbols of movement through space. In this, the Futurist stage was closer to realizing the principle of dynamism than were the Futurist painters. The use of various illogical and unconnected stage actions such as dancing, juggling, hopping, jumping and others, reflect the translation of the principle of object movement, dynamism, which the painters were struggling with in such works as Boccioni's *States of Mind: Those Who Go. . . .* (pp. 50-4)

In a sintesi by Emilio Settimelli called *Passatism* the author used the device of nondevelopmental dialogue in a manner which clearly prefigures the use of this device by the writers associated with the Theatre of the Absurd, as well as earlier groups.

> ACT 1:
>
> (*An old man and old woman are seated at a table, facing each other. Nearby is a calendar.*)
>
> MAN. How are you?
>
> WOMAN. Not bad. And you?
>
> MAN. Not bad. (*Pause*) What a beautiful day tomorrow will be! (*Pause*) Let's tear out the page, as usual: 10 January 1860. (*Pause*) Did you have a good digestion?
>
> WOMAN. Not bad.
>
> MAN. Did you overcome your dyspepsia?
>
> WOMAN. I ate rather well and digested well. How happy I am!
>
> MAN. How happy I am! (*Darkness*)
>
> ACT 2:
>
> (*Same scene, same arrangement*)
>
> MAN. How are you?
>
> WOMAN. Not bad. And you?
>
> MAN. Not bad. (*Pause*) What a beautiful day tomorrow will be! (*Pause*) Let's tear out the page as usual: 10 January 1880. (*Pause*) Did you have a good digestion?
>
> WOMAN. Not bad.
>
> MAN. Did you overcome your dyspepsia?
>
> WOMAN. I ate rather well and digested well. How happy I am!
>
> MAN. How happy I am! (*Darkness*)
>
> ACT 3:
>
> (*Same scene, same arrangement*)

MAN. How are you?

WOMAN. Not bad. And you?

MAN. Not bad. (*Pause*) What a beautiful day tomorrow will be! (*Pause*) Let's tear out the page, as usual: 10 January 1910.

WOMAN. Oh, God! What a pain in the heart! I'm dying . . . (*Falls over and remains immobile*).

MAN. Oh, God! What a pain in the heart! I'm dying . . . (*Falls over and remains immobile*).

CURTAIN

In this short and enigmatic piece, the questions raised are not answered. Who are these people? What is their raison d'etre? What is the author trying to do? Instead the audience is left with a visual image which involves the passage of time as symbolized by the calendar and the death of two people whose life had no apparent consequence. The dialogue contains none of the substance and information which would render a thematic idea intelligible to the audience. It simply repeats a series of commonplace exchanges which have no significance beyond that of everyday pleasantries.

Following the publication of the *Futurist Synthetic Theatre Manifesto,* Marinetti and the Futurist playwrights and poets continued developing these principles. They wrote numerous 'sintesi' which were performed by travelling groups of actors and they reiterated in later manifestos the basic concepts and accomplishments of their theatre.

In 1915, as soon as Italy entered the war, Marinetti, Corrà, Balla, Russolo and Sant'Elia joined the Volunteer Cyclists. Boccioni joined the cavalry. Communication between Marinetti and the members of the movement who were not engaged in the war was carried out by mail, telephone and telegraph. Although the movement kept up a stunning outpouring of publications, performances, and gallery shows throughout the war, Futurism underwent changes during and after the war years which can most logically be attributed to Marinetti's absence as a guiding force and to the changes in the movement's membership. In the areas of painting and sculpture these changes were fatal to the strength of the movement in Italy and abroad. . . . (pp. 54-7)

In the development of Futurist theatre the changes which began in 1915 (after Marinetti's departure to the front) were both subtle and important in terms of the international reputation of the movement. Futurist theatre works had been primarily concerned with the relationship between the actor and the audience and with political and ideological ideas to be expressed by the actor. Moreover, the Futurists viewed their theatre as a political and philosophical arena where they could voice their programs in a variety of ways. The intellectual and entertainment possibilities of the theatre had been developed without the use of traditional scenography. Marinetti had defined the performance space as a continuation of the auditorium so that it more completely included both actors and spectators. The men who took over the leadership of the theatre after Marinetti left had a different point of view.

The two men who found themselves in charge of the Futurist theatre in May 1915 were Enrico Prampolini (1894-1960) and Fortunato Depero (1892-1960). Both were accomplished painters who had been with the movement for several years, but whose main interest was directed toward the development of a Futurist scenography capable of expressing the complexities of modern life and celebrating the wonders of the technological age. In this their efforts were compatible with the general impulse of the *Foundation Manifesto* and manifestos which came after it. Prampolini and Depero began exploring the possibilities of mechanical scenography, thus moving away from the most basic concepts of *The Variety Theatre Manifesto* and *The Futurist Synthetic Theatre Manifesto.* What had begun as a means of reforming the stage picture became instead a reform of the theatre itself. (p. 57)

Prampolini's manifesto [*Futurist Scenography*], written four months after the *Futurist Synthetic Theatre Manifesto,* was clear and concise in outlining the nature of the new Futurist stage. However, in tone and spirit it was unlike the other manifestos. Moreover, it was not primarily concerned with the same aims which Marinetti set forth for the movement. There was no war rhetoric, no appeals for the revelation of man's inner core. Prampolini was more preoccupied with elevating his profession and bringing new values to scenography; Futurist devices served that purpose. Due to the works of Prampolini and Depero, the innovations made in stage decor between 1916 and 1929 have been regarded by most historians as the seminal contributions of Futurist Theatre.

Essentially, Prampolini suggested five central concepts. The stage picture was to become part of the stage action, no longer a static passive background against which stage action occurred. Therefore, the stage space would become an important concern of the theatre producer instead of being largely ignored in favor of the actor. The space was envisioned as having dynamic potential; that is, technological progress had provided the scenographer with the means to produce illuminations electrically which could be used to fill the stage space. These illuminations in conjunction with gases, both of which were possible in a variety of colors, would "interact and compenetrate" in endless combinations which would stir the audience with new electric sensations. Finally, the dynamic stage would render the actor unnecessary.

The elimination of the actor from the stage was in contradiction to the principles which Marinetti had developed in his theatre manifestos. Moreover, these two hypotheses could not be resolved without compromise. Evidence suggests that due to the financial and practical difficulties of constructing the theatre space Prampolini described, any conflict of interest was avoided and dissolved over the decade between 1916-1926. Although both Prampolini and Depero continued to publish documents advertising and restating their ideas for a mechanized theatre space, the designs which they rendered for Futurist performances usually achieved a compromise. Using the vocabularies of Cubism and Futurism, they developed geometricality as the dominant aspect of their designs. The modification of the performer to this geometry complemented the design.

For example, Prampolini designed a set for a 'sintesi' by Buzzi called *Parallelepiped* in 1921. The set, . . . while it convincingly utilizes variations of cubic forms to define and modify the acting space, does not produce 'electro-chemical architecture, powerfully vitalized by chromatic emanations from a luminous source.' Nevertheless, in 1921 Prampolini's design was indicative of the work of an innovative group of scenographers who had moved away from the prevalent styles of naturalism and symbolism. Prampolini has separated the forestage and backstage by using the act curtain in a straightforward manner which makes no pretence of being illusory. His free-standing geometric constructions suggested instability, a lack of equilibrium and confusion of depth. Moreover, Prampolini broke up the acting space in a subtle manner by creating illogical spatial relationships between actors and set. By running his orthogonal axes against the traditional perspective, he achieved a startling conflict between the upstage and downstage heights of set and performer.

The most obvious manifestation of the compromise between an automated and a live theatre occurred in the area of Futurist costume design. In a document dated 1915 Depero described the mechanical costume-type which was subsequently utilized in numerous forms in Futurist performance.

> Apparition-like costume equivalent (magical, mechanical) to *complex simultaneity of forms—colors—onomatopoeia—sounds and noises*. Constructed on a framework of metallic wire—light—forms of transparent material—brightly colored.
>
> The framework will be made so as to open and close itself, that is to say, it must appear like a normal Futurist costume but the jacket opens by clicking one's heels; various movements with one's arms, hands, feet, legs, or raising one's hat, etc . . . will open certain fanlike contrivances like tongs, etc. . . . simultaneously with luminous Apparitions in bursts and rhythms of noiselike instruments.
>
> The costumes for the Futurist abstract and dynamic theatre to come will be constructed on this very new principle of Depero's that was inaugurated by Marinetti at the extraordinary Depero-Balla Exposition of 1915.

The mechanical costume was original and the characteristic humor and extravagance of Depero's idea were particularly Futurist. Futurist humor, despite the overbearing tone of many Futurist publications, was consistently noted for its raucousness and true spontaneity.

Following the publication of Prampolini's manifesto in 1915, *Notes on the Theatre* by Depero appeared in the Italian press between 1915 and 1917. Although he echoed some of Prampolini's concepts, Depero introduced new devices to be used in Futurist scenography. (pp. 60-2)

Depero's *Notes* expressed a fundamental preoccupation with the cinema which absorbed most of the Futurists. Distinctions between stage and film were seen only in the speed with which film could impress the spectator with sensations, and in the film, the Futurists admired the potential for simultaneity, variety and surprise—all three concepts of the utmost importance. Hence, film was immediately perceived as a 'powerful means of artistic creation . . . it is necessary to add to theatre everything that is suggested by cinematography.' The Futurists were among the first theatre workers to contend with the new media, film, which was so obviously related to theatre but also in competition with it. Their enthusiastic incorporation of cinematic techniques and cinema itself into the vocabulary of the stage fostered a period of healthy interaction between the two performance forms. However, Depero clearly recognized the growing popularity of film posed a threat to the survival of the theatre. The Futurists chose to imitate and outdo the film; an objective which has proven unattainable.

The other central proposition of Depero's *Notes* concerned movable scenery. Movable scenery was a further development of Prampolini's concept of 'electrochemical architecture' with a more practical application. Depero envisioned a stage with its typical accoutrements capable of a variety of movements to create an active stage space. Among his examples of the mechanized stage scene he mentions 'Sensational news and dramatic situations may create typographic scenery, those luminous advertising walls. . . .' The use of multiple media or 'mixed media' was inherent in the use of the typographic revolution in literature and in Balla's set for *Printing Press*. Once the potential for incorporating letters and words into non-literary forms was introduced, the translation of that device into a usable scenographic form was inevitable for the Futurists. The use of several types of visual communication used in conjunction was another manifestation of the principle of simultaneity, one which was later employed by other avant garde theatre groups.

The earliest production to accomplish many of Prampolini's and Depero's most revolutionary goals was designed and executed by Balla in 1917 for Serge Diaghilev's Ballet Russes. In this production, *Feu d'artifice,* most of the major concepts articulated by Depero and Prampolini were realized in a production which astounded and delighted audiences first in Rome and later in Paris. (pp. 65-6)

In 1918 Marinetti returned from the front lines. The war in Italy was over except for the signing of the final documents. Among the changes that awaited him in Milan, the change in the political climate of Italy was the greatest. The Russian Revolution had begun; its impact on Italy was enormous. The battle for control was well underway in 1918 and Marinetti lost no time choosing sides. He had been a friend of Benito Mussolini, the young pacifist journalist, now the leader of the Italian Fasceti, who had finally renounced his Socialist friends and joined the nationalists and Futurists in 1915, and it was with Mussolini that Marinetti allied himself.

Mussolini was shrewd and calculating in his use of his friend Marinetti. During the next six years, while Il Duce was establishing and then stabilizing his control, Marinetti performed innumerable services for him and conducted many successful campaigns to swing the people over to Mussolini's camp. After his success was ensured, Mussolini repaid his friend by appointing him to a meaningless bureaucratic job and mocking the buffoonery and brashness of Marinetti's campaign. Mussolini supported the Futurist theatre and other areas of the movement, however, by regarding them as more or less the national voice of the government in the arts. The association between Fascism and Futurism in the minds of many critics ultimately proved to be the proverbial "kiss of death" for the Futurist movement, although the alliance proved fortuitous in one respect. Through Mussolini's support, the Futurists were able to build an ambitious Experimental Theatre, which included the most impressive mechanical devices available anywhere. This marvelous theatre was located in the Baths of Septimus Severus, a dungeon-like cellar under Mussolini's home in Rome. *Theatre Magazine* had a representative in Rome who regularly attended productions at the Experimental Theatre in 1924-25. Maxim Gordon described the theatre in the September 1925 issue:

> In the cellar of the Palazzo Titoni, the modern home of Mussolini, there were still to be seen a few years back the ruins of the Baths of Septimus Severus. It was this highly connotative, if dilapidated, interior which the Futurists took for their Teatro Sperimentale and the Casa d'Arte, run by Anton Bragaglia in connection with the theatre. The transformation is at once magical and ironic. In place of the crumbling masonry and debris which remained as relics of the ante-Christian era, we now find symmetrical columns and arches, twisted iron scrolls, fantastic lamps, nonrepresentative paintings and cubistic furniture. The theatre, the gallery and the adjoining restaurant present an unusual arrangement of unexpected angles and curious curves, an interior as far removed as possible from any suggestion of the past.

That same year, while the Futurists were entertaining an international public in their theatre in Rome, Prampolini was awarded the first prize for stage design at the International Exposition of Decorative Arts in Paris. His entry was financed by the government, and was an elaborate mechanical model of the Magnetic Theatre.

The Magnetic Theatre was a complicated construction of wheels, platforms, geometric solids, spheres and wires which were to 'replace the actors as focus for the performance.' Prampolini described the Magnetic Theatre in 1926. The structure was:

> . . . made up of a mass of plastic constructions in action which rises from the centre of the theatrical hollow instead of the periphery of the "scenic-arc." Auxiliary moving constructions rise, first on a square movable platform, standing on an elevator. On this in turn is erected a *moving, rolling platform* going in the opposite direction from the first, and likewise carrying other *planes* and *auxiliary volumes*. To these plastic constructions, *ascending, rotating* and *shifting* movements are given, in accordance with necessity. The scenic action of the chromatic light, an essential element of interaction in creating the scenic personality of space, unfolds parallel to the scenic development of these moving constructions. Its function is to give *spiritual life* to

the environment or setting, while measuring time in *scenic space*. This chromatic ladder will be made with apparatuses of *projection, refraction, and diffusion*.

The Magnetic Theatre was a completely abstract machine which would use space and mass, movement, light and sound to create a performance. The performance created by the shifting and moving light which fell upon the parts of the machine was supposed to restore a 'spiritual virginity to scenic matter.' With the Magnetic Theatre Prampolini brought to a culmination the ideas which he had articulated with Depero and Balla in 1915.

The Magnetic Theatre Machine demonstrated the contradictions between two distinct viewpoints. Prampolini and Depero created machinery which permitted the audience to move around the outside of a performance, on an ambulatory, but which permitted no interaction between audience and event. This procedure was in contrast to Marinetti, who had argued that the audience and event must be integrated.

Marinetti reasserted his original position in his final theatre-related manifesto, *The Total Theatre Manifesto*, which he published after retiring from the government position he held. The *Total Theatre Manifesto* of 1933 was perhaps his most intriguing and profound vision. Furthermore, evidence suggests that it was his last major contribution until his death in 1944.

In the *Total Theatre Manifesto* Marinetti pulls together the two major facets of the Futurist theatre into a single, cohesive statement which was to include every aspect and every possibility which had been suggested over the last twenty years. Here was the resolution of architecture, machine, actor and audience. (pp. 66-70)

The Futurist movement had an impact on nearly every development of modern art, directly or indirectly, and provided an important stimulus to the writing, staging and design of drama. Translations of the *Synthetic Theatre Manifesto* appeared within eight weeks of its publication. The activities which began with Futurism were incorporated with many interesting and consequential modifications into every major theatre experiment of this century. Marinetti and others of the movement travelled extensively, speaking, debating and presenting Futurist ideas in the artistic centers of Europe. The well documented trips to Russia and England in 1913-14 were two which had particularly interesting results in the formation of Russian Futurism and the English movement Vorticism.

In Zurich, the Dadaists capitalized on most of the pre-war Futurist proposals and techniques in launching their movement. Many of the Surrealists have asserted the primacy of Futurism as an influence on their development. In Germany, the Bauhaus' collaboration was demonstrably cognizant of and intrigued by many of the Futurists' activities and publications. In this country, the Living Newspaper technique of the Thirties was an adaptation of Marinetti's Total Theatre concept which advocated projecting "startling or important newspaper headlines" around a circular auditorium. Thorton Wilder was present at a number of Futurist performances in 1921 from which he drew the seminal concepts which are visually identifiable in his plays.

More recently, fisificolla-bodymadness has erupted in numerous artistic manifestations from Jackson Pollack's "Action Painting" to the action built into the Happenings and Events of the early 1960's.

Ideas and theories which described a total theatre have been articulated since Aristotle. The accomplishment of Futurism was to update the vocabularies of all the arts to meet the demands of the twentieth century. The Futurists pulled the boundaries of each discipline out of shape and overlapped them, one upon another, causing a stimulating flow of ideas among artists. They observed no rules or conventions except the rule of moving ahead, of never being satisfied with what they had done. They were, often, unable to produce a satisfactory synthesis of theory and practice. Nevertheless, in most of their endeavors they were far ahead of the rest of the world, at least theoretically. Indeed, we have not yet seen the end of the explorations which their work suggested in painting, architecture, theatre, music, film or literature. Perhaps their most important legacy was their gift for serious commitment combined with an eloquent sense of the bizarre which has impregnated the arts of the twentieth century. (pp. 74-5)

> *Christiana J. Taylor, in her* Futurism: Politics, Painting and Performance, *UMI Research Press, 1979, 108 p.*

Michael Kirby and Victoria Nes Kirby

[*In the following excerpt from their study* Futurist Performance, *the critics discuss the techniques of Futurist synthetic theater and examine major* syntesi, *the movement's most significant dramatic form. For a general discussion of Futurist theater by Michael Kirby, see excerpt dated 1971 in* TCLC, *Vol. 10, pp. 317-20.*]

The most important plays of the Futurists took the form of very short pieces called *sintesi*. Marinetti, Pratella, Pino Masnata, and others wrote plays and operas of extended length, but the *sintesi* embody all of the major Futurist contributions in this area. During 1915 and 1916 several acting companies toured Italy presenting programs of *sintesi*; they included the companies of Gualtiero Tumiati, Annibale Ninchi, Ettore Berti, Luigi Zoncada, and Ettore Petrolini. . . . [The] basic concepts of this type of performance were elucidated in a manifesto [excerpted above]: *The Futurist Synthetic Theatre*, written by Marinetti, Emilio Settimelli, and Bruno Corra; it is dated both January 11, 1915, and February 18, 1915.

The most obvious characteristic of the *sintesi* was its length. "Synthetic," it was flatly stated in the manifesto, meant "very brief": although most were somewhat longer, some of the scripts would take only a minute, or even less, to perform. This could be considered their one defining characteristic; however, the term became very popular, at least among the Futurists, and was occasionally attached to rather long works.

As explained by the manifesto, brevity was, most simply, a distillation, condensation, or compression of traditional drama. In keeping with the Futurist concern with speed and motion, the proper work of the playwright was seen as "synthesizing facts and ideas into the least number of words"; his pieces were to be "rapid and concise."

Actually, this compressed brevity was one of the aspects of nightclubs, circuses, and music halls that had been praised two years earlier in *The Variety Theatre* manifesto [excerpted above]. The variety theatre, it had been pointed out, "explains in an incisive and rapid manner the most sentimental and abstruse problems," and there one sees "heaps of events dispatched in haste." Not only did Marinetti approve in *The Variety Theatre* of "the execution of *Parsifal* in forty minutes that is now in preparation for a large London music hall," but he suggested "representing, for example, in a single evening all the Greek, French and Italian tragedies condensed and comically mixed up" and reducing "the whole of Shakespeare to a single act."

When *The Synthetic Theatre* manifesto specifically advised the world to "abolish farce, vaudeville, sketches, comedy, drama, and tragedy, in order to create in their place numerous forms of Futurist theatre," the concepts of brevity and condensation had become more subtle and elaborate. The distillation or compression of existing dramatic works was only the crudest and most obvious form of synthesis. Now what was to be compressed and synthesized was the diversity of life itself, a diversity "present *for a moment* in a tram, in a café, at a station, and which remains filmed on our minds as dynamic, fragmentary symphonies of gestures, words, noises, and lights." The writers of *The Synthetic Theatre* might have been talking about the well-established *parole in libertà* rather than drama.

As with all Futurist art, the Synthetic Theatre can be clarified and, at least in part, explained in terms of its rejection of traditional forms. In this case, it was the conventions of exposition, structure, and characterization that, among other things, were rejected. In an extended analysis of the current techniques of playwriting, *The Synthetic Theatre* manifesto scorned the practice of "introducing only a tenth of the conceptions in the first act, five tenths in the second, four tenths in the third"; it claimed that it was "STUPID to be subjected to the impositions of *crescendo, exposition,* and *the final climax,*" and it mocked the public that "from habit and by infantile instinct, wishes to see how the character of a person emerges from a series of events." The age-old dichotomy between heroes and villains and the contingent processes of projection and identification were dismissed as "the primitiveness of the crowd that wishes to see the agreeable person exalted and the disagreeable one defeated." But most important of all the Futurists rejected the "minute logic" that holds together traditional theatre and is the binding force in its structure; they dismissed the notion that the public must *"always completely understand the whys and wherefores of every scenic action."*

Like the other aspects of Futurist art and performance, however, the Synthetic Theatre was not merely a rejection of traditional concepts. If the brevity of the *sintesi* can be seen in part as a reaction against a theatre that was considered "monotonous and depressing" and in which the public was "in the disgusting attitude of a group of loafers who sip their distress and their pity, spying on the very slow agony of a horse fallen on the pavement," the short length of the new plays also had its positive side. Above all, the compression of the *sintesi* was seen as a means of intensifying the direct impact of the performance. *The Synthetic Theatre* manifesto might well have influenced Artaud's thought when it called for "synthetic expressions of cerebral energy" creating "a specialized reality that violently assaults the nerves." Unlike the "long-winded, analytical, pedantically psychological, explanatory, diluted, meticulous, static" traditional theatre, the new Synthetic Theatre moved away from information and logic and toward direct sensory appeal. According to the Futurists, "reality vibrates around us, hitting us with *bursts of fragments* with events amongst them, embedded one within the other, confused, entangled, chaotic." Although there is a somewhat telegraphic list in the manifesto indicating how these goals were being achieved in practice, the best way to understand how they were to take actual theatrical form is to look at the *sintesi* themselves.

There is a tremendous formal and stylistic diversity among so-called *sintesi*. In part this diversity is intentional and programmatic. Marinetti himself was quite catholic and eclectic, and the Futurists saw no need to develop a single style of performance. *The Synthetic Theatre* manifesto spoke of their discoveries in a variety of areas: "in the subconscious, in undefined forces, in pure abstraction, in pure cerebralism, in pure fantasy, in breaking records, and physical madness." The acceptance of one avenue of investigation—that of the unconscious, for example, that would eventually lead to Surrealism—did not preclude the investigation of other areas. But along with the more original forms, almost every trend that was then current in playwriting can be found represented in the *sintesi*. Calling a piece a *"sintesi"* was not a stylistic qualification.

Traditional standards of "verisimilitude" and "the photographic" were among those attacked in *The Synthetic Theatre*, and, with very few exceptions, the *sintesi* rejected literal reality and naturalism. This in itself was no innovation, however: many of the *sintesi*, as well as some of the longer Futurist works, were influenced by Symbolism. But all of the *sintesi*, the innovative as well as the derivative, did tend to be nonnaturalistic. In their stylistic diversity, this tendency and their "very brief" length are the only defining characteristics that we have. Of course the common nonrealistic approach was not a rejection of reality itself, like all nonrealistic artists, the Futurists felt that imitation was superficial and that they were in touch with "reality" of a more meaningful kind.

The emphasis on compression in the *sintesi*, and their relationship to variety theatre, sometimes reduced the brief plays to a kind of staged "gag" or pun. *Bachelor Apartment (La garçonnière)* by the sculptor Umberto Boccioni is an example of this type of *sintesi*. It may be seen to contain a certain compression of character and a shock element that were important to the Futurists, but basically its impact depends on the humor of a sudden reversal when an apparently unseducible woman becomes the seducer herself. Indeed, a number of writers borrow Papini's

view that the *sintesi* can be traced back to a very short play by Verlaine in which a man enters to find a couple embracing, shoots them dead, and is astonished to discover that he has killed the wrong couple. But short humorous skits are much older than Verlaine. Comedy acts and variety shows would have easily provided many examples of the humorous reversal. And very few of the *sintesi* actually show this form. The great majority of them are basically serious, even when an element of humor is involved. It is clear that almost all of them were intended for something more than mere entertainment.

The *sintesi* [of the Italian Futurists] may be divided into two general categories or groups. Some seem to have been written programmatically in response to the specific demands of *The Synthetic Theatre* manifesto, and others developed from existing theatrical styles. In the first group, the plays give the impression of being formed "externally" by the aesthetic rules and standards elucidated by the Futurist movement. In the second category, the development is more "internal," intuitively adapting current forms and techniques to Futurist ends. This distinction is primarily a practical one. It facilitates analysis and discussion. In actuality, works do not always fall easily and completely into one category or the other. Moreover, it should be noted that "internal" and "external" do not connote value. Neither approach is, in itself, good or bad. But there are many ways in which a work of art can develop, and the importance of the manifesto, with its power to objectify and promulgate aesthetic standards and goals, should not be overlooked.

If *The Synthetic Theatre* manifesto established reduction and compression as the basic requirements of the *sintesi*, these qualities could be achieved in a variety of ways. The simplest and most obvious method was to "condense" a long-existing work. *Parsifal* or one of Shakespeare's dramas could be cut down to play in a much shorter time. Marinetti himself demonstrated this approach during his trip to Russia in 1914—before *The Synthetic Theatre* manifesto was written—when he visited one of Vsevelod Meyerhold's classes. As the Russian director described it:

> He [Marinetti] suggested to a group which had just performed *Antony and Cleopatra* for him (three actors and four "proscenium servants") the theme of *Othello* for improvisation. After a three-minute discussion on stage of the tragedy's salient features, the group performed a three-minute résumé of it.

Giuseppe Steiner's *"Saul" by Alfieri (Il "Saul" di Alfieri)*, published six years later, is another example of this approach. Taking the best-known work of Italy's most famous tragedian, the *Saul* written in 1782 by Vittorio Alfieri, Steiner kept the five-act structure, but some of his "acts" are only two lines long. In a few very brief vignettes, the characters and even the story become surprisingly clear.

The compression of time that is contingent to an approach such as Steiner's could also be clarified, systematized, and focused until it became the main point of a presentation. It is interesting to compare *Old Age (Passatismo)* and *Sempronio's Lunch (Il pranzo di Sempronio)*, both coauthored by Corra and Settimelli. Each uses a different method of compressing time. In the former, the passage of fifty years is indicated, in three brief scenes, by a calendar and by lines of dialogue referring to the date. In the latter play, a much more sophisticated treatment that would be difficult to stage, Sempronio goes from the age of five to the age of ninety in five short scenes; space is also compressed as he moves from country to country, his appearance changing as he gets older, but the single action of eating a meal runs through all the scenes, creating a powerful unifying image.

At one extreme, the compression of the *sintesi* moved it completely away from story and characterization. The play became merely an image, a brief stage action that did not depend upon the interplay of individual characters. Since the exchange of information between the fictional figures and its extended retention and elaboration were not central to these pieces, some of them did not use any dialogue. Mario Dessy's *Madness* (*La pazzia*) is the image of a motion-picture audience driven mad by progressive insanity in the film they are watching. *The Troop Train* (*La tradotta*), by the same author, is a slightly symbolic vignette that contrasts a beautiful woman with soldiers on their way to the front. Although no dialogue is provided by Dessy in either play, they are far from silent, and the voices of the actors play an important part in the total image.

A second important tenet of Futurist theory that formed certain *sintesi* was the emphasis on simultaneity. The earliest example, published in 1915, was a play by Marinetti himself with the simple title of *Simultaneity* (*Simultaneità*). Two entirely different places and their particular inhabitants occupy the same stage at the same time. The life of a beautiful cocotte "penetrates," to use Marinetti's word, the life of a bourgeois family. For most of the play, the occupants of one "world" are completely unaware of those in the other, although the cocotte's dressing table occupies part of the family's living room.

The following year Marinetti developed the concept of simultaneity even further in *The Communicating Vases* (*I Vasi Communicanti*). (Later the same title was used for a book by André Breton, the leader of the Surrealists.) In this play, three different, unrelated locations occupy the stage, which is divided by two partitions, and the action goes on in all three at the same time. It is interesting that in both of these plays Marinetti chose to fuse the disparate ambiences at the end: the cocotte suddenly enters the other world of the bourgeois living room, and, in *The Communicating Vases*, soldiers actually break through the partitions between the areas, moving from one to the other. *The Synthetic Theatre* manifesto had spoken of the "race with cinematography," and the use of simultaneity undoubtedly derived in part from an attempt to parallel in stage terms the way in which motion pictures moved instantaneously from one locale to another, eliminating distance while compressing time.

Waiting (*Attesa*) by Mario Dessy, published in his 1919 book *Your Husband Doesn't Work? . . . Change Him!*, is an example of simultaneity in which the script is written in two columns to indicate the coordination of two physi-

cally unrelated actions. Dessy's play, which has certain symbolic overtones, gains formal strength by comparing two similar actions: in each a single man is waiting for a woman who does not arrive.

Another element of Futurist doctrine that shaped certain performances was the emphasis in *The Variety Theatre* and *The Synthetic Theatre* manifestos on a more direct and noncontemplative involvement of the spectators with the presentation. *The Synthetic Theatre* manifesto said that the Futurists would "eliminate the preconceptions of the stage by flinging a net of sensations between the stage and the public, scenic action will invade the orchestra and the spectators." The influence of this concept on the writing of scripts is quite clear in *Gray + Red + Violet + Orange* (*Grigio + rosso + violetto + arancione*) by Corra and Settimelli: the subtitle of the play is "Net of Sensations."

Gray + Red + Violet + Orange was produced by Ettore Petrolini during his tour of Brazil in 1921, although the name was shortened to *Gray + Red + Orange* on a poster announcing the program at the Antarctica Theatre Casino in Rio de Janiero. The play changes suddenly from a realistic drama in the fourth-wall tradition to one involving the audience, at least as subject matter, when an actor accuses a spectator in the front row of murder. The empathy called for and exploited by traditional theatre is underlined by the early excessive suffering of the protagonist, who then converts the observer's state of mind into one of self-consciousness by turning attention to the audience.

Petrolini and Cangiullo carried the direct involvement of the audience to a physical level in *Radioscopia,* which was also in the repertory during the tour of Brazil. Too long, at a running time of forty minutes, to be called a *sintesi,* the "simultaneous penetration" mixed spectators and performers. At its initial presentation in Naples in 1917—a performance attended by Benito Mussolini—actors were scattered throughout the auditorium, eliminating rigid spatial distinctions between presentation and audience.

Unlike the accusatory actor in *Gray + Red + Violet + Orange,* the leading character in *The Great Remedy* (*La grande cura*) by Marinetti actually comes down from the stage to "almost graze" the spectators in the front row with her hands. As Marinetti describes it, "the first row of seats is occupied by very beautiful women, abundantly décolleté." He probably intended them to be "planted" members of the company rather than real spectators, but the use of the audience as an element in the performance is still clear.

The role of the audience becomes active and central in Cangiullo's *Lights!* (*Luce!*), published in *Dinamo* in March, 1919. Planted performers definitely were to be used in this piece. With the auditorium completely in darkness, the actors—who were not to be recognized as such—were, by their own example, to provoke the spectators into demanding light. Indeed, acting in the house rather than on the stage and actual physical involvement and participation of members of the audience were to make up the entire performance: when the excitement reached its peak, the lights were finally to come on—and the curtain was to fall. This short but significant piece could be related to Dada and to later neo-Dada performances; it is also an example of Cangiullo's interest in mixing spectators and performers and in searching for new types of theatrical experience. In it he made a simple theatrical "object" out of the emotional audience, eliminating—along with character, place, and anecdote—the formal concept of "a presentation."

Earlier, a very strange and unusual attempt to increase the involvement of the spectator had been embodied by Arnaldo Ginna—who was using the name Arnaldo Corradini at that time—and Emilio Settimelli in *From the Window* (*Dalla finestra*), published in 1915. The spectators were to "place themselves, by self-hypnotism, in the place of a paralyzed person" and watch the presentation, as if through a window, without moving or saying anything. Each member of the audience was to hypnotize himself into believing that the two actors in the piece were his or her father and sister. How this was to be done, or even how the concept was to be communicated to the spectators, is not clear. Perhaps instructions were to be published in the program. But, unlike the audience-oriented plays involving self-consciousness and physical involvement, *From the Window* can be seen as an attempt to carry the traditional psychic mechanisms of empathy and projection to an extreme degree. The observer is really to believe and to care about what he sees on stage. It also demonstrates that these traditional devices, like self-hypnotism, require the spectator's cooperation and mental effort.

Compression, simultaneity, and the involvement of the audience in the performance were demands of the Futurist manifestos that gave form to their *sintesi*; other concepts in the published writings provided particular content for certain of the plays. The basic rejection of accepted theatrical devices and techniques in the manifestos can be seen mirrored in several *sintesi* that satirize or parody traditional drama. *Dissonance* (*Dissonanza*) by Bruno Corra and Emilio Settimelli makes fun of the historical romance by exaggerating the elaborate declamatory style: a gentleman in contemporary clothes intrudes on a supposed scene of thirteenth-century dalliance in order, in part, to emphasize its artificiality.

Corra and Settimelli also parodied the grandiose emotions and strident rhetoric of traditional drama in *Toward Victory* (*Verso la conquista*) published, as was *Dissonance,* in 1915. The concept of the all-powerful and successful hero is scornfully debunked when the protagonist, on his way "toward victory," slips on a fig skin and is killed falling downstairs.

Corra also teamed with his brother Arnaldo Corradini (Ginna) to write *Alternation of Character* (*Alternazione di carattere*), an early *sintesi* that attacks traditional theatre in a less obvious and more formally interesting way. Aiming at the well-established concept of consistent characterization, *The Synthetic Theatre* scorned the "analytical, pedantically psychological" approach of drama designed to satisfy the "infantile instinct" of the public that wanted "to see how the character of a person emerges from a series of events." The two Futurist brothers contradicted the traditional approach in *Alternation of Character* by creating a husband and wife who are completely inconsistent and change with each line of dialogue.

Corra and Settimelli also wrote two *sintesi* that, without the same specific conventions to attack and without the corrective use of humor, were nihilistic and somewhat bitter. *Faced with the Infinite* (*Davanti all'infinito*) presents a young philosopher who sees no important difference between reading the paper and shooting himself; choosing one, he commits suicide. In the aptly titled *Negative Act* (*Atto negativo*) an unidentified man angrily walks on stage, tells the members of the audience that he has nothing to say to them, and calls for the curtain to be brought down. Of course it is too obvious, and perhaps misleading, to refer to these plays as negative. They are negative only in their philosophy. As statements of that philosophy, a philosophy that is not typical of Futurism in general, they are strong and positive representations. Published in 1915, the year before Hugo Ball opened the Cabaret Voltaire in Zürich, they seem to be clear forerunners of what was to become recognized as the Dada spirit of aesthetic nihilism.

Nor can these plays really be considered to be without humor. They manifest a kind of black humor as they deny completely our expectations about what a play is. We may even laugh at the suddenness with which they end their own existence, making the compression of the *sintesi* into a rejection of the drama itself.

Closely related to *Faced with the Infinite* and, especially, to *Negative Act* are two extremely short *sintesi* by Francesco Cangiullo entitled *Detonation* (*Detonazione*) and *There Is No Dog* (*Non c'è un cane*). Published in the same 1915 collection, they, too, may be seen as indications of how the attitudes necessary for the Dada movement were clearly established with Futurism, but they do not have quite the same aggressive nihilism of the pieces by Corra and Settimelli. No actors appear in either play. "A bullet" is the only "character" in *Detonation*. The curtain goes up to reveal a scene representing a deserted road on a cold winter night. After a moment, a shot is heard, and the curtain falls.

In *There Is No Dog,* the scene is the same. A dog walks across the road. The play ends. Both *sintesi* are examples of the play-as-an-image carried to an extreme. The images are fleeting, nondeveloping, and somberly evocative. They are simple, bare, and direct statements rather than didactic demonstrations, like *Faced with the Infinite,* or audience provocations, like *Negative Act.*

A final group of *sintesi* whose content is clearly related to the proposals of the Futurist manifestos is that in which the Futurists themselves play a part. Paolo Buzzi's *sintesi* *The Futurist Prize* (*Il premio di futurismo*) is a kind of dramatized manifesto summarizing in a humorous way the views of Futurists in the various arts. When the prize of an airplane is to be awarded to the artist most truly representative of Futurism, the members of the jury explain why one discipline or another should be considered most worthy, but they agree to give the award to a man who, by replacing damaged parts of his body, has actually become mechanical to a great extent.

The Arrest (*L'arresto*) by Marinetti gives an interesting and apparently accurate view of how the Futurist plays were sometimes performed. It takes place in "an elegant room, with chandeliers"; a small stage has been set up in the room, and the audience of intellectuals and socialites is sitting in armchairs and standing along the walls. In the context of a play-within-a-play, Marinetti develops the theme of the virile, war-loving and combat-experienced Futurists opposed to passéist and effetely intellectual critics.

Historians have seen the wish, in the basic *Foundation and Manifesto of Futurism* of 1909, to "destroy the museums" as a proto-Dada attitude; *Runio clacla,* published by Marinetti in the 1916 collection of *sintesi,* demonstrates that the Futurists meant to be as ruthless with their own work as with the creations of other artists. When Balla is awarded a prize in the play, he gives it to a hunchback, and, shouting "Runio clacla," he and the other Futurists destroy all of the paintings in his exhibition.

The Arrest carefully avoided mentioning the names of the characters. The "First Spectator" has forgotten the name of the "celebrated [Futurist] painter" who is playing the part of the Captain in the play-within-a-play. But Balla is a character in *Runio clacla.* Marinetti and Boccioni appear as characters in Marinetti's play *The Dormice (I ghiri)*: as they were in real life, they are shown as soldiers fighting the Austrians during World War I. *The Dormice* was published in the 1916 collection of *sintesi,* before a fall from his horse killed Boccioni on August 17, 1916, while he was still in the service. Since the Futurists sometimes performed in their own pieces, one wonders whether Boccioni, Marinetti, and Balla were intended to, or ever did, play themselves in these *sintesi.*

The same is true of Cangiullo, who appears as a character in his own *The Paunch of the Vase (La pancia del vaso)*, published in *Roma futurista* on April 25, 1920. Cangiullo refers to himself in the first person—"I throw it on the table, light a cigarette and exit"—giving strength to the feeling that he at least hoped to play the part himself. Indeed, since the play hinges to a great extent upon the identity of the "I" figure, it would only be fully effective if the relationship to the author was clearly understood or if Cangiullo portrayed himself for spectators who recognized him.

At any rate, this Futurist attitude toward characterization is one of the elements in their work that seems to have influenced Luigi Pirandello. Not only did the Futurists attack the consistent, well-developed character, but they presented stage figures that, in playing themselves, were more real than traditional representations. This questioning of characterization and the offering of new alternatives can be seen as establishing a theatrical context from which Pirandello, who knew the work of the Futurists, developed.

Futurism also influenced Pirandello by making the audience part of the performance, creating both an increased awareness of fourth-wall conventions and heightening requirements for "belief" or "the suspension of disbelief." Simultaneity, which sometimes bordered on paradox, and even the nihilism of some *sintesi* in which one alternative

is as good as another can be seen as additional factors contributing to the development of Pirandello and the Theatre of the Grotesque.

If certain of the *sintesi* can be discussed most easily in terms of the demands of the Futurist manifestos, others can be analyzed best in terms of their objective style. As has been mentioned, both of these approaches are somewhat arbitrary. To relate a play to particular concepts in the manifestos does not mean that it was actually written in reaction to the manifestos. It is merely as if this were true. The first collection of *sintesi* was apparently published after *The Synthetic Theatre* manifesto, but some of them were written and performed before the manifesto was published, and the exact dates of composition are mostly unknown. It is safe to say that almost all of the *sintesi* followed the publication of *The Variety Theatre,* but some of them contributed concepts and terminology to the later manifesto.

All of the *sintesi* could, of course, be analyzed both in terms of their relation to the manifestos and in terms of their style. It is quite obvious that the completely abstract or alogical plays, for example, could also be related to the demands in *The Synthetic Theatre* for "autonomous" performances, "pure abstraction" and "pure cerebralism." Thus a discussion of the *sintesi* in terms of stylistic categories is primarily for convenience. An examination of style is important, however, to illustrate the range of Futurist work and to suggest a certain development of theatrical thought. Although historical progression or development is indicated by such an approach, it is not intended to be taken literally. Many different styles were developing simultaneously in Futurism, and a clear line of historical growth, with one style clearly leading to another, is impossible to document. But, again, it is as if this were true. Perhaps the development or progression was only within the minds of individual artists who tended to follow the same line of aesthetic growth. At any rate, a spectrum of styles can be laid out in which a logical and consistent development can be traced, even though the actual history was much more complicated and obscure.

At the base of this hypothetical history of stylistic development lies Symbolism, a form inherited by the Futurists from Maeterlinck and Andreyev. At least two branches can be seen to develop from Symbolism. One moves toward the irrational, illogical, and absurd, and the other emphasizes formal elements to create semi-abstract and totally alogical performances.

Nocturnal (Notturno) by Francesco Balilla Pratella, the Futurist composer, was one of the earliest *sintesi.* Produced, along with other works, by Ettore Berti's company in January and February, 1915, and subtitled a "Dramatized State of Mind," it was basically a Symbolist piece. The "state of mind" concept that appeared so frequently in Futurist performance was directly derived from Symbolism, which attempted to portray not surface reality but the more intangible aspects of life. Mood, atmosphere, and a sense of mystery were important elements of Symbolism; like *Nocturnal,* many *sintesi* took place at night, and the characters performed actions, like counting the stars, that were both realistic and symbolic. The huge glass bell jar that contains a nude woman in Volt's *Flirt* is not intended to be taken literally but as the representation of a state of mind or of certain sociopsychological conditions of existence.

In Symbolism, characters became abstractions representing types, categories, or concepts. Personal names and idiosyncratic personality traits would interfere with *Flirt's* presentation of "states of mind": the performers are referred to as "He" and "She." "The Artist" and "The Critic" in Boccioni's *Genius and Culture* (*Genio e coltura*) represent all artists and all critics. The "Lady" in Buzzi's *Parallelepiped* (*Parallelepipedo*) is not a woman, but death. Death was a rather popular figure in Symbolist works.

In the same way, place or location in Symbolist drama was not particular or realistically detailed. Since abstractions and types do not need a practical environment in which to function, Symbolist plays frequently gave no indication of where they were taking place. The armchair and the bell jar in *Flirt* relate to character rather than to a specific location. They exist on a neutral ground that gives no indication of a unifying environment. The three characters in *Genius and Culture* are related, in the same way, to elements of decor that are emblematic of their categories. "The Critic," for example, is sitting at "a table overburdened with books and papers." But the three different types of stage furnishing are realistically unrelated to each other and "float," as it were, in an unspecified limbo. If ideas and concepts are represented, rather than people and situations, no particular environment or place is needed, although a sense of place, usually manifest through mood or atmosphere, is retained.

From one point of view, Marinetti's "drama of objects," in which inanimate things moved and spoke, could be considered an extension of Symbolism. If "states of mind" such as inhibition/frustration and objective concepts such as death could be personified on stage, it would seem that furniture, too, could take on life. The romantic and somewhat gloomy darkness of *The Little Theatre of Love* (*Il teatrino dell'amore*) is reminiscent of Symbolist atmosphere, but the use of nonhuman characters, however, is quite different. When the furniture speaks, it is to offer specific details about the weather, the offstage activities of people, and its own state of being. Anthropomorphic comments are used to create a very particular and exact environment. In the same way, *They Are Coming* (*Vengono*) by Marinetti uses people rather than concept characters and an individualized place rather than an emblematic one. The movement of the furniture that climaxes the *sintesi* can be contrasted with the revelation at the end of *Parallelepiped* that "The Lady" is death. Although both plays develop out of a milieu that is recognizably representational, Marinetti's *sintesi* does not provide an intellectual explanation or answer. As in Surrealism, another, more powerful, reality takes over and asserts itself. Like the protagonists of Ionesco's *The Chairs,* Marinetti's people are helpless when faced with animate furniture that contradicts the accepted laws of existence.

Thus we find in the Futurist *sintesi* the development of elements that were to lead directly to Dada, Surrealism, and the Theatre of the Absurd. The grotesque illogical humor

of plays such as Cangiullo's *The Paunch of the Vase* and the exaggerated, physical, anti-establishment satire of *sintesi* like Marinetti's *Runio clacla* can be clearly traced to the later works. *Vagrant Madmen* (*Pazzi girovaghi*) by Chiti and Settimelli approaches the irrational from a somewhat Symbolist orientation, creating a stage world peopled only by two psychotics, but *The Body That Ascends* (*Il corpo che sale*) by Umberto Boccioni focuses on the effect of an irrational occurrence in an everyday context, creating a basically surreal image.

At the same time, we can see developing in Futurism a tendency toward the abstract and alogical. Symbolism, like Realism and Naturalism, was fundamentally a logical form of theatre. The logical process is additive: one unit of information is joined to another in a consistent context. Symbolism was not always explicit, favoring ambiguity and suggestion as it did, but it accumulated connotative detail to arrive at an intellectually coherent statement.

Illogic, on the other hand, is a process of disruption and contradiction. Rather than "adding up," it "subtracts." The illogical elements of Futurist *sintesi* that later developed into Dada, Surrealism, and the Theatre of the Absurd work against expectancy, against probability, and against their context of logicality.

A third alternative, alogical theatre, is neither logical nor illogical. Alogical structure can be seen in a play like Marinetti's *Feet* (*Le basi*). Published in the January-February, 1915, supplement to *Gli avvenimenti, Feet* consists of seven short scenes in which the audience sees only the performers' feet, although it can hear their voices. A photograph that still exists of a production in 1915 indicates that all of the actors, or at least their legs and feet, appeared on stage at the same time, the upper parts of their bodies hidden by the curtain, which was raised only a short way. The important point, however, is that one vignette does not explain another. The sections do not "add up" in an intellectual sense.

Feet may be compared with *Amore pedestre* (*Pedestrian Love*), a short film made by Marcel Fabre in 1914. Running only about seven minutes, the film tells the story of a man who follows a woman onto a streetcar, where he flirts with her. A love note is intercepted by the woman's boyfriend (or husband), a soldier. The man and the soldier fight a duel. The man is wounded, but, after the soldier drives off in a car, the woman comes to him, and they go off together. In telling this whole story, the camera shows only feet. In the last shot, we see the feet of the man and woman turned toward each other; apparently they are embracing. The woman's skirt falls down around her ankles, she steps out of it, and the couple walks toward the bed that can be seen in the background. The important point is not the similarity between *Amore pedestre* and *Feet* but their differences. Fabre tells a story; Marinetti's does not. Fabre's piece develops to a climax; Marinetti's does not. Fabre's intent is merely humorous entertainment; Marinetti, even though he makes use of humor, is attempting to create a more subtle and profound experience.

Hands (*Le mani*) by Marinetti and Bruno Corra, also published in 1915 and perhaps written before *Feet,* is structurally similar. In it only the hands of the actors can be seen above a curtain stretched across the stage. Twenty different isolated images are presented in sequence: two hands shaking each other in greeting, hands praying, two hands writing at different speeds, a hand scratching, a hand with a revolver, a fist punching, a caressing female hand, and so forth. The use of only hands or feet gives a kind of unity to these pieces that is formal, imagistic, and isomorphic rather than literary. The expressive possibilities and, so to speak, the visual language involved are presented for their own sake rather than being used to create narrative development.

Whereas *Feet* retains the elements of place and interaction of characters and *Hands* makes use of specific human gestures in their alogical structures, other *sintesi* like Depero's *Colors* (*Colori*) tend toward the elimination of all human qualities. Depero's "abstract theatrical synthesis" seems intended to create the stage equivalent of a nonobjective painting. Four three-dimensional shapes are moved by strings like giant puppets. Each a single color—gray, red, white, and black—they are seen within the blue cube of the stage. Each of the shapes "speaks," but it is in a pure sound language that is a vocal equivalent of music.

Fillia's *Mechanical Sensuality* (*Sensualità meccanica*) is quite similar to Depero's *sintesi*. It is an actorless performance that presents moving, geometrical, monochrome shapes against a pure architectural ground. But because the shapes, in part, use actual words when they speak, they take on a degree of personification or characterization that is not present in *Colors*.

If completely alogical plays can be compared to abstract painting and sculpture, however, there are many that are not completely alogical and may be thought of as semiabstract or semi-alogical. Just as a semi-abstract painting retains certain references to representational reality, the semi-alogical play retains representational elements. But in both the painting and the play, the predominant aesthetic emphasis is on the formal qualities of the work. Representation merely serves as a framework or point of origin for these formal elaborations and is subservient to them.

In analyzing the degree of representation in a performance, both detail and continuity through the dimension of time must be considered. The varying degrees to which the *sintesi* used representational detail can be illustrated by their elimination of the sense of place and by their use of abstract or invented language. The tendency away from representational time structures in the plays is seen in their approaches to the interaction of characters and to narrative.

Symbolism frequently did away with specific place. But the mood, atmosphere, or feeling of place still existed. The spectator felt that the performers were in an environment quite different from that of the audience. In certain of the Futurist *sintesi* even this poetic, nonspecific sense of place was eliminated, and the place of the action was the stage itself. *To Understand Weeping* (*Per comprendere il pianto*) by Giacomo Balla establishes a purely formal stage, half red and half green, that is without pretense or atmosphere.

Much, if not all, of the action in *The Battle of the Backdrops* (*Lotta di fondali*) by Marinetti refers directly to the curtains hung at the rear of the stage, and the play occurs in its own stage space rather than in an imaginary one. In *The Lady-Killer and the Four Seasons* (*Il donnaiuolo e le 4 stagioni*) by Cangiullo, the audience also is addressed directly, helping to establish the concrete reality of the stage as a real place rather than an imaginative one; although the relation of at least two of the four actresses to an imaginary place is quite specific, a single unified environment is never created, and the real stage remains as a ground for all of the isolated actions.

The degree of representation in a play also can be measured in the language that is used, but invented language is not necessarily completely nonrepresentational. The satirical and sarcastic Dadaistic chant from which *Runio clacla* takes its title could be quite close to actual utterances of the Futurists. Although certain aspects of the play are obviously exaggerated and symbolic, the invented phrases retain a strong representational quality in their context. Nor is invented language abstract or nonrepresentational in Mario Carli's *States of Mind* (*Stati d'animo*). The characters exist in a single unified place, a café, and they speak to each other. Although they speak, for the most part, words created by Carli, their behavior remains realistic, and the effect is somewhat like listening to people speak a foreign language: We can often gain a general understanding of what they are saying—and of their "states of mind"—without knowing the language.

A more abstract use of language occurs in *Words* (*Parole*) by Remo Chiti, even though none of the vocalizations is invented. The source and context of the lines are clear. A large crowd of people is waiting outside of a gate; the beginning and end of each sentence disappear in the general tumult, and are lost. The phrases we hear are perfectly clear, but their meaning cannot be understood because they are incomplete. We receive fragmentary impressions and suggestions. Phrases do not fit together or explain each other. Meaning does not accumulate, and the effect tends toward abstraction.

The degree to which invented language retains representational character in *To Understand Weeping* can be seen by comparing it with the abstract vocalizations in *Colors*. The two men in Balla's play talk to each other: most of their speech are meaningless sounds and numbers, although certain phrases can be understood literally, providing an emotional context and situation that frames the artificial vocabulary and controls its interpretation. On the other hand, since the nonhuman moving shapes in Depero's *Colors* do not talk to each other, express particular emotions, or play a scene, the invented language can remain as totally nonrepresentational as music.

The same range can be seen in the work of Balla himself, who showed an involvement with abstract language in many of his performance pieces. His *Discussion of Futurism by Two Sudanese Critics* (*Discussione di due critici Sudanesi sul futurismo*, 1914) was performed by Balla, Cangiullo, and Marinetti, apparently at the Sprovieri Gallery in Rome about the time of *Piedigrotta*. The piece employed a piano, probably played by Cangiullo, and a guitar, played by Balla. Balla's notes suggest the "dialogue," which may have been improvised to a great extent:

> Farcionisgnaco gurninfuturo bordubalotapompimagnusa sfacataca mimitirichita plucu sbumu farufutusmaca sgnacgnacgnac chr chr chr stechestecheteretete maumauzizitititititititi.

Judging from the title, the "discussion" still retained a degree of representation. When thought of as being the speech of Africans—the performers undoubtedly elaborated on this idea with gestures, facial expressions, and, perhaps, costumes—the piece resembles a humorous cabaret act, but it helped to create the artistic climate that was to produce Dada.

In the same year, 1914, Balla produced another work that used representational sound of an entirely different kind. Each of the twelve performers in *Printing Press* (*Macchina tipografica*) became part of a machine, moving rhythmically and repeating a particular sound: "lalalala," "ftftftft," "riorioriorio," and so forth. It was not language that was represented, however abstractly, but the sounds of machinery.

Parts of Balla's *Disconcerted States of Mind* (*Sconcertazione di stati d'animo,* 1916) seem to have abandoned representation completely, although the title suggests subjective reference. Four performers "dressed differently" stand in front of a white background. In the first of four sections, which are separated from each other by pauses, they each repeat loudly a single number. Speaking simultaneously again in the second section, they say a single letter over and over (or perhaps Balla intended them to make the sounds indicated by the letters). In the third section, each of the four performs a simple everyday action: looking at his watch, blowing his nose, etc. Again the actions are done simultaneously. The last section makes use of particular representational sounds ("no, no, no, no . . ."), and the proper emotions and attitudes ("denial") are indicated in the script. Each of the sections, like the sharply-defined areas of pure color in a painting by Mondrian, was self-contained and had its own particular and pronounced quality. Thus Balla created a performance that, while making no use of an imaginary place, created and juxtaposed visual and auditory textures or patterns by combining pure sound, simple movements, and basic emotional expressions.

Of course these elements of place and language exist in the context of time. But we may pick out other aspects of a play, such as the interaction of the characters and the sequential structure, that are more intrinsically involved with time. Even though life is merely sequential, and selection is required to derive a story or a plot from it, narrative may be considered as the basic representational form of durational structure in a performance. In this dimension, then, a work is nonrepresentational to the degree that it eschews narrative or story-line structure.

In a story, one thing leads to another. The storyline of *Weariness* (*Stanchezza*), written in 1916 by Angelo Rognoni, is internalized, narrating the progressive subjective states of a man falling asleep, but it is still a story. In a plotted story, the relationship is even stronger, and one thing causes another. But in many Futurist *sintesi* story and plot are ignored. As in *Colors,* one thing merely precedes, or follows, another.

Narrative structure can easily sustain itself over long periods of time, but short images may make use of other unifying devices and formal structures. *Vowel Refrains* (*Storneli vocali*) by Cangiullo merely presents, in a somewhat symbolic way, the five vowel sounds. The unity is imagistic rather than narrative. *The Lady-Killer and the Four Seasons* gives an entirely visual personification of abstract categories. Its unity is conceptual rather than causative.

The sense of place is one thing that creates imaginary time in performance. A single place is assumed to have a single consistent time. By eliminating place, such plays as *Synthesis of Syntheses* (*Sintesi delle sintesi*) by Guglielmo Jannelli and Luciano Nicastro tend to weaken the narrative or story-line potential of their images. But causality is also a factor, and even without a definite sense of place, one image may be felt to cause or to be caused by another, thereby creating a plotlike time structure. In the *sintesi* by Jannelli and Nicastro, a revolver shot is followed by "confused screams," and it is not difficult to assume that one has caused the other. But in other *sintesi,* and in other parts of *Synthesis of Syntheses,* causal connections are very slight or nonexistent, and we have already seen that no such representational sequence exists in *sintesi* such as *Hands* and *Feet.*

Story or plot continuity may, of course, be clear and obvious, or it may be tenuous, indirect, and suggested. As narrative moves away from the explicit, it may be considered to become semi-abstract or relatively nonrepresentational. *Lights* (*Luci*) by Marinetti is basically a sequence of images all employing light in one way or another. Thus the structure, in making use of a single repeated element, seems, like *Hands* and *Feet,* to be isomorphic and completely formal. But the traces of an ill-fated love story can be perceived in the "poetic" implications of the images. Even though the light images are clearly separated from each other by blackouts, and there is no interaction between the two performers, the traces of story, plot, and situation remain. The work is not completely abstract or alogical.

The degree of interaction between the characters in a play can also be seen as a measure of abstraction or representation. In *sintesi* such as *The Battle of the Backdrops, The Lady-Killer and the Four Seasons,* and *Vowel Refrains,* any exchange between characters that could create a sense of place and causality is completely absent. This isolation of the characters tends to objectify the action and remove it from the areas of fantasy and imagination. As in the other measures of representation, the traditional realistic connections between things are weakened or eliminated in the *sintesi* as they move toward total abstraction and nonrepresentation. (pp. 41-65)

Michael Kirby and Victoria Nes Kirby, in their Futurist Performance. *E. P. Dutton, 1971.*

FUTURIST ART

Alfred H. Barr, Jr.

[*An American art critic, Barr was the founding director of the Museum of Modern Art in New York. Through the museum he made accessible to the American public a wide breadth of modern artwork, and in his writing he elucidated the works of such modern artists as Pablo Picasso and Henri Matisse. In the following excerpt, Barr surveys the major works and exhibitions of Italian Futurism in the visual arts.*]

Marinetti's call to arms [in *The Founding and Manifesto of Futurism* of 1909, excerpted above] aroused considerable interest in Paris and, as he had hoped, it electrified the youthful Milanese. The band of Futurist writers grew and was soon joined by three young painters, Boccioni, Carrà and Russolo. They had known each other for over a year and were already united in revolt against the stale air of artistic Milan where the Lombard divisionists were still considered too radical for academic tolerance. Carlo Carrà, born in 1881, had worked with the two best painters in Milan, the realist Tallone and the poetic Previati. Umberto Boccioni, born in Calabria in 1882, had studied with the most advanced painter in Rome, the divisionist Giacomo Balla. In 1904, with his master Balla and his fellow student Gino Severini, Boccioni had helped organize the first Roman *salon des refusés*. In 1907, he settled in Milan and in January, 1909, conspired with Carrà and Luigi Russolo to put on a rebel section in the staid annual exhibition of the society *Famiglia artistica*.

About a year later, after discussions with Marinetti, Boccioni, Carrà and Russolo began work on their own manifesto. Boccioni wrote his friends Balla in Rome and Severini in Paris and got them to join with the Milanese trio in signing their proclamation, dated February 11, 1910:

Manifesto of the Futurist Painters

To the young artists of Italy!

By associating our ideals with those of the futurist poets we are launching a cry of rebellion.

We want rabidly to fight the fanatical, lifeless and snobbish cult of the past which is fed by the deplorable existence of museums. . . .

For other countries Italy still seems the land of the dead, a huge Pompeii white with graves. But actually Italy is coming alive and her political rebirth is now followed by her intellectual rebirth. In the country of illiterates schools multiply; in the country of *dolce far niente* countless factories roar; in the country of traditional esthetics inspirations sparkling with novelty are taking flight today. . . .

Art is vital only when it is grounded in its environment. Our ancestors drew their artistic material from the religious atmosphere that weighed upon their souls and in the same way we must draw our inspiration from the tangible miracles of contemporary life, from the iron net of speed that envelops the earth, from ocean liners, from dreadnoughts, from marvelous flights that plough the skies, from the dark daring of underwater navigators, from the anguished struggle in the conquest of the unknown. And can we remain insensitive to the frenzied activities of great capital cities, to the new psychology of night life, to the hectic figures of the *viveur,* the *cocotte,* the *apache* and the intoxicated? . . .

We propose:

 . . . To exalt every form of originality even if reckless, even if over-violent. . . .

To consider art critics useless and harmful. . . .

To rebel against the tyranny of the words "harmony" and "good taste," expressions so elastic that with them one might easily demolish the work of Rembrandt, Goya and Rodin. . . .

To render and glorify the life of today, incessantly and tumultuously transformed by the victories of science. . . .

A month later, March 8, 1910, at the big Chiarella theatre in Turin, the three Milanese painters took part with Marinetti in their first "Futurist Evening." Boccioni read their new Manifesto to an outraged public which had already hissed verses from Dante's *Divine Comedy* under the mistaken impression that they too were Futurist poetry. Carrà then denounced the Italian critics "who didn't know the difference between Cézanne and Ettore Tito" and the evening ended in a riot. Other evenings followed in Milan and other cities. At Bologna, Carrà was nearly struck by the back of a bench hurled from a balcony. In Treviso the Futurists were rescued from a furious citizenry by the police. Marinetti bearded the Austrians in Trieste, and, with the three painters, assaulted d'Annunzio's Venice in the manifesto *Contro Venezia passatista*. (D'Annunzio countered by making the hero of his new novel an airplane pilot.)

A month after the Turin riot, the five artists signed an explanatory statement, dated April 11:

Technical Manifesto of Futurist Painting

 . . . Our thirst for truth can no longer be assuaged by traditional form and color!

A gesture for us will no longer be an *arrested moment* within the universal dynamism: it will be, definitely, *dynamic sensation* itself. . . .

Everything is moving, everything is running, everything is whirling. A figure never stands passively before us, but appears and disappears constantly. Thanks to the persistence of images on the retina, forms in movement are multiplied, deformed, follow one another like vibrations in the space through which they pass. Thus a running horse does not have four legs: he has twenty and their movements are triangular. . . .

The sixteen people around you in a moving tram are one, ten, four, three: they are still and they move; they come and go, they rattle along the street, they are devoured by a patch of sunlight, they sit down again—persistent symbols of universal vibration. And sometimes on the cheek of the person we are speaking to on the street we see a horse passing by at a distance. Our bodies penetrate the couches on which we sit, the couches penetrate us, just as the tram going by enters the houses which, in their turn, fall upon the tram and become amalgamated with it.

. . . Painters have always shown us figures and objects arranged in front of us. We are going to put the spectator at the center of the picture.

We proclaim . . . that universal dynamism must be rendered as dynamic sensation; that movement and light destroy the substance of objects.

We are fighting . . . against the superficial and elementary archaism based on flat tints which reduces painting to an impotent synthesis, infantile and grotesque; against the nude in painting which has become as boring and nauseating as adultery in literature.

We are the primitives of a new and completely transformed sensibility.

After reading these manifestoes so full of youthful bombast, Bergsonian metaphysics, reckless iconoclasm and defiant patriotism, the early paintings of the Milanese Futurists—at least what is left of them—seem an anticlimax. Almost all the Carràs and Russolos of 1910 have, in fact, disappeared. There are a few Boccionis of Milanese industrial suburbs or small excited crowd scenes painted in a meticulous, neo-impressionist, or divisionist dot technique. And there is *The City Rises,* Boccioni's panorama of building construction, the energies of modern technology symbolized not by machines as one might expect from the Futurist manifestoes, but by two colossal horses and their drivers straining at their work. The large drawing gives some idea of how the forms in this painting seem fused in a kind of flowing radiance, as if painted with an electric brush.

The *Street Pavers,* somewhat later in style, combines divisionist breaking up of light into color spots with cubist breaking up of form into angular planes.

After more demonstrations which included a riotous evening in Rome, the trio held their second show in Milan at the Ricordi Pavilion in the early summer of 1911. A list of the exhibition is not available, but the show probably included two large works by Boccioni, *The City Rises* and *The Laugh,* a garish night-life scene in which the round gaping face of a belly-laughing woman seems to shatter tables, shirt fronts, glasses and bright gowns into a fantasmagoria of color sliced by light rays. Boccioni's chief new work comprised three canvases illustrating *States of Mind.* The large preliminary drawings reveal a rather obvious and naïve use of abstract lines for symbolic and emotional effects. In *The Farewells,* whirling, twisting lines amplify the figures and gestures of the leave-takers. In *Those Who Go,* sharp blade-shaped lines streak across the surface veiling half-seen fragments of the faces of the travelers, while telegraph poles, trees and houses flicker by, merging with the inside of the train along the lines of the paragraph in the *Technical Manifesto* which describes the interior-exterior of a tram in motion. In the third drawing, the fig-

ures of those left behind walk slowly away from the station through curtains of drooping, dejected lines.

The canvases themselves were repainted after a trip to Paris in the fall. By comparison with the drawings, the paintings in their revised version are more developed and less obvious. They well demonstrate the Futurist effort to present simultaneously subjective feeling and the complex sensations of movement or flux.

Carrà's large Futurist painting, the *Funeral of the Anarchist Galli,* was also finished in 1911. In his autobiography he describes how, in 1904, he was watching the funeral of the assassinated radical on its way to the Musocco Cemetery. A riot broke out against the squadron of mounted police protecting the procession.

Without wishing to, I found myself in the center of the struggle. I saw the bier covered with the red flag careening on the shoulders of the pallbearers. I saw the horses rear skittishly, canes and lances clashing, so that it seemed to me that the coffin would fall at any moment and be trampled by the horses.

It was this experience which led him, six years later, to contribute to the *Technical Manifesto* the phrase, "we are going to put the spectator at the center of the picture"— though Boccioni also claims credit for this idea. The Futurist use of broken silhouettes, interpenetrating lights and shades and the flickering fan-shaped patterns of flailing weapons contributes to the frenzied kinesthesia of the painting. Yet, fundamentally, in its main lines and masses Carrà's *Funeral* is as classically organized as a fifteenth-century battle piece by Paolo Uccello.

Somewhat later in 1911 Carrà painted *The Tram,* which he originally called, *What the Tram Said to Me.* Again the sense of the simultaneity of movement and the sensation of inner and outer space are fused by the fragmentation of forms, lines and color surfaces.

The exhibition at the Ricordi Pavilion produced some blunt criticism by Soffici in *La voce.* The Florentine, with seven years of Paris behind him, said the Futurists grossly exaggerated their own importance and called their paintings half-baked in comparison with the work of contemporary French masters whose work he accused them of garbling. The Futurists—Marinetti, Boccioni, Russolo and Carrà—took the next train to Florence and found Soffici, Papini and the rest of *La voce* at the Café Giubbe Rosse. Boccioni hit Soffici and started a fight. They were all taken to the police station, but were released only to renew the brawl in the station the next morning as the Futurists boarded the train back to Milan.

Soffici's criticisms were confirmed by Severini who came down from Paris a few months later. Though he had signed the 1910 manifestoes at Boccioni's persuasion, he found the paintings of the Futurists pretentious, literary and uncertain in style. He insisted that they must come to Paris to make themselves *au courant* with modernism at its source. Together they persuaded Marinetti to pay for the trip, and later in the fall they all arrived in Paris for a reconnaissance. In Severini's company they saw cubist pictures and their painters first hand. At the same time

Riot in the Galleria *(1910) by Boccioni.*

they made arrangements with Félix Fénéon, the manager of the important Bernheim Jeune Gallery, for a great exhibition to be held early in the new year. When they returned to Milan they painted furiously to prepare for the crucial test.

The exhibition opened February 5, 1912 with a stormy oration by Marinetti before a large gathering of the Paris *avant-garde,* many of whom had previously read the various Futurist manifestoes. The French were aware that the Futurists were mounting a frontal assault on French hegemony in the arts; and they were offended by the aggressive belligerence of the Italians. Apollinaire and Salmon took the Futurists fairly seriously, but other critics were condescending or hostile. Modigliani was outraged; Picasso, contemptuous. Yet the general uproar gave the Milanese a sense of success. Carrà's *Funeral of the Anarchist Galli* was reproduced on the front page of *Le journal* and the publicity was considerable. Severini, however, was embarrassed by what seemed to him provincial chauvinism on the part of his friends, but he found their paintings better integrated in style than those he had criticized in Milan.

Besides the *Funeral,* Carrà showed *The Jolting of a Cab, What the Tram Said to Me, The Milan Station* and several paintings which seemed more static and cubist than Futurist. Boccioni showed the repainted *States of Mind, The Street Enters the House, The City Rises, Forces of the Street,* and *Simultaneous Vision.* Russolo exhibited *A Tram in Motion,* and his most famous work, *The Revolt.* The largest painting in the show was the *Pan-Pan at the Monaco* by Severini himself, who for the first time was showing with his fellow Futurists. He had been working

for two years on this kaleidoscopic panorama of a night club, using flat, angular fragments of color. He also showed *Recollections of the Voyage,* a composite picture of trains, trams and buildings, and the *Boulevard,* which well illustrates his early Futurist style.

Although the Paris exhibition was not received with critical enthusiasm, it aroused popular curiosity throughout Europe. From Paris it went to London, accompanied by Boccioni and Marinetti. On the 10th of March, an hour before the press review of the London show, Boccioni wrote to his friend Vico Baer in Milan:

> The Paris show has proved to all Europe the existence of a new movement animated by a formidable enthusiasm. . . . My preface to the catalog aroused so much interest that 17,000 copies were printed. The English catalog is fine too. They have added explanations of every painting. . . . which will be useful to these *bestie di Inglesi*—these stupid Englishmen—as Benvenuto Cellini used to call them. Anyway, the public is imbecile in all countries, and just as it does not understand in Italy, it does not understand here, and it does not understand in France.
>
> Those here abroad who know Italy and the infantile, ignoble, vulgar condition of its esthetic standards, cannot understand how we have been able to escape from the mud puddle, and thereby, with one leap, put Italian art side by side with French.

From London the exhibition went to Berlin under the auspices of the Sturm Gallery. In Berlin all the remaining paintings were sold, but the exhibition, totaling thirty-four canvases, was kept together for subsequent showings in Brussels, Hamburg, Amsterdam, The Hague, Munich, Vienna, Budapest, Frankfurt, Breslau, Wiesbaden, Zurich and Dresden. In the middle of the tour, the Futurists were invited to take part in the "Armory Show" in New York, held early in 1913, but they refused because they wanted separate galleries with a separate box office. Their work was not to be shown in America until the San Francisco Exposition of 1915.

Boccioni did not accompany the exhibition on its grand tour, but returned from Berlin to Paris where he renewed his interest in sculpture. By the end of spring he had gone back to Milan in spite of Severini's insistence that all the Futurists should leave Italy to seek their artistic fortunes in the great competitive arena of the French capital. Marinetti, meanwhile, had gone east to enjoy the Balkan War which inspired his most famous poem, *Zang-tumb-tuum; or, The Siege of Adrianople.*

Back in Milan, the Futurists found that their international renown had not deeply impressed their fellow countrymen. Soffici, perhaps a little jealous of the Paris show, wrote another attack in *La voce,* accusing the Futurists of charlatanism, professional vulgarity and of using Belgian and American publicity methods. Yet the article was kinder than the piece of a year before which had led to the battle of the Café Giubbe Rosse. Though he proclaimed that the Paris show was mostly a *succès de scandale,* he admitted that it had helped break down the legend of

Italy's living in her cultural past. Severini, who had been introduced to Soffici by Picasso, now renewed their acquaintance in Tuscany, and before the end of the year a coalition between the Milanese and Florentine vanguards had taken place, thanks partly to Severini's diplomacy. Papini and Soffici actually deserted *La voce* and founded a new magazine, *Lacerba,* which passed rapidly from tolerance of Futurism to enthusiastic participation. Thereafter, for a year and a half, *Lacerba* was the chief Futurist organ.

In February, 1913, the combined Milanese and Florentine forces put on an exhibition in Rome, and a Futurist Evening at the Costanzi Theatre where they were greeted with a "nutritious shower of missiles *più o meno alimentari*" ["more or less nourishing"]. The Roman exhibition, one of the best of all Futurist shows, included the mature work of Severini, the three Milanese and, for the first time, Balla and Soffici.

Boccioni showed six canvases including *Materia,* his major work of 1912, a complex painting in which the imposing figure of his mother, sitting with colossal folded hands, dominates, and at the same time is absorbed into her environment, the interior of the room, the window, the balcony and a row of houses across the street beyond. *Elasticity,* with its cantering horse and rider seen against a background of factories and high-tension poles, is less ambitious but better integrated.

Carrà's paintings of 1912 grew closer to the static analytical cubism of Picasso and Braque, though his Futurist masterpiece, *The Milan Galleria,* involves some suggestion of orthodox Futurist commotion. The quality and restraint of Carrà's painting of this time quite belie the Futurist rebellion against "harmony" and "good taste." Soffici, the new recruit, also contributed work which seems more cubist than Futurist. Russolo showed *The Fog,* Balla, the *Girl* × *Balcony* and the *Leash in Motion.*

Balla, although he had signed the 1910 manifestoes, had developed his style in the comparative isolation of Rome. The *Girl* × *Balcony* shows that he had not yet freed himself from Signac-like neo-impressionist spot painting. The study for the feet in the *Girl* × *Balcony* suggests that his technique of kinetic suggestion is derived directly from the "geometrical chronophotographs" of figures in motion such as were made by E. J. Marey in Paris as early as 1883 and widely publicized. Balla's kinetic researches are clarified in the *Leash in Motion,* one of the most famous, original and entertaining of all Futurist paintings.

Among Severini's six pictures was his masterwork, the *Dynamic Hieroglyphic of the Bal Tabarin,* painted in Faenza in the summer of 1912. In it are still a few passages which seem naïve and out of style, but on the whole the *Bal Tabarin* wonderfully assimilates and expresses the tinsel whirl of a Paris cabaret. The sequins glued to the canvas, Severini writes, had a respectable precedent in the jewel-encrusted halo of a fourteenth-century Saint Peter in the Brera, which Apollinaire mentioned to him. Severini's sequins themselves may have anticipated cubist collages by several months. Two years before, however, the cubists had begun to use isolated words and letters in their com-

positions. Severini, of course, knew their work but with typically Futurist concern for subject matter he scatters such words as VALSE, BOWLING, POLKA through his *Bal Tabarin* as integral and positive elements in the representation of the scene. Later, words and images are used in almost equal balance by Severini and Carrà in some of their war pictures and by Marinetti in his war poems.

The exhibition in Rome marks a high point in the development of Futurist painting, indeed of Futurism as an art movement. The show traveled as a whole to Rotterdam and selections from it were shown in Berlin and elsewhere, including Balla's *Leash in Motion* and Severini's *Bal Tabarin* which was sold in London. Many young artists of talent and some older men were attracted to the Futurist standard, and Futurism's influence grew stronger throughout Europe. Even the French critics and artists were now not only more respectful, they even borrowed Futurist critical and pictorial ideas, usually without giving credit. All through 1913 *Lacerba's* pages were full of new manifestoes and polemical articles by Boccioni, Carrà, Marinetti, Soffici and Papini. Russolo published his manifesto on the *Futurist Art of Noises* and followed it with performances on his noise-machine in Paris and London as well as in Italy. Pratella, whose manifesto of Futurist music had appeared in 1910, conducted a Futurist symphony in Rome. Carrà was asked by Diaghilew and Strawinsky to design a ballet. Severini had a successful one-man show in London. Most important of all, Boccioni held his first exhibition of Futurist sculpture in Paris. The Futurists staged violent evenings at Genoa, Venice, Mantua, Padua, the series coming to a climax in Florence on December 12 at the Teatro Verdi where Carrà's "smoking" was soiled by a direct hit of *"pasta asciutta"* ["dry pasta"].

Among the memorable Futurist paintings of 1913 are Severini's train compositions. . . . The use of chevron or wedge-shaped forms to suggest speed and force had however been initiated by Russolo in 1911 in his striking *Revolt.* Throughout 1913 Balla also experimented successfully with the suggestion of speed in a series of automobile pictures which began with the earlier *Speeding Automobile.* Balla's *Swifts,* sub-titled "Paths of Movement + Dynamic Sequences," combines exterior and interior, moving and static objects by fusing kinetic series of birds in flight with the window frame and suggestions of roof tiles and gutters.

Boccioni painted the *Dynamism of a Cyclist . . .* and the *Dynamism of a Human Body.* To these may be added the best known of his drawings, *Muscular Dynamism.* These three pictures belong fundamentally to the long series of studies of the human figure in action, striding, running, cycling, which pre-occupied Boccioni more than any other subject. In painting, these researches are climaxed by the huge *Football Player* of 1913. More notable, however, than any of these pictures is the series of striding figures in sculpture which he completed in the same year.

Boccioni's theories of sculpture, announced in the *Technical Manifesto of Futurist Sculpture,* April 11, 1912, were just as elaborate as his painting theories. They were also more prophetic of future developments, far more than he himself could realize in his two short years of work as a sculptor. In the manifesto he condemns, of course, the oppressive weight of the Greeks and Michelangelo upon the contemporary sculpture of France, Belgium and Italy. He scorns the archaistic and primitivist tendencies in Central European sculpture. He rejects the academic insistence upon the nude human figure and proposes sculpture which would integrate the complex elements and emotions of contemporary life. He dismisses his older contemporaries Meunier, Bourdelle, Rodin, but praises with real sympathy the plastic fluidity and freedom of Medardo Rosso. He proposes a sculpture of movement and atmosphere, the abolition of the silhouette, the extension of natural forms into space and the use of *polimateria,* that is, the abandonment of the traditionally "noble" materials of bronze and marble for glass, wood, cardboard, concrete, horsehair, leather, cloth, mirrors, electric lights, in various combinations. He foresees sculpture not only of forms in movement but sculpture itself mechanically mobile.

Boccioni's own sculpture falls into two periods, before and after his visits to Paris in the winter of 1911-12. The early work is ambitiously complex. *Head + House + Light,* now destroyed, was very closely related to the painting *Materia,* but the fusion of the woman's figure with a balcony and a house across the street together with rays of light result in a grotesque conglomeration, courageous but too doctrinaire. In Paris in March of 1912 Severini had taken him to the studios of Archipenko, Brancusi and Duchamp-Villon. Although his own ideas were more radical than theirs, their more traditional and less pictorial sculpture may have persuaded Boccioni to return to more manageable problems.

Back in Milan, he began the series of striding figures. The first, *Synthesis of the Human Dynamism,* still includes miscellaneous fragments of environment such as window mullions. In 1913 he abandoned these accessories, clarifying his forms in three successive figures, the *Spiral Expansion of Muscles in Movement,* the *Muscles in Velocity* and the climactic *Unique Forms of Continuity in Space.* This last figure well embodies Boccioni's theory that "sculpture should bring to life the object by making visible its prolongation into space. The circumscribed lines of the enclosed statue should be abolished. The figure must be opened up and fused in space." The muscles of the *Continuity* figure are forced into streamlined shapes as if under the distorting pressure of supersonic speed. The sense of gravity is further diminished by the flaming spiral of the figure when seen from the front.

A still life of 1912, the *Development of a Bottle in Space,* demonstrates Boccioni's dictum that "there is more truth in the intersection of the planes of a book with the corners of a table . . . than in all the twisting of muscles in all the breasts and thighs of the heroes and venuses which inspired the idiotic sculpture of our time."

Boccioni took his ten pieces of sculpture and twenty drawings to Paris for a show at the Galerie La Boëtie in June, 1913. At the opening he spoke in faltering French which Severini helped to interpret to an audience more sympathetic and respectful than that which had greeted Marinetti at the general exhibition of Futurist painting fifteen

months before. Though influenced somewhat by cubism, [some of Severini's drawings] seem more advanced than any sculpture of the period in which they were done; and the *Continuità* remains one of the brilliant achievements of early twentieth-century art.

Futurism as a movement continued to gain ground in Italy during 1914. Adding still another art to the movement, the architect Antonio Sant' Elia published his manifesto *L'architettura futurista* in *Lacerba* of August 1, 1914, together with remarkably prophetic projects for skyscrapers with terraced setbacks several years before the zoning law brought about similar designs in New York. And Boccioni published his *Pittura, scultura futuriste,* the authoritative source-book on early Futurist art.

In his paintings Boccioni, abandoning the expression of violent movement, worked on the traditional theme of the figure seated at a café table, adding light rays and psychological atmosphere which were lacking in cubist paintings of similar subjects. Severini began a series of highly abstract compositions painted in a whirl of gay, rainbow colors, among them the *Dancer—Helix—Sea.* Carrà and Soffici, however, were more and more influenced by cubism. They assimilated collage techniques with greater skill and sensibility than any but the best Paris cubists. Indeed Carrà recalls that in the spring of 1914 he was offered a contract by Kahnweiler, discriminating dealer of Picasso, Braque and Gris.

The outbreak of the European war in August, 1914, aroused the Futurists to even more violent activity. Boccioni had written in the catalog of the Paris exhibition of February, 1912, "If our paintings are Futurist, it is because they represent the result of ethical, esthetic, political and social concepts which are absolutely Futurist." To the faithful, Futurism was a way of life devoted, among other things, to the patriotic aggrandizement of Italy. The Futurists were anti-German and, of course, anti-Austrian. They were pro-French politically and through strong personal associations, particularly in the cases of Marinetti, Soffici and Severini. Consequently they threw themselves with the utmost energy and enthusiasm into the cause of Italian intervention on the side of the Allies. As a result of public demonstrations, they were several times arrested and jailed (once with Mussolini, in Rome) and when Italy finally entered the war in April, 1915, most of the Futurists responded wholeheartedly and courageously to the call to arms. Russolo and Boccioni enlisted in the artillery. Marinetti was wounded and twice decorated. Sant'Elia was killed. (pp. 8-15)

Boccioni was hit and invalided to a base hospital at Verona. There, one day in the summer of 1916, before he was fully recovered, and under circumstances of extreme romantic irony, he was killed in a riding accident.

"The War is a motor for art," Carrà proclaimed in his book *Guerrapittura* published in 1915 and signed Carrrà —with one extra consonant, two extra accents and a growl. And between political demonstrations and military service, the Milaneseᵖ Futurists produced a number of drawings such as Carrà's *Cannon at a Gallop* or Boccioni's *Charge of Lancers,* brushed on a collage of war news clippings. But it was Severini who made the best Futurist pictures of the war, perhaps because he took no active part in it. During 1915 he lived near a station on the outskirts of Paris where he could see ammunition and Red Cross trains moving to and from the front. The *Armored Train* was probably painted at this time. The drawing, *Flying over Rheims,* must be one of the first air-view pictures by a well-known modern artist. Earlier in his life Severini had wanted to be an aviator.

Yet, in spite of the stimulation of the War, the original group of Futurist artists was disintegrating. By the end of 1914, Boccioni had begun to desert Futurism for a more static and traditional technique. His last important work, the portrait of his friend the great pianist Busoni, was completed in 1916 not long before his death, in a style very close to Cézanne. Carrà's ardor as a Futurist painter was also cooling. In 1915 he forsook Futurism in his painting; in 1916 he contributed articles in praise of Giotto and Uccello to *La voce* which had revived as a rival to *Lacerba*; and early in 1917 he became a collaborator of de Chirico in *pittura metafisica,* a movement entirely anti-Futurist in spirit. In 1915, Papini, the publisher of *Lacerba,* and Soffici, too, formally repudiated Futurism, going back, as Marinetti scornfully expressed it, to *"passatismo."* However, Balla remained faithful; and Rosai and then Sironi . . . joined the movement briefly. In Paris, after his Futurist war pictures of 1915, Severini accompanied Picasso back to a kind of neo-classic style, at least in his figure painting. It is true that as late as 1917, Carrà and Severini signed themselves as Futurists in one-man shows, the former in Milan, the latter in Alfred Stieglitz' Gallery in New York. But their allegiance was vestigial. When Marinetti emerged from the war to ally himself with his fellow interventionist, Mussolini, none of the original band of artists was with him save only Balla.

Futurism undoubtedly involved some of the same elements as Fascism: chauvinism for instance, admiration for war and military courage, enthusiasm for technology and machinery—"modernolatry"—to use Boccioni's word. But, fundamentally, Futurism was anarchic, not Fascist. Once Fascism was in power, the love of freedom, of perpetual revolt against the stale and conventional which had characterized early Futurism, was no longer politically valuable within the discipline of the totalitarian state. A second generation of Futurists grew up around Marinetti, painted, wrote manifestoes, demonstrated and were accorded some official recognition. A few of them were men of talent but their activities seem marginal and their achievements minor in quality beside those of the original Futurists. More congenial to the Fascist régime—and far better rewarded by it—were the *Novecentisti* who . . . rode the general wave of reaction and isolationism by painting old-masterish figures and landscapes, often with solemn references to the Italian Renaissance or Imperial Rome.

Throughout Europe, however, the influence of early Futurism was perhaps greater than that of any movement save cubism. Often dismissed by the French as a rather tasteless and provincial back eddy of cubism, Futurism was in principle, a repudiation of the static, puristic and quasi-academic elements in the Paris movement. Quite deliberately Boccioni insisted upon the importance of subject matter and overt emotion which the *fauve* and cubist movements had almost eliminated in favor of an art of pure esthetic values. A number of Paris artists and critics felt the impact of Futurism. In 1913 Apollinaire himself contributed a manifesto, "L'antitradizione futurista," to *Lacerba.* And the Dadaists of 1916 turned to the Futurists for valuable precedent in iconoclastic agitation and as well for their later rejection of the dogmas of the *Section d'or* cubists. Through the Dadaists, the irrational element in Futurism passed on to Paris Surrealism in the early 1920's. Futurism also influenced the Berlin *Sturm* group before 1915, the Berlin Dadaists such as George Grosz after 1917, the British Vorticists of 1914, the Central European Activists, and Americans such as Weber and Stella.

Marinetti had lectured in Moscow in 1914 and it was in Russia both before and after the Revolutions of 1917 that Futurism flourished most vigorously. The kinetic effects in Malevich's painting of 1912-13 and later in the work of Burliuk, the dynamic-mechanical, multimaterial esthetics of Tatlin's constructions, the general machinolatry of the theatre, the poetry of Mayakovsky, all were in large part latently or avowedly Futurist in inspiration. But Futurism soon shared the fate of other modern movements in the U.S.S.R. As in Nazi Germany ten years later, they were discouraged and then suppressed by a regime which feared any sign of individual freedom or of nonconformity with popular taste as exploited by authoritarian politicians. (pp. 15-16)

Alfred H. Barr, Jr., "Early Futurism," in Twentieth-Century Italian Art *by James Thrall Soby and Alfred H. Barr, Jr., 1949. Reprint by Arno Press, 1972, pp. 7-16.*

Roger Fry

[*A member of the Bloomsbury Group, Fry was one of the most important English art critics of the early twentieth century, serving as director of the Metropolitan Museum of Art in New York from 1905 to 1910 and as the editor of* Burlington *magazine from 1910 to 1919. He is remembered in particular as a champion of the post-Impressionists and is credited with introducing their works, as well as those of the Fauvists, to England with his unprecedented "Post-Impressionist" exhibitions held in London in 1910 and 1912. In the following excerpt from a review of an exhibition of Futurist paintings at the Sackville Gallery in London in March 1912, Fry comments on Futurist theory and practice in art.*]

At the Sackville Gallery is to be seen a small collection of work by [the Futurist] group of Italian painters. The catalogue contains a manifesto of their aims and beliefs. This, at least in the English translation, is by no means closely reasoned or clearly expressed; it might have been better to allow us the assistance of the original Italian.

It is interesting to find painters who regard their art as a necessary expression of a complete attitude to life. Whatever one thinks about the content of their strangely Nihilistic creed, one must admit that they hold it with a kind of religious fervor, and that they endeavor to find an expression for it in their art. Fortunately, too, their dogmas appear to allow of great variety of treatment or method, so that, as yet, no stereotyped formula has been evolved, and each of those artists pursues his researches along individual lines. None the less, admitting as one may the sincerity and courage of these artists and their serious endeavor to make of art a genuine expression of spiritual experience, I cannot accept without qualification their rash boast of complete and absolute originality, even supposing that such a thing were in itself desirable. Rather what strikes one is the prevalence in their work of a somewhat tired convention, one that never had much value and which lost with the freshness of novelty almost all its charm, the convention of Chéret, Besnard, and Boldini. It is quite true that the Futurist arranges his forms upon peculiar and original principles, breaking them up into fragments as though they were seen through the refracting prisms of a lighthouse, but the forms retain, even in this fragmentary condition, their well-worn familiarity.

Apparently what is common to the group is the belief in psychological painting. The idea of this is to paint not any particular external scene, but, turning the observation within, to paint the images which float across the *camera obscura* of the brain. And these images are to be made prominent in proportion to their significance, while their relations one to another have the spacelessness, the mere contiguity of mental visions. Thus, in rendering the state of mind of a journey, the artist jumbles together a number of more or less complete images of the home and friends he is leaving, of the country seen from the carriage window, and of anticipations of his journey's end [depicted in Boccioni's *States of Mind* series: *The Farewell, Those Who Stay,* and *Those Who Go*].

These pictures are certainly more entertaining and interesting than one would expect to result from such an idea, and one or two of the painters, notably Boccioni (in his later works) and Severini, do manage to give a vivid pictorial echo of the vague complex of mental visions. If once they give up preconceived ideas of what sort of totality a picture ought to represent, most people would, I think, admit the verisimilitude of several of these pictures— would own that they do correspond in a curiously exact way to certain conditions of consciousness. Unfortunately, the result is much more of a psychological or scientific curiosity than a work of art, and for this reason that the states of mind which these artists investigate are not really at all interesting states of mind, but just those states of quite ordinary practical life when the images that beset us have no particular value or significance for the imagination.

The idea of painting from the mental image is no new one, though it is one that artists might well practise more than they do. Blake roundly declared that to draw from anything but a mental image was vain folly; but he drew from mental images only when, stimulated by some emotional exaltation, they attained to coherence and continuity of texture. Probably a great many of Rembrandt's sketches are the result of distinct mental imagery, but it was a men-

tal imagery stimulated by reading the poetical prose of the Bible. The fact is that mental visions, though they tend always to be more distinctly colored by the visionaries' own personality than external visions, are almost as various in their quality, and are, as often as not, merely accidental and meaningless. Doubtless the Futurists aim at giving them meaning by their relations to one another, and in this they aim at a direct symbolism of form and color. Here, I think, they have got hold of a good idea, but one which it will be very hard to carry out; as yet their work seems for the most part too merely ingenious, too scientific and theoretic, too little inspired by concrete emotion. It is the work of bold and ingenious theorists expressing themselves in painted images rather than of men to whom paint is the natural, inevitable mode of self-revelation. One artist of the group, Severini, stands out, however, as an exception. He has a genuine and personal feeling for colors and pattern, and the quality of his paint is that of an unmistakable artist. His *Pan Pan* is a brilliant piece of design, and really does, to some extent, justify the curious methods adopted, in that it conveys at once a general idea of the scene and of the mental exasperation which it provokes. For all its apparently chaotic confusion, it is not without the order of a genuine feeling for design. Here, as elsewhere, the worst fault is a tendency to lapse into an old and commonplace convention in individual forms.

His *Yellow Dancers* is another charming design. The statement in the catalogue that it exemplifies the destruction of form and color by brilliant light, shows the curious scientific obsession of these people. Such a fact is æsthetically quite irrelevant, and the picture is good enough to appeal on its own merits. The same is true of his *Black Cats,* a novel and curious color harmony, which gains nothing from the purely autobiographical note in the catalogue. Whether Signor Severini arrived at his design by reading Edgar Allan Poe or not is immaterial; the spectator is only concerned with the result which, in this case, is certainly justified.

No amount of successful exposition of theory will make bad painting of any value, and, on the other hand, a good picture is none the worse because the artist thinks he painted it to prove a theory, only in that case the theory has served its turn before the picture was painted, and no one need be troubled with it again.

Apart from individual failures and successes, one result of these efforts stands out as having some possibilities for the future of pictorial design, namely, the effort to prove that it is not necessary that the images of a picture should have any fixed spatial relation to one another except that dictated by the needs of pure design. That, in fact, their relation to one another may be directly expressive of their imaginative importance.

In thus endeavoring to relate things not according to their actual spatial conditions but according to their imaginative purpose in the design, the Futurists are, no doubt all unconsciously, taking up once again the pictorial language of early art, for it was thus that Cimabue arranged his diminutive angels around the vast figure of the Virgin in the Rucellai *Madonna.*

What the Futurists have yet to learn, if their dogmas still retain the power of growth, is that great design depends upon emotion, and that, too, of a positive kind, which is nearer to love than hate. As yet the positive elements in their creed, their love of speed and of mechanism, have failed to produce that lyrical intensity of mood which alone might enable the spectator to share their feelings. (pp. 945-46)

> Roger Fry, "The Futurists," in The Nation, New York, Vol. X, No. 23, March 9, 1912, pp. 945-46.

Marianne W. Martin

[In the following excerpt, Martin examines Futurist painting theory and its sources.]

Marinetti had made only one specific reference to the plastic arts in the First Manifesto, apart from his notorious elevation of the automobile over the *Victory of Samothrace* in the aesthetic hierarchy. After comparing museums to cemeteries, he warned the artist of the overpowering effect past works of art could have on fragile creative sensibilities and bid them stay away from museums. But one wistful concession mitigated the tone of total iconoclasm: 'Let us make one visit a year [to the museums] just as one goes to see one's dead once a year . . . Let us even place flowers at the foot of *La gioconda* once a year.'

In their first manifesto of February 1910, the painters adopted Marinetti's therapeutic statements as part of their general dependence on his First Manifesto, adding little that was new and specifically relevant to painting. They advocated a more honest and aggressive approach to art, denouncing the easy success won by catering to popular taste. The artist was to 'Sweep the ideal camp of art free of all previously exploited motifs and subjects'. But apart from general directions to express the changing modern world, the artist was still left in the dark as to the kind of art the Futurist painters really had in mind. The single clue was given in their second point: 'Profoundly to despise all forms of imitation.' This warning evidently applied not only to art of the past, but to imitation of various current forms of drawing-room realism and earnest social realism as well. Not until the appearance of the technical manifesto two months later were the characteristics of Futurist painting finally itemized and the means of their realization discussed. The fundamental premise is stated metaphorically at the beginning of the manifesto, and repeated more simply, with a slightly different emphasis, at its conclusion: 'For us the gesture will no longer be an *arrested moment* of the universal dynamism: it will clearly be the *dynamic sensation* itself made eternal . . . the universal dynamism must be rendered as dynamic sensation.' These sentences establish the two interlocking directions which Futurist painting and, in a broad sense, all Futurist art was to take. It was (1) to concern itself with the emotional expression of the vital impulse as revealed through 'gesture'; (2) to present the temporal extension of this perception. In other words, Futurist dynamism was to be rendered in terms both of psychic and physical phenomena.

The Futurist painters were undoubtedly aware that they

had established difficult requirements, and having blithely tossed academic rules and methods to the winds, they looked to science both for example and inspiration. 'Today's science, [which] discards its past [achievements], responds to the material necessities of our time; similarly, art, disowning its past, must meet the intellectual needs of our time.' They drew especially upon the much discussed psychophysics and psychophysiology of visual perception for analogues which could be explored in representations of their new dynamic image of the world. For instance, the phenomenon of after-sensation of seen movement largely accounts for their chief proposition that: 'Everything moves, everything runs, everything changes rapidly. A figure is never motionless before our eyes, but continuously appears and disappears. Because of the persistence of the image upon the retina, moving objects are multiplied, deformed, succeed each other like vibrations within the space through which they run. Therefore a race horse does not have four legs; it has twenty and their movements are triangular.' Irradiation and the various types of geometrical optical illusions could produce effects such as those described below. While these recall certain ideas suggested by the canvases of Van Gogh or Munch they anticipated the more daring ones of the German Expressionists: 'Space no longer exists: a rain-drenched street illuminated by electric lights will form an abyss down to the centre of the earth. The sun is thousands of miles away from us, yet does not the house in front of us appear to be set into the solar disk?' Because the perception of light and movement thus destroys the apparent autonomy and inviolability of objects in space, and hence conventional concepts of space, the artist's attention was to be called to startling spectacles like the following:

> The sixteen people around you in a moving tram are one, ten, four, three; they stand still and move; they come and go, they leap into the street, are swallowed up by a zone of sunlight and then come back and sit down . . . And sometimes we see on the cheek of the person to whom we are talking a horse which passes by in the distance. Our bodies penetrate the benches on which we sit and the benches penetrate our bodies, just as the passing tram penetrates the houses which in their turn hurl themselves upon the tram and merge with it.

That the Futurist painters concerned themselves with such phenomena is suggested by Boccioni's and Carrà's accounts of specific experiences which reportedly formed the basis for some of the manifesto's propositions.

The artists' search for a new experience and interpretation of the universe was accompanied by a desire to provide fresh angles for perception of their work. Like Marinetti, they believed themselves to be situated at the heart of the world and recommended a corresponding position for the spectator 'in the centre of the picture'. In this projected transposition of the artist (and the spectator) into the creative core of life, they were reflecting the Futurist desire to regain a leading position in society. In the purely artistic sense, the painters were trying to break down the traditional psychological distance between the aesthetic object and the spectator. Their principle was that of empathy, which at the time had theoretical spokesmen in France,

Germany and Italy. It is based on the hypothesis of an unconscious physical response to, and consequent psychological identification with, the object contemplated.

Such unorthodox modes of seeing and representation obviously demanded an untrammelled consciousness. The Futurists considered themselves 'the Primitives of a new and completely transformed sensibility', and called for a similar spiritual purity in the spectator: 'To conceive and understand the novel beauties of a modern painting, the soul must again become chaste; the eye must free itself from the veil with which atavism and culture have covered it and look to nature and not the museum . . . as the unique control.'

This brings up the attitude of the Futurist painters towards 'artistic truth', 'nature', and 'reality'. Although their views were not yet clearly formulated they subscribed to an aesthetic relativism in keeping with their philosophy of dynamism: 'Everything in art is convention, and the truths of yesterday are today, for us, pure lies.' The artist was the subjective transmitter of an ever-changing truth which was, however, subject to the laws of nature. They prescribed 'sincerity and virginity in the interpretation of nature'; but they did not mean to say that the artist should paint what was commonly accepted as visual reality. Instead he was told to draw upon an internal, conceptual image of reality and was reminded 'that the portrait in order to be a work of art neither must nor can resemble the sitter, and that the painter carries within himself all the landscapes which he wishes to create'.

Some of the actual technical problems of executing Futurist dynamism were also taken up in the manifesto, as promised in the title. The expectations aroused by the painters' grandiloquent claim in the first paragraphs, that traditional form and colour would no longer suffice, are later somewhat deflated by the recommendation of *complementarismo congenito,* a form of Divisionism, as the basic technique. Today it is not entirely clear as to how 'innate complementarism' was understood in the early days of the movement. The manifesto explained that 'we conceive of divisionism not as a technical *process* which can be methodically learned and applied. To the modern painter divisionism must mean *innate complementarism* which we deem essential and inevitable.' From this vague definition, and from their comparison of *complementarismo congenito* to free verse, it appears that what the artists had in mind was more than a specific technique, but a general rejection of academic formulae which inhibited spontaneous perception and the free flow of emotional expression. Thus the innate optical and physiological reactions implicit in Divisionism were regarded as mere points of departure. The Futurists evidently wished to explore other instinctive perceptive processes in their creations and may well have hoped to draw upon the findings of the then fashionable parapsychology. Hence *complementarismo congenito* may partly have been conceived as an occult spiritual experience bringing the artist in closer touch with the universal forces. Their own statements support such an approach: 'Who can still believe in the opacity of bodies,' they asked, 'when our sharpened and multiplied sensibility allows us to perceive the obscure disclosures of me-

diumistic phenomena? Why should we continue to create without taking into account our perceptive powers [*potenza visiva*] which can give results analogous to those of X rays?'

The more general technical recommendations were less equivocal. The painters dismissed 'the false *avvenirismo* of the secessionists and independents, new academicians of all countries . . . [and] the superficial and elementary archaism based on flat colours which reduces painting to an impotent synthesis, both childish and grotesque . . . [the latter being a reference to the *stile liberty,* and] the patina and varnish of the false old masters'. Above all they wanted to exclude 'the nude in painting', which would rob the academy of its chief stock-in-trade. This principle also made explicit the pantheism of Futurist dynamism. When man was portrayed, he was to be dressed in modern clothes, whose 'musicality of line and fold have for us an emotive and symbolic power equal to that which the nude held for the ancients'. But man was deprived of the monopoly on psychic states with which he had been endowed by the humanist tradition. His passion and anguish were to be of no more interest to the artist than those of any other bundle of molecules, for example 'an electric lamp which suffers, writhes and shrieks with the most heart-rending expressions of colour'. This declaration opened the way to the less romantic conception of animated matter which characterized later Futurist art and theory in particular.

. . . . .

Futurist painting theory as outlined in the technical manifesto was in essence an adaptation of Impressionism leavened by Symbolist and other current ideas. These debts were fully and repeatedly acknowledged, especially by Boccioni in his 1914 *Pittura scultura futuriste,* in which he declared: 'our [technical] manifesto was founded on Impressionism'. But with characteristic shrewdness he minimized Futurism's dependence by asserting that 'today there does not exist in Europe or in the world a trend in painting or sculpture . . . which is not derived from French Impressionism.'

None of the signatories of the painting manifestos could claim an intimate knowledge of French art comparable to Marinetti's in the field of literature. But a key to local interpretations upon which they could have drawn when formulating their artistic precepts is supplied by the writings of Ardengo Soffici. One of the first important articles on French art by this painter-critic to be published in his native country was devoted to Cézanne; it appeared in *Vita d'arte* in 1908 and was one of numerous statements to result from the large Cézanne retrospective at the 1907 Salon d'Automne in Paris. Soffici seems to have based himself on Maurice Denis' Symbolist interpretation of Cézanne of that year. He presented the painter as an impassioned seeker of truth and made Cézanne's method sound like an anticipation of the aggressive, expressionist vitalism postulated by the Futurists. Cézanne's art was seen as 'a philosophy in action . . . Because nature appears as a colossal hieroglyph to a spirit starved for the absolute, which only an enraptured soul can decipher, Cézanne wished to assault and violate [nature], exploring her to the blood and bone.'

Soffici's critique of Impressionism—even more suggestive to the groping Futurists—was printed during 1909 in *La voce* and climaxed in April 1910 by the first French Impressionist exhibition and Medardo Rosso's first one-man show in Italy. Soffici revealed again an essentially Symbolist approach, but he now invoked the radical, unorthodox authority of Jules Laforgue rather than following later and weaker Symbolist critics. Laforgue was singled out as one of the exceptional few who truly understood Impressionism and the movement's bold rejection of absolute and objective standards of beauty. Soffici underlined the poet's interpretation of Impressionism as a revolutionary effort with Laforgue's celebrated declaration of artistic independence, which must have struck a loud chord in the Futurists' anarchic spirits: 'Every man is . . . a keyboard on which the external world plays in a certain manner. My keyboard is perpetually changing and there is not another identical to mine . . . All keyboards are legitimate.'

To Soffici, as to Edmond Duranty before him, the Impressionists were 'the primitives of a new epoch'. He praised especially their transformation of the academic concept of '*disegno* . . . [into] a mystical writing . . . suitable to the transposition and translation of sentiments which objects evoke in the sensibility of the person contemplating them'. This foreshadows the Futurists' empathetic identification with the objective world. Soffici also admired the Impressionists' daring *mise en cadre* ["framing"], explaining that this resulted from the suggestion of an infinite expansion beyond the frame, the unexpected juxtaposition of objects and, above all, the interdependence of objects and surroundings. By the giving of equal importance to every constituent of the picture, the '*ambiente*' became a dominant expressive element.

This last point was again much stressed in Soffici's provocative discussion of Medardo Rosso—also of 1909—in which he elaborated upon the sculptor's own ideas. Rosso, as transcribed by Soffici, held 'that sculpture should not be condemned to produce solely beautiful forms isolated in space and enclosed by definite, static, certain lines; forms are thus almost imprisoned in a profile of immobility, shaved off from the whirling centre of universal life, remaining there stiff and still to be examined from all sides by curious spectators'. The sculptor demanded therefore that a piece of sculpture should be conceived not only as a part of the life surrounding it, but that its suggested movements should express the greater cosmic rhythms as well. 'The movements of a figure must not stop with the lines of its contour, . . . but the intensity of the play of values and the protrusions and lines of the work should impel it into space, spreading out to infinity the way an electric wave emitted by a well-constructed machine flies out to rejoin the eternal force of the universe.' It is a short step from such a concept of the union of works of art with the universal flux to Futurist dynamism as illustrated in the images of the technical manifesto, particularly since Rosso maintained that 'nothing is material in space'.

Following in the footsteps of his Impressionist masters, Rosso apparently relied on contemporary expositions of the psychology of visual perception to support his ideas. The seriousness with which he explored these leads may have been suggestive to the Milanese artists. For example, Rosso described the inconstancy of visual sensations and suggested that such changeability was indicative of 'the movements of life'. Man was considered as only one integral, but not dominant, part of the total environment and thus subject to its variability of appearance. Rosso in fact made man a dependent element: 'We are mere consequences of the objects which surround us', he once said. Hence the proud, self-sufficient, and technically free-standing isolation of the antique nude did not appeal to him any more than to his Futurist heirs and he hoped for its exclusion from the contemporary sculptural vocabulary.

Soffici's tribute to Rosso and his efforts on the artist's behalf undoubtedly inspired the Futurist painters to follow suit. Rosso was included among those Italian artists whom they defended in their first manifesto. That they knew Soffici's writings is proved by a telegram they sent to him on 19 May 1910, with congratulations on his courageous propaganda for Rosso and the Impressionists. The message shows that they had followed his activities and those of the *La voce* group for some time.

. . . . .

The Futurist painters did not have to go far afield to learn about the technical principles of Divisionism, since Milan had its own eloquent spokesman in Gaetano Previati, whose two volumes on painting had appeared in 1905 and 1906. Late in 1907 Boccioni noted in his diary that he was reading Previati and felt 'humbled in the presence of so much technical erudition . . [and wondered] how to do it . . . where, when to study all that chemistry and physics?' Previati's books must have held a place in Italian artistic circles comparable to that of Chevreul's *De la loi du contraste simultané des couleurs* in France. Because of the later date, Previati was able to include recent findings in optics and the psychology of visual perception, making his books veritable compendia of opinion on the subject.

Previati's writings contain valuable sources for the ideas incorporated by the Futurist painters into the technical manifesto. The first chapter in *I principii scientifici del divisionismo* is especially rich in influential passages. There Previati dealt with 'Visione oculare e visione soggetiva', including short discussions of some of the general and individually variable determinants of the appearance of the object, such as binocular vision, geometrical illusions, irradiation, astigmatism, diplopia, and so on. Although he stressed the importance of these researches for the artist, Previati, like the Futurists, insisted that the 'subjective sensations . . . open the doors of art'. But Previati, unlike his French compeer Seurat, did not in his writings examine the psychic effects of the artist's formal uses of colour, line and shape. Yet abundant literature on this subject was available to the Futurists. While Seurat relied in part on Charles Henry's theories of *dynamogénie* in his attempt to enhance the emotional expressiveness of his work, the Futurists must have known of the related concept of empathy possibly through Croce's discussion of Lipps' researches, or through Berenson's notion of tactile values, or even through Bergson's *Essai sur les données immédiates de la conscience.*

. . . . .

The impassioned Futurists were not satisfied by the relative restraint with which their older mentors employed and advocated expressionist principles. They wanted their works of art to be such forceful vehicles of emotions and sensations that the spectator would be completely absorbed by them. In spite of important dissimilarities, Matisse's dream of 'an art . . . like a good armchair' has therefore certain characteristics in common with the highly evocative creations envisaged by the Futurists. The artists' translation of Marinetti's precepts into painterly terminology retains the exaggeratedly Fauve spirit of his First Manifesto and suggests some knowledge of Fauve painting. 'Our pictorial sensations can no longer be whispered. We shall make them sing and shout on our canvases which will blare forth [with] deafening and triumphant fanfares', said the painters, pointing out

> that beneath our skin brown does not course, but . . . yellow sparkles, red blazes, and . . . green, blue and violet dance voluptuously and caressingly there . . . The pallor of a woman's face who is looking at a jeweller's shop window is more iridescent than all the prisms of the jewels which bewitch her . . . Your eyes accustomed to dimness will be opened to the most radiant visions of light. The shadows which we shall paint will be more luminous than the highlights of our predecessors; and our pictures, compared to those stored in museums, will be as a refulgent day to a gloomy night.

Boccioni later confirmed that their theory presumed a Fauve approach and that their technical manifesto was a 'synthesized Impressionism made more violent, the only possible neo- and post-Impressionism for us who were in a hurry; a kind of theoretical *Matisse* which was hastily to prepare our plastic consciousness [and] our pictorial evolution'.

In their attempt to transpose Futurist dynamism into a workable pictorial theory, the painters not only drew near Fauvism but posited a vision of objects and space which approached the 'Cubist' mode of depicting a state of flux. Some of Picasso's and Braque's tangential followers—Gleizes, Metzinger, Léger, Delaunay, and others—eagerly received the technical manifesto when it appeared in Paris, because its explicit statements bolstered their own still uncertain efforts which derived in part from similar social and philosophical convictions. It is more difficult to say whether Futurist theory had at this time any effect on Picasso and Braque themselves. Their development followed a very isolated course in these early years.

There is no indication that the Milanese painters were familiar with any Cubist work or statement about it before the summer of 1911. But because the Futurists' precepts were part of the general European intellectual climate, Boccioni's claim made in the preface to their Parisian exhibition catalogue seems generally justified: 'Our experiments and our achievements have followed a different route, but one in some ways parallel to that followed by the Post-Impressionists, Synthetists and Cubists in France, guided by their masters Picasso, Braque, Derain, Metzinger, LeFauconnier, Gleizes, Léger, Lhote, etc.' Their work itself further corroborates this statement and helps to explain why the Futurists were able to make such amazingly rapid and imaginative use of the formal vocabulary of Cubism. (pp. 50-60)

> *Marianne W. Martin, in her* Futurist Art and Theory: 1909-1915, *1968. Reprint by Hacker Art Books, 1978, 336 p.*

FUTURIST MUSIC

Rodney J. Payton

[In the following excerpt, Payton assesses the Futurist contribution to twentieth-century music.]

[The Italian Futurist movement] was originally a literary group, and its poetic and dramatic experiments foreshadowed much that is fashionable today in literature. Even less known is the musical side of the movement, yet the Futurists were just as daring in music as they were in the visual arts and literature. During the years 1911-12 the two Futurist musicians, Francesco Balilla Pratella and Luigi Russolo, published their radical manifestos, gave many concerts, and invented a number of new instruments that are spiritual ancestors to the very latest synthesizers. Today Pratella and Russolo are largely forgotten; a few journal articles, an occasional passing reference, is all they have received from scholarship. They deserve better. In their own time their experiments were no less an affront to contemporary sensibility than *Le sacre du printemps,* and until their efforts are recognized and evaluated we cannot say we have an adequate picture of the early twentieth century or understand how deep are the roots of some of our contemporary artistic expression.

William W. Austin, in *Music in the Twentieth Century,* makes a comment which reflects the general state of scholarship as it relates to Futurist music:

> The art of noises, now called "bruitisme," was introduced by Marinetti into the group of painters and poets that rallied in 1916 with the slogan "Dada" whence its fame reëchoed in histories and dictionaries. No composers were directly associated with Dada. The terms "futurism" and "Dadaism" have been loosely applied to composers as staid as Richard Strauss. They are seldom illuminating in talk about music.

Now, Futurism and Dadaism were actually separate things. Dadaism did indeed originate in 1916, in Switzerland, and Futurism dates from 1909 in Italy, where Marinetti was its founder. But in 1916 the Futurist leader, an ardent patriot who was then an officer in the Italian army, had other concerns than the international group of war resisters who called themselves "dada." As for the term *Futurism,* it may seem to lack usefulness because, rather than being used to refer to the efforts of the musicians of the Italian movement, Pratella and Russolo, it has, as Mr.

Austin reports, often been used as a catch-all term for almost any avant-garde effort. (pp. 25-6)

One possible reason why the title *Futurist* should have escaped the Italian group, in the field of music at least, is that Pratella's and Russolo's primarily nationalistic concerns had kept the two from being generally recognized by an international public. But how had composers themselves reacted to the Futurist stimulus? The trail begins with the publication of Busoni's essay "Futurism in Music" in *Pan* of September, 1912. Busoni quotes Pratella's 1912 musical manifesto and reacts favorably to it: "That is right. It pleases me, and I stood on this side long ago, if only as a theorist." He concludes by wondering if the Futurists have the talent for the task. Due to the resistance of conservative circles to the radical fringe, this article created some resentment. In 1917 the Austrian Hans Pfitzner published his *Futuristengefahr*, which accused Busoni of *being* a Futurist. Busoni was moved to defend himself.

Other composers were at least aware of the Futurists, and some have left their comments and opinions. One of these, Igor Stravinsky, who heard the music of Russolo and Pratella in 1915, recalled the encounter some forty years later [see Further Reading]:

> On one of my Milanese visits Marinetti and Russolo, a genial quiet man but with wild hair and beard, and Pratella, another noisemaker, put me through a demonstration of their "futurist music." Five phonographs standing on five tables in a large and otherwise empty room emitted digestive noises, static, etc., remarkably like the *musique concrete* of seven or eight years ago (so perhaps they were futurists after all; or perhaps futurisms aren't progressive enough). I pretended to be enthusiastic and told them that sets of five phonographs with such music, mass produced, would surely sell like Steinway Grand Pianos.
>
> (pp. 27-8)

Thus musical Futurism knew, and was known by, composers from all of Europe. In general, its history followed the lines of development of Futurism itself, thanks to the magnificent organizing abilities of the *caposcuola* ["movement's founder"] Filippo Tommaso Marinetti (1876-1944). Officially, Futurist music celebrated the new urban environment with its speed, noises, and machines. The actual course of musical Futurism can be charted by studying its two composers' different responses to this idea. Luigi Russolo (1885-1947) was a true believer in this aesthetic. Francesco Balilla Pratella (1880-1955), on the other hand, while subordinating himself for a time to these ideals, retained his own original personality and lived out an artistic history which goes beyond that of Futurism. Born at Lugo di Romagna, Pratella remained an enthusiastic proponent of Romagnese culture all his life—notwithstanding his Futurist period. By 1909, when Pratella was twenty-nine, he had written two operas on traditional Romagnese themes, *Lilia* and *La sina d'vargöun*, both of which won prizes in competitions and were produced. *La sina*, in particular, attained some critical notice,

and it was the work which attracted Marinetti's attention. (p. 30)

Pratella met Marinetti on August 20, 1910, at Imola during a concert in which some of Pratella's music was played. By that time, of course, *Il primo manifesto del futurismo*, *Il manifesto della pittura futurista*, and *Il manifesto technico della pittura futurista* had already been published, and to judge from the tone of these documents, all inspired by Marinetti, the subject of the opera certainly would not have been attractive to the Futurists. (In fact there is one conclusion of the *Manifesto technico* which would seem to label *La sina's* plot as definitely *passatista*: "Against the nude in painting, as nauseous and as tedious as adultery in literature.") However, Pratella's reforming zeal made him attractive to the Futurists and the Futurists attractive to him. In his memoirs Pratella says: "The condition of my art at that time and my particular state of mind, so to say, predisposed my spirit to abandon itself to the persuasive fascination of promises and salutary liberation which the ideas and practical actions of the Marinetti group emitted." The actual introduction of Marinetti and Pratella was accomplished by Luigi Donati, a journalist of Oriani, who knew both Marinetti and Pratella, the latter because of the success of *La sina*. The conversation was evidently amiable. Pratella records in his memoirs: "From then on we were faithful friends, and so we have remained. We reciprocally tolerate one another, notwithstanding the changed times and events and the evolution of ideas and principles." (p. 31)

Il manifesto dei musicisti futuristi was quickly followed by *Il manifesto technico della musica futurista*, on March 11, 1911, and by *La distruzione della quadratura* on July 18, 1912. These three works form the backbone of Futurist musical polemic and have very much the flavor of the other Futurist manifestos, in particular those signed by the painters connected with the movement. This unanimity is probably due to the iron editorial fist of Marinetti, who maintained considerable control over the polemics of the movement.

The three manifestos form the basis of a complete musical aesthetic program. *Il manifesto dei musicisti futuristi* is a dramatically written attack on the *passato* of contemporary Italian composers and their tendency to perpetuate the musical forms of the past rather than attempt what is new and truly creative. *Il manifesto technico* places the blame for Italy's unprogressive attitudes on conservatories and teachers who inhibit experimentation for their own benefit and explains that the new Futurist music will be rhythmically free and microtonal. *La distruzione della quadratura* presents Pratella's notational system designed to free music from repeated rhythmic pulses.

By the time of the publication of *La distruzione della quadratura* Pratella's theoretical program was substantially complete. What was needed now was an example of music composed to conform to the program, and Pratella was not long in providing it. *Inno alla vita, musica futurista per orchestra* was first performed in February, 1913, and again in March. Pratella tells of both occasions in his *Autobiografia*:

Russolo (left) and assistant with noise intoners.

My first true direct contact with the public, as a Futurist musician, took place at the Teatro Costanzi di Roma on two evenings, February 21 and March 9, 1913, with the first and second performances of my *Musica futurista* with the great orchestra of the Teatro Costanzi itself under my direction.

The first performance on February 21, reserved by the Mocchi firm of impressarios for season ticket holders and those who were invited, went off fairly well: applause, ironic comments, discussions in a loud voice, but nothing more, and these were reserved for the aggressive and polemic addresses of Marinetti, Boccioni, Carrà and Russolo.

At the second performance on March 9 pandemonium broke loose. . . .

The spectacle was opened by me with my *Musica futurista per orchestra,* which proceeded to the end amidst an infernal clamor, made up of whistles, applause, cries, acclamations, and invectives. The public seemed driven insane, and the frantic mass boiled and from time to time exploded in rage resembling a mass of burning lava during a volcanic eruption. Some threw upon the orchestra and also on me, the conductor, an uninterrupted shower of garbage, of fruit, of chestnut cakes; others shouted themselves hoarse crying every kind of thing; some protested not being able to hear; some became exalted, others infuriated, some laughed and enjoyed themselves, others quarreled and started rows,

with frequent blows between friends and enemies.

Finally, as if God willed the music, without which most people would not even have heard it, I turned towards the public, made a beautiful smile of thanks to friends and of mirth to enemies, and then went up to the stage where I found Marinetti, who was pronouncing in a loud voice some strange formula of exorcism to which he attributed a great mystical power like a magical mascot, and woe to anyone who contradicted him.

These performances evidently supplied the impulse which brought Luigi Russolo onto the Futurist musical scene. Russolo, flamboyant inventor of the *intonarumori* and other marvels, painter and eventual mystic, would be precisely the sort of disciple Pratella and Marinetti might have wished for. Where Pratella could promote real reform with subtle polemic, Russolo could truly *believe.* A brilliant man, he faced the world pragmatically; if a program like that described in Pratella's manifestos existed, it existed to be acted on. A little ingenuity would make it all a reality. The scope of his vision was staggering. Witness this passage from the conclusions to his manifesto "L'arte dei rumori":

> 8. Let us therefore invite young musicians of genius and audacity to listen attentively to all noises. . . . Our increased perceptivity, which has already acquired futurist eyes, will then have futurist ears. Thus the motors and machines of industrial cities may someday be intelligently

pitched, so as to make of every factory an intoxicating orchestra of noises.

(pp. 32-5)

In 1910 he joined Marinetti and the Futurist movement and with Carlo Carrà, Giacomo Balla, Umberto Boccioni, Arnoldo Bonzagni, and Romolo Romani signed the *Manifesto della pittura futurista.* Russolo's career as a Futurist painter continued until 1913, when he issued *L'arte dei rumori* and officially joined Pratella in musical Futurism. The document is in the form of an open letter:

> My Dear Balilla Pratella, Great Futuristic composer:
>
> In the crowded Costanzi Theater, in Rome, while I was listening with my futurist friends Marinetti, Boccioni, and Balla to the orchestral performance of your overwhelming MUSICA FUTURISTA, there came to my mind the idea of a new art: The Art of Noises, a logical consequence of your marvelous innovations.

Thus was the concept of *rumorismo* presented to the public, but it is important to note that while Russolo proclaims the "art of noises" to be a logical outcome of Pratella's efforts, Pratella himself does not specifically advocate any such innovation in any of his manifestos. Indeed, it is tempting to speculate that the appearance of the *L'arte dei rumori* was conceived and masterminded by the *caposcuola* himself, F. T. Marinetti. This speculation is prompted by Pratella's specific denial of any interest in "a rapport between music and machines." In addition, there exists a letter from Marinetti to Pratella which seems to indicate that the *intonarumori* were Marinetti's passion, not necessarily Pratella's.

> Work with great confidence. Do not hold back, not forgetting that all, absolutely *all extravagances are obtainable* by you. I will mention, almost insist on, the necessity of confusing everyone and always going forward. Not forgetting, moreover, your most important intention, it seems proper to me, to introduce into the orchestra of your *Aviatore Dro,* two, three, four, or five or even more of Russolo's *intonarumori.* This is of enormous importance, I think, because while Russolo prepares a complete orchestra of *intonarumori,* you absolutely must, it seems to me (in one part of your new work, perhaps best in the finale of the second act) create the first example of a mixed orchestra or, better, of a *conventional orchestra enriched with intonarumori.* Think about all this. I believe this innovation is absolutely necessary to your work, from your personal point of view as an innovator and from the point of view of Futurism. One would then be able to frankly define you as the first musician who has with his genius revolutionized the orchestra, courageously leaping the gap that separates Futurism from *passatismo* in music. You know that I see exactly, and that I am armed with great discernment.

Whatever the source of Russolo's innovations and the ideas for the applications of this theory, his own dedication to them is not subject to debate. He continued to work

on various noise instruments, occasionally giving concerts until the 1920s, when he turned to Eastern mysticism.

L'arte dei rumori, dated March 11, 1913, agrees theoretically with Pratella's manifestos in that it views the history of music in terms of a purely melodic art which only gradually evolved the idea of vertical organizations:

> The Middle Ages . . . [regarded] music from the point of view of *linear development in time.* . . . In a word, the medieval conception of music was horizontal, not vertical. An interest in the simultaneous union of difficult sounds, that is, in the chord as a complex sound, developed gradually, passing from the perfect consonance, with a few incidental dissonances, to the complex and persistent dissonances which characterize the music of today.

One of the problems faced by the composer or theorist seeking to renovate the art of music, according to Russolo, is that the circumstances surrounding the birth of music were such that a mystic character was assigned to the art:

> *Noises* being so scarce, the first *musical sounds* which man succeeded in drawing from a hollow reed or from a stretched string were a new, astonishing, miraculous discovery. By primitive peoples musical sound was ascribed to the gods, regarded as holy, and entrusted to the sole care of the priests, who made use of it to enrich their rites with mystery. Thus was born the conception of a musical sound as a thing having an independent existence, a thing different from life and unconnected with it. From this conception resulted an idea of music as a world of fantasy superimposed upon reality, a world inviolate and sacred. It will be readily understood how this idea of music must inevitably have impeded its progress, as compared with that of the other arts.

As the machine has proliferated and added noise to the environment, says Russolo, human response to sound itself has changed:

> . . . the machine today has created so many varieties of noise that pure musical sound—with its poverty and its monotony—no longer awakens any emotion in the hearer.

Russolo is careful to note that not all noises are by any means disagreeable: "I need scarcely enumerate all the small and delicate noises which are pleasing to the ear." Modern man needs more and more complex sounds, and this is a need that can be met by Futurist musicians, as Russolo states in his conclusions:

> 1. Futurist musicians must constantly broaden and enrich the field of sound. This is a need of our senses. Indeed, we note in present-day composers of genius a tendency towards the most complex dissonances. Moving further and further away from pure musical sound, they have almost reached the noise-sound. This need and this tendency can only be satisfied *by the supplementary use of noise and its substitution for musical sounds.*

In order to use the richness of noise creatively, noise must be controllable. This can be accomplished by determining the predominating pitch or pitches of a given noise:

> Every noise has a note—sometimes even a chord—that predominates in the ensemble of its irregular vibrations. Because of this characteristic note, it becomes possible to fix the pitch of a given noise, that is, to give it not a single pitch but a variety of pitches, without losing its characteristic quality—its distinguishing timbre.

That the modern ear requires more complex sounds (noises) is important, but more important is an assertion relating to the very function of music:

> Every manifestation of life is accompanied by noise. Noise is therefore familiar to our ears and has the power to remind us immediately of life itself. Musical sound, a thing extraneous to life and independent of it, . . . has become to our ears what a too familiar face is to our eyes. Noise, on the other hand, which comes to us confused and irregular as life itself, never reveals itself wholly but reserves for us innumerable surprises. We are convinced, therefore, that by selecting, coordinating and controlling noises we shall enrich mankind with a new and unsuspected source of pleasure.

However, in spite of the fact that noise reminds one forcefully of life itself, Russolo categorically moves beyond mere programmatic imitation of natural sound:

> . . . the Art of Noises must not limit itself to reproductive imitation. It will reach its greatest emotional power through the purely acoustic enjoyment which the inspiration of the artist will contrive to evoke from combinations of noises.

Russolo lists the six families of noises proper to the Futurist orchestra: booms, whistles, whispers, screams, percussive sounds, and the voices of men and animals.

Russolo must have been working on these instruments, which were to be called *intonarumori,* by the time of the manifesto's publication or immediately thereafter, since the first demonstration of a single *intonarumore* was held at the Teatro Stocchi in Modena on June 2, 1913, only three months after the publication of *L'arte dei rumori.* The instrument demonstrated was a *scoppiatore* (crackler), which, according to Russolo's "Gl'intonarumori futuristi," imitated the sound of an internal combustion engine. In his article Russolo takes the opportunity to state again the aesthetic considerations behind the art of noises in response, he says, to the lack of understanding of his program by the foreign press. He proceeds to a description of the workings of his machines:

> It was . . . necessary . . . that these instruments, *intonarumori,* be as simple as possible, and it is in precisely this that we have succeeded perfectly. It is enough to say that a single stretched diaphragm, correctly positioned, will produce by variations in tension a scale of more than ten whole tones with all the divisions of semitone, quarter tone and of even smaller fractions.
>
> . . . Varying, then, [the manufacture and] the

way of exciting the diaphragm, one obtains yet a different sound *as to type and as to timbre,* always preserving, naturally, the possibility of varying the pitch. So far we have used four different means of excitation and have already completed the relative instruments.

> The first makes the *scoppio* [explosive] sound like an automobile engine; the second makes the *crepitio* [crackling] sound like rifle fire; the third makes the *ronzio* [hum] sound like a dynamo; the fourth makes different kinds of *stropiccii* [stamping, shuffling of feet].

> In these instruments the simple movement of a graduated lever suffices to give the noise the pitch that one wants, even in the smallest fraction. Just as easily regulated is the rhythm of every single noise, making it easy to calculate the beat, be it equal or unequal. . . .

> Research is already complete to obtain noises (always, understand, tunable)—of the first series listed in the *Manifesto,* the *rombi* [rumbles], the *tuoni* [thunderers,] and the *scrosci* [crushers]; of the second series, the *sibili* [whistlers]; of the third, the *gorgoglii* [gurglers]; of the fourth, the *stridoni* [screamers], and the *fruscii* [rustlers]. For these noises the instruments are already being built: *rombatore, tuonatore, scrosciatore, gorgogliatore.*

Russolo concludes the article by emphasizing again that the music of the *intonarumori* is not to be merely imitative.

During the period between the printing of "Gl'intonarumori futuristi" and the first concert given at Teatro del Verme in Milan on April 21, 1914, Russolo published two more theoretical articles in *Lacerba.* The first of these, "Conquista totale dell'enarmonismo mediante gl'intonarumori futuristi," seconds Pratella's assertion, in *Il manifesto technico,* that "*enarmonia* gives us the possibility of rendering the natural and instinctive intonations and modulations of enharmonic intervals presently impossible, given the artificiality of a tempered scale which we wish to overcome." Russolo believes not only that, when the sounds of nature change pitch, they invariably do so by "enharmonic gradation" but that the world of machines is no different:

> Equally, if we pass from natural sounds into the infinitely richer world of the sounds of machines, we again find that all the sounds produced by rotary motion are in their crescendo or diminuendo constantly enharmonic . . . examples: the dynamo and the electric motor.

Furthermore, the human ear is quite capable of hearing these microintervals, even those as small as one eighth of a tone. Since these sounds exist and are natural, and since they are easily perceptible to the ear, it behooves Futurism to enlarge the field of music with them "as it has enlarged the field of painting with *dinamismo,* poetry with *immaginazione senza fili* and free words, music with *antigrazioso* and the abolition of any rhythmic system." The *intonarumori* are the means by which Futurism will accomplish the task:

> In fact, in the construction of the *intonarumori*

we have attempted not only the possibility of changing the sound-noise by whole and half steps but also by any gradation between one tone and another.

We have succeeded perfectly in obtaining any fraction, however small, of pitch.

Enarmonismo is today, thanks to the *intonarumori,* a musical reality.

Russolo's second article in *Lacerba,* which appeared on March 1, 1914, is entitled "Grafia enarmonica per gl'intonarumori futuristi." It includes an example from *Rete di rumori, Risveglio di una città,* and this seven-measure excerpt is the only available specimen of Russolo's own work for *intonarumori.* In spite of Russolo's seeming determination to embrace all of Pratella's polemic program, the excerpt does not include any rhythmic innovations derived from Pratella. It is somewhat surprising that there is only one instance of a quarter tone in the excerpt.

Russolo's concert in Milan at the Teatro del Verme was given on April 21, 1914. In *L'intransigeant* of Paris, Marinetti wrote an account of the occasion. He reports on how the Futurists responded to the large number of unruly *passéistes* among the audience.

> For an hour, the Futurists offered passive resistance. But an extraordinary thing happened just at the start of *Network of Noise No. 4:* five Futurists—Boccioni, Carrà, Amando Mazza, Piatti and myself—descended from the stage, crossed the orchestra pit, and, right in the center of the hall, using their fists and canes, attacked the "passéistes," who appeared to be stultified and intoxicated with reactionary rage. The battle lasted fully half an hour. During all this time Luigi Russolo continued to conduct imperturbably the nineteen bruiteurs on the stage. It was a display of an amazing harmonic arrangement of bloody faces and infernal mêlée. . . . The performing artists were suddenly divided into two groups: one group continued to play, while the other went down into the hall to combat the hostile and rioting audience. It is thus that an escort in the desert protects the caravan against the Touaregs. It is thus that the infantry sharpshooters provide cover for the construction of a military pontoon. Our skill in boxing and our fighting spirit enables us to emerge from the skirmish with but a few bruises. But the "passéistes" suffered eleven wounded, who had to be taken to a first-aid station for treatment.

In the May 15, 1914, issue of *Lacerba* there appeared a short article, "Gl'intonarumori nell'orchestra," and a short composition for *intonarumori* and orchestra, *Gioia saggio di orchestra mista,* both by Pratella. The piece is printed in a piano score plus parts for *scoppiatori* ["cracklers"] and *ronzatori* ["buzzers"]. In the article Pratello acknowledges his debt to Russolo. He ends his remarks by speaking of the role of the *intonarumori:*

> As one can easily see, the *intonarumori* in practice lose any sense of objective reality; they move from an objective reality, to stand aloof from it immediately, coming to form a new abstract re-

ality—the *abstract expressive* element of a state of mind. Their timbre does not join itself to the other *sound elements* as heterogeneous material, but joins as a new *sound element, emotional* and essentially *musical.*

One has the feeling that the *Saggio* might be the direct result of Marinetti's urgings, but, be that as it may, the two forces in Futurist music were now officially unified, even though no compositions were ever produced by the two musicians in collaboration and even though Pratella was to use the *intonarumori* for little more than sound effects in his opera *L'Aviatore Dro,* which was performed only in 1920.

The third concert of Russolo's *intonarumori* took place in the Politeama theater in Genoa on May 20, 1914. It was evidently held in a more genial atmosphere. Maria Russolo, the widow of the master, quotes him:

> At the Politeama of Genoa, the evening of May 20, 1914, followed a performance with the same orchestra. The conduct of the Genoese public was not as unreasonable and indecorous as that of Milan. . . . The Genoese had the rare good sense *to want to hear.* They did not lack troublemakers, but the majority made them keep silent. Thus the Genoese public could get a general idea of that which is my orchestra.

The chance to hear Futurist music was afforded London audiences on June 15, 1914, at the London Coliseum, where Russolo and his *intonarumori* were presented. This took place during the time when the Futurist painters were on exhibition at London's Dore Gallery. Little information is available about the concert, since it does not seem to have had the same impact on British cultural life as Futurist polemic implied. The review of the concert in the London *Times* is indulgent, but hardly laudatory:

> . . . the curtain rose upon an orchestra of weird funnel-shaped instruments directed by Signor Luigi Russolo.

> It is impossible to say that the first of the "noise-spirals" performed "The Awakening of a Great City," was as exhilarating as Futurist art usually is; on the contrary, it rather resembled the sounds heard in the rigging of a Channel-steamer during a bad crossing, and it was, perhaps, unwise of the players—or should we call them the "noisicians?"—to proceed with their second piece, "A Meeting of Motor-cars and Aeroplanes," after the pathetic cries of "No more!" which greeted them from all the excited quarters of the auditorium.

These six occasions, Pratella's two concerts in February and March of 1913, and Russolo's four concerts on June 2, 1913, April 21 and May 20, 1914, and the Coliseum concert (or, possibly, concerts) in June of 1914 constitute the Futurists' chief musical exposure in the years before the war. It is hoped that with a knowledge of this record and on the basis of the documentary evidence scholars will recognize that musical Futurism, in combination with the other artistic aspects of the movement, forms an important and fertile part of the cultural history of the twentieth century. It seems particularly significant that the Futurists were the first group to be aware of the possibilities of a larger technological aesthetic. Long before *musique concrète* the Futurists were attempting to enlarge the vocabulary of sounds available to the composer; long before the Surrealists they demonstrated how categorical might be the imperative of *épater les bourgeoisie* ["shock the bourgeoisie"] in achieving an artistic objective. Before the Fascists they showed how to use art as propaganda, and before almost anyone they practiced an art of violence demonstrating the use of art as a weapon against the past, against the present, in short, violence as art and art as violence. However unhappily, this motive has had its way not only in music, painting, and the other arts but also in the world of political action. (pp. 36-45)

Rodney J. Payton, "The Music of Futurism: Concerts and Polemics," in The Musical Quarterly, *Vol. LXII, No. 1, January, 1976, pp. 25-45.*

FUTURIST ARCHITECTURE

Reyner Banham

[*Banham was an English critic and educator who wrote extensively on modern architecture and was particularly interested in the interrelationship of art and technology. In the following excerpt, he discusses the chief proponent of Futurist architecture, Antonio Sant'Elia, and evaluates the significance of his drawings and design concepts.*]

The application of the term 'Futurist' to the opinions and designs of Antonio Sant'Elia has been contested with legalistic enthusiasm by Italian scholars since 1955, but only on biographical grounds, not in terms of the ideas involved. The biographical facts are not in doubt and may be briefly stated. Sant'Elia was born in Como in 1888, and was thus a little younger than the masters of the Twenties. His studies, first in Milan, and later at the University of Bologna, were interrupted by a period of apprenticeship to the Villoresi Canal Company, and of service in the works department of the commune of Milan. On his return from Bologna to Milan in 1912 he set up as an architect, but most of his time seems to have been taken up in work for other offices, and no buildings designed under his own name appear to survive with any certainty.

[Alberto Sartoris in *L'architetto Antonio Sant'Elia*] has stated that Sant'Elia was in touch with the Futurists from the time of his return, and this has not been questioned in the recent polemics. In 1912, 1913 and 1914 he made a number (possibly several hundred) of imaginative drawings of buildings and town-planning ideas, and a group of these under the title of the *Città nuova* were shown at an exhibition of the group *Nuove Tendenze* in May 1914. In the catalogue of this exhibition there appeared, over Sant'Elia's name, a *Messaggio* on the problems of Modern architecture: and a reworked version of this *Messaggio* ap-

peared on the canonical eleventh day of July 1914, as the Manifesto of Futurist architecture, still over the name of Sant'Elia, and without other signatories. After the outbreak of War, Sant'Elia, like Marinetti and Boccioni volunteered for the Army, even before Italy entered the fighting. Eventually he died a hero's death in the battle of Monfalcone in October 1916, two months after Boccioni. His name and reputation were nurtured with unusual care by Marinetti, who, for instance, brought his work to the attention of the Dutch *de Stijl* group in 1917, but it is this Marinettian connection that seems to have provoked the recent attempts to diminish the importance, even to deny the existence, of Sant'Elia's Futurist affiliations.

The argument hinges upon the differences between the texts of the *Messaggio* and the Manifesto. Neither now appears to have been actually written by Sant'Elia himself, even the *Messaggio* having been worked up, apparently, by Ugo Nebbia from ideas expounded to him by the architect 'alle quali perfettamente aderivo'. If Nebbia's word is to be trusted—and even the anti-Marinettians appear to trust it—then a scrutiny of the text of the *Messaggio* should not only give a fair view of the ideas that were indisputably Sant'Elia's own, but also make it possible to evaluate their relationship to Futurism, without any suspicion of Marinetti's interference, such as exists with the Manifesto. . . . By any standard of historical judgement [the *Messaggio*] would be a remarkable document to have been produced early in 1914, because it puts together the predisposing causes and the newly emergent ideas of the pre-War epoch in a manner which did not become general until the War was over, and—more important—it takes up attitudes to those predisposing causes according to those new ideas. Thus, the second paragraph rejects the architecture of the past, the third takes a view of the past that Choisy could have approved (and probably inspired), the fourth explains why the past must be rejected, and the fifth explains that rejection further in terms of concepts that derive mostly from nineteenth-century Rationalist sources, or from the moralising tradition of England. This kind of revaluation of older bodies of ideas, accepting much of what they had to say as true, but recasting them in new frames of reference that often completely altered their meaning, was to become the common ground of mainstream ideas in the Twenties—for instance, the reworking of Guadet's idea of elementary composition in terms of asymmetrical planning, or the use of Choisy's own insistence on the importance of technique to make nonsense of his proposition that the technical aids available to modern architects were those of the Gothic or even the prehistoric world.

But Sant'Elia does more than this. He anticipates, in the second of his affirmations, the anti-Functionalist mood of Le Corbusier and Gropius in the Twenties, and in taking up Berlage's view on the impropriety of adding decoration to structure, he moves forward to a position abreast of that adopted by Adolf Loos in *Ornament und Verbrechen*. That he knew Loos's work is entirely possible, but the possibility at once raises the problem of the connection with Futurism. There is a distinct streak of Viennese late Art Nouveau about some of Sant'Elia's earliest surviving designs, such as the project for the cemetery at Monza, of

1912, executed in collaboration with Italo Paternostro. But well before the compilation of the *Messaggio* this quality had disappeared, replaced by a bold glyptic starkness, more extreme than that of any of his contemporaries, even Poelzig, and far beyond anything being done in Vienna by anyone except possibly Loos himself. But there are no stylistic resemblances to Loos at all, and the indications are that by the time Sant'Elia evolved this undecorated style of his own, he was out of direct touch with Vienna—if he had ever been in touch at all.

On the other hand, Marinetti and the Futurists provided a direct line of contact with Paris, where Georges Besson's translation of *Ornament und Verbrechen* had appeared in 1913, and with *Der Sturm* which had reprinted the essay in 1912. If it is maintained that Sant'Elia was not a Futurist at the time the *Messaggio* was composed, these two links with Loos are, presumably impossible. However, in spite of the fact that the words *Futurist* and *Futurism* do not appear in the *Messaggio,* it is difficult to construe it as anything but a work Futurist in spirit, form and inspiration. The Futurist spirit is manifest in its rejection of the past, of Monumentality and Classicism, its insistence on the revolutionary changes in cultural life wrought by science and technique. It is Futurist too in the vehemence of its opinions, and in its form, complete with positive and negative propositions at its end. Above all it contains numerous ideas, echoes and partial quotations from existing Futurist publications.

Thus, the 'new ideal of beauty' connects it with the Foundation Manifesto of Futurism, the 'masses' it fascinated connect it with those 'men of the people' to whom Marinetti attributed the gift of mechanical prophecy in *Le futurisme*. The proposed new materials to replace wood, stone and brick are directly comparable to the new materials (in some cases they are identical) proposed by Boccioni to replace marble and bronze in the Manifesto on sculpture, the insistence on dynamism is endemic in Futurist writing, while in the final affirmation the contrast between the inspiration of the ancients and the inspiration proper to a Modernist is simply a reworking of Boccioni's pronouncements on the same subjects, though with the curious and significant modification of 'world of religion that weighed upon their souls' to 'elements of the natural world'—where Boccioni saw the church as the inspiration of the great art of the past, Sant'Elia presumably saw tree-trunks as the inspiration of Doric, branches as the inspiration of Gothic, and foliage as the inspiration of most of the ornament known to ancient architecture.

Even so, the sentiment remains Futurist, and the document as a whole stands too close to Futurism in every respect to be capable of consideration under any other heading. Furthermore, the most elaborate of Sant'Elia's sketches of 1913 and 1914 underline the Futurist quality of his inspiration at the time. In order of increasing complexity, rather than chronology, these sketches begin with simple and almost abstract exercises in architectonic form, tall structures titled *Dinamismo architettonico* and occasionally given the functional justification of lighthouses. Their shapes are bare and smooth, rectangular or semicircular in plan, often battered back in section to give a tapering silhouette, their vertical emphasis uninterrupted by string-courses or cornices, but reinforced by boldly marked vertical arrises. Though nothing designed by him in this idiom was ever built, the monument to the War-dead (and to Sant'Elia himself) in Como was worked up from drawings of this type by Enrico Prampolini and Giuseppe Terragni, and—allowing for the fact that Sant'Elia himself could never, presumably, have designed a monument—gives a fair idea of the plastic qualities he intended in these sketches.

The next order of complexity in his designs is represented by single buildings for relatively uncomplicated functions. These include all the types of buildings that Marinetti had indicated in *Le futurisme:* villas open to the breeze and the horizon (and one of them visibly influenced by Wright), large apartment houses (though the best-known designs for blocks of flats from Sant'Elia's circle were by the Swiss, Mario Chiattone), great meeting halls (sometimes labelled theatres) and others, such as airship hangars, bridges, factories, and power-stations. In most of these projects, all of them presented in perspectives and very few indeed in plan, the emphasis is on the same elements as appear in the simpler sketches—battered walls, canted buttresses, square podia or basements, and strong semicircular projections, either as apses, or in ranks along the side of the building, the buttresses too being used repetitively in this way. The most striking of all these designs are those for power-stations, which embrace the most grandiose vertical rhetoric in some, an unassuming simplicity in others, and in one, the geometrical rigour of the forms and their mode of grouping is such that only the date 1913 under Sant'Elia's signature and a slight Art Nouveau border would give one to suppose that it had not been done in the late Twenties or even the Thirties.

The most complex of all his sketches are the fragments of town-planning schemes which were put into fairly precise draughtsmanship, as against his usual free-hand style, for exhibition in May 1914. The original inspiration of these projects would appear to have been the proposal to rebuild Milan Central Station, first mooted in 1906, which involved moving it back to its present site, thus creating (*a*) the broad avenue of the present Viale Vittor Pisani and (*b*) the need for a traffic underpass beneath the tracks, such as now exists. The earliest of his Central Station projects exhibit both of these features, with the manifestly Futurist addition that the Viale is shown decked over to provide a landing strip for aircraft between its two ranks of skyscrapers—a suicidal project which reappears along with a good deal more of Sant'Elia, in Le Corbusier.

But this particular design is conceived in loosely modelled curved masses, unlike the precise forms of the projects of late 1913, and equally unlike the neatly-detailed, sharp-arrised forms of the Central Station as it appeared re-drawn in 1914. These carefully rendered presentation drawings, are united both in style of draughtsmanship, and the style of the buildings they represent, with the rest of the *Città nuova* series that were exhibited with them, and Sant'Elia's version of Milan in the year 2,000, though fragmentary, is held together by a basic unity of style, and—even more important—a basic unity of vision.

LA CITTÀ FUTURISTA. — Casamento, con ascensori esterni, galleria, passaggio coperto, su 3 piani stradali (linea tramviaria, strada per automobili, passerella metallica) fari e telegrafia senza fili.

Architectural drawing by Sant'Elia for his 1914 collection Città nuova.

Sant'Elia sees his city as based in a complex network of transport services, in some drawings as much as seven levels deep, much as he had proposed in his observations on streets in the Manifesto. Out of this three-dimensional grid of communications rise the buildings, usually *a gradinate,* that is, with the floors stepped back one behind the other towards the top. The floors are of equal, or even increasing depth from back to front, however, and the overhangs at the back are taken up by the rising curve of a parabolic arch whose other half supports the back of the building's twin, which is backed up against it, leaving a tunnel for transport and services between them. The lift-shafts are on the façades, and, rising vertically, stand well clear of the upper floors, to which they are connected by bridges of ever-increasing length as one goes up. This device, which fulfils, again, a proposition in the *Messaggio,* was probably suggested to him by the lifts on the shores of Lake Como rising from landing stages, and connected back to points on the mountainside by bridges.

He appears to have envisaged his city as consisting of knots of building of this type, connected by the network of multi-level circulation at their feet. The resemblance to Boccioni's 'field' concept of space, with bodies connected by geometrical fields of force is very striking, as is the reappearance of purely superficial Boccionisms like the illuminated advertising that appears on the roof of some of these projects. Yet in this minor device of designing the advertising as part of the building, he was a pioneer of later developments, as much as he was in his fully three-

dimensional view of town-planning problems. On both counts, the comparison with Tony Garnier is instructive. Garnier has skyline advertising over the principal hotel of his *Cité industrielle* but it looks like an afterthought attached to a broadly Classical design, even though he was probably the first architect to recognise that such advertising had its place. Similarly, in spite of the fact that he was also the first architect to recognise that the planning of industrial towns had its special problems, his conclusions, though published later than Sant'Elia's, are less radical, less well integrated, and were to prove less influential, even though lip-service was often paid to them.

After 1918 it was to be the Sant'Elian concept of the multi-level tower city that held sway in men's imaginations, and the wide distribution of his ideas on the subject seems to have been almost entirely due to the energetic promotion of Sant'Elia's memory by Marinetti. It is fair to say that his reputation is largely of Marinetti's making, outside Italy at least, not only because Marinetti circulated his work to groups like *de Stijl* and *Der Sturm,* but also because some of the most widely admired opinions associated with his name are only to be found in the disputed Manifesto, not in the *Messaggio,* which hardly anyone outside Italy ever saw.

It is generally agreed that the Manifesto is largely Marinetti's responsibility, but there is still some confusion about how much he actually wrote. The differences between the two texts are of two kinds. Firstly, alterations, which consist mostly of inserting the words Futurist or Futurism on the slightest pretext, and leaving the *Messaggio* otherwise almost untouched, and secondly, the addition of new paragraphs at the head of the text, and among the propositions at the end. The authorship of the four new paragraphs at the head is obscure; they do not read like Marinetti, and Sant'Elia's reported objections to the text of the Manifesto were to the additions at the end, not those at the beginning. They do not, in fact, add much to the argument, and their flavour can be adequately typified by the first

> Since the eighteenth century there has been no architecture at all. A bewildering mix-up of the most varied elements of style, employed in masking the skeletons of Modern buildings is called Modern architecture. The new beauty of steel and concrete is being profaned by the superimposition of carnival-style decorative incrustations justified neither by antiquity of the constructional methods nor by our own tastes, drawing their sources from ancient Egypt, India and Byzantium . . .

and so forth, mostly a rhetorical expansion of the sentiments of the body of the *Messaggio,* with even stronger echoes of Loos.

However, the additions at the end are more to the point, the first of them now reading, after 'I combat and despise'

> All *avant-garde* pseudo-architecture from Austria, Hungary, Germany and America

which is simply Marinettian politics and makes his hand very clear in this last part. The next three negative propositions are virtually unchanged, the fifth has been dropped. The first two positive propositions are unchanged apart from the insertion of *Futurist* instead of *new:* the third proposition has been dismissed to fourth to make way for a new one reading

> That oblique and elliptical lines are dynamic by their very nature, have an emotive power a thousand times greater than that of horizontals and verticals, and there can be no dynamically integrated architecture without them.

It is difficult to see how Sant'Elia could have disagreed with this since it is a logical extension of his own disapproval of cubic forms, etc. He had no need to disapprove of the next two since they were his own unaltered, except for the usual insertion of the word *Futurist* for *new*, but he might conceivably have objected to the last three, all added, though his status as a pioneer and prophet of the Twenties would be slightly diminished thereby, since these, apart from the patent 'advertisement' in the last paragraph, contain the most forward-looking ideas to which his name has ever been attached, viz.

> That architecture as the art of disposing the forms of a building according to pre-established laws is finished.

> That architecture must be understood as the power freely and boldly to harmonise environment and man, that is, to render the world of things a projection of the world of the spirit.

> That from an architecture so conceived no stock answers, plastic or linear, could arise, because the fundamental characteristics of Futurist architecture will be expendability and transience. Our houses will last less time than we do, and every generation will have to make its own. This constant renewal of the architectonic environment will contribute to the victory of Futurism, already asserting itself through *les mots en liberté*, plastic dynamism, music without bars, the art of noise, through all of which we fight without quarter against *passéist* cowardice.

Since the idea that every generation must make its own house is by far the best known to which Sant'Elia's name attaches, it appears that his international reputation is indeed of Marinetti's making.

Whether or not he was a Futurist, the possibility of a Futurist architecture perished with Sant'Elia in 1916 just as the development of Futurist painting expired, for certain, with the death of Boccioni in the same year. The most interesting sketches made by Mario Chiattone, Sant'Elia's fellow architect in the *Nuove Tendenze* group, all seem to have been made before the middle of the War, in spite of the fact that he lived until 1957. After 1918, Virgilio Marchi, one of the 'Bar Bragaglia' circle of Roman Futurists converted some Roman remains in the Via Avignonesi into the aforementioned Bar, and an experimental theatre a piece of restoration that shows how far Marchi had receded from the position adopted by Sant'Elia, even while paying lip-service to his name. The recession is underscored by the merely modish style of this work, and further underlined by the text and illustrations of a small

book on *Architettura futurista* that Marchi published about this time. The sketches have some affinities with the work of such Berlin Expressionists as Otto Bartning, but without his structural sense, and achieve their nadir in a project for the 'adaptation of an existing structure to Futurism'—a piece of applied decoration that would have appalled Sant'Elia, spread over a raw concrete skeleton that he would have admired.

But Marchi's inanities are only typical of the downfall of the movement as a whole. Robbed of its most active and substantial members by deaths and resignations, robbed of relevance by a world that had been rendered forcibly Futurist by the War, robbed of independence of manoeuvre by too close an involvement with the Fascist revolution, it had become an object of ridicule. Only Marinetti and Balla survived of the old brigade, the ten years they had given themselves to achieve their aims having expired in 1919. Yet they had, in fact, achieved most of their aims. The bulk of their irredentist claims had been satisfied, barring Trieste; parliamentary government had been ridiculed and overthrown; the comic-opera politics and backstage barbarities of the Fascist régime were, so to speak, part of the original specification for a virile and bellicose Italy. Though the official eyes of that Italy were fixed too often on the Roman past, rather than the Milanese future, the Futurists' small place in the hierarchy did help to make progressive architecture possible, and even produce some patronage for it, in the Twenties and Thirties— Terragni's work in and around Como being to some extent a conscious assumption of the mantle of Sant'Elia, but couched in the established idiom of the International Style that had been created in other countries.

Yet it was in those other countries that the Futurists had most fully achieved their aims. As Marinetti sank deeper into political buffoonery, the ideas that he and his circle had propagated before 1914 became more and more part of the inalienable common ground of mainstream developments in Modern architecture. . . . (pp. 127-36)

> *Reyner Banham, "Sant'Elia and Futurist Architecture," in his* Theory and Design in the First Machine Age, *Frederick A. Praeger, Publishers, 1960, pp. 127-37.*

FUTURISM AND POLITICS

Judy Davies

[*In the following excerpt, Davies expounds on the politics of Italian Futurism, focusing on the movement's relationship to Benito Mussolini and the early development of Fascism in Italy.*]

On the Fascist electoral list of November 1919 [in Italy] the name of Filippo Tommaso Marinetti appears after that of Benito Mussolini. From the distant vantage-point of today it looks as though the avant-garde group that prided itself on the notorious slogan, 'war—only hygiene of the world', had found a fitting outlet for its energies under the banner of a man who would take Italy into twenty years of right-wing dictatorship. The reality of the situation was a good deal more complex.

The first complexity involves Mussolini's early political career. For he began as a Marxist and came to occupy a prominent position within the Italian Socialist Party. Towards the end of 1914 Mussolini was ousted from the editorship of the socialist paper *Avanti!* and expelled from the Party, having gradually come to favour intervention on the *entente* side in the First World War. His concept of a 'revolutionary' war, capable of politicising the masses and preparing the way for fundamental changes in social organisation, was incompatible with the orthodox internationalist position of Socialist colleagues; but it was nonetheless still a notion fuelled by leftist ideology. Peculiarities of national history made the Italy of the new century a fertile terrain for 'aberrant' left-wing theorising; and in fact the early Fascism which evolved in Milan retained a left-wing character.

Here we encounter further difficulties. Futurism's insistence on Italian supremacy and its cult of youth and energy would lead one to assume that Marinetti and his friends were anything but responsive to the Left. Yet Lenin himself saw in the founder of Futurism a real power for revolution; and Gramsci, writing to Trotsky, expresses his approval, though admittedly he is referring to the cultural impact of the Movement in pre-war days. But the supreme and awkward fact remains: Marinetti chose to part company with Fascism in May 1920. In later years, when the sphere of his activities had become more exclusively artistic, he repaired the damage, insisting that Futurism expressed the 'dynamic' spirit of Fascism. Yet following the 1920 Congress Marinetti remained aloof from the Fascists for some three years, just when the political movement was unequivocally emerging as Fascist in nature as well as name. Though Futurism wished to see society 'deregulated' and individual creativity released, its radicalism was so thoroughly interlaced with nationalist rhetoric and so patently disdainful of the real conditions of life in most of Italy that there seems little choice retrospectively but to class it as an extravagant, right-wing phenomenon. How then did Marinetti and his followers come to align themselves with a political movement whose original members came on the whole from a dissident or interventionist Left? And why did they remain within that movement only as long as its policies retained traces of a left-wing provenance?

In attempting to answer these questions, I shall begin by discussing Futurism's ideology as it emerges from the more imaginative pronouncements of the movement, and then outline its political policies. . . . But first, by way of introduction, I offer a brief chronicle of some salient events surrounding the Marinetti-Mussolini alliance:

> *February 1909* Marinetti publishes the *Founding Manifesto of Futurism* in *Le Figaro*. He includes the following 'articles': 'Courage, audacity, and revolt will be essential elements of our poetry.' 'Except in struggle there is no more

beauty. No work without an aggressive character can be a masterpiece. Poetry must be conceived as a violent attack on unknown forces, to reduce and prostrate them before man.' 'We will glorify war—the world's only hygiene—militarism, patriotism, the destructive gesture of the freedom-bringer, beautiful ideas worth dying for, and scorn for women.'

January 1910 The first Futurist 'evening' takes place in Trieste (at that time under Austrian rule).

1909 and 1911 Futurist political manifestos for elections and one supporting Italy's colonial campaign in Libya. Mussolini is imprisoned for anti-war agitation.

September 1914 Anti-Austrian demonstration by the Futurists in Milan.

December 1914 Mussolini founds *Il popolo d'Italia* and the Autonomous Fascio for Revolutionary Action.

Spring 1915 Mussolini is arrested with the Futurists Marinetti, Settimelli, and Carrà after interventionist speech-making. But the interventionist campaign succeeds, and Italy declares war on Germany and Austria-Hungary.

February 1918 First publication of the *Manifesto of the Italian Futurist Party.*

November 1918 The Futurist Mario Carli founds The Association for Italian Arditi (shock-troops). Futurist groups (*fasci*) are set up in various Italian cities.

January 1919 Marinetti and Mussolini involved in violent disruption at the Scala Theatre, Milan, while Bissolati (the reformist socialist and 1914 interventionist) attempts to expound a policy of reducing Italy's post-war territorial claims.

March 1919 Foundation of Fascism at Piazza San Sepolcro, Milan. Adherents include members of the Futurist *fasci,* of the Arditi Association, dissident or independent socialists, revolutionary and nationalist syndicalists, radical republicans.

April 1919 'The Battle of Via Mercanti'. Marinetti and Mussolini are present during anti-socialist incidents culminating in the destruction of offices of *Avanti!* (the paper Mussolini had formerly edited).

June 1919 *Il popolo d'Italia* publishes the Fascist programme.

October First Fascist Congress. Marinetti speaks on the necessity of removing the Papacy from Italy (*svaticanamento*). Electoral campaigning by Mussolini and Marinetti.

November 1919 Failure of Fascism at elections (4,567 votes out of a possible 270,000). Arrest and imprisonment of Mussolini and Marinetti after arms are discovered at Fascist and Arditi headquarters.

May 1920 Futurists withdraw from Fascism.

It is on these early developments that I shall focus, leaving aside the events that followed Mussolini's rise to power and Marinetti's return to the fold. This denigrator of cultural institutions was eventually to become a member of the Fascist Academy, and he remained loyal to Mussolini for the rest of his life. He co-operated in the assimilation of Futurism by the regime; and in so doing he forfeited the movement's avant-garde status. If it is the case that true avant-gardes can exist only under liberal systems of government which permit plurality of opinion and freedom of expression, it is also the case that they cannot effectively survive the toleration of an authoritarian one, for conflict is their life-blood.

As the events listed above show, both Marinetti and Mussolini were prepared to take their battles on to the street, at risk of violence and illegality. The common ground on which these two Milanese residents first met was interventionism; and the Great War—a first-hand, front-line experience for their generation—remained a catalyst of action and a polariser of opinion in the circles they frequented. It was, for instance, the combatant associations founded by Carli, and shortly afterwards, in Milan, by Ferruccio Vecchi, that provided political Futurism with a 'shadow' organisation as well as potential adherents. As for the fairly heterogeneous group that met at Piazza San Sepolcro, it consisted of men who at the very least had welcomed Italy's intervention in the war, and now wished to see that participation pay off in political terms.

From the outset Futurism displays the activism and the agonism that Poggioli has seen as constitutive of avant-garde movements [see Further Reading]. *The Founding Manifesto* [excerpted above] sets the polemical, frenzied tone for all its successors. But all that passion for 'dynamic' technological society—for machines and factories, for 'multicoloured, polyphonic tides of revolution in modern capitals'—is accompanied by a readiness for self-immolation. In a land the Futurists see as fossilised by its cultural traditions and its scholarly mentality, the exuberant creativity that they seek seems locatable only in the instant which is *now,* and on the extreme periphery of experience. Futurism looks to a Dionysiac moment of heroism that releases the self from human limitations. Marinetti is willing to find it in ideas 'worth dying for', or in that murderous onslaught of even newer generations on the Futurists which he jubilantly predicts. Futurism abolishes all notion of history as an ascending series. Reality for Marinetti involves an oscillating cycle of parricide and suicide; its 'perpetual becoming' is achieved by the unceasing struggle of the individual with himself. 'Overcome yourself, or cease to be', as he writes later, in Nietzschean mood.

The first manifesto appeared in that phase of Italian life dominated by the pragmatic politics of the Liberal Prime Minister, Giovanni Giolitti. Beneath Futurism's calculated outrageousness, there are subtexts which betray something of the predicament of intellectuals in that period. Because of her late unification and economic backwardness, Italy was not a country that had been able to allow herself much in the way of cultural radicalism. But by 1909 things had changed. Where Italy had been predominantly an agricultural nation, she was belatedly industrialising, at least in the north, and had a fast-developing economy. But that prosperity was relative; her *per capita* income for 1911-13 was only just over half of Germany's, for instance, and less than one third of Britain's. It was a situation that at best made for fragile confidence. At worst Italians were caught between assertive desires and feelings of inferiority. Futurism lived out this conflict with particularly dramatic intensity.

It was of course clear, especially in a city like Milan, that the vitality of the nation lay with the creators of wealth, the industrial bourgeoisie. Futurism's machine aesthetic and its brave visions of a technological future represent a homage to industrial enterprise. The manifesto *Destruction of Syntax* (May 1913) takes stock of the 'complete renewal of human sensibility' brought about by scientific discoveries, and notes that modern patriotism is 'the heroic idealization of a people's commercial, industrial and artistic solidarity'. The trouble, however, with the entrepreneur is not only that the value-system generated by his economic potency may tend in due course to become settled and stifling, but that it is a value-system in which men remain subject to individual exploitation while all glory goes to their artefacts. This ambiguous situation the Futurists nevertheless welcome in a spirit of 'willed optimism'.

This is only half the story. In reality the Futurist intellectual, who correctly pinpoints the true site of social change and its extraordinarily accelerated rhythms, also has to confront the possibility (and the fear) that art in these new circumstances is irrelevant. Thus when the Futurists abandoned the shadowy margins where artists had traditionally engaged in contemplation and took up a position in the neon glare of the marketplace, it was a move that was fundamentally defensive. All the quantifications and demystifications to be found in the 1914 Corradini-Settimelli manifesto, *Weights, Measures and Prices of Artistic Genius,* for example, are anti-bourgeois (and anti-art) in one sense; but in another they speak the language of bourgeois capitalism, and seek its shelter. Nor is this the Futurists' only ambivalence.

If one strategy for protecting the interests of artists in a new mass-producing environment is to accommodate to it by treating artists as the makers of market products, another is to indulge in unashamed self-aggrandisement. Futurism publicly and persistently celebrates its own creative 'genius'; and in this it is hard to tell whether it viewed itself as audaciously bohemian or hardheadedly commercial. In any event it sees in what it calls genius not only the power to trigger energetic reactions between subject and object, text and context, but also that of determining the nature of the object itself. At one level, then, there is an orientation in Futurism to what is happening 'out there' in the real world; at another there is the flamboyant, theatrical narcissism which disguises a sense of vulnerability. Both factors are conducive to the artist's eruption into the 'real', political world. The activism of the movement works out on the formal plane in its lasting experimental verve. On the practical plane it translates first into those theatrical 'happenings', the Futurist *serate* ["evening performances"], in which art is deemed to be created in the instant of confrontation. And the *serate*, always provocative as a phenomenon and seldom without some specific political content, easily become the pro-war rallies of 1914-15, such as that drawn by Cangiullo. His *Milan-Demonstration* makes the crowds in the cathedral square spell out the names of Mussolini and Marinetti in adjacent left-hand lines.

The notion of an instantaneous, ephemeral art is of course markedly anti-humanist; the radicalism of the rejection being reflected in the passage from free verse to free word-tables. Graphic elements, words, syllables, arithmetical and typographical signs explode in 'simultaneity' across the page, formal equivalents of an outlook that refuses history and reason. Futurism, like other avant-garde movements, tends to regard creativity as belonging to a primordial stratum of the psyche, one long mortified by cultural and moral prejudice. Its anti-humanist stance liberated what had been seen as anti-human, in particular the erotic and the aggressive. Yet in glorifying war as a hygiene, Marinetti at first tries to claim a mystical and apolitical stance. In a manifesto probably written in 1909 he insists that Futurist 'patriotism and love of war have nothing to do with ideology': without them there is quite simply 'nothing but decadence and death'. He sees them as part of a heroic morality that seeks to potentiate the human, not to deny it. But of course his notion of heroism is inadequate all along—and precisely because it cannot be realised in strictly human terms.

The Futurists seem to have repressed a pessimism about modern living that was more openly acknowledged elsewhere—from the Expressionists to Eliot. Scientific advances and their industrial applications after all brought not only a sense of exhilaration but one of threat. New powers were available to men, but the whole configuration of their society was being changed: the individual was submerged in the anonymous urban mass, the realm of the natural was shrinking. In their 'artificial optimism' the Futurists, however, refuse all disquiet on this score. It is crucial that they choose instead to view human nature itself as incomplete: fulfilled only as far as it can be made to evolve towards 'a non-human and mechanical type', one 'constructed for omnipresent speed' and 'naturally cruel, omniscient and aggressive'. This Machine-Man ideal offers the foundation for an aesthetic theory (requiring, for instance, the 'suppression of the I in literature' and a 'lyrical obsession with matter'; but also represents an ideological position. For if creativity and apotheosis in men comes about only through struggle against their own mortality, in the modern context that struggle can only mean war on an industrial scale.

All this may seem obvious when we consider the enthusiasm of Futurists for the wars of their time. But Marinetti's love-affair with notoriety on the one hand, and ordinary considerations of *realpolitik* on the other, may cloud the issue. The most telling observations can be made therefore, not in texts that deal directly with Tripoli, Adrianopolis or the Carso, but in areas more or less uncontaminated by activist rhetoric or political motive. In such an area lies a short Marinettian text of 1911: it is titled *Electric War* and subtitled 'Futurist Vision-Hypothesis'. The chaotic nihilism of a piece like *Let's Kill the Moonlight* gives way here to a fantasy of control and efficiency. Electricity has turned the whole Italian countryside into an automated agricultural factory. Men in flying machines (which hardly ever touch down) regulate the accelerated processes of nature achieved in this controlled environment, watching while before their very eyes 'forests grow fantastically towards the moon'. The humming landscape brings superproductivity. Hunger, poverty, social and economic problems, the drudgery of labour are at an end. This is the reign of intelligence. However, disputes over markets for the superabundance of products are the prelude to electric war. Machines with elephantine proboscies suck vacuums in the air, bombarding the unbreathable emptiness with 'great tangles of irritated lightning'.

The forecasts are far enough off target to let us enjoy the detail of these quaintly vigorous imaginings. But the fact remains that for Marinetti there is no earthly paradise without war. As [Edoardo Sanguineti comments in *Ideologia e linguaggio*, 1970], 'industrial war is not just the hygiene of the world, but its truth: the ultimate truth of nature and history'.

Electric War reveals in allegory how fundamental to Marinetti is the connection between productivity and bellicosity, or, to put it another way, between capitalist expansion and aggressive nationalism. The productivism of the movement bulks so large in its thinking that the image of the nation as factory survives into the post-war period. Later Futurist texts, like Depero's 'Skyscrapers', still celebrate what industry has created: the modern consumer city, built of iron and glass and crowded with restaurants, hotels, cinemas. And Marinetti, deeply observant of capitalist orthodoxy, writes: 'Patriotism for us is simply the sublimation of that respectful loyalty that good and prosperous businessmen inspire in their employees'. The Futurist writer Volt identifies politics largely with economics, and wants union representation on his proposed legislative body determined not by size of membership, but by *'the importance of the economic function* the union exercises in the country'.

After 1918, when Futurism was at its most 'democratic' and politically engaged, the political mileage in continuing to preach the joys of warfare was clearly limited (even though victory had brought Italy territorial gains). The other half of the productivity/bellicosity nexus was in trouble too, because of Italy's badly disrupted economy. Improvement in individual standards of living had in any case been a matter of deep indifference to Marinetti (who ploughed his own fortune into Futurism); and even he had had to concede that Italy, compared with other nations, was poor in natural resources. The result is that Marinetti becomes evasive on the key notion of imperialism. A certain sense of realism now causes him to advance the idea of Italy as representing, in relation to other nations, 'a super-brilliant minority composed entirely of individuals above the human average for their creative, innovative, improvisational powers'. The resultant 'democracy', he continues, 'will inevitably find itself in competition with the majority formed by the other nations, for whom numbers signify merely the more or less blind masses, that is to say, the democracy of the unaware'. The once bellicose Marinetti has fallen back on the idea of a purely spiritual hegemony.

Now it is evident that Futurism's entry into the political arena and the mass participation it envisages in a Futurist Democracy are determined by the experience of war. 'It is the first time in history', Marinetti enthuses, 'that it has fallen to the lot of more than four million citizens of a single nation to have undergone in a mere four years a total, intensive education, learning by fire, by heroism and death. . . . Marvellous spectacle of a whole army leaving for war practically unaware and returning politicized and worthy to govern'. Behind Futurism's political hopes lies the invigorating memory of everyday bravery in the trenches. But its optimism foundered badly. The goal of activating the masses, as the disastrous 1919 elections proved, was not so easily attained.

It seems likely that this moment of electoral defeat produced a further transformation in Marinetti's thinking, and ultimately caused him to withdraw from active politics. *Beyond Communism,* begun in prison a month after the elections of November 1919, is not an overtly dispirited work, though it has its pessimistic notes. But it is subtly reactionary, a work which in some respects points the way forward for Fascism.

Where *Futurist Democracy* of 1919 had been chiefly concerned to elaborate the policies of the party founded in 1918, and to stigmatise the attitudes of Italy's ruling classes, *Beyond Communism* retreats to Utopia and is often lyrical in tone. Its main impulse is to resuscitate the possibility of that disinterested heroism which belonged to early Futurism. Once again a modulation in attitude takes place, presumably because the magical transition from industrial plentitude to the heroic discharge of surfeit—such as was figured in *Electric War*—is inconceivable in the context of post-war depression. Moreover the masses have refused to follow where Marinetti (and Mussolini) led; and so we return to the exaltation of a spiritual aristocracy. The 'heroic citizen' of *Beyond Communism* is in fact none other than the Futurist artist. The distinguishing features of the old pre-war movement reappear: pride in anarchic self-determination, a libertarianism now extended to the abolition of law-courts and police, the familiar horror of all levelling influences, with communism replacing socialism as target. Significant is the following: 'We hear all around shouts of "everyone will have enough to eat, everyone will be rich". We shout instead "everyone will be strong: a genius" '. When the material base shows its cracks, all that remains is the gratuitous heroism of the avant-garde.

In political terms, Marinetti is talking about leadership. He no longer really believes in *Futurist Democracy's* 'race of geniuses', and this has a curious twofold effect. For the first time he acknowledges the waste lands of capitalism, the 'harsh, gloomy, stale and agitated rhythms of everyday living'; and he ascribes to art the function of a counterbalance: 'We shall not have an earthly paradise, but the economic hell will be rejoiced and calmed by countless festivals of art'. Even more important, in his re-emergent elitism, he distinguishes between those who have the 'right to create the Italian revolution and those who must submit to its conception and realization'. Compare this with the assertion of *Futurist Democracy,* so short a time before, that Italy is made up of forty million individuals, 'all of them intelligent and capable of autonomy'. And who now can be the artificers of the 'becoming-progress-revolution of the race'? Why, members of the *piccola borghesia* ["lower middle class"], that class caught between capital and labour which was eventually to be the backbone of Fascism. Marinetti writes:

> In all countries and particularly in Italy, the distinction between the proletariat and the bourgeoisie is a false one . . . There are . . . so-called members of the rich bourgeoisie who work much harder than the working class; and workers who work as little as possible. . . . It is absurd to call that formidable mass of intelligent hard-working young men from the middle classes a rotten and moribund bourgeoisie. . . . They . . . are all anxious to outdo, by assiduous labour, the modest economic standing of their fathers. They went through war as lieutenants and captains, and to-day, not in the least exhausted, they are ready to take up their effort in life with heroism.

There is a marked similarity between the insistence of Marinetti on economic striving and on the futility of class distinctions, and Mussolini's own vision of inter-class collaboration for the sake of national productivity, which he expressed at the Congress of May 1920:

> The bourgeoisie has technical and moral value: there are parasitical elements in the bourgeoisie just as there are in the proletariat. It will be a great step forward therefore to make the values of the proletariat and the bourgeoisie coincide. It is collaboration between the producing proletariat and the producing bourgeoisie alone that will take our civilization forward.

This parallel takes us back to the paradoxes of the Futurist-Fascist alliance, it being precisely at the 1920 Congress that Marinetti abandoned the Fascist Party. To understand this, we must look more closely at Futurist policies, and at the left-wing connotations of early Fascism into which they fed.

As far as those policies are concerned the war is a watershed. Though the few brief manifestos issued between 1909 and 1913 become gradually more specific, polemical generalities of a predictable kind remain the order of the day. More than once, for instance, the Futurists declare that 'the word ITALY must dominate the word LIBERTY'. The choice of Trieste as the venue for the first *serata futurista,* on the other hand, seems more focused. It meant that the movement espoused the cause of the *terre irredente,* those 'unredeemed lands' with their partly Italian-speaking population which at the time were part of the Austro-Hungarian Empire. Yet one can hardly avoid the thought that the Futurists may have been just as concerned to offer that challenge to the political establishment which is so vital to an avant-garde movement as with the unfinished business of the Risorgimento. The fact is that since the signing of the Triple Alliance with Austria and Germany in 1882, official Italy had been effectively muzzled on the question of this territory, so that Futurism was tapping a source of rebelliousness sufficiently widespread in northern Italy to give buoyancy to the movement, but able also to attract the equally desirable disapproval of the establishment.

In any case we are dealing with attitudes, not a coherent set of policies capable of enactment. The latter came only when the old supine Italy had become Italy-at-war, filling Marinetti's imagination with a new vision of his compatriots. The scale of participation must have seemed a fulfilment beyond every expectation of his activist dreams; and it is the resulting excitement and optimism that gives to the *Manifesto of the Futurist Party* of 1918 its unexpectedly democratic character. Much of this Manifesto found an echo in the two programmes of the *fasci di combattimento,* which appeared in *Il popolo d'Italia* a few months after the San Sepolcro meeting and in necessary amplification of its generic statements. For convenience I summarise the Futurist programme below, italicising elements which find some equivalent in the statements of the *fasci:*

> *Universal suffrage* and *proportional representation; a 'technical' parliament with strong representation by industry, agriculture, engineering and commerce; abolition of the Senate* (or its replacement by twenty young elected members to serve as an *eccitatorio* or stimulant to government). 'Socialization' of land, with *allocations to veterans, purchase or exproportion of underexploited areas, encouragement to co-operatives,* both *agricultural* and industrial. Land reclamation, *improved communications, systematic exploitation of natural resources.* Nationalization of waterways, waterworks and mines; modernization and industrialization of towns. *Progressive taxation, wealth tax, confiscation of two-thirds of war profits.* Elimination of conscription in favour of a small, professional army. Military skills and sport to be taught in schools; elimination of illiteracy, penal sanctions for non-attendance at *lay* elementary *schools.* Legal aid, elected judiciary, freedom to strike, of association, of press. *Eight-hour working day, minimum wages,* equal pay for men and women; *worker and veteran pension schemes,* collective wage bargaining, welfare benefits. *Radical reform of bureaucracy and its hierarchial career-structure, decentralization. Anticlericalism* and the introduction of divorce.

On the evidence of summer 1919, there is no denying the radical and leftist orientation of Fascism at this early stage. But a certain truculence in tone, an insistence on the Italian character of the social revolution proposed (even more pronounced in the Futurist Party Manifesto), gives today's reader pause. Distinctions of left and right in fact do little to illuminate the complicated situation that obtained in Italy; and the wisdom of hindsight discerns with ease what the passions of the day made obscure. The curious vagaries of Mussolini's early career have often been interpreted superficially. Irritating contradictions can be all too conveniently dismissed as consonant with Mussolini's

proven lack of integrity and his opportunism; or else regarded as all of a piece with a political doctrine that prided itself on having burst free of rationalist constraint, and was not noted for the distinction of its intellectuals. Other commentators, in what is perhaps an effort to redress the balance, argue that Mussolini's early Fascism at least was an illegitimate offspring of Marxism itself, born at a time when odd liaisons were by no means rare. The connections between Futurism and Fascism, as well as the oddnesses internal to the two movements, need to be seen against the background of their peculiarly hybrid theoretical ancestry. It was this that made the strange partnership possible.

To clarify this complex issue, we may consider their divergent reactions to the Libyan War of 1911. This colonial campaign found enthusiastic support among the Futurists, but was duly condemned by Mussolini and Italian Socialism, for whom it involved a reactionary strengthening of the military and the throne. Yet there were others of Marxist extraction—revolutionary socialists and syndicalists, expelled from the Party in 1906 during its more moderate, reformist phase—who supported the Libyan venture. Their support was based on the consideration that colonial expansion was acceptable where it was conducive to that maturing of the economic base which was an indispensable preliminary to the socialist revolution. It seemed to some, moreover, that the internationalism of socialist doctrine was likely to remain a chimera until all nations had reached the same stage of economic development. Syndicalists like Arturo Labriola, Olivetti and Orano believed that the masses could best be mobilised through a proletarian and revolutionary nationalism that would bring this economic advance. It was further argued that, since the Italian bourgeoisie still had its historic responsibility to discharge, the interests of its entrepreneurial sectors (as opposed to the landed gentry) temporarily coincided with those of the proletariat.

This was a distortion of Marxism, a 'Marxist heresy', owing its existence to Italy's relative backwardness, and corresponding to a persecuted feeling among Italians that they needed to compress into the shortest possible span the hundred years during which the other nations had expanded and industrialised while Italy, as it seemed, had stood and watched: only then could she meet her neighbours on an equal footing. So it was that there existed in Italy by 1911 a left-wing rationale for imperialism.

These same expansionist views appear—much more predictably—in the nationalist thinking that also emerged in the first decade of the century. This new 'revolutionary' nationalism eschewed old-style patriotic appeals. To talk of king and country where a people included so many labourers without stake of ownership was futile. Instead it was argued that radical economic regeneration alone could bring about a rebirth and a truly Italian way of life. Colonial possessions were desirable not only because they could staunch what one nationalist called the 'haemorrhage' of emigration, but precisely because of their regenerative potential.

So it was that while the aims of revolutionary socialists and syndicalists on the one hand and the 'new' nationalists on the other remained antagonistic, the two groupings nonetheless shared an emphasis on economic expansion. Both also believed in the role of an elite capable of articulating and focusing the stirrings of the masses; both based their strategies on an *anticipated* future rather than on existing material conditions; and both despised representative parliamentary democracy as a sham—which is less surprising when we reflect that until 1912 less than a quarter of the population was enfranchised.

These coincidences suggest something of the extraordinary blurring of political distinctions that occurs in the period. Futurism itself shares in the points of convergence I have outlined. Even if, for example, it always treated socialist doctrine disparagingly, calling it a recipe for 'belly-filling' cowardice, this does not preclude a debt to the theory of syndicalism. That theory supplemented the determinist view of economic history with the notion that ethical consciousness also plays its part in processes of change. Did Marinetti have Sorel's heroic 'mobilizing myths' in mind when he coined his slogan on war? It seems clear at any rate that Futurism's anti-parliamentarianism, its scorn for the traditional, opportunistic conduct of politics, its libertarianism are as much inspired by syndicalism as nationalism.

In an environment where strange debts are regularly contracted, where terms like 'proletarian nationalism' and 'nationalist syndicalism' have a meaning, no policy of Milanese Fascism can be said to derive simply or in line of direct descent from the Futurist Party. But if Marinetti's influence in the field of policy was probably less than is sometimes assumed, it seems to have exerted itself on the self-image of the *fasci*. Mussolini was willing to see them not as a party, but as a movement, an ideological avant-garde. And in that same summer of 1919, reading the following pronouncement by Mussolini, Marinetti must have been gratified to note the impact of artistic vision on political blueprint:

> Fascism is anti-academic. It refuses political deals. It has no statutes or rules . . . It does not tolerate endless speeches. . . . On the issue of workers' demands it is in line with nationalist syndicalism . . . Fascism is antipus [ie. anti-PSI—Italian Socialist Party], but because it is productivist it is not and cannot be antiproletarian.

Sant'Elia, Boccioni, and Marinetti in uniform during the First World War.

> Fascism is . . . pragmatic, it has no preconceptions nor distant goals. It makes none of the usual promises of an ideal world, leaving that sort of chatter to the herd of card-carriers. It doesn't presume to exist for ever, or even for long. . . . Once we decide that the solution to the fundamental problems troubling Italy to-day has been reached, Fascism won't cling to life . . . but will know how to die a glorious death, without protest or pomp. If Youth from the trenches, and students, flow into the Fasci . . . it's because there are no mouldering ideas in the Fasci, no venerable greybeards, no conventional scale of values: there is youth, energy and faith. Fascism will always be a movement that belongs to a minority. It cannot spread outside the cities, but soon . . . the forthcoming national rally will draw together in concord and libertarian unity of action this formidable grouping of new energies.

Fascism is here closer to a revolutionary Left than to the so-called revolutionary nationalist Right; and in its agonism, its heroic irrationalism, its urban elitism, its insistence on youth and energy, it speaks the purist avant-garde idiom. Mussolini could allow himself such recklessness precisely because the *fasci* represented to him no more than a temporary anchorage that kept him in the political swim. A bloc moulded from the official interventionist left was what he really wished to lead. After the defeat of Milanese Fascism in November 1919 (arguably caused in part by a too great overlap of some of its policies with those of socialism), and after Mussolini failed to engineer his bloc, the movement found that its new adherents tended to come from the provinces, and that its best chances of survival lay in more 'realistic' directions. This was no longer the moment to speak of abolishing senate, monarchy or papacy. 'Unpatriotic', socialist-inspired strikes proliferated and the *fasci* no longer talked of going out to meet Labour, but of rigorously opposing those confrontations 'in which purely economic motivation has become subject to the mystifications of calculating demagogues'.

At the May Congress of 1920 Marinetti resisted this turn of events, apparently criticising the current position on strike action, as well as deploring the conciliatory stance now being adopted by Fascism in relation to monarch and Pope. When he came to record the schism between the two movements in "Futurism and Fascism" (1924), he made no mention, however, of having espoused the workers' cause. Any reference to conflict provoked by Futurist attitudes which looked left-wing, even if they might more accurately be described as anarchic and libertarian, would have been totally inappropriate: for by this time Marinetti had come to heel, and was anxious to demonstrate that Futurism was Fascism's precursor. In explaining the break with Fascism, he therefore mentioned only the issues of the monarchy and the Vatican. It may also have been the impulse to defend the movement he had founded that caused him to tell the story as he did, for it permitted him, even as he claimed that as yet Fascism had only realised Futurism's 'minimalist programme', to make a last-ditch bid for that front-line territory of the avant-garde which in reality was well and truly lost.

Perhaps there is more to that moment of defection and Marinetti's explanation of it. If the really coercive reason for his bowing out was indeed the desire to see Italy free of monarch and Pope, he had certainly picked issues that were politically suicidal. In so doing he offered an oblique indication that at the heart of his dissent lay the failure of Fascism to embrace a radicalism that was total and uncompromising. In later years there would no longer be any doubt about the subordination of Marinetti the visionary to Mussolini the dictator. But in 1920, when Fascism ceased to be an *eccitatorio* ["exciter"], a thorn in the flesh of the old body politic, and looked to its future, Futurism briefly acted out the old agonistic ideal. (pp. 82-97)

> *Judy Davies, "The Futures Market: Marinetti and the Fascists of Milan," in* Visions and Blueprints: Avant-Garde Culture and Radical Politics in Early Twentieth-Century Europe, *edited by Edward Timms and Peter Collier, Manchester University Press, 1988, pp. 82-97.*

REPUTATION AND SIGNIFICANCE

Janko Lavrin

[*Lavrin was a Yugoslavian-born English journalist, educator, and critic who specialized in nineteenth-century Russian literature and in modern drama. In the following essay from his* Aspects of Modernism: From Wilde to Pirandello, *he offers a retrospective assessment of the Futurist movement.*]

What one still remembers of the hey-day of futurism (between 1910 and 1915) is mainly a series of scandals connected with futurist gatherings, exhibitions and publications. At present it would be rather difficult to point out a single futurist book or even painting (in spite of such names as Severini and Boccioni) of real significance. Yet the movement itself was significant enough. With all its warlike dilettantism mistaken for novelty, and its impudence mistaken for courage, it proved a useful and even a necessary ferment which exercised a definite influence upon the recent development of art and literature. It helped to modify the technique of the verse (particularly of the *vers libre*); it left its traces in certain aspects of modern prose (disruption of the syntax), painting, sculpture, and even in modern architecture—since Le Corbusier and other similar innovators had been anticipated by the talented futurist Sant'Elia who was killed on the Italian front in 1916.

All things considered, futurism as an independent movement may now be defunct; but a number of post-war currents bore, and partly still bear, its stamp, not to mention the new lease of life it received in the poetry of revolutionary Russia. Far from being the casual outcome of a clique, it concealed behind its extravagances a number of features which were typical of the *Zeitgeist* and which anticipated quite a few disturbing phenomena. For the root of futurism is to be sought beyond, or at least apart from, mere art. It was not so much an aesthetic as a spiritual and social manifestation. And as such it certainly deserves a retrospective scrutiny—a proceeding which can be of value only in so far as it throws some light upon larger and more important issues of the present-day inner crisis.

The safest approach, in this case, is to let futurism speak for itself. Even those readers who are not familiar with the books of its founder Marinetti, can gather all its tenets from the "Initial Manifesto" attached to the catalogue of the Italian futurist paintings, exhibited in the Sackville Gallery in 1912. Here are some of them, signed by Marinetti himself.

> The essential elements of our poetry shall be courage, daring and rebellion.

> Literature has hitherto glorified thoughtful immobility, ecstasy and sleep; we shall extol aggressive movement, feverish insomnia, the double quick step, the somersault, the box on the ear, the fisticuff.

> We declare that the world's splendour has been enriched by a new beauty: the beauty of speed. A racing motor car, its frame adorned with great pipes, like snakes with explosive breath . . . a roaring motor car, which looks as though running on shrapnel, is more beautiful than the *Victory of Samothrace.*

> We wish to glorify War—the only health giver of the world—militarism, patriotism, the destructive arm of the Anarchist, the beautiful ideas that kill, the contempt for woman.

> We wish to destroy the museums, the libraries; we fight against moralism, feminism and all opportunistic and utilitarian meannesses.

> We shall sing the great crowds in the excitement of labour, pleasure of rebellion; of the multi-coloured and polyphonic surf of revolutions in modern capital cities; of the nocturnal vibration of arsenals and workshops beneath their violent electric moons; of the greedy stations swallowing smoking snakes; of factories suspended from the clouds by their strings of smoke; of bridges leaping like gymnasts over the diabolical cutlery of sunbathed rivers; of adventurous liners scenting the horizon; of broad-chested locomotives prancing on the rails, like huge steel horses bridled with long tubes; and of the gliding flight of aeroplanes, the sound of whose screw is like the flapping of flags in the applause of an enthusiastic crowd.

> To admire an old picture is to pour out sensitiveness into a funeral urn, instead of casting it forward in violent gushes of creation and action. . . . Set fire to the shelves of libraries! Deviate the course of the canals to flood the cellars of the museums! Oh! may the glorious canvasses drift helplessly! Seize pickaxes and hammers! Sap the foundations of the venerable cities!

> Look at us! Our heart does not feel the slightest weariness! For it is fed with fire, hatred and

speed! . . . That surprises you? It is because you do not remember even having lived! We stand upon the summit of the world and once more we cast our challenge to the stars!

What is as conspicuous in the quoted passages as the ideas themselves is the bombastic accent, the false rhetoric with its countless exclamation marks. Instead of power one feels in them only an hysterical "will to power" which asserts itself through a ruthless negation, as well as through the cult of those very elements of modern life which display aggressiveness, violence, and a purely quantitative external strength—the strength of speed and of the machine. The ideas are of course second hand. So much so that it is even unnecessary to mention their sources. Yet underneath it all one can detect a few traits and tendencies worth discussing even after the span of time which separates us from the futurist manifestoes.

One of such outstanding features is the brutal affirmation of the masculine as against the feminine principle in art and literature, and this is more important than it looks. For there is no doubt that both literature and art in Europe have been largely dominated (since the beginning of the romantic era) by the "feminine" impulse. Hence their anti-intellectual, that is, emotional, sensuous and "musical" character, full of refined nerves on the one hand, and of an exaggerated interest in adultery and sex on the other. Hence also the passivity of so many artists—the tender passivity of natures who are unable to cope with the hard realities and are therefore on the look-out for "ivory towers" which would shelter them from life. A kind of collective "mother-complex" seems to hover over a large area of modern sensibility, and the reaction against it on the part of the futurists has been salutary, in spite of all its extravagances. Unfortunately, they have made the mistake of emphasizing the opposite, i.e., the masculine principle with an equal or even greater one-sidedness.

This in itself is enough to put one on one's guard: to make one suspect that the futurists were in essence but romantic decadents who wanted to overcome their decadence by a reversal of everything from which they themselves suffered together with their age. Herein we may find, perhaps, even an explanation of their creative poverty. For the exaggerated masculine principle in culture leads to the same sterility as an exclusive emphasis on the feminine element, and is moreover considerably less "interesting", less subtle. And is not a negation of cultural traditions in itself a sign of fear, of impotence? Those individuals only who are unable to digest the past and to overcome it through a creative effort of their own, are likely to turn with all the greater violence against that past the more they are oppressed by its wealth. Unable to find an adequate strength to master it, they instinctively wish to turn it into a *tabula rasa*.

Such was the actual aim of Marinetti and his colleagues when they began to preach that it was enough to rebel against the traditions and destroy all *passéisme* in order to secure a great, an intense future.

The fact that futurism enjoyed a particular vogue in Italy is in itself significant, because it raises, from a wider angle, the question of cultural inheritance. Of all European countries Italy can boast of a greater cultural heritage than she is able to assimilate for her further creative efforts. Her present seems to be poor from her very wealth—the wealth of the past. While suffocating under its weight, she is still too much fascinated by it not to sponge on her past at the expense of her future. To reject such "sponging" does not mean however to reject cultural continuity. It is precisely in this context that the relationship between the past and the future becomes very complicated. But instead of facing these complications, Marinetti shirked them and made a short cut towards a brutally "simplified" type of man and of culture.

Confusing novelty with originality, and vitality with aggressiveness, he debased not only the idea of artistic creation, but also that of the human Ego, which he reduced to its primitive biological and zoological impulses. Instead of integrating the chaotic modern consciousness, he only lowered it deliberately and dogmatically. An apotheosis of the aggressive male on the one hand, and of the aggressive nation or state on the other; the exaltation of quantitative mechanical achievements, as well as the worship of sport for its own sake, of speed and of the machine—such were the elements necessary for the futurist conception of man and life.

Like the romantics of old, the futurists too indulged in simplifications, but whereas the romantics fled (from a hated present) back to the past, the futurists volunteered for an "intensified" future. Their cry for speed—for a greater and greater speed—and their chase for novelty was also prompted by a hectic desire to escape from the present. A further analysis shows that the very essence of futurism contains a romantic kernel, in spite of its surface negation of all romantic elements. It is largely based on Bergson's irrational idea of "flux" and of "creative evolution", interpreted in a purely external mechanical way, as the St. Vitus dance of modern speed.

Art itself was identified by Marinetti as speed and novelty. But as each novelty can only be momentary in a life looked upon as speed, such an idea of art actually abolishes art and substitutes for it something entirely different. Besides, when it comes to artistic creation, the futurists only illustrate through their works their own ready-made theories of art. Moreover, like the aesthetes they confuse the plane of art with the plane of life, but from the other end: if the aesthetes wanted to impose art upon life, the futurists were even more anxious to impose life upon art by means of mixing up both. In a manifesto signed by the principal futurist painters we read the following declaration:

> With the desire to interpret the aesthetic emotions by blending, so to speak, the painted canvas with the soul of the spectator, we have declared that the latter *must in future be placed in the centre of the picture.* . . . If we paint the phases of a riot, the crowd bustling with uplifted fists and noisy onslaughts of cavalry are translated upon the canvas in sheaves of lines corresponding with all the conflicting forces, following the general law of the picture. These *force-lines* must encircle and involve the spectator so that he will in a manner be forced to struggle himself with the persons in the picture. . . .

The public must also be convinced that in order to understand aesthetic sensations to which one is not accustomed, it is necessary to forget entirely one's intellectual culture, not in order to *assimilate* the work of art, but *to deliver one's self up to it* heart and soul.

Such a confusion of art and life on the part of the futurists is, however, trifling if compared with their ominous substitution of mechanical civilization for culture. Owing to Oswald Spengler's cheap generalizations (in his *Decline of the West*), the distinction between the two is now a commonplace, although it was first made, not by Spengler, but by the German savant F. A. Wolf (of Homeric fame) at least a hundred years before him. Spengler's conclusion that after its period of maturity each culture is bound to pass into mere civilization, can be replaced with a greater amount of logic by the statement that culture and civilization co-exist as two complementary and yet antagonistic factors (like soul and body in an individual); and that the aforementioned transition takes place only when the balance between the two has been destroyed by a much too accelerated development of the purely mechanical factors of life. Now the problem our age has to face is not Spengler's dogmatic fatalism, but the question as to whether there are any means and ways of *consciously* regulating, or restoring, that balance between the elements of culture and of civilization, which in less complicated ages took care of itself unconsciously. Such a problem becomes urgent, since both America and Europe have practically destroyed culture by an excess of external mechanical civilization run amok.

What then can be more indicative than the attempt of the futurists to transfer the whole of art and literature from the plane of culture to the plane of such a civilization! The attempt was new in its deliberateness and intolerant exclusiveness. Apart from this, however, they have added nothing new to our inventory. Even their "new" poetry, glorifying the machines, masses and factories, can be found long before them—in Walt Whitman. Whatever elements the futurists may have taken from Whitman, that inwardness of his which Jules Romains blended (in his *unanimisme*) with an almost mystical conception of the group-soul, was inaccessible to them. On the other hand, the ecstatic worship of speed and of the machine has actually degenerated, with some of them, into a kind of sentimentality in which the picturesque groves, shepherds and nightingales of old are replaced by power-plants, airmen and factory whistles.

Speed has already been turned into a religion. The next step will be to deify the Machine and find in it a substitute for God (O'Neill's play, *Dynamo,* echoes such fetishism). And to crown it all, a few years ago Marinetti even founded in Italy a "Society for the Prevention of Cruelty to Machines". Its highly laudable object seems to be to watch that "poor old machines", which are no longer able to earn their living, should not be treated in the same rough way in which their human operators are usually treated, once they have reached the same age and the same degree of decrepitude.

However grotesque this touch may be, it shows that futur-

ism itself has become senile and a matter of the past. (pp. 183-93)

Janko Lavrin, "The Futurist Interlude," in his Aspects of Modernism: From Wilde to Pirandello, *1935. Reprinted by Books for Libraries Press, Inc., 1968; distributed by Arno Press, Inc., pp. 183-93.*

Jane Rye

[*In the following excerpt, Rye assesses the impact of Italian Futurism on subsequent international avant-garde movements in literature, drama, and the fine arts.*]

Futurism was undoubtedly an important source of ideas for contemporary painting in Europe, but most artists, understandably in view of the Italians' boastfulness and arrogant claims, were reluctant to acknowledge its influence. This was particularly true in France, where Futurism tended to be seen as a presumptuous attack on French artistic supremacy. The Futurists had their supporters there, including Félix Fenéon, and even Apollinaire, champion and theorist of Cubism, at first so scathing, came round sufficiently to write a free-word manifesto called *The Futurist Anti-tradition*. He was obviously impressed by Futurism, and in 'The Futurists Plagiarized in France' of 1913 Boccioni accused him, with some justice, of ascribing their ideas to Orphism. Delaunay is indeed an artist whose work seems in many ways close to Futurism; the Futurists certainly profited by his example, but the influence was probably not all one way, although he, like others, angrily repudiated any association with them.

The movement met with much more whole-hearted enthusiasm, however, in Germany. The Expressionists Franz Marc and August Macke were particularly impressed: 'We shall envy Italy her sons and shall hang their works in our galleries', Marc wrote in *Der Sturm;* and Macke declared that 'Modern painting can bypass these ideas even less than Picasso'. Here their works were accepted unquestioningly as an important part of the modern movement.

Although Futurist theories were absorbed into the work of artists and writers in France and Germany, it was in Russia that the most vigorous off-shoot of Futurism grew up. Marinetti's Foundation Manifesto was apparently translated and published there very soon after its appearance in *Le Figaro* and was widely discussed. The movement was at first a literary one, led by the poet Mayakovsky and the painter and poet David Burliuk, and groups were established in Moscow and Petersburg. The Russian Futurists, however, did not wish to be associated with Marinetti's movement, and felt no need of its support. On the occasion of Marinetti's second visit to the country (the date of his first is uncertain) in 1914, those who welcomed him were accused by Klebnikov and Benedict Livsic of 'forcing Asia to bend its noble neck beneath the yoke of Europe', and Mayakovsky and others published a letter in the newspaper *Nov* in which they denied 'any debt to the Italian Futurists'.

Their manifesto of 1912 entitled *A Slap in the Face of Pub-*

lic Taste (signed by David Burliuk, Vladimir Mayakovsky and the poets Kruchenikh and Klebnikov) reveals that they had at least absorbed Marinetti's style of propaganda. In it they called for 'throwing Pushkin, Dostoevsky and Tolstoy overboard from the steamer of modern times'; they condemned the lingering traces of 'good sense' and 'good taste' in their own works, and expressed their belief in the 'new beauty of the self-sufficient and autonomous word'.

Some influence of Futurist ideas can also be seen in the works of the group of painters, including David Burliuk, Michael Larionov and Natalia Gontcharova, Alexandra Exter and Olga Rosanova, who were closely associated with the poets. Russia differed from Italy, however, in that the state of painting there at the time of the advent of Futurism was very much alive. Artists had for some time been in close contact with the latest trends in France and Germany, and Futurism was absorbed along with Cubism, Orphism and German Expressionism. They were already much more mature than the Italians, and could assimilate new ideas into their painting more completely. Whereas the Italians wanted to cut themselves off as completely as possible from their artistic heritage, the Russians drew much inspiration from their own folk art.

The short-lived movement of Larionov and Gontcharova which they called Rayonnism, was described by its authors as 'a synthesis of Cubism, Futurism and Orphism'. The Rayonnist Manifesto was published in 1913, although most of their works in this style had been produced in the previous two years. 'We declare: the genius of our days to be: trousers, jackets, shoes, tramways, buses, aeroplanes, railways, magnificent ships—what an enchantment—what a great epoch unrivalled in world history.' 'The style of Rayonnist painting promoted by us is concerned with spatial forms which are obtained through the crossing of reflected rays from various objects, and forms which are singled out by the artist.' These rays ('conventionally represented on the surface by a line of colour') can be seen as a version of the Italian Futurists' 'lines of force'. Of these two Gontcharova, with paintings such as *The Machine's Engine* and *The Cyclist,* comes closest to the themes which occupied the Italians.

Another work in which Cubist forms are animated to convey movement and mechanical rhythms is Kasimir Malevich's picture *Scissor Grinder* of 1912; but although the Italian Futurists may have opened the way to such a use of Cubist technique, it is handled with much greater assurance and skill than their own attempts, and at the same time without their expressionist preoccupations.

Like the Italians, the Russian Futurists also drew the attention of the public to themselves through their provocative and often violent behaviour. They went about wearing extraordinary costumes in brilliant colours, painted themselves with flowers and words and strange designs, and held Futurist entertainments similar to those with which Marinetti kept himself before the public eye in Italy, in which 'Non-sense' verses and manifestoes were declaimed, and plays performed. And as in Italy, these occasions frequently ended in brawls and the intervention of the police.

The Russian Futurists echoed the Italians in their conviction that the artist must no longer be cut off from life, but had a part to play. The Italian artists had wanted to 're-enter life at all costs'; 'Art in Life!' was the slogan of the future Constructivists. In Italy the inspiration of the Futurist movement was the desire to create a new Italy; and in Russia the advent of the revolution in 1917 brought about a state of mind in Russian artists which seems to be almost the essence of Futurism. 'We do not need', wrote Mayakovsky in a passage that brings to mind the first Futurist manifesto, 'a dead mausoleum of art where dead works are worshipped, but a living factory of—the human spirit—in the streets, in the tramways, in the factories, workshops and workers' homes.' The symphonies of factory sirens would surely have delighted Luigi Russolo, with his conviction that a new music should be made from the noises of the modern industrial city. Something of the Italians' love of constant change, movement and excitement can be felt in the description of Tatlin's *Monument to the Third International:* 'Least of all must you stand or sit in this building; you must be mechanically transported up, down, carried along willy-nilly; in front of you will flash the firm, laconic phrases of an announcer-agitator, further on the latest news, decree, decision, the latest invention will be announced . . . creation, only creation.'

In 1915 Balla and the newcomer to Futurism Fortunato Depero published a manifesto called *The Futurist Reconstruction of the Universe* which anticipates the Constructivism of Rodchenko and Pevsner, and Gabo's kinetic models of the 1920s. The manifesto explains Balla's concept of 'plastic complexes', which was both the culmination of Boccioni's experiments in sculpture and the beginning of the mechanical preoccupations of the 'second Futurism' of the postwar period.

> Balla began with the study of the velocity of automobiles and discovered their laws and essential lines of force. After more than twenty pictures dealing with this investigation he realized that the single plane of the canvas did not allow the suggestion of the dynamic volume of speed in depth. Balla felt the need of constructing with wires, cardboard planes, cloth and tissue-paper etc. the first dynamic plastic complex.

None of these works survive, although some have been reconstructed from illustrations in the manifesto. Anticipating the Russians' later rejection of 'physical mass as an element of plasticity', they were to be

> 1. ABSTRACT. 2. DYNAMIC. Relative motion (cinematographic) + absolute motion. 3. HIGHLY TRANSPARENT. For the speed and volatility of the plastic complex, which must appear and disappear. 4. HIGHLY COLOURED and HIGHLY LUMINOUS (by means of internal lights). 5. AUTONOMOUS, that is resembling nothing but themselves. 6. TRANSFORMABLE. 7. DRAMATIC. 8. VOLATILE. 9. ODOROUS. 10. NOISY . . . 11. EXPLODING, simultaneously appearing and disappearing in bursts.

Italian Futurist experiments in the expressive use of typography also foreshadow the work of El Lissitsky and others in the early years of the Revolution, and there are close connections between the two countries in the field of the theatre. 'Russian stage-design', wrote the Minister for Culture, Lunacharsky, 'has been directly influenced by Italian Futurism.' The Italians really began to develop their ideas about the theatre after the Great War when the 'first Futurism' with which this account deals was over, and the 'second Futurism' grew up around the figures of Balla, Prampolini, Depero, Bragaglia and others, but Marinetti's most important writings on the subject, *The Variety Theatre* and *The Futurist Synthetic Synthetic Theatre* were published in 1913 and 1915 respectively. Alexandra Exter, an important pioneer in the Russian theatre, is known to have visited Italy several times and to have been in touch with Boccioni (who experimented in this field) and the other Futurists, and her development of the system of 'Synthetic Theatre' in the productions of the Kamerny Theatre from 1916 presumably reflects their ideas. The Italian experiments with stage design were a continuation, broadly speaking, of the painters' aim of putting the spectator 'in the centre of the picture' and centred round ways of involving the audience in the action, ideas developed in the twenties in Meyerhold's Constructivist productions.

Futurism also had a stimulating effect on English art. It was much discussed in English literary and artistic circles, newspapers were full of it, and literary reviews devoted whole numbers to its discussion. Marinetti visited the country several times, and his visits were enlivened by the usual incidents and dissensions. In 1911 he challenged the journalist Francis McCullagh to a duel for accusing the Italians of piracy in their campaign in Tripoli. In 1914 Russolo gave a recital on his 'Noise organ' at the Coliseum. The recital was not a success: 'it must have sounded magnificent to him, for he beamed, but a little way back in the auditorium all one heard was the faintest of buzzes'. But such events inevitably created something of a stir.

In 1914 Marinetti was welcomed by the painter C. R. W. Nevinson (who was a friend of Severini) and Wyndham Lewis at a banquet attended by sixty guests including Harold Monro, Laurence Housman, and R. Wilenski, during which 'Marinetti recited a poem about the siege of Adrianople with various kinds of onomatopoeic noises and crashes in free verse, while all the time the band downstairs played "You made me love you. I didn't want to do it".' Marinetti lectured the English on their national vices and virtues; he admired their 'indomitable and bellicose patriotism', and their passion for boxing ('simple, brutal and swift'), but condemned 'the lymphatic ideology of your deplorable Ruskin . . . with his nostalgia for Homeric cheeses . . . with his hatred of the machine' and 'the obsessional cult of our past [which has] entirely perverted your judgement of contemporary Italy'. During this visit Nevinson wrote a Futurist manifesto entitled *Vital English Art,* signed by himself and Marinetti. It was published in *The Times,* the *Observer* and the *Daily Mail,* and was scattered down on audiences at the theatre. Battle was to be waged against

> Worship of tradition and the conservatism of Academies, the commercial acquiescence of English artists, the effeminacy of their art. The pessimistic, sceptical and narrow views of the En-

glish public, who stupidly prefer the pretty-pretty, the commonplace, the soft, sweet and mediocre. The sickly revivals of mediaevalism, the Garden Cities with their curfews and artificial battlements, the Maypole Morris dancers, Aestheticism, Oscar Wilde, the pre-Raphaelites, neo-Primitives, and Paris. The perverted snob who ignores all English originality and daring but welcomes eagerly all foreign originality and daring . . . The indifference of the King, the State and the politicians towards all arts. The English notion that Art is a useless pastime, only fit for women and school-girls, that artists are poor deluded fools to be pitied and protected, and Art a ridiculous complaint, a mere topic for table-talk. The sentimentality with which you load your pictures, to compensate, perhaps for your praiseworthy utter lack of sentimentality in life. The Mania for immortality. A masterpiece must disappear with its author. . . .

The manifesto ended with a call for an English art 'that is strong, virile and anti-sentimental' and an explosion of Futurist excitement: 'Forward! Hurrah for motors! Hurrah for speed! Hurrah for draughts! Hurrah for lightning!'

Wyndham Lewis hastened to disclaim any connection with this manifesto, and resolutely declined, despite Marinetti's coaxing, to call himself a Futurist. Nevertheless, his movement, Vorticism, was the most important offshoot of Futurism in England. Lewis called Vorticism a 'counter-*putsch'* to Futurism, but his magazine *Blast,* which appeared in July 1914 and July 1915, clearly reflects Marinetti's propagandist style, and the general tone of Futurist writings. It contained poems, plays, manifestoes and 'outbursts of one sort and another', and illustrated the works of Lewis himself, together with those of Wadsworth, Gaudier-Brzeska, William Roberts, Epstein and others of the Vorticist Group. Vorticism, Wyndham Lewis later wrote, 'hustled the cultural Britannia, stepping up that cautious pace with which she prefers to advance'; it was the first school of abstract painting in England, based on Cubism, 'hard, clean and plastic', but combining it with the Futurist concept of dynamic movement. The Vorticist Group held an exhibition in 1915, in which David Bomberg took part, but in painting the movement did not survive the Great War. Nevinson's paintings of the war are influenced by Futurism, but for him, as for so many others, Futurism was only a brief phase of his youthful development. Vorticism was also a literary movement; its major manifesto, *The Great Vortex,* was signed by writers as well as artists, including Richard Aldington and Ezra Pound, who invented the movement's name. Pound vouches for the lasting importance of Futurism in literature in this surprisingly generous tribute: 'Marinetti and Futurism have given a great impetus to all European literature. The movement to which Joyce, Eliot and myself have given birth in London would not have existed without Futurism.'

The Dada movement which grew up in Switzerland in 1915 has also acknowledged its debt to Futurism. 'Like all new-born movements,' writes Hans Richter, one of the original members of the group, 'we were convinced that the world began anew with us; but in fact we had swallowed Futurism—bones, feathers and all.' By 1915, as we have seen, the spirit of the Italian Futurists had begun to flag, and the group to break up; the Dadaists seem to have taken over where the Futurists left off.

'Proto-Dada' elements had made their appearance in the writings of Marinetti and his followers quite early on. The 'anti-art' mood can be seen in Russolo's *Art of Noises,* a musical response to Marinetti's exhortations in his 1912 *Manifesto of Futurist Literature* to make use of 'all brutal sounds, all expressive screams of the violent life which surrounds us . . . [to produce] the "ugly" . . . and to Kill solemnity everywhere'. A similar spirit is evident in the tone of Carrà's *Painting of Sounds, Noises and Smells,* and in the poet Aldo Palazzeschi's manifesto *Il controdolore* in which man is encouraged to discover the maximum amount of laughter in grief, and 'the man who suffers, the man who dies are the largest sources for human joy'. Perhaps the most direct anticipation of Dadaism was contained in Marinetti's *Variety Theatre* manifesto, which advocated the systematic prostitution of all classic art on the stage: a Beethoven symphony played backwards; all Shakespeare reduced to one act, etc.

Marinetti contributed to *Cabaret Voltaire,* the first Dada brochure, in 1916, and he and Tristan Tzara remained in close contact. The Dada *soirée,* with its reading of 'Bruitist' and 'Simultaneist' poems and its cabaret technique, was more or less identical with the Futurist entertainments with which Marinetti had been outraging the public for years. The Futurist spirit can be seen clearly in this description of the Bruitist poem (*Dadaist Manifesto,* Berlin 1918): 'The Bruitist poem represents a streetcar as it is, the essence of the streetcar with the yawning of Schulze the *rentier,* and the screeching of brakes', and indeed the combining of poetry and noises, and the simultaneous reading of poems were both taken over from Futurism. The Dadaists also made great use of the Futurist manifesto, declaimed from the stage or distributed as broadsheets, and the layout of these documents, and of Dada posters, employs the typographical devices invented by the Futurists. Hans Richter also gives Futurism as the source of the Dada phonetic poem, which he says originated in Marinetti's 'parole in libertà' ["words-in-freedom"], and of Dada's photomontage, which, he writes, 'was basically no more than a "correct" application of the "realistic" Futurist principle of assembling suggestive documentary items to produce an all-embracing, dynamic pattern of the interpenetrating aspects of reality'. But the most striking similarity between the two movements is the desire to shock, to do violence to bourgeois sensibilities. (pp. 129-51)

A journalist once described Marinetti as 'the caffeine of Europe', and Futurism left its mark on literature and art rather through the stimulating effect of its theories than the example of the works it produced. It helped to awaken in artists and writers a new sense of the aesthetic possibilities of the modern world; it expressed the widespread contemporary reaction against what Ezra Pound called the 'emotional slither' of romanticism. In a letter of 1914 [see *TCLC,* Vol. 10, pp. 314-15] D. H. Lawrence writes of Futurism: 'I like it because it is the applying to emotions of the purging of the old forms and sentimentalities. I like it

for its saying—enough of this sickly cant, let us be honest and stick by what is in us.'

In his *Foundation Manifesto* Marinetti had given the Futurists ten years to achieve their ends. In the event the movement was over before that time was up. For better or worse they had helped to put Italy politically on the map; and they had certainly brought her, with a splash, into the mainstream of European art.

In their insistence on breaking down the barriers between the individual arts; their belief that any materials, however unconventional, could be used in the creation of works of art, and that these works would quickly be made obsolete by new inventions; their idea of 'the art of the becoming, the perishable, the transitory and the expendable'; and their over-all realization that new artistic forms were needed to express the new conditions of life, the Futurists not only expressed a feeling that was in the air at the time, but anticipated a whole line of development which is still unfolding today. They were so fruitful of original ideas, so occupied with the business of expressing them in words and making them widely known, and so side-tracked by their feelings of artistic and national inferiority, that it is little wonder that it was left for others to put their theories into practice. (pp. 153-55)

> *Jane Rye, in her* Futurism, *Studio Vista, 1972, 159 p.*

FURTHER READING

I. Anthologies

Apollonio, Umbro, ed. *The Documents of Twentieth-Century Art: Futurist Manifestos.* Translated by Robert Brain, et al. New York: Viking Press, 1973, 232 p.

    Collects statements of intent by Marinetti, Boccioni, Carrà, Balla, Pratella, Russolo, Sant'Elia, Prampolini, and others, with an introduction by Apollonio discussing Futurism's history and aesthetic tenets.

Kirby, Michael, and Kirby, Victoria Nes. *Futurist Performance.* 1971. Reprint. New York: PAJ Publications, 1986, 335 p.

    Critical study accompanied by a number of translated Italian Futurist dramas and manifestos. For the authors' discussion of Futurist synthetic theater, see excerpt above; for Michael Kirby's general analysis of Futurist drama, see *TCLC,* Vol. 10, pp. 317-20.

Stefanile, Felix, ed. *The Blue Moustache: Some Futurist Poets.* Translated by Felix Stefanile. Manchester: Carcanet New Press, 1981, 59 p.

    Contains English translations of poems by eleven Italian Futurists with a foreword offering brief thematic commentary on the works.

II. Secondary Sources

Andreoli-deVillers, Jean-Pierre. *Futurism and the Arts: A*

Bibliography, 1959-73. Toronto: University of Toronto Press, 1975, 189 p.

> Extensive bibliography of Italian Futurism and international futurism covering all relevant artistic and literary media as well as related fields and movements.

Ballerini, Luigi. "60 Years of Visual Writing." In *Italian Visual Poetry, 1912-72,* edited by Luigi Ballerini, pp. 5-9. New York: Instituto Italiano di Cultura, 1973.

> Exhibition catalog devoted to the Italian Futurist contribution to visual poetry, asserting that the movement "brought about the elimination of the century-old dichotomy of content and form, extolling the act of 'making' over and above all the other elements of artistic experience."

Ballo, Guido. "Futurism." In his *Modern Italian Painting: From Futurism to the Present Day,* translated by Barbara Wall, pp. 14-20. New York: Frederick A. Praeger, 1958.

> Discusses the individual styles of the major figures in Futurist painting. The book also includes more than 200 reproductions of works by Futurist and other modern Italian artists.

Banham, Reyner. "Futurism for Keeps." *Arts Magazine* 35, No. 3 (December 1960): 33-9.

> Asserts the significance of Italian Futurism as a multimedia movement, and argues that Futurism "looks to be the one constant and permanent line of inspiration in twentieth-century art."

————. "Futurism: The Foundation Manifesto" and "Futurism: Theory and Development." In his *Theory and Design in the First Machine Age,* pp. 99-105, 106-26. New York: Frederick A. Praeger, 1960.

> Addresses *The Founding and Manifesto of Futurism* and the development of Futurist aesthetics, particularly in relation to Cubism in art. Banham's essay, "Sant'Elia and Futurist Architecture," is excerpted above.

Bohn, Willard. "The Futurist Experience." In his *The Aesthetics of Visual Poetry, 1914-1928,* pp. 29-45. Cambridge: Cambridge University Press, 1986.

> Focuses on Italian Futurist pictorial poetry as exemplified by *Rapporta di un nottambulo milanese* by Carlo Carrà, and *Bicchier d'acqua* and *Al buffet della stazione* by Ardengo Soffici.

Bradbury, Malcolm, and McFarlane, James, eds. *Modernism, 1890-1930.* New York: Penguin Books, 1976, 684 p.

> Contains two essays addressing Italian Futurism: "Russian Futurism" by G. M. Hyde, which contrasts the Italian movement with that in Russian poetry, and "Italian Futurism" by Judy Rawson, which outlines the movement's political and aesthetic tenets in literature and the visual arts (see excerpt in *TCLC,* Vol. 10, pp. 324-26).

Cambon, Glauco. "The Poetics of Futurism: Iconoclasm and Idolatry." *Mediterranean Review* 11, No. 4 (Summer 1972): 61-7.

> Describes Italian Futurism as "a movement which insisted on absolute iconoclasm and yet, through Marinetti's own work and propaganda, proved in the last resort the impossibility of such an iconoclasm."

Carrieri, Raffaele. *Futurism.* Translated by Leslie van Rensselaer White. Milan: Edizioni del Milione, 1963, 187 p.

> Major survey of the Italian movement in the visual arts through World War I, profiling the lives and works of major Futurist artists and offering an extensive number of large-format reproductions of their artwork.

Carroll, Donald, and Lucie-Smith, Edward. "Cubism/Futurism." In their *Movements in Modern Art,* pp. 13-47. New York: Horizon Press, 1973.

> Interview format in which Lucie-Smith outlines the origins of modern art and parallels French Cubism and Italian Futurism, esteeming the influence of Futurist theory on later movements.

Chipp, Herschel B., ed. *Theories of Modern Art: A Source Book by Artists and Critics.* Berkeley and Los Angeles: University of California Press, 1968, 664 p.

> Includes an introductory survey of Italian Futurism by Joshua C. Taylor and reprints English translations of several Futurist manifestos.

Dashwood, Julie R. "Futurism and Fascism." *Italian Studies* XXVII (1972): 91-103.

> Outlines the aesthetic and political creed of Italian Futurism and argues that it influenced the early Fascist movement in Italy, although noting that "there was no lasting political contact between the two movements."

————. "The Italian Futurist Theatre." In *Theories in Drama: Drama and Society,* edited by James Redmond, pp. 129-46. Cambridge: Cambridge University Press, 1979.

> Traces the development of Futurist drama and scenography through the 1920s.

Davies, Judy. "Mechanical Millennium: Sant'Elia and the Poetry of Futurism." In *Unreal City: Urban Experience in Modern European Literature and Art,* edited by Edward Timms and David Kelley, pp. 65-79. Manchester: Manchester University Press, 1985.

> Discusses the portrayal of the modern city in the manifestos and poetry of Marinetti and in the architectural design concepts of Sant'Elia.

Deák, František. "Two Manifestos: The Influence of Italian Futurism in Russia." *The Drama Review* 19, No. 4 (December 1975): 88-94.

> Discusses the influence of the aesthetics expressed in Marinetti's manifesto *The Variety Theater* and Enrico Prampolini's *Futurist Scenography* on Russian theater from 1917 to 1929.

Egbert, Donald Drew. "Futurism and Anarcho-Syndicalism." In his *Social Radicalism and the Arts,* pp. 273-85. New York: Alfred A. Knopf, 1970.

> Argues that Italian Futurism was sympathetic to the precepts of revolutionary anarchism, although divergent in its emphasis on nationalism and militarism.

Ferrua, Pietro. "Futurism in Brazil." *Neohelicon* V, No. 2 (1977): 185-94.

> Notes the role of Italian Futurism in shaping literary Modernism in Brazil.

Fraina, Louis C. "The Social Significance of Futurism." *The New Review* 1, No. 23 (December 1913): 964-70.

> Examines the relationship of Futurism to the economic and sociopolitical conditions of turn-of-the-century Italy.

Gordon, Maxim. "The Italian Futurists." *Theatre Magazine* XLII, No. 294 (September 1925): 22, 50.

Discusses Futurist drama, scenography, and music, focusing on the movement's post–World War I period.

Hulten, Pontus, ed. *Futurism and Futurisms.* Translated by Asterisco, et al. New York: Abbeville Press, 1986, 639 p.
Exhibition catalog offering an essay by Hulten, "Futurist Prophecies," that discusses the influence of Italian Futurism in the visual arts on early twentieth-century avant-garde movements.

Huneker, James. "The Italian Futurist Painters." In his *Ivory Apes and Peacocks,* pp. 262-74. New York: Charles Scribner's Sons, 1915.
Discusses the literary aspect of Futurism in the visual arts and questions the originality of the movement's aesthetic philosophy.

Ilie, Paul. "Futurism in Spain." *Criticism* VI, No. 3 (Summer 1964): 201-11.
Elaborates on the negative reception of Italian Futurist theory in art and literature by vanguard cultural movements in early twentieth-century Spain.

Kaun, Alexander S. "Futurism and Pseudo-Futurism." *The Little Review* I, No. 4 (June 1914): 12-18.
Evaluates Futurism as an international phenomenon, focusing on the poems and personality of Marinetti and the aesthetics of Russian futurist poets.

Kirby, E. T. "Futurism and the Theatre of the Future." In his *Total Theatre: A Critical Anthology,* pp. 85-124. New York: E. P. Dutton & Co., 1969, 280 p.
Contains a reprinted essay by Joseph Cary outlining the influence of Italian Futurist dramatic theory on French avant-garde playwrights, and another by L. Moholy-Nagy examining attempts by Futurist, Dadaist, and Surrealist concepts in drama to achieve a "theatre of totality." Also included are manifestos on theater by Marinetti and on scenography by Enrico Prampolini.

Kozloff, Max. *Cubism/Futurism.* New York: Charterhouse, 1973, 234 p.
Discusses the exhibition history, aesthetics, and major techniques of Italian Futurist painting, emphasizing Cubism's influence on the movement.

Kramer, Hilton. "Futurism Today." *Arts Magazine* 36, No. 1 (October 1961): 22-9.
Denigrates a Futurist exhibition held at New York's Museum of Modern Art in 1961, deeming Italian Futurist artwork "a posture of bafflement, of helpless anxiety and unfocused excitement." Joshua C. Taylor's exhibition catalog and study of the exhibition is cited below.

Lawton, Anna. "Russian and Italian Futurist Manifestoes." *Slavic and East European Journal* 20, No. 4 (Winter 1976): 405-20.
Argues the influence of Italian Futurist poetics on that of the Russian movement, giving "particular attention to the stylistic parallels in their respective manifestoes."

Lewis, Wyndham. "The Melodrama of Modernity." *Blast,* No. 1 (20 June 1914): 143-44.
Condemns Italian Futurist painting and sculpture, although offering individual praise for the paintings of Giacomo Balla.

———. *Wyndham Lewis on Art: Collected Writings, 1913-*
1956, edited by Walter Michel and C. J. Fox, pp. 28ff. New York: Funk & Wagnalls, 1969.
Contains negative commentary on Italian Futurism, especially directed against Marinetti's glorification of technology.

Martin, Marianne W. "Futurism, Unanimism and Apollinaire." *Art Journal* 28, No. 3 (Spring 1969): 258-68.
Compares Italian Futurism in art and literature with the literary concept of unanimism in works by French author Jules Romains (1885-1972), and suggests the Futurists' influence on the poetry and art criticism of Guillaume Apollinaire (1880-1918).

Mitchell, Bonner. "Italian Futurism and French Neo-Classicism." *Kentucky Foreign Language Quarterly* XI, No. 1 (1964): 14-23.
Parallels the two movements in literature, particularly in relation to the early twentieth-century nationalistic trend in European thought.

Poggioli, Renato. "Agonism and Futurism." In his *The Theory of the Avant-Garde,* translated by Gerald Fitzgerald, pp. 60-77. Cambridge, Mass.: Belknap Press of Harvard University Press, 1968.
Characterizes the worldview of Futurism in its Italian and international manifestations, relating it to nihilism and agonism.

Rischbieter, Henning, et al. "The Futurists." In *Art and the Stage in the 20th Century: Painters and Sculptors Work for the Theater,* edited by Henning Rischbieter, translated by Michael Bullock, pp. 68-75. Greenwich, Conn.: New York Graphic Society, 1968.
Includes Rischbieter's "Futurism and the Theater," which stresses the conflation of artistic media in Italian Futurist drama, several reprinted manifestos on Futurist performance, a brief memoir by Carlo Carrà of Futurist *serate,* and an essay by Gilberto Clavel on "Depero's Plastic Theater."

Rizzo, Gino. "Futurism, Pirandello and the Contemporary Theatre." In *Altro Polo: A Volume of Italian Studies,* edited by Silvio Trambaiolo and Nerida Newbigin, pp. 91-105. Sydney: Frederick May Foundation for Italian Studies, 1978.
Outlines the role of Italian Futurist theater on the aesthetics of Italian dramatist Luigi Pirandello (1867–1936), focusing on the movement's initiation of untraditional approaches to the concepts of dramatic authorship and the audience-actor dichotomy.

Rosenberg, Harold. "Futurism." In his *Art on the Edge: Creators and Situations,* pp. 181-89. New York: Macmillan, 1975.
Evaluates Italian Futurism in the visual arts, stressing the movement's relationship to subsequent avant-garde movements.

Rosenblum, Robert. "Cubism and the Italian Futurists." In his *Cubism and Twentieth-Century Art,* pp. 203-16. New York: Harry N. Abrams, 1976.
Discusses the Italian movement's adaptation of Cubist aesthetics in the visual arts through 1915, analyzing numerous representative Futurist works.

Samuel, Horace B. "The Future of Futurism." *The Fortnightly Review* n.s. 99, No. DLVI (1 April 1913): 725-40.
Examines paintings by Italian Futurists, offers an over-

view of Marinetti's works, and notes the influence of Futurism's forbears, particularly the German philosopher Friedrich Nietzsche (1844-1900).

Scharf, Aaron. "Futurism = States of Mind + States of Matter." *Studio International* 173, No. 889 (May 1967): 244-49.
Suggests artistic prototypes for the treatment of dynamic movement in Italian Futurist painting and sculpture.

Sharkey, Stephen R., and Dombroski, Robert S. "Revolution, Myth and Mythical Politics: The Futurist Solution." *Journal of European Studies* VI, No. 24 (December 1976): 231-47.
Parallels the aesthetic and political philosophy of Italian Futurism with the political program of Fascism in Italy, positing a shared mythic structure.

Soby, James Thrall. "Italy: Two Movements, Two Paintings." In his *Contemporary Painters,* pp. 104-14. New York: Museum of Modern Art, 1948.
Reprints a 1946 essay comparing Futurism and the subsequent *pittura metafisica* movement in Italian painting and sculpture.

The Solomon R. Guggenheim Museum. *Futurism: A Modern Focus.* New York: Solomon R. Guggenheim Foundation, 1973, 251 p.
Exhibition catalog containing Linda Shearer's essay "Beyond Futurism: The Winston/Malbin Collection," which discusses the Italian Futurist influence on subsequent avant-garde movements in the arts; Marianne W. Martin's essay "Futurism Now," treating the philosophy and techniques of Futurist painting through 1916; and numerous reproductions of works by major Futurist artists.

Stravinsky, Igor, and Craft, Robert. *Conversations with Igor Stravinsky,* pp. 103ff. Garden City, N.Y.: Doubleday & Co., 1959.
Includes an anecdotal account by Russian-born American composer Stravinsky recalling his contact with Italian Futurists and their art and music.

Taylor, Joshua C. *Futurism.* New York: Museum of Modern Art, 1961, 154 p.
Exhibition catalog offering Taylor's discussion of Italian Futurist aesthetics, exhibition history, and artwork. Appendixes feature manifestos in translation, several relevant letters by Boccioni, and a selected bibliography.

————. "Futurism: The Avant-Garde as a Way of Life." *ARTnews Annual: The Avant Garde* XXXIV (1968): 80-7.
Examines the interplay between Italian Futurist theory and art, and analyzes its sociopolitical implications.

Wees, William C. " 'England Has Need of These Foreign Auxiliaries': Futurism in England, 1910-13" and " 'Time for Definition': Futurism in England, 1914." In his *Vorticism and the English Avant-Garde,* pp. 87-101, 103-18. Toronto: University of Toronto Press, 1972.
Charts the reception of Italian Futurist aesthetics by avant-garde artists in England via Futurist art exhibitions and Marinetti's lectures in London before World War I.

Weisstein, Ulrich. "Futurism in Germany and England: Two Flashes in the Pan?" *Revue des langues vivantes / Tijdschrift voor levende talen* XLIV, No. 6 (1978): 467-97.
Elaborates on the impact of Italian Futurist aesthetics on avant-garde authors and painters in England, Germany, and the United States.

Wright, Willard Huntington. "Futurism." In his *Modern Painting: Its Tendency and Meaning,* pp. 263-76. New York: Dodd, Mead and Co., 1922.
Examines the objectives of Italian Futurist painting, faulting Futurist works for creating "visual confusion," although acknowledging the influence of Futurist theory in art.

The Literature of the Holocaust

INTRODUCTION

Arguably the most horrifying example of human brutality in recorded history, the Holocaust refers to the period between 1933 and 1945 when the National Socialist, or Nazi, forces of Germany murdered more than six million people of Jewish descent. Envisioned by Nazi leader Adolf Hitler, the persecution of the Jewish population began in Germany with the withdrawal of their legal and civil rights, followed closely by their expulsion from the country. Hitler's "final solution"—his attempt to totally eradicate the Jewish people through mass executions—commenced with the outbreak of World War II and Germany's subsequent military occupation of much of Europe. Jewish Europeans, along with gypsies, homosexuals, and other "asocials," were confined within urban ghettos then transported to such concentration camps as Auschwitz, Treblinka, and Dachau, where a life of appalling squalor, starvation, and degradation preceded death in gas chambers or before firing squads. While the Allied victory in 1945 ended these atrocities, the Holocaust continues to raise profound questions concerning the moral, theological, and psychological assumptions of the civilized world.

In the years immediately following the Holocaust, writers remained largely silent concerning the concentration camps. T. W. Adorno, the renowned German sociologist, declared: "No poetry after Auschwitz," a statement which reflected the prevailing opinion that language could not fully encompass the insanity of the death camps. Therefore, attempts to address the Holocaust through literature were perceived as futile acts that further demeaned those who had suffered or died. Yet, an increasingly vocal group of survivors and others have asserted that silence perpetuated the Nazi crimes, and they have called upon artists and writers to confront the Holocaust and its legacy so that humanity might understand and ultimately overcome its basest tendencies.

Considered among the most poignant works to be published in response to this imperative are the diaries of Holocaust victims, which had been hidden or smuggled out of Nazi-occupied countries years earlier. As in the most famous of these records, Anne Frank's *The Diary of a Young Girl*, overwhelming statistics are humanized through the diarist's growing understanding of and struggle against the forces of destruction. A significant contribution to Holocaust literature has also been made by memoirists, including Elie Wiesel, Alexander Donat, and Samuel Pisar. Memoirs, unlike diaries, document the daily struggle of survivors against their memories and feelings of guilt for having survived when so many did not. Critics and readers generally approach these eyewitness accounts with what Alvin H. Rosenfeld has termed a "transfiguring sense of awe." This reverence for historical truth in Holocaust literature highlights the problems confronting writers who attempt to base works of fiction on the events of the Holocaust. According to commentators, the reality of the Holocaust exceeded the imagination of novelists, poets, and dramatists and so cannot be adequately expressed in their work. However, critics also recognize the importance of authors who accept the challenge of overcoming the Holocaust's alienating irreality to draw the reader or audience into its perverse moral landscape. Nelly Sachs, Primo Levi, and the many anonymous poets who wrote in the ghettos are recognized for their invention of new metaphors to adequately impart the Jewish experience during the Holocaust years. Survivors such as Elie Wiesel, Arnost Lustig, and André Schwartz-Bart as well as some writers who did not suffer internment personally, including Saul Bellow and Isaac Bashevis Singer, are esteemed for novels that successfully synthesize historical truth and the imagination to become what Lawrence L. Langer has referred to as "factual fictions." Similarly, the stylized works of such playwrights as Charlotte Delbo and George Tabori create environments that are considered to more accurately reflect the atmosphere of the concentration camps than many naturalistic representations of Nazi atrocities.

Despite the passage of years, the Holocaust remains in the forefront of modern consciousness through the continuing efforts of writers. Their many poems, memoirs, and novels offer fragments that together may approach the enormity of the event while continually compelling individuals and nations to reassess human morality. Richard Exner has asserted: "Writing can never solve the question of why and how such an event as the Holocaust occurred, but it is the duty of writers to further and to keep alive our awareness of that event. . . . In other words [post-Holocaust writers] must commemorate for fear we might forget why we almost have not survived."

REPRESENTATIVE WORKS*

Aichinger, Ilse
  Herod's Children   (novel)   1963
Amichai, Yehuda
  Not of This Time, Not of This Place   (poetry)   1968
Andersch, Alfred
  Efraim's Book   (novel)   1970
Barkai, Meyer
  The Fighting Ghettos   (memoir)   1962
Becker, Jurek
  Jacob the Liar   (novel)   1975
Bellow, Saul
  Mr. Sammler's Planet   (novel)   1970
Berg, Mary
  Warsaw Ghetto   (diary)   1945
Bettelheim, Bruno

The Informed Heart   (memoir)   1960
Bor, Josef
   The Terezin Requiem   (memoir)   1963
Borowski, Tadeusz
   This Way for the Gas, Ladies and Gentlemen   (short stories)   1967
Bryks, Rachmil
   Ghetto Factory 76   (poetry)   1967
Celan, Paul
   Selected Poems   (poetry)   1972
Delbo, Charlotte
   None of Us Will Return   (memoir)   1969
   Who Will Carry the Word?   (drama)   1974
Des Pres, Terrence
   The Survivor: An Anatomy of Life in the Death Camps   (memoir)   1976
Donat, Alexander
   The Holocaust Kingdom   (memoir)   1965
Eliach, Yaffa, and Assaf, Uri
   The Last Jew   (drama)   1977
Epstein, Leslie
   King of the Jews   (novel)   1979
Feldman, Irving
   The Pripet Marshes, and Other Poems   (poetry)   1965
Flinker, Moses
   Young Moshe's Diary: The Spiritual Torment of a Jewish Boy in Nazi Europe   (diary)   1965
Frank, Anne
   The Diary of a Young Girl   (diary)   1952
Frankl, Viktor
   Man's Search for Meaning: An Introduction to Logotherapy   (memoir)   1963
Friedländer, Saul
   When Memory Comes   (memoir)   1978
Gary, Romain
   The Dance of Ghengis Cohn   (novel)   1968
Gershon, Karen
   Selected Poems   (poetry)   1966
Glatstein, Jacob
   The Selected Poems of Jacob Glatstein   (poetry)   1972
Goldstein, Charles
   The Bunker   (memoir)   1973
Gray, Martin
   For Those I Loved   (memoir)   1972
Green, Gerald
   Holocaust   (novel)   1979
Hecht, Anthony
   The Hard Hours   (poetry)   1967
Heimler, Eugene
   Night of the Mist   (memoir)   1960
Hersey, John
   The Wall   (novel)   1950
Heyen, William
   The Swastika Poems   (poetry)   1977
Hoess, Rudolph
   Commandant of Auschwitz: The Autobiography of Rudolph Hoess   (memoir)   1960
Kaniuk, Yoram
   Adam Resurrected   (novel)   1971
Kaplan, Chaim A.
   Scroll of Agony   (diary)   1965; also published as *The Warsaw Diary of Chaim Kaplan,*   1973

Karmel, Ilona
   An Estate of Memory   (novel)   1969
Katz, Josef
   One Who Came Back: The Diary of a Jewish Survivor   (memoir)   1973
Katznelson, Yitzhak
   Vittel Diary   (diary)   1972
Ka-Tztenik
   Atrocity   (novel)   1963
   House of Dolls   (novel)   1969
   Star Eternal   (novel)   1971
   Sunrise over Hell   (novel)   1977
Klein, A. M.
   Collected Poems   (poetry)   1974
Klein, Gerda Weissman
   All But My Life   (memoir)   1957
Kolmar, Gertrud
   Dark Soliloquy: The Selected Poems of Gertrud Kolmar   (poetry)   1975
Kosinski, Jerzy
   The Painted Bird   (novel)   1965
   Steps   (novel)   1969
Kovner, Abba
   A Canopy in the Desert   (poetry)   1973
Kuznetsov, A. Anatoli
   Babi Yar   (memoir)   1971
Lampell, Millard
   The Wall   (drama)   1961
Langfus, Anna
   The Whole Land Brimstone   (novel)   1962
   The Lost Shore   (novel)   1963
Levi, Primo
   The Reawakening   (memoir)   1965
   Survival in Auschwitz   (memoir)   1969
   Shema: Collected Poems of Primo Levi   (poetry)   1976
Lieberman, Harold and Edith L.
   Throne of Straw   (drama)   1973
Lind, Jakov
   Soul of Wood, and Other Stories   (short stories)   1964
   Landscape in Concrete   (novel)   1966
   Counting My Steps   (novel)   1969
   Numbers   (novel)   1972
Lustig, Arnost
   A Prayer for Katerina Horovitzova   (novel)   1973
   Darkness Casts No Shadow   (novel)   1977
   Night and Hope   (short stories)   1977
   Diamonds of the Night   (novel)   1978
   Dita Saxova   (novel)   1983
   The Unloved: From the Diary of Perla S.   (novel)   1985
Miller, Arthur
   Incident at Vichy   (drama)   1965
Miłosz, Czesław
   Selected Poems   (poetry)   1973
Morgenstern, Soma
   The Third Pillar   (novel)   1955
Pisar, Samuel
   Of Blood and Hope   (memoir)   1979
Radnoti, Miklos
   Clouded Sky   (poetry)   1972
Rawicz, Piotr

Blood from the Sky   (novel)   1964
Reznikoff, Charles
   Holocaust   (poetry)   1975
Ringelblum, Emmanuel
   Notes from the Warsaw Ghetto   (diary)   1958
Rosen, Donia
   The Forest My Friend   (memoir)   1971
Rosen, Norma
   Touching Evil   (novel)   1969
Rousset, David
   The Other Kingdom   (memoir)   1947
Różewicz, Tadeusz
   "The Survivor," and Other Poems   (poetry)   1976
Rudnicki, Adolf
   The Alive and the Dead Sea   (short stories)   1957
Sachs, Nelly
   O the Chimneys   (poetry)   1967
   The Seeker, and Other Poems   (poetry)   1970
Sartre, Jean-Paul
   The Condemned of Altona   (drama)   1961
Schaeffer, Susan Fromberg
   Anya   (novel)   1974
Schwartz-Bart, André
   The Last of the Just   (novel)   1960
Semprun, Jorge
   The Long Voyage   (novel)   1964
Shapell, Nathan
   Witness to the Truth   (memoir)   1974
Shaw, Robert
   The Man in the Glass Booth   (drama)   1967
Singer, Isaac Bashevis
   Enemies: A Love Story   (novel)   1972
Singer, Israel Joshua
   The Carnovsky Family   (novel)   1943
Sobol, Joshua
   The Ghetto   (drama)   1988
Steiner, George
   The Voyage to San Cristobal of A. H.   (novella)   1979
Styron, William
   Sophie's Choice   (novel)   1979
Tabori, George
   The Cannibals   (drama)   1968
Thomas, D. M.
   The White Hotel   (novel)   1981
Uris, Leon
   Mila 18   (novel)   1961
   QB VII   (novel)   1970
von Kardoff, Ursula
   Diary of a Nightmare   (diary)   1966
Wells, Leon W.
   The Janowska Road   (memoir)   1963
Wiesel, Elie
   Night   (memoir)   1960
   Dawn   (novel)   1961
   The Accident   (novel)   1962
   The Town Beyond the Wall   (novel)   1964
   The Gates of the Forest   (novel)   1966
   A Beggar in Jerusalem   (novel)   1970
   The Oath   (novel)   1973
   Zalmen; or, The Madness of God   (drama)   1974
   The Trial of God   (drama)   1979
   The Testament   (novel)   1981

The Fifth Son   (novel)   1985
Wincelberg, Shimon
   Resort 76   (drama)   1969

*This list contains only works in English or in English translation.

HISTORICAL OVERVIEW

David Weinberg and Byron L. Sherwin

[*Weinberg is an American historian and an executive committee member of the National Holocaust Resource Center. His works include* A Community on Trial: The Jews of Paris in the 1930s *(1977) and* The Challenge of Modern Jewish Emancipation *(1979). Sherwin, a rabbi and professor of Jewish theology, has written several critical studies, among them* Jerzy Kosinski: Literary Alarmclock *(1982) and* The Golem Legend: Origins and Implications *(1985). In the following essay, Weinberg and Sherwin briefly summarize the events that encompass the Holocaust.*]

The National Socialist Workers Party (NSDAP) or Nazi Party had its origins in the violent political atmosphere of Bavaria in the immediate post–World War I period. At first, its appeal was restricted to a handful of eccentric nationalists, racists, and war veterans who found its platform of extreme nationalism and social reform a reflection of their own hostility toward Weimar politics and society. By 1921, however, the Nazis had a new leader, Adolf Hitler, committed to transforming the fringe party into a mass movement. Thriving on popular insecurity and hostility toward the Weimar regime, the Nazi party grew slowly but determinedly in the 1920's. After the unsuccessful Beer Hall *putsch* in Munich in 1923, the Nazis made their first entry into national politics in 1924, garnering three percent of the vote and sending fourteen representatives to the *Reichstag* or National Assembly. An upswing in economic conditions saw a Nazi reversal in the 1928 elections, the party gaining only 2.6 percent of the vote and twelve seats. The onset of the Depression, however, enabled the Nazis to make impressive gains in 1930, receiving 18.3 percent of the vote and electing 107 representatives. Though never able to secure an absolute majority in the *Reichstag,* (the party actually suffered a slight reversal in the 1932 elections), the Nazis played a pivotal role in obstructing parliamentary activity during the waning years of Weimar. The appointment of Adolf Hitler as Chancellor in January 1933 climaxed the Nazi drive for power and sounded the death knell for the Republic. The conservative and nationalist forces that brought Hitler to power were convinced that they would be able to manipulate him for their own ends. They were sadly mistaken. Far from a willing servant of others, Hitler and the Nazis soon showed their determination to carry out their program despite opposition at home and abroad.

Most observers in 1933 assumed that Hitler would judiciously "forget" his anti-Semitic tirades upon his accession to power. Instead, anti-Semitism became the central focus of the Nazi regime. What had previously been only propaganda now became, in the hands of a totalitarian State, a determined policy to eliminate the Jew, root and branch, from German and later European life. There were three major stages in the Third Reich's plan to solve the "Jewish problem"—expulsion, ghettoization, and the "Final Solution"—extermination. Though it is unclear whether all three policies were fully envisioned before the Nazis came to power, there is little doubt that once the Third Reich committed itself to a policy of racial anti-Semitism, the progression from expulsion to annihilation was inevitable.

Expulsion of the Jews was preceded by withdrawal of their legal and civil equality and by social and economic segregation. As early as April 1933, the Nazis had declared a general economic boycott against German Jews. Within the year, Jews were dismissed from the army, universities, the government, and the judiciary. The public burning of books by Jewish authors signalled the official exclusion of Jews from German cultural life. Legislation was passed in the first two years to prevent social and economic interchange between German and Jew, culminating in the Nuremberg Laws of September 1935 which denied German citizenship to Jews and prohibited marriage and sexual intercourse between Jews and Aryans. Legal restrictions were accompanied by a massive propaganda campaign depicting the Jew as an alien in the German midst and a corruptor of Aryan values and beliefs. Effectively excluded from all aspects of German society, Jews were declared non-citizens and could now be expelled from the Third Reich.

Tens of thousands of Jews left Germany in the first years of Nazi rule. After the passage of the Nuremberg Laws, emigration became official government policy with the result that many Jews were forced to leave property and personal belongings behind. The tragic plight of German Jewish refugees was highlighted by the desperate act of Hermann Grynspann, a young Jew who assassinated a German official in Paris in November 1938 after hearing of his parents' internment in a refugee camp on the German-Polish border. In retaliation, the German government initiated the so-called *Kristallnacht*—Night of the Broken Glass (November 9-10)—during which Germans set fire to synagogues and Jewish businesses in the major cities of Germany.

Of the close to 600,000 Jews in Germany upon Hitler's accession to power, more than half managed to escape before the implementation of the "Final Solution." After the *Anschluss* or annexation of Austria by Germany in 1938, 120,000 of the 185,000 Jews living in Austria also fled westward. Although efforts were made by international Jewish relief organizations to alleviate the refugees' plight, they were stymied by the refusal of most countries to accept Jewish immigrants. At an international conference called by President Franklin Roosevelt and held in Evian, Switzerland in 1938, representatives from nation after nation rose to explain why they could not and would not accept Jewish refugees. The tragic fate of the *St. Louis*, a German ship carrying Jewish refugees which in 1939 was denied entrance into Cuba and the United States and only at the last moment found temporary refuge for its passengers in France, Belgium, and England, highlighted the failure of the western nations to respond to Nazi anti-Semitism.

The advent of World War II in September 1939 marked a new stage in the Nazi plan to eliminate Jewry. In conquering the greater part of Poland, the Third Reich inherited a population of some three million Jews. Expulsion was no longer feasible. More importantly, Hitler and the Nazis viewed the War as a struggle to the death between Aryan and Jew. There could be no room for compromise with the racial enemy. Jews in conquered territories had to be "concentrated" in preparation for the "Final Solution."

The policy of forced concentration or ghettoization was initiated in September 1939 with instructions given to local Nazi officials in occupied Poland to transfer Jews living in scattered villages to the larger Jewish settlements, such as Lodz and Warsaw. By the winter of 1940, over a half a million Jews were living in the sealed-off ghetto of Warsaw, an area of no more than a few square city blocks. With ghettoization came restrictive measures isolating Jews from the outside world and further aggravating their miserable living conditions. After being forbidden to trade with Poles living outside the ghetto walls, Jews were forced to leave the ghetto and work in Nazi-controlled factories and plants. The *Judenrate* or Jewish Councils established under Nazi auspices could do little to counter the hunger and disease caused by inadequate food supplies and medical services. For example, it is estimated that over 100,000 Warsaw Ghetto residents died of hunger and disease before the mass deportations of July 1942.

The third and final stage of the Nazi solution to the "Jewish problem" began with the German invasion of the Soviet Union in June 1941. Hitler had envisioned the attack upon Russia as part of a master plan to destroy "Judaeo-Bolshevism," the last stage in his crusade against world Jewry. Not surprisingly, the Nazi invasion was accompanied by the wholesale slaughter of Jews. The massacres were carried out by the so-called *Einsatzgruppen* or Operational Brigades who first crossed over into Polish territory occupied by Russia in September 1939 and then carried their murderous campaign into the heartland of the Soviet Union. "Killing operations" followed a set pattern. Jews were marched to the outskirts of their village, forced to dig a mass grave, and then shot. All in all, the *Einsatzgruppen* murdered over two million Jews.

For Nazis committed to the total annihilation of Jewry, such operations were deemed insufficient. It would take too long to eliminate the Jewish population of Europe through mass shootings. There were also disturbing reports of "inefficiency" in the killing operations—wasted bullets, disobedient soldiers, escaping Jews. In January 1942, a meeting was held in the Berlin suburb of Wannsee (The Wannsee Conference) to coordinate plans for the "Final Solution" of the "Jewish problem" within Nazi-occupied Europe. Mobile gas ovens had been used occasionally during *Einsatzgruppen* operations. They were now to become the major implement in the destruction of European Jewry.

Within months after the Wannsee Conference, death camps were established to carry out the Nazi plan. The major camps—Chelmno, Auschwitz, Belzec, Sobibor, Treblinka, and Maidanek—were set up in strategic areas of occupied Poland close to major concentrations of Jews. Thus Treblinka was the final destination of Warsaw Jewry after the *aktion* or roundup of July 1942 while Lublin and Lvov Jews arrived in Belzec in March 1942. Auschwitz, the most infamous of the death camps, served as the killing center for Jews transported from other countries conquered by the Nazis.

Besides these six major centers for mass murder, the Nazis also set up hundreds of labor camps in Poland and in Germany where Jewish and non-Jewish prisoners were forced to produce material necessary for the Nazi war effort. In addition to the extermination camps and labor camps, concentration camps had been established in the early 1930's for "enemies of the Reich." While Buchenwald was the best known of these camps, scores of concentration camps were sprinkled across Nazi-occupied Europe.

The Nazis also set up Theresienstadt, situated near Prague, as a "model" camp where representatives of international relief organizations and foreign governments were shown the "humane" conditions under which Jews were allegedly being interned. Though not actually killing centers, such camps took a heavy toll of Jewish internees. Tens of thousands died from disease and starvation while hundreds of thousands eventually met their deaths after being transported to Auschwitz and Treblinka, no longer needed as slave laborers or "model" prisoners.

In almost every case, Nazi conquest was quickly followed by the deportation of Jews. In western Europe, however, Nazi efforts to round up Jews sometimes met with resistance from the local non-Jewish population. Denmark, where only about 500 of the nearly 7000 Jewish residents were deported, is the most memorable example of non-Jewish efforts to save Jews. In other countries with larger Jewish populations, the picture was less clear.

There were few attempts to defend Jews in eastern and southeastern Europe. Indeed, in some cases, local residents outdid their Nazi occupiers in brutalities against Jewish citizens. In areas such as Slovakia, Hungary, Rumania, and Croatia, local and national government officials actively aided German administrators in the roundup and deportation of Jews until the desire to join the winning Allied cause in 1944 led them to back down. The active collaboration of government leaders in the "Final Solution" is revealed in the grim figures of murder and death: about 55,000 of the 75,000 Jews in Yugoslavia, over 70,000 of the 90,000 Jews of Slovakia, about 425,000 of the nearly 850,000 Jews of Rumania and 450,000 of the almost 650,000 Jews of Hungary. By far, the most decimated community was that of Poland. The center of world Jewish culture and learning before World War II, only about 400,000 of the approximately 3,300,000 Jews in Poland in 1939 survived the Holocaust. The murderous activities of the Nazi occupying forces were not limited to Ashkenazic Jewry. Once a center of Sephardic Jewish life, the Greek Jewish community lost over 60,000 of its 75,000 members in the Holocaust, including almost the entire population of Salonika, its most vibrant and populous settlement.

Given the brutal efficiency of the Nazi extermination machine and the active collaboration of many non-Jews, it was almost impossible for Jews to resist the Nazi onslaught. Powerless, cut off from the rest of the world, lacking arms, despised by both Nazi occupier and local resident, and steeped in a historical tradition that emphasized passive acceptance of one's fate, the Jewish communities of Europe were no match for the massive might of the Third Reich. And yet, despite incredible odds, Jews resisted. The example of the uprising in the Warsaw Ghetto in April 1943 is only one of the many recorded examples of armed defense in the face of the Nazi enemy. Hopelessly outmanned and lacking arms, the unseasoned troops of the Warsaw resistance held out for weeks as Nazi soldiers were forced to take each street and each house. Revolts even occurred in death camps such as Treblinka and Sobibor, desperate efforts in the closing days of war to counter the frantic attempts by Nazi officials to complete their program of annihilation. More common was the creation of underground movements among Jewish youth in cities such as Warsaw, Bialystok, and Vilna to ferret Jews out of and smuggle arms into various ghetto communities.

Yet, for all the recorded incidents of heroic defense, there were countless examples of resistance that went unrecorded and even unnoticed. The smuggling of food into the starving ghettos, the hiding of wanted Jews, the continuance of religious and cultural life, the maintenance of educational institutions—all represented an attempt to maintain Jewish identity and Jewish life itself in the face of the concerted effort by the Nazis to destroy Jewry and Judaism. Those Jews who marched to their deaths with dignity, despite efforts to dehumanize them, manifested a form of resistance which is too often ignored in discussions of the Holocaust.

The liberation of the death camps in 1945 did not mark the end of the Jewish tragedy. The European Jewish population had been reduced by two-thirds and world Jewry by one-third, yet murders continued as Jews attempting to return to their homes in Poland were viciously attacked by local residents. Equally tragic was the plight of the *heimlosen*—the nearly 250,000 stateless Jews who did not want to return to their former residences but were denied admittance to new homes. The successful struggle by nearly 100,000 Jews to emigrate to Palestine in the years 1940-1948 lies beyond our concerns but it is an important component of the history of the Holocaust. Other Jews would eventually find refuge in western countries but only after years of anxious waiting in displaced persons' camps.

Though Jews were the primary targets of the Nazis' plan for mass murder, members of other specific social, religious and ethnic groups, considered "enemies of the Reich," were also earmarked for persecution and extermination. The Allied armies represented the external enemies of the Reich which had to be conquered. However, others within Nazi-occupied Europe, were construed by the Nazi leadership to be "internal enemies of the Reich." For complete victory, these "internal enemies" also had to be subdued. While the Jew represented the primary "internal enemy," who must be destroyed to insure German survival and Nazi victory, others were also considered "a-social elements," "unproductive," "useless mouths to feed," and as having "lives unworthy of being lived."

In the very same month in which the war against the external enemies of the Reich began, Hitler signed an order aimed at destroying "unproductive" people, mostly non-Jewish Germans. This decree initiated the "Euthanasia Program," designated by the code T-4 (referring to 4 Tiergartenstrasse in Berlin where the operation originated).

Under the guise of a program for the health care of the physically and mentally disabled, T-4 was actually a program for the mass murder of the insane, mongoloids and retarded children. Eventually, political dissidents and random victims were also sent to their deaths.

The Euthanasia Program, in a sense, was a "dry run" for the extermination of Jews a few years later. Many of the personnel later used to staff the Nazi extermination centers received their "training" in the T-4 program. Franz Stangl, Commandant of Treblinka, is one notable example.

The killing process was carried out in secrecy. People were arrested by police with warrants issued by courts of law. Physicians "certified" the "illnesses" of candidates for destruction. Families, more often than not, trusted the "authorities."

Euphemisms helped to obscure the actual aim of the program. For example, the "Health Department" administered it. Transports to death were provided by the "Charitable Foundation for the Transport of the Ill." The operation itself was called "The General Foundation for Institutional Care."

Doctors and nurses greeted the "patients" at "hospitals" and "sanitoria." The "patients" were put at ease. Their temperatures were taken. Within a few hours, patients were informed that as part of the admissions process, they would have to take showers. These rooms which had the appearance of showers were actually gas chambers. Carbon monoxide asphyxiated the victims. Their remains were cremated so as to obscure evidence regarding the manner of their deaths. A form letter notified their family that death was from "natural causes." Often, the family of the deceased was given the option of buying the "ashes" of the victim.

Despite the guise of secrecy surrounding the actual activities of the Euthanasia Program, the German people eventually discerned its true intent. Public protests were made by Germans, including Nazi party members and Church leaders. In the summer of 1941, Hitler's train was jeered as "patients" were being "loaded" onto a nearby train. On August 24, 1941, possibly as a result of these protests, Hitler ordered a halt to the T-4 program. It is not clear as to how many non-Jewish Germans and Austrians were murdered in this manner. At the Nuremberg trials, the number of victims was estimated at 275,000. Other, lower estimates, range between 50,000 and 80,000. What is significant is that at the height of Hitler's power, protest against a supposedly "secret" program appeared to have been efficacious. No such protest regarding mass murder of the Jews was forthcoming from the German people.

A second group marked for mass murder by Nazi eugenic policies was the Gypsies. The Nuremberg Laws of 1935 specifically defined the Gypsies as non-Aryans. In 1937, Laws against Crime labeled the Gypsies as "a-socials." In 1939, the "resettlement" of the Gypsies was put under the jurisdiction of Adolf Eichmann.

Thousands of Gypsies were transported to concentration camps such as Buchenwald, to ghettos such as the Warsaw Ghetto and to extermination centers such as Auschwitz. Upon their arrival at extermination centers, Gypsies were often murdered at once, without any "selection" process. In addition, Gypsies were often used as subjects for medical experiments. Besides death from disease, starvation, medical experiments and gassing, thousands of Gypsies were murdered by the "mobile killing units" (*Einsatzgruppen*). The actual number of Gypsies murdered is impossible to ascertain. Figures vary from 100,000 to 400,000.

A third group marked for persecution by the Nazis was the Jehovah Witnesses. Considered "a-social" because they would not take an oath of allegiance to Hitler, say "Heil Hitler," or serve in the armed forces, massive arrests of Witnesses occurred in 1936. Many were taken to Buchenwald. Nazi propaganda identified the Witnesses as "defeatists," and as collaborators with Judaism and with the "Jewish World Conspiracy." In fact, the Witnesses were only being faithful to their religious convictions which forbade all but minimal recognition of temporal, political powers. These convictions did not permit them to take oaths recognizing any sovereignty, except the sovereignty of God's Kingdom.

In 1937, Witnesses came under the administration of the Gestapo. Rather than being perceived as a religious group, they were considered a dangerous, a-social and criminal enemy of the State. Religious, personal or moral opposition to the *Fuhrer* was considered a political crime.

In 1938 and 1939, Witnesses were given the option of taking the oath of loyalty to the State and of joining the armed forces, but they refused to comply. Of the 6,034 Witnesses in Germany, 5,911 were arrested. Many were brutally tortured. Approximately 2,000 were murdered. One may claim, with some justification, that the Witnesses were the only *religious* group persecuted by the Nazis for their religious convictions.

A fourth group persecuted by the Nazis was homosexuals. Categorized as "a-socials," homosexuals and those suspected of homosexuality were arrested and sent to penal colonies as slave laborers and to concentration camps, Buchenwald in particular, where many died. As the War progressed, many more were transported to extermination camps. Sparse data regarding the fate of homosexuals under the Nazis is presently available. One cannot even offer a viable estimate as to the number of homosexuals persecuted and murdered by the Nazis.

The fifth and largest group destined for slavery and extermination by the Nazis was the Slavs. Included within this group were Russians, Ukrainians, Byelorussians, Serbians, Bulgarians, Slovaks, Croats, Poles and all Slavic-language-speaking peoples.

Heinrich Himmler had told his SS generals that thirty million Slavs would have to be killed. The plan for the Slavs was to be one of "delayed genocide." Considered a "racially inferior" group, the Slavs were supposed to undergo massive sterilization and to be enslaved to support the Aryan race as a prelude to genocide. Though this plan was not completely implemented, its partial execution led to the enslavement and murder of millions of Slavs.

While some Slavic countries such as Bulgaria were allied with Germany, and while members of some Slavic groups such as Ukrainians were utilized by the Nazis as militia, helpful in the military war effort and in the mass murder of Jews, other Slavic groups—especially Poles and Russians—were enslaved and systematically murdered by the millions.

Himmler had declared that it was the mission of the German people to destroy the Polish people. He predicted the "disappearance of the Poles from the world." To a significant degree, Himmler's prediction came true. Besides the massive hardships endured by the Polish people under Nazi occupation, about 5,000,000 non-Jewish Poles were forced into slave labor by the Nazis. Furthermore, about 2,200,000 non-Jewish Poles were systematically murdered.

The number of Poles—Jews and non-Jews—in German-occupied Poland was about 22,000,000. Of these, about 3,000,000 Jewish Poles and 2,200,000 non-Jewish Poles were murdered. Adding the 5,200,000 enslaved Poles, it emerges that almost one of every two Poles in Nazi-occupied Poland was either enslaved or murdered by the Nazis.

In addition to being considered racially inferior, Russian Slavs were held guilty of the "sociological crime" of Bolshevism. Hitler perceived his war with Russia as a struggle to the death between two antithetical ideologies: Nazism and Communism. Therefore, Hitler maintained, no rules of law ought to apply in the battle against the Russians. The Russian "beasts" must be murdered. Russian prisoners of war, especially "Asiatic" Russians, were not to be sent to Prisoner of War Camps, but to extermination camps. It has been estimated that more than 4,000,000 Soviet prisoners perished in the execution of this policy. While many died of starvation and exposure, many were systematically murdered in extermination centers in a manner not unlike other Slavs, Jews and Gypsies, and by the *Einsatzgruppen*.

Thus, the Holocaust emerges as a particularly, but not exclusively, Jewish tragedy. In the narrow sense, the Holocaust was a specific disaster which befell Jews, Slavs and others. In the broadest sense, it was a horror which implicates all human beings. Each of us is a potential murderer, bystander, or victim. Consequently, study of the Holocaust is not only an attempt at historical understanding, but a frightening exercise in self-knowledge. (pp. 12-20)

David Weinberg and Byron L. Sherwin, "The Holocaust: A Historical Overview," in Encountering the Holocaust: An Interdisciplinary Survey, *edited by Byron L. Sherwin and Susan G. Ament, Impact Press, 1979, pp. 12-22.*

CRITICAL OVERVIEW

Alvin H. Rosenfeld

[*A respected editor and educator, Rosenfeld has written numerous scholarly articles on American poetry, Jewish writers, and the literature of the Holocaust, as well as the critical study* Imagining Hitler *(1985). In the following essay, he introduces the critical issues surrounding Holocaust literature.*]

Just what is Holocaust literature? By that I mean a literature that is more than topical, as, say, a literature of the sea or a literature of warfare might be considered merely topical. For if by Holocaust literature all we have in mind is a large but loosely arranged collection of novels, poems, essays, and plays about a *subject*, even one so enormous and unnerving as the Nazi genocide against the Jews, then our concerns, while interesting and legitimate enough, are not truly compelling. Topical studies of all kinds—of the family, of slavery, of the environment, of World War I or World War II—abound today, and while they can be individually engaging, their value does not and cannot transcend the limitations inherent in their definitions *as* topical literatures.

By contrast—and the contrast must be conceived of as being one of the first degree—Holocaust literature occupies another sphere of study, one that is not only topical in interest but that extends so far as to force us to contemplate what may be fundamental changes in our modes of perception and expression, our altered way of being-in-the-world. Just as we designate and give validity to such concepts as "the Renaissance Mind" and "Romantic Sensibility" and "the Victorian Temper" to indicate earlier shifts in awareness and expression, so, too, should we begin to see that Holocaust literature is an attempt to express a new order of consciousness, a recognizable shift in being. The human imagination after Auschwitz is simply not the same as it was before. Put another way, the addition to our vocabulary of the very word Auschwitz means that today we *know* things that before could not even be imagined. Stunned by the awesomeness and pressure of event, the imagination comes to one of its periodic endings; undoubtedly, it also stands at the threshold of new and more difficult beginnings. Holocaust literature, situated at this point of threshold, is a chronicle of the human spirit's most turbulent strivings with an immense historical and metaphysical weight.

I use the term "human spirit" quite deliberately here, acknowledging in full the awkwardness and imprecision inherent in the term, because I cannot but conceive of Holo-

caust literature, when taken in its most encompassing definition, except as an attempt to retrieve some ongoing
life—posit a future tense—for whatever it is of human definition that remains to us. The bodies—that is to say, the
people—are gone and cannot be rescued back to life; neither can meaning in the old sense, nor absolute faith, nor
old-fashioned humanism, nor even the senses intact. Yet
writing itself, as we know from such a strongly determined
work as Chaim Kaplan's diary, succeeded as an effective
counterforce to nihilism, not so much an answer to death
as an answer to barbarism, a last-ditch means of approximating and preserving the human in the face of a vicious-
ness poised to destroy it. As a result, the vicious and the
barbarous could win only partial victories, destroy the living but not altogether submerge life. What remains is less
than what perished but more than that which wanted to
conquer and prevail. We do have the books while the night
has nothing but itself.

Given these considerations, what can we say about the attitude that denies the validity or even the possibility of a
literature of the Holocaust? In one of its earliest and by
now most famous formulations, that of the eminent critic
T. W. Adorno [in *Noten zur Literatur III*], this position
states that it is not only impossible but perhaps even immoral to attempt to write about the Holocaust. Adorno
had poetry specifically in mind, moreover, perhaps just a
single poem, the "Todesfuge" of Paul Celan, which struck
him as being incongruously, and perhaps even obscenely,
lyrical. As it happens, this poem is one of the great documents of Holocaust literature, but to Adorno it was hopelessly out of touch with its subject, as, he surmised, all
such literature seemed destined to be. That judgment is
echoed by the German critic Reinhard Baumgart, who objects to Holocaust literature on the grounds that it imposes
artificial meaning on mass suffering, and, "by removing
some of the horror, commits a grave injustice against the
victims" [*Literatur für Zeitgenossen*]. The point has also
been reaffirmed in a recent pronouncement of denunciation by Michael Wyschogrod: "I firmly believe that art is
not appropriate to the holocaust. Art takes the sting out
of suffering. . . . It is therefore forbidden to make fiction
of the holocaust. . . . Any attempt to transform the holocaust into art demeans the holocaust and must result in
poor art" [*Response* 25 (Spring 1975)].

Those who would know and could best judge the truth of
this assertion—the artists themselves—have, on occasion,
spoken similarly, even if out of a different ground and for
different reasons. Thus Elie Wiesel, whose writings perhaps more than any other's attest to the continuing possibility of Holocaust literature, has newly and pointedly
spoken of its utter impossibility:

> One generation later, it can still be said and must
> now be affirmed: There is no such thing as a liter-
> ature of the Holocaust, nor can there be. The
> very expression is a contradiction in terms.
> Auschwitz negates any form of literature, as it
> defies all systems, all doctrines. . . . A novel
> about Auschwitz is not a novel, or else it is not
> about Auschwitz. The very attempt to write
> such a novel is blasphemy. . . . [*Sh'ma* (31 Oc-
> tober 1975)].

The fact that such a view is put before us by an Elie Wiesel—and only that fact—renders it understandable and respectable, even if not acceptable. We know, for more than
a dozen books by Elie Wiesel alone have now told us, that
the Holocaust demands speech even as it threatens to impose silence. But to let silence prevail would be tanta-
mount to granting Hitler one more posthumous victory.
If it is a blasphemy, then, to attempt to write about the
Holocaust, and an injustice against the victims, how much
greater the injustice and more terrible the blasphemy to
remain silent.

What really is involved here is the deep anguish and immense frustration of the writer who confronts a subject
that belittles and threatens to overwhelm the resources of
his language. The writer's position is, in this respect, analogous to that of the man of faith, who is likewise beset by
frustration and anguish and, in just those moments when
his spirit may yearn for the fullness of Presence, is forced
to acknowledge the emptiness and silence of an imposed
Absence. The life centers of the self—intelligence, imagination, assertiveness—undergo paralysis in such moments, which, if prolonged, have the effect of a total detachment or the profoundest despair. Yet to indulge in silence is to court madness or death. At just those points
where, through some abiding and still operative reflex of
language, silence converts once more into words—even
into words about silence—Holocaust literature is born. Its
birth must be seen as a miracle of some sort, not only an
overcoming of mute despair but an assertion and affirmation of faith.

Faith in what? In some cases, perhaps in nothing more
than human tenacity, the sheer standing fast of life in the
face of a brutal death; in other cases, faith in the will to
reject a final and wicked obliteration; in still others, faith
in the persistent and all but uncanny strength of character
to search out and find new beginnings. Given these dimensions of its existence and power, Holocaust literature, with
all its acknowledged difficulties and imperfections, can be
seen as occupying not only a legitimate place in modern
letters but a central place. Long after much else in contemporary literature is forgotten, future generations of readers
will continue to answer—by their very presence *as* readers—the question that ends Chaim Kaplan's diary: "If my
life ends—what will become of my diary?" It will stand
to the ages—and not by itself alone but with other accounts of what happened to man in the ghettos and camps
of Europe—as a testament of our times.

If it is possible to reply to the view that would deny the
existence or validity of Holocaust literature, it is much
harder to know how to read such literature confidently or
to assess it adequately. The problems are many and, in
some cases, hardly manageable at all. There is the question
of knowing how to respond to and comprehend the kinds
of material that come before us. The stress here must fall
on "kinds" because it is almost certain that we confront
the works of survivors in markedly different ways than we
do the works of those who perished, just as we assume still
another reading stance for writings about the Holocaust
by those who were not there. Knowing what we do
know—but what the authors themselves could not when

they wrote—about the ultimate fates of Chaim Kaplan or Emmanuel Ringelblum or Moshe Flinker, we do not take up their books with the same expectations and read them with the same kinds of responses as we do, say, the books of Primo Levi or Alexander Donat or Elie Wiesel. The difference is not reducible solely to the dimension of tragic irony implicit in the writings of the first group but absent from those of the second; nor is it just that we read, react to, and interpret the dead with a greater deference or solemnity than the living, for within the context of Holocaust literature the living often carry a knowledge of death more terrible in its intimacy than that ever recorded in the writings of the victims. Who, in fact, are the real victims here, the dead or those cursed back into life again, guilt-ridden and condemned by a fate that would not take them?

Is it not the case that the most lacerating writings often belong to those who survived, not perished in, the Holocaust? The concern here is with the problem of survivorship and with trying to determine the reader's role in Holocaust literature, a role that seems more difficult and anguished when confronting the living than the dead. When, for instance, we read the diary of young Moshe Flinker or Ringelblum's notebooks, we inevitably "complete" the narrative by bringing to the text material that it itself does not contain; we do that almost by reflex, filling in and interpreting with knowledge gained through biographical or historical notes. That is a wrenching but still possible act for the sympathetic imagination to perform. Oddly enough, the fact that it is we who are asked to perform it, and not the authors themselves, makes reading them somewhat more bearable, somewhat more possible. When, however, the task of not only recording but also interpreting, judging, and ever again suffering through the agony falls to a living writer—as it clearly does in the works of Elie Wiesel—then we no longer are talking about acts of sympathetic imagination but something else, something that we do not have a name for and hardly know how to grasp. The nightmare, in a word, is never-ending, and repeats itself over and over again.

It is not for nothing that the Holocaust seems to expel certain writers from its provenance after a single book, that they are, from this standpoint, one-book authors. Did the curse of obsessive recurrence lift from them (consider, for example, the writing careers of André Schwarz-Bart or Jerzy Kosinski) or merely change its terms? If they have found their way to new fictional territory, what was the purchase price for their release? Why can Elie Wiesel or Katzetnik or Arnost Lustig not pay it? These are problems—among other things, readers' problems—that we do not understand and have hardly even begun to take note of.

Here is a simple test: read Anne Frank's diary—one of the best known but, as such things go, one of the "easiest" and most antiseptic works of Holocaust literature—and then read Ernst Schnabel's *Anne Frank: A Profile in Courage,* which "completes" the work by supplying the details of the young girl's ending in Auschwitz and Bergen-Belsen. You will never again be able to rid your understanding of the original text of dimensions of terror, degradation, and

Anne Frank.

despair that it itself does not contain. We need, but do not have, a suitable hermeneutics to explain that phenomenon and render it intelligible, just as we need, but do not have, a working theory of the miraculous to explain the mere existence of other texts. That certain books have come down to us at all is nothing short of astonishing, and we can never distance ourselves from an accompanying and transfiguring sense of awe as we encounter them. A manuscript written secretly and at the daily risk of life in the Warsaw ghetto; buried in milk tins or transmitted through the ghetto walls at the last moment; finally transmitted to us—such a manuscript begins to carry with it the aura of a holy text. Surely we do not take it in our hands and read it as we do those books that reach us through the normal channels of composition and publication. But how *do* we read it? At this point in the study of Holocaust literature, the question remains open-ended.

As the years pass and direct access to events becomes impossible, the question of what constitutes legitimacy within the contexts of Holocaust literature promises to become increasingly important. The complexity of this issue has recently been heightened by Emil Fackenheim's suggestion that eyewitness accounts of events may at times be less credible than studies made after the fact and by people at some distance from it. Although Fackenheim was incarcerated briefly at Sachsenhausen and thus was given firsthand knowledge of that camp, it was not until he read a study of Sachsenhausen years later, he admits, that he felt he truly understood what had taken place there and what he himself had experienced.

The issue in this case is not analogous to the one that always obtains when a personal and perhaps emotionally colored account of experience is weighed against the cooler and more objective kinds of information gathered after the fact by the working historian. For, as Fackenheim came to understand only much later, a built-in feature of the Nazi camp system was "deception of the victims," rendering accounts of the eyewitness in many cases less than reliable. The fictitious element of camp life—its pervasive irreality—was calculated to confuse and disarm the rational faculties, making the camp prisoners more pliable to their masters and hence more vulnerable to the diabolical system in which they were entrapped.

What does Fackenheim's case suggest about the relationship between proximity and authority in writings about the Holocaust? Normally, we are willing to grant a greater validity to the accounts of those who were there, and, in some measure, to withhold it from—or grant it only reluctantly to—the writings of those who were not. Fackenheim's questions may bring us to revise these notions and to reevaluate our measures not only of historical truth but of imaginative penetration and narrative effect as well.

And what about the truth of endings—writers' endings? Because Paul Celan or Tadeusz Borowski terminated their lives as they did, is it not the case that we are almost forced into a reader's stance *vis-à-vis* their stories and poems that we otherwise would not have and indeed do not want? Was suicide in each case an inevitable outcome of their work, a final and desperate conclusion to it, ultimately even a bitter evaluation of it? Was the self-destructive act of the man only and not of the writer? That such questions raise themselves at all means that we read these writers under a shadow of some kind—a different kind, incidentally, than the one that now hangs over the work of Sylvia Plath or John Berryman. (While their suicides also mediate between us and their books, one senses no historical determinism behind the personal anguish that must have led them to take their lives; the pressure to which they succumbed seems to have been biographically generated, its pain not larger than that of the single life.)

Kafka said that we are usually too easy on ourselves as readers, that we should choose books that ask more of us than we normally are willing to give. "We must have those books," he wrote, "which come upon us like ill-fortune, and distress us deeply, like the death of one we love better than ourselves, like suicide. A book must be an ice-axe to break the sea frozen inside us." To make that formulation, Kafka must have been a great reader, as well as a great hungerer (in his case the two are really one), and yet, despite all his intense suffering and estrangement, he was spared the worst that the twentieth century was to bring upon writers such as Celan and Borowski. Had Kafka known them, could he still have spoken in the terms just cited above? When, in a writer's life, suicide becomes not a metaphor for something but the thing itself, we grow more cautious and defensive as readers and do not so readily welcome the kinds of hard blows that Kafka exhorts

upon us. Better to read warily and keep the seas of empathy inside us safely frozen a while longer.

By now the point should be clear: we lack a phenomenology of reading Holocaust literature, a series of maps that will guide us on our way as we pick up and variously try to comprehend the writings of the victims, the survivors, the survivors-who-become-victims, and the kinds-of-survivors, those who were never there but know more than the outlines of the place. Until we devise such maps, our understanding of Holocaust literature will be only partial, well below that which belongs to full knowledge.

One conclusion to these questions is that we are yet to develop the kind of practical criticism that will allow us to read, interpret, and evaluate Holocaust literature with any precision or confidence. Older criticisms of whatever orientation or variety—Freudian, Marxist, formalist, structuralist, or linguistic—will not do here for any number of reasons. The largest is that the conception of man, or world view, embodied in psychoanalysis or dialectical theory or theories of aesthetic autonomy had almost no place in the ghettos and camps, which were governed by forces of an altogether different and far less refined nature. As a result, it would seem a radical misapplication of method and intentions to search through literary accounts of Auschwitz or the Warsaw Ghetto for covert Oedipal symbols, class struggle, revealing patterns of imagery and symbolism, mythic analogies, or deep grammatical structures. Auschwitz no more readily reduces to these considerations than does death itself.

Nor will it do to confine understanding within a framework of literary history that would tend to see Holocaust literature as part of the literature of warfare-in-general or even of World War II. There are novels eligible for such study, including Irwin Shaw's *The Young Lions,* Norman Mailer's *The Naked and the Dead,* and Herman Wouk's *The Caine Mutiny.* The distinction between these works and the works we shall be addressing—a hard one that needs to be held firmly in mind—has an illuminating parallel within historical writings about the period. In [*The Second World War,* a popular history] . . . written by A. J. P. Taylor, for instance, I find a total of two pages out of two hundred and thirty-five devoted to the Holocaust, this despite the fact that the author concludes his four-paragraph summary by stating that "the memory of Oświęcim and the other murder camps will remain when all the other achievements of the Nazi Empire are forgotten." Given that view—a correct one—it seems shocking at first that Taylor would mention the Holocaust only, as it were, in passing. And yet he is not entirely wrong to do so, for to do otherwise would be to see the war against the Jews as an integral part of World War II. More and more it seems that it was not, neither in intention, nor in kind, nor in outcome. The war against the Jews may have occupied some of the same dimensions of time and space as World War II, but it was not always fought as a logical part of that war, nor can the literature it generated be compared to or profitably studied with the topical literature of the Second World War. Holocaust literature is simply and complexly something else, as the cataclysm that triggered it was something else, and not part of the general storm that swept over Europe four decades ago.

In referring to such extreme cases we tend to use the language of weather, but the analogy with earthquakes and storms will finally not hold; nor will most other analogies. That precisely is part of the problem. It supports the view that we must make distinctions between the literature of the Holocaust and the literature of general warfare. This is not to belittle those books that belong to this other literature or to suggest that the Great Wars of our century did not pose their own problems for writers. Clearly they did. The First World War in particular came with an enormous jolt and hardly presented itself to the grasping intelligence in neatly formed and easily apprehensible ways. Hemingway wrote that among the casualties of that war were "the words sacred, glorious, and sacrifice and the expression in vain," that these were words he "could not stand to hear," and that "finally only the names of places had dignity." Hemingway's loss was huge, the collapse of a whole idealistic code that once sustained life by giving it a measure of purpose and honor. In reading his fiction of the Great War, it does not take much to realize that Hemingway was saying farewell to far more than arms.

To what, though, was the young Elie Wiesel saying farewell when, in an often quoted and by now famous passage from *Night,* he wrote that he will never forget the flames that turned the bodies of children "into wreaths of smoke beneath a silent blue sky," the flames that consumed his faith forever? What was his loss when, in turning the pages of an album of Holocaust photographs, he made this monstrous discovery:

> At every page, in front of every image, I stop to catch my breath. And I tell myself: This is the end, they have reached the last limit; what follows can only be less horrible; surely it is impossible to invent suffering more naked, cruelty more refined. Moments later I admit my error: I underestimated the assassin's ingenuity. The progression into the inhuman transcends the exploration of the human. Evil, more than good, suggests infinity.

For that plunge to the bottom of a final knowledge, we simply have no analogy, except perhaps to hell—a possibility that we shall have occasion to pursue a little later. For now, though, I think we must accept as a given the proposition that the Holocaust was something new in the world, without likeness or kind, a truth that was set forth years ago in a forceful and memorable poem by Uri Zvi Greenberg:

> Are there other analogies to this, our disaster
>   that came to us at their hands?
> There are no other analogies (all words are
>   shades of shadow)—
> Therein lies the horrifying phrase: No other
>   analogies!
> For every cruel torture that man may yet do to
>   man in a Gentile country—
> He who comes to compare will state: He was tor-
>   tured like a Jew.
> Every fright, every terror, every loneliness, every
>   chagrin,

> Every murmuring, weeping in the world
> He who compares will say: This analogy is of the
>   Jewish kind.

There have been attempts to find analogies—with Job, with the destruction of the Second Temple, with the *Akedah* (the binding of Isaac), with the concepts of *Kiddush ha-Shem* (martyrdom) or the Thirty-Six Righteous Men who uphold the world—and, to the extent that such allusions and antecedents have allowed certain writers at least a partial grasp of the tragedy, it would seem that we must qualify the notion that the Holocaust was altogether without parallels. On closer examination, however, it emerges in almost all cases that the gains in perspective are only temporary and provisional, for what inevitably emerges in Holocaust literature is that such analogies are introduced only to reveal their inadequacy, and they are in turn either refuted or rejected as being unworkable. Schwarz-Bart, for instance, ultimately shows us the *exhaustion* of the tradition of the *Lamed-Vov* rather than its continuing usefulness, just as Elie Wiesel will time and again adopt the stance of a Job only to find that it will not serve. In the end, he will have to stand alone, rooted in a solitary ground that became his in the moment when he was struck by the isolating knowledge that "the Holocaust defies reference, analogy" [*Legends of Our Time*]. It must have been this realization more than any other that led Wiesel to remark that "by its nature, the Holocaust defies literature" [*One Generation After*].

As Wiesel's case shows, the implications of a literature without analogy are frightening in the extreme, for our whole conception of literature insists on recognizing its antecedents and, as such, affirms that writing grows as much from within a tradition as from within an individual. That is, a poem or a novel is not a new and wholly undetermined thing—a sudden and unprecedented appearance in the world—but bears some necessary relationship to other poems and novels that have gone before and, in some sense, have sired it. While every good piece of writing must be, in its way, an original act of creation, all literature is formed as much from reactions to an antecedent literature as from more direct or unmediated reaction to life. A poem descends from other poems, a novel from other novels, a play from other plays. Whether we know it or not, we read and understand literature exactly in this way, with implicit reference to and analogy with prior texts. Indeed, we could not begin to read at all, nor could writers write, if that were not so. Our whole fund of literacy, in short, comes into play in reading.

Yet when we confront those texts that are our concern here, we sooner or later find ourselves without these expected and necessary moorings in a familiar literary landscape, and, as a result, it is sometimes hardly possible to know how to proceed. Lost in a place whose dimensions we cannot easily recognize, let alone acknowledge as our own, we strive for orientation through intimacy with the common and familiar things of the world, but grasp only fog. The object in our hands looks like a book but seems to have turned into something else.

Some contrasting examples from past literature can be instructive here. Even a casual reader of Edgar Allan Poe or Franz Kafka, for instance, knows that a literature of terror and radical estrangement is not exclusively a product of the post–World War II decades. Read Poe's "The Pit and the Pendulum" or Kafka's "In the Penal Colony" and you will have all the terror you might want. Poe, in particular, relished macabre sensations and "the exquisite terror of the soul," and was gifted at finding precise literary correlatives for them. That is why still to this day the best of his stories possess the power to "thrill" and "haunt" us with simulations of extreme psychic torment. It was his subject, and he went about developing it with all the props and atmospherics of the Gothic romance or early symbolist fiction—a whole catalogue of literary horrors that will please and stimulate the imagination with fright. Yet at no time in reading Poe do we ever come to believe that the fantasy world we are invited to enter—his "dream kingdom"—is the "real" world, the phenomenal world of our day-to-day existence. We know that Poe is inventing, that at his best he is a gifted inventor, that his literary inventions possess a stark psychological power and can grip us, at times, mightily. In short, we pretty well know how to read him.

Kafka is a deeper and more complicated writer, one who is still far enough ahead of us to render his works less accessible to full and confident understanding. In his case, we may recognize affinities with an antecedent literature of the grotesque or absurd, but to read him in these terms does not carry us very far, just as it will not finally do to reduce his more enigmatic parables and stories to the critical categories of symbolism or expressionism or surrealism. While Kafka seems to embody elements of all of these, he simultaneously transcends them, so that in the end he is only what we have come to call, inadequately and at the risk of tautology, "Kafkaesque." Let us admit that we have not yet entirely caught up with him and, as a result, he is a far more dangerous writer for us than Poe.

Nevertheless, even in Kafka's case—as, say, in "In the Penal Colony" or "The Metamorphosis"—we are never led to abandon altogether our hold on a normative, stabilizing sense of things, on the saving power of the mundane. We may be released by his fiction into a universe of absurd and frightening proportions, but it is a highly composed universe, and while few would welcome a prolonged residence there, it is not a totally alien place. Kafka possessed the power, in fact, to domesticate us rather easily to his strange but familiar world, and we can cross back and forth between it and what we perhaps too comfortably call "reality" without paying an ultimate price in credulity. In its depictions of a mechanized or technological terror, of a reigning injustice, of brutal and systematic and causeless punishment, of an accepted guilt and passivity before annihilation, "In the Penal Colony" is an uncanny prefiguration of Holocaust literature, a premonitory text. Nevertheless, in reading it we are still a step or two away from a direct knowledge of *history* as Holocaust, and no reader of the novella would confuse the infernal torture machine that is its elaborate centerpiece with the actual machinery of Auschwitz or Treblinka, just as no reader of "The Metamorphosis" would accept Gregor Samsa's transformation into a giant insect as a change that could ever actually overtake him. We accept these intricate literary devices as complex acts of initiation—a series of bridges that we must cross to enter the Kafkaesque world—and once we acknowledge them as such, we are usually content to let the stories take over and develop in their own terms. Since we do not read Kafka within predominantly realistic or naturalistic frameworks, credulity is not unduly strained by these inventions, which we recognize as the components of a profoundly disturbing but nevertheless fictional universe.

What happens, though, when we enter *l'univers concentrationnaire* and come upon the kind of metamorphosis cited earlier, one in which living children are suddenly transformed into wreaths of smoke? What is our interpretive frame of reference for that? One finds nothing like it in Poe or Kafka or any other writer I know, including the Marquis de Sade. Since it is altogether too disorienting to acknowledge such writing as a piece of realism, one perhaps tries initially to shift the terms into the language of dreams—of some inverted symbolism or dark allegory. Yet these are evasive gestures, strategies of defense, and ultimately they must be abandoned in order to perform a reluctant and all but impossible act—reading—which in this case means acknowledging a truth that we do not want to be true. How, after all, can we accept a realism more extreme than any surrealism yet invented? It is one thing to grant Kafka the artistic liberty he needs to write "The Metamorphosis," changing a man into a bug, but it is something else again entirely—and altogether too much for rational belief—when Elie Wiesel writes of children being metamorphosed into smoke. Yet that is what is presented to us in *Night,* presented moreover in such a way as to permit us to read it on one level only—the literal one—the level of plainly declared, unencumbered truth. This, we are told, is what happened. It has no symbolic dimensions, carries no allegorical weight, possesses no apparent or covert meaning. Do not think about it in terms of Ovid or Poe or Kafka, for the mythical or metaphorical aspects of their writings do not come into play here; nor does anything else you have ever read before. Know only one thing—the truth of what happened—which sounds like this: "Not far from us, flames were leaping up from a ditch, gigantic flames. They were burning something. A lorry drew up at the pit and delivered—little children. Babies! Yes, I saw it—saw it with my own eyes . . . those children in the flames."

Has there ever before been a literature more dispiriting and forlorn, more scandalous than this? Who would not erase it at once from memory? Yet we must stay with these words, or with others like them, in an effort to determine one of the distinguishing characteristics of Holocaust literature.

In order to do that, I turn briefly from prose to poetry and present two short poems. The first was written in the nineteenth century by Henry David Thoreau; the second, written closer to our own day, is by the Yiddish poet Jacob Glatstein. The poems both carry the same title: "Smoke." Here is Thoreau's:

> Light-winged Smoke, Icarian bird,
> Melting thy pinions in thy upward flight,
> Lark without song, and messenger of dawn,

Circling above the hamlets as thy nest;
Or else, departing dream, and shadowy form
Of midnight vision, gathering up thy skirts;
By night star-veiling, and by day
Darkening the light and blotting out the sun;
Go thou my incense upward from this hearth,
And ask the gods to pardon this clear flame.

Among the first observations one makes about this poem is that, in writing it, Thoreau had little interest in smoke as smoke but rather was attracted to it as the base for his transfiguring imagination, which loved to dissolve phenomena into fanciful patterns of thought. The poem, that is to say, employs its central figure in a clearly metaphorical sense, likening the smoke to other things—to birds, to the mythical Icarus, to dreams and clouds, finally to incense. Through this series of delicate imagistic changes, the poem develops the author's sense of the fugitive and transient quality of life. It is a finely wrought if uncomplicated poem, one that holds closely to classical patterns of poetic rhetoric, and therefore presents no particular problems to interpretation.

Compare it to Glatstein's "Smoke" ("Roikh" in the original Yiddish), given below in an English translation:

From the crematory flue
A Jew aspires to the Holy One.
And when the smoke of him is gone,
His wife and children filter through.
Above us, in the height of sky,
Saintly billows weep and wait.
God, wherever you may be,
There all of us are also not.

This, too, is a fine poem, but what is it saying? In the opening lines it describes a Jew ascending to his God through a chimney, followed soon after by his wife and children passing upward in the same way. The poem says that they do so by turning into smoke; moreover, it says so with a certain jauntiness of rhythm—the hippety-hop of nursery school jingles—and the playfulness of rhyme. Is it a children's poem of some kind? It is not inconceivable that a reader who chances upon this poem a hundred years from now might ask such questions, for there are elements here that call them forth. They do so, however, only to disabuse us rather quickly of our innocence, for before very long we would see that the sprightliness of rhythm and rhyme serves as a trap, the apparent lightheartedness only a lure to draw us forward into the poem's deadly center.

In searching to locate this center, we are soon brought to see that the entire poem is predicated upon the author's certain knowledge that we will recognize and be able to name the crime that resides behind or before words, in the silence that the poem was written to break. The unspoken but unmistakable ground of this poem, that is to say, is the Holocaust.

Now we have just looked at a poem about smoke and recognized that it served as a source of considerable metaphorical richness and variety. Thoreau changed the smoke into birds and clouds and religious incense, into a whole flock of wafting and melting and dissolving images. Glatstein, far from doing that, does the opposite: he changes the Jew into smoke. Worse yet—and at this point

the poem turns into something else, something new in the history of poetry—he does so in a way that has nothing at all to do with metaphor, a disabling fact that he forces upon us from the start. To read this poem at all, we must disown the figurative use of language, then, and interpret literally: the Jew has become smoke and a similar fate will overtake his wife and children. Thereafter Glatstein will add a religious dimension to his poem, at which point we recognize play of another kind, that of Jewish speculative theology. The poem ends, in fact, on a note of theological paradox: the destroyed Jews will become absent company for an Absent God. Their "aspiration," or ascent, however, must not be understood in the first place in terms of paradox or fantasy or anything else that would detract from the brutal literalness of their end. For an exact parallel to their fate, recall that casual but unforgettable moment in Hochhuth's *The Deputy* when the Doctor remarks, quite matter-of-factly, that "On Tuesday, I piped the sister of Sigmund Freud up the chimney."

It is all too strange but, at the same time, it is powerfully affecting. The poem, as we come to realize, is an assertion about a negation, a double negation: that of man and that of God. Both in this poem *are not*. Is there also a triple negation implied, the third loss being that of poetry itself? For what kind of poetry can we have that eschews the metaphorical use of language? The answer to this question compels us to recognize one of the deepest and most distinguishing characteristics of Holocaust literature and to state what may be one of its abiding laws: there are no metaphors for Auschwitz, just as Auschwitz is not a metaphor for anything else. Why is that the case? Because the flames were real flames, the ashes only ashes, the smoke always and only smoke. If one wants "meaning" out of that, it can only be this: at Auschwitz humanity incinerated its own heart. Otherwise the burnings do not lend themselves to metaphor, simile, or symbol—to likeness or association with anything else. They can only "be" or "mean" what they in fact were: the death of the Jews.

The only knowledge we are left with, then, is this: in our own day, annihilation overleapt the bounds of metaphor and was enacted on earth. Is it possible to make poetry out of that? Insofar as it is a poem that has led us to the question, the answer, clearly, must be yes. Poetry—in this instance, a something about nothing, an assertion about a negation—survives to remind us of all that has been destroyed. And also to remind us of what has not been destroyed, for while it is true that Holocaust literature is nothing if not language in a condition of severe diminishment and decline, it is still capable of articulating powerful truths—if none other, then those that reflect life in its diminishment and decline. We have lost so much, but not yet the power to register what it is that has been taken from us.

Surely that is one of the major functions of Holocaust literature, to register and record the enormity of human loss. "For me," as Elie Wiesel once stated it, "writing is a *matzeva,* an invisible tombstone, erected to the memory of the dead unburied" [*Legends of Our Time*]. There is no denying the nobility of that conception of art or the importance of its execution. Yet a tombstone is at best only a minor literary genre, and part of the problem for Wiesel as a writer, as for all writers of the Holocaust, is to discover the literary forms most appropriate to representing the extremities of dehumanization and heroism that together begin to define what the Holocaust was.

In this connection, we must begin by recognizing that even before the advent of a literature of the Holocaust, the major literary genres were in a weakened state of flux and great uncertainty. Holocaust literature, which places its own heavy burdens on literary forms of all kinds, arrived, in fact, at a time when considerable doubt was already being raised about the ongoing viability of the narrative, dramatic, and lyrical modes. While it is not possible here to rehearse the troubled state of modern fiction, drama, and poetry, it can be stated that a large part of the trouble derives from an increasingly felt imbalance between what the world daily offers us as raw data and the mind's ability to make sense of it through its own conceptual and inventive capacities. In the ghettos and camps of Europe "reality" underwent so radical a distortion as to disarm and render no longer trustworthy the normal cognitive and expressive powers. As a result, reason seemed to give way to madness, as language did time and again to silence. When those thresholds dissolve, literature—a product of the composed mind and senses—is reduced to screams and whimpers: it decomposes. And there is no escaping the fact that, in part, Holocaust literature is a literature of decomposition. "No, this is not life!" runs the familiar refrain in Chaim Kaplan's diary. Although Kaplan had lived in Warsaw for forty years and must have come to know it well, its transformation under Nazi rule into a city of madness and slaughter disoriented him almost totally. "At times," he writes, "it seems to me that I am in an alien land, entirely unknown to me." At other times his sense of displacement exceeds anything even resembling the terrestrial, so that it appears "the ghetto was suspended over nothingness."

That strain of irreality runs throughout Holocaust literature and continually undermines it. "Today at this very moment as I sit writing at a table, I am not convinced that these things really happened." The confession in this instance is Primo Levi's [from *Survival in Auschwitz*], but it speaks a common truth, one known to all writers of the Holocaust and one as well that quite obviously subverts the writer's enterprise. For what literary means—what mere words—could possibly compete with the extravagant inventiveness of Nazism? In that time when day was ruled over by the twisted sun of the swastika and night by the dominant black of the Death's Head, life itself became a kind of macabre theatre. Nazism was far more than that, of course, was nothing less than an unrestrained plague of steel and flame, but it also worked in more subtle ways, preparing its ultimate terror by intermediary steps of manipulative distortion and deception. In this respect it might legitimately be grasped within the terms of literary fabrication, terms that a Joseph Goebbels or a Leni Riefenstahl were intimate with. Moreover, it is not difficult to locate the imaginative sources of this aspect of its genius. George Steiner pointed to them quite specifically and also quite accurately, I think, when he argued that Nazism was a literal staging of hell on earth, a perception confirmed by virtually all writers of Holocaust literature. Hell as a prototype of the ghettos and death camps—that, it seems, was Christianity's distinctive contribution to the Final Solution, although one would hope to understand it as a Christianity turned against itself, in rebellion against itself and its own deepest principles.

In this paradigm of ethical and religious subversion, we may be able to discover a literary paradigm as well, one that is constant enough in Holocaust literature to constitute another of its governing laws. To grasp it, we must understand the revisionary and essentially antithetical nature of so much of Holocaust writing, which not only mimics and parodies but finally refutes and rejects its direct literary antecedents. The *Bildungsroman,* as Lawrence Langer has demonstrated, is one of these. In such a book as *Night,* the traditional pattern of successfully initiating a young boy into social life and his own maturity is altogether reversed. Primo Levi's *Survival in Auschwitz,* which chronicles the devolution of a man, is a more complicated instance of the same thing. In both cases one sees not only the reversal of a familiar literary pattern but also a repudiation of the philosophical basis on which it rests. We recall Wiesel's pronouncement of the death of the idea of man. With the crumbling of that idea, all narrative forms that posit the reality of persons—rational, educable, morally responsible beings—are undermined and perhaps even invalidated. Yet such personal narratives of the Holocaust as the two just mentioned necessarily depend upon the traditional means of memoir, autobiography, and *Bildungsroman,* even though the stories they relate rewind the progress of growth backwards—from life toward death. I do not know that Wiesel and Levi consciously chose to counterpoint their terrifying accounts of dehumanization against forms that are essentially civilized and humane, but the effects of such a jarring contrast are unmistakable and strongly felt in their books.

In the case of Paul Celan, it is clear that an attitude of repudiation was specifically developed as a technique for writing post-Holocaust poetry. The evidence, as Jerry Glenn has shown [in his critical study *Paul Celan*] is everywhere—in the ironically destructive allusions to the Song of Songs and Goethe's Faust in "Todesfuge"; in the radical undoing of Hölderlin's famous hymn "Patmos" in "Tenebrae"; in denial of the Genesis account of God's creation of man in "Psalm." In each of these cases (and many similar to them could be brought forward), Celan employs a technique of literary subversion that the German critic Götz Wienold has called a "*Widerruf*" [*Poetica,* 1968]. We have no precise English equivalent for the term— "repudiation" comes closest—but it is not difficult to explain.

Consider, for instance, this line from Chaim Kaplan's diary [*The Warsaw Diary of Chaim Kaplan*]: "The enemy of Israel neither sleeps nor slumbers." Kaplan wrote that, almost certainly, not out of a mood of blasphemy but as an expression of genuine religious despair. It appears in his pages in an entry dated "October 12, 1940/End of Yom Kippur, 5701." On that very day the edict to establish the ghetto went into effect. The year before, at the end of Yom Kippur, 5700, Kaplan noted in his diary that "on the Day of Atonement the enemy displayed even greater might than usual," employing its artillery to destroy and kill at random. In the intervening year the bombardments got only worse, and it became clear to Kaplan that Warsaw Jewry was to face complete destruction. "Is this the way the Almighty looks after His dear ones?" he asks. "Has Israel no God?" He could not admit that, so on Yom Kippur, 5701, he gathered with his fellow Jews, "like Marranos in the fifteenth century," to pray secretly and illegally for God's forgiveness and mercy. What Jewish Warsaw received, however, was not the protection of the Guardian of Israel but the ghetto edict, which then and there effectively sealed the fate of hundreds of thousands of Polish Jews. Kaplan's profound shock at this reversal registers in that terrible line—"The enemy of Israel neither sleeps nor slumbers"—a radical rewriting of Psalm 121:4 that shows, in only a few words, a whole sustaining faith come crashing down. The entry for "October 24, 1940/The night of Simhat Torah, 5701" brings the matter to its bitter conclusion: "But he who sits in Heaven laughs."

In Kaplan's case, it would make no sense to identify such expressions of forlornness and raw pain as examples of conscious "technique," if by that we imply a sustained literary method. Kaplan, a highly literate Jew, composed his diary in Hebrew and quite naturally thought in a language pervaded by Biblical and Talmudic passages. These influences never drop from his prose, but as he witnessed the level of Nazi barbarism rise in the ghetto, they undergo inversion, substitution, and reversals. In brief, they are destabilized, demoralized, subverted. Writing under this kind of pressure becomes counter-commentary.

The Yiddish poet Jacob Glatstein, like Celan, adopted these changes deliberately and developed them technically in his poems. I suspect that André Schwarz-Bart worked somewhat similarly in writing *The Last of the Just,* a novel that should be understood as an exhaustion not only of the Jewish tradition of the *Lamed-Vov* but of the Christian traditions of the saint's life and the *imitatio Christi* as well. In *The Painted Bird* Jerzy Kosinski will appropriate some of the language of the New Testament and Christian liturgy only to undermine it and invalidate its claims to permanent religious truth. Rolf Hochhuth will do the same in his highly charged and controversial play, which, among other things, offers itself as a contemporary rewriting of the lives of the Popes.

The common element in all these examples is the employment of the literary text as refutation and repudiation, a denial not only of an antecedent literary assertion but also of its implicit premises and explicit affirmations. In the main, Holocaust literature relies for its expression on the received languages and the established literary forms. It does so, however, in the profoundly revisionary way that we have been noticing, turning earlier literary models against themselves and, in the process, overturning the reigning conceptions of man and his world that speak in and through the major writings of our literary traditions. Levi, cognizant of these reversals and denials, suggests where they might lead us when he asks, "Our stories, . . . all different and all full of a tragic, disturbing necessity, . . . are they not themselves stories of a new

Bible?" If we agree that they are, then Holocaust literature is at its heart of hearts revelatory in some new way, although of what we do not yet know.

There is something preposterous and even obscene about the notion of gross evil being inspiring, yet more than anything else, it is this crime, simultaneously searing and illuminating, that has inflicted the writer's vocation on the novelists and poets of the Holocaust. That it is an infliction is no longer open to doubt, for all survivors of this catastrophe who venture to write about it confess a disfiguration or impairment of one kind or another—a lapse in vision, a muteness of voice, other vaguer disturbances of the sensorium. Think of how badly mutilated Ernie Levy is, how some of Celan's poems break down into stammering, how pervasive the fear of blinding is in Kosinski's writings, how often Elie Wiesel's survivors seem to be struck dumb. For a summarizing example, think most of all of that frightening line in one of Nelly Sachs's late poems—the most costly *ars poetica* I know—"This can be put on paper only / with one eyed ripped out." No one touched by the Holocaust is ever whole again—that much this literature makes clear.

Yet that is not the whole truth, for while crime is impairing, it is also powerfully vivifying, exposing the world as never before in all of its most frightful detail. It is as if the fires that consumed so many also carried with them a kind of wicked illumination. Yitzhak Katznelson's description of his own pain, pairing as it does infirmity and insight, is paradigmatic: "These last four years I have been shocked and confused at what is being perpetrated so brazenly before the whole world. For nearly a year now, I feel like one broken both in body and mind. . . . My emotions are benumbed. . . . There are, however, terrible moments when I am acutely alert, when shafts of light pierce and hurt me like sharp needles" [*Vittel Diary*]. The Holocaust has worked on its authors in a double way, then, simultaneously disabling them and enlarging their vision, so that they see with an almost prophetic exactness. Holocaust writers, in short, are one-eyed seers, men possessed of a double knowledge: cursed into knowing how perverse the human being can be to create such barbarism and blessed by knowing how strong he can be to survive it.

Saul Bellow expands upon this phenomenon in fine detail in his characterization of Artur Sammler, [the title character of *Mr. Sammler's Planet*], who is, I believe, a prototype of the Holocaust writer. A widower who lost his wife to the Nazis, Sammler himself survives Hitler by escaping from a mass grave and then hiding out in the forests, cellars, and cemeteries of Poland. Struck in the eye by a German gun butt, he suffers a visual obstruction, but at the same time the very nature of his experience has enlarged his sight, vivifying all things and allowing him to make the subtlest kinds of distinctions among them. His vocation, in other words, is that of a seer, a man of unusual perception whose observations carry the ring of authority.

But, given the damage done to Mr. Sammler's sight, does he qualify as a trustworthy seer? From where or what does he derive his authority? He will raise this question himself more than once: "Of course since Poland, nineteen thirty-nine, my judgments are different. Altered. Like my eyesight." To one of his interlocutors Sammler even apologizes for his "deformity," acknowledging that the abnormality of his experience during the war years brings him sometimes to suspect his own judgments: "My lot has been extreme. . . . One cannot come out intact."

Nevertheless, when it comes to determining "the true stature of a human being," Artur Sammler's point of view is fully informed and his vision the most delicate of recording systems. That is the case because after his experiences, he is able to look at life as one who has been inside death. His survival removed from him all distortions imposed by the fear of death and, in this sense, granted him not so much an exceptional vision but the only one that can properly see and assess life in the post-Holocaust period.

Such vision, as one soon comes to recognize in reading the Holocaust writers, has been purchased at an unusually high price. Physical injury, visual impairment, linguistic incapacity, the moral discouragements of listener lassitude and reader reluctance—what kind of literature can develop against such extreme countervailing forces? The answer is, a literature of fragments, of partial and provisional forms, no one of which by itself can suffice to express the Holocaust, but the totality of which begins to accumulate and register a coherent and powerful effect. On this one point all writers agree: the most that can ever be said individually will be nothing more than a beginning, a small opening into a large and barely imaginable truth. Historical research can begin to identify and gather some of the pieces, but literary forms that aim to be more encompassing and synthesizing inevitably come up against their limitations and fail, as they must, whenever inclusiveness or comprehensiveness is wanted. We have had no Milton or Tolstoy of the Holocaust and should not soon await one; in fact, it is wiser to discourage expectation of a literature of epic scope and look instead to its opposite, to the shards and fragments that reveal, in their separateness and brokenness, the uncountable small tragedies that together add up to something larger than the tragic sense implies.

If every broken head is a fragment of divinity . . . then the most we can do as readers intent on glimpsing something close to wholeness is to assemble some of the shattered pieces. To make such an admission is not to deny the validity of a more holistic approach to knowledge or to discourage historical or critical efforts at integration, but rather to underline the importance of reading Holocaust writings as part of a composite literature, more impressive in the sum of its parts than as separate statements. The corporate impact far surpasses at this stage what any individual work can do.

If this view of Holocaust literature is correct, then one should read it with an ear attuned to its collective voices rather than to more isolated instances of expressive genius. To be sure, each of the writers we shall be concerned with may have written out his story or that of others in ways that are in some manner singular and distinct. Nevertheless, while amidst the general horror we are able to recognize individuated styles and concerns, for the most part we respond to them and learn from them as representative voices of a collective fate. The specific details of living and dying can never be lost or overlooked, but within the common features of this literature they do not easily overleap the boundaries of shared experience that a common history defines. . . . [This] is especially true for the documentary literature, so much of which reaches us in diaries, journals, and memoirs that seem to be more the consecutive and often repetitive chapters of an ongoing, multi-authored story than the discrete narratives of single personalities. The individual cry is always recognizable, but as it echoes across a continent it is the assemblage of pain and rebellion that impresses itself upon us more than anything else. To hear it otherwise is in this instance to hear falsely. (pp. 12-34)

Alvin H. Rosenfeld, "The Problematics of Holocaust Literature," in his A Double Dying: Reflections on Holocaust Literature, *Indiana University Press, 1980, pp. 12-34.*

DIARIES AND MEMOIRS

Irving Halperin

[*An American educator, Halperin is the author of* Here I Am: A Jew in Today's Germany *(1971). In the following essay, he examines meaning and despair in the memoirs of Holocaust survivors.*]

> We stumbled on in the darkness, over big stones and through large puddles, along the one road leading from the camp. The accompanying guards kept shouting at us and driving us with the butts of their rifles. Anyone with very sore feet supported himself on his neighbor's arm. Hardly a word was spoken; the icy wind did not encourage talk. Hiding his mouth behind his up-turned collar, the man marching next to me whispered suddenly: "If our wives could see us now! I do hope they are better off in their camps and don't know what is happening to us."
>
> That brought thoughts of my own wife to mind. And as we stumbled on for miles, slipping on icy spots, supporting each other time and again, dragging one another up and onward, nothing was said, but we both knew: each of us was thinking of his wife. Occasionally I looked at the sky, where the stars were fading and the pink light of the morning was beginning to spread behind a dark bank of clouds. But my mind clung to my wife's image, imagining it with uncanny acuteness. I heard her answering me, saw her smile, her frank and encouraging look. Real or not, her look was then more luminous than the sun which was beginning to rise.
> —Viktor Frankl, *From Death-Camp to Existentialism*

So our nights drag on. The dream of Tantalus and the dream of the story are woven into a texture of more indistinct images: the suffering of the day, composed of hunger, blows, cold, exhaustion, fear and promiscuity, turns at nighttime into shapeless nightmares of unheard-of violence, which in free life would only occur during a fever. One wakes up at every moment, frozen with terror, shaking in every limb, under the impression of an order shouted out by a voice full of anger in a language not understood. The procession to the bucket and the thud of bare heels on the wooden floor turns into another symbolic procession: it is us again, grey and identical, small as ants, yet so huge as to reach up to the stars, bound one against the other, countless, covering the plain as far as the horizon; sometimes melting into a single substance, a sorrowful turmoil in which we all feel ourselves trapped and suffocated; sometimes marching in a circle, without beginning or end, with a blinding giddiness and a sea of nausea rising from the praecordia to the gullet; until hunger or cold or the fullness of our bladders turn our dreams into their customary forms.

—Primo Levi, *If This Is a Man*

Felled to the ground, stunned with blows, the old man cried:

"Meir. Meir, my boy! Don't you recognize me? I'm your father . . . you're hurting me . . . you're killing your father! I've got some bread . . . for you too . . . for you too . . . "

He collapsed. His fist was still clenched around a small piece. He tried to carry it to his mouth. But the other one threw himself upon him and snatched it. The old man again whispered something, let out a rattle, and died amid the general indifference. His son searched him, took the bread, and began to devour it. He was not able to get very far. Two men had seen and hurled themselves upon him. Others joined in. When they withdrew, next to me were two corpses, side by side, the father and the son.

I was fifteen years old.

—Elie Wiesel, *Night*

I learnt that within me, as in others, the murderer and the humanitarian exist side by side; the weak child with the voracious male. That I am not in any way superior, that I am not different from others, that I am but a link in the great chain, was among the greatest discoveries of my life. From then on I resolved to support those who fell, even as I had been supported. When someone was despicable, greedy and selfish, I remembered all the occasions when I, too, had been despicable, greedy and selfish. Buchenwald taught me to be tolerant of myself, and by that means tolerant to others.

It may be that I would have learnt this without the lesson of Buchenwald. But I would have learnt it much later—perhaps too late.

—Eugene Heimler, *Night of the Mist*

Four statements by four authors and two essential points of view: to survive as a prisoner in the camps one had to descend to the level of animals; and, conversely, despite the brutalizing conditions in the camps, it was possible for a prisoner to be impressively human. There is, of course,

nothing unique about this two-sided observation. One would expect that there were as many different kinds of behavior among the prisoners as there were environmental differences from camp to camp; for example, it was generally easier for a prisoner in a so-called model camp like Sachsenhausen to maintain a semblance of composure than for prisoners who were exposed to substantially greater hardships and pressures in Auschwitz. All this is to underscore the self-evident: so many prisoners, so many conditions. Therefore it is not for us to assert cavalierly that this or that former prisoner conducted himself commendably whereas this or that prisoner carried on badly. Especially those of us who were spared the ordeal of being "there" have not earned the right to make such value judgments.

Then why the opening four quotations and the above statement about the two essential points of view they represent? For one, this arrangement is intended to provide a principle of organization for some key issues in the personal narratives. Also, the views represented by the above quotations underscore the opposing evaluations of some survivor-writers as they look back at the past: those, on the one hand, who contend that in a time when men bestially defiled and disfigured the bodies and spirits of other men, suicide or madness or nihilism for any self-respecting person would have been understandable. They aver that there was no such thing as "transcending" one's suffering in the camps, that the Nazis were beasts and they made beasts of the prisoners. And, on the other hand, those survivor-writers who believe that many of the oppressed in the camps were ennobled by their suffering.

What follows, then, is an examination of some widely acclaimed personal narratives. In this genre I include Elie Wiesel's autobiographical novel, *Night,* whose point of view and essential manner is that of personal narration.

Such an unbearably depressing body of literature. But are there any places in it that "lift up" the reader? In affirmative response to this question, we can look to *From Death-Camp to Existentialism,* by Viktor Frankl, a professor of psychiatry and neurology at the University of Vienna, who was imprisoned for three years at Auschwitz and other camps. A number of incidents in this important book point up the spiritual resources of some remarkable human beings. First, there is the unforgettable scene where Frankl buoys up the spirits of his fellow prisoners. This incident happened at a time when the morale of the men in his hut was at a dangerously low point. Hungry and cold, plagued by lice, illnesses, and severe depression, they despaired of going on; it seemed to them that their suffering was senseless, that it would be better to give up, die, and be done with the daily torture. From such despair the next step downward was to become a Mussulman, a member of the living dead, they who were almost beyond pain. In this dark moment a senior block warden, knowing of Frankl's background as a psychiatrist, persuaded him to offer his disconsolate comrades a "medical care for their souls."

One evening after work, Frankl spoke to them. He sought to instill in them a justification, a moral sanction for attempting to live through their unbearable circumstances.

He encouraged them to bear their suffering with whatever dignity was possible; to be, in short, as Dostoevsky used the phrase—and Frankl frequently alludes to it—worthy of their suffering. As the present was a nightmare, he began by speaking to them of the past and future.

Frankl himself is ailing, hungry, cold, despondent; so he is scarcely in a frame of mind to minister to others. Yet he says that their situation, though extremely grave, is not altogether futile; some of them will survive; they need to "hold on" and hope for the best. But it would not have taken an extraordinary man to say this much to them. Inmates of the camps frequently exhorted one another to hold on, to *iberlebyn* (to remain alive). What makes Frankl's exhortation distinctive is the depth and power of his remarks. Even if they perish, he suggests, whatever they have experienced in the past is not lost.

> Again I quoted a poet—to avoid sounding like a preacher myself—who had written, *"Was Du erlebst, kann keine Macht der Welt Dir rauben."* (What you have experienced, no power on earth can take from you.) Not only our experiences, but all we have done . . . and all we have suffered, all this is not lost, though it is past; we have brought it into being. Having been is also a kind of being, and perhaps the surest kind.

Then he returns to the present, to their situation in the camp. His comrades lie motionless, listening attentively, as he goes on to speak of the spiritual challenge before each man: the necessity to be "worthy" of one's suffering and to find some meaning in their situation.

> I told my comrades . . . that human life, under any circumstances, never ceases to have a meaning, and that this infinite meaning of life includes suffering and dying, privation and death. I asked the poor creatures who listened to me attentively in the darkness of the hut to face up to the seriousness of our position. They must not lose hope but should keep their courage in the certainty that the hopelessness of our struggle did not detract from its dignity and meaning. I said that someone looks down on each of us in difficult hours—a friend, a wife, somebody alive or dead, or a God—and he would not expect us to disappoint him. He would hope to find us suffering proudly—not miserably—knowing how to die.

"Knowing how to die . . . " How remarkable! To encourage one another to die with dignity in, of all places, an extermination camp! His words invoke accounts of observant Jews who went to their deaths in the gas chambers with heads high, backs straight, singing *Ani Maamin* ("I Believe"). So, too, in *The Holocaust Kingdom*, Lena Donat recalls the way in which some Greek Jewish women went to the gas chambers:

> When they went to their deaths they sang the "Hatikvah," the song of an old people which has always carried the vision of Zion in its heart. Since then every time I hear "Hatikvah" I always see them, the dregs of human misery, and I know that through mankind flows a stream of eternity greater and more powerful than individual deaths.

What was the immediate result of Frankl's remarks to his comrades? He remembers that at the conclusion of his words, he saw "the miserable figures of my friends limping toward me to thank me with tears in their eyes." Frankl does not consider this response an occasion for self-congratulation; for in the sentence directly following the one just cited, he adds: "But I have to confess here that only too rarely had I the inner strength to make contact with my companions in suffering and that I must have missed many opportunities for doing so."

How are we to view this incident? Men are ill, in pain; they need food, warmth. Frankl offers them only words—yet the words touch responsive chords in them, and they come forward to express their gratitude. In other parts of the camp, the SS are sadistically humiliating, torturing, murdering. Defenseless men and women are shot; Germans dispose of thousands with phenol injections; prisoners are hanged on the courtyard gallows; the infamous camp official, Boger, employs his "typewriter" [a form of torture] with zeal. These are the cultured and civilized Germans. By contrast, Frankl and his comrades, these "subhumans," probe into the farthest reaches of the spirit while the "superior" Aryans lash out with truncheons and fists. So that when Frankl's comrades come toward him with tears of gratitude in their eyes, one can grasp why there was a genuine release of spiritual elation in Auschwitz.

There are other equally moving incidents in the book. To dwell lovingly on the image of one's wife and to take immense pleasure from seeing the forms of nature, these, too, were ways of giving meaning to one's wretched existence in the camps. Such observation and reflection helped Frankl to find a *why* to live, for—to recall Nietzsche's saying: "He who has a *why* to live for can bear almost any *how*."

One "why" was through love. Although he had no way of knowing where she was—or whether she was even still alive—Frankl often thought of his wife. Nothing, he avows, could diminish the strength of his love.

> Had I known then that my wife was dead, I think that I would still have given myself, undisturbed by that knowledge, to the contemplation of her image, and that my mental conversation with her would have been just as vivid and just as satisfying. "Set me like a seal upon thy heart, love is as strong as death."

In the camp, men are proficient in the means of hate, Nazi-style, and yet Frankl wills to love! He is mercilessly beaten with the butts of rifles, forced to walk for miles through darkness and over ice; and yet, astonishingly, his mind clings to an image of his wife. Sometimes the intensity and radiance of this image makes it more real than the all too palpable landmarks of fences, huts, watchtowers, crematoria. And once, in a particularly black moment, Frankl feels he has grasped the deeper meaning of human love.

> A thought transfixed me: for the first time in my life I saw the truth as it is set into song by so many poets, proclaimed as the final wisdom by so many thinkers. The truth—that love is the ultimate and the highest goal to which man can aspire. Then I grasped the meaning of the greatest

secret that human poetry and human thought and belief have to impart: *The salvation of man is through love and in love.* I understood how a man who has nothing left in this world still may know bliss, be it only for a brief moment, in the contemplation of his beloved.

The point is that it was in Auschwitz, in *anus mundi,* as the Nazis referred to it, he perceived this truth; before then it apparently had been for him only a theoretical generalization. Thus, in the greatest extermination center of recorded history, Frankl experienced on his very pulses the validity of love as the "final wisdom."

Just as it is remarkable that his devotion transcended the physical absence of his wife, so, too, not even the coldest winter days nor the abuse of the guards could blunt his feelings for her. He would recall her face, voice, and this would help to sustain him through cycles of exhaustion, hunger, depression. On one occasion, a freezing winter dawn, as he was at work in a trench under the surveillance of a sadistic guard, he seems to have had a mystical experience.

> For hours I stood hacking at the icy ground. The guard passed by, insulting me, and once again I communed with my beloved. More and more I felt that she was present, that she was with me; I had the feeling that I was able to touch her, able to stretch out my hand and grasp hers. The feeling was very strong: she was *there.* Then, at that very moment, a bird flew down silently and perched just in front of me, on the heap of soil which I had dug up from the ditch, and looked steadily at me.

Still, what is one such inspiring moment, it may be asked, against the twelve years of destruction? For every such transcendent experience there were thousands of banal ones. The day-by-day "banality" of people being reduced to Mussulmen, dehumanized, and destroyed. Is it "mystical" to expire in a gas chamber? or to be shot down at the Black Wall of Auschwitz? or burned alive in a ditch?

And yet it would be unfortunate if the significance of this incident were minimized. For prior to its occurrence, Frankl had despaired that his suffering was meaningless. He and his fellow prisoners were clad in rags; they stood hacking away at the icy ground; gloom enveloped him, and he felt that death drew near. Altogether, the moment was no less grim than the one in which Camus's Sisyphus finds himself before his decision to keep rolling a stone up the hill. Precisely then, when his suffering was at a nadir, Frankl came to reflect on an image of his wife. And while he was "conversing silently" with her, he heard a "Yes," as though in response to the question: Is there any meaning to all this?

A moment later, as though to indicate some sign under the "miserable gray" sky, a light went on in a distant farmhouse. The "Yes" and the light were immediately followed by the appearance of the bird. All these "responses" to Frankl's question served to shape his belief in an ultimate higher meaning of human existence; and he felt he had found a "why" to live for.

As Frankl's inner life became more intensely attuned to memories of his wife and to the spiritual needs of his comrades, he apparently became more open to the beauty of the physical world beyond the barbed wire. On one occasion he was moved by a view of the mountains of Salzburg with their summits glowing in the distance. Another time he was arrested by an especially beautiful sunset.

> One evening, when we were already resting on the floor of our hut, dead tired, soup bowls in hand, a fellow prisoner rushed in and asked us to run out to the assembly grounds and see the wonderful sunset. Standing outside we saw sinister clouds glowing in the west and the whole sky alive with clouds of ever-changing shapes and colors, from steel blue to blood red. The desolate grey mud huts provided a sharp contrast, while the puddles on the muddy ground reflected the glowing sky. Then, after minutes of moving silence, one prisoner said to another, "How beautiful the world *could* be!"

Here the sky was as a light shining through the darkness, and the peacefulness and beauty of nature appeared to him as evidence of the essential health of the universe.

The astonishing capacity of human beings! The prisoners were hungry and cold, plagued by illness, harassed by guards, and yet they would respond powerfully to a sunset, the song of a lark, a flowering meadow. In reflecting on this capacity for such response, one begins to follow Nietzsche's words—"That which does not kill me makes me stronger."

Ultimately, then, Frankl came to see his ordeal in Auschwitz as a spiritual challenge that he wanted to be "worthy" of. Determined to "get through" and not to "go around" his suffering, he, in effect, said to himself: This apparently is how my lot must be for a time; it is important to be of good courage.

> When a man finds that it is his destiny to suffer, he will have to accept his suffering as his task; . . . the fact that even in suffering he is unique and alone in the universe. No one can relieve him of his suffering or suffer in his place. His unique opportunity lies in the way in which he bears his burden.

He had come to view his imprisonment not as something abnormal, tangential to his existence, but rather as a spiritual test—a test that had to be squarely confronted with toughness of mind, compassion for the anguish of one's comrades, and trust in the ultimate meaning of the ordeal. In the face of all that was Auschwitz, the will to believe that something significant might be taking place within oneself was an extraordinary expression of spiritual freedom, and within this perspective, Frankl's experiences as a prisoner are instructive for contemporary readers who wish to probe the moral center of Holocaust literature.

It is important to point out the spiritual resistance of survivors like Frankl. It is well to realize that there were men in the camps who lifted up their fellow sufferers, who were moved by sunsets, the sight of flowers growing beside barbed wire. Although we have mountains of evidence documenting what was destroyed during the twelve Hitler years, we are far from glutted by accounts, like Frankl's, of the ways in which men remained impressively human.

But—and this is a big word here—just as it is important to know that some prisoners could not be spiritually broken by their imprisonment, so, too, it is well to realize that we have been discussing an exceptional man; few are capable of Frankl's iron-willed resolve—and ability—to conduct himself with dignity and courage in Auschwitz. Almost at the poles from Frankl's affirmative, will-to-meaning perspective is a view which has been preeminently represented by Primo Levi, the celebrated Italian-Jewish writer, in *If This Is a Man:*

> We do not believe in the most obvious and facile deduction: that man is fundamentally brutal, egoistic and stupid in his conduct once every civilized institution is taken away, and that the Häftling is consequently nothing but a man without inhibitions. We believe, rather, that the only conclusion to be drawn is that in the face of driving necessity and physical disabilities many social habits and instincts are reduced to silence.

" . . . many social habits and instincts are reduced to silence." What exactly is meant here? *What* social habits did Levi see "reduced to silence" in Auschwitz? His observations therein began with his arrival at the camp in early 1944; he was then twenty-four. Overnight he found himself in a nether universe where blows, cold, hunger, and death were the order of the day. A year later he took stock of his circumstances; and no writer on the Holocaust has written a more somber statement on how such an experience alters a man.

> This time last year I was a free man: an outlaw but free, I had a name and a family, I had an eager and restless mind, an agile and healthy body. I used to think of many, far-away things: of my work, of the end of the war, of good and evil, of the nature of things and of the laws which govern human actions; and also of the mountains, of singing and loving, of music, of poetry. I had an enormous, deep-rooted foolish faith in the benevolence of fate; to kill and to die seemed extraneous literary things to me. My days were both cheerful and sad, but I regretted them equally, they were all full and positive; and the future stood before me as a great treasure. Today the only thing left of the life of these days is what one needs to suffer hunger and cold; I am not even alive enough to know how to kill myself.

Levi soon realized that to exist from day to day in Auschwitz, one had to make compromises with one's usual standards of ethics and morality. Prisoners were encouraged by the camp officials to feel that each man had to look after only Number One. Their captors had taken almost everything away from them—their clothing, hair, and even their names; the Nazis often referred to them merely by the numbers tattooed on their flesh. Indeed, the only thing the Nazis could not take away from them was their resolve to hang on, as long as possible, to a sense of their own identity.

In such circumstances survival often depended, Levi observed, on being cunning, selfish, ruthless; sometimes it depended, alas, on serving as an informer. To resist the pressures that turned the resigned into Mussulmen, one had to wear an inner armor that was resistant to pity and, above all, hope; for hope could be still another source of disappointment and pain. Rather, the imprisoned were constrained to become inwardly as hard as steel so that they would not break. In Primo Levi's words:

> One has to fight against the current; to battle every day and every hour against exhaustion, hunger, cold and the resulting inertia; to resist enemies and have no pity for rivals; to sharpen one's wits, build up one's patience, strengthen one's will power. Or else, to throttle all dignity and kill all conscience, to climb down into the arena as a beast against other beasts, to let oneself be guided by those unsuspected subterranean forces which sustain families and individuals in cruel times.

Which is to say that the suffering of the prisoners did not make for saints; brutalized, starving men compromised their usual moral principles for a piece of bread.

The narrator of Elie Wiesel's *Night* similarly became aware of the necessity for "aberration" and "compromise" in Buna. He too encountered few saints behind barbed wire. The majority of his fellow prisoners were bowed down by their suffering until they were "cringing like beaten dogs." For how many men could have maintained their self-respect in a place where the starving fought each other—sometimes even a son against a father—for a few crumbs of bread? Nor was Eliezer, the narrator, himself free from "aberrations." When, for example, his father was struck by a Gypsy, Eliezer said nothing, did nothing. To have avenged the insult to his father by striking the Gypsy would have been a blow for his self-respect, but it also would have cost Eliezer's life. Again, when his father lay dying and with his last breath called for him, Eliezer admits he did not reply, fearing to draw attention to himself from camp officials; moreover, he was relieved to be freed of the "dead weight" burden his ailing father had become for him.

> . . . at the same moment this thought came into my mind: "Don't let me find him! If only I could get rid of this dead weight, so that I could use all my strength to struggle for my own survival, and only worry about myself." Immediately I felt ashamed of myself, ashamed forever.

But if he had been relieved of a "burden," not so of guilt. "I abandoned him"—this is the self-accusation that would never leave him.

Thus in the world of the Lager, where men had to be "less than human," where aberration and compromise were the rule, not the exception, where men found it wise not to try to "understand" what was happening to them, certain traditional social habits and values were, of necessity, "reduced to silence." Within this perspective, then, Levi poses the question, "Would it have made sense for a prisoner to adhere to a well defined and structured system of ethics and morals?" His answer is in the negative. What the world outside the camp considered virtue was not desirable from Levi's viewpoint or from that of his fellow prisoners. In the Lager the words "good," "evil," "just," and "unjust" lost their familiar meanings; Auschwitz and Buchenwald were hardly ideal settings for maintaining moral absolutes. If ever there was a time and place when the practice of an ethical relativism or situational ethics could have been justified, it was in the Lager.

The question bitterly raised by Levi at the end of his narrative is—"Are these, the survivors of Auschwitz, actually *men?*" The last chapter describes the miserable conditions confronting Levi and his comrades after the Germans had fled and while they were waiting for the Russians to arrive. Everywhere, prisoners, "starving specters," "unshaven with hollow eyes, greyish skeleton bones in rags" lay dying from typhus, pneumonia, scarlet fever, dysentery, and tuberculosis. Allied bombs had cut off the water and electricity supplies. Latrines were overflowing, for no one had the strength to look after their maintenance. During below-zero weather, the central heating system was inoperative and windows were broken in some of the huts. Even those who were comparatively well felt inert and helpless. Levi saw "ragged, decrepit, skeleton-like" prisoners dragging themselves over "the frozen soil, like an invasion of worms." Many corpses lay exposed in the snow; and others, "rigid as wood," rested on bunks in the huts. In the wards of the camp infirmary, lying in frozen excrement, patients continually cried out for help that could not be given to them. Some men died slowly, torturously, and in the grip of delirium. Levi describes one such death, that of a fifty-year-old Hungarian chemist.

> Following a last interminable dream of acceptance and slavery he began to murmur: "Jawohl" with every breath, regularly and continuously like a machine, "Jawohl," at every collapsing of his wretched frame, thousands of times, enough to make one want to shake him, to suffocate him, at least to make him change the word.
>
> I never understood so clearly as at that moment how laborious is the death of a man.

I have deliberately underscored the details of the misery that gripped Levi and his comrades as they waited some ten days for the Russians to arrive. Perhaps it would be well if these details were to be repeated again and again, like the words of a dirge, for they are emblematic of the anguish that men inflicted upon men in our time. The post-Auschwitz reader who was not "there" feebly tries to imagine how it must have been during that period of waiting. How the prisoners must have lain in their bunks, wondering whether they could hold on until the Russians arrived. Some may not have wanted to think too much about the promised liberation, because hope could turn to unbearable disappointment and fresh pain. Supposing the Germans staged a successful counterattack, stopped the advancing Russians, and came back to the camp? So then one morning they would awake to see that the watchtowers were again manned by Germans.

It is not too surprising, then, that in such an inferno some would prefer death to life. . . . After having been witness to the most degrading scenes of the twentieth century, many prisoners did not want to return to the "civilized" world. Enough! they must have cried out from the depths of their agony and given up the fierce daily struggle for clinging to life. Untouchables in their own eyes and in the eyes of others, they may have eventually looked to death as a merciful deliverer.

And yet here one recalls Frankl thinking lovingly of his wife while working, on a winter dawn, in a ditch. The ground is icy, the guard hurls insults at Frankl, but the latter is sustained by dwelling on an image of his wife. By comparison, it is a rare moment in Levi's *If This Is a Man* when prisoners are actually shown thinking of their loved ones. The most notable exception to this condition occurs once when Levi and his hutmates have had an unexpected windfall—an extra portion of rancid soup and turnips. They eat, feel content, and *then only* are "able to think of our mothers and wives, which usually does not happen." Did not often happen when a prisoner was starving, because then he barely had enough strength to think about one thing—bread.

Given the nature of his experiences, there is wisdom and courage in Levi's reluctance to reach for moral absolutes or "transcending" experiences. Not for him discourses on "love," "meaning," "beauty." Perhaps his morality is the stark honesty with which he documents the view that to survive in Auschwitz one had to become *less* than human. For we recognize the terrible clarity of what he says to us at the end of his book: There is no "meaning" to be gleaned from this wanton destruction; it was all cruelly senseless. And that finally we were liberated does not mean that we won a victory over our oppressors. In the end, though freed, we were defeated; in reality the Germans, though vanquished, emerged the victors. They "won" because by the time the day of liberation came, we had already been reduced to the state of animals. Hence the tone of what must be one of the most profoundly disquieting passages in Holocaust literature.

> We lay in a world of death and phantoms. The last trace of civilization had vanished around and inside us. The work of bestial degradation, begun by the victorious Germans, had been carried to its conclusion by the Germans in defeat.
>
> It is man who kills, man who creates or suffers injustice; it is no longer man who, having lost all restraint, shares his bed with a corpse. Whoever waits for his neighbor to die in order to take his piece of bread is, albeit guiltless, further from the model of thinking man than the most primitive pigmy or the most vicious sadist.

There can be no more tragic commentary than Levi's on what was done by men to men in our time. When the prisoners pounced like beasts upon the bread that was given them, their liberators could not have readily pictured that these half skeletons had once spoken of Truth and Beauty, Goodness and Justice. So, too, in describing the liberation at Buchenwald, Eliezer of Wiesel's *Night* bitterly laments: "Our first act as free men was to throw ourselves onto the provisions. We thought only of that. Not of revenge, not of our families. Nothing but bread."

The liberated had come through cold, starvation, torture,

and yet, in any ultimate reckoning, they had not really been freed. Many would long be enchained by recurring feelings of guilt and shame for having survived. Survived? In body, yes, but internally they would still be back in the camps. Hence the next to last sentence of *Night,* when Eliezer first looks at himself in a mirror after the Buchenwald liberation: "From the depths of the mirror, a corpse gazed back at me."

That survivors like Levi and Wiesel cannot forget should not be surprising. If Anatoly Kuznetsov, who was never in a concentration camp or walled ghetto, fell into a "comatose state of endless nightmares" [*The New York Times Book Review* (9 April 1967)] when he began to write his novel on the mass murders at Babi Yar, how much more reason there is for those who were imprisoned behind barbed wire to be haunted by the past.

Bodies in calcium chloride, infants killed by lethal injections and placed in boxes, prisoners sharing their bunks with corpses, prisoners stealing bread from the sick and dying—this is what some of the survivors remember, looking back on their days in the camps. By contrast, Frankl remembers how his comrades and he responded to sunsets, to the singing of Italian arias. How, following his liberation, he walked through the country for miles, hearing the joyous sounds of larks; and that at some point during this walk he looked up at the sky and then went down on his knees, thinking: "I called to the Lord from my narrow prison and He answered me in the freedom of space." Frankl's rebirth in the fields needs to be valued for what it says about the capacity of human beings to weather despair and loss and still seek spiritual resurrection.

But saying that much is not to stipulate that Frankl's religious experience ought to call forth from the reader an entirely affirmative response; his spiritual achievement here has to be seen in scale. For, surely, the center of Holocaust literature is not concerned with a few remarkable men who may have transcended their suffering but rather with the millions who were destroyed. Resurrection may follow death, the phoenix may rise from the ashes, but paeans of praise to human endurance and spiritual resistance cannot turn ashes back into warm, living bodies.

Still, any balanced computation of the tragic facts must include recognition of some extraordinary ways in which the oppressed turned a human face to one another. Neither Primo Levi nor Elie Wiesel, grim as their reports are, denies the crucial importance of human relationships in the camps; indeed, they point out that to the extent the prisoners helped one another their ordeal was given a semblance of meaning. True, but not the kind of meaning that evolved from meditating on an image of one's beloved or from being moved by a sunset or from giving a "pep talk" to one's despondent fellow prisoners; rather, the meaning derived from responding compassionately to the needs of one's comrades-in-suffering. Hence in *Night* the advice given by a Polish prisoner at Auschwitz to newly arrived inmates:

> Let there be comradeship among you. We are all brothers, and we are all suffering the same fate. The same smoke floats over all our heads. Help one another.

And when the veteran has finished speaking, Eliezer thinks: "The first human words."

In the last days of Auschwitz, Primo Levi, as we indicated earlier, existed in a "world of death and phantoms"; starving prisoners waited to steal a piece of bread from the weak and defenseless; in the dispensary, the sick and dying lay beside corpses; the bodies of the dead rose out of ditches, latrines overflowed . . . Nothing in Dante's *Inferno* is more terrifying than these scenes in the Lager. Even so, embittered as Levi is by the knowledge of what men did to men during that time, the last words of his book describe the healing influence of human friendship. We see Levi and his friends Arthur and Charles by a stove at night, smoking cigarettes made of herbs, and listening to the sounds of gunfire in the distance. "In the middle of this endless plain, frozen and full of war, we felt at peace with ourselves and with the world." Sitting with his friends by the stove, Levi felt that they were beginning to change from Häftlings (prisoners) to men again. In Levi's words:

> Part of our existence lies in the feelings of those near to us. This is why the experience of someone who has lived for days during which man was merely a thing in the eyes of man is nonhuman. We three were for the most part immune from it, and we owe each other mutual gratitude.

Giving to others—this, too, is the last word of Eugene Heimler's *Night of the Mist.* Heimler was twenty-one when the Germans invaded Hungary in the spring of 1944. His father was arrested and never seen again. His wife and family were deported to Auschwitz and died there. Heimler survived Buchenwald and other camps.

Before his imprisonment, Heimler felt—and apparently with good reason—that Hungarian Christians treated him, a Jew, as though he were a second-class citizen. Looked upon as an inferior person, he came to think of himself as one. Perhaps in an attempt to compensate for his frequent sense of being rejected by others, he became very competitive and sought to "show the world" that he was "twice as good" as those who looked down at him.

In Buchenwald he outgrew this immature need. There he learned that he had to answer to no one but himself. From the beginning of his internment, he was thrown back upon his own resources; and the more these supported him the more he developed a sense of self-esteem. But before such awareness came to him, he was lashed by self-loathing. He felt shame in observing himself "scheming how to get a bigger chunk of bread." It shamed him also that he had become so hardened that even the "sight of people lying in their congealed blood in the ditch beneath the electric fence had ceased to quicken my pulse." He witnessed savage beatings when his fists were "no longer itching to get at the murderers." Nor was his self-esteem enhanced by the fact that he had become, in his own words, a "whore's pimp"; he made love to a Gypsy girl, and in exchange for his embraces she gave him bread, margarine, and jam.

What gave him a measure of self-respect was his determination to remain alive, to outlive his captors, so that one day he could bear witness against them.

This resolve helped Heimler to "hang on" from day to

day; and, gradually, as he came to see that he was being tested by Buchenwald, his inner strength was revealed to him. He discovered not only the positive values of his own life but also the deeper ways in which he was spiritually bound to other men.

> It was in Buchenwald that I learned, from Jews, Christians, Moslems, and pagans, from Englishmen, Serbs, Rumanians, Czechs, Frenchmen, Belgians, Dutch, Russians, Greeks, Albanians, Poles and Italians that I was only one more suffering insignificant man. . . . I learned that within me, as in others, the murderer and the humanitarian exist side by side; the weak child with the voracious male. That I am not in any way superior, that I am not different from others, that I am but a link in the great chain, was among the greatest discoveries of my life.

In time, having come to accept his own worth as a man, he was able to accept the worth of others and to feel responsible for their welfare.

How, then, did he transform this recognition into deeds, a readiness to help others? In one instance he helped an old man. The man and Heimler were among a group of prisoners who had been forced to evacuate Buchenwald as the liberating Allied armies advanced. During the enforced march, the prisoners were deprived of food for three days. When finally the guards doled out a portion of boiled rice, the old man was too weakened to fight for a place in the queue. Heimler intervened, fighting off other prisoners, who had become like wild beasts at the sight of food, until a place was made for the old man. Concluding his account of that incident, Heimler writes: "When the food was given out and my turn came I gave the first plate to him, and not until I had watched him licking it clean as he sat by the roadside did I eat my own food."

In another instance, he elected to be the protector of sixteen young boys who had been brought to Buchenwald. Heimler probably saved their lives—but for his intervention, they very likely would have gone to the gas chambers—by getting permission from an SS officer to let them peel potatoes in the camp's kitchen. Working with these children before the ovens, he would attempt to feed their inquiring minds. He would speak to them about "democracy, about the world we hoped for after the war—a world where one would have enough to eat and be able to roam the streets freely, where everybody would be able to think what he liked and say what he thought. . . . "

At night in the barracks, they would ask him such questions as "whether there had ever lived another Hitler who had destroyed other people by fiery furnaces"; and they wanted to know also about the "differences between Judaism and Christianity, and whether Jesus was really the Son of God." In being their teacher, Heimler felt the power of his humanity; and thus, by his actions, by his extraordinary moral force, he had earned the right to respond to the question posed by a fellow prisoner, Dr. Ekstein: "Tell me, on what does it depend whether a man remains a man?"

Heimler had resolved to survive so that he could bear witness, and finally one day the German guards were gone, fleeing for their lives before the advancing Allied forces. He was free. But at first the liberation was of the body and not yet of the spirit. He was too numbed, exhausted, to grasp the fact that he was really free. During his imprisonment he had died a thousand deaths, and now that liberation had finally come he was not ready to turn his face toward a new life.

Then one day he walked in a large field under a clear sky; a vast silence was above and around him, like the "silence such as there must have been before the days of creation, before the heavens and the stars and this chaotic yet law-abiding world were formed." What apparently happened in that moment is powerfully described by Heimler in one of the most mystical and moving passages in Holocaust literature:

> Then I began to cry. I fell down on to the deep brown earth and breathed in the smell of the fields, and it was good. And the silence was broken by the whisper of the wind, by the song of the birds and by the distant lowing of the cows in far-off meadows. Somewhere a dog was barking. And it was good.
>
> I was part of the world and of the present again, and my tears had meaning because I had lost everything except my life. I knew that all the people I loved were dead. I knew that the freedom I had gained would be difficult to bear, and that it would be long before I found peace once more. I realized that I should go on searching for love.

As he was lying in the field, a young girl came up to him. She appeared frightened, wanted to know what he was doing there. Then she saw the triangle of the political prisoner on his jacket and understood.

> She knelt down beside me in the field, and slowly, without either of us uttering a word, tears gathered in her eyes, and soon our tears were intermingled on the earth. Then she spoke again in broken German; "I love you." "I love you, too," I said. We gazed at each other, two young people unable to speak, but our hearts crying out to each other in a language louder than words. Then we kissed—and it was the first kiss of love I had received or given since Eva had died. There was no desire of flesh in this kiss, only desire of the soul, a pure desire for unity between man and woman. It was the kiss of a long-lost sister, a re-discovered mother, a wife who over the years has become part of oneself.
>
> She went as she had come, but suddenly she stopped. "What is your name?" When I told her she repeated it: "Jancsi, Jancsi." Then she said "Yarnicsku" in Czech and slipped away and I never saw her again.
>
> But I returned from that field like a newly awakened man who has just seen the world and knows that he is part of it and belongs to it. I felt that the funeral of my dear ones had begun, and I recognized the birth of my freedom.

Frankl speaking to fellow prisoners of his hut, attempting to lift up their morale; Heimler in Buchenwald ministering to sixteen children; Frankl kneeling in the fields and offering thanksgiving to God for his deliverance from the camps; Heimler's mystical experience in the presence of the young girl. Compare these scenes with the endings of *Night* and *If This Is a Man:* Eliezer's corpselike face staring back at him in the mirror; the accumulating bodies in Levi's hut.

Given these differences, how should one conclude this investigation? It would be comforting to end by paying tribute to those prisoners who apparently were "worthy" of their suffering. But I doubt that ending on a bright note would be appropriate. Still, one need not go to the other extreme by asserting that there are no lessons to be derived from the reading of these accounts. Perhaps all that should be said is that almost any man, even those with exceptional inner strength, could be dehumanized. That resolution and courage did not necessarily prevail against starvation, cold, disease, beatings. That even thoughtful and intelligent men did not find meaning in their sufferings or find them spiritually "challenging." And that many who survived did so at considerable expense to their humanity.

There is perhaps one slim consolation: despite the general condition that each man was fiercely alone in the struggle for survival, some prisoners apparently drew sustenance from their kinship with others. Their captors had almost succeeded in turning them into animals but through the grace of those who ministered to their needs, or who were helped by them, they came to feel like men again. In so doing they recognized the value of Alyosha's words to the boys at the end of *The Brothers Karamazov:* "Help one another."

And yet there can be no truly substantive consolation. We may assume the instances of human goodness during the Hitler era; nevertheless, a hard light needs to be focused and kept on the suffering and loss and brutality. Men died by the millions, and words in memoriam to the spiritual achievements of a few remarkable men are as nothing against that indictment. Studies on the Holocaust cannot resurrect the dead. The communities they once comprised are destroyed. Many of the survivors are marked for life. Nothing can alter those tragic facts. (pp. 22-45)

> *Irving Halperin, "Meaning and Despair in the Literature of the Survivors," in his* Messengers from the Dead: Literature of the Holocaust, *The Westminster Press, 1970, pp. 22-45.*

Hamida Bosmajian

[*Bosmajian is a German-born American educator, editor, and critic. In the following excerpt from her* Metaphors of Evil: Contemporary German Literature and the Shadow of Nazism, *she discusses presentation of the self in autobiographical accounts of the Holocaust.*]

The destiny of the concentrationary universe is inconceivably remote. Measureless expanses of laws and offices, of meandering corridors and stacks of papers, where a whole genus of office workers, preoccupied and pale, lives and dies, human typewriters, isolating the camp and letting nothing leak through to the outside world except a vague and awesome terror of inhuman realms. At the center of this empire, forever invisible, a brain unifies and controls all the police resources of the Reich—and Europe—and dominates with absolute will every possible aspect of the camps—the brain of Himmler and his intimates.

David Rousset, philosopher, French resistance worker, and inmate of three concentration camps, mythologizes here [in an excerpt from *The Other Kingdom*], the bureaucracy behind the camps into the Kafkaesque cosmos of the concentrationary universe. In this universe the unspeakable event came about through the will of the Führer and through words used in laws, propaganda slogans, and obscene expletives. Words created the reality of the SS state and the other kingdom, the camp. It was precisely that power of words that Himmler feared when he told a group of SS men that the events in the camps must remain "a never recorded and never to be recorded glorious page of our history" [Leon Poliakov and Joseph Wulf, *Das dritte Reich und die Juden*]. Totalitarian will wants to abolish its movement through historical time; and if Himmler had had his way, millions of Jews and other undesirables would have disappeared without any verbal record into the crematoriums and burial pits, into the abyss of unrecorded time. It was not to be. Words and the symbolic structures that the human mind shapes through them became the nemesis of the Nazis, for few historical atrocities have ever been as thoroughly documented, analyzed, and written about as the concentrationary universe.

The diary or autobiography of the victim-survivor as witness is written in a language whose familiarity of phrase makes the unspeakable situation accessible to the reader. It is a language that is outer-directed in its historical and ethical orientation and as such seems to be the antithesis to the intense inner-directedness of the hermetic language in the poetry of Nelly Sachs and Paul Celan. Yet, because each of the works to be discussed in this chapter is an expression of the same historical event as perceived by different personalities, the social aspects of language are more or less subtly subverted by the displacements, memory screens, and projections with which the victim-survivor manages to cope with the unspeakable situation. Thus, each diary or autobiography also has a centripetal movement which makes it a unique and self-contained linguistic universe. As records, Chaim Kaplan's *Warsaw Diary* and Odd Nansen's *Day after Day* seem to use familiar language that fixes experiences immediately after they occur. The language of Elie Wiesel's *Night* while still outer-directed by the familiarity of its metaphors, becomes much more centripetal, primarily because of the central image of the eyes into which the memory of the unspeakable situation contracts. Such contraction is also present in Tadeusz Borowski's short stories, whose language fluctuates between intensely realistic and objectified descriptions of human behavior at Auschwitz and demonically apocalyptic image constellations through which the narrator defends himself against the memory of Auschwitz. Nevertheless, given the pattern of the historical experience of the camp, the narrative of diarist and autobiographer follows lines that can be summarized as an ironic and perverse inversion of the conventional quest pattern, an inversion that markedly affects the traditional definition of autobiography.

In a sense, all the works to be discussed here are defenses against horror; for even as the memory of horror is being retained, horror is given shape, is being controlled by the autobiographer. Horror is a response that comes suddenly over those whose beings are still somehow intact, and it threatens those beings with physical and psychological disintegration unless defenses are soon established. Therefore, horror particularly overwhelmed the newcomer who suddenly entered the antiworld of the camp. Old timers became used to the horror to a certain extent and developed what Erich Kahler calls "the splitting of consciousness," a transpersonal objective perception that allowed them to withdraw as much as possible from the experience of their own pain and the pain of others [*The Tower and the Abyss*]. This splitting of consciousness is, of course, applicable to victims and persecutors alike, as well as to most of us as we turn away from the recurring horrors of historical time and retract our steps from the abyss.

The ritual of daily routine is one of the first means preventing the individual from succumbing to the experience of horror. The camp, an anarchic world of chaos and death where anything was possible, had at the same time a predictable and rigid routine; part of that routine was the daily ritual of roll call, whose main function was to terrorize the prisoner into rigid attention in summer heat or winter cold. In his record of and meditation about events, the diarist responds to the immediacy of the moment, while the autobiographer recalls such moments through memory and reflection from a more distant point of view in time. Thus, the literature which sprang from the experience of the camps inevitably contributed to the shaping of a myth of the camp experience, the myth of a secular hell. Today, what was once so very real has already taken on the aura of something distant, of a "once upon a time" horror story, a metaphor and myth of evil.

The autobiographer and diarist are witnesses who, in order to retain memory and somehow give that memory meaning, record out of a sense of personal need. Yet they realize that they cannot do justice either to reality or its victims. Like the historian, the autobiographer is finally no mere accumulator of facts but, rather, a creator of symbolic patterns that synthesize and articulate experience. Language was instrumental in the catastrophic creation of the camp world, and the language of the survivor becomes the means of coping with that catastrophe by containing its chaos within a book. The metaphors of antiworlds as applied to the camp and the prisoner's horribly ironic quest in that world are two conventional means with which the survivor-victim can comprehend and communicate catastrophic experiences.

"In extremely varied cultural contexts," writes Eliade, "we constantly find the same cosmological schema and the same ritual scenario: settling a territory is equivalent to founding a world" [*The Sacred and the Profane*]. The Warsaw Ghetto, Treblinka, and Auschwitz were such staked-out territories in conquered Poland. Here settlements were established that were the antithesis of the sheltering nest, the refuge, the loved, sacred place that is the clearing in the wilderness, the form out of chaos. Instead, the camp became the obscene place with all the perverted sacredness that attaches itself to the obscene. It was a tabooed place, an autonomous state existing in time but simultaneously outside of time. Because it was so alien, the outsider could repress its existence even though the camp always depended on outside contact. Eugen Kogon [in *Der SS-Staat*] points to the perverted Darwinism of the camps and their absolute lack of justice, the first requisite of an ordered state: "The concentration camp was a world in and of itself—an order into which man was thrown with all his virtues and vices (more vices than virtues) to fight for bare existence and mere survival." This separate and secret place fulfilled its function not only as a center for the destruction of life but also as a means to spread anxiety and terror through the land, feelings much stronger than those of the traditional fear of hell. For no matter how much the indifferent person suppressed the knowledge of the camp, he or she knew that it was very real. It was the nadir of the new Reich envisioned by the Nazis, and at the bottom of its hierarchy were the Jews, who had been defined as the epitome of evil.

At one point, all accounts of the concentrationary universe attempt to convey the physical reality of camp or ghetto either through analogy with the Christian, especially Dantean, concept of hell or through analogy with the utopian polis of reason and light to which camp and ghetto are the kakotopian counterpart. Nightmare and dream of European thought are thus demythologized by being displaced into historical reality, thereby returning to the point of origin from whence they generated: the fear of disintegration, death. Before the victims met death, they were *durch den Schmutz gezogen* (pulled through the dirt) so that, by appearing physically dirty and deprived, their emaciated bodies looked as if they had done something wrong, looked like criminals in need of punishment. As a cloacal hell, the camp received all those whom the Nazis considered the excrement of Europe. The camp, as anus of the world, turned the Jews, as Richard Rubinstein and others noted, into feces, the devil's food, his gold and weapon. At the same time, the anal, aggressive world of the camp was a world of boredom and indifference, of the banality of evil. Oppressor and oppressed were in the same evil ditches, Dante's *malebolge*, getting used to it and chewing the cud of death endlessly with the same dull motions. Only a few of the damned managed to save remnants of human dignity, while many either vented their aggressive feelings away from the oppressor towards their fellow sufferers or resigned themselves to the death-in-life state of the *Mussulmann*, a Moslem, in the sense of being indifferent or fatalistic. The breakdown of the inferno analogy occurs, however, when we ask who the sinners in this inferno were. From the Nazi point of view, they were the inmates, but for us they are the Nazis who, like Dante's sinners, have proven themselves incapable of raising sin and guilt into a consciousness of fault.

As a parody of the secular utopian city, the camp mocked the ideas of progress so prevalent in advanced industrial societies. It mocked the tradition of the Greek polis and the yearning for the New Jerusalem, envisioned by the victim over and against suffering; and it mocked Nuremberg, the city of Nazi party rallies impeccably organized and punctuated by the marching boot as an expression of the "Triumph of the Will." As the antipode of the city as progressive community, Auschwitz, with its vast complex of industries, exploited every part of the human being and finally reduced the human body itself to products. The monuments of the kakotopian city—the furnace, the pit, the chimneys of the crematoriums—were, to the newcomer, images of horror to which many eventually became indifferent. Escape, as the taunting remarks of the Nazis reveal, was possible only through the chimneys, a grotesque parody of what Eliade has defined as the fundamental mystical experience, namely, the transcendence of the human condition through the two-fold image of breaking the roof and flight. As Nelly Sachs and Paul Celan say so often, Israel's body found its grave as smoke in air. That smoke, however, did not leave Auschwitz but hung as a polluted cloud over the camp and became, along with the miasma of the surrounding swamp, an indelible figuration of evil in the experience and memory of humankind.

In all the works to be discussed here, the lived experience of the inmate is expressed in terms of an archetypal quest pattern. Deportation was a perverted and ironic quest journey into an externalized dark night for body and soul that ended for most in a meaningless death, at best offering a word, a phrase, or a muted insight to those who survived. As the territorial definition of the camp became the antithesis to the ideal city, the "quest" became the antithesis to the process of individuation. The radical of every quest is the struggle of life against death, but the deportee could engage in this quest only if he or she was given time to struggle. Yet the quest metaphor in concentration camp literature is an expression of the rage for order, a very real and necessary illusion with which the individual can reconstruct the accumulations of the past as he projects patterns for life into the void of the future. Nevertheless, we choose our memories, especially when we have been victimized by traumatic experiences. Experience is thus made dense in *Dichtung* (fiction) that reverberates with intimations of the *Wahrheit* (the truth of reality). Literature created by former concentration camp inmates is, therefore, grounded in the experience of historical reality and controlled through the choice and condensation of certain events in that experience. Because reality swallowed the individual so totally, it, rather than the individual, provided the pattern along which the diaries and autobiographies are written. First, there is life before the ordeal, an innocent and ignorant life expressed poignantly in the notion of business as usual. After the victims have been collected comes the journey in the cattle wagon where they begin to intimate what is in store for them. Arrival at the camp provokes an illusion of reprieve: "Thank God this terrible journey is over." The self is almost immediately traumatized and, if it survives this stage, attempts to establish a pattern for survival. The final stage is liberation and the demands it makes on the former inmate to cope with the fact of survival. All this is, of course, deeply ironic, for the people forced to go on this quest were ordinary men and women who had no desire for heroics or any sort of challenge to their bodies and souls. Hence, so many deluded themselves that nothing could really happen to them, an all too human delusion that persisted to the moment of deportation and even to the moment of selection in the camp.

If the prisoner survived initial selection as well as the trauma of being brutally initiated into the camp world, he or she (though women had fewer chances of survival) would begin a process of adjustment in the camp until the status of "old timer" had been achieved. All records point out how prisoner and persecutor alike were dehumanized, how all human responses, especially emotions, were deadened. The *Mussulmann* no longer lifted his feet while walking but glided along like an automaton; the camp had swallowed him and any concept of selfhood. The SS man, as powerful as the *Mussulmann* was powerless, shared with the latter the quality of an automaton. As [William Grenzman, in *The Third Reich*] pointed out, the SS man who accepted the idea of the superman "must abandon all moral order; he condemns himself to act as an automaton. And it has frequently been demonstrated that he did not even find it unpleasant to be in motion like an automaton." While the *Mussulmann* had been voided of all will power, the will to power in the SS officer contracted into tensed rigidity and at best projected bored indifference or discharged itself in willful and brutal acts of gratuitous violence.

Absolute power and absolute powerlessness offer temptations that are unthinkable to the individual in ordinary circumstances. The persecutor is allowed to vent aggression by almost any means against the powerless, whose abjectness is to him in and of itself a provocation; and the powerless will on occasion do anything to regain a reprieve from death. Compared to the numbers that died, only a fraction carried away the prize of life. Even this was not unambiguous, for survival itself affects the individual with a sense of stain. Hence, all autobiographical accounts of the camp experience express the writer's need to gain relief, perhaps only temporarily, through the confession of the experience. Sometimes the confession attempts to metamorphose the camp experience into a hell through which one had to pass in order to eventually work for a progressive, secular paradise. Examples of such autobiographical statements are David Rousset's *The Other Kingdom* and Bruno Bettelheim's *The Informed Heart*. The autobiographies I have chosen to discuss offer no externally defined set of values through which the writer could make life liveable after the extreme situation. Rather, they reveal the individual in an often agonizing search for meaning, for the extreme situation had challenged if not destroyed all belief. The diaries reveal this search on a day to day basis as the human being is caught in and has to form an attitude to each moment.

Traditional autobiography reveals much introspection and self-analysis. In James Olney's words [in *Metaphors of the Self*], the reader of an autobiography looks for "a characteristic way of perceiving, of organizing and of understanding, an individual way of feeling and expressing that one can somehow relate to oneself." The implication is that we are to ourselves the center of the world and reflect the manifoldness of that world in the metaphors of the self. Autobiographies of former concentration camp inmates also show a characteristic way of perceiving and organizing experience. The extreme situation, however, is one into which the individual is cast and which bears down upon him with sudden, tremendous physical and psychological pressures. Ordinary pressures such as familial tensions and conflicts or identity crises disappear as the individual is thrown into an environment that threatens to consume him. The destructive reality of the concentrationary universe cannot be incorporated and absorbed by the human being as can less problematical situations. The concentration camp inmate had to make a concerted effort to preserve in the core of his or her being some contrasting way of thinking that at least maintained a remnant of selfhood. This inner core had to remain detached from the world of the camp; as a result, the autobiographer does not reveal himself with the depth into which an autobiographer delves under more normal circumstances. He cannot reveal himself because he cannot identify with and incorporate the world in which he lived into his own being. At least he cannot do so rationally.

James Olney writes in his study on autobiography, "If a man suffers a sudden shock or fright, then, whether or not he acts 'out of character', I think most people would agree from experience, that for the moment he is not his normal self. Extreme pain and extreme anger can also, in a sense, cause an apparent disjunction of selfhood." For the concentration camp inmate this disjunction became a state of being. In order to survive he had to adjust himself with incredible speed to a situation into which he was literally thrown and which was totally alien to him. A disjunction between his present and former self took place; later, after his liberation, he had to further modify his self and screen his memories. While imprisoned he had to be constantly aware of everything around him and yet pretend to see nothing. If he wanted to remain somehow intact and not become a *Mussulmann*, he had to observe himself sideways, that is, askance and with a certain sense of disapproval. For this reason, all accounts by former inmates must by necessity be an identification with a world of stain and guilt; it cannot be otherwise no matter how much that identification is screened. The choice of rhetorical form often makes it appear as if the individual is totally detached. This is particularly true when that form is rational, descriptive, and professes to be objective, as, for example, in Kogon's *The SS State*. Rational structuring prevents the identification with a guilty world; but the more personal and emotional an account becomes, as in the case of Wiesel's *Night,* the more the world of stain and guilt is absorbed by the individual and threatens to destroy him.

Defined as a defilement, the inmate was subjected to verbal and physical rituals of uncleanliness by the Nazis. Some accepted the definition they were given, others asked the question "Have we really sinned more than other people?" Still others developed the apparently cooperative yet observant self that retained, in spite of the split, some sense of personhood. These became guilty, not through the accusations of the Nazis, but by what they saw within themselves, in others, and in the environment. The drive for survival caused a sense, if not of sin, then of guilt. This sense of guilt was internalized and developed after liberation, unless totally repressed, into consciousness and conscience. With these two qualities man becomes again the measure of himself. As [Paul] Ricoeur asserts [in *The Symbolism of Evil*], "The promotion of guilt marks the entry of man into the circle of condemnation; the meaning of that condemnation appears only after the event to the 'justified' conscience; it is granted to that conscience to understand its past condemnation as a sort of pedagogy; but to a conscience still kept under the guard of the law, its meaning is unknown." Thus, an inmate could look on while someone was being strangled with the handle of a shovel. After liberation, the survivor-victim will give such moments ethical connotations they did not have when they occurred, but which they need to have so that the justified conscience can transcend callousness.

The autobiographers and diarists I will discuss dwell little on their personal physical and mental agonies, not only for the above reasons but also because dwelling on such suffering would make the autobiographer guilty against those who succumbed. Also, very few autobiographers admit to any depths the feelings of hate and frustrated aggression they felt for the Nazis. Such emotions were real; but because they could not be directed against the oppressor, they turned towards fellow inmates or reflected back to the person who felt them. Though the former inmate may have expiated or repressed his experience, he is not free of it since he is driven to record his memories and reflections in a book. This confessional quality is shared by the inmate with more traditional autobiographies. "Most autobiographies," writes Northrop Frye [in *The Anatomy of Criticism*], "are inspired by a creative, and therefore fictional impulse to select only those events and experiences in a writer's life that go to build up an integrated pattern. This pattern may be something larger than himself with which he has come to identify himself, or simply the coherence of his character and attitude. We may call this very important form of prose fiction the confession form."

We have come full circle. The world of the camp with all its associations of fault was created through language. It became real; but as reality it blinded the individual who found himself in its historical time, a time where continual fear of annihilation deadened feelings and blocked most positive emotions. Many survivors could not talk or write about their experiences until several years later. As the antiworld and the prisoner's quest in it are brought into the consciousness and light of speech, the sufferer reveals his own consciousness and conscience and gains, at least momentarily, symbolic power over memory.

The writing of a diary requires at least a shell of privacy for a few moments during the day. In the camps, such a shell was denied to almost everybody, and this total lack of privacy contributed much to the suffering of the inmates. Among the few diaries that have come to us from women and men in the extreme situation are Odd Nansen's *Day after Day* and Chaim Kaplan's *Warsaw Diary,* both distinguished by their intense perceptions and sensitive language. Both writers were habitual diarists; and after both became caught in the extreme situation, this habit not only provided relief in a personal sense but became a crucial device to retain the immediacy of the moment. Kaplan never had the chance to reread his diary after the evil time had passed. But Nansen had that chance, and when he read his diary for the first time, he was surprised at the tricks memory had already begun to play with him: "Much was worse than I seemed to remember. And yet I know that words are too pale to describe most of it. And another thing: What my companions and I saw and experienced is little and pale in comparison with what many, many others saw and lived through in the worst camps." Kaplan records how the community of the ghetto is subjected to ever increasing constriction until the inhabitants find their only escape in death, the final destination of the diarist himself. Nansen's record is primarily that of a man who remained at the periphery of the extreme situation because of his privileged position as a Norwegian and who struggled to remain a decent man by channeling his consciousness and guilt into empathy with those whose suffering exceeded his.

Both writers could isolate themselves spatially from the horror of ghetto or camp. Nansen, who was arrested in January 1942 and who stayed in Sachsenhausen and Neuengamme from 1943-1945, had some privacy as a Norwegian and kept his diary hidden inside hollowed-out bread boards. Kaplan had his room in an apartment from which he could view the chaos in the streets of the ghetto. When Kaplan's diary ends, this protective shell is taken from him, and time, which liberates Nansen, destroys him. Both writers are intensely aware of time and are driven to record and shape historical vicissitudes, thus attempting to make them somehow meaningful. Kaplan is especially conscious of his mission: "I sense within me the magnitude of this hour, and my responsibility toward it, and I have an inner awareness that I am fulfilling a national obligation, a historic obligation that I am not free to relinquish. My words are not rewritten; momentary reflexes shape them. Perhaps their value lies in this. Be it as it may, I am sure that Providence sent me to fulfill this mission. My record will serve as source material for the future historian."

Unlike Kaplan's communal mission, Nansen's motive is at first a private one. Unable to write the truth about the camps to his wife, he records what he sees so that she will be able to understand him later. In his postscript, however, he realizes that the diary transcended the private motive and became a record against forgetfulness that all should read. He has little hope for the future, for hardly anywhere does he see evidence of man acting with civilizing love, the only means towards a better way of life as far as Nansen is concerned. The enemy of this love is not hate but the indifference among humankind: "The worst you can commit today, against yourself and society, is to forget what happened and sink back into indifference. What happened was worse than you have any idea of—and it was the indifference of mankind that let it take place!" Both diarists write in spite of the final impotence of the word. When we have read their chronicles of wasted time, we realize that, though the moments in time were chaotic, they converge once again into an overall pattern in the diaries, namely, the time before the extreme situation, the camp world and humankind's adjustment to it, and the end of bondage either through death or liberation.

Nansen is the perfect example of an individual who looks askance at himself. Because of his privileged status, he and his fellow Norwegians smugly define themselves as a group over and against those less fortunate than they. Moreover, in order to maintain privilege, they actively participate in anti-Semitism since it is profitable and easily cooperated with: "And so we lounge our own way, grocers in spirit and, in fact, Jews as that word is understood when we use it as a term of abuse—and we nearly always do, not least in this place. At any rate, one would suppose we'd be above that. But no! we howl with the Germans and with others: 'Verdammte Juden!' " Nansen's rigorous criticism of himself and others shows that he is fully aware of what the right attitude ought to be. To compensate for his privilege and failings, Nansen develops a compulsive need to go to the Jewish quarters in order to learn about greater miseries and to hear, at least second hand, about the horrors of Auschwitz. Imprisoned in one of the lesser circles of hell, he wants to remain the man of conscience who feels compelled to learn about the lower depths so as not to become guilty of what he considers the worst moral evil, indifference and sloth.

On 11 February 1945 he decides to make his attitude visible in spite of the risks; he wants to act, to help, and only discovers his own helplessness. His next day's entry expresses a deep sense of futility and a sense of shame for having been praised for his impotent gesture: "The language is exhausted. I have exhausted myself. There are no words left to describe the horrors I have seen with my own eyes. How am I to give even a reflection of the hell I plunged in yesterday?" "Dante's inferno could not have been worse" when nearly one thousand Jews arrived, attacked the garbage cans, and were beaten down by young hoods of a *Sonderabteilung* of the *Wehrmacht* (soldiers imprisoned most likely because of theft). In an ecstasy of violence the young men become "living devils" and "roaring lions" as they beat, laughing fiendishly, the bleeding skeletons. Nansen, the man of consciousness and conscience, leaves his comfortable periphery and goes into the circle of the damned in order to aid one of them: "I went over to him, took him under the arms and raised him. He was light as a child." Nansen realizes that his action is no more than a pitiful gesture because all are doomed. Nevertheless, his act is recognized with astonishment, for the Jew and his friend cannot believe that a Norwegian would aid them:

> They simply stared at me, both of them, with big surprised eyes, then he raised his arm with an effort, as though mastering all his failing strength; his hand reached the level of my head; there he let it sink, and slowly his bony hand slid down over my face. It was his last caress, and he gurgled something which his friend translated with: "He says you are a decent man." Then he collapsed along the wall and on to the ground, and I think he died there and then, but I don't know, for I was hurrying off with my face burning. "A *decent man!* " I who hadn't even dared to try to stop his tormentor. I who hadn't even dared to risk my own skin by going into the camp and collecting food for those starving skeletons! "A *decent man!* " If only I could ever raise myself up again from this shadow-life in this sink of degradation, and be a decent man!

The human response to his futile attempt evokes in Nansen a deep sense of shame over undeserved praise and the realization that it is impossible to ever love one's neighbor enough. It becomes clear to Nansen that, under certain circumstances, the simplest human gesture merely contrasts more violently to the lovelessness of the world.

Nansen always describes the evil of the camps in human terms and avoids abstraction by focusing on the specific moment, the specific individual through whom evil manifests itself. He notes that, while we often exaggerate events in ordinary life, in the world of the camp events told from mouth to mouth do "by no means always grow worse in reality": "The plain fact is that reality is stronger, more dramatic, and far more gruesome than one can grasp on hearing it recapitulated; normal human imagination falls short, therefore a second-hand account is always paler and more plausible." Nansen is a person who remains capable of experiencing horror. Whenever he thinks that the sights around him have become habitual, he is shocked again into consciousness.

Among Nansen's last and most disturbing impressions is a Jewish child who had worked as an errand boy at Auschwitz and to whom the horror of destruction had become so habitual that he no longer experienced it as such. He is less than ten years old, and his angelic face, which is at the same time a mockery of the divine child, robs Nansen of his last illusions over the possibility of innocence. Completely in the know about death and destruction and yet remaining grotesquely innocent, the child is a riddle to the decent man: "Death and destruction, murder, torture and all the deviltry of man are familiar to him. Such was his world picture—the only one he had a chance of forming. He knew nothing of life—and death—but what he had seen in Hell! Yet I couldn't make out any stamp, in that little face, of all the horrors he has lived among." The child knows how to please, but his hands are in constant nervous motion and unconsciously reveal the effect hell has had on him. His prereflective consciousness has absorbed the world, but to Nansen to whom the death and corruption of that world indicate the absolute moral failing of man, the child's acceptance of horror is shocking. He attempts to instruct the boy morally but realizes that it would take years "to save his little soul." After the desire to create a better world for this boy momentarily overwhelms him, he realizes that this, too, would be futile. All that is left is the impression he had of the child: "Even though I am pretty thoroughly hardened by this life here and in the German concentration camps altogether, and used to hearing both this and that, these little smiling replies of his came down on me like bombs."

On 27-28 April 1945 Nansen is free in Denmark, and the last entry of his diary is that of a stunned man who has lost his power of words and is "out of contact with reality." Asked to write to his wife, he comments, "One might have thought it would be easy. . . . But no, it seemed to me impossible, insuperable! Every word became a great intrusive toad, and Kari and the children, all that is dear to me, all that I have been longing for for years with all my soul, more remote than ever. I felt like crying with despair and rage." As life becomes ordinary again, the person who has been in the extreme situation remains locked in the closed circuit of his memories, unable to share them with anyone. For this reason, Nansen attempts to universalize the experience in his postscript, expanding the concentration camp to a global community of guilt and suffering. "Can you picture it?" he often asks the reader, to whom he offers the "front of human kindness" as the only battleground against misery and guilt.

Unlike Nansen's chronicle, Chaim Kaplan's *Warsaw Diary* is unfinished and open-ended but leaves the reader with an overpowering sense of conclusiveness as the author's impending deportation and inevitable death (in 1943) encroach upon the record. Kaplan's diary reveals an introverted and reflective elderly man, a man who, however, keeps his own experiences in the background in order to fully perceive and reflect upon the myriad manifestations of the ghetto from its inception to its eventual dissolution. Caught in that time and place, Kaplan could not know all the facts that brought about this particular reality for the Jews in Warsaw. When reading his book, one gets the lasting impression of a man sitting in his room in the Warsaw Ghetto of conquered Poland during the Second World War, a war fought by three contending powers: the old democratic world, fascism, and communism. Surrounding this set of boxed-in aggressions is a silent and indifferent universe to which Kaplan often directs his gaze and question in vain. In his final reference to the once benign force of the cosmos, he concludes, "In these two days the emptiness of the ghetto has been filled with cries and wails. If they found no way to the God of Israel it is a sign that He doesn't exist."

Beginning with his entry of 1 September 1939, Kaplan is conscious that a new era in history has begun and that it is the beginning of the end for Nazism and perhaps for the Jews unless the free nations rise and defend their liberty. He thus projects the definite beginning, middle, and end of the ordeal, after which humankind will move once again into the light of freedom, democracy, or the formation of the State of Israel. At present, however, a darkness that gains symbolic dimensions reigns in a blacked-out Warsaw: "Great Warsaw, from its center to its suburbs, is cloaked in a terrible darkness, comparable to the plague that was visited upon Egypt—darkness so thick that it can be felt." People hide in their houses so that "our noisy gay city seems to have stopped breathing." As yet Kaplan is unaware that this is only the beginning, for this lack of air and breath will become a state of being as the ghetto is built and more and more people are forced to exist on its narrowing ground. At that point Kaplan writes, "I do not exaggerate when I say that we have reached a state of lack of breath. There simply is no air. Every minute is like a thousand years. Every day is like a never ending eternity." Time ceases to exist for the Jews as they are forced into a converging point of suffering where they can only make labyrinthian turns but no progression. As Kaplan perceives the stark reality of the ghetto, as its gruesome images bear down upon him, his comprehensive faculties force rigidity and chaos into traditional metaphors whose familiarity functions to make the present comprehensible to him and somewhat accessible to his future readers.

The metaphor of the forbidden city, the cloaca of humanity, the antithesis to Eden, becomes the historical actuality of the Warsaw Ghetto which condenses into a demonic epiphany. Time reveals the circles of hell, for before it becomes a roofless prison, it seems as if the ghetto might lead to "a Jewish state with all the attributes that pertain to any state" as people try to establish the routine of business as usual. In the spring of 1942, however, Kaplan is keenly aware that Eden is outside where "there are trees and beautiful ploughed fields, forests and streams, hills and valleys, 'full of splendor, they radiate brightness.'" This is a world from which the ghetto dweller is infinitely distant, a vision of pastoral innocence from which he may be separated by a mere fence: "It is now three years since we have seen the grass growing and the flowers in blossom. Even before we were shoved into the ghetto we were forbidden to enter the city parks. Inside the parks there was space and breath. Outside, the Jewish children—beautiful little ones, the children of the masses—would find a place for their games and toys on the stone sidewalks outside the fence. Within the limits of the ghetto there is not a single garden. . . . We have been robbed of every tree and flower."

As time moves from one point of constriction to another, Kaplan believes repeatedly that he and his fellow sufferers have reached the nadir of their ordeal and that the upward turn of their existence must come soon; for "on the very day the Temple was destroyed, the Messiah was born." The metaphor of hell is both end and beginning. After Warsaw has been bombarded he writes, "Dante's description of the Inferno is mild compared to the inferno raging in the streets of Warsaw." After the ghetto has been closed and the point of constriction narrowed, Kaplan wonders if the sight of external evil is not some objective correlative to an inner condition: "I gazed at the Dantean scenes of Warsaw, and could not stop thinking: are we really guiltier than any nation? Have we sinned more than any other people? Will we really die? Are we doomed to total destruction? Nobody in the world is concerned for us, nobody shares our plight." The metaphor of hell explains nothing, for the ghetto's inhabitants have obviously sinned no more or less than other people. Kaplan does not know that the constriction furthers the aims of the Nazis to eventually destroy all inhabitants. The reader perceives the terrible irony whenever Kaplan wonders about the future or when he complains that the Nazis have turned off the gas. In the beginning of his chronicle, he writes, "I have seen Warsaw in its utter devastation. Woe is me!" But after innumerable miseries have come to pass, he concludes, "Blessed is the eye which has not beheld all this." The mere absence of the sight of evil defines the good life.

The roads of the ghetto, too, take on a metaphorical quality as people move backward and forward in frantic activity that eventually leads nowhere. In the early days, "the streets have begun to resemble a fair. . . . everywhere selling and bargaining, trade and barter are going on under the sky," as all give themselves to the illusion that business can go on as usual. As time passes, it becomes clear that these streets are not the arteries that bring the stuff of life to a body politic but are intestinal labyrinths wherein human beings are drained of life until they can be carted off as waste. In the winter of 1942, the last winter in the ghetto, Kaplan perceives the cloacal city: "Frozen water and sewage pipes have forced us to make latrines out of stairways and yards. We are surrounded by stinking filth, and when the spring thaw melts the frozen dung heaps who knows what ghastly diseases will be let loose on us then?" Even at night the streets are silently crowded, as "the whole ghetto seems like some eerie underworld inhabited by ghosts intent on strange pursuits." But these ghosts no longer care for each other, locked in their own misery: "There is crowding and congestion on the sidewalks. One person shoves another on the side and shoulder without malice and without any apology. . . . They all share the same fate. In everyone's face the terrible happenings of which he himself is subject are reflected. A certain silent sorrow is cast on all faces." Finally, all normal conduct ceases, the dead begin to line the streets, and the living scurry into hideaways whenever a Nazi walks the streets looking for a victim. Wholesale destruction has begun; however, the exact form it will take remains a rumor. When Kaplan prepares himself to go to the collection point, the reader becomes fully aware that the ghetto is "suspended over nothingness," that only death reigns: "There is the silence of death in the streets of the ghetto all through the day. The fear of death is in the eyes of the few people who pass by on the sidewalk opposite our window. Everyone presses himself against the wall and draws into himself so that they will not detect his existence or his presence."

The *Warsaw Diary* reveals to us a walled-in humanity with all its frailties and occasional goodness. The evils of ordinary life become intensified in this microcosm as the rich hoard luxuries and the poor roam greedily through the streets until death overtakes them both. Kaplan does not spare his people invectives, and only rarely does he set a memorial for a good man. It is hard to be a good man in the ghetto. Outside, the Poles generally support the anti-Semitic measures of the Nazis who have unleashed all the brutality of absolute power. Kaplan defines the Nazis as beasts and psychopaths: "A poison of diseased hatred permeates the blood of the Nazis, and therefore all their stupid decrees, the fruits of this hatred, are doomed to failure. Such an awareness saves us from despair." In spite of external evidence, Kaplan cannot afford to admit that the deeds of the Nazis are manifestations of human potential for evil. Here the language used by the victim is similar to but differently motivated than the language used by the oppressor. The familiar associative cluster of images by which evil is seen as permeating the biological being of the evil-doer is used by Kaplan to "save us from despair." To admit that the Nazis are human would mean that they be included in the humanity of the ghetto dweller who by definition would then have to admit the possibility of atrocious depravity within himself; such an admission would lead to despair. Language alone provides the powerless with the futile magic of exorcism and with the secret knowledge that the oppressor will fail.

Language is impotent but is also the only means to preserve at least an inkling of the agony of actual experience. As Kaplan states in his purpose sentences, "It is difficult to write, but I consider it an obligation and am determined to fulfill it. I will write a scroll of agony in order to remember the past in the future." Self-contained as a scroll whose content is antithetical to the law content of the Torah, Kaplan's diary is a defense against the overwhelming influence of a reality that chokes his breath and cannot possibly be contained in a book. Kaplan does not indulge in self-revelations; we know nothing about his hunger, his pains, or his fear of death. Often he reacts angrily at the evil time but remains open and vulnerable to it in order to recreate it. Shortly before he will be sent to Treblinka, his last concern is for his diary: "If my life ends, what will become of my diary?" It is the concern of a parent who, in continual agony, gave birth to a child, the link with the future; and, in order to reach the empathetic thou which will receive the child, the writer shapes his work through familiar language. Implicit in that language, however, is also the problem of repetition and compulsion as the metaphors of Eden and hell, of every man and man as beast catching us in circles of associations.

"Humankind cannot bear very much reality." When applied to the autobiographies about the concentrationary universe, T. S. Eliot's insight in "Burnt Norton" defines not a Platonic reality, but a reality in which body and soul were annihilated to the body's carbon. Lawrence Langer quotes Elie Wiesel as saying that the event of the holocaust "seems unreal as if it occurred on a different planet," and he adds, "Perhaps what we tell about what happened and what really happened has nothing to do with the other." The autobiographer, who has not used the extreme situation as an infernal experience from whose center of gravity he was led to a "progressive" vision of future humanity, is more often than not the artist and can offer only a consciousness of negation, a downward transcendence of profoundest irony.

In Elie Wiesel's *Night* and in Borowski's collection of short stories, the illusion of reprieve of the diarist writing in his defined space is absent. The autobiographer of the concentration camp is a survivor who has received an extended reprieve from death, but that reprieve has not liberated him. As a matter of fact, it can contribute to make life so unlivable that the survivor seeks death through suicide, as Borowski did on 1 July 1951. With compulsive repetitiveness, the autobiographer must return to the memory of deprivation even as that memory is bound to take on fictional aspects, one of the main reasons why Wiesel and Borowski use a first person narrative in which the narrator's name varies slightly from the author's—Elie becomes Eliezer, Tadeusz becomes Tadek. The self looks askance at itself in that time, and the reader is aware of the distance between narrator and author. In *Night* that distance is created between the fifteen-year-old boy who runs to the synagogue of his village "to weep over the destruction of the Temple" at a time when the Nazis are closing in on Hungary and the adult writer-narrator who reflects on that illusory innocence. Tadek and Tadeusz Borowski are less distant from each other; both are young adults, and both agree on the universal implications of Auschwitz. Both autobiographers were swallowed by the experience no matter what defenses they attempted to construct. The reader knows that Auschwitz forced itself into the struggling, vulnerable, and open consciousness of two young

human beings and brought about a physical and psychological suffocation and paralysis, leading each consciousness to a point of constriction in its memory from which it tries to extricate, but cannot liberate itself, through art. Wiesel retraces the ground of deprivation because of the love and guilt he feels over the loss of his family, and he does so by shaping his recollections in terms of a parodic quest pattern. Borowski, a political prisoner at Auschwitz, survived because he cooperated. His stories, while they can be arranged to give the illusion of beginning, middle, and end, are really memory shards in which he retraces his guilt, reacts aggressively against it, and mocks himself profoundly as an artist in a world of stone.

Since Lawrence Langer has written an extensive analysis of the parody of the quest in Wiesel's *Night* [in *The Holocaust and the Literary Imagination;* see Further Reading], I will focus mainly on how metaphors of evil define Eliezer's experience in Auschwitz as well as the rupture of dialogue between himself and the god of his fathers. Both writers describe the extreme situation in accessible language. Wiesel's language is influenced by his religious education, and it is able to provoke in the reader a deep feeling of sorrow. Borowski's language, however, stuns the relief that comes with tears. He attempts mimesis through cool understatement and the juxtaposition of opposites, or he reflects with brutal irony or flagrant aggression against this world of stone. I will analyze Borowski's constricted memory points in the short story "This Way for the Gas, Ladies and Gentlemen" and in the sketches "A Visit" and "The World of Stone."

In *Night,* time ends for young Eliezer in the spring of 1944 when he and his family are torn from their idyllic world in Sighet and transported to Auschwitz. His mother and sister die immediately, and Eliezer begins work in the Buna factories. During the evacuation of Auschwitz, Eliezer, his father, and a multitude of prisoners are driven on the run through a raging blizzard, eventually herded into open cattle wagons which transport them to Buchenwald. It is there that his father, the mainstay of Eliezer's existence, dies. On the eve of 28 January 1945 (the first date since he left Sighet), time begins again for Eliezer as he looks at his dying father for the last time and climbs into the bunk above him. The next morning his father is gone: "They must have taken him away before dawn and carried him to the crematory. He may still have been breathing. There were no prayers at his grave." If time before the concentrationary universe was one of Edenic innocence and ignorance, time after the experience defines knowledge of a world so totally fallen that, for Eliezer, at least there is no hope for redemption after liberation. He is locked in his memory of the antiworld: "From the depths of the mirror a corpse gazed at me. The look in his eyes, as they stared into mine, has never left me." Wiesel's autobiography is about the origin of that look.

The language of *Night* is deceptively simple, language that gives the reader the illusion of understanding the unspeakable situation. The familiar linguistic signals, however, reverberate and urge the discovery of a revelation of experience and truth behind the image as sign. It is the language of a religious imagination, demonstrated in the first chapter by the passion with which Eliezer studied not only the law of the Talmud but also the mysticism of the Kabbalah. In the final analysis, *Night* is not an attempt to realistically detail the experience of Auschwitz but rather to show how that experience transformed the religious personality's relation to God. The relation to God is brought about through the language of prayer, as Moché, the mystic Beadle of Sighet, tells Eliezer: "Man raises himself towards God by the questions he asks of Him . . . that is the true dialogue. Man questions God and God answers. But we don't understand His answers. We can't understand them. Because they come from the depths of the soul, and they stay there until death. You will find the true answers, Eliezer, only within yourself."

This is the most important thematic statement in *Night.* It defines the complex inner-outer relationship of the ego to the larger self; it defines the narrator and his language, in which the familiar phrase "depth of the soul" becomes a leitmotif. Charged with affirmation or negation, the phrase is used in all crucial moments of Eliezer's experience. Moché is unaware of the problems his definition can and will cause the boy; he is unaware that the "true dialogue" will be a monologue, a failure of communication. In Wiesel's autobiography, the creature finds himself in a catastrophic creation and concludes that the creator must have withdrawn defensively from that chaos. The creature, too, after viewing and absorbing the chaos, withdraws with defensive aggressiveness into a rigid posture. As Harold Bloom points out in *Kabbalah and Criticism,* "Such a concentration sets up defensive reactions in the self, making the subsequent creation a catastrophe, and rendering . . . representation a hopeless quest." The narrator's defensive reaction is that he, unlike the Creator, does not want his linguistic creation to be catastrophic but wants to shape it with a rage for order by means of a language that is obviously defective in its "imagery of limitation." Yet the familiar order of the narrator's linguistic cosmos reverberates, and the reader, receptive to these reverberations, will break the familiar vessels of the images in *Night* and approximate the catastrophe that underlies them. Such approximation necessarily involves a misreading; for the reader's defenses against the catastrophe in *Night* are likewise provoked, and the true dialogue becomes impossible.

Eliezer's experience at Auschwitz-Buna is shaped by the gradual stripping from him of everything he loves. There is the blind struggle for existence at all cost, but along with it the meaning for life is lost. As the boy deteriorates physically, as he is stripped of his flesh, he loses his potential for love as a force in a meaningful life. To be sure, this takes a long time, for love is strong. But in the end, however, only emptiness remains. During the first selection upon his arrival at Birkenau, he is as yet unaware that the stripping process has begun—"men to the left, women to the right." His mother and sister disappear forever. His father, who was somewhat on the periphery of Eliezer's world in Sighet, now becomes for him the fulcrum, the one stable point with which Eliezer can align himself even after his commitment to his father becomes hardly more than a conditioned reflex.

The reader of *Night* has to remain conscious of the fact that the events Eliezer witnesses in the inferno are experienced by him as a child. Although he is not innocent in the sense of being unreflective (for he had studied and interpreted the scriptures too much), he is still innocent in that the world into which he is cast is at first totally alien and incomprehensible to him. The child is father of the man and as such holds the promise for the future. In the concentration camps, that future was demolished and the innocence of the child perverted. The child in the camp did not only hear stories about evil such as the destruction of the Temple, over which he could weep with the empathy that distance permits, but the child lived in what has become for the twentieth century a myth of evil. The camp was never a metaphor for the child. His first consciousness of evil is aroused by the sight of infant damnation that pales all images of the slaughter of the innocent: a lorry filled with babies is emptied into a burning pit. "In the depths of my heart, I bade farewell to my father, to the whole universe; and in spite of myself, the words formed themselves and issued from my lips: ' . . . May His name be blessed and magnified . . . '." Eliezer can still pray, prayer that has already become a reflex action.

Eliezer's rebellion against God is initiated by witnessing two hangings. The first, the execution of a heroic Polish youth, affects him hardly at all; the second, the hanging of an angelic-looking child, affects him deeply. On the eve of Rosh Hashanah, however, when hundreds of men prostrate themselves with love before their invisible and powerful God, "like trees before the tempest," Eliezer accuses God of breaking His covenant with men. He does not deny the existence of God; he contracts away from God, as God has withdrawn from him: "My eyes were open and I was alone—terribly alone in a world without God and without man. Without love or mercy. I had ceased to be anything but ashes, yet I felt myself stronger than the Almighty to whom my life had been tied for so long." Until now, his ego had identified with the archetypal symbols of his religion which he had projected, not only as an energy within "the depths of his soul," but also as existing externally. As a religious but powerless human being, he felt empathy at the sight of suffering, an onrush of powerful emotion that ought to be felt by the all-powerful god he had projected. Since the god remains silent, no matter how much the believer demonstrates love, Eliezer rejects the god through his ego's expression of will. With hope gone, his will makes him strong and allows him to say no to a cosmic system that is contradicted by the reality of Auschwitz. He turns to his weak, earthly father instead and achieves with him a wordless moment of perfect communion of love, a primal communication of touch assuring that the other is really there.

Even the bond with the earthly father is threatened, however, by the temptation that he might be better off without him. This temptation develops during the evacuation of Auschwitz as the inmates are forced to run through the snow and are eventually transported, snow and ice encrusted, on open cattle wagons. Torn between the need to protect and reject his parent, Eliezer projects images of how other sons treat their fathers. The most horrible of these images occurs in the cattle wagon when a nameless son, crazed with starvation, creeps towards his father who is chewing a crust of bread. He beats his father down only to be himself killed by his starving fellow prisoners. Eliezer, however, saves his father from being thrown out as dead from the cattle wagon, but increasingly these rescues become the prolonging of a death of which the son does not want to be guilty. He can never give enough love to keep his father alive; love is no longer enough, just as hate will not suffice to avenge the camp experience. He will be left with guilt because he survives, but at the time of his father's death he only feels drained: "And, in the depths of my being, in the recesses of my weakened conscience could I have searched it, I might perhaps have found something like—free at last!"

Having struggled between life and death for so long, he looks into a mirror at the end of his ordeal: "From the depths of the mirror, a corpse gazed back at me. The look in his eyes, as they stared into mine, has never left me." The image communicates the demonic epiphany of a Narcissus locked into the closed circuit of experiences that have robbed him of all interest in and love for life. He cannot love the world, and, since the world is reflected in his eyes, he cannot love himself. But Wiesel writes "a corpse" and "his eyes," and this implies that the reflection is expe-

rienced as *the other,* a life-saving disjunction which turns the camp experience at that moment into memory and all which the process of memory entails. The look in the mirror holds a memory of a loveless world, but it is in memory of a loved family who died in the camp that the book is created. In the re-creation of the struggle to maintain love and in the eventual defeat of love, the catastrophe is once more enacted: the mother once more carries the sister to the gas chamber, God is once more rejected, the father dies once more. But this time it happens in a verbal structure, in a record that preserves and stalls forgetfulness. *Night* is an homage to such love and its struggle; it is also, however, a denial of forgiveness and expiation, for the look of the corpse never leaves the autobiographer who incorporated the world of Auschwitz into his very being.

In Tadeusz Borowski's "This Way for the Gas, Ladies and Gentlemen," we see again how a young man, the narrator Tadek, incorporated Auschwitz. Tadek is not a religious person; there arises no rebellious energy against his god from the depths of his being. Instead, after having had to deny his question "Are we good people?" throughout an interminable day during which he fought his nausea through three transports of victims, he succumbs finally to the momentary relief of a violent vomiting. This release

A United States Army photograph taken in April 1945 that shows Elie Wiesel (circled) in the Buchenwald camp.

387

parallels Eliezer's rebellion from the depths of his being; however, Eliezer's guilt concentrates primarily on his father, Tadek, who works at the ramp, actively participates in sending thousands to their deaths. Yet the nonmetaphysically inclined Tadek also arrives at metaphysical intimations; for the magnitude of decreation around him evokes such resonances in "This Way for the Gas," internalizes them in "A Visit," and disgorges them in aggressive apocalyptic visions in "The World of Stone."

The uncreating world of the concentrationary universe is a world of lies and deceit, as is already evident in the title of "This Way for the Gas, Ladies and Gentlemen," and is confirmed as the reader becomes conscious of the fact that within the twenty pages of this short story 15,000 people have been gassed. Speed intensifies throughout the narrative as Tadek races through the account of his participation in preparing the victims of three transports for their deaths. In the beginning he and his compeers seem to eagerly await the first transport, for also at the ramp is "Canada," the land of plenty, where the inmates get supplies for survival. The narrator's tone is objective, casual, and cynical. A detachment of inmates does not hesitate to drink the water intended for the people on the transport. The oppressors, while highly visible, remain anonymous officers, SS men, guards. Anonymity protects persecutors and cooperative victims alike. An eager busy-ness pervades the ramp: crews are given work instructions, "motor cycles drive up, delivering SS officers, bemedalled, glittering with brass . . . some have brought their briefcases, others held thin flexible whips. This gives them an air of military readiness and agility" as they talk about home and families. "We lie against the rails in the narrow streaks of shade, breathe unevenly, occasionally exchange a few words in our various tongues, and gaze listlessly at the majestic men in green uniforms, at the green leaves, and at the church steeple of a distant village." Complicity is established through the air of expectancy between the two groups and is repressed with an attitude of negligent apathy. Typical of Borowski's style is the climactic but ironic use of parallelisms. The church steeple obviously points to something that transcends this world. But whatever that might be, it has no contact with the two groups of men who conspire within this confined, narrow ground of evil.

If the camp is "sealed off tight," the wagons of the transport intensify constriction; when "the bolts crack, the doors fall open," and the people and their belongings spill from the wagon. As they breathe the fresh air with relief, however, they inhale with it the illusion of reprieve that the SS and the work crew try to maintain. One SS man is particularly courteous as he urges good will and cooperation, but his whip flies as a woman, caught in the illusion of reprieve, attempts to recover her purse. She is destined for the gas chamber, for behind her walks her little girl affectionately calling her "Mamele" and thus defining her as a mother. It was too bothersome to separate mothers from children, no matter how "workable" the mothers might be.

After the wagons have been emptied, the inmates must clean up the "Schweinerei" (pig's mess); the physical and moral stain must appear to have been removed. Among the human refuse in the wagon, Tadek finds "squashed, trampled infants, naked little monsters, with enormous heads and bloated belies. We carry them out like chickens, holding several in each hand. 'Don't take them to the trucks, pass them on to the women,' says the SS man, lighting his cigarette. His cigarette lighter is not working properly; he examines it carefully." Pity is consistently undercut as the narrator moves from infants to monsters, to chickens, and to the seemingly unaffected diversionary attitude of the SS man who sees but does not choose to see. Shocked, the women refuse to take the little bodies; but a tall, grey-haired woman accepts them and addresses Tadek as "my poor boy," a personalized phrase that overwhelms him, not with tears, but with intense, physical fatigue and with the refusal to look at people individually. When he addresses a fellow inmate, his words spill forth aggressively: "I feel no pity. I am not sorry they are going to the gas chamber. Damn them all! I could throw myself at them and beat them with my fists. . . ." His compeer assures him that such an attitude is almost healthy.

With the arrival of the second transport brutality increases and deception diminishes. A woman, aware that she would go to the gas chamber if defined as a mother, denies her child but is killed by a Russian inmate. As Tadek once again struggles with nausea, there emerges from the train a girl that belongs to another time and world. She "descends lightly from the train, hops to the gravel, looks around inquiringly as if somewhat surprised. Her soft, blond hair has fallen on her shoulders in a torrent." Her wise and mature look defines her as in the know as she insists on going to the gas chamber. She is a totally absurd but true appearance of personhood and dignity in this world of deceit; her knowledge, however, leads her to seek death. Once again, only the human being can contain such knowledge, for there is no god who contains or refuses to contain so much suffering.

This is particularly evident after Tadek has cleaned up the wagons of the second transport and rests against the rails: "The sun has leaned low over the horizon and illuminates the ramp with a reddish glow: the shadows of the trees have become elongated, ghostlike. In the silence that settles over nature at this time of day, the human cries seem to rise all the way to the sky." No ear will receive the cries that rise from this constricted and seemingly eternal narrow ground. Tadek, who sees all this, describes it in a language resonant with religious connotations, a language similar to the images of Nelly Sachs in "Landscape of Screams"; for the precision of Borowski's attempt to imitate reality and Sachs's precise use of the literalness of the word approximate each other.

Sachs also refers to the "woe tendrils of the smallest children" in her poem, and just such a tendril of sound is emitted from a motherless little girl who falls out of the window of the third transport:

> Stunned, she lies still for a moment, then stands up and begins walking around in a circle, faster and faster, waving her rigid arms in the air, breathing loudly and spasmodically, whining in a faint voice. Her mind has given way in the in-

ferno inside the train. The whining is hard on the nerves: an SS man approaches calmly, his heavy boot strikes between her shoulders. She falls. Holding her down with his foot, he draws his revolver, fires once, then again. She remains face down, kicking the gravel with her feet, until she stiffens. They proceed to unseal the train.

Tadek, as nervously tense as the SS, appears to approve of this action, but shortly afterwards, when a corpse's fingers close around his hand, he screams, breaks down, and vomits. In a final image he describes the translucent morning sky against which "great columns of smoke rise from the crematoria and merge above into a huge black river . . . ," the black milk of morning that the voices of Celan's "Todesfuge" drink and drink. Contrasting with this image of dissolution is the rigidity of "a heavily armed SS detachment. . . . The men march briskly, in step, shoulder to shoulder, one mass one will."

Nausea is a momentary and illusory relief for a man who has made such a world part of his being that his sense of ego has been lost. In the sketches "A Visit" and "The World of Stone," Tadek describes the state of such a man after liberation. He admits in "A Visit" that "I have never been able to look at myself," a realization which Wiesel communicated through the eyes of the corpse, the unfamiliar other that rose from the depths of the mirror. Self-knowledge is a myth for the former concentration camp inmate, for his self is constituted of what he saw. "A Visit" is a visit of the people who claimed his kinship, as is evident in the twice-repeated whisper of a dying man: "Brother, brother." Tadek had to fail as his brother's keeper, for he had thousands of brothers and sisters who claimed his kinship. As the repetition of "I saw, I saw, I saw" reveals, Tadek has only been able to fulfill the final request of the victims, namely, that he remember what happened. He is now housed in his memory but is unhoused in his present world as he sits "in someone else's room," where in a moment he will feel "homesick for the people I saw then." He can visit them all, and they will be his visitation. Because he is defined through them alone, because there is no room for self-knowledge, his consciousness is nothing but a house for the memory of the victims. The world that once swallowed him is now contained within him.

In "The World of Stone" the alienated narrator reacts aggressively against the "intimate immensity" (Bachelard) of himself as the anagogic container of the world of Auschwitz. Growing within him "like a foetus inside a womb" is the terrible knowledge and foreboding that "the Infinite Universe is inflating at incredible speed." He wants to retain it like "a miser," afraid that solid matter will dissolve into emptiness like a "fleeting sound." Demonic knowledge crowds and pressures the confines of his being, a knowledge that cannot be transformed into the logos of speech because it would not generate an individualized creation; rather, it would generate a chaos of emptiness, reminiscent of smoke and air or the cries that rose all the way to the sky from the ground of Auschwitz.

With this knowledge in him, he walks "on hot summer afternoons . . . long, lonely strolls throught the poorest districts of my city," where he enjoys inhaling "the stale crumb-dry dust of the ruins." At minimum subsistence level, life is returning to the illusion of normality, an illusion he does not want to share. Instead he falls into a demonic reverie in which he expresses his terrible knowledge through a futile exorcism:

> Through half-open eyes I see with satisfaction that once again a gust of the cosmic gale has blown the crowd into the air, all the way up to the treetops, sucked the human bodies into a huge whirlpool, twisted their lips open with terror, mingled the children's rosy cheeks with the hairy chests of the men, entwined the clenched fists with strips of women's dresses, thrown snow-white thighs on the top, like foam, with hats and fragments of heads tangled in hair-like seaweed peeping from below. And I see that this weird snarl, this gigantic stew concocted out of the human crowd, flows along the street, down the gutter, and seeps into space with a loud gurgle, like water into a sewer.

The visionary with his half-open eyes reacts aggressively to the blindness of the outside world and to the pressure of memory which becomes so dense that it seems as if his physical being has coagulated and stiffened. Where he once took in the world with "wide-open, astonished eyes," he is now the demonic daydreamer caught between repression and emergence of memory; he transforms the horizontal life of the sidewalk into an apocalypse which satisfies him because it affirms that the world of his memory is the real world. His vision of a cosmic gale is, however, no divine pneuma. Rather, it is a funneled sucking into an upward-downward transcendence wherein human beings once more are as contorted as the victims of the gas chamber. The center of this whirlpool is again a point of constriction "that seeps into space with a loud gurgle, like water into a sewer." Humanity is waste water, but only as a simile. It seeps into space, the universe he feared would slip through his hands like water, and disappears with a loud gurgle that will be no more than a fleeting sound.

Tadek is left with the choice of chaos as void or a world of stone, the latter symbolized by the "massive cool building made of granite" where he works. But granite does not protect him; he knows it "cannot keep the world from swelling and bursting like an over-ripe pomegranate, leaving behind but a handful of contracted, grey, dry ashes," an image which is a grotesque inversion of Mallarmé's "Afternoon of a Faun." In Borowski's world of stone there may be a volcanic eruption of aggression, there may be ashes, but no queen of love visits the daydreamer.

Tadek concludes that, because the world has not yet blown away, he intends to write and "grasp the true significance of the events and people I have seen." His matter is great and worthy of "an immortal epic," but the act of writing would mean a concession to the illusion of normality in which he does not want to participate. Tadek and the other victim-survivors of the concentrationary universe have not left us, who are still caught in the illusion of reprieve, the conclusive comfort of a great epic. They have left us partial visions, short stories, sketches, and fragments and retained "with a miser's piercing anxiety" the world which swallowed them and which they swallowed with open eyes. (pp. 27-54)

> *Hamida Bosmajian, "The Rage for Order: Autobiographical Accounts of the Self in the Nightmare of History," in her* Metaphors of Evil: Contemporary German Literature and the Shadow of Nazism, *University of Iowa Press, 1979, pp. 27-54.*

Joseph Sungolowsky

[*Sungolowsky is a Belgian-born American critic and educator. In the following excerpt, he determines the defining characteristics of Holocaust autobiography by examining four representative memoirs:* Night *(1958), by Elie Wiesel;* When Memory Comes *(1978), by Saul Friedländer; and* Of Blood and Hope *(1979) and* La ressource humaine *(1983), by Samuel Pisar.*]

The history of the destruction of European Jewry by the Nazis has relied heavily upon the accounts written by survivors, which will probably remain a prime source of information concerning the magnitude of the catastrophe. Autobiography written as a result of experiences lived during the Holocaust is therefore an integral part of its literature. Since such literature cannot be linked to any of the norms of literary art, it has been termed a literature of "atrocity" or "decomposition." Holocaust autobiography inherits, therefore, the problematic aspect of both autobiography and the literature of the Holocaust. (p. 131)

Autobiography is generally written in midlife by an author who has achieved fame thanks to previous works which have been recognized for their value, or by an individual who has played a significant role in public life. Saul Friedländer was 46 years old when *When Memory Comes* was published. At that time, he had gained an international reputation as a historian of Nazism. Samuel Pisar was 50 when he wrote *Of Blood and Hope*. He is also the author of *Coexistence and Commerce* (1970), an impressive political and economic treatise advocating trade relations between East and West, especially as a means to ease the Cold War. He, too, has achieved recognition as a political scientist, as an advisor to governments, and as an international lawyer.

Writing autobiography at an earlier age or as a first book is considered an exception. Elie Wiesel's *Night* is such an exception. He recounts how fortuitous his career as a writer was in its beginnings, especially considering that he might not have survived the concentration camps at all. Upon his liberation, he vowed not to speak of his experience for at least ten years. It was the French novelist François Mauriac who persuaded him to tell his story, and Wiesel adds that at the time Mauriac was as well-known as he was obscure. Thus, at the age of 28, Wiesel published his autobiographical narrative concerning his experience in the concentration camps, first in Yiddish under the title *Un die velt hot geshvigen*, subsequently in French under the title *La nuit*. In 1976, Wiesel stated that *Night* could have remained his one and only book; indeed, when he began to write fiction, the French critic René Lalou wondered how Wiesel could have undertaken to write any-

thing else after *Night*. Clearly, at the time Wiesel published *Night*, he lacked the fame as an author of previous works usually expected of an autobiography, as indicated by Philippe Lejeune and Georges May.

An autobiography is deemed authentic when there is identity between the name of the author appearing on the title page and the narrator of the story. In *Night*, Wiesel relates that during a rollcall in Auschwitz, he heard a man crying out: "Who among you is Wiesel from Sighet?" He turned out to be a relative that had been deported from Antwerp. Subsequently, Wiesel is called by his first name "Eliezer" by that relative, by Juliek, a fellow-inmate, and by his father. Friedländer refers to his name several times in the course of his narrative. He recalls how difficult it was for him to get accustomed to his new first-name "Paul-Henri" given to him in the Catholic boarding school in France, as he was called "Pavel" or "Pawlicek," the diminutive given to him by his family. He names himself again when he recalls his stay, in 1950, with an uncle who directed an institution for mentally ill children. One of them tried to communicate with him during a fit, and all he could say was "Herr Friedländer." (Friedländer sees in this incident an example of the unlocking of the inner world which he experienced himself when he began to write his book.)

Pisar names himself throughout *Of Blood and Hope*. Upon returning to Auschwitz as a member of a delegation to a commemorative ceremony, he describes himself as follows: "a reincarnated Samuel Pisar clothed simply in his respectable attire of international lawyer, scholar, American citizen had to step into the light and avow once more that once, not so long ago, he had crawled in the pain, the filth and the degradation of the factories of death." Later on, he quotes Solzhenitsyn commenting upon his views on coexistence between East and West: "Pisar is one of the few to see clearly."

Autobiography is considered genuine when the author states, either in the text itself or in connection with it, that his intent has indeed been autobiographical. Lejeune [in *L'autobiographie en France*] calls such a statement an "autobiographical pact"—an agreement between author and reader according to which the reader is assured that he is reading the truth.

Upon the publication of his book, Friedländer told an interviewer that he wrote it as a result of an "inner necessity," and he discussed its main themes: his childhood, his life as a youngster in a Catholic boarding school after he was separated from his parents during the war, his discovery of Zionism and his views on Israel where he lives. In the preface to the French edition of his book, Pisar explains that in order to write it he had to revive from within the depths of his self the tragic episodes of his life which represent such a sharp contrast with his "reincarnation" as a brilliant public figure. Pisar's subsequent book intitled *La ressource humaine* is of a similar intent. It opens as follows: "I sleep with eyes half-closed. I have done so for the last forty years. Even since I entered the precincts of Auschwitz." Wiesel's autobiographical pact was established twenty years after the publication of *Night*, when he told an interviewer: "*Night*, my first narrative, was an autobiographical story, a kind of testimony of one witness speaking of his own life, his own death" [*Harry James Cargas in Conversation with Elie Wiesel*].

Autobiography is written in order to come to terms with oneself. Recapturing the past is, therefore, the most common preoccupation of the autobiographer. This motivation is repeatedly stressed by Saul Friedländer whose childhood was shattered by the events of the war. Recounting his suicide attempt after he was separated from his parents, he wonders whether he is the same person or even the same Jew "if there were such a thing as a collective Jew." When he tries to seek out a former schoolmate 35 years later, he suspects that this impulse is dictated by the "need for synthesis . . . that no longer excludes anything." Therefore, in order to recapture the past, his sole recourse is to write, for "writing retraces the contours of the past . . . , it does at least preserve a presence." In measuring the distance between past and present, Friedländer realizes that he has retained a reticence toward people, a tendency to passivity, moral preoccupations and self-examination inculcated to him by the "taboos" of his former Catholic education.

In searching for himself, the autobiographer may indulge in narcissism and conceit. Pisar hardly avoids these temptations. Self-glorification is a pervasive theme in both of his autobiographical books. He dwells extensively upon his close relationships with world celebrities, on his brilliance as a political scientist whose advice is sought by statesmen, on his participation in international conferences where he is eagerly listened to, on his talent at handling the affairs of renowned movie stars. However, such vanity seems deliberate, for Pisar never fails to stress the contrast between his present success and his former condition as a concentration camp inmate. He often recalls "the young boy with a shaven head, pale skin tightly drawn over his face, and an almost broken body." In *La ressource humaine,* he writes. "I carry the immense privilege of a double experience. That of a sub-human thrown in the deepest hell of the century and that of an individual treasured by the great and productive cultures of this planet that are still free."

Autobiography is written as a testimony, especially when the author has lived a particular moment of history that must not be forgotten. Such was Elie Wiesel's intent when he wrote *Night.* For him, "Auschwitz was a unique phenomenon, a unique event, like the revelation at Sinai." Had it not been for the war, he would not have become a storyteller but would have written on philosophy, the Bible, and the Talmud. He recalls that as he looked at himself in the mirror after his liberation, he realized how much he had changed and decided that someone had to write about that change. Although he had vowed to remain silent for ten years, he had absorbed "the obsession to tell the tale." He states: "I knew that anyone who remained alive had to become a story-teller, a messenger, had to speak up."

Autobiography may also be written to educate. The autobiographer wishes his reader to learn from his experience. In the preface to the French edition of *Blood and Hope,* Pisar writes that he did not mean to write a narrative describing the atrocities of the Holocaust or an abstract ideo-

logical work on the subject, but: "to forget those four hellish years spent in the most loathsome trashcan of history." For him, the danger of a thermonuclear war is a mere repetition of the former madness. He writes, therefore, to educate the youth of today. "They need to arm themselves against the tragedies, the hypocrisies, the false gods of history." In *La ressource humaine,* Pisar further explores the means by which a third world war can be avoided. The autobiographical element is present in it again, and with the same educational intent. He relates that while he was about to enter the gas chamber, he escaped from the line, seized a brush and pail, and began scrubbing the floor of the waiting room much to the liking of the guards. He is convinced, therefore, that the world possesses likewise the resources to avoid a nuclear war.

No matter how sincere or truthful the autobiographer intends to be, he must face the technical and literary problems related to the writing. Such problems are even more acute in the case of Holocaust autobiography. Before they write autobiography, authors will make sure that a reasonable amount of time has elapsed between the events they wish to relate and the actual writing. Such "distanciation" ensures orderliness to the narrative. In the case of Holocaust autobiography, the waiting period is not only technical but also emotional. Elie Wiesel states that he feared being unable to live up to the past, "of saying the wrong things, of saying too much or too little." He therefore decided to wait ten years before writing. Friedländer stated that he had unsuccessfully attempted to write his account fifteen years earlier. Pisar waited about 35 years before he decided to write.

With the best faith or memory in the world, it is impossible to re-create in writing a reality long gone by. In this respect, Holocaust autobiographers are even more frustrated. They constantly suspect that whatever the form and content of their narrative, they have not succeeded in conveying the past adequately. Wiesel feels that, while *Night* is the center of his work, "what happened during that night . . . will not be revealed" [Cargas]. In the midst of writing, Friedländer feels "deeply discouraged." He writes: "I will never be able to express what I want to say; these lines, often clumsy, are very far removed, I know, from my memories, and even my memories retrieve only sparse fragments of my parents' existence, of their world, of the time when I was a child." At the conclusion of his book, he is still wondering whether he has succeeded "in setting down even so much as a tiny part of what [he] wanted to express." However, since they represent an attempt to recapture whatever is retained of the past, such memories, as fragmented as they may be, remain invaluable. As put by Leon Wieseltier, they are "all the more illuminating, because memory is the consciousness of things and events that have not yet disappeared completely into knowledge" [*New York Review of Books* (25 October 1979)].

No matter how truthful the autobiographer tries to be, he cannot avoid having recourse to fictional or literary devices. Indeed, autobiography is necessarily linked to related literary genres such as the novel, the theater, the diary, or the chronicle. Thus, despite Theodore W. Adorno's contention that it is barbaric to write literature after Auschwitz, the Holocaust writer or autobiographer must engage in a "writing experience" if he wishes to express himself.

The terse language of Wiesel's *Night* is occasionally broken by harrowing scenes such as that of Madame Shachter gone mad in the cattle car or by dialogues such as those that take place between himself and his erstwhile master Moshe-the-Beadle or with his dying father. Fantasy is present when he depicts his native Sighet as "an open tomb" after its Jews have been rounded up. He uses irony when he recalls that a fellow inmate has faith in Hitler because he has kept all his promises to the Jewish people. Images express the author's feelings. Gallows set up in the assembly place in preparation of a hanging appear to him as "three black crows," and the violin of a fellow inmate who has died after playing a Beethoven concerto lies beside him like "a strange overwhelming little corpse." The grotesque best portrays his fellow inmates, "Pour mountebanks, wider than they were tall, more dead than alive; poor clowns, their ghostlike faces emerging from piles of prison clothes! Buffoons!"

While Friedländer and Pisar are not writers in the artistic sense of the word, they cannot avoid resorting to literary devices. On page 78 of *When Memory Comes,* Friedländer writes in a footnote: "All the names associated with my stay in Montluçon, the Indre and Sweden are fictitious," clearly a technique widely used by discretion-conscious autobiographers and by authors of autobiographical novels. The universe of the concentration camp has imprinted on Pisar's mind indelible images and myths. Upon visiting the naval base at Norfolk, Virginia, he is impressed by the latest inventions in warfare such as the nuclear aircraft carriers. The white star which adorns one of them reminds him of the same emblem on the American tank that liberated him. Witnessing the array of these formidable weapons meant to be used in a third world war, he cannot help but seeing in them a "nuclear gas chamber."

According to Georges May, reproducing letters and evoking historical episodes and personalities enliven autobiography and enhance its authenticity. Friedländer reproduces correspondence related to his childhood in France. There are letters written by his mother to the guardian to whose care she entrusted him, by his father to the director of the Catholic school authorizing her to baptize the child; and he reproduces the last letter written by both parents from the train that took them to the death camp. There are letters written by himself after the Liberation to his new guardians inquiring about the fate of his parents and eventually informing them that he would not return home since he had decided to leave for the newly born State of Israel. Retracing the stages of his ascent from a subhuman survivor to his present position, Pisar rarely misses an opportunity to name the celebrities with whom he associated. As a student in Australia, he took walks with Prime Minister Menzies. At Harvard, Ralph Nader and Zaki Yamani were his classmates. During a ceremony in Auschwitz, he stood next to Giscard d'Estaing of France and Gierek of Poland. At the World Gathering of Holocaust Survivors, he stood next to Begin. *Of Blood and Hope* includes a centerfold where he is pictured with Kissinger, Arthur Rubinstein, etc. Mitterand agrees with his views on coexistence between East and West. He is the lawyer of Richard Burton, Ava Gardner, and Catherine Deneuve.

While autobiography may choose to embrace a greater or smaller part of one's life, Holocaust autobiography will essentially deal with the period marked by the events of the Nazi genocide. Just as any autobiography related to a troubled historical period acquires an added significance, so does Holocaust autobiography exert a unique fascination upon the reader because of its central motive.

Like many autobiographers who try to resurrect their happy past, Wiesel, Pisar, and Friedländer dwell upon their childhood as they recall their native towns, their families, and their early schooling shortly before the outbreak of the war. Wiesel and Pisar are sons of educated fathers who were actively involved in Jewish communal affairs. While Friedländer's father had not retained much from his early Jewish education, he was not indifferent to his origins. At the age of 12, Wiesel was eager to study the Kabbalah with his enigmatic teacher Moshe-the-Beadle in his native Sighet. Pisar's native city, Bialystok, is a "vibrant center of Jewish cultural life," where socialism and Zionism mingle and vie with the study of Torah. As he studies for his Bar Mitzvah, which takes place in the ghetto, he realizes that the persecutions which beset the Jewish people throughout its history had forged its very identity. For Friedländer the child, his native Prague is a city of legends, especially that of the Golem, the robot built by the sixteenth-century Rabbi Loewe to protect the endangered Jews of the city. While attending the English school in that city, Friedländer becomes aware of his Jewishness as he is invited to leave catechism classes and told to attend instead Jewish religious instruction.

These evocations of childhood are all the more dramatic as they abruptly came to an end. As he completes the recollection of his early childhood, Friedländer writes: "I hesitate somehow to leave this calm and, when all is said and done, happy period of my life." What follows in the writings of all three authors are scenes of departures. When Wiesel's family must join the roundup of Jews in Sighet, he sees his father weeping for the first time. Looking at his little sister, Tzipora, he notices that "the bundle on her back was too heavy for her." On the eve of the family's departure from Prague, Friedländer is ceremoniously given a ring by his father so that he may not forget his native city. What is concealed from him is that they are fleeing the Nazis. Before leaving the house for the ghetto of Bialystok, Pisar's father gathers his family in the drawing-room, lights a big fire in the fireplace, throws in it the most cherished mementoes of the family and states: "We are living our last moments in our home. We don't know when we will return. We don't know who will move in here after we are gone."

As painful as it may be to both author and reader, these autobiographical writings attempt to come to grips with the hard reality of the concentrationary universe. If *Night* has become a classic, it is because it remains one of the most concise and factual eyewitness accounts of the horrors. Wiesel goes into such details as the early disbelief of the victims ("The yellow star? Oh! well, what of it?" says his own father), the anguish of those who have been marked by death by Mengele in the course of a selection and Wiesel's own joy at having escaped it, the careless trampling of inmates by their own comrades in the course of the agonizing death marches.

The opening pages of Pisar's *Of Blood and Hope* are dedicated to a rather detailed account of his life in the concentration camps. Among the numerous descriptions of his experiences is a shattering portrait of a dying inmate, called "Musulman" in concentration camp terminology. Such an individual who had succeeded in escaping many a selection, once given that label by his own fellow-inmates, "was left feeling he had exhausted his last reserves of strength and hope," and would drop lifeless while no one cared. However, most of his experiences as a former inmate are related in the light of his activities as a political or economic advisor. When he addresses a session of the Bundestag in Bonn, he finds irony in the fact that his previous dialogue with the Germans was a one sided: "caps off, caps on!" coming from his guards. He feels that it is utterly dangerous to subject economy to a nondemocratic regime. Under Nazism, such an alliance led to the I. G. Farben phenomenon which treated human beings as "an expandable raw material . . . from which all vital force was first extracted, was then treated with Zyklon B gas so that it could yield its secondary products: gold teeth and fillings for the Reichsbank, hair for the mattresses, grease for the soap and skin for the lampshades." The struggle for inalienable human rights must go on. In the concentration camps, many died with the conviction that no one would ever learn of their utter suffering, while today violations of human rights anywhere are swiftly publicized to the world at large.

Unlike Wiesel and Pisar, Friedländer did not experience concentration-camp life. Yet, the Holocaust remains a central theme of his book. He relates how he narrowly escaped a transport of children rounded up by the French police as a result of an agreement between the Vichy government and the Nazis. As for other typical aspects of the Holocaust, one might say that he attempts to live them vicariously. As an adult, he visits the village on the French-Swiss border where his parents were kept from crossing into Switzerland, handed over to the French police, and returned to a concentration camp in France while awaiting deportation. Upon the anniversary of the Warsaw ghetto uprising, he meditates about a story told by a survivor concerning a boy begging for a piece of bread in the ghetto and dying before he could reach the piece thrown to him by the narrator from his window. Eight years before the release of *Shoah*, the film by Claude Lanzman, Friedländer relates the detailed testimony concerning the destruction of the Jews at Treblinka given by a former SS guard to Lanzman. He writes that he must leave the room when he hears a former SS officer telling about the burning of villages in Russia where he served. He is appalled when Admiral Dönitz, Hitler's successor, tells him that he knew nothing of the extermination of the Jews, and when he does research in Germany, he feels the urge to pack up and leave. Yet, Friedländer admits that he is unable to fathom

the reality of Belzec and Maidanek. He writes: "The veil between the events and me had not been rent. I had lived on the edges of the catastrophe . . . and despite all my efforts, I remained in my own eyes not so much a victim as a spectator."

"Autobiography," writes Georges May, "is capable of absorbing the most diverse material, to assimilate it and to change it into autobiography" [*L'autobiographie*]. Inasmuch as Holocaust autobiography deals with the events of one of the greatest upheavals of the twentieth century and the most traumatic destruction of the Jewish people, it is natural that autobiographers reflect upon the impact of those events on their personality, on the destiny of the Jewish people and on the post-Holocaust world.

Confession is an essential ingredient of autobiography. Its degree of sincerity remains the sole prerogative of the autobiographer who can choose to shield himself behind his own writing. In Wiesel's *Night*, the frankness of his confession serves as a testimony to the extent of the dehumanization he has reached as a result of his concentration-camp life. While he has been separated forever from his mother and sister upon arrival in Auschwitz, he has managed to stay with his father. Both have miraculously escaped selection for death on several occasions. Yet, the survival instinct has overtaken him in the face of his dying father. When a guard tells him that in the camp "there are no fathers, no brothers, no friends," he thinks in his innermost heart that the guard is right but does not dare admit it. When he wakes up the next morning (less than four months before the Liberation) to find his father dead, he thinks "something like—free at last." Henceforth, Wiesel's life is devoid of meaning. *Night* concludes with the episode of the author looking at himself in the mirror. He writes: "a corpse gazed at me. The look in his eyes as they stared into mine has never left me." As indicated by Ellen Fine [in *Legacy of Night: The Literary Universe of Elie Wiesel*], the shift from the first to the third person in that sentence points to the "fragmented self," and, as indicated by Wiesel himself, that sight was to determine his career as a "writer-witness."[Cargas].

Friedländer informs us of the psychological effects the separation from his parents has had on his childhood. An immediate result of it is his attempted suicide followed by nightmarish fits of fever during which he is vainly looking for his mother in rolling trains. Passing by the hospital where his father lay sick, he wonders, "if one of the glass doors wouldn't suddenly open and [my] mother or father lean out over the edge of the terrace to signal discreetly to [me]." Without news from his parents, he becomes very devout, worshipping especially the Virgin Mary for he rediscovered in her "something of the presence of a mother." When he does not see his parents return after the Liberation, anxiety overtakes him, and he describes in detail its physiological and psychological effects. To this day, the adult remains unsettled by his past. He writes: "In my heart of hearts, I still feel a strange attraction, mingled with profound repulsion, for this phase of my childhood."

The Holocaust causes all three writers to question God's ways. One of the main themes of *Night* is Wiesel's shattered faith. When he recalls his arrival in Auschwitz, he writes the now famous words: "Never shall I forget those flames which consumed my faith forever." He subsequently doubts God's justice, argues with God on Rosh-Hashanah, eats on Yom Kippur as an act of defiance against God, and feels that God Himself is hanging on the gallows when he witnesses the hanging of a child. In fact, the "Trial of God" obsesses Wiesel throughout his work. Without being specifically preoccupied with metaphysics in their account, both Friedländer and Pisar seem nevertheless to take God to task. In the last letter written to his guardian, Friedländer's parents express the wish that God may repay and bless her, which prompts the author's comment: "What God was meant?" Upon being separated forever from his mother and sister, Pisar, too, raises his fist to heaven "in a blasphemous cry towards the Almighty."

Many inmates were able to survive by means of "spiritual resistance"—by clinging to an ideal which would keep them from being destroyed against all odds. For Pisar, such an ideal was friendship in the camps with Ben, a childhood friend, and with Nico, "a resourceful older ally in the daily struggle against death." Having escaped death on several occasions, it is they that he seeks out and it is with them that he is ultimately reunited until they were liberated. For Pisar, this lasting friendship not only meant that they had endured the Holocaust together but also proved that "man can overcome, if he has the courage not to despair."

Having reasonably distanced themselves from the events of the Holocaust before they engaged into autobiographical writing, Friedländer and Pisar are able to put their experience in perspective and, therefore, reflect upon Jewish destiny and identity and express views on the post-Holocaust world.

If, as a child, Friedländer is fascinated by the legend of the Golem or by the sacrifice of Isaac, to the adult, the former symbolizes Jewish "perpetual restlessness" and the latter Jewish obedience to "some mysterious destiny." Upon discovering Zionism after the war, he becomes convinced that a state is needed so that the Jewish people may never again go to the slaughter like sheep. Recalling that his father had waited to become a refugee in France to tell him the Hannukah story, he realizes that his father had rediscovered a "permanent and lasting" feeling of kinship to the community only as a result of the crisis. He himself observes sincere Jewish prayer while living with a religious guardian after the war, experiences a genuine feeling of Jewishness upon discovering Hasidism in the books of Martin Buber, and, on the occasion of Yom Kippur 1977, he states that one can hardly define the Jewish people without the Jewish religion. As an Israeli, Friedländer would like to see his country at peace. He wonders, therefore, whether Israel fails "to accept compromise at the proper moment." He acknowledges, however, that the Jewish people has always been engaged in an "endless quest" which is symbolic of that pursued by mankind as a whole. Therefore, Friedländer surmises that Israel is not likely to alter the course of Jewish history.

Pisar views Jewish destiny and the post-Holocaust world solely with the eyes of a survivor. He concludes the account of a family trip to Masada, the historic symbol of Jewish resistance, with the words "No more Auschwitz, no more Masada." The existence of the State of Israel and the freedom of Soviet Jews are causes that are very close to his heart. The sight of Israeli soldiers praying at the Wailing Wall they had just conquered during the Six-Day War convinces him that "the trains headed for Treblinka, Maidanek and Auschwitz had finally reached their destination." He is indignant at the UN resolution which equates Zionism with racism. It causes him to question his own survival and to realize that perhaps "there was no way to escape from the mentality of the ghettos and the camps after all." Therefore, Israel must remain the ultimate "haven for survivors," especially in the light of recent attacks upon Jews in Europe, which show that the Jew remains prime target. He is heartened by the fact that a Jewish community continues to exist in the Soviet Union sixty five years after the revolution. As a member of an American delegation to a conference on *détente* that took place in Kiev in 1971, he daringly confronts the Russians with their persistant anti-Semitic policy. Introducing himself as a survivor, he criticizes them for requiring that the word JEW be inscribed on the identity cards of Soviet Jews and for failing to recognize Babi Yar as the burial place of thousands of Jews killed by the Nazis. Nevertheless, Pisar remains unequivocally committed to the idea of peaceful coexistence, which is the underlying idea of his autobiographical writings. When he is reminded that, as a survivor, he ought to advocate a militant attitude toward the Russians, he replies that firmness and open mindedness in dealing with them are not incompatible.

Meant as a stark narrative of the events and despite the ten-year period that preceded its writing, Wiesel's *Night* is devoid of reflections extraneous to his experiences in the concentration camps. He has stated that, except for *Night,* his other works are not autobiographical, although he occasionally brings into them "autobiographical data and moods." Yet, Wiesel has emphasized the importance of *Night* as the foundation of his subsequent works. He states: "*Night,* my first narrative, was an autobiographical story, a kind of testimony of one witness speaking of his own life, his own death. All kinds of options were available: suicide, madness, killing, political action, hate, friendship. I note all these options: faith, rejection of faith, blasphemy, atheism, denial, rejection of man, despair, and in each book I explore one aspect. In *Dawn,* I explore the political action; in *The Accident,* suicide; in *The Town Beyond the Wall,* madness; in *The Gates of the Forest,* faith and friendship; in *A Beggar in Jerusalem,* history, the return. All the stories are one story except that I build them in concentric circles. The center is the same and is in *Night.*" Such a position illustrates Philippe Lejeune's concept of "autobiographical space." Indeed, according to Lejeune, it is not always possible to derive the total image of a writer solely on the basis of a work explicitly declared to be autobiographical. Such an image is to be sought rather in the totality of his work which cannot fail to contain autobiographical data. Reflections on Jewish destiny and identity and on the post-Holocaust world are surely the very essence of Wiesel's writings whether they take the form of fiction, tales, plays, or essays.

Autobiography does not necessarily encompass a whole

life. Many autobiographers choose to write about a part of it which they deem significant enough to reflect a profound if not crucial human experience. The Holocaust illustrates this aspect of autobiographical writing. As recognized authors in their respective fields, Wiesel, Friedländer, and Pisar feel a compelling need at one point or another in their lives to tell of their experiences. Whether they write to settle the past, to testify or to educate, they mobilize a variety of devices and themes available to the autobiographer who seeks to share his experiences with the reader. As the Holocaust continues to be represented in an ever-growing multiplicity of forms, autobiography remains a fascinating means to express it. It is noteworthy, therefore, that the Holocaust autobiographer encounters consciously or not many of the problems faced by any autobiographer. However, in the case of the Holocaust autobiographer, such problems become even more crucial because of the nature of the material he is dealing with. Autobiography universalizes one's life. In the hands of the writers examined in this study, Holocaust autobiography not only serves as an invaluable testimony of events that must never be forgotten, but also strengthens the feeling of all those who wish to identify with the victims of the greatest crime that ever took place amidst modern civilization. (p. 131-43)

> *Joseph Sungolowsky, "Holocaust and Autobiography: Wiesel, Friedländer, Pisar," in* Reflections of the Holocaust in Art and Literature, *edited by Randolph L. Braham, Social Science Monographs and The Csengeri Institute for Holocaust Studies of the Graduate School and University Center of the City University of New York, 1990, pp. 131-46.*

NOVELS AND SHORT STORIES

Josephine Knopp

[*Knopp is the director of research for the National Institute on the Holocaust and is the author of* The Trial of Judaism *(1971), a study of contemporary Jewish literature. In the following excerpt, she surveys major novels and short stories arising from the Holocaust.*]

Many victims of the Holocaust have published accounts of their experience. Impelled largely by the need to get the story to light, they feared that the tale might otherwise be lost with the slaughtered. Although all of these accounts are historically important, many are of only marginal literary interest (except insofar as they provide the underpinnings of the genre by offering a basis for comparison with Holocaust writings of real depth and power). Despite this, the story of victimization and occasional survival so deeply moves us that the absence of literary refinement seems irrelevant. That literary criticism does indeed play an important role becomes clear upon confrontation with those Holocaust works of surpassing literary merit. In fact, genuine literary skill, even when applied to the Holocaust, has a special power to convey these enormities.

The problem of distinguishing the writings of literary value among the many that have emerged from the Holocaust is beyond the scope of the present discussion. (The other side of this coin is the fact that a large number of works of undeniable literary merit must be omitted from the discussion, although many of these will be cited.) In any event, in the realm of Holocaust literature the issue of literary quality *per se,* usually regarded as the *sine qua non* of criticism, yields to the deeper questions implicit in T. W. Adorno's succinct proposition: "no poetry after Auschwitz . . . ," the questions whether the Holocaust is amenable to meaningful literary treatment at all and whether the attempt at such treatment should be made. The credibility of an affirmative response to the first of these questions, at least, continues to grow with the rapidly expanding canon of effective literary works dealing with the Holocaust and its aftermath, in a variety of languages, many of them now available in English. That Adorno probably did not intend his dictum to be taken too literally can be read from his own statement that the magnitude of the horror does indeed demand a voice, but a voice that will not betray it by a descent to cynicism. Requiring that the metaphor serve as a memorial to the event, at the same time he cannot avoid the feeling that "language itself had been damaged, possibly beyond creative repair, by the politics of terror and mass-murder." Adorno's position on this issue involves a dilemma reflected as well in the words of Elie Wiesel—perhaps the most important of the literary figures to emerge from the Holocaust—who has repeatedly acknowledged the dual and contradictory demands imposed by the Holocaust: response and silence.

Though Adorno and Wiesel describe essentially the same paradox, the basis for the contradiction differs markedly in the two men. As Lawrence Langer describes so well, Adorno sees "something disagreeable, almost dishonorable, in the conversion of the suffering of the victims into works of art, which are then . . . thrown as fodder to the world . . . that murdered them. . . . Adorno appeals here not to latent sadistic impulses, but to the pleasures inherent in artistic response." Langer goes on to isolate a problem belonging uniquely to the art created in response to the Holocaust and one that surely counts among the deepest problems arising in the entire critical sphere: "The prospect of art denying what it seeks to affirm (the hideous chaos of dehumanization during the Holocaust) raises a spectre of paradox for the critic, the reader, and the artist himself, that is not easily circumvented." Thus for Adorno, the tension between silence and literary response arises primarily from aesthetic considerations, grounded in questions concerning the very nature and purpose of art.

For Wiesel, by contrast, the contradiction has its roots in theological considerations, touching upon the nature of God and man, and especially upon the historical relationship between God and Israel. As one imbued from childhood with biblical and talmudic lore, the product of an Orthodox Jewish background, Wiesel views the Holocaust from within the framework of Jewish history and tradition, linking it with Sinai and Masada, his works at the same time illuminating its uniqueness within that framework. (Wiesel, indeed, would be the last to suggest anything that denies the historical uniqueness of the Holocaust.) For the theologically serious Jew, Sinai remains as clouded in mystery as God himself, a subject for study and discussion, but one destined ultimately to remain impervious to rational scrutiny. A serious Jew—and one with mystical leanings at that—Wiesel finds himself similarly overwhelmed by the impossibility of explaining the Holocaust and especially God's role in the event. "Perhaps some day," he has said, "someone will explain how, on the level of man, Auschwitz was possible; but on the level of God, it will forever remain the most disturbing of mysteries." If the problem of theodicy engendered by the Holocaust is insoluble, perhaps solutions should not be attempted at all; perhaps response is futile and the stance of the survivor (and with him the rest of us) should be a lapse into silence.

However, for one preoccupied with the power and necessity of silence in the face of the Holocaust, Wiesel has written remarkably often of the event, perhaps producing the largest canon on the subject by any single writer. And, of course, he is far from alone in his literary response. The nature of man mandates the continuing quest for an unattainable knowledge of the events of Sinai and the Holocaust, and none finds the mandate more imperative than does the creative artist, who must pursue the apprehension of "truth," wherever that may lead. The act of writing is, furthermore, in itself a "counterforce to nihilism," an attack upon barbarism, and an attempt to restore an articulate life, after Auschwitz. Hence the works of Holocaust literature which—in literary analogy to "Russell's paradox"—themselves question the possibility of creating a meaningful Holocaust literature and the wisdom of making the attempt.

Even if one admits to the hopelessness of achieving real comprehension and one settles for the lesser goal of description, a serious problem remains inherent in the unprecedented nature of the events described. Langer has observed that "all serious art undoubtedly aspires toward the revelation of a new sense of reality," but Holocaust literature has "the curious advantage of having such a 'new' reality already available, pressing with equal force on the conscious and . . . preconscious life of the artist, and seeking only a way of being convincingly presented to an audience of contemporary readers." The problem then for the writer who adopts the Holocaust as a domain for literary scrutiny is in a sense the reverse of the usual problem confronting the would-be creator of imaginative literature, who strives to imbue his work—whether or not the subject is based upon actual events—with sufficient fantasy to warrant that appellation. Indeed, the Holocaust writer— virtually alone among writers—faces the difficulty of making a factual subject believable, of informing the actuality he describes with an aura of reality acceptable as such to his readers. He must somehow break through the barrier of nonacceptance engendered by an absence of that shared experience and sensibility upon which other writers may rely.

Among the group of writers who have successfully accom-

plished this, Wiesel, Andre Schwarz-Bart, Jerzy Kosinski, and Jakov Lind are generally acknowledged as outstanding examples. Schwarz-Bart, like Wiesel, reaches for the indispensable core of experience shared with his audience by placing the Holocaust within a (relatively familiar) super-structure of Jewish history and tradition. Kosinski and Lind, on the other hand, deal with the events of the Holocaust in isolation, presenting their lunacy directly and unsupported by a surrounding ambience of familiarity, logic or sanity. Drawing the reader into their unfamiliar world, they force him to accept its inverted logic and to perceive events from within a wholly altered framework of reality. These four writers are drawn together, however, by their common bond of survivorship, all of them having been victims of the Holocaust in their childhood years. Indeed, most who have written of the event are its survivors, a fact not surprising in view of the difficulties, already noted, in creating literature based upon it at all. The writer not directly touched must surely experience the same difficulty—greatly magnified and intensified—in moving across the threshold of ordinary reality into the special and distorted reality of the Holocaust Universe that besets the reader of Holocaust literature. In writing about the poet Sylvia Plath, George Steiner has in fact gone well beyond the observation of this difficulty to challenge the very right of the nonsurvivor to create a work of art based upon the Holocaust, to take on what he calls the "death-rig of Auschwitz." "What extraterritorial right," Steiner asks, in reference to Sylvia Plath's poetic "overdraft," does one have "to draw on the reserves of animate horror in the ash and the children's shoes? . . . Do any of us have the license to locate our personal disasters, raw as they may be, in Auschwitz?" Despite the objection raised by Steiner— and reiterated by other critics—some writers without direct experience of the Holocaust have indeed attempted to assimilate the event into the fabric of their imaginative works; these include Sylvia Plath, of course, and the poet Anthony Hecht, as well as the American novelists John Hersey, Leon Uris, Gerald Green, Bernard Malamud, and (in *Mr. Sammler's Planet*) Saul Bellow.

Green's *Holocaust,* in essence an historical novel conceived and executed upon a large scale, views the evolution of the Nazi "Final Solution" within the context of World War II. Tracing the varied fates of the members of the Jewish Weiss family of Berlin, as well as the career of the SS officer Dorf, the work provides a broad external perspective upon the Holocaust—even if it does not offer deep or original insights into those events. In a general way, the novel is historically accurate, enough so to serve as a factual introduction to a difficult subject for a large and possibly skeptical audience.

Bellow's work affords a good example of the uses to which Holocaust material may be applied by writers who are "outsiders," not themselves survivors. Limitations upon the function of this material in the fiction of such writers is suggested by a comparison of Bellow's Sammler with the creation of an "insider," the protagonist of Wiesel's novel *The Accident.* Both are Jewish survivors of Hitler's Europe living in New York after the War, yet the two men differ markedly in spirit. For Wiesel's character, survival has become the central experience; among the living he feels himself a "messenger of the dead," life itself being too great a burden to bear. In the case of Sammler—though the Holocaust has left its mark, though he speaks of himself as a survivor, not the man he was before the War—there is the sense of a life shaped primarily by other, more normal and benevolent forces. Despite the setting of *The Accident*—New York after the War—its protagonist continues to be obsessed by the enormities inflicted upon him in an earlier time and a different place, and the novel, like all of Wiesel's, emerges as a response to the Holocaust and to the far-reaching consequences it has had for those touched by this perverted new reality. By contrast, Bellow's survivor-as-protagonist immerses himself in the new (and essentially normal) life he has established in the New World; *Mr. Sammler's Planet* does not treat the consequences of survivorship for the reestablishment of normalcy—as does *The Accident*—but deals rather with the reactions of a survivor to the new life he finds. Hence this work is, as Bellow intends it to be, an examination of contemporary Jewish-American life and morality through the eyes of one who knows it well, yet has the objectivity born of an earlier life first molded by a different culture and milieu and then destroyed, together with the world that nurtured it.

The American writers Norma Rosen and Susan Fromberg Schaeffer are two outsiders who—in the face of George Steiner's dictum and despite the difficulties we have already indicated—have produced novels with the specific and sole intention of responding to the Holocaust. Rosen's *Touching Evil* and Schaeffer's *Anya* are highly disparate works, differing radically in technique and substance, but firmly linked by this common intention. *Anya,* set for the most part in the Holocaust itself, attempts to re-create the unprecedented events and the bizarre atmosphere surrounding them, while Rosen's novel takes place in present-day New York and deals with the implications of the Holocaust for succeeding generations. In a *Midstream* article Rosen herself raises serious artistic questions about such an undertaking: "But how was the Holocaust to be written about? How could the virtues of fiction—indirection, irony, ambivalence—be used to make art out of this unspeakable occurrence?" Beyond raising these literary problems she expresses attendant doubts—which are far from trivial—of a philosophical/theological nature: "To make bad art would be unforgivable. Even to make good art would be in another way unforgivable. Because that would be transcendence. And it was not the right time for transcendence—it was far too soon, and maybe it would never be time." With Rosen's suggestion that "the best response to the Holocaust might be silence, or an endless scream—neither one makes art," we are back upon the familiar ground of the Adorno-Wiesel dilemma, especially in view of the prior existence of her own *Touching Evil.* Though she expresses the dilemma even more explicitly with the claim that "for the American Jewish writer, the Holocaust as subject was a double bind, as nearly impossible to write about as to avoid writing about," the fact remains that few American writers—Jewish or not—have approached the Holocaust in their fiction in as serious a way as have Schaeffer and Rosen.

Norma Rosen has expressed the view—one certainly wor-

thy of serious discussion—that "the Holocaust is the central occurrence of the twentieth century, that it cannot therefore be more so for Jews and Jewish writers." Indeed, *Touching Evil* is constructed upon this concept, with the protagonists Jean and Hattie, non-Jewish Americans living in New York. The two women touch the evil of the Holocaust, become vicariously caught up in the death camp experience, through watching the Eichmann trial on television, which soon becomes a daily ritual, faithfully observed. Commenting upon her own work, Rosen reveals that to her "it seemed right . . . that the woman in my novel [Jean] should be determined that nothing in her life would, after she learned of the existence of the death camps, be as before." The other woman, Hattie, is pregnant and, once again in Rosen's words, "obsessed by the fear of what is passed on in the cycles of human generations." That these women are not Jewish plays a significant role in the author's design of the novel and her hopes for its impact upon the reader: "Clearly, a Jew might respond this way to the Eichmann trial. Non-Jews *ought* to respond in the same way and in my book at least, they would."

Rosen's reach for universality extends to the novel's New York setting, which, with the fearful residents locked into their apartments, serves as a metaphor for the fear-ridden ghettos of Eastern Europe. The metaphor is strengthened by the continuing demolition of Jean's neighborhood in the path of urban renewal, the white X's on the windows of those vacant buildings already marked for the inevitable destruction calling forth some of the horror of the Nazi destruction of the ghettos and their inhabitants. Toward the end of the novel Hattie, Jean's younger counterpart, gives birth to a child, complaining later of the careless treatment—she perceives it as brutal—which she and the other women in the maternity ward experienced. Hattie interprets her hospital experiences within the framework of her newly found awareness of the Nazi evil, becoming "in her hallucination, [symbolic of] the women who gave birth in the camps" and experiencing "the 'taking in' of the knowledge of the Holocaust." (pp. 268-73)

In contradistinction to Norma Rosen, who takes a literary gamble in serving the need for response to the Holocaust by building *Touching Evil* upon her concept of "witness-through-the-imagination," Susan Schaeffer reacts to this need by offering in *Anya* a written oral history, the true story of a real survivor based upon tape-recorded interviews between author and subject. Through this device and by presenting the story as a first person narration through Anya herself, Schaeffer overcomes the difficulties inherent in her lack of firsthand knowledge of the Nazi terror, thereby creating an effective novel of the Holocaust. Schaeffer ultimately succeeds in identifying with the survivor virtually to the point of obliterating the distinction between author and narrator, of fusing outsider and survivor into a single consciousness.

The work begins as a *Bildungsroman,* chronicling the life and fortunes of Anya, a member of a wealthy and assimilated Jewish family in Vilna who enjoys a happy, comfortable childhood, later enrolling as a medical student at the University after overcoming the handicap of her Jewish background by virtue of outstanding academic achievement. Though the Holocaust sweeps up Anya, together with her entire family, in the German invasion of Poland, she senses from the outset her destiny to survive. Long after the War's end she reflects upon her fate, revealing an ambivalent obsession with survival that pervades much of Holocaust writing: "I believe there was something that wanted to keep me alive. . . . I was chosen to live or doomed to live, depending upon my mood for the day."

What strikes one most is the author's almost offhand manner: the fact, made clear by Anya's matter-of-fact description, that the participants—Jew and Gentile, victim and persecutor—do not find remarkable the Jew's role as the object of violence, that indeed violent anti-Judaism is accepted as normative behavior. Schaeffer never deviates from her understated style nor does she lapse into moral considerations upon the events as they occur. Perhaps for this reason Anya long avoids the guilt associated with survival in the midst of mass death, and only in the brief epilogue, describing her life in New York since the time of her arrival after the War, does that guilt become an important component of her personality. Instead of her earlier optimism and resourcefulness in the face of mortal danger, Anya reveals an inability to force the years of suffering from her consciousness. "I was a person who loved, who trusted, who never accepted defeat," she tells us. "And now I am not whole. There are chunks of flesh the war bit from me; my clothes cover them." Thus Anya's assumption that with liberation from the Germans there can be nothing further to fear proves no less a delusion than Hattie's hallucinatory terror. For she has failed to reckon with memory, to take into account the future effects of suffering so profound "that it teaches you you can never forget; you can only repeat and repeat." Jean and Hattie undeniably confront evil, but evil that can be put aside to allow room for normal life and thoughts of the future, while for Anya the future, preempted by the horrors of her past, has lost both hope and meaning.

The case of the novelists I. B. Singer and I. J. Singer does not fit neatly into a dichotomy between Holocaust "insiders" and "outsiders" since the two brothers were nurtured upon the rich Eastern European Yiddish culture destroyed by the Nazis, but they left it behind for the safety of America before the destruction began. Thus, while they cannot speak with firsthand authority about the events of the Holocaust itself, their work does offer a perspective informed by intimate knowledge, in its manifold complexity, of the world destroyed.

An instructive example is I. J. Singer's novel *The Family Carnovsky,* which traces the historic diaspora experience through several generations of a single family, illuminating the Jewish sensibility within the framework of the specific historicity provided by the Holocaust. In this work the Jew, as immigrant and as Holocaust survivor, is a victim of exile—ironically, both from a life-granting environment and from imminent death and destruction. With the history of the Carnovsky family as a vehicle, Singer exposes a good deal of the recent (and, indeed, not-so-recent) history of the Jewish people as a whole, presenting the

eventual genocide as a consequence, in part, of historical Christian anti-Semitism and Jewish self-hate.

These two forces impinge prominently upon the life of David Carnovsky, a Polish *shtetl* Jew who settles in Germany, "the source of all goodness, knowledge, and light," where he seeks a life of enlightenment and movement in the larger society. Indeed, in Berlin David turns from the ways of the Polish Hasidim he disdains and establishes himself among the "distinguished descendants of long-settled German Jewry"—followers of Moses Mendelssohn—avoiding the "raggedy Eastern Jews" for which his wife Leah still yearns. In David, Singer suggests an essential link between the direction taken by the German-Jewish community in its efforts to merge into the surrounding German culture and the catastrophe that was to follow. This is not to suggest that the author is blind to the shortcomings of life in the *shtetl:* the superstition, the restraining customs and rituals, the inhibiting aversion to new ideas. Nevertheless, he condemns—at least by implication—the loss of Jewish traditions, the break with the Jewish past, as a factor in the Holocaust to come.

In Berlin David Carnovsky becomes a leading spokesman of "enlightened" Jewry, whose rejection of the Eastern European Jews results not only from the attractions of the larger society, but from a kind of anti-Semitic self-rejection as well. (pp. 273-75)

The second section of the novel introduces Solomon Burak, a Jewish storekeeper living in Berlin, a man who insists upon maintaining his ethnic identity with the Eastern European *shtetl* from which he emerged. In contrast to David Carnovsky and the Jews of his circle, Burak refuses to submerge his Jewishness or to conceal his origins. He does not change his name or drop his native Yiddish. To many of his fellow Jews in Berlin, Burak represents all that they seek to leave behind, an example of "typical Jewish impudence calculated to antagonize the gentiles. . . . They were uneasy because of people like him, who with their names, conduct and business tactics caused the gentiles to lump them, the long settled and German assimilated Jews, in the same category." It is interesting that this same denial of origins through rejection of Yiddish culture is described—in a post-Holocaust setting, however—by Philip Roth in "Eli, the Fanatic," a story in which a group of young Holocaust survivors cause embarrassment to the prosperous Jews of a suburban community in New York. In each instance members of the established Jewish community betray an unworthy cowardice, revealing themselves willing to abandon fellow Jews in need in order to preserve a fragile security built largely upon a separation from their own history.

This rejection of Jewish history explains the outrage of David Carnovsky's circle at Burak's success in buying his family out of the internment camps established by Germany to contain Polish immigrants during the First World War. Carnovsky—rich, respected, and a former Pole himself—feels that he "can't afford to get involved" to aid those Jews recently arrived from Poland, despite his wish to do so. But David's response to his own helplessness in this situation amounts to a profound reappraisal of his earlier involvement with the Jewish Enlightenment. He comes to believe that "the Melnitz Rabbi had been right after all. The ways of the philosopher led only to evil. It began with the enlightenment . . . it ended with apostasy. As it had happened with Moses Mendelssohn's descendents, it was happening with his. If Georg would not himself convert, his children surely would."

David's change of heart finds further justification in the altered social climate of Berlin following the World War—ably described by Singer—in the lawless bands of youths roaming the streets "screaming for Jewish blood," promising "dire revenge against the traitors of the *Vaterland.*" The Jews are denounced—in traditional and familiar terms—as Christ killers, conspirators, devils in the disguise of ordinary people. But if the elder Carnovsky has grown sensitive to the dangers of assimilation, his son Georg—its victim—has not. Georg suffers the torments of growing up within conflicting Jewish and German traditions, rejecting the one and denied full access to the other, and his marriage to a Gentile woman serves only to alienate him further from both worlds. In him the notion of the enlightened "universal man" has become a mockery, a cruel and humorless joke, for, viewing himself as a free thinker, Georg remains a Jew to the world at large, subject to the sporadic anti-Semitic outbursts of a Gentile world. Nevertheless, like the earlier generation of German Jews during World War I, he maintains confidence in his credentials as a true German, naively believing himself immune to the Nazi onslaught when Hitler comes to power.

The final section of *The Family Carnovsky* depicts the life of Jegor Carnovsky, the son of Georg and grandson of David. Jegor is not merely an anti-Semite, despising his Jewish father, but one eager to further the Nazi war upon his father's people. David, now returned to the practice of traditional Judaism, understands the attitudes of his grandson as a sharp rebuke to the assimilationist practices of his own generation of Jews in Germany, as the inexorable consequence of Enlightenment thought. Jegor, indeed, expresses the ultimate form of Jewish self-hatred, going far beyond the simple wish to conceal his Jewish origins, to the point of willingness to participate in the destruction of the people and the culture of his father. Through the escalating self-rejection of successive Carnovsky generations, Singer suggests a possible role of the German Jews in their own destruction. Yet, in the end, with Jegor's return to the house of his father—despite the boy's flirtation with Nazism—the author seems to imply that Jewish history cannot easily be discarded, that—particularly under the cloud of anti-Semitism—Jews will seek out and identify with their origins. The implication remains as well that "enlightened Jew" is a contradiction in terms, that the path of Moses Mendelssohn inevitably leads to apostasy and eventual destruction for the Jew. (pp. 276-77)

Like *Anya, The Family Carnovsky* does not end with the escape of the protagonists from the Nazis, but depicts their lives in America, where the sense of exile persists. Now safe, they have nonetheless become—in the phrase of Karl Shapiro's preface to his *Poems of a Jew*—"man left over, after everything that can happen has happened."

Enemies: A Love Story by I. B. Singer also focuses upon the lives of these survivor-exiles in New York after the War. The life stories here are of Jews trapped in the Diaspora, cut off from a *shtetl* culture that has been destroyed, people irretrievably damaged, alive but not whole after the Holocaust. Both Singer brothers suggest the impossibility of transporting intact—from one world to another—the multifaceted European Jewish culture, which necessarily undergoes a profound change with the migration.

With Jurek Becker's *Jacob the Liar,* we approach those Holocaust works produced by the Holocaust survivors themselves. Becker, now a resident of East Berlin, was born in Poland in 1937, later forced into a ghetto, and finally transported from there to a Nazi death camp. Despite these early experiences and despite the somber subject matter of *Jacob the Liar,* Becker evokes in this work humor of a kind almost never found in the literature of survivors. The work suggests nothing of the religious searchings of Wiesel and Schwarz-Bart, little of Kosinski and Lind's reconstruction of the horrors they have experienced, and none of the Christian-Jewish encounter that we find in Wiesel's later work, especially in *The Oath.*

Becker makes no attempt to salvage the remains, to seek reasons, to explain. Instead, *Jacob the Liar* presents a microcosm of Jewish life in the ghetto, not so much "under" Nazi authority as "with" Nazi authority. It is as if we had before us a world inhabited by "Lilliputian" Jews watched over by Nazi "big people," not malevolent or evil, but simply in a position of power and responsibility. Though they are unequal in stature, the lives of the Jewish prisoners of the ghetto and their German overseers are intertwined, the existence of each dependent upon that of the other, in a symbiosis of victim and executioner that has been remarked upon in a number of Holocaust writings. Here the Germans do not view the Jews as vermin to be exterminated, but rather as one might look upon dwarfs in a circus— as human freaks. As freaks, the Jews pose the problem of how the Germans ought to treat them; yet the reader is not allowed to forget that Auschwitz is the certain end which all of the inhabitants of the ghetto face. Until the final transport by freight train, however, the ghetto remains alive and—for the most part—intact, and it is the nature and quality of this life upon which Becker focuses the reader's attention.

Jacob's story is a simple one. A resident of the Nazi-controlled ghetto, purely by chance he overhears a few brief remarks indicating that Russian troops are close by and advancing. Jacob shares the good news with Mischa, who is on the verge of suicide and desperately in need of encouragement. To prevent Mischa from taking his own life, Jacob adds credibility to his rumor with an innocent lie: "I know—I have a radio." The virtual impossibility for a Jew to have a radio in the ghetto somehow does not dampen Mischa's belief, nor that of the other Jews of the ghetto, among whom the news spreads rapidly. They believe in Jacob's radio because, like Mischa, they must believe in order to preserve sanity and the will to go on living. Indeed, the radio brings about a profound change in the ghetto, whose residents go to Jacob for daily reports of the outside world, and especially news of the progress of the Russian troops. Unable to disappoint his friends, Jacob forces himself each day to an "act of creation," finding a new way to tell the same story so that hope would not die. Forced to defend this behavior toward his fellow Jews, Jacob justifies it on the grounds that "I try to use my very last means to keep them from simply lying down and croaking, with words, you understand. . . . Because I have nothing else, you see!"

Under the circumstances, Jacob's life becomes dominated by two fears—that the Germans might learn of the radio and that the Jews would stop believing in its existence. These fears eventually weary Jacob to the point that he can no longer bear the lie in solitude, and in his state of fatigue he reveals the secret to Kowalski, an old friend. Kowalski, having invested his last bit of hope in the advancing Russian troops, promptly throws himself onto the electrified barbed wire which surrounds the ghetto. In response, Jacob's despair deepens, as he realizes the untenable position into which he has maneuvered himself. Kowalski's suicide brings home clearly the dangerous double bind with which he must now live: while it is risky to continue to promulgate the lie, it is catastrophic to reveal the truth.

The charade continues, and the radio becomes the focal point of the novel, an inanimate "protagonist" about which Becker develops a series of vignettes concerning the ghetto residents, whose lives center more and more upon the outside "news" they receive from Jacob. One of these stories is of special interest since it reveals the sense of humor which lies at the heart of the novel. Jacob assumes the responsibility of caring for Lena, a young girl whose parents were transported one night to Auschwitz. Living with Jacob, Lena becomes curious about the radio, since she has never yet seen one in her young life. She looks through Jacob's things, finding a lantern which she decides must be the precious radio itself. As she has heard that a radio "talks," she speaks to the lantern, hoping for a response, and the ingenious Jacob devises a way to have the lantern answer her. Of course, contrast with the surrounding tragedy serves to emphasize the hilarity of this scene.

Humor is not the only characteristic of Becker's writing that sets him apart from the majority of writers on the Holocaust. He has, in addition, an intimate and disarmingly simple approach to his characters that allows the reader almost to forget from time to time that the world described is one of insanity, degradation, and horror. For the imminent, all-pervasive death receives muted treatment by Becker, without rage or outcry, without metaphysical speculation or vows of revenge. His perspective on the German enemy is equally understated and unusual. No need for the reader to recoil, Becker seems to imply, for they too are human. Jews die quietly, with a suggestion of heroism, of human dignity preserved, in their silence, as in the case of Herschl Stamm, a pious Jew who reveals a heroic side to his character. Yet the author suggests some disapproval at the absence of widespread, organized resistance in the ghetto against the prevailing evil social order imposed by the Nazis. But, finally, the passive resistance of ordinary people like Jacob, with their will to go on in the face of terrors unknown to earlier generations, amounts to resistance against the Nazis just as meaningful

as armed uprising, and perhaps more profound as a statement of the power of the human will.

Like Becker's novel and like *Anya,* Ka-Tzetnik's *House of Dolls* chronicles the daily struggle of young Polish Jews to survive the degradations imposed upon them by the Nazis. Forced from her home into a ghetto, the schoolgirl Daniella eventually finds herself in a German labor camp. Because she is young and attractive, she does not share the manual labor done by the majority of the inmates, but serves rather in the "Doll House," established to fulfill the sexual desires of the German soldiers. The girls of the Doll House must serve their German masters with enthusiasm, the slightest indication of less than full attention to their work resulting in a much dreaded "report." In contrast to Anya, Daniella does not survive the experience, preferring finally to die in a heroic gesture of defiance, infuriated to the point of madness by the death of her beloved Harry, while her friend and fellow inmate Fella remains alive at the end.

Clever and resourceful, a tough survivor reminiscent of Anya, Fella—the reader is certain—will live to carry out the mission entrusted to her by Daniella: the delivery of a notebook and locket to Daniella's brother in Niederwalden. Indeed, the mission itself lends new purpose to a life drained of all significance beyond the instinct for survival. However, Anya's example serves to warn against the inference that Fella has found somehow the alchemist's secret for transmuting enormity into joy, death into meaning. Fella's mission can help her move more easily through the remaining days of torment perhaps, but it cannot erase the scars of survival. As Harry points out, in the Holocaust Universe "everything is mixed up. Life and death in one brew. A hereafter that's not here, not after. Fraud and hoax." Much as the thought violates our usual notions, we are forced to entertain the possibility, at least, that for the Holocaust victims, survival is not preferable to death, an idea which finds literary implications in Alvin Rosenfeld's observation that "within the context of Holocaust Literature the living often carry a knowledge of death more terrible in its intimacy than that ever recorded in the writings of the [dead] victims." These remarks shed some light upon *House of Dolls,* written by the survivor Ka-Tzetnik whose very pen name contains the number branded into his flesh by the Nazis and translates roughly as "Internee 135633." Rosenfeld pursues the idea further by raising a question which yields some insight into the fates of Daniella and Fella, one asked time and again in the writings of those who survived and implicit as well in the epilogue to *Anya:* "Who, in fact, *are* the real victims here, the dead or those cursed back into life again, guilt-ridden and condemned by a fate that would not take them?"

The ambiguity of survival provides the central idea about which Arnost Lustig, himself a survivor of Theresienstadt (Terezin), has constructed his story "The Return," from the collection *Night and Hope.* The story opens upon Hynek Tausig, a Jew who has escaped removal to the Theresienstadt Ghetto by hiding from the Germans during the roundup. Though his identification papers give him a new identity, Tausig walks the streets of Prague fearful of detection. Miserable, tired, and hungry, his fear impels him finally to rejoin his fellow Jews by slipping into the ghetto, where he finds a measure of contentment—despite the loss of freedom and cruel beatings—in the company of other Jews and in the knowledge that he will no longer need to hide. But Tausig eventually grows unhappy in the ghetto, reacting against its miserable conditions and the loss of dignity, despising his fellow Jews—and himself—for their fear and subservience, yet knowing that they cannot behave otherwise. Ultimately, he finds within himself that will to live which permeates *Anya* (and the autobiographical works of Kosinski and Lind), escaping from the certain death of the ghetto into the uncertain world outside to take up life once again under his false identity, and to struggle daily with that overwhelming fear of detection with which the story began.

"Rose Street" is another story from *Night and Hope* which hints at the possible implication, through passivity, of the Jews in their own fate. In this tale the elderly Elizabeth Feiner, bringing to mind Hannah Arendt's famous denunciation of the *Judenrat,* suggests that by not cooperating so readily with the Nazis, perhaps by refusing or merely "neglecting" to conform to German regulations, the Jews might shorten the War and with it, their misery. But Elizabeth Feiner has her own method to resist "the onslaught on human dignity that the present time brought with it"—silence, the refusal to speak or cry out in face of unspeakable horror, a response which runs as a thread throughout Wiesel's works and indeed forms the basis for the plot of *The Oath.* Mrs. Feiner remains silent during a brutal beating at the hands of First Officer Herz and she finally dies in silence, refusing to yield to the pain and dehumanization which comprise the Nazi answer to "the Jewish question."

Within the domain of Holocaust Literature, this story is unusual in its partial shift of narrative viewpoint away from the victims to Herz and his driver Binde. Binde, in particular, arrests our attention for his silent disapproval of the way in which Herz mistreats the old woman, who somehow touches him, who reminds him, curiously, of his stepbrother. Binde's spark of decency finds expression in his feeling that Elizabeth Feiner is "a mediator between him and his future peace of mind." He brings her food, at great risk to himself, in an attempt to win her trust and salve his conscience, only to be met by a wary and suspicious silence. Later he assumes even greater risk, preventing the final humiliation to Mrs. Feiner by shooting a dog ordered to attack her. But Binde's actions, though heroic under the circumstances, serve more to highlight the brutal level to which the Nazis have sunk than they do to salvage the humanity of the German nation. Binde, representing a small minority among the Nazis, cannot save Mrs. Feiner—or the other Jews of the ghetto—from a horrible death inflicted by his compatriots, who have created the conditions which make impossible all but the weakest assertion of his humane instincts.

The role of the *Judenrat* in the fate of European Jewry is suggested in "Stephen and Anne," a story from the same collection, whose theme is that of awakening youthful love crushed by the circumstances of ghetto life. In "Blue Flames" Lustig focuses more intently upon this aspect of

the tragedy, enlarging his treatment of the *Judenrat* to the status of theme. The story centers upon the relationship between Ignatz Marmulstaub, a member of the Jewish Council of Elders, and Herr von Holler, commandant of the ghetto. Holler confers favors upon Marmulstaub—in particular, keeping him alive—in order to turn to advantage his position as Council member. Although Marmulstaub is a coward, promoting his own interests even at the expense of his fellow Jews, the story cannot be read as a blanket condemnation of *Judenrat* members. Indeed, Lustig draws important distinctions, providing Lowenbach as counterfoil to Marmulstaub. Convinced that those in the forthcoming "labor transport" from the ghetto are never to return, Lowenbach, as head of the Council, withholds the signature that Holler—constrained by the rules of the Nazi bureaucracy—requires before the shipment can begin. Holler responds by summoning Marmulstaub to deputize for the imprisoned Lowenbach and to provide the needed signature. Too fearful to follow the heroic lead of his fellow Council member, Marmulstaub signs the paper and rationalizes his action on the grounds that "Holler had to call somebody." Lowenbach does not actually appear in the story, but his presence is powerful throughout, serving as background and silent rebuke to Marmulstaub's self-serving behavior. The same can be said of the young man, Woodpecker, who—calling to mind Elizabeth Feiner—emulates Lowenbach's refusal to cooperate, at first resisting with silence, and ultimately losing his life in a suicidal attempt to counter Nazi bullets with the axle of a carriage.

Woodpecker and Lowenbach, Mrs. Feiner and Tausig—all of these in their own ways rebel against the Nazi authority, choosing to maintain dignity and humanity, even at the expense of their lives. Their examples suggest a potential for Jewish resistance to the Nazis which, though perhaps not fully exploited, did occasionally make itself felt under virtually impossible circumstances. Indeed, the seven interconnected stories of *Night and Hope* demonstrate that in the face of the teror and misery of the Theresienstadt Ghetto a semblance of life did nevertheless carry on there, and it is Lustig's gift to recapture the spirit of this life for us. Focused closely upon the actions and fate of a few, the stories—however limited in intent—have sufficient cumulative impact to convey vividly the strengths and foibles of the victims and the complex interrelationships between them and their tormentors. Lustig's writings share with *Anya* and the works of Ka-Tzetnik—as they do with Wiesel's autobiographical *Night*—the force of actuality. The perceptive reader does not need to be told explicitly that the events described actually took place, that the characters depicted are real ones, however shattering one may find the acceptance of such truth.

Night and Hope, like many other works emerging from the Holocaust, batters the senses with the events of the present, describing the real actions of real people and leaving to the reader the inferences implicit in the situations described.

The same can be said of Lustig's novel *A Prayer for Katerina Horovitzova,* to my knowledge the only Holocaust work in which American Jews play a major role. The story, based upon an actual episode documented at Yad Vashem, concerns twenty American Jews taken prisoner by the Nazis after being trapped in Italy. These twenty men have been brought to Poland under the "protection" of a Nazi bureaucrat, Mr. Friedrich Brenske, to a concentration camp where they are held. Brenske has undertaken negotiations with the object—so the Americans are led to believe—of securing their release in exchange for a fortune in Swiss currency.

Katerina's life enters the negotiations when Herman Cohen, spokesman for the American group, overhears her plea to her father as she is being forced onto a death transport: "But I don't want to die. . . . " The figure of Katerina—like the American group—is based upon fact, modeled after an American-born Jewish ballerina of great beauty who was caught in Poland by the Nazis and sent to Auschwitz. Already on her way to the gas chambers, she so overwhelmed the guard with her beauty that he spared her life. Ultimately she was shot to death after wresting a gun from one of the guards and killing several. (See Borowski's "The Death of Schillinger," also based upon the story of this anonymous heroine.)

Although Lustig's novel contains little "action" in the conventional sense, the author brings to the work a manifold perspective successfully combining various levels of meaning. Katerina eagerly leaps at Mr. Cohen's offer of help, yet she cannot free herself of guilt rooted in her "reprieve." She acknowledges her cowardice under the threat of death, but, confronting death, in the end she emerges as a heroine. For their part, the Americans delude themselves with the belief that even warfare has rules to which both sides adhere. Gradually, painfully, Lustig exposes to light what the reader fears from the outset, that this belief is naive and unrealistic, that under Nazi rule the fate of Jews—regardless of their citizenship—is immutably sealed.

Especially significant in this connection is the failure of the American government to intercede on behalf of the group of twenty, who are "grossly rejected by their own authorities." Indeed, while Lustig does not formulate the notion explicitly, the suggestion nevertheless remains of a link between Hitler's successful campaign to destroy European Jewry and the silence of the world, of the Allied governments in particular.

As he does in *Night and Hope,* in *Katerina* Lustig has something significant to reveal concerning Jewish compliance and Jewish resistance. Finally understanding clearly and without self-deception that she is on the brink of death, Katerina seizes the gun of a Nazi officer and shoots several of the soldiers. Her behavior in death contrasts sharply with the passivity of the Americans, whose nudity—they have been forced to disrobe in preparation for the gas chamber—symbolizes an underlying moral nakedness, exposed in part by the diabolical, highly cultivated Nazi talent for dehumanization. Even more striking is the reaction of Brenske's commandos—Jewish inmates of long standing—who, though armed, fail to turn against their tormenters, instead aiming their "guns at the 19 men and one woman who stood huddled together," thus earning a

brief respite from the fear of death and keeping alive a desperate and slim hope of survival.

But it is not Lustig's purpose to condemn these victims who remain passive or participate actively in their own extermination. Rather, he has undertaken the more difficult and subtle task of exposing to view the complexities inherent in the moral/psychological issues touching upon compliance and resistance among those exposed daily to physical torture and moral degradation. With regard to the Americans, Brenske understands that "a lot of people more vigilant and less credulous than they had been had also been lured from the path of judgement and reason. Mr. Brenske was an expert at the job." The Jewish tailor who acted as a commando upon Brenske's orders "understood a lot; there was a lot he didn't understand and there was a lot which had been inevitable," just as Brenske realized "that blood and blood relationships alone are never decisive. . . . It was strength that counted, rather, and the realization of which side has the superiority and power and who will be the one to present the bill when the rebellion is over." In view of the complete Jewish powerlessness during the Holocaust, exacerbated by the silence of Hitler's enemies—Lustig may be suggesting—even the scattered, spontaneous resistance of individual victims such as Katerina and the people of *Night and Hope,* albeit restricted in scope, is a tribute to the human spirit.

The theme of resistance against impossible odds is taken up on alarger scale in Lustig's autobiographical novel *Darkness Casts No Shadow,* which tells the story of two

Arnost Lustig.

teenaged boys who escape from a death transport and struggle for survival by hiding in the woods. The central episode of the work describes the boys' encounter with a German housewife, from whom they demand food. Though they understand well that the protection of their own lives dictates killing the woman, the boys cannot bring themselves to carry out the act, in part because she has a young child. They perceive that the will to live carries with it "the multiplied determination to kill . . . stronger than you are, but as long as you live, you can try to resist it." Indeed, they feel that there are "situations when . . . it would almost be better to be killed . . . than to kill." This resistance to killing has its inevitable consequence, as the woman reports the incident to the village authorities. Ultimately the boys are hunted down and executed by the old men of the village, men too old for the *Wehrmacht,* who want nonetheless to participate in the new dream—the work of the great German Reich.

Darkness Casts No Shadow is far from a self-conscious exploration of courage and morality in opposition to an all-pervasive and overwhelming evil; yet its sparse, elegantly executed narrative effectively carries the force and message of such an essay. Here, as elsewhere in his writings, Lustig has focused upon a narrowly circumscribed segment of Holocaust life, evidently believing—and with some justice—that assimilation of the larger picture is best left to the historians. Still, the behavior of two adolescent boys in this one small episode has universal implications, not about death, but about humane life, informed by the knowledge that "conscience is like your heart—you can't carve off a piece and expect the rest to function as before."

Jerzy Kosinski's *The Painted Bird,* similarly, emphasizes the immediate, but the narrative thread is overlaid with a quality of fantasy generated in part by the author's deliberate ambiguity concerning the protagonist's identity and the locale of his actions. (The fact that the events of *The Painted Bird* are even conceivable as actuality reveals the extent to which the Holocaust has altered our notions of reality by diminishing the scope of the impossible.) We are told only that "in the fall of 1939, a six-year-old boy from a large city in Eastern Europe was sent by his parents, like thousands of other children, to the shelter of a distant village" to the east, that in the War's disruption the parents lost contact with the boy, and that he "was considered a Gypsy or Jewish stray" by the villagers, who therefore could aid him only by risking severe penalties at the hands of the Germans. The work describes the boy's movement from village to village throughout the War, his exposure to bestiality and random, senseless violence, and his eventual liberation from the ordeal by Russian troops advancing westward during the War's concluding days.

The marked differences between Lustig's characters and this boy without family, past, name or language explain, in part, the off-center, disturbing atmosphere that Kosinski creates in this work. If we do not know in great detail the backgrounds of the people in *Night and Hope,* we nevertheless do have a grasp of the general outlines of their history. The contrast is even more striking when comparisons are made with Anya or Ka-Tzetnik's Daniella, whose history and family relationships receive detailed exposure,

and who succeed in carrying with them—even into the ghetto and concentration camp—some of the artifacts and ambience of their past lives. Because of his youth, Kosinski's youngster remembers little of his past and dwells on it only at the beginning of the work, in anticipation of a reunion with his parents. But this expectation, crowded out by the immediate demands of bare survival, soon fades from his thoughts, leaving him to move from adventure to adventure, mute and in isolation. After the book's opening pages the boy remains sealed off from his past, establishing only short-lived human contacts, and these only from the necessity imposed by harsh circumstances.

The action of *The Painted Bird* is far removed from the ghettos and death camps described in much of Holocaust Literature; yet, the work succeeds in recreating the atmosphere of the Nazi universe of terror by depicting events which are equally devastating in their threat to destroy the boy's humanity. In this novel, indeed, Kosinski appears to mount an effective challenge—possibly the only one up to now—to what Alvin Rosenfeld understands as one of the "abiding laws" of Holocaust Literature: "there are no metaphors for Auschwitz" [see Critical Overview above]. (Whether *The Painted Bird* will remain an isolated exception to prove Rosenfeld's rule remains, of course, to be seen.) Auschwitz, however, haunts the periphery of Kosinski's fictive world, a silent, though powerfully disturbing presence, a backdrop against which the primitive animalistic villagers act out their lives of violence and inarticulate superstition. Acutely aware of the contents and destination of the German death-camp trains which periodically move across their landscape, they believed that "the Lord was using the Germans as His instrument of justice," justly punishing the Jews "for the shameful crimes of their ancestors, for refuting the only True Faith, for mercilessly killing Christian babies and drinking their blood."

The boy, finding shelter where he can, moves from one peasant to another, mutely absorbing the scenes of death and bestiality which he confronts daily, his own life beset with constant pain and danger. One episode is particularly overpowering in its horror, as the boy witnesses the punishment a drunken miller inflicts upon a plowboy who lusts after his wife. The miller pushes the plowboy against a wall and gouges out his eye with an iron spoon. His terrible revenge as yet incomplete, the miller keeps the victim pinned against the wall and plunges the spoon into the other eye "which sprang out even faster." In an interview between Kosinski and Lawrence Langer (as quoted in Langer's *The Holocaust and the Literary Imagination*), the author attempts to explain the tendency of readers to reject this passage in his novel. Citing the instance of a woman who could not read through the episode, Kosinski wonders why she finds the eye-gouging too terrible to confront although she can contemplate the even worse realities of the gas chambers and concentration camps. His explanation of this phenomenon casts a good deal of light upon the literary and psychological considerations underlying the central design of *The Painted Bird:*

> The concentration camp as such is a symbol you can live with very well. We do. It doesn't really perform any specific function. It's not as close to us as the eyesight is. When you describe the

atrocity of the concentration camp you are immediately reminding the reader that this is not his reality. . . . But when you describe the eyes being gouged out, you don't make it easier for the reader, he cannot help feeling his own eyes disappearing somehow, becoming blind.

The Painted Bird does indeed achieve its powerful effect through a succession of bizarre and violent incidents which evoke horror, a literary device that moves toward a re-creation of the atmosphere of Auschwitz without attempting to recreate Auschwitz itself. The life which the boy suffers has the expected result: having grown up with violence, he condones it and resorts to it. As Langer has observed, the boy's understanding of revenge as a mark of the true human being points to a reading of the novel as an intentional parody of the traditional *Bildungsroman*. Revealing in this connection is the contrast with *Anya*, which might be considered an incomplete *Bildungsroman*, describing a career interrupted precisely when it is about to mature into productivity. At the time of the German invasion Anya is an adult, with a firm grasp upon life, the values and goals instilled during her childhood already internalized, and indeed she retains her basic decency even in the ghetto and the concentration camp. Kosinski's boy, on the other hand, has nowhere to turn for humane guidance or example, the Holocaust itself acting as the societal framework—if one may use that term—within which he begins his growth to maturity. Not surprisingly, the values he has absorbed are a distortion, a parody of those that society normally attempts to inculcate. Only twelve years old at the War's end, as a result of his intimate knowledge of physical and moral degradation, he is violent and barely controllable, mute despite his need to communicate. Ultimately, the boy is reunited with his parents and he regains the power of speech as well, but optimism about his future is misplaced for, as the epilogue of *Anya* makes clear, liberation does not guarantee a return to prewar sensibilities, and the Holocaust survivor, indeed, may find impossible genuine liberation from the memory of his ordeal.

That the world has emerged from the Holocaust a radically altered place, its basic values and assumptions displaced beyond the point of return by the Nazi exploration in new regions of terror, is implicit in the final pages of *The Painted Bird,* suggested by the boy's great difficulty in readjusting to a measure of normalcy. The message becomes more explicit in Kosinski's later novel, *Steps,* a collection of loosely interrelated vignettes not describing a world going mad—as does *The Painted Bird*—but rather a world already in the throes of madness. In this sense *Steps* carries the central idea of *The Painted Bird* to its logical (or, rather, logically illogical) conclusion, surrounding the reader in an ambience bizarre enough to create a sense of disjunction from the familiar, yet too familiar to be dismissed as pure fantasy. As in the earlier work, the plot of *Steps* focuses largely upon bestiality, violence, and degraded, manipulative sexuality—but with an important difference. While the events in *The Painted Bird* shock the sense with their immediacy, often forcing one to turn away from the horror projected in its pages (the eye-gouging episode is a good example), those in *Steps* are presented in a detached fashion, calculated to make them appear unremarkable, almost acceptable as normal human behavior.

The consequent tension established between surface appearance and underlying substance, between style of presentation and events presented, explains in large measure the power of *Steps* to disturb profoundly—if not immediately, then after reflection upon the implications for civilized society of Kosinski's fictive vision. In the sense that *Steps* is farther removed than is *The Painted Bird* from the actual events of the Holocaust out of which its world-view grows, it is a "second generation" work of Holocaust Literature, belonging among those artistic attempts to apprehend and assess a universe damaged, perhaps irremediably, by the knowledge of Auschwitz, rather than among those works grappling with Auschwitz itself.

The same may be said of much of the fiction—as opposed to the autobiographical works—of Jakov Lind, a Viennese Jew who survived the Nazi years in Germany itself, aided by false identity papers and an "Aryan" appearance. Lind's background of wartime life under an assumed identity, described in *Counting My Steps* and *Numbers,* explains the distance from the ghettos and concentration camps that his fiction shares with that of Kosinski. Even these autobiographies, like *The Painted Bird,* offer only the exterior view of the events of the Holocaust to which Lind, in his isolation from the great mass of Jewish victims, was himself exposed. This relatively distanced position, however, lies at the heart of Lind's uniqueness as a Holocaust writer and explains some of the intrinsic interest of his work. *Counting My Steps* and *Numbers,* as autobiography, do, indeed, depict reality, but reality of a kind quite different from that exposed in *Anya, Night and Hope, House of Dolls,* or Wiesel's *Night.* In fact, Lind's life history brings to light the possibilities, however limited, for approximating normal existence in the midst of the Holocaust, for establishing a life outside of that death-in-life planned and executed by the Nazis as response to the "Jewish question."

These possibilities were realized for the teenaged Lind in the wake of his impulsive—and retroactively courageous—decision to ignore German orders to report for deportation with the Jews of Amsterdam. Instead, he separated himself from family and friends, going underground in search of freedom and sexual partners, to emerge later in the guise of ordinary Dutch citizen, Jan Overbeek, with papers entitling him to work to support himself. As Michael Berenbaum suggests, "Lind's life experience" contrasts with that of Anne Frank—who was about the same age—in illustrating the alternatives "available to one who faces his fear and admits to himself the magnitude of the problem." Indeed, Lind tends to be extremely critical of those Jews who, unable to face their situation directly and paralyzed by fear and disbelief, did little to save themselves from deportation and eventual death. Lind's frequently expressed ambivalence toward his Jewishness arises from revulsion against the kind of fear that reinforces powerlessness instead of combating it, the kind of fear that he associates with being Jewish: "My roots are in fear and fear is the marrow of my bones." Having himself survived by struggling in the face of fear and powerlessness, he reacts against what is—in his perception—the weakness of the vast majority of his fellow Jews, who could not—or simply did not—follow the same course of action. In Berenbaum's view Lind's career provides a small measure of evidence in support of the condemnation of the *Judenrat* and the Jewish willingness to cooperate with its leadership expressed in Hannah Arendt's claim that the total number of Jewish victims of the Nazis would have been reduced greatly "if the Jewish people had really been unorganized and leaderless."

As a Jew who finds fault with his own people while managing to "pass" among the Nazis, Lind is doubly an outsider, at home nowhere. This holds true even in Israel after his liberation, where he finds himself "turned back into Jan Overbeek on a visit to the Jews. Only more anti-Semitic than most Dutchmen." Lind's status as permanent (or, at least, long-term) outsider lends a special character to his fiction, adding an edge of objectivity to his description of chaos and abetting his violation—carried out repeatedly and with great effect—of the boundaries between sanity and madness, between historical truth and literary imagination. Lind presents his perception of the post-Holocaust era as a time in which such traditional distinctions no longer apply, having become largely irrelevant or meaningless. The first line of the title story in the collection *Soul of Wood*, rivaling in its searing effect the famous opening of Camus's *The Stranger*, illustrates the point: "Those who had no papers entitling them to live lined up to die." The reader who grasps at the hope that Lind's shattering conception is rooted only in the author's fantasy is very shortly disabused of that notion, alerted by the reference to freight cars packed with dying people, the alternative, more bearable interpretation swept away with a single reference to Auschwitz: "In the little town of Oswiecim they were taken off the train by men in uniform and cremated the same day."

As does most of Lind's fiction, *Soul of Wood* explores the state of mind that made Auschwitz possible and the resulting damage to the human spirit as revealed in both victim and executioner, rather than the events of the Holocaust itself. After his parents die on the way to Auschwitz, the crippled protagonist Anton Barth—even his eyelids were paralyzed—is removed by the faithful servant Wohlbrecht to a hut in the mountains, there presumably to starve or to be killed by forest animals, if the Nazis do not find him first. But Anton does not die in his isolation; miraculously, he survives a stag's attack, to develop the complete use of his body and voice. However, in order to survive in isolation, Anton is compelled to join a herd of deer, learning to live, eat, and run as the deer do, and, indeed, becoming the leader of the herd. Thus, upon his return to the hut at the War's end, an amazed Wohlbrecht finds Anton Barth whole in body but animal in spirit, deriving nourishment from hay but revolted by bread. Lind's transmutation of victim into beast is but one instance of a theme occurring frequently in the literature of the Holocaust—Schwarz-Bart's *The Last of the Just* and Kaniuk's *Adam Resurrected* come immediately to mind—an aspect of the new reality that the Nazi period has unleashed. The literary antecedent of this theme is to be sought in Kafka, for whom, however, the notion undoubtedly has significance more as symbolism for man's condition than as depiction of literal reality. The post-Holocaust writer, on the other hand, knows that Kafka's stunning conception has mean-

ing beyond and outside of the symbolic, matching closely a reality that the Holocaust survivor has experienced firsthand.

Anton's transformation serves as a metaphor for Lind's own survival, made possible by the protective coloration of a new identity. Clearly, survival for Anton, as for Lind himself, depends upon an altered state of being, a descent from the usual self, which is doomed, to life upon a new level at which physical survival becomes possible. Thus, as we have noted in connection with *Anya*, survival, in itself, is far from an unalloyed good, tainted with the experience and memory of bestiality. Indeed bestiality pervades Lind's post-Holocaust fictive world, a place where modern-day cannibals ride Western European trains dressed in ordinary business attire and recruit potential victims, where nudists who drink fresh blood and eat their own children seem unexceptional. To our eternal horror, it is a place where the inverted logic of the Holocaust Universe has made mass murder of humans more acceptable than petty theft—a violation of "good breeding"—or the killing of squirrels and rabbits. After all, Bachmann tells us in *Landscape in Concrete*, "men can defend themselves, but what can animals do in this world without steel and dynamite? . . . Men are men, they have reason and weapons."

The descent of the executioner to the bestial along with the victim is a commonplace of Holocaust Literature, but in the novel *Landscape in Concrete* Lind achieves an unusual and graphic treatment of this theme by employing the narrative viewpoint of the Nazis themselves in place of the more commonly adopted viewpoint of the victims. This literary strategy, available to Lind because of his unusual experience of survival in Germany, gives the author an internal view of the actions and motivations of the Nazis that has generally not emerged in the writings of those who were trapped in ghettos and concentration camps. The work, describing the chaotic state of the German mentality during the declining days of the War, emphasizes the human indifference to human suffering, the devolution of mass slaughter to the routine and tedious, the "banality"—to use Hannah Arendt's term—of extermination through technology. It stresses as well a theme which is prominent in Lind's autobiographical works—the madness of defenseless passivity in a violent world.

In the end, however, it is not merely the victims of the Nazis who find themselves defenseless, as the executioners are themselves trapped in the Holocaust they have unleashed upon the world. The final pages of *Landscape in Concrete* describe an air raid and its aftermath, a sequence of events evolving into a metaphor for nothing less than the destruction of civilization as we know it. At the end, there remains only "the gray ocean of an extinguished landscape, a colorless and bare" stillness yielding no sign of the human or, indeed, of life in any form. The descent into nothingness is complete and irretrievable, it is "too late for help . . . remedy is nothing but a word, stale medicine, nothing can revive dead cells."

If the title of Lind's novel can serve as a clue to the mood of hopelessness in its final pages, the title of Yoram Kaniuk's *Adam Resurrected* is, similarly, an indication of the message its author intends to project. Like Lind, Kaniuk depicts a post-Holocaust world beset by madness, a reality distorted and misshapen by the enormity of events past but not forgotten. However, in contradistinction to Lind, for Kaniuk the madness is balanced by an ameliorating hope, the hope found in the "resurrection" of Adam, at the novel's end, from the inferno of insanity which he suffers throughout the work.

As with Lind's Anton Barth, the physical survival of Adam Stein has entailed a degradation of spirit from the human to the animal. Imprisoned in a Nazi extermination camp, Adam—a well-known clown before the War—was forced to provide humorous diversion for the benefit of the camp commandant while his fellow Jews, his own wife and daughter among them, marched to the gas chambers. This experience irreparably subverts Adam's humanity in his own eyes, and in the eyes of the Nazis, and in response he assumes the role of a dog, chewing on bones, eschewing human speech in favor of a remarkably doglike series of growls and barks, snapping and biting, and running on all fours, all to the great amusement of Commandant Klein. In keeping with the familiar pattern of survival, Adam's release from the camp at the War's end does not, in itself, provide an antidote to the spiritual poison methodically forced into his system by the Nazis. Indeed, the bulk of the novel's action centers upon an asylum for the insane near the Dead Sea, where, within his person, Adam as patient acts out the deep-rooted conflict between the world of normal human intercourse and the diabolical legacy of the Holocaust, struggling with the contradictory claims imposed by the need to reestablish sanity and the desire to preserve madness, the longing to forget and the impossibility of suppressing the past.

While Lind's writing has theological implications only in the sense of complete negation, Kaniuk's novel—beyond the obvious reference contained in its title—raises that bitter challenge to Judaism and the God of Israel which the works of Schwarz-Bart and Wiesel develop into a major and sustained theme. At the same time Kaniuk condemns the mainstream Western European civilization upon which the hopes of so many had been focused, but which in the end spawned the methodical slaughter of millions of innocents. With a searing irony, Kaniuk suggests that Adam found security in the Nazi camp because his classmates from the university designed and built it, that he understood where he was because "the culture which made Adam Stein also made the Camp." Kaniuk discredits the faith that Western civilization has traditionally invested in a scientific approach to the world, falling back instead upon the irrational power—bordering on the mystical—of Adam Stein as individual genius. Significantly, the persistent attempts by Dr. Gross to cure Adam's insanity prove futile, and in the end Adam—deliberately frustrating the psychiatrist's efforts—brings about his own "resurrection," not by application of scientific principles, but rather through the instinctual but difficult act of reaching out to another human being in distress. In helping David to throw off his doghood and become a whole child once again, Adam, in fact, succeeds in discarding the bestiality lying at the core of his own spiritual illness. In Kaniuk's world, then, science has proved itself—in Nazi hands—an

effective weapon in promoting death, yet helpless in the face of the overpowering need to restore life.

Kaniuk's work shares with the writings of Wiesel a consideration of the efficacy of clinical madness as a response to the Holocaust, with *Anya* a depiction of the permanent emotional damage with which a survivor is burdened, and with both Kosinski and Lind a nightmare vision of the post-Holocaust world, a world in which sanity and madness are barely distinguishable. In several important respects it parallels Andre Schwarz-Bart's novel *The Last of the Just,* which also deals with the problem of human descent to the bestial within the context of the Holocaust. Indeed, the two works employ the identical image— metamorphosis of victim into dog—as the burden of humanity becomes unbearable. Though Schwarz-Bart's protagonist, Ernie Levy, does not survive the Nazi terror physically, as does Adam Stein, nevertheless his deeply sensitive humanity emerges intact, though profoundly altered by martyrdom. Adam, as victim, avoids martyrdom by exchanging his humanity for bare survival (ultimately regaining it only when the humanity of another is at stake), while Ernie Levy inverts the bargain to become a genuine martyr to man's spirituality. Ultimately, the lives of both emerge as testimony to the ambiguity inherent in man's nature, to the clash of self-destructive and self-fulfilling elements within the individual human being.

To find an appropriate context for his perception of the Jewish confrontation with the Holocaust, Schwarz-Bart turns to the legend of the *Lamed-Vov Zaddikim,* the thirty-six Just Men whose existence justifies the survival of Mankind within God's universe. In *The Last of the Just* he employs the legend as unifying theme and leitmotif, as a framework about which the intricate strands of plot are woven. Ernie Levy, the protagonist, is a twentieth century *Lamed-Vov,* descended from the Rabbi Yom Tov Levy, who was martyred by his own hand during the pogrom in York in 1185. Benjamin, Ernie's father, responds to a tragic Jewish past closely reflected in the history of his own family by opposing God, concluding that a Just Man is worth nothing either in this world or the next, that the suffering of the world and the *Lamed-Vov* "goes for nothing."

Travelling to Germany, Benjamin becomes intimately acquainted with the lacerating effects of Christian anti-Judaic teachings in his encounter with Yankel, the sole survivor of a pogrom who buried his entire village when it was over. No longer able to believe in God, Yankel turns his back on his people "to avoid spending his life on all fours." Benjamin later witnesses the return of an apostate seeking admission once again to the synagogue, confessing that . . . he had "wanted to live as the Christians do because he was ashamed to remain Jewish." As the congregation considers an appropriate penalty, Benjamin insists that the man has suffered enough already, quoting the words of the fifteenth century Rabbi Israel Isserlein: "he who returns to Judaism . . . imposes upon himself a continual penance." The extent to which persecution has influenced the Jews' view of themselves, with profound effects upon the Jewish community, is suggested in Benjamin's unanswered call for "one among us who never thought about" taking on "the advantages and felicities of Christianity." In the end Benjamin himself remains suspended between apostasy and tradition, neither turning away from Judaism completely nor able to accept the goodness of God or the efficacy of the *Lamed-Vov.* (pp. 278-93)

Another work which views the Holocaust in the light of Jewish history and tradition is Soma Morgenstern's *The Third Pillar,* which takes as its setting a "small half-burned bordertown" in Eastern Europe on the day of its liberation from Nazi occupation by the Russian army. The action of the novel centers upon the trial of a group of captured German Storm Troopers. Convened in the old synagogue of the town—erected, significantly, upon the ruins of a far older one destroyed by Chmelnitzsky—the trial functions as a literary framework for the narrative, which is biblical in tone and overlaid with religious mysticism. Within the context of the Holocaust, however, the trial emerges as more than a convenient—and particularly apt—narrative technique. It is, in fact, the civilized expression, consonant with principles both of secular and Jewish law, of the victim's overwhelming need to bring the defilers of humanity to justice and thus to seek a measure of redemption for mankind.

The trial is conducted by one called "The Messenger," a stranger of unknown origin and background ("in a certain sense I may be said to be Jewish"), who appears in the town on the day of its liberation. Although the few Jewish survivors of the town step forward to tell their stories indicting the Nazi prisoners—and with them the entire German nation—the most telling witness is an inanimate object, an innocent-looking but mysterious box that assumes mystical qualities as the plot unfolds. At the novel's opening "three Christian publicans" (one of whom later reveals himself as a Jew in disguise) find the box—apparently the property of the German army—and take it to the nearby synagogue after they find themselves unable to open it, despite their vigorous efforts. In the course of the trial that later unfolds, it is revealed that the box contains soap made by the Germans from the body of Jochanan, the pious thirteen-year-old son of the town's Torah scribe. With this revelation, it becomes clear that the dead themselves have returned to bear witness against their murderers, that any defense of the Nazis has become unthinkable.

The titular third pillar, the "pillar of blood" forged from Jewish sacrifice at Nazi hands, like the biblical pillars of fire and smoke, is to lead the Jewish people to their redemption, "through all the wildernesses into the Holy Land." Thus Morgenstern appears to suggest—as others have as well—that the founding of the State of Israel, the fulfillment of the biblical promise to establish the descendants of Abraham "in their land, that they be no more cast forth from their land," functions as a response to, perhaps a mitigation of, the annihilation of European Jewry. On the other hand, it can be, and has been, argued that the unprecedented destruction inflicted during the Holocaust was too high a price in blood for the Jewish people to pay, even to achieve the establishment of the Jewish national homeland. Elie Wiesel, whose entire career as a creative artist has been a response to the Holocaust, rejects the sug-

gestion that Israel is an answer to the Holocaust and, in fact, as a survivor he refuses to acknowledge any lesson at all to be drawn from the event, despite its clear significance for Jewish history. Yet Wiesel shares with Morgenstern a preoccupation with religious mysticism and a perspective upon the Holocaust shaped by an acute awareness of the historical role played by the confrontation of the Jewish people with the effects of Christian dogma and the teachings of the church.

The two writers share as well in their use of the trial as a literary device to cry out against the demons raised by the Holocaust. However, while Morgenstern devotes virtually his entire novel to a trial in which the Nazis stand accused and condemned, Wiesel shifts the emphasis away from the executioners and puts God Himself on trial. An explicit instance occurs toward the end of *The Gates of the Forest,* in a Nazi concentration camp. One of the four rabbis summons the other three to convoke a special court to put God on trial, to accuse Him of murder, of "destroying his people and the Law he gave them from Mount Sinai. . . . The trial proceeded in due legal form with witnesses for both sides. . . . The unanimous verdict: 'guilty.' "

As witness to the Holocaust Wiesel remains firmly within the Judaic tradition—established by Abraham, Moses, Jeremiah, and Job—of condemnation of God for failure to intercede on behalf of His creatures. Indeed, Wiesel's first five works can be read as a sustained developing revolt against God from within a Jewish context. Jewish tradition provides not only adequate precedents for such revolt, but legal and moral sanction as well, in the covenant with God into which the Jewish people entered: "We are to protect His Torah, and He, in turn, assumes responsibility for Israel's presence in the world. . . . when our physical existence was threatened we simply reminded God of His duties and promises deriving from the covenant." Against this background the reality of Auschwitz confronts the Jew with a dilemma, an "absurdity" which cannot be easily dismissed and which stubbornly refuses to dissipate of its own accord. Since the Jewish God is "Lord of actual history," the Jew must conclude that God was somehow part of Auschwitz, thus calling into question the continued validity of the covenant itself. Clearly, any recognition that the covenant might no longer be operative would strike a devastating blow at the very foundations of Judaism and leave the theologically serious Jew isolated, to struggle in an unaccustomed loneliness with an indifferent, or worse, hostile universe. After Auschwitz, he is joined to the French existentialists in confronting the absurdity of the universe, an absurdity engendered and given substance by the Holocaust and signaling the breakdown of the covenant. The only possible response that remains within the framework of Judaism is rebellion against God, a denunciation of God that at the same time demands that He fulfill His contractual obligation. This is the religious/moral context within which Wiesel attempts to apprehend and assimilate the events of the Holocaust.

In his early works Wiesel's role as witness to the Holocaust predominates, perhaps in response to the survivor's fear that the tale would not be told or, if told, not believed.

Hence, the autobiography *Night* exposes to view the inner life of the young Jewish inmate of a German concentration camp, while *Dawn* and *The Accident* are largely autobiographical works describing the torment that this survivor endures after liberation. As with other Holocaust writers, for Wiesel survival itself carries with it a stigma, engendering guilt and a sense that the survivor is no longer of the living, that he is—in Wiesel's phrase—"a messenger of death." If the enormities of the concentration camp experience lead Eliezer/Elisha, Wiesel's protagonist, to reject God in *Night*, the torment of survival brings him to question seriously and reject the Jewish moral commitment in *Dawn* and *The Accident*, not, however, without the sense that in violating the traditional Jewish code of morality he has violated his own being: "I've killed. I've killed Elisha." The rebellion against Jewish tradition, begun in the Nazi concentration camp of *Night* and continued in *Dawn* through Elisha's killing of a fellow human creature, reaches a climax in *The Accident* in the protagonist's act of attempted suicide. For the sacredness of life, God's gift to mankind, is basic to Judaism and, in fact, arguably the most basic tenet of the Jewish faith. Thus the Jew is not free to argue, as does Camus, that "there is but one truly serious philosophical problem, and that is suicide." It is not for the Jew to judge "whether"—in the words of Camus—"life is or is not worth living"; only the God of Israel, as Creator and Giver of Life, is to determine when life is to end. In Wiesel's Jewish context, therefore, the suicide attempt takes on significance as a kind of ultimate defiance of God, explainable only on the basis of a recognition, in reaction to Auschwitz, that God encompasses evil as well as good, that in violating His covenant with Man, God has not only withdrawn His protection, but has left man free of the restraints of His Laws and Commandments.

Wiesel's hero has thus come to share the attitude which characterizes Camus's protagonist, Meursault, at the beginning of *The Stranger*—a sense of the absurdity of the world and the pointlessness of human existence. In contrast to Meursault, however, Wiesel's character is obsessed by the relationship of man to God, never losing his belief in God's presence in the world, even while bitterly denouncing God's injustice toward man. While Meursault appears to have no past, living in a kind of timeless present devoid of history and human attachments, the narrator of *The Accident* cannot forget his past despite the horror of the memory, because "I am my past. If it is buried, I'm buried with it." He is at great pains to explain his desire to die, to make understood the tragedy of those "living-dead," who came back after merely lasting through the Holocaust, devoid of joy, hope, or delusions about the future.

The Town Beyond the Wall represents a new point of view in Wiesel's writing, emphasizing the culpability of man for the crimes of the Holocaust and indicting the indifferent observers equally with the executioners. Here the problem is couched primarily in terms of man's cruelty and indifference to his fellows, and the solution is sought within man as well. Indeed, in this work Wiesel clearly seeks response to the Holocaust in the secular existential philosophy of Camus. Following Albert Camus, Wiesel suggests

that man's proper stance in the face of suffering entails a rejection of suicide and madness; it involves struggling against indifference, assuming responsibility for one's fellow man, retaining an essential core of humanity at all costs.

In contrast to the Jewish victims of his childhood, who were unable or unwilling either to surrender faith or to acknowledge the possibility of evil within God, the protagonist of *The Town Beyond the Wall*—now named Michael—frees himself to take positive action by refusing to shrink from these alternatives. Michael's ultimate victory over the tortures and loneliness of imprisonment comes about, not through prayer, which he rejects in spite of the danger of heading to perdition, but by extending his help to another human being, the demented young prisoner whose life he saves, whose mind he struggles with all his being to bring out of its catatonic state. The struggle to cure the boy saves Michael because it is a meaningful protest against the world's indifference, and thus, as for Adam Stein, an effective antidote to clinical madness. As Byron Sherwin has pointed out, Michael does in fact display a kind of madness in *Town Beyond the Wall*, the "moral madness" (in the sense of A. J. Heschel) of the ancient Hebrew prophets, which entails remaining human and retaining a concern for others in a world in which the social norm is hate and indifference. It is in this sense that Sherwin interprets the novel's epitaph from Dostoevsky: "I have a plan: to go mad." The moral madman is closely linked in spirit to the "absurd man," in the sense of Camus; both are able to face the world's absurdity unflinchingly, with aversion perhaps, but without denial. Where the absurd man may succeed in doing this on the basis of a rational decision, executed by force of will, the moral madman, like the Hebrew prophets, often acts upon inner compulsion, unable to do otherwise. The end result is the same in either case—that genuine confrontation with the absurd advocated in *The Myth of Sisyphus*.

Moral madness reappears as a theme of some importance in Wiesel's succeeding novel *The Gates of the Forest*. At the beginning of the work it is not the young protagonist Gregor, but Gabriel, his philosopher-teacher, who displays moral madness by reacting with laughter to the horrors of the War. Gabriel clings to this position even in the face of death; exposing himself to capture in order to save Gregor, he bursts into overwhelming laughter at the very moment he falls into the hands of the German soldiers. A similar response to enormity is urged upon Gabriel—in New York after the War—by the Hasidic Rebbe, who renews the emphasis, so prominent in *Night*, upon the implication of God in evil, but with a difference. Here there is a new awareness that the recognition of God's guilt is, in itself, not a viable solution to the problem of evil in the world, that there must be a constructive response from man as well. That response, Wiesel suggests, can be expressed in the Hasidic way of prayer and joy, through clinging to God until he is forced to recognize once again his covenantal responsibility for the preservation of the Jewish people. Thus, Wiesel's protest against God is such that it allows him to remain a Jew, "within God"—in Wiesel's phrase. The object of this protest is not nihilism, not denial of God, but the very opposite—the reestablishment of God's order in a world which has witnessed the destruction of order. The boy of *Night,* who vows never to "forget those flames which consumed my faith forever," gives way to the man of *The Gates of the Forest,* who understands that "God's final victory . . . lies in man's inability to reject Him."

The Gates of the Forest provides the first instance within Wiesel's canon in which traditional Christian dogma concerning the historical role of the Jewish people assumes more than minor importance; this novel, indeed, marks only the beginning of an increasing preoccupation with that theme in the author's more recent writings. Wiesel's attention to the function of Christian attitudes in Jewish tragedy—especially in *The Oath*—where it serves as a framework supporting the entire plot—suggests that in the teachings of the Church, he has found (as have a number of Christian theologians in recent years) a clue toward understanding man's participation, whether active or passive, in Auschwitz. His recent work develops and builds upon the notion that men were freed to commit and accept the enormities of the Holocaust in part by the accumulation of centuries of Christian retribution against those among Jesus' people who did not accept him as Messiah.

Two episodes in *The Gates of the Forest* have particular interest in this connection. The first of these describes a school play performed in a Hungarian village upon the subject—"hatred of the Jews and its justification." During the performance the figure of Judas Iscariot—played, ironically, by Gregor, a Jew hiding from the Germans by posing as a mute Gentile—comes under verbal and physical attack as the other actors and the audience are carried away by hatred. As it happens, in his role of deaf-mute, Gregor has heard confessions of many guilty secrets by the villagers, who saw in him a completely safe confessor, one who could carry no tales. In danger of his life, Gregor briefly considers a public exposure of the villagers, who would then, he reasons, turn their hatred from him and toward each other. That Gregor rejects this plan in favor of a far more difficult and dangerous course of action indicates that this Jew-as-Judas, at least, is no betrayer. The impression seems unavoidable that Wiesel is attempting to reach a new understanding of the relationship between Judas and his master here, one that raises questions concerning the traditional Christian view of the betrayal, not only about the motivation of Judas, but about that of Jesus as well.

The second episode involves the village priest, who is harboring a Jewish fugitive. Having saved the Jew from capture by the Germans, he decides it is time to apply himself to the man's soul as well. The priest urges the Jew to accept Jesus, insisting that the trials of the Jewish people would end with their collective repentance. The Jew rejects the priest and his theology: "Stop thinking about our salvation and perhaps the cemeteries won't be so full of Jews." Unable to bear the Jew's dismissal of Jesus as Messiah, and indeed of the Hebraic God Himself, the priest loses control of his anger, ordering the man out of the house—and to certain death.

Consonant with Wiesel's reexamination of the figure of Judas is his reconsideration of the fundamental problem

of the Crucifixion, from a Jewish perspective, in a brief episode in *A Beggar in Jerusalem.* The scene relates a conversation between the dying Jesus and one called Shlomo, who makes it clear to Jesus that he is not to be accepted as the Messiah by future generations of Jews: "You think you are suffering for my sake and for my brothers, yet we are the ones who will be made to suffer for you, because of you." Through Shlomo, Wiesel expresses his sympathy for Jesus and a grasp of the moral dilemma posed for him by the "actions his followers would undertake in his name to spread his word . . . the innumerable victims persecuted and crushed under the sign of his law." Wiesel perceives with Emil Fackenheim that "the returning Christ would have gone to Auschwitz . . . involuntarily if not voluntarily." His artistic perception as expressed here foreshadows a significant theological insight: it is not in Jesus as man and prophet, but rather in the Church's conception of Jesus as Messiah that the genesis of Christian anti-Semitism is to be found.

In *The Oath,* Wiesel makes his most extensive attempt to date to gauge the role of Christian doctrine in the formulation of the "Final Solution of the Jewish question," removing the major plot action to the Eastern European village of Kolvillàg in the 1920's—well before Hitler's rise to power—in order to add a new dimension to his understanding of the Holocaust by viewing the future from the perspective of the tragic Jewish past. The plot is set into motion by the confrontation in the present between two victims of past Jewish persecutions: Azriel, sole survivor of the pogrom in Kolvillàg some fifty years earlier, and a young man who shares in the agony of survival by virtue of his being the child of survivors of the Holocaust. The encounter between the two reveals that they are linked not only by the Jewish history of suffering but in their personal fates as well. It becomes apparent that only Azriel can prevent the young man's "abdication" from a life of despair, and only by revealing the secrets which he and the dead victims of the pogrom had sworn under oath not to reveal. After fifty years of silence Azriel, as the sole survivor and link between the victims of Kolvillàg and the living present, speaks out in order to avoid "not suffering but . . . indifference to suffering." Azriel relates the circumstances leading to the final destruction of the Jewish community of Kolvillàg, and with his tale as vehicle, *The Oath* emerges as a quasi-theological inquest into the Christian roots of anti-Semitism. Through the novel's dramatic action, Wiesel examines the consequences of confrontation between the teachings of Judaism and traditional Christian dogma relating to the Jews, and in so doing he raises a number of serious and difficult problems that challenge both Jewish and Christian theology in the post-Holocaust era.

Azriel's story incorporates into the present the medieval accusation of ritual murder—the Jews of Kolvillàg are held responsible for the disappearance of a Christian youth—thus linking the circumstances leading to the destruction of Kolvillàg and, by implication, those surrounding the Holocaust itself with the pogroms of the Middle Ages. While the tale of "ritual murder" is central to the implication of Christianity in the Holocaust, the consequences for Judaic thought issue from the theological debate between the Rebbe and Moshe. Arguing within the framework of traditional *halacha* (Jewish law), the Rebbe opposes Moshe's offer of martyrdom, which can be justified only when the Torah itself is in danger. Moshe's counter-argument cuts deeper, reaching for another level of understanding of the covenant and describing the dilemma of the theologically serious Jew threatened with pogrom: "We must save the divine Law even if it places us in contradiction to the Law . . . Without Jews there would be no Torah. . . . They are inextricably bound." Moshe understands the paradox inherent in affirming God's presence during the Kolvillàg pogrom, that such affirmation would imply concomitant damnation of God for his complicity in the evil of the pogrom. Yet in characteristically mystical fashion, Moshe demands that the Jews of Kolvillàg remain Jews, continuing to praise God, but in "silence" rather than as witnesses. He concludes that despite the importance in Jewish history of the witness to disaster, of the "survivor-story-teller," they must now "adopt a new way: silence . . . we shall testify no more." Moshe's exhortation of his fellow Jews to remain with God does not in itself break new theological ground, reflecting rather the theological insight achieved in Wiesel's earlier work: man's need to define himself in relationship to God continues undiminished, even after Auschwitz. However—and we shall enlarge upon this presently—*The Oath* does offer fresh possibilities for assimilating the knowledge of God's implication in evil, despite Wiesel's assertion elsewhere of the impossibility of understanding Auschwitz on the level of God.

At the same time, the recognition with which *The Oath* is informed—clearer than elsewhere in Wiesel's writings—of the implication in Jewish suffering of Christian doctrine and Christian institutions, of the "love of God turned into hate of man," as Wiesel puts it, contributes to the possibility of comprehending Auschwitz on the level of man. This recognition is expressed in part through the concern with the history of Christian atrocity against the Jews displayed by Shmuel, who immerses himself in martyrology in an attempt to gain a better understanding of what is to come. In continuing to act as chronicler and witness, Shmuel rejects Moshe's oath, which has as its purpose the rupture of continuity in Jewish history, the abolition of suffering through an attack upon the history of suffering. This opposition of responses in Moshe and Shmuel serves as a focal point in the novel for the tension between the survivor's desire to remain silent and his need to record the event. This theme is a familiar one in the works of Wiesel, reflecting the author's personal dilemma as survivor, his feeling, often expressed, that the Holocaust demands response yet imposes silence. However, in *The Oath,* for the first time in Wiesel's fiction, this theme emerges as a central problem of the novel. Like Wiesel himself, Shmuel chooses to continue to serve as witness to history. Initiating Azriel into the tradition of the Book, he fulfills his chosen role, discharges his obligation to link Jewish past and future, denies the validity of Moshe's position.

With the killing already begun, the priest and the Bishop "decided this was the time to debate orthodoxy and heresy," giving credence to the Rebbe's position that "Help

Elie Wiesel.

cannot come from the other side. A Jew must not expect anything from Christians, man must not expect anything from man. Consolation can and must come only from God." Consolation perhaps, but not rescue, and this is the heart of the difficulty Wiesel experiences in understanding the Holocaust on the level of God. Christian churchmen have not intervened on behalf of the Jews, but neither has the God of Israel, who, according to Jewish tradition, is bound to do so by virtue of the covenant. While Wiesel's earlier novels respond to this inherent paradox by declaring God guilty of complicity in evil, *The Oath* reaches toward a resolution within the Talmudic tradition of *Hester Panim,* the Hiding of the Divine Face, a point of view foreshadowed, however, in a legend appended to *The Town Beyond the Wall,* relating how God and man exchanged places, "so neither . . . was ever again what he seemed to be." Thus God may forfeit omnipotence and become, like man, not indifferent to history, but unable to control it, powerless to combat man's destructive impulse. The legend suggests that in observing helplessly the suffering of man, God suffers with him as well, since "the liberation of the one was bound to the liberation of the other."

In contrast to Wiesel, who has consistently admitted his inability to reconcile the Holocaust with the traditional Jewish view of the God of history and the covenant, Nelly Sachs in the verse drama *Eli* has employed the notion of *Hester Panim* in an attempt to achieve precisely such a reconciliation. *Eli* presents a plea for the survivors of the Holocaust to "re-establish their relationship to God and to regain his attention—in effect to bring him out of hiding" and an examination of the thesis that through prayer this can, in fact, be accomplished. While Wiesel does not go nearly this far in establishing upon *Hester Panim* a theological vantage point from which to view God's silence during the Holocaust, in *The Oath* he seems to weigh seriously the possibilities for understanding inherent in the concept. Illustrative are the Rebbe's questioning in the face of a pogrom, whether God "could be turning His Face away from His people," and Moshe's understanding—on his own terms, in terms of silence—of God's role in the affairs of men: "rather than speak, God listens; rather than intervene and decide, He waits and judges only later."

Though Wiesel implies, through Moshe, that God may have no choice in the Hiding of the Face, the suggestion remains as well that God is implicated in evil by virtue of his ambivalence: "Satan is more than evil," Moshe declares, "he is evil disguised as good, the link between the two . . . his place is at God's right. An awesome concept, leading to horror. How is one to distinguish God in evil, Satan in good?" Moshe's perception of the ambiguous and elusive nature of God's role in good and evil finds its counterpart in "the perplexing duality of the knowledge of God"—as theologian Eliezer Berkovits puts it—that confronts the Jew of faith after the Holocaust:

> He [the Jew of faith] knows of the numerous revelations of the divine presence as he knows of the overlong phrases of God's absence. . . . But he also knows that God's absence, even at Auschwitz, is not absolute. . . . There were many who found him even in his hiding.

Between Berkovits and Wiesel there is an essential convergence of overall outlook, a unanimity in stressing the interconnectedness of all of Jewish history, the unbroken continuity of Jewish tradition. Shmuel's immersion in the study of the atrocities punctuating Jewish history, Moshe's teaching that "nothing in Jewish tradition was unconnected," find their counterpart in the observation of Berkovits that "a straight line leads from the first act of Christian oppression against the Jews and Judaism in the fourth century to the Holocaust in the twentieth."

Kolvillàg is a Jewish Everytown, whose destruction links past pogroms with future Holocaust. As he watched the town burn—destroying both Jew and Christian, both victim and executioner in a powerful evocation of the indivisibility of violence—Azriel, the sole survivor, the indispensable link needed to maintain the continuity of Jewish history, understood that he had just glimpsed the future. Kolvillàg provides a backdrop against which Azriel can view the Holocaust to come in terms of the accumulation of past events, but his view of the future is only one side of a dual truth. A description of the other is provided by Berkovits:

> The rabbis of the Talmud could speak of the silence of God at the time of the destruction of the Temple . . . and yet remain true to His word, because . . . Israel survived, remained historically viable, full of future expectation.

Azriel not only survives, but he survives to rescue the young Jew from self-destruction, to maintain Jewish continuity in *that* man's future by passing on to him, through

the tale of Kolvillàg and its victims, the role of witness inherited from Shmuel. Like Azriel, who was saved from the flames of Kolvillàg in order to testify as witness, this young Jew no longer has the right to die. In spite of his initial reluctance, Azriel ultimately has rejected silence in favor of history, understanding the nature of man's encounter with God not as Moshe understood it, but as did his father Shmuel. As witness to future generations, Azriel becomes the fictive counterpart of his creator, carrying out the role that Wiesel, as writer and survivor, has taken upon himself. (pp. 295-305)

> *Josephine Knopp and Arnost Lustig, "Holocaust Literature II: Novels and Short Stories," in* Encountering the Holocaust: An Interdisciplinary Survey, *edited by Byron L. Sherwin and Susan G. Ament, Impact Press, 1979, pp. 267-315.*

S. Lillian Kremer

[*Kremer is an American critic and educator. In the following essay, she observes that in the late 1960s Jewish-American fiction writers first began to employ the Holocaust as a significant subject in their works.*]

Historians, artists, and critics who contemplate the imaginative integration of the Holocaust in fiction recognize its pitfalls. Some critics argue that Holocaust literature unavoidably diminishes the suffering that victims endured. Some believe that only eyewitness accounts are valid. Hannah Arendt, who has written brilliantly on the nature of totalitarianism, believes the horror of life in the concentration camps can never be fully embraced by the imagination, "for the very reason that it stands outside of life and death" [*The Origins of Totalitarianism*]. T. W. Adorno's dictum, "No poetry after Auschwitz," has haunted many. Elie Wiesel and George Steiner have at various times identified silence as the deepest form of respect for the Holocaust victims. Yet the literary careers of both Wiesel and Steiner testify to the paradox of Holocaust-imposed silence and compelled speech. Six million Jewish victims must not be consigned to oblivion. The murdered must be mourned and remembered.

Representative of the immediate postwar American intellectual response to the "age of enormity" is Isaac Rosenfeld's 1948 recognition of the problematics of Holocaust comprehension.

> We still don't understand what happened to the Jews of Europe, and perhaps we never will. There have been books, magazine and newspaper articles, eyewitness accounts, letters, diaries, documents certified by the highest authorities on the life in ghettos and concentration camps, slave factories and extermination centers under the Germans. By now we know all there is to know. But it hasn't helped; we still don't understand. It is too painful for the majority—besides, who wants to understand? [*The New Leader*, 1948]

Rosenfeld realized that mankind has, in the Holocaust era, surpassed its historic notions of good and evil, that the

Holocaust initiated a condition of "terror beyond evil." In the same year, Lionel Trilling addressed the inadequacy of literary response to the Holocaust, even in light of growing knowledge of Holocaust history. Trilling, like Elie Wiesel and the Yiddish poet Uri Zvi Greenberg, recognized that there are no adequate analogues to the Holocaust in history or literature:

> Society's resistance to the discovery of depravity has ceased; now everyone knows that Thackeray was wrong, Swift right. The world and the soul have split open of themselves and are all agape for our revolted inspection. The simple eye of the camera shows us, at Belsen and Buchenwald, horrors that quite surpass Swift's powers, a vision of life turned back to its corrupted elements which is more disgusting than any that Shakespeare could contrive, a cannibalism more literal and fantastic than that which Montaigne ascribed to organized society. A characteristic activity of mind is therefore no longer needed. Indeed, before what we now know the mind stops; the great psychological fact of our time which we all observe with baffled wonder and shame is that there is no possible way of responding to Belsen and Buchenwald. The activity of mind fails before the incommunicability of man's suffering [*The Liberal Imagination*].

Alfred Kazin speaks for many American Jews when he writes [in *New York Jew*] of the intrusion of the Holocaust in his consciousness, describing it as the "nightmare that would bring everything else into question, that will haunt me to my last breath." Few Jews have escaped some version of Kazin's nightmare of himself, his parents, his family, his neighbors, and his friends: "fuel for flames, dying by a single flame that burned us all up at once." Kazin's nightmare is a manifestation of George Steiner's observation that "Jews everywhere have been maimed by the European catastrophe, that the massacre has left all who survived (even if they were nowhere near the actual scene) off balance" [see Further Reading].

During the late 1960s, a significant change occurred in Jewish-American Holocaust fiction. Early in the decade Holocaust delineation was virtually absent from Jewish-American literature, and by decade's end it was an ever present, though subdued, component of the fiction. [In *After the Tradition*], Robert Alter lamented, "With all the restless probing into the implications of the Holocaust that continues to go on in Jewish intellectual forums . . . it gives one pause to note how rarely American Jewish fiction has attempted to come to terms . . . with the European catastrophe." Three years later, Lothar Kahn observed [in *Congress Bi-Weekly*, 1969], "No Jewish writer . . . has written a book without the memory of Auschwitz propelling him to issue warnings, implied or specific, against the Holocaust." The sixties marked the beginning of widespread American interest in Holocaust literature and the ensuing decades have witnessed the development of a substantial body of work.

The writers treated [here] did not directly experience the ghettos, camps, and killing centers. That innocence, however, does not deny them the privilege of writing about the Holocaust. Authority is not limited to those with personal suffering. Nor is authenticity guaranteed by personal suffering. Emil Fackenheim, who was incarcerated at Sachsenhausen, asserts that it was not until years later—when he read a study of that camp—that he felt he truly understood his own experience and what had occurred there. Deception of the victims was such an integral part of the administrative policies in the camps that it is possible historical accounts could contain information hidden from camp inmates. Authority may be achieved from the will of the artist to learn and shape the material. . . . [Although these writers] have not directly shared the Jewish experience in Europe in 1939-1945, they share the historic burden of Jewish history. Tradition commands all Jews to consider themselves figuratively present at Sinai to receive the Torah. Contemporary Jews increasingly feel that, geography aside, they were present at Auschwitz. American Jews carry the psychological burden of Auschwitz and Chelmno and Dachau and Bergen-Belsen and Treblinka and all the other Nazi death factories where their relatives died brutal deaths.

A year before the 1948 commentaries of Rosenfeld and Trilling, Saul Bellow's *The Victim,* a novel whose symbolic underpinnings are delineated in Holocaust images, was published. Although Bellow's approach is muted and includes only one overt Holocaust reference, he addressed the topic while focusing the novel on the related topic of anti-Semitism. Despite their psychological association with the *Shoah,* many Jewish American writers began to write Holocaust literature in the sixties after the Europeans. Perhaps as nonparticipants, Americans believed it would have been presumptuous to deal with subject matter they did not experience directly. Perhaps they believed it was too soon to approach the topic without the benefit of adequate historic analysis. Perhaps since Jewish writers had only recently gained acceptance by the literary establishment, they were unwilling to broach a topic as controversial as the Holocaust.

What accounts for the intensification of the treatment of the Holocaust in Jewish-American fiction at the end of the sixties and through the seventies and eighties? The trial of Adolf Eichmann in Jerusalem and the 1967 Arab-Israeli Six Day War appear to have stimulated American interest in the Holocaust. The Eichmann trial, the intellectual debate aroused by Hannah Arendt's analysis of the trial, and her "banality of evil" thesis again brought Holocaust crimes to the forefront of American Jewish thought. Several Israeli writers who "derived their authority from their participation in the War of Independence in 1948" [Alan Mintz; see Further Reading] departed from customary national themes and finally confronted the Holocaust following the Eichmann trial. The post-Eichmann transformation from Holocaust silence to expression in Israeli literature was paralleled in American writing.

The 1967 joint Arab attack on Israel and its concomitant Nazi-style threats to annihilate Israel provided another catalyst for the development of imaginative Holocaust literature. Since the 1967 and 1973 Arab-Israeli wars, petrol politics has helped fuel international anti-Israeli propaganda, and once again in the twentieth century a large segment of the Jewish people is threatened with extinction.

The unthinkable is again thinkable and is the articulated policy of most of Israel's geographic neighbors. When Jean Paul Sartre linked Zionists with Nazis, and a coalition of Third World and Communist countries in the United Nations branded Israel a racist society, Jews were even more threatened by hostile forces. Nations that appeased Hitler in the thirties and forties acquiesce in the seventies and eighties to Middle Eastern terrorists; anti-Semitism is, therefore, again on the rise, leading scholars and artists to renewed interest in the Holocaust. With the revival of Nazi rhetoric—even in America, where Jews believe they are safe and assimilated, just as German Jews believed half a century ago—many have been moved to think and some to write in the Holocaust framework. Whatever the reason, or aggregate of reasons, we now have in American literature an admirable body of fiction addressing the Holocaust. Although it is interesting to speculate about the confluence of causes that have generated American Jewish Holocaust literature in recent decades, from its historic inception the Holocaust has haunted the Jewish American imagination, and its expression was long overdue.

Historically the German annihilation of Jews is widely interpreted both as the logical outcome of a two-thousand year old European, anti-Jewish tradition nourished by the Christian churches and as a drastic new policy formulated according to a racial doctrine, which asserted that the superior Aryan race had to rid itself of the debasing presence of the inferior Jewish race. After 1933, hatred of Jews was raised to the level of law. *Rassenkunde*—racial science—dominated Germany's intellectual climate and infiltrated every segment of national life during the Hitler era. Religion, science, philosophy, law, economics, and history recast their old premises to acknowledge the danger of the "Jewish poison." Historians generally concur that the success of the war against European Jewry is substantially attributable to the continent's historic Christian anti-Semitism as manifested in anti-Jewish edicts, expulsions, pogroms, and mass murders—all rationalized by the need to keep Christian Europe free from Jewish influence.

Determinist racial theory, contending that human destiny is decreed by nature and expressed in race and that history is determined by the iron fist of race, is bankrupt and has come to naught. As Hitler came to power, the emptiness of Nazi ideology was revealed in rule by brute force and by exploitation of conquered peoples rather than viable social, economic, and political philosophy. Perhaps for these reasons, novelists give minor attention to Nazi racial theory, focusing instead on the Christian attitude toward Jews throughout European history as a primary element in the success of Nazi propaganda and its *Judenrein* objectives. The causal relationship between historic Christian anti-Semitism and the Holocaust is a recurrent subject of American Holocaust literature. Rather than emphasize the distinction between Christian and Nazi anti-Jewish policies, the novelists more often dramatize their similarities to demonstrate the acceptability of the Final Solution in Christian Europe. The writers also make clear the significance of the strategies of Christian anti-Semitism in the implementation of the Final Solution. Each of the authors [discussed here] portray the major catastrophes of Jewish history in the Diaspora as annunciations of the Holocaust. Although the novelists acknowledge distinctions in the racial and technological aspects of Nazi genocide and Christian anti-Jewish persecutions, they persistently raise the moral implications of Christian anti-Semitism as a source of Western acquiescence to Germany's war against the Jews and as explanation for the zealous role of non-Germans in facilitating the slaughter of the Jews.

Like the handful of Christian scholars and theologians, such as Henry Cargas and Robert Drinan, who have acknowledged Christian Holocaust culpability, the novelists allude to the similarity of Martin Luther's assertion, "next to the devil life has no enemy more cruel, more venomous and violent than a true Jew," and Hitler's statement in *Mein Kampf,* "I believe that I am today acting in accordance with the will of the Almighty Creator: by defending myself against the Jew I am fighting for the work of the Lord." Like the historian [Nora Levin, who in *The Holocaust*] describes Hitler "reechoing the medieval Christian stereotype of the Jew as criminal, parasite, evil incarnate, aiming at world conquest," the novelists show the analogy between the church's historic efforts to protect the Christian community from Jewish teaching and the German desire for racial purity. Nazi rhetoric is perceived as latter-day racist revision of traditional religious bigotry. Parallels are drawn between the church and Nazi persecutions of the Jews, including the progression from book burnings to human burnings; visual differentiation of Jews from the general population by requiring identifying badges; prohibitions against intermarriage; exclusion from businesses, schools, and professions, and the social and cultural activities of the community; ghettoization; and finally mass murders.

The Holocaust gave rise to unique categories of fictional characters, often classified by their attitudes or job statuses in the concentrationary hierarchy. Wallant's Nazerman, a *sonderkommando* who had to shovel the corpses from the gas chambers into the crematorium, is troubled by memories of brutal *kapos* who herded men to labor; others remember the lessons learned from the *muslims,* the living dead, who were unable or lacked incentive to practice techniques that might keep them from joining the ranks in the death selections, such as personal sanitation, a spritely walk or rouging the cheeks in order to look healthier. Leslie Epstein takes the fullest opportunity to explore Jewish and German functionaries, the Jewish ghetto elder and his Nazi-instituted Jewish Council members, Jewish police, resistance smugglers, organizers, fighters, and ghetto workers. A recurring character in the fiction of Malamud and Ozick is the survivor-mentor, whose function is to instruct untutored and lapsed American Jews in the significance of Jewish history, ethics, and sacred literature—or in Potok's and Ozick's cases, to teach in American religious communities. A related role is Wallant's and Bellow's use of survivor as judge and critic of contemporary life. Not infrequently, in the worlds of Ozick, Potok, and Malamud, these survivor-mentors resemble stock figures in Yiddish literature and folklore, and *lamed-vov tzaddikim* (the thirty-six hidden saints), the Hasidic *tzaddik* (righteous model) or the *rebbe*. Malamud's last Mohican, a *schnorrer* (mendicant) survivor, teaches an American artist Jewish history, Potok's boy fashions an imaginary *golem* to fight Nazis, and Ozick invokes Rabbi Akiva's *Bene Brak.*

Typically Jewish-American Holocaust literature focuses on the Jewish victims of Nazism and consigns the Germans to verbal oblivion. Concentration on the victims rather than the perpetrators of the crime adheres to the archetypal tradition of Jewish commemorative liturgy, which mourns martyrs and relegates villains to a tangential reference at best, possibly stemming from the liturgical petition to "blot out the names of our enemies." Aside from the historic figures who administer Epstein's ghetto and Elman's references to Eichmann's contrivance of the Brand and Kastner negotiations in 1944, Germans remain peripheral ghosts in Jewish-American Holocaust literature.

Struggle for survival during the Holocaust and during the postwar era constitute significant parallel themes in American fiction. Although American Holocaust fiction devotes considerably less attention to the description and dramatization of Nazi brutality than the works of Europeans and Israelis who directly endured the Nazi terror, dramatic presentation, memory, and nightmare are devices Americans frequently employ to depict the horrors of starvation, disease, excremental filth, medical experimentation, sadism, deportations, and death selections. After witnessing the asphyxiation of his fellow ghettoites in a mobile gas chamber and their subsequent stripping of gold teeth and hair, Epstein's protagonist struggles to maintain his sanity. Elman's protagonist is deceived in his good faith negotiations to barter his property and wealth for the safe passage of his family out of Hungary. Unlike Epstein and Elman who set their novels in the Holocaust era, most of the writers in this study use recollection and nightmare to record survivors' endurance of Holocaust humiliation and pain. Wallant's protagonist dreams of the surgery he suffered without benefit of anesthetic, remembers witnessing his wife's rape and his countryman's electrocution, and recalls being forced to move the corpses of his family and friends from the gas chamber to the crematorium. Bellow's protagonist speaks of escaping from a mass grave and hiding in a forest from Polish partisans who preferred to complete the Nazi genocidal objective rather than have Jews survive in Poland. Singer's protagonist frequently recalls his concealment in a haystack, and Ozick's recalls his fugitive fears in a convent cellar and barn. Through direct dramatic convention and indirect retrospective revery, American fiction charts the history of degradation that characterized the survival struggle in Nazi controlled Europe.

The more common and extensive treatment of survival in American fiction is devoted to the problems of postwar survival trauma. After overcoming the horrendous difficulties in the ghettos and camps, survivors suffered from both physical and psychological wounds. Extended postwar physical and psychological debilitation appears in Bellow's *Mr. Sammler's Planet;* Wallant's *The Pawnbroker;* Singer's *Enemies, Shosha,* "The Cafeteria," "Hanka," and "The Mentor"; Malamud's "The German Refugee"; Ozick's *The Cannibal Galaxy;* Elman's *The 28th Day of*

Elul; Cohen's *In the Days of Simon Stern;* Steiner's *The Portage to San Cristobal of A. H.;* and Potok's *In the Beginning* and "The Dark Place Inside." In addition to depicting the survivors' long-term, Holocaust-generated physical ailments, the writers focus on the depression that stems from the guilt many feel for outliving families and friends; the recurrent nightmares and memories of Holocaust indignities, betrayals, and torture; the loss of faith and rejection of obligatory duties and rituals; and the failure to resume prewar ambitions and professions. Malamud's literary critic loses the ability to communicate in his native language; Wallant's Cracow University professor becomes a pawnbroker; Bellow's artist degenerates into a painter and sculptor of the grotesque; Ozick's aspiring astronomer becomes a mediocre educational administrator; Singer's Talmudic prodigy descends to hack essayist. Others suffer identity and religious crises, impairment of the capacity to love and trust others, death or disorientation of the creative impulse. Many are trapped by their Holocaust experiences. Some continue to manifest wartime behavior, such as searching for places of concealment; others dream of revenge; and still others interpret postwar violence in light of Holocaust knowledge. Each of the survivor-protagonists manifests alienation and suffers unbidden memories, nightmares, and psychological disquiet. "More recent novels with immigrant-survivor protagonists are likely to stress the homelessness of the immigrant, his separation from Americans who have not experienced near-death and qualified rebirth as he has" [Dorothy Bilik; see Further Reading]. This phenomenon appears in the histories of Wallant's, Bellow's, Cohen's, and Singer's protagonists. Unlike the immigrants of American-Jewish fiction set in the pre-Holocaust period, the post-Holocaust immigrants do not seek assimilation and acculturation, but continue instead to grapple with the European past and often labor to preserve their Jewish particularity, history, and tradition.

American Holocaust fiction demonstrates the constant change in the human condition and the perspective wrought in the Holocaust crucible. Although all survivors suffer Holocaust trauma, some engage in a regenerative process that takes the form of rebuilding Judaism and the Jewish community in America and Israel. Central to the concerns of the religious survivors is the preservation and transmission of the Jewish past. Potok's yeshiva teachers and scholars try to build new centers of Jewish learning in America and Steiner's Israeli Nazi hunters try to bring Nazis to justice and retain the Holocaust in the historic record opposing forces that would diminish or deny its significance. In the fictional worlds of Cohen, Ozick, and Potok, preservation and transmission of the Jewish sacred legacy is essential to the witness's testimony. Enoch Vand begins to study the Torah and the Talmud, Joseph Brill develops a dual Hebrew/Western curriculum, and Bleilip returns to the orthodoxy he scorned. Potok's rabbis and writers are strengthened in their devotion to Jewish practices and learning: Simon Stern builds a survivors' compound on the Akiva model. Even prewar Anglophile Sammler manifests renewed interest in Jewish particularity and history. Singer's Communists, Socialists, and secular intellectuals often recant and return to the values of Jewish orthodoxy or ethics. In one way or another, these protagonists respond to the Holocaust tragedy by revitalizing their Jewish identities and commitments. They become committed to "increased emphasis on Jewishness and traditionalism . . . [as] part of the post-Holocaust sensibility" [Bilik].

Wallant, Bellow, Singer, Steiner, and Cohen create survivor communities that function like a Greek chorus, amplifying the tragic hero's positions and commenting on the actions and opinions of the principal dramatic figures. This device has been particularly valuable for enlarging the Holocaust canvases beyond the protagonist's experience and in incorporating the diversity of Holocaust history and the national peculiarities and operations of distinctive ghettos and camps. Thus, through the extended survivor community, Wallant deals with the Buchenwald and Bergen-Belsen camps; Bellow with the Lodz Ghetto and Buchenwald, in addition to Polish forest partisan units; Singer with the Nazi occupations of Poland and Russia; Steiner with the German, British, French, and Russian spheres of influence as well as various ghettos and camps experienced by a team of Nazi hunters; and Cohen with the French, Austrian, and German experiences.

A minor theme in the fiction is the interpretation of the Holocaust in light of the establishment of an independent Jewish homeland in Israel, the second major event of twentieth-century Jewish history. Although the American novelists neither link the two events politically, suggesting that Israel's birth was an acceptable outcome of the Holocaust, nor suggest that the meaning of the Holocaust is found in the creation of a Jewish state, they often link the perils of contemporary Israeli survival to the threats in the Nazi era to European Jewry. Analogies are often drawn either in character dialogue or authorial voice between Nazi and Arab anti-Jewish rhetoric and propaganda. Bellow, Singer, Steiner, and Elman set portions of their Holocaust narratives in Israel and introduce Israeli Holocaust survivors who parallel Arab rhetoric, war, and terrorist policies to those of the Nazis and proudly contrast Israeli military assertiveness with historic Jewish diasporan passivity in the face of anti-Semitism. Even the non-Israeli Jewish characters in this fiction interpret Israeli political and military policies regarding security according to Holocaust history. Although the topic of Jewish immigration to Israel is generally given short shrift in American fiction, it is a concern of the Holocaust fiction, appearing as a political theme in Bellow's, Elman's, and Steiner's works, and as political and spiritual themes in Singer's and Potok's works.

A related subject of American Holocaust fiction is the post *Shoah* status of theodicy and Judaism. Called into question are the three pillars of historic Judaism: God, Torah, and the Jewish people. The Holocaust, more than any other event in Jewish history, taxes the Jew's faith in a just and merciful God and provokes questions about the nature of God, the covenant between God and Israel, and the nature of man. Since the covenant implies a moral partnership between God and His people, the Jew asserts his moral position in these protestations. Jews question the meaning of Jewish identity in our time, whether traditional Jewish responses to evil and persecution are still viable

options, and what kind of Judaism is appropriate in the post-Holocaust era.

Jewish novelists write as descendants of the biblical protestors and interrogators of divine purpose. Judaism has a tradition of theological protest dating from the biblical histories of Job, Abraham, Moses, and Jeremiah. Elie Wiesel uses the metaphor of a trial in *The Gates of the Forest,* a tale of four rabbis who convene a court in their concentration camp to confront God with His sins. The prosecutor announces his intent "to convict God of murder, for He is destroying His people and the Law He gave them from Mt. Sinai." Not unexpectedly, the judges return a guilty verdict. Without the formal trial structure, I. B. Singer also incorporates the theme of judging the Almighty for Holocaust sins. Several characters in *Enemies, A Love Story* and the heroine of "The Mentor" try to convict the passive deity. Chaim Potok's Israeli Holocaust survivor and George Steiner's Nazi hunter also indict God of crimes against the Jewish people. Richard Elman's Yagodah, a secularist, asks the pertinent questions without the benefit of traditional Judaic learning.

Representative of the major Jewish Holocaust theological and philosophical responses are questioning and protest against God's inaction in the face of injustice. Contemporary theses promulgated by Richard Rubenstein, Emil Fackenheim, Eliezar Berkovits, and Irving Greenberg derive from the biblical and prophetic tradition. Although the moderns categorically reject *mi-penei hata' einu,* an explanation that posits catastrophe as just retribution for sin, they differ widely in their conclusions. Rubenstein argues that the only response to the death camps is rejection of God, posits the meaninglessness of existence in a universe in which there is neither divine plan nor divine concern, and proposes that the human condition reflects no transcendental purpose. Instead of a covenantal bond, Rubenstein urges a strong commitment to the survival of the Jewish people. Emil Fackenheim insists on reaffirming God and Judaism, arguing that to do otherwise would give Hitler a posthumous victory. Eliezar Berkovits accepts the uniqueness of the Holocaust in the magnitude of its destruction, but rejects the notion of a consequent unique theological dilemma, since Jewry has throughout its history suffered terrible persecutions and retained faith. Irving Greenberg accepts Holocaust-wrought vacillation between moments of faith and renunciation.

In *After Auschwitz: Radical Theology and Contemporary Judaism,* Rubenstein denies divine will and the world and history as manifestations of divine purpose. Rejecting God and the traditional Jewish theological framework, Rubenstein affirms instead the existential belief that people must create meaning and value. He argues further that with the "death of God," the significance of the community of Israel is more important: "It is precisely because human existence is tragic, ultimately hopeless, and without meaning that we treasure our religious community." For Rubenstein the post-Holocaust Jewish identity is fashioned in "the shared vicissitudes of history, culture, and psychological perspective." One finds the characters expounding this view in "The Mentor," *The 28th Day of Elul, The Portage to San Cristobal of A. H.,* and "The Last Mohican."

In *God's Presence in History,* Emil Fackenheim rejects the Rubenstein thesis, countering that a more appropriate response to the Holocaust is to keep God and Israel together. Also rejecting the *mi-penei hata' einu* theory of retribution for sins, Fackenheim does not seek to explain the Holocaust because its enormity transcends all traditional explanations of suffering and evil. In his postwar reappraisal of Judaism, Fackenheim finds Jewish liberal belief in the perfectability of man invalid, but still affirms the orthodox position on the centrality of God in human history and the covenantal bond between God and Israel. Fackenheim's acceptance of the covenant is based on a reading of Jewish history that distinguishes central events as "root" experiences and "epoch making events":

> The most powerful incidents, such as those connected with the Exodus from Egypt and the giving of the Torah at Sinai, actually created the religious identity of the Jewish people. These creative extraordinary happenings Fackenheim calls "root experiences." [They] are historical events of such a formative character that they continue to influence all future "presents" of the people. . . these past moments legislate to every future era. . . . They belong to the collective memory of the people and continue to claim the allegiance of the nation. . . . [They] provide the accessibility of Divine Presence in the here and now . . . thus the Jew is "assured that the saving God of the past saves still."

Distinguished from the "root experiences" are those occasions Fackenheim calls "epoch making events," which are not formative in that they do not create the essentials of Jewish faith

> but rather they are crises that challenge the "root experiences" through new situations, which test the resiliency and generality of "root experiences" to answer to new and unprecedented conditions and realities. For example, the destruction of the First and Second Temples severely tested whether or not the commanding and saving Presence of God could be maintained.

The Holocaust is an "epoch making event." Yet Fackenheim contends "the Jew must still affirm the continued proximity of God in Jewish history . . . and he must affirm the present reality of the people's 'root experience' of a commanding God (at Sinai) now commanding Israel from within the Holocaust itself." The religious Jews in the fictions of Potok, Singer, and Ozick share these thoughts without expressing them in Fackenheimian vocabulary. This view is at the heart of Singer's *Shosha,* Ozick's "Bloodshed" and *Cannibal Galaxy,* Cohen's *In the Days of Simon Stern,* and Potok's *In the Beginning.*

Fackenheim takes the Jobian position, "Though He slay me, yet shall I trust in Him," (Job 13:15) and his rationale is that Jews are under a sacred obligation to survive as Jews. Jews are "forbidden to despair of the God of Israel, lest Judaism perish" and Hitler be granted a posthumous victory. For Fackenheim, the God of deliverance is affirmed in the establishment and maintenance of the State of Israel. What Auschwitz denies, Israel affirms and provides living testimony to God's continued presence in history. Bellow's Sammler and Malamud's Bok come to similar conclusions in secular terms and the religious devotees in the fiction of Potok, Ozick, Singer, and Cohen express these convictions in terms more closely associated with, although not necessarily derivative of, Fackenheim.

In *Faith after the Holocaust,* Eliezar Berkovits searches the tradition for concepts to help deal with the death camps. He joins Rubenstein and Fackenheim in rejecting the *mi-penei hata' einu* thesis, arguing that it is "an injustice absolute," but adds, "It was an injustice countenanced by God." He arrives at this belief through the tradition's explanation of God's tolerance of evil known as *hester panim* (Hiding of the Face of God), postulating that occasionally God inexplicably turns His face from man and that such hiddenness is necessary for man to exercise free will, because only by withdrawing from history and abstaining from intervention in the human condition, despite great injustice and evil, does God facilitate freedom of choice. Thus, God suffers evil humanity while allowing the innocent and good to suffer. For Berkovits, this view of theodicy permits the Jew to continue to believe in the deity despite Holocaust reality. Elman's Alex Yagodah arrives at a similar position at the close of his theological debate. Berkovits further insists that the Holocaust not be treated as an isolated event in Jewish history; he agrees that it must be analyzed within the framework of past Jewish experience. Although Berkovits acknowledges that the Holocaust, like previous persecutions of Jewry, poses questions about God's providential presence and moral perfection, he disputes the notion that it represents a novum in Jewish history whose essential distinctness creates a new problem for religious faith different from previous persecutions. The continued existence of Jewry in the face of its long history of suffering is, for Berkovits, proof that God exists despite His periodic concealment. The Jew must assess God not simply on the basis of His Holocaust passivity but upon consideration of all history, including the redemptive joy of rebuilt Zion, the "ingathering of the exiles," in the ancient homeland. Concurring with Fackenheim, Berkovits believes that just as Auschwitz is evidence of the self-concealed God, the rebirth of Israel as a Jewish state and its survival are evidence of "a smile on the face of God." Illustrating this proposition, I. B. Singer's survivor-penitent, Shapiro, advances from denunciation of the silent God of the Holocaust era to his spiritual return to a loving God in the rebuilt Zion.

In the essay "Cloud of Smoke, Pillar of Fire: Judaism, Christianity, and Modernity After the Holocaust," Irving Greenberg inquires where God was during Auschwitz and whether His silence was another instance of hiding His face or whether He ceased to be the God of trust. Greenberg argues that even if we are able to retain belief in the caring biblical God after the Holocaust, such affirmation is problematic and inconstant, comprising "moment faiths." Like Elie Wiesel, Greenberg acknowledges that since the death camps, there are times when "the flames and smoke of the burning children blot out faith," but these moments of doubt are interspersed with moments of faith. The tension between these polarities of doubt and faith constitutes a major thematic interest in American

Holocaust fiction and may be seen in the fiction of Bellow, Ozick, Singer, and Malamud.

The Jewish messianic and mystical interpretation that catastrophe requires greater human effort to repair in the face of the hidden God also finds expression in American literature. Lurianic kabbalists respond to Divine self-exile with a call for *tikkun* (a continual act of human repair and restoration) by means of proper *kavanah* (intention, devotion, meditation). Human assistance in the achievement of God's purpose is an intricate part of the kabbalistic response to evil. The view that the interruption of divine duty does not excuse human covenantal responsibility finds vital expression in the fiction of I. B. Singer, Bernard Malamud, Arthur Cohen, Cynthia Ozick, Saul Bellow, and Chaim Potok.

The moral dilemma of whether to speak or remain reverentially silent in tribute to the Holocaust victims is resolved in this fiction on the side of the sacred duty to bear witness. Unlike Israeli writers of the *Palmach* generation—those who fought in the War of Independence, who sought to write an Israeli rather than a Diasporan literature, who sought to separate themselves from the passive ethos of European Jewry, and who experienced the conflict between longing to forget the Holocaust and compulsion to remember—for the Americans, bearing witness and the act of Holocaust transmission itself are central Holocaust themes. After writing six novels on the Holocaust, Elie Wiesel explored the dilemma in *The Oath* and examined the possibility that it might have been better to have remained silent in the face of such evil. Silence might have been the more powerful witness. *The Oath* chronicles his conviction that if a single life is saved by telling the Holocaust story, he is morally obliged to speak, even if in so doing he violates an earlier oath to keep silent, as did the narrator. The novelists represented in this study do not grapple with the dilemma of speech or silence. They and their protagonists are morally committed to bearing witness. If there is any dissent, it is in the manner of articulation. Indeed, some survivor-characters assert that the essential purpose of surviving is to bear witness. So significant is the role of survivor-witness that characters are specifically designated as scribes, journalists, and teachers. Arthur Cohen's book is narrated by Nathan, the scribe who brings to his *hurban* narration the dedication of a Torahic scribe. His vision is panoramic, placing the Holocaust in the context of ancient and modern persecutions of the Jews. Bellow's Sammler abandons writing about aesthetics to concentrate on spiritual studies. On the occasion of the Six Day War, he is compelled to write a journalistic account of the event. Singer's writer-protagonists record the lives of the dead, chronicle *shtetl* memories to commemorate the Holocaust dead, or act as interpreters or facilitators through whom survivors may tell their histories. Cynthia Ozick's Enoch Vand literally documents the Holocaust in his role as a U.S. government record keeper. In "The Suitcase," witness testimony is the vehicle for the direct confrontation of a Jew and German. In "Levitation" and *The Messiah of Stockholm* oral history is given. Steiner's Nazi hunters bear witness by bringing Nazis to trial. Malamud and Potok create survivor-mentors to transmit Holocaust history, Jewish values, and

learning. Epstein approaches the issue visually creating an artist and two photographers who record for posterity life and death in the ghetto. As each writer bears witness to the uniqueness of the Holocaust, a dual sense of mission emerges. Not only do they attest to the historic record and commemorate the dead, each warns humanity of its capacity for genocide.

How does literature—an art form people use to bring order to chaos, to impose form on the formless, to explore the vagaries of human thought and emotion—give form and structure to the atrocities of a schematic, mechanized, and socially organized program of annihilation that denies the human values literature celebrates? To structure a creative response to a destructive force is an anomaly. Nothing about the Holocaust is aesthetic. It is a denial of the creative instinct. Just as the Holocaust was beyond normal human experience, so too the imaginative recreation of it demands, many believe, a language and literature somehow different from that which expressed pre-Holocaust suffering. The aesthetic problem is to find language appropriate to the Nazi universe, language to convey a bureaucracy of evil. Literature has long explored evil; it has traced the careers of Machiavellian villains such as Tamberlaine, Macbeth, and Richard III; it has treated obsessive megalomaniacs such as Ahab and Rappaccini, but never before has humanity, and literature, encountered evil in the magnitude of the Holocaust. Such desolation, it has been argued, required a new artistic style, a new language. "The difficulty," as A. Alverez suggests [see Further Reading], "is to find language for this world without values, with its meticulously controlled lunacy and bureaucracy of suffering." Although there may be no adequate Holocaust aesthetic, there is nonetheless the experience that demands artistic rendition and writers have struggled to create a language and literature to convey some measure of the Holocaust trauma.

The writer's problem is to devise a means of presenting material for which there is no adequate analogue in human history and a subject that many believe is beyond art. There is no archetypal or familiar model, no literary touchstone, no exemplar for Holocaust fiction. Documentary realism would be a mere repetition of the archivists and historians. Writers had to devise methods for fusing documentary matter with refashioned conventional literary models to convey the image of man and the social order wrought by the Holocaust. American writers learned from their European and Israeli colleagues and from the patterns of behavior and responses to extreme experiences described by diarists, archivists, historians, and social scientists and integrated the documentary material with artistic vision. American Holocaust fiction is a literature of hindsight. The creative writers immersed themselves in the voluminous testimonials and diaries that were retrieved from hiding places, ghettos, camps and those that were written after the war in the histories and documents published by Holocaust researchers. Survivors have provided materials novelists have diligently studied—eyewitness accounts of the genocidal capacity of humankind, as well as its capacity to endure.

In his description of Yiddish writers' responses to the catastrophe [in *Against the Apocalypse*], David Roskies argues that they had "basically two approaches to draw upon from the fund of ancient and modern sources; one that imploded history, and the other that made the Holocaust the center of apocalypse." A similar principle may be noted in Jewish-American Holocaust fiction, with Singer, Ozick, Cohen, and Potok on the first side of the equation and Malamud, Wallant, Elman, Epstein, Steiner, and Bellow on the second. Writers steeped in Jewish history could draw upon the centuries-long history of persecution suffered by European Jews. Because the Nazis followed church precedent with the imposition of yellow badges, the defiling of Torah scrolls, the burning of synagogues, the public humiliation of rabbis, the establishment of Jewish ghettos, the expropriation of Jewish property, and the mass expulsions and murders, and because the Nazis followed historic precedent in coordinating their violence with the Jewish calendar, some novelists invoke historic persecutions as referents and correspondents—albeit on a smaller scale—to the modern disaster. Writers sensitive to Jewish history commonly invoke the paradigms of destruction and desecration as imprecise evocations of Holocaust loss. Thus, Singer invokes the Chmielnicki and Petlurian Massacres and villains such as Pharoah and Haman; Cohen invokes the Spanish Inquisition and Ozick the plight of the Marranos and persecutions in the time of Akiva; and Malamud invokes the blood libel persecution. Representative of this approach is Arthur Cohen's vast compendium of Jewish history, his disjointed narrative style interrupted by essay entries, philosophic digressions, stories within stories, and parables, all used to create a background for viewing the Holocaust in the historic context of traditional European anti-Semitism. Andre Schwartz-Bart's use of Jewish history in *The Last of the Just,* from tenth-century persecutions through the Nazi slaughter, finds its counterpart in Ozick's *Cannibal Galaxy,* with its allusions to *midrashic* Akiva, Uriah, and Zechariah stories, her Egyptian references, and *Ta'anit* lessons. At the opposite extreme is Leslie Epstein who has little interest in traditional Judaism, but a deep interest in the Holocaust and a particular fascination with the personality of Chaim Rumkowski, the model for his ghetto elder. Aside from one scene evoking medieval, church-orchestrated anti-Semitism, Epstein essentially apprehends the Holocaust as its own archetype, and rather than compare it with other historic anti-Jewish persecutions, he introduces a catalogue of literary genres—the Greek satyr play, the medieval morality play, and Renaissance drama—to evoke the cultural context of evil; and he fuses that atmosphere with the Lodz Ghetto as a touchstone of Nazi reality.

History is a creative resource throughout American Holocaust fiction, reflecting the artist's primary loyalty to fact while allowing either the fusion or superimposition of specific events to convey an imaginative response. Incorporation of historic figures into the fictional context is a successful device in American Holocaust literature. Saul Bellow and Leslie Epstein examine the flamboyant and enigmatic elder of the Lodz Ghetto, Chaim Rumkowski; Bellow dramatizes in a brief vignette the simultaneous tragedy and absurdity of the Nazi universe, and Epstein structures his novel around the career of the elder. Epstein fuses invented scenes with episodes from the Warsaw, Lodz, and Vilna ghettos reported in Leonard Tushnet's *Pavement of Hell.* He dramatizes ghetto starvation, slave labor, public beatings, the display of tortured bodies as object lessons, public executions, and mass murders. Aside from John Hersey's *The Wall,* it is difficult to identify American fiction that is as heavily dependent and true to the histories and documents chronicling the ghetto experience as is *King of the Jews.* Cynthia Ozick's description of the roundup of Parisian Jews owes much to *Vichy France and the Jews,* and her fantasy about the recovery of the Bruno Schulz manuscript is based on the historic account of one German's protection and another's murder of the novelist. Similarly, Richard Elman's treatment of the Hungarian situation in 1944 reflects a close reading of the Hungarian section in Raul Hilberg's *The Destruction of the European Jews.* Although his incorporation of historic figures is limited to references to the Joel Brand case and the work of Rudolf Kastner and his unsuccessful negotiations with the Allies to exchange war supplies for the lives of thousands of Hungarian Jews, Elman's work focuses on the systematic isolation of Hungarian Jews in 1944 through restrictive legislation and deportations. Elman depicts rape, expropriation of civil rights, and human branding. Despite its faulty chronology, Elman's medical examination and tattooing session suggests the same dehumanization that Primo Levi's *Haftling* 174517 feels, recognizing "Nothing belongs to us anymore, they have taken away our clothes, our shoes, even our hair. . . . They will even take away our name."

Whereas Epstein and Elman dramatize these events because their work is set in the European sphere during the Holocaust, those whose narratives are set in America use symbolism, memory, nightmare, or survivor dialogue to evoke the same events. "Perhaps," as A. Alverez noted, "the most convincing way [of delineating the concentrationary world] is that by which dreams express anguish: by displacement, disguise, and indirection." Illustrative of the successful use of the dream device to create Holocaust reality is Bellow's creation in *The Victim* of a disorientation and entrapment nightmare, which assaults the senses with an immediacy and brutality that imitates Holocaust violence. Wallant also uses the dream device in his nightmare series in *The Pawnbroker:* the transport dream in which parents helplessly witness their child drowning in excrement, nightmares in which the protagonist is subjected to surgical experimentation without the benefit of anesthetic, and others in which he is witness to an electrocution and his wife's enforced whoredom. Throughout *The Pawnbroker,* Nazerman's nightmare memories are juxtaposed with American ghetto scenes at key stressful moments to suggest the brutality and sadistic attitude of Germans toward their Jewish victims. Potok uses both dreams and a stream of consciousness reverie to convey an American's response to newspaper photographs of Buchenwald. Writers often turn to the dream device both to convey the displacement, confusion, indirection, and incoherence of the victim during the Nazi period and to serve as a barometer measuring the failure of the victim to repress the past.

In contrast to the indirection of dream and involuntary memory, direct speeches focusing on Nazi crimes are offered by Cohen's survivor-narrator, Nathan of Gaza, who records the history of starvation, disease, and illness among the inmates of Auschwitz; Ozick's Vand, who documents the various camp death tolls for American intelligence services; and Steiner's Nazi hunter, who iterates a long catalogue of Nazi atrocities in his prosecution of Hitler. Similarly, Sammler's recurring recollections of a massacre in front of an open mass grave serve as a persistent reminder of Nazi atrocities.

Although there is no equal in these works for the surreal quality of Jerzy Kosinski's *The Painted Bird* and Gunter Gras's *Tin Drum,* fantasy occasionally appears in American Holocaust fiction. Examples of the use of fantasy are found in I. B. Singer's "The Cafeteria," in which the ghosts of Hitler's henchmen are summoned; in "A Wedding in Brownsville," where the dead Jews of an East-European village are revived; Bellow's creation in *Mr. Sammler's Planet* of a mad scene dramatizing Bruch's Buchenwald-generated psychic disturbances; Ozick's levitation scene; Cohen's projection of a modern Spanish Inquisition; and Steiner's resurrection of Hitler.

Whereas some Europeans felt they had to disrupt conventional literary forms to write Holocaust literature, the Americans often used traditional Jewish and Western forms. Western forms often highlight the connections between Holocaust brutality and the civilization where the brutality took shape and was sustained. Illustrative of this method is Epstein's introduction of Greek, medieval, and Shakespearean models to render his themes of political corruption and radical evil. Conversely, in writings from the Hebrew and Yiddish traditions, American writers found conventions and language appropriate to the unique Holocaust sufferings of the Jews. Ozick and Cohen introduce the Hebrew *midrashic* legend, Singer and Potok lamentation liturgy, biblical allusions, Hasidic implications of restoration, and covenant theology to place the Holocaust in the historic context of Jewish martyrdom. A comparative study of methods of Holocaust delineation reveals that Americans share the elegiac, lamentative tone and its parodic countercommentary commonly found in the writing of Jewish European and Israeli writers. Arthur Cohen, Cynthia Ozick, I. B. Singer, and Chaim Potok draw on traditional Hebraic responses to national catastrophe, invoking the collective Jewish memory. These novelists are knowledgeable heirs of the rabbinic literature; their touchstones are Jewish theology and history. Their characters are often located in communities whose values are ultimately Jewish rather than secular. They are more often firmly rooted in the Jewish cultural and religious contexts, and they express themselves in biblical, *midrashic,* mystical, and messianic themes when responding to the *Shoah.* They speak in authentic Jewish voices. Adherence to the collective history distinguishes the characters of these authors from the characters in the works of Elman and Wallant, who are generally secular and assimilated rather than religiously or culturally Jewish. In the Holocaust fiction of the latter, attention is focused on the suffering of the individual, whereas in the former, the suffering individual translates his plight into the collective experience, because he is much more attuned to Jewish history. Readers of Cohen's *In the Days of Simon Stern* and Ozick's *The Can-*

nibal Galaxy learn of the history of Jewish martyrology, as one also does in Andre Schwarz-Bart's *The Last of the Just.* Simon Stern and Joseph Brill understand that their destinies are tied to the Jewish people and to Jewish history. They are culturally bound to Jewish civilization despite their diasporan location. Bellow's Arthur Sammler, on the other hand, represents assimilated Jews arbitrarily subjected to catastrophe in Europe because of an accident of Jewish birth, who later choose Jewish association as part of their Holocaust witness. In Elman's trilogy, the characters consistently evidence their lack of Jewish education. Aside from Lilo's countercommentary prayer-parody, biblical allusion is superimposed by the novelist using the omniscient voice, rather than imaginatively integrated as in the fiction of Singer, Cohen, and Ozick. In place of Jewish cultural loss sustained in the Holocaust, Bellow, Wallant, and Malamud stress historic data, concentrating on the political, social, and psychological ramifications of the Holocaust.

Among the most effective techniques Americans borrowed from Hebrew and Yiddish Holocaust literature is countercommentary. In *Against the Apocalypse,* David Roskies explicates the fascination of secular Jewish writers with collective catastrophe through the use of parody and the inversion of sacred texts, which emphasizes the subversion of God's principles in the historic context. Thus, the violation of the text mirrors the violation of the covenant. The prayer-parodies in the fiction of Singer and Elman reveal this attitude. Lilo's *Kaddish* achieves the same forceful expression of anguish that is rendered in the Yiddish and Hebrew writers' irreverent use of the sacred text, and it functions as they do: "to imitate the sacrilege, [to disrupt] the received order of the text in the same way as the enemy, . . . disrupted the order of the world." Roskies offers an important distinction between those who use parody constructively and destructively, arguing that the use of parody is present in

> anger deflected through the hallowed texts, a highly mediated and ritualized form of anger. By making the text seem for a while crazy and corrupt, the individual sufferer expands its meaning, allowing subsequent sufferers to enter the breach.

Generally the pattern that follows this inversion is an ode of defiant affirmation, which is clearly present in Lilo's passage, a passage whose sequence mimics prayer allowing her to maintain faith even as the promise is subverted. The angry commentators of the twentieth century share the dismay of the Hebrew poet who played on sound and sense, transposing the traditional petition "Who is like You, O Lord, among the mighty" (*elim*) (Exodus 15:11) to "Who is like You among the mute" (*illemim*) to register dissatisfaction with the silent God.

A related phenomenon in Holocaust literature that Lawrence Langer and Alvin Rosenfeld have noted is the revisionary and antithetical tendency in European Holocaust writing to refute and reject literary antecedents. Langer demonstrates the Holocaust-wrought subversion of the *Bildungsroman* in Wiesel's *Night,* which inverts the traditional pattern of initiating a young boy into society;

Rosenfeld addresses a similar reversal in Primo Levi's *Survival in Auschwitz*, which renders the concentrationary goal of dehumanization and debasement of prisoners. Rosenfeld reads these literary inversions as repudiations of the antecedent literature and culture, "a denial not only of an antecedent literary assertion but also of its implicit premises and explicit affirmations." Perhaps because Americans were not victims, one finds little of that tendency in American writers who remain reluctant to parody literary forms in Holocaust fiction. On the contrary, American writers often use traditional forms and devices, in addition to subversion and parody, to dramatize the connections between the Holocaust and its antecedents in European culture. Leslie Epstein introduces a contemporary, wagon-staged morality play to correlate Christian and Nazi anti-Semitism and incorporates a Greek satyr play to expose Nazi corruption. Rather than suggesting disillusionment with traditional literary forms or the failure of literature to posit rational, humane, moral and ethical ideals, Epstein incorporates these celebrated forms either to emphasize German corruption or, as in the case of his superb production of a ghetto *Macbeth*, to dramatize the capacity of art to inspire human compassion in the midst of moral decay. Epstein's technique here is illustrative of Jewish American writers' shared antiapocalyptic vision. They write as witnesses against Nazism and witnesses for humanistic values normally associated with literature, even in an age of atrocity.

Whereas survivor-writers bear witness in literature to their direct experience, American writers bear "witness through the imagination," as Norma Rosen observed in her *Midstream* essay, "The Holocaust and the American-Jewish Novelist." American writers join their European and Israeli colleagues as "the generation that bears the scar without the wound, sustaining memory without direct experience. It is this generation that has the obligation, self-imposed and self-accepted . . . to describe a meaning and wrest instruction from the historical." [Arthur A. Cohen, *The Tremendum: A Theological Interpretation of the Holocaust*] (pp. 13-35)

> *S. Lillian Kremer, in an introduction to her* Witness through the Imagination: Jewish American Holocaust Literature, *Wayne State University Press, 1989, pp. 13-35.*

Lawrence L. Langer

[*An American critic and educator, Langer has written and edited numerous studies of the Holocaust, including* The Holocaust and the Literary Imagination *(1975),* Confronting the Holocaust: The Impact of Elie Wiesel *(1978), and* The Holocaust and the Human Spirit *(1982). In the following essay, "Fictional Facts and Factual Fictions: History in Holocaust Literature," Langer focuses on William Styron's* Sophie's Choice *(1979) and Saul Bellow's* Mr. Sammler's Planet *(1970).*]

I call this essay fictional facts and factual fictions in order to suggest a symbiotic kinship between actual and imaginative truth in the literature of the Holocaust. One of the many tasks of Holocaust criticism is to clarify the complex bond, in the minds of both author and audience, linking the oppressions of history to the impressions of art. Normally, the artist is free, and indeed expected, to manipulate reality in any way his vision sees fit. The imagination seizes experience, drops it into its crucible, allows it to ferment, and offers the results to a tolerant and often eager public. Few readers today fault Tolstoy's art for being "unfair" to Napoleon in *War and Peace*, any more than they censure Hawthorne for adapting Puritan values to the needs of his theme in various stories and novels. But Rolf Hochhuth roused a storm of controversy when he dramatized the "facts" of Pope Pius XII's attitude toward the Jews, thus making of it a fictional fact that forced audiences to acknowledge the tension between actual and imagined truth. Similarly, in *King of the Jews*, Leslie Epstein antagonized many by transforming the "facts" of Chaim Rumkowski's leadership in the Lodz ghetto into the extravagant antics of I.C. Trumpelman. Somehow, they felt, the imagined tone of comedy and farce seemed inappropriate to the actual details of the atrocity it sought to illuminate. The same, of course, has been said repeatedly of Lina Wertmüller's film *Seven Beauties*, which offends the memory and sensibilities of viewers who anticipate greater fidelity to the realities of the concentration camp ordeal.

When the Holocaust is the theme, history imposes limitations on the supposed flexibility of artistic license. We are confronted by the perplexing challenge of the reversal of normal creative procedure: instead of Holocaust fictions liberating the facts and expanding the range of their implications, Holocaust facts enclose the fictions, drawing the reader into an ever narrower area of association, where history and art stand guard over their respective territories, wary of abuses that either may commit upon the other.

The problem is not exclusively the reader's or author's. Essentially, the problem is time's, and eventually time will solve it. What will happen, for example, when the specific details of the atrocities at Babi Yar and Auschwitz are forgotten, when their associations with the Holocaust have passed beyond historical memory and they become mere place names as obscure to their audiences as Borodino and Tagliamento are to Tolstoy's and Hemingway's readers today? In time, in other words, the boundaries separating the historical moment from its imaginative rendition will be blurred, and it will no longer matter so much whether fictional facts, tied to the actual deeds of history, have become factual fictions, monuments to artistic vision that require no defense or justification, but stand or fall on the strength of their aesthetic mastery of material.

But today it still matters, because the urgency of the historical event continues to exert its mysterious power over modern consciousness. A fictional Napoleon no longer triggers an alarm, but the presence of Rudolf Hoess, commandant of Auschwitz, in Willilam Styron's *Sophie's Choice*, sets off sirens of wary constraint. One admires the imaginative courage, if not the results, of George Steiner's effort to write a fiction whose central fact is that Israeli agents have discovered an aged Adolf Hitler, very much alive, deep in a South American jungle. Reading that novella, *The Voyage to San Cristobal of A. H.*, imposes almost impossible burdens on the audience's willing suspension of disbelief, confronted as it is simultaneously with the historical fact of Hitler's death and his artistic resurrection, a burden that would be negligible if Steiner's intention were not so serious and the figure were not so centrally identified with the experience of the Holocaust. By re-creating a Holocaust personality whose motives still have not been firmly established (to say nothing of being understood) in *fact,* Steiner establishes a wall of resistance to block the passage leading from history to art. Once the historical Hitler becomes a fictional fact, he inadvertently joins the fraternity of men; then (since his creator eschews melodrama), we are forced to face him in fiction as we were reluctant to do in fact. The factual fiction, in other words, becomes a figure we do not want to confront, partly because the real man is still so much more vivid to our imagination than his invented counterpart, and partly because the fact and the fiction constantly war with each other for higher priority. The Holocaust in fact resists displacement by the Holocaust in fiction, as if the artist were guilty of some unprincipled violation of a sacred shrine. This may help to explain Adorno's early cry, constantly repeated by others though later modified by him, that to write poetry after Auschwitz is barbaric.

How may we account for this resistance? If the Holocaust were an event that lent itself to heroic portraiture, or the legendary tone of epic, or even to the conventional tale of purification through suffering—and of course much Holocaust literature limits itself to expressing just such traditional themes—then this problem, I think, would not exist. Literature generalizes human experience, while the events of atrocity we call the Holocaust insist on their singularity. The imagination seeks to link the two, to find a bridge through metaphor, image, a language of connection. But the Holocaust has impurified language in a way that prevents this from happening. [In "The Second Life of Holocaust Imagery," (*Witness,* 1987)] Norma Rosen quotes a line from a poem by Eugene Montale—"I've sniffed on the wind the burnt fragrance / of sweet rolls from the ovens"—and suggests that no one today can register those images without some form of associative despair. The catalogue of such terms is long, and if they do not deplete available vocabulary, they certainly limit the writer's control of their use: train, track, boxcar, smoke, chimney, ghetto, roundup, deport, roll call, organize, camp, block, oven, furnace, gas, shower—even arrival and departure. They are not a lingo (though some unique terms like kapo and musselman and Canada appeared, with many more emerging from the longer Gulag experience that Solzhenitsyn writes of), but ordinary language that normally empowers the writer to give rebirth in literature to the tensions and conflicts of life.

How do we verbalize the enigma of a language that alienates even as it struggles to connect? We can avoid the problem, as many do, by choosing a language of consolation and transforming the Holocaust experience into a story of Jewish resistance and survival, pretending that these terms at least permit the universalization of the ordeal. But those who confront that ordeal with unabashed frankness will have to acknowledge that in its scope it was little more than, and never *will* be much more than a story

of Jewish murder. Since the *factual* fact is so dismal and unedifying, how are we to face the fictional fact that lifts it out of its original bedrock in history (where, four decades later, we still probe for its "meanings" in the layers of time), and translates it into an artificial setting? How can we expect the mind to adjust from the real horror to its portrayal in art, while simultaneously accepting the premise that nothing essential has been lost or changed in the process?

Sometimes I think this is too much to ask, of writer *or* audience. Except for the brief episode near the end of André Schwarz-Bart's *Last of the Just,* I know of no fictional moment set *inside* a gas chamber (though probably others exist). Making a fictional fact of that factual fact raises the specter of the resultant factual fiction's becoming "only" a fictional fiction, by which I mean that for the sake of art, the imagination raises the event to the level of imagined experience and somehow constricts instead of illuminating the implications of that dehumanizing trial. Art in its essence asks us to see life other than it literally was, since all art, even the most objective naturalism, requires selection and composition, and this alters the purity (or in this case the impurity) of the original historical moment. A wholly imagined fictional episode, or one unrelated to a sustained trauma like the Holocaust, faces no such constraints. Hence the temptation is to defer to tradition by heroizing the victim by identifying him or her with familiar forms of suffering and well-known gestures of resistance, or villainizing the persecutor through familiar expressions of cruelty. But these are evasive tactics too.

Another task of Holocaust criticism is to address the implications and consequences of these dilemmas. Some writers are more sensitive to the issue than others. Wishing the life of his heroine in *The White Hotel* to end at Babi Yar, D. M. Thomas—wisely, I think—does not try to reconstruct that episode as a purely imaginative act because he knows, perhaps through instinct, that the Holocaust raises questions of narrative authority few other historical occasions confront us with. Moreover, since the intersection of history with fiction, actual with imaginative truth, is one of the themes of Thomas's novel, introducing a literal eyewitness account of Babi Yar into the text reinforces the issue he is exploring. He takes most of the description of the catastrophe of Babi Yar from Anatoli Kuznetsov's non-fiction novel of the same name. As a young boy, Kuznetsov lived in Kiev and experienced some of the events surrounding the executions at Babi Yar. But even he felt the need for a more reliable narrative authority and, as he tells us, used the account of a survivor, Dina Mironovna Pronicheva. "She is the only eyewitness to come out of it," he says (inaccurately, as it turns out), "and I am now going to tell her story, as I wrote it down from her own words, without adding anything of my own." Curiously, this is a familiar formula to anyone conversant with the history of the novel. Unwilling to be accused of frivolous fabrications, some early novelists habitually fell back on such disclaimers, as if invented narratives would somehow seem less authentic than so-called authoritative testimony. Ironically—for some writers, at any rate—the Holocaust has revived an ancient tradition. Perhaps this accounts for the popularity of one form of Holocaust literature, the documentary novel, represented not only by Kuznetsov's work, but also by Jean-François Steiner's *Treblinka* and Thomas Kenneally's *Schindler's List.*

Thomas's purpose, however, is not to give us an authoritative account of Babi Yar, but to find a fitting dramatic conclusion to the life of his heroine and erstwhile patient of Sigmund Freud, the fictional Lisa Erdmann. The reader, already compelled to identify her character with historical reality by the presence of Freud in the novel, has the merging of her story into fictional fact confirmed by her fate at Babi Yar. "No one could have imagined the scene," she thinks as the executions continue, "because it was happening."

Facts we *know* because they have happened; fictions we only imagine. But the facts of Babi Yar are "unimaginable," and this is why what I call fictional facts play such an important role in our response to and understanding of the Holocaust. By creating an imagined context for Dina Pronicheva's experience at Babi Yar, Thomas makes accessible to the imagination what might have seemed intractable material. But at the same time, he alters the narrative of the real survivor, Dina Pronicheva, whose ordeal is transmitted by Kuznetsov; and in so doing, he creates what I call a factual fiction, since there never was a Lisa Erdmann, so that her "perception" of Babi Yar is an invention. The reader searching for information about or insight into Babi Yar by reading *The White Hotel* runs the same risk as one turning to John Hersey's *The Wall* to learn about the Warsaw ghetto. Art intervenes almost inevitably to mute the impact of history, just as Thomas chose to end his novel with a fantasy that at the very least qualifies the finality of the anguish represented by the real Babi Yar. Although *The White Hotel* is not exclusively a Holocaust novel, the extermination of the Jews is the denouement of its fictional milieu. The concluding fantasy of transcendence, and perhaps of redemption, wholly a product of the imagination, cannot undo the historical horror of the prior episode at Babi Yar. Whether this is the point, or the missed point, of the narrative, each reader must decide in the privacy of his or her critical engagement with the text.

Babi Yar is an episode, a mass execution, perceived through the eyes of a victim, whose own source, we now know, was primarily the testimony of an actual survivor, Dina Pronicheva. In William Styron's *Sophie's Choice* the commandant of Auschwitz, Rudolf Hoess, is a character, with a wife, children, a home, friends, normal desires, while the "episode" of Auschwitz, with its mass executions, forms only the periphery of the narrative. The fictional facts of Hoess's tenure at Auschwitz come from his *Autobiography,* his various war-crimes trial testimonies, and Styron's own visit to the site of the deathcamp. The factual fictions, however, are far more crucial in this work: the motives, the dialogue, the gestures, the portrait not of Commandant Hoess, but of Hoess the private human being, whose primary task almost incidentally happens to be the construction of the gas chambers and crematoria of Auschwitz-Birkenau and the murder of its Jewish inmates. Between one and two million of them perished

there, by his own estimation (though not in the pages of this novel).

Far more challenging than Sophie's manufactured choice—sending her daughter to her death in order to save her son (a decision which any informed reader would know lay beyond the control of Auschwitz's victims, Jewish or not)—far more challenging than Sophie's choiceless choice is *Styron's* choice: to assault our historical consciousness of Hoess the mass murderer with his own conception of Hoess the man, and to expect the resulting fictional facts to be persuasive. If they are not—and I think they are not—the fault lies both with Styron and the tyranny of history, which at this moment in time demands to know not how decent and polite Hoess might have been when he wasn't killing Jews and Poles, but how a man otherwise decent and polite—questionable designations, at best—so effortlessly advanced the cause of genocide.

The factual fictions of Styron's narrative, solely on his own creative authority, would have us believe that Commandant Hoess might apologize to Polish prisoner Sophie for violating his promise by failing to produce her son for her to see. Or that Commandant Hoess, destroyer of Jews and Poles, would not object to the humiliation of vowing to that same Polish prisoner, seriously, not ironically: "You have my assurance and word as a German officer, my word of honor." Styron's boldness in characterizing Hoess matches Steiner's in uncovering Hitler "alive" after all these years: but what fresh understanding of Nazi mentality emerges from their imaginative forays? Is it a revelation that Hoess suffers from migraines; or is exasperated by bureaucratic interference from Berlin; or that he is beholden to former Prussian mannerisms; or admires his Arabian stallion's spontaneity? In attempting to imagine Hoess as someone other than a creature of melodrama, a monster of iniquity, Styron has created an unremarkable figure almost totally dissociated from the deeds that led to his execution after the war. The consequences of those deeds, which engage the reader's consciousness with as much energy as the factual fictions about Hoess in the novel distract it, solicit something more than the familiar outlines of characterization that Styron offers us, something akin to the bizarre contradictions that drive the more complex nature of Nathan.

Literature may not provide sufficient model or inspiration for personages like Rudolf Hoess, but history compounds the dilemma by also hemming in Styron, in spite of himself. He cannot approach Hoess with the same psychological freedom that he does Nathan; yet to do otherwise is to create a wooden creature whose responses in fiction neither illuminate nor are justified by his actions in fact. *Sophie's Choice* is a classic example of the kinship linking the two, constraining instead of freeing the potential for insight inherent in the bond. We cannot say to the reader: take Hoess for what he is, a character in a novel who need not shed light on his real-life prototype. Such a demand would trivialize history, the victims, the critical imagination, the whole macabre enterprise of genocide. But if a character's representational authority does not emerge from the context of the fiction, how are we to respond to him? We return to the intersection of fiction and fact, history and imagination, and that defiant event we call the Holocaust, which the creative faculty will not dismiss but cannot enclose because the limbo it inhabits is shrouded in such uncertain gloom.

Up to this point I have tried to confirm the difficulty, not to say the impossibility, of making a historical figure the center of consciousness in a piece of Holocaust literature. Whether we are thinking of Hitler, Hoess, Chaim Rumkowski, Pope Pius XII, or any other major participant in the catastrophe, the memory of their actual role intrudes on all attempts to dramatize it and erodes the authenticity of their fictional presence. I am convinced that many decades must pass before art will be able to displace memory as the measure of literary success. The most effective Holocaust fictions, like Piotr Rawicz's *Blood from the Sky,* Jorge Semprun's *The Long Voyage,* Tadeusz Borowski's *This Way for the Gas, Ladies and Gentlemen,* Ida Fink's *A Scrap of Time,* and Aharon Appelfeld's various novels, while not ignoring the specific historical context, turn their imaginative beacons on the problem of tone and point of view, angle of vision, centers of consciousness through which the essential atrocity may be filtered. Although fictionalized historical material may alienate the reader, an adequately imagined *invented* center of consciousness can draw him against his will into the net of atrocity, where his own sense of normal reality struggles to escape from the lure. To balance the theoretical discussion in the first part of this essay, I would like to turn now to two texts (one of them, by design, discussed earlier, but with a different emphasis) in order to assess the use of centers of consciousness as bulwarks against the invasion by Holocaust facts of Holocaust fictions.

Although Saul Bellow's *Mister Sammler's Planet* and Styron's *Sophie's Choice* are not Holocaust novels in the sense of some of the aforementioned works, the title figures in both have had their encounters with mass murder and atrocity. Their lives thereafter have been unalterably affected by their ordeals. Mr. Sammler sees himself as a *"past* person," as "a man who had come back," who "had rejoined life," though moments of his Holocaust ordeal trickle into the present through his own perceiving consciousness at various points in the narrative. He is his own conduit into the foreground of the novel's action, our only source of authority for the history of the Holocaust "then" and its impact during subsequent years on the mind and vision of Sammler the survivor now.

Sophie is a survivor too, though we shall have to ask how her encounter with atrocity differs from Sammler's. By adopting Stingo as his narrator, Styron prevents Sophie from internalizing her experience as Sammler does, thus excluding the reader from direct access to the inner process whereby she adjusts the background of her ordeal in Poland and Auschwitz to the foreground of her postwar years in Brooklyn. Sophie offers us only oral testimony; Stingo is the perceiving consciousness, and as an aspiring writer, he seems less interested, his assertions to the contrary notwithstanding, in the "meaning" of Auschwitz than in the literary re-creation of Sophie's story and the gradual revelation of her "secret"—the choice between her children, imposed on her by a Nazi doctor at Ausch-

witz. Stingo thus duplicates in his own career as a fledgling writer the conflict between fictional facts and factual fictions that beset Styron as author of *Sophie's Choice.* Unfortunately, his efforts to achieve equilibrium are no more successful than his creator's.

The Holocaust background of *Sophie's Choice* is thus Sophie's Holocaust experience, the anguish of the loss of her children, her friends, her health, her self-esteem. That experience evolves slowly into the foreground of the novel through the strict shaping control of Stingo's consciousness, but the evolution is so often disrupted by discordant or farcical concerns that the link joining background to foreground ultimately shatters, never to be repaired. These eccentric matters include Stingo's obsessive fantasies about a final resting place for his wayward organ; Nathan's brutal, lunatic antics; and Sophie's determination to master the intricacies of American, and particularly Southern, literary rhetoric. To have a Polish immigrant who mistakes the elementary distinction between seersucker and other kinds of suckers diligently poring over Malcolm Cowley's *Portable Faulkner* or the concise novels of Thomas Wolfe is to strain the reader's credulity. As a writer, Stingo is bound and trapped by his literary commitment to create a portrait of Sophie that is more stylized than human, projecting for us his own version of what a southern American writer might have imagined Sophie to be. The novel is less about Sophie's experience in Auschwitz and her encounter with Commandant Hoess than it is about Stingo's unflagging determination to make literature out of them.

Whether Styron had serious or parodistic intentions with Stingo, the results, for readers interested in the uses of Holocaust facts in fiction, are the same. Striving for literary effects turns out to be incompatible with Sophie's choice between her children, improbable as that was, forced on Sophie by the equally improbable Dr. Jemand von Niemand. But Stingo is unable to restrain his impulse to stylistic embellishment. He taints the purity of Sophie's already melodramatic scream, "I can't choose! I can't choose!" with his private commentary that "Tormented angels never screamed so loudly above hell's pandemonium." The compulsion to transform painful human moments into cosmic gestures through stylistic effects like this one makes the Holocaust a gratuitous literary event to be "written up" by an aspiring novelist like Stingo. This *separates* the history from the fiction by advertising the effort to absorb one into the other.

One other example should suffice to make this point. As Sophie's "battered memory" struggles for the last time to face the implications of her children's fate, Stingo again buries her efforts beneath the writer's mound of rhetoric: "She paused to look out through the night at the dark shore of the Virginia of our destination, removed by staggering dimensions of time and space from her own benighted, cursed, and—to me even at that moment—incomprehensible history." One purpose of literary art, especially when confronting the Holocaust, is to encourage a perceiving consciousness to make comprehensible the incomprehensible, but Stingo's penchant for inflated style intervenes repeatedly at crucial potential moments of recognition like these, diverting the reader's attention from Sophie's trial to the writer's resolve to *render* it.

One might expect that Stingo, having extracted from Sophie her ultimate painful revelation, would have devoted himself to sympathy for the victim. But though Sophie's heart may have turned to stone, her body, to Stingo's delight, has retained its sumptuous sinuosity. Indeed, his failure as a perceiving consciousness is that he mistakes a climax for a denouement. On the page following Sophie's confession about her children's fate, Stingo's curiosity about her story is replaced by a night of erotic calisthenics that make one wonder where the focus of his interest has lain all along. What are we to make of this narrator, to say nothing of his narrative, which can literally juxtapose death in the gas chamber with lavish descriptions of the varieties of his sexual experience with Sophie? One longs to believe that here too Styron is indulging in parody; but once more, whether he is or not, the results are the same: to mock, to diminish, to negate the authenticity of Sophie's anguish in Auschwitz. Indeed, Stingo parodies Sophie and himself when he describes his last spasm of pleasure in Sophie's mouth in language reminiscent of her response to Dr. Jemand von Niemand's cruel challenge to her to choose between her children. Stingo says of himself: "I verged on a scream, or a prayer, and my vision went blank, and I gratefully perished." So close to her Auschwitz narrative, such evocation of Sophie's language savors of the indecent. Her "oral testimony" itself has collapsed into a bizarre form of sexual parody, as speech disintegrates into suction.

In attempting to write a serious novel about the Holocaust using Stingo as narrator, Styron created for himself insuperable obstacles. Stingo's priapic sensibility, his obsession with tumescence, combined with his platitudinous anti-Semitic instincts, disqualify him for the literary task he chooses—to tell Sophie's story convincingly and sympathetically. The evidence is strewn throughout the narrative. Though Styron may have been indulging in some ethnic "humor" by having his narrator endlessly identify Jews with bagels, Manischewitz, and halvah, or longing to bury his nose in Leslie Lapidus's "damp Jewish bosom," or feeling pleased with the clever turn of phrase that alludes to "window-shopping Hadassah matrons," or asking regretfully "Why, instead of the floundering, broke, unpublished writer that I was, couldn't I be an attractive, intelligent, well-paid Jewish urologist with a sexy wife?"—whatever Styron's intentions, such tiresome facility for stereotyping eventually undermines Stingo's qualifications for the serious business of narrating and interpreting Sophie's Auschwitz background. And a parody of Sophie's ordeal would not be worth telling—certainly not worthy of Styron's talent as a writer. However Styron feels personally about these matters, his real choice of Stingo as perceiving consciousness proves fatal to our appreciation of Sophie's fictional choice in the novel. Stingo's failure betrays Styron's—and vice versa.

Saul Bellow will have none of the romantic sentimentalism that enables Stingo to speak of SS Doctor Jemand von Niemand as "a failed believer seeking redemption, groping for renewed faith." Unlike Stingo, who magnifies the drama of Sophie's ordeal at every opportunity, Mr. Sammler is modest about what he has endured. It was not, he thinks, an achievement: "There was no special merit, there was no wizardry. There was only suffocation escaped." The search for some intellectual, emotional, and spiritual "air" to liberate Sammler's consciousness from this stifling heritage constitutes the burden of the novel, and if his quest is not entirely successful, the fault is history's, not his. History, in the form of his Holocaust encounter with a mass grave, has estranged Sammler from his earlier enthusiasm for the utopian vision of H.G. Wells; it has also alienated him from the student generation of the sixties, which hoots him off the platform at Columbia, unaware of the genesis of his present condition of mind and hence totally unsympathetic to his position. Sammler is able to bring his Holocaust experience into the foreground of his *own* consciousness, and he does this throughout the novel; but he can bring it into no one else's, so must bear his memories and their consequences alone.

As a survivor, Sammler thinks near the end of the narrative, "he still has consciousness, earthliness, human actuality." But instead of gaining him entrance to the community of men, these qualities isolate Sammler, since they issue from an exclusive background that he cannot share with others. Sammler consistently deflates the heroic and dramatic possibilities of his encounter with the pit, going so far as to suggest that only chance preserved his life: "If there had been another foot of dirt," he thinks. "Perhaps others *had* been buried alive in that ditch." But this is not the stuff of romantic defiance and energy that the younger generation around Sammler thrives on; it offers a view diametrically opposed to the enthusiastic schemes of his daughter, his nephew, and his former son-in-law, schemes heedless of the ordeal Sammler has survived. *They* still dream of molding the future; Sammler has been shaped by his past.

And while he has not lapsed into the pessimism of his namesake, Arthur Schopenhauer, Mr. Sammler speaks of the "luxury of nonintimidation by doom" as if he were fighting a rearguard action against the gloomy momentum of modern history. Between the pickpocket's phallic assertiveness against Sammler in the novel's opening episode (a sour if unintended commentary on Stingo's adolescent faith in the power of tumescence) and Eisen's gratuitous violence against the same culprit near the novel's end, Sammler gathers his musings and meditations to find some small justification for his belief that the earth might still be, as he calls it, a "glorious planet." This is in spite of his simultaneous perception that everything was being done by its inhabitants "to make it intolerable to abide here, an unconscious collaboration of all souls spreading madness and poison." Because he himself has had to kill in order to survive, because he has had impressed on him not only the idea but also the experience of life as a mausoleum, Sammler develops internal resistance to the threat of becoming a "bad joke of the self," a threat that both Sophie and Stingo (and Styron?) succumb to when they allow sexual acrobatics to displace sober confrontation with the possibility of the universe as mausoleum. Bellow excludes from his vision the incongruity, not to say the inconsistency of character, that Styron incorporates, thus acknowledging a continuity between Holocaust past and post-Holocaust present that Stingo seems immune to. From the "harsh surgery" of immersion in mass dying, Sammler reflects, one "cannot come out intact." "I assume I am one of you," he volunteers to his audience, "But also I am not." This dual vision constitutes the essence of his perception, what we might call his "good eye" and "bad eye" seeing, the fusion of background and foreground that characterizes his peculiar point of view.

In the end, the main difference between Stingo and Sammler is that Stingo is unable to avoid experiencing Sophie's encounter with atrocity as a writer rather than as a fellow human being. Sammler, on the other hand, has endured the Holocaust in all his creatureliness; his human actuality, as he thinks, is a blend of earthliness and consciousness. Stingo reserves his own encounter with the symbolic grave for the closing paragraphs of *Sophie's Choice,* but his allusion gives away the literary inspiration that has been guiding his investigation from the beginning. Falling asleep on the beach at Coney Island, he tells us, he had "abominable dreams—which seemed to be a compendium of all the tales of Edgar Allan Poe." One would think that Sophie's experience might be enough to shape his nightmares. He views reality through his literary heritage: "All night long I had the sensation of helplessness, speechlessness, and inability to move or cry out against the inexorable weight of the earth as it was flung in *thud-thud-thud*ing rhythm against my rigidly paralyzed, supine body, a living cadaver being prepared for burial in the sands of Egypt."

What Styron has given us in Stingo is the immense, overwhelming egoism of the literary imagination. Sammler condenses into two words—"suffocation escaped"—the ponderous distance between living cadavers in the landscape of Poe and his own escape from "the sand clay and stones of Poland." Stingo's last legacy, to no one's surprise, is some lines from a poem, acknowledging his dream of death but affirming nonetheless *"in glory, the bright, the morning star."* The novel's last words, "excellent and fair," are also from a poem—this time by Emily Dickinson. Are we to assume that literary vision so easily displaces Holocaust fact in the foreground of our imagination?

Once again, Mr. Sammler's concluding aspirations are more modest. The scene of his life has shifted from a mass grave and a mausoleum to a morgue, where the body of his friend Elya Gruner lies in the repose of death. For Sammler, life has become a post-mortem on the implications of his survival; so perhaps it is fitting that his last reflections should be on the fate that links all human beings—the corpse Elya Gruner mirrors our common destiny. Sammler's last gesture of tribute and commemoration is not literary, but human, humbling rather than assertive, even self-effacing: it is the legacy of an aging man, even as the Holocaust is the legacy of an aging planet. What Sammler "knows" in the novel's closing words is, as he had thought earlier, "To be so powerless was death." He does indeed see himself as a *"past* person," someone "between the human and the non-human states, between content and emptiness, between full and void, meaning and not-meaning, between this world and no world." He meditates

on the limits within which life on the post-Holocaust planet fluctuates, a shrinking area where Mr. Sammler's melancholy memories leave some space for the decently human and the humanly decent. Holocaust fact and literary fiction share the constraints of these limits. The novels of Bellow and Styron reflect the difficulty of maintaining an equilibrium between them. (pp. 117-29)

> *Lawrence L. Langer, "Fictional Facts and Factual Fictions: History in Holocaust Literature," in* Reflections of the Holocaust in Art and Literature, *edited by Randolph L. Braham, Social Science Monographs and The Csengeri Institute for Holocaust Studies of the Graduate School and University Center of the City University of New York, 1990, pp. 117-29.*

POETRY

Brian Murdoch

[*In the following essay, Murdoch traces the use of Holocaust imagery in poetry from the Yiddish lyrics composed in the ghettos and camps to the works of such poets as Sylvia Plath and Paul Celan.*]

Within the extensive criticism that has by now arisen on the poetry of Sylvia Plath and on the *Ariel* poems in particular, the poet's use of a set of images deriving from the Nazi concentration camps has for the most part been discussed without consideration of its social and aesthetic acceptability. One critic, however, George Steiner, has seen in this imagery problems that might be raised with the works of other post-war lyric poets, or indeed with other genres. Speaking of these images of Sylvia Plath's poetic "overdraft," Steiner asks, "Does any writer . . . other than an actual survivor, have the right to put on this death-rig? Auschwitz and Belsen lodge at the center of our current lives and sensibilities like the energized, malignant void of a Gnostic vision of damnation. The imagination touches on them at its peril. . . .What extraterritorial right had Sylvia Plath . . . to draw on the reserves of animate horror in the ash and the children's shoes? . . . Do any of us have license to locate our personal disasters, raw as these may be, in Auschwitz?" [*The Cambridge Mind,* eds. Eric Homberger, William Janeway, and Simon Schama].

Steiner's extension of the problem beyond Sylvia Plath to a more general query is significant, and the question is a legitimate one. Can so great a horror be reconciled with aesthetic creativity at all, and more especially with a genre as potentially fragile as the lyric?

In the same context, Steiner refers to "T. W. Adorno's dictum 'no poetry after Auschwitz' " and to those "European poets who felt that language itself had been damaged, possibly beyond creative repair, by the politics of terror and mass-murder." Adorno's attitude is not as clear-cut as the "dictum" makes it seem, but his development of the point is relevant as a partial answer to the question posed by Steiner. In the essay in which he discusses the point in the greatest detail—his essay dealing with *engagement* in the lyric—Adorno insists that he does not wish "to modify to any extent the comment that the writing of lyric poetry after Auschwitz is barbaric; for it embodies in negative terms that impulse which is at the root of *engagé* literature. The question posed by one of the characters in *Morts sans sepultres,* 'Is there any reason for living when there are people around capable of beating you until your very bones break?' is the same question as 'Should art exist at all?' or 'Does social regression not force a spiritual regression as far as *engagé* literature is concerned?' But Enzensberger's rejoinder is also valid: poetry has to stand by this verdict, has to *be* that way, just so that it does not, by dint of its existence after Auschwitz, collapse in the face of cynicism. Its very situation is a paradox" [*Noten zur Literatur, III*].

For Adorno, the magnitude of the horror demands a voice that will not betray it in cynicism: an *engagé* lyric emerges as the ideal mode. Sylvia Plath's poetry is, however, not *engagé* in any real sense: it does not even (consciously, at least) fulfill Adorno's requirement that the lyric serve as a memorial in this context, a function which he sums up by adapting Pascal: "on ne doit plus dormir." For Sylvia Plath, the imagery exists for itself alone. The metaphor has become purely aesthetic and has lost its social function.

Whether Steiner's question has, or indeed even requires, an answer in any orthodox sense is debatable. But it is possible to explain, at least partially, Sylvia Plath's use of this imagery, even if it cannot perhaps be justified. In spite of the poets who did feel that the Hitlerian era had so greatly damaged creative language, there is a wide range of otherwise conventional lyric that employs imagery drawn from the experience of the time, and Sylvia Plath may be seen as the final stage in a development of such imagery. The term "development" needs in this context perhaps a word of qualification: there is no diachronic *tradition* involved, but rather a series of transformations of the imagery based on the concentration camps, transformations that may be arranged to form a line of development. But the poets whose work is relevant here are with few exceptions quite independent of one another, and there is no question of direct influence one on the other.

Steiner is right in placing the knowledge of Auschwitz and Belsen at the center of modern thought. The death camps have given rise to prose and to drama: for the novel, one recalls Romain Gary's extraordinary *Dance of Genghis Cohn,* for the drama, Rolf Hochhuth's *Deputy,* two works written from very different standpoints, and both with universal applications that transcend their nevertheless clear roles as memorials to the events themselves. One might cite more examples from the shorter prose genres, such as the essay. . . . Auschwitz, as a symbol for the death camps, undergoes transformations in the lyric, with reference to individual works by poets of widely differing cultural backgrounds, levels of social *engagement,* and aesthetic intent.

The roots of the development of the death-camp imagery go back further than the works alluded to by Steiner or by Adorno. The genesis of the imagery is found in the writings of poets who were involved with the events themselves, at the time the camps themselves were operating. Some of the poets were survivors, some were not. This is not a literature that is simply *engagé*: it is a lyric of total involvement, rather than of intellectual *engagement* as exemplified, to take an example from Sartre, by Zola's Dreyfus letter.

In *Voices of a People,* a study of the Yiddish folk song, Ruth Rubin devotes an entire chapter to the lyrics that arose during the Nazi period. The mere existence of such songs is significant: even in the face of such horror, the quest for poetic order proves as strong as the experience of literary fragmentation. (pp. 123-25)

By and large, the songs cited by Rubin fall into two groups, and the division is an important one. There are songs of defiance, sometimes military and physical, more often spiritual:

> Lomir zayn freylech un zogn zich vitsn,
> Mir veln noch hitlern shive noch zitsn.

> Let us be gay and tell jokes,
> We'll yet live to see Hitler dead.

A further example of this defiant tone is the "Es brent" ("It's burning") of Modche Gebirtig, who died in 1942 in the Cracow ghetto.

The second type of lyric to emerge from this period is more purely poetic, elegiac, descriptive of the situation as it was, with only occasional glances toward a future and with only occasional thought as to the reason for the suffering. Already in these descriptive songs appear some of the central images of the tradition as it is to continue. The trains, for example, are, predictably, a dominant motif from this early stage. For example,

> Lokomotiv, du shvartser, bizt zich geforn,
> Host kayn birkenau mich bald avekgefirt. . . .

> Black locomotive, you rode and rode,
> Till you brought me to Birkenau. . . .

> S'loyfn, s'yogn di mashinen
> Un es fayft der tsug. . . .

> Fast fly the wheels of the train
> And the engine whistle blows. . . .

> S'hobn di getos fun der provints
> Gegebn fir toyznt korbones,
> Un opgefirt hot men di zachn fun zey
> Tsurik in di zelbe vagones.

> The ghettos of the province
> Gave up four thousand martyrs,
> And their clothes were brought back
> In the same freight cars.

> Bashraybn kon es nit kayn feder,
> Vi es dreyen zich di reder,
> Men firt di yidn oyf kidesh-hashem,
> Kayn treblinke, kayn treblinke.

> No pen can ever describe

How the wheels go round and round.
As the Jews are being martyred,
Going, going to Treblinka.

There are various reasons for the emergence of this motif as such a central one, both historical and poetic—as a contextual symbol and as a rhythmic one—and these must be discussed in detail later.

Other motifs that will reappear are found in this early and frequently anonymous poetry. An interesting instance is the insistence on music as an accompaniment to the misery, a kind of introverted *danse macabre:*

> Shpilt, shpilt, strunes fun payn,
> Shpilt-zhe mir a yidishn nign.

> Play, play, strings of pain,
> Play me a Jewish tune.

This emphasis on creativity as a means of keeping the spirits up, which in itself can be seen as central to the entire concept of a poetry of Auschwitz, persists. It finds, perhaps, its defiant *reductio ad absurdum* in the title and the opening scenes of Gary's *Dance of Genghis Cohn.*

The line "Bashraybn kon es nit kayn feder" ("No pen can ever describe it") in the last of the four songs cited together above is of course an axiom here. As a poetical motif it represents the ultimate realization of the rhetorical "tongue cannot tell." The answer is a corresponding focus on small points, or on individual victims, because the larger issues are *too* large. The Yiddish poet H. Leivick (1888-1962), who was not himself in the camps but collected songs from survivors there after the war, has a poem called "Treblinka Grass Song," for example. This is related in part to the insistence on the train motif, as the attention is more frequently concentrated on the inanimate, rather than on the animate sufferings of the actual victims.

Many of the anonymous songs noted by Rubin are without doubt *ad hoc* productions arising from the varying circumstances. There is, however, a formalized Yiddish poetry even within the world of the Nazi persecutions. An intrinsically interesting example is the structured cycle *Ghetto Factory 76* of Rachmil Bryks, written in the Lodz ghetto in 1943/44 and discovered in manuscript after the war was over, when it was sent to the poet, by then in New York. Some of it was set to music by William Gunther. Although the bulk of the work is not relevant to the present context as such, the closing lines may be cited:

> Damf, damf!
> Gants batrib
> ayngehilt
> in giftikn damf
> s'damft gift-geshtank.

> Steam, steam!
> The whole place
> filled
> with poison-steam
> steaming poison-stink.

As a single example of the personally involved poet creating lyrics from and about his own experience of the era, we may take the work of the Vilna poet Abraham Sutzkever. Born in 1913 and now living in Israel, Sutzkever spent the period of Nazi occupation of Poland first in the Vilna ghetto, then in the Resistance. His experiences, transformed into lyrics, were published in collections such as that entitled *Yidishe gas (Jews' Lane)*. A poem not in this collection, however, may stand as the epitome of much of the imagery that persists far beyond the Vilna ghetto. His poem "A vogn shikh" ("A Freight Car of Shoes") was written in Vilna on 7 January 1943. The poem is in a simple ballad form, with an initial strophe that is repeated at the close of the poem. The poet hears the rhythm of the train wheels, a rhythm which continues metrically throughout the poem, and wonders what the train is carrying:

> Di reder yogn, yogn,
> vos bringen zay mit zikh?
> Zay bringen mir a vogn
> mit tsaplendike shikh.

> The wheels are pounding, pounding,
> what are they bringing?
> They are bringing me a freight-car
> full of jolting shoes.

The language ("di reder yogn . . . ") already calls to mind some of the folk poetry cited from Rubin's collection. The concentration is on small inanimate objects—shoes—in the inanimate train. The poet considers the individual shoes from the pile, seeing a bride's shoe, children's shoes (an early instance, then, of the motif that Steiner cites as commonplace in 1969), and eventually his mother's shoes, all being taken to Berlin. The reference to the mother's shoes in the last full verse may be cited as an example of the simplicity of the whole:

> kh'derken mayn mames shikh!
> Zi flegt zay bloyz oyf shabes
> arovftsien oyf zikh

> I recognize my mother's shoes!
> She only used to put them on
> on the Sabbath.

The question posed by the poet in the fifth strophe is, however, the most important:

> Ikh darf nit fregn vemes,
> nor s'tut in harts a ris:
> o, zogt mir, shikh, dem emes,
> vu zenen zay, di fis?

> There is no one I can ask,
> but it pains me in my heart:
> o shoes, tell me the truth,
> where are they, the feet?

The first line states the rhetorical topos of impossibility: there is quite literally no one left to reply, and asking the shoes is ironic. The inanimate objects are all that is left. There are large numbers of these shoes, but through them we see individual people: the bride, the lady, the mother. Only the children's shoes are in the plural.

The train is there in fact and in the rhythm ("vuhin, vuhin, vuhin," "where to, where to, where to"), and the sound is taken up by the clicking of the shoes together. The eternal running of the wheels is also echoed in the repeat of the initial strophe. At the same time, this repeat might also serve to indicate a general inevitability, an eternal return of suffering, particularly in a Jewish context, but also in general. The technique is a familiar one in the ballad.

The same focus on small things is found elsewhere in Sutzkever's poetry, although not all of his work, even the ghetto poems, is purely elegiac. Sometimes there is an optimistic emphasis on the survivors, even on the orphans, and this is at its clearest in his later poems in Israel. In his earlier work there is also sometimes a defiant note, as in a well-known poem, "Di blayene platn fun roms drukeray" ("The Lead Plates of the Rome Press"), which celebrates the occasion when the lead plates from which the Vilna editions of the Talmud had been printed were melted into bullets by the partisans.

One final comment might be made about "A vogn shikh." There is here perhaps an echo of the *danse macabre* motif; the piles of shoes click together in the rhythm of the train, it is true, but they suggest to the poet a dance:

> di shikh—a fule kupe,
> vi mentshen in a tants.
> the shoes—a full car-load,
> like the people in a dance.

This in its turn links with the bride's shoes and the wedding/holiday motif connected with them by the poet.

What remains, however, is the *fact* of the poem. Although totally involved, Sutzkever's verse is not fragmented in any sense, certainly not "damaged beyond creative repair." One might see elements of this fragmentation in Bryk's *Ghetto Factory 76,* but it is not there in Sutzkever, any more than it is there in the folk songs cited by Rubin. Catastrophe may indeed also lead to an *increased* emphasis on form, as Sutzkever's use of the ballad, surely the least fragmented of poetic forms, offers proof that poetic transformation may still play a normative role even in the face of such intense suffering. Here the language and the form are as simple as each other, and there is no question of cynicism of betrayal. The "enormity of the facts" has not "stomped the life out of the language" [Steiner].

With the consideration of poems by writers such as Sutzkever, the biographical approach is valid, and the fact that these poems are written in Yiddish, the language of the doomed East European Jews, is itself important. There is, however, a poetry of Auschwitz in other languages, poems written by those who escaped the holocaust—poems especially in German, the other language that is of particular relevance to the subject matter. In his study of postwar German poetry [*German Poetry, 1944-1948*], Leonard Forster refers not only to the lyrics that arose from the events of the war itself (the reflection, for example, of the saturation bombing of German cities in the lyrics of Paula von Preradović and others) but also to "the voices . . . of men and women of German speech for whom the catastrophe in their lives was not the series of disasters between Stalingrad and the Rhine crossings, but had begun ten years earlier with the passing of the Nürnberg Decrees and culminated in the horrors of Auschwitz and Theresienstadt."

Forster refers to a number of poets, Jews and non-Jews, and discovers that there is a genre of "KZ-Lyrik" ("con-

centration-camp lyrics"). Again the titles strike one: "Kupfer-Koberwitz, *Gedichte aus Dachau* [*Poems from Dachau*] (Stuttgart, n.d.)" is a case in point. Of the names mentioned by Forster—Kurt Oser, Henri Sternberg, Albrecht Haushofer—it is the name of Nelly Sachs that has remained most prominent.

Nelly Sachs was also, although less directly, involved in the era. She escaped from Germany to Sweden in 1940 at the age of 48, but her Auschwitz poems were written in Sweden while the war was still on and the camps still in operation. The poems are mainly collected under the title *In den Wohnungen des Todes* (*In the Habitations of Death*) and may be linked with *Eli,* her mystery play, written at the same time. The central symbol of the camps is again an inanimate object, this time one closer to the horror: it is the chimney rather than the trains, the last stage of the "final solution" rather than the first. Nelly Sachs links this dominant image with the triad smoke/dust/ash, the components of which become familiar in later poetry. The opening poem of the collection in question begins:

> O die Schornsteine
> Auf den sinnreich erdachten Wohnungen des
>   Todes,
> Als Israels Leib zog aufgelöst in Rauch
> Durch die Luft. . . .
>
> O the chimneys
> On the ingeniously devised habitations of death
> When Israel's body drifted as smoke
> Through the air. . . .

The ash and the smoke become dominant in their own right later in the collection. Sometimes the allusions are concealed, as in "Mit dem aschgrau ziehenden Horizont der Angst" ("With the ash-grey receding horizon of fear"). Sometimes they are quite plain, as in "da du in Asche gefallen" ("where you turned to ashes") or "Als eure Formen zu Asche versanken" ("When your forms turned to ashes").

Several of the points raised in these brief citations parallel the Yiddish poetry. The technology of the holocaust is one of its striking features, and Rubin cites a Yiddish poem that alludes to this in ironic terms: . . .

> In tsvantsigstn yorhundert di tsivilizatsie iz
>   groys,
> Di technik dergreycht hot ir tsil:
> A roshe hitler gekumen iz tsu der macht—
> Er tut mit di yidn vos er vil.
>
> Farbrenen in treblinke di yidn mit gaz—
>
> In the twentieth century civilisation is great,
> Technical progress has achieved its goal:
> A tyrant Hitler came to power—
> And does with the Jews as he pleases.
>
> He burns the Jews in Treblinka with gas—

There is also a reference to the ash, to cite one of many, in a concrete sense in a Yiddish poem written much later than these poems of Nelly Sachs. For Itsik Manger (1901-1969) in his brief "Maidanek," the ash is real; it is not concealed in a compound adjective, as it is in the example

Drawings by an unknown prisoner of Dachau concentration camp; given by survivors to Dr. Marcus J. Smith, the first American Army physician to enter the camp after its liberation.

from Nelly Sachs ("aschgrau") and as it frequently is in the work of postwar poets. Rather, Manger writes:

> Der alter Elihu ha-nevi
> Glet di hoyfns ash. . . .
>
> The old man, the prophet Elijah
> Smooths the pile of ashes. . . .

Nelly Sachs pays attention too to the natural surroundings, to the watching stones, for example, recalling the grass at Treblinka.

Abraham Sutzkever's personal involvement in "A vogn shikh" is effected at the sight of his mother's shoes. Nelly Sachs adopts the same technique but involves herself more intensely, taking on the role in one of her poems of a dead child. Here the central figure is a single victim: the enormity of the slaughter is hinted at only in the series of choruses in the collection—choruses of shadows, of orphans.

The imagery of the chimneys not only appears in her poems but also dominates Nelly Sach's play *Eli*. In the latter, we encounter an attitude that is not entirely elegiac, just as we did with Sutzkever. The note of hope is more metaphysical than it is in the Yiddish poet, although it is

there with Sutzkever, too. In *Eli*, the chimney is equated with the camp commandant, but from the chimney arises the sound of the *sh'ma:*

> Hör O Israel—
> Er unser Gott—
> Er, der Eine—
>
> Hear, O Israel—
> He, our God—
> He, the One—

The scene in question begins with the same image as the first poem of the *Habitations of Death,* with the smoke of Israel's bodies, now also Israel's freedom. The last point links most coherently with Sutzkever. But the dominance here is not of the chimney but of the *sh'ma,* which perhaps provides a *raison d'être* for the poetry as a whole. It is the acceptance of a divine plan, a perception of the metaphysical which would be, in Christian terms, not an Augustinian teleology, mancentered and ominiscient, but rather an uncomprehending respect for providence.

Historically one stage further from the camps themselves is the work of Paul Celan (1920-1970), again a Jew and again writing in German. Much critical attention has been paid to his "Todesfuge" ("Fugue of Death"), to which Steiner also refers. The poem appeared in 1952. It is, therefore, a poem written with hindsight, a product of the post-Auschwitz situation, although Celan was of course involved in that era. In language "Todesfuge" shows at first sight some of the fragmentation that sometimes comes as a corollary of the situation, but this fragmentation is by no means as dominant as it appears.

The first sign of the fragmentation of language is the lack here of formal punctuation. This, however, may perhaps be linked with already familiar motifs. The meter of the work has been the subject of debate, and pertinent distinctions have been drawn between the natural rhythm of the poem and formal prosodic analysis. In formal terms, the judgment of L. L. Duroche, that the meter is basically amphibrachic and not dactylic, is certainly correct; but what is far more important is the inexorable quality of the rhythm as such, its "irresistible forward movement" [*Modern Language Notes*, 1967]. We may hear in this the rhythm of the trains to the camps as clearly as, or even more clearly than, we hear it in Sutzkever's ballad meter.

Celan's rhythms are not consistent, although syntactically they might have been made to be regular. This irregularity contributes greatly toward the effect of the rhythm of a train, giving a periodicity that recalls the varying measures between the gaps in the rails. This periodicity was exploited in a German prose poem by Wolfgang Borchert (who died in 1947), with which Celan may have been familiar. Borchert's "Eisenbahnen, nachmittags und nachts" ("Railroads, in the Afternoon and at Night") turns varying train rhythms into words, and it is the variation that we can hear in Celan's poem. Thus, the lines

> Ein Mann wohnt im Haus und speilt mit den
> Schlangen der schreibt
> der schreibt wenn es dunkelt nach Deutschland
> dein goldenes Haar Margarete
> Dein aschenes Haar Sulamith wir schaufeln ein
> Grab in den Lüften da liegt man nicht eng

> A man's in the house he plays with the serpents
> he writes
> he writes home to Germany evenings the gold of
> your hair Margarete
> Your ash-colored hair Shulamite we're digging
> a grave in the air where there's plenty of room

are certainly amphibrachic but contain occasional and marked metrical ellipses, which are particularly apparent when they fall at the end of a line, since the lines frequently run on. This use of ellipsis makes for a definite pause of greater or lesser intensity (that after "Haus," for example, is less strong than that after "Sulamith," which is the end of a syntactic grouping). The placing of the pauses is careful. Syntactically, "im Haus" might have been *im Hause,* which would have provided an extra and metrically regulating unstressed syllable. Conversely, the plural of *Luft* ("in den Lüften") is unusual, but the syllable is required in this case.

Contextually, the poem forms part of what may by now be regarded as a tradition, although some of the metaphors here are unusual. The ash recurs, this time in the hair of the Shulamite, rather than in concrete form. The

making of graves in the air recalls Nelly Sachs, and it links with the ash motif, stressing the finality of the situation rather than the horror of its present.

Again the death scenes themselves are not described. There is in the lyric no counterpart to the actuality of the horror found in other genres—in the essay, for example, written well after the events, by Itsik Manger, in which the death camps are viewed in terms of a novel by Kafka:

> Iberzets kafkas "shlos" oyf daytsher virklekh-
> kayt un du host kontsentratsielager, gaz-kamern
> un daytshe oygn vos kukn durkh shaybelekh.
> Zay kukn tsu dikh, zay zeen dikh, zay vern
> greser, du otemst arayn in zikh di gazn, du
> shtikst zikh. . . . Du vilst a geshray ton. . . .
> Nor du knost nisht. Tsu shpet. . . .

> Translate Kafka's *Castle* into German reality
> and you get the concentration camps and the gas
> chambers, and German eyes looking at you
> through the peepholes. They look at you, see
> you, grow bigger, you breathe in the gasses, you
> choke. . . . You want to scream. . . . But you
> cannot. Too late. . . .

Another major motif in Celan's poem that remains a constant is that of the *danse macabre,* which is here given an even more ironic twist. The Jews, dying in the camps, play at their own funeral. The German overseer commands:. . . .

> . . . stecht tiefer ins Erdrich ihr einen ihr and-
> ern singet und spielt
> er greift nach dem Eisen im Gurt er schwingts
> seine Augen sind blau
> stecht tiefer die Spaten ihr einen ihr andern
> spielt weiter zum Tanz auf. . . .

> [He shouts] go deeper cut into the earth there
> you men you others play up now and sing
> He goes for the club at his side he swings it his
> eyes they are blue
> the spades must cut deeper you men there the
> rest of you play for the dance now. . . .

Duroche links this motif with Psalm 137:1-4 as well as with the actual events in the camps. There is, however, no verbal connection and little close connection of content between the psalm and these lines. What seems more likely is the suggestion made recently by Leonard Forster that the dance motif here links with Heine's "Sklavenschiff" ("Slave Ship"), a poem that Celan may well have known, in which slaves are forced to dance and play to keep alive, thus ensuring a profit for their owner.

That these things did happen is, of course, more valid than possible literary sources. But if Heine was a source, even an indirect one, rather than the psalmist, then the poem is more pessimistic than Duroche would admit. The final lines,

> dein goldenes Haar Margarete
> dein aschenes Haar Sulamith

> the gold of your hair Margarete
> your ash-colored hair Shulamite,

might then be read as the stopping of the train, a finality which the ashen hair of the Shulamite underlines, rather than as some sort of redemption through the *Ewig-Weibliche*. In any event, the dance motif is a despairing version of the playing-for-encouragement in some of the ghetto songs and a more poignant live variation on the macabre dance of Sutzkever's shoes.

Pessimistic or not, "Todesfuge" is still an expression by an involved survivor of the experience transformed into poetic terms. The symbolism of the final outcome—here the ashen hair of the Shulamite—is a stage removed from the reality of Sutzkever's shoes. In other respects, however, Celan's feeling of personal involvement is stronger than that of the Yiddish poet in this poem, closer to that of Nelly Sachs in her assumption of the role of the dead child. The entire poem is written from *within* the situation: . . .

> Schwarze Milch der Frühe wir trinken sie
>   abends
> wir trinken sie mittages und morgens wir trinken
>   sie nachts
> wir trinken und trinken. . . .

> Black milk of the morning we drink it at evening
> we drink it at midday and early we drink it at
>   night
> we drink it and drink it. . . .

The anaphoric "wir" expresses perhaps a Jewish identity of suffering (implied too by Nelly Sachs) even though the events as such are now past. That Jewish poets should feel this kind of involvement and express it in this fashion is of course understandable, but this identification with the victims, this role, becomes a familiar framework for the use of the motifs later.

Celan's language is fragmented to an extent. But this is by no means as apparent as it is in the writings of the German expressionists after World War I. One need but glance at a poem by August Stramm, by Yvan Goll, or later at some of the more extravagant offerings of Dadaism and the school of the Absurd to realize that Celan's is a far more conservative clinging to language than might be expected. The rhythm gives a tight formality to his poem, and the title itself, implying the most rigid of musical forms, also imposes a rigidity; this is taken up in the fugal repetitions within the work (which again, incidentally, echo Borchert) and perhaps symbolizes again the eternal repetition of suffering.

Yevgeny Yevtushenko's "Babi Yar" is as well known internationally as Celan's "Todesfuge"—possibly better known, in view of the use made of it by Shostakovich in the Thirteenth Symphony. There are several translations. The poem, which was written in 1962, commemorates the killing of tens of thousands of Jews at Babi Yar, a ravine near Kiev in the Ukraine, in September 1941. The incident was, as it happens, first dealt with by the Soviet Yiddish writer Itsik Kipnis in 1944, and more recently it has been the subject of a controversial "documentary novel" by Anatoly Kuznetsov. The mass murder here is not exactly like that of the killings in the camps, although the themes are closely linked. The standpoint of the poem, however, is also different from those encountered so far, for the event has become history. Yevtushenko is erecting a monument; his poem has as its starting point the fact that there is no memorial over Babi Yar.

Now, all historical writing rests on variable determinants of the present of the history—or historical poem. "Historical inquiry is an affair (1) of selection and arrangement, and (2) is controlled by the dominant problems and conceptions of the culture of the period in which it was written" [John Dewey, *Logic: The Theory of Inquiry*]. The question of historical standpoint, further, becomes more complex the closer we come to our own time. There is now, for example, something that approaches a consensus of opinion on the verifiable facts of the battle of Roncesvalles in 1778 although contemporary comments varied—the Arab chronicles have little enough in common with the *Chanson de Roland*. But opinion and cultural-social standpoints will differ more plainly with more recent events, even when there is a certain amount of historical distance already involved. Considerations of this sort play a role in determining the development of the death-camp imagery in the lyric.

Yevtushenko's poem is *engagé* in two senses. His poem is a memorial, but it also combines an attack on anti-Semitism in general with elements of Soviet nationalism. As far as the latter point is concerned, "Babi Yar" is a means to an end. Yevtushenko, while sincerely *engagé*, is not *involved* in the same way as Sutzkever, Sachs, or Celan. He is not a Jew: indeed, part of the point of the work rests upon this fact. The point is, further, made explicit, and this poetical disclaimer recurs in other non-Jewish poetry on the theme. The tradition, then, passes from *Erlebnisdichtung* to a more purely intellectual *Gedankenlyrik*.

Some of the techniques of the poem are familiar, however. Even though many thousands died at Babi Yar, there are only one or two references to the extent of the killing, such as where the poet sees himself standing "nad tisyachami tisyach pogrebennikh" ("over the thousands and thousands buried"). For the most part, Yevtushenko follows the patterns noted so far, electing to focus on a few (archetypal) individuals. In this case, the examples cover the whole history of Jewish suffering rather than only the incident at Babi Yar, however. Yevtushenko speaks then of the "mal'chik v Belostoke" (the "boy in Bialystok") and of Anne Frank, the best-known epitome of the incomprehensible figure of six million.

Again the moment and method of death plays no part. There is a certain amount of graphic narrative of past Jewish oppressions, but apart from the adjective "rasstrelyanniy" ("shot down") applied to the victims at Babi Yar, the fact that the events are over is in the foreground: "Nad Babim Yarom shelest dikikh trav" ("The rustle of wild grasses over Babi Yar"). This echoes again the grasses at Treblinka. But Leivick's grass was too close to the event and sought a solution, crying for help. For Yevtushenko the grass has become a comment in itself. Nature judges (as, implicitly, do the stones in Nelly Sachs's choruses):

> "Derev'ya smotryat grozno,
>   po-sudeyski. . . .

> The trees watch sternly,
> in the guise of judges. . . .

One link between the Jewish poems of involvement and Yevtushenko's poem is the question of poetic identification with the victims. The Russian poet, like Celan, uses the device of anaphora in this context, but he replaces the first person plural with the first person singular. This is not a corporate identity (nor even a feeling of collective responsibility proper) but a personal association that is somewhat tentative. The identification cannot be as total as Celan's was. The repeated phrase is "mne kazhetsya" ("it seems to me")

> Mne kazhetsya seychas—
> ya yudey. . . .

> Now it seems to me—
> that I'm a Judaean. . . .

> Mne kazhetsya, chto Dreyfus—
> eto ya.

> It seems that Dreyfus—
> that is who I am.

> Mne kazhetsya—
> ya mal'chik v Belostoke.

> It seems to me—
> that I'm a boy in Bialystok.

> Mne kazhetsya—
> ya—eto Anna Frank.

> It seems to me—
> that I am Anne Frank.

This changes to a positive assumption of the role when the poet turns to the events at Babi Yar:. . . .

> Ya—
> kazhdiy zdes' rasstrelyanniy starik.
> Ya—
> kazhidy zdes' rasstrelyanniy rebyonok.

> I—
> am each one of the old men gunned down here.
> I—
> am each one of the boys gunned down here.

Even in the earlier, distanced passages, however, the adoption of the role is clear after the initial "It seems." This is especially true of the passage dealing with the boy in Bialystok, who sees his mother beaten in the name of Russia. The emotional appeal is that of Sutzkever's reference to his mother's shoes, with the difference that Yevtushenko has to make another step, has to visualize himself in the role and then imagine his mother. He also has to visualize his own people as the perpetrators of the crime.

Metrical questions do not concern us here. There are no trains, for example, and the context is somewhat different. The poem is, however, regular in rhythm and rhyme. There is again no fragmentation. (Yevtushenko is of course setting up a monument, which demands some technical formality.)

Yevtushenko's *engagement* presents certain problems. Where does the emphasis fall? Sutzkever, Sachs, and Celan write *engagé* lyrics made so by the poets' very exis-

tence, *involved* lyrics, but Yevtushenko makes explicit two points. In the simplest terms, he is as much "for" Russia as he is "against" anti-Semitism and the forces that gave rise to Babi Yar and then left the site unmarked. This double *engagement* becomes clear at the end of the poem. The poet expressly disclaims any Jewish blood, but he *is* a Russian, and it is Russia that concludes the poem. The work, then, is essentially concerned with the reaction of the Russianness in Yevtushenko to the events at Babi Yar. In his last lines, Yevtushenko shows perhaps an awareness of the same scruples that Steiner voices about the validity of Sylvia Plath's poetic identification with the victims. Yevtushenko's voiced awareness of the point—as well as his *engagement*—justifies his playing of the role, however, and it is interesting that the Russian poet should show some consciousness of this fictional involvement, whether it is accepted as valid or not:

> Evreyskoy krovi net v krovi moey.
> No nenavisten zloboy zaskoryzloy
> ya vsem antisemitam,
> kak evrey.
> I potomu—
> ya nastoyashchiy russkiy!

> There is no Jewish blood in my blood.
> But I am hated with fierce passion
> by all anti-Semites
> as if a Jew.
> And for that reason—
> I am a real Russian!

In some respects, this kind of *engagement* (even ignoring the present state of Soviet-Jewish relations) might be felt to be more worthy of Steiner's objections than the personal poetry of Sylvia Plath. One might compare with it other *engagé* poems that make use of the tragic metaphors of the camps in an even more clearly political context, shorn, often, even of the memorial function noted by Adorno. One might adduce not only lyric examples but also more straightforward political essays.

Several examples are afforded by the poetically very uneven but politically very interesting volume of verse published in 1957 as a memorial to the executed Rosenbergs. The poems involved are by and large angry rather than elegiac:

> Ilse Koch lives
> But Ethel Rosenberg must die. . . .

The connection with the Auschwitz imagery is sometimes crude, even offensive:

> "What was the color of the smoke
> From Ethel Rosenberg's head?"
>
> . . . . .
> It was exactly the same color
> As the smoke that rose
> Over the crematoria
> In Buchenwald, Dachau.

Less than a decade after Nelly Sachs's poems were published, the smoke has taken on a new role.

That the Rosenbergs were themselves Jews and that their execution was on a Saturday provided ample opportunity for the link. The volume did, in fact, contain a large number of translations from the Yiddish and poems by Jewish writers. It is interesting to note, however, that the same images have been used more recently in discussion of the political situation of Blacks in the United States, rather than Jews. A recent example was provided by an essay in the *New York Review of Books,* in which James Baldwin referred to Black militants in terms of the victims of the Nazi camps. His work provoked an angry response from some quarters, including an "Open Letter to James Baldwin" from Shlomo Katz, editor of the Jewish periodical *Midstream.* Katz's essay poses what is essentially Steiner's question. What right has James Baldwin to assume, even vicariously, this "death-rig"?

The arguments as such, which continued at various levels in a wide range of printed sources, are not relevant to the present study, nor is it the task of an outsider to comment on the relative extents of historical suffering. But it is significant that there was a precedent for the use of the Auschwitz imagery in a political context—a precedent in the Rosenberg poems, even if the Rosenberg case and that described by Baldwin are by no means the same. An ironic comment on the Baldwin-Katz controversy itself is that the first poem in the Rosenberg volume was contributed by W. E. B. DuBois and contains the lines:

> To us shriek five thousand blacks
> Lynched without trial
> And hundred thousands mobbed
> The millions dead in useless war.

In spite of the controversy (and let it be admitted that in prose the use of the imagery is all too often less than appropriate, although in some of these cases the sincerity of the user must be considered), there are of course similarities between Black and Jewish history that lead to the cultural overlap of images. The difference is primarily that the Hitlerian oppression was closer in time, more concentrated, and more horrifyingly technological than slavery. The slave ships have already come to be regarded—one suspects even by many modern Black writers—in much the same historical light as, say, the terrible crusade against the Albigensians. It is predictable that modern Black poetry should turn to the Auschwitz imagery as fresher than a set of images based on the years of slavery. Thus Gwendolyn Brooks, in "Loam Norton," a poem which parodies Psalm 23, seems to link the Jewish and the Black experience in general terms. After a reference to "Belsen and Dachau," she continues:

> The Lord was their shepherd
> Yet did they want.
> Joyfully would they have lain in jungles or pastures,
> walked beside waters. Their gaunt
> souls were not restored, their souls were banished.
> In the shadow valley
> They feared the evil, whether with or without God.
> They were comforted by no Rod,
> no Staff, but flayed by, O besieged by, shot aplenty.
> The prepared table was the rot or curd of the day.

> Annointings were of lice. . . .

"Loam Norton" is interesting further for the fact that it is essentially elegiac, rather than militant.

Sylvia Plath, who wrote her last poems shortly after the appearance of Yevtushenko's "Babi Yar," represents a final stage of development of the Auschwitz imagery, although her work predates much of the Black poetry mentioned above. Her poetry is without any *engagement,* appropriate or not, and there is no personal justification for her use of the imagery. It is simply the logical aesthetic step into the pure image. The only really surprising feature is the relatively short time in which this step has been accomplished.

It is difficult to separate Sylvia Plath's poetry from her biography—this has become a topos of Plath criticism. It is, however, significant that this kind of biographical positivism has played a part in the evaluations of many of the poems that employ the death-camp imagery, and we are perhaps as justified in looking at Sylvia Plath's own sufferings as a touchstone for her sincerity and lack of cynicism as we are in discussing the background of Abraham Sutzkever as an introduction to his work.

The poem that is most relevant here is the one that has received the bulk of critical attention, "Daddy." Studies of the poem have pointed out, for example, the regularity of its rhythms, nursery rhyme in essence but recalling also the (irregular) beat of the train wheels heard in Celan's "Todesfuge." There are further examples of the same point in other poems from the *Ariel* collection, such as "Getting There," but in "Daddy" Sylvia Plath overtly refers to

> An engine, an engine
> Chuffing me off like a Jew,
> A Jew to Dachau, Auschwitz, Belsen.

The lines merit close consideration: the double meaning of "chuffing me off" (echoing the Shakesperian "shuffling off"?) calls to mind the smoke/air motifs in Sachs and Celan, although the camps have not yet been reached, as it were.

The question of poetic identification is also of concern here. As in Yevtushenko's poem, this identification is tentative, a gradual assumption of the role. The lines cited above continue, "I begin to talk like a Jew." And after the simile, "I think I may well be a Jew." This is then echoed in the next strophe, which ends "I may be a bit of a Jew" and also contains a rare allusion to those other victims of the camps, the Gypsies.

Other poems in the *Ariel* collection take the identification further. In the very personal "Lady Lazarus," from which Steiner takes the title of one of his own essays ("Dying is an Art"), we encounter images, in the first person, of the order of:

> A sort of walking miracle, my skin
> Bright as a Nazi lampshade,
> My right foot
>
> A paperweight
> My face a featureless, fine

Jew linen.

Then, later in the same poem:

> I am your opus,
> I am your valuable,
> The pure gold baby
>
> That melts to a shriek.
> I turn and burn.

In some ways, Sylvia Plath comes closer to the horror, even though not directly caught up in it historically, than many of the more involved poets. It is interesting too that she uses the same evocative words out of context: the ash, for example, is prominent at the end of "Lady Lazarus." Here, however, the positive note struck by Nelly Sachs as the *sh'ma* rises above the smoke becomes pessimistic in the personal context. From the ash, from the suffering, the poet will rise again but be doomed implicitly, like Lazarus, to the pain of dying once again in other circumstances:

> Out of the ash
> I rise with my red hair
> And I eat men like air.

Although the reference to the red hair is personal, there is perhaps a conscious echo of Celan's "Todesfuge" here in the combination ash/hair/air.

For the most part, Sylvia Plath concentrates on the inanimate remainders of the suffering rather than the actuality (apart from lines like "I turn and burn"), referring not to the shoes, but to

> A cake of soap,
> A wedding ring,
> A gold filling. . . .

Still, she does imbue these with a sense of horror when the gold "melts to a shriek," a line noted for its effectiveness by Steiner, or in the references to the grisly pastimes of Ilse Koch, as much an antitype as Anne Frank is a type.

Some conclusions may perhaps be drawn about the nature of death-camp imagery in the lyric. The various poets differ in standpoint, but the motifs themselves remain similar. Some of the motifs are obvious, and primary among them is that of the sound and motion of the trains. This comes about for various reasons: the trains are, in the first instance, what those who avoided the camps would recall. Further, the trains symbolize the inevitability of the mechanized journey to death. The train is the infernal machine of tragedy made literal. Its inhuman necessity might of course be found with similar connotations of pathos elsewhere in literature, but here it reaches horrible proportions. Except perhaps in the world of the popular song, trains are most frequently associated with departure, sometimes into the unknown. One thinks of forms as disparate as the blues and some of the novels and short stories of Heinrich Böll.

The question of rhythm is important here, and the forceful beat of the train may well act as a counter to the fragmentation of language. It might perhaps be argued that any regular or fairly regular rhythm could suggest a train, but, most of the cases adduced make overt reference to the trains. It is worth noting, furthermore, that a train can be evoked in the lyric without the rhythm and the forward motion that is so much a part of the death-camp imagery. G. Guder cites in a recent study of "Industrie-Lyrik" in Germany the lines by Josef Büscher:

> Du hast kein Ziel.
> Längst sind die Weichen gestellt.
> Du hast keine Wahl.
> Schienenzwang.
>
> You have no goal.
> The points were set long ago.
> You have no choice.
> Predetermined rails.

Guder points out how the (untranslatable) last word of the German text "conjures up the criss-cross complex of diverging railway lines." The difference between this sort of imagery and the Auschwitz imagery we have been discussing is the intellectual distance between the train wheels in a boogie bass and those in Honneger's *Pacific 231*.

The journey to the camps, then, is a theme. So too is what is left after the killings: the ash, the smoke, the shoes. We are not shown the human struggle with catastrophe, for it would be impossible to give any impression of the numbers. One tragic central figure is possible, we can accompany Mary Stuart practically to the block, but the numbers are overwhelming here. Only in some prose and drama is there any approach to individual or collective fates. Hochhuth's *Deputy* shows some individual figures in the camps (although the central figure, Father Riccardo, is of course not a Jew), and the techniques of Erwin Piscator, using documentary film as a background, give some idea of the real events.

But the ash has become the symbol, not the gas. When individuals are mentioned, then they are archetypal: Anne Frank is the chief example, the difficulty with this sort of focus on one figure being that the others like Anne Frank may be forgotten through concentration on the one case. Sachs and Yevtushenko do make some allusion to the numbers involved, but mostly the mere names of the camps are evocation enough. There are only occasional divergences from this pattern, as when another Soviet-Yiddish poet, Isaac Katzenelson writes of

> . . .Jews! Jews! Jews! Numberless and more—
> Three hundred fifty thousand Jews of Warsaw,
>   herded for massacres;
> The old ones shot down on the town cemetery,
>   all others led away
> To the Treblinkas. And Milla Street is crowded
>   with freight-cars.

The danger is, of course, that the numbers might become even more incomprehensible within the creative confines of the lyric.

The question of whether genocide is ever a proper theme for artistic creativity is relevant of itself, and one answer is that of Adorno: the memorial function. In fact, the Nazi extermination of the Jews is rare as a literary theme of this nature. Other horrors can be recounted, but few have given rise to similar traditions, not even Hiroshima. There are some literary treatments of earlier genocides, although they are rarely lyric: Peter Shaffer's *Royal Hunt of the Sun* or, in the eighteenth century, Kotzebue's *Die Spanier in Peru* are concerned with the systematic murder of the Aztecs by the conquistadores, but as far as the lyric is concerned, Heine's satirical *Vitzliputzli* is a rare handling of the theme. Individual novels come to mind—Zoe Oldenbourg's medieval novels, Franz Werfel's *Vierzig Tage des Musa Dagh,* some recent works dealing with the massacres of the North American Indians—but again none is really part of a tradition, tragic though they may be.

Catastrophic wars generate lyrical outcries: the Thirty Years' War (Gryphius) and World War I (Stramm, Sassoon, Owen) are examples. To return to the Black experience, the slower miseries of slavery have found some expression in verse, beginning with the very mannered poetry of slaves and their descendants, such as Phyllis Wheatley (ca. 1753-1784), George Moses Horton (1797-1883) or Paul Dunbar (1872-1906). . . .One might also cite the spiritual, such as "Nobody Knows the Trouble I've Seen." But more recent Black poetry is militant rather than elegiac. (pp. 125-44)

There are elegiac poems identifying with the Black past, such as Leslie M. Collins' "Soliloqui,"

> My sorrow knows no pattern, no end
> As I hang from a Georgia pine, flogged and
>   lynched,
> Alone . . .

or less directly in the late Melvin B. Tolson's "Dark Symphony,"

> Black slaves singing *One More River to Cross*
> In the torture tombs of slave-ships. . . .

But these are a minority. Nor has the slave ship become a symbol *outside* Black poetry, certainly not with any sense of identification. Heine's "Sklavenschiff" has been mentioned, but Heine does not involve himself, keeping rather his satirical distance. Indeed, the poetic identification, the adoption of the role of victim, is generally uncommon, implying as it perhaps does a quasi-Franciscan assumption of stigmata.

Why, then, does it happen with the Jewish fate under the Nazis? That the actual roots of the tradition are Yiddish and Jewish is the answer, perhaps—giving rise to a simple Goethean catharsis in literature, the awareness that

> . . . wenn der Mensch in seiner Qual
>   verstummt
> Gab mir ein Gott zu sagen, wie ich leide.

> . . . When man grows silent in the depths of
>   pain,
> A God let me transform pain into words.

It is less easy to decide whether the assumption of the role when one has no "right" to do so is acceptable or not. One may well be concerned—as Shlomo Katz was in his argument with James Baldwin—with the devaluation of the suffering. One must of course guard against this, against uses that are deliberately cynical or merely careless, more than against those that are sincere, if perhaps unjustified. The fears of Enzensberger and Adorno about cynicism have in fact become a theme in modern lyric in their own right, interestingly enough, in Germany. Hochhuth's *Dep-*

uty is a dramatic example of a German attempting to come to terms with the horrors, but there are actual references to cynicism in the lyric.

Two examples may be cited from a collection of lyrics published in 1966 and comprising lyrics by German-speaking poets most of whom were born during or after the war. Thus, Andreas Reimann, born in 1946 and now living in the German Democratic Republic, can refer in his formally impressive "Elegie in Buchenwald" to the fact that

> Da dröhnen die autotüren
> schon wie zynismensalut.

> The car doors make a noise there
> that is already like a cynical salvo.

The very preservation of Buchenwald has lost meaning, and the mechanical aspects of the horror have turned into museum pieces as remote as medieval torture chambers:

> Noch unter der galgenfeste,
> dem knarrenden spinnenskelett,
> lagern gefühllos die gäste.

> And still under the gallows, under
> the rattling spidery skeleton,
> the guests wait, without feelings.

Their hearts are "immun gegen leiden" ("immune to suffering") and once again, only nature has the memory: the wind weeps "aschtränen" ("tears of ash"), a verbal and contextual echo of the earlier poems, particularly those in German by Sachs and Celan.

The same cynicism is criticized in Ulrich Otto Berger's (b. 1941) "Auschwitz." The short poem opens with the statement:

> Der Volksmund weiss zu erzählen:
> Ein gebranntes Kind scheut das Feuer.

> From the mouth of the people comes the com-
>   ment:
> A burnt child fears the fire.

The choice of the proverb links with the ash/fire motif once again, but here the fire is in a hearth, a supposedly comforting symbol, which gradually turns into the imagery of the camps:

> Kinder und Kindeskinder
> machten Abzählreime draus
> und Rauchzeilen,
> damit schneller wurde zu deutscher Erde,
> was nicht deutsche Asche sein durfte.

> Children and their children's children
> make counting-out rhymes out of it
> and lines of smoke,
> to turn more quickly into German earth
> what was not allowed to be German ashes.

The final *sententia* makes the point clear with a circular return to the opening lines:

> Der Volksmund weiss heute zu erzählen
> mehr als einen Witz über Auschwitz.

> From the mouth of the people nowadays
> comes more than one joke about Auschwitz.

The poems by Reimann and Berger may be seen as part of the development in an *engagé* sense, good examples of the lyric used as a conscious memorial to the events. They may, further, give a clue to the reasons behind the transformations that the idea of the holocaust has undergone. Although these two writers feel a connection with the Hitlerian period, they are at some distance from it, and time and distance seem to be the main transforming factors. The distance across the Atlantic appears to have played a great role. Steiner stresses Sylvia Plath's personal distance from the actual events, and it is through poets like her that the idea of Auschwitz may become a literary (and even lyric) tradition, a metaphor that may today still suggest insensitivity.

There is no reason, however, why the assumption of the "death-rig" should not be honorable, even when there is no memorial intended. Sylvia Plath uses the imagery to underline her own suffering, but a symbol must always carry a concrete meaning of its own. The initial cognitive response provoked by Sylvia Plath's use of Auschwitz imagery serves as a memorial in its own right. One must not cross the borderline between cynicism and sincerity; but if there are jokes about Auschwitz in the *Volksmund,* the common currency, there are none in the lyric, certainly not in the lyric of Sylvia Plath. The notion of the "great tragic metaphor" is Steiner's, and it is in effect an answer to his own questions about the Auschwitz imagery in the lyric. (pp. 144-46)

> *Brian Murdoch, "Transformations of the Holocaust: Auschwitz in Modern Lyric Poetry," in* Comparative Literature Studies, *Vol. XI, No. 2, June, 1974, pp. 123-50.*

Frieda W. Aaron

[*In the following essay, Aaron surveys the major themes of the poetry written by Holocaust victims.*]

An inherent human need is to bring order to chaos, to render the incomprehensible intelligible; hence the primordial mythopoeic compulsion. In the three decades since the Holocaust, a profusion of myths and abstractions of theories has been postulated to explain the carnage. To be sure, an inquiry into the causes of the catastrophe is the proper and necessary subject of history and mimetic art; but what is disquieting is the plethora of social scientists, novelists, playwrights, and filmmakers who trample "where angels fear to tread," misinterpreting evidence, revising history, and perverting the truth.

The frightening phenomenon is that neither the honest inquiries into the causes of the Holocaust nor the reductionisms that exploit it mitigate the suspicion that the edifice, and perhaps even the very foundation of Western civilization, has gone up with the smoke of the immolated Jews. For what is civilization, what are its determinants if not a stream of events generated by the dialectic of antecedent and contemporaneous processes? It is this that produces a continuum within which accepted and established beliefs, customs, and laws are transmitted from one generation to the next, from one cultural type to another. The Holocaust established such a continuum, an archetype against which various bloodlettings around the globe seem to be tacitly measured. Since none exceeds the barbarity of the Holocaust, they are willy-nilly included in the purview of the acceptable and permissible. If the world was initially shocked by the exposure of the concentrationary world, it quickly learned to live in peace and equanimity with the unthinkable.

It seems that the Holocaustal lava continues to erode the foundation of the human community in the third decade after the fact, leaving an increasingly deeper chasm between our feet in which, to echo Dostoevsky, "everything is permissible." This crisis, flagrantly manifested in the licentious policies of great and small nations, in the unconscionable behavior of groups and individuals, is eloquently articulated in the contemporary literature of despair and atrocity.

In view of this one wonders how the condemned, immured in the ghettos and concentration camps, apprehended the cosmic chaos—a scheme in which Dante's imagined "Frozen Lake" was translated into the palpable fires of Maidanek and Auschwitz. One further wonders what kind of literature was produced there and what significance it might have in countering the current vulgarization of the Holocaust.

Astonishing as it may be, literary activity was vital and widespread in the ghettos, in hiding, among the partisans, on the "Aryan" side, and even in some of the concentration camps. Indeed, after waves of mass deportations to death centers, those who temporarily hugged life in the various places feverishly turned to writing. Spontaneous literary activity not only continued but actually increased, when one would expect language to evaporate, to turn to ashes in the conflagration of gas chambers and crematoria. As the poet Michal Borwicz writes:

> After each deportation action—when the narrow ghetto streets echoed with a cry of bleeding silence, when the dwellings blew with the emptiness of many thousand martyrs, and the furniture and belongings were confiscated by the Germans—the thresholds, floors, and sidewalks were strewn with tatters and scraps of plundered property. In the midst of it, it was easy to find handwritten slips of paper. Ripped out of drawers and hiding places by the German marauders, these notes, devoid of material value, were trampled by them in utter disdain [*Pieśń ujdzie calo*].

The flowering of literature in the crucible of the Holocaust world reflected an urgent determination to leave a testament for posterity. It was, furthermore, a quest for reaffirmation of traditional values and all that constituted Judaic culture. Hence the greater the threat to the physical and cultural existence of the condemned, the more feverish was their literary activity. What kind of literature did they produce? What linguistic approaches were employed to articulate the unspeakable? What were the dominant themes?

Although the writers availed themselves of the entire spectrum of literary genres, the most popular one was poetry.

That this poetry is probably the richest of the Holocaust literature should not be surprising. For poetry—perhaps because it provides, more often than any other literary genre, the most precise correlatives for states of consciousness—was the first vehicle of reaction against Nazi barbarism. Moreover, the poets, writing from "the heart of darkness," reflect an immediacy of experience that is untainted by the remembering processes of memory. Nothing but total recall could unveil the truth articulated in this body of literature. For as Janusz Korczak notes, "Reminiscences hinge on our immediate experience. Reminiscing we lie unconsciously" [*Ghetto Diary*]. Yet this naked immediacy of truth has been glaringly neglected by Holocaust scholarship. In fact, little of this work has been translated—perhaps because the bulk of it was written in Yiddish and Polish, both somewhat esoteric languages.

Interestingly, the first to respond to the Nazi assault were the Yiddish and the Polish-Jewish poets. Apparently they knew that the objective chronicler of events needs the complement of a truth that transcends historical fact: the truth of the poet. For it is the poet who explores the thing felt subcutaneously and who lays bare the existential response to life, to hope, to terror, to despair, to heroism, to death. The most cogent articulation of this idea appears in Chaim Kaplan's *Warsaw Diary:*

> Who will immortalize our troubles? The national splendor inherent in religious poetry is not expressed in newspaper reports. . . .A catastrophe that becomes part of poetry . . . spreads among the people and is transmitted to future generations. A poet who clothes adversity in poetic form immortalizes it in an everlasting monument. And this monument provides historic material from which future generations are nourished.

There is yet another much simpler and more pragmatic reason for the popularity of the poetic idiom. Since paper and pencil were not readily available, especially in the concentration camps, poetry was easier to compose in the mind and easier to commit to memory than was prose.

Often these poems were sung to popular and banal melodies. The juxtaposition between the highly charged concentrationary poetry and the sentimental tunes was startling. The irony was especially corrosive when the carefully wrought poetic diction of despair or hope and moral or political didacticism stood in sharp contrast to a vulgar love tune. This dissonance made more emphatic the chasm between the landscape of endless terror and a world where sentimental love songs were still being crooned in night clubs.

Not all the poetry was marked by the same quality of literary excellence. An abundance of literary neophites, moved by a compulsion to bear witness, resolved to record the apocalyptic events for posterity. Thus occurred a spontaneous explosion of folk poetry—a kind of *Urdichtung* as well as balladry, the chief of which was the *kina* or *kluglid* (dirge). The latter is reflected in the following Polish song written and very popular in the Warsaw Ghetto:

> The universe collapses in ruins,
> Immolated in a vast conflagration.

> Nothing can save it,
> All drowns in devastation.

Although the young poet witnesses the literal incineration of her world, she cannot fathom it. Nor can she comprehend the vast cosmic silence that envelops her burning world:

> O, people where is your conscience?
> Where are your hearts?
> Where is divine essence?

This simple rhyming lament, devoid as it is of any other aesthetic compulsion, expresses the doubt that the victims could endure the agony and terror much longer. It further affirms the impossible task of recording the suffering. Yet this poet, like all the others, writes.

The dominant idiom, notably among the Yiddish threnodists, derived from the surfeit of Jewish literature of destruction. In the crucible of the Holocaustal world, even such avowed secularists as the Yiddish writing Abraham Sutzkever and Yitzhak Katzenelson and the Polish-Jewish Wladyslaw Szlengel turned to it, seeking in the paradigm of liturgical threnodies a vehicle for expressing the unspeakable. This poetry, therefore, takes its historical analogue, lexicon, and form from the Book of Lamentations and Jeremiah as well as from the iconography of pogroms. Of course the resonances inherent in Yiddish poetry are closer to the liturgical literature than are the poems written in Polish.

Yitzhak Katznelson's poetry, notably his epic poem, *The Song of the Murdered Jewish People,* resonates with such liturgical influences:

> *Ani ha-gever,* I am the man who watched, who saw
> How my children, my women, my young and old were thrown
> Like stones, like logs, into wagons
> Brutally beaten, rudely abused.

This strophe, one of many, reflects yet another phenomenon: the dissolution of the demarcation lines between personal and communal grief. For the "children . . . women . . . young and old," the poet laments, are not only his two murdered sons and wife, but the entire murdered Jewish people. In this Katzenelson adheres to the traditional Jewish canon that tends to eschew the singling out of the individual victim, but rather invokes the memory of communal suffering.

Moreover, as an eyewitness, the poet of this epic becomes the interpretive mediator whose poetic mimesis produces an abiding fusion of lyricism of agony and objective chronology of events. This jeremiad, like many of its kind, is therefore a synthesis of personal responses to the Draconic laws and detailed documentation.

The structure too is hybrid, combining an identifiable pattern of external archetectonics (fifteen cantos, fifteen four-line stanzas each) with an internal arrangement that defies any known design. Only those who have knowledge of the chronology of the events can decode the inner substance. The disjunctive internal structure is primarily revealed in the dissolution of time. The chronological order of events

Emanuel Ringelblum, archivist of the Warsaw ghetto, with his son Uri in a photograph taken before the war. Both were killed in Warsaw in 1944.

is suspended in surreal timelessness, and the cantos are held together by the displaced logic of nightmares. The recounting of the sequence of events dissolves in a lament, and the words tumble out in the distraught confusion of uncontrollable weeping. The tension arising from the poem's disjunctiveness and its apparent concern with the primacy of careful documentation heightens its eloquence. *The Song of the Murdered Jewish People* is a monumental elegy and a national testament of the beginning and end of the "Last Jews on Europe's Soil":

> Woe is unto me, nobody is left. . . .There was
> a people and it is no more . . . There was a
> people and it's . . . gone.
> What a tale. It began in the Bible and lasted till
> now . . . A very sad tale.
> A tale that began with *Amalek* and concluded
> with the far crueler Germans . . .

The torment and the bereavement of the condemned were expressed not only in transtemporal eschatological elegies. A wide spectrum of modernist trends informed the work of many poets, both Yiddish and Polish speaking ones. The bankruptcy of language (intimations of which were already a commonplace in the interwar period) caused them to seek a tongue within the wave of modernist influences, just as it did within the framework of traditional and biblical archetypes. Hence, many poems exhibit unusual patterns that repudiate standard grammatic structures, punctuations, and strophic archetectonics. The poem "Szpital obozowy" ("Camp Hospital"), written in the Gross-Rosen concentration camp by the Polish Jew Jozef Bau, manifests this predilection. The structure of the poem reveals three strophes of uneven length. The unrhymed verses are marked by a dissonant rhythm and fragmented diction.

On the shelf-bunks lie
emaciated, glistening with sweat's enamel
dying "Mussulmen."

With heavy, monotonous step
of creaking hours,
treads
the length and breadth of the barak-tent
in the blood-stained apron of a medic . . .
the "capo-watch"
—and counts the last minutes
—and figures who soon will
be released:
. . . these yes . . . those not yet,
. . . these yes . . . those tomorrow
   morning . . .

Sees; fever consumes
the not yet lice devoured skeletons
displayed for death to buy,
and stares out the window;—in the nearby
chimney, lightly roasted souls
dance a spectral minuet with the black smoke.
   . . . then crosses out the numbers, jots down
      some footnotes:
"died voluntarily."

The convincing verisimilitude with which great poets were able to transcribe the human condition into art derived from the availability of familiar images. However, the kaleidoscope of imagery accrued over the millennia, as well as language itself, was hardly applicable to a knowledge that had no antecedents and no analogues. Nevertheless, the poets knew that language was often all they had in the flood of blood. They also knew that the paradox of language, as Paul Celan expressed it, was that "it had to find sustenance in its own inability to explain. . . .Sustenance was often found in the adherence to simple, standard devices of versification, in the unadorned, naked language that deliberately eschewed metaphor. Yet, these seeming palimpsests are replete with imagery—imagery, however, that does not lie in the realm of recognizable human experience. Unsymbolic and concrete, unimaginative and *sachlich,* the images mean what they are; for they arise from the spectral reality of the concentrationary world, from "the daily *dread* of experience"—to paraphrase James Joyce. An example of this is another of Jozef Bau's poems "Glod" ("Hunger") written in Plaszow, a slave labor camp near Cracow:

Flour coagulated into a loaf of cement
—condensed wages for a day's anguish
—that's bread

Eight stomachs creeping through the eyes
divide it into eight even parts,
the exactness of each crumb;
—that's the godhead
to which the thought prays
through the triple barbed-wire wall

. . . and farther beyond that braid
of wires and anguish, apparently a world exists.
But we, check-mated
by watch-tower
machine guns—know it not,
our temples are branded: "check-mate."

This compelling articulation of hunger is almost completely devoid of extrinsic imagery. The sole superimposed metaphor is the word "cement" to which the daily bread of the denizens in Plaszow is likened. That the coveted bread is metamorphosed into the very godhead by the most excruciating of tortures, starvation, is not an extravagant conceit, but rather a faithful recording of fact. For in the Holocaustal world, a planet expelled from the universe, a slice of cementlike bread was often perceived as the only redemption to which body and soul bowed in reverence and supplication. Indeed, starvation here is so intense that there is a veritable dissolution of selfhood. The austere language has lost one of its essential words: "man," and consciousness is a disembodied sensation of hunger, a stomach "creeping through the eyes." In this godless realm, the victims are condemned to death not only by starvation, but also by the machine guns poised in the numerous watchtowers that dot the triple barbed wire walls. This image, too, derives from the language of concentrationary realism.

The modes of aesthetic stylization used to convey the brutalization and moral chaos suggest that a considerable body of the poetry written in the Holocaust constitutes a new poetic genre, one that evolved from, and is thus peculiar to, the historicity of the apocalyptic events. The register of common language with its accretion of idiomatic expressions was in a continuous process of change, reflecting the growing barbarism. Syntax, style, and symbol were subject to endless changes. Since the self-contained, discrete concentrationary organisms produced their own hierarchy of human relations, they often rendered traditional mores and epistemological modalities obsolete. In the surreality of this world neologisms were a commonplace, and familiar terminology either lost its meaning or else was invested with derisive connotations. Not only was common language informed by Nazi-Deutsch, but by ghetto and concentration camp slang of both Yiddish and Polish derivation as well. Rubinsztajn, the famous Warsaw Ghetto madman-clown and master punster, was particularly adept at coining new words and making droll puns. Here is one of his pithy apothegms in the Yiddish slang of Warsaw:

> Ah groshn is goonish,
> Ah tsvayer is goonish,
> Ah drayer is goonish,
> Ah fihrer zol paygern.

> (A penny is worthless, twopence is worthless, three worthless, four—which in the Warsaw slang sounded like the Führer—let the fihrer drop dead.)

The historicity of the poetry written in the Holocaustal dominion is not only a function of the growing barbarism, but also of the inner vision and, above all, the cultural retina of each poet. Some poets, writing in European languages, straddle two cultures, the Jewish and the non-Jewish. This ontological and cultural divisibility is not the experience of those poets who are indivisibly anchored in the Jewish culture and the Yiddish language. Poets like Czeslav Milosz, who experienced the devastation as Christians, present yet another vision of the violated world.

Polish-Jewish poets often express a bereavement alien to the sensibilities of the Yiddish poets. The assimilated writers, suddenly wrested from their non-Jewish heritage and catapulted into the ghettos, agonize over this cultural truncation. The early poetry is especially replete with adumbrations of this cultural wrench. Later poetry seems to eschew this concern, possibly because of the inverse relationship between the growing atrocities and the intensified sense of Jewish identity. Cogent formulations of these divergent perceptions inform Wladyslaw Szlengel's "Windows Facing the Aryan Side," an early poem, and "Counter Attack," a late one.

"Windows Facing the Aryan Side" establishes the extent to which the Jew, who formerly lived side by side with his Polish neighbor, is now irrevocably separated from the world outside the ghetto. The window of the poet's Warsaw Ghetto room faces not only the Aryan side but also the famous Krasinski Park. Yet looking out the window and feasting his eyes on the Aryan trees is strongly forbidden. He is a "Jewish worm and a Jewish mole," and it is "just and right" that he "should and must be blind." At night, however, the poet rushes to his window, "ravenously gazing and stealing snatches of darkened Warsaw." The poet's longing for his beloved city is intensified and spiritualized by memory. The crescendo cataloguing of the attributes of Warsaw ends on a cadence of bitter resignation and realization that the city and his friends are indifferent to his fervent incantations and invocations. Their ways have parted. Friendship has sunk into an irretrievable swamp, as "Telefon," another of Szlengel's poems, indicates. The world, the culture, the life, the people he once knew are lost forever.

In "Counter Attack," on the other hand, Szlengel's concern is only with Jewish heritage and the Jewish future. Hence, he is determined to infuse his fellow Jews with renewed pride in their Jewishness. He further seeks to extricate his people from historical casuality of acquiescence in the face of atrocity. Since the *shtetl* Jew had little recourse to law or justice, he was often forced to resist total destruction by appeasement. Szlengel now rejects this moral imperative; and his fiery poem echoes the prophetic eschatology of Isaiah. Like the ancient Hebrew prophet, Szlengel, the reborn Jew, rejects redemption through a policy of appeasement. "Counter Attack" becomes a clarion call for armed resistance and reflects the vital political role poetry played in the concentrationary universe. Written after the January 1943 insurrection, it was a vehicle of inspiration of the Warsaw Ghetto uprising in April of the same year. The poem's closing lines lay bare the desperate exaltation and hopeless grandeur of the fighting Jews of the Warsaw Ghetto:

> Hear oh German Gods
> How Jews in the "wild" houses pray,
> Clenching in the fist a stick, a stone.
> We beg you, oh God, for a bloody battle,
> We implore You for a violent death.
> Let us not see, before we expire,
> The stretch of the train tracks,
> But let the precise aim of the hand, oh Lord,
> Stain their livid uniform with blood,
> Before the mute groan shreds our throats,
> Let us see our simple human fear in their
> Haughty hands, in their whip-wielding paws.

From Niska, Mila, Muranowska Streets,
Like scarlet blood-flowers,
Bloom the flames of our gun-barrels.
This is our resurrection! This is our counter at-
    tack!
The intoxication of battle!
The alleys of Dzika and Ostrowska
Are our partisan forests.
The block numbers, medals of the Jewish war,
Quiver on our breasts.
The cry, "Revolt," flashes in scarlet
Like a bellowing . . . battering ram.

The shock sustained by the victims often produced a crisis of faith, though rarely absolute apostasy. In the works of many poets, God is inscrutable, unreachable, and unaccountable. Terror, chimneys, and death consecrated by divine will are an organic part of the cosmic chaos. In other poetry, the religious despair is transformed into outright blasphemy. The poets express the suspicion that the omnipotent, just, and wise God of their fathers has turned his back on his children either because of their sinfulness or because God Himself has been reduced to craven pusillanimity in the shadow of the hailing Nazi arm. He is, therefore, no longer able to protect his chosen people. In the first case God's wisdom and justice are challenged, for a punishment that calls for living children to be thrown into flames exceeds any conceivable form of sin. In the second case God is charged with bad faith, for He mislead his people into believing in his omnipotence and his promise of ultimate redemption. Thus in some poems, Szlengel's for example, the universe is stood on its head, and it is God who, on Judgment Day, is judged by his children. The logic of such an inversion has its antecedents in Hasidic and rabbinic literature. The right to judge God is implicit in the relationship between God and Israel—a relationship established by God's insistence that Israel accept his covenant. Thus:

> In Jewish law, God can be tried for his crimes because he is a party to an agreement. . . .In this respect he is a "person" in Jewish law. The trials of God narrated by Hasidic literature [and] Holocaust literature . . . are not only aggadically [theologically] defensible, but halakhically viable. As man is required to bear witness before God, he may also bear witness against God. [Byron Sherwin; see Rosenfeld entry in Further Reading]

In his passionately bitter poem, "It's High Time," Szlengel charges God not only with breaking the agreement, but he also accuses Him of handing his faithful and penitent children into the hands of the brutal murderers and into the ovens of Treblinka. That in the distant past, Szlengel vituperates, "God delivered His children from Egypt and brought them to their land will change nothing!" For God cannot be absolved of his terrible sin of indifference when his children were sacrificed on the altars of the world with his name on their lips. Now in a paroxysm of cruelty, God has abandoned them to the terror of the ghetto and death in Treblinka. For this barbarous betrayal and the recantation of the covenant, Szlengel thunders at God:

> We'll pay You back! We'll pay You back! . . .

And when the executioner will chase and force
    You,
Drive and push you onto the gas chamber floor,
And seal behind you the hermetic door,
The vapors will choke You, You'll see,
You'll scream and weep and try to flee—
And when Your death agony will end,
You'll be dragged and in a monstrous pit land.
Then they'll tear out your stars—the gold teeth
    from Your flesh—
Then they will burn You.
    And You will be ash.

Although this bitter invective has its roots in traditional liturgy, notably in the right to judge God for his trespasses—his breaching of the covenant—Szlengel's language stands in contrast to the poem's paradigms. He deliberately uses slang, especially ghetto slang, and Yiddishisms to destroy the perfect diction of preconcentrationary poetry. His poems are for and about the condemned, the exhausted, and he makes emphatic the inappropriateness of lofty poetic standards.

Poetry in the Holocaustal world was a vital and viable means of articulating the entire range of intellectual principles and states of consciousness. These articulations, as indicated, include political, philosophical, and religious concerns. Poetry was also a vehicle of moral and cultural sustenance and an expression of spiritual defiance that helped to keep the spirit of the condemned from dying. Since it articulated for many their thoughts and feelings, this literary genre was often an indispensable means of catharsis. Moreover, it was an expression of moral revulsion and opposition against the oppressor. Above all, it was a vital affirmation of life—an attempt to sunder the walls of an unbearable world and to walk toward the future.

Abraham Sutzkever's "The First Night in the Ghetto" is such an affirmation. For it transcends the moral bewilderment of the young poet whose integrity of youth has been savagely violated. The first night in the ghetto is an evocation of the first night in the grave. The poet is, however, reassured by a neighbor that in the end one gets accustomed even to that. In this, Sutzkever reflects the traditional pacifism of European Judaism, which had to adjust to calamity in order to save the community, the individual, the religion, and the culture. But the poet has it "up to his throat," as he lies near death under a gutter of a building in ruins, a building previously occupied by Jewish tenants, all of whom are now dead. Only he, a piece of "ember betrayed by the last spark precipitously extinguished," is left, and so are "the bricks in the ruins." "Roaring bricks / torn out with chunks of flesh from the walls." Black poison oozes from the gutter drop by drop in the irreality of this world. "Suddenly each drop becomes an eye" and the gutter "a telescope," through which the poet gazes at yesterday's luminous sky and at yesterday's stars, notably at "the after-Sabbath star / that my mother's lips used to bless: *gut vokh.*"

Resuscitated by the firmament and his mother's star, the poet declares in existential terms: "I must live, for my mother's good star is alive." This affirmation of life, variously orchestrated in Sutzkever's poetry as well as in that of most other poets of that period, is not only an act of personal survival but one of cultural continuity as well. Such a phenomenology of continuity is the imperative associated with the consecration of life (*kiddush ha-hayym*). In different times the prototypic obligation was martyrdom in the name of God (*kiddush ha-Shem*). The eschatological justification of this shift of imperatives derives from the fact that only a "dying ember" is left of the Jewish community in Europe. The primacy of individual survival is metaphysically linked to Jewish continuity, which is in itself redemptive. Often the struggle to stay alive was less for oneself than for the mother, father, or child who were killed. To reiterate, "I must live, for my mother's good star is alive." The "dying ember" (a central image in "The First Night in the Ghetto"), Sutzkever intimates, will be ignited again; and his dead mother's star "among the familiar, living stars of my town" is a symbol of abiding Jewish continuity that is unextinguishable.

There is yet another purpose in rekindling the "dying ember"—namely, to bear witness lest there be a sweeping and final obliteration of the very memory of European Jewry. The prototype of the "dying ember" as historical witness is a medieval fragment that, according to Sidra DeKoven Ezrahi,

> has survived from the Hebrew lamentation literature of the fourteenth century, written by a man who returned to his hometown after a trip only to discover that a pogrom had wiped out every inhabitant and destroyed all the holy books, exept one Bible. This one remaining man, who refers to himself as the "last ember," wrote a brief account of the destruction of his town on the pages of the one remaining Bible [see Ezrahi entry in Further Reading].

The flowering of poetry even in the darkest of pits has its roots in the tradition of the "dying ember's" sacred duty to leave a chapter of martyrology for posterity. This testimonial or documentation poetry records the community's response to the unfolding destruction. As a day-to-day chronicle, it attests not only to the growing horrors but also to the diverse modes of resistance. This poetry unveils the vitality of the underground culture, replete with clandestine schools on all levels, libraries, theaters, and ingenious support systems without which no survival would have been possible. Even the poems of the children reflect the testimonial purpose of this writing, for they and their adult counterparts, like the biblical poets, knew that it was imperative to leave a record for posterity.

Moreover, poetry was used as a call for assistance from abroad. In the spring of 1944 a slim anthology of poetry entitled *Z Otchlani* (*From the Abyss*)—containing the works of Czeslaw Milosz, the Nobel Laureate, and Jan Kott, the famous Shakespearean scholar, among others—was smuggled out on microfilm to England by the underground National Jewish Committee. The anthology found its way to New York in November 1944.

The fervid poetic activity was coupled with an equally fervid attempt to save the manuscripts from destruction by depositing them in hermetically sealed containers and burying them in the ground. Abraham Sutzkever's *Kerndlekh Vayts* (*Grains of Wheat*) articulates this fever-

ish activity. In the imaginative world of the poet, the manuscripts he hides in the earth become grains of wheat sown for an uncertain future. When overcome with despair, he recalls an Egyptian tale about a king who ordered his servants to fill a gold urn with grains of wheat. This urn was deposited in the pyramid built for the king. Nine thousand years later, when the seeds were unearthed, they blossomed into golden wheat. In pensive tones the poet muses:

> Perhaps in destiny's hour
> Even these words may
> Suddenly grow into flower
> In the light of the day.
>
> And like the prehistoric seed
> Transformed into sheafs of wheat—
> My words will belong
> To my people, the eternal throng.

Indeed, Sutzkever's poetry, written both in the Vilna Ghetto and in the forests where he joined the partisans, saw "the light of the day." Unfortunately this cannot be said for most of the literature written in the Holocaust dominion, although some of it miraculously survived. Most of the poets, however, both well known and anonymous, perished. (pp. 119-31)

Frieda W. Aaron, "Poetry in the Holocaust Dominion," in Perspectives on the Holocaust, *edited by Randolph L. Braham, Kluwer-Nijhoff Publishing, 1983, pp. 119-31.*

DRAMA

Yaffa Eliach

[*Born in Poland, Eliach is the founder of the Center for Holocaust Studies at the City University of New York and is herself a survivor of the Holocaust. Her extensive writings on the subject include* The Liberators (1981), *a historical study of the Allied liberation of the concentration camps;* Hasidic Tales of the Holocaust (1982), *a short story collection; and* The Last Jew (1975), *an award-winning play written with Uri Assaf. In the following excerpt, Eliach discusses plays based on the Holocaust by European and Israeli dramatists.*]

The playwright, writing on the Holocaust, shares identical difficulties with the novelist and the poet. He, too, must transform the unspeakable atrocities of the Hitlerian era into words. He, too, must travel from documentation to art, from the horrors of the Holocaust to their imaginative realization in literature. His creative task does not stop here, for he must carry the literary imagination one step beyond the written word, to its visual realization on stage. The playwright brings a cycle to a close in the artistic realization on stage of the concentration camp universe. Between the artist and the audience there is no longer a word on a page but a controlled visual reality. The playwright's task may well be the most difficult and vulnerable one. The playwright cannot hope to find guidance in Western or Jewish tradition. The mass anonymity of the victims, the overwhelming atrocities, have a precedent neither in Western drama nor in Jewish literature, where drama is a relative newcomer to millenia-old literary traditions. Can the medium of the stage convey the message of Auschwitz without minimizing or distorting the reality of that huge European wasteland?

In *The Theatre and Its Double,* Antonin Artaud (1896-1948) charts a new course for the theatre. His views have had a powerful impact upon the aesthetics of contemporary drama. The book was published in 1938, before Hitler's atrocities assumed monstrous proportions. Artaud argued for a return to drama as a primitive rite concerned with elemental human needs and emotions. Drama must protest artificial values imposed by a rationalistic culture. Such drama will repudiate established conventions and forms of the modern theatre with its reliance on text, speech, plot, psychological analysis and the proscenium arch, in favor of a purely irrational assemblage of sounds where gestures symbolize ideas and effigies and bizarre objects signify cosmic forces hostile to man. Audiences must be subjected to the maximum theatrical experience in order to undermine their assurance and revive latent forces in themselves and ranging outside of them. To make the theatre believable, providing "the heart and the senses that kind of concrete bite which true sensation requires," Artaud advocated the exteriorization of a depth of latent cruelty by means of which all the perverse possibilities of the mind, whether of an individual or a people, are localized. On the eve of the war Artaud wrote as if he sensed the atrocities of World War II with his artistic intuition.

Artaud's avant-garde theories offer new vistas in the attempt to cope with the Holocaust on stage. Nevertheless, the challenge to the artist remains monumental. Relatively few playwrights attempt to approach the subject and even fewer theatres dare to product Holocaust plays. The European playwrights, especially in Western Europe, have taken the lead. The New York and London stage also made significant contributions. The Israeli theatre, subsidized by the national and municipal governments, has made only a token attempt to promote Holocaust related drama. Yet despite the small volume of Holocaust plays written in Europe and Israel, major trends and themes have emerged among European and Israeli playwrights.

The European playwright seems to be more preoccupied with the artist's ability to recreate the Holocaust reality on stage, to transform the documentation of the post-World War II trials into drama, to locate the guilt of the individual, the nation and civilization during the Holocaust. Jose Szajna, director of the Polish Studio Theatre, produced *Replika*. It looks and sounds like a fulfillment of Artaud's theory. *Replika* is a wordless odyssey through the Holocaust. The stage is filled with bizarre objects, effigies, piles of clothing and shoes. *Replika* attempts to re-create Auschwitz, to reproduce man's indomitable spirit, tempered by the inhumanity directed against him by himself.

Charlotte Delbo in *Till Human Voices Wake Us,* also simi-

larly does not spare the public the concentration camp universe with its sights, sounds and language. It is all enacted on stage. The all-female cast emphasizes to the on-lookers that the least they can do is to endure and comprehend the action on stage so that they may prevent it from becoming a reality again. As a playwright Delbo assumes the position of an eyewitness, a survivor who was spared so that she may tell the unbelievable stories of her survival which survivors themselves do not comprehend.

Louis Novas Terrara (Newlander) in his *Yom Kippur,* carries his depiction of the Holocaust to an extreme in the attempt to re-create a replica of the authentic concentration camp universe. The strange, authentic reality of the "other planet" makes events in the play probable and possible. Peter Weiss' *The Investigation,* is a reproduction of the Auschwitz trials held in Frankfurt, Germany, during 1964-1965. The trials are presented in the form of an oratorio with 11 cantos. Weiss documents the negative achievements of all civilization. Barbaric, lawless acts unfold on an austere stage with no attempt to reconstruct a court room. There is no personal drama in the play, and all questions and answers are delivered in a monotone. Guilt is an essential element in the play; it is diffused through the Nazi ranks and even taints the victims. The Western world is guilty, tormentor and victim alike.

Rolf Hochhuth in the *Deputy,* locates the guilt with the individual. He especially singles out Pope Pious XII, Christ's deputy on earth, for censure. Hochhuth stigmatizes the Pope for failing to protest, and for remaining silent while six million Jews were murdered. The Pope is blamed as an individual who failed to use his powerful position. The blame falls upon a person rather than an institution. Father Riccardo Fontana and Kurt Gerstein also acted as individuals. They were guided by deep personal convictions that Man must exercise his fundamental freedom and that Man is, indeed, his brother's keeper. The play's theatrical power stems from the author's use of heightened verse dialogue mixing colloquialism with ecclesiastical and Nazi party jargon.

Weiss and Hochhuth based their dramas upon actual events. Whereas Weiss is unyielding in his insistence on unmitigated evil, Hochhuth succeeds in the transformation of an historical event into a theatrical experience.

European playwrights who have tried to depict the atrocities of the Holocaust usually confront it directly. Friedrich Durrenmatt, on the other hand, resorts to cynicism and tragic-comedy. There are ways of bringing Auschwitz to the audience without bringing the death camp to the stage but by inventing parallel situations. *The Visit,* in which the grotesque revenge of a rich, old lady exposes her native town in a garish, satirical light is a fine example. Durrenmatt justifies his dramatic technique in his essay, "Theatre Problems" (1955), as being the only one valid for this apocalyptically absurd age, an age in which we are all collectively guilty, enmeshed in the sins of our fathers and of our father's fathers. This is not our guilt but, rather, our misfortune. Comedy alone is suitable for us.

Max Frisch in *The Fire Risers,* also resorts to comedy and parables to attack the complacent irresponsibility of the average citizen who appeases and encourages the amoral. Every man's behavior in an incendiary world is criminal. One of Frisch's greatest plays is *Andora,* a tragedy about anti-Semitism and the destructiveness of complacency and prejudice. Unlike Durrenmatt, who establishes a detachment from his characters, Frisch is involved with them.

The major themes which dominate European plays are almost absent from the Holocaust plays written in Israel. The few plays written in Israel after the Holocaust are not based upon extensive documentation like *The Deputy,* nor are they exclusively from the realm of the imagination like *Mr. Runaway.* They are rather taken from the survivor's experiences and post-Holocaust reality. The Israeli playwright is concerned with the fate of the survivor, his ability or inability to cope with reality, and the central place of Israel in his life. Israel is viewed as the only positive force and solution for the Jewish survivor and for others who seek justice.

For the Israeli playwright, because of his Jewish literary background, and the unique position of the Jew during the Holocaust, coping with the Holocaust in drama is virtually an overwhelming task. The Jewish author comes from a literary tradition in which, for the most part, the suffering of an individual is submerged, diffused and transformed into national suffering and consciousness of the past, present and future. The biblical book of *Lamentations,* describing the greatest Jewish catastrophe prior to the Holocaust, the destruction of the Temple, does not mention a single protagonist, a single victim. It is the national collective suffering of a people and a city in which the individual and the nation become one. The suffering, exalted, individual hero, the basic element of a drama, is totally absent. This is in sharp contrast to the Greek and New Testament tradition which focuses always on the solitary figure of the sacrificial victim: the Hanged Man, Christ or Oedipus. The figures of Oedipus, Christ, Hamlet and Lear dominated European stages for centuries. The Israeli author, who may be better equipped to cope with the anonymity of the victims, is at a distinctive disadvantage as a dramatist.

Unlike the European playwright, the Israeli playwright is physically removed from Europe, from the sights, sounds, and languages of the Holocaust. The physical landscape of Auschwitz is not a factor in his daily life. For the Israeli writing on the Holocaust, Auschwitz is a source of constant mental anguish, the anguish of an historical victim. His guilt cannot be dominant, for as a Jew it was not his civilization which produced Auschwitz; neither is he a tormented, guilt ridden heir to that civilization. His people was neither executioner nor bystander, but victim. When writing about the victim, the Israeli playwright seems to prefer the survivor who settled in Israel and not the victim within the concentration camp universe. The survivor who demonstrates a quest for life, normalcy and nationhood lives in the post-Holocaust era. Perhaps the Israeli playwright is guided by an ancient, optimistic Jewish literary tradition. The book of *Lamentations* ends on a hopeful note, a promise at the end of catastrophe and calamity. For Jewish Holocaust drama such a stance is a severe limitation. It is within these old-new Jewish literary traditions

and Israeli reality that the Israeli playwright tries to come to terms with the Holocaust.

Yehuda Amichai's *Bells and Trains,* is a powerful short radio play. It is about the visit of Hans Wolf, now Yohanan, to an old-age home in his native town Singburg. The old-age home was built by the German government "out of a guilty feeling." It is a paradise of ghosts in the midst of a German town where many of its thriving businessmen were former S.S. and Gestapo men. In the background the church bells toll and the trains run on their punctual schedule. The old live by those painful sounds and their ghastly memories. Aunt Henrietta points out to her visitors the inhabitants of the old-age home.

> In the rocking chair is Doctor Rieger, the dentist . . . Nine of his family died there . . . Mrs. Gruenfeld's three brothers were also burned . . . That's Herr Levin. Both his sons were shot the same day.

Each old person with his own dead. Hans feels that he is like Orpheus who descends to hell to fetch his dead. He wants to bring his aunt to Jerusalem, but she belongs in Singburg among the living dead. The old-age home assumes the symbolic dimensions of the death of Jewish civilization in Europe, while the visitor from Jerusalem represents the continuity of Jewish life.

Gavriel Dagan's play *The Reunion* also takes place in Europe, but the theme is distinctly Israeli: "Why didn't the victim resist?" As with the German playwright Sylvanus, Dagan's major concern is the audience. He aims to show his viewers that, under similar conditions, they would have behaved the same way. For Sylvanus in *Dr. Korczak and the Children,* the theme was collaboration. For Dagan it is resistance. He tries to prove to the audience that Jewish resistance within the Nazi system was almost impossible. To convey the message to the audience he turns a friendly gathering between the playwright and his friends in a hotel suite in Central Europe in 1970 into a nightmarish experience. Within minutes the guests comply with their oppressors and do not offer any resistance, in a cleverly staged play within a play.

Leah Goldberg's *Lady of the Castle* also takes place in Europe. Michael Zand, a librarian from the land of Israel, and Dr. Dora Ringel, a social worker for the Youth Aliyah, are in Europe in 1947 on separate missions. Zand hopes to trace rare Jewish manuscripts scattered by the Germans, while Dora is in search of Jewish children in monasteries, nunneries and other hiding places. They are forced by a raging storm to spend the night in the manor where Zand had been looking for manuscripts. The watchman reluctantly allows them to spend the night in the manor. During the evening an ideological discussion develops among the three. Each represents a different theological trend of the forties. During the course of the conversation, they learn that the watchman is a Count, the former owner of the manor, who, after the Communist takeover, became a watchman. During World War II, the castle served as a Gestapo headquarters and the Count was one of the most prominent members of the Resistance.

When Zand is left alone in the library he touches an old

cuckoo clock. The clock strikes ten. A secret door open in the wall and a beautiful, bewildered young girl appears. Zand learns that her name is Lena and that she was saved by the Count during World War II. She lives in constant fear in her secret hiding place, thinking that the war is still going on. The Count did not tell Lena that the war had ended more than two years ago. She is all that is left to the Count in his lonely, crumbling world and he clings to her even if the price demands deceiving the only person that he loves. The girl, the Lady of the manor, lives in an imaginary world in which she is a prisoner. Zand and Dora urge her to leave the manor and start a new life in the Land of Israel among her people and her peers.

It is a very simple plot, a mixture of ideological overtones and fairy tale touches. Neither the structure nor the language reflect the fine poetic style of Leah Goldberg. In Israel, the play is a favorite. The fairy tale element appeals to the younger generation since it lacks the usual morbidity associated with the Holocaust. The librarian and the social worker are true to life characters of the late forties and early fifties and are familiar to a segment of the Israeli population. The theme, rescue of Jewish children after the War, is also a familiar subject. Thousands of similar episodes took place in real life. It is a pleasant play about the Holocaust in which the horrors of the Holocaust are absent and the more profound questions are not asked. The play was staged in New York but was not a critical success.

Ben-Zion Tomer's play *Children of the Shadows,* begins thematically where Leah Goldberg's play ends, with the attempt of a young boy, a survivor, to rebuild his life. He came to the Land of Israel at the age of fourteen with the "Teheran children," who had managed to survive on their own in the Russian-Asiatic countryside. Unlike George Kaiser in his play *The Raft of the Medusa* (1943) and William Golding in his novel *The Lord of the Flies,* Tomer is not interested in the children's savage struggle for survival, but rather in their attempt to achieve normalcy in the post-Holocaust reality.

Yoram, the main protagonist of the play, is twenty-eight years old. He was fourteen when he came to the Land of Israel. In his attempt to acculturate and assimilate into Kibbutz reality, he denies his past, changes his name from Yossele to Yoram, and severs all ties with friends and family. He succeeds and even marries a "sabra," a native Israeli, named Nurit. In the fifties, the wave of new immigrants brings to Israel his family and friends and other Holocaust survivors. The past starts to haunt him day and night. His wife, Nurit, despite her efforts, finds it very difficult to cope with the "dark side" of her husband about which she never knew.

Both Nurit and Yoram are followed by a mysterious stranger. He is a homeless, lonely, half-crazed man, who sleeps on a bench on the Tel-Aviv boardwalk. The only man to whom he occasionally responds is a balloon seller who is also a survivor. The mysterious stranger refers to himself as "Medusa—a kind of jellyfish who has no words."

Yoram discovers that Medusa is Dr. Sigmund Rabi-nowitz, his brother-in-law, who prior to the War, was a famous humanist and authority on Renaissance art. He lost his family during the war and paid a high price for his own survival—Sigmund cooperated with the Nazis.

In the final confrontation between Yoram and Sigmund, Tomer delivers the finest dialogue of the play. When Yoram demands an explanation, Sigmund replies:

> You want to understand, to understand . . . Here you will find the story of a certain commandant of a concentration camp . . . A boyhood friend of mine . . . A German . . . We studied together at Heidelberg . . . A humanist . . . He had a special way of torturing me: once a week he would invite me to discuss with him the future of humanity. Once he said to me: You Jews have given us Marx, Freud, Einstein, Heine . . . But only Heine grasped the essential thing about German temperament . . . that we've remained fire-worshippers to this day. I want you to understand that I was a human being, and the most terrible thing of all was that they were human too . . .

Unlike Yoram, Sigmund is unable to forget and is unable to reconcile his pre-Holocaust humanism with his own behavior during the Holocaust and his post-Holocaust existence. Even madness is no escape. His guilt is overpowering and his only way out is suicide. (pp. 37-46)

Tomer is not interested in German guilt, a theme so common in German and European plays. His main concern is the Jewish survivor's struggle with rehabilitation. For a country like Israel, where Holocaust survivors comprise a high percentage of the population, this was one of the most difficult problems. In Tomer's play young survivors, like Yoram and Helenka, are afraid of life: yet, youth is in their favor and they are able to overcome. Tomer seems to imply that "normalcy" for the adult survivor is a difficult task, beyond realization. Sigmund finds the solution in the waves of the sea. Another survivor sells balloons, a symbolic occupation of nothingness. Israeli society and its attempt to "absorb" the survivors is marginal to the play and is represented by Nurit and the couple's friend, Dubi.

In *The Last Jew* by Uri Assaf and Yaffa Eliach, the lives of two generations are constantly marred by the trauma of the Holocaust. Vladimir, a convert to Judaism, is the son of a collaborator who murdered the Jews of Eisyski in 1941 and his wife Bluma is the daughter of the Last Jew. Both Vladimir and Bluma emigrated to Israel from the Soviet Union and are psychiatrists in a mental institution. Yigal Sinai is an Israeli Intelligence officer who screens Russian immigrants. The older generation is represented by Schneiderman, Bluma's father, the sole adult Jewish survivor of Eisyski who continued to live in the town for thirty years, and Levangorski, Schneiderman's business associate who is Vladimir's father and a former Nazi collaborator. Nachummadman and Maphtir-Yonah are two lunatic survivors from Eisyski living in a mental institution in Israel under Vladimir's care.

Each protagonist from his own perspective, experiences the guilt, pride, penance, revenge and shame forced upon him by the events of the Holocaust. The play constantly shifts between the dead and the living, between Eisyski and Israel; flashbacks are dominant. The two madmen are unwilling to accept reality. They choose the asylum out of sound calculations and convenience. There, within its walls, they recreate their shtetl, Eisyski, with its East European lore and folklore. They are constantly busy in the construction of a strange surrealistic vehicle inspired by Ezekiel's divine chariot. Their "passengers" are nine life-size effigies of their town's nine dead notables. They always await the arrival of the mysterious coachman, the tenth man. When Schneiderman, a former coachman, arrives at the hospital on a visit, the confrontation reaches its peak.

The younger generation has the misfortune of being their father's children. As eloquently stated by Durrenmatt, they cannot escape their father's world which is now their own. Bluma fights for some share of normalcy, love and justice. Vladimir is torn between guilt and penance, between Christian concepts and Jewish aspirations. He is forever marked with the sign of Cain as the murderer's son. Yigal Sinai, the Israeli officer, is committed to the idea that his generation will never allow the Holocaust to happen in Israel. In a confrontation between Nachum-madman and Sinai, after a ceremony on "Heroes and Martyrs Day," the madman bursts out in a frenzied speech:

> What do you know about the Holocaust? We are the Holocaust. This is what they say every year at the ceremony. People like us should be locked up behind bars, right? Because we shout and we always shout one thing, only one thing . . . And this is why it is better that we should be behind walls, all the year round, all the years, and once a year, at your convenience . . . you allow us to shout, to scream loudly, to open all the wounds, so that all may see them, smell them and listen. But it must be dignified, right? So that you may say, "Massada shall never fall again!" So for that purpose you set aside a special day, a special ceremony for the dignified scream. One day a year to be what indeed we truly are, the remainder of the other 364 days.

Can one indeed cope with the Holocaust 365 days every year, especially in a country with a large population of survivors, with a constant flow of new immigrants who re-open old wounds, and with hordes of hostile millions on the borders calling for annihilation? Survival is a fundamental issue. What price did one have to pay "there" for one's own survival? Was survival mere chance, with fate on the crossroads directing "left and right?" Did only the Schneidermans survive? Are the characters of *The Last Jew* mere individuals involved in their daily personal affairs?

> There is no doubt that each character in the play has not only its own personal existence but is intensely symbolic. . . . Each is a defined archetype and as such the meaning of his activities and behavior is different from characters in a regular play.

In *The Last Jew* there is continuity between the pre-

Holocaust past and the post-Holocaust future. The world of the fathers, their ghosts and guilt, still haunts and torments the lives of their sons and daughters. The latter attempt to build a better and safer world than the one they witnessed as young children, a Europe filled with dead bodies and decimated cities.

Most of the plays written by Israeli playwrights deal with the aspects of the Holocaust which are relevant to the Israeli experience rather than with the universal dimensions of the theme. Yet provincialism is not unique to Israeli Holocaust-related plays alone, but rather reflects the state of the Israeli theatre in general.

Since 1977 there seems to have been a silent switch in the presentation of the Holocaust in the public media. There is less focus on the concentration camp universe, destroyed cities, war crimes and trials. The focus now appears to be on the more flamboyant aspects of the Hitler era, Nazi leadership and Hitler himself. Within the span of less than half a year, four books on Hitler were published and two were more than one thousand pages long. One may attribute this to a new generation born after the Hitlerian era, physically and emotionally less scarred by the events of World War II. Its members are fascinated with the Third Reich and try to come to terms with the ghosts that clearly haunt them, as heirs to the legacy of the oppressors, collaborators and victims.

The screen, and to a lesser extent the theatre, also seems to be following this trend. The limelight is focused on Hitler and Germany's top leadership during World War II, as in the rock opera *Der Führer*, just completed by three young Germans.

One rock opera with sixty participants and Hitler as its superstar does not clearly set a new trend. Yet it introduces a new element in Holocaust drama—heroic, Wagnerian-like characters as protagonists, heroes totally removed from the realities of the concentration camp universe and World War II. One hopes that this will become a passing vogue and that this trendy rock opera, a reflection of the current fascination with Hitler, will not be the beginning of an outpouring of Holocaust plays with flamboyant Nazi heroes, but rather an indication that the time may be ripe for dramatists to make a more aggressive attempt to come to terms with the Holocaust period.

The playwright, more than other artists, needs historical latitude and an ample range of time and space. Unlike poetry and diaries, the number of plays written under siege is miniscule. Even a generation after the Holocaust the harvest of plays is rather unimpressive when compared with other areas of literature. When the artist confronts the empty page, he writes, consciously or subconsciously, for an individual reader. It is an intimate relationship between two individuals. The playwright writes for an audience. He creates a reality to be judged in public by a public, a reality over which he, the author, loses some measure of control to the actors and director. Due to the overpowering, paralyzing impact of the Holocaust, any drama on this theme remains a risky adventure for the playwright, audience and theatre. (pp. 46-9)

Yaffa Eliach, "The Holocaust in Hebrew

Drama," in Jewish Book Annual, Vol. 36, *No. 5739, 1978-79, pp. 37-49.*

Robert Skloot

[*Skloot is an American educator and theater director. In the following excerpt, he analyzes the concerns that dominate dramatic treatments of the Holocaust.*]

In general, playwrights of the Theatre of the Holocaust are motivated by five objectives, often simultaneously pursued: 1) to pay homage to the victims, if not as individuals then as a group; 2) to educate audiences to the facts of history; 3) to produce an emotional response to those facts; 4) to raise certain moral questions for audiences to discuss and reflect upon; and 5) to draw a lesson from the events re-created. What makes their work different from attempts to deal with other tragic themes, war for example, is their conviction that the Holocaust was a *unique* historical (and theological, political, and social) event, an event unlike anything else in the long and often tragic story of Western civilization.

The question of the uniqueness of the Holocaust is a controversial one. On one hand are those who argue that the attempted extermination of the Jews and other "unwanted" groups was merely another chapter in humanity's dark record, although an action which was carried out with an uncommon efficiency. Advocates of this viewpoint find parallels with other historical events. The Nazi objective of keeping pure the "master race" was political as well as racial; the camps and ghettos, we are reminded, did produce war materiel. The Holocaust, so this argument runs, differs in scale but not in essence from other genocidal activity.

On the other hand are the larger number of survivors and observers who regard the Holocaust as the seminal contemporary event in both Jewish and world history, an event against which our present morality may be measured, and our future predicted. The historian Nora Levin has written: "In Nazi Germany, mass murder became a civic virtue. In the years from 1933 to 1945 there was a quantum leap in the history of human destructiveness. . . . The Holocaust challenges us to reverse this process, if we can, to regain our humanity and restore the old taboos or live in a world with models for unlimited evil" ["Reflections on the Holocaust," lecture delivered 16 October 1977]. Levin and many others argue that when considered *in its totality* the Holocaust is without historical parallel; the fanatical barbarity, the technological efficiency, the virulent political and racial ideology, the world's insensitivity, and the virtual inconceivability of the size of the human slaughter, when taken together, describe an event unlike any other before or since. In this second view, the Holocaust, by altering the course of human history, raises profound and dire implications for the future of the entire world.

In accepting the Holocaust as unique, historians, artists, and audiences are greeted by another problem: the danger in metaphorical or analogical discussion. For if the Holocaust is a unique event, what it is compared to or symbolized by can be chosen only with the greatest sensitivity and depicted with the greatest precision. An inapt comparison could degrade the victims' suffering or courage, or diminish the respect due them. On the simplest level we see this problem in the often indiscriminate use of the term Holocaust itself, to refer to the consequences of floods, fires, riots, road accidents, multiple suicides, or bankruptcies. In the highly charged atmosphere which often surrounds depictions or discussions of the Holocaust (especially when survivors are present), responsible artists attempt the task of definition with an extreme consciousness of risk, for an inappropriate analogy or a failure of language is liable to expose the artist to accusations of falsification, trivialization, insensitivity, hypocrisy, or betrayal—aesthetic criticism on moral grounds. Protecting against the debasement of language is the job of every artist, but artists of the Holocaust must exercise a special kind of vigilance so that the full horrifying power of the word is preserved.

The search for a style and a form for the Holocaust experience, with all the challenges, responsibilities, and risks it entails, is yet more difficult in the theatre, because of all the arts theatre is the most public and the most *real.* By presenting verbal and visual action in a perpetual present moment, the theatre creates an experience which *lives* before other people; performed by live actors during a time shared with an audience, a live performance has an impact and effectiveness which is immediate and powerful. While other art forms presuppose a more passive relationship between the art object and the audience, the theatre's temporal and physical nature evokes immediate and intense interaction, permitting less evasion by encouraging greater subjective involvement. In this way history is made to live again in the most palpable of ways.

Another critical problem confronting playwrights who wish to deal with the Holocaust centers on the use of realism, a late nineteenth-century theatrical form which is still most common in contemporary drama. Born out of an attraction to rationalism and materialism, a belief in social progress, an urge to correct societal abuse of the unfortunate, and readiness to exploit the popular fascination with theatrical replication, realism succeeded extraordinarily well so long as it lodged itself in drawing rooms and preoccupied itself with the salutary possibilities of a scientifically regulated future and the evils of social misconduct. During the generation of its greatest success (1880-1914), realistic playwrights were often able scenically and textually to describe contemporary affairs in a complex vision of "life as it is lived." This characteristic became realism's legacy to the movies and television, the appearance of which did much to relieve theatre of the arbitrary standard of truth to life by which it had come to be judged.

Dramatic realism never lacked for critics, and the theatrical movements which followed it in our century attacked realism with vigor and conviction, usually on the grounds that it presented not more truth, but considerably less. And when we remember that realism, philosophically and formally, was predicated on objectivity and rationalism, it becomes increasingly clear why some artists and critics reject as inappropriate any realistic treatment of the most hope-defying and irrational event of modern times. . . .

[This argument is advanced] by Susan Sontag: "To simulate atrocities convincingly is to risk making the audience passive, reinforcing witless stereotypes, confirming distance, and creating meretricious fascination. . . . Like its simulation as fiction, the display of atrocity in the form of photographic evidence risks being tacitly pornographic" [*New York Review of Books,* 1980].

Still, realism in the theatre is not so easily dismissed, if only because the dangers of abstraction are also considerable. Also, the presence of the live actor always makes realistic demands on the playwright. Whatever the approach taken by the dramatist, a commitment to *some kind* of stage reality must be made from the earliest moments of conception; the playwright must decide what picture of the world of the Holocaust is to be visually presented and spatially concretized in the production of his or her script. But since the world of the ghettos and concentration camps is impossible to duplicate on the stage, the writer on the Holocaust is caught in a dilemma: how to give stage images their full burden of meaning without making them unrecognizable through abstraction or untruthful through replication. In reaction to just this situation, criticism of the Theatre of the Holocaust often makes two opposite arguments: that a realistic approach is a falsification of the subject and that an abstract approach is a betrayal of it. In truth, there is no single correct style for the Theatre of the Holocaust, and we should be cautious of those who insist on only one kind of treatment.

In their search for the forms to achieve their individual objectives, it is not surprising that playwrights of the Theatre of the Holocaust have employed a wide range of dramatic modes. Peter Weiss's *The Investigation* attempts a documentary style, Nellie Sachs's *Eli* is an extended poem in dramatic form, Erwin Sylvanus's *Dr. Korczak and the Children,* one of the best plays on the Holocaust theme, makes use of Pirandellian techniques, and George Tabori's *The Cannibals* . . . presents a surreal, nightmarish world where the actors assume the presences not only of victims, but of oppressors, insects, idiots, and even God.

It is true, however, that many other Holocaust plays retain a realistic base, because that is what people know best; audiences accept the form most readily because it is most "lifelike." Although the tension which develops between acceptance of the form and simultaneous revulsion with the content is likely to be intellectually unsettling and emotionally unendurable, the opposite strategy of deliberately distorting reality in an attempt to present the theme more accurately runs another sort of risk: losing sight of the "facts," and, with them, of the Holocaust's historical uniqueness.

In responding to this problem, playwrights have often tried to create believable environments by "softening" the depiction of ghetto or camp life; one method is to exclude or reduce the appearance of the Nazi oppressors and instead to focus on their victims. The dramatization of Anne Frank's *Diary* does without the Germans as actual stage presences; similarly, Shimon Wincelberg's *Resort 76* and Charlotte Delbo's *Who Will Carry the Word?* avoid actually showing the Nazis on stage. In Harold and Edith Lieberman's *Throne of Straw,* we see a German officer in the first scene, but only his civilian factotum thereafter; the central conflicts of the play occur among the Jewish victims. Arthur Miller's *Incident At Vichy* does not graphically picture the horrors of the Holocaust but rather implies them through events in the waiting room of the Vichy police station where the detainees' deportation and destruction is prefigured and symbolized (as when the silent, elderly Jew is cruelly separated from his most prized and only possession, a feather pillow, which is torn apart on stage).

Among other better-known Holocaust plays, Rolf Hochhuth's *The Deputy,* about the Catholic Church's response to the destruction of European Jewry, comes close to an actual depiction of the brutality of the Holocaust experience, especially in the concentration camp setting of act 5. But Hochhuth uses abstraction in his story too, distorting and allegorizing historical fact. So does Jean-Paul Sartre in *The Condemned of Altona,* which tells of a corrupt and decadent German family working out its war guilt. Sartre's is one of the few plays of importance which appear to relate the "German side" of the Holocaust story; however, as the playwright later admitted, *Altona* wasn't about the Holocaust at all, but about the war between France and Algeria a decade after the Holocaust. (Here is a fine example of the problem of the "diminishing analogy," cited earlier.) Both these plays are stylistic hybrids internally at odds with themselves. The same can be said of Martin Sherman's *Bent,* which deals with the problems of homosexuals in Nazi Germany, and of Robert Shaw's *The Man in the Glass Booth,* a story about a man who is both a Nazi and a Jew, which seems to care more for theatrical shock than intellectual coherency. Ultimately, these four playwrights (Hochhuth, Sartre, Sherman, and Shaw) fall short of the artistic success they seek for two reasons: they are unable to satisfyingly integrate their various styles, and they tend toward sensationalism by reducing and exploiting the Holocaust in order to favor their own religious, national, sexual, or psychological commitments.

Nevertheless, although the specific points of view of the playwrights vary considerably in the Theatre of the Holocaust, the point of departure is always the same: the historical event itself. It is important to realize how strongly the playwrights of this group rely not only on history but on the *idea* of history to give their imaginative creations an additional measure of stature, conviction, and even, for some, respectability. Thus, Hochhuth published an extensive and meticulous historical essay to accompany his massive play about Pope Pius XII, in order to give it more credibility and himself more ready evidence to call to *The Deputy*'s defense in case it was attacked (which it was). Sartre published interviews and essays separately from his plays and made historical points to anticipate and counteract audience ambivalence or hostility toward the Gerlach family. The protagonist of Shaw's psychological fantasy, the schizophrenic Goldman-Dorff, is clearly modeled on the figure of Adolf Eichmann, Hitler's chief assistant in charge of extermination of the Jews. Erwin Sylvanus focuses on one of the Holocaust's most celebrated heroes, Janusz Korczak, the Polish orphanage director who *chose* to go to his death along with "his children"; in this short play Sylvanus continually shatters the realistic description of character and the realistic use of space so that our confrontation with Korczak's "history" will be more powerful. Anne Frank, of course, was among the most famous victims of the Holocaust, and her simple story has achieved universal recognition. (pp. 14-20)

[Both] *Throne of Straw* and *Resort 76* explicitly draw upon the lives of Jews in the ghetto of Lodz, Poland, under the harsh rule of Mordechai Chaim Rumkowski to whom the Germans delegated certain administrative powers. The Liebermans contrast the last years of Rumkowski's life with the last years of the fictional but representative Wolf family in order to convey their moral understanding of Rumkowski's notorious career. In *The Cannibals,* George Tabori's characters, two survivors and the sons of those who perished in one of the barracks of a concentration camp, create through sound effects and vaudeville turns the world of the Holocaust as Tabori sees it; our knowing that the play is dedicated to the memory of Tabori's father Cornelius, "a small eater" who died in Auschwitz, gives his characters greater power over us. And Charlotte Delbo, one of the few playwrights who was a survivor of the camps, although striving for anonymity for her individual characters, lets us know in her book *Le convoi du 24 Janvier* (1965) that their history is real: of the 230 women in her group who were deported to Auschwitz, only forty-nine lived to see their liberation.

The creative efforts of all the playwrights reflect many different perspectives on the Holocaust experience and are written so as to express their understanding of the historical facts and individual interpretations of those facts; by their nature, the plays are not history, but they would not stand apart from history. Although we can learn about history from them, their significance is that they search for meaning, or at least intelligibility, in an event which, from nearly every angle, shelters some kind of profound truth about us all. To complete their search they must re-create an historical event by creating a fully imagined, internally coherent, and completely believable theatrical one. That is why, when we assess their historical content and their stylistic approach, the plays stand or fall on the basis of their own moral passion, honesty of emotion, and theatrical skill.

> A dramatist does not deal in the same kind of truth as an historian. He is concerned with its possibilities as much as or more than with its probabilities or its certainties. Unlike the historian, what he looks for in history is the raw material, whether of fact or of legend or even mere unrealized potentialities out of which he can fashion an action which on stage will carry its own conviction [R., *Encounter,* 1967].

The plays of the "Theatre of the Holocaust" assume many forms because from the raw material can be drawn differing interpretations of the same historical event, and because no single form can accurately portray that event. In addition, the known facts concern the playwrights less than the possibilities those facts suggest. Imaginatively searching out possibilities, and finding a form in which to express them, is nowhere more painful or demanding than in the Theatre of the Holocaust: yet, confronted by a terrifying and incontrovertible history, subjected to unrelent-

ing pressures from themselves and others, there still are playwrights willing to try to wrest some kind of meaning from the Holocaust experience. Their efforts are needed: for the solemn truth is that only one generation after the systematic and deliberate destruction of whole races and entire nations, the full meaning of those times still eludes us. An important reason why the literature of the Holocaust continues to proliferate is that the tasks it has taken upon itself remain unfinished. (pp. 20-2)

> *Robert Skloot, in an introduction to* The Theatre of the Holocaust: Four Plays, *edited by Robert Skloot, The University of Wisconsin Press, 1982, pp. 3-37.*

FURTHER READING

I. Anthologies

Dawidowicz, Lucy S., ed. *A Holocaust Reader.* New York: Behrman House, 1976, 397 p.
> Collection of eyewitness accounts by victims of the Holocaust.

Friedlander, Albert H. *Out of the Whirlwind: A Reader of Holocaust Literature.* New York: Schocken Books, 1976, 536 p.
> Extensive selection of excerpts from novels, diaries, and poems by such authors as Alexander Donat, Primo Levi, and Elie Wiesel.

Lévy, Isaac Jack. *And the World Stood Silent: Sephardic Poetry of the Holocaust.* Urbana: University of Illinois Press, 1989, 228 p.
> Anthology of poetry concerning the Holocaust by Jewish authors of Spanish or Portuguese descent.

II. Secondary Sources

Aaron, Frieda W. *Bearing the Unbearable: Yiddish and Polish Poetry in the Ghettos and Concentration Camps.* Albany: State University of New York Press, 1990, 242 p.
> Study of poetry written by Polish Jews in response to Nazi atrocities.

Abramson, Glenda. "The Plays of the Holocaust." In her *Modern Hebrew Drama,* pp. 116-40. New York: St. Martin's Press, 1979.
> Explication of Leah Goldberg's *The Chatelaine,* Ben-Zion Tomer's *The Children of the Shadow,* Aharon Meged's *Hannah Senesh,* and other Hebrew plays about the Holocaust.

Alexander, Edward. "The Holocaust in Jewish Novels." *Jewish Book Annual* 35, No. 5738 (1977-78): 25-32.
> Explores how Jewish writers of different nationalities and generations perceive the Holocaust.

———. *The Resonance of Dust: Essays on Holocaust Literature and Jewish Fate.* Columbus: Ohio State University Press, 1979, 256 p.
> Survey of Holocaust literature that addresses the rela-

tionship between the Holocaust, the course of Jewish history, and the future of the Jewish people.

Alter, Robert. *Defenses of the Imagination: Jewish Writers and Modern Historical Crisis.* Philadelphia: The Jewish Publication Society of America, 1977, 262 p.

Examines how Jewish writers give meaning to the Holocaust and other catastrophic events through art.

Alvarez, A. "The Literature of the Holocaust." In his *Beyond All This Fiddle,* pp. 22-33. London: Penguin Press, 1968.

Investigation of how such authors as Elie Wiesel and Tadeusz Borowski effectively convey the universal implications of the Holocaust as well as the immediate suffering of its victims.

Berger, Alan L. *Crisis and Covenant: The Holocaust in American Jewish Fiction.* Albany: State University of New York Press, 1985, 226 p.

Critiques the response of authors including Saul Bellow, Cynthia Ozick, and Philip Roth to the religious and philosophical implications of the Holocaust.

Bilik, Dorothy Seidman. *Immigrant-Survivors: Post-Holocaust Consciousness in Recent Jewish American Fiction.* Middletown, Conn.: Wesleyan University Press, 1981, 216 p.

Posits that "the immigrant-survivors in America bridge the historical and psychological distance between the modern Jewish American writer and the somber events that the writer confronts through the fictive imagination."

Cargas, Harry James, ed. *When God and Man Failed: Non-Jewish Views of the Holocaust.* New York: Macmillan Publishing, 1981, 238 p.

Collection of essays by non-Jewish authors that includes criticism on Holocaust literature by Cargas and Thomas A. Idinopulos.

Cernyak-Spatz, Susan E. *German Holocaust Literature.* New York: Peter Lang, 1985, 144 p.

Analyzes Holocaust literature written by Jewish and non-Jewish Germans in the decades following World War II. Cernyak-Spatz maintains that a movement away from stereotypical characterizations coincides with "the gradual assumption of responsibility for the events by the whole nation."

Exner, Richard. "Some Reflections on Holocaust and Post-Holocaust Writing." *World Literature Today* 60, No. 3 (Summer 1986): 402-06.

Posits that those writers not directly affected by the Holocaust must nevertheless take into account its moral and philosophical implications.

Ezrahi, Sidra DeKoven. *By Words Alone: The Holocaust in Literature.* Chicago: University of Chicago Press, 1980, 262 p.

Literary history of the Holocaust legacy.

Farnham, James F. "Holocaust Literature for Children: The Presentation of Evil." *University of Hartford Studies in Literature* 18, Nos. 2-3 (1986): 55-62.

Argues that Holocaust literature for children should present the dehumanizing effects of racism and prejudice while affirming the positive aspects of human nature.

Fine, Ellen S. "The Surviving Voice: Literature of the Holocaust." In *Perspectives on the Holocaust,* edited by Randolph

L. Braham, pp. 105-17. Boston: Kluwer-Nijhoff Publishing, 1983.

Asserts that the poignancy of memoirs and diaries by Holocaust victims dispels claims that silence is the only appropriate response to Nazi atrocities.

Foley, Barbara. "Fact, Fiction, Fascism: Testimony and Mimesis in Holocaust Narratives." *Comparative Literature* 34, No. 4 (Fall 1982): 330-60.

Asserts that a synthesis of the memoir and the novel best expresses the Holocaust experience.

Harrison, Barbara. "Howl Like the Wolves." *Children's Literature* 15 (1987): 67-90.

Examines Holocaust literature for children.

Kohn, Murray J. *The Voice of My Blood Cries Out: The Holocaust As Reflected in Hebrew Poetry.* New York: Shengold Publishers, 1979, 224 p.

Explores how Hebrew poets express the shock, despair, guilt, and loss of faith experienced by Holocaust survivors.

Langer, Lawrence L. *The Holocaust and the Literary Imagination.* New Haven: Yale University Press, 1975, 300 p.

Among the first in-depth studies of Holocaust literature.

——. *Versions of Survival: The Holocaust and the Human Spirit.* Albany: State University of New York Press, 1982, 267 p.

Uses the works of Elie Wiesel, Gertrud Kolmar, Nelly Sachs, and others to examine how the concept of humanity has been altered by the Holocaust.

——. "Family Dilemmas in Holocaust Literature." *Michigan Quarterly Review* 26, No. 2 (Spring 1987): 387-99.

Contends that by reading accounts of the agonizing decisions faced by Jewish families during the Holocaust, readers will better comprehend the morally dislocated world of the concentration camp.

Mandel, Eli. "Auschwitz: Poetry of Alienation." *Canadian Literature* 100 (Spring 1984): 213-18.

Recounts his attempt to communicate the horrors of Auschwitz through poetry.

Mendelsohn, Leonard M. "The Survival of the Spirit in Holocaust Literature for and about Children." In *Triumphs of the Spirit in Children's Literature,* edited by Francelia Butler and Richard Rotert, pp. 76-87. Hamden, Conn.: Shoe String Press, 1986.

Argues that children's literature of the Holocaust confirms the survival, if not the triumph, of the human spirit.

Mintz, Alan. "Survivors and Bystanders." In his *Hurban: Responses to Catastrophe in Hebrew Literature,* pp. 157-269. New York: Columbia University Press, 1984.

Explores the treatment of the Holocaust in Israeli literature and discusses works by Uri Zvi Greenberg and Aharon Appelfeld.

Patraka, Vivian M. "Contemporary Drama, Fascism, and the Holocaust." *Theatre Journal* 39, No. 1 (March 1987): 65-77.

Examines how such playwrights as Charlotte Delbo, David Hare, and George Tabori transform the historical fact of the Holocaust into a dramatic discourse.

Pawel, Ernst. "Fiction of the Holocaust." *Midstream* 16, No. 6 (June-July 1970): 14-26.

> Brief survey of Holocaust narratives in which Pawel concludes that fiction cannot adequately convey the full horror of the concentration camp.

Rosen, Norma. "The Holocaust and the American-Jewish Novelist." *Midstream* 20, No. 8 (October 1974): 54-62.

> Investigates why only a few American novelists have addressed the Holocaust in their work.

Rosenfeld, Alvin H. "The Fascination of Abomination." In his *Imagining Hitler,* pp. 42-60. Bloomington: Indiana University Press, 1985.

> Examines how Hitler and his "final solution" have affected both serious and popular literature.

————, and Greenberg, Irving, eds. *Confronting the Holocaust: The Impact of Elie Wiesel.* Bloomington: Indiana University Press, 1978, 239 p.

> Critical anthology discussing Wiesel's important contribution to the understanding of the Holocaust.

Rubin, Ruth. "The Struggle to Survive." In her *Voices of a People: Yiddish Folk Song,* pp. 423-61. New York: Thomas Yoseloff, 1963.

> Analyzes the lyrics of Yiddish songs composed in the ghettos and concentration camps.

Steiner, George. "A Kind of Survivor." In his *Language and Silence: Essays on Language, Literature, and the Inhuman,* pp. 140-54. New York: Atheneum, 1967.

> Argues that the Holocaust irreversibly debased the German language.

Yuter, Alan J. *The Holocaust in Hebrew Literature: From Genocide to Rebirth.* Port Washington, N.Y.: Associated Faculty Press, 1983, 137 p.

> Survey of individual Israeli authors who have published works on the Holocaust, including Ka-Tzetnik, Amos Oz, and Aharon Appelfeld.

Twentieth-Century
Literary Criticism

Cumulative Indexes
Volumes 1-42

This Index Includes References to Entries in These Gale Series

Contemporary Literary Criticism presents excerpts of criticism on the works of novelists, poets, dramatists, short story writers, scriptwriters, and other creative writers who are now living or who have died since 1960. Cumulative indexes to authors and nationalities are included, as well as an index to titles discussed in the individual volume.

Twentieth-Century Literary Criticism contains critical excerpts by the most significant commentators on poets, novelists, short story writers, dramatists, and philosophers who died between 1900 and 1960. Indexes to authors, nationalities, and titles discussed are included in each new volume.

Nineteenth-Century Literature Criticism offers significant passages from criticism on authors who died between 1800 and 1899. Indexes to authors, nationalities, and titles discussed are included in each new volume.

Literature Criticism from 1400 to 1800 compiles significant passages from the most noteworthy criticism on authors of the fifteenth through the eighteenth centuries. Cumulative indexes to authors, nationalities, and titles discussed are included in each new volume.

Classical and Medieval Literature Criticism offers excerpts of criticism on the works of world authors from classical antiquity through the fourteenth century. Cumulative indexes to authors, titles and critics are included in each volume.

Short Story Criticism combines excerpts of criticism on short fiction by writers of all eras and nationalities. Cumulative indexes to authors, nationalities, and titles discussed are included in each new volume.

Poetry Criticism presents excerpts of criticism on the works of poets from all eras, movements, and nationalities.

Children's Literature Review includes excerpts from reviews, criticism, and commentary on works of authors and illustrators who create books for children. Cumulative indexes to authors, nationalities, and titles discussed are included in each new volume.

Contemporary Authors Series encompasses five related series. *Contemporary Authors* provides biographical and bibliographical information on more than 92,000 writers of fiction, nonfiction, poetry, journalism, drama, film, and other related fields. Each new volume contains sketches on authors not previously covered in the series. *Contemporary Authors New Revision Series* provides completely updated information on active authors covered in previously published volumes of *CA*. Only entries requiring significant change are revised for *CA New Revision Series*. *Contemporary Authors Permanent Series* consists of updated listings for deceased and inactive authors removed from the original volumes 9-36 when those volumes were revised. *Contemporary Authors Autobiography Series* presents specially commissioned autobiographies by leading contemporary writers. *Contemporary Authors Bibliographical Series* contains primary and secondary bibliographies as well as analytical bibliographical essays by authorities on major modern authors.

Dictionary of Literary Biography encompasses three related series. *Dictionary of Literary Biography* furnishes illustrated overviews of authors' lives and works and places them in the larger perspective of literary history. *Dictionary of Literary Biography Documentary Series* illuminates the careers of major figures through a selection of literary documents, including letters, notebook and diary entries, interviews, book reviews, and photographs. *Dictionary of Literary Biography Yearbook* summarizes the past year's literary activity with articles on genres, major prizes, conferences, and other timely subjects and includes updated and new entries on individual authors. A cumulative index to authors and articles is included in each new volume. *Concise Dictionary of Literary Biography,* a six-volume series, collects revised and updated sketches on major American authors that were originally presented in *Dictionary of Literary Biography.*

Something about the Author Series encompasses three related series. *Something about the Author* contains heavily illustrated biographical sketches on authors and illustrators of juvenile and young adult literature from all eras. *Something about the Author Autobiography Series* presents specially commissioned autobiographies by prominent authors and illustrators of books for children and young adults. *Authors and Artists for Young Adults* provides high school and junior high school students with profiles of their favorite creative artists in the media of print, film, television, drama, song lyrics, and cartoons.

Yesterday's Authors of Books for Children contains heavily illustrated entries on children's writers who died before 1961. Complete in two volumes.

Literary Criticism Series
Cumulative Author Index

This index lists all author entries in the Gale Literary Criticism Series and includes cross-references to other Gale sources. References in the index are identified as follows:

AAYA: *Authors & Artists for Young Adults*, Volumes 1-6
CAAS: *Contemporary Authors Autobiography Series*, Volumes 1-13
CA: *Contemporary Authors* (original series), Volumes 1-132
CABS: *Contemporary Authors Bibliographical Series*, Volumes 1-3
CANR: *Contemporary Authors New Revision Series*, Volumes 1-33
CAP: *Contemporary Authors Permanent Series*, Volumes 1-2
CA-R: *Contemporary Authors* (revised editions), Volumes 1-44
CDALB: *Concise Dictionary of American Literary Biography*, Volumes 1-6
CLC: *Contemporary Literary Criticism*, Volumes 1-66
CLR: *Children's Literature Review*, Volumes 1-24
CMLC: *Classical and Medieval Literature Criticism*, Volumes 1-7
DC: *Drama Criticism*, Volume 1
DLB: *Dictionary of Literary Biography*, Volumes 1-104
DLB-DS: *Dictionary of Literary Biography Documentary Series*, Volumes 1-8
DLB-Y: *Dictionary of Literary Biography Yearbook*, Volumes 1980-1988
LC: *Literature Criticism from 1400 to 1800*, Volumes 1-16
NCLC: *Nineteenth-Century Literature Criticism*, Volumes 1-32
PC: *Poetry Criticism*, Volumes 1-2
SAAS: *Something about the Author Autobiography Series*, Volumes 1-12
SATA: *Something about the Author*, Volumes 1-64
SSC: *Short Story Criticism*, Volumes 1-8
TCLC: *Twentieth-Century Literary Criticism*, Volumes 1-42
YABC: *Yesterday's Authors of Books for Children*, Volumes 1-2

Aiken, Conrad (Potter)
    1889-1973 .... **CLC 1, 3, 5, 10, 52**
    See also CANR 4; CA 5-8R;
        obituary CA 45-48; SATA 3, 30; DLB 9,
        45

Aiken, Joan (Delano)   1924- .... **CLC 35**
    See also CLR 1, 19; CANR 4; CA 9-12R;
        SAAS 1; SATA 2, 30

Ainsworth, William Harrison
    1805-1882 .... **NCLC 13**
    See also SATA 24; DLB 21

Ajar, Emile   1914-1980
    See Gary, Romain

Akhmadulina, Bella (Akhatovna)
    1937- .... **CLC 53**
    See also CA 65-68

Akhmatova, Anna
    1888-1966 .... **CLC 11, 25, 64; PC 2**
    See also CAP 1; CA 19-20;
        obituary CA 25-28R

Aksakov, Sergei Timofeyvich
    1791-1859 .... **NCLC 2**

Aksenov, Vassily (Pavlovich)   1932-
    See Aksyonov, Vasily (Pavlovich)

Aksyonov, Vasily (Pavlovich)
    1932- .... **CLC 22, 37**
    See also CANR 12; CA 53-56

Akutagawa Ryunosuke
    1892-1927 .... **TCLC 16**
    See also CA 117

Alain   1868-1951 .... **TCLC 41**
    See also Chartier, Emile-Auguste

Alain-Fournier   1886-1914 .... **TCLC 6**
    See also Fournier, Henri Alban
    See also DLB 65

Alarcon, Pedro Antonio de
    1833-1891 .... **NCLC 1**

Alas (y Urena), Leopoldo (Enrique Garcia)
    1852-1901 .... **TCLC 29**
    See also CA 113

Albee, Edward (Franklin III)
    1928- ... **CLC 1, 2, 3, 5, 9, 11, 13, 25, 53**
    See also CANR 8; CA 5-8R; DLB 7;
        CDALB 1941-1968

Alberti, Rafael   1902- .... **CLC 7**
    See also CA 85-88

Alcott, Amos Bronson   1799-1888 .. **NCLC 1**
    See also DLB 1

Alcott, Louisa May   1832-1888 .... **NCLC 6**
    See also CLR 1; YABC 1; DLB 1, 42, 79;
        CDALB 1865-1917

Aldanov, Mark   1887-1957 .... **TCLC 23**
    See also CA 118

Aldington, Richard   1892-1962..... **CLC 49**
    See also CA 85-88; DLB 20, 36

Aldiss, Brian W(ilson)
    1925- .... **CLC 5, 14, 40**
    See also CAAS 2; CANR 5; CA 5-8R;
        SATA 34; DLB 14

Alegria, Fernando   1918-.......... **CLC 57**
    See also CANR 5; CA 11-12R

Aleixandre, Vicente   1898-1984 ... **CLC 9, 36**
    See also CANR 26; CA 85-88;
        obituary CA 114

Alepoudelis, Odysseus   1911-
    See Elytis, Odysseus

Aleshkovsky, Yuz   1929-.......... **CLC 44**
    See also CA 121, 128

Alexander, Lloyd (Chudley)   1924- .. **CLC 35**
    See also CLR 1, 5; CANR 1; CA 1-4R;
        SATA 3, 49; DLB 52

Alfau, Felipe   1902-.............. **CLC 66**

Alger, Horatio, Jr.   1832-1899 ..... **NCLC 8**
    See also SATA 16; DLB 42

Algren, Nelson   1909-1981 .... **CLC 4, 10, 33**
    See also CANR 20; CA 13-16R;
        obituary CA 103; DLB 9; DLB-Y 81, 82;
        CDALB 1941-1968

Alighieri, Dante   1265-1321 .... **CMLC 3**

Allard, Janet   1975-.............. **CLC 59**

Allen, Edward   1948-.............. **CLC 59**

Allen, Roland   1939-
    See Ayckbourn, Alan

Allen, Woody   1935-........... **CLC 16, 52**
    See also CANR 27; CA 33-36R; DLB 44

Allende, Isabel   1942- .... **CLC 39, 57**
    See also CA 125

Alleyne, Carla D.   1975?-.......... **CLC 65**

Allingham, Margery (Louise)
    1904-1966 .... **CLC 19**
    See also CANR 4; CA 5-8R;
        obituary CA 25-28R; DLB 77

Allingham, William   1824-1889 ... **NCLC 25**
    See also DLB 35

Allston, Washington   1779-1843.... **NCLC 2**
    See also DLB 1

Almedingen, E. M.   1898-1971...... **CLC 12**
    See also Almedingen, Martha Edith von
    See also SATA 3

Almedingen, Martha Edith von   1898-1971
    See Almedingen, E. M.
    See also CANR 1; CA 1-4R

Alonso, Damaso   1898-............ **CLC 14**
    See also CA 110; obituary CA 130

Alta   1942-....................... **CLC 19**
    See also CA 57-60

Alter, Robert B(ernard)   1935-...... **CLC 34**
    See also CANR 1; CA 49-52

Alther, Lisa   1944-.............. **CLC 7, 41**
    See also CANR 12; CA 65-68

Altman, Robert   1925-............. **CLC 16**
    See also CA 73-76

Alvarez, A(lfred)   1929-........... **CLC 5, 13**
    See also CANR 3; CA 1-4R; DLB 14, 40

Alvarez, Alejandro Rodriguez   1903-1965
    See Casona, Alejandro
    See also obituary CA 93-96

Amado, Jorge   1912-........... **CLC 13, 40**
    See also CA 77-80

Ambler, Eric   1909-............. **CLC 4, 6, 9**
    See also CANR 7; CA 9-12R; DLB 77

Amichai, Yehuda   1924- ...... **CLC 9, 22, 57**
    See also CA 85-88

Amiel, Henri Frederic   1821-1881 .. **NCLC 4**

Amis, Kingsley (William)
    1922- ...... **CLC 1, 2, 3, 5, 8, 13, 40, 44**
    See also CANR 8; CA 9-12R; DLB 15, 27

Amis, Martin   1949- .... **CLC 4, 9, 38, 62**
    See also CANR 8, 27; CA 65-68; DLB 14

Ammons, A(rchie) R(andolph)
    1926- .... **CLC 2, 3, 5, 8, 9, 25, 57**
    See also CANR 6; CA 9-12R; DLB 5

Anand, Mulk Raj   1905-........... **CLC 23**
    See also CA 65-68

Anaya, Rudolfo A(lfonso)   1937- .... **CLC 23**
    See also CAAS 4; CANR 1; CA 45-48;
        DLB 82

Andersen, Hans Christian
    1805-1875 .... **NCLC 7; SSC 6**
    See also CLR 6; YABC 1, 1

Anderson, Jessica (Margaret Queale)
    19??-......................... **CLC 37**
    See also CANR 4; CA 9-12R

Anderson, Jon (Victor)   1940- .... **CLC 9**
    See also CANR 20; CA 25-28R

Anderson, Lindsay   1923-.......... **CLC 20**
    See also CA 125

Anderson, Maxwell   1888-1959 ..... **TCLC 2**
    See also CA 105; DLB 7

Anderson, Poul (William)   1926- .... **CLC 15**
    See also CAAS 2; CANR 2, 15; CA 1-4R;
        SATA 39; DLB 8

Anderson, Robert (Woodruff)
    1917-....................... **CLC 23**
    See also CA 21-24R; DLB 7

Anderson, Roberta Joan   1943-
    See Mitchell, Joni

Anderson, Sherwood
    1876-1941 ...... **TCLC 1, 10, 24; SSC 1**
    See also CAAS 3; CA 104, 121; DLB 4, 9;
        DLB-DS 1

Andrade, Carlos Drummond de
    1902-1987 .... **CLC 18**
    See also CA 123

Andrewes, Lancelot   1555-1626 .... **LC 5**

Andrews, Cicily Fairfield   1892-1983
    See West, Rebecca

Andreyev, Leonid (Nikolaevich)
    1871-1919 .... **TCLC 3**
    See also CA 104

Andrezel, Pierre   1885-1962
    See Dinesen, Isak; Blixen, Karen
        (Christentze Dinesen)

Andric, Ivo   1892-1975 .... **CLC 8**
    See also CA 81-84; obituary CA 57-60

Angelique, Pierre   1897-1962
    See Bataille, Georges

Angell, Roger   1920-.............. **CLC 26**
    See also CANR 13; CA 57-60

Angelou, Maya   1928-....... **CLC 12, 35, 64**
    See also CANR 19; CA 65-68; SATA 49;
        DLB 38

Annensky, Innokenty   1856-1909 ... **TCLC 14**
    See also CA 110

Anouilh, Jean (Marie Lucien Pierre)
    1910-1987 ...... **CLC 1, 3, 8, 13, 40, 50**
    See also CA 17-20R; obituary CA 123

Anthony, Florence   1947-
    See Ai

Anthony (Jacob), Piers 1934- ...... **CLC 35**
See also Jacob, Piers A(nthony)
D(illingham)
See also DLB 8

Antoninus, Brother 1912-
See Everson, William (Oliver)

Antonioni, Michelangelo 1912- ..... **CLC 20**
See also CA 73-76

Antschel, Paul 1920-1970. ..... **CLC 10, 19**
See also Celan, Paul
See also CA 85-88

Anwar, Chairil 1922-1949 .... **TCLC 22**
See also CA 121

Apollinaire, Guillaume
1880-1918 .... **TCLC 3, 8**
See also Kostrowitzki, Wilhelm Apollinaris
de

Appelfeld, Aharon 1932- .... **CLC 23, 47**
See also CA 112

Apple, Max (Isaac) 1941-....... **CLC 9, 33**
See also CANR 19; CA 81-84

Appleman, Philip (Dean) 1926- ..... **CLC 51**
See also CANR 6; CA 13-16R

Apuleius, (Lucius) (Madaurensis)
125?-175?.................. **CMLC 1**

Aquin, Hubert 1929-1977.......... **CLC 15**
See also CA 105; DLB 53

Aragon, Louis 1897-1982........ **CLC 3, 22**
See also CA 69-72; obituary CA 108;
DLB 72

Arbuthnot, John 1667-1735.......... **LC 1**

Archer, Jeffrey (Howard) 1940- .... **CLC 28**
See also CANR 22; CA 77-80

Archer, Jules 1915- .... **CLC 12**
See also CANR 6; CA 9-12R; SAAS 5;
SATA 4

Arden, John 1930- .... **CLC 6, 13, 15**
See also CAAS 4; CA 13-16R; DLB 13

Arenas, Reinaldo 1943- .... **CLC 41**
See also CA 124, 128

Arendt, Hannah 1906-1975 .... **CLC 66**
See also CA 19-20R; obituary CA 61-64

Aretino, Pietro 1492-1556.......... **LC 12**

Arguedas, Jose Maria
1911-1969 .... **CLC 10, 18**
See also CA 89-92

Argueta, Manlio 1936-............ **CLC 31**

Ariosto, Ludovico 1474-1533......... **LC 6**

Aristophanes
c. 450 B. C.-c. 385 B. C. ...... **CMLC 4**

Arlt, Roberto 1900-1942 .... **TCLC 29**
See also CA 123

Armah, Ayi Kwei 1939-......... **CLC 5, 33**
See also CANR 21; CA 61-64

Armatrading, Joan 1950-.......... **CLC 17**
See also CA 114

Arnim, Achim von (Ludwig Joachim von
Arnim) 1781-1831 .... **NCLC 5**
See also DLB 90

Arnold, Matthew 1822-1888 ... **NCLC 6, 29**
See also DLB 32, 57

Arnold, Thomas 1795-1842 ...... **NCLC 18**
See also DLB 55

Arnow, Harriette (Louisa Simpson)
1908-1986 .... **CLC 2, 7, 18**
See also CANR 14; CA 9-12R;
obituary CA 118; SATA 42, 47; DLB 6

Arp, Jean 1887-1966................ **CLC 5**
See also CA 81-84; obituary CA 25-28R

Arquette, Lois S(teinmetz) 1934-
See Duncan (Steinmetz Arquette), Lois
See also SATA 1

Arrabal, Fernando 1932- ... **CLC 2, 9, 18, 58**
See also CANR 15; CA 9-12R

Arrick, Fran 19??- .... **CLC 30**

Artaud, Antonin 1896-1948 ..... **TCLC 3, 36**
See also CA 104

Arthur, Ruth M(abel) 1905-1979.... **CLC 12**
See also CANR 4; CA 9-12R;
obituary CA 85-88; SATA 7;
obituary SATA 26

Artsybashev, Mikhail Petrarch
1878-1927 .... **TCLC 31**

Arundel, Honor (Morfydd)
1919-1973 .... **CLC 17**
See also CAP 2; CA 21-22;
obituary CA 41-44R; SATA 4;
obituary SATA 24

Asch, Sholem 1880-1957 .... **TCLC 3**
See also CA 105

Ashbery, John (Lawrence)
1927- ... **CLC 2, 3, 4, 6, 9, 13, 15, 25, 41**
See also CANR 9; CA 5-8R; DLB 5;
DLB-Y 81

Ashton-Warner, Sylvia (Constance)
1908-1984 .... **CLC 19**
See also CA 69-72; obituary CA 112

Asimov, Isaac 1920-.... **CLC 1, 3, 9, 19, 26**
See also CLR 12; CANR 2, 19; CA 1-4R;
SATA 1, 26; DLB 8

Astley, Thea (Beatrice May)
1925- .... **CLC 41**
See also CANR 11; CA 65-68

Aston, James 1906-1964
See White, T(erence) H(anbury)

Asturias, Miguel Angel
1899-1974 .... **CLC 3, 8, 13**
See also CAP 2; CA 25-28;
obituary CA 49-52

Atheling, William, Jr. 1921-1975
See Blish, James (Benjamin)

Atherton, Gertrude (Franklin Horn)
1857-1948 .... **TCLC 2**
See also CA 104; DLB 9, 78

Atwood, Margaret (Eleanor)
1939- .... **CLC 2, 3, 4, 8, 13, 15, 25, 44;**
SSC 2
See also CANR 3, 24; CA 49-52; SATA 50;
DLB 53

Aubin, Penelope 1685-1731? .... **LC 9**
See also DLB 39

Auchincloss, Louis (Stanton)
1917- .... **CLC 4, 6, 9, 18, 45**
See also CANR 6; CA 1-4R; DLB 2;
DLB-Y 80

Auden, W(ystan) H(ugh)
1907-1973 ..... **CLC 1, 2, 3, 4, 6, 9, 11,**
14, 43; PC 1
See also CANR 5; CA 9-12R;
obituary CA 45-48; DLB 10, 20

Audiberti, Jacques 1899-1965 ...... **CLC 38**
See also obituary CA 25-28R

Auel, Jean M(arie) 1936-.......... **CLC 31**
See also CANR 21; CA 103

Augier, Emile 1820-1889 .... **NCLC 31**

Augustine, St. 354-430........... **CMLC 6**

Austen, Jane 1775-1817.... **NCLC 1, 13, 19**

Auster, Paul 1947- .... **CLC 47**
See also CANR 23; CA 69-72

Austin, Mary (Hunter)
1868-1934 .... **TCLC 25**
See also CA 109; DLB 9

Averroes 1126-1198 .... **CMLC 7**

Avison, Margaret 1918-.......... **CLC 2, 4**
See also CA 17-20R; DLB 53

Ayckbourn, Alan 1939- .... **CLC 5, 8, 18, 33**
See also CA 21-24R; DLB 13

Aydy, Catherine 1937-
See Tennant, Emma

Ayme, Marcel (Andre) 1902-1967... **CLC 11**
See also CA 89-92; DLB 72

Ayrton, Michael 1921-1975......... **CLC 7**
See also CANR 9, 21; CA 5-8R;
obituary CA 61-64

Azorin 1874-1967 .... **CLC 11**
See also Martinez Ruiz, Jose

Azuela, Mariano 1873-1952........ **TCLC 3**
See also CA 104

"Bab" 1836-1911
See Gilbert, (Sir) W(illiam) S(chwenck)

Babel, Isaak (Emmanuilovich)
1894-1941 .... **TCLC 2, 13**
See also CA 104

Babits, Mihaly 1883-1941 .... **TCLC 14**
See also CA 114

Bacchelli, Riccardo 1891-1985 ..... **CLC 19**
See also CA 29-32R; obituary CA 117

Bach, Richard (David) 1936-....... **CLC 14**
See also CANR 18; CA 9-12R; SATA 13

Bachman, Richard 1947-
See King, Stephen (Edwin)

Bacovia, George 1881-1957 .... **TCLC 24**

Bagehot, Walter 1826-1877 ...... **NCLC 10**
See also DLB 55

Bagnold, Enid 1889-1981.......... **CLC 25**
See also CANR 5; CA 5-8R;
obituary CA 103; SATA 1, 25; DLB 13

Bagryana, Elisaveta 1893-......... **CLC 10**

Bailey, Paul 1937- .... **CLC 45**
See also CANR 16; CA 21-24R; DLB 14

Baillie, Joanna 1762-1851 .... **NCLC 2**

Bainbridge, Beryl
1933- .... **CLC 4, 5, 8, 10, 14, 18, 22, 62**
See also CANR 24; CA 21-24R; DLB 14

Baker, Elliott 1922-............. **CLC 8, 61**
See also CANR 2; CA 45-48

Baker, Nicholson 1957-........... **CLC 61**

Boyle, Thomas Coraghessan
1948- . . . . CLC 36, 55
See also CA 120; DLB-Y 86

Brackenridge, Hugh Henry
1748-1816 . . . . NCLC 7
See also DLB 11, 37

Bradbury, Edward P. 1939-
See Moorcock, Michael

Bradbury, Malcolm (Stanley)
1932- . . . . CLC 32, 61
See also CANR 1; CA 1-4R; DLB 14

Bradbury, Ray(mond Douglas)
1920- . . . . CLC 1, 3, 10, 15, 42
See also CANR 2; CA 1-4R; SATA 11;
DLB 2, 8

Bradford, Gamaliel 1863-1932 . . . . . TCLC 36
See also DLB 17

Bradley, David (Henry), Jr. 1950- . . CLC 23
See also CANR 26; CA 104; DLB 33

Bradley, John Ed 1959- . . . . CLC 55

Bradley, Marion Zimmer 1930- . . . . . CLC 30
See also CANR 7; CA 57-60; DLB 8

Bradstreet, Anne 1612-1672 . . . . LC 4
See also DLB 24; CDALB 1640-1865

Bragg, Melvyn 1939- . . . . CLC 10
See also CANR 10; CA 57-60; DLB 14

Braine, John (Gerard)
1922-1986 . . . . CLC 1, 3, 41
See also CANR 1; CA 1-4R;
obituary CA 120; DLB 15; DLB-Y 86

Brammer, Billy Lee 1930?-1978
See Brammer, William

Brammer, William 1930?-1978 . . . . . CLC 31
See also obituary CA 77-80

Brancati, Vitaliano 1907-1954 . . . . . TCLC 12
See also CA 109

Brancato, Robin F(idler) 1936- . . . . . CLC 35
See also CANR 11; CA 69-72; SATA 23

Brand, Millen 1906-1980 . . . . CLC 7
See also CA 21-24R; obituary CA 97-100

Branden, Barbara 19??- . . . . CLC 44

Brandes, Georg (Morris Cohen)
1842-1927 . . . . TCLC 10
See also CA 105

Brandys, Kazimierz 1916- . . . . CLC 62

Branley, Franklyn M(ansfield)
1915- . . . . CLC 21
See also CLR 13; CANR 14; CA 33-36R;
SATA 4

Brathwaite, Edward 1930- . . . . CLC 11
See also CANR 11; CA 25-28R; DLB 53

Brautigan, Richard (Gary)
1935-1984 . . . . CLC 1, 3, 5, 9, 12, 34, 42
See also CA 53-56; obituary CA 113;
SATA 56; DLB 2, 5; DLB-Y 80, 84

Brecht, (Eugen) Bertolt (Friedrich)
1898-1956 . . . . TCLC 1, 6, 13, 35
See also CA 104; DLB 56

Bremer, Fredrika 1801-1865 . . . . . NCLC 11

Brennan, Christopher John
1870-1932 . . . . TCLC 17
See also CA 117

Brennan, Maeve 1917- . . . . CLC 5
See also CA 81-84

Brentano, Clemens (Maria)
1778-1842 . . . . NCLC 1
See also DLB 90

Brenton, Howard 1942- . . . . CLC 31
See also CA 69-72; DLB 13

Breslin, James 1930-
See Breslin, Jimmy
See also CA 73-76

Breslin, Jimmy 1930- . . . . CLC 4, 43
See also Breslin, James

Bresson, Robert 1907- . . . . CLC 16
See also CA 110

Breton, Andre 1896-1966 . . . CLC 2, 9, 15, 54
See also CAP 2; CA 19-20;
obituary CA 25-28R; DLB 65

Breytenbach, Breyten 1939- . . . . . CLC 23, 37
See also CA 113, 129

Bridgers, Sue Ellen 1942- . . . . CLC 26
See also CANR 11; CA 65-68; SAAS 1;
SATA 22; DLB 52

Bridges, Robert 1844-1930 . . . . TCLC 1
See also CA 104; DLB 19

Bridie, James 1888-1951 . . . . TCLC 3
See also Mavor, Osborne Henry
See also DLB 10

Brin, David 1950- . . . . CLC 34
See also CANR 24; CA 102

Brink, Andre (Philippus)
1935- . . . . CLC 18, 36
See also CA 104

Brinsmead, H(esba) F(ay) 1922- . . . . CLC 21
See also CANR 10; CA 21-24R; SAAS 5;
SATA 18

Brittain, Vera (Mary) 1893?-1970 . . . CLC 23
See also CAP 1; CA 15-16;
obituary CA 25-28R

Broch, Hermann 1886-1951 . . . . . . TCLC 20
See also CA 117; DLB 85

Brock, Rose 1923-
See Hansen, Joseph

Brodkey, Harold 1930- . . . . CLC 56
See also CA 111

Brodsky, Iosif Alexandrovich 1940-
See Brodsky, Joseph (Alexandrovich)
See also CA 41-44R

Brodsky, Joseph (Alexandrovich)
1940- . . . . CLC 4, 6, 13, 36, 50
See also Brodsky, Iosif Alexandrovich

Brodsky, Michael (Mark) 1948- . . . . CLC 19
See also CANR 18; CA 102

Bromell, Henry 1947- . . . . CLC 5
See also CANR 9; CA 53-56

Bromfield, Louis (Brucker)
1896-1956 . . . . TCLC 11
See also CA 107; DLB 4, 9

Broner, E(sther) M(asserman)
1930- . . . . CLC 19
See also CANR 8, 25; CA 17-20R; DLB 28

Bronk, William 1918- . . . . CLC 10
See also CANR 23; CA 89-92

Bronte, Anne 1820-1849 . . . . NCLC 4
See also DLB 21

Bronte, Charlotte 1816-1855 . . . . NCLC 3, 8
See also DLB 21

Bronte, (Jane) Emily 1818-1848 . . NCLC 16
See also DLB 21, 32

Brooke, Frances 1724-1789 . . . . LC 6
See also DLB 39

Brooke, Henry 1703?-1783 . . . . LC 1
See also DLB 39

Brooke, Rupert (Chawner)
1887-1915 . . . . TCLC 2, 7
See also CA 104; DLB 19

Brooke-Rose, Christine 1926- . . . . . . CLC 40
See also CA 13-16R; DLB 14

Brookner, Anita 1928- . . . . . . CLC 32, 34, 51
See also CA 114, 120; DLB-Y 87

Brooks, Cleanth 1906- . . . . CLC 24
See also CA 17-20R; DLB 63

Brooks, Gwendolyn
1917- . . . . CLC 1, 2, 4, 5, 15, 49
See also CANR 1; CA 1-4R; SATA 6;
DLB 5, 76; CDALB 1941-1968

Brooks, Mel 1926- . . . . CLC 12
See also Kaminsky, Melvin
See also CA 65-68; DLB 26

Brooks, Peter 1938- . . . . CLC 34
See also CANR 1; CA 45-48

Brooks, Van Wyck 1886-1963 . . . . . . CLC 29
See also CANR 6; CA 1-4R; DLB 45, 63

Brophy, Brigid (Antonia)
1929- . . . . CLC 6, 11, 29
See also CAAS 4; CANR 25; CA 5-8R;
DLB 14

Brosman, Catharine Savage 1934- . . . . CLC 9
See also CANR 21; CA 61-64

Broughton, T(homas) Alan 1936- . . . CLC 19
See also CANR 2, 23; CA 45-48

Broumas, Olga 1949- . . . . CLC 10
See also CANR 20; CA 85-88

Brown, Charles Brockden
1771-1810 . . . . NCLC 22
See also DLB 37, 59, 73;
CDALB 1640-1865

Brown, Christy 1932-1981 . . . . CLC 63
See also CA 105; obituary CA 104

Brown, Claude 1937- . . . . CLC 30
See also CA 73-76

Brown, Dee (Alexander) 1908- . . CLC 18, 47
See also CAAS 6; CANR 11; CA 13-16R;
SATA 5; DLB-Y 80

Brown, George Douglas 1869-1902
See Douglas, George

Brown, George Mackay 1921- . . . . CLC 5, 28
See also CAAS 6; CANR 12; CA 21-24R;
SATA 35; DLB 14, 27

Brown, Rita Mae 1944- . . . . CLC 18, 43
See also CANR 2, 11; CA 45-48

Brown, Rosellen 1939- . . . . CLC 32
See also CANR 14; CA 77-80

Brown, Sterling A(llen)
1901-1989 . . . . CLC 1, 23, 59
See also CANR 26; CA 85-88;
obituary CA 27; DLB 48, 51, 63

Brown, William Wells
1816?-1884 . . . . NCLC 2; DC 1
See also DLB 3, 50

Chappell, Fred 1936- .... CLC 40
  See also CAAS 4; CANR 8; CA 5-8R;
  DLB 6

Char, Rene (Emile)
  1907-1988 .... CLC 9, 11, 14, 55
  See also CA 13-16R; obituary CA 124

Charles I 1600-1649 .... LC 13

Chartier, Emile-Auguste 1868-1951
  See Alain

Charyn, Jerome 1937- .... CLC 5, 8, 18
  See also CAAS 1; CANR 7; CA 5-8R;
  DLB-Y 83

Chase, Mary (Coyle) 1907-1981 ...... DC 1
  See also CA 77-80, 105; SATA 17, 29

Chase, Mary Ellen 1887-1973 .... CLC 2
  See also CAP 1; CA 15-16;
  obituary CA 41-44R; SATA 10

Chateaubriand, Francois Rene de
  1768-1848 .... NCLC 3

Chatier, Emile-Auguste 1868-1951
  See Alain

Chatterji, Bankim Chandra
  1838-1894 .... NCLC 19

Chatterji, Saratchandra
  1876-1938 .... TCLC 13
  See also CA 109

Chatterton, Thomas 1752-1770 .... LC 3

Chatwin, (Charles) Bruce
  1940-1989 .... CLC 28, 57, 59
  See also CA 85-88,; obituary CA 127

Chayefsky, Paddy 1923-1981 .... CLC 23
  See also CA 9-12R; obituary CA 104;
  DLB 7, 44; DLB-Y 81

Chayefsky, Sidney 1923-1981
  See Chayefsky, Paddy
  See also CANR 18

Chedid, Andree 1920- .... CLC 47

Cheever, John
  1912-1982 ..... CLC 3, 7, 8, 11, 15, 25,
                    64; SSC 1
  See also CANR 5, 27; CA 5-8R;
  obituary CA 106; CABS 1; DLB 2;
  DLB-Y 80, 82; CDALB 1941-1968

Cheever, Susan 1943- .... CLC 18, 48
  See also CA 103; DLB-Y 82

Chekhov, Anton (Pavlovich)
  1860-1904 ...... TCLC 3, 10, 31; SSC 2
  See also CA 104, 124

Chernyshevsky, Nikolay Gavrilovich
  1828-1889 .... NCLC 1

Cherry, Caroline Janice 1942-
  See Cherryh, C. J.

Cherryh, C. J. 1942- .... CLC 35
  See also CANR 10; CA 65-68; DLB-Y 80

Chesnutt, Charles Waddell
  1858-1932 .... TCLC 5, 39; SSC 7
  See also CA 106, 125; DLB 12, 50, 78

Chester, Alfred 1929?-1971 .... CLC 49
  See also obituary CA 33-36R

Chesterton, G(ilbert) K(eith)
  1874-1936 .... TCLC 1, 6; SSC 1
  See also CA 104; SATA 27; DLB 10, 19,
  34, 70

Ch'ien Chung-shu 1910- .... CLC 22

Child, Lydia Maria 1802-1880 .... NCLC 6
  See also DLB 1, 74

Child, Philip 1898-1978 .... CLC 19
  See also CAP 1; CA 13-14; SATA 47

Childress, Alice 1920-. .... CLC 12, 15
  See also CLR 14; CANR 3; CA 45-48;
  SATA 7, 48; DLB 7, 38

Chislett, (Margaret) Anne 1943?- ... CLC 34

Chitty, (Sir) Thomas Willes 1926- .. CLC 11
  See Hinde, Thomas
  See also CA 5-8R

Chomette, Rene 1898-1981
  See Clair, Rene
  See also obituary CA 103

Chopin, Kate (O'Flaherty)
  1851-1904 .... TCLC 5, 14; SSC 8
  See also CA 122; brief entry CA 104;
  DLB 12, 78; CDALB 1865-1917

Christie, (Dame) Agatha (Mary Clarissa)
  1890-1976 ...... CLC 1, 6, 8, 12, 39, 48
  See also CANR 10; CA 17-20R;
  obituary CA 61-64; SATA 36; DLB 13

Christie, (Ann) Philippa 1920-
  See Pearce, (Ann) Philippa
  See also CANR 4; CA 7-8

Christine de Pizan 1365?-1431?. ...... LC 9

Chulkov, Mikhail Dmitrievich
  1743-1792 .... LC 2

Churchill, Caryl 1938- .... CLC 31, 55
  See also CANR 22; CA 102; DLB 13

Churchill, Charles 1731?-1764........ LC 3

Chute, Carolyn 1947- .... CLC 39
  See also CA 123

Ciardi, John (Anthony)
  1916-1986 .... CLC 10, 40, 44
  See also CAAS 2; CANR 5; CA 5-8R;
  obituary CA 118; SATA 1, 46; DLB 5;
  DLB-Y 86

Cicero, Marcus Tullius
  106 B.C.-43 B.C.............. CMLC 3

Cimino, Michael 1943?- .... CLC 16
  See also CA 105

Cioran, E. M. 1911- .... CLC 64
  See also CA 25-28R

Clair, Rene 1898-1981 .... CLC 20
  See also Chomette, Rene

Clampitt, Amy 19??- .... CLC 32
  See also CA 110

Clancy, Tom 1947- .... CLC 45
  See also CA 125

Clare, John 1793-1864 .... NCLC 9
  See also DLB 55

Clark, (Robert) Brian 1932-........ CLC 29
  See also CA 41-44R

Clark, Eleanor 1913- .... CLC 5, 19
  See also CA 9-12R; DLB 6

Clark, John Pepper 1935- .... CLC 38
  See also CANR 16; CA 65-68

Clark, Mavis Thorpe 1912?- .... CLC 12
  See also CANR 8; CA 57-60; SAAS 5;
  SATA 8

Clark, Walter Van Tilburg
  1909-1971 .... CLC 28
  See also CA 9-12R; obituary CA 33-36R;
  SATA 8; DLB 9

Clarke, Arthur C(harles)
  1917- ...... CLC 1, 4, 13, 18, 35; SSC 3
  See also CANR 2; CA 1-4R; SATA 13

Clarke, Austin 1896-1974........ CLC 6, 9
  See also CANR 14; CAP 2; CA 29-32;
  obituary CA 49-52; DLB 10, 20, 53

Clarke, Austin (Ardinel) C(hesterfield)
  1934- .... CLC 8, 53
  See also CANR 14; CA 25-28R; DLB 53

Clarke, Gillian 1937- .... CLC 61
  See also CA 106; DLB 40

Clarke, Marcus (Andrew Hislop)
  1846-1881 .... NCLC 19

Clarke, Shirley 1925- .... CLC 16

Clash, The .... CLC 30

Claudel, Paul (Louis Charles Marie)
  1868-1955 .... TCLC 2, 10
  See also CA 104

Clavell, James (duMaresq)
  1924- .... CLC 6, 25
  See also CANR 26; CA 25-28R

Clayman. Gregory 1974?-.......... CLC 65

Cleaver, (Leroy) Eldridge 1935- .... CLC 30
  See also CANR 16; CA 21-24R

Cleese, John 1939-............... CLC 21
  See also Monty Python
  See also CA 112, 116

Cleland, John 1709-1789 .... LC 2
  See also DLB 39

Clemens, Samuel Langhorne
  1835-1910 ...... TCLC 6, 12, 19; SSC 6
  See also Twain, Mark
  See also YABC 2; CA 104; DLB 11, 12, 23,
  64, 74; CDALB 1865-1917

Cliff, Jimmy 1948- .... CLC 21

Clifton, Lucille (Thelma)
  1936- .... CLC 19, 66
  See also CLR 5; CANR 2, 24; CA 49-52;
  SATA 20; DLB 5, 41

Clough, Arthur Hugh 1819-1861.. NCLC 27
  See also DLB 32

Clutha, Janet Paterson Frame 1924-
  See Frame (Clutha), Janet (Paterson)
  See also CANR 2; CA 1-4R

Coburn, D(onald) L(ee) 1938- ...... CLC 10
  See also CA 89-92

Cocteau, Jean (Maurice Eugene Clement)
  1889-1963 .... CLC 1, 8, 15, 16, 43
  See also CAP 2; CA 25-28; DLB 65

Codrescu, Andrei 1946- .... CLC 46
  See also CANR 13; CA 33-36R

Coetzee, J(ohn) M. 1940-.... CLC 23, 33, 66
  See also CA 77-80

Cohen, Arthur A(llen)
  1928-1986 .... CLC 7, 31
  See also CANR 1, 17; CA 1-4R;
  obituary CA 120; DLB 28

Cohen, Leonard (Norman)
  1934- .... CLC 3, 38
  See also CANR 14; CA 21-24R; DLB 53

Author Index

Eigner, Larry 1927- .... CLC 9
See also Eigner, Laurence (Joel)
See also DLB 5

Eigner, Laurence (Joel) 1927-
See Eigner, Larry
See also CANR 6; CA 9-12R

Eiseley, Loren (Corey) 1907-1977.... CLC 7
See also CANR 6; CA 1-4R;
obituary CA 73-76

Eisenstadt, Jill 1963- .... CLC 50

Ekeloef, Gunnar (Bengt) 1907-1968
See Ekelof, Gunnar (Bengt)
See also obituary CA 25-28R

Ekelof, Gunnar (Bengt) 1907-1968 .. CLC 27
See also Ekeloef, Gunnar (Bengt)

Ekwensi, Cyprian (Odiatu Duaka)
1921- .... CLC 4
See also CANR 18; CA 29-32R

Eliade, Mircea 1907-1986 .... CLC 19
See also CA 65-68; obituary CA 119

Eliot, George 1819-1880.... NCLC 4, 13, 23
See also DLB 21, 35, 55

Eliot, John 1604-1690 .... LC 5
See also DLB 24

Eliot, T(homas) S(tearns)
1888-1965 .... CLC 1, 2, 3, 6, 9, 10, 13,
15, 24, 34, 41, 55, 57
See also CA 5-8R; obituary CA 25-28R;
DLB 7, 10, 45, 63; DLB-Y 88

Elizabeth 1866-1941 .... TCLC 41
See also Russell, Mary Annette Beauchamp

Elkin, Stanley (Lawrence)
1930- .... CLC 4, 6, 9, 14, 27, 51
See also CANR 8; CA 9-12R; DLB 2, 28;
DLB-Y 80

Elledge, Scott 19??- .... CLC 34

Elliott, George P(aul) 1918-1980..... CLC 2
See also CANR 2; CA 1-4R;
obituary CA 97-100

Elliott, Janice 1931- .... CLC 47
See also CANR 8; CA 13-16R; DLB 14

Elliott, Sumner Locke 1917- .... CLC 38
See also CANR 2, 21; CA 5-8R

Ellis, A. E. 19??- .... CLC 7

Ellis, Alice Thomas 19??- .... CLC 40

Ellis, Bret Easton 1964- .... CLC 39
See also CA 118, 123

Ellis, (Henry) Havelock
1859-1939 .... TCLC 14
See also CA 109

Ellis, Trey 1964- .... CLC 55

Ellison, Harlan (Jay) 1934- ... CLC 1, 13, 42
See also CANR 5; CA 5-8R; DLB 8

Ellison, Ralph (Waldo)
1914- .... CLC 1, 3, 11, 54
See also CANR 24; CA 9-12R; DLB 2, 76;
CDALB 1941-1968

Ellmann, Lucy 1956- .... CLC 61
See also CA 128

Ellmann, Richard (David)
1918-1987 .... CLC 50
See also CANR 2; CA 1-4R;
obituary CA 122; DLB-Y 87

Elman, Richard 1934- .... CLC 19
See also CAAS 3; CA 17-20R

Eluard, Paul 1895-1952 .... TCLC 7, 41
See also Grindel, Eugene

Elyot, (Sir) Thomas 1490?-1546 ..... LC 11

Elytis, Odysseus 1911- .... CLC 15, 49
See also CA 102

Emecheta, (Florence Onye) Buchi
1944- .... CLC 14, 48
See also CA 81-84

Emerson, Ralph Waldo
1803-1882 .... NCLC 1
See also DLB 1, 59, 73; CDALB 1640-1865

Empson, William
1906-1984 .... CLC 3, 8, 19, 33, 34
See also CA 17-20R; obituary CA 112;
DLB 20

Enchi, Fumiko (Veda) 1905-1986 ... CLC 31
See also obituary CA 121

Ende, Michael 1930- .... CLC 31
See also CLR 14; CA 118, 124; SATA 42;
DLB 75

Endo, Shusaku 1923- ..... CLC 7, 14, 19, 54
See also CANR 21; CA 29-32R

Engel, Marian 1933-1985......... CLC 36
See also CANR 12; CA 25-28R; DLB 53

Engelhardt, Frederick 1911-1986
See Hubbard, L(afayette) Ron(ald)

Enright, D(ennis) J(oseph)
1920- .... CLC 4, 8, 31
See also CANR 1; CA 1-4R; SATA 25;
DLB 27

Enzensberger, Hans Magnus
1929- .... CLC 43
See also CA 116, 119

Ephron, Nora 1941- .... CLC 17, 31
See also CANR 12; CA 65-68

Epstein, Daniel Mark 1948- .... CLC 7
See also CANR 2; CA 49-52

Epstein, Jacob 1956- .... CLC 19
See also CA 114

Epstein, Joseph 1937- .... CLC 39
See also CA 112, 119

Epstein, Leslie 1938- .... CLC 27
See also CANR 23; CA 73-76

Equiano, Olaudah 1745?-1797 ...... LC 16
See also DLB 37, 50

Erasmus, Desiderius 1469?-1536..... LC 16

Erdman, Paul E(mil) 1932- .... CLC 25
See also CANR 13; CA 61-64

Erdrich, Louise 1954- .... CLC 39, 54
See also CA 114

Erenburg, Ilya (Grigoryevich) 1891-1967
See Ehrenburg, Ilya (Grigoryevich)

Erickson, Steve 1950- .... CLC 64
See also CA 129

Eseki, Bruno 1919-
See Mphahlele, Ezekiel

Esenin, Sergei (Aleksandrovich)
1895-1925 .... TCLC 4
See also CA 104

Eshleman, Clayton 1935- .... CLC 7
See also CAAS 6; CA 33-36R; DLB 5

Espriu, Salvador 1913-1985........ CLC 9
See also obituary CA 115

Estleman, Loren D. 1952- .... CLC 48
See also CA 85-88

Evans, Marian 1819-1880
See Eliot, George

Evans, Mary Ann 1819-1880
See Eliot, George

Evarts, Esther 1900-1972
See Benson, Sally

Everett, Percival L. 1957?- .... CLC 57
See also CA 129

Everson, Ronald G(ilmour) 1903- ... CLC 27
See also CA 17-20R; DLB 88

Everson, William (Oliver)
1912- .... CLC 1, 5, 14
See also CANR 20; CA 9-12R; DLB 5, 16

Evtushenko, Evgenii (Aleksandrovich) 1933-
See Yevtushenko, Yevgeny

Ewart, Gavin (Buchanan)
1916- .... CLC 13, 46
See also CANR 17; CA 89-92; DLB 40

Ewers, Hanns Heinz 1871-1943 ... TCLC 12
See also CA 109

Ewing, Frederick R. 1918-
See Sturgeon, Theodore (Hamilton)

Exley, Frederick (Earl) 1929- .... CLC 6, 11
See also CA 81-84; DLB-Y 81

Ezekiel, Nissim 1924- .... CLC 61
See also CA 61-64

Ezekiel, Tish O'Dowd 1943- .... CLC 34

Fagen, Donald 1948- .... CLC 26

Fair, Ronald L. 1932- .... CLC 18
See also CANR 25; CA 69-72; DLB 33

Fairbairns, Zoe (Ann) 1948-   CLC 32
See also CANR 21; CA 103

Fairfield, Cicily Isabel 1892-1983
See West, Rebecca

Fallaci, Oriana 1930- .... CLC 11
See also CANR 15; CA 77-80

Faludy, George 1913- .... CLC 42
See also CA 21-24R

Fante, John 1909-1983............ CLC 60
See also CANR 23; CA 69-72;
obituary CA 109; DLB-Y 83

Farah, Nuruddin 1945- .... CLC 53
See also CA 106

Fargue, Leon-Paul 1876-1947 ..... TCLC 11
See also CA 109

Farigoule, Louis 1885-1972
See Romains, Jules

Farina, Richard 1937?-1966........ CLC 9
See also CA 81-84; obituary CA 25-28R

Farley, Walter 1920- .... CLC 17
See also CANR 8; CA 17-20R; SATA 2, 43;
DLB 22

Farmer, Philip Jose 1918- .... CLC 1, 19
See also CANR 4; CA 1-4R; DLB 8

Farrell, J(ames) G(ordon)
1935-1979 .... CLC 6
See also CA 73-76; obituary CA 89-92;
DLB 14

Fournier, Pierre 1916- .... **CLC 11**
See also Gascar, Pierre
See also CANR 16; CA 89-92

Fowles, John (Robert)
1926- .... **CLC 1, 2, 3, 4, 6, 9, 10, 15, 33**
See also CANR 25; CA 5-8R; SATA 22;
DLB 14

Fox, Paula 1923- .... **CLC 2, 8**
See also CLR 1; CANR 20; CA 73-76;
SATA 17; DLB 52

Fox, William Price (Jr.) 1926- ..... **CLC 22**
See also CANR 11; CA 17-20R; DLB 2;
DLB-Y 81

Foxe, John 1516?-1587............. **LC 14**

Frame (Clutha), Janet (Paterson)
1924- .... **CLC 2, 3, 6, 22, 66**
See also Clutha, Janet Paterson Frame

France, Anatole 1844-1924 .... **TCLC 9**
See also Thibault, Jacques Anatole Francois

Francis, Claude 19??- .... **CLC 50**

Francis, Dick 1920- .... **CLC 2, 22, 42**
See also CANR 9; CA 5-8R; DLB 87

Francis, Robert (Churchill)
1901-1987 .... **CLC 15**
See also CANR 1; CA 1-4R;
obituary CA 123

Frank, Anne 1929-1945 .... **TCLC 17**
See also CA 113; SATA 42

Frank, Elizabeth 1945- .... **CLC 39**
See also CA 121, 126

Franklin, (Stella Maria Sarah) Miles
1879-1954 .... **TCLC 7**
See also CA 104

Fraser, Antonia (Pakenham)
1932- .... **CLC 32**
See also CA 85-88; SATA 32

Fraser, George MacDonald 1925- .... **CLC 7**
See also CANR 2; CA 45-48

Fraser, Sylvia 1935- .... **CLC 64**
See also CANR 1, 16; CA 45-48

Frayn, Michael 1933- ..... **CLC 3, 7, 31, 47**
See also CA 5-8R; DLB 13, 14

Fraze, Candida 19??- .... **CLC 50**
See also CA 125

Frazer, Sir James George
1854-1941 .... **TCLC 32**
See also CA 118

Frazier, Ian 1951- .... **CLC 46**
See also CA 130

Frederic, Harold 1856-1898...... **NCLC 10**
See also DLB 12, 23

Frederick the Great 1712-1786 ...... **LC 14**

Fredman, Russell (Bruce) 1929-
See also CLR 20

Fredro, Aleksander 1793-1876..... **NCLC 8**

Freeling, Nicolas 1927- .... **CLC 38**
See also CANR 1, 17; CA 49-52; DLB 87

Freeman, Douglas Southall
1886-1953 .... **TCLC 11**
See also CA 109; DLB 17

Freeman, Judith 1946- .... **CLC 55**

Freeman, Mary (Eleanor) Wilkins
1852-1930 .... **TCLC 9; SSC 1**
See also CA 106; DLB 12, 78

Freeman, R(ichard) Austin
1862-1943 .... **TCLC 21**
See also CA 113; DLB 70

French, Marilyn 1929- ...... **CLC 10, 18, 60**
See also CANR 3; CA 69-72

Freneau, Philip Morin 1752-1832.. **NCLC 1**
See also DLB 37, 43

Friedman, B(ernard) H(arper)
1926- .... **CLC 7**
See also CANR 3; CA 1-4R

Friedman, Bruce Jay 1930- .... **CLC 3, 5, 56**
See also CANR 25; CA 9-12R; DLB 2, 28

Friel, Brian 1929- .... **CLC 5, 42, 59**
See also CA 21-24R; DLB 13

Friis-Baastad, Babbis (Ellinor)
1921-1970 .... **CLC 12**
See also CA 17-20R; SATA 7

Frisch, Max (Rudolf)
1911- .... **CLC 3, 9, 14, 18, 32, 44**
See also CA 85-88; DLB 69

Fromentin, Eugene (Samuel Auguste)
1820-1876 .... **NCLC 10**

Frost, Robert (Lee)
1874-1963 ... **CLC 1, 3, 4, 9, 10, 13, 15,**
26, 34, 44; PC 1
See also CA 89-92; SATA 14; DLB 54;
DLB-DS 7; CDALB 1917-1929

Fry, Christopher 1907- .... **CLC 2, 10, 14**
See also CANR 9; CA 17-20R; DLB 13

Frye, (Herman) Northrop 1912- .... **CLC 24**
See also CANR 8; CA 5-8R; DLB 67, 68

Fuchs, Daniel 1909- .... **CLC 8, 22**
See also CAAS 5; CA 81-84; DLB 9, 26, 28

Fuchs, Daniel 1934- .... **CLC 34**
See also CANR 14; CA 37-40R

Fuentes, Carlos
1928- ...... **CLC 3, 8, 10, 13, 22, 41, 60**
See also CANR 10; CA 69-72

Fugard, Athol 1932- ... **CLC 5, 9, 14, 25, 40**
See also CA 85-88

Fugard, Sheila 1932- .... **CLC 48**
See also CA 125

Fuller, Charles (H., Jr.)
1939- .... **CLC 25; DC 1**
See also CA 108, 112; DLB 38

Fuller, John (Leopold) 1937- .... **CLC 62**
See also CANR 9; CA 21-22R; DLB 40

Fuller, (Sarah) Margaret
1810-1850 .... **NCLC 5**
See also Ossoli, Sarah Margaret (Fuller
marchesa d')
See also DLB 1, 59, 73; CDALB 1640-1865

Fuller, Roy (Broadbent) 1912- .... **CLC 4, 28**
See also CA 5-8R; DLB 15, 20

Fulton, Alice 1952- .... **CLC 52**
See also CA 116

Furphy, Joseph 1843-1912 .... **TCLC 25**

Futrelle, Jacques 1875-1912 ...... **TCLC 19**
See also CA 113

Gaboriau, Emile 1835-1873 ...... **NCLC 14**

Gadda, Carlo Emilio 1893-1973 .... **CLC 11**
See also CA 89-92

Gaddis, William
1922- .... **CLC 1, 3, 6, 8, 10, 19, 43**
See also CAAS 4; CANR 21; CA 17-20R;
DLB 2

Gaines, Ernest J. 1933- ...... **CLC 3, 11, 18**
See also CANR 6, 24; CA 9-12R; DLB 2,
33; DLB-Y 80

Gale, Zona 1874-1938 .... **TCLC 7**
See also CA 105; DLB 9, 78

Gallagher, Tess 1943- .... **CLC 18, 63**
See also CA 106

Gallant, Mavis
1922- .... **CLC 7, 18, 38; SSC 5**
See also CA 69-72; DLB 53

Gallant, Roy A(rthur) 1924- .... **CLC 17**
See also CANR 4; CA 5-8R; SATA 4

Gallico, Paul (William) 1897-1976 ... **CLC 2**
See also CA 5-8R; obituary CA 69-72;
SATA 13; DLB 9

Galsworthy, John 1867-1933 ...... **TCLC 1**
See also CA 104; DLB 10, 34

Galt, John 1779-1839............. **NCLC 1**

Galvin, James 1951- .... **CLC 38**
See also CANR 26; CA 108

Gamboa, Frederico 1864-1939..... **TCLC 36**

Gann, Ernest K(ellogg) 1910- ...... **CLC 23**
See also CANR 1; CA 1-4R

Garcia Lorca, Federico
1899-1936 .... **TCLC 1, 7**
See also CA 104

Garcia Marquez, Gabriel (Jose)
1928- ... **CLC 2, 3, 8, 10, 15, 27, 47, 55;**
SSC 8
See also CANR 10, 28; CA 33-36R;
AAYA 3

Gardam, Jane 1928- .... **CLC 43**
See also CLR 12; CANR 2, 18; CA 49-52;
SATA 28, 39; DLB 14

Gardner, Herb 1934- .... **CLC 44**

Gardner, John (Champlin, Jr.)
1933-1982 .... **CLC 2, 3, 5, 7, 8, 10, 18,**
28, 34; SSC 7
See also CA 65-68; obituary CA 107;
obituary SATA 31, 40; DLB 2; DLB-Y 82

Gardner, John (Edmund) 1926- ..... **CLC 30**
See also CANR 15; CA 103

Garfield, Leon 1921- .... **CLC 12**
See also CA 17-20R; SATA 1, 32

Garland, (Hannibal) Hamlin
1860-1940 .... **TCLC 3**
See also CA 104; DLB 12, 71, 78

Garneau, Hector (de) Saint Denys
1912-1943 .... **TCLC 13**
See also CA 111; DLB 88

Garner, Alan 1935- .... **CLC 17**
See also CLR 20; CANR 15; CA 73-76;
SATA 18

Garner, Hugh 1913-1979 .... **CLC 13**
See also CA 69-72; DLB 68

Garnett, David 1892-1981 .... **CLC 3**
See also CANR 17; CA 5-8R;
obituary CA 103; DLB 34

Golding, William (Gerald)
　　1911-..... **CLC 1, 2, 3, 8, 10, 17, 27, 58**
　　See also CANR 13; CA 5-8R; DLB 15

Goldman, Emma 1869-1940...... **TCLC 13**
　　See also CA 110

Goldman, William (W.) 1931-.... **CLC 1, 48**
　　See also CA 9-12R; DLB 44

Goldmann, Lucien 1913-1970 ..... **CLC 24**
　　See also CAP 2; CA 25-28

Goldoni, Carlo 1707-1793 .... **LC 4**

Goldsberry, Steven 1949-......... **CLC 34**

Goldsmith, Oliver 1728?-1774....... **LC 2**
　　See also SATA 26; DLB 39

Gombrowicz, Witold
　　1904-1969 .... **CLC 4, 7, 11, 49**
　　See also CAP 2; CA 19-20;
　　obituary CA 25-28R

Gomez de la Serna, Ramon
　　1888-1963 .... **CLC 9**
　　See also obituary CA 116

Goncharov, Ivan Alexandrovich
　　1812-1891 .... **NCLC 1**

Goncourt, Edmond (Louis Antoine Huot) de
　　1822-1896 .... **NCLC 7**

Goncourt, Jules (Alfred Huot) de
　　1830-1870 .... **NCLC 7**

Gontier, Fernande 19??-......... **CLC 50**

Goodman, Paul 1911-1972.... **CLC 1, 2, 4, 7**
　　See also CAP 2; CA 19-20;
　　obituary CA 37-40R

Gordimer, Nadine
　　1923-....... **CLC 3, 5, 7, 10, 18, 33, 51**
　　See also CANR 3; CA 5-8R

Gordon, Adam Lindsay
　　1833-1870 .... **NCLC 21**

Gordon, Caroline
　　1895-1981 .... **CLC 6, 13, 29**
　　See also CAP 1; CA 11-12;
　　obituary CA 103; DLB 4, 9; DLB-Y 81

Gordon, Charles William 1860-1937
　　See Conner, Ralph
　　See also CA 109

Gordon, Mary (Catherine)
　　1949-..................... **CLC 13, 22**
　　See also CA 102; DLB 6; DLB-Y 81

Gordon, Sol 1923-............... **CLC 26**
　　See also CANR 4; CA 53-56; SATA 11

Gordone, Charles 1925-.......... **CLC 1, 4**
　　See also CA 93-96; DLB 7

Gorenko, Anna Andreyevna 1889?-1966
　　See Akhmatova, Anna

Gorky, Maxim 1868-1936 .... **TCLC 8**
　　See also Peshkov, Alexei Maximovich

Goryan, Sirak 1908-1981
　　See Saroyan, William

Gosse, Edmund (William)
　　1849-1928 .... **TCLC 28**
　　See also CA 117; DLB 57

Gotlieb, Phyllis (Fay Bloom)
　　1926-..................... **CLC 18**
　　See also CANR 7; CA 13-16R; DLB 88

Gould, Lois 1938?-............. **CLC 4, 10**
　　See also CA 77-80

Gourmont, Remy de 1858-1915.... **TCLC 17**
　　See also CA 109

Govier, Katherine 1948-........... **CLC 51**
　　See also CANR 18; CA 101

Goyen, (Charles) William
　　1915-1983 .... **CLC 5, 8, 14, 40**
　　See also CANR 6; CA 5-8R;
　　obituary CA 110; DLB 2; DLB-Y 83

Goytisolo, Juan 1931- .... **CLC 5, 10, 23**
　　See also CA 85-88

Gozzi, (Conte) Carlo 1720-1806 .. **NCLC 23**

Grabbe, Christian Dietrich
　　1801-1836 .... **NCLC 2**

Grace, Patricia 1937-............. **CLC 56**

Gracian y Morales, Baltasar
　　1601-1658 .... **LC 15**

Gracq, Julien 1910- .... **CLC 11, 48**
　　See also Poirier, Louis
　　See also DLB 83

Grade, Chaim 1910-1982 .... **CLC 10**
　　See also CA 93-96; obituary CA 107

Graham, Jorie 1951-............. **CLC 48**
　　See also CA 111

Graham, R(obert) B(ontine) Cunninghame
　　1852-1936 .... **TCLC 19**

Graham, W(illiam) S(ydney)
　　1918-1986 .... **CLC 29**
　　See also CA 73-76; obituary CA 118;
　　DLB 20

Graham, Winston (Mawdsley)
　　1910-..................... **CLC 23**
　　See also CANR 2, 22; CA 49-52;
　　obituary CA 118

Granville-Barker, Harley
　　1877-1946 .... **TCLC 2**
　　See also CA 104

Grass, Gunter (Wilhelm)
　　1927-... **CLC 1, 2, 4, 6, 11, 15, 22, 32, 49**
　　See also CANR 20; CA 13-16R; DLB 75

Grau, Shirley Ann 1929-......... **CLC 4, 9**
　　See also CANR 22; CA 89-92; DLB 2

Graves, Richard Perceval 1945-.... **CLC 44**
　　See also CANR 9, 26; CA 65-68

Graves, Robert (von Ranke)
　　1895-1985 ... **CLC 1, 2, 6, 11, 39, 44, 45**
　　See also CANR 5; CA 5-8R;
　　obituary CA 117; SATA 45; DLB 20;
　　DLB-Y 85

Gray, Alasdair 1934- .... **CLC 41**
　　See also CA 123

Gray, Amlin 1946-............... **CLC 29**

Gray, Francine du Plessix 1930-.... **CLC 22**
　　See also CAAS 2; CANR 11; CA 61-64

Gray, John (Henry) 1866-1934 .... **TCLC 19**
　　See also CA 119

Gray, Simon (James Holliday)
　　1936-.................... **CLC 9, 14, 36**
　　See also CAAS 3; CA 21-24R; DLB 13

Gray, Spalding 1941-............. **CLC 49**

Gray, Thomas 1716-1771....... **LC 4; PC 2**

Grayson, Richard (A.) 1951-....... **CLC 38**
　　See also CANR 14; CA 85-88

Greeley, Andrew M(oran) 1928-.... **CLC 28**
　　See also CAAS 7; CANR 7; CA 5-8R

Green, Hannah 1932-......... **CLC 3, 7, 30**
　　See also Greenberg, Joanne
　　See also CA 73-76

Green, Henry 1905-1974 .... **CLC 2, 13**
　　See also Yorke, Henry Vincent
　　See also DLB 15

Green, Julien (Hartridge) 1900- .. **CLC 3, 11**
　　See also CA 21-24R; DLB 4, 72

Green, Paul (Eliot) 1894-1981...... **CLC 25**
　　See also CANR 3; CA 5-8R;
　　obituary CA 103; DLB 7, 9; DLB-Y 81

Greenberg, Ivan 1908-1973
　　See Rahv, Philip
　　See also CA 85-88

Greenberg, Joanne (Goldenberg)
　　1932-.................. **CLC 3, 7, 30**
　　See also Green, Hannah
　　See also CANR 14; CA 5-8R; SATA 25

Greenberg, Richard 1959?- .... **CLC 57**

Greene, Bette 1934-............... **CLC 30**
　　See also CLR 2; CANR 4; CA 53-56;
　　SATA 8

Greene, Gael 19??-................. **CLC 8**
　　See also CANR 10; CA 13-16R

Greene, Graham (Henry)
　　1904- ..... **CLC 1, 3, 6, 9, 14, 18, 27, 37**
　　See also CA 13-16R; SATA 20; DLB 13, 15;
　　DLB-Y 85

Gregor, Arthur 1923-............. **CLC 9**
　　See also CANR 11; CA 25-28R; SATA 36

Gregory, Lady (Isabella Augusta Persse)
　　1852-1932 .... **TCLC 1**
　　See also CA 104; DLB 10

Grendon, Stephen 1909-1971
　　See Derleth, August (William)

Grenville, Kate 1950-............. **CLC 61**
　　See also CA 118

Greve, Felix Paul Berthold Friedrich
　　1879-1948
　　See Grove, Frederick Philip
　　See also CA 104

Grey, (Pearl) Zane 1872?-1939 ..... **TCLC 6**
　　See also CA 104; DLB 9

Grieg, (Johan) Nordahl (Brun)
　　1902-1943 .... **TCLC 10**
　　See also CA 107

Grieve, C(hristopher) M(urray) 1892-1978
　　See MacDiarmid, Hugh
　　See also CA 5-8R; obituary CA 85-88

Griffin, Gerald 1803-1840 .... **NCLC 7**

Griffin, Peter 1942- .... **CLC 39**

Griffiths, Trevor 1935-......... **CLC 13, 52**
　　See also CA 97-100; DLB 13

Grigson, Geoffrey (Edward Harvey)
　　1905-1985 .... **CLC 7, 39**
　　See also CANR 20; CA 25-28R;
　　obituary CA 118; DLB 27

Grillparzer, Franz 1791-1872...... **NCLC 1**

Grimke, Charlotte L(ottie) Forten 1837-1914
　　See Forten (Grimke), Charlotte L(ottie)
　　See also CA 117, 124

Harris, Joel Chandler   1848-1908 ... **TCLC 2**
See also YABC 1; CA 104; DLB 11, 23, 42,
78, 91

Harris, John (Wyndham Parkes Lucas)
Beynon   1903-1969 .... **CLC 19**
See also Wyndham, John
See also CA 102; obituary CA 89-92

Harris, MacDonald   1921- .... **CLC 9**
See also Heiney, Donald (William)

Harris, Mark   1922- .... **CLC 19**
See also CAAS 3; CANR 2; CA 5-8R;
DLB 2; DLB-Y 80

Harris, (Theodore) Wilson   1921-.... **CLC 25**
See also CANR 11, 27; CA 65-68

Harrison, Harry (Max)   1925-...... **CLC 42**
See also CANR 5, 21; CA 1-4R; SATA 4;
DLB 8

Harrison, James (Thomas)   1937- ... **CLC 66**
See also Harrison, Jim
See also CANR 8; CA 13-16R

Harrison, Jim   1937-......... **CLC 6, 14, 33**
See also Harrison, James (Thomas)
See also DLB-Y 82

Harrison, Tony   1937-............. **CLC 43**
See also CA 65-68; DLB 40

Harriss, Will(ard Irvin)   1922-...... **CLC 34**
See also CA 111

Hart, Moss   1904-1961 .... **CLC 66**
See also Conrad, Robert Arnold
See also obituary CA 89-92; DLB 7

Harte, (Francis) Bret(t)
1836?-1902......... **TCLC 1, 25; SSC 8**
See also brief entry CA 104; SATA 26;
DLB 12, 64, 74, 79; CDALB 1865-1917

Hartley, L(eslie) P(oles)
1895-1972 .... **CLC 2, 22**
See also CA 45-48; obituary CA 37-40R;
DLB 15

Hartman, Geoffrey H.   1929-....... **CLC 27**
See also CA 117, 125; DLB 67

Haruf, Kent   19??-............... **CLC 34**

Harwood, Ronald   1934-.......... **CLC 32**
See also CANR 4; CA 1-4R; DLB 13

Hasek, Jaroslav (Matej Frantisek)
1883-1923 .... **TCLC 4**
See also CA 104, 129

Hass, Robert   1941-............ **CLC 18, 39**
See also CANR 30; CA 111

Hastings, Selina   19??- .... **CLC 44**

Hauptmann, Gerhart (Johann Robert)
1862-1946 .... **TCLC 4**
See also CA 104; DLB 66

Havel, Vaclav   1936-........ **CLC 25, 58, 65**
See also CA 104

Haviaras, Stratis   1935- .... **CLC 33**
See also CA 105

Hawkes, John (Clendennin Burne, Jr.)
1925-...... **CLC 1, 2, 3, 4, 7, 9, 14, 15,
27, 49**
See also CANR 2; CA 1-4R; DLB 2, 7;
DLB-Y 80

Hawking, Stephen (William)
1948-....................... **CLC 63**
See also CA 126, 129

Hawthorne, Julian   1846-1934 ..... **TCLC 25**

Hawthorne, Nathaniel
1804-1864 ... **NCLC 2, 10, 17, 23; SSC 3**
See also YABC 2; DLB 1, 74;
CDALB 1640-1865

Hayashi Fumiko   1904-1951 ...... **TCLC 27**

Haycraft, Anna   19??-
See Ellis, Alice Thomas
See also CA 122

Hayden, Robert (Earl)
1913-1980 .... **CLC 5, 9, 14, 37**
See also BLC 2; CANR 24; CA 69-72;
obituary CA 97-100; CABS 2; SATA 19;
obituary SATA 26; DLB 5, 76;
CDALB 1941-1968

Hayman, Ronald   1932-............ **CLC 44**
See also CANR 18; CA 25-28R

Haywood, Eliza (Fowler)   1693?-1756.. **LC 1**
See also DLB 39

Hazlitt, William   1778-1830 ...... **NCLC 29**

Hazzard, Shirley   1931- .... **CLC 18**
See also CANR 4; CA 9-12R; DLB-Y 82

H(ilda) D(oolittle)
1886-1961 .... **CLC 3, 8, 14, 31, 34**
See also Doolittle, Hilda

Head, Bessie   1937-1986........... **CLC 25**
See also BLC 2; CANR 25; CA 29-32R;
obituary CA 119

Headon, (Nicky) Topper   1956?- .... **CLC 30**
See also The Clash

Heaney, Seamus (Justin)
1939- .... **CLC 5, 7, 14, 25, 37**
See also CANR 25; CA 85-88; DLB 40

Hearn, (Patricio) Lafcadio (Tessima Carlos)
1850-1904 .... **TCLC 9**
See also CA 105; DLB 12, 78

Hearne, Vicki   1946-.............. **CLC 56**

Hearon, Shelby   1931-............. **CLC 63**
See also CANR 18; CA 25-28

Heat Moon, William Least   1939-... **CLC 29**

Hebert, Anne   1916- .... **CLC 4, 13, 29**
See also CA 85-88; DLB 68

Hecht, Anthony (Evan)
1923- .... **CLC 8, 13, 19**
See also CANR 6; CA 9-12R; DLB 5

Hecht, Ben   1894-1964 .... **CLC 8**
See also CA 85-88; DLB 7, 9, 25, 26, 28, 86

Hedayat, Sadeq   1903-1951........ **TCLC 21**
See also CA 120

Heidegger, Martin   1889-1976 ...... **CLC 24**
See also CA 81-84; obituary CA 65-68

Heidenstam, (Karl Gustaf) Verner von
1859-1940 .... **TCLC 5**
See also CA 104

Heifner, Jack   1946-.............. **CLC 11**
See also CA 105

Heijermans, Herman   1864-1924 ... **TCLC 24**
See also CA 123

Heilbrun, Carolyn G(old)   1926-..... **CLC 25**
See also CANR 1, 28; CA 45-48

Heine, Harry   1797-1856
See Heine, Heinrich

Heine, Heinrich   1797-1856 .... **NCLC 4**
See also DLB 90

Heinemann, Larry C(urtiss)   1944- .. **CLC 50**
See also CA 110

Heiney, Donald (William)   1921-..... **CLC 9**
See also Harris, MacDonald
See also CANR 3; CA 1-4R

Heinlein, Robert A(nson)
1907-1988 ...... **CLC 1, 3, 8, 14, 26, 55**
See also CANR 1, 20; CA 1-4R;
obituary CA 125; SATA 9, 56; DLB 8

Heller, Joseph
1923- .... **CLC 1, 3, 5, 8, 11, 36, 63**
See also CANR 8; CA 5-8R; CABS 1;
DLB 2, 28; DLB-Y 80

Hellman, Lillian (Florence)
1905?-1984..... **CLC 2, 4, 8, 14, 18, 34,
44, 52; DC 1**
See also CA 13-16R; obituary CA 112;
DLB 7; DLB-Y 84

Helprin, Mark   1947- ..... **CLC 7, 10, 22, 32**
See also CA 81-84; DLB-Y 85

Hemans, Felicia   1793-1835 ...... **NCLC 29**

Hemingway, Ernest (Miller)
1899-1961 ... **CLC 1, 3, 6, 8, 10, 13, 19,
30, 34, 39, 41, 44, 50, 61; SSC 1**
See also CA 77-80; DLB 4, 9; DLB-Y 81,
87; DLB-DS 1; CDALB 1917-1929

Hempel, Amy   1951-.............. **CLC 39**
See also CA 118

Henley, Beth   1952-.............. **CLC 23**
See also Henley, Elizabeth Becker
See also CABS 3; DLB-Y 86

Henley, Elizabeth Becker   1952-
See Henley, Beth
See also CA 107

Henley, William Ernest
1849-1903 .... **TCLC 8**
See also CA 105; DLB 19

Hennissart, Martha
See Lathen, Emma
See also CA 85-88

Henry, O.   1862-1910 ... **TCLC 1, 19; SSC 5**
See also Porter, William Sydney
See also YABC 2; CA 104; DLB 12, 78, 79;
CDALB 1865-1917

Henry VIII   1491-1547............. **LC 10**

Hentoff, Nat(han Irving)   1925-..... **CLC 26**
See also CLR 1; CAAS 6; CANR 5, 25;
CA 1-4R; SATA 27, 42; AAYA 4

Heppenstall, (John) Rayner
1911-1981 .... **CLC 10**
See also CANR 29; CA 1-4R;
obituary CA 103

Herbert, Frank (Patrick)
1920-1986 .... **CLC 12, 23, 35, 44**
See also CANR 5; CA 53-56;
obituary CA 118; SATA 9, 37, 47; DLB 8

Herbert, Zbigniew   1924- .... **CLC 9, 43**
See also CA 89-92

Herbst, Josephine   1897-1969....... **CLC 34**
See also CA 5-8R; obituary CA 25-28R;
DLB 9

Herder, Johann Gottfried von
1744-1803 .... **NCLC 8**

Jones, Diana Wynne   1934- . . . . CLC 26
See also CLR 23; CANR 4, 26; CA 49-52;
SAAS 7; SATA 9

Jones, Gayl   1949- . . . . CLC 6, 9
See also BLC 2; CANR 27; CA 77-80;
DLB 33

Jones, James   1921-1977 . . . . CLC 1, 3, 10, 39
See also CANR 6; CA 1-4R;
obituary CA 69-72; DLB 2

Jones, (Everett) LeRoi
1934- . . . . CLC 1, 2, 3, 5, 10, 14, 33
See also Baraka, Amiri; Baraka, Imamu
Amiri
See also CA 21-24R

Jones, Louis B.   19??- . . . . CLC 65

Jones, Madison (Percy, Jr.)   1925- . . . CLC 4
See also CAAS 11; CANR 7; CA 13-16R

Jones, Mervyn   1922- . . . . CLC 10, 52
See also CAAS 5; CANR 1; CA 45-48

Jones, Mick   1956?- . . . . CLC 30
See also The Clash

Jones, Nettie   19??- . . . . CLC 34

Jones, Preston   1936-1979 . . . . CLC 10
See also CA 73-76; obituary CA 89-92;
DLB 7

Jones, Robert F(rancis)   1934- . . . . CLC 7
See also CANR 2; CA 49-52

Jones, Rod   1953- . . . . CLC 50
See also CA 128

Jones, Terry   1942?- . . . . CLC 21
See also Monty Python
See also CA 112, 116; SATA 51

Jong, Erica   1942- . . . . CLC 4, 6, 8, 18
See also CANR 26; CA 73-76; DLB 2, 5, 28

Jonson, Ben(jamin)   1572-1637 . . . . LC 6
See also DLB 62

Jordan, June   1936- . . . . CLC 5, 11, 23
See also CLR 10; CANR 25; CA 33-36R;
SATA 4; DLB 38; AAYA 2

Jordan, Pat(rick M.)   1941- . . . . CLC 37
See also CANR 25; CA 33-36R

Josipovici, Gabriel (David)
1940- . . . . CLC 6, 43
See also CAAS 8; CA 37-40R; DLB 14

Joubert, Joseph   1754-1824 . . . . NCLC 9

Jouve, Pierre Jean   1887-1976 . . . . . . CLC 47
See also obituary CA 65-68

Joyce, James (Augustine Aloysius)
1882-1941 . . . . . . TCLC 3, 8, 16, 26, 35;
SSC 3
See also CA 104, 126; DLB 10, 19, 36

Jozsef, Attila   1905-1937 . . . . TCLC 22
See also CA 116

Juana Ines de la Cruz   1651?-1695 . . . . LC 5

Julian of Norwich   1342?-1416? . . . . . . LC 6

Just, Ward S(wift)   1935- . . . . CLC 4, 27
See also CA 25-28R

Justice, Donald (Rodney)   1925- . . CLC 6, 19
See also CANR 26; CA 5-8R; DLB-Y 83

Kacew, Romain   1914-1980
See Gary, Romain
See also CA 108; obituary CA 102

Kacewgary, Romain   1914-1980
See Gary, Romain

Kadare, Ismail   1936- . . . . CLC 52

Kadohata, Cynthia   19??- . . . . CLC 59

Kafka, Franz
1883-1924 . . . . TCLC 2, 6, 13, 29; SSC 5
See also CA 105, 126; DLB 81

Kahn, Roger   1927- . . . . CLC 30
See also CA 25-28R; SATA 37

Kaiser, (Friedrich Karl) Georg
1878-1945 . . . . TCLC 9
See also CA 106

Kaletski, Alexander   1946- . . . . CLC 39
See also CA 118

Kallman, Chester (Simon)
1921-1975 . . . . CLC 2
See also CANR 3; CA 45-48;
obituary CA 53-56

Kaminsky, Melvin   1926-
See Brooks, Mel
See also CANR 16; CA 65-68

Kaminsky, Stuart   1934- . . . . CLC 59
See also CANR 29; CA 73-76

Kane, Paul   1941-
See Simon, Paul

Kanin, Garson   1912- . . . . CLC 22
See also CANR 7; CA 5-8R; DLB 7

Kaniuk, Yoram   1930- . . . . CLC 19

Kant, Immanuel   1724-1804 . . . . . . NCLC 27

Kantor, MacKinlay   1904-1977 . . . . . . CLC 7
See also CA 61-64; obituary CA 73-76;
DLB 9

Kaplan, David Michael   1946- . . . . . . CLC 50

Kaplan, James   19??- . . . . CLC 59

Karamzin, Nikolai Mikhailovich
1766-1826 . . . . NCLC 3

Karapanou, Margarita   1946- . . . . CLC 13
See also CA 101

Karl, Frederick R(obert)   1927- . . . . . CLC 34
See also CANR 3; CA 5-8R

Kassef, Romain   1914-1980
See Gary, Romain

Katz, Steve   1935- . . . . CLC 47
See also CANR 12; CA 25-28R; DLB-Y 83

Kauffman, Janet   1945- . . . . CLC 42
See also CA 117; DLB-Y 86

Kaufman, Bob (Garnell)
1925-1986 . . . . CLC 49
See also CANR 22; CA 41-44R;
obituary CA 118; DLB 16, 41

Kaufman, George S(imon)
1889-1961 . . . . CLC 38
See also CA 108; obituary CA 93-96; DLB 7

Kaufman, Sue   1926-1977 . . . . CLC 3, 8
See also Barondess, Sue K(aufman)

Kavan, Anna   1904-1968 . . . . CLC 5, 13
See also Edmonds, Helen (Woods)
See also CANR 6; CA 5-8R

Kavanagh, Patrick (Joseph Gregory)
1905-1967 . . . . CLC 22
See also CA 123; obituary CA 25-28R;
DLB 15, 20

Kawabata, Yasunari
1899-1972 . . . . CLC 2, 5, 9, 18
See also CA 93-96; obituary CA 33-36R

Kaye, M(ary) M(argaret)   1909?- . . . . CLC 28
See also CANR 24; CA 89-92

Kaye, Mollie   1909?-
See Kaye, M(ary) M(argaret)

Kaye-Smith, Sheila   1887-1956 . . . . . TCLC 20
See also CA 118; DLB 36

Kazan, Elia   1909- . . . . CLC 6, 16, 63
See also CA 21-24R

Kazantzakis, Nikos
1885?-1957 . . . . TCLC 2, 5, 33
See also CA 105

Kazin, Alfred   1915- . . . . CLC 34, 38
See also CAAS 7; CANR 1; CA 1-4R;
DLB 67

Keane, Mary Nesta (Skrine)   1904-
See Keane, Molly
See also CA 108, 114

Keane, Molly   1904- . . . . CLC 31
See also Keane, Mary Nesta (Skrine)

Keates, Jonathan   19??- . . . . CLC 34

Keaton, Buster   1895-1966 . . . . CLC 20

Keaton, Joseph Francis   1895-1966
See Keaton, Buster

Keats, John   1795-1821 . . . . . . NCLC 8; PC 1

Keene, Donald   1922- . . . . CLC 34
See also CANR 5; CA 1-4R

Keillor, Garrison   1942- . . . . CLC 40
See also Keillor, Gary (Edward)
See also CA 111; SATA 58; DLB-Y 87;
AAYA 2

Keillor, Gary (Edward)
See Keillor, Garrison
See also CA 111, 117

Kell, Joseph   1917-
See Burgess (Wilson, John) Anthony

Keller, Gottfried   1819-1890 . . . . NCLC 2

Kellerman, Jonathan (S.)   1949- . . . . . CLC 44
See also CANR 29; CA 106

Kelley, William Melvin   1937- . . . . . . CLC 22
See also CANR 27; CA 77-80; DLB 33

Kellogg, Marjorie   1922- . . . . CLC 2
See also CA 81-84

Kelly, M. T.   1947- . . . . CLC 55
See also CANR 19; CA 97-100

Kelman, James   1946- . . . . CLC 58

Kemal, Yashar   1922- . . . . CLC 14, 29
See also CA 89-92

Kemble, Fanny   1809-1893 . . . . NCLC 18
See also DLB 32

Kemelman, Harry   1908- . . . . CLC 2
See also CANR 6; CA 9-12R; DLB 28

Kempe, Margery   1373?-1440? . . . . LC 6

Kempis, Thomas á   1380-1471 . . . . LC 11

Kendall, Henry   1839-1882 . . . . NCLC 12

Keneally, Thomas (Michael)
1935- . . . . . . CLC 5, 8, 10, 14, 19, 27, 43
See also CANR 10; CA 85-88

Kotzebue, August (Friedrich Ferdinand) von
   1761-1819 .... NCLC 25

Kotzwinkle, William   1938- ... CLC 5, 14, 35
   See also CLR 6; CANR 3; CA 45-48;
   SATA 24

Kozol, Jonathan   1936-............ CLC 17
   See also CANR 16; CA 61-64

Kozoll, Michael   1940?-............ CLC 35

Kramer, Kathryn   19??-............ CLC 34

Kramer, Larry   1935- .... CLC 42
   See also CA 124, 126

Krasicki, Ignacy   1735-1801 .... NCLC 8

Krasinski, Zygmunt   1812-1859 .... NCLC 4

Kraus, Karl   1874-1936............ TCLC 5
   See also CA 104

Kreve, Vincas   1882-1954 .... TCLC 27

Kristofferson, Kris   1936-......... CLC 26
   See also CA 104

Krizanc, John   1956-.............. CLC 57

Krleza, Miroslav   1893-1981........ CLC 8
   See also CA 97-100; obituary CA 105

Kroetsch, Robert (Paul)
   1927- .... CLC 5, 23, 57
   See also CANR 8; CA 17-20R; DLB 53

Kroetz, Franz Xaver   1946- .... CLC 41
   See also CA 130

Kropotkin, Peter   1842-1921....... TCLC 36
   See also CA 119

Krotkov, Yuri   1917-.............. CLC 19
   See also CA 102

Krumgold, Joseph (Quincy)
   1908-1980 .... CLC 12
   See also CANR 7; CA 9-12R;
   obituary CA 101; SATA 1, 48;
   obituary SATA 23

Krutch, Joseph Wood   1893-1970.... CLC 24
   See also CANR 4; CA 1-4R;
   obituary CA 25-28R; DLB 63

Krylov, Ivan Andreevich
   1768?-1844............... NCLC 1

Kubin, Alfred   1877-1959 .... TCLC 23
   See also CA 112; DLB 81

Kubrick, Stanley   1928-........... CLC 16
   See also CA 81-84; DLB 26

Kumin, Maxine (Winokur)
   1925- ....CLC 5, 13, 28
   See also CAAS 8; CANR 1, 21; CA 1-4R;
   SATA 12; DLB 5

Kundera, Milan   1929- ..... CLC 4, 9, 19, 32
   See also CANR 19; CA 85-88; AAYA 2

Kunitz, Stanley J(asspon)
   1905- .... CLC 6, 11, 14
   See also CANR 26; CA 41-44R; DLB 48

Kunze, Reiner   1933-.............. CLC 10
   See also CA 93-96; DLB 75

Kuprin, Aleksandr (Ivanovich)
   1870-1938 .... TCLC 5
   See also CA 104

Kureishi, Hanif   1954-............. CLC 64

Kurosawa, Akira   1910-............ CLC 16
   See also CA 101

Kuttner, Henry   1915-1958........ TCLC 10
   See also CA 107; DLB 8

Kuzma, Greg   1944-................ CLC 7
   See also CA 33-36R

Kuzmin, Mikhail   1872?-1936...... TCLC 40

Labrunie, Gerard   1808-1855
   See Nerval, Gerard de

Laclos, Pierre Ambroise Francois Choderlos
   de   1741-1803 .... NCLC 4

La Fayette, Marie (Madelaine Pioche de la
   Vergne, Comtesse) de
   1634-1693 .... LC 2

Lafayette, Rene
   See Hubbard, L(afayette) Ron(ald)

Laforgue, Jules   1860-1887........ NCLC 5

Lagerkvist, Par (Fabian)
   1891-1974........CLC 7, 10, 13, 54
   See also CA 85-88; obituary CA 49-52

Lagerlof, Selma (Ottiliana Lovisa)
   1858-1940................TCLC 4, 36
   See also CLR 7; CA 108; SATA 15

La Guma, (Justin) Alex(ander)
   1925-1985 .... CLC 19
   See also CANR 25; CA 49-52;
   obituary CA 118

Lamartine, Alphonse (Marie Louis Prat) de
   1790-1869 .... NCLC 11

Lamb, Charles   1775-1834........ NCLC 10
   See also SATA 17

Lamming, George (William)
   1927- .... CLC 2, 4, 66
   See also BLC 2; CANR 26; CA 85-88

LaMoore, Louis Dearborn   1908?-
   See L'Amour, Louis (Dearborn)

L'Amour, Louis (Dearborn)
   1908-1988 .... CLC 25, 55
   See also CANR 3, 25; CA 1-4R;
   obituary CA 125; DLB-Y 80

Lampedusa, (Prince) Giuseppe (Maria
   Fabrizio) Tomasi di
   1896-1957 .... TCLC 13
   See also CA 111

Lampman, Archibald   1861-1899 .. NCLC 25
   See also DLB 92

Lancaster, Bruce   1896-1963........ CLC 36
   See also CAP 1; CA 9-12; SATA 9

Landis, John (David)   1950-........ CLC 26
   See also CA 112, 122

Landolfi, Tommaso   1908-1979... CLC 11, 49
   See also CA 127; obituary CA 117

Landon, Letitia Elizabeth
   1802-1838 .... NCLC 15

Landor, Walter Savage
   1775-1864 .... NCLC 14

Landwirth, Heinz   1927-
   See Lind, Jakov
   See also CANR 7; CA 11-12R

Lane, Patrick   1939-.............. CLC 25
   See also CA 97-100; DLB 53

Lang, Andrew   1844-1912........ TCLC 16
   See also CA 114; SATA 16

Lang, Fritz   1890-1976 .... CLC 20
   See also CANR 30; CA 77-80;
   obituary CA 69-72

Langer, Elinor   1939- .... CLC 34
   See also CA 121

Lanier, Sidney   1842-1881 .... NCLC 6
   See also SATA 18; DLB 64

Lanyer, Aemilia   1569-1645 .... LC 10

Lao Tzu   c. 6th-3rd century B.C.... CMLC 7

Lapine, James   1949-.............. CLC 39
   See also CA 123, 130

Larbaud, Valery   1881-1957 .... TCLC 9
   See also CA 106

Lardner, Ring(gold Wilmer)
   1885-1933 .... TCLC 2, 14
   See also CA 104; DLB 11, 25, 86;
   CDALB 1917-1929

Larkin, Philip (Arthur)
   1922-1985 ... CLC 3, 5, 8, 9, 13, 18, 33,
                            39, 64
   See also CANR 24; CA 5-8R;
   obituary CA 117; DLB 27

Larra (y Sanchez de Castro), Mariano Jose de
   1809-1837 .... NCLC 17

Larsen, Eric   1941- .... CLC 55

Larsen, Nella   1891-1964 .... CLC 37
   See also BLC 2; CA 125; DLB 51

Larson, Charles R(aymond)   1938-... CLC 31
   See also CANR 4; CA 53-56

Latham, Jean Lee   1902-........... CLC 12
   See also CANR 7; CA 5-8R; SATA 2

Lathen, Emma .... CLC 2
   See also Hennissart, Martha; Latsis, Mary
   J(ane)

Latsis, Mary J(ane)................. CLC 2
   See also Lathen, Emma
   See also CA 85-88

Lattimore, Richmond (Alexander)
   1906-1984 .... CLC 3
   See also CANR 1; CA 1-4R;
   obituary CA 112

Laughlin, James   1914-............ CLC 49
   See also CANR 9; CA 21-24R; DLB 48

Laurence, (Jean) Margaret (Wemyss)
   1926-1987 .. CLC 3, 6, 13, 50, 62; SSC 7
   See also CA 5-8R; obituary CA 121;
   SATA 50; DLB 53

Laurent, Antoine   1952- .... CLC 50

Lautreamont, Comte de
   1846-1870 .... NCLC 12

Lavin, Mary   1912-...... CLC 4, 18; SSC 4
   See also CA 9-12R; DLB 15

Lawler, Raymond (Evenor)   1922-... CLC 58
   See also CA 103

Lawrence, D(avid) H(erbert)
   1885-1930 .... TCLC 2, 9, 16, 33; SSC 4
   See also CA 104, 121; DLB 10, 19, 36

Lawrence, T(homas) E(dward)
   1888-1935 .... TCLC 18
   See also CA 115

Lawson, Henry (Archibald Hertzberg)
   1867-1922 .... TCLC 27
   See also CA 120

Laxness, Halldor (Kiljan)   1902- .... CLC 25
   See also Gudjonsson, Halldor Kiljan

Laye, Camara   1928-1980........ CLC 4, 38
   See also BLC 2.; CANR 25; CA 85-88;
   obituary CA 97-100

Layton, Irving (Peter) 1912- ..... **CLC 2, 15**
See also CANR 2; CA 1-4R; DLB 88

Lazarus, Emma 1849-1887....... **NCLC 8**

Leacock, Stephen (Butler)
1869-1944 .... **TCLC 2**
See also CA 104; DLB 92

Lear, Edward 1812-1888 .... **NCLC 3**
See also CLR 1; SATA 18; DLB 32

Lear, Norman (Milton) 1922- ...... **CLC 12**
See also CA 73-76

Leavis, F(rank) R(aymond)
1895-1978 .... **CLC 24**
See also CA 21-24R; obituary CA 77-80

Leavitt, David 1961?- .... **CLC 34**
See also CA 116, 122

Lebowitz, Fran(ces Ann)
1951?- .... **CLC 11, 36**
See also CANR 14; CA 81-84

Le Carre, John 1931- ... **CLC 3, 5, 9, 15, 28**
See also Cornwell, David (John Moore)
See also DLB 87

Le Clezio, J(ean) M(arie) G(ustave)
1940- .... **CLC 31**
See also CA 116, 128; DLB 83

Leconte de Lisle, Charles-Marie-Rene
1818-1894 .... **NCLC 29**

Leduc, Violette 1907-1972........ **CLC 22**
See also CAP 1; CA 13-14;
obituary CA 33-36R

Ledwidge, Francis 1887-1917...... **TCLC 23**
See also CA 123; DLB 20

Lee, Andrea 1953- .... **CLC 36**
See also BLC 2; CA 125

Lee, Andrew 1917-
See Auchincloss, Louis (Stanton)

Lee, Don L. 1942-................. **CLC 2**
See also Madhubuti, Haki R.
See also CA 73-76

Lee, George Washington
1894-1976 .... **CLC 52**
See also BLC 2; CA 125; DLB 51

Lee, (Nelle) Harper 1926- ...... **CLC 12, 60**
See also CA 13-16R; SATA 11; DLB 6;
CDALB 1941-1968

Lee, Lawrence 1903- .... **CLC 34**
See also CA 25-28R

Lee, Manfred B(ennington)
1905-1971 .... **CLC 11**
See also Queen, Ellery
See also CANR 2; CA 1-4R;
obituary CA 29-32R

Lee, Stan 1922-................... **CLC 17**
See also CA 108, 111

Lee, Tanith 1947-................. **CLC 46**
See also CA 37-40R; SATA 8

Lee, Vernon 1856-1935 .... **TCLC 5**
See also Paget, Violet
See also DLB 57

Lee-Hamilton, Eugene (Jacob)
1845-1907 .... **TCLC 22**
See also CA 117

Leet, Judith 1935- .... **CLC 11**

Le Fanu, Joseph Sheridan
1814-1873 .... **NCLC 9**
See also DLB 21, 70

Leffland, Ella 1931- .... **CLC 19**
See also CA 29-32R; DLB-Y 84

Leger, (Marie-Rene) Alexis Saint-Leger
1887-1975 .... **CLC 11**
See also Perse, St.-John
See also CA 13-16R; obituary CA 61-64

Le Guin, Ursula K(roeber)
1929- .... **CLC 8, 13, 22, 45**
See also CLR 3; CANR 9; CA 21-24R;
SATA 4, 52; DLB 8, 52;
CDALB 1968-1987

Lehmann, Rosamond (Nina) 1901- ... **CLC 5**
See also CANR 8; CA 77-80; DLB 15

Leiber, Fritz (Reuter, Jr.) 1910-.... **CLC 25**
See also CANR 2; CA 45-48; SATA 45;
DLB 8

Leimbach, Marti 1963-............ **CLC 65**

Leino, Eino 1878-1926.......... **TCLC 24**

Leiris, Michel 1901-............. **CLC 61**
See also CA 119, 128

Leithauser, Brad 1953-............ **CLC 27**
See also CANR 27; CA 107

Lelchuk, Alan 1938-.............. **CLC 5**
See also CANR 1; CA 45-48

Lem, Stanislaw 1921-........ **CLC 8, 15, 40**
See also CAAS 1; CA 105

Lemann, Nancy 1956-............. **CLC 39**
See also CA 118

Lemonnier, (Antoine Louis) Camille
1844-1913 .... **TCLC 22**
See also CA 121

Lenau, Nikolaus 1802-1850...... **NCLC 16**

L'Engle, Madeleine 1918- .... **CLC 12**
See also CLR 1, 14; CANR 3, 21; CA 1-4R;
SATA 1, 27; DLB 52; AAYA 1

Lengyel, Jozsef 1896-1975.......... **CLC 7**
See also CA 85-88; obituary CA 57-60

Lennon, John (Ono)
1940-1980 .... **CLC 12, 35**
See also CA 102

Lennon, John Winston 1940-1980
See Lennon, John (Ono)

Lennox, Charlotte Ramsay
1729?-1804 .... **NCLC 23**
See also DLB 39

Lentricchia, Frank (Jr.) 1940-...... **CLC 34**
See also CANR 19; CA 25-28R

Lenz, Siegfried 1926-............. **CLC 27**
See also CA 89-92; DLB 75

Leonard, Elmore 1925-........ **CLC 28, 34**
See also CANR 12, 28; CA 81-84

Leonard, Hugh 1926-............. **CLC 19**
See also Byrne, John Keyes
See also DLB 13

Leopardi, (Conte) Giacomo (Talegardo
Francesco di Sales Saverio Pietro)
1798-1837 .... **NCLC 22**

Lerman, Eleanor 1952-............ **CLC 9**
See also CA 85-88

Lerman, Rhoda 1936-............. **CLC 56**
See also CA 49-52

Lermontov, Mikhail Yuryevich
1814-1841 .... **NCLC 5**

Leroux, Gaston 1868-1927....... **TCLC 25**
See also CA 108

Lesage, Alain-Rene 1668-1747....... **LC 2**

Leskov, Nikolai (Semyonovich)
1831-1895 .... **NCLC 25**

Lessing, Doris (May)
1919- .... **CLC 1, 2, 3, 6, 10, 15, 22, 40;**
SSC 6
See also CA 9-12R; DLB 15; DLB-Y 85

Lessing, Gotthold Ephraim
1729-1781 .... **LC 8**

Lester, Richard 1932-............. **CLC 20**

Lever, Charles (James)
1806-1872 .... **NCLC 23**
See also DLB 21

Leverson, Ada 1865-1936........ **TCLC 18**
See also CA 117

Levertov, Denise
1923- ...... **CLC 1, 2, 3, 5, 8, 15, 28, 66**
See also CANR 3, 29; CA 1-4R; DLB 5

Levi, Peter (Chad Tiger) 1931- ..... **CLC 41**
See also CA 5-8R; DLB 40

Levi, Primo 1919-1987........ **CLC 37, 50**
See also CANR 12; CA 13-16R;
obituary CA 122

Levin, Ira 1929- .... **CLC 3, 6**
See also CANR 17; CA 21-24R

Levin, Meyer 1905-1981 .... **CLC 7**
See also CANR 15; CA 9-12R;
obituary CA 104; SATA 21;
obituary SATA 27; DLB 9, 28; DLB-Y 81

Levine, Norman 1924-............ **CLC 54**
See also CANR 14; CA 73-76; DLB 88

Levine, Philip 1928-... **CLC 2, 4, 5, 9, 14, 33**
See also CANR 9; CA 9-12R; DLB 5

Levinson, Deirdre 1931-........... **CLC 49**
See also CA 73-76

Levi-Strauss, Claude 1908- .... **CLC 38**
See also CANR 6; CA 1-4R

Levitin, Sonia 1934-.............. **CLC 17**
See also CANR 14; CA 29-32R; SAAS 2;
SATA 4

Lewes, George Henry
1817-1878 .... **NCLC 25**
See also DLB 55

Lewis, Alun 1915-1944............ **TCLC 3**
See also CA 104; DLB 20

Lewis, C(ecil) Day 1904-1972
See Day Lewis, C(ecil)

Lewis, C(live) S(taples)
1898-1963 .... **CLC 1, 3, 6, 14, 27**
See also CLR 3; CA 81-84; SATA 13;
DLB 15

Lewis (Winters), Janet 1899-....... **CLC 41**
See also Winters, Janet Lewis
See also CANR 29; CAP 1; CA 9-10R;
DLB-Y 87

Lewis, Matthew Gregory
1775-1818 .... **NCLC 11**
See also DLB 39

Lytton, Edward Bulwer 1803-1873
See Bulwer-Lytton, (Lord) Edward (George
Earle Lytton)
See also SATA 23

Maas, Peter 1929- .... **CLC 29**
See also CA 93-96

Macaulay, (Dame Emile) Rose
1881-1958 .... **TCLC 7**
See also CA 104; DLB 36

MacBeth, George (Mann)
1932- .... **CLC 2, 5, 9**
See also CA 25-28R; SATA 4; DLB 40

MacCaig, Norman (Alexander)
1910- .... **CLC 36**
See also CANR 3; CA 9-12R; DLB 27

MacCarthy, Desmond 1877-1952 .. **TCLC 36**

MacDermot, Thomas H. 1870-1933
See Redcam, Tom

MacDiarmid, Hugh
1892-1978 .... **CLC 2, 4, 11, 19, 63**
See also Grieve, C(hristopher) M(urray)
See also DLB 20

Macdonald, Cynthia 1928- ...... **CLC 13, 19**
See also CANR 4; CA 49-52

MacDonald, George 1824-1905 ..... **TCLC 9**
See also CA 106; SATA 33; DLB 18

MacDonald, John D(ann)
1916-1986 .... **CLC 3, 27, 44**
See also CANR 1, 19; CA 1-4R;
obituary CA 121; DLB 8; DLB-Y 86

Macdonald, (John) Ross
1915-1983 ...... **CLC 1, 2, 3, 14, 34, 41**
See also Millar, Kenneth
See also DLB-DS 6

MacEwen, Gwendolyn (Margaret)
1941-1987 .... **CLC 13, 55**
See also CANR 7, 22; CA 9-12R;
obituary CA 124; SATA 50, 55; DLB 53

Machado (y Ruiz), Antonio
1875-1939 .... **TCLC 3**
See also CA 104

Machado de Assis, (Joaquim Maria)
1839-1908 .... **TCLC 10**
See also BLC 2; brief entry CA 107

Machen, Arthur (Llewellyn Jones)
1863-1947 .... **TCLC 4**
See also CA 104; DLB 36

Machiavelli, Niccolo 1469-1527 ...... **LC 8**

MacInnes, Colin 1914-1976 ...... **CLC 4, 23**
See also CANR 21; CA 69-72;
obituary CA 65-68; DLB 14

MacInnes, Helen (Clark)
1907-1985 .... **CLC 27, 39**
See also CANR 1, 28; CA 1-4R;
obituary CA 65-68, 117; SATA 22, 44;
DLB 87

Macintosh, Elizabeth 1897-1952
See Tey, Josephine
See also CA 110

Mackenzie, (Edward Montague) Compton
1883-1972 .... **CLC 18**
See also CAP 2; CA 21-22;
obituary CA 37-40R; DLB 34

Mac Laverty, Bernard 1942- .... **CLC 31**
See also CA 116, 118

MacLean, Alistair (Stuart)
1922-1987 .... **CLC 3, 13, 50, 63**
See also CANR 28; CA 57-60;
obituary CA 121; SATA 23, 50

MacLeish, Archibald
1892-1982 .... **CLC 3, 8, 14**
See also CA 9-12R; obituary CA 106;
DLB 4, 7, 45; DLB-Y 82

MacLennan, (John) Hugh
1907- .... **CLC 2, 14**
See also CA 5-8R; DLB 68

MacLeod, Alistair 1936- .... **CLC 56**
See also CA 123; DLB 60

Macleod, Fiona 1855-1905
See Sharp, William

MacNeice, (Frederick) Louis
1907-1963 .... **CLC 1, 4, 10, 53**
See also CA 85-88; DLB 10, 20

Macpherson, (Jean) Jay 1931- ...... **CLC 14**
See also CA 5-8R; DLB 53

MacShane, Frank 1927- .... **CLC 39**
See also CANR 3; CA 11-12R

Macumber, Mari 1896-1966
See Sandoz, Mari (Susette)

Madach, Imre 1823-1864 .... **NCLC 19**

Madden, (Jerry) David 1933- .... **CLC 5, 15**
See also CAAS 3; CANR 4; CA 1-4R;
DLB 6

Madhubuti, Haki R. 1942- .... **CLC 6**
See also Lee, Don L.
See also BLC 2; CANR 24; CA 73-76;
DLB 5, 41; DLB-DS 8

Maeterlinck, Maurice 1862-1949 ... **TCLC 3**
See also CA 104

Mafouz, Naguib 1912-
See Mahfuz, Najib

Maginn, William 1794-1842 .... **NCLC 8**

Mahapatra, Jayanta 1928- .... **CLC 33**
See also CAAS 9; CANR 15; CA 73-76

Mahfuz Najib 1912- .... **CLC 52, 55**
See also DLB-Y 88

Mahon, Derek 1941- .... **CLC 27**
See also CA 113, 128; DLB 40

Mailer, Norman
1923- ...... **CLC 1, 2, 3, 4, 5, 8, 11, 14,
28, 39**
See also CANR 28; CA 9-12R; CABS 1;
DLB 2, 16, 28; DLB-Y 80, 83;
DLB-DS 3; CDALB 1968-1987

Maillet, Antonine 1929- .... **CLC 54**
See also CA 115, 120; DLB 60

Mais, Roger 1905-1955 .... **TCLC 8**
See also CA 105, 124

Maitland, Sara (Louise) 1950- ...... **CLC 49**
See also CANR 13; CA 69-72

Major, Clarence 1936- .... **CLC 3, 19, 48**
See also BLC 2; CAAS 6; CANR 13, 25;
CA 21-24R; DLB 33

Major, Kevin 1949- .... **CLC 26**
See also CLR 11; CANR 21; CA 97-100;
SATA 32; DLB 60

Malamud, Bernard
1914-1986 ..... **CLC 1, 2, 3, 5, 8, 9, 11,
18, 27, 44**
See also CANR 28; CA 5-8R;
obituary CA 118; CABS 1; DLB 2, 28;
DLB-Y 80, 86; CDALB 1941-1968

Malcolm X 1925-1965
See Little, Malcolm

Malherbe, Francois de 1555-1628 ..... **LC 5**

Mallarme, Stephane 1842-1898 .... **NCLC 4**

Mallet-Joris, Francoise 1930- ...... **CLC 11**
See also CANR 17; CA 65-68; DLB 83

Maloff, Saul 1922- .... **CLC 5**
See also CA 33-36R

Malone, Louis 1907-1963
See MacNeice, (Frederick) Louis

Malone, Michael (Christopher)
1942- .... **CLC 43**
See also CANR 14; CA 77-80

Malory, (Sir) Thomas ?-1471 .... **LC 11**
See also SATA 33, 59

Malouf, David 1934- .... **CLC 28**

Malraux, (Georges-) Andre
1901-1976 ...... **CLC 1, 4, 9, 13, 15, 57**
See also CAP 2; CA 21-24;
obituary CA 69-72; DLB 72

Malzberg, Barry N. 1939- .... **CLC 7**
See also CAAS 4; CANR 16; CA 61-64;
DLB 8

Mamet, David (Alan)
1947- .... **CLC 9, 15, 34, 46**
See also CANR 15; CA 81-84, 124;
CABS 3; DLB 7; AAYA 3

Mamoulian, Rouben 1898- .... **CLC 16**
See also CA 25-28R; obituary CA 124

Mandelstam, Osip (Emilievich)
1891?-1938? .... **TCLC 2, 6**
See also CA 104

Mander, Jane 1877-1949 .... **TCLC 31**

Mandiargues, Andre Pieyre de
1909- .... **CLC 41**
See also CA 103; DLB 83

Mangan, James Clarence
1803-1849 .... **NCLC 27**

Manley, (Mary) Delariviere
1672?-1724 .... **LC 1**
See also DLB 39, 80

Mann, (Luiz) Heinrich 1871-1950... **TCLC 9**
See also CA 106; DLB 66

Mann, Thomas
1875-1955 ...... **TCLC 2, 8, 14, 21, 35;
SSC 5**
See also CA 104, 128; DLB 66

Manning, Frederic 1882-1935 ..... **TCLC 25**
See also CA 124

Manning, Olivia 1915-1980 ...... **CLC 5, 19**
See also CANR 29; CA 5-8R;
obituary CA 101

Mano, D. Keith 1942- .... **CLC 2, 10**
See also CAAS 6; CANR 26; CA 25-28R;
DLB 6

Mansfield, Katherine
1888-1923 .... **TCLC 2, 8, 39**
See also CA 104

Manso, Peter   1940- . . . .   **CLC 39**
  See also CA 29-32R

Manzoni, Alessandro   1785-1873 . .   **NCLC 29**

Mapu, Abraham (ben Jekutiel)
  1808-1867 . . . .   **NCLC 18**

Marat, Jean Paul   1743-1793 . . . .   **LC 10**

Marcel, Gabriel (Honore)
  1889-1973 . . . .   **CLC 15**
  See also CA 102; obituary CA 45-48

Marchbanks, Samuel   1913-
  See Davies, (William) Robertson

Marie de l'Incarnation   1599-1672. . . .   **LC 10**

Marinetti, F(ilippo) T(ommaso)
  1876-1944 . . . .   **TCLC 10**
  See also CA 107

Marivaux, Pierre Carlet de Chamblain de
  (1688-1763) . . . .   **LC 4**

Markandaya, Kamala   1924- . . . . . .   **CLC 8, 38**
  See also Taylor, Kamala (Purnaiya)

Markfield, Wallace (Arthur)   1926- . . .   **CLC 8**
  See also CAAS 3; CA 69-72; DLB 2, 28

Markham, Robert   1922-
  See Amis, Kingsley (William)

Marks, J.   1942-
  See Highwater, Jamake

Marley, Bob   1945-1981 . . . .   **CLC 17**
  See also Marley, Robert Nesta

Marley, Robert Nesta   1945-1981
  See Marley, Bob
  See also CA 107; obituary CA 103

Marlowe, Christopher   1564-1593 . . . . .   **DC 1**
  See also DLB 62

Marmontel, Jean-Francois
  1723-1799 . . . .   **LC 2**

Marquand, John P(hillips)
  1893-1960 . . . .   **CLC 2, 10**
  See also CA 85-88; DLB 9

Marquez, Gabriel Garcia   1928-
  See Garcia Marquez, Gabriel

Marquis, Don(ald Robert Perry)
  1878-1937 . . . .   **TCLC 7**
  See also CA 104; DLB 11, 25

Marryat, Frederick   1792-1848 . . . .   **NCLC 3**
  See also DLB 21

Marsh, (Dame Edith) Ngaio
  1899-1982 . . . .   **CLC 7, 53**
  See also CANR 6; CA 9-12R; DLB 77

Marshall, Garry   1935?- . . . .   **CLC 17**
  See also CA 111; AAYA 3

Marshall, Paule   1929- . . . . .   **CLC 27; SSC 3**
  See also BLC 2; CANR 25; CA 77-80;
  DLB 33

Marsten, Richard   1926-
  See Hunter, Evan

Martin, Steve   1945?- . . . .   **CLC 30**
  See also CANR 30; CA 97-100

Martin du Gard, Roger
  1881-1958 . . . .   **TCLC 24**
  See also CA 118; DLB 65

Martineau, Harriet   1802-1876. . . .   **NCLC 26**
  See also YABC 2; DLB 21, 55

Martinez Ruiz, Jose   1874-1967
  See Azorin
  See also CA 93-96

Martinez Sierra, Gregorio
  1881-1947 . . . .   **TCLC 6**
  See also CA 104, 115

Martinez Sierra, Maria (de la O'LeJarraga)
  1880?-1974. . . . .   **TCLC 6**
  See also obituary CA 115

Martinson, Harry (Edmund)
  1904-1978 . . . .   **CLC 14**
  See also CA 77-80

Marvell, Andrew   1621-1678. . . . .   **LC 4**

Marx, Karl (Heinrich)
  1818-1883 . . . .   **NCLC 17**

Masaoka Shiki   1867-1902 . . . .   **TCLC 18**

Masefield, John (Edward)
  1878-1967 . . . .   **CLC 11, 47**
  See also CAP 2; CA 19-20;
  obituary CA 25-28R; SATA 19; DLB 10,
  19

Maso, Carole   19??- . . . .   **CLC 44**

Mason, Bobbie Ann
  1940- . . . .   **CLC 28, 43; SSC 4**
  See also CANR 11; CA 53-56; SAAS 1;
  DLB-Y 87

Mason, Nick   1945- . . . .   **CLC 35**
  See also Pink Floyd

Mason, Tally   1909-1971
  See Derleth, August (William)

Masters, Edgar Lee
  1868?-1950. . . . .   **TCLC 2, 25; PC 1**
  See also CA 104; DLB 54;
  CDALB 1865-1917

Masters, Hilary   1928- . . . .   **CLC 48**
  See also CANR 13; CA 25-28R

Mastrosimone, William   19??- . . . . . .   **CLC 36**

Matheson, Richard (Burton)
  1926- . . . .   **CLC 37**
  See also CA 97-100; DLB 8, 44

Mathews, Harry   1930- . . . .   **CLC 6, 52**
  See also CAAS 6; CANR 18; CA 21-24R

Mathias, Roland (Glyn)   1915- . . . . . .   **CLC 45**
  See also CANR 19; CA 97-100; DLB 27

Matthews, Greg   1949- . . . .   **CLC 45**

Matthews, William   1942- . . . .   **CLC 40**
  See also CANR 12; CA 29-32R; DLB 5

Matthias, John (Edward)   1941- . . . . . .   **CLC 9**
  See also CA 33-36R

Matthiessen, Peter
  1927- . . . .   **CLC 5, 7, 11, 32, 64**
  See also CANR 21; CA 9-12R; SATA 27;
  DLB 6

Maturin, Charles Robert
  1780?-1824. . . . .   **NCLC 6**

Matute, Ana Maria   1925- . . . .   **CLC 11**
  See also CA 89-92

Maugham, W(illiam) Somerset
  1874-1965 . . . .   **CLC 1, 11, 15; SSC 8**
  See also CA 5-8R; obituary CA 25-28R;
  SATA 54; DLB 10, 36, 77, 100

Maupassant, (Henri Rene Albert) Guy de
  1850-1893 . . . .   **NCLC 1; SSC 1**

Mauriac, Claude   1914- . . . .   **CLC 9**
  See also CA 89-92; DLB 83

Mauriac, Francois (Charles)
  1885-1970 . . . .   **CLC 4, 9, 56**
  See also CAP 2; CA 25-28; DLB 65

Mavor, Osborne Henry   1888-1951
  See Bridie, James
  See also CA 104

Maxwell, William (Keepers, Jr.)
  1908- . . . .   **CLC 19**
  See also CA 93-96; DLB-Y 80

May, Elaine   1932- . . . .   **CLC 16**
  See also CA 124; DLB 44

Mayakovsky, Vladimir (Vladimirovich)
  1893-1930 . . . .   **TCLC 4, 18**
  See also CA 104

Mayhew, Henry   1812-1887 . . . . . .   **NCLC 31**
  See also DLB 18, 55

Maynard, Joyce   1953- . . . .   **CLC 23**
  See also CA 111, 129

Mayne, William (James Carter)
  1928- . . . .   **CLC 12**
  See also CA 9-12R; SATA 6

Mayo, Jim   1908?-
  See L'Amour, Louis (Dearborn)

Maysles, Albert   1926- and Maysles, David
  1926- . . . .   **CLC 16**
  See also CA 29-32R

Maysles, Albert   1926- . . . .   **CLC 16**
  See also Maysles, Albert and Maysles,
  David
  See also CA 29-32R

Maysles, David   1932- . . . .   **CLC 16**
  See also Maysles, Albert and Maysles,
  David

Mazer, Norma Fox   1931- . . . .   **CLC 26**
  See also CLR 23; CANR 12; CA 69-72;
  SAAS 1; SATA 24

McAuley, James (Phillip)
  1917-1976 . . . .   **CLC 45**
  See also CA 97-100

McBain, Ed   1926-
  See Hunter, Evan

McBrien, William   1930- . . . .   **CLC 44**
  See also CA 107

McCaffrey, Anne   1926- . . . .   **CLC 17**
  See also CANR 15; CA 25-28R; SATA 8;
  DLB 8

McCarthy, Cormac   1933- . . . .   **CLC 4, 57**
  See also CANR 10; CA 13-16R; DLB 6

McCarthy, Mary (Therese)
  1912-1989- . . .   **CLC 1, 3, 5, 14, 24, 39, 59**
  See also CANR 16; CA 5-8R;
  obituary CA 129; DLB 2; DLB-Y 81

McCartney, (James) Paul
  1942- . . . .   **CLC 12, 35**

McCauley, Stephen   19??- . . . .   **CLC 50**

McClure, Michael   1932- . . . .   **CLC 6, 10**
  See also CANR 17; CA 21-24R; DLB 16

McCorkle, Jill (Collins)   1958- . . . . . .   **CLC 51**
  See also CA 121; DLB-Y 87

McCourt, James   1941- . . . .   **CLC 5**
  See also CA 57-60

Miller, Henry (Valentine)
 1891-1980 .... **CLC 1, 2, 4, 9, 14, 43**
 See also CA 9-12R; obituary CA 97-100;
 DLB 4, 9; DLB-Y 80; CDALB 1929-1941

Miller, Jason 1939?-............... **CLC 2**
 See also CA 73-76; DLB 7

Miller, Sue 19??-................. **CLC 44**

Miller, Walter M(ichael), Jr.
 1923-...................... **CLC 4, 30**
 See also CA 85-88; DLB 8

Millhauser, Steven 1943-....... **CLC 21, 54**
 See also CA 108, 110, 111; DLB 2

Millin, Sarah Gertrude 1889-1968 .. **CLC 49**
 See also CA 102; obituary CA 93-96

Milne, A(lan) A(lexander)
 1882-1956 .... **TCLC 6**
 See also CLR 1; YABC 1; CA 104;
 DLB 10, 77

Milner, Ron(ald) 1938-............ **CLC 56**
 See also BLC 2; CANR 24; CA 73-76;
 DLB 38

Milosz Czeslaw
 1911-.......... **CLC 5, 11, 22, 31, 56**
 See also CANR 23; CA 81-84

Milton, John 1608-1674............. **LC 9**

Miner, Valerie (Jane) 1947-....... **CLC 40**
 See also CA 97-100

Minot, Susan 1956- .... **CLC 44**

Minus, Ed 1938-................. **CLC 39**

Miro (Ferrer), Gabriel (Francisco Victor)
 1879-1930 .... **TCLC 5**
 See also CA 104

Mishima, Yukio
 1925-1970 .... **CLC 2, 4, 6, 9, 27; DC 1;**
           SSC 4
 See also Hiraoka, Kimitake

Mistral, Gabriela 1889-1957 .... **TCLC 2**
 See also CA 104

Mitchell, James Leslie 1901-1935
 See Gibbon, Lewis Grassic
 See also CA 104; DLB 15

Mitchell, Joni 1943-.............. **CLC 12**
 See also CA 112

Mitchell (Marsh), Margaret (Munnerlyn)
 1900-1949 .... **TCLC 11**
 See also CA 109, 125; DLB 9

Mitchell, S. Weir 1829-1914 ...... **TCLC 36**

Mitchell, W(illiam) O(rmond)
 1914- .... **CLC 25**
 See also CANR 15; CA 77-80; DLB 88

Mitford, Mary Russell 1787-1855.. **NCLC 4**

Mitford, Nancy 1904-1973......... **CLC 44**
 See also CA 9-12R

Miyamoto Yuriko 1899-1951...... **TCLC 37**

Mo, Timothy 1950-............... **CLC 46**
 See also CA 117

Modarressi, Taghi 1931- .... **CLC 44**
 See also CA 121

Modiano, Patrick (Jean) 1945- ..... **CLC 18**
 See also CANR 17; CA 85-88; DLB 83

Mofolo, Thomas (Mokopu)
 1876-1948 .... **TCLC 22**
 See also BLC 2; brief entry CA 121

Mohr, Nicholasa 1935-............ **CLC 12**
 See also CLR 22; CANR 1; CA 49-52;
 SAAS 8; SATA 8

Mojtabai, A(nn) G(race)
 1938-................ **CLC 5, 9, 15, 29**
 See also CA 85-88

Moliere 1622-1673 .... **LC 10**

Molnar, Ferenc 1878-1952....... **TCLC 20**
 See also CA 109

Momaday, N(avarre) Scott
 1934-...................... **CLC 2, 19**
 See also CANR 14; CA 25-28R; SATA 30,
 48

Monroe, Harriet 1860-1936....... **TCLC 12**
 See also CA 109; DLB 54, 91

Montagu, Elizabeth 1720-1800 .... **NCLC 7**

Montagu, Lady Mary (Pierrepont) Wortley
 1689-1762 .... **LC 9**

Montague, John (Patrick)
 1929-................. **CLC 13, 46**
 See also CANR 9; CA 9-12R; DLB 40

Montaigne, Michel (Eyqucm) de
 1533-1592 .... **LC 8**

Montale, Eugenio 1896-1981... **CLC 7, 9, 18**
 See also CANR 30; CA 17-20R;
 obituary CA 104

Montesquieu, Charles-Louis de Secondat
 1689-1755 .... **LC 7**

Montgomery, Marion (H., Jr.)
 1925-..................... **CLC 7**
 See also CANR 3; CA 1-4R; DLB 6

Montgomery, Robert Bruce 1921-1978
 See Crispin, Edmund
 See also CA 104

Montherlant, Henri (Milon) de
 1896-1972 .... **CLC 8, 19**
 See also CA 85-88; obituary CA 37-40R;
 DLB 72

Monty Python.................... **CLC 21**

Moodie, Susanna (Strickland)
 1803-1885 .... **NCLC 14**

Mooney, Ted 1951-............... **CLC 25**

Moorcock, Michael (John)
 1939-................. **CLC 5, 27, 58**
 See also CAAS 5; CANR 2, 17; CA 45-48;
 DLB 14

Moore, Brian
 1921-......... **CLC 1, 3, 5, 7, 8, 19, 32**
 See also CANR 1, 25; CA 1-4R

Moore, George (Augustus)
 1852-1933 .... **TCLC 7**
 See also CA 104; DLB 10, 18, 57

Moore, Lorrie 1957-........... **CLC 39, 45**
 See also Moore, Marie Lorena

Moore, Marianne (Craig)
 1887-1972 ... **CLC 1, 2, 4, 8, 10, 13, 19,**
             47
 See also CANR 3; CA 1-4R;
 obituary CA 33-36R; SATA 20; DLB 45;
 CDALB 1929-1941

Moore, Marie Lorena 1957-
 See Moore, Lorrie
 See also CA 116

Moore, Thomas 1779-1852....... **NCLC 6**

Morand, Paul 1888-1976 .... **CLC 41**
 See also obituary CA 69-72; DLB 65

Morante, Elsa 1918-1985........ **CLC 8, 47**
 See also CA 85-88; obituary CA 117

Moravia, Alberto
 1907- .... **CLC 2, 7, 11, 18, 27, 46**
 See also Pincherle, Alberto

More, Hannah 1745-1833 .... **NCLC 27**

More, Henry 1614-1687............. **LC 9**

More, (Sir) Thomas 1478-1535 ...... **LC 10**

Moreas, Jean 1856-1910 .... **TCLC 18**

Morgan, Berry 1919-.............. **CLC 6**
 See also CA 49-52; DLB 6

Morgan, Edwin (George) 1920-..... **CLC 31**
 See also CANR 3; CA 7-8R; DLB 27

Morgan, (George) Frederick
 1922-...................... **CLC 23**
 See also CANR 21; CA 17-20R

Morgan, Janet 1945- .... **CLC 39**
 See also CA 65-68

Morgan, Lady 1776?-1859 .... **NCLC 29**

Morgan, Robin 1941-.............. **CLC 2**
 See also CA 69-72

Morgan, Seth 1949-1990 .... **CLC 65**
 See also CA 132

Morgenstern, Christian (Otto Josef Wolfgang)
 1871-1914................... **TCLC 8**
 See also CA 105

Moricz, Zsigmond 1879-1942 ..... **TCLC 33**

Morike, Eduard (Friedrich)
 1804-1875 .... **NCLC 10**

Mori Ogai 1862-1922............ **TCLC 14**
 See also Mori Rintaro

Mori Rintaro 1862-1922
 See Mori Ogai
 See also CA 110

Moritz, Karl Philipp 1756-1793 ...... **LC 2**

Morris, Julian 1916-
 See West, Morris L.

Morris, Steveland Judkins 1950-
 See Wonder, Stevie
 See also CA 111

Morris, William 1834-1896 .... **NCLC 4**
 See also DLB 18, 35, 57

Morris, Wright (Marion)
 1910-.......... **CLC 1, 3, 7, 18, 37**
 See also CANR 21; CA 9-12R; DLB 2;
 DLB-Y 81

Morrison, James Douglas 1943-1971
 See Morrison, Jim
 See also CA 73-76

Morrison, Jim 1943-1971.......... **CLC 17**
 See also Morrison, James Douglas

Morrison, Toni 1931-..... **CLC 4, 10, 22, 55**
 See also BLC 2; CANR 27; CA 29-32R;
 SATA 57; DLB 6, 33; DLB-Y 81;
 CDALB 1968-1987; AAYA 1

Morrison, Van 1945- .... **CLC 21**
 See also CA 116

Mortimer, John (Clifford)
 1923-.................... **CLC 28, 43**
 See also CANR 21; CA 13-16R; DLB 13

Mortimer, Penelope (Ruth) 1918-.... **CLC 5**
See also CA 57-60

Mosher, Howard Frank 19??-...... **CLC 62**

Mosley, Nicholas 1923-............. **CLC 43**
See also CA 69-72; DLB 14

Moss, Howard
1922-1987 .... **CLC 7, 14, 45, 50**
See also CANR 1; CA 1-4R;
obituary CA 123; DLB 5

Motion, Andrew (Peter) 1952-...... **CLC 47**
See also DLB 40

Motley, Willard (Francis)
1912-1965 .... **CLC 18**
See also CA 117; obituary CA 106; DLB 76

Mott, Michael (Charles Alston)
1930-..................... **CLC 15, 34**
See also CAAS 7; CANR 7, 29; CA 5-8R

Mowat, Farley (McGill) 1921-..... **CLC 26**
See also CLR 20; CANR 4, 24; CA 1-4R;
SATA 3, 55; DLB 68; AAYA 1

Mphahlele, Es'kia 1919-
See Mphahlele, Ezekiel

Mphahlele, Ezekiel 1919-.......... **CLC 25**
See also BLC 2; CANR 26; CA 81-84

Mqhayi, S(amuel) E(dward) K(rune Loliwe)
1875-1945 .... **TCLC 25**
See also BLC 2

Mrozek, Slawomir 1930-........ **CLC 3, 13**
See also CAAS 10; CANR 29; CA 13-16R

Mtwa, Percy 19??-............... **CLC 47**

Mueller, Lisel 1924-........... **CLC 13, 51**
See also CA 93-96

Muir, Edwin 1887-1959 .... **TCLC 2**
See also CA 104; DLB 20

Muir, John 1838-1914 .... **TCLC 28**

Mujica Lainez, Manuel
1910-1984 .... **CLC 31**
See also CA 81-84; obituary CA 112

Mukherjee, Bharati 1940-........ **CLC 53**
See also CA 107; DLB 60

Muldoon, Paul 1951-............. **CLC 32**
See also CA 113, 129; DLB 40

Mulisch, Harry (Kurt Victor)
1927-..................... **CLC 42**
See also CANR 6, 26; CA 9-12R

Mull, Martin 1943-.............. **CLC 17**
See also CA 105

Munford, Robert 1737?-1783......... **LC 5**
See also DLB 31

Munro, Alice (Laidlaw)
1931-........ **CLC 6, 10, 19, 50; SSC 3**
See also CA 33-36R; SATA 29; DLB 53

Munro, H(ector) H(ugh) 1870-1916
See Saki
See also CA 104; DLB 34

Murasaki, Lady c. 11th century-... **CMLC 1**

Murdoch, (Jean) Iris
1919-...... **CLC 1, 2, 3, 4, 6, 8, 11, 15,
22, 31, 51**
See also CANR 8; CA 13-16R; DLB 14

Murphy, Richard 1927-........... **CLC 41**
See also CA 29-32R; DLB 40

Murphy, Sylvia 19??-............ **CLC 34**

Murphy, Thomas (Bernard) 1935-... **CLC 51**
See also CA 101

Murray, Les(lie) A(llan) 1938-..... **CLC 40**
See also CANR 11, 27; CA 21-24R

Murry, John Middleton
1889-1957 .... **TCLC 16**
See also CA 118

Musgrave, Susan 1951-........ **CLC 13, 54**
See also CA 69-72

Musil, Robert (Edler von)
1880-1942 .... **TCLC 12**
See also CA 109; DLB 81

Musset, (Louis Charles) Alfred de
1810-1857 .... **NCLC 7**

Myers, Walter Dean 1937-........ **CLC 35**
See also BLC 2; CLR 4, 16; CANR 20;
CA 33-36R; SAAS 2; SATA 27, 41;
DLB 33; AAYA 4

Nabokov, Vladimir (Vladimirovich)
1899-1977 .... **CLC 1, 2, 3, 6, 8, 11, 15,
23, 44, 46, 64**
See also CANR 20; CA 5-8R;
obituary CA 69-72; DLB 2; DLB-Y 80;
DLB-DS 3; CDALB 1941-1968

Nagy, Laszlo 1925-1978........... **CLC 7**
See also CA 129; obituary CA 112

Naipaul, Shiva(dhar Srinivasa)
1945-1985 .... **CLC 32, 39**
See also CA 110, 112; obituary CA 116;
DLB-Y 85

Naipaul, V(idiadhar) S(urajprasad)
1932-.......... **CLC 4, 7, 9, 13, 18, 37**
See also CANR 1; CA 1-4R; DLB-Y 85

Nakos, Ioulia 1899?-
See Nakos, Lilika

Nakos, Lilika 1899?-............. **CLC 29**

Nakou, Lilika 1899?-
See Nakos, Lilika

Narayan, R(asipuram) K(rishnaswami)
1906-................. **CLC 7, 28, 47**
See also CA 81-84

Nash, (Frediric) Ogden 1902-1971 .. **CLC 23**
See also CAP 1; CA 13-14;
obituary CA 29-32R; SATA 2, 46;
DLB 11

Nathan, George Jean 1882-1958 ... **TCLC 18**
See also CA 114

Natsume, Kinnosuke 1867-1916
See Natsume, Soseki
See also CA 104

Natsume, Soseki 1867-1916..... **TCLC 2, 10**
See also Natsume, Kinnosuke

Natti, (Mary) Lee 1919-
See Kingman, (Mary) Lee
See also CANR 2; CA 7-8R

Naylor, Gloria 1950-.......... **CLC 28, 52**
See also BLC 3; CANR 27; CA 107;
AAYA 6

Neff, Debra 1972-................ **CLC 59**

Neihardt, John G(neisenau)
1881-1973 .... **CLC 32**
See also CAP 1; CA 13-14; DLB 9, 54

Nekrasov, Nikolai Alekseevich
1821-1878 .... **NCLC 11**

Nelligan, Emile 1879-1941........ **TCLC 14**
See also CA 114; DLB 92

Nelson, Willie 1933-.............. **CLC 17**
See also CA 107

Nemerov, Howard 1920- .... **CLC 2, 6, 9, 36**
See also CANR 1, 27; CA 1-4R; CABS 2;
DLB 5, 6; DLB-Y 83

Neruda, Pablo
1904-1973 ..... **CLC 1, 2, 5, 7, 9, 28, 62**
See also CAP 2; CA 19-20;
obituary CA 45-48

Nerval, Gerard de 1808-1855...... **NCLC 1**

Nervo, (Jose) Amado (Ruiz de)
1870-1919 .... **TCLC 11**
See also CA 109

Neufeld, John (Arthur) 1938- ...... **CLC 17**
See also CANR 11; CA 25-28R; SAAS 3;
SATA 6

Neville, Emily Cheney 1919-....... **CLC 12**
See also CANR 3; CA 5-8R; SAAS 2;
SATA 1

Newbound, Bernard Slade 1930-
See Slade, Bernard
See also CA 81-84

Newby, P(ercy) H(oward)
1918-..................... **CLC 2, 13**
See also CA 5-8R; DLB 15

Newlove, Donald 1928- .... **CLC 6**
See also CANR 25; CA 29-32R

Newlove, John (Herbert) 1938-..... **CLC 14**
See also CANR 9, 25; CA 21-24R

Newman, Charles 1938-.......... **CLC 2, 8**
See also CA 21-24R

Newman, Edwin (Harold) 1919- .... **CLC 14**
See also CANR 5; CA 69-72

Newton, Suzanne 1936-.......... **CLC 35**
See also CANR 14; CA 41-44R; SATA 5

Ngema, Mbongeni 1955- .... **CLC 57**

Ngugi, James (Thiong'o)
1938-................. **CLC 3, 7, 13, 36**
See also Ngugi wa Thiong'o; Wa Thiong'o,
Ngugi
See also CANR 27; CA 81-84

Ngugi wa Thiong'o 1938-... **CLC 3, 7, 13, 36**
See also Ngugi, James (Thiong'o); Wa
Thiong'o, Ngugi
See also BLC 2

Nichol, B(arrie) P(hillip) 1944-..... **CLC 18**
See also CA 53-56; DLB 53

Nichols, John (Treadwell) 1940-.... **CLC 38**
See also CAAS 2; CANR 6; CA 9-12R;
DLB-Y 82

Nichols, Peter (Richard)
1927-................... **CLC 5, 36, 65**
See also CANR 33; CA 104; DLB 13

Nicolas, F.R.E. 1927-
See Freeling, Nicolas

Niedecker, Lorine 1903-1970.... **CLC 10, 42**
See also CAP 2; CA 25-28; DLB 48

Nietzsche, Friedrich (Wilhelm)
1844-1900 .... **TCLC 10, 18**
See also CA 107, 121

Nievo, Ippolito 1831-1861 .... **NCLC 22**

Nightingale, Anne Redmon   1943-
    See Redmon (Nightingale), Anne
    See also CA 103

Nin, Anais
        1903-1977 ..... **CLC 1, 4, 8, 11, 14, 60**
    See also CANR 22; CA 13-16R;
        obituary CA 69-72; DLB 2, 4

Nissenson, Hugh   1933-........... **CLC 4, 9**
    See also CANR 27; CA 17-20R; DLB 28

Niven, Larry   1938-................. **CLC 8**
    See also Niven, Laurence Van Cott
    See also DLB 8

Niven, Laurence Van Cott   1938-
    See Niven, Larry
    See also CANR 14; CA 21-24R

Nixon, Agnes Eckhardt   1927-...... **CLC 21**
    See also CA 110

Nizan, Paul   1905-1940........... **TCLC 40**
    See also DLB 72

Nkosi, Lewis   1936-................ **CLC 45**
    See also BLC 2; CANR 27; CA 65-68

Nodier, (Jean) Charles (Emmanuel)
        1780-1844 .... **NCLC 19**

Nolan, Christopher   1965-.......... **CLC 58**
    See also CA 111

Nordhoff, Charles   1887-1947...... **TCLC 23**
    See also CA 108; SATA 23; DLB 9

Norman, Marsha   1947- .... **CLC 28**
    See also CA 105; CABS 3; DLB-Y 84

Norris, (Benjamin) Frank(lin)
        1870-1902 .... **TCLC 24**
    See also CA 110; DLB 12, 71;
        CDALB 1865-1917

Norris, Leslie   1921- .... **CLC 14**
    See also CANR 14; CAP 1; CA 11-12;
        DLB 27

North, Andrew   1912-
    See Norton, Andre

North, Christopher   1785-1854
    See Wilson, John

Norton, Alice Mary   1912-
    See Norton, Andre
    See also CANR 2; CA 1-4R; SATA 1, 43

Norton, Andre   1912- .... **CLC 12**
    See also Norton, Mary Alice
    See also DLB 8, 52

Norway, Nevil Shute   1899-1960
    See Shute (Norway), Nevil
    See also CA 102; obituary CA 93-96

Norwid, Cyprian Kamil
        1821-1883 .... **NCLC 17**

Nossack, Hans Erich   1901-1978 ..... **CLC 6**
    See also CA 93-96; obituary CA 85-88;
        DLB 69

Nova, Craig   1945-.............. **CLC 7, 31**
    See also CANR 2; CA 45-48

Novak, Joseph   1933-
    See Kosinski, Jerzy (Nikodem)

Novalis   1772-1801 .... **NCLC 13**

Nowlan, Alden (Albert)   1933-...... **CLC 15**
    See also CANR 5; CA 9-12R; DLB 53

Noyes, Alfred   1880-1958 .... **TCLC 7**
    See also CA 104; DLB 20

Nunn, Kem   19??-................ **CLC 34**

Nye, Robert   1939- .... **CLC 13, 42**
    See also CANR 29; CA 33-36R; SATA 6;
        DLB 14

Nyro, Laura   1947- .... **CLC 17**

Oates, Joyce Carol
        1938- ..... **CLC 1, 2, 3, 6, 9, 11, 15, 19,
                            33, 52; SSC 6**
    See also CANR 25; CA 5-8R; DLB 2, 5;
        DLB-Y 81; CDALB 1968-1987

O'Brien, Darcy   1939-............. **CLC 11**
    See also CANR 8; CA 21-24R

O'Brien, Edna
        1936- .... **CLC 3, 5, 8, 13, 36, 65**
    See also CANR 6; CA 1-4R; DLB 14

O'Brien, Fitz-James   1828?-1862.. **NCLC 21**
    See also DLB 74

O'Brien, Flann
        1911-1966 .... **CLC 1, 4, 5, 7, 10, 47**
    See also O Nuallain, Brian

O'Brien, Richard   19??-............ **CLC 17**
    See also CA 124

O'Brien, (William) Tim(othy)
        1946- .... **CLC 7, 19, 40**
    See also CA 85-88; DLB-Y 80

Obstfelder, Sigbjorn   1866-1900.... **TCLC 23**
    See also CA 123

O'Casey, Sean
        1880-1964 .... **CLC 1, 5, 9, 11, 15**
    See also CA 89-92; DLB 10

Ochs, Phil   1940-1976 .... **CLC 17**
    See also obituary CA 65-68

O'Connor, Edwin (Greene)
        1918-1968 .... **CLC 14**
    See also CA 93-96; obituary CA 25-28R

O'Connor, (Mary) Flannery
        1925-1964 ... **CLC 1, 2, 3, 6, 10, 13, 15,
                            21, 66; SSC 1**
    See also CANR 3; CA 1-4R; DLB 2;
        DLB-Y 80; CDALB 1941-1968

O'Connor, Frank
        1903-1966 .... **CLC 14, 23; SSC 5**
    See also O'Donovan, Michael (John)
    See also CA 93-96

O'Dell, Scott   1903-................ **CLC 30**
    See also CLR 1, 16; CANR 12; CA 61-64;
        SATA 12; DLB 52

Odets, Clifford   1906-1963 .... **CLC 2, 28**
    See also CA 85-88; DLB 7, 26

O'Donovan, Michael (John)
        1903-1966 .... **CLC 14**
    See also O'Connor, Frank
    See also CA 93-96

Oe, Kenzaburo   1935-.......... **CLC 10, 36**
    See also CA 97-100

O'Faolain, Julia   1932-....... **CLC 6, 19, 47**
    See also CAAS 2; CANR 12; CA 81-84;
        DLB 14

O'Faolain, Sean   1900-..... **CLC 1, 7, 14, 32**
    See also CANR 12; CA 61-64; DLB 15

O'Flaherty, Liam
        1896-1984 .... **CLC 5, 34; SSC 6**
    See also CA 101; obituary CA 113; DLB 36;
        DLB-Y 84

O'Grady, Standish (James)
        1846-1928 .... **TCLC 5**
    See also CA 104

O'Grady, Timothy   1951-......... **CLC 59**

O'Hara, Frank   1926-1966 ..... **CLC 2, 5, 13**
    See also CA 9-12R; obituary CA 25-28R;
        DLB 5, 16; CDALB 1929-1941

O'Hara, John (Henry)
        1905-1970 ...... **CLC 1, 2, 3, 6, 11, 42**
    See also CA 5-8R; obituary CA 25-28R;
        DLB 9; DLB-DS 2; CDALB 1929-1941

O'Hara Family
    See Banim, John and Banim, Michael

O'Hehir, Diana   1922-............. **CLC 41**
    See also CA 93-96

Okigbo, Christopher (Ifenayichukwu)
        1932-1967 .... **CLC 25**
    See also BLC 2; CA 77-80

Olds, Sharon   1942-............ **CLC 32, 39**
    See also CANR 18; CA 101

Olesha, Yuri (Karlovich)
        1899-1960 .... **CLC 8**
    See also CA 85-88

Oliphant, Margaret (Oliphant Wilson)
        1828-1897 .... **NCLC 11**
    See also DLB 18

Oliver, Mary   1935-............ **CLC 19, 34**
    See also CANR 9; CA 21-24R; DLB 5

Olivier, (Baron) Laurence (Kerr)
        1907-...................... **CLC 20**
    See also CA 111, 129

Olsen, Tillie   1913-............. **CLC 4, 13**
    See also CANR 1; CA 1-4R; DLB 28;
        DLB-Y 80

Olson, Charles (John)
        1910-1970 ..... **CLC 1, 2, 5, 6, 9, 11, 29**
    See also CAP 1; CA 15-16;
        obituary CA 25-28R; CABS 2; DLB 5, 16

Olson, Theodore   1937-
    See Olson, Toby

Olson, Toby   1937- .... **CLC 28**
    See also CANR 9; CA 65-68

Ondaatje, (Philip) Michael
        1943-................. **CLC 14, 29, 51**
    See also CA 77-80; DLB 60

Oneal, Elizabeth   1934-............ **CLC 30**
    See also Oneal, Zibby
    See also CLR 13; CA 106; SATA 30

Oneal, Zibby   1934-............... **CLC 30**
    See also Oneal, Elizabeth

O'Neill, Eugene (Gladstone)
        1888-1953 .... **TCLC 1, 6, 27**
    See also CA 110; DLB 7;
        CDALB 1929-1941

Onetti, Juan Carlos   1909-....... **CLC 7, 10**
    See also CA 85-88

O'Nolan, Brian   1911-1966
    See O'Brien, Flann

O Nuallain, Brian   1911-1966
    See O'Brien, Flann
    See also CAP 2; CA 21-22;
        obituary CA 25-28R

Oppen, George   1908-1984 .... **CLC 7, 13, 34**
    See also CANR 8; CA 13-16R;
        obituary CA 113; DLB 5

Percy, Walker
1916-1990 ... **CLC 2, 3, 6, 8, 14, 18, 47, 65**
See also CANR 1, 23; CA 1-4R;
obituary CA 131; DLB 2; DLB-Y 80

Perec, Georges 1936-1982 .... **CLC 56**
See also DLB 83

Pereda, Jose Maria de
1833-1906 .... **TCLC 16**

Perelman, S(idney) J(oseph)
1904-1979 ... **CLC 3, 5, 9, 15, 23, 44, 49**
See also CANR 18; CA 73-76;
obituary CA 89-92; DLB 11, 44

Peret, Benjamin 1899-1959 .... **TCLC 20**
See also CA 117

Peretz, Isaac Leib 1852?-1915..... **TCLC 16**
See also CA 109

Perez, Galdos Benito 1853-1920 ... **TCLC 27**
See also CA 125

Perrault, Charles 1628-1703 .... **LC 2**
See also SATA 25

Perse, St.-John 1887-1975.... **CLC 4, 11, 46**
See also Leger, (Marie-Rene) Alexis
Saint-Leger

Pesetsky, Bette 1932-............. **CLC 28**

Peshkov, Alexei Maximovich 1868-1936
See Gorky, Maxim
See also CA 105

Pessoa, Fernando (Antonio Nogueira)
1888-1935 .... **TCLC 27**
See also CA 125

Peterkin, Julia (Mood) 1880-1961... **CLC 31**
See also CA 102; DLB 9

Peters, Joan K. 1945-............. **CLC 39**

Peters, Robert L(ouis) 1924-........ **CLC 7**
See also CAAS 8; CA 13-16R

Petofi, Sandor 1823-1849........ **NCLC 21**

Petrakis, Harry Mark 1923-........ **CLC 3**
See also CANR 4, 30; CA 9-12R

Petrov, Evgeny 1902-1942........ **TCLC 21**

Petry, Ann (Lane) 1908- ...... **CLC 1, 7, 18**
See also CLR 12; CAAS 6; CANR 4;
CA 5-8R; SATA 5; DLB 76

Petursson, Halligrimur 1614-1674 .... **LC 8**

Philipson, Morris (H.) 1926-....... **CLC 53**
See also CANR 4; CA 1-4R

Phillips, Jayne Anne 1952- ..... **CLC 15, 33**
See also CANR 24; CA 101; DLB-Y 80

Phillips, Robert (Schaeffer) 1938-... **CLC 28**
See also CANR 8; CA 17-20R

Pica, Peter 1925-
See Aldiss, Brian W(ilson)

Piccolo, Lucio 1901-1969.......... **CLC 13**
See also CA 97-100

Pickthall, Marjorie (Lowry Christie)
1883-1922 .... **TCLC 21**
See also CA 107; DLB 92

Pico della Mirandola, Giovanni
1463-1494 .... **LC 15**

Piercy, Marge
1936- .... **CLC 3, 6, 14, 18, 27, 62**
See also CAAS 1; CANR 13; CA 21-24R

Pilnyak, Boris 1894-1937?........ **TCLC 23**

Pincherle, Alberto 1907- .... **CLC 11, 18**
See also Moravia, Alberto
See also CA 25-28R

Pineda, Cecile 1942-.............. **CLC 39**
See also CA 118

Pinero, Miguel (Gomez)
1946-1988 .... **CLC 4, 55**
See also CANR 29; CA 61-64;
obituary CA 125

Pinero, Sir Arthur Wing
1855-1934 .... **TCLC 32**
See also CA 110; DLB 10

Pinget, Robert 1919- .... **CLC 7, 13, 37**
See also CA 85-88; DLB 83

Pink Floyd...................... **CLC 35**

Pinkney, Edward 1802-1828 ..... **NCLC 31**

Pinkwater, D(aniel) M(anus)
1941- .... **CLC 35**
See also Pinkwater, Manus
See also CLR 4; CANR 12; CA 29-32R;
SAAS 3; SATA 46; AAYA 1

Pinkwater, Manus 1941-
See Pinkwater, D(aniel) M(anus)
See also SATA 8

Pinsky, Robert 1940-........ **CLC 9, 19, 38**
See also CAAS 4; CA 29-32R; DLB-Y 82

Pinter, Harold
1930- ..... **CLC 1, 3, 6, 9, 11, 15, 27, 58**
See also CA 5-8R; DLB 13

Pirandello, Luigi 1867-1936..... **TCLC 4, 29**
See also CA 104

Pirsig, Robert M(aynard) 1928- ... **CLC 4, 6**
See also CA 53-56; SATA 39

Pisarev, Dmitry Ivanovich
1840-1868 .... **NCLC 25**

Pix, Mary (Griffith) 1666-1709....... **LC 8**
See also DLB 80

Plaidy, Jean 1906-
See Hibbert, Eleanor (Burford)

Plant, Robert 1948- .... **CLC 12**

Plante, David (Robert)
1940- .... **CLC 7, 23, 38**
See also CANR 12; CA 37-40R; DLB-Y 83

Plath, Sylvia
1932-1963 .... **CLC 1, 2, 3, 5, 9, 11, 14, 17, 50, 51, 62; PC 1**
See also CAP 2; CA 19-20; DLB 5, 6;
CDALB 1941-1968

Platonov, Andrei (Platonovich)
1899-1951 .... **TCLC 14**
See also Klimentov, Andrei Platonovich
See also CA 108

Platt, Kin 1911- .... **CLC 26**
See also CANR 11; CA 17-20R; SATA 21

Plimpton, George (Ames) 1927-..... **CLC 36**
See also CA 21-24R; SATA 10

Plomer, William (Charles Franklin)
1903-1973 .... **CLC 4, 8**
See also CAP 2; CA 21-22; SATA 24;
DLB 20

Plumly, Stanley (Ross) 1939- ...... **CLC 33**
See also CA 108, 110; DLB 5

Poe, Edgar Allan
1809-1849 ... **NCLC 1, 16; PC 1; SSC 1**
See also SATA 23; DLB 3, 59, 73, 74;
CDALB 1640-1865

Pohl, Frederik 1919- .... **CLC 18**
See also CAAS 1; CANR 11; CA 61-64;
SATA 24; DLB 8

Poirier, Louis 1910-
See Gracq, Julien
See also CA 122, 126

Poitier, Sidney 1924?-............. **CLC 26**
See also CA 117

Polanski, Roman 1933-............ **CLC 16**
See also CA 77-80

Poliakoff, Stephen 1952-.......... **CLC 38**
See also CA 106; DLB 13

Police, The...................... **CLC 26**

Pollitt, Katha 1949-.............. **CLC 28**
See also CA 120, 122

Pollock, Sharon 19??-............. **CLC 50**
See also DLB 60

Pomerance, Bernard 1940-......... **CLC 13**
See also CA 101

Ponge, Francis (Jean Gaston Alfred)
1899- .... **CLC 6, 18**
See also CA 85-88; obituary CA 126

Pontoppidan, Henrik 1857-1943 ... **TCLC 29**
See also obituary CA 126

Poole, Josephine 1933-............ **CLC 17**
See also CANR 10; CA 21-24R; SAAS 2;
SATA 5

Popa, Vasko 1922-................ **CLC 19**
See also CA 112

Pope, Alexander 1688-1744.......... **LC 3**

Porter, Gene Stratton 1863-1924 , , **TCLC 21**
See also CA 112

Porter, Katherine Anne
1890-1980 ..... **CLC 1, 3, 7, 10, 13, 15, 27; SSC 4**
See also CANR 1; CA 1-4R;
obituary CA 101; obituary SATA 23, 39;
DLB 4, 9; DLB-Y 80

Porter, Peter (Neville Frederick)
1929- .... **CLC 5, 13, 33**
See also CA 85-88; DLB 40

Porter, William Sydney 1862-1910
See Henry, O.
See also YABC 2; CA 104; DLB 12, 78, 79;
CDALB 1865-1917

Post, Melville D. 1871-1930 ...... **TCLC 39**
See also brief entry CA 110

Potok, Chaim 1929-....... **CLC 2, 7, 14, 26**
See also CANR 19; CA 17-20R; SATA 33;
DLB 28

Potter, Dennis (Christopher George)
1935- .... **CLC 58**
See also CA 107

Pound, Ezra (Loomis)
1885-1972 ..... **CLC 1, 2, 3, 4, 5, 7, 10, 13, 18, 34, 48, 50**
See also CA 5-8R; obituary CA 37-40R;
DLB 4, 45, 63; CDALB 1917-1929

Povod, Reinaldo 1959-........... **CLC 44**

Powell, Adam Clayton, Jr. 1908-1972
    See also BLC 2; CA 102;
    obituary CA 33-36R

Powell, Anthony (Dymoke)
    1905- . . . . CLC 1, 3, 7, 9, 10, 31
    See also CANR 1; CA 1-4R; DLB 15

Powell, Dawn 1897-1965 . . . . CLC 66
    See also CA 5-8R

Powell, Padgett 1952- . . . . CLC 34
    See also CA 126

Powers, J(ames) F(arl)
    1917- . . . . CLC 1, 4, 8, 57; SSC 4
    See also CANR 2; CA 1-4R

Powers, John J(ames) 1945-
    See Powers, John R.

Powers, John R. 1945- . . . . CLC 66
    See also Powers, John J(ames)
    See also CA 69-72

Pownall, David 1938- . . . . CLC 10
    See also CA 89-92; DLB 14

Powys, John Cowper
    1872-1963 . . . . CLC 7, 9, 15, 46
    See also CA 85-88; DLB 15

Powys, T(heodore) F(rancis)
    1875-1953 . . . . TCLC 9
    See also CA 106; DLB 36

Prager, Emily 1952- . . . . CLC 56

Pratt, E(dwin) J(ohn) 1883-1964 . . . . CLC 19
    See also obituary CA 93-96; DLB 92

Premchand 1880-1936 . . . . TCLC 21

Preussler, Otfried 1923- . . . . CLC 17
    See also CA 77-80; SATA 24

Prevert, Jacques (Henri Marie)
    1900-1977 . . . . CLC 15
    See also CANR 29; CA 77-80;
    obituary CA 69-72; obituary SATA 30

Prevost, Abbe (Antoine Francois)
    1697-1763 . . . . LC 1

Price, (Edward) Reynolds
    1933- . . . . CLC 3, 6, 13, 43, 50, 63
    See also CANR 1; CA 1-4R; DLB 2

Price, Richard 1949- . . . . CLC 6, 12
    See also CANR 3; CA 49-52; DLB-Y 81

Prichard, Katharine Susannah
    1883-1969 . . . . CLC 46
    See also CAP 1; CA 11-12

Priestley, J(ohn) B(oynton)
    1894-1984 . . . . CLC 2, 5, 9, 34
    See also CA 9-12R; obituary CA 113;
    DLB 10, 34, 77; DLB-Y 84

Prince (Rogers Nelson) 1958?- . . . . . CLC 35

Prince, F(rank) T(empleton) 1912- . . CLC 22
    See also CA 101; DLB 20

Prior, Matthew 1664-1721. . . . . LC 4

Pritchard, William H(arrison)
    1932- . . . . CLC 34
    See also CANR 23; CA 65-68

Pritchett, V(ictor) S(awdon)
    1900- . . . . CLC 5, 13, 15, 41
    See also CA 61-64; DLB 15

Probst, Mark 1925- . . . . CLC 59
    See also CA 130

Procaccino, Michael 1946-
    See Cristofer, Michael

Prokosch, Frederic 1908-1989 . . . . CLC 4, 48
    See also CA 73-76; obituary CA 128;
    DLB 48

Prose, Francine 1947- . . . . CLC 45
    See also CA 109, 112

Proust, Marcel 1871-1922 . . TCLC 7, 13, 33
    See also CA 104, 120; DLB 65

Pryor, Richard 1940- . . . . CLC 26
    See also CA 122

Przybyszewski, Stanislaw
    1868-1927 . . . . TCLC 36
    See also DLB 66

Puig, Manuel
    1932-1990 . . . . CLC 3, 5, 10, 28, 65
    See also CANR 2, 32; CA 45-48

Purdy, A(lfred) W(ellington)
    1918- . . . . CLC 3, 6, 14, 50
    See also CA 81-84

Purdy, James (Amos)
    1923- . . . . CLC 2, 4, 10, 28, 52
    See also CAAS 1; CANR 19; CA 33-36R;
    DLB 2

Pushkin, Alexander (Sergeyevich)
    1799-1837 . . . . NCLC 3, 27

P'u Sung-ling 1640-1715 . . . . LC 3

Puzo, Mario 1920- . . . . CLC 1, 2, 6, 36
    See also CANR 4; CA 65-68; DLB 6

Pym, Barbara (Mary Crampton)
    1913-1980 . . . . CLC 13, 19, 37
    See also CANR 13; CAP 1; CA 13-14;
    obituary CA 97-100; DLB 14; DLB-Y 87

Pynchon, Thomas (Ruggles, Jr.)
    1937- . . . . . CLC 2, 3, 6, 9, 11, 18, 33, 62
    See also CANR 22; CA 17-20R; DLB 2

Quarrington, Paul 1954?- . . . . CLC 65
    See also CA 129

Quasimodo, Salvatore 1901-1968 . . . CLC 10
    See also CAP 1; CA 15-16;
    obituary CA 25-28R

Queen, Ellery 1905-1982 . . . . CLC 3, 11
    See also Dannay, Frederic; Lee, Manfred
    B(ennington)

Queneau, Raymond
    1903-1976 . . . . CLC 2, 5, 10, 42
    See also CA 77-80; obituary CA 69-72;
    DLB 72

Quin, Ann (Marie) 1936-1973 . . . . . . CLC 6
    See also CA 9-12R; obituary CA 45-48;
    DLB 14

Quinn, Simon 1942-
    See Smith, Martin Cruz
    See also CANR 6, 23; CA 85-88

Quiroga, Horacio (Sylvestre)
    1878-1937 . . . . TCLC 20
    See also CA 117

Quoirez, Francoise 1935-
    See Sagan, Francoise
    See also CANR 6; CA 49-52

Rabe, David (William) 1940- . . . CLC 4, 8, 33
    See also CA 85-88; CABS 3; DLB 7

Rabelais, Francois 1494?-1553. . . . . . . LC 5

Rabinovitch, Sholem 1859-1916
    See Aleichem, Sholom
    See also CA 104

Rachen, Kurt von 1911-1986
    See Hubbard, L(afayette) Ron(ald)

Radcliffe, Ann (Ward) 1764-1823 . . NCLC 6
    See also DLB 39

Radiguet, Raymond 1903-1923 . . . . TCLC 29
    See also DLB 65

Radnoti, Miklos 1909-1944 . . . . TCLC 16
    See also CA 118

Rado, James 1939- . . . . CLC 17
    See also CA 105

Radomski, James 1932-
    See Rado, James

Radvanyi, Netty Reiling 1900-1983
    See Seghers, Anna
    See also CA 85-88; obituary CA 110

Rae, Ben 1935-
    See Griffiths, Trevor

Raeburn, John 1941- . . . . CLC 34
    See also CA 57-60

Ragni, Gerome 1942- . . . . CLC 17
    See also CA 105

Rahv, Philip 1908-1973 . . . . CLC 24
    See also Greenberg, Ivan

Raine, Craig 1944- . . . . CLC 32
    See also CANR 29; CA 108; DLB 40

Raine, Kathleen (Jessie) 1908- . . . CLC 7, 45
    See also CA 85-88; DLB 20

Rainis, Janis 1865-1929 . . . . TCLC 29

Rakosi, Carl 1903- . . . . CLC 47
    See also Rawley, Callman
    See also CAAS 5

Ramos, Graciliano 1892-1953 . . . . . TCLC 32

Rampersad, Arnold 19??- . . . . CLC 44

Ramuz, Charles-Ferdinand
    1878-1947 . . . . TCLC 33

Rand, Ayn 1905-1982 . . . . CLC 3, 30, 44
    See also CANR 27; CA 13-16R;
    obituary CA 105

Randall, Dudley (Felker) 1914- . . . . . . CLC 1
    See also CANR 23; CA 25-28R; DLB 41

Ransom, John Crowe
    1888-1974 . . . . CLC 2, 4, 5, 11, 24
    See also CANR 6; CA 5-8R;
    obituary CA 49-52; DLB 45, 63

Rao, Raja 1909- . . . . CLC 25, 56
    See also CA 73-76

Raphael, Frederic (Michael)
    1931- . . . . CLC 2, 14
    See also CANR 1; CA 1-4R; DLB 14

Rathbone, Julian 1935- . . . . CLC 41
    See also CA 101

Rattigan, Terence (Mervyn)
    1911-1977 . . . . CLC 7
    See also CA 85-88; obituary CA 73-76;
    DLB 13

Ratushinskaya, Irina 1954- . . . . CLC 54
    See also CA 129

Raven, Simon (Arthur Noel)
    1927- . . . . CLC 14
    See also CA 81-84

Rawley, Callman 1903-
    See Rakosi, Carl
    See also CANR 12; CA 21-24R

Author Index

Roberts, (Sir) Charles G(eorge) D(ouglas)
1860-1943 . . . . TCLC 8
See also CA 105; SATA 29; DLB 92

Roberts, Kate 1891-1985 . . . . CLC 15
See also CA 107; obituary CA 116

Roberts, Keith (John Kingston)
1935- . . . . CLC 14
See also CA 25-28R

Roberts, Kenneth 1885-1957 . . . . . . TCLC 23
See also CA 109; DLB 9

Roberts, Michele (B.) 1949- . . . . CLC 48
See also CA 115

Robinson, Edwin Arlington
1869-1935 . . . . TCLC 5; PC 1
See also CA 104; DLB 54;
CDALB 1865-1917

Robinson, Henry Crabb
1775-1867 . . . . NCLC 15

Robinson, Jill 1936- . . . . CLC 10
See also CA 102

Robinson, Kim Stanley 19??- . . . . CLC 34
See also CA 126

Robinson, Marilynne 1944- . . . . CLC 25
See also CA 116

Robinson, Smokey 1940- . . . . CLC 21

Robinson, William 1940-
See Robinson, Smokey
See also CA 116

Robison, Mary 1949- . . . . CLC 42
See also CA 113, 116

Roddenberry, Gene 1921- . . . . CLC 17
See also CANR 110; SATA 45

Rodgers, Mary 1931- . . . . CLC 12
See also CLR 20; CANR 8; CA 49-52;
SATA 8

Rodgers, W(illiam) R(obert)
1909-1969 . . . . CLC 7
See also CA 85-88; DLB 20

Rodman, Howard 19??- . . . . CLC 65

Rodriguez, Claudio 1934- . . . . CLC 10

Roethke, Theodore (Huebner)
1908-1963 . . . . . . CLC 1, 3, 8, 11, 19, 46
See also CA 81-84; CABS 2; SAAS 1;
DLB 5; CDALB 1941-1968

Rogers, Sam 1943-
See Shepard, Sam

Rogers, Thomas (Hunton) 1931- . . . . CLC 57
See also CA 89-92

Rogers, Will(iam Penn Adair)
1879-1935 . . . . TCLC 8
See also CA 105; DLB 11

Rogin, Gilbert 1929- . . . . CLC 18
See also CANR 15; CA 65-68

Rohan, Koda 1867-1947 . . . . TCLC 22
See also CA 121

Rohmer, Eric 1920- . . . . CLC 16
See also Scherer, Jean-Marie Maurice

Rohmer, Sax 1883-1959 . . . . TCLC 28
See also Ward, Arthur Henry Sarsfield
See also CA 108; DLB 70

Roiphe, Anne (Richardson)
1935- . . . . CLC 3, 9
See also CA 89-92; DLB-Y 80

Rolfe, Frederick (William Serafino Austin
Lewis Mary) 1860-1913 . . . . . . TCLC 12
See also CA 107; DLB 34

Rolland, Romain 1866-1944 . . . . TCLC 23
See also CA 118; DLB 65

Rolvaag, O(le) E(dvart)
1876-1931 . . . . TCLC 17
See also CA 117; DLB 9

Romains, Jules 1885-1972 . . . . CLC 7
See also CA 85-88

Romero, Jose Ruben 1890-1952 . . . TCLC 14
See also CA 114

Ronsard, Pierre de 1524-1585 . . . . LC 6

Rooke, Leon 1934- . . . . CLC 25, 34
See also CANR 23; CA 25-28R

Roper, William 1498-1578 . . . . LC 10

Rosa, Joao Guimaraes 1908-1967 . . . CLC 23
See also obituary CA 89-92

Rosen, Richard (Dean) 1949- . . . . CLC 39
See also CA 77-80

Rosenberg, Isaac 1890-1918 . . . . TCLC 12
See also CA 107; DLB 20

Rosenblatt, Joe 1933- . . . . CLC 15
See also Rosenblatt, Joseph

Rosenblatt, Joseph 1933-
See Rosenblatt, Joe
See also CA 89-92

Rosenfeld, Samuel 1896-1963
See Tzara, Tristan
See also obituary CA 89-92

Rosenthal, M(acha) L(ouis) 1917- . . . CLC 28
See also CAAS 6; CANR 4; CA 1-4R;
SATA 59; DLB 5

Ross, (James) Sinclair 1908- . . . . CLC 13
See also CA 73-76; DLB 88

Rossetti, Christina Georgina
1830-1894 . . . . NCLC 2
See also SATA 20; DLB 35

Rossetti, Dante Gabriel
1828-1882 . . . . NCLC 4
See also DLB 35

Rossetti, Gabriel Charles Dante 1828-1882
See Rossetti, Dante Gabriel

Rossner, Judith (Perelman)
1935- . . . . CLC 6, 9, 29
See also CANR 18; CA 17-20R; DLB 6

Rostand, Edmond (Eugene Alexis)
1868-1918 . . . . TCLC 6, 37
See also CA 104, 126

Roth, Henry 1906- . . . . CLC 2, 6, 11
See also CAP 1; CA 11-12; DLB 28

Roth, Joseph 1894-1939 . . . . TCLC 33
See also DLB 85

Roth, Philip (Milton)
1933- . . . . . . CLC 1, 2, 3, 4, 6, 9, 15, 22,
31, 47, 66
See also CANR 1, 22; CA 1-4R; DLB 2, 28;
DLB-Y 82; CDALB 1968-1988

Rothenberg, James 1931- . . . . CLC 57

Rothenberg, Jerome 1931- . . . . CLC 6, 57
See also CANR 1; CA 45-48; DLB 5

Roumain, Jacques 1907-1944 . . . . . . TCLC 19
See also CA 117

Rourke, Constance (Mayfield)
1885-1941 . . . . TCLC 12
See also YABC 1; CA 107

Rousseau, Jean-Baptiste 1671-1741 . . . LC 9

Rousseau, Jean-Jacques 1712-1778 . . . LC 14

Roussel, Raymond 1877-1933 . . . . . TCLC 20
See also CA 117

Rovit, Earl (Herbert) 1927- . . . . CLC 7
See also CANR 12; CA 5-8R

Rowe, Nicholas 1674-1718 . . . . LC 8

Rowson, Susanna Haswell
1762-1824 . . . . NCLC 5
See also DLB 37

Roy, Gabrielle 1909-1983 . . . . CLC 10, 14
See also CANR 5; CA 53-56;
obituary CA 110; DLB 68

Rozewicz, Tadeusz 1921- . . . . CLC 9, 23
See also CA 108

Ruark, Gibbons 1941- . . . . CLC 3
See also CANR 14; CA 33-36R

Rubens, Bernice 192?- . . . . CLC 19, 31
See also CA 25-28R; DLB 14

Rudkin, (James) David 1936- . . . . . . CLC 14
See also CA 89-92; DLB 13

Rudnik, Raphael 1933- . . . . CLC 7
See also CA 29-32R

Ruiz, Jose Martinez 1874-1967
See Azorin

Rukeyser, Muriel
1913-1980 . . . . CLC 6, 10, 15, 27
See also CANR 26; CA 5-8R;
obituary CA 93-96; obituary SATA 22;
DLB 48

Rule, Jane (Vance) 1931- . . . . CLC 27
See also CANR 12; CA 25-28R; DLB 60

Rulfo, Juan 1918-1986 . . . . CLC 8
See also CANR 26; CA 85-88;
obituary CA 118

Runyon, (Alfred) Damon
1880-1946 . . . . TCLC 10
See also CA 107; DLB 11

Rush, Norman 1933- . . . . CLC 44
See also CA 121, 126

Rushdie, (Ahmed) Salman
1947- . . . . CLC 23, 31, 55, 59
See also CA 108, 111

Rushforth, Peter (Scott) 1945- . . . . . CLC 19
See also CA 101

Ruskin, John 1819-1900 . . . . TCLC 20
See also CA 114; SATA 24; DLB 55

Russ, Joanna 1937- . . . . CLC 15
See also CANR 11; CA 25-28R; DLB 8

Russell, George William 1867-1935
See A. E.
See also CA 104

Russell, (Henry) Ken(neth Alfred)
1927- . . . . CLC 16
See also CA 105

Russell, Mary Annette Beauchamp 1866-1941
See Elizabeth

Russell, Willy 1947- . . . . CLC 60

Rutherford, Mark 1831-1913 . . . . . . TCLC 25
See also CA 121; DLB 18

Ruyslinck, Ward 1929- . . . . CLC 14

Ryan, Cornelius (John) 1920-1974 . . . CLC 7
See also CA 69-72; obituary CA 53-56

Ryan, Michael 1946- . . . . CLC 65
See also CA 49-52; DLB-Y 82

Rybakov, Anatoli 1911?- . . . . CLC 23, 53
See also CA 126

Ryder, Jonathan 1927-
See Ludlum, Robert

Ryga, George 1932- . . . . CLC 14
See also CA 101; obituary CA 124; DLB 60

Séviné, Marquise de Marie de
    Rabutin-Chantal 1626-1696. . . . . LC 11

Saba, Umberto 1883-1957 . . . . TCLC 33

Sabato, Ernesto 1911- . . . . CLC 10, 23
See also CA 97-100

Sacher-Masoch, Leopold von
    1836?-1895. . . . . NCLC 31

Sachs, Marilyn (Stickle) 1927- . . . . . CLC 35
See also CLR 2; CANR 13; CA 17-20R;
    SAAS 2; SATA 3, 52

Sachs, Nelly 1891-1970 . . . . CLC 14
See also CAP 2; CA 17-18;
    obituary CA 25-28R

Sackler, Howard (Oliver)
    1929-1982 . . . . CLC 14
See also CA 61-64; obituary CA 108; DLB 7

Sade, Donatien Alphonse Francois, Comte de
    1740-1814 . . . . NCLC 3

Sadoff, Ira 1945- . . . . CLC 9
See also CANR 5, 21; CA 53-56

Safire, William 1929- . . . . CLC 10
See also CA 17-20R

Sagan, Carl (Edward) 1934- . . . . CLC 30
See also CANR 11; CA 25-28R; SATA 58

Sagan, Francoise
    1935- . . . . CLC 3, 6, 9, 17, 36
See also Quoirez, Francoise
See also CANR 6; DLB 83

Sahgal, Nayantara (Pandit) 1927-. . . CLC 41
See also CANR 11; CA 9-12R

Saint, H(arry) F. 1941- . . . . CLC 50

Sainte-Beuve, Charles Augustin
    1804-1869 . . . . NCLC 5

Sainte-Marie, Beverly 1941-1972?
See Sainte-Marie, Buffy
See also CA 107

Sainte-Marie, Buffy 1941- . . . . CLC 17
See also Sainte-Marie, Beverly

Saint-Exupery, Antoine (Jean Baptiste Marie
    Roger) de 1900-1944 . . . . TCLC 2
See also CLR 10; CA 108; SATA 20;
    DLB 72

Saintsbury, George 1845-1933. . . . . TCLC 31
See also DLB 57

Sait Faik (Abasiyanik)
    1906-1954 . . . . TCLC 23

Saki 1870-1916. . . . . TCLC 3
See also Munro, H(ector) H(ugh)
See also CA 104

Salama, Hannu 1936- . . . . CLC 18

Salamanca, J(ack) R(ichard)
    1922- . . . . CLC 4, 15
See also CA 25-28R

Salinas, Pedro 1891-1951. . . . . TCLC 17
See also CA 117

Salinger, J(erome) D(avid)
    1919- . . . . CLC 1, 3, 8, 12, 56; SSC 2
See also CA 5-8R; DLB 2;
    CDALB 1941-1968

Salter, James 1925- . . . . CLC 7, 52, 59
See also CA 73-76

Saltus, Edgar (Evertson)
    1855-1921 . . . . TCLC 8
See also CA 105

Saltykov, Mikhail Evgrafovich
    1826-1889 . . . . NCLC 16

Samarakis, Antonis 1919- . . . . CLC 5
See also CA 25-28R

Sanchez, Florencio 1875-1910. . . . . TCLC 37

Sanchez, Luis Rafael 1936- . . . . CLC 23

Sanchez, Sonia 1934- . . . . CLC 5
See also CANR 24; CA 33-36R; SATA 22;
    DLB 41

Sand, George 1804-1876. . . . . NCLC 2

Sandburg, Carl (August)
    1878-1967 . . . CLC 1, 4, 10, 15, 35; PC 2
See also CA 5-8R; obituary CA 25-28R;
    SATA 8; DLB 17, 54; CDALB 1865-1917

Sandburg, Charles August 1878-1967
See Sandburg, Carl (August)

Sanders, (James) Ed(ward) 1939- . . . CLC 53
See also CANR 13; CA 15-16R, 103;
    DLB 16

Sanders, Lawrence 1920- . . . . CLC 41
See also CA 81-84

Sandoz, Mari (Susette) 1896-1966 . . CLC 28
See also CANR 17; CA 1-4R;
    obituary CA 25-28R; SATA 5; DLB 9

Saner, Reg(inald Anthony) 1931- . . . . CLC 9
See also CA 65-68

Sannazaro, Jacopo 1456?-1530 . . . . . . LC 8

Sansom, William 1912-1976. . . . . . CLC 2, 6
See also CA 5-8R; obituary CA 65-68

Santayana, George 1863-1952. . . . . TCLC 40
See also CA 115; DLB 54, 71

Santiago, Danny 1911- . . . . CLC 33
See also CA 125

Santmyer, Helen Hooven
    1895-1986 . . . . CLC 33
See also CANR 15; CA 1-4R;
    obituary CA 118; DLB-Y 84

Santos, Bienvenido N(uqui) 1911-. . . CLC 22
See also CANR 19; CA 101

Sappho c. 6th-century B.C.- . . . . CMLC 3

Sarduy, Severo 1937- . . . . CLC 6
See also CA 89-92

Sargeson, Frank 1903-1982 . . . . CLC 31
See also CA 106, 25-28R; obituary CA 106

Sarmiento, Felix Ruben Garcia 1867-1916
See Dario, Ruben
See also CA 104

Saroyan, William
    1908-1981 . . . . . CLC 1, 8, 10, 29, 34, 56
See also CA 5-8R; obituary CA 103;
    SATA 23; obituary SATA 24; DLB 7, 9;
    DLB-Y 81

Sarraute, Nathalie
    1902- . . . . CLC 1, 2, 4, 8, 10, 31
See also CANR 23; CA 9-12R; DLB 83

Sarton, Eleanore Marie 1912-
See Sarton, (Eleanor) May

Sarton, (Eleanor) May
    1912- . . . . CLC 4, 14, 49
See also CANR 1; CA 1-4R; SATA 36;
    DLB 48; DLB-Y 81

Sartre, Jean-Paul (Charles Aymard)
    1905-1980 . . . CLC 1, 4, 7, 9, 13, 18, 24,
                                            44, 50, 52
See also CANR 21; CA 9-12R;
    obituary CA 97-100; DLB 72

Sassoon, Siegfried (Lorraine)
    1886-1967 . . . . CLC 36
See also CA 104; obituary CA 25-28R;
    DLB 20

Saul, John (W. III) 1942- . . . . CLC 46
See also CANR 16; CA 81-84

Saura, Carlos 1932- . . . . CLC 20
See also CA 114

Sauser-Hall, Frederic-Louis
    1887-1961 . . . . CLC 18
See also Cendrars, Blaise
See also CA 102; obituary CA 93-96

Savage, Thomas 1915- . . . . CLC 40
See also CA 126

Savan, Glenn 19??- . . . . CLC 50

Sayers, Dorothy L(eigh)
    1893-1957 . . . . TCLC 2, 15
See also CA 104, 119; DLB 10, 36, 77

Sayers, Valerie 19??- . . . . CLC 50

Sayles, John (Thomas)
    1950- . . . . CLC 7, 10, 14
See also CA 57-60; DLB 44

Scammell, Michael 19??- . . . . CLC 34

Scannell, Vernon 1922- . . . . CLC 49
See also CANR 8; CA 5-8R; DLB 27

Schaeffer, Susan Fromberg
    1941- . . . . CLC 6, 11, 22
See also CANR 18; CA 49-52; SATA 22;
    DLB 28

Schell, Jonathan 1943- . . . . CLC 35
See also CANR 12; CA 73-76

Schelling, Friedrich Wilhelm Joseph von
    1775-1854 . . . . NCLC 30
See also DLB 90

Scherer, Jean-Marie Maurice 1920-
See Rohmer, Eric
See also CA 110

Schevill, James (Erwin) 1920- . . . . . . CLC 7
See also CA 5-8R

Schisgal, Murray (Joseph) 1926- . . . . . CLC 6
See also CA 21-24R

Schlee, Ann 1934- . . . . CLC 35
See also CA 101; SATA 36, 44

Schlegel, August Wilhelm von
    1767-1845 . . . . NCLC 15

Shawn, Wallace 1943- .... **CLC 41**
See also CA 112

Sheed, Wilfrid (John Joseph)
1930- .... **CLC 2, 4, 10, 53**
See also CA 65-68; DLB 6

Sheffey, Asa 1913-1980
See Hayden, Robert (Earl)

Sheldon, Alice (Hastings) B(radley)
1915-1987
See Tiptree, James, Jr.
See also CA 108; obituary CA 122

Shelley, Mary Wollstonecraft Godwin
1797-1851 .... **NCLC 14**
See also SATA 29

Shelley, Percy Bysshe
1792-1822 .... **NCLC 18**

Shepard, Jim 19??- .... **CLC 36**

Shepard, Lucius 19??- .... **CLC 34**
See also CA 128

Shepard, Sam
1943- .... **CLC 4, 6, 17, 34, 41, 44**
See also CANR 22; CA 69-72; DLB 7

Shepherd, Michael 1927-
See Ludlum, Robert

Sherburne, Zoa (Morin) 1912- ...... **CLC 30**
See also CANR 3; CA 1-4R; SATA 3

Sheridan, Frances 1724-1766 .... **LC 7**
See also DLB 39, 84

Sheridan, Richard Brinsley
1751-1816 .... **NCLC 5; DC 1**
See also DLB 89

Sherman, Jonathan Marc 1970?- .... **CLC 55**

Sherman, Martin 19??- .... **CLC 19**
See also CA 116

Sherwin, Judith Johnson 1936- ... **CLC 7, 15**
See also CA 25-28R

Sherwood, Robert E(mmet)
1896-1955 .... **TCLC 3**
See also CA 104; DLB 7, 26

Shiel, M(atthew) P(hipps)
1865-1947 .... **TCLC 8**
See also CA 106

Shiga, Naoya 1883-1971 .... **CLC 33**
See also CA 101; obituary CA 33-36R

Shimazaki, Haruki 1872-1943
See Shimazaki, Toson
See also CA 105

Shimazaki, Toson 1872-1943 .... **TCLC 5**
See also Shimazaki, Haruki

Sholokhov, Mikhail (Aleksandrovich)
1905-1984 .... **CLC 7, 15**
See also CA 101; obituary CA 112;
SATA 36

Sholom Aleichem 1859-1916 .... **TCLC 1, 35**
See also Rabinovitch, Sholem

Shreve, Susan Richards 1939- ...... **CLC 23**
See also CAAS 5; CANR 5; CA 49-52;
SATA 41, 46

Shue, Larry 1946-1985 .... **CLC 52**
See also obituary CA 117

Shulman, Alix Kates 1932- ...... **CLC 2, 10**
See also CA 29-32R; SATA 7

Shuster, Joe 1914- .... **CLC 21**

Shute (Norway), Nevil 1899-1960 ... **CLC 30**
See also Norway, Nevil Shute
See also CA 102; obituary CA 93-96

Shuttle, Penelope (Diane) 1947- ..... **CLC 7**
See also CA 93-96; DLB 14, 40

Siegel, Jerome 1914- .... **CLC 21**
See also CA 116

Sienkiewicz, Henryk (Adam Aleksander Pius)
1846-1916 .... **TCLC 3**
See also CA 104

Sigal, Clancy 1926- .... **CLC 7**
See also CA 1-4R

Sigourney, Lydia (Howard Huntley)
1791-1865 .... **NCLC 21**
See also DLB 1, 42, 73

Siguenza y Gongora, Carlos de
1645-1700 .... **LC 8**

Sigurjonsson, Johann 1880-1919 ... **TCLC 27**

Sikelianos, Angelos 1884-1951 .... **TCLC 39**

Silkin, Jon 1930- .... **CLC 2, 6, 43**
See also CAAS 5; CA 5-8R; DLB 27

Silko, Leslie Marmon 1948- .... **CLC 23**
See also CA 115, 122

Sillanpaa, Franz Eemil 1888-1964... **CLC 19**
See also CA 129; obituary CA 93-96

Sillitoe, Alan
1928- .... **CLC 1, 3, 6, 10, 19, 57**
See also CAAS 2; CANR 8, 26; CA 9-12R;
DLB 14

Silone, Ignazio 1900-1978 .... **CLC 4**
See also CAAS 2; CANR 26; CAP 2;
CA 25-28, 11-12R,; obituary CA 81-84

Silver, Joan Micklin 1935- .... **CLC 20**
See also CA 114, 121

Silverberg, Robert 1935- .... **CLC 7**
See also CAAS 3; CANR 1, 20; CA 1-4R;
SATA 13; DLB 8

Silverstein, Alvin 1933- .... **CLC 17**
See also CANR 2; CA 49-52; SATA 8

Silverstein, Virginia B(arbara Opshelor)
1937- .... **CLC 17**
See also CANR 2; CA 49-52; SATA 8

Simak, Clifford D(onald)
1904-1988 .... **CLC 1, 55**
See also CANR 1; CA 1-4R;
obituary CA 125; DLB 8

Simenon, Georges (Jacques Christian)
1903-1989 .... **CLC 1, 2, 3, 8, 18, 47**
See also CA 85-88; obituary CA 129;
DLB 72

Simenon, Paul 1956?-
See The Clash

Simic, Charles 1938- .... **CLC 6, 9, 22, 49**
See also CAAS 4; CANR 12; CA 29-32R

Simmons, Charles (Paul) 1924- ..... **CLC 57**
See also CA 89-92

Simmons, Dan 1948- .... **CLC 44**

Simmons, James (Stewart Alexander)
1933- .... **CLC 43**
See also CA 105; DLB 40

Simms, William Gilmore
1806-1870 .... **NCLC 3**
See also DLB 3, 30, 59, 73

Simon, Carly 1945- .... **CLC 26**
See also CA 105

Simon, Claude (Henri Eugene)
1913- .... **CLC 4, 9, 15, 39**
See also CA 89-92; DLB 83

Simon, (Marvin) Neil
1927- .... **CLC 6, 11, 31, 39**
See also CA 21-24R; DLB 7

Simon, Paul 1941- .... **CLC 17**
See also CA 116

Simonon, Paul 1956?-
See The Clash

Simpson, Louis (Aston Marantz)
1923- .... **CLC 4, 7, 9, 32**
See also CAAS 4; CANR 1; CA 1-4R;
DLB 5

Simpson, Mona (Elizabeth) 1957- ... **CLC 44**
See also CA 122

Simpson, N(orman) F(rederick)
1919- .... **CLC 29**
See also CA 11-14R; DLB 13

Sinclair, Andrew (Annandale)
1935- .... **CLC 2, 14**
See also CAAS 5; CANR 14; CA 9-12R;
DLB 14

Sinclair, Mary Amelia St. Clair 1865?-1946
See Sinclair, May
See also CA 104

Sinclair, May 1865?-1946 ...... **TCLC 3, 11**
See also Sinclair, Mary Amelia St. Clair
See also DLB 36

Sinclair, Upton (Beall)
1878-1968 .... **CLC 1, 11, 15, 63**
See also CANR 7; CA 5-8R;
obituary CA 25-28R; SATA 9; DLB 9

Singer, Isaac Bashevis
1904- .... **CLC 1, 3, 6, 9, 11, 15, 23, 38;
SSC 3**
See also CLR 1; CANR 1; CA 1-4R;
SATA 3, 27, DLB 6, 28, 52;
CDALB 1941-1968

Singer, Israel Joshua 1893-1944 ... **TCLC 33**

Singh, Khushwant 1915- .... **CLC 11**
See also CANR 6; CA 9-12R

Sinyavsky, Andrei (Donatevich)
1925- .... **CLC 8**
See also CA 85-88

Sirin, V.
See Nabokov, Vladimir (Vladimirovich)

Sissman, L(ouis) E(dward)
1928-1976 .... **CLC 9, 18**
See also CANR 13; CA 21-24R;
obituary CA 65-68; DLB 5

Sisson, C(harles) H(ubert) 1914- ..... **CLC 8**
See also CAAS 3; CANR 3; CA 1-4R;
DLB 27

Sitwell, (Dame) Edith 1887-1964... **CLC 2, 9**
See also CA 9-12R; DLB 20

Sjoewall, Maj 1935-
See Wahloo, Per
See also CA 61-64, 65-68

Sjowall, Maj 1935-
See Wahloo, Per

Skelton, Robin 1925- .... **CLC 13**
See also CAAS 5; CA 5-8R; DLB 27, 53

Spurling, Hilary 1940-........... **CLC 34**
See also CANR 25; CA 104

Squires, (James) Radcliffe 1917-.... **CLC 51**
See also CANR 6, 21; CA 1-4R

Stael-Holstein, Anne Louise Germaine Necker, Baronne de 1766-1817....... **NCLC 3**

Stafford, Jean 1915-1979...... **CLC 4, 7, 19**
See also CANR 3; CA 1-4R;
obituary CA 85-88; obituary SATA 22;
DLB 2

Stafford, William (Edgar)
1914-................... **CLC 4, 7, 29**
See also CAAS 3; CANR 5, 22; CA 5-8R;
DLB 5

Stannard, Martin 1947-........... **CLC 44**

Stanton, Maura 1946- .... **CLC 9**
See also CANR 15; CA 89-92

Stapledon, (William) Olaf
1886-1950 .... **TCLC 22**
See also CA 111; DLB 15

Starbuck, George (Edwin) 1931-.... **CLC 53**
See also CANR 23; CA 21-22R

Stark, Richard 1933-
See Westlake, Donald E(dwin)

Stead, Christina (Ellen)
1902-1983 .... **CLC 2, 5, 8, 32**
See also CA 13-16R, obituary CA 109

Steele, Timothy (Reid) 1948-....... **CLC 45**
See also CANR 16; CA 93-96

Steffens, (Joseph) Lincoln
1866-1936 .... **TCLC 20**
See also CA 117; SAAS 1

Stegner, Wallace (Earle) 1909-... **CLC 9, 49**
See also CANR 1, 21; CA 1-4R; DLB 9

Stein, Gertrude 1874-1946... **TCLC 1, 6, 28**
See also CA 104; DLB 4, 54, 86;
CDALB 1917-1929

Steinbeck, John (Ernst)
1902-1968 ..... **CLC 1, 5, 9, 13, 21, 34,**
45, 59
See also CANR 1; CA 1-4R;
obituary CA 25-28R; SATA 9; DLB 7, 9;
DLB-DS 2; CDALB 1929-1941

Steinem, Gloria 1934-............. **CLC 63**
See also CANR 28; CA 53-56

Steiner, George 1929-............. **CLC 24**
See also CA 73-76; DLB 67

Steiner, Rudolf(us Josephus Laurentius)
1861-1925 .... **TCLC 13**
See also CA 107

Stendhal 1783-1842............. **NCLC 23**

Stephen, Leslie 1832-1904....... **TCLC 23**
See also CANR 9; CA 21-24R, 123;
DLB 57

Stephens, James 1882?-1950 .... **TCLC 4**
See also CA 104; DLB 19

Stephens, Reed
See Donaldson, Stephen R.

Steptoe, Lydia 1892-1982
See Barnes, Djuna

Sterchi, Beat 1949-.............. **CLC 65**

Sterling, George 1869-1926....... **TCLC 20**
See also CA 117; DLB 54

Stern, Gerald 1925- .... **CLC 40**
See also CA 81-84

Stern, Richard G(ustave) 1928-... **CLC 4, 39**
See also CANR 1, 25; CA 1-4R; DLB 87

Sternberg, Jonas 1894-1969
See Sternberg, Josef von

Sternberg, Josef von 1894-1969..... **CLC 20**
See also CA 81-84

Sterne, Laurence 1713-1768......... **LC 2**
See also DLB 39

Sternheim, (William Adolf) Carl
1878-1942 .... **TCLC 8**
See also CA 105

Stevens, Mark 19??-.............. **CLC 34**

Stevens, Wallace 1879-1955..... **TCLC 3, 12**
See also CA 104, 124; DLB 54

Stevenson, Anne (Katharine)
1933-.................... **CLC 7, 33**
See also Elvin, Anne Katharine Stevenson
See also CANR 9; CA 17-18R; DLB 40

Stevenson, Robert Louis
1850-1894 .... **NCLC 5, 14**
See also CLR 10, 11; YABC 2; DLB 18, 57

Stewart, J(ohn) I(nnes) M(ackintosh)
1906-................... **CLC 7, 14, 32**
See also CAAS 3; CA 85-88

Stewart, Mary (Florence Elinor)
1916-..................... **CLC 7, 35**
See also CANR 1; CA 1-4R; SATA 12

Stewart, Will 1908-
See Williamson, Jack
See also CANR 23; CA 17-18R

Still, James 1906-................. **CLC 49**
See also CANR 10, 26; CA 65-68;
SATA 29; DLB 9

Sting 1951-
See The Police

Stitt, Milan 1941-................ **CLC 29**
See also CA 69-72

Stoker, Abraham
See Stoker, Bram
See also CA 105; SATA 29

Stoker, Bram 1847-1912 .... **TCLC 8**
See also Stoker, Abraham
See also SATA 29; DLB 36, 70

Stolz, Mary (Slattery) 1920-....... **CLC 12**
See also CANR 13; CA 5-8R; SAAS 3;
SATA 10

Stone, Irving 1903-1989........... **CLC 7**
See also CAAS 3; CANR 1; CA 1-4R, 129;
SATA 3

Stone, Robert (Anthony)
1937?- .... **CLC 5, 23, 42**
See also CANR 23; CA 85-88

Stoppard, Tom
1937-... **CLC 1, 3, 4, 5, 8, 15, 29, 34, 63**
See also CA 81-84; DLB 13; DLB-Y 85

Storey, David (Malcolm)
1933-.................. **CLC 2, 4, 5, 8**
See also CA 81-84; DLB 13, 14

Storm, Hyemeyohsts 1935-......... **CLC 3**
See also CA 81-84

Storm, (Hans) Theodor (Woldsen)
1817-1888 .... **NCLC 1**

Storni, Alfonsina 1892-1938 .... **TCLC 5**
See also CA 104

Stout, Rex (Todhunter) 1886-1975 ... **CLC 3**
See also CA 61-64

Stow, (Julian) Randolph 1935- .. **CLC 23, 48**
See also CA 13-16R

Stowe, Harriet (Elizabeth) Beecher
1811-1896 .... **NCLC 3**
See also YABC 1; DLB 1, 12, 42, 74;
CDALB 1865-1917

Strachey, (Giles) Lytton
1880-1932 .... **TCLC 12**
See also CA 110

Strand, Mark 1934-......... **CLC 6, 18, 41**
See also CA 21-24R; SATA 41; DLB 5

Straub, Peter (Francis) 1943- ...... **CLC 28**
See also CA 85-88; DLB-Y 84

Strauss, Botho 1944-............. **CLC 22**

Straussler, Tomas 1937-
See Stoppard, Tom

Streatfeild, (Mary) Noel 1897- .... **CLC 21**
See also CA 81-84; obituary CA 120;
SATA 20, 48

Stribling, T(homas) S(igismund)
1881-1965 .... **CLC 23**
See also obituary CA 107; DLB 9

Strindberg, (Johan) August
1849-1912 .... **TCLC 1, 8, 21**
See also CA 104

Stringer, Arthur 1874-1950 .... **TCLC 37**
See also DLB 92

Strugatskii, Arkadii (Natanovich)
1925-..................... **CLC 27**
See also CA 106

Strugatskii, Boris (Natanovich)
1933-..................... **CLC 27**
See also CA 106

Strummer, Joe 1953?-
See The Clash

Stuart, (Hilton) Jesse
1906-1984 .... **CLC 1, 8, 11, 14, 34**
See also CA 5-8R; obituary CA 112;
SATA 2; obituary SATA 36; DLB 9, 48;
DLB-Y 84

Sturgeon, Theodore (Hamilton)
1918-1985 .... **CLC 22, 39**
See also CA 81-84; obituary CA 116;
DLB 8; DLB-Y 85

Styron, William
1925-.......... **CLC 1, 3, 5, 11, 15, 60**
See also CANR 6; CA 5-8R; DLB 2;
DLB-Y 80; CDALB 1968-1987

Sudermann, Hermann 1857-1928 .. **TCLC 15**
See also CA 107

Sue, Eugene 1804-1857 .... **NCLC 1**

Sukenick, Ronald 1932-..... **CLC 3, 4, 6, 48**
See also CAAS 8; CA 25-28R; DLB-Y 81

Suknaski, Andrew 1942- .... **CLC 19**
See also CA 101; DLB 53

Sully Prudhomme, Rene
1839-1907 .... **TCLC 31**

Su Man-shu 1884-1918.......... **TCLC 24**
See also CA 123

Summers, Andrew James 1942-
See The Police

Summers, Andy 1942-
See The Police

Summers, Hollis (Spurgeon, Jr.)
1916- .... CLC 10
See also CANR 3; CA 5-8R; DLB 6

Summers, (Alphonsus Joseph-Mary Augustus)
Montague 1880-1948 .... TCLC 16
See also CA 118

Sumner, Gordon Matthew 1951-
See The Police

Surtees, Robert Smith
1805-1864 .... NCLC 14
See also DLB 21

Susann, Jacqueline 1921-1974 .... CLC 3
See also CA 65-68; obituary CA 53-56

Suskind, Patrick 1949- .... CLC 44

Sutcliff, Rosemary 1920- .... CLC 26
See also CLR 1; CA 5-8R; SATA 6, 44

Sutro, Alfred 1863-1933 .... TCLC 6
See also CA 105; DLB 10

Sutton, Henry 1935-
See Slavitt, David (R.)

Svevo, Italo 1861-1928 .... TCLC 2, 35
See also Schmitz, Ettore

Swados, Elizabeth 1951- .... CLC 12
See also CA 97-100

Swados, Harvey 1920-1972 .... CLC 5
See also CANR 6; CA 5-8R;
obituary CA 37-40R; DLB 2

Swarthout, Glendon (Fred) 1918- ... CLC 35
See also CANR 1; CA 1-4R; SATA 26

Swenson, May 1919-1989 ..... CLC 4, 14, 61
See also CA 5-8R; obituary CA 130;
SATA 15; DLB 5

Swift, Graham 1949- .... CLC 41
See also CA 117, 122

Swift, Jonathan 1667-1745 .... LC 1
See also SATA 19; DLB 39

Swinburne, Algernon Charles
1837-1909 .... TCLC 8, 36
See also CA 105; DLB 35, 57

Swinfen, Ann 19??- .... CLC 34

Swinnerton, Frank (Arthur)
1884-1982 .... CLC 31
See also obituary CA 108; DLB 34

Symons, Arthur (William)
1865-1945 .... TCLC 11
See also CA 107; DLB 19, 57

Symons, Julian (Gustave)
1912- .... CLC 2, 14, 32
See also CAAS 3; CANR 3; CA 49-52;
DLB 87

Synge, (Edmund) John Millington
1871-1909 .... TCLC 6, 37
See also CA 104; DLB 10, 19

Syruc, J. 1911-
See Milosz, Czeslaw

Szirtes, George 1948- .... CLC 46
See also CANR 27; CA 109

Tabori, George 1914- .... CLC 19
See also CANR 4; CA 49-52

Tagore, (Sir) Rabindranath
1861-1941 .... TCLC 3
See also Thakura, Ravindranatha
See also CA 120

Taine, Hippolyte Adolphe
1828-1893 .... NCLC 15

Talese, Gaetano 1932-
See Talese, Gay

Talese, Gay 1932- .... CLC 37
See also CANR 9; CA 1-4R

Tallent, Elizabeth (Ann) 1954- ..... CLC 45
See also CA 117

Tally, Ted 1952- .... CLC 42
See also CA 120, 124

Tamayo y Baus, Manuel
1829-1898 .... NCLC 1

Tammsaare, A(nton) H(ansen)
1878-1940 .... TCLC 27

Tan, Amy 1952- .... CLC 59

Tanizaki, Jun'ichiro
1886-1965 .... CLC 8, 14, 28
See also CA 93-96; obituary CA 25-28R

Tarbell, Ida 1857-1944 .... TCLC 40
See also CA 122; DLB 47

Tarkington, (Newton) Booth
1869-1946 .... TCLC 9
See also CA 110; SATA 17; DLB 9

Tasso, Torquato 1544-1595 .... LC 5

Tate, (John Orley) Allen
1899-1979 .... CLC 2, 4, 6, 9, 11, 14, 24
See also CA 5-8R; obituary CA 85-88;
DLB 4, 45, 63

Tate, James 1943- .... CLC 2, 6, 25
See also CA 21-24R; DLB 5

Tavel, Ronald 1940- .... CLC 6
See also CA 21-24R

Taylor, C(ecil) P(hillip) 1929-1981 .. CLC 27
See also CA 25-28R; obituary CA 105

Taylor, Edward 1644?-1729 .... LC 11
See also DLB 24

Taylor, Eleanor Ross 1920- .... CLC 5
See also CA 81-84

Taylor, Elizabeth 1912-1975 ... CLC 2, 4, 29
See also CANR 9; CA 13-16R; SATA 13

Taylor, Henry (Splawn) 1917- ...... CLC 44
See also CAAS 7; CA 33-36R; DLB 5

Taylor, Kamala (Purnaiya) 1924-
See Markandaya, Kamala
See also CA 77-80

Taylor, Mildred D(elois) 1943- ..... CLC 21
See also CLR 9; CANR 25; CA 85-88;
SAAS 5; SATA 15; DLB 52

Taylor, Peter (Hillsman)
1917- .... CLC 1, 4, 18, 37, 44, 50
See also CANR 9; CA 13-16R; DLB-Y 81

Taylor, Robert Lewis 1912- .... CLC 14
See also CANR 3; CA 1-4R; SATA 10

Teasdale, Sara 1884-1933 .... TCLC 4
See also CA 104; SATA 32; DLB 45

Tegner, Esaias 1782-1846 .... NCLC 2

Teilhard de Chardin, (Marie Joseph) Pierre
1881-1955 .... TCLC 9
See also CA 105

Tennant, Emma 1937- .... CLC 13, 52
See also CAAS 9; CANR 10; CA 65-68;
DLB 14

Tennyson, Alfred 1809-1892 ..... NCLC 30
See also DLB 32

Teran, Lisa St. Aubin de 19??- ..... CLC 36

Terkel, Louis 1912-
See Terkel, Studs
See also CANR 18; CA 57-60

Terkel, Studs 1912- .... CLC 38
See also Terkel, Louis

Terry, Megan 1932- .... CLC 19
See also CA 77-80; CABS 3; DLB 7

Tertz, Abram 1925-
See Sinyavsky, Andrei (Donatevich)

Tesich, Steve 1943?- .... CLC 40
See also CA 105; DLB-Y 83

Tesich, Stoyan 1943?-
See Tesich, Steve

Teternikov, Fyodor Kuzmich 1863-1927
See Sologub, Fyodor
See also CA 104

Tevis, Walter 1928-1984 .... CLC 42
See also CA 113

Tey, Josephine 1897-1952 .... TCLC 14
See also Mackintosh, Elizabeth

Thackeray, William Makepeace
1811-1863 .... NCLC 5, 14, 22
See also SATA 23; DLB 21, 55

Thakura, Ravindranatha 1861-1941
See Tagore, (Sir) Rabindranath
See also CA 104

Thelwell, Michael (Miles) 1939- .... CLC 22
See also CA 101

Theroux, Alexander (Louis)
1939- .... CLC 2, 25
See also CANR 20; CA 85-88

Theroux, Paul
1941- .... CLC 5, 8, 11, 15, 28, 46
See also CANR 20; CA 33-36R; SATA 44;
DLB 2

Thesen, Sharon 1946- .... CLC 56

Thibault, Jacques Anatole Francois
1844-1924
See France, Anatole
See also CA 106

Thiele, Colin (Milton) 1920- .... CLC 17
See also CANR 12; CA 29-32R; SAAS 2;
SATA 14

Thomas, Audrey (Grace)
1935- .... CLC 7, 13, 37
See also CA 21-24R; DLB 60

Thomas, D(onald) M(ichael)
1935- .... CLC 13, 22, 31
See also CANR 17; CA 61-64; DLB 40

Thomas, Dylan (Marlais)
1914-1953 ..... TCLC 1, 8; PC 2; SSC 3
See also CA 104, 120; SATA 60; DLB 13,
20

Thomas, Edward (Philip)
1878-1917 .... TCLC 10
See also CA 106; DLB 19

Thomas, John Peter 1928-
See Thomas, Piri

Thomas, Joyce Carol 1938- . . . . **CLC 35**
See also CLR 19; CA 113, 116; SAAS 7;
SATA 40; DLB 33

Thomas, Lewis 1913- . . . . **CLC 35**
See also CA 85-88

Thomas, Piri 1928- . . . . **CLC 17**
See also CA 73-76

Thomas, R(onald) S(tuart)
1913- . . . . **CLC 6, 13, 48**
See also CAAS 4; CA 89-92; DLB 27

Thomas, Ross (Elmore) 1926- . . . . . . **CLC 39**
See also CANR 22; CA 33-36R

Thompson, Ernest 1860-1946
See Seton, Ernest (Evan) Thompson

Thompson, Francis (Joseph)
1859-1907 . . . . **TCLC 4**
See also CA 104; DLB 19

Thompson, Hunter S(tockton)
1939- . . . . **CLC 9, 17, 40**
See also CANR 23; CA 17-20R

Thompson, Judith 1954- . . . . **CLC 39**

Thomson, James 1700-1748 . . . . **LC 16**
See also DLB 95

Thomson, James 1834-1882 . . . . . . **NCLC 18**
See also DLB 35

Thoreau, Henry David
1817-1862 . . . . **NCLC 7, 21**
See also DLB 1; CDALB 1640-1865

Thurber, James (Grover)
1894-1961 . . . . **CLC 5, 11, 25; SSC 1**
See also CANR 17; CA 73-76; SATA 13;
DLB 4, 11, 22

Thurman, Wallace 1902-1934 . . . . . . **TCLC 6**
See also CA 104, 124; DLB 51

Tieck, (Johann) Ludwig
1773-1853 . . . . **NCLC 5**
See also DLB 90

Tilghman, Christopher 1948?- . . . . . . **CLC 65**

Tillinghast, Richard 1940- . . . . **CLC 29**
See also CANR 26; CA 29-32R

Timrod, Henry 1828-1867 . . . . **NCLC 25**

Tindall, Gillian 1938- . . . . **CLC 7**
See also CANR 11; CA 21-24R

Tiptree, James, Jr. 1915-1987 . . . **CLC 48, 50**
See also Sheldon, Alice (Hastings) B(radley)
See also DLB 8

Tocqueville, Alexis (Charles Henri Maurice
Clerel, Comte) de 1805-1859 . . **NCLC 7**

Tolkien, J(ohn) R(onald) R(euel)
1892-1973 . . . . **CLC 1, 2, 3, 8, 12, 38**
See also CAP 2; CA 17-18;
obituary CA 45-48; SATA 2, 24, 32;
obituary SATA 24; DLB 15

Toller, Ernst 1893-1939 . . . . **TCLC 10**
See also CA 107

Tolson, Melvin B(eaunorus)
1900?-1966 . . . . **CLC 36**
See also CA 124; obituary CA 89-92;
DLB 48, 124

Tolstoy, (Count) Alexey Nikolayevich
1883-1945 . . . . **TCLC 18**
See also CA 107

Tolstoy, (Count) Leo (Lev Nikolaevich)
1828-1910 . . . . **TCLC 4, 11, 17, 28**
See also CA 104, 123; SATA 26

Tomlin, Lily 1939- . . . . **CLC 17**

Tomlin, Mary Jean 1939-
See Tomlin, Lily
See also CA 117

Tomlinson, (Alfred) Charles
1927- . . . . **CLC 2, 4, 6, 13, 45**
See also CA 5-8R; DLB 40

Toole, John Kennedy
1937-1969 . . . . **CLC 19, 64**
See also CA 104; DLB-Y 81

Toomer, Jean
1894-1967 . . . . . **CLC 1, 4, 13, 22; SSC 1**
See also CA 85-88; DLB 45, 51

Torrey, E. Fuller 19??- . . . . **CLC 34**
See also CA 119

Tournier, Michel 1924- . . . . . . **CLC 6, 23, 36**
See also CANR 3; CA 49-52; SATA 23;
DLB 83

Townsend, Sue 1946- . . . . **CLC 61**
See also CA 119, 127; SATA 48, 55

Townshend, Peter (Dennis Blandford)
1945- . . . . **CLC 17, 42**
See also CA 107

Tozzi, Federigo 1883-1920 . . . . **TCLC 31**

Traill, Catharine Parr
1802-1899 . . . . **NCLC 31**
See also DLB 99

Trakl, Georg 1887-1914 . . . . **TCLC 5**
See also CA 104

Transtromer, Tomas (Gosta)
1931- . . . . **CLC 52, 65**
See also CA 129; brief entry CA 117

Traven, B. 1890-1969 . . . . **CLC 8, 11**
See also CAP 2; CA 19-20;
obituary CA 25-28R; DLB 9, 56

Tremain, Rose 1943- . . . . **CLC 42**
See also CA 97-100; DLB 14

Tremblay, Michel 1942- . . . . **CLC 29**
See also CA 116; DLB 60

Trevanian 1925- . . . . **CLC 29**
See also CA 108

Trevor, William 1928- . . . . . **CLC 7, 9, 14, 25**
See also Cox, William Trevor
See also DLB 14

Trifonov, Yuri (Valentinovich)
1925-1981 . . . . **CLC 45**
See also obituary CA 103, 126

Trilling, Lionel 1905-1975 . . . . **CLC 9, 11, 24**
See also CANR 10; CA 9-12R;
obituary CA 61-64; DLB 28, 63

Trogdon, William 1939-
See Heat Moon, William Least
See also CA 115, 119

Trollope, Anthony 1815-1882 . . . . . **NCLC 6**
See also SATA 22; DLB 21, 57

Trollope, Frances 1780-1863 . . . . . **NCLC 30**
See also DLB 21

Trotsky, Leon (Davidovich)
1879-1940 . . . . **TCLC 22**
See also CA 118

Trotter (Cockburn), Catharine
1679-1749 . . . . **LC 8**
See also DLB 84

Trow, George W. S. 1943- . . . . **CLC 52**
See also CA 126

Troyat, Henri 1911- . . . . **CLC 23**
See also CANR 2; CA 45-48

Trudeau, G(arretson) B(eekman) 1948-
See Trudeau, Garry
See also CA 81-84; SATA 35

Trudeau, Garry 1948- . . . . **CLC 12**
See also Trudeau, G(arretson) B(eekman)

Truffaut, Francois 1932-1984 . . . . **CLC 20**
See also CA 81-84; obituary CA 113

Trumbo, Dalton 1905-1976 . . . . **CLC 19**
See also CANR 10; CA 21-24R;
obituary CA 69-72; DLB 26

Trumbull, John 1750-1831 . . . . **NCLC 30**
See also DLB 31

Tryon, Thomas 1926- . . . . **CLC 3, 11**
See also CA 29-32R

Ts'ao Hsueh-ch'in 1715?-1763 . . . . **LC 1**

Tsushima Shuji 1909-1948
See Dazai Osamu
See also CA 107

Tsvetaeva (Efron), Marina (Ivanovna)
1892-1941 . . . . **TCLC 7, 35**
See also CA 104, 128

Tunis, John R(oberts) 1889-1975 . . . **CLC 12**
See also CA 61-64; SATA 30, 37; DLB 22

Tuohy, Frank 1925- . . . . **CLC 37**
See also DLB 14

Tuohy, John Francis 1925-
See Tuohy, Frank
See also CANR 3; CA 5-8R

Turco, Lewis (Putnam) 1934- . . . **CLC 11, 63**
See also CANR 24; CA 13-16R; DLB-Y 84

Turgenev, Ivan
1818-1883 . . . . **NCLC 21; SSC 7**

Turner, Frederick 1943- . . . . **CLC 48**
See also CANR 12; CA 73-76; DLB 40

Tutuola, Amos 1920- . . . . **CLC 5, 14, 29**
See also CA 9-12R

Twain, Mark
1835-1910 . . . **TCLC 6, 12, 19, 36; SSC 6**
See also Clemens, Samuel Langhorne
See also YABC 2; DLB 11, 12, 23, 64, 74

Tyler, Anne
1941- . . . . **CLC 7, 11, 18, 28, 44, 59**
See also CANR 11; CA 9-12R; SATA 7;
DLB 6; DLB-Y 82

Tyler, Royall 1757-1826 . . . . **NCLC 3**
See also DLB 37

Tynan (Hinkson), Katharine
1861-1931 . . . . **TCLC 3**
See also CA 104

Tytell, John 1939- . . . . **CLC 50**
See also CA 29-32R

Tzara, Tristan 1896-1963 . . . . **CLC 47**
See also Rosenfeld, Samuel

Uhry, Alfred 1947?- . . . . **CLC 55**
See also CA 127

Wahloo, Peter 1926-1975
See Wahloo, Per

Wain, John (Barrington)
1925- .... **CLC 2, 11, 15, 46**
See also CAAS 4; CANR 23; CA 5-8R;
DLB 15, 27

Wajda, Andrzej 1926-............. **CLC 16**
See also CA 102

Wakefield, Dan 1932-.............. **CLC 7**
See also CAAS 7; CA 21-24R

Wakoski, Diane
1937- .... **CLC 2, 4, 7, 9, 11, 40**
See also CAAS 1; CANR 9; CA 13-16R;
DLB 5

Walcott, Derek (Alton)
1930- .... **CLC 2, 4, 9, 14, 25, 42**
See also CANR 26; CA 89-92; DLB-Y 81

Waldman, Anne 1945- .... **CLC 7**
See also CA 37-40R; DLB 16

Waldo, Edward Hamilton 1918-
See Sturgeon, Theodore (Hamilton)

Walker, Alice
1944- ...... **CLC 5, 6, 9, 19, 27, 46, 58;
SSC 5**
See also CANR 9, 27; CA 37-40R;
SATA 31; DLB 6, 33; CDALB 1968-1988

Walker, David Harry 1911-........ **CLC 14**
See also CANR 1; CA 1-4R; SATA 8

Walker, Edward Joseph 1934-
See Walker, Ted
See also CANR 12; CA 21-24R

Walker, George F. 1947-....... **CLC 44, 61**
See also CANR 21; CA 103; DLB 60

Walker, Joseph A. 1935-.......... **CLC 19**
See also CANR 26; CA 89-92; DLB 38

Walker, Margaret (Abigail)
1915- .... **CLC 1, 6**
See also CANR 26; CA 73-76; DLB 76

Walker, Ted 1934- .... **CLC 13**
See also Walker, Edward Joseph
See also DLB 40

Wallace, David Foster 1962-....... **CLC 50**

Wallace, Irving 1916-........... **CLC 7, 13**
See also CAAS 1; CANR 1; CA 1-4R

Wallant, Edward Lewis
1926-1962 .... **CLC 5, 10**
See also CANR 22; CA 1-4R; DLB 2, 28

Walpole, Horace 1717-1797.......... **LC 2**
See also DLB 39

Walpole, (Sir) Hugh (Seymour)
1884-1941 .... **TCLC 5**
See also CA 104; DLB 34

Walser, Martin 1927-............. **CLC 27**
See also CANR 8; CA 57-60; DLB 75

Walser, Robert 1878-1956....... **TCLC 18**
See also CA 118; DLB 66

Walsh, Gillian Paton 1939-
See Walsh, Jill Paton
See also CA 37-40R; SATA 4

Walsh, Jill Paton 1939-........... **CLC 35**
See also CLR 2; SAAS 3

Wambaugh, Joseph (Aloysius, Jr.)
1937-....................... **CLC 3, 18**
See also CA 33-36R; DLB 6; DLB-Y 83

Ward, Arthur Henry Sarsfield 1883-1959
See Rohmer, Sax
See also CA 108

Ward, Douglas Turner 1930-....... **CLC 19**
See also CA 81-84; DLB 7, 38

Warhol, Andy 1928-1987.......... **CLC 20**
See also CA 89-92; obituary CA 121

Warner, Francis (Robert le Plastrier)
1937- .... **CLC 14**
See also CANR 11; CA 53-56

Warner, Marina 1946-............. **CLC 59**
See also CANR 21; CA 65-68

Warner, Rex (Ernest) 1905-1986.... **CLC 45**
See also CA 89-92; obituary CA 119;
DLB 15

Warner, Susan 1819-1885 .... **NCLC 31**
See also DLB 3, 42

Warner, Sylvia Townsend
1893-1978 .... **CLC 7, 19**
See also CANR 16; CA 61-64;
obituary CA 77-80; DLB 34

Warren, Mercy Otis 1728-1814... **NCLC 13**
See also DLB 31

Warren, Robert Penn
1905-1989 ... **CLC 1, 4, 6, 8, 10, 13, 18,
39, 53, 59; SSC 4**
See also CANR 10; CA 13-16R. 129. 130;
SATA 46; DLB 2, 48; DLB-Y 80;
CDALB 1968-1987

Warton, Thomas 1728-1790........ **LC 15**

Washington, Booker T(aliaferro)
1856-1915 .... **TCLC 10**
See also CA 114, 125; SATA 28

Wassermann, Jakob 1873-1934..... **TCLC 6**
See also CA 104; DLB 66

Wasserstein, Wendy 1950-...... **CLC 32, 59**
See also CA 121; CABS 3

Waterhouse, Keith (Spencer)
1929- .... **CLC 47**
See also CA 5-8R; DLB 13, 15

Waters, Roger 1944-
See Pink Floyd

Wa Thiong'o, Ngugi
1938- .... **CLC 3, 7, 13, 36**
See also Ngugi, James (Thiong'o); Ngugi wa
Thiong'o

Watkins, Paul 1964-.............. **CLC 55**

Watkins, Vernon (Phillips)
1906-1967 .... **CLC 43**
See also CAP 1; CA 9-10;
obituary CA 25-28R; DLB 20

Waugh, Auberon (Alexander) 1939-.. **CLC 7**
See also CANR 6, 22; CA 45-48; DLB 14

Waugh, Evelyn (Arthur St. John)
1903-1966 ... **CLC 1, 3, 8, 13, 19, 27, 44**
See also CANR 22; CA 85-88;
obituary CA 25-28R; DLB 15

Waugh, Harriet 1944- .... **CLC 6**
See also CANR 22; CA 85-88

Webb, Beatrice (Potter)
1858-1943 .... **TCLC 22**
See also CA 117

Webb, Charles (Richard) 1939-...... **CLC 7**
See also CA 25-28R

Webb, James H(enry), Jr. 1946-.... **CLC 22**
See also CA 81-84

Webb, Mary (Gladys Meredith)
1881-1927 .... **TCLC 24**
See also CA 123; DLB 34

Webb, Phyllis 1927-............... **CLC 18**
See also CANR 23; CA 104; DLB 53

Webb, Sidney (James)
1859-1947 .... **TCLC 22**
See also CA 117

Webber, Andrew Lloyd 1948-...... **CLC 21**

Weber, Lenora Mattingly
1895-1971 .... **CLC 12**
See also CAP 1; CA 19-20;
obituary CA 29-32R; SATA 2;
obituary SATA 26

Webster, Noah 1758-1843 .... **NCLC 30**
See also DLB 1, 37, 42, 43, 73

Wedekind, (Benjamin) Frank(lin)
1864-1918 .... **TCLC 7**
See also CA 104

Weidman, Jerome 1913-............ **CLC 7**
See also CANR 1; CA 1-4R; DLB 28

Weil, Simone 1909-1943.......... **TCLC 23**
See also CA 117

Weinstein, Nathan Wallenstein 1903?-1940
See West, Nathanael
See also CA 104

Weir, Peter 1944-................. **CLC 20**
See also CA 113, 123

Weiss, Peter (Ulrich)
1916-1982 .... **CLC 3, 15, 51**
See also CANR 3; CA 45-48;
obituary CA 106; DLB 69

Weiss, Theodore (Russell)
1916- .... **CLC 3, 8, 14**
See also CAAS 2; CA 9-12R; DLB 5

Welch, (Maurice) Denton
1915-1948 .... **TCLC 22**
See also CA 121

Welch, James 1940-......... **CLC 6, 14, 52**
See also CA 85-88

Weldon, Fay
1933-.......... **CLC 6, 9, 11, 19, 36, 59**
See also CANR 16; CA 21-24R; DLB 14

Wellek, Rene 1903-................ **CLC 28**
See also CAAS 7; CANR 8; CA 5-8R;
DLB 63

Weller, Michael 1942-.......... **CLC 10, 53**
See also CA 85-88

Weller, Paul 1958-................ **CLC 26**

Wellershoff, Dieter 1925-.......... **CLC 46**
See also CANR 16; CA 89-92

Welles, (George) Orson
1915-1985 .... **CLC 20**
See also CA 93-96; obituary CA 117

Wellman, Mac 1945- .... **CLC 65**

Wellman, Manly Wade 1903-1986 .. **CLC 49**
See also CANR 6, 16; CA 1-4R;
obituary CA 118; SATA 6, 47

Wells, Carolyn 1862-1942 .... **TCLC 35**
See also CA 113; DLB 11

Literary Criticism Series
Cumulative Topic Index

This index lists all topic entries in the Gale Literary Criticism Series *Contemporary Literary Criticism, Literature Criticism from 1400 to 1800, Nineteenth-Century Literature Criticism,* and *Twentieth-Century Literary Criticism.*

TCLC Cumulative Nationality Index

Nationality Index

AMERICAN

Adams, Henry **4**
Agee, James **1, 19**
Anderson, Maxwell **2**
Anderson, Sherwood **1, 10, 24**
Atherton, Gertrude **2**
Austin, Mary **25**
Barry, Philip **11**
Baum, L. Frank **7**
Beard, Charles A. **15**
Belasco, David **3**
Benchley, Robert **1**
Benét, Stephen Vincent **7**
Benét, William Rose **28**
Bierce, Ambrose **1, 7**
Black Elk **33**
Bourne, Randolph S. **16**
Bradford, Gamaliel **36**
Bromfield, Louis **11**
Burroughs, Edgar Rice **2, 32**
Cabell, James Branch **6**
Cable, George Washington **4**
Cather, Willa **1, 11, 31**
Chambers, Robert W. **41**
Chandler, Raymond **1, 7**
Chapman, John Jay **7**
Chesnutt, Charles Waddell **5, 39**
Chopin, Kate **5, 14**
Comstock, Anthony **13**
Cotter, Joseph Seamon, Sr. **28**
Crane, Hart **2, 5**
Crane, Stephen **11, 17, 32**
Crawford, F. Marion **10**
Crothers, Rachel **19**
Cullen, Countee **4, 37**
Davis, Rebecca Harding **6**
Davis, Richard Harding **24**
Day, Clarence **25**
DeVoto, Bernard **29**

Dreiser, Theodore **10, 18, 35**
Dunbar, Paul Laurence **2, 12**
Dunne, Finley Peter **28**
Fisher, Rudolph **11**
Fitzgerald, F. Scott **1, 6, 14, 28**
Fletcher, John Gould **35**
Forten, Charlotte L. **16**
Freeman, Douglas Southall **11**
Freeman, Mary Wilkins **9**
Futrelle, Jacques **19**
Gale, Zona **7**
Garland, Hamlin **3**
Gilman, Charlotte Perkins **9, 37**
Glasgow, Ellen **2, 7**
Goldman, Emma **13**
Grey, Zane **6**
Guiney, Louise Imogen **41**
Hall, James Norman **23**
Harper, Frances Ellen Watkins **14**
Harris, Joel Chandler **2**
Harte, Bret **1, 25**
Hawthorne, Julian **25**
Hearn, Lafcadio **9**
Henry, O. **1, 19**
Hergesheimer, Joseph **11**
Higginson, Thomas Wentworth **36**
Hopkins, Pauline Elizabeth **28**
Howard, Robert E. **8**
Howe, Julia Ward **21**
Howells, William Dean **7, 17, 41**
James, Henry **2, 11, 24, 40**
James, William **15, 32**
Jewett, Sarah Orne **1, 22**
Johnson, James Weldon **3, 19**
Kornbluth, C. M. **8**
Kuttner, Henry **10**
Lardner, Ring **2, 14**
Lewis, Sinclair **4, 13, 23, 39**
Lewisohn, Ludwig **19**

Lindsay, Vachel **17**
London, Jack **9, 15, 39**
Lovecraft, H. P. **4, 22**
Lowell, Amy **1, 8**
Marquis, Don **7**
Masters, Edgar Lee **2, 25**
McCoy, Horace **28**
McKay, Claude **7, 41**
Mencken, H. L. **13**
Millay, Edna St. Vincent **4**
Mitchell, Margaret **11**
Mitchell, S. Weir **36**
Monroe, Harriet **12**
Muir, John **28**
Nathan, George Jean **18**
Nordhoff, Charles **23**
Norris, Frank **24**
O'Neill, Eugene **1, 6, 27**
Oskison, John M. **35**
Porter, Gene Stratton **21**
Post, Melville **39**
Rawlings, Marjorie Kinnan **4**
Reed, John **9**
Roberts, Kenneth **23**
Robinson, Edwin Arlington **5**
Rogers, Will **8**
Rölvaag, O. E. **17**
Rourke, Constance **12**
Runyon, Damon **10**
Saltus, Edgar **8**
Santayana, George **40**
Sherwood, Robert E. **3**
Slesinger, Tess **10**
Steffens, Lincoln **20**
Stein, Gertrude **1, 6, 28**
Sterling, George **20**
Stevens, Wallace **3, 12**
Tarbell, Ida **40**
Tarkington, Booth **9**

509

Nationality Index